City Crime Rankings 2010–2011

Other titles in the State Fact Finder series

Crime State Rankings

Education State Rankings

Health Care State Rankings

State Rankings

City Crime Rankings 2010–2011

Crime in Metropolitan America

Kathleen O'Leary Morgan

and

Scott Morgan

with

Rachel Boba

CQ PRESS

A Division of SAGE

Washington, D.C.

CQ Press
2300 N Street, NW, Suite 800
Washington, DC 20037

Phone: 202-729-1900; toll-free, 1-866-4CQ-PRESS (1-866-427-7737)

Web: www.cqpress.com

Cover design: Silverander Communications

∞ The paper used in this publication exceeds the requirements of the American National Standard for Information Sciences—Permanence of Paper for Printed Library Materials, ANSI Z39.48-1992.

Printed and bound in the United States of America

14 13 12 11 10 1 2 3 4 5

ISBN: 978-1-60871-016-4

Contents

Detailed Table of Contents

I. METROPOLITAN AREA CRIME STATISTICS

II. CITY CRIME STATISTICS (FOR CITIES WITH POPULATIONS OF 75,000 AND LARGER)

III. METROPOLITAN AND CITY POPULATIONS

APPENDIX

Introduction and Methodology

City Crime Rankings 2010–2011 analyzes the latest (2009) FBI crime statistics for U.S. metropolitan areas and cities with populations of 75,000 or more. *City Crime Rankings* begins by describing the data and methodology used in the rankings; it then provides a comparative analysis of cities and metropolitan areas, a distribution analysis of comparison scores and rates, and additional information and caveats regarding the analyzed data. The data and their limitations, the methodology, and the results of the comparative analysis of six types of reported crime are discussed. Also presented are charts illustrating the distribution of values for selected analyses along with the related statistics for the median, mean, standard deviation, minimum value, and maximum value. Lastly, the definitions of crimes based on the FBI's coding system are presented with supporting facts and caveats that provide context to the numbers presented in this volume.

The two main sections of the book, Metropolitan Area Crime Statistics and City Crime Statistics, report the statistics for 370 metropolitan areas and 411 cities with populations of 75,000 or more. Each section has forty tables, presented in both alphabetical and rank order, that compare the actual numbers of reported crimes, crime rates, and percent changes over periods of one year (2008 to 2009) and five years (2005 to 2009). Each table spans four pages with the first two pages displaying the metro areas and cities in alphabetical order, and the third and fourth pages displaying them in rank order. In addition, City Crime Statistics presents the actual numbers, rates, and percent change in police officers employed per capita by law enforcement agencies in each city.

To be included in this edition, cities must have reported crime data to the FBI for 2009. Metropolitan areas must have met two criteria: first, their central city or cities must have submitted twelve months of data in 2009 and, second, at least 75 percent of all law enforcement agencies located in a specific metro area must have reported crime statistics for 2009. (The cities and metro areas not meeting these requirements were excluded from this edition of *City Crime Rankings* and are listed in the Missing Cities and Metro Areas section.)

The Metropolitan and City Populations Appendix presents population data for the cities and metro areas included in *City Crime Rankings*. The section consists of a description for each metropolitan area, including a listing of cities and counties; a county index for 2009; tables illustrating rates for each reported crime category for the past twenty years, with an examination of national trends and perspective of crime in the United States; and a summary of the 2009 national, metropolitan, and city crime statistics.

Purpose of This Book

The purpose of *City Crime Rankings* is to serve as a resource for researchers, city and law enforcement officials, and the community. The book provides the means by which individuals can compare local communities to other similar communities through contrast with the national level of reported crime—more specifically, crime rates per 100,000 persons for individual types of reported crime, for violent and property crime categories, and for overall crime.

In editions prior to the 2008–2009 edition, the terms "safest" and "dangerous" were used to describe the cities and metropolitan areas with lowest and highest rankings in the comparative analysis, respectively. Even though the rankings are still provided, these terms are no longer used because perceptions of safety and danger are just that—perceptions. The data analyzed here are "reported crime" and population, which together constitute only two factors considered when determining safety or risk of crime victimization. Thus, the analyses in this book are purely descriptive. At no time do we attempt to explain *why* reported crime rates are higher or lower from one community to the next. These explanations—currently sought by criminologists and other social science researchers—are beyond the scope of this book.

Consequently, to enhance the usefulness of *City Crime Rankings,* a new section was introduced in the 2008–2009 edition and is continued in this edition. The Distribution Analysis section (see page xii) provides histograms of the comparison score and reported crime rate distributions as well as such measures of central tendency as median, mean, standard deviation, and minimum and maximum values for each distribution. Because the rank ordering of scores and crime rates does not illustrate the relative difference between metro areas' and cities' values, this analysis is provided so the reader can better understand how the values are distributed and where a particular metro area's or city's ranking falls in comparison to others.

These statistics are used in a variety of ways, by a range of audiences, including the following:

- Law enforcement agencies use them to help identify crime problems for further study (POP Center, 2010).
- City governments compare their cities' crime levels to those of other jurisdictions to determine how their rates appear in comparison.
- The federal government uses this type of analysis to allocate grant funding (Bauer, 2004).
- The media draw upon these results when reporting and comparing crime rates across cities and years.

In addition, it is important to examine the statistics of a city along with its metro area when using *City Crime Rankings*. Although a city's scores and rates are useful for understanding the crime levels within the boundaries of that city and making comparisons to other law enforcement jurisdictions, criminals and opportunities for crime do not adhere to city boundaries, but rather spill over to adjacent (metro) areas. In fact, crime rates and comparison scores tend to be lower in metro areas than in individual cities because many of the more populous cities are geographically small and include central business, retail, and industrial areas where residential population is low. These nonresidential areas contain more victims and targets (for example, commuters, merchandise, vehicles) than do residential areas, so their crime rates appear higher when population is used as the denominator in the calculation of the crime rate. Researchers who study low population areas within cities often use other denominators to determine rates, such as number of vehicles parked in lots for auto theft, number of businesses for commercial burglary, or square footage of retail establishments for shoplifting and theft (Boba, 2008).

However, these variables are not easily obtained for all U.S. cities. By expanding the geographic unit from city to metro area to include business, retail, industrial, and residential areas, using population of the entire area as a basis for determining rate becomes more practical. Thus, combining a major city with its suburbs provides an overall view of how crime is present in interrelated communities. For example, the city of West Palm Beach, FL, has a relatively low population but contains a large number of retail, commercial, and tourist locations and is the principal city in a much larger, more diverse metropolitan area. The table below presents population, comparison scores, and rates for the city of West Palm Beach, FL, and the West Palm Beach, FL, Metropolitan Division (MD) for 2009. As shown, there is a large difference between the city and its metro area for each variable. Thus, city statistics and metro area statistics both serve useful purposes and should be considered together when examining a city situated within a metro area.

The Data and Their Limitations

The data featured in *City Crime Rankings* come from the FBI publication *Crime in the United States,* which is available every fall of a given year (for example, September 2010) and presents information for the previous year (for example, 2009). This report is based on data collected through the Uniform Crime Reporting (UCR) Program, which began in 1930. The purpose of the UCR Program has been to develop reliable information about crime reported to law enforcement that can be used by law enforcement as well as by criminologists, sociologists, legislators, municipal planners, and the media for a variety of research and planning purposes (FBI, 2010). The program is voluntary, yet in 2009 nearly 18,000 city, university and college, county, state, tribal, and federal law enforcement agencies provided information representing 96.3 percent of the population.

Although law enforcement agencies collect common information on crimes reported to and discovered by them, each state has slightly different criminal laws, and each law enforcement agency has its own policies and procedures for recording activity. This makes it very difficult to compare statistics across agencies. To classify criminal activity consistently, the UCR Program was created. This program provides national standards for the uniform classification of crimes and arrests (for further details, visit the FBI's Web site at www.fbi.gov/ucr). Notably, the UCR crime definitions are distinct and do not conform to federal or state laws.

There are well-documented criticisms of the UCR data that must be considered when using these data for any purpose. But while the nature of the data and their limitations should be understood, they should not preclude researchers, practitioners, and others from using the data to understand crime and guide policy decisions. The following is a brief discussion of the major issues and concerns surrounding UCR data.

While individual law enforcement agencies classify reported crimes based on the laws of their own states and jurisdictions, these agencies reclassify these crimes according to UCR definitions when reporting them and provide aggregate counts of a) particular crimes (known as Part I crimes: murder, rape, robbery, aggravated assault, burglary, larceny-theft, motor vehicle theft, and arson) and b) arrests for all crimes. Note that the FBI does not report the aggregate counts of Part II crimes—including simple assault, fraud, prostitution, and DUI—it reports only the arrests that occur. Thus, when statistics about reported violent and property crime are published in this or any other book or article, they are only based on the eight Part I crimes.

In addition, UCR reporting requires the use of a hierarchical coding system that means if two crimes happen during one incident, only one is counted. For example, if one person is the victim of both rape and robbery, only the rape will be counted, or if a car is stolen out of a locked garage, it is considered a

	Population	Comparison Score	Overall Crime Rate	Violent Crime Rate	Property Crime Rate
West Palm Beach, FL	100,763	120.66	6,222.5	898.1	5,324.4
West Palm Beach, FL MD	1,269,333	33.73	4,727.7	633.7	4,094.0

burglary, not a burglary and an auto theft. The UCR Program has specific rules for coding that are not detailed here; however, the result is that the actual number of reported crimes might be underestimated in that the number of incidents is counted and not the number of unique crimes that occur.

The factor of actual versus reported crime is probably the most important one to consider when interpreting statistics based on UCR data. That is, the data provided to the FBI contain only those crimes reported or known to law enforcement as opposed to all crime that has actually occurred. We know from victimization surveys that not all crimes are reported to law enforcement (BJS, 2010) and that different types of crimes are reported at different levels. The Bureau of Justice Statistics estimates from the National Crime Victimization Survey that violent crime is reported 40 to 50 percent of the time and that property crime is reported 30 to 40 percent of the time (BJS, 2010). When UCR data are analyzed, we must recognize that the data do not represent the actual amount of crime. However, if the data are collected accurately and consistently, they can be used, with caution, to make comparisons across geographic areas and over time.

Additional criticisms of the UCR data include inaccuracy due to inputting errors and handling of missing data (Maltz, 1999; Lynch and Jarvis, 2008); pressure on some law enforcement agencies to "doctor" the numbers; and the use of aggregate numbers that mask other factors such as time of day, location, and circumstance of the crime (for example, whether the crime is committed by a stranger or family member). Yet, the UCR data are the most comprehensive and consistently collected data on crime in the United States. In most cases, analysis of UCR data begins the conversation, and additional in-depth analysis of crime in local areas is required to really understand the nature and context of crime problems (Boba, 2008).

Methodology

As noted above, the crimes tracked by the UCR Program include the violent crimes of murder, rape, robbery, and aggravated assault and the property crimes of burglary, larceny-theft, motor vehicle theft, and arson. These are also sometimes known as "Crime Index" offenses; the index is simply the total of the eight main offense categories. The FBI discontinued use of this measure in 2004 because the agency's officials and advisory board of criminologists concluded that the index was no longer a true indicator of crime. The primary concern was that the Crime Index was inflated by a high number of larceny-thefts, which account for nearly 60 percent of reported crime, thereby diminishing the focus on more serious but less frequently reported offenses, such as aggravated assault and rape. The consensus of the FBI and its advisory groups was that the Crime Index no longer served its purpose and that a more meaningful index should be developed.

While the FBI considers how it will replace the Crime Index, *City Crime Rankings* continues to provide total crime numbers, rates, and trends for U.S. cities and metropolitan areas as a service to readers. We offer a cautionary note, however, that in 2009, larceny-theft comprised 59.5 percent of all reported crimes.

Our analyses are conducted on two geographic units, the city and the metropolitan statistical area (MSA) as provided by the FBI. The cities included in these analyses are those with populations of 75,000 or more. According to the FBI in 2009,

> each MSA contains a principal city or urbanized area with a population of at least 50,000 inhabitants. MSAs include the principal city; the county in which the city is located; and other adjacent counties that have, as defined by the OMB, a high degree of economic and social integration with the principal city and county as measured through commuting. In the UCR Program, counties within an MSA are considered metropolitan. In addition, MSAs may cross state boundaries.

The methodology used to produce the statistics presented in this book is fairly straightforward. In the first analysis, a score is calculated for each metropolitan area and city; this score is a summary of the percent differences of the reported crime rate from the national rate of six crime types (excluding larceny-theft and arson). Because this formula is unique to this book, it is described in detail below. The rest of the analyses are simple calculations of reported crime rates per 100,000 population and percent change for one year and five years. Lastly, all the analyses present a ranking that is a simple sort of the values computed for the analysis and numbered from highest to lowest. In case of a tie, the rankings are listed alphabetically. Parentheses indicate negative numbers and rates (except in the data distribution charts). Data reported as "NA" are not available or could not be calculated. The national totals and rates appearing at the top of each table are for the entire United States, including both metropolitan and nonmetropolitan areas. Specific totals for metropolitan areas and larger cities are provided in the Appendix.

"Comparison Score" Methodology

The methodology for determining the city and metro area comparison crime rate rankings involves a multistep process in which the reported crimes per 100,000 population rate are compared to the national reported crimes per 100,000 population rate and then indexed to create a summary score and ranking across six areas of reported violent and property crime. The methodology used for this edition of the book has been used for the past twelve editions and is described here in detail.

Reported crime rates per 100,000 population in 2009 across six crime categories—murder, rape, robbery, aggravated assault, burglary, and motor vehicle theft—were examined in this analysis. Larceny-theft was removed from this analysis because of the aforementioned concerns noted by the FBI and others. Cities with populations of 75,000 or more that reported data for the six categories of crime measured were included in the analysis. There is no population minimum for metropolitan areas. In all, 400 cities and 347 metro areas were included in the results.

The following are steps for the "comparison score" calculation and examples that illustrate the calculations:

1. For each of the six categories of reported crime, the crime rate per 100,000 residents of a city or metropolitan area is calculated from the reported crime and population data provided to the FBI by local law enforcement agencies for a particular type of crime. In the example below, the calculation for murder is 2 divided by 150,000 multiplied by

Example: City A, Population 150,000

	Murder	Rape	Robbery	Aggravated Assault	Burglary	Motor Vehicle Theft
Reported Crime Count	2	39	170	230	1,499	653
Rate per 100,000	1.33	26.00	113.33	153.33	999.33	435.33

Example: City A, Population 150,000

	Murder	Rape	Robbery	Aggravated Assault	Burglary	Motor Vehicle Theft
City Rate	1.33	26.00	113.33	153.33	999.33	435.33
National Rate	5.6	30.0	147.6	283.8	722.5	363.3
Percent Difference	(76.25)	(13.33)	(23.22)	(45.97)	38.32	19.83

Example: City A, Population 150,000

	Murder	Rape	Robbery	Aggravated Assault	Burglary	Motor Vehicle Theft
Percent Difference	(76.25)	(13.33)	(23.22)	(45.97)	38.32	19.83
Weighting Factor	.1667	.1667	.1667	.1667	.1667	.1667
Resulting Score	(12.71)	(2.22)	(3.87)	(7.66)	6.39	3.31

100,000, which results in a 1.33 per capita reported crime rate per 100,000 people for that year.

2. The percent difference between the metro area/city rate and the national rate for each of the six crimes is then computed. The use of percent difference for each crime separately eliminates weighting more frequent crimes more heavily (for example, a city may have 1 murder and 1,500 burglaries). Negative numbers are displayed in parentheses here and throughout the analysis tables. The formula for this calculation is:

$$\frac{\text{Metro Area/City Rate} - \text{National Rate}}{\text{National Rate}} \times 100$$

3. The number is then scaled to be one-sixth of the index to make it comparable to scores in the previous editions of this book. A number of years ago, each of the six crimes was weighted, based on the results of a telephone survey that determined which crimes were of greatest concern to Americans. The polls indicated that most Americans believed crimes such as burglary are more likely to happen in their lives than more serious crimes such as murder. Thus, burglary received the highest weight, and murder received the lowest weight in the formula. In subsequent years, the polling was discontinued and, consequently, the weights were eliminated. However, equal weight is assigned to the crimes during this step in the analysis, so that future scores will be more closely comparable to the scores with the weighted factors.
4. The final comparison score for each metro area and city is the sum of the individual scores for the six crimes. In this case, the sum is –16.76. The interpretation of these scores is that the higher a metro area/city score, the further above the national score; the lower the score, the further below the national score; and a score of zero is equal to the national score.
5. The scores are then sorted from highest to lowest to produce the rankings. Note that the rankings do not indicate the actual difference between the scores, only their order. The 17th annual Metropolitan and Cities Crime Rates tables on pages xx–xxvii provide the results of the metro area and city scores. The Metropolitan and Cities Comparison Score Distribution Analyses for 2009 on pages xiii–xvi provide the results of the distribution of these scores.

This methodology results in a score for each metro area and city that compares its rate to the national rates, providing a means to gauge crime trends in communities.

References

Bauer, L. (2004). *Local Law Enforcement Block Grant Program, 1996–2004*. Technical Report. Washington, DC: Bureau of Justice Statistics.

Boba, R. (2008). *Crime Analysis with Crime Mapping*. Thousand Oaks, CA: SAGE Publications.

Bureau of Justice Statistics [BJS] (2008). *Percent of Total Crime Reported to the Police*. Retrieved from www.ojp.usdoj.gov/bjs/glance/tables/reportingtypetab.htm.

Center for Problem-Oriented Policing (2010). Retrieved from www.popcenter.org.

FBI (2010). *Area Definitions*. Retrieved from www.fbi.gov/ucr/cius2009/about/area_definitions.html.

Lynch, J. P., and Jarvis, J. P. (2008). Missing data and imputation in the Uniform Crime Reports and the effects on national estimates. *Journal of Contemporary Criminal Justice* 24: 69–85.

Maltz, M. (2009). *Bridging gaps in police crime data*. Technical Report. Washington, DC: Bureau of Justice Statistics.

Distribution Analysis

The charts in this section depict the distributions of the comparison scores as well as the individual and collective reported crime rates shown in *City Crime Rankings* to provide a mechanism of comparison beyond the rankings included in each analysis. The histograms in this section illustrate the distribution of values for the comparison score analyses as well as the overall, violent, and property crime rate analyses. Along with each histogram, measures of central tendency, such as median, mean, standard deviation, and minimum and maximum values, are reported to provide further description of each distribution.

In each histogram (formatted as area charts for easier viewing), the values of the scores or rates are shown along the bottom (x-axis) and the frequency of cases (that is, metro areas or cities) are shown along the left (y-axis). The values along the bottom are ranges for which the frequency of cases is totaled. These ranges and frequencies are different for each distribution, in this case, each histogram.

The median indicates the middle value of the distribution, which means that 50 percent of the metro areas or cities have scores or rates above that value, and 50 percent have scores or rates below it. The mean is the average value of the distribution, and the standard deviation, described generally, is the measure of spread of all the values from the mean. The minimum and maximum values are the lowest and highest values of the distribution, respectively.

These statistics are based on a normal curve, so one standard deviation above and below the mean contains 68 percent of the distribution, two standard deviations above and below the mean contain 95 percent of the distribution, and three standard deviations above and below the mean contain 99.7 percent of the distribution. The use of these statistics is purely descriptive, but it does help the reader assess the distribution as a whole as well as illustrate where an individual value sits in terms of all the other values. For example, if a score is two or three standard deviations above or below the mean, it may be considered an outlier because it falls with only 5 percent or .3 percent of the values, respectively.

Figure 1 depicts the comparison scores for metro areas in 2009. The median is –9.0, the mean is –4.5, the standard deviation is 37.9, the minimum value is –78.0, and the maximum value is 169.7. These statistics are interpreted as follows:

- The lowest comparison score for metro areas is –78.0.
- The highest comparison score for metro areas is 169.7.
- The range of scores (maximum minus minimum) is 247.7.
- 50 percent of the metro areas have comparison scores lower than –9.0, and 50 percent have scores higher than –9.0.
- The average comparison score for metro areas is –4.5 and the standard deviation is 37.9.
- 68 percent of the metro areas have scores between –42.4 and 33.4.
- 95 percent of the metro areas have scores between –80.3 and 71.3.
- 99.7 percent of the metro areas have scores between –118.2 and 109.2. (The fact that the lower end of this range (–118.2) and the previous range (–80.3) are less than the minimum value of the distribution (–78.0) indicates the distribution is skewed.)

Assessing the score of –34.54 for San Marcos, CA, for example, reveals that it is in the lower 50 percent of all the scores (below the median) and falls within the first standard deviation of the mean with 68 percent of the other scores (between –42.4 and 33.4).

The remainder of this section presents charts and statistics for both metropolitan areas and cities in the categories listed here:

1. Comparison Score
2. Overall Crime
3. Violent Crime
4. Property Crime

A word of caution: these distribution analysis charts and statistics are provided to help the reader understand the nature of the values within each analysis, but the analyses are still based on data that must be interpreted within the constraints noted earlier. These charts are only descriptions of the data and do not provide predictions or explanations of why these values are different.

Missing Cities and Metropolitan Areas

To be included in the comparative analysis, cities and metro areas must report data for six crime categories: murder, rape,

Figure 1 Metropolitan Areas Comparison Score Distribution Analysis for 2009

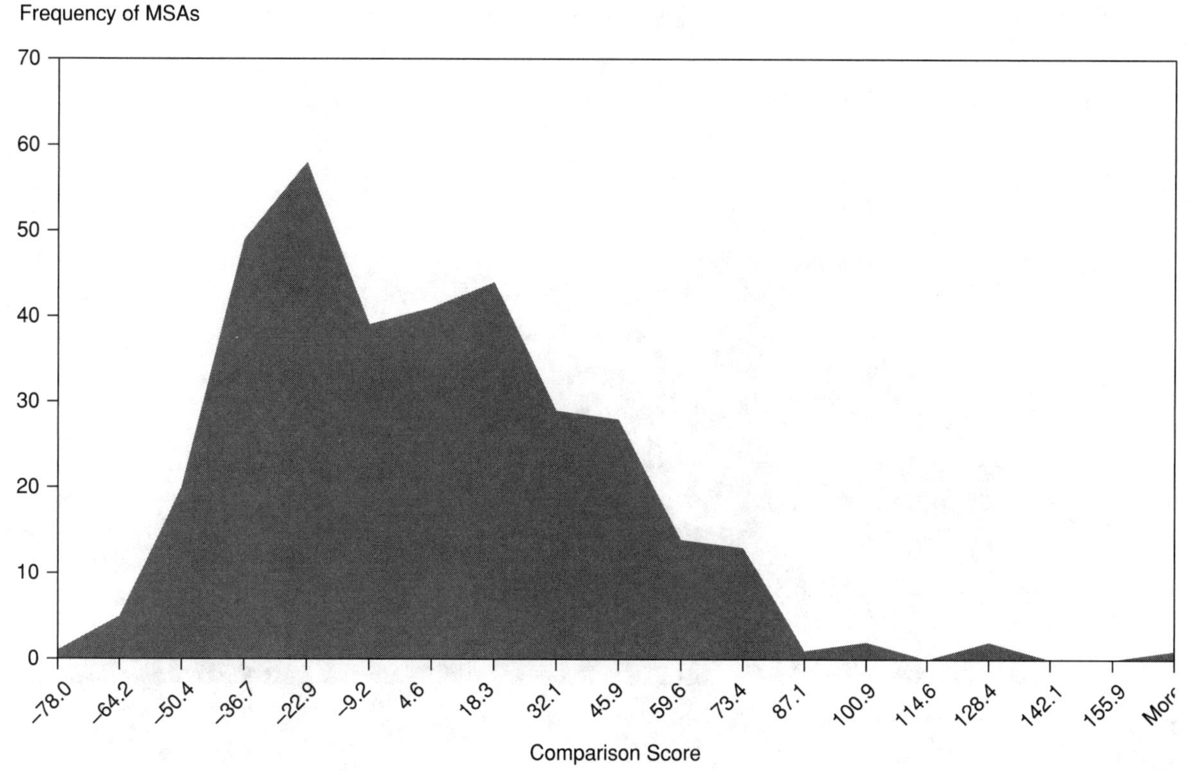

Figure 2 Cities Areas Comparison Score Distribution Analysis for 2009

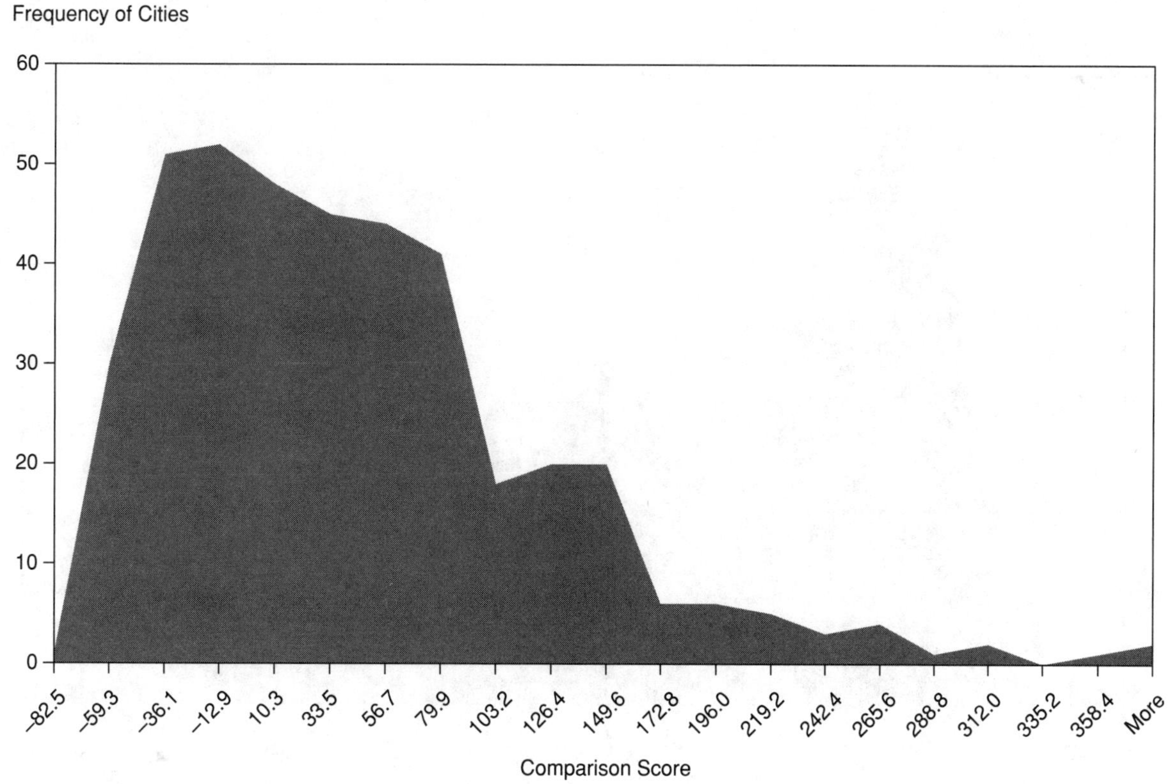

Figure 3 Metropolitan Areas Overall Reported Crime Rate Distribution Analysis for 2009

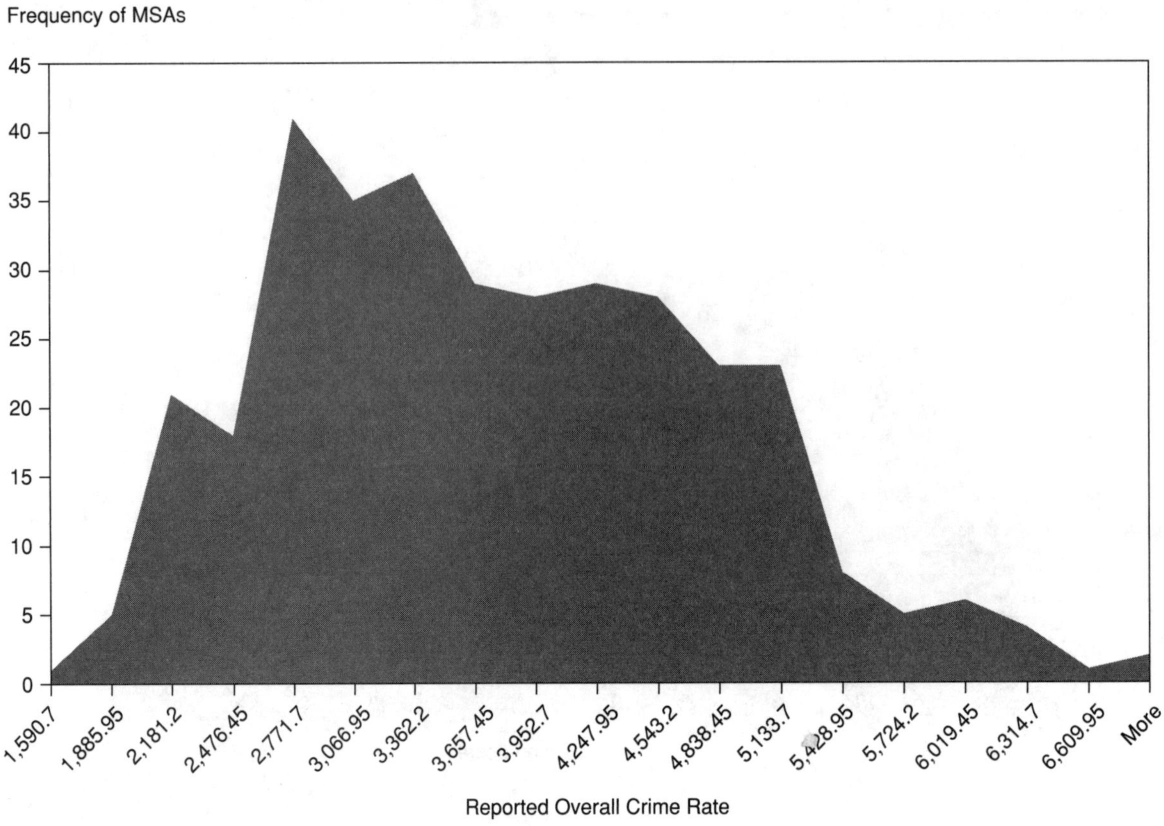

Figure 4 Cities Overall Reported Crime Rate Distribution Analysis for 2009

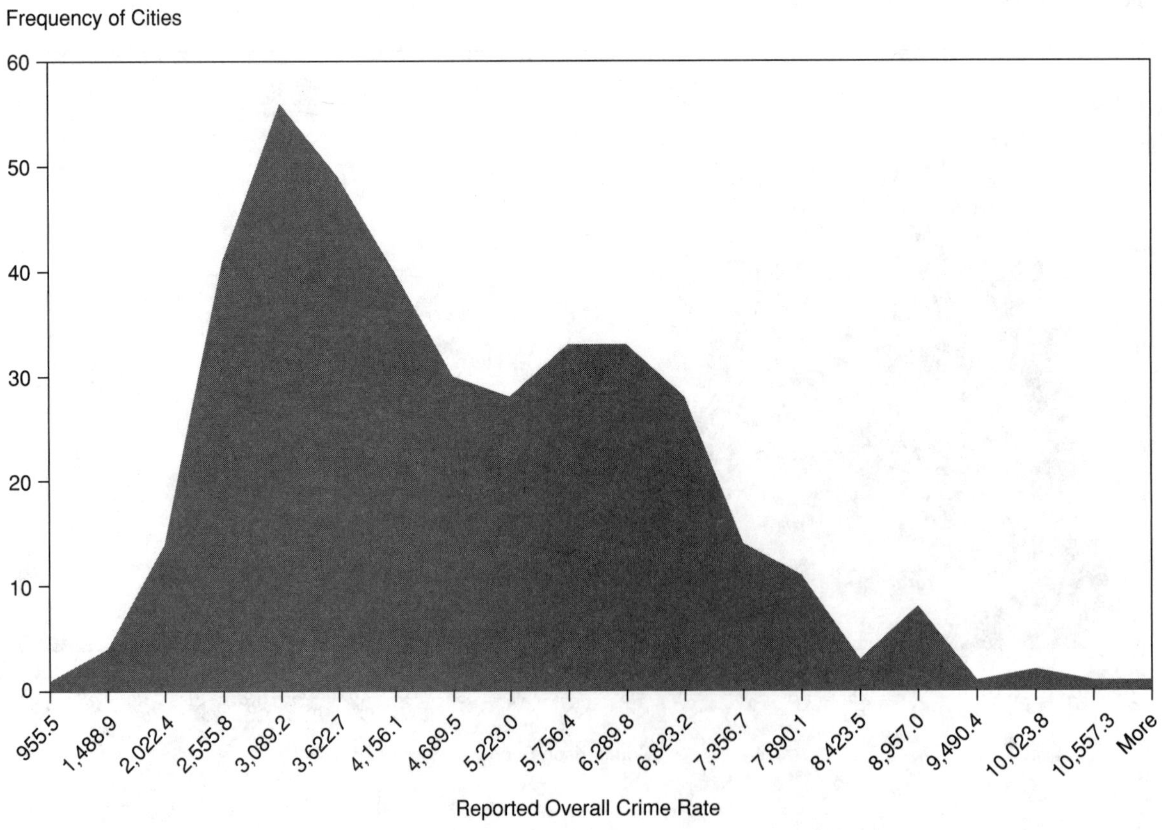

Figure 5 Metropolitan Areas Reported Violent Crime Rate Distribution Analysis for 2009

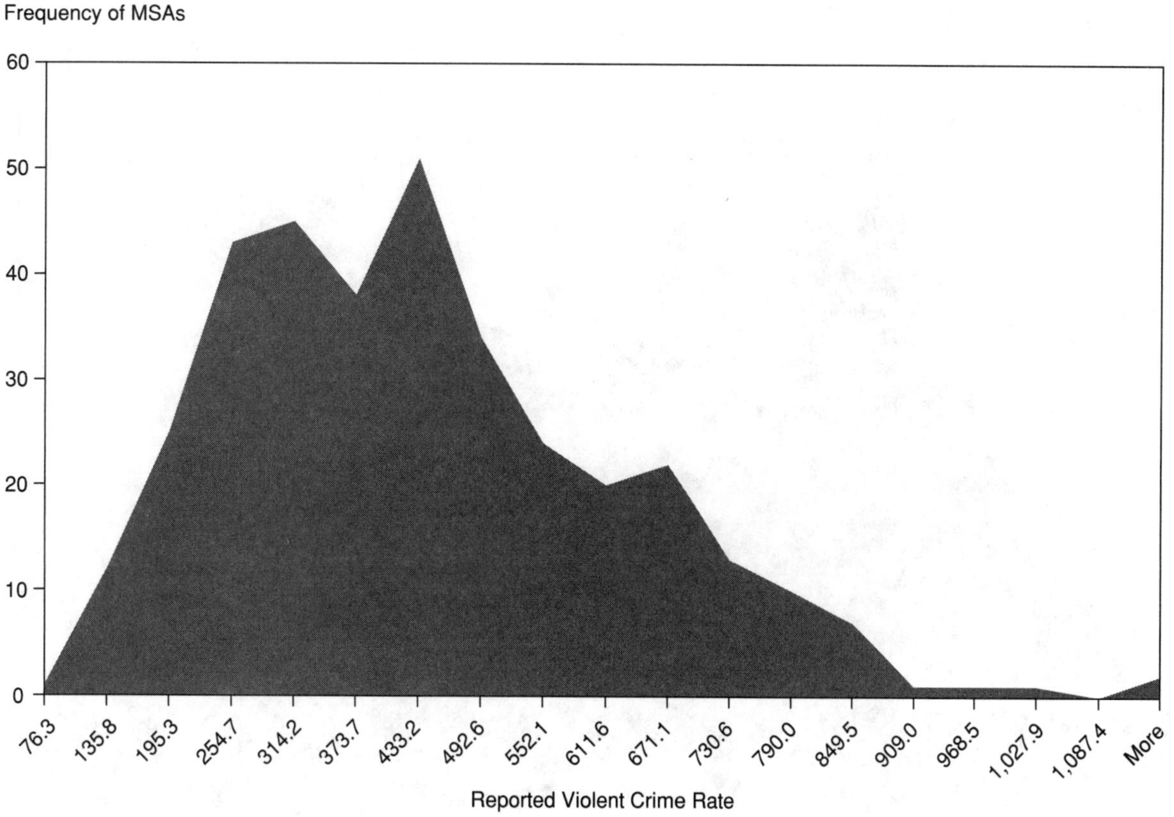

Figure 6 Cities Reported Violent Crime Rate Distribution Analysis for 2009

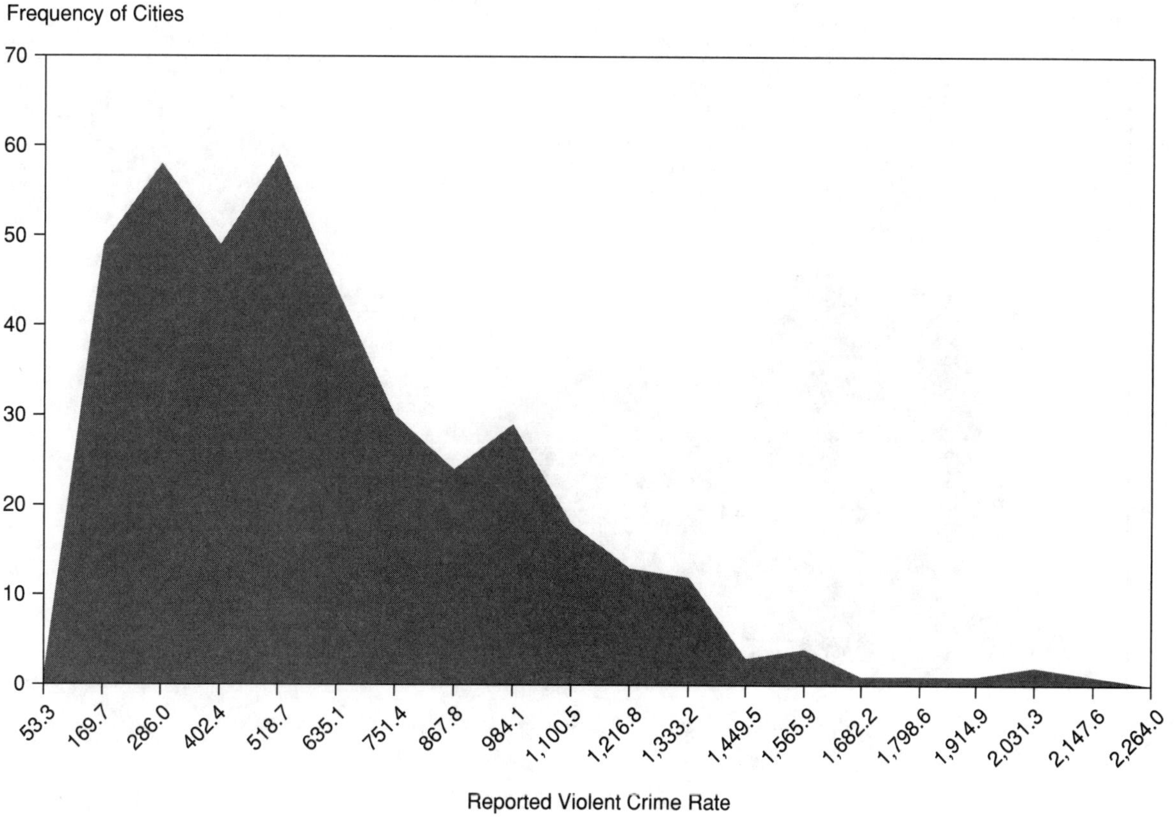

Figure 7 Metropolitan Areas Reported Property Crime Rate Distribution Analysis for 2009

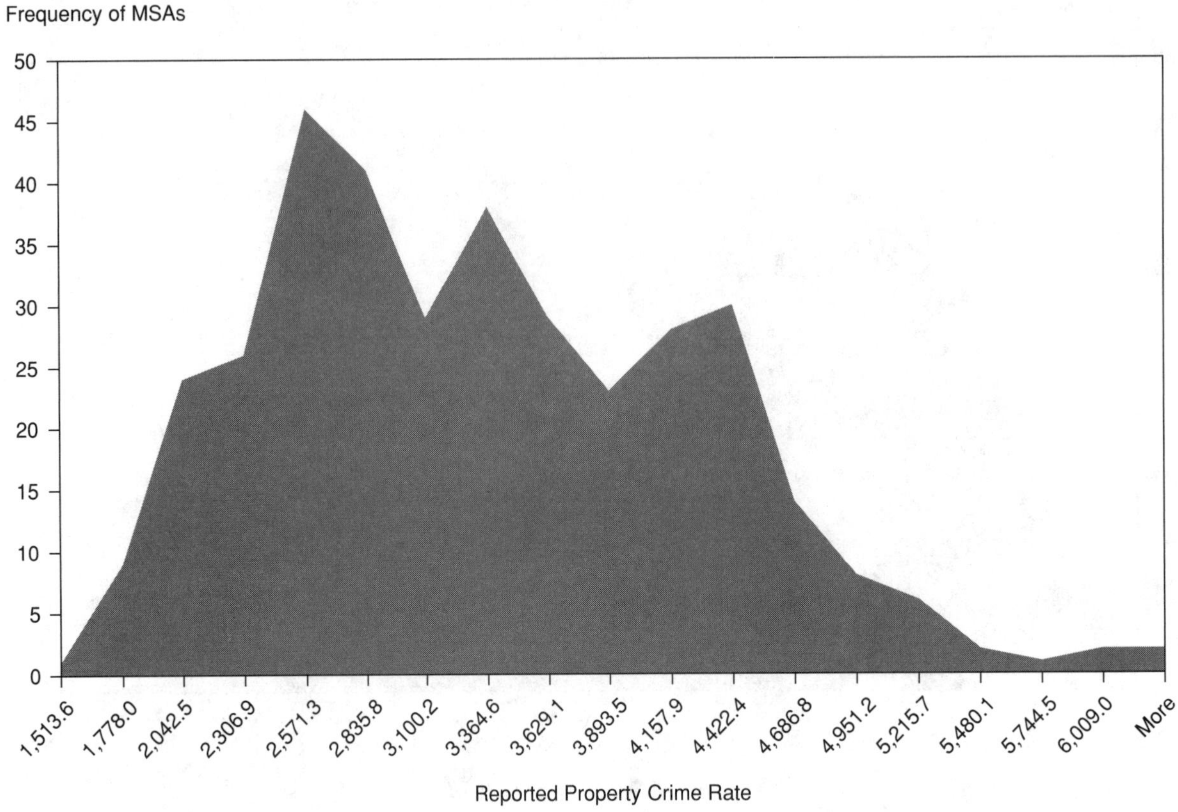

Figure 8 Cities Reported Property Crime Rate Distribution Analysis for 2009

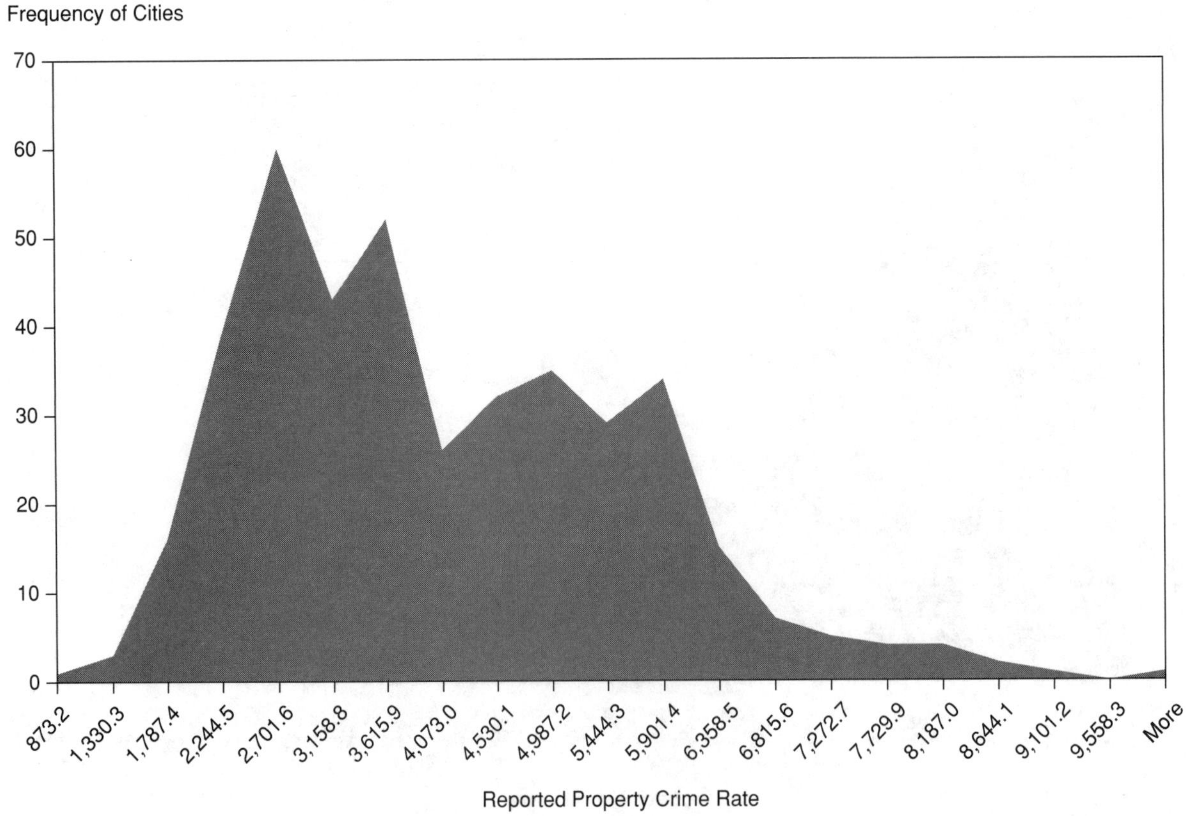

robbery, aggravated assault, burglary, and motor vehicle theft. All metro areas and all cities with populations of 75,000 or more that reported crime data to the FBI were included. A number of cities and metropolitan areas did not report complete crime information for 2009. This information is delineated below.

Missing Cities

The data collection method used by the states of Illinois and Minnesota for the offense of forcible rape did not meet the Federal Bureau of Investigation's Uniform Crime Reporting (UCR) guidelines in 2009 (Rockford, IL; Minneapolis, MN; and St. Paul, MN, are exceptions). Given that the rape numbers were not available, the following cities are not included in the comparative analysis: in Illinois: Aurora, Chicago, Decatur, Elgin, Joliet, Naperville, Peoria, and Springfield; in Minnesota: Bloomington, Duluth, and Rochester.

The FBI did not report crime data for eleven other cities with populations larger than 75,000. Crime statistics for these cities were unavailable for a number of reasons, ranging from general reporting difficulties and computer issues to changes in reporting systems. Below is a list of cities with populations greater than 75,000 (according to the U.S. Census Bureau) for which no information was available in the FBI's 2009 Uniform Crime Report. These cities are: Augusta, GA; Champaign, IL; Cicero, IL; Deltona, FL; Evanston, IL; Greenville, NC; Lowell, MA; Newport News, VA; Parma, OH; Waukegan, IL; and Yakima, WA.

Missing Metropolitan Areas

For crime figures to be reported for a metropolitan area, twelve months of complete data must be submitted for 75 percent of agencies and for the principal city or cities within that area. A number of metropolitan areas are not included in the comparative analysis because of missing data for specific offenses. As noted, forcible rape statistics were not available for metropolitan areas in Illinois and Minnesota. Aggravated assault data were not reported for the Auburn, AL; Decatur, AL; Dothan, AL; El Centro, CA; Ithaca, NY; Oklahoma City, OK; Shreveport-Bossier, LA; and Wilmington, NC, metro areas. Burglary statistics were not available for Charleston–North Charleston, SC; Kansas City, MO-KS; and New Orleans, LA, metro areas. Another group of metropolitan areas was not included in the comparative analysis because the FBI did not report data for these areas in its 2009 *Crime in the United States* report. These metropolitan areas are: Canton-Massillon, OH; Greenville, NC; Greenville-Mauldin-Easley, SC; Hanford-Corcoran, CA; Huntington-Ashland, WV-KY-OH; Johnstown, PA; Joplin, MO; Monroe, LA; Myrtle Beach–North Myrtle Beach–Conway, SC; Parkersburg-Marietta-Vienna, WV-OH; Terre Haute, IN; Virginia Beach–Norfolk–Newport News, VA-NC; Weirton-Steubenville, WV-OH; and Yakima, WA.

An Overview of 2009 Crime

Final data for 2009 reported in the Federal Bureau of Investigation's (FBI) annual *Crime in the United States* show that an estimated 1,318,398 violent crimes and 9,320,971 property crimes were reported to the police. The data also show that incidents of both reported violent and property crimes decreased in 2009 from 2008 by 5.3 percent and 4.6 percent, respectively. In addition, the rate per 100,000 persons decreased from 2008 to 2009 by 6.1 percent for reported violent crime and 4.6 percent for reported property crime. This overview provides definitions, basic facts, and brief summaries about violent crime and property crime, as well as their subcategories, as they occurred in 2009. Also included here is a statistical overview specifically of the police officers serving the nation's cities.

Total Crime and Changes in the UCR Program

Crimes are reported by police agencies to the FBI as part of the Uniform Crime Reporting (UCR) Program. Nearly 18,000 city, county, college and university, state, tribal, and federal law enforcement agencies participated in the program in 2009. Law enforcement agencies active in the program represented 96.3 percent of the total U.S. population in 2009.

Larcenies and thefts accounted for 59.5 percent of crimes, burglaries accounted for 20.7 percent, aggravated assaults for 7.6 percent, motor vehicle thefts for 7.5 percent, robberies for 3.8 percent, forcible rapes for 0.8 percent, and murders for 0.14 percent. The 2009 total crime rate of 3,465.5 crimes per 100,000 people is 5.5 percent lower than in 2008.

Violent Crime

Violent crimes include offenses of murder, forcible rape, robbery, and aggravated assault. A total of 1,318,398 such crimes were committed in 2009. Of these, 61.2 percent were aggravated assaults, 31 percent were robberies, 6.7 percent were forcible rapes, and 1.2 percent were murders. The 2009 national violent crime rate was 429.4 violent crimes per 100,000 population, a 6.1 percent decrease from 2008.

Five- and ten-year trends show the 2009 violent crime rate was 8.4 percent lower than it was in 2005 and 15.2 percent lower than in 2000. Actual numbers of violent crimes dropped 5.2 percent from 2005 levels and were 7.5 percent lower than in 2000.

Among those violent crimes for which weapons information was available, firearms were involved in 67.1 percent of murders, 42.6 percent of robberies, and 20.9 percent of aggravated assaults.

Murder

Murder and nonnegligent manslaughter, as defined by the FBI, involve the willful (nonnegligent) killing of one human being by another. Down 8.1 percent from 2008, the national murder rate in 2009 was 5.0 murders per 100,000 population, or 15,241 murders total. Five-year trends show the 2009 murder rate was 12.1 percent lower than in 2005. A ten-year comparison of murder rates shows a drop of 10.4 percent from levels recorded in 2000.

Of those murders for which complete weapons data were available, 67.1 percent involved firearms. FBI data showed that 14.8 percent of murders were committed in conjunction with felonies or suspected felonies such as robberies, drug deals, and rapes. Among murders for which the relationship between the victim and offender was known, strangers committed slightly more than 22 percent of those murders in 2009. Approximately 77 percent of murder victims were male, 48.2 percent were white, and 48.1 percent were black.

New Orleans, LA, had the highest murder rate in 2009. The city's murder rate of 51.7 murders per 100,000 population was well above the national rate of 5.0 murders per 100,000 population.

Forcible Rape

The FBI defines forcible rape as the carnal knowledge of a female forcibly and against her will. While the definition includes assaults or attempts to commit rape by force or threat of force, it does not include statutory rape (without force) or other sex offenses. There is quite a bit of controversy surrounding this definition. Most states and the District of Columbia collect data for both male and female rapes; however, the UCR data reflects the narrower female-only definition. Sexual attacks on males are counted as aggravated assaults or sex offenses, depending on the circumstances and extent of injuries.

An estimated 56.6 of every 100,000 females in the United States were reported rape victims in 2009. Although the FBI's definition of rape is limited to female victims, the 2009 national rape rate of 28.7 per 100,000 applies to the entire U.S. population, both males and females. This national rape rate dropped 3.5 percent from levels recorded in 2008 and decreased 9.8 percent from 2005 levels.

A total of 88,097 rapes were reported to the FBI by law enforcement agencies in 2009. Of that total, 93.0 percent constituted rapes by force. The remainder included attempts or assaults to commit forcible rape.

Robbery

Robbery is the taking or attempt to take anything by force or threat of force. The 408,217 robberies that occurred in 2009 represented a decrease of 8.0 percent from levels recorded in 2008. The national rate of 133.0 robberies per 100,000 population is lower as well, having decreased 8.8 percent from 2008.

The average dollar loss per robbery was $1,244. Banks lost an average of $4,029 per robbery. Forty-three percent of robberies occurred on streets or highways, 21.5 percent took place in commercial establishments, 16.9 percent were at residences, and 2.2 percent were at banks. The remaining robbery locations were termed "miscellaneous."

Firearms of various types were used in 42.6 percent of robberies in 2009. Strong-arm tactics were used in 41.1 percent of robberies, knives or cutting instruments were used in 7.7 percent, and other dangerous weapons were involved in the remaining 8.7 percent.

Aggravated Assault

Aggravated assault is the unlawful attack by one person upon another for the purpose of inflicting severe bodily injury. This type of assault usually involves the use of a dangerous weapon. The FBI aggravated assault data includes attempts.

The 806,843 aggravated assaults that occurred in 2009 represent a 4.2 percent decrease from 2008 levels. The nation's 2009 rate of 262.8 aggravated assaults per 100,000 population is a 5.0 percent decrease from 2008. Aggravated assault rates fell 9.6 percent from 2005 levels and 18.9 percent from 2000 levels.

Assailants chose a variety of weapons with which to carry out their attacks in 2009. Slightly more than 33.5 percent of assaults were committed with blunt objects (for example, clubs), 26.9 percent with "personal weapons" (for example, hands or feet), 20.9 percent with firearms, and 18.7 percent with knives.

Property Crime

Property crime includes the crimes of burglary, larceny-theft, motor vehicle theft, and arson. These offenses involve the taking of money or property, but there is no force or threat of force against the victims. While arson is considered a property crime, data for arson offenses are not included in this book. The vast majority of crimes committed in the United States are property crimes; in 2009 they accounted for approximately 87.6 percent of all crimes reported.

A total of 9,320,971 property crimes occurred in the United States in 2009. The national property crime rate measured 3,036.1 property crimes per 100,000 population. Property crime decreased from 2008 to 2009 in both number and rate: the number of property crimes fell 4.6 percent from 2008, while the rate decreased 5.5 percent. Five-year trends show that property crime rates decreased 11.5 percent from 2005. A ten-year comparison shows a decline of 16.1 percent from 2000.

Property crimes accounted for an estimated $15.2 billion in losses in 2009. Larceny-thefts accounted for 67.9 percent of all property crimes, burglaries for 23.6 percent, and motor vehicle thefts for 8.5 percent.

Burglary

Burglary is defined as the unlawful entry of a structure to commit a felony or theft. The use of force to gain entry is not required for an offense to be classified as burglary. The FBI tracks data for three types of burglaries: forcible entry, unlawful entry in which no force is used, and attempted forcible entry. Burglary accounted for 23.6 percent of the estimated number of property crimes committed in 2009.

A total of 2,199,125 burglaries were reported in 2009. The year's burglary rate of 716.3 burglaries per 100,000 population is 2.2 percent lower than in 2008. Five- and ten-year trends show that burglary rates have decreased 1.5 percent since 2005 and 1.7 percent since 2000.

Burglaries of residential properties accounted for 72.6 percent of all burglary offenses. Burglary offenses cost victims an estimated $4.6 billion in lost property. The average dollar loss per burglary offense was $2,096.

Larceny-Theft

Larceny-theft is the unlawful taking of property from another person. It includes crimes such as shoplifting, pick-pocketing, purse-snatching, thefts from motor vehicles, thefts of motor vehicle parts and accessories, and bicycle thefts. No use of force, violence, or fraud is involved in these offenses. This category does not include embezzlement, "con" games, forgery, or the writing of "bad" checks.

A total of 6,327,230 thefts occurred in 2009, down 4.0 percent from 2008. This number represents 67.9 percent of property crimes reported for the year. The national rate of 2,060.9

larcenies and thefts per 100,000 population represents a 4.8 percent decrease from 2008 levels. Five- and ten-year trends show that larceny-theft rates have decreased 9.9 percent since 2005 and are down 16.8 percent from 2000.

The average value of property stolen in 2009 was $864. Total losses from larceny-thefts measured $5.5 billion.

Motor Vehicle Theft

The motor vehicle theft category includes the stealing of automobiles, trucks, buses, motorcycles, motor scooters, snowmobiles, etc. The definition does not include the taking of a motor vehicle for temporary use by those persons having lawful access to the vehicle.

A total of 794,616 motor vehicle thefts were committed in 2009. This represents a 17.1 percent decrease from 2008. The national rate of 258.8 vehicles stolen per 100,000 population represents a decrease of 17.8 percent from the prior year.

The total estimated value of these thefts was $5.2 billion, or an average of $6,505 per stolen vehicle. Automobiles were the most frequently stolen vehicle type, accounting for 72.1 percent of all those stolen.

Police Officers

Nationwide, a total of 706,886 sworn police officers were on the job in 2009, with an additional 314,570 civilian employees assisting. This equates to 2.4 full-time officers per 1,000 population.

Only police officers on each city's primary police force are reported in this volume. Many cities have a number of overlapping law enforcement agencies. For example, New York City has its Transit Police, Port Authority Police, and officials in other special law enforcement agencies. Those officers are not covered in *City Crime Rankings*.

Miscellaneous Notes Regarding City and Metro Crime Data

- 2009 crime statistics are not comparable to previous years' data for all cities in Michigan and Kentucky; Des Moines, IA; Little Rock, AR; and Olathe, KS. Accordingly, one- and five-year crime rate trends are not available for these cities.
- 2009 crime statistics are not comparable to previous years' data for these metro areas: Hattiesburg, MS; Lawton, OK; Little Rock, AR; Oklahoma City, OK; Springfield, MO; Sumter, SC; and Wausau, WI. As a result, one- and five-year trends are not available for these metro areas.
- The population estimates reported in *City Crime Rankings 2010–2011* are provided by the FBI. These estimates sometimes differ from those reported by the U.S. Census Bureau.
- Forcible rape data reported to the Uniform Crime Reporting (UCR) Program by the states of Illinois (with the exception of Rockford) and Minnesota (with the exception of Minneapolis and St. Paul) were not in accordance with national UCR guidelines. Therefore, these numbers are not available for cities and metro areas in these two states.
- Larceny-theft theft data were not reported for the cities of Toledo, OH, and Tucson, AZ, because they did not meet UCR guidelines. Thus this information, as well as property crime statistics, is not available for these cities.
- Reporting for one or more crimes did not meet UCR guidelines for the metro areas of Charleston–North Charleston, SC; Decatur, AL; Dothan, AL; El Centro, CA; Hattiesburg, MS; Ithaca, NY; Kansas City, MO-KS; Mobile, AL; New Orleans, LA; Oklahoma City, OK; Shreveport–Bossier City, LA; Toledo, OH; Tucson, AZ; and Wilmington, NC. Thus this information is listed as not available for these areas.
- The Hamilton Township, NJ, data are for the township located in Mercer County.
- Honolulu, HI, has a combined city-county government. Therefore, the population and crime data provided in this book include areas outside the principal city of Honolulu.
- Indianapolis, IN, crime and population data include Marion County.
- Charlotte, NC, crime and population data include Mecklenburg County.
- Louisville, KY, data include offenses reported by the Louisville and Jefferson County Police Departments.
- Las Vegas, NV, has a metropolitan police department, and its crime and population numbers include areas outside of the principal city of Las Vegas.
- Savannah, GA, crime and population data include Chatham County.
- Toms River Township, NJ, was formerly known as Dover Township.
- The population shown for the city of Mobile, AL, includes 55,995 inhabitants from the jurisdiction of the Mobile County Sheriff's Department.
- *City Crime Rankings 2010–2011* also provides rankings for Metropolitan Divisions (MDs). These are subdivisions of eleven large Metropolitan Statistical Areas (MSAs).

2010 Metropolitan Crime Rate Rankings*

RANK	METROPOLITAN AREA	SCORE
274	Abilene, TX	26.81
201	Akron, OH	(0.06)
73	Albany-Schenectady-Troy, NY	(37.42)
286	Albany, GA	32.00
328	Albuquerque, NM	58.95
273	Alexandria, LA	26.55
66	Allentown, PA-NJ	(40.32)
56	Altoona, PA	(41.42)
296	Amarillo, TX	38.14
37	Ames, IA	(46.94)
330	Anchorage, AK	61.64
83	Anderson, IN	(34.82)
283	Anderson, SC	31.37
146	Ann Arbor, MI	(20.50)
320	Anniston-Oxford, AL	53.79
5	Appleton, WI	(67.82)
95	Asheville, NC	(32.40)
215	Athens-Clarke County, GA	4.94
256	Atlanta, GA	17.89
239	Atlantic City, NJ	12.43
NA	Auburn, AL**	NA
302	Augusta, GA-SC	41.61
147	Austin-Round Rock, TX	(19.93)
327	Bakersfield, CA	57.73
314	Baltimore-Towson, MD	44.93
20	Bangor, ME	(55.97)
174	Barnstable Town, MA	(9.03)
323	Baton Rouge, LA	55.56
326	Battle Creek, MI	56.77
167	Bay City, MI	(12.53)
270	Beaumont-Port Arthur, TX	25.47
120	Bellingham, WA	(25.94)
26	Bend, OR	(51.82)
38	Bethesda-Frederick, MD M.D.	(46.74)
76	Billings, MT	(36.35)
64	Binghamton, NY	(40.33)
313	Birmingham-Hoover, AL	44.91
53	Bismarck, ND	(43.22)
102	Blacksburg, VA	(29.64)
108	Bloomington, IN	(28.87)
46	Boise City-Nampa, ID	(45.29)
110	Boston (greater), MA-NH	(27.89)
199	Boston-Quincy, MA M.D.	(0.52)
48	Boulder, CO	(44.93)
134	Bowling Green, KY	(22.87)
186	Bremerton-Silverdale, WA	(3.91)
88	Bridgeport-Stamford, CT	(33.60)
145	Brownsville-Harlingen, TX	(20.83)
337	Brunswick, GA	70.06
221	Buffalo-Niagara Falls, NY	7.42
21	Burlington-South Burlington, VT	(54.92)
190	Burlington, NC	(2.49)
33	Cambridge-Newton, MA M.D.	(48.93)
123	Camden, NJ M.D.	(25.08)
203	Cape Coral-Fort Myers, FL	1.58
99	Cape Girardeau, MO-IL	(29.98)
24	Carson City, NV	(53.55)
78	Casper, WY	(35.69)
42	Cedar Rapids, IA	(45.81)
NA	Charleston-North Charleston, SC**	NA
222	Charleston, WV	7.50
261	Charlotte-Gastonia, NC-SC	19.81
43	Charlottesville, VA	(45.74)
250	Chattanooga, TN-GA	15.42
109	Cheyenne, WY	(28.04)
230	Chico, CA	9.59
175	Cincinnati-Middletown, OH-KY-IN	(8.69)
228	Clarksville, TN-KY	9.28
251	Cleveland-Elyria-Mentor, OH	15.82
178	Cleveland, TN	(7.48)
156	Coeur d'Alene, ID	(17.25)
192	College Station-Bryan, TX	(1.35)
225	Colorado Springs, CO	8.57
103	Columbia, MO	(29.63)
306	Columbia, SC	42.49
325	Columbus, GA-AL	56.35
13	Columbus, IN	(59.23)
269	Columbus, OH	25.17
277	Corpus Christi, TX	28.44
14	Corvallis, OR	(59.11)
112	Crestview-Fort Walton Beach, FL	(27.13)
127	Cumberland, MD-WV	(24.07)
243	Dallas (greater), TX	13.74
255	Dallas-Plano-Irving, TX M.D.	17.55
67	Dalton, GA	(39.92)
NA	Danville, IL**	NA
128	Danville, VA	(24.00)
207	Dayton, OH	1.99
NA	Decatur, AL**	NA
NA	Decatur, IL**	NA
237	Deltona-Daytona Beach, FL	11.43
196	Denver-Aurora, CO	(0.91)
100	Des Moines-West Des Moines, IA	(29.86)
324	Detroit (greater), MI	55.74
347	Detroit-Livonia-Dearborn, MI M.D.	169.66
NA	Dothan, AL**	NA
238	Dover, DE	11.83
79	Dubuque, IA	(35.67)
NA	Duluth, MN-WI**	NA
242	Durham-Chapel Hill, NC	13.41
7	Eau Claire, WI	(63.86)
8	Edison, NJ M.D.	(63.56)
NA	El Centro, CA**	NA
151	El Paso, TX	(18.02)
32	Elizabethtown, KY	(49.20)
92	Elkhart-Goshen, IN	(33.28)
29	Elmira, NY	(49.98)
114	Erie, PA	(27.00)
179	Eugene-Springfield, OR	(7.16)
61	Evansville, IN-KY	(40.63)
NA	Fargo, ND-MN**	NA
307	Farmington, NM	42.74
121	Fayetteville, AR-MO	(25.51)
331	Fayetteville, NC	62.29
152	Flagstaff, AZ	(17.74)
341	Flint, MI	73.08
129	Florence-Muscle Shoals, AL	(23.92)
333	Florence, SC	64.60
15	Fond du Lac, WI	(58.81)
98	Fort Collins-Loveland, CO	(30.08)
244	Fort Lauderdale, FL M.D.	13.76
173	Fort Smith, AR-OK	(9.11)
131	Fort Wayne, IN	(23.21)
216	Fort Worth-Arlington, TX M.D.	5.76
293	Fresno, CA	35.29
198	Gadsden, AL	(0.70)
304	Gainesville, FL	42.16
57	Gainesville, GA	(41.39)
1	Glens Falls, NY	(77.96)
287	Goldsboro, NC	32.67
NA	Grand Forks, ND-MN**	NA
142	Grand Junction, CO	(21.24)
158	Grand Rapids-Wyoming, MI	(16.75)
136	Great Falls, MT	(22.39)
86	Greeley, CO	(34.13)
34	Green Bay, WI	(48.61)
246	Greensboro-High Point, NC	14.27
184	Gulfport-Biloxi, MS	(5.45)
35	Hagerstown-Martinsburg, MD-WV	(47.43)
122	Harrisburg-Carlisle, PA	(25.30)
10	Harrisonburg, VA	(60.66)
139	Hartford, CT	(22.11)
152	Hattiesburg, MS	(17.74)
155	Hickory, NC	(17.66)
258	Hinesville, GA	19.13
41	Holland-Grand Haven, MI	(46.16)
160	Honolulu, HI	(15.70)
342	Hot Springs, AR	78.80
193	Houma, LA	(1.24)
321	Houston, TX	54.38
226	Huntsville, AL	8.75
70	Idaho Falls, ID	(39.17)
295	Indianapolis, IN	37.00
55	Iowa City, IA	(42.79)
NA	Ithaca, NY**	NA
305	Jacksonville, FL	42.23
240	Jacksonville, NC	12.50
208	Jackson, MI	2.83
297	Jackson, MS	38.61
335	Jackson, TN	67.83
80	Janesville, WI	(35.59)
68	Jefferson City, MO	(39.76)
141	Johnson City, TN	(21.59)
204	Jonesboro, AR	1.69
233	Kalamazoo-Portage, MI	10.96
NA	Kansas City, MO-KS**	NA
93	Kennewick-Pasco-Richland, WA	(33.13)
166	Killeen-Temple-Fort Hood, TX	(12.77)
157	Kingsport, TN-VA	(16.84)
16	Kingston, NY	(58.74)
219	Knoxville, TN	6.92
45	Kokomo, IN	(45.50)
NA	La Crosse, WI-MN**	NA
36	Lafayette, IN	(47.13)
280	Lafayette, LA	29.49
344	Lake Charles, LA	89.90
111	Lake Havasu City-Kingman, AZ	(27.71)
217	Lakeland, FL	5.85
22	Lancaster, PA	(54.71)
163	Lansing-East Lansing, MI	(14.18)

Note: All listings are for Metropolitan Statistical Areas (M.S.A.s) except for those ending with "M.D." Listings with "M.D." are Metropolitan Divisions which are smaller parts of eleven large M.S.A.s. See explanatory note at beginning of metropolitan area section.

Alpha Order - Metro Area (continued)

RANK	METROPOLITAN AREA	SCORE
315	Laredo, TX	46.14
168	Las Cruces, NM	(11.93)
340	Las Vegas-Paradise, NV	71.34
165	Lawrence, KS	(13.37)
343	Lawton, OK	89.72
28	Lebanon, PA	(50.06)
23	Lewiston-Auburn, ME	(54.03)
51	Lewiston, ID-WA	(44.39)
170	Lexington-Fayette, KY	(9.80)
312	Lima, OH	44.81
137	Lincoln, NE	(22.36)
339	Little Rock, AR	70.73
2	Logan, UT-ID	(73.37)
310	Longview, TX	43.46
171	Longview, WA	(9.79)
275	Los Angeles County, CA M.D.	27.37
236	Los Angeles (greater), CA	11.40
195	Louisville, KY-IN	(1.18)
318	Lubbock, TX	50.77
49	Lynchburg, VA	(44.87)
299	Macon, GA	40.58
183	Madera, CA	(5.47)
31	Madison, WI	(49.51)
39	Manchester-Nashua, NH	(46.50)
135	Manhattan, KS	(22.52)
NA	Mankato-North Mankato, MN**	NA
124	Mansfield, OH	(24.89)
234	McAllen-Edinburg-Mission, TX	11.23
19	Medford, OR	(56.02)
345	Memphis, TN-MS-AR	117.58
311	Merced, CA	44.16
300	Miami (greater), FL	40.86
332	Miami-Dade County, FL M.D.	63.89
104	Michigan City-La Porte, IN	(29.48)
161	Midland, TX	(14.86)
230	Milwaukee, WI	9.59
NA	Minneapolis-St. Paul, MN-WI**	NA
51	Missoula, MT	(44.39)
329	Mobile, AL	59.76
319	Modesto, CA	51.55
133	Monroe, MI	(22.97)
281	Montgomery, AL	31.03
62	Morgantown, WV	(40.54)
118	Morristown, TN	(26.31)
143	Mount Vernon-Anacortes, WA	(21.22)
197	Muncie, IN	(0.90)
211	Muskegon-Norton Shores, MI	3.06
84	Napa, CA	(34.39)
71	Naples-Marco Island, FL	(38.78)
264	Nashville-Davidson, TN	21.15
11	Nassau-Suffolk, NY M.D.	(60.17)
180	New Haven-Milford, CT	(6.66)
NA	New Orleans, LA**	NA
96	New York (greater), NY-NJ-PA	(32.09)
130	New York-W. Plains NY-NJ M.D.	(23.73)
181	Newark-Union, NJ-PA M.D.	(6.14)
182	Niles-Benton Harbor, MI	(5.55)
241	North Port-Bradenton-Sarasota, FL	13.34
149	Norwich-New London, CT	(18.95)
336	Oakland-Fremont, CA M.D.	68.46
206	Ocala, FL	1.79
107	Ocean City, NJ	(28.93)
276	Odessa, TX	27.42

RANK	METROPOLITAN AREA	SCORE
27	Ogden-Clearfield, UT	(50.22)
NA	Oklahoma City, OK**	NA
119	Olympia, WA	(26.17)
208	Omaha-Council Bluffs, NE-IA	2.83
289	Orlando, FL	33.20
12	Oshkosh-Neenah, WI	(59.38)
54	Owensboro, KY	(43.18)
60	Oxnard-Thousand Oaks, CA	(40.95)
235	Palm Bay-Melbourne, FL	11.25
87	Palm Coast, FL	(33.97)
272	Panama City-Lynn Haven, FL	26.12
194	Pascagoula, MS	(1.22)
85	Peabody, MA M.D.	(34.29)
263	Pensacola, FL	20.53
254	Philadelphia (greater) PA-NJ-MD-DE	17.25
282	Philadelphia, PA M.D.	31.08
232	Phoenix-Mesa-Scottsdale, AZ	10.26
346	Pine Bluff, AR	123.32
105	Pittsburgh, PA	(29.13)
126	Pittsfield, MA	(24.37)
47	Pocatello, ID	(45.20)
162	Port St. Lucie, FL	(14.36)
140	Portland-Vancouver, OR-WA	(21.98)
30	Portland, ME	(49.85)
25	Poughkeepsie, NY	(53.50)
40	Prescott, AZ	(46.23)
150	Providence-New Bedford, RI-MA	(18.77)
4	Provo-Orem, UT	(68.08)
265	Pueblo, CO	21.31
63	Punta Gorda, FL	(40.47)
101	Racine, WI	(29.69)
90	Raleigh-Cary, NC	(33.51)
202	Rapid City, SD	0.17
116	Reading, PA	(26.42)
253	Redding, CA	17.15
218	Reno-Sparks, NV	5.96
148	Richmond, VA	(19.89)
227	Riverside-San Bernardino, CA	9.24
97	Roanoke, VA	(30.25)
NA	Rochester, MN**	NA
106	Rochester, NY	(29.08)
6	Rockingham County, NH M.D.	(65.20)
317	Rocky Mount, NC	47.81
169	Rome, GA	(10.32)
260	Sacramento, CA	19.31
322	Saginaw, MI	54.90
115	Salem, OR	(26.59)
316	Salinas, CA	46.29
303	Salisbury, MD	41.65
212	Salt Lake City, UT	3.09
267	San Angelo, TX	23.18
278	San Antonio, TX	29.03
189	San Diego, CA	(2.74)
309	San Francisco (greater), CA	43.40
224	San Francisco-S. Mateo, CA M.D.	8.34
144	San Jose, CA	(20.95)
74	San Luis Obispo, CA	(37.25)
69	Sandusky, OH	(39.58)
58	Santa Ana-Anaheim, CA M.D.	(41.29)
154	Santa Barbara-Santa Maria, CA	(17.68)
210	Santa Cruz-Watsonville, CA	3.01
301	Santa Fe, NM	40.95
125	Santa Rosa-Petaluma, CA	(24.53)

RANK	METROPOLITAN AREA	SCORE
290	Savannah, GA	33.28
82	Scranton--Wilkes-Barre, PA	(35.37)
187	Seattle-Bellevue-Everett, WA M.D.	(3.50)
214	Seattle-Tacoma-Bellevue, WA	4.72
117	Sebastian-Vero Beach, FL	(26.36)
17	Sheboygan, WI	(58.68)
81	Sherman-Denison, TX	(35.56)
NA	Shreveport-Bossier City, LA**	NA
75	Sioux City, IA-NE-SD	(37.18)
89	Sioux Falls, SD	(33.58)
229	South Bend-Mishawaka, IN-MI	9.41
262	Spartanburg, SC	19.91
205	Spokane, WA	1.70
220	Springfield, MA	7.23
177	Springfield, MO	(8.03)
191	Springfield, OH	(1.66)
3	State College, PA	(69.34)
334	Stockton, CA	66.33
NA	St. Cloud, MN**	NA
9	St. George, UT	(61.54)
159	St. Joseph, MO-KS	(16.37)
NA	St. Louis, MO-IL**	NA
298	Sumter, SC	38.92
91	Syracuse, NY	(33.30)
284	Tacoma, WA M.D.	31.41
292	Tallahassee, FL	35.16
252	Tampa-St Petersburg, FL	16.58
338	Texarkana, TX-Texarkana, AR	70.23
294	Toledo, OH	36.05
249	Topeka, KS	15.34
164	Trenton-Ewing, NJ	(13.49)
259	Tucson, AZ	19.21
308	Tulsa, OK	43.30
268	Tuscaloosa, AL	23.55
200	Tyler, TX	(0.29)
50	Utica-Rome, NY	(44.69)
257	Valdosta, GA	18.09
285	Vallejo-Fairfield, CA	31.47
247	Victoria, TX	14.60
213	Vineland, NJ	3.18
291	Visalia-Porterville, CA	34.48
271	Waco, TX	25.71
138	Warner Robins, GA	(22.20)
94	Warren-Farmington Hills, MI M.D.	(32.88)
185	Washington (greater) DC-VA-MD-WV	(3.96)
223	Washington, DC-VA-MD-WV M.D.	7.76
172	Waterloo-Cedar Falls, IA	(9.25)
18	Wausau, WI	(56.85)
59	Wenatchee, WA	(41.28)
288	West Palm Beach, FL M.D.	32.73
64	Wheeling, WV-OH	(40.33)
245	Wichita Falls, TX	14.16
279	Wichita, KS	29.41
44	Williamsport, PA	(45.51)
248	Wilmington, DE-MD-NJ M.D.	15.28
NA	Wilmington, NC**	NA
72	Winchester, VA-WV	(37.74)
266	Winston-Salem, NC	21.92
112	Worcester, MA	(27.13)
77	York-Hanover, PA	(35.73)
188	Youngstown, OH-PA	(3.37)
132	Yuba City, CA	(23.03)
176	Yuma, AZ	(8.57)

Source: CQ Press using reported data from the F.B.I. "Crime in the United States 2009"

*Includes murder, rape, robbery, aggravated assault, burglary, and motor vehicle theft. A negative score (in parentheses) indicates a composite crime number below the national rate, a positive number is above the national rate. **Not available.

Rank Order - Metro Area

2010 Metropolitan Crime Rate Rankings* (continued)

RANK	METROPOLITAN AREA	SCORE
1	Glens Falls, NY	(77.96)
2	Logan, UT-ID	(73.37)
3	State College, PA	(69.34)
4	Provo-Orem, UT	(68.08)
5	Appleton, WI	(67.82)
6	Rockingham County, NH M.D.	(65.20)
7	Eau Claire, WI	(63.86)
8	Edison, NJ M.D.	(63.56)
9	St. George, UT	(61.54)
10	Harrisonburg, VA	(60.66)
11	Nassau-Suffolk, NY M.D.	(60.17)
12	Oshkosh-Neenah, WI	(59.38)
13	Columbus, IN	(59.23)
14	Corvallis, OR	(59.11)
15	Fond du Lac, WI	(58.81)
16	Kingston, NY	(58.74)
17	Sheboygan, WI	(58.68)
18	Wausau, WI	(56.85)
19	Medford, OR	(56.02)
20	Bangor, ME	(55.97)
21	Burlington-South Burlington, VT	(54.92)
22	Lancaster, PA	(54.71)
23	Lewiston-Auburn, ME	(54.03)
24	Carson City, NV	(53.55)
25	Poughkeepsie, NY	(53.50)
26	Bend, OR	(51.82)
27	Ogden-Clearfield, UT	(50.22)
28	Lebanon, PA	(50.06)
29	Elmira, NY	(49.98)
30	Portland, ME	(49.85)
31	Madison, WI	(49.51)
32	Elizabethtown, KY	(49.20)
33	Cambridge-Newton, MA M.D.	(48.93)
34	Green Bay, WI	(48.61)
35	Hagerstown-Martinsburg, MD-WV	(47.43)
36	Lafayette, IN	(47.13)
37	Ames, IA	(46.94)
38	Bethesda-Frederick, MD M.D.	(46.74)
39	Manchester-Nashua, NH	(46.50)
40	Prescott, AZ	(46.23)
41	Holland-Grand Haven, MI	(46.16)
42	Cedar Rapids, IA	(45.81)
43	Charlottesville, VA	(45.74)
44	Williamsport, PA	(45.51)
45	Kokomo, IN	(45.50)
46	Boise City-Nampa, ID	(45.29)
47	Pocatello, ID	(45.20)
48	Boulder, CO	(44.93)
49	Lynchburg, VA	(44.87)
50	Utica-Rome, NY	(44.69)
51	Lewiston, ID-WA	(44.39)
51	Missoula, MT	(44.39)
53	Bismarck, ND	(43.22)
54	Owensboro, KY	(43.18)
55	Iowa City, IA	(42.79)
56	Altoona, PA	(41.42)
57	Gainesville, GA	(41.39)
58	Santa Ana-Anaheim, CA M.D.	(41.29)
59	Wenatchee, WA	(41.28)
60	Oxnard-Thousand Oaks, CA	(40.95)
61	Evansville, IN-KY	(40.63)
62	Morgantown, WV	(40.54)
63	Punta Gorda, FL	(40.47)
64	Binghamton, NY	(40.33)
64	Wheeling, WV-OH	(40.33)
66	Allentown, PA-NJ	(40.32)
67	Dalton, GA	(39.92)
68	Jefferson City, MO	(39.76)
69	Sandusky, OH	(39.58)
70	Idaho Falls, ID	(39.17)
71	Naples-Marco Island, FL	(38.78)
72	Winchester, VA-WV	(37.74)
73	Albany-Schenectady-Troy, NY	(37.42)
74	San Luis Obispo, CA	(37.25)
75	Sioux City, IA-NE-SD	(37.18)
76	Billings, MT	(36.35)
77	York-Hanover, PA	(35.73)
78	Casper, WY	(35.69)
79	Dubuque, IA	(35.67)
80	Janesville, WI	(35.59)
81	Sherman-Denison, TX	(35.56)
82	Scranton--Wilkes-Barre, PA	(35.37)
83	Anderson, IN	(34.82)
84	Napa, CA	(34.39)
85	Peabody, MA M.D.	(34.29)
86	Greeley, CO	(34.13)
87	Palm Coast, FL	(33.97)
88	Bridgeport-Stamford, CT	(33.60)
89	Sioux Falls, SD	(33.58)
90	Raleigh-Cary, NC	(33.51)
91	Syracuse, NY	(33.30)
92	Elkhart-Goshen, IN	(33.28)
93	Kennewick-Pasco-Richland, WA	(33.13)
94	Warren-Farmington Hills, MI M.D.	(32.88)
95	Asheville, NC	(32.40)
96	New York (greater), NY-NJ-PA	(32.09)
97	Roanoke, VA	(30.25)
98	Fort Collins-Loveland, CO	(30.08)
99	Cape Girardeau, MO-IL	(29.98)
100	Des Moines-West Des Moines, IA	(29.86)
101	Racine, WI	(29.69)
102	Blacksburg, VA	(29.64)
103	Columbia, MO	(29.63)
104	Michigan City-La Porte, IN	(29.48)
105	Pittsburgh, PA	(29.13)
106	Rochester, NY	(29.08)
107	Ocean City, NJ	(28.93)
108	Bloomington, IN	(28.87)
109	Cheyenne, WY	(28.04)
110	Boston (greater), MA-NH	(27.89)
111	Lake Havasu City-Kingman, AZ	(27.71)
112	Crestview-Fort Walton Beach, FL	(27.13)
112	Worcester, MA	(27.13)
114	Erie, PA	(27.00)
115	Salem, OR	(26.59)
116	Reading, PA	(26.42)
117	Sebastian-Vero Beach, FL	(26.36)
118	Morristown, TN	(26.31)
119	Olympia, WA	(26.17)
120	Bellingham, WA	(25.94)
121	Fayetteville, AR-MO	(25.51)
122	Harrisburg-Carlisle, PA	(25.30)
123	Camden, NJ M.D.	(25.08)
124	Mansfield, OH	(24.89)
125	Santa Rosa-Petaluma, CA	(24.53)
126	Pittsfield, MA	(24.37)
127	Cumberland, MD-WV	(24.07)
128	Danville, VA	(24.00)
129	Florence-Muscle Shoals, AL	(23.92)
130	New York-W. Plains NY-NJ M.D.	(23.73)
131	Fort Wayne, IN	(23.21)
132	Yuba City, CA	(23.03)
133	Monroe, MI	(22.97)
134	Bowling Green, KY	(22.87)
135	Manhattan, KS	(22.52)
136	Great Falls, MT	(22.39)
137	Lincoln, NE	(22.36)
138	Warner Robins, GA	(22.20)
139	Hartford, CT	(22.11)
140	Portland-Vancouver, OR-WA	(21.98)
141	Johnson City, TN	(21.59)
142	Grand Junction, CO	(21.24)
143	Mount Vernon-Anacortes, WA	(21.22)
144	San Jose, CA	(20.95)
145	Brownsville-Harlingen, TX	(20.83)
146	Ann Arbor, MI	(20.50)
147	Austin-Round Rock, TX	(19.93)
148	Richmond, VA	(19.89)
149	Norwich-New London, CT	(18.95)
150	Providence-New Bedford, RI-MA	(18.77)
151	El Paso, TX	(18.02)
152	Flagstaff, AZ	(17.74)
152	Hattiesburg, MS	(17.74)
154	Santa Barbara-Santa Maria, CA	(17.68)
155	Hickory, NC	(17.66)
156	Coeur d'Alene, ID	(17.25)
157	Kingsport, TN-VA	(16.84)
158	Grand Rapids-Wyoming, MI	(16.75)
159	St. Joseph, MO-KS	(16.37)
160	Honolulu, HI	(15.70)
161	Midland, TX	(14.86)
162	Port St. Lucie, FL	(14.36)
163	Lansing-East Lansing, MI	(14.18)
164	Trenton-Ewing, NJ	(13.49)
165	Lawrence, KS	(13.37)
166	Killeen-Temple-Fort Hood, TX	(12.77)
167	Bay City, MI	(12.53)
168	Las Cruces, NM	(11.93)
169	Rome, GA	(10.32)
170	Lexington-Fayette, KY	(9.80)
171	Longview, WA	(9.79)
172	Waterloo-Cedar Falls, IA	(9.25)
173	Fort Smith, AR-OK	(9.11)
174	Barnstable Town, MA	(9.03)
175	Cincinnati-Middletown, OH-KY-IN	(8.69)
176	Yuma, AZ	(8.57)
177	Springfield, MO	(8.03)
178	Cleveland, TN	(7.48)
179	Eugene-Springfield, OR	(7.16)
180	New Haven-Milford, CT	(6.66)

Note: All listings are for Metropolitan Statistical Areas (M.S.A.s) except for those ending with "M.D." Listings with "M.D." are Metropolitan Divisions which are smaller parts of eleven large M.S.A.s. See explanatory note at beginning of metropolitan area section.

RANK	METROPOLITAN AREA	SCORE
181	Newark-Union, NJ-PA M.D.	(6.14)
182	Niles-Benton Harbor, MI	(5.55)
183	Madera, CA	(5.47)
184	Gulfport-Biloxi, MS	(5.45)
185	Washington (greater) DC-VA-MD-WV	(3.96)
186	Bremerton-Silverdale, WA	(3.91)
187	Seattle-Bellevue-Everett, WA M.D.	(3.50)
188	Youngstown, OH-PA	(3.37)
189	San Diego, CA	(2.74)
190	Burlington, NC	(2.49)
191	Springfield, OH	(1.66)
192	College Station-Bryan, TX	(1.35)
193	Houma, LA	(1.24)
194	Pascagoula, MS	(1.22)
195	Louisville, KY-IN	(1.18)
196	Denver-Aurora, CO	(0.91)
197	Muncie, IN	(0.90)
198	Gadsden, AL	(0.70)
199	Boston-Quincy, MA M.D.	(0.52)
200	Tyler, TX	(0.29)
201	Akron, OH	(0.06)
202	Rapid City, SD	0.17
203	Cape Coral-Fort Myers, FL	1.58
204	Jonesboro, AR	1.69
205	Spokane, WA	1.70
206	Ocala, FL	1.79
207	Dayton, OH	1.99
208	Jackson, MI	2.83
208	Omaha-Council Bluffs, NE-IA	2.83
210	Santa Cruz-Watsonville, CA	3.01
211	Muskegon-Norton Shores, MI	3.06
212	Salt Lake City, UT	3.09
213	Vineland, NJ	3.18
214	Seattle-Tacoma-Bellevue, WA	4.72
215	Athens-Clarke County, GA	4.94
216	Fort Worth-Arlington, TX M.D.	5.76
217	Lakeland, FL	5.85
218	Reno-Sparks, NV	5.96
219	Knoxville, TN	6.92
220	Springfield, MA	7.23
221	Buffalo-Niagara Falls, NY	7.42
222	Charleston, WV	7.50
223	Washington, DC-VA-MD-WV M.D.	7.76
224	San Francisco-S. Mateo, CA M.D.	8.34
225	Colorado Springs, CO	8.57
226	Huntsville, AL	8.75
227	Riverside-San Bernardino, CA	9.24
228	Clarksville, TN-KY	9.28
229	South Bend-Mishawaka, IN-MI	9.41
230	Chico, CA	9.59
230	Milwaukee, WI	9.59
232	Phoenix-Mesa-Scottsdale, AZ	10.26
233	Kalamazoo-Portage, MI	10.96
234	McAllen-Edinburg-Mission, TX	11.23
235	Palm Bay-Melbourne, FL	11.25
236	Los Angeles (greater), CA	11.40
237	Deltona-Daytona Beach, FL	11.43
238	Dover, DE	11.83
239	Atlantic City, NJ	12.43
240	Jacksonville, NC	12.50
241	North Port-Bradenton-Sarasota, FL	13.34
242	Durham-Chapel Hill, NC	13.41
243	Dallas (greater), TX	13.74

RANK	METROPOLITAN AREA	SCORE
244	Fort Lauderdale, FL M.D.	13.76
245	Wichita Falls, TX	14.16
246	Greensboro-High Point, NC	14.27
247	Victoria, TX	14.60
248	Wilmington, DE-MD-NJ M.D.	15.28
249	Topeka, KS	15.34
250	Chattanooga, TN-GA	15.42
251	Cleveland-Elyria-Mentor, OH	15.82
252	Tampa-St Petersburg, FL	16.58
253	Redding, CA	17.15
254	Philadelphia (greater) PA-NJ-MD-DE	17.25
255	Dallas-Plano-Irving, TX M.D.	17.55
256	Atlanta, GA	17.89
257	Valdosta, GA	18.09
258	Hinesville, GA	19.13
259	Tucson, AZ	19.21
260	Sacramento, CA	19.31
261	Charlotte-Gastonia, NC-SC	19.81
262	Spartanburg, SC	19.91
263	Pensacola, FL	20.53
264	Nashville-Davidson, TN	21.15
265	Pueblo, CO	21.31
266	Winston-Salem, NC	21.92
267	San Angelo, TX	23.18
268	Tuscaloosa, AL	23.55
269	Columbus, OH	25.17
270	Beaumont-Port Arthur, TX	25.47
271	Waco, TX	25.71
272	Panama City-Lynn Haven, FL	26.12
273	Alexandria, LA	26.55
274	Abilene, TX	26.81
275	Los Angeles County, CA M.D.	27.37
276	Odessa, TX	27.42
277	Corpus Christi, TX	28.44
278	San Antonio, TX	29.03
279	Wichita, KS	29.41
280	Lafayette, LA	29.49
281	Montgomery, AL	31.03
282	Philadelphia, PA M.D.	31.08
283	Anderson, SC	31.37
284	Tacoma, WA M.D.	31.41
285	Vallejo-Fairfield, CA	31.47
286	Albany, GA	32.00
287	Goldsboro, NC	32.67
288	West Palm Beach, FL M.D.	32.73
289	Orlando, FL	33.20
290	Savannah, GA	33.28
291	Visalia-Porterville, CA	34.48
292	Tallahassee, FL	35.16
293	Fresno, CA	35.29
294	Toledo, OH	36.05
295	Indianapolis, IN	37.00
296	Amarillo, TX	38.14
297	Jackson, MS	38.61
298	Sumter, SC	38.92
299	Macon, GA	40.58
300	Miami (greater), FL	40.86
301	Santa Fe, NM	40.95
302	Augusta, GA-SC	41.61
303	Salisbury, MD	41.65
304	Gainesville, FL	42.16
305	Jacksonville, FL	42.23
306	Columbia, SC	42.49

RANK	METROPOLITAN AREA	SCORE
307	Farmington, NM	42.74
308	Tulsa, OK	43.30
309	San Francisco (greater), CA	43.40
310	Longview, TX	43.46
311	Merced, CA	44.16
312	Lima, OH	44.81
313	Birmingham-Hoover, AL	44.91
314	Baltimore-Towson, MD	44.93
315	Laredo, TX	46.14
316	Salinas, CA	46.29
317	Rocky Mount, NC	47.81
318	Lubbock, TX	50.77
319	Modesto, CA	51.55
320	Anniston-Oxford, AL	53.79
321	Houston, TX	54.38
322	Saginaw, MI	54.90
323	Baton Rouge, LA	55.56
324	Detroit (greater), MI	55.74
325	Columbus, GA-AL	56.35
326	Battle Creek, MI	56.77
327	Bakersfield, CA	57.73
328	Albuquerque, NM	58.95
329	Mobile, AL	59.76
330	Anchorage, AK	61.64
331	Fayetteville, NC	62.29
332	Miami-Dade County, FL M.D.	63.89
333	Florence, SC	64.60
334	Stockton, CA	66.33
335	Jackson, TN	67.83
336	Oakland-Fremont, CA M.D.	68.46
337	Brunswick, GA	70.06
338	Texarkana, TX-Texarkana, AR	70.23
339	Little Rock, AR	70.73
340	Las Vegas-Paradise, NV	71.34
341	Flint, MI	73.08
342	Hot Springs, AR	78.80
343	Lawton, OK	89.72
344	Lake Charles, LA	89.90
345	Memphis, TN-MS-AR	117.58
346	Pine Bluff, AR	123.32
347	Detroit-Livonia-Dearborn, MI M.D.	169.66
NA	Auburn, AL**	NA
NA	Charleston-North Charleston, SC**	NA
NA	Danville, IL**	NA
NA	Decatur, AL**	NA
NA	Decatur, IL**	NA
NA	Dothan, AL**	NA
NA	Duluth, MN-WI**	NA
NA	El Centro, CA**	NA
NA	Fargo, ND-MN**	NA
NA	Grand Forks, ND-MN**	NA
NA	Ithaca, NY**	NA
NA	Kansas City, MO-KS**	NA
NA	La Crosse, WI-MN**	NA
NA	Mankato-North Mankato, MN**	NA
NA	Minneapolis-St. Paul, MN-WI**	NA
NA	New Orleans, LA**	NA
NA	Oklahoma City, OK**	NA
NA	Rochester, MN**	NA
NA	Shreveport-Bossier City, LA**	NA
NA	St. Cloud, MN**	NA
NA	St. Louis, MO-IL**	NA
NA	Wilmington, NC**	NA

Source: CQ Press using reported data from the F.B.I. "Crime in the United States 2009"

*Includes murder, rape, robbery, aggravated assault, burglary, and motor vehicle theft. A negative score (in parentheses) indicates a composite crime number below the national rate, a positive number is above the national rate. **Not available.

2010 City Crime Rate Rankings*

RANK	CITY	SCORE
265	Abilene, TX	53.73
354	Akron, OH	132.09
345	Albany, GA	122.01
317	Albany, NY	86.77
324	Albuquerque, NM	97.30
60	Alexandria, VA	(45.87)
100	Alhambra, CA	(30.48)
331	Allentown, PA	104.78
21	Allen, TX	(65.35)
281	Amarillo, TX	64.84
6	Amherst, NY	(76.00)
121	Anaheim, CA	(20.27)
286	Anchorage, AK	67.83
59	Ann Arbor, MI	(46.11)
310	Antioch, CA	78.35
232	Arlington, TX	35.63
65	Arvada, CO	(43.35)
233	Athens-Clarke, GA	36.30
376	Atlanta, GA	168.53
230	Aurora, CO	35.04
NA	Aurora, IL**	NA
198	Austin, TX	16.99
219	Avondale, AZ	30.66
278	Bakersfield, CA	61.45
186	Baldwin Park, CA	11.54
390	Baltimore, MD	241.64
385	Baton Rouge, LA	205.59
305	Beaumont, TX	76.81
50	Beaverton, OR	(49.35)
46	Bellevue, WA	(52.40)
119	Bellingham, WA	(20.41)
26	Bend, OR	(62.36)
290	Berkeley, CA	69.88
103	Billings, MT	(28.22)
391	Birmingham, AL	244.83
NA	Bloomington, MN**	NA
101	Boca Raton, FL	(29.59)
83	Boise, ID	(35.75)
288	Boston, MA	68.56
105	Boulder, CO	(27.63)
22	Brick Twnshp, NJ	(64.81)
341	Bridgeport, CT	120.38
328	Brockton, MA	98.96
64	Broken Arrow, OK	(44.95)
97	Brownsville, TX	(31.50)
145	Buena Park, CA	(9.45)
384	Buffalo, NY	202.43
94	Burbank, CA	(32.45)
122	Cambridge, MA	(20.05)
399	Camden, NJ	374.33
41	Canton Twnshp, MI	(54.96)
364	Canton, OH	140.82
53	Cape Coral, FL	(48.07)
102	Carlsbad, CA	(28.50)
104	Carrollton, TX	(27.73)
195	Carson, CA	15.05
8	Cary, NC	(74.76)
123	Cedar Rapids, IA	(19.96)
23	Centennial, CO	(63.53)
81	Chandler, AZ	(36.21)
188	Charleston, SC	12.08
283	Charlotte, NC	66.25
334	Chattanooga, TN	107.67
54	Cheektowaga, NY	(48.00)
128	Chesapeake, VA	(16.56)
NA	Chicago, IL**	NA
187	Chico, CA	11.60
80	Chino, CA	(36.56)

RANK	CITY	SCORE
155	Chula Vista, CA	(5.79)
377	Cincinnati, OH	182.09
189	Citrus Heights, CA	12.41
5	Clarkstown, NY	(76.17)
269	Clarksville, TN	55.23
238	Clearwater, FL	38.13
394	Cleveland, OH	260.60
61	Clifton, NJ	(45.78)
89	Clinton Twnshp, MI	(34.14)
98	Clovis, CA	(31.43)
108	College Station, TX	(26.33)
1	Colonie, NY	(82.49)
226	Colorado Springs, CO	31.76
143	Columbia, MO	(9.95)
336	Columbia, SC	110.86
323	Columbus, GA	94.14
352	Columbus, OH	127.21
393	Compton, CA	260.13
177	Concord, CA	6.61
43	Coral Springs, FL	(53.65)
95	Corona, CA	(31.99)
259	Corpus Christi, TX	51.37
85	Costa Mesa, CA	(35.09)
75	Cranston, RI	(38.84)
349	Dallas, TX	125.48
74	Daly City, CA	(39.25)
57	Danbury, CT	(47.05)
221	Davenport, IA	31.22
175	Davie, FL	6.49
381	Dayton, OH	191.14
202	Dearborn, MI	17.86
NA	Decatur, IL**	NA
112	Denton, TX	(23.25)
260	Denver, CO	52.04
236	Des Moines, IA	36.99
398	Detroit, MI	356.44
214	Downey, CA	28.31
NA	Duluth, MN**	NA
284	Durham, NC	66.68
48	Edison Twnshp, NJ	(49.93)
34	Edmond, OK	(57.08)
207	El Cajon, CA	21.44
203	El Monte, CA	18.69
126	El Paso, TX	(17.91)
NA	Elgin, IL**	NA
330	Elizabeth, NJ	101.86
127	Elk Grove, CA	(17.18)
209	Erie, PA	22.23
185	Escondido, CA	11.49
208	Eugene, OR	21.62
167	Evansville, IN	1.22
282	Everett, WA	66.12
181	Fairfield, CA	9.36
313	Fall River, MA	80.80
149	Fargo, ND	(7.89)
30	Farmington Hills, MI	(60.43)
162	Fayetteville, AR	(2.40)
337	Fayetteville, NC	116.74
270	Federal Way, WA	56.33
397	Flint, MI	310.31
172	Fontana, CA	4.79
141	Fort Collins, CO	(12.07)
300	Fort Lauderdale, FL	74.72
273	Fort Smith, AR	58.49
173	Fort Wayne, IN	4.88
252	Fort Worth, TX	47.62
86	Fremont, CA	(34.92)
268	Fresno, CA	55.12
14	Frisco, TX	(67.76)

RANK	CITY	SCORE
135	Fullerton, CA	(12.68)
315	Gainesville, FL	82.14
113	Garden Grove, CA	(22.66)
158	Garland, TX	(4.94)
392	Gary, IN	250.48
17	Gilbert, AZ	(66.29)
242	Glendale, AZ	39.69
34	Glendale, CA	(57.08)
220	Grand Prairie, TX	30.82
256	Grand Rapids, MI	49.62
20	Greece, NY	(65.89)
154	Greeley, CO	(6.14)
157	Green Bay, WI	(5.06)
316	Greensboro, NC	82.89
176	Gresham, OR	6.59
33	Hamilton Twnshp, NJ	(57.37)
339	Hammond, IN	119.68
152	Hampton, VA	(7.38)
382	Hartford, CT	192.15
280	Hawthorne, CA	62.54
276	Hayward, CA	60.79
84	Henderson, NV	(35.38)
130	Hesperia, CA	(15.47)
174	Hialeah, FL	5.61
225	High Point, NC	31.69
66	Hillsboro, OR	(42.56)
228	Hollywood, FL	33.97
129	Honolulu, HI	(15.70)
356	Houston, TX	133.55
39	Huntington Beach, CA	(55.43)
292	Huntsville, AL	71.06
241	Independence, MO	39.44
372	Indianapolis, IN	154.46
224	Indio, CA	31.68
357	Inglewood, CA	134.13
10	Irvine, CA	(72.95)
137	Irving, TX	(12.37)
312	Jacksonville, FL	78.95
183	Jacksonville, NC	10.52
387	Jackson, MS	218.91
267	Jersey City, NJ	53.96
NA	Joliet, IL**	NA
369	Kansas City, KS	145.72
380	Kansas City, MO	186.01
117	Kenosha, WI	(20.93)
301	Kent, WA	75.01
234	Killeen, TX	36.37
348	Knoxville, TN	124.51
294	Lafayette, LA	71.67
7	Lake Forest, CA	(75.34)
215	Lakeland, FL	28.34
169	Lakewood, CA	3.01
211	Lakewood, CO	24.78
237	Lancaster, CA	37.07
321	Lansing, MI	92.28
257	Laredo, TX	50.07
171	Las Cruces, NM	4.66
325	Las Vegas, NV	97.54
156	Lawrence, KS	(5.09)
347	Lawton, OK	123.63
38	Lee's Summit, MO	(55.71)
114	Lewisville, TX	(22.26)
191	Lexington, KY	13.64
134	Lincoln, NE	(13.10)
386	Little Rock, AR	213.99
96	Livermore, CA	(31.80)
90	Livonia, MI	(33.96)
263	Long Beach, CA	52.74
72	Longmont, CO	(39.45)

Alpha Order - City (continued)

RANK	CITY	SCORE
335	Longview, TX	110.54
243	Los Angeles, CA	39.86
254	Louisville, KY	47.87
279	Lubbock, TX	62.46
258	Lynn, MA	50.83
363	Macon, GA	140.07
99	Madison, WI	(31.00)
178	Manchester, NH	6.67
110	McAllen, TX	(24.20)
51	McKinney, TX	(49.32)
285	Melbourne, FL	67.50
389	Memphis, TN	236.32
275	Merced, CA	60.11
147	Mesa, AZ	(8.70)
190	Mesquite, TX	12.42
359	Miami Beach, FL	135.59
361	Miami Gardens, FL	138.05
350	Miami, FL	126.34
153	Midland, TX	(6.66)
358	Milwaukee, WI	134.25
353	Minneapolis, MN	127.47
206	Miramar, FL	20.91
4	Mission Viejo, CA	(79.97)
36	Missouri City, TX	(56.32)
295	Mobile, AL	72.36
293	Modesto, CA	71.08
302	Montgomery, AL	75.55
191	Moreno Valley, CA	13.64
222	Murfreesboro, TN	31.24
24	Murrieta, CA	(62.67)
93	Nampa, ID	(32.74)
NA	Naperville, IL**	NA
55	Nashua, NH	(47.74)
326	Nashville, TN	98.00
343	New Bedford, MA	120.96
383	New Haven, CT	196.86
388	New Orleans, LA	226.95
132	New York, NY	(14.48)
378	Newark, NJ	182.29
31	Newport Beach, CA	(59.87)
9	Newton, MA	(74.64)
298	Norfolk, VA	74.66
70	Norman, OK	(41.74)
338	North Charleston, SC	119.00
253	North Las Vegas, NV	47.70
231	Norwalk, CA	35.22
116	Norwalk, CT	(21.31)
396	Oakland, CA	308.29
142	Oceanside, CA	(10.72)
229	Odessa, TX	34.38
2	O'Fallon, MO	(82.05)
204	Ogden, UT	18.79
351	Oklahoma City, OK	126.96
49	Olathe, KS	(49.57)
239	Omaha, NE	38.76
182	Ontario, CA	9.83
27	Orange, CA	(62.13)
11	Orem, UT	(70.43)
355	Orlando, FL	132.45
44	Overland Park, KS	(53.11)
150	Oxnard, CA	(7.68)
144	Palm Bay, FL	(9.52)
201	Palmdale, CA	17.67
111	Pasadena, CA	(23.26)
193	Pasadena, TX	14.14
303	Paterson, NJ	76.14
42	Pearland, TX	(54.80)
78	Pembroke Pines, FL	(37.71)

RANK	CITY	SCORE
125	Peoria, AZ	(18.14)
NA	Peoria, IL**	NA
371	Philadelphia, PA	153.91
266	Phoenix, AZ	53.78
319	Pittsburgh, PA	87.99
52	Plano, TX	(48.85)
163	Plantation, FL	(2.28)
277	Pomona, CA	61.06
318	Pompano Beach, FL	87.33
62	Port St. Lucie, FL	(45.39)
227	Portland, OR	32.67
306	Portsmouth, VA	77.26
314	Providence, RI	81.92
37	Provo, UT	(55.96)
289	Pueblo, CO	69.24
120	Quincy, MA	(20.34)
216	Racine, WI	28.38
165	Raleigh, NC	(1.43)
3	Ramapo, NY	(81.16)
56	Rancho Cucamon., CA	(47.51)
360	Reading, PA	137.59
223	Redding, CA	31.28
213	Reno, NV	28.18
248	Rialto, CA	44.96
88	Richardson, TX	(34.52)
395	Richmond, CA	287.15
322	Richmond, VA	93.80
76	Rio Rancho, NM	(38.82)
210	Riverside, CA	23.75
247	Roanoke, VA	44.65
NA	Rochester, MN**	NA
340	Rochester, NY	120.32
365	Rockford, IL	140.87
79	Roseville, CA	(37.52)
92	Roswell, GA	(33.81)
25	Round Rock, TX	(62.37)
329	Sacramento, CA	100.12
169	Salem, OR	3.01
344	Salinas, CA	121.94
296	Salt Lake City, UT	72.38
217	San Angelo, TX	29.39
264	San Antonio, TX	53.44
367	San Bernardino, CA	145.46
180	San Diego, CA	8.80
271	San Francisco, CA	56.57
164	San Jose, CA	(1.62)
291	San Leandro, CA	71.00
87	San Marcos, CA	(34.54)
91	San Mateo, CA	(33.83)
160	Sandy Springs, GA	(3.83)
69	Sandy, UT	(41.78)
205	Santa Ana, CA	20.00
151	Santa Barbara, CA	(7.54)
106	Santa Clara, CA	(26.74)
67	Santa Clarita, CA	(42.08)
251	Santa Maria, CA	46.86
148	Santa Monica, CA	(8.10)
159	Santa Rosa, CA	(4.72)
297	Savannah, GA	72.95
58	Scottsdale, AZ	(46.72)
244	Seattle, WA	40.93
332	Shreveport, LA	106.77
16	Simi Valley, CA	(66.62)
140	Sioux City, IA	(12.12)
136	Sioux Falls, SD	(12.50)
124	Somerville, MA	(18.17)
333	South Bend, IN	107.34
320	South Gate, CA	88.03

RANK	CITY	SCORE
235	Southfield, MI	36.51
194	Sparks, NV	15.01
109	Spokane Valley, WA	(25.59)
287	Spokane, WA	67.99
NA	Springfield, IL**	NA
366	Springfield, MA	142.58
311	Springfield, MO	78.55
77	Stamford, CT	(37.96)
39	Sterling Heights, MI	(55.43)
362	Stockton, CA	138.10
19	St. George, UT	(65.97)
184	St. Joseph, MO	11.39
400	St. Louis, MO	381.62
298	St. Paul, MN	74.66
370	St. Petersburg, FL	148.42
146	Suffolk, VA	(9.31)
12	Sugar Land, TX	(69.32)
32	Sunnyvale, CA	(58.87)
133	Sunrise, FL	(13.35)
29	Surprise, AZ	(61.26)
327	Syracuse, NY	98.34
346	Tacoma, WA	122.13
309	Tallahassee, FL	77.80
246	Tampa, FL	43.97
47	Temecula, CA	(50.68)
196	Tempe, AZ	15.45
138	Thornton, CO	(12.20)
18	Thousand Oaks, CA	(65.99)
374	Toledo, OH	157.14
15	Toms River Twnshp, NJ	(66.78)
255	Topeka, KS	49.30
63	Torrance, CA	(45.36)
115	Tracy, CA	(21.65)
375	Trenton, NJ	165.08
13	Troy, MI	(68.26)
274	Tucson, AZ	58.84
373	Tulsa, OK	155.51
218	Tuscaloosa, AL	29.54
200	Tyler, TX	17.66
161	Upper Darby Twnshp, PA	(3.01)
68	Vacaville, CA	(41.89)
368	Vallejo, CA	145.65
212	Vancouver, WA	27.06
118	Ventura, CA	(20.76)
272	Victorville, CA	57.22
72	Virginia Beach, VA	(39.45)
240	Visalia, CA	38.90
166	Vista, CA	0.26
262	Waco, TX	52.36
250	Warren, MI	46.20
45	Warwick, RI	(52.96)
379	Washington, DC	183.50
168	Waterbury, CT	2.05
179	West Covina, CA	7.07
82	West Jordan, UT	(36.20)
342	West Palm Beach, FL	120.66
249	West Valley, UT	45.36
199	Westland, MI	17.38
71	Westminster, CA	(39.75)
107	Westminster, CO	(26.72)
139	Whittier, CA	(12.17)
261	Wichita Falls, TX	52.07
307	Wichita, KS	77.61
304	Wilmington, NC	76.28
308	Winston-Salem, NC	77.74
28	Woodbridge Twnshp, NJ	(61.79)
245	Worcester, MA	41.99
131	Yonkers, NY	(14.84)
197	Yuma, AZ	15.77

Source: CQ Press using reported data from the F.B.I. "Crime in the United States 2009"

*Includes murder, rape, robbery, aggravated assault, burglary, and motor vehicle theft. A negative score (in parentheses) indicates a composite crime number below the national rate, a positive number is above the national rate. **Not available.

2010 City Crime Rate Rankings* (continued)

RANK	CITY	SCORE
1	Colonie, NY	(82.49)
2	O'Fallon, MO	(82.05)
3	Ramapo, NY	(81.16)
4	Mission Viejo, CA	(79.97)
5	Clarkstown, NY	(76.17)
6	Amherst, NY	(76.00)
7	Lake Forest, CA	(75.34)
8	Cary, NC	(74.76)
9	Newton, MA	(74.64)
10	Irvine, CA	(72.95)
11	Orem, UT	(70.43)
12	Sugar Land, TX	(69.32)
13	Troy, MI	(68.26)
14	Frisco, TX	(67.76)
15	Toms River Twnshp, NJ	(66.78)
16	Simi Valley, CA	(66.62)
17	Gilbert, AZ	(66.29)
18	Thousand Oaks, CA	(65.99)
19	St. George, UT	(65.97)
20	Greece, NY	(65.89)
21	Allen, TX	(65.35)
22	Brick Twnshp, NJ	(64.81)
23	Centennial, CO	(63.53)
24	Murrieta, CA	(62.67)
25	Round Rock, TX	(62.37)
26	Bend, OR	(62.36)
27	Orange, CA	(62.13)
28	Woodbridge Twnshp, NJ	(61.79)
29	Surprise, AZ	(61.26)
30	Farmington Hills, MI	(60.43)
31	Newport Beach, CA	(59.87)
32	Sunnyvale, CA	(58.87)
33	Hamilton Twnshp, NJ	(57.37)
34	Edmond, OK	(57.08)
34	Glendale, CA	(57.08)
36	Missouri City, TX	(56.32)
37	Provo, UT	(55.96)
38	Lee's Summit, MO	(55.71)
39	Huntington Beach, CA	(55.43)
39	Sterling Heights, MI	(55.43)
41	Canton Twnshp, MI	(54.96)
42	Pearland, TX	(54.80)
43	Coral Springs, FL	(53.65)
44	Overland Park, KS	(53.11)
45	Warwick, RI	(52.96)
46	Bellevue, WA	(52.40)
47	Temecula, CA	(50.68)
48	Edison Twnshp, NJ	(49.93)
49	Olathe, KS	(49.57)
50	Beaverton, OR	(49.35)
51	McKinney, TX	(49.32)
52	Plano, TX	(48.85)
53	Cape Coral, FL	(48.07)
54	Cheektowaga, NY	(48.00)
55	Nashua, NH	(47.74)
56	Rancho Cucamon., CA	(47.51)
57	Danbury, CT	(47.05)
58	Scottsdale, AZ	(46.72)
59	Ann Arbor, MI	(46.11)
60	Alexandria, VA	(45.87)
61	Clifton, NJ	(45.78)
62	Port St. Lucie, FL	(45.39)
63	Torrance, CA	(45.36)
64	Broken Arrow, OK	(44.95)
65	Arvada, CO	(43.35)
66	Hillsboro, OR	(42.56)
67	Santa Clarita, CA	(42.08)
68	Vacaville, CA	(41.89)
69	Sandy, UT	(41.78)
70	Norman, OK	(41.74)
71	Westminster, CA	(39.75)
72	Longmont, CO	(39.45)
72	Virginia Beach, VA	(39.45)
74	Daly City, CA	(39.25)
75	Cranston, RI	(38.84)
76	Rio Rancho, NM	(38.82)
77	Stamford, CT	(37.96)
78	Pembroke Pines, FL	(37.71)
79	Roseville, CA	(37.52)
80	Chino, CA	(36.56)
81	Chandler, AZ	(36.21)
82	West Jordan, UT	(36.20)
83	Boise, ID	(35.75)
84	Henderson, NV	(35.38)
85	Costa Mesa, CA	(35.09)
86	Fremont, CA	(34.92)
87	San Marcos, CA	(34.54)
88	Richardson, TX	(34.52)
89	Clinton Twnshp, MI	(34.14)
90	Livonia, MI	(33.96)
91	San Mateo, CA	(33.83)
92	Roswell, GA	(33.81)
93	Nampa, ID	(32.74)
94	Burbank, CA	(32.45)
95	Corona, CA	(31.99)
96	Livermore, CA	(31.80)
97	Brownsville, TX	(31.50)
98	Clovis, CA	(31.43)
99	Madison, WI	(31.00)
100	Alhambra, CA	(30.48)
101	Boca Raton, FL	(29.59)
102	Carlsbad, CA	(28.50)
103	Billings, MT	(28.22)
104	Carrollton, TX	(27.73)
105	Boulder, CO	(27.63)
106	Santa Clara, CA	(26.74)
107	Westminster, CO	(26.72)
108	College Station, TX	(26.33)
109	Spokane Valley, WA	(25.59)
110	McAllen, TX	(24.20)
111	Pasadena, CA	(23.26)
112	Denton, TX	(23.25)
113	Garden Grove, CA	(22.66)
114	Lewisville, TX	(22.26)
115	Tracy, CA	(21.65)
116	Norwalk, CT	(21.31)
117	Kenosha, WI	(20.93)
118	Ventura, CA	(20.76)
119	Bellingham, WA	(20.41)
120	Quincy, MA	(20.34)
121	Anaheim, CA	(20.27)
122	Cambridge, MA	(20.05)
123	Cedar Rapids, IA	(19.96)
124	Somerville, MA	(18.17)
125	Peoria, AZ	(18.14)
126	El Paso, TX	(17.91)
127	Elk Grove, CA	(17.18)
128	Chesapeake, VA	(16.56)
129	Honolulu, HI	(15.70)
130	Hesperia, CA	(15.47)
131	Yonkers, NY	(14.84)
132	New York, NY	(14.48)
133	Sunrise, FL	(13.35)
134	Lincoln, NE	(13.10)
135	Fullerton, CA	(12.68)
136	Sioux Falls, SD	(12.50)
137	Irving, TX	(12.37)
138	Thornton, CO	(12.20)
139	Whittier, CA	(12.17)
140	Sioux City, IA	(12.12)
141	Fort Collins, CO	(12.07)
142	Oceanside, CA	(10.72)
143	Columbia, MO	(9.95)
144	Palm Bay, FL	(9.52)
145	Buena Park, CA	(9.45)
146	Suffolk, VA	(9.31)
147	Mesa, AZ	(8.70)
148	Santa Monica, CA	(8.10)
149	Fargo, ND	(7.89)
150	Oxnard, CA	(7.68)
151	Santa Barbara, CA	(7.54)
152	Hampton, VA	(7.38)
153	Midland, TX	(6.66)
154	Greeley, CO	(6.14)
155	Chula Vista, CA	(5.79)
156	Lawrence, KS	(5.09)
157	Green Bay, WI	(5.06)
158	Garland, TX	(4.94)
159	Santa Rosa, CA	(4.72)
160	Sandy Springs, GA	(3.83)
161	Upper Darby Twnshp, PA	(3.01)
162	Fayetteville, AR	(2.40)
163	Plantation, FL	(2.28)
164	San Jose, CA	(1.62)
165	Raleigh, NC	(1.43)
166	Vista, CA	0.26
167	Evansville, IN	1.22
168	Waterbury, CT	2.05
169	Salem, OR	3.01
169	Lakewood, CA	3.01
171	Las Cruces, NM	4.66
172	Fontana, CA	4.79
173	Fort Wayne, IN	4.88
174	Hialeah, FL	5.61
175	Davie, FL	6.49
176	Gresham, OR	6.59
177	Concord, CA	6.61
178	Manchester, NH	6.67
179	West Covina, CA	7.07
180	San Diego, CA	8.80
181	Fairfield, CA	9.36
182	Ontario, CA	9.83
183	Jacksonville, NC	10.52
184	St. Joseph, MO	11.39
185	Escondido, CA	11.49
186	Baldwin Park, CA	11.54
187	Chico, CA	11.60
188	Charleston, SC	12.08
189	Citrus Heights, CA	12.41
190	Mesquite, TX	12.42
191	Lexington, KY	13.64
191	Moreno Valley, CA	13.64
193	Pasadena, TX	14.14
194	Sparks, NV	15.01
195	Carson, CA	15.05
196	Tempe, AZ	15.45
197	Yuma, AZ	15.77
198	Austin, TX	16.99
199	Westland, MI	17.38
200	Tyler, TX	17.66
201	Palmdale, CA	17.67
202	Dearborn, MI	17.86
203	El Monte, CA	18.69
204	Ogden, UT	18.79
205	Santa Ana, CA	20.00
206	Miramar, FL	20.91

RANK	CITY	SCORE
207	El Cajon, CA	21.44
208	Eugene, OR	21.62
209	Erie, PA	22.23
210	Riverside, CA	23.75
211	Lakewood, CO	24.78
212	Vancouver, WA	27.06
213	Reno, NV	28.18
214	Downey, CA	28.31
215	Lakeland, FL	28.34
216	Racine, WI	28.38
217	San Angelo, TX	29.39
218	Tuscaloosa, AL	29.54
219	Avondale, AZ	30.66
220	Grand Prairie, TX	30.82
221	Davenport, IA	31.22
222	Murfreesboro, TN	31.24
223	Redding, CA	31.28
224	Indio, CA	31.68
225	High Point, NC	31.69
226	Colorado Springs, CO	31.76
227	Portland, OR	32.67
228	Hollywood, FL	33.97
229	Odessa, TX	34.38
230	Aurora, CO	35.04
231	Norwalk, CA	35.22
232	Arlington, TX	35.63
233	Athens-Clarke, GA	36.30
234	Killeen, TX	36.37
235	Southfield, MI	36.51
236	Des Moines, IA	36.99
237	Lancaster, CA	37.07
238	Clearwater, FL	38.13
239	Omaha, NE	38.76
240	Visalia, CA	38.90
241	Independence, MO	39.44
242	Glendale, AZ	39.69
243	Los Angeles, CA	39.86
244	Seattle, WA	40.93
245	Worcester, MA	41.99
246	Tampa, FL	43.97
247	Roanoke, VA	44.65
248	Rialto, CA	44.96
249	West Valley, UT	45.36
250	Warren, MI	46.20
251	Santa Maria, CA	46.86
252	Fort Worth, TX	47.62
253	North Las Vegas, NV	47.70
254	Louisville, KY	47.87
255	Topeka, KS	49.30
256	Grand Rapids, MI	49.62
257	Laredo, TX	50.07
258	Lynn, MA	50.83
259	Corpus Christi, TX	51.37
260	Denver, CO	52.04
261	Wichita Falls, TX	52.07
262	Waco, TX	52.36
263	Long Beach, CA	52.74
264	San Antonio, TX	53.44
265	Abilene, TX	53.73
266	Phoenix, AZ	53.78
267	Jersey City, NJ	53.96
268	Fresno, CA	55.12
269	Clarksville, TN	55.23
270	Federal Way, WA	56.33
271	San Francisco, CA	56.57
272	Victorville, CA	57.22
273	Fort Smith, AR	58.49
274	Tucson, AZ	58.84

RANK	CITY	SCORE
275	Merced, CA	60.11
276	Hayward, CA	60.79
277	Pomona, CA	61.06
278	Bakersfield, CA	61.45
279	Lubbock, TX	62.46
280	Hawthorne, CA	62.54
281	Amarillo, TX	64.84
282	Everett, WA	66.12
283	Charlotte, NC	66.25
284	Durham, NC	66.68
285	Melbourne, FL	67.50
286	Anchorage, AK	67.83
287	Spokane, WA	67.99
288	Boston, MA	68.56
289	Pueblo, CO	69.24
290	Berkeley, CA	69.88
291	San Leandro, CA	71.00
292	Huntsville, AL	71.06
293	Modesto, CA	71.08
294	Lafayette, LA	71.67
295	Mobile, AL	72.36
296	Salt Lake City, UT	72.38
297	Savannah, GA	72.95
298	Norfolk, VA	74.66
298	St. Paul, MN	74.66
300	Fort Lauderdale, FL	74.72
301	Kent, WA	75.01
302	Montgomery, AL	75.55
303	Paterson, NJ	76.14
304	Wilmington, NC	76.28
305	Beaumont, TX	76.81
306	Portsmouth, VA	77.26
307	Wichita, KS	77.61
308	Winston-Salem, NC	77.74
309	Tallahassee, FL	77.80
310	Antioch, CA	78.35
311	Springfield, MO	78.55
312	Jacksonville, FL	78.95
313	Fall River, MA	80.80
314	Providence, RI	81.92
315	Gainesville, FL	82.14
316	Greensboro, NC	82.89
317	Albany, NY	86.77
318	Pompano Beach, FL	87.33
319	Pittsburgh, PA	87.99
320	South Gate, CA	88.03
321	Lansing, MI	92.28
322	Richmond, VA	93.80
323	Columbus, GA	94.14
324	Albuquerque, NM	97.30
325	Las Vegas, NV	97.54
326	Nashville, TN	98.00
327	Syracuse, NY	98.34
328	Brockton, MA	98.96
329	Sacramento, CA	100.12
330	Elizabeth, NJ	101.86
331	Allentown, PA	104.78
332	Shreveport, LA	106.77
333	South Bend, IN	107.34
334	Chattanooga, TN	107.67
335	Longview, TX	110.54
336	Columbia, SC	110.86
337	Fayetteville, NC	116.74
338	North Charleston, SC	119.00
339	Hammond, IN	119.68
340	Rochester, NY	120.32
341	Bridgeport, CT	120.38
342	West Palm Beach, FL	120.66

RANK	CITY	SCORE
343	New Bedford, MA	120.96
344	Salinas, CA	121.94
345	Albany, GA	122.01
346	Tacoma, WA	122.13
347	Lawton, OK	123.63
348	Knoxville, TN	124.51
349	Dallas, TX	125.48
350	Miami, FL	126.34
351	Oklahoma City, OK	126.96
352	Columbus, OH	127.21
353	Minneapolis, MN	127.47
354	Akron, OH	132.09
355	Orlando, FL	132.45
356	Houston, TX	133.55
357	Inglewood, CA	134.13
358	Milwaukee, WI	134.25
359	Miami Beach, FL	135.59
360	Reading, PA	137.59
361	Miami Gardens, FL	138.05
362	Stockton, CA	138.10
363	Macon, GA	140.07
364	Canton, OH	140.82
365	Rockford, IL	140.87
366	Springfield, MA	142.58
367	San Bernardino, CA	145.46
368	Vallejo, CA	145.65
369	Kansas City, KS	145.72
370	St. Petersburg, FL	148.42
371	Philadelphia, PA	153.91
372	Indianapolis, IN	154.46
373	Tulsa, OK	155.51
374	Toledo, OH	157.14
375	Trenton, NJ	165.08
376	Atlanta, GA	168.53
377	Cincinnati, OH	182.09
378	Newark, NJ	182.29
379	Washington, DC	183.50
380	Kansas City, MO	186.01
381	Dayton, OH	191.14
382	Hartford, CT	192.15
383	New Haven, CT	196.86
384	Buffalo, NY	202.43
385	Baton Rouge, LA	205.59
386	Little Rock, AR	213.99
387	Jackson, MS	218.91
388	New Orleans, LA	226.95
389	Memphis, TN	236.32
390	Baltimore, MD	241.64
391	Birmingham, AL	244.83
392	Gary, IN	250.48
393	Compton, CA	260.13
394	Cleveland, OH	260.60
395	Richmond, CA	287.15
396	Oakland, CA	308.29
397	Flint, MI	310.31
398	Detroit, MI	356.44
399	Camden, NJ	374.33
400	St. Louis, MO	381.62
NA	Aurora, IL**	NA
NA	Bloomington, MN**	NA
NA	Chicago, IL**	NA
NA	Decatur, IL**	NA
NA	Duluth, MN**	NA
NA	Elgin, IL**	NA
NA	Joliet, IL**	NA
NA	Naperville, IL**	NA
NA	Peoria, IL**	NA
NA	Rochester, MN**	NA
NA	Springfield, IL**	NA

Source: CQ Press using reported data from the F.B.I. "Crime in the United States 2009"

*Includes murder, rape, robbery, aggravated assault, burglary, and motor vehicle theft. A negative score (in parentheses) indicates a composite crime number below the national rate, a positive number is above the national rate. **Not available.

I. Metropolitan Area Crime Statistics

Please note the following for Tables 1 through 40 and 85 through 87:

- All listings are for Metropolitan Statistical Areas (M.S.A.s) except for those ending with "M.D."
- Listings with "M.D." are Metropolitan Divisions, which are smaller parts of eleven large M.S.A.s. These eleven M.S.A.s further divided into M.D.s are identified using "(greater)" following the metropolitan area name.
- For example, the "Dallas (greater)" M.S.A. includes the two M.D.s of Dallas-Plano-Irving and Fort Worth-Arlington. The data for the M.D.s are included in the data for the overall M.S.A.

1. Crimes in 2009
National Total = 10,639,369 Crimes*

RANK	METROPOLITAN AREA	CRIMES
224	Abilene, TX	6,348
88	Akron, OH	25,412
92	Albany-Schenectady-Troy, NY	24,528
190	Albany, GA	8,097
59	Albuquerque, NM	42,993
189	Alexandria, LA	8,117
104	Allentown, PA-NJ	21,057
323	Altoona, PA	2,717
140	Amarillo, TX	13,525
331	Ames, IA	2,508
136	Anchorage, AK	13,816
270	Anderson, IN	4,853
185	Anderson, SC	9,070
171	Ann Arbor, MI	10,470
225	Anniston-Oxford, AL	6,295
273	Appleton, WI	4,703
160	Asheville, NC	11,112
187	Athens-Clarke County, GA	8,403
8	Atlanta, GA	218,690
167	Atlantic City, NJ	10,763
NA	Auburn, AL**	NA
86	Augusta, GA-SC	27,219
39	Austin-Round Rock, TX	74,718
68	Bakersfield, CA	36,337
24	Baltimore-Towson, MD	108,220
258	Bangor, ME	5,151
192	Barnstable Town, MA	8,050
65	Baton Rouge, LA	39,194
226	Battle Creek, MI	6,270
320	Bay City, MI	2,932
121	Beaumont-Port Arthur, TX	16,939
200	Bellingham, WA	7,432
278	Bend, OR	4,435
80	Bethesda-Frederick, MD M.D.	30,971
232	Billings, MT	6,017
216	Binghamton, NY	6,647
50	Birmingham-Hoover, AL	57,331
332	Bismarck, ND	2,460
277	Blacksburg, VA	4,461
240	Bloomington, IN	5,895
139	Boise City-Nampa, ID	13,648
22	Boston (greater), MA-NH	116,966
51	Boston-Quincy, MA M.D.	57,121
196	Boulder, CO	7,853
285	Bowling Green, KY	4,183
204	Bremerton-Silverdale, WA	7,225
111	Bridgeport-Stamford, CT	20,033
109	Brownsville-Harlingen, TX	20,411
247	Brunswick, GA	5,620
64	Buffalo-Niagara Falls, NY	39,757
211	Burlington-South Burlington, VT	6,749
221	Burlington, NC	6,479
75	Cambridge-Newton, MA M.D.	32,536
70	Camden, NJ M.D.	35,390
108	Cape Coral-Fort Myers, FL	20,501
305	Cape Girardeau, MO-IL	3,379
344	Carson City, NV	1,331
314	Casper, WY	3,117
197	Cedar Rapids, IA	7,757
NA	Charleston-North Charleston, SC**	NA
161	Charleston, WV	10,990
36	Charlotte-Gastonia, NC-SC	77,629
248	Charlottesville, VA	5,611
87	Chattanooga, TN-GA	25,592
316	Cheyenne, WY	3,064
203	Chico, CA	7,270
33	Cincinnati-Middletown, OH-KY-IN	79,440
183	Clarksville, TN-KY	9,148
41	Cleveland-Elyria-Mentor, OH	68,381
288	Cleveland, TN	4,120
284	Coeur d'Alene, ID	4,195
177	College Station-Bryan, TX	10,052
106	Colorado Springs, CO	20,646
238	Columbia, MO	5,918
71	Columbia, SC	35,254
113	Columbus, GA-AL	19,209
324	Columbus, IN	2,694
29	Columbus, OH	83,784
95	Corpus Christi, TX	23,612
336	Corvallis, OR	2,395
243	Crestview-Fort Walton Beach, FL	5,704
310	Cumberland, MD-WV	3,211
6	Dallas (greater), TX	278,856
10	Dallas-Plano-Irving, TX M.D.	182,732
279	Dalton, GA	4,296
NA	Danville, IL**	NA
312	Danville, VA	3,171
78	Dayton, OH	31,355
NA	Decatur, AL**	NA
NA	Decatur, IL**	NA
103	Deltona-Daytona Beach, FL	21,121
32	Denver-Aurora, CO	80,209
120	Des Moines-West Des Moines, IA	17,146
14	Detroit (greater), MI	164,189
25	Detroit-Livonia-Dearborn, MI M.D.	105,284
NA	Dothan, AL**	NA
215	Dover, DE	6,665
330	Dubuque, IA	2,542
NA	Duluth, MN-WI**	NA
100	Durham-Chapel Hill, NC	22,200
304	Eau Claire, WI	3,442
56	Edison, NJ M.D.	47,241
NA	El Centro, CA**	NA
89	El Paso, TX	25,212
336	Elizabethtown, KY	2,395
249	Elkhart-Goshen, IN	5,603
339	Elmira, NY	2,123
201	Erie, PA	7,357
132	Eugene-Springfield, OR	15,295
172	Evansville, IN-KY	10,433
NA	Fargo, ND-MN**	NA
292	Farmington, NM	3,951
150	Fayetteville, AR-MO	12,776
99	Fayetteville, NC	22,653
272	Flagstaff, AZ	4,821
112	Flint, MI	19,540
268	Florence-Muscle Shoals, AL	4,887
155	Florence, SC	11,870
342	Fond du Lac, WI	1,935
184	Fort Collins-Loveland, CO	9,073
35	Fort Lauderdale, FL M.D.	79,130
168	Fort Smith, AR-OK	10,668
153	Fort Wayne, IN	12,597
28	Fort Worth-Arlington, TX M.D.	96,124
63	Fresno, CA	39,846
290	Gadsden, AL	4,101
148	Gainesville, FL	13,157
269	Gainesville, GA	4,857
338	Glens Falls, NY	2,210
251	Goldsboro, NC	5,516
NA	Grand Forks, ND-MN**	NA
266	Grand Junction, CO	4,951
90	Grand Rapids-Wyoming, MI	24,725
320	Great Falls, MT	2,932
209	Greeley, CO	6,815
220	Green Bay, WI	6,498
73	Greensboro-High Point, NC	34,228
166	Gulfport-Biloxi, MS	10,772
212	Hagerstown-Martinsburg, MD-WV	6,719
146	Harrisburg-Carlisle, PA	13,200
341	Harrisonburg, VA	2,007
81	Hartford, CT	30,726
NA	Hattiesburg, MS**	NA
143	Hickory, NC	13,261
319	Hinesville, GA	2,982
263	Holland-Grand Haven, MI	5,022
69	Honolulu, HI	35,912
208	Hot Springs, AR	6,831
198	Houma, LA	7,544
4	Houston, TX	282,846
124	Huntsville, AL	16,209
317	Idaho Falls, ID	3,059
37	Indianapolis, IN	77,610
306	Iowa City, IA	3,343
NA	Ithaca, NY**	NA
43	Jacksonville, FL	66,304
217	Jacksonville, NC	6,640
271	Jackson, MI	4,832
97	Jackson, MS	23,150
219	Jackson, TN	6,506
264	Janesville, WI	5,004
298	Jefferson City, MO	3,712
228	Johnson City, TN	6,230
260	Jonesboro, AR	5,034
149	Kalamazoo-Portage, MI	12,879
NA	Kansas City, MO-KS**	NA
213	Kennewick-Pasco-Richland, WA	6,671
141	Killeen-Temple-Fort Hood, TX	13,411
158	Kingsport, TN-VA	11,542
294	Kingston, NY	3,885
84	Knoxville, TN	28,254
300	Kokomo, IN	3,513
NA	La Crosse, WI-MN**	NA
233	Lafayette, IN	6,007
135	Lafayette, LA	13,999
170	Lake Charles, LA	10,525
205	Lake Havasu City-Kingman, AZ	7,203
91	Lakeland, FL	24,616
165	Lancaster, PA	10,774
137	Lansing-East Lansing, MI	13,741

Note: All listings are for Metropolitan Statistical Areas (M.S.A.s) except for those ending with "M.D." Listings with "M.D." are Metropolitan Divisions which are smaller parts of eleven large M.S.A.s. See explanatory note at beginning of metropolitan area section.

Alpha Order - Metro Area (continued)

RANK	METROPOLITAN AREA	CRIMES
130	Laredo, TX	15,511
199	Las Cruces, NM	7,503
38	Las Vegas-Paradise, NV	76,964
250	Lawrence, KS	5,566
222	Lawton, OK	6,464
335	Lebanon, PA	2,419
325	Lewiston-Auburn, ME	2,664
343	Lewiston, ID-WA	1,930
115	Lexington-Fayette, KY	18,044
259	Lima, OH	5,064
156	Lincoln, NE	11,845
60	Little Rock, AR	41,596
340	Logan, UT-ID	2,022
164	Longview, TX	10,787
289	Longview, WA	4,111
3	Los Angeles County, CA M.D.	296,707
2	Los Angeles (greater), CA	364,830
58	Louisville, KY-IN	46,451
123	Lubbock, TX	16,771
254	Lynchburg, VA	5,358
154	Macon, GA	12,420
296	Madera, CA	3,855
125	Madison, WI	16,199
175	Manchester-Nashua, NH	10,096
311	Manhattan, KS	3,191
NA	Mankato-North Mankato, MN**	NA
257	Mansfield, OH	5,172
61	McAllen-Edinburg-Mission, TX	40,347
252	Medford, OR	5,461
31	Memphis, TN-MS-AR	80,782
178	Merced, CA	9,968
5	Miami (greater), FL	281,792
16	Miami-Dade County, FL M.D.	142,651
281	Michigan City-La Porte, IN	4,258
262	Midland, TX	5,027
45	Milwaukee, WI	64,057
NA	Minneapolis-St. Paul, MN-WI**	NA
318	Missoula, MT	3,039
98	Mobile, AL	23,029
93	Modesto, CA	24,298
291	Monroe, MI	3,996
122	Montgomery, AL	16,887
308	Morgantown, WV	3,242
267	Morristown, TN	4,925
244	Mount Vernon-Anacortes, WA	5,700
297	Muncie, IN	3,797
195	Muskegon-Norton Shores, MI	7,992
301	Napa, CA	3,509
206	Naples-Marco Island, FL	6,911
46	Nashville-Davidson, TN	63,593
53	Nassau-Suffolk, NY M.D.	54,281
82	New Haven-Milford, CT	29,546
NA	New Orleans, LA**	NA
1	New York (greater), NY-NJ-PA	406,748
7	New York-W. Plains NY-NJ M.D.	255,228
54	Newark-Union, NJ-PA M.D.	49,998
253	Niles-Benton Harbor, MI	5,420
79	North Port-Bradenton-Sarasota, FL	31,212
286	Norwich-New London, CT	4,156
26	Oakland-Fremont, CA M.D.	102,859
173	Ocala, FL	10,391
275	Ocean City, NJ	4,510
218	Odessa, TX	6,557

RANK	METROPOLITAN AREA	CRIMES
129	Ogden-Clearfield, UT	15,521
NA	Oklahoma City, OK**	NA
191	Olympia, WA	8,068
76	Omaha-Council Bluffs, NE-IA	31,858
27	Orlando, FL	97,705
280	Oshkosh-Neenah, WI	4,278
306	Owensboro, KY	3,343
119	Oxnard-Thousand Oaks, CA	17,350
102	Palm Bay-Melbourne, FL	21,592
328	Palm Coast, FL	2,587
188	Panama City-Lynn Haven, FL	8,154
241	Pascagoula, MS	5,723
114	Peabody, MA M.D.	18,681
118	Pensacola, FL	17,699
9	Philadelphia (greater) PA-NJ-MD-DE	191,833
19	Philadelphia, PA M.D.	129,123
11	Phoenix-Mesa-Scottsdale, AZ	174,335
236	Pine Bluff, AR	5,955
52	Pittsburgh, PA	56,050
303	Pittsfield, MA	3,484
327	Pocatello, ID	2,638
144	Port St. Lucie, FL	13,260
40	Portland-Vancouver, OR-WA	71,600
145	Portland, ME	13,239
133	Poughkeepsie, NY	15,144
255	Prescott, AZ	5,247
57	Providence-New Bedford, RI-MA	47,106
151	Provo-Orem, UT	12,700
246	Pueblo, CO	5,639
274	Punta Gorda, FL	4,623
227	Racine, WI	6,233
74	Raleigh-Cary, NC	32,858
295	Rapid City, SD	3,860
162	Reading, PA	10,861
237	Redding, CA	5,920
126	Reno-Sparks, NV	15,727
67	Richmond, VA	37,516
18	Riverside-San Bernardino, CA	136,626
181	Roanoke, VA	9,363
NA	Rochester, MN**	NA
77	Rochester, NY	31,630
186	Rockingham County, NH M.D.	8,628
202	Rocky Mount, NC	7,351
299	Rome, GA	3,519
34	Sacramento, CA	79,241
193	Saginaw, MI	8,033
147	Salem, OR	13,191
142	Salinas, CA	13,322
234	Salisbury, MD	5,997
49	Salt Lake City, UT	57,360
261	San Angelo, TX	5,031
20	San Antonio, TX	123,359
30	San Diego, CA	82,513
13	San Francisco (greater), CA	168,071
44	San Francisco-S. Mateo, CA M.D.	65,212
55	San Jose, CA	49,121
213	San Luis Obispo, CA	6,671
329	Sandusky, OH	2,545
42	Santa Ana-Anaheim, CA M.D.	68,123
163	Santa Barbara-Santa Maria, CA	10,806
174	Santa Cruz-Watsonville, CA	10,274
223	Santa Fe, NM	6,383
159	Santa Rosa-Petaluma, CA	11,367

RANK	METROPOLITAN AREA	CRIMES
127	Savannah, GA	15,658
138	Scranton--Wilkes-Barre, PA	13,673
23	Seattle-Bellevue-Everett, WA M.D.	111,058
15	Seattle-Tacoma-Bellevue, WA	150,062
276	Sebastian-Vero Beach, FL	4,484
315	Sheboygan, WI	3,100
282	Sherman-Denison, TX	4,224
NA	Shreveport-Bossier City, LA**	NA
293	Sioux City, IA-NE-SD	3,937
239	Sioux Falls, SD	5,899
134	South Bend-Mishawaka, IN-MI	14,150
152	Spartanburg, SC	12,615
101	Spokane, WA	21,845
94	Springfield, MA	23,636
105	Springfield, MO	20,889
229	Springfield, OH	6,147
322	State College, PA	2,860
72	Stockton, CA	34,303
NA	St. Cloud, MN**	NA
326	St. George, UT	2,642
256	St. Joseph, MO-KS	5,220
NA	St. Louis, MO-IL**	NA
287	Sumter, SC	4,128
117	Syracuse, NY	17,870
66	Tacoma, WA M.D.	39,004
128	Tallahassee, FL	15,620
21	Tampa-St Petersburg, FL	122,522
210	Texarkana, TX-Texarkana, AR	6,787
NA	Toledo, OH**	NA
176	Topeka, KS	10,056
180	Trenton-Ewing, NJ	9,378
NA	Tucson, AZ**	NA
62	Tulsa, OK	40,126
169	Tuscaloosa, AL	10,538
182	Tyler, TX	9,182
194	Utica-Rome, NY	7,999
245	Valdosta, GA	5,658
131	Vallejo-Fairfield, CA	15,334
235	Victoria, TX	5,976
230	Vineland, NJ	6,119
116	Visalia-Porterville, CA	17,911
157	Waco, TX	11,671
242	Warner Robins, GA	5,721
48	Warren-Farmington Hills, MI M.D.	58,905
12	Washington (greater) DC-VA-MD-WV	170,463
17	Washington, DC-VA-MD-WV M.D.	139,492
265	Waterloo-Cedar Falls, IA	4,977
333	Wausau, WI	2,453
302	Wenatchee, WA	3,503
47	West Palm Beach, FL M.D.	60,011
313	Wheeling, WV-OH	3,136
207	Wichita Falls, TX	6,908
83	Wichita, KS	28,953
334	Williamsport, PA	2,439
85	Wilmington, DE-MD-NJ M.D.	27,320
NA	Wilmington, NC**	NA
309	Winchester, VA-WV	3,221
96	Winston-Salem, NC	23,321
107	Worcester, MA	20,594
179	York-Hanover, PA	9,924
110	Youngstown, OH-PA	20,316
283	Yuba City, CA	4,212
231	Yuma, AZ	6,104

Source: CQ Press using reported data from the F.B.I. "Crime in the United States 2009"
*Includes murder, rape, robbery, aggravated assault, burglary, larceny-theft, and motor vehicle theft.
**Not available.

1. Crimes in 2009 (continued)
National Total = 10,639,369 Crimes*

RANK	METROPOLITAN AREA	CRIMES
1	New York (greater), NY-NJ-PA	406,748
2	Los Angeles (greater), CA	364,830
3	Los Angeles County, CA M.D.	296,707
4	Houston, TX	282,846
5	Miami (greater), FL	281,792
6	Dallas (greater), TX	278,856
7	New York-W. Plains NY-NJ M.D.	255,228
8	Atlanta, GA	218,690
9	Philadelphia (greater) PA-NJ-MD-DE	191,833
10	Dallas-Plano-Irving, TX M.D.	182,732
11	Phoenix-Mesa-Scottsdale, AZ	174,335
12	Washington (greater) DC-VA-MD-WV	170,463
13	San Francisco (greater), CA	168,071
14	Detroit (greater), MI	164,189
15	Seattle-Tacoma-Bellevue, WA	150,062
16	Miami-Dade County, FL M.D.	142,651
17	Washington, DC-VA-MD-WV M.D.	139,492
18	Riverside-San Bernardino, CA	136,626
19	Philadelphia, PA M.D.	129,123
20	San Antonio, TX	123,359
21	Tampa-St Petersburg, FL	122,522
22	Boston (greater), MA-NH	116,966
23	Seattle-Bellevue-Everett, WA M.D.	111,058
24	Baltimore-Towson, MD	108,220
25	Detroit-Livonia-Dearborn, MI M.D.	105,284
26	Oakland-Fremont, CA M.D.	102,859
27	Orlando, FL	97,705
28	Fort Worth-Arlington, TX M.D.	96,124
29	Columbus, OH	83,784
30	San Diego, CA	82,513
31	Memphis, TN-MS-AR	80,782
32	Denver-Aurora, CO	80,209
33	Cincinnati-Middletown, OH-KY-IN	79,440
34	Sacramento, CA	79,241
35	Fort Lauderdale, FL M.D.	79,130
36	Charlotte-Gastonia, NC-SC	77,629
37	Indianapolis, IN	77,610
38	Las Vegas-Paradise, NV	76,964
39	Austin-Round Rock, TX	74,718
40	Portland-Vancouver, OR-WA	71,600
41	Cleveland-Elyria-Mentor, OH	68,381
42	Santa Ana-Anaheim, CA M.D.	68,123
43	Jacksonville, FL	66,304
44	San Francisco-S. Mateo, CA M.D.	65,212
45	Milwaukee, WI	64,057
46	Nashville-Davidson, TN	63,593
47	West Palm Beach, FL M.D.	60,011
48	Warren-Farmington Hills, MI M.D.	58,905
49	Salt Lake City, UT	57,360
50	Birmingham-Hoover, AL	57,331
51	Boston-Quincy, MA M.D.	57,121
52	Pittsburgh, PA	56,050
53	Nassau-Suffolk, NY M.D.	54,281
54	Newark-Union, NJ-PA M.D.	49,998
55	San Jose, CA	49,121
56	Edison, NJ M.D.	47,241
57	Providence-New Bedford, RI-MA	47,106
58	Louisville, KY-IN	46,451
59	Albuquerque, NM	42,993
60	Little Rock, AR	41,596
61	McAllen-Edinburg-Mission, TX	40,347
62	Tulsa, OK	40,126
63	Fresno, CA	39,846
64	Buffalo-Niagara Falls, NY	39,757
65	Baton Rouge, LA	39,194
66	Tacoma, WA M.D.	39,004
67	Richmond, VA	37,516
68	Bakersfield, CA	36,337
69	Honolulu, HI	35,912
70	Camden, NJ M.D.	35,390
71	Columbia, SC	35,254
72	Stockton, CA	34,303
73	Greensboro-High Point, NC	34,228
74	Raleigh-Cary, NC	32,858
75	Cambridge-Newton, MA M.D.	32,536
76	Omaha-Council Bluffs, NE-IA	31,858
77	Rochester, NY	31,630
78	Dayton, OH	31,355
79	North Port-Bradenton-Sarasota, FL	31,212
80	Bethesda-Frederick, MD M.D.	30,971
81	Hartford, CT	30,726
82	New Haven-Milford, CT	29,546
83	Wichita, KS	28,953
84	Knoxville, TN	28,254
85	Wilmington, DE-MD-NJ M.D.	27,320
86	Augusta, GA-SC	27,219
87	Chattanooga, TN-GA	25,592
88	Akron, OH	25,412
89	El Paso, TX	25,212
90	Grand Rapids-Wyoming, MI	24,725
91	Lakeland, FL	24,616
92	Albany-Schenectady-Troy, NY	24,528
93	Modesto, CA	24,298
94	Springfield, MA	23,636
95	Corpus Christi, TX	23,612
96	Winston-Salem, NC	23,321
97	Jackson, MS	23,150
98	Mobile, AL	23,029
99	Fayetteville, NC	22,653
100	Durham-Chapel Hill, NC	22,200
101	Spokane, WA	21,845
102	Palm Bay-Melbourne, FL	21,592
103	Deltona-Daytona Beach, FL	21,121
104	Allentown, PA-NJ	21,057
105	Springfield, MO	20,889
106	Colorado Springs, CO	20,646
107	Worcester, MA	20,594
108	Cape Coral-Fort Myers, FL	20,501
109	Brownsville-Harlingen, TX	20,411
110	Youngstown, OH-PA	20,316
111	Bridgeport-Stamford, CT	20,033
112	Flint, MI	19,540
113	Columbus, GA-AL	19,209
114	Peabody, MA M.D.	18,681
115	Lexington-Fayette, KY	18,044
116	Visalia-Porterville, CA	17,911
117	Syracuse, NY	17,870
118	Pensacola, FL	17,699
119	Oxnard-Thousand Oaks, CA	17,350
120	Des Moines-West Des Moines, IA	17,146
121	Beaumont-Port Arthur, TX	16,939
122	Montgomery, AL	16,887
123	Lubbock, TX	16,771
124	Huntsville, AL	16,209
125	Madison, WI	16,199
126	Reno-Sparks, NV	15,727
127	Savannah, GA	15,658
128	Tallahassee, FL	15,620
129	Ogden-Clearfield, UT	15,521
130	Laredo, TX	15,511
131	Vallejo-Fairfield, CA	15,334
132	Eugene-Springfield, OR	15,295
133	Poughkeepsie, NY	15,144
134	South Bend-Mishawaka, IN-MI	14,150
135	Lafayette, LA	13,999
136	Anchorage, AK	13,816
137	Lansing-East Lansing, MI	13,741
138	Scranton--Wilkes-Barre, PA	13,673
139	Boise City-Nampa, ID	13,648
140	Amarillo, TX	13,525
141	Killeen-Temple-Fort Hood, TX	13,411
142	Salinas, CA	13,322
143	Hickory, NC	13,261
144	Port St. Lucie, FL	13,260
145	Portland, ME	13,239
146	Harrisburg-Carlisle, PA	13,200
147	Salem, OR	13,191
148	Gainesville, FL	13,157
149	Kalamazoo-Portage, MI	12,879
150	Fayetteville, AR-MO	12,776
151	Provo-Orem, UT	12,700
152	Spartanburg, SC	12,615
153	Fort Wayne, IN	12,597
154	Macon, GA	12,420
155	Florence, SC	11,870
156	Lincoln, NE	11,845
157	Waco, TX	11,671
158	Kingsport, TN-VA	11,542
159	Santa Rosa-Petaluma, CA	11,367
160	Asheville, NC	11,112
161	Charleston, WV	10,990
162	Reading, PA	10,861
163	Santa Barbara-Santa Maria, CA	10,806
164	Longview, TX	10,787
165	Lancaster, PA	10,774
166	Gulfport-Biloxi, MS	10,772
167	Atlantic City, NJ	10,763
168	Fort Smith, AR-OK	10,668
169	Tuscaloosa, AL	10,538
170	Lake Charles, LA	10,525
171	Ann Arbor, MI	10,470
172	Evansville, IN-KY	10,433
173	Ocala, FL	10,391
174	Santa Cruz-Watsonville, CA	10,274
175	Manchester-Nashua, NH	10,096
176	Topeka, KS	10,056
177	College Station-Bryan, TX	10,052
178	Merced, CA	9,968
179	York-Hanover, PA	9,924
180	Trenton-Ewing, NJ	9,378

Note: All listings are for Metropolitan Statistical Areas (M.S.A.s) except for those ending with "M.D." Listings with "M.D." are Metropolitan Divisions which are smaller parts of eleven large M.S.A.s. See explanatory note at beginning of metropolitan area section.

Rank Order - Metro Area (continued)

RANK	METROPOLITAN AREA	CRIMES
181	Roanoke, VA	9,363
182	Tyler, TX	9,182
183	Clarksville, TN-KY	9,148
184	Fort Collins-Loveland, CO	9,073
185	Anderson, SC	9,070
186	Rockingham County, NH M.D.	8,628
187	Athens-Clarke County, GA	8,403
188	Panama City-Lynn Haven, FL	8,154
189	Alexandria, LA	8,117
190	Albany, GA	8,097
191	Olympia, WA	8,068
192	Barnstable Town, MA	8,050
193	Saginaw, MI	8,033
194	Utica-Rome, NY	7,999
195	Muskegon-Norton Shores, MI	7,992
196	Boulder, CO	7,853
197	Cedar Rapids, IA	7,757
198	Houma, LA	7,544
199	Las Cruces, NM	7,503
200	Bellingham, WA	7,432
201	Erie, PA	7,357
202	Rocky Mount, NC	7,351
203	Chico, CA	7,270
204	Bremerton-Silverdale, WA	7,225
205	Lake Havasu City-Kingman, AZ	7,203
206	Naples-Marco Island, FL	6,911
207	Wichita Falls, TX	6,908
208	Hot Springs, AR	6,831
209	Greeley, CO	6,815
210	Texarkana, TX-Texarkana, AR	6,787
211	Burlington-South Burlington, VT	6,749
212	Hagerstown-Martinsburg, MD-WV	6,719
213	Kennewick-Pasco-Richland, WA	6,671
213	San Luis Obispo, CA	6,671
215	Dover, DE	6,665
216	Binghamton, NY	6,647
217	Jacksonville, NC	6,640
218	Odessa, TX	6,557
219	Jackson, TN	6,506
220	Green Bay, WI	6,498
221	Burlington, NC	6,479
222	Lawton, OK	6,464
223	Santa Fe, NM	6,383
224	Abilene, TX	6,348
225	Anniston-Oxford, AL	6,295
226	Battle Creek, MI	6,270
227	Racine, WI	6,233
228	Johnson City, TN	6,230
229	Springfield, OH	6,147
230	Vineland, NJ	6,119
231	Yuma, AZ	6,104
232	Billings, MT	6,017
233	Lafayette, IN	6,007
234	Salisbury, MD	5,997
235	Victoria, TX	5,976
236	Pine Bluff, AR	5,955
237	Redding, CA	5,920
238	Columbia, MO	5,918
239	Sioux Falls, SD	5,899
240	Bloomington, IN	5,895
241	Pascagoula, MS	5,723
242	Warner Robins, GA	5,721
243	Crestview-Fort Walton Beach, FL	5,704

RANK	METROPOLITAN AREA	CRIMES
244	Mount Vernon-Anacortes, WA	5,700
245	Valdosta, GA	5,658
246	Pueblo, CO	5,639
247	Brunswick, GA	5,620
248	Charlottesville, VA	5,611
249	Elkhart-Goshen, IN	5,603
250	Lawrence, KS	5,566
251	Goldsboro, NC	5,516
252	Medford, OR	5,461
253	Niles-Benton Harbor, MI	5,420
254	Lynchburg, VA	5,358
255	Prescott, AZ	5,247
256	St. Joseph, MO-KS	5,220
257	Mansfield, OH	5,172
258	Bangor, ME	5,151
259	Lima, OH	5,064
260	Jonesboro, AR	5,034
261	San Angelo, TX	5,031
262	Midland, TX	5,027
263	Holland-Grand Haven, MI	5,022
264	Janesville, WI	5,004
265	Waterloo-Cedar Falls, IA	4,977
266	Grand Junction, CO	4,951
267	Morristown, TN	4,925
268	Florence-Muscle Shoals, AL	4,887
269	Gainesville, GA	4,857
270	Anderson, IN	4,853
271	Jackson, MI	4,832
272	Flagstaff, AZ	4,821
273	Appleton, WI	4,703
274	Punta Gorda, FL	4,623
275	Ocean City, NJ	4,510
276	Sebastian-Vero Beach, FL	4,484
277	Blacksburg, VA	4,461
278	Bend, OR	4,435
279	Dalton, GA	4,296
280	Oshkosh-Neenah, WI	4,278
281	Michigan City-La Porte, IN	4,258
282	Sherman-Denison, TX	4,224
283	Yuba City, CA	4,212
284	Coeur d'Alene, ID	4,195
285	Bowling Green, KY	4,183
286	Norwich-New London, CT	4,156
287	Sumter, SC	4,128
288	Cleveland, TN	4,120
289	Longview, WA	4,111
290	Gadsden, AL	4,101
291	Monroe, MI	3,996
292	Farmington, NM	3,951
293	Sioux City, IA-NE-SD	3,937
294	Kingston, NY	3,885
295	Rapid City, SD	3,860
296	Madera, CA	3,855
297	Muncie, IN	3,797
298	Jefferson City, MO	3,712
299	Rome, GA	3,519
300	Kokomo, IN	3,513
301	Napa, CA	3,509
302	Wenatchee, WA	3,503
303	Pittsfield, MA	3,484
304	Eau Claire, WI	3,442
305	Cape Girardeau, MO-IL	3,379
306	Iowa City, IA	3,343

RANK	METROPOLITAN AREA	CRIMES
306	Owensboro, KY	3,343
308	Morgantown, WV	3,242
309	Winchester, VA-WV	3,221
310	Cumberland, MD-WV	3,211
311	Manhattan, KS	3,191
312	Danville, VA	3,171
313	Wheeling, WV-OH	3,136
314	Casper, WY	3,117
315	Sheboygan, WI	3,100
316	Cheyenne, WY	3,064
317	Idaho Falls, ID	3,059
318	Missoula, MT	3,039
319	Hinesville, GA	2,982
320	Bay City, MI	2,932
320	Great Falls, MT	2,932
322	State College, PA	2,860
323	Altoona, PA	2,717
324	Columbus, IN	2,694
325	Lewiston-Auburn, ME	2,664
326	St. George, UT	2,642
327	Pocatello, ID	2,638
328	Palm Coast, FL	2,587
329	Sandusky, OH	2,545
330	Dubuque, IA	2,542
331	Ames, IA	2,508
332	Bismarck, ND	2,460
333	Wausau, WI	2,453
334	Williamsport, PA	2,439
335	Lebanon, PA	2,419
336	Corvallis, OR	2,395
336	Elizabethtown, KY	2,395
338	Glens Falls, NY	2,210
339	Elmira, NY	2,123
340	Logan, UT-ID	2,022
341	Harrisonburg, VA	2,007
342	Fond du Lac, WI	1,935
343	Lewiston, ID-WA	1,930
344	Carson City, NV	1,331
NA	Auburn, AL**	NA
NA	Charleston-North Charleston, SC**	NA
NA	Danville, IL**	NA
NA	Decatur, AL**	NA
NA	Decatur, IL**	NA
NA	Dothan, AL**	NA
NA	Duluth, MN-WI**	NA
NA	El Centro, CA**	NA
NA	Fargo, ND-MN**	NA
NA	Grand Forks, ND-MN**	NA
NA	Hattiesburg, MS**	NA
NA	Ithaca, NY**	NA
NA	Kansas City, MO-KS**	NA
NA	La Crosse, WI-MN**	NA
NA	Mankato-North Mankato, MN**	NA
NA	Minneapolis-St. Paul, MN-WI**	NA
NA	New Orleans, LA**	NA
NA	Oklahoma City, OK**	NA
NA	Rochester, MN**	NA
NA	Shreveport-Bossier City, LA**	NA
NA	St. Cloud, MN**	NA
NA	St. Louis, MO-IL**	NA
NA	Toledo, OH**	NA
NA	Tucson, AZ**	NA
NA	Wilmington, NC**	NA

Source: CQ Press using reported data from the F.B.I. "Crime in the United States 2009"
*Includes murder, rape, robbery, aggravated assault, burglary, larceny-theft, and motor vehicle theft.
**Not available.

2. Crime Rate in 2009

National Rate = 3,465.5 Crimes per 100,000 Population*

RANK	METROPOLITAN AREA	RATE
127	Abilene, TX	3,976.7
161	Akron, OH	3,625.5
249	Albany-Schenectady-Troy, NY	2,863.0
45	Albany, GA	4,902.3
38	Albuquerque, NM	4,986.5
24	Alexandria, LA	5,236.8
285	Allentown, PA-NJ	2,575.2
320	Altoona, PA	2,172.4
17	Amarillo, TX	5,497.1
248	Ames, IA	2,869.6
74	Anchorage, AK	4,525.6
155	Anderson, IN	3,689.8
47	Anderson, SC	4,881.7
235	Ann Arbor, MI	3,003.4
16	Anniston-Oxford, AL	5,514.4
330	Appleton, WI	2,122.2
271	Asheville, NC	2,686.9
88	Athens-Clarke County, GA	4,397.3
126	Atlanta, GA	3,980.2
132	Atlantic City, NJ	3,948.3
NA	Auburn, AL**	NA
32	Augusta, GA-SC	5,061.6
90	Austin-Round Rock, TX	4,380.9
80	Bakersfield, CA	4,461.2
118	Baltimore-Towson, MD	4,018.4
179	Bangor, ME	3,462.3
168	Barnstable Town, MA	3,588.9
39	Baton Rouge, LA	4,975.6
66	Battle Creek, MI	4,641.9
261	Bay City, MI	2,745.9
78	Beaumont-Port Arthur, TX	4,481.4
154	Bellingham, WA	3,693.9
267	Bend, OR	2,710.2
282	Bethesda-Frederick, MD M.D.	2,593.3
135	Billings, MT	3,921.4
265	Binghamton, NY	2,720.1
31	Birmingham-Hoover, AL	5,070.2
311	Bismarck, ND	2,300.1
255	Blacksburg, VA	2,793.2
209	Bloomington, IN	3,183.2
316	Boise City-Nampa, ID	2,222.7
291	Boston (greater), MA-NH	2,550.2
239	Boston-Quincy, MA M.D.	2,986.9
276	Boulder, CO	2,651.7
177	Bowling Green, KY	3,493.3
240	Bremerton-Silverdale, WA	2,985.2
312	Bridgeport-Stamford, CT	2,281.6
28	Brownsville-Harlingen, TX	5,103.3
19	Brunswick, GA	5,428.6
172	Buffalo-Niagara Falls, NY	3,552.6
201	Burlington-South Burlington, VT	3,226.1
97	Burlington, NC	4,312.1
322	Cambridge-Newton, MA M.D.	2,162.9
253	Camden, NJ M.D.	2,815.1
186	Cape Coral-Fort Myers, FL	3,376.3
166	Cape Girardeau, MO-IL	3,605.7
303	Carson City, NV	2,443.9
108	Casper, WY	4,164.0
232	Cedar Rapids, IA	3,016.9
NA	Charleston-North Charleston, SC**	NA
165	Charleston, WV	3,615.3
84	Charlotte-Gastonia, NC-SC	4,430.4
251	Charlottesville, VA	2,841.2
46	Chattanooga, TN-GA	4,885.9
181	Cheyenne, WY	3,429.0
193	Chico, CA	3,282.5
159	Cincinnati-Middletown, OH-KY-IN	3,647.2
180	Clarksville, TN-KY	3,448.2
196	Cleveland-Elyria-Mentor, OH	3,266.8
160	Cleveland, TN	3,632.9
238	Coeur d'Alene, ID	2,987.7
54	College Station-Bryan, TX	4,780.2
192	Colorado Springs, CO	3,287.2
171	Columbia, MO	3,555.1
57	Columbia, SC	4,753.6
2	Columbus, GA-AL	6,678.9
174	Columbus, IN	3,549.3
64	Columbus, OH	4,661.2
14	Corpus Christi, TX	5,659.6
245	Corvallis, OR	2,916.6
208	Crestview-Fort Walton Beach, FL	3,184.8
199	Cumberland, MD-WV	3,239.1
95	Dallas (greater), TX	4,323.5
104	Dallas-Plano-Irving, TX M.D.	4,220.1
212	Dalton, GA	3,179.8
NA	Danville, IL**	NA
236	Danville, VA	2,999.4
147	Dayton, OH	3,742.2
NA	Decatur, AL**	NA
NA	Decatur, IL**	NA
103	Deltona-Daytona Beach, FL	4,225.4
214	Denver-Aurora, CO	3,144.4
228	Des Moines-West Des Moines, IA	3,037.8
149	Detroit (greater), MI	3,727.8
18	Detroit-Livonia-Dearborn, MI M.D.	5,454.1
NA	Dothan, AL**	NA
107	Dover, DE	4,186.1
263	Dubuque, IA	2,733.8
NA	Duluth, MN-WI**	NA
81	Durham-Chapel Hill, NC	4,455.4
325	Eau Claire, WI	2,153.7
334	Edison, NJ M.D.	2,018.3
NA	El Centro, CA**	NA
187	El Paso, TX	3,361.8
331	Elizabethtown, KY	2,120.1
257	Elkhart-Goshen, IN	2,783.6
305	Elmira, NY	2,428.2
279	Erie, PA	2,630.2
89	Eugene-Springfield, OR	4,388.5
242	Evansville, IN-KY	2,966.6
NA	Fargo, ND-MN**	NA
206	Farmington, NM	3,191.2
256	Fayetteville, AR-MO	2,790.6
4	Fayetteville, NC	6,310.3
146	Flagstaff, AZ	3,752.9
70	Flint, MI	4,584.9
184	Florence-Muscle Shoals, AL	3,381.6
10	Florence, SC	5,884.8
336	Fond du Lac, WI	1,942.1
226	Fort Collins-Loveland, CO	3,043.5
75	Fort Lauderdale, FL M.D.	4,523.1
162	Fort Smith, AR-OK	3,624.7
227	Fort Wayne, IN	3,041.7
73	Fort Worth-Arlington, TX M.D.	4,534.8
94	Fresno, CA	4,337.1
130	Gadsden, AL	3,952.4
30	Gainesville, FL	5,075.1
288	Gainesville, GA	2,561.1
342	Glens Falls, NY	1,710.0
49	Goldsboro, NC	4,843.3
NA	Grand Forks, ND-MN**	NA
185	Grand Junction, CO	3,377.1
211	Grand Rapids-Wyoming, MI	3,179.9
170	Great Falls, MT	3,567.2
277	Greeley, CO	2,631.2
328	Green Bay, WI	2,130.2
53	Greensboro-High Point, NC	4,794.6
68	Gulfport-Biloxi, MS	4,610.9
297	Hagerstown-Martinsburg, MD-WV	2,490.6
300	Harrisburg-Carlisle, PA	2,467.5
343	Harrisonburg, VA	1,672.0
225	Hartford, CT	3,049.7
NA	Hattiesburg, MS**	NA
163	Hickory, NC	3,623.9
98	Hinesville, GA	4,293.3
337	Holland-Grand Haven, MI	1,918.8
128	Honolulu, HI	3,958.9
1	Hot Springs, AR	6,905.2
151	Houma, LA	3,713.0
50	Houston, TX	4,827.6
119	Huntsville, AL	4,015.5
302	Idaho Falls, ID	2,446.1
82	Indianapolis, IN	4,455.0
317	Iowa City, IA	2,209.8
NA	Ithaca, NY**	NA
36	Jacksonville, FL	5,004.1
131	Jacksonville, NC	3,949.7
231	Jackson, MI	3,025.8
100	Jackson, MS	4,269.2
13	Jackson, TN	5,726.4
219	Janesville, WI	3,107.9
292	Jefferson City, MO	2,524.3
213	Johnson City, TN	3,145.3
101	Jonesboro, AR	4,232.7
125	Kalamazoo-Portage, MI	3,983.1
NA	Kansas City, MO-KS**	NA
260	Kennewick-Pasco-Richland, WA	2,747.3
178	Killeen-Temple-Fort Hood, TX	3,482.1
142	Kingsport, TN-VA	3,766.9
326	Kingston, NY	2,134.2
117	Knoxville, TN	4,024.6
175	Kokomo, IN	3,540.5
NA	La Crosse, WI-MN**	NA
223	Lafayette, IN	3,082.9
23	Lafayette, LA	5,321.9
20	Lake Charles, LA	5,423.4
164	Lake Havasu City-Kingman, AZ	3,618.9
106	Lakeland, FL	4,193.1
329	Lancaster, PA	2,124.3
229	Lansing-East Lansing, MI	3,034.4

Note: All listings are for Metropolitan Statistical Areas (M.S.A.s) except for those ending with "M.D." Listings with "M.D." are Metropolitan Divisions which are smaller parts of eleven large M.S.A.s. See explanatory note at beginning of metropolitan area section.

Alpha Order - Metro Area (continued)

RANK	METROPOLITAN AREA	RATE
3	Laredo, TX	6,397.7
158	Las Cruces, NM	3,653.8
115	Las Vegas-Paradise, NV	4,042.4
55	Lawrence, KS	4,773.5
11	Lawton, OK	5,764.2
340	Lebanon, PA	1,857.2
298	Lewiston-Auburn, ME	2,489.6
210	Lewiston, ID-WA	3,182.9
139	Lexington-Fayette, KY	3,832.3
52	Lima, OH	4,817.8
129	Lincoln, NE	3,955.4
7	Little Rock, AR	6,068.9
344	Logan, UT-ID	1,590.7
25	Longview, TX	5,231.4
122	Longview, WA	3,998.4
234	Los Angeles County, CA M.D.	3,008.0
252	Los Angeles (greater), CA	2,832.2
153	Louisville, KY-IN	3,697.6
6	Lubbock, TX	6,136.7
324	Lynchburg, VA	2,154.4
22	Macon, GA	5,382.4
290	Madera, CA	2,555.4
250	Madison, WI	2,851.9
296	Manchester-Nashua, NH	2,497.1
284	Manhattan, KS	2,581.8
NA	Mankato-North Mankato, MN**	NA
110	Mansfield, OH	4,139.1
21	McAllen-Edinburg-Mission, TX	5,402.9
270	Medford, OR	2,690.1
5	Memphis, TN-MS-AR	6,218.7
123	Merced, CA	3,996.3
27	Miami (greater), FL	5,122.4
12	Miami-Dade County, FL M.D.	5,746.5
140	Michigan City-La Porte, IN	3,830.7
141	Midland, TX	3,828.9
111	Milwaukee, WI	4,122.4
NA	Minneapolis-St. Paul, MN-WI**	NA
254	Missoula, MT	2,798.7
15	Mobile, AL	5,633.1
61	Modesto, CA	4,707.1
281	Monroe, MI	2,610.5
72	Montgomery, AL	4,565.9
266	Morgantown, WV	2,711.1
169	Morristown, TN	3,574.2
59	Mount Vernon-Anacortes, WA	4,732.7
190	Muncie, IN	3,318.1
69	Muskegon-Norton Shores, MI	4,591.3
280	Napa, CA	2,618.7
323	Naples-Marco Island, FL	2,159.0
120	Nashville-Davidson, TN	4,012.9
338	Nassau-Suffolk, NY M.D.	1,888.1
150	New Haven-Milford, CT	3,717.9
NA	New Orleans, LA**	NA
327	New York (greater), NY-NJ-PA	2,132.4
318	New York-W. Plains NY-NJ M.D.	2,174.6
309	Newark-Union, NJ-PA M.D.	2,355.2
182	Niles-Benton Harbor, MI	3,419.5
76	North Port-Bradenton-Sarasota, FL	4,502.8
237	Norwich-New London, CT	2,998.3
113	Oakland-Fremont, CA M.D.	4,102.9
221	Ocala, FL	3,097.8
58	Ocean City, NJ	4,742.4
44	Odessa, TX	4,915.3

RANK	METROPOLITAN AREA	RATE
247	Ogden-Clearfield, UT	2,878.2
NA	Oklahoma City, OK**	NA
204	Olympia, WA	3,212.7
145	Omaha-Council Bluffs, NE-IA	3,758.1
63	Orlando, FL	4,680.9
278	Oshkosh-Neenah, WI	2,631.1
243	Owensboro, KY	2,951.8
321	Oxnard-Thousand Oaks, CA	2,169.6
121	Palm Bay-Melbourne, FL	4,008.2
272	Palm Coast, FL	2,677.7
41	Panama City-Lynn Haven, FL	4,962.1
148	Pascagoula, MS	3,730.4
295	Peabody, MA M.D.	2,499.8
136	Pensacola, FL	3,899.4
203	Philadelphia (greater) PA-NJ-MD-DE	3,213.1
202	Philadelphia, PA M.D.	3,219.2
124	Phoenix-Mesa-Scottsdale, AZ	3,996.1
9	Pine Bluff, AR	5,934.9
307	Pittsburgh, PA	2,386.4
275	Pittsfield, MA	2,653.5
241	Pocatello, ID	2,972.8
200	Port St. Lucie, FL	3,226.7
205	Portland-Vancouver, OR-WA	3,197.5
287	Portland, ME	2,566.3
315	Poughkeepsie, NY	2,233.7
306	Prescott, AZ	2,397.0
244	Providence-New Bedford, RI-MA	2,931.2
313	Provo-Orem, UT	2,269.6
173	Pueblo, CO	3,552.1
222	Punta Gorda, FL	3,089.4
220	Racine, WI	3,107.0
246	Raleigh-Cary, NC	2,913.2
217	Rapid City, SD	3,115.3
274	Reading, PA	2,662.1
197	Redding, CA	3,261.5
144	Reno-Sparks, NV	3,760.3
233	Richmond, VA	3,012.3
198	Riverside-San Bernardino, CA	3,246.7
216	Roanoke, VA	3,117.4
NA	Rochester, MN**	NA
224	Rochester, NY	3,062.2
333	Rockingham County, NH M.D.	2,042.1
37	Rocky Mount, NC	5,001.2
157	Rome, GA	3,660.1
152	Sacramento, CA	3,703.7
116	Saginaw, MI	4,037.8
189	Salem, OR	3,330.3
195	Salinas, CA	3,270.0
43	Salisbury, MD	4,915.4
29	Salt Lake City, UT	5,089.9
71	San Angelo, TX	4,569.3
8	San Antonio, TX	5,953.5
262	San Diego, CA	2,740.5
134	San Francisco (greater), CA	3,931.0
156	San Francisco-S. Mateo, CA M.D.	3,687.4
269	San Jose, CA	2,696.0
294	San Luis Obispo, CA	2,504.3
191	Sandusky, OH	3,304.6
314	Santa Ana-Anaheim, CA M.D.	2,257.3
273	Santa Barbara-Santa Maria, CA	2,670.7
114	Santa Cruz-Watsonville, CA	4,077.6
91	Santa Fe, NM	4,372.4
304	Santa Rosa-Petaluma, CA	2,440.1

RANK	METROPOLITAN AREA	RATE
67	Savannah, GA	4,633.8
299	Scranton--Wilkes-Barre, PA	2,488.7
99	Seattle-Bellevue-Everett, WA M.D.	4,273.3
86	Seattle-Tacoma-Bellevue, WA	4,415.1
188	Sebastian-Vero Beach, FL	3,360.8
268	Sheboygan, WI	2,702.6
176	Sherman-Denison, TX	3,524.9
NA	Shreveport-Bossier City, LA**	NA
259	Sioux City, IA-NE-SD	2,750.7
301	Sioux Falls, SD	2,465.6
79	South Bend-Mishawaka, IN-MI	4,462.4
85	Spartanburg, SC	4,419.8
65	Spokane, WA	4,642.2
183	Springfield, MA	3,387.8
51	Springfield, MO	4,823.1
87	Springfield, OH	4,398.5
335	State College, PA	1,956.6
34	Stockton, CA	5,024.0
NA	St. Cloud, MN**	NA
341	St. George, UT	1,844.0
112	St. Joseph, MO-KS	4,121.6
NA	St. Louis, MO-IL**	NA
133	Sumter, SC	3,943.7
258	Syracuse, NY	2,779.4
48	Tacoma, WA M.D.	4,875.8
93	Tallahassee, FL	4,358.5
83	Tampa-St Petersburg, FL	4,453.8
40	Texarkana, TX-Texarkana, AR	4,974.3
NA	Toledo, OH**	NA
92	Topeka, KS	4,364.5
289	Trenton-Ewing, NJ	2,560.7
NA	Tucson, AZ**	NA
96	Tulsa, OK	4,323.4
33	Tuscaloosa, AL	5,036.0
77	Tyler, TX	4,488.2
264	Utica-Rome, NY	2,729.3
105	Valdosta, GA	4,210.6
143	Vallejo-Fairfield, CA	3,764.9
26	Victoria, TX	5,208.5
138	Vineland, NJ	3,873.7
109	Visalia-Porterville, CA	4,148.8
35	Waco, TX	5,023.6
102	Warner Robins, GA	4,230.0
308	Warren-Farmington Hills, MI M.D.	2,381.0
215	Washington (greater) DC-VA-MD-WV	3,126.5
194	Washington, DC-VA-MD-WV M.D.	3,276.0
230	Waterloo-Cedar Falls, IA	3,033.9
339	Wausau, WI	1,865.8
207	Wenatchee, WA	3,188.4
60	West Palm Beach, FL M.D.	4,727.7
319	Wheeling, WV-OH	2,172.6
62	Wichita Falls, TX	4,698.8
56	Wichita, KS	4,761.9
332	Williamsport, PA	2,091.6
137	Wilmington, DE-MD-NJ M.D.	3,890.9
NA	Wilmington, NC**	NA
286	Winchester, VA-WV	2,574.5
42	Winston-Salem, NC	4,918.4
283	Worcester, MA	2,589.4
310	York-Hanover, PA	2,304.7
167	Youngstown, OH-PA	3,604.0
293	Yuba City, CA	2,509.4
218	Yuma, AZ	3,111.2

Source: CQ Press using reported data from the F.B.I. "Crime in the United States 2009"

*Includes murder, rape, robbery, aggravated assault, burglary, larceny-theft, and motor vehicle theft.

**Not available.

2. Crime Rate in 2009 (continued)
National Rate = 3,465.5 Crimes per 100,000 Population*

RANK	METROPOLITAN AREA	RATE
1	Hot Springs, AR	6,905.2
2	Columbus, GA-AL	6,678.9
3	Laredo, TX	6,397.7
4	Fayetteville, NC	6,310.3
5	Memphis, TN-MS-AR	6,218.7
6	Lubbock, TX	6,136.7
7	Little Rock, AR	6,068.9
8	San Antonio, TX	5,953.5
9	Pine Bluff, AR	5,934.9
10	Florence, SC	5,884.8
11	Lawton, OK	5,764.2
12	Miami-Dade County, FL M.D.	5,746.5
13	Jackson, TN	5,726.4
14	Corpus Christi, TX	5,659.6
15	Mobile, AL	5,633.1
16	Anniston-Oxford, AL	5,514.4
17	Amarillo, TX	5,497.1
18	Detroit-Livonia-Dearborn, MI M.D.	5,454.1
19	Brunswick, GA	5,428.6
20	Lake Charles, LA	5,423.4
21	McAllen-Edinburg-Mission, TX	5,402.9
22	Macon, GA	5,382.4
23	Lafayette, LA	5,321.9
24	Alexandria, LA	5,236.8
25	Longview, TX	5,231.4
26	Victoria, TX	5,208.5
27	Miami (greater), FL	5,122.4
28	Brownsville-Harlingen, TX	5,103.3
29	Salt Lake City, UT	5,089.9
30	Gainesville, FL	5,075.1
31	Birmingham-Hoover, AL	5,070.2
32	Augusta, GA-SC	5,061.6
33	Tuscaloosa, AL	5,036.0
34	Stockton, CA	5,024.0
35	Waco, TX	5,023.6
36	Jacksonville, FL	5,004.1
37	Rocky Mount, NC	5,001.2
38	Albuquerque, NM	4,986.5
39	Baton Rouge, LA	4,975.6
40	Texarkana, TX-Texarkana, AR	4,974.3
41	Panama City-Lynn Haven, FL	4,962.1
42	Winston-Salem, NC	4,918.4
43	Salisbury, MD	4,915.4
44	Odessa, TX	4,915.3
45	Albany, GA	4,902.3
46	Chattanooga, TN-GA	4,885.9
47	Anderson, SC	4,881.7
48	Tacoma, WA M.D.	4,875.8
49	Goldsboro, NC	4,843.3
50	Houston, TX	4,827.6
51	Springfield, MO	4,823.1
52	Lima, OH	4,817.8
53	Greensboro-High Point, NC	4,794.6
54	College Station-Bryan, TX	4,780.2
55	Lawrence, KS	4,773.5
56	Wichita, KS	4,761.9
57	Columbia, SC	4,753.6
58	Ocean City, NJ	4,742.4
59	Mount Vernon-Anacortes, WA	4,732.7
60	West Palm Beach, FL M.D.	4,727.7
61	Modesto, CA	4,707.1
62	Wichita Falls, TX	4,698.8
63	Orlando, FL	4,680.9
64	Columbus, OH	4,661.2
65	Spokane, WA	4,642.2
66	Battle Creek, MI	4,641.9
67	Savannah, GA	4,633.8
68	Gulfport-Biloxi, MS	4,610.9
69	Muskegon-Norton Shores, MI	4,591.3
70	Flint, MI	4,584.9
71	San Angelo, TX	4,569.3
72	Montgomery, AL	4,565.9
73	Fort Worth-Arlington, TX M.D.	4,534.8
74	Anchorage, AK	4,525.6
75	Fort Lauderdale, FL M.D.	4,523.1
76	North Port-Bradenton-Sarasota, FL	4,502.8
77	Tyler, TX	4,488.2
78	Beaumont-Port Arthur, TX	4,481.4
79	South Bend-Mishawaka, IN-MI	4,462.4
80	Bakersfield, CA	4,461.2
81	Durham-Chapel Hill, NC	4,455.4
82	Indianapolis, IN	4,455.0
83	Tampa-St Petersburg, FL	4,453.8
84	Charlotte-Gastonia, NC-SC	4,430.4
85	Spartanburg, SC	4,419.8
86	Seattle-Tacoma-Bellevue, WA	4,415.1
87	Springfield, OH	4,398.5
88	Athens-Clarke County, GA	4,397.3
89	Eugene-Springfield, OR	4,388.5
90	Austin-Round Rock, TX	4,380.9
91	Santa Fe, NM	4,372.4
92	Topeka, KS	4,364.5
93	Tallahassee, FL	4,358.5
94	Fresno, CA	4,337.1
95	Dallas (greater), TX	4,323.5
96	Tulsa, OK	4,323.4
97	Burlington, NC	4,312.1
98	Hinesville, GA	4,293.3
99	Seattle-Bellevue-Everett, WA M.D.	4,273.3
100	Jackson, MS	4,269.2
101	Jonesboro, AR	4,232.7
102	Warner Robins, GA	4,230.0
103	Deltona-Daytona Beach, FL	4,225.4
104	Dallas-Plano-Irving, TX M.D.	4,220.1
105	Valdosta, GA	4,210.6
106	Lakeland, FL	4,193.1
107	Dover, DE	4,186.1
108	Casper, WY	4,164.0
109	Visalia-Porterville, CA	4,148.8
110	Mansfield, OH	4,139.1
111	Milwaukee, WI	4,122.4
112	St. Joseph, MO-KS	4,121.6
113	Oakland-Fremont, CA M.D.	4,102.9
114	Santa Cruz-Watsonville, CA	4,077.6
115	Las Vegas-Paradise, NV	4,042.4
116	Saginaw, MI	4,037.8
117	Knoxville, TN	4,024.6
118	Baltimore-Towson, MD	4,018.4
119	Huntsville, AL	4,015.5
120	Nashville-Davidson, TN	4,012.9
121	Palm Bay-Melbourne, FL	4,008.2
122	Longview, WA	3,998.4
123	Merced, CA	3,996.3
124	Phoenix-Mesa-Scottsdale, AZ	3,996.1
125	Kalamazoo-Portage, MI	3,983.1
126	Atlanta, GA	3,980.2
127	Abilene, TX	3,976.7
128	Honolulu, HI	3,958.9
129	Lincoln, NE	3,955.4
130	Gadsden, AL	3,952.4
131	Jacksonville, NC	3,949.7
132	Atlantic City, NJ	3,948.3
133	Sumter, SC	3,943.7
134	San Francisco (greater), CA	3,931.0
135	Billings, MT	3,921.4
136	Pensacola, FL	3,899.4
137	Wilmington, DE-MD-NJ M.D.	3,890.9
138	Vineland, NJ	3,873.7
139	Lexington-Fayette, KY	3,832.3
140	Michigan City-La Porte, IN	3,830.7
141	Midland, TX	3,828.9
142	Kingsport, TN-VA	3,766.9
143	Vallejo-Fairfield, CA	3,764.9
144	Reno-Sparks, NV	3,760.3
145	Omaha-Council Bluffs, NE-IA	3,758.1
146	Flagstaff, AZ	3,752.9
147	Dayton, OH	3,742.2
148	Pascagoula, MS	3,730.4
149	Detroit (greater), MI	3,727.8
150	New Haven-Milford, CT	3,717.9
151	Houma, LA	3,713.0
152	Sacramento, CA	3,703.7
153	Louisville, KY-IN	3,697.6
154	Bellingham, WA	3,693.9
155	Anderson, IN	3,689.8
156	San Francisco-S. Mateo, CA M.D.	3,687.4
157	Rome, GA	3,660.1
158	Las Cruces, NM	3,653.8
159	Cincinnati-Middletown, OH-KY-IN	3,647.2
160	Cleveland, TN	3,632.9
161	Akron, OH	3,625.5
162	Fort Smith, AR-OK	3,624.7
163	Hickory, NC	3,623.9
164	Lake Havasu City-Kingman, AZ	3,618.9
165	Charleston, WV	3,615.3
166	Cape Girardeau, MO-IL	3,605.7
167	Youngstown, OH-PA	3,604.0
168	Barnstable Town, MA	3,588.9
169	Morristown, TN	3,574.2
170	Great Falls, MT	3,567.2
171	Columbia, MO	3,555.1
172	Buffalo-Niagara Falls, NY	3,552.6
173	Pueblo, CO	3,552.1
174	Columbus, IN	3,549.3
175	Kokomo, IN	3,540.5
176	Sherman-Denison, TX	3,524.9
177	Bowling Green, KY	3,493.3
178	Killeen-Temple-Fort Hood, TX	3,482.1
179	Bangor, ME	3,462.3
180	Clarksville, TN-KY	3,448.2

Note: All listings are for Metropolitan Statistical Areas (M.S.A.s) except for those ending with "M.D." Listings with "M.D." are Metropolitan Divisions which are smaller parts of eleven large M.S.A.s. See explanatory note at beginning of metropolitan area section.

RANK	METROPOLITAN AREA	RATE
181	Cheyenne, WY	3,429.0
182	Niles-Benton Harbor, MI	3,419.5
183	Springfield, MA	3,387.8
184	Florence-Muscle Shoals, AL	3,381.6
185	Grand Junction, CO	3,377.1
186	Cape Coral-Fort Myers, FL	3,376.3
187	El Paso, TX	3,361.8
188	Sebastian-Vero Beach, FL	3,360.8
189	Salem, OR	3,330.3
190	Muncie, IN	3,318.1
191	Sandusky, OH	3,304.6
192	Colorado Springs, CO	3,287.2
193	Chico, CA	3,282.5
194	Washington, DC-VA-MD-WV M.D.	3,276.0
195	Salinas, CA	3,270.0
196	Cleveland-Elyria-Mentor, OH	3,266.8
197	Redding, CA	3,261.5
198	Riverside-San Bernardino, CA	3,246.7
199	Cumberland, MD-WV	3,239.1
200	Port St. Lucie, FL	3,226.7
201	Burlington-South Burlington, VT	3,226.1
202	Philadelphia, PA M.D.	3,219.2
203	Philadelphia (greater) PA-NJ-MD-DE	3,213.1
204	Olympia, WA	3,212.7
205	Portland-Vancouver, OR-WA	3,197.5
206	Farmington, NM	3,191.2
207	Wenatchee, WA	3,188.4
208	Crestview-Fort Walton Beach, FL	3,184.8
209	Bloomington, IN	3,183.2
210	Lewiston, ID-WA	3,182.9
211	Grand Rapids-Wyoming, MI	3,179.9
212	Dalton, GA	3,179.8
213	Johnson City, TN	3,145.3
214	Denver-Aurora, CO	3,144.4
215	Washington (greater) DC-VA-MD-WV	3,126.5
216	Roanoke, VA	3,117.4
217	Rapid City, SD	3,115.3
218	Yuma, AZ	3,111.2
219	Janesville, WI	3,107.9
220	Racine, WI	3,107.0
221	Ocala, FL	3,097.8
222	Punta Gorda, FL	3,089.4
223	Lafayette, IN	3,082.9
224	Rochester, NY	3,062.2
225	Hartford, CT	3,049.7
226	Fort Collins-Loveland, CO	3,043.5
227	Fort Wayne, IN	3,041.7
228	Des Moines-West Des Moines, IA	3,037.8
229	Lansing-East Lansing, MI	3,034.4
230	Waterloo-Cedar Falls, IA	3,033.9
231	Jackson, MI	3,025.8
232	Cedar Rapids, IA	3,016.9
233	Richmond, VA	3,012.3
234	Los Angeles County, CA M.D.	3,008.0
235	Ann Arbor, MI	3,003.4
236	Danville, VA	2,999.4
237	Norwich-New London, CT	2,998.3
238	Coeur d'Alene, ID	2,987.7
239	Boston-Quincy, MA M.D.	2,986.9
240	Bremerton-Silverdale, WA	2,985.2
241	Pocatello, ID	2,972.8
242	Evansville, IN-KY	2,966.6
243	Owensboro, KY	2,951.8

RANK	METROPOLITAN AREA	RATE
244	Providence-New Bedford, RI-MA	2,931.2
245	Corvallis, OR	2,916.6
246	Raleigh-Cary, NC	2,913.2
247	Ogden-Clearfield, UT	2,878.2
248	Ames, IA	2,869.6
249	Albany-Schenectady-Troy, NY	2,863.0
250	Madison, WI	2,851.9
251	Charlottesville, VA	2,841.2
252	Los Angeles (greater), CA	2,832.2
253	Camden, NJ M.D.	2,815.1
254	Missoula, MT	2,798.7
255	Blacksburg, VA	2,793.2
256	Fayetteville, AR-MO	2,790.6
257	Elkhart-Goshen, IN	2,783.6
258	Syracuse, NY	2,779.4
259	Sioux City, IA-NE-SD	2,750.7
260	Kennewick-Pasco-Richland, WA	2,747.3
261	Bay City, MI	2,745.9
262	San Diego, CA	2,740.5
263	Dubuque, IA	2,733.8
264	Utica-Rome, NY	2,729.3
265	Binghamton, NY	2,720.1
266	Morgantown, WV	2,711.1
267	Bend, OR	2,710.2
268	Sheboygan, WI	2,702.6
269	San Jose, CA	2,696.0
270	Medford, OR	2,690.1
271	Asheville, NC	2,686.9
272	Palm Coast, FL	2,677.7
273	Santa Barbara-Santa Maria, CA	2,670.7
274	Reading, PA	2,662.1
275	Pittsfield, MA	2,653.5
276	Boulder, CO	2,651.7
277	Greeley, CO	2,631.2
278	Oshkosh-Neenah, WI	2,631.1
279	Erie, PA	2,630.2
280	Napa, CA	2,618.7
281	Monroe, MI	2,610.5
282	Bethesda-Frederick, MD M.D.	2,593.3
283	Worcester, MA	2,589.4
284	Manhattan, KS	2,581.8
285	Allentown, PA-NJ	2,575.2
286	Winchester, VA-WV	2,574.5
287	Portland, ME	2,566.3
288	Gainesville, GA	2,561.1
289	Trenton-Ewing, NJ	2,560.7
290	Madera, CA	2,555.4
291	Boston (greater), MA-NH	2,550.2
292	Jefferson City, MO	2,524.3
293	Yuba City, CA	2,509.4
294	San Luis Obispo, CA	2,504.3
295	Peabody, MA M.D.	2,499.8
296	Manchester-Nashua, NH	2,497.1
297	Hagerstown-Martinsburg, MD-WV	2,490.6
298	Lewiston-Auburn, ME	2,489.6
299	Scranton--Wilkes-Barre, PA	2,488.7
300	Harrisburg-Carlisle, PA	2,467.5
301	Sioux Falls, SD	2,465.6
302	Idaho Falls, ID	2,446.1
303	Carson City, NV	2,443.9
304	Santa Rosa-Petaluma, CA	2,440.1
305	Elmira, NY	2,428.2
306	Prescott, AZ	2,397.0

RANK	METROPOLITAN AREA	RATE
307	Pittsburgh, PA	2,386.4
308	Warren-Farmington Hills, MI M.D.	2,381.0
309	Newark-Union, NJ-PA M.D.	2,355.2
310	York-Hanover, PA	2,304.7
311	Bismarck, ND	2,300.1
312	Bridgeport-Stamford, CT	2,281.6
313	Provo-Orem, UT	2,269.6
314	Santa Ana-Anaheim, CA M.D.	2,257.3
315	Poughkeepsie, NY	2,233.7
316	Boise City-Nampa, ID	2,222.7
317	Iowa City, IA	2,209.8
318	New York-W. Plains NY-NJ M.D.	2,174.6
319	Wheeling, WV-OH	2,172.6
320	Altoona, PA	2,172.4
321	Oxnard-Thousand Oaks, CA	2,169.6
322	Cambridge-Newton, MA M.D.	2,162.9
323	Naples-Marco Island, FL	2,159.0
324	Lynchburg, VA	2,154.4
325	Eau Claire, WI	2,153.7
326	Kingston, NY	2,134.2
327	New York (greater), NY-NJ-PA	2,132.4
328	Green Bay, WI	2,130.2
329	Lancaster, PA	2,124.3
330	Appleton, WI	2,122.2
331	Elizabethtown, KY	2,120.1
332	Williamsport, PA	2,091.6
333	Rockingham County, NH M.D.	2,042.1
334	Edison, NJ M.D.	2,018.3
335	State College, PA	1,956.6
336	Fond du Lac, WI	1,942.1
337	Holland-Grand Haven, MI	1,918.8
338	Nassau-Suffolk, NY M.D.	1,888.1
339	Wausau, WI	1,865.8
340	Lebanon, PA	1,857.2
341	St. George, UT	1,844.0
342	Glens Falls, NY	1,710.0
343	Harrisonburg, VA	1,672.0
344	Logan, UT-ID	1,590.7
NA	Auburn, AL**	NA
NA	Charleston-North Charleston, SC**	NA
NA	Danville, IL**	NA
NA	Decatur, AL**	NA
NA	Decatur, IL**	NA
NA	Dothan, AL**	NA
NA	Duluth, MN-WI**	NA
NA	El Centro, CA**	NA
NA	Fargo, ND-MN**	NA
NA	Grand Forks, ND-MN**	NA
NA	Hattiesburg, MS**	NA
NA	Ithaca, NY**	NA
NA	Kansas City, MO-KS**	NA
NA	La Crosse, WI-MN**	NA
NA	Mankato-North Mankato, MN**	NA
NA	Minneapolis-St. Paul, MN-WI**	NA
NA	New Orleans, LA**	NA
NA	Oklahoma City, OK**	NA
NA	Rochester, MN**	NA
NA	Shreveport-Bossier City, LA**	NA
NA	St. Cloud, MN**	NA
NA	St. Louis, MO-IL**	NA
NA	Toledo, OH**	NA
NA	Tucson, AZ**	NA
NA	Wilmington, NC**	NA

Source: CQ Press using reported data from the F.B.I. "Crime in the United States 2009"
*Includes murder, rape, robbery, aggravated assault, burglary, larceny-theft, and motor vehicle theft.
**Not available.

3. Percent Change in Crime Rate: 2008 to 2009
National Percent Change = 5.5% Decrease*

RANK	METROPOLITAN AREA	% CHANGE
13	Abilene, TX	8.4
76	Akron, OH	(0.9)
83	Albany-Schenectady-Troy, NY	(1.3)
NA	Albany, GA**	NA
262	Albuquerque, NM	(12.6)
NA	Alexandria, LA**	NA
225	Allentown, PA-NJ	(9.5)
236	Altoona, PA	(10.3)
22	Amarillo, TX	5.8
110	Ames, IA	(3.5)
24	Anchorage, AK	5.2
NA	Anderson, IN**	NA
NA	Anderson, SC**	NA
105	Ann Arbor, MI	(3.0)
NA	Anniston-Oxford, AL**	NA
281	Appleton, WI	(19.6)
269	Asheville, NC	(14.8)
267	Athens-Clarke County, GA	(14.6)
252	Atlanta, GA	(11.5)
NA	Atlantic City, NJ**	NA
NA	Auburn, AL**	NA
NA	Augusta, GA-SC**	NA
37	Austin-Round Rock, TX	3.1
91	Bakersfield, CA	(1.8)
193	Baltimore-Towson, MD	(7.3)
33	Bangor, ME	4.1
26	Barnstable Town, MA	5.1
NA	Baton Rouge, LA**	NA
180	Battle Creek, MI	(6.6)
NA	Bay City, MI**	NA
52	Beaumont-Port Arthur, TX	1.7
138	Bellingham, WA	(4.9)
264	Bend, OR	(13.8)
203	Bethesda-Frederick, MD M.D.	(8.1)
17	Billings, MT	6.9
234	Binghamton, NY	(10.2)
138	Birmingham-Hoover, AL	(4.9)
109	Bismarck, ND	(3.4)
156	Blacksburg, VA	(5.4)
6	Bloomington, IN	12.7
248	Boise City-Nampa, ID	(11.0)
121	Boston (greater), MA-NH	(3.9)
124	Boston-Quincy, MA M.D.	(4.2)
NA	Boulder, CO**	NA
NA	Bowling Green, KY**	NA
160	Bremerton-Silverdale, WA	(5.6)
155	Bridgeport-Stamford, CT	(5.3)
110	Brownsville-Harlingen, TX	(3.5)
NA	Brunswick, GA**	NA
83	Buffalo-Niagara Falls, NY	(1.3)
NA	Burlington-South Burlington, VT**	NA
125	Burlington, NC	(4.4)
187	Cambridge-Newton, MA M.D.	(6.9)
226	Camden, NJ M.D.	(9.7)
273	Cape Coral-Fort Myers, FL	(15.1)
131	Cape Girardeau, MO-IL	(4.6)
251	Carson City, NV	(11.3)
39	Casper, WY	2.8
138	Cedar Rapids, IA	(4.9)
NA	Charleston-North Charleston, SC**	NA
125	Charleston, WV	(4.4)
279	Charlotte-Gastonia, NC-SC	(16.8)
39	Charlottesville, VA	2.8
NA	Chattanooga, TN-GA**	NA
220	Cheyenne, WY	(9.4)
121	Chico, CA	(3.9)
NA	Cincinnati-Middletown, OH-KY-IN**	NA
NA	Clarksville, TN-KY**	NA
NA	Cleveland-Elyria-Mentor, OH**	NA
226	Cleveland, TN	(9.7)
NA	Coeur d'Alene, ID**	NA
19	College Station-Bryan, TX	6.5
198	Colorado Springs, CO	(7.5)
79	Columbia, MO	(1.1)
65	Columbia, SC	0.2
42	Columbus, GA-AL	2.3
14	Columbus, IN	8.3
88	Columbus, OH	(1.5)
180	Corpus Christi, TX	(6.6)
3	Corvallis, OR	16.3
NA	Crestview-Fort Walton Beach, FL**	NA
46	Cumberland, MD-WV	2.1
125	Dallas (greater), TX	(4.4)
168	Dallas-Plano-Irving, TX M.D.	(5.9)
93	Dalton, GA	(2.1)
NA	Danville, IL**	NA
268	Danville, VA	(14.7)
107	Dayton, OH	(3.3)
NA	Decatur, AL**	NA
NA	Decatur, IL**	NA
134	Deltona-Daytona Beach, FL	(4.7)
104	Denver-Aurora, CO	(2.9)
NA	Des Moines-West Des Moines, IA**	NA
NA	Detroit (greater), MI**	NA
NA	Detroit-Livonia-Dearborn, MI M.D.**	NA
NA	Dothan, AL**	NA
54	Dover, DE	1.4
107	Dubuque, IA	(3.3)
NA	Duluth, MN-WI**	NA
177	Durham-Chapel Hill, NC	(6.5)
143	Eau Claire, WI	(5.0)
168	Edison, NJ M.D.	(5.9)
NA	El Centro, CA**	NA
149	El Paso, TX	(5.2)
NA	Elizabethtown, KY**	NA
284	Elkhart-Goshen, IN	(25.6)
213	Elmira, NY	(8.9)
149	Erie, PA	(5.2)
266	Eugene-Springfield, OR	(13.9)
NA	Evansville, IN-KY**	NA
NA	Fargo, ND-MN**	NA
NA	Farmington, NM**	NA
59	Fayetteville, AR-MO	0.7
177	Fayetteville, NC	(6.5)
246	Flagstaff, AZ	(10.8)
NA	Flint, MI**	NA
278	Florence-Muscle Shoals, AL	(16.4)
202	Florence, SC	(7.9)
185	Fond du Lac, WI	(6.8)
70	Fort Collins-Loveland, CO	(0.3)
118	Fort Lauderdale, FL M.D.	(3.7)
10	Fort Smith, AR-OK	10.3
208	Fort Wayne, IN	(8.4)
83	Fort Worth-Arlington, TX M.D.	(1.3)
149	Fresno, CA	(5.2)
98	Gadsden, AL	(2.5)
59	Gainesville, FL	0.7
NA	Gainesville, GA**	NA
257	Glens Falls, NY	(12.0)
210	Goldsboro, NC	(8.7)
NA	Grand Forks, ND-MN**	NA
54	Grand Junction, CO	1.4
NA	Grand Rapids-Wyoming, MI**	NA
257	Great Falls, MT	(12.0)
205	Greeley, CO	(8.2)
277	Green Bay, WI	(16.3)
193	Greensboro-High Point, NC	(7.3)
NA	Gulfport-Biloxi, MS**	NA
203	Hagerstown-Martinsburg, MD-WV	(8.1)
105	Harrisburg-Carlisle, PA	(3.0)
79	Harrisonburg, VA	(1.1)
115	Hartford, CT	(3.6)
NA	Hattiesburg, MS**	NA
118	Hickory, NC	(3.7)
79	Hinesville, GA	(1.1)
NA	Holland-Grand Haven, MI**	NA
30	Honolulu, HI	4.4
138	Hot Springs, AR	(4.9)
42	Houma, LA	2.3
16	Houston, TX	7.3
214	Huntsville, AL	(9.0)
172	Idaho Falls, ID	(6.3)
131	Indianapolis, IN	(4.6)
193	Iowa City, IA	(7.3)
NA	Ithaca, NY**	NA
243	Jacksonville, FL	(10.7)
69	Jacksonville, NC	(0.1)
NA	Jackson, MI**	NA
53	Jackson, MS	1.5
158	Jackson, TN	(5.5)
269	Janesville, WI	(14.8)
NA	Jefferson City, MO**	NA
100	Johnson City, TN	(2.6)
120	Jonesboro, AR	(3.8)
NA	Kalamazoo-Portage, MI**	NA
NA	Kansas City, MO-KS**	NA
143	Kennewick-Pasco-Richland, WA	(5.0)
100	Killeen-Temple-Fort Hood, TX	(2.6)
75	Kingsport, TN-VA	(0.8)
21	Kingston, NY	6.0
135	Knoxville, TN	(4.8)
234	Kokomo, IN	(10.2)
NA	La Crosse, WI-MN**	NA
59	Lafayette, IN	0.7
5	Lafayette, LA	12.9
NA	Lake Charles, LA**	NA
125	Lake Havasu City-Kingman, AZ	(4.4)
208	Lakeland, FL	(8.4)
197	Lancaster, PA	(7.4)
NA	Lansing-East Lansing, MI**	NA

Note: All listings are for Metropolitan Statistical Areas (M.S.A.s) except for those ending with "M.D." Listings with "M.D." are Metropolitan Divisions which are smaller parts of eleven large M.S.A.s. See explanatory note at beginning of metropolitan area section.

Alpha Order - Metro Area (continued)

RANK	METROPOLITAN AREA	% CHANGE
162	Laredo, TX	(5.7)
58	Las Cruces, NM	0.8
236	Las Vegas-Paradise, NV	(10.3)
156	Lawrence, KS	(5.4)
NA	Lawton, OK**	NA
190	Lebanon, PA	(7.1)
56	Lewiston-Auburn, ME	1.2
15	Lewiston, ID-WA	7.6
NA	Lexington-Fayette, KY**	NA
185	Lima, OH	(6.8)
149	Lincoln, NE	(5.2)
NA	Little Rock, AR**	NA
191	Logan, UT-ID	(7.2)
62	Longview, TX	0.6
78	Longview, WA	(1.0)
188	Los Angeles County, CA M.D.	(7.0)
182	Los Angeles (greater), CA	(6.7)
NA	Louisville, KY-IN**	NA
34	Lubbock, TX	3.7
254	Lynchburg, VA	(11.7)
217	Macon, GA	(9.2)
138	Madera, CA	(4.9)
172	Madison, WI	(6.3)
NA	Manchester-Nashua, NH**	NA
275	Manhattan, KS	(15.8)
NA	Mankato-North Mankato, MN**	NA
110	Mansfield, OH	(3.5)
12	McAllen-Edinburg-Mission, TX	8.6
182	Medford, OR	(6.7)
241	Memphis, TN-MS-AR	(10.6)
166	Merced, CA	(5.8)
193	Miami (greater), FL	(7.3)
247	Miami-Dade County, FL M.D.	(10.9)
226	Michigan City-La Porte, IN	(9.7)
29	Midland, TX	4.6
166	Milwaukee, WI	(5.8)
NA	Minneapolis-St. Paul, MN-WI**	NA
260	Missoula, MT	(12.3)
27	Mobile, AL	5.0
176	Modesto, CA	(6.4)
NA	Monroe, MI**	NA
231	Montgomery, AL	(10.0)
NA	Morgantown, WV**	NA
240	Morristown, TN	(10.5)
66	Mount Vernon-Anacortes, WA	0.1
93	Muncie, IN	(2.1)
NA	Muskegon-Norton Shores, MI**	NA
269	Napa, CA	(14.8)
168	Naples-Marco Island, FL	(5.9)
212	Nashville-Davidson, TN	(8.8)
71	Nassau-Suffolk, NY M.D.	(0.5)
NA	New Haven-Milford, CT**	NA
NA	New Orleans, LA**	NA
162	New York (greater), NY-NJ-PA	(5.7)
162	New York-W. Plains NY-NJ M.D.	(5.7)
243	Newark-Union, NJ-PA M.D.	(10.7)
NA	Niles-Benton Harbor, MI**	NA
NA	North Port-Bradenton-Sarasota, FL**	NA
19	Norwich-New London, CT	6.5
210	Oakland-Fremont, CA M.D.	(8.7)
92	Ocala, FL	(1.9)
206	Ocean City, NJ	(8.3)
17	Odessa, TX	6.9

RANK	METROPOLITAN AREA	% CHANGE
67	Ogden-Clearfield, UT	0.0
NA	Oklahoma City, OK**	NA
260	Olympia, WA	(12.3)
115	Omaha-Council Bluffs, NE-IA	(3.6)
252	Orlando, FL	(11.5)
67	Oshkosh-Neenah, WI	0.0
NA	Owensboro, KY**	NA
135	Oxnard-Thousand Oaks, CA	(4.8)
115	Palm Bay-Melbourne, FL	(3.6)
46	Palm Coast, FL	2.1
31	Panama City-Lynn Haven, FL	4.3
42	Pascagoula, MS	2.3
79	Peabody, MA M.D.	(1.1)
57	Pensacola, FL	1.1
248	Philadelphia (greater) PA-NJ-MD-DE	(11.0)
254	Philadelphia, PA M.D.	(11.7)
274	Phoenix-Mesa-Scottsdale, AZ	(15.2)
259	Pine Bluff, AR	(12.1)
160	Pittsburgh, PA	(5.6)
88	Pittsfield, MA	(1.5)
130	Pocatello, ID	(4.5)
241	Port St. Lucie, FL	(10.6)
232	Portland-Vancouver, OR-WA	(10.1)
63	Portland, ME	0.3
125	Poughkeepsie, NY	(4.4)
220	Prescott, AZ	(9.4)
188	Providence-New Bedford, RI-MA	(7.0)
177	Provo-Orem, UT	(6.5)
NA	Pueblo, CO**	NA
272	Punta Gorda, FL	(15.0)
236	Racine, WI	(10.3)
NA	Raleigh-Cary, NC**	NA
76	Rapid City, SD	(0.9)
191	Reading, PA	(7.2)
135	Redding, CA	(4.8)
250	Reno-Sparks, NV	(11.1)
146	Richmond, VA	(5.1)
200	Riverside-San Bernardino, CA	(7.7)
98	Roanoke, VA	(2.5)
NA	Rochester, MN**	NA
50	Rochester, NY	1.8
38	Rockingham County, NH M.D.	3.0
NA	Rocky Mount, NC**	NA
NA	Rome, GA**	NA
121	Sacramento, CA	(3.9)
NA	Saginaw, MI**	NA
229	Salem, OR	(9.8)
83	Salinas, CA	(1.3)
50	Salisbury, MD	1.8
63	Salt Lake City, UT	0.3
146	San Angelo, TX	(5.1)
206	San Antonio, TX	(8.3)
276	San Diego, CA	(16.0)
201	San Francisco (greater), CA	(7.8)
171	San Francisco-S. Mateo, CA M.D.	(6.2)
88	San Jose, CA	(1.5)
149	San Luis Obispo, CA	(5.2)
263	Sandusky, OH	(13.0)
146	Santa Ana-Anaheim, CA M.D.	(5.1)
103	Santa Barbara-Santa Maria, CA	(2.8)
7	Santa Cruz-Watsonville, CA	11.7
1	Santa Fe, NM	21.5
24	Santa Rosa-Petaluma, CA	5.2

RANK	METROPOLITAN AREA	% CHANGE
143	Savannah, GA	(5.0)
110	Scranton--Wilkes-Barre, PA	(3.5)
NA	Seattle-Bellevue-Everett, WA M.D.**	NA
NA	Seattle-Tacoma-Bellevue, WA**	NA
172	Sebastian-Vero Beach, FL	(6.3)
158	Sheboygan, WI	(5.5)
9	Sherman-Denison, TX	10.5
NA	Shreveport-Bossier City, LA**	NA
28	Sioux City, IA-NE-SD	4.7
8	Sioux Falls, SD	11.0
NA	South Bend-Mishawaka, IN-MI**	NA
243	Spartanburg, SC	(10.7)
11	Spokane, WA	9.8
102	Springfield, MA	(2.7)
NA	Springfield, MO**	NA
172	Springfield, OH	(6.3)
34	State College, PA	3.7
264	Stockton, CA	(13.8)
NA	St. Cloud, MN**	NA
283	St. George, UT	(24.4)
48	St. Joseph, MO-KS	1.9
NA	St. Louis, MO-IL**	NA
NA	Sumter, SC**	NA
41	Syracuse, NY	2.5
NA	Tacoma, WA M.D.**	NA
217	Tallahassee, FL	(9.2)
182	Tampa-St Petersburg, FL	(6.7)
42	Texarkana, TX-Texarkana, AR	2.3
NA	Toledo, OH**	NA
214	Topeka, KS	(9.0)
96	Trenton-Ewing, NJ	(2.3)
NA	Tucson, AZ**	NA
71	Tulsa, OK	(0.5)
96	Tuscaloosa, AL	(2.3)
4	Tyler, TX	14.9
48	Utica-Rome, NY	1.9
23	Valdosta, GA	5.7
236	Vallejo-Fairfield, CA	(10.3)
2	Victoria, TX	16.7
254	Vineland, NJ	(11.7)
199	Visalia-Porterville, CA	(7.6)
149	Waco, TX	(5.2)
232	Warner Robins, GA	(10.1)
NA	Warren-Farmington Hills, MI M.D.**	NA
216	Washington (greater) DC-VA-MD-WV	(9.1)
219	Washington, DC-VA-MD-WV M.D.	(9.3)
87	Waterloo-Cedar Falls, IA	(1.4)
NA	Wausau, WI**	NA
32	Wenatchee, WA	4.2
131	West Palm Beach, FL M.D.	(4.6)
93	Wheeling, WV-OH	(2.1)
280	Wichita Falls, TX	(17.8)
110	Wichita, KS	(3.5)
162	Williamsport, PA	(5.7)
220	Wilmington, DE-MD-NJ M.D.	(9.4)
NA	Wilmington, NC**	NA
220	Winchester, VA-WV	(9.4)
229	Winston-Salem, NC	(9.8)
36	Worcester, MA	3.3
220	York-Hanover, PA	(9.4)
74	Youngstown, OH-PA	(0.6)
282	Yuba City, CA	(24.3)
71	Yuma, AZ	(0.5)

Source: CQ Press using reported data from the F.B.I. "Crime in the United States 2009"

*Includes murder, rape, robbery, aggravated assault, burglary, larceny-theft, and motor vehicle theft.

**Not available.

3. Percent Change in Crime Rate: 2008 to 2009 (continued)
National Percent Change = 5.5% Decrease*

RANK	METROPOLITAN AREA	% CHANGE
1	Santa Fe, NM	21.5
2	Victoria, TX	16.7
3	Corvallis, OR	16.3
4	Tyler, TX	14.9
5	Lafayette, LA	12.9
6	Bloomington, IN	12.7
7	Santa Cruz-Watsonville, CA	11.7
8	Sioux Falls, SD	11.0
9	Sherman-Denison, TX	10.5
10	Fort Smith, AR-OK	10.3
11	Spokane, WA	9.8
12	McAllen-Edinburg-Mission, TX	8.6
13	Abilene, TX	8.4
14	Columbus, IN	8.3
15	Lewiston, ID-WA	7.6
16	Houston, TX	7.3
17	Billings, MT	6.9
17	Odessa, TX	6.9
19	College Station-Bryan, TX	6.5
19	Norwich-New London, CT	6.5
21	Kingston, NY	6.0
22	Amarillo, TX	5.8
23	Valdosta, GA	5.7
24	Anchorage, AK	5.2
24	Santa Rosa-Petaluma, CA	5.2
26	Barnstable Town, MA	5.1
27	Mobile, AL	5.0
28	Sioux City, IA-NE-SD	4.7
29	Midland, TX	4.6
30	Honolulu, HI	4.4
31	Panama City-Lynn Haven, FL	4.3
32	Wenatchee, WA	4.2
33	Bangor, ME	4.1
34	Lubbock, TX	3.7
34	State College, PA	3.7
36	Worcester, MA	3.3
37	Austin-Round Rock, TX	3.1
38	Rockingham County, NH M.D.	3.0
39	Casper, WY	2.8
39	Charlottesville, VA	2.8
41	Syracuse, NY	2.5
42	Columbus, GA-AL	2.3
42	Houma, LA	2.3
42	Pascagoula, MS	2.3
42	Texarkana, TX-Texarkana, AR	2.3
46	Cumberland, MD-WV	2.1
46	Palm Coast, FL	2.1
48	St. Joseph, MO-KS	1.9
48	Utica-Rome, NY	1.9
50	Rochester, NY	1.8
50	Salisbury, MD	1.8
52	Beaumont-Port Arthur, TX	1.7
53	Jackson, MS	1.5
54	Dover, DE	1.4
54	Grand Junction, CO	1.4
56	Lewiston-Auburn, ME	1.2
57	Pensacola, FL	1.1
58	Las Cruces, NM	0.8
59	Fayetteville, AR-MO	0.7
59	Gainesville, FL	0.7
59	Lafayette, IN	0.7
62	Longview, TX	0.6
63	Portland, ME	0.3
63	Salt Lake City, UT	0.3
65	Columbia, SC	0.2
66	Mount Vernon-Anacortes, WA	0.1
67	Ogden-Clearfield, UT	0.0
67	Oshkosh-Neenah, WI	0.0
69	Jacksonville, NC	(0.1)
70	Fort Collins-Loveland, CO	(0.3)
71	Nassau-Suffolk, NY M.D.	(0.5)
71	Tulsa, OK	(0.5)
71	Yuma, AZ	(0.5)
74	Youngstown, OH-PA	(0.6)
75	Kingsport, TN-VA	(0.8)
76	Akron, OH	(0.9)
76	Rapid City, SD	(0.9)
78	Longview, WA	(1.0)
79	Columbia, MO	(1.1)
79	Harrisonburg, VA	(1.1)
79	Hinesville, GA	(1.1)
79	Peabody, MA M.D.	(1.1)
83	Albany-Schenectady-Troy, NY	(1.3)
83	Buffalo-Niagara Falls, NY	(1.3)
83	Fort Worth-Arlington, TX M.D.	(1.3)
83	Salinas, CA	(1.3)
87	Waterloo-Cedar Falls, IA	(1.4)
88	Columbus, OH	(1.5)
88	Pittsfield, MA	(1.5)
88	San Jose, CA	(1.5)
91	Bakersfield, CA	(1.8)
92	Ocala, FL	(1.9)
93	Dalton, GA	(2.1)
93	Muncie, IN	(2.1)
93	Wheeling, WV-OH	(2.1)
96	Trenton-Ewing, NJ	(2.3)
96	Tuscaloosa, AL	(2.3)
98	Gadsden, AL	(2.5)
98	Roanoke, VA	(2.5)
100	Johnson City, TN	(2.6)
100	Killeen-Temple-Fort Hood, TX	(2.6)
102	Springfield, MA	(2.7)
103	Santa Barbara-Santa Maria, CA	(2.8)
104	Denver-Aurora, CO	(2.9)
105	Ann Arbor, MI	(3.0)
105	Harrisburg-Carlisle, PA	(3.0)
107	Dayton, OH	(3.3)
107	Dubuque, IA	(3.3)
109	Bismarck, ND	(3.4)
110	Ames, IA	(3.5)
110	Brownsville-Harlingen, TX	(3.5)
110	Mansfield, OH	(3.5)
110	Scranton--Wilkes-Barre, PA	(3.5)
110	Wichita, KS	(3.5)
115	Hartford, CT	(3.6)
115	Omaha-Council Bluffs, NE-IA	(3.6)
115	Palm Bay-Melbourne, FL	(3.6)
118	Fort Lauderdale, FL M.D.	(3.7)
118	Hickory, NC	(3.7)
120	Jonesboro, AR	(3.8)
121	Boston (greater), MA-NH	(3.9)
121	Chico, CA	(3.9)
121	Sacramento, CA	(3.9)
124	Boston-Quincy, MA M.D.	(4.2)
125	Burlington, NC	(4.4)
125	Charleston, WV	(4.4)
125	Dallas (greater), TX	(4.4)
125	Lake Havasu City-Kingman, AZ	(4.4)
125	Poughkeepsie, NY	(4.4)
130	Pocatello, ID	(4.5)
131	Cape Girardeau, MO-IL	(4.6)
131	Indianapolis, IN	(4.6)
131	West Palm Beach, FL M.D.	(4.6)
134	Deltona-Daytona Beach, FL	(4.7)
135	Knoxville, TN	(4.8)
135	Oxnard-Thousand Oaks, CA	(4.8)
135	Redding, CA	(4.8)
138	Bellingham, WA	(4.9)
138	Birmingham-Hoover, AL	(4.9)
138	Cedar Rapids, IA	(4.9)
138	Hot Springs, AR	(4.9)
138	Madera, CA	(4.9)
143	Eau Claire, WI	(5.0)
143	Kennewick-Pasco-Richland, WA	(5.0)
143	Savannah, GA	(5.0)
146	Richmond, VA	(5.1)
146	San Angelo, TX	(5.1)
146	Santa Ana-Anaheim, CA M.D.	(5.1)
149	El Paso, TX	(5.2)
149	Erie, PA	(5.2)
149	Fresno, CA	(5.2)
149	Lincoln, NE	(5.2)
149	San Luis Obispo, CA	(5.2)
149	Waco, TX	(5.2)
155	Bridgeport-Stamford, CT	(5.3)
156	Blacksburg, VA	(5.4)
156	Lawrence, KS	(5.4)
158	Jackson, TN	(5.5)
158	Sheboygan, WI	(5.5)
160	Bremerton-Silverdale, WA	(5.6)
160	Pittsburgh, PA	(5.6)
162	Laredo, TX	(5.7)
162	New York (greater), NY-NJ-PA	(5.7)
162	New York-W. Plains NY-NJ M.D.	(5.7)
162	Williamsport, PA	(5.7)
166	Merced, CA	(5.8)
166	Milwaukee, WI	(5.8)
168	Dallas-Plano-Irving, TX M.D.	(5.9)
168	Edison, NJ M.D.	(5.9)
168	Naples-Marco Island, FL	(5.9)
171	San Francisco-S. Mateo, CA M.D.	(6.2)
172	Idaho Falls, ID	(6.3)
172	Madison, WI	(6.3)
172	Sebastian-Vero Beach, FL	(6.3)
172	Springfield, OH	(6.3)
176	Modesto, CA	(6.4)
177	Durham-Chapel Hill, NC	(6.5)
177	Fayetteville, NC	(6.5)
177	Provo-Orem, UT	(6.5)
180	Battle Creek, MI	(6.6)

Note: All listings are for Metropolitan Statistical Areas (M.S.A.s) except for those ending with "M.D." Listings with "M.D." are Metropolitan Divisions which are smaller parts of eleven large M.S.A.s. See explanatory note at beginning of metropolitan area section.

Rank Order - Metro Area (continued)

RANK	METROPOLITAN AREA	% CHANGE
180	Corpus Christi, TX	(6.6)
182	Los Angeles (greater), CA	(6.7)
182	Medford, OR	(6.7)
182	Tampa-St Petersburg, FL	(6.7)
185	Fond du Lac, WI	(6.8)
185	Lima, OH	(6.8)
187	Cambridge-Newton, MA M.D.	(6.9)
188	Los Angeles County, CA M.D.	(7.0)
188	Providence-New Bedford, RI-MA	(7.0)
190	Lebanon, PA	(7.1)
191	Logan, UT-ID	(7.2)
191	Reading, PA	(7.2)
193	Baltimore-Towson, MD	(7.3)
193	Greensboro-High Point, NC	(7.3)
193	Iowa City, IA	(7.3)
193	Miami (greater), FL	(7.3)
197	Lancaster, PA	(7.4)
198	Colorado Springs, CO	(7.5)
199	Visalia-Porterville, CA	(7.6)
200	Riverside-San Bernardino, CA	(7.7)
201	San Francisco (greater), CA	(7.8)
202	Florence, SC	(7.9)
203	Bethesda-Frederick, MD M.D.	(8.1)
203	Hagerstown-Martinsburg, MD-WV	(8.1)
205	Greeley, CO	(8.2)
206	Ocean City, NJ	(8.3)
206	San Antonio, TX	(8.3)
208	Fort Wayne, IN	(8.4)
208	Lakeland, FL	(8.4)
210	Goldsboro, NC	(8.7)
210	Oakland-Fremont, CA M.D.	(8.7)
212	Nashville-Davidson, TN	(8.8)
213	Elmira, NY	(8.9)
214	Huntsville, AL	(9.0)
214	Topeka, KS	(9.0)
216	Washington (greater) DC-VA-MD-WV	(9.1)
217	Macon, GA	(9.2)
217	Tallahassee, FL	(9.2)
219	Washington, DC-VA-MD-WV M.D.	(9.3)
220	Cheyenne, WY	(9.4)
220	Prescott, AZ	(9.4)
220	Wilmington, DE-MD-NJ M.D.	(9.4)
220	Winchester, VA-WV	(9.4)
220	York-Hanover, PA	(9.4)
225	Allentown, PA-NJ	(9.5)
226	Camden, NJ M.D.	(9.7)
226	Cleveland, TN	(9.7)
226	Michigan City-La Porte, IN	(9.7)
229	Salem, OR	(9.8)
229	Winston-Salem, NC	(9.8)
231	Montgomery, AL	(10.0)
232	Portland-Vancouver, OR-WA	(10.1)
232	Warner Robins, GA	(10.1)
234	Binghamton, NY	(10.2)
234	Kokomo, IN	(10.2)
236	Altoona, PA	(10.3)
236	Las Vegas-Paradise, NV	(10.3)
236	Racine, WI	(10.3)
236	Vallejo-Fairfield, CA	(10.3)
240	Morristown, TN	(10.5)
241	Memphis, TN-MS-AR	(10.6)
241	Port St. Lucie, FL	(10.6)
243	Jacksonville, FL	(10.7)
243	Newark-Union, NJ-PA M.D.	(10.7)
243	Spartanburg, SC	(10.7)
246	Flagstaff, AZ	(10.8)
247	Miami-Dade County, FL M.D.	(10.9)
248	Boise City-Nampa, ID	(11.0)
248	Philadelphia (greater) PA-NJ-MD-DE	(11.0)
250	Reno-Sparks, NV	(11.1)
251	Carson City, NV	(11.3)
252	Atlanta, GA	(11.5)
252	Orlando, FL	(11.5)
254	Lynchburg, VA	(11.7)
254	Philadelphia, PA M.D.	(11.7)
254	Vineland, NJ	(11.7)
257	Glens Falls, NY	(12.0)
257	Great Falls, MT	(12.0)
259	Pine Bluff, AR	(12.1)
260	Missoula, MT	(12.3)
260	Olympia, WA	(12.3)
262	Albuquerque, NM	(12.6)
263	Sandusky, OH	(13.0)
264	Bend, OR	(13.8)
264	Stockton, CA	(13.8)
266	Eugene-Springfield, OR	(13.9)
267	Athens-Clarke County, GA	(14.6)
268	Danville, VA	(14.7)
269	Asheville, NC	(14.8)
269	Janesville, WI	(14.8)
269	Napa, CA	(14.8)
272	Punta Gorda, FL	(15.0)
273	Cape Coral-Fort Myers, FL	(15.1)
274	Phoenix-Mesa-Scottsdale, AZ	(15.2)
275	Manhattan, KS	(15.8)
276	San Diego, CA	(16.0)
277	Green Bay, WI	(16.3)
278	Florence-Muscle Shoals, AL	(16.4)
279	Charlotte-Gastonia, NC-SC	(16.8)
280	Wichita Falls, TX	(17.8)
281	Appleton, WI	(19.6)
282	Yuba City, CA	(24.3)
283	St. George, UT	(24.4)
284	Elkhart-Goshen, IN	(25.6)
NA	Albany, GA**	NA
NA	Alexandria, LA**	NA
NA	Anderson, IN**	NA
NA	Anderson, SC**	NA
NA	Anniston-Oxford, AL**	NA
NA	Atlantic City, NJ**	NA
NA	Auburn, AL**	NA
NA	Augusta, GA-SC**	NA
NA	Baton Rouge, LA**	NA
NA	Bay City, MI**	NA
NA	Boulder, CO**	NA
NA	Bowling Green, KY**	NA
NA	Brunswick, GA**	NA
NA	Burlington-South Burlington, VT**	NA
NA	Charleston-North Charleston, SC**	NA
NA	Chattanooga, TN-GA**	NA
NA	Cincinnati-Middletown, OH-KY-IN**	NA
NA	Clarksville, TN-KY**	NA
NA	Cleveland-Elyria-Mentor, OH**	NA
NA	Coeur d'Alene, ID**	NA
NA	Crestview-Fort Walton Beach, FL**	NA
NA	Danville, IL**	NA
NA	Decatur, AL**	NA
NA	Decatur, IL**	NA
NA	Des Moines-West Des Moines, IA**	NA
NA	Detroit (greater), MI**	NA
NA	Detroit-Livonia-Dearborn, MI M.D.**	NA
NA	Dothan, AL**	NA
NA	Duluth, MN-WI**	NA
NA	El Centro, CA**	NA
NA	Elizabethtown, KY**	NA
NA	Evansville, IN-KY**	NA
NA	Fargo, ND-MN**	NA
NA	Farmington, NM**	NA
NA	Flint, MI**	NA
NA	Gainesville, GA**	NA
NA	Grand Forks, ND-MN**	NA
NA	Grand Rapids-Wyoming, MI**	NA
NA	Gulfport-Biloxi, MS**	NA
NA	Hattiesburg, MS**	NA
NA	Holland-Grand Haven, MI**	NA
NA	Ithaca, NY**	NA
NA	Jackson, MI**	NA
NA	Jefferson City, MO**	NA
NA	Kalamazoo-Portage, MI**	NA
NA	Kansas City, MO-KS**	NA
NA	La Crosse, WI-MN**	NA
NA	Lake Charles, LA**	NA
NA	Lansing-East Lansing, MI**	NA
NA	Lawton, OK**	NA
NA	Lexington-Fayette, KY**	NA
NA	Little Rock, AR**	NA
NA	Louisville, KY-IN**	NA
NA	Manchester-Nashua, NH**	NA
NA	Mankato-North Mankato, MN**	NA
NA	Minneapolis-St. Paul, MN-WI**	NA
NA	Monroe, MI**	NA
NA	Morgantown, WV**	NA
NA	Muskegon-Norton Shores, MI**	NA
NA	New Haven-Milford, CT**	NA
NA	New Orleans, LA**	NA
NA	Niles-Benton Harbor, MI**	NA
NA	North Port-Bradenton-Sarasota, FL**	NA
NA	Oklahoma City, OK**	NA
NA	Owensboro, KY**	NA
NA	Pueblo, CO**	NA
NA	Raleigh-Cary, NC**	NA
NA	Rochester, MN**	NA
NA	Rocky Mount, NC**	NA
NA	Rome, GA**	NA
NA	Saginaw, MI**	NA
NA	Seattle-Bellevue-Everett, WA M.D.**	NA
NA	Seattle-Tacoma-Bellevue, WA**	NA
NA	Shreveport-Bossier City, LA**	NA
NA	South Bend-Mishawaka, IN-MI**	NA
NA	Springfield, MO**	NA
NA	St. Cloud, MN**	NA
NA	St. Louis, MO-IL**	NA
NA	Sumter, SC**	NA
NA	Tacoma, WA M.D.**	NA
NA	Toledo, OH**	NA
NA	Tucson, AZ**	NA
NA	Warren-Farmington Hills, MI M.D.**	NA
NA	Wausau, WI**	NA
NA	Wilmington, NC**	NA

Source: CQ Press using reported data from the F.B.I. "Crime in the United States 2009"
*Includes murder, rape, robbery, aggravated assault, burglary, larceny-theft, and motor vehicle theft.
**Not available.

4. Percent Change in Crime Rate: 2005 to 2009
National Percent Change = 11.2% Decrease*

RANK	METROPOLITAN AREA	% CHANGE
103	Abilene, TX	(6.3)
121	Akron, OH	(7.7)
93	Albany-Schenectady-Troy, NY	(5.4)
12	Albany, GA	10.6
179	Albuquerque, NM	(13.3)
137	Alexandria, LA	(9.2)
141	Allentown, PA-NJ	(9.7)
224	Altoona, PA	(19.6)
130	Amarillo, TX	(8.8)
70	Ames, IA	(2.3)
144	Anchorage, AK	(10.0)
15	Anderson, IN	10.4
176	Anderson, SC	(13.1)
144	Ann Arbor, MI	(10.0)
NA	Anniston-Oxford, AL**	NA
95	Appleton, WI	(5.8)
249	Asheville, NC	(23.8)
64	Athens-Clarke County, GA	(1.2)
182	Atlanta, GA	(13.6)
166	Atlantic City, NJ	(12.5)
NA	Auburn, AL**	NA
32	Augusta, GA-SC	3.1
68	Austin-Round Rock, TX	(2.2)
170	Bakersfield, CA	(12.9)
108	Baltimore-Towson, MD	(6.7)
3	Bangor, ME	17.9
1	Barnstable Town, MA	30.6
128	Baton Rouge, LA	(8.6)
87	Battle Creek, MI	(4.6)
NA	Bay City, MI**	NA
157	Beaumont-Port Arthur, TX	(11.2)
274	Bellingham, WA	(32.2)
282	Bend, OR	(41.1)
45	Bethesda-Frederick, MD M.D.	1.4
219	Billings, MT	(18.7)
41	Binghamton, NY	1.8
NA	Birmingham-Hoover, AL**	NA
61	Bismarck, ND	(0.5)
72	Blacksburg, VA	(2.7)
12	Bloomington, IN	10.6
NA	Boise City-Nampa, ID**	NA
75	Boston (greater), MA-NH	(3.0)
132	Boston-Quincy, MA M.D.	(9.0)
NA	Boulder, CO**	NA
NA	Bowling Green, KY**	NA
140	Bremerton-Silverdale, WA	(9.5)
143	Bridgeport-Stamford, CT	(9.9)
117	Brownsville-Harlingen, TX	(7.3)
27	Brunswick, GA	4.0
50	Buffalo-Niagara Falls, NY	0.7
NA	Burlington-South Burlington, VT**	NA
80	Burlington, NC	(4.2)
48	Cambridge-Newton, MA M.D.	0.9
66	Camden, NJ M.D.	(1.9)
215	Cape Coral-Fort Myers, FL	(17.7)
NA	Cape Girardeau, MO-IL**	NA
220	Carson City, NV	(18.8)
208	Casper, WY	(16.9)
161	Cedar Rapids, IA	(11.4)
NA	Charleston-North Charleston, SC**	NA
224	Charleston, WV	(19.6)
259	Charlotte-Gastonia, NC-SC	(26.3)
78	Charlottesville, VA	(3.8)
103	Chattanooga, TN-GA	(6.3)
151	Cheyenne, WY	(10.6)
174	Chico, CA	(13.0)
NA	Cincinnati-Middletown, OH-KY-IN**	NA
NA	Clarksville, TN-KY**	NA
NA	Cleveland-Elyria-Mentor, OH**	NA
NA	Cleveland, TN**	NA
222	Coeur d'Alene, ID	(19.5)
106	College Station-Bryan, TX	(6.4)
265	Colorado Springs, CO	(28.3)
35	Columbia, MO	2.7
54	Columbia, SC	0.3
10	Columbus, GA-AL	13.4
179	Columbus, IN	(13.3)
162	Columbus, OH	(11.5)
216	Corpus Christi, TX	(18.0)
254	Corvallis, OR	(25.0)
NA	Crestview-Fort Walton Beach, FL**	NA
7	Cumberland, MD-WV	15.3
217	Dallas (greater), TX	(18.1)
235	Dallas-Plano-Irving, TX M.D.	(20.4)
NA	Dalton, GA**	NA
NA	Danville, IL**	NA
22	Danville, VA	7.2
127	Dayton, OH	(8.3)
NA	Decatur, AL**	NA
NA	Decatur, IL**	NA
NA	Deltona-Daytona Beach, FL**	NA
279	Denver-Aurora, CO	(35.9)
NA	Des Moines-West Des Moines, IA**	NA
NA	Detroit (greater), MI**	NA
NA	Detroit-Livonia-Dearborn, MI M.D.**	NA
NA	Dothan, AL**	NA
4	Dover, DE	15.9
44	Dubuque, IA	1.5
NA	Duluth, MN-WI**	NA
152	Durham-Chapel Hill, NC	(10.7)
150	Eau Claire, WI	(10.4)
65	Edison, NJ M.D.	(1.5)
NA	El Centro, CA**	NA
83	El Paso, TX	(4.3)
NA	Elizabethtown, KY**	NA
267	Elkhart-Goshen, IN	(29.0)
243	Elmira, NY	(23.0)
5	Erie, PA	15.6
248	Eugene-Springfield, OR	(23.7)
NA	Evansville, IN-KY**	NA
NA	Fargo, ND-MN**	NA
NA	Farmington, NM**	NA
214	Fayetteville, AR-MO	(17.4)
35	Fayetteville, NC	2.7
269	Flagstaff, AZ	(29.9)
NA	Flint, MI**	NA
NA	Florence-Muscle Shoals, AL**	NA
201	Florence, SC	(16.2)
59	Fond du Lac, WI	(0.4)
103	Fort Collins-Loveland, CO	(6.3)
23	Fort Lauderdale, FL M.D.	6.6
128	Fort Smith, AR-OK	(8.6)
181	Fort Wayne, IN	(13.5)
177	Fort Worth-Arlington, TX M.D.	(13.2)
234	Fresno, CA	(20.3)
226	Gadsden, AL	(19.7)
42	Gainesville, FL	1.7
277	Gainesville, GA	(33.3)
NA	Glens Falls, NY**	NA
39	Goldsboro, NC	2.2
NA	Grand Forks, ND-MN**	NA
243	Grand Junction, CO	(23.0)
NA	Grand Rapids-Wyoming, MI**	NA
263	Great Falls, MT	(27.9)
286	Greeley, CO	(46.0)
200	Green Bay, WI	(16.1)
97	Greensboro-High Point, NC	(5.9)
NA	Gulfport-Biloxi, MS**	NA
74	Hagerstown-Martinsburg, MD-WV	(2.9)
154	Harrisburg-Carlisle, PA	(11.0)
58	Harrisonburg, VA	(0.3)
174	Hartford, CT	(13.0)
NA	Hattiesburg, MS**	NA
113	Hickory, NC	(7.2)
37	Hinesville, GA	2.5
NA	Holland-Grand Haven, MI**	NA
230	Honolulu, HI	(20.0)
205	Hot Springs, AR	(16.5)
147	Houma, LA	(10.1)
67	Houston, TX	(2.1)
251	Huntsville, AL	(24.6)
185	Idaho Falls, ID	(13.7)
113	Indianapolis, IN	(7.2)
126	Iowa City, IA	(8.2)
NA	Ithaca, NY**	NA
89	Jacksonville, FL	(4.8)
NA	Jacksonville, NC**	NA
NA	Jackson, MI**	NA
45	Jackson, MS	1.4
177	Jackson, TN	(13.2)
238	Janesville, WI	(20.7)
198	Jefferson City, MO	(15.8)
252	Johnson City, TN	(24.8)
243	Jonesboro, AR	(23.0)
NA	Kalamazoo-Portage, MI**	NA
NA	Kansas City, MO-KS**	NA
271	Kennewick-Pasco-Richland, WA	(30.7)
187	Killeen-Temple-Fort Hood, TX	(14.3)
83	Kingsport, TN-VA	(4.3)
108	Kingston, NY	(6.7)
102	Knoxville, TN	(6.2)
239	Kokomo, IN	(21.4)
NA	La Crosse, WI-MN**	NA
121	Lafayette, IN	(7.7)
18	Lafayette, LA	9.2
29	Lake Charles, LA	3.6
NA	Lake Havasu City-Kingman, AZ**	NA
124	Lakeland, FL	(8.1)
158	Lancaster, PA	(11.3)
NA	Lansing-East Lansing, MI**	NA

Note: All listings are for Metropolitan Statistical Areas (M.S.A.s) except for those ending with "M.D." Listings with "M.D." are Metropolitan Divisions which are smaller parts of eleven large M.S.A.s. See explanatory note at beginning of metropolitan area section.

RANK	METROPOLITAN AREA	% CHANGE
40	Laredo, TX	2.0
52	Las Cruces, NM	0.6
247	Las Vegas-Paradise, NV	(23.6)
17	Lawrence, KS	9.7
NA	Lawton, OK**	NA
250	Lebanon, PA	(24.4)
158	Lewiston-Auburn, ME	(11.3)
199	Lewiston, ID-WA	(15.9)
NA	Lexington-Fayette, KY**	NA
59	Lima, OH	(0.4)
261	Lincoln, NE	(26.6)
NA	Little Rock, AR**	NA
211	Logan, UT-ID	(17.2)
77	Longview, TX	(3.6)
280	Longview, WA	(37.6)
189	Los Angeles County, CA M.D.	(14.6)
192	Los Angeles (greater), CA	(14.9)
NA	Louisville, KY-IN**	NA
83	Lubbock, TX	(4.3)
70	Lynchburg, VA	(2.3)
222	Macon, GA	(19.5)
259	Madera, CA	(26.3)
113	Madison, WI	(7.2)
8	Manchester-Nashua, NH	14.0
NA	Manhattan, KS**	NA
NA	Mankato-North Mankato, MN**	NA
163	Mansfield, OH	(11.7)
94	McAllen-Edinburg-Mission, TX	(5.5)
278	Medford, OR	(35.8)
189	Memphis, TN-MS-AR	(14.6)
170	Merced, CA	(12.9)
76	Miami (greater), FL	(3.2)
123	Miami-Dade County, FL M.D.	(8.0)
97	Michigan City-La Porte, IN	(5.9)
56	Midland, TX	0.2
29	Milwaukee, WI	3.6
NA	Minneapolis-St. Paul, MN-WI**	NA
285	Missoula, MT	(42.6)
11	Mobile, AL	11.5
240	Modesto, CA	(22.0)
NA	Monroe, MI**	NA
193	Montgomery, AL	(15.0)
34	Morgantown, WV	2.9
106	Morristown, TN	(6.4)
281	Mount Vernon-Anacortes, WA	(38.4)
79	Muncie, IN	(4.0)
NA	Muskegon-Norton Shores, MI**	NA
111	Napa, CA	(6.9)
196	Naples-Marco Island, FL	(15.5)
233	Nashville-Davidson, TN	(20.2)
54	Nassau-Suffolk, NY M.D.	0.3
NA	New Haven-Milford, CT**	NA
NA	New Orleans, LA**	NA
164	New York (greater), NY-NJ-PA	(12.2)
188	New York-W. Plains NY-NJ M.D.	(14.5)
227	Newark-Union, NJ-PA M.D.	(19.8)
NA	Niles-Benton Harbor, MI**	NA
NA	North Port-Bradenton-Sarasota, FL**	NA
33	Norwich-New London, CT	3.0
167	Oakland-Fremont, CA M.D.	(12.6)
182	Ocala, FL	(13.6)
57	Ocean City, NJ	(0.1)
16	Odessa, TX	10.0

RANK	METROPOLITAN AREA	% CHANGE
170	Ogden-Clearfield, UT	(12.9)
NA	Oklahoma City, OK**	NA
235	Olympia, WA	(20.4)
218	Omaha-Council Bluffs, NE-IA	(18.4)
131	Orlando, FL	(8.9)
9	Oshkosh-Neenah, WI	13.8
NA	Owensboro, KY**	NA
118	Oxnard-Thousand Oaks, CA	(7.4)
25	Palm Bay-Melbourne, FL	4.6
NA	Palm Coast, FL**	NA
37	Panama City-Lynn Haven, FL	2.5
91	Pascagoula, MS	(5.3)
NA	Peabody, MA M.D.**	NA
31	Pensacola, FL	3.3
86	Philadelphia (greater) PA-NJ-MD-DE	(4.4)
110	Philadelphia, PA M.D.	(6.8)
270	Phoenix-Mesa-Scottsdale, AZ	(30.5)
100	Pine Bluff, AR	(6.1)
189	Pittsburgh, PA	(14.6)
12	Pittsfield, MA	10.6
169	Pocatello, ID	(12.7)
120	Port St. Lucie, FL	(7.5)
276	Portland-Vancouver, OR-WA	(32.5)
62	Portland, ME	(0.8)
28	Poughkeepsie, NY	3.7
264	Prescott, AZ	(28.2)
NA	Providence-New Bedford, RI-MA**	NA
266	Provo-Orem, UT	(28.8)
284	Pueblo, CO	(42.3)
167	Punta Gorda, FL	(12.6)
208	Racine, WI	(16.9)
149	Raleigh-Cary, NC	(10.3)
111	Rapid City, SD	(6.9)
201	Reading, PA	(16.2)
194	Redding, CA	(15.1)
220	Reno-Sparks, NV	(18.8)
NA	Richmond, VA**	NA
241	Riverside-San Bernardino, CA	(22.1)
201	Roanoke, VA	(16.2)
NA	Rochester, MN**	NA
118	Rochester, NY	(7.4)
2	Rockingham County, NH M.D.	18.9
99	Rocky Mount, NC	(6.0)
272	Rome, GA	(30.9)
232	Sacramento, CA	(20.1)
NA	Saginaw, MI**	NA
275	Salem, OR	(32.4)
211	Salinas, CA	(17.2)
80	Salisbury, MD	(4.2)
139	Salt Lake City, UT	(9.4)
228	San Angelo, TX	(19.9)
43	San Antonio, TX	1.6
262	San Diego, CA	(27.4)
158	San Francisco (greater), CA	(11.3)
132	San Francisco-S. Mateo, CA M.D.	(9.0)
132	San Jose, CA	(9.0)
152	San Luis Obispo, CA	(10.7)
210	Sandusky, OH	(17.0)
197	Santa Ana-Anaheim, CA M.D.	(15.7)
91	Santa Barbara-Santa Maria, CA	(5.3)
142	Santa Cruz-Watsonville, CA	(9.8)
62	Santa Fe, NM	(0.8)
237	Santa Rosa-Petaluma, CA	(20.5)

RANK	METROPOLITAN AREA	% CHANGE
170	Savannah, GA	(12.9)
124	Scranton--Wilkes-Barre, PA	(8.1)
256	Seattle-Bellevue-Everett, WA M.D.	(25.3)
246	Seattle-Tacoma-Bellevue, WA	(23.3)
144	Sebastian-Vero Beach, FL	(10.0)
53	Sheboygan, WI	0.5
165	Sherman-Denison, TX	(12.3)
NA	Shreveport-Bossier City, LA**	NA
195	Sioux City, IA-NE-SD	(15.4)
95	Sioux Falls, SD	(5.8)
NA	South Bend-Mishawaka, IN-MI**	NA
186	Spartanburg, SC	(14.0)
73	Spokane, WA	(2.8)
132	Springfield, MA	(9.0)
NA	Springfield, MO**	NA
273	Springfield, OH	(32.0)
113	State College, PA	(7.2)
242	Stockton, CA	(22.7)
NA	St. Cloud, MN**	NA
268	St. George, UT	(29.7)
100	St. Joseph, MO-KS	(6.1)
NA	St. Louis, MO-IL**	NA
NA	Sumter, SC**	NA
47	Syracuse, NY	1.2
207	Tacoma, WA M.D.	(16.7)
132	Tallahassee, FL	(9.0)
138	Tampa-St Petersburg, FL	(9.3)
68	Texarkana, TX-Texarkana, AR	(2.2)
NA	Toledo, OH**	NA
258	Topeka, KS	(25.6)
205	Trenton-Ewing, NJ	(16.5)
NA	Tucson, AZ**	NA
155	Tulsa, OK	(11.1)
NA	Tuscaloosa, AL**	NA
49	Tyler, TX	0.8
18	Utica-Rome, NY	9.2
228	Valdosta, GA	(19.9)
NA	Vallejo-Fairfield, CA**	NA
5	Victoria, TX	15.6
230	Vineland, NJ	(20.0)
NA	Visalia-Porterville, CA**	NA
213	Waco, TX	(17.3)
25	Warner Robins, GA	4.6
NA	Warren-Farmington Hills, MI M.D.**	NA
155	Washington (greater) DC-VA-MD-WV	(11.1)
182	Washington, DC-VA-MD-WV M.D.	(13.6)
80	Waterloo-Cedar Falls, IA	(4.2)
NA	Wausau, WI**	NA
256	Wenatchee, WA	(25.3)
88	West Palm Beach, FL M.D.	(4.7)
21	Wheeling, WV-OH	7.9
252	Wichita Falls, TX	(24.8)
NA	Wichita, KS**	NA
147	Williamsport, PA	(10.1)
24	Wilmington, DE-MD-NJ M.D.	4.9
NA	Wilmington, NC**	NA
90	Winchester, VA-WV	(5.1)
50	Winston-Salem, NC	0.7
20	Worcester, MA	8.9
201	York-Hanover, PA	(16.2)
NA	Youngstown, OH-PA**	NA
283	Yuba City, CA	(41.6)
255	Yuma, AZ	(25.2)

Source: CQ Press using reported data from the F.B.I. "Crime in the United States 2009"
*Includes murder, rape, robbery, aggravated assault, burglary, larceny-theft, and motor vehicle theft.
**Not available.

4. Percent Change in Crime Rate: 2005 to 2009 (continued)
National Percent Change = 11.2% Decrease*

RANK	METROPOLITAN AREA	% CHANGE
1	Barnstable Town, MA	30.6
2	Rockingham County, NH M.D.	18.9
3	Bangor, ME	17.9
4	Dover, DE	15.9
5	Erie, PA	15.6
5	Victoria, TX	15.6
7	Cumberland, MD-WV	15.3
8	Manchester-Nashua, NH	14.0
9	Oshkosh-Neenah, WI	13.8
10	Columbus, GA-AL	13.4
11	Mobile, AL	11.5
12	Albany, GA	10.6
12	Bloomington, IN	10.6
12	Pittsfield, MA	10.6
15	Anderson, IN	10.4
16	Odessa, TX	10.0
17	Lawrence, KS	9.7
18	Lafayette, LA	9.2
18	Utica-Rome, NY	9.2
20	Worcester, MA	8.9
21	Wheeling, WV-OH	7.9
22	Danville, VA	7.2
23	Fort Lauderdale, FL M.D.	6.6
24	Wilmington, DE-MD-NJ M.D.	4.9
25	Palm Bay-Melbourne, FL	4.6
25	Warner Robins, GA	4.6
27	Brunswick, GA	4.0
28	Poughkeepsie, NY	3.7
29	Lake Charles, LA	3.6
29	Milwaukee, WI	3.6
31	Pensacola, FL	3.3
32	Augusta, GA-SC	3.1
33	Norwich-New London, CT	3.0
34	Morgantown, WV	2.9
35	Columbia, MO	2.7
35	Fayetteville, NC	2.7
37	Hinesville, GA	2.5
37	Panama City-Lynn Haven, FL	2.5
39	Goldsboro, NC	2.2
40	Laredo, TX	2.0
41	Binghamton, NY	1.8
42	Gainesville, FL	1.7
43	San Antonio, TX	1.6
44	Dubuque, IA	1.5
45	Bethesda-Frederick, MD M.D.	1.4
45	Jackson, MS	1.4
47	Syracuse, NY	1.2
48	Cambridge-Newton, MA M.D.	0.9
49	Tyler, TX	0.8
50	Buffalo-Niagara Falls, NY	0.7
50	Winston-Salem, NC	0.7
52	Las Cruces, NM	0.6
53	Sheboygan, WI	0.5
54	Columbia, SC	0.3
54	Nassau-Suffolk, NY M.D.	0.3
56	Midland, TX	0.2
57	Ocean City, NJ	(0.1)
58	Harrisonburg, VA	(0.3)
59	Fond du Lac, WI	(0.4)
59	Lima, OH	(0.4)
61	Bismarck, ND	(0.5)
62	Portland, ME	(0.8)
62	Santa Fe, NM	(0.8)
64	Athens-Clarke County, GA	(1.2)
65	Edison, NJ M.D.	(1.5)
66	Camden, NJ M.D.	(1.9)
67	Houston, TX	(2.1)
68	Austin-Round Rock, TX	(2.2)
68	Texarkana, TX-Texarkana, AR	(2.2)
70	Ames, IA	(2.3)
70	Lynchburg, VA	(2.3)
72	Blacksburg, VA	(2.7)
73	Spokane, WA	(2.8)
74	Hagerstown-Martinsburg, MD-WV	(2.9)
75	Boston (greater), MA-NH	(3.0)
76	Miami (greater), FL	(3.2)
77	Longview, TX	(3.6)
78	Charlottesville, VA	(3.8)
79	Muncie, IN	(4.0)
80	Burlington, NC	(4.2)
80	Salisbury, MD	(4.2)
80	Waterloo-Cedar Falls, IA	(4.2)
83	El Paso, TX	(4.3)
83	Kingsport, TN-VA	(4.3)
83	Lubbock, TX	(4.3)
86	Philadelphia (greater) PA-NJ-MD-DE	(4.4)
87	Battle Creek, MI	(4.6)
88	West Palm Beach, FL M.D.	(4.7)
89	Jacksonville, FL	(4.8)
90	Winchester, VA-WV	(5.1)
91	Pascagoula, MS	(5.3)
91	Santa Barbara-Santa Maria, CA	(5.3)
93	Albany-Schenectady-Troy, NY	(5.4)
94	McAllen-Edinburg-Mission, TX	(5.5)
95	Appleton, WI	(5.8)
95	Sioux Falls, SD	(5.8)
97	Greensboro-High Point, NC	(5.9)
97	Michigan City-La Porte, IN	(5.9)
99	Rocky Mount, NC	(6.0)
100	Pine Bluff, AR	(6.1)
100	St. Joseph, MO-KS	(6.1)
102	Knoxville, TN	(6.2)
103	Abilene, TX	(6.3)
103	Chattanooga, TN-GA	(6.3)
103	Fort Collins-Loveland, CO	(6.3)
106	College Station-Bryan, TX	(6.4)
106	Morristown, TN	(6.4)
108	Baltimore-Towson, MD	(6.7)
108	Kingston, NY	(6.7)
110	Philadelphia, PA M.D.	(6.8)
111	Napa, CA	(6.9)
111	Rapid City, SD	(6.9)
113	Hickory, NC	(7.2)
113	Indianapolis, IN	(7.2)
113	Madison, WI	(7.2)
113	State College, PA	(7.2)
117	Brownsville-Harlingen, TX	(7.3)
118	Oxnard-Thousand Oaks, CA	(7.4)
118	Rochester, NY	(7.4)
120	Port St. Lucie, FL	(7.5)
121	Akron, OH	(7.7)
121	Lafayette, IN	(7.7)
123	Miami-Dade County, FL M.D.	(8.0)
124	Lakeland, FL	(8.1)
124	Scranton--Wilkes-Barre, PA	(8.1)
126	Iowa City, IA	(8.2)
127	Dayton, OH	(8.3)
128	Baton Rouge, LA	(8.6)
128	Fort Smith, AR-OK	(8.6)
130	Amarillo, TX	(8.8)
131	Orlando, FL	(8.9)
132	Boston-Quincy, MA M.D.	(9.0)
132	San Francisco-S. Mateo, CA M.D.	(9.0)
132	San Jose, CA	(9.0)
132	Springfield, MA	(9.0)
132	Tallahassee, FL	(9.0)
137	Alexandria, LA	(9.2)
138	Tampa-St Petersburg, FL	(9.3)
139	Salt Lake City, UT	(9.4)
140	Bremerton-Silverdale, WA	(9.5)
141	Allentown, PA-NJ	(9.7)
142	Santa Cruz-Watsonville, CA	(9.8)
143	Bridgeport-Stamford, CT	(9.9)
144	Anchorage, AK	(10.0)
144	Ann Arbor, MI	(10.0)
144	Sebastian-Vero Beach, FL	(10.0)
147	Houma, LA	(10.1)
147	Williamsport, PA	(10.1)
149	Raleigh-Cary, NC	(10.3)
150	Eau Claire, WI	(10.4)
151	Cheyenne, WY	(10.6)
152	Durham-Chapel Hill, NC	(10.7)
152	San Luis Obispo, CA	(10.7)
154	Harrisburg-Carlisle, PA	(11.0)
155	Tulsa, OK	(11.1)
155	Washington (greater) DC-VA-MD-WV	(11.1)
157	Beaumont-Port Arthur, TX	(11.2)
158	Lancaster, PA	(11.3)
158	Lewiston-Auburn, ME	(11.3)
158	San Francisco (greater), CA	(11.3)
161	Cedar Rapids, IA	(11.4)
162	Columbus, OH	(11.5)
163	Mansfield, OH	(11.7)
164	New York (greater), NY-NJ-PA	(12.2)
165	Sherman-Denison, TX	(12.3)
166	Atlantic City, NJ	(12.5)
167	Oakland-Fremont, CA M.D.	(12.6)
167	Punta Gorda, FL	(12.6)
169	Pocatello, ID	(12.7)
170	Bakersfield, CA	(12.9)
170	Merced, CA	(12.9)
170	Ogden-Clearfield, UT	(12.9)
170	Savannah, GA	(12.9)
174	Chico, CA	(13.0)
174	Hartford, CT	(13.0)
176	Anderson, SC	(13.1)
177	Fort Worth-Arlington, TX M.D.	(13.2)
177	Jackson, TN	(13.2)
179	Albuquerque, NM	(13.3)
179	Columbus, IN	(13.3)

Note: All listings are for Metropolitan Statistical Areas (M.S.A.s) except for those ending with "M.D." Listings with "M.D." are Metropolitan Divisions which are smaller parts of eleven large M.S.A.s. See explanatory note at beginning of metropolitan area section.

Rank Order - Metro Area (continued)

RANK	METROPOLITAN AREA	% CHANGE
181	Fort Wayne, IN	(13.5)
182	Atlanta, GA	(13.6)
182	Ocala, FL	(13.6)
182	Washington, DC-VA-MD-WV M.D.	(13.6)
185	Idaho Falls, ID	(13.7)
186	Spartanburg, SC	(14.0)
187	Killeen-Temple-Fort Hood, TX	(14.3)
188	New York-W. Plains NY-NJ M.D.	(14.5)
189	Los Angeles County, CA M.D.	(14.6)
189	Memphis, TN-MS-AR	(14.6)
189	Pittsburgh, PA	(14.6)
192	Los Angeles (greater), CA	(14.9)
193	Montgomery, AL	(15.0)
194	Redding, CA	(15.1)
195	Sioux City, IA-NE-SD	(15.4)
196	Naples-Marco Island, FL	(15.5)
197	Santa Ana-Anaheim, CA M.D.	(15.7)
198	Jefferson City, MO	(15.8)
199	Lewiston, ID-WA	(15.9)
200	Green Bay, WI	(16.1)
201	Florence, SC	(16.2)
201	Reading, PA	(16.2)
201	Roanoke, VA	(16.2)
201	York-Hanover, PA	(16.2)
205	Hot Springs, AR	(16.5)
205	Trenton-Ewing, NJ	(16.5)
207	Tacoma, WA M.D.	(16.7)
208	Casper, WY	(16.9)
208	Racine, WI	(16.9)
210	Sandusky, OH	(17.0)
211	Logan, UT-ID	(17.2)
211	Salinas, CA	(17.2)
213	Waco, TX	(17.3)
214	Fayetteville, AR-MO	(17.4)
215	Cape Coral-Fort Myers, FL	(17.7)
216	Corpus Christi, TX	(18.0)
217	Dallas (greater), TX	(18.1)
218	Omaha-Council Bluffs, NE-IA	(18.4)
219	Billings, MT	(18.7)
220	Carson City, NV	(18.8)
220	Reno-Sparks, NV	(18.8)
222	Coeur d'Alene, ID	(19.5)
222	Macon, GA	(19.5)
224	Altoona, PA	(19.6)
224	Charleston, WV	(19.6)
226	Gadsden, AL	(19.7)
227	Newark-Union, NJ-PA M.D.	(19.8)
228	San Angelo, TX	(19.9)
228	Valdosta, GA	(19.9)
230	Honolulu, HI	(20.0)
230	Vineland, NJ	(20.0)
232	Sacramento, CA	(20.1)
233	Nashville-Davidson, TN	(20.2)
234	Fresno, CA	(20.3)
235	Dallas-Plano-Irving, TX M.D.	(20.4)
235	Olympia, WA	(20.4)
237	Santa Rosa-Petaluma, CA	(20.5)
238	Janesville, WI	(20.7)
239	Kokomo, IN	(21.4)
240	Modesto, CA	(22.0)
241	Riverside-San Bernardino, CA	(22.1)
242	Stockton, CA	(22.7)
243	Elmira, NY	(23.0)

RANK	METROPOLITAN AREA	% CHANGE
243	Grand Junction, CO	(23.0)
243	Jonesboro, AR	(23.0)
246	Seattle-Tacoma-Bellevue, WA	(23.3)
247	Las Vegas-Paradise, NV	(23.6)
248	Eugene-Springfield, OR	(23.7)
249	Asheville, NC	(23.8)
250	Lebanon, PA	(24.4)
251	Huntsville, AL	(24.6)
252	Johnson City, TN	(24.8)
252	Wichita Falls, TX	(24.8)
254	Corvallis, OR	(25.0)
255	Yuma, AZ	(25.2)
256	Seattle-Bellevue-Everett, WA M.D.	(25.3)
256	Wenatchee, WA	(25.3)
258	Topeka, KS	(25.6)
259	Charlotte-Gastonia, NC-SC	(26.3)
259	Madera, CA	(26.3)
261	Lincoln, NE	(26.6)
262	San Diego, CA	(27.4)
263	Great Falls, MT	(27.9)
264	Prescott, AZ	(28.2)
265	Colorado Springs, CO	(28.3)
266	Provo-Orem, UT	(28.8)
267	Elkhart-Goshen, IN	(29.0)
268	St. George, UT	(29.7)
269	Flagstaff, AZ	(29.9)
270	Phoenix-Mesa-Scottsdale, AZ	(30.5)
271	Kennewick-Pasco-Richland, WA	(30.7)
272	Rome, GA	(30.9)
273	Springfield, OH	(32.0)
274	Bellingham, WA	(32.2)
275	Salem, OR	(32.4)
276	Portland-Vancouver, OR-WA	(32.5)
277	Gainesville, GA	(33.3)
278	Medford, OR	(35.8)
279	Denver-Aurora, CO	(35.9)
280	Longview, WA	(37.6)
281	Mount Vernon-Anacortes, WA	(38.4)
282	Bend, OR	(41.1)
283	Yuba City, CA	(41.6)
284	Pueblo, CO	(42.3)
285	Missoula, MT	(42.6)
286	Greeley, CO	(46.0)
NA	Anniston-Oxford, AL**	NA
NA	Auburn, AL**	NA
NA	Bay City, MI**	NA
NA	Birmingham-Hoover, AL**	NA
NA	Boise City-Nampa, ID**	NA
NA	Boulder, CO**	NA
NA	Bowling Green, KY**	NA
NA	Burlington-South Burlington, VT**	NA
NA	Cape Girardeau, MO-IL**	NA
NA	Charleston-North Charleston, SC**	NA
NA	Cincinnati-Middletown, OH-KY-IN**	NA
NA	Clarksville, TN-KY**	NA
NA	Cleveland-Elyria-Mentor, OH**	NA
NA	Cleveland, TN**	NA
NA	Crestview-Fort Walton Beach, FL**	NA
NA	Dalton, GA**	NA
NA	Danville, IL**	NA
NA	Decatur, AL**	NA
NA	Decatur, IL**	NA
NA	Deltona-Daytona Beach, FL**	NA

RANK	METROPOLITAN AREA	% CHANGE
NA	Des Moines-West Des Moines, IA**	NA
NA	Detroit (greater), MI**	NA
NA	Detroit-Livonia-Dearborn, MI M.D.**	NA
NA	Dothan, AL**	NA
NA	Duluth, MN-WI**	NA
NA	El Centro, CA**	NA
NA	Elizabethtown, KY**	NA
NA	Evansville, IN-KY**	NA
NA	Fargo, ND-MN**	NA
NA	Farmington, NM**	NA
NA	Flint, MI**	NA
NA	Florence-Muscle Shoals, AL**	NA
NA	Glens Falls, NY**	NA
NA	Grand Forks, ND-MN**	NA
NA	Grand Rapids-Wyoming, MI**	NA
NA	Gulfport-Biloxi, MS**	NA
NA	Hattiesburg, MS**	NA
NA	Holland-Grand Haven, MI**	NA
NA	Ithaca, NY**	NA
NA	Jacksonville, NC**	NA
NA	Jackson, MI**	NA
NA	Kalamazoo-Portage, MI**	NA
NA	Kansas City, MO-KS**	NA
NA	La Crosse, WI-MN**	NA
NA	Lake Havasu City-Kingman, AZ**	NA
NA	Lansing-East Lansing, MI**	NA
NA	Lawton, OK**	NA
NA	Lexington-Fayette, KY**	NA
NA	Little Rock, AR**	NA
NA	Louisville, KY-IN**	NA
NA	Manhattan, KS**	NA
NA	Mankato-North Mankato, MN**	NA
NA	Minneapolis-St. Paul, MN-WI**	NA
NA	Monroe, MI**	NA
NA	Muskegon-Norton Shores, MI**	NA
NA	New Haven-Milford, CT**	NA
NA	New Orleans, LA**	NA
NA	Niles-Benton Harbor, MI**	NA
NA	North Port-Bradenton-Sarasota, FL**	NA
NA	Oklahoma City, OK**	NA
NA	Owensboro, KY**	NA
NA	Palm Coast, FL**	NA
NA	Peabody, MA M.D.**	NA
NA	Providence-New Bedford, RI-MA**	NA
NA	Richmond, VA**	NA
NA	Rochester, MN**	NA
NA	Saginaw, MI**	NA
NA	Shreveport-Bossier City, LA**	NA
NA	South Bend-Mishawaka, IN-MI**	NA
NA	Springfield, MO**	NA
NA	St. Cloud, MN**	NA
NA	St. Louis, MO-IL**	NA
NA	Sumter, SC**	NA
NA	Toledo, OH**	NA
NA	Tucson, AZ**	NA
NA	Tuscaloosa, AL**	NA
NA	Vallejo-Fairfield, CA**	NA
NA	Visalia-Porterville, CA**	NA
NA	Warren-Farmington Hills, MI M.D.**	NA
NA	Wausau, WI**	NA
NA	Wichita, KS**	NA
NA	Wilmington, NC**	NA
NA	Youngstown, OH-PA**	NA

Source: CQ Press using reported data from the F.B.I. "Crime in the United States 2009"
*Includes murder, rape, robbery, aggravated assault, burglary, larceny-theft, and motor vehicle theft.
**Not available.

5. Violent Crimes in 2009
National Total = 1,318,398 Violent Crimes*

RANK	METROPOLITAN AREA	CRIMES
216	Abilene, TX	741
111	Akron, OH	2,503
106	Albany-Schenectady-Troy, NY	2,655
190	Albany, GA	957
59	Albuquerque, NM	5,625
178	Alexandria, LA	1,039
127	Allentown, PA-NJ	1,992
298	Altoona, PA	349
142	Amarillo, TX	1,661
320	Ames, IA	228
107	Anchorage, AK	2,606
330	Anderson, IN	204
166	Anderson, SC	1,214
173	Ann Arbor, MI	1,122
209	Anniston-Oxford, AL	829
315	Appleton, WI	256
191	Asheville, NC	948
219	Athens-Clarke County, GA	732
11	Atlanta, GA	24,161
148	Atlantic City, NJ	1,465
NA	Auburn, AL**	NA
114	Augusta, GA-SC	2,232
52	Austin-Round Rock, TX	6,074
65	Bakersfield, CA	4,892
16	Baltimore-Towson, MD	19,456
346	Bangor, ME	124
177	Barnstable Town, MA	1,044
61	Baton Rouge, LA	5,493
195	Battle Creek, MI	927
304	Bay City, MI	337
123	Beaumont-Port Arthur, TX	2,021
273	Bellingham, WA	443
299	Bend, OR	346
96	Bethesda-Frederick, MD M.D.	2,955
297	Billings, MT	355
262	Binghamton, NY	481
53	Birmingham-Hoover, AL	6,045
323	Bismarck, ND	221
307	Blacksburg, VA	319
254	Bloomington, IN	512
152	Boise City-Nampa, ID	1,440
18	Boston (greater), MA-NH	18,357
29	Boston-Quincy, MA M.D.	11,068
220	Boulder, CO	719
313	Bowling Green, KY	261
174	Bremerton-Silverdale, WA	1,069
100	Bridgeport-Stamford, CT	2,792
157	Brownsville-Harlingen, TX	1,337
214	Brunswick, GA	801
57	Buffalo-Niagara Falls, NY	5,759
305	Burlington-South Burlington, VT	332
230	Burlington, NC	677
72	Cambridge-Newton, MA M.D.	4,221
69	Camden, NJ M.D.	4,474
109	Cape Coral-Fort Myers, FL	2,561
295	Cape Girardeau, MO-IL	363
337	Carson City, NV	180
339	Casper, WY	163
250	Cedar Rapids, IA	531
73	Charleston-North Charleston, SC	4,066
158	Charleston, WV	1,330
36	Charlotte-Gastonia, NC-SC	9,255
280	Charlottesville, VA	426
90	Chattanooga, TN-GA	3,090
337	Cheyenne, WY	180
193	Chico, CA	932
47	Cincinnati-Middletown, OH-KY-IN	7,444
169	Clarksville, TN-KY	1,167
39	Cleveland-Elyria-Mentor, OH	8,973
217	Cleveland, TN	735
261	Coeur d'Alene, ID	482
201	College Station-Bryan, TX	894
98	Colorado Springs, CO	2,837
232	Columbia, MO	670
58	Columbia, SC	5,643
147	Columbus, GA-AL	1,500
350	Columbus, IN	82
50	Columbus, OH	6,658
103	Corpus Christi, TX	2,739
347	Corvallis, OR	103
251	Crestview-Fort Walton Beach, FL	528
269	Cumberland, MD-WV	455
9	Dallas (greater), TX	26,495
20	Dallas-Plano-Irving, TX M.D.	17,355
288	Dalton, GA	396
NA	Danville, IL**	NA
317	Danville, VA	235
99	Dayton, OH	2,793
NA	Decatur, AL**	NA
NA	Decatur, IL**	NA
101	Deltona-Daytona Beach, FL	2,762
40	Denver-Aurora, CO	8,848
146	Des Moines-West Des Moines, IA	1,554
8	Detroit (greater), MI	28,929
13	Detroit-Livonia-Dearborn, MI M.D.	22,002
NA	Dothan, AL**	NA
184	Dover, DE	1,007
296	Dubuque, IA	360
NA	Duluth, MN-WI**	NA
116	Durham-Chapel Hill, NC	2,206
332	Eau Claire, WI	193
77	Edison, NJ M.D.	3,831
NA	El Centro, CA**	NA
87	El Paso, TX	3,303
301	Elizabethtown, KY	341
314	Elkhart-Goshen, IN	260
342	Elmira, NY	161
224	Erie, PA	694
175	Eugene-Springfield, OR	1,057
210	Evansville, IN-KY	827
NA	Fargo, ND-MN**	NA
197	Farmington, NM	919
154	Fayetteville, AR-MO	1,400
126	Fayetteville, NC	1,998
282	Flagstaff, AZ	425
88	Flint, MI	3,288
277	Florence-Muscle Shoals, AL	432
145	Florence, SC	1,558
340	Fond du Lac, WI	162
213	Fort Collins-Loveland, CO	807
35	Fort Lauderdale, FL M.D.	9,562
162	Fort Smith, AR-OK	1,270
181	Fort Wayne, IN	1,020
38	Fort Worth-Arlington, TX M.D.	9,140
66	Fresno, CA	4,694
294	Gadsden, AL	367
122	Gainesville, FL	2,052
300	Gainesville, GA	342
345	Glens Falls, NY	137
253	Goldsboro, NC	515
NA	Grand Forks, ND-MN**	NA
275	Grand Junction, CO	440
97	Grand Rapids-Wyoming, MI	2,954
319	Great Falls, MT	230
221	Greeley, CO	711
245	Green Bay, WI	577
85	Greensboro-High Point, NC	3,421
246	Gulfport-Biloxi, MS	565
234	Hagerstown-Martinsburg, MD-WV	641
139	Harrisburg-Carlisle, PA	1,726
334	Harrisonburg, VA	184
94	Hartford, CT	2,965
312	Hattiesburg, MS	262
185	Hickory, NC	999
306	Hinesville, GA	325
270	Holland-Grand Haven, MI	454
110	Honolulu, HI	2,537
238	Hot Springs, AR	625
199	Houma, LA	896
5	Houston, TX	41,409
144	Huntsville, AL	1,637
293	Idaho Falls, ID	368
31	Indianapolis, IN	10,938
274	Iowa City, IA	442
NA	Ithaca, NY**	NA
37	Jacksonville, FL	9,218
247	Jacksonville, NC	561
229	Jackson, MI	678
118	Jackson, MS	2,120
211	Jackson, TN	813
287	Janesville, WI	398
267	Jefferson City, MO	462
228	Johnson City, TN	679
266	Jonesboro, AR	465
153	Kalamazoo-Portage, MI	1,417
30	Kansas City, MO-KS	11,044
233	Kennewick-Pasco-Richland, WA	659
159	Killeen-Temple-Fort Hood, TX	1,308
170	Kingsport, TN-VA	1,158
272	Kingston, NY	445
84	Knoxville, TN	3,471
331	Kokomo, IN	199
NA	La Crosse, WI-MN**	NA
264	Lafayette, IN	471
125	Lafayette, LA	2,020
149	Lake Charles, LA	1,452
268	Lake Havasu City-Kingman, AZ	456
104	Lakeland, FL	2,734
208	Lancaster, PA	842
135	Lansing-East Lansing, MI	1,849

Note: All listings are for Metropolitan Statistical Areas (M.S.A.s) except for those ending with "M.D." Listings with "M.D." are Metropolitan Divisions which are smaller parts of eleven large M.S.A.s. See explanatory note at beginning of metropolitan area section.

Alpha Order - Metro Area (continued)

RANK	METROPOLITAN AREA	CRIMES
155	Laredo, TX	1,395
207	Las Cruces, NM	843
24	Las Vegas-Paradise, NV	15,439
259	Lawrence, KS	485
172	Lawton, OK	1,142
323	Lebanon, PA	221
340	Lewiston-Auburn, ME	162
349	Lewiston, ID-WA	97
120	Lexington-Fayette, KY	2,073
248	Lima, OH	558
167	Lincoln, NE	1,200
62	Little Rock, AR	5,410
348	Logan, UT-ID	98
171	Longview, TX	1,156
326	Longview, WA	218
4	Los Angeles County, CA M.D.	54,747
2	Los Angeles (greater), CA	62,176
67	Louisville, KY-IN	4,653
113	Lubbock, TX	2,315
231	Lynchburg, VA	671
183	Macon, GA	1,016
227	Madera, CA	685
160	Madison, WI	1,296
199	Manchester-Nashua, NH	896
278	Manhattan, KS	428
NA	Mankato-North Mankato, MN**	NA
316	Mansfield, OH	243
91	McAllen-Edinburg-Mission, TX	3,036
288	Medford, OR	396
25	Memphis, TN-MS-AR	14,898
143	Merced, CA	1,658
6	Miami (greater), FL	37,403
15	Miami-Dade County, FL M.D.	19,797
328	Michigan City-La Porte, IN	213
265	Midland, TX	468
46	Milwaukee, WI	7,679
NA	Minneapolis-St. Paul, MN-WI**	NA
310	Missoula, MT	274
95	Mobile, AL	2,963
105	Modesto, CA	2,721
302	Monroe, MI	340
156	Montgomery, AL	1,374
284	Morgantown, WV	411
260	Morristown, TN	483
318	Mount Vernon-Anacortes, WA	231
276	Muncie, IN	434
218	Muskegon-Norton Shores, MI	734
290	Napa, CA	393
176	Naples-Marco Island, FL	1,050
33	Nashville-Davidson, TN	10,450
64	Nassau-Suffolk, NY M.D.	5,229
82	New Haven-Milford, CT	3,572
51	New Orleans, LA	6,458
1	New York (greater), NY-NJ-PA	72,842
3	New York-W. Plains NY-NJ M.D.	55,679
43	Newark-Union, NJ-PA M.D.	8,103
236	Niles-Benton Harbor, MI	632
74	North Port-Bradenton-Sarasota, FL	4,053
244	Norwich-New London, CT	578
23	Oakland-Fremont, CA M.D.	15,446
130	Ocala, FL	1,911
311	Ocean City, NJ	266
201	Odessa, TX	894

RANK	METROPOLITAN AREA	CRIMES
203	Ogden-Clearfield, UT	882
NA	Oklahoma City, OK**	NA
239	Olympia, WA	616
86	Omaha-Council Bluffs, NE-IA	3,339
26	Orlando, FL	14,253
292	Oshkosh-Neenah, WI	383
344	Owensboro, KY	157
123	Oxnard-Thousand Oaks, CA	2,021
81	Palm Bay-Melbourne, FL	3,617
309	Palm Coast, FL	296
187	Panama City-Lynn Haven, FL	990
283	Pascagoula, MS	416
108	Peabody, MA M.D.	2,572
93	Pensacola, FL	2,968
7	Philadelphia (greater) PA-NJ-MD-DE	34,364
10	Philadelphia, PA M.D.	25,450
21	Phoenix-Mesa-Scottsdale, AZ	17,174
206	Pine Bluff, AR	852
44	Pittsburgh, PA	8,053
249	Pittsfield, MA	556
325	Pocatello, ID	219
140	Port St. Lucie, FL	1,701
55	Portland-Vancouver, OR-WA	6,012
226	Portland, ME	693
133	Poughkeepsie, NY	1,865
222	Prescott, AZ	697
54	Providence-New Bedford, RI-MA	6,020
279	Provo-Orem, UT	427
194	Pueblo, CO	929
263	Punta Gorda, FL	472
242	Racine, WI	591
89	Raleigh-Cary, NC	3,138
291	Rapid City, SD	386
164	Reading, PA	1,254
161	Redding, CA	1,280
117	Reno-Sparks, NV	2,166
79	Richmond, VA	3,652
19	Riverside-San Bernardino, CA	17,416
198	Roanoke, VA	899
NA	Rochester, MN**	NA
92	Rochester, NY	3,022
257	Rockingham County, NH M.D.	496
188	Rocky Mount, NC	986
280	Rome, GA	426
32	Sacramento, CA	10,880
134	Saginaw, MI	1,852
192	Salem, OR	934
119	Salinas, CA	2,118
180	Salisbury, MD	1,027
75	Salt Lake City, UT	3,919
286	San Angelo, TX	406
34	San Antonio, TX	9,731
28	San Diego, CA	12,775
12	San Francisco (greater), CA	24,072
42	San Francisco-S. Mateo, CA M.D.	8,626
63	San Jose, CA	5,259
224	San Luis Obispo, CA	694
333	Sandusky, OH	190
48	Santa Ana-Anaheim, CA M.D.	7,429
131	Santa Barbara-Santa Maria, CA	1,897
165	Santa Cruz-Watsonville, CA	1,215
236	Santa Fe, NM	632
129	Santa Rosa-Petaluma, CA	1,917

RANK	METROPOLITAN AREA	CRIMES
150	Savannah, GA	1,448
151	Scranton--Wilkes-Barre, PA	1,444
41	Seattle-Bellevue-Everett, WA M.D.	8,833
27	Seattle-Tacoma-Bellevue, WA	13,061
271	Sebastian-Vero Beach, FL	450
343	Sheboygan, WI	159
302	Sherman-Denison, TX	340
NA	Shreveport-Bossier City, LA**	NA
285	Sioux City, IA-NE-SD	407
256	Sioux Falls, SD	507
168	South Bend-Mishawaka, IN-MI	1,176
138	Spartanburg, SC	1,744
137	Spokane, WA	1,775
78	Springfield, MA	3,706
136	Springfield, MO	1,833
258	Springfield, OH	489
336	State College, PA	183
60	Stockton, CA	5,531
NA	St. Cloud, MN**	NA
334	St. George, UT	184
252	St. Joseph, MO-KS	518
NA	St. Louis, MO-IL**	NA
223	Sumter, SC	695
128	Syracuse, NY	1,925
71	Tacoma, WA M.D.	4,228
102	Tallahassee, FL	2,748
22	Tampa-St Petersburg, FL	16,200
179	Texarkana, TX-Texarkana, AR	1,029
80	Toledo, OH	3,623
189	Topeka, KS	960
141	Trenton-Ewing, NJ	1,677
68	Tucson, AZ	4,481
56	Tulsa, OK	5,768
186	Tuscaloosa, AL	992
204	Tyler, TX	879
212	Utica-Rome, NY	812
243	Valdosta, GA	590
121	Vallejo-Fairfield, CA	2,064
235	Victoria, TX	639
205	Vineland, NJ	859
115	Visalia-Porterville, CA	2,230
163	Waco, TX	1,263
255	Warner Robins, GA	509
49	Warren-Farmington Hills, MI M.D.	6,927
14	Washington (greater) DC-VA-MD-WV	21,942
17	Washington, DC-VA-MD-WV M.D.	18,987
196	Waterloo-Cedar Falls, IA	922
329	Wausau, WI	206
327	Wenatchee, WA	215
45	West Palm Beach, FL M.D.	8,044
307	Wheeling, WV-OH	319
241	Wichita Falls, TX	592
76	Wichita, KS	3,905
322	Williamsport, PA	226
70	Wilmington, DE-MD-NJ M.D.	4,440
NA	Wilmington, NC**	NA
321	Winchester, VA-WV	227
112	Winston-Salem, NC	2,421
83	Worcester, MA	3,504
182	York-Hanover, PA	1,018
132	Youngstown, OH-PA	1,870
240	Yuba City, CA	595
215	Yuma, AZ	771

Source: Reported data from the F.B.I. "Crime in the United States 2009"
*Violent crimes are offenses of murder, forcible rape, robbery, and aggravated assault.
**Not available.

5. Violent Crimes in 2009 (continued)
National Total = 1,318,398 Violent Crimes*

RANK	METROPOLITAN AREA	CRIMES
1	New York (greater), NY-NJ-PA	72,842
2	Los Angeles (greater), CA	62,176
3	New York-W. Plains NY-NJ M.D.	55,679
4	Los Angeles County, CA M.D.	54,747
5	Houston, TX	41,409
6	Miami (greater), FL	37,403
7	Philadelphia (greater) PA-NJ-MD-DE	34,364
8	Detroit (greater), MI	28,929
9	Dallas (greater), TX	26,495
10	Philadelphia, PA M.D.	25,450
11	Atlanta, GA	24,161
12	San Francisco (greater), CA	24,072
13	Detroit-Livonia-Dearborn, MI M.D.	22,002
14	Washington (greater) DC-VA-MD-WV	21,942
15	Miami-Dade County, FL M.D.	19,797
16	Baltimore-Towson, MD	19,456
17	Washington, DC-VA-MD-WV M.D.	18,987
18	Boston (greater), MA-NH	18,357
19	Riverside-San Bernardino, CA	17,416
20	Dallas-Plano-Irving, TX M.D.	17,355
21	Phoenix-Mesa-Scottsdale, AZ	17,174
22	Tampa-St Petersburg, FL	16,200
23	Oakland-Fremont, CA M.D.	15,446
24	Las Vegas-Paradise, NV	15,439
25	Memphis, TN-MS-AR	14,898
26	Orlando, FL	14,253
27	Seattle-Tacoma-Bellevue, WA	13,061
28	San Diego, CA	12,775
29	Boston-Quincy, MA M.D.	11,068
30	Kansas City, MO-KS	11,044
31	Indianapolis, IN	10,938
32	Sacramento, CA	10,880
33	Nashville-Davidson, TN	10,450
34	San Antonio, TX	9,731
35	Fort Lauderdale, FL M.D.	9,562
36	Charlotte-Gastonia, NC-SC	9,255
37	Jacksonville, FL	9,218
38	Fort Worth-Arlington, TX M.D.	9,140
39	Cleveland-Elyria-Mentor, OH	8,973
40	Denver-Aurora, CO	8,848
41	Seattle-Bellevue-Everett, WA M.D.	8,833
42	San Francisco-S. Mateo, CA M.D.	8,626
43	Newark-Union, NJ-PA M.D.	8,103
44	Pittsburgh, PA	8,053
45	West Palm Beach, FL M.D.	8,044
46	Milwaukee, WI	7,679
47	Cincinnati-Middletown, OH-KY-IN	7,444
48	Santa Ana-Anaheim, CA M.D.	7,429
49	Warren-Farmington Hills, MI M.D.	6,927
50	Columbus, OH	6,658
51	New Orleans, LA	6,458
52	Austin-Round Rock, TX	6,074
53	Birmingham-Hoover, AL	6,045
54	Providence-New Bedford, RI-MA	6,020
55	Portland-Vancouver, OR-WA	6,012
56	Tulsa, OK	5,768
57	Buffalo-Niagara Falls, NY	5,759
58	Columbia, SC	5,643
59	Albuquerque, NM	5,625
60	Stockton, CA	5,531
61	Baton Rouge, LA	5,493
62	Little Rock, AR	5,410
63	San Jose, CA	5,259
64	Nassau-Suffolk, NY M.D.	5,229
65	Bakersfield, CA	4,892
66	Fresno, CA	4,694
67	Louisville, KY-IN	4,653
68	Tucson, AZ	4,481
69	Camden, NJ M.D.	4,474
70	Wilmington, DE-MD-NJ M.D.	4,440
71	Tacoma, WA M.D.	4,228
72	Cambridge-Newton, MA M.D.	4,221
73	Charleston-North Charleston, SC	4,066
74	North Port-Bradenton-Sarasota, FL	4,053
75	Salt Lake City, UT	3,919
76	Wichita, KS	3,905
77	Edison, NJ M.D.	3,831
78	Springfield, MA	3,706
79	Richmond, VA	3,652
80	Toledo, OH	3,623
81	Palm Bay-Melbourne, FL	3,617
82	New Haven-Milford, CT	3,572
83	Worcester, MA	3,504
84	Knoxville, TN	3,471
85	Greensboro-High Point, NC	3,421
86	Omaha-Council Bluffs, NE-IA	3,339
87	El Paso, TX	3,303
88	Flint, MI	3,288
89	Raleigh-Cary, NC	3,138
90	Chattanooga, TN-GA	3,090
91	McAllen-Edinburg-Mission, TX	3,036
92	Rochester, NY	3,022
93	Pensacola, FL	2,968
94	Hartford, CT	2,965
95	Mobile, AL	2,963
96	Bethesda-Frederick, MD M.D.	2,955
97	Grand Rapids-Wyoming, MI	2,954
98	Colorado Springs, CO	2,837
99	Dayton, OH	2,793
100	Bridgeport-Stamford, CT	2,792
101	Deltona-Daytona Beach, FL	2,762
102	Tallahassee, FL	2,748
103	Corpus Christi, TX	2,739
104	Lakeland, FL	2,734
105	Modesto, CA	2,721
106	Albany-Schenectady-Troy, NY	2,655
107	Anchorage, AK	2,606
108	Peabody, MA M.D.	2,572
109	Cape Coral-Fort Myers, FL	2,561
110	Honolulu, HI	2,537
111	Akron, OH	2,503
112	Winston-Salem, NC	2,421
113	Lubbock, TX	2,315
114	Augusta, GA-SC	2,232
115	Visalia-Porterville, CA	2,230
116	Durham-Chapel Hill, NC	2,206
117	Reno-Sparks, NV	2,166
118	Jackson, MS	2,120
119	Salinas, CA	2,118
120	Lexington-Fayette, KY	2,073
121	Vallejo-Fairfield, CA	2,064
122	Gainesville, FL	2,052
123	Beaumont-Port Arthur, TX	2,021
123	Oxnard-Thousand Oaks, CA	2,021
125	Lafayette, LA	2,020
126	Fayetteville, NC	1,998
127	Allentown, PA-NJ	1,992
128	Syracuse, NY	1,925
129	Santa Rosa-Petaluma, CA	1,917
130	Ocala, FL	1,911
131	Santa Barbara-Santa Maria, CA	1,897
132	Youngstown, OH-PA	1,870
133	Poughkeepsie, NY	1,865
134	Saginaw, MI	1,852
135	Lansing-East Lansing, MI	1,849
136	Springfield, MO	1,833
137	Spokane, WA	1,775
138	Spartanburg, SC	1,744
139	Harrisburg-Carlisle, PA	1,726
140	Port St. Lucie, FL	1,701
141	Trenton-Ewing, NJ	1,677
142	Amarillo, TX	1,661
143	Merced, CA	1,658
144	Huntsville, AL	1,637
145	Florence, SC	1,558
146	Des Moines-West Des Moines, IA	1,554
147	Columbus, GA-AL	1,500
148	Atlantic City, NJ	1,465
149	Lake Charles, LA	1,452
150	Savannah, GA	1,448
151	Scranton--Wilkes-Barre, PA	1,444
152	Boise City-Nampa, ID	1,440
153	Kalamazoo-Portage, MI	1,417
154	Fayetteville, AR-MO	1,400
155	Laredo, TX	1,395
156	Montgomery, AL	1,374
157	Brownsville-Harlingen, TX	1,337
158	Charleston, WV	1,330
159	Killeen-Temple-Fort Hood, TX	1,308
160	Madison, WI	1,296
161	Redding, CA	1,280
162	Fort Smith, AR-OK	1,270
163	Waco, TX	1,263
164	Reading, PA	1,254
165	Santa Cruz-Watsonville, CA	1,215
166	Anderson, SC	1,214
167	Lincoln, NE	1,200
168	South Bend-Mishawaka, IN-MI	1,176
169	Clarksville, TN-KY	1,167
170	Kingsport, TN-VA	1,158
171	Longview, TX	1,156
172	Lawton, OK	1,142
173	Ann Arbor, MI	1,122
174	Bremerton-Silverdale, WA	1,069
175	Eugene-Springfield, OR	1,057
176	Naples-Marco Island, FL	1,050
177	Barnstable Town, MA	1,044
178	Alexandria, LA	1,039
179	Texarkana, TX-Texarkana, AR	1,029
180	Salisbury, MD	1,027

Note: All listings are for Metropolitan Statistical Areas (M.S.A.s) except for those ending with "M.D." Listings with "M.D." are Metropolitan Divisions which are smaller parts of eleven large M.S.A.s. See explanatory note at beginning of metropolitan area section.

RANK	METROPOLITAN AREA	CRIMES
181	Fort Wayne, IN	1,020
182	York-Hanover, PA	1,018
183	Macon, GA	1,016
184	Dover, DE	1,007
185	Hickory, NC	999
186	Tuscaloosa, AL	992
187	Panama City-Lynn Haven, FL	990
188	Rocky Mount, NC	986
189	Topeka, KS	960
190	Albany, GA	957
191	Asheville, NC	948
192	Salem, OR	934
193	Chico, CA	932
194	Pueblo, CO	929
195	Battle Creek, MI	927
196	Waterloo-Cedar Falls, IA	922
197	Farmington, NM	919
198	Roanoke, VA	899
199	Houma, LA	896
199	Manchester-Nashua, NH	896
201	College Station-Bryan, TX	894
201	Odessa, TX	894
203	Ogden-Clearfield, UT	882
204	Tyler, TX	879
205	Vineland, NJ	859
206	Pine Bluff, AR	852
207	Las Cruces, NM	843
208	Lancaster, PA	842
209	Anniston-Oxford, AL	829
210	Evansville, IN-KY	827
211	Jackson, TN	813
212	Utica-Rome, NY	812
213	Fort Collins-Loveland, CO	807
214	Brunswick, GA	801
215	Yuma, AZ	771
216	Abilene, TX	741
217	Cleveland, TN	735
218	Muskegon-Norton Shores, MI	734
219	Athens-Clarke County, GA	732
220	Boulder, CO	719
221	Greeley, CO	711
222	Prescott, AZ	697
223	Sumter, SC	695
224	Erie, PA	694
224	San Luis Obispo, CA	694
226	Portland, ME	693
227	Madera, CA	685
228	Johnson City, TN	679
229	Jackson, MI	678
230	Burlington, NC	677
231	Lynchburg, VA	671
232	Columbia, MO	670
233	Kennewick-Pasco-Richland, WA	659
234	Hagerstown-Martinsburg, MD-WV	641
235	Victoria, TX	639
236	Niles-Benton Harbor, MI	632
236	Santa Fe, NM	632
238	Hot Springs, AR	625
239	Olympia, WA	616
240	Yuba City, CA	595
241	Wichita Falls, TX	592
242	Racine, WI	591
243	Valdosta, GA	590

RANK	METROPOLITAN AREA	CRIMES
244	Norwich-New London, CT	578
245	Green Bay, WI	577
246	Gulfport-Biloxi, MS	565
247	Jacksonville, NC	561
248	Lima, OH	558
249	Pittsfield, MA	556
250	Cedar Rapids, IA	531
251	Crestview-Fort Walton Beach, FL	528
252	St. Joseph, MO-KS	518
253	Goldsboro, NC	515
254	Bloomington, IN	512
255	Warner Robins, GA	509
256	Sioux Falls, SD	507
257	Rockingham County, NH M.D.	496
258	Springfield, OH	489
259	Lawrence, KS	485
260	Morristown, TN	483
261	Coeur d'Alene, ID	482
262	Binghamton, NY	481
263	Punta Gorda, FL	472
264	Lafayette, IN	471
265	Midland, TX	468
266	Jonesboro, AR	465
267	Jefferson City, MO	462
268	Lake Havasu City-Kingman, AZ	456
269	Cumberland, MD-WV	455
270	Holland-Grand Haven, MI	454
271	Sebastian-Vero Beach, FL	450
272	Kingston, NY	445
273	Bellingham, WA	443
274	Iowa City, IA	442
275	Grand Junction, CO	440
276	Muncie, IN	434
277	Florence-Muscle Shoals, AL	432
278	Manhattan, KS	428
279	Provo-Orem, UT	427
280	Charlottesville, VA	426
280	Rome, GA	426
282	Flagstaff, AZ	425
283	Pascagoula, MS	416
284	Morgantown, WV	411
285	Sioux City, IA-NE-SD	407
286	San Angelo, TX	406
287	Janesville, WI	398
288	Dalton, GA	396
288	Medford, OR	396
290	Napa, CA	393
291	Rapid City, SD	386
292	Oshkosh-Neenah, WI	383
293	Idaho Falls, ID	368
294	Gadsden, AL	367
295	Cape Girardeau, MO-IL	363
296	Dubuque, IA	360
297	Billings, MT	355
298	Altoona, PA	349
299	Bend, OR	346
300	Gainesville, GA	342
301	Elizabethtown, KY	341
302	Monroe, MI	340
302	Sherman-Denison, TX	340
304	Bay City, MI	337
305	Burlington-South Burlington, VT	332
306	Hinesville, GA	325

RANK	METROPOLITAN AREA	CRIMES
307	Blacksburg, VA	319
307	Wheeling, WV-OH	319
309	Palm Coast, FL	296
310	Missoula, MT	274
311	Ocean City, NJ	266
312	Hattiesburg, MS	262
313	Bowling Green, KY	261
314	Elkhart-Goshen, IN	260
315	Appleton, WI	256
316	Mansfield, OH	243
317	Danville, VA	235
318	Mount Vernon-Anacortes, WA	231
319	Great Falls, MT	230
320	Ames, IA	228
321	Winchester, VA-WV	227
322	Williamsport, PA	226
323	Bismarck, ND	221
323	Lebanon, PA	221
325	Pocatello, ID	219
326	Longview, WA	218
327	Wenatchee, WA	215
328	Michigan City-La Porte, IN	213
329	Wausau, WI	206
330	Anderson, IN	204
331	Kokomo, IN	199
332	Eau Claire, WI	193
333	Sandusky, OH	190
334	Harrisonburg, VA	184
334	St. George, UT	184
336	State College, PA	183
337	Carson City, NV	180
337	Cheyenne, WY	180
339	Casper, WY	163
340	Fond du Lac, WI	162
340	Lewiston-Auburn, ME	162
342	Elmira, NY	161
343	Sheboygan, WI	159
344	Owensboro, KY	157
345	Glens Falls, NY	137
346	Bangor, ME	124
347	Corvallis, OR	103
348	Logan, UT-ID	98
349	Lewiston, ID-WA	97
350	Columbus, IN	82
NA	Auburn, AL**	NA
NA	Danville, IL**	NA
NA	Decatur, AL**	NA
NA	Decatur, IL**	NA
NA	Dothan, AL**	NA
NA	Duluth, MN-WI**	NA
NA	El Centro, CA**	NA
NA	Fargo, ND-MN**	NA
NA	Grand Forks, ND-MN**	NA
NA	Ithaca, NY**	NA
NA	La Crosse, WI-MN**	NA
NA	Mankato-North Mankato, MN**	NA
NA	Minneapolis-St. Paul, MN-WI**	NA
NA	Oklahoma City, OK**	NA
NA	Rochester, MN**	NA
NA	Shreveport-Bossier City, LA**	NA
NA	St. Cloud, MN**	NA
NA	St. Louis, MO-IL**	NA
NA	Wilmington, NC**	NA

Source: Reported data from the F.B.I. "Crime in the United States 2009"

*Violent crimes are offenses of murder, forcible rape, robbery, and aggravated assault.

**Not available.

6. Violent Crime Rate in 2009
National Rate = 429.4 Violent Crimes per 100,000 Population*

RANK	METROPOLITAN AREA	RATE
113	Abilene, TX	464.2
192	Akron, OH	357.1
227	Albany-Schenectady-Troy, NY	309.9
65	Albany, GA	579.4
46	Albuquerque, NM	652.4
37	Alexandria, LA	670.3
281	Allentown, PA-NJ	243.6
254	Altoona, PA	279.0
34	Amarillo, TX	675.1
268	Ames, IA	260.9
5	Anchorage, AK	853.6
333	Anderson, IN	155.1
45	Anderson, SC	653.4
220	Ann Arbor, MI	321.9
23	Anniston-Oxford, AL	726.2
345	Appleton, WI	115.5
292	Asheville, NC	229.2
178	Athens-Clarke County, GA	383.1
131	Atlanta, GA	439.7
82	Atlantic City, NJ	537.4
NA	Auburn, AL**	NA
153	Augusta, GA-SC	415.1
194	Austin-Round Rock, TX	356.1
60	Bakersfield, CA	600.6
25	Baltimore-Towson, MD	722.4
348	Bangor, ME	83.3
112	Barnstable Town, MA	465.4
29	Baton Rouge, LA	697.3
31	Battle Creek, MI	686.3
223	Bay City, MI	315.6
84	Beaumont-Port Arthur, TX	534.7
299	Bellingham, WA	220.2
305	Bend, OR	211.4
273	Bethesda-Frederick, MD M.D.	247.4
291	Billings, MT	231.4
311	Binghamton, NY	196.8
85	Birmingham-Hoover, AL	534.6
306	Bismarck, ND	206.6
310	Blacksburg, VA	199.7
257	Bloomington, IN	276.5
290	Boise City-Nampa, ID	234.5
168	Boston (greater), MA-NH	400.2
66	Boston-Quincy, MA M.D.	578.8
282	Boulder, CO	242.8
300	Bowling Green, KY	218.0
124	Bremerton-Silverdale, WA	441.7
222	Bridgeport-Stamford, CT	318.0
212	Brownsville-Harlingen, TX	334.3
14	Brunswick, GA	773.7
95	Buffalo-Niagara Falls, NY	514.6
331	Burlington-South Burlington, VT	158.7
119	Burlington, NC	450.6
249	Cambridge-Newton, MA M.D.	280.6
195	Camden, NJ M.D.	355.9
147	Cape Coral-Fort Myers, FL	421.8
175	Cape Girardeau, MO-IL	387.4
217	Carson City, NV	330.5
301	Casper, WY	217.8
307	Cedar Rapids, IA	206.5
56	Charleston-North Charleston, SC	616.3
135	Charleston, WV	437.5
89	Charlotte-Gastonia, NC-SC	528.2
302	Charlottesville, VA	215.7
61	Chattanooga, TN-GA	589.9
308	Cheyenne, WY	201.4
149	Chico, CA	420.8
208	Cincinnati-Middletown, OH-KY-IN	341.8
130	Clarksville, TN-KY	439.9
140	Cleveland-Elyria-Mentor, OH	428.7
47	Cleveland, TN	648.1
205	Coeur d'Alene, ID	343.3
142	College Station-Bryan, TX	425.1
118	Colorado Springs, CO	451.7
164	Columbia, MO	402.5
19	Columbia, SC	760.9
91	Columbus, GA-AL	521.5
346	Columbus, IN	108.0
189	Columbus, OH	370.4
43	Corpus Christi, TX	656.5
341	Corvallis, OR	125.4
237	Crestview-Fort Walton Beach, FL	294.8
114	Cumberland, MD-WV	459.0
157	Dallas (greater), TX	410.8
166	Dallas-Plano-Irving, TX M.D.	400.8
243	Dalton, GA	293.1
NA	Danville, IL**	NA
295	Danville, VA	222.3
214	Dayton, OH	333.3
NA	Decatur, AL**	NA
NA	Decatur, IL**	NA
77	Deltona-Daytona Beach, FL	552.6
201	Denver-Aurora, CO	346.9
258	Des Moines-West Des Moines, IA	275.3
42	Detroit (greater), MI	656.8
2	Detroit-Livonia-Dearborn, MI M.D.	1,139.8
NA	Dothan, AL**	NA
51	Dover, DE	632.5
176	Dubuque, IA	387.2
NA	Duluth, MN-WI**	NA
123	Durham-Chapel Hill, NC	442.7
343	Eau Claire, WI	120.8
327	Edison, NJ M.D.	163.7
NA	El Centro, CA**	NA
127	El Paso, TX	440.4
232	Elizabethtown, KY	301.9
339	Elkhart-Goshen, IN	129.2
319	Elmira, NY	184.1
272	Erie, PA	248.1
231	Eugene-Springfield, OR	303.3
289	Evansville, IN-KY	235.2
NA	Fargo, ND-MN**	NA
22	Farmington, NM	742.3
230	Fayetteville, AR-MO	305.8
75	Fayetteville, NC	556.6
216	Flagstaff, AZ	330.8
16	Flint, MI	771.5
236	Florence-Muscle Shoals, AL	298.9
15	Florence, SC	772.4
329	Fond du Lac, WI	162.6
264	Fort Collins-Loveland, CO	270.7
79	Fort Lauderdale, FL M.D.	546.6
137	Fort Smith, AR-OK	431.5
277	Fort Wayne, IN	246.3
138	Fort Worth-Arlington, TX M.D.	431.2
96	Fresno, CA	510.9
197	Gadsden, AL	353.7
12	Gainesville, FL	791.5
323	Gainesville, GA	180.3
347	Glens Falls, NY	106.0
117	Goldsboro, NC	452.2
NA	Grand Forks, ND-MN**	NA
233	Grand Junction, CO	300.1
181	Grand Rapids-Wyoming, MI	379.9
251	Great Falls, MT	279.8
260	Greeley, CO	274.5
318	Green Bay, WI	189.2
105	Greensboro-High Point, NC	479.2
283	Gulfport-Biloxi, MS	241.8
285	Hagerstown-Martinsburg, MD-WV	237.6
219	Harrisburg-Carlisle, PA	322.6
334	Harrisonburg, VA	153.3
239	Hartford, CT	294.3
320	Hattiesburg, MS	183.4
261	Hickory, NC	273.0
110	Hinesville, GA	467.9
324	Holland-Grand Haven, MI	173.5
252	Honolulu, HI	279.7
53	Hot Springs, AR	631.8
125	Houma, LA	441.0
27	Houston, TX	706.8
162	Huntsville, AL	405.5
239	Idaho Falls, ID	294.3
54	Indianapolis, IN	627.9
245	Iowa City, IA	292.2
NA	Ithaca, NY**	NA
30	Jacksonville, FL	695.7
213	Jacksonville, NC	333.7
143	Jackson, MI	424.6
173	Jackson, MS	391.0
26	Jackson, TN	715.6
274	Janesville, WI	247.2
225	Jefferson City, MO	314.2
207	Johnson City, TN	342.8
173	Jonesboro, AR	391.0
134	Kalamazoo-Portage, MI	438.2
83	Kansas City, MO-KS	535.9
262	Kennewick-Pasco-Richland, WA	271.4
210	Killeen-Temple-Fort Hood, TX	339.6
183	Kingsport, TN-VA	377.9
280	Kingston, NY	244.5
100	Knoxville, TN	494.4
309	Kokomo, IN	200.6
NA	La Crosse, WI-MN**	NA
284	Lafayette, IN	241.7
17	Lafayette, LA	767.9
21	Lake Charles, LA	748.2
293	Lake Havasu City-Kingman, AZ	229.1
111	Lakeland, FL	465.7
326	Lancaster, PA	166.0
160	Lansing-East Lansing, MI	408.3

Note: All listings are for Metropolitan Statistical Areas (M.S.A.s) except for those ending with "M.D." Listings with "M.D." are Metropolitan Divisions which are smaller parts of eleven large M.S.A.s. See explanatory note at beginning of metropolitan area section.

Alpha Order - Metro Area (continued)

RANK	METROPOLITAN AREA	RATE
68	Laredo, TX	575.4
158	Las Cruces, NM	410.5
9	Las Vegas-Paradise, NV	810.9
152	Lawrence, KS	415.9
3	Lawton, OK	1,018.4
325	Lebanon, PA	169.7
335	Lewiston-Auburn, ME	151.4
330	Lewiston, ID-WA	160.0
128	Lexington-Fayette, KY	440.3
87	Lima, OH	530.9
167	Lincoln, NE	400.7
13	Little Rock, AR	789.3
349	Logan, UT-ID	77.1
72	Longview, TX	560.6
303	Longview, WA	212.0
76	Los Angeles County, CA M.D.	555.0
103	Los Angeles (greater), CA	482.7
189	Louisville, KY-IN	370.4
7	Lubbock, TX	847.1
265	Lynchburg, VA	269.8
128	Macon, GA	440.3
116	Madera, CA	454.1
294	Madison, WI	228.2
297	Manchester-Nashua, NH	221.6
202	Manhattan, KS	346.3
NA	Mankato-North Mankato, MN**	NA
314	Mansfield, OH	194.5
161	McAllen-Edinburg-Mission, TX	406.6
313	Medford, OR	195.1
1	Memphis, TN-MS-AR	1,146.9
39	Merced, CA	664.7
33	Miami (greater), FL	679.9
11	Miami-Dade County, FL M.D.	797.5
317	Michigan City-La Porte, IN	191.6
193	Midland, TX	356.5
101	Milwaukee, WI	494.2
NA	Minneapolis-St. Paul, MN-WI**	NA
271	Missoula, MT	252.3
24	Mobile, AL	724.8
90	Modesto, CA	527.1
296	Monroe, MI	222.1
187	Montgomery, AL	371.5
204	Morgantown, WV	343.7
198	Morristown, TN	350.5
316	Mount Vernon-Anacortes, WA	191.8
182	Muncie, IN	379.3
148	Muskegon-Norton Shores, MI	421.7
241	Napa, CA	293.3
218	Naples-Marco Island, FL	328.0
41	Nashville-Davidson, TN	659.4
321	Nassau-Suffolk, NY M.D.	181.9
120	New Haven-Milford, CT	449.5
78	New Orleans, LA	547.7
179	New York (greater), NY-NJ-PA	381.9
106	New York-W. Plains NY-NJ M.D.	474.4
180	Newark-Union, NJ-PA M.D.	381.7
169	Niles-Benton Harbor, MI	398.7
64	North Port-Bradenton-Sarasota, FL	584.7
150	Norwich-New London, CT	417.0
57	Oakland-Fremont, CA M.D.	616.1
69	Ocala, FL	569.7
252	Ocean City, NJ	279.7
38	Odessa, TX	670.2

RANK	METROPOLITAN AREA	RATE
328	Ogden-Clearfield, UT	163.6
NA	Oklahoma City, OK**	NA
279	Olympia, WA	245.3
170	Omaha-Council Bluffs, NE-IA	393.9
32	Orlando, FL	682.8
288	Oshkosh-Neenah, WI	235.6
336	Owensboro, KY	138.6
270	Oxnard-Thousand Oaks, CA	252.7
35	Palm Bay-Melbourne, FL	671.4
229	Palm Coast, FL	306.4
59	Panama City-Lynn Haven, FL	602.5
263	Pascagoula, MS	271.2
203	Peabody, MA M.D.	344.2
44	Pensacola, FL	653.9
67	Philadelphia (greater) PA-NJ-MD-DE	575.6
49	Philadelphia, PA M.D.	634.5
171	Phoenix-Mesa-Scottsdale, AZ	393.7
6	Pine Bluff, AR	849.1
206	Pittsburgh, PA	342.9
145	Pittsfield, MA	423.5
275	Pocatello, ID	246.8
154	Port St. Lucie, FL	413.9
266	Portland-Vancouver, OR-WA	268.5
338	Portland, ME	134.3
259	Poughkeepsie, NY	275.1
221	Prescott, AZ	318.4
186	Providence-New Bedford, RI-MA	374.6
350	Provo-Orem, UT	76.3
63	Pueblo, CO	585.2
224	Punta Gorda, FL	315.4
238	Racine, WI	294.6
255	Raleigh-Cary, NC	278.2
226	Rapid City, SD	311.5
228	Reading, PA	307.4
28	Redding, CA	705.2
93	Reno-Sparks, NV	517.9
242	Richmond, VA	293.2
154	Riverside-San Bernardino, CA	413.9
235	Roanoke, VA	299.3
NA	Rochester, MN**	NA
244	Rochester, NY	292.6
344	Rockingham County, NH M.D.	117.4
36	Rocky Mount, NC	670.8
122	Rome, GA	443.1
98	Sacramento, CA	508.5
4	Saginaw, MI	930.9
287	Salem, OR	235.8
92	Salinas, CA	519.9
8	Salisbury, MD	841.8
200	Salt Lake City, UT	347.8
191	San Angelo, TX	368.7
108	San Antonio, TX	469.6
144	San Diego, CA	424.3
70	San Francisco (greater), CA	563.0
102	San Francisco-S. Mateo, CA M.D.	487.8
246	San Jose, CA	288.6
269	San Luis Obispo, CA	260.5
276	Sandusky, OH	246.7
278	Santa Ana-Anaheim, CA M.D.	246.2
109	Santa Barbara-Santa Maria, CA	468.8
104	Santa Cruz-Watsonville, CA	482.2
136	Santa Fe, NM	432.9
156	Santa Rosa-Petaluma, CA	411.5

RANK	METROPOLITAN AREA	RATE
141	Savannah, GA	428.5
267	Scranton--Wilkes-Barre, PA	262.8
209	Seattle-Bellevue-Everett, WA M.D.	339.9
177	Seattle-Tacoma-Bellevue, WA	384.3
211	Sebastian-Vero Beach, FL	337.3
336	Sheboygan, WI	138.6
248	Sherman-Denison, TX	283.7
NA	Shreveport-Bossier City, LA**	NA
247	Sioux City, IA-NE-SD	284.4
304	Sioux Falls, SD	211.9
188	South Bend-Mishawaka, IN-MI	370.9
58	Spartanburg, SC	611.0
184	Spokane, WA	377.2
86	Springfield, MA	531.2
146	Springfield, MO	423.2
199	Springfield, OH	349.9
342	State College, PA	125.2
10	Stockton, CA	810.1
NA	St. Cloud, MN**	NA
340	St. George, UT	128.4
159	St. Joseph, MO-KS	409.0
NA	St. Louis, MO-IL**	NA
40	Sumter, SC	664.0
234	Syracuse, NY	299.4
88	Tacoma, WA M.D.	528.5
18	Tallahassee, FL	766.8
62	Tampa-St Petersburg, FL	588.9
20	Texarkana, TX-Texarkana, AR	754.2
73	Toledo, OH	557.4
151	Topeka, KS	416.7
115	Trenton-Ewing, NJ	457.9
132	Tucson, AZ	439.2
55	Tulsa, OK	621.5
107	Tuscaloosa, AL	474.1
139	Tyler, TX	429.7
256	Utica-Rome, NY	277.1
133	Valdosta, GA	439.1
99	Vallejo-Fairfield, CA	506.8
74	Victoria, TX	556.9
80	Vineland, NJ	543.8
94	Visalia-Porterville, CA	516.5
81	Waco, TX	543.6
185	Warner Robins, GA	376.3
250	Warren-Farmington Hills, MI M.D.	280.0
165	Washington (greater) DC-VA-MD-WV	402.4
121	Washington, DC-VA-MD-WV M.D.	445.9
71	Waterloo-Cedar Falls, IA	562.0
332	Wausau, WI	156.7
312	Wenatchee, WA	195.7
50	West Palm Beach, FL M.D.	633.7
298	Wheeling, WV-OH	221.0
163	Wichita Falls, TX	402.7
48	Wichita, KS	642.3
315	Williamsport, PA	193.8
52	Wilmington, DE-MD-NJ M.D.	632.3
NA	Wilmington, NC**	NA
322	Winchester, VA-WV	181.4
97	Winston-Salem, NC	510.6
126	Worcester, MA	440.6
286	York-Hanover, PA	236.4
215	Youngstown, OH-PA	331.7
196	Yuba City, CA	354.5
172	Yuma, AZ	393.0

Source: Reported data from the F.B.I. "Crime in the United States 2009"
*Violent crimes are offenses of murder, forcible rape, robbery, and aggravated assault.
**Not available.

6. Violent Crime Rate in 2009 (continued)
National Rate = 429.4 Violent Crimes per 100,000 Population*

RANK	METROPOLITAN AREA	RATE
1	Memphis, TN-MS-AR	1,146.9
2	Detroit-Livonia-Dearborn, MI M.D.	1,139.8
3	Lawton, OK	1,018.4
4	Saginaw, MI	930.9
5	Anchorage, AK	853.6
6	Pine Bluff, AR	849.1
7	Lubbock, TX	847.1
8	Salisbury, MD	841.8
9	Las Vegas-Paradise, NV	810.9
10	Stockton, CA	810.1
11	Miami-Dade County, FL M.D.	797.5
12	Gainesville, FL	791.5
13	Little Rock, AR	789.3
14	Brunswick, GA	773.7
15	Florence, SC	772.4
16	Flint, MI	771.5
17	Lafayette, LA	767.9
18	Tallahassee, FL	766.8
19	Columbia, SC	760.9
20	Texarkana, TX-Texarkana, AR	754.2
21	Lake Charles, LA	748.2
22	Farmington, NM	742.3
23	Anniston-Oxford, AL	726.2
24	Mobile, AL	724.8
25	Baltimore-Towson, MD	722.4
26	Jackson, TN	715.6
27	Houston, TX	706.8
28	Redding, CA	705.2
29	Baton Rouge, LA	697.3
30	Jacksonville, FL	695.7
31	Battle Creek, MI	686.3
32	Orlando, FL	682.8
33	Miami (greater), FL	679.9
34	Amarillo, TX	675.1
35	Palm Bay-Melbourne, FL	671.4
36	Rocky Mount, NC	670.8
37	Alexandria, LA	670.3
38	Odessa, TX	670.2
39	Merced, CA	664.7
40	Sumter, SC	664.0
41	Nashville-Davidson, TN	659.4
42	Detroit (greater), MI	656.8
43	Corpus Christi, TX	656.5
44	Pensacola, FL	653.9
45	Anderson, SC	653.4
46	Albuquerque, NM	652.4
47	Cleveland, TN	648.1
48	Wichita, KS	642.3
49	Philadelphia, PA M.D.	634.5
50	West Palm Beach, FL M.D.	633.7
51	Dover, DE	632.5
52	Wilmington, DE-MD-NJ M.D.	632.3
53	Hot Springs, AR	631.8
54	Indianapolis, IN	627.9
55	Tulsa, OK	621.5
56	Charleston-North Charleston, SC	616.3
57	Oakland-Fremont, CA M.D.	616.1
58	Spartanburg, SC	611.0
59	Panama City-Lynn Haven, FL	602.5
60	Bakersfield, CA	600.6
61	Chattanooga, TN-GA	589.9
62	Tampa-St Petersburg, FL	588.9
63	Pueblo, CO	585.2
64	North Port-Bradenton-Sarasota, FL	584.7
65	Albany, GA	579.4
66	Boston-Quincy, MA M.D.	578.8
67	Philadelphia (greater) PA-NJ-MD-DE	575.6
68	Laredo, TX	575.4
69	Ocala, FL	569.7
70	San Francisco (greater), CA	563.0
71	Waterloo-Cedar Falls, IA	562.0
72	Longview, TX	560.6
73	Toledo, OH	557.4
74	Victoria, TX	556.9
75	Fayetteville, NC	556.6
76	Los Angeles County, CA M.D.	555.0
77	Deltona-Daytona Beach, FL	552.6
78	New Orleans, LA	547.7
79	Fort Lauderdale, FL M.D.	546.6
80	Vineland, NJ	543.8
81	Waco, TX	543.6
82	Atlantic City, NJ	537.4
83	Kansas City, MO-KS	535.9
84	Beaumont-Port Arthur, TX	534.7
85	Birmingham-Hoover, AL	534.6
86	Springfield, MA	531.2
87	Lima, OH	530.9
88	Tacoma, WA M.D.	528.5
89	Charlotte-Gastonia, NC-SC	528.2
90	Modesto, CA	527.1
91	Columbus, GA-AL	521.5
92	Salinas, CA	519.9
93	Reno-Sparks, NV	517.9
94	Visalia-Porterville, CA	516.5
95	Buffalo-Niagara Falls, NY	514.6
96	Fresno, CA	510.9
97	Winston-Salem, NC	510.6
98	Sacramento, CA	508.5
99	Vallejo-Fairfield, CA	506.8
100	Knoxville, TN	494.4
101	Milwaukee, WI	494.2
102	San Francisco-S. Mateo, CA M.D.	487.8
103	Los Angeles (greater), CA	482.7
104	Santa Cruz-Watsonville, CA	482.2
105	Greensboro-High Point, NC	479.2
106	New York-W. Plains NY-NJ M.D.	474.4
107	Tuscaloosa, AL	474.1
108	San Antonio, TX	469.6
109	Santa Barbara-Santa Maria, CA	468.8
110	Hinesville, GA	467.9
111	Lakeland, FL	465.7
112	Barnstable Town, MA	465.4
113	Abilene, TX	464.2
114	Cumberland, MD-WV	459.0
115	Trenton-Ewing, NJ	457.9
116	Madera, CA	454.1
117	Goldsboro, NC	452.2
118	Colorado Springs, CO	451.7
119	Burlington, NC	450.6
120	New Haven-Milford, CT	449.5
121	Washington, DC-VA-MD-WV M.D.	445.9
122	Rome, GA	443.1
123	Durham-Chapel Hill, NC	442.7
124	Bremerton-Silverdale, WA	441.7
125	Houma, LA	441.0
126	Worcester, MA	440.6
127	El Paso, TX	440.4
128	Lexington-Fayette, KY	440.3
128	Macon, GA	440.3
130	Clarksville, TN-KY	439.9
131	Atlanta, GA	439.7
132	Tucson, AZ	439.2
133	Valdosta, GA	439.1
134	Kalamazoo-Portage, MI	438.2
135	Charleston, WV	437.5
136	Santa Fe, NM	432.9
137	Fort Smith, AR-OK	431.5
138	Fort Worth-Arlington, TX M.D.	431.2
139	Tyler, TX	429.7
140	Cleveland-Elyria-Mentor, OH	428.7
141	Savannah, GA	428.5
142	College Station-Bryan, TX	425.1
143	Jackson, MI	424.6
144	San Diego, CA	424.3
145	Pittsfield, MA	423.5
146	Springfield, MO	423.2
147	Cape Coral-Fort Myers, FL	421.8
148	Muskegon-Norton Shores, MI	421.7
149	Chico, CA	420.8
150	Norwich-New London, CT	417.0
151	Topeka, KS	416.7
152	Lawrence, KS	415.9
153	Augusta, GA-SC	415.1
154	Port St. Lucie, FL	413.9
154	Riverside-San Bernardino, CA	413.9
156	Santa Rosa-Petaluma, CA	411.5
157	Dallas (greater), TX	410.8
158	Las Cruces, NM	410.5
159	St. Joseph, MO-KS	409.0
160	Lansing-East Lansing, MI	408.3
161	McAllen-Edinburg-Mission, TX	406.6
162	Huntsville, AL	405.5
163	Wichita Falls, TX	402.7
164	Columbia, MO	402.5
165	Washington (greater) DC-VA-MD-WV	402.4
166	Dallas-Plano-Irving, TX M.D.	400.8
167	Lincoln, NE	400.7
168	Boston (greater), MA-NH	400.2
169	Niles-Benton Harbor, MI	398.7
170	Omaha-Council Bluffs, NE-IA	393.9
171	Phoenix-Mesa-Scottsdale, AZ	393.7
172	Yuma, AZ	393.0
173	Jackson, MS	391.0
173	Jonesboro, AR	391.0
175	Cape Girardeau, MO-IL	387.4
176	Dubuque, IA	387.2
177	Seattle-Tacoma-Bellevue, WA	384.3
178	Athens-Clarke County, GA	383.1
179	New York (greater), NY-NJ-PA	381.9
180	Newark-Union, NJ-PA M.D.	381.7

Note: All listings are for Metropolitan Statistical Areas (M.S.A.s) except for those ending with "M.D." Listings with "M.D." are Metropolitan Divisions which are smaller parts of eleven large M.S.A.s. See explanatory note at beginning of metropolitan area section.

Rank Order - Metro Area (continued)

RANK	METROPOLITAN AREA	RATE
181	Grand Rapids-Wyoming, MI	379.9
182	Muncie, IN	379.3
183	Kingsport, TN-VA	377.9
184	Spokane, WA	377.2
185	Warner Robins, GA	376.3
186	Providence-New Bedford, RI-MA	374.6
187	Montgomery, AL	371.5
188	South Bend-Mishawaka, IN-MI	370.9
189	Columbus, OH	370.4
189	Louisville, KY-IN	370.4
191	San Angelo, TX	368.7
192	Akron, OH	357.1
193	Midland, TX	356.5
194	Austin-Round Rock, TX	356.1
195	Camden, NJ M.D.	355.9
196	Yuba City, CA	354.5
197	Gadsden, AL	353.7
198	Morristown, TN	350.5
199	Springfield, OH	349.9
200	Salt Lake City, UT	347.8
201	Denver-Aurora, CO	346.9
202	Manhattan, KS	346.3
203	Peabody, MA M.D.	344.2
204	Morgantown, WV	343.7
205	Coeur d'Alene, ID	343.3
206	Pittsburgh, PA	342.9
207	Johnson City, TN	342.8
208	Cincinnati-Middletown, OH-KY-IN	341.8
209	Seattle-Bellevue-Everett, WA M.D.	339.9
210	Killeen-Temple-Fort Hood, TX	339.6
211	Sebastian-Vero Beach, FL	337.3
212	Brownsville-Harlingen, TX	334.3
213	Jacksonville, NC	333.7
214	Dayton, OH	333.3
215	Youngstown, OH-PA	331.7
216	Flagstaff, AZ	330.8
217	Carson City, NV	330.5
218	Naples-Marco Island, FL	328.0
219	Harrisburg-Carlisle, PA	322.6
220	Ann Arbor, MI	321.9
221	Prescott, AZ	318.4
222	Bridgeport-Stamford, CT	318.0
223	Bay City, MI	315.6
224	Punta Gorda, FL	315.4
225	Jefferson City, MO	314.2
226	Rapid City, SD	311.5
227	Albany-Schenectady-Troy, NY	309.9
228	Reading, PA	307.4
229	Palm Coast, FL	306.4
230	Fayetteville, AR-MO	305.8
231	Eugene-Springfield, OR	303.3
232	Elizabethtown, KY	301.9
233	Grand Junction, CO	300.1
234	Syracuse, NY	299.4
235	Roanoke, VA	299.3
236	Florence-Muscle Shoals, AL	298.9
237	Crestview-Fort Walton Beach, FL	294.8
238	Racine, WI	294.6
239	Hartford, CT	294.3
239	Idaho Falls, ID	294.3
241	Napa, CA	293.3
242	Richmond, VA	293.2
243	Dalton, GA	293.1
244	Rochester, NY	292.6
245	Iowa City, IA	292.2
246	San Jose, CA	288.6
247	Sioux City, IA-NE-SD	284.4
248	Sherman-Denison, TX	283.7
249	Cambridge-Newton, MA M.D.	280.6
250	Warren-Farmington Hills, MI M.D.	280.0
251	Great Falls, MT	279.8
252	Honolulu, HI	279.7
252	Ocean City, NJ	279.7
254	Altoona, PA	279.0
255	Raleigh-Cary, NC	278.2
256	Utica-Rome, NY	277.1
257	Bloomington, IN	276.5
258	Des Moines-West Des Moines, IA	275.3
259	Poughkeepsie, NY	275.1
260	Greeley, CO	274.5
261	Hickory, NC	273.0
262	Kennewick-Pasco-Richland, WA	271.4
263	Pascagoula, MS	271.2
264	Fort Collins-Loveland, CO	270.7
265	Lynchburg, VA	269.8
266	Portland-Vancouver, OR-WA	268.5
267	Scranton--Wilkes-Barre, PA	262.8
268	Ames, IA	260.9
269	San Luis Obispo, CA	260.5
270	Oxnard-Thousand Oaks, CA	252.7
271	Missoula, MT	252.3
272	Erie, PA	248.1
273	Bethesda-Frederick, MD M.D.	247.4
274	Janesville, WI	247.2
275	Pocatello, ID	246.8
276	Sandusky, OH	246.7
277	Fort Wayne, IN	246.3
278	Santa Ana-Anaheim, CA M.D.	246.2
279	Olympia, WA	245.3
280	Kingston, NY	244.5
281	Allentown, PA-NJ	243.6
282	Boulder, CO	242.8
283	Gulfport-Biloxi, MS	241.8
284	Lafayette, IN	241.7
285	Hagerstown-Martinsburg, MD-WV	237.6
286	York-Hanover, PA	236.4
287	Salem, OR	235.8
288	Oshkosh-Neenah, WI	235.6
289	Evansville, IN-KY	235.2
290	Boise City-Nampa, ID	234.5
291	Billings, MT	231.4
292	Asheville, NC	229.2
293	Lake Havasu City-Kingman, AZ	229.1
294	Madison, WI	228.2
295	Danville, VA	222.3
296	Monroe, MI	222.1
297	Manchester-Nashua, NH	221.6
298	Wheeling, WV-OH	221.0
299	Bellingham, WA	220.2
300	Bowling Green, KY	218.0
301	Casper, WY	217.8
302	Charlottesville, VA	215.7
303	Longview, WA	212.0
304	Sioux Falls, SD	211.9
305	Bend, OR	211.4
306	Bismarck, ND	206.6
307	Cedar Rapids, IA	206.5
308	Cheyenne, WY	201.4
309	Kokomo, IN	200.6
310	Blacksburg, VA	199.7
311	Binghamton, NY	196.8
312	Wenatchee, WA	195.7
313	Medford, OR	195.1
314	Mansfield, OH	194.5
315	Williamsport, PA	193.8
316	Mount Vernon-Anacortes, WA	191.8
317	Michigan City-La Porte, IN	191.6
318	Green Bay, WI	189.2
319	Elmira, NY	184.1
320	Hattiesburg, MS	183.4
321	Nassau-Suffolk, NY M.D.	181.9
322	Winchester, VA-WV	181.4
323	Gainesville, GA	180.3
324	Holland-Grand Haven, MI	173.5
325	Lebanon, PA	169.7
326	Lancaster, PA	166.0
327	Edison, NJ M.D.	163.7
328	Ogden-Clearfield, UT	163.6
329	Fond du Lac, WI	162.6
330	Lewiston, ID-WA	160.0
331	Burlington-South Burlington, VT	158.7
332	Wausau, WI	156.7
333	Anderson, IN	155.1
334	Harrisonburg, VA	153.3
335	Lewiston-Auburn, ME	151.4
336	Owensboro, KY	138.6
336	Sheboygan, WI	138.6
338	Portland, ME	134.3
339	Elkhart-Goshen, IN	129.2
340	St. George, UT	128.4
341	Corvallis, OR	125.4
342	State College, PA	125.2
343	Eau Claire, WI	120.8
344	Rockingham County, NH M.D.	117.4
345	Appleton, WI	115.5
346	Columbus, IN	108.0
347	Glens Falls, NY	106.0
348	Bangor, ME	83.3
349	Logan, UT-ID	77.1
350	Provo-Orem, UT	76.3
NA	Auburn, AL**	NA
NA	Danville, IL**	NA
NA	Decatur, AL**	NA
NA	Decatur, IL**	NA
NA	Dothan, AL**	NA
NA	Duluth, MN-WI**	NA
NA	El Centro, CA**	NA
NA	Fargo, ND-MN**	NA
NA	Grand Forks, ND-MN**	NA
NA	Ithaca, NY**	NA
NA	La Crosse, WI-MN**	NA
NA	Mankato-North Mankato, MN**	NA
NA	Minneapolis-St. Paul, MN-WI**	NA
NA	Oklahoma City, OK**	NA
NA	Rochester, MN**	NA
NA	Shreveport-Bossier City, LA**	NA
NA	St. Cloud, MN**	NA
NA	St. Louis, MO-IL**	NA
NA	Wilmington, NC**	NA

Source: Reported data from the F.B.I. "Crime in the United States 2009"

*Violent crimes are offenses of murder, forcible rape, robbery, and aggravated assault.

**Not available.

7. Percent Change in Violent Crime Rate: 2008 to 2009
National Percent Change = 6.1% Decrease*

RANK	METROPOLITAN AREA	% CHANGE
61	Abilene, TX	3.2
63	Akron, OH	2.9
151	Albany-Schenectady-Troy, NY	(5.5)
NA	Albany, GA**	NA
271	Albuquerque, NM	(18.3)
NA	Alexandria, LA**	NA
102	Allentown, PA-NJ	(1.7)
159	Altoona, PA	(6.0)
44	Amarillo, TX	5.8
197	Ames, IA	(8.9)
176	Anchorage, AK	(7.5)
NA	Anderson, IN**	NA
92	Anderson, SC	(0.4)
252	Ann Arbor, MI	(14.5)
NA	Anniston-Oxford, AL**	NA
88	Appleton, WI	0.0
274	Asheville, NC	(19.3)
163	Athens-Clarke County, GA	(6.5)
233	Atlanta, GA	(12.2)
23	Atlantic City, NJ	10.6
NA	Auburn, AL**	NA
NA	Augusta, GA-SC**	NA
62	Austin-Round Rock, TX	3.1
55	Bakersfield, CA	4.3
144	Baltimore-Towson, MD	(5.1)
27	Bangor, ME	9.6
37	Barnstable Town, MA	7.0
21	Baton Rouge, LA	12.0
158	Battle Creek, MI	(5.9)
NA	Bay City, MI**	NA
97	Beaumont-Port Arthur, TX	(1.3)
111	Bellingham, WA	(2.5)
13	Bend, OR	16.7
137	Bethesda-Frederick, MD M.D.	(4.3)
128	Billings, MT	(3.8)
267	Binghamton, NY	(16.9)
209	Birmingham-Hoover, AL	(10.0)
114	Bismarck, ND	(2.6)
233	Blacksburg, VA	(12.2)
4	Bloomington, IN	34.7
98	Boise City-Nampa, ID	(1.4)
72	Boston (greater), MA-NH	1.4
71	Boston-Quincy, MA M.D.	1.7
NA	Boulder, CO**	NA
NA	Bowling Green, KY**	NA
142	Bremerton-Silverdale, WA	(4.9)
116	Bridgeport-Stamford, CT	(2.8)
276	Brownsville-Harlingen, TX	(20.9)
NA	Brunswick, GA**	NA
50	Buffalo-Niagara Falls, NY	5.2
NA	Burlington-South Burlington, VT**	NA
141	Burlington, NC	(4.6)
56	Cambridge-Newton, MA M.D.	4.0
108	Camden, NJ M.D.	(2.3)
209	Cape Coral-Fort Myers, FL	(10.0)
47	Cape Girardeau, MO-IL	5.7
279	Carson City, NV	(22.3)
269	Casper, WY	(17.8)
92	Cedar Rapids, IA	(0.4)
252	Charleston-North Charleston, SC	(14.5)
56	Charleston, WV	4.0
275	Charlotte-Gastonia, NC-SC	(20.1)
76	Charlottesville, VA	1.3
NA	Chattanooga, TN-GA**	NA
137	Cheyenne, WY	(4.3)
23	Chico, CA	10.6
NA	Cincinnati-Middletown, OH-KY-IN**	NA
NA	Clarksville, TN-KY**	NA
NA	Cleveland-Elyria-Mentor, OH**	NA
180	Cleveland, TN	(7.9)
NA	Coeur d'Alene, ID**	NA
250	College Station-Bryan, TX	(14.1)
132	Colorado Springs, CO	(4.0)
7	Columbia, MO	22.0
70	Columbia, SC	1.8
151	Columbus, GA-AL	(5.5)
15	Columbus, IN	14.2
198	Columbus, OH	(9.1)
58	Corpus Christi, TX	3.9
164	Corvallis, OR	(6.7)
NA	Crestview-Fort Walton Beach, FL**	NA
79	Cumberland, MD-WV	0.9
212	Dallas (greater), TX	(10.2)
225	Dallas-Plano-Irving, TX M.D.	(11.6)
240	Dalton, GA	(12.6)
NA	Danville, IL**	NA
288	Danville, VA	(30.8)
170	Dayton, OH	(7.2)
NA	Decatur, AL**	NA
NA	Decatur, IL**	NA
164	Deltona-Daytona Beach, FL	(6.7)
119	Denver-Aurora, CO	(3.3)
NA	Des Moines-West Des Moines, IA**	NA
NA	Detroit (greater), MI**	NA
NA	Detroit-Livonia-Dearborn, MI M.D.**	NA
NA	Dothan, AL**	NA
148	Dover, DE	(5.4)
245	Dubuque, IA	(13.7)
NA	Duluth, MN-WI**	NA
246	Durham-Chapel Hill, NC	(13.9)
11	Eau Claire, WI	20.0
122	Edison, NJ M.D.	(3.5)
NA	El Centro, CA**	NA
80	El Paso, TX	0.8
NA	Elizabethtown, KY**	NA
269	Elkhart-Goshen, IN	(17.8)
276	Elmira, NY	(20.9)
272	Erie, PA	(18.8)
172	Eugene-Springfield, OR	(7.3)
NA	Evansville, IN-KY**	NA
NA	Fargo, ND-MN**	NA
NA	Farmington, NM**	NA
105	Fayetteville, AR-MO	(2.0)
281	Fayetteville, NC	(23.8)
222	Flagstaff, AZ	(11.2)
NA	Flint, MI**	NA
284	Florence-Muscle Shoals, AL	(25.0)
280	Florence, SC	(23.0)
283	Fond du Lac, WI	(24.2)
87	Fort Collins-Loveland, CO	0.1
207	Fort Lauderdale, FL M.D.	(9.9)
139	Fort Smith, AR-OK	(4.4)
25	Fort Wayne, IN	10.2
172	Fort Worth-Arlington, TX M.D.	(7.3)
33	Fresno, CA	8.2
196	Gadsden, AL	(8.8)
95	Gainesville, FL	(0.9)
NA	Gainesville, GA**	NA
290	Glens Falls, NY	(39.6)
167	Goldsboro, NC	(7.0)
NA	Grand Forks, ND-MN**	NA
220	Grand Junction, CO	(10.9)
NA	Grand Rapids-Wyoming, MI**	NA
29	Great Falls, MT	9.4
225	Greeley, CO	(11.6)
146	Green Bay, WI	(5.2)
178	Greensboro-High Point, NC	(7.7)
NA	Gulfport-Biloxi, MS**	NA
238	Hagerstown-Martinsburg, MD-WV	(12.4)
82	Harrisburg-Carlisle, PA	0.6
48	Harrisonburg, VA	5.4
96	Hartford, CT	(1.1)
NA	Hattiesburg, MS**	NA
106	Hickory, NC	(2.1)
44	Hinesville, GA	5.8
NA	Holland-Grand Haven, MI**	NA
100	Honolulu, HI	(1.5)
134	Hot Springs, AR	(4.2)
116	Houma, LA	(2.8)
65	Houston, TX	2.7
128	Huntsville, AL	(3.8)
58	Idaho Falls, ID	3.9
101	Indianapolis, IN	(1.6)
77	Iowa City, IA	1.2
NA	Ithaca, NY**	NA
256	Jacksonville, FL	(15.3)
186	Jacksonville, NC	(8.3)
NA	Jackson, MI**	NA
134	Jackson, MS	(4.2)
237	Jackson, TN	(12.3)
89	Janesville, WI	(0.1)
NA	Jefferson City, MO**	NA
160	Johnson City, TN	(6.3)
83	Jonesboro, AR	0.5
NA	Kalamazoo-Portage, MI**	NA
NA	Kansas City, MO-KS**	NA
39	Kennewick-Pasco-Richland, WA	6.7
262	Killeen-Temple-Fort Hood, TX	(15.8)
50	Kingsport, TN-VA	5.2
122	Kingston, NY	(3.5)
111	Knoxville, TN	(2.5)
286	Kokomo, IN	(28.4)
NA	La Crosse, WI-MN**	NA
68	Lafayette, IN	2.1
65	Lafayette, LA	2.7
NA	Lake Charles, LA**	NA
72	Lake Havasu City-Kingman, AZ	1.4
147	Lakeland, FL	(5.3)
241	Lancaster, PA	(13.2)
NA	Lansing-East Lansing, MI**	NA

Note: All listings are for Metropolitan Statistical Areas (M.S.A.s) except for those ending with "M.D." Listings with "M.D." are Metropolitan Divisions which are smaller parts of eleven large M.S.A.s. See explanatory note at beginning of metropolitan area section.

Alpha Order - Metro Area (continued)

RANK	METROPOLITAN AREA	% CHANGE
139	Laredo, TX	(4.4)
144	Las Cruces, NM	(5.1)
122	Las Vegas-Paradise, NV	(3.5)
54	Lawrence, KS	4.9
NA	Lawton, OK**	NA
287	Lebanon, PA	(28.8)
78	Lewiston-Auburn, ME	1.0
32	Lewiston, ID-WA	8.3
NA	Lexington-Fayette, KY**	NA
130	Lima, OH	(3.9)
209	Lincoln, NE	(10.0)
NA	Little Rock, AR**	NA
43	Logan, UT-ID	5.9
227	Longview, TX	(11.7)
285	Longview, WA	(27.5)
187	Los Angeles County, CA M.D.	(8.4)
179	Los Angeles (greater), CA	(7.8)
NA	Louisville, KY-IN**	NA
81	Lubbock, TX	0.7
12	Lynchburg, VA	19.1
273	Macon, GA	(18.9)
198	Madera, CA	(9.1)
151	Madison, WI	(5.5)
NA	Manchester-Nashua, NH**	NA
182	Manhattan, KS	(8.0)
NA	Mankato-North Mankato, MN**	NA
94	Mansfield, OH	(0.5)
18	McAllen-Edinburg-Mission, TX	12.9
254	Medford, OR	(14.7)
143	Memphis, TN-MS-AR	(5.0)
36	Merced, CA	7.4
222	Miami (greater), FL	(11.2)
248	Miami-Dade County, FL M.D.	(14.0)
103	Michigan City-La Porte, IN	(1.8)
230	Midland, TX	(12.0)
201	Milwaukee, WI	(9.3)
NA	Minneapolis-St. Paul, MN-WI**	NA
187	Missoula, MT	(8.4)
1	Mobile, AL	51.8
126	Modesto, CA	(3.7)
NA	Monroe, MI**	NA
28	Montgomery, AL	9.5
NA	Morgantown, WV**	NA
203	Morristown, TN	(9.4)
164	Mount Vernon-Anacortes, WA	(6.7)
20	Muncie, IN	12.1
NA	Muskegon-Norton Shores, MI**	NA
291	Napa, CA	(53.1)
215	Naples-Marco Island, FL	(10.4)
260	Nashville-Davidson, TN	(15.6)
35	Nassau-Suffolk, NY M.D.	7.6
NA	New Haven-Milford, CT**	NA
230	New Orleans, LA	(12.0)
134	New York (greater), NY-NJ-PA	(4.2)
151	New York-W. Plains NY-NJ M.D.	(5.5)
118	Newark-Union, NJ-PA M.D.	(3.1)
NA	Niles-Benton Harbor, MI**	NA
NA	North Port-Bradenton-Sarasota, FL**	NA
8	Norwich-New London, CT	20.3
230	Oakland-Fremont, CA M.D.	(12.0)
206	Ocala, FL	(9.5)
248	Ocean City, NJ	(14.0)
18	Odessa, TX	12.9
60	Ogden-Clearfield, UT	3.3
NA	Oklahoma City, OK**	NA
148	Olympia, WA	(5.4)
155	Omaha-Council Bluffs, NE-IA	(5.6)
266	Orlando, FL	(16.8)
10	Oshkosh-Neenah, WI	20.1
NA	Owensboro, KY**	NA
148	Oxnard-Thousand Oaks, CA	(5.4)
108	Palm Bay-Melbourne, FL	(2.3)
53	Palm Coast, FL	5.1
185	Panama City-Lynn Haven, FL	(8.2)
26	Pascagoula, MS	10.1
107	Peabody, MA M.D.	(2.2)
98	Pensacola, FL	(1.4)
187	Philadelphia (greater) PA-NJ-MD-DE	(8.4)
207	Philadelphia, PA M.D.	(9.9)
243	Phoenix-Mesa-Scottsdale, AZ	(13.5)
218	Pine Bluff, AR	(10.5)
176	Pittsburgh, PA	(7.5)
44	Pittsfield, MA	5.8
241	Pocatello, ID	(13.2)
260	Port St. Lucie, FL	(15.6)
187	Portland-Vancouver, OR-WA	(8.4)
91	Portland, ME	(0.3)
132	Poughkeepsie, NY	(4.0)
182	Prescott, AZ	(8.0)
72	Providence-New Bedford, RI-MA	1.4
265	Provo-Orem, UT	(16.5)
NA	Pueblo, CO**	NA
203	Punta Gorda, FL	(9.4)
212	Racine, WI	(10.2)
NA	Raleigh-Cary, NC**	NA
282	Rapid City, SD	(24.0)
167	Reading, PA	(7.0)
31	Redding, CA	8.5
126	Reno-Sparks, NV	(3.7)
263	Richmond, VA	(16.3)
180	Riverside-San Bernardino, CA	(7.9)
227	Roanoke, VA	(11.7)
NA	Rochester, MN**	NA
215	Rochester, NY	(10.4)
201	Rockingham County, NH M.D.	(9.3)
NA	Rocky Mount, NC**	NA
NA	Rome, GA**	NA
111	Sacramento, CA	(2.5)
NA	Saginaw, MI**	NA
125	Salem, OR	(3.6)
37	Salinas, CA	7.0
187	Salisbury, MD	(8.4)
90	Salt Lake City, UT	(0.2)
84	San Angelo, TX	0.4
268	San Antonio, TX	(17.7)
103	San Diego, CA	(1.8)
224	San Francisco (greater), CA	(11.5)
215	San Francisco-S. Mateo, CA M.D.	(10.4)
192	San Jose, CA	(8.6)
233	San Luis Obispo, CA	(12.2)
278	Sandusky, OH	(22.1)
119	Santa Ana-Anaheim, CA M.D.	(3.3)
15	Santa Barbara-Santa Maria, CA	14.2
119	Santa Cruz-Watsonville, CA	(3.3)
30	Santa Fe, NM	8.6
160	Santa Rosa-Petaluma, CA	(6.3)
246	Savannah, GA	(13.9)
85	Scranton--Wilkes-Barre, PA	0.3
NA	Seattle-Bellevue-Everett, WA M.D.**	NA
NA	Seattle-Tacoma-Bellevue, WA**	NA
155	Sebastian-Vero Beach, FL	(5.6)
4	Sheboygan, WI	34.7
72	Sherman-Denison, TX	1.4
NA	Shreveport-Bossier City, LA**	NA
65	Sioux City, IA-NE-SD	2.7
263	Sioux Falls, SD	(16.3)
NA	South Bend-Mishawaka, IN-MI**	NA
195	Spartanburg, SC	(8.7)
200	Spokane, WA	(9.2)
130	Springfield, MA	(3.9)
NA	Springfield, MO**	NA
2	Springfield, OH	42.0
3	State College, PA	36.1
214	Stockton, CA	(10.3)
NA	St. Cloud, MN**	NA
289	St. George, UT	(32.1)
14	St. Joseph, MO-KS	16.0
NA	St. Louis, MO-IL**	NA
NA	Sumter, SC**	NA
115	Syracuse, NY	(2.7)
NA	Tacoma, WA M.D.**	NA
251	Tallahassee, FL	(14.3)
220	Tampa-St Petersburg, FL	(10.9)
244	Texarkana, TX-Texarkana, AR	(13.6)
192	Toledo, OH	(8.6)
22	Topeka, KS	10.9
17	Trenton-Ewing, NJ	13.3
256	Tucson, AZ	(15.3)
203	Tulsa, OK	(9.4)
167	Tuscaloosa, AL	(7.0)
239	Tyler, TX	(12.5)
157	Utica-Rome, NY	(5.7)
49	Valdosta, GA	5.3
233	Vallejo-Fairfield, CA	(12.2)
34	Victoria, TX	7.9
259	Vineland, NJ	(15.5)
110	Visalia-Porterville, CA	(2.4)
227	Waco, TX	(11.7)
41	Warner Robins, GA	6.3
NA	Warren-Farmington Hills, MI M.D.**	NA
184	Washington (greater) DC-VA-MD-WV	(8.1)
192	Washington, DC-VA-MD-WV M.D.	(8.6)
9	Waterloo-Cedar Falls, IA	20.2
NA	Wausau, WI**	NA
63	Wenatchee, WA	2.9
170	West Palm Beach, FL M.D.	(7.2)
68	Wheeling, WV-OH	2.1
160	Wichita Falls, TX	(6.3)
50	Wichita, KS	5.2
6	Williamsport, PA	25.3
172	Wilmington, DE-MD-NJ M.D.	(7.3)
NA	Wilmington, NC**	NA
219	Winchester, VA-WV	(10.6)
258	Winston-Salem, NC	(15.4)
40	Worcester, MA	6.6
172	York-Hanover, PA	(7.3)
85	Youngstown, OH-PA	0.3
255	Yuba City, CA	(15.0)
41	Yuma, AZ	6.3

Source: CQ Press using reported data from the F.B.I. "Crime in the United States 2009"
*Violent crimes are offenses of murder, forcible rape, robbery, and aggravated assault.
**Not available.

7. Percent Change in Violent Crime Rate: 2008 to 2009 (continued)
National Percent Change = 6.1% Decrease*

RANK	METROPOLITAN AREA	% CHANGE	RANK	METROPOLITAN AREA	% CHANGE	RANK	METROPOLITAN AREA	% CHANGE
1	Mobile, AL	51.8	61	Abilene, TX	3.2	119	Santa Cruz-Watsonville, CA	(3.3)
2	Springfield, OH	42.0	62	Austin-Round Rock, TX	3.1	122	Edison, NJ M.D.	(3.5)
3	State College, PA	36.1	63	Akron, OH	2.9	122	Kingston, NY	(3.5)
4	Bloomington, IN	34.7	63	Wenatchee, WA	2.9	122	Las Vegas-Paradise, NV	(3.5)
4	Sheboygan, WI	34.7	65	Houston, TX	2.7	125	Salem, OR	(3.6)
6	Williamsport, PA	25.3	65	Lafayette, LA	2.7	126	Modesto, CA	(3.7)
7	Columbia, MO	22.0	65	Sioux City, IA-NE-SD	2.7	126	Reno-Sparks, NV	(3.7)
8	Norwich-New London, CT	20.3	68	Lafayette, IN	2.1	128	Billings, MT	(3.8)
9	Waterloo-Cedar Falls, IA	20.2	68	Wheeling, WV-OH	2.1	128	Huntsville, AL	(3.8)
10	Oshkosh-Neenah, WI	20.1	70	Columbia, SC	1.8	130	Lima, OH	(3.9)
11	Eau Claire, WI	20.0	71	Boston-Quincy, MA M.D.	1.7	130	Springfield, MA	(3.9)
12	Lynchburg, VA	19.1	72	Boston (greater), MA-NH	1.4	132	Colorado Springs, CO	(4.0)
13	Bend, OR	16.7	72	Lake Havasu City-Kingman, AZ	1.4	132	Poughkeepsie, NY	(4.0)
14	St. Joseph, MO-KS	16.0	72	Providence-New Bedford, RI-MA	1.4	134	Hot Springs, AR	(4.2)
15	Columbus, IN	14.2	72	Sherman-Denison, TX	1.4	134	Jackson, MS	(4.2)
15	Santa Barbara-Santa Maria, CA	14.2	76	Charlottesville, VA	1.3	134	New York (greater), NY-NJ-PA	(4.2)
17	Trenton-Ewing, NJ	13.3	77	Iowa City, IA	1.2	137	Bethesda-Frederick, MD M.D.	(4.3)
18	McAllen-Edinburg-Mission, TX	12.9	78	Lewiston-Auburn, ME	1.0	137	Cheyenne, WY	(4.3)
18	Odessa, TX	12.9	79	Cumberland, MD-WV	0.9	139	Fort Smith, AR-OK	(4.4)
20	Muncie, IN	12.1	80	El Paso, TX	0.8	139	Laredo, TX	(4.4)
21	Baton Rouge, LA	12.0	81	Lubbock, TX	0.7	141	Burlington, NC	(4.6)
22	Topeka, KS	10.9	82	Harrisburg-Carlisle, PA	0.6	142	Bremerton-Silverdale, WA	(4.9)
23	Atlantic City, NJ	10.6	83	Jonesboro, AR	0.5	143	Memphis, TN-MS-AR	(5.0)
23	Chico, CA	10.6	84	San Angelo, TX	0.4	144	Baltimore-Towson, MD	(5.1)
25	Fort Wayne, IN	10.2	85	Scranton--Wilkes-Barre, PA	0.3	144	Las Cruces, NM	(5.1)
26	Pascagoula, MS	10.1	85	Youngstown, OH-PA	0.3	146	Green Bay, WI	(5.2)
27	Bangor, ME	9.6	87	Fort Collins-Loveland, CO	0.1	147	Lakeland, FL	(5.3)
28	Montgomery, AL	9.5	88	Appleton, WI	0.0	148	Dover, DE	(5.4)
29	Great Falls, MT	9.4	89	Janesville, WI	(0.1)	148	Olympia, WA	(5.4)
30	Santa Fe, NM	8.6	90	Salt Lake City, UT	(0.2)	148	Oxnard-Thousand Oaks, CA	(5.4)
31	Redding, CA	8.5	91	Portland, ME	(0.3)	151	Albany-Schenectady-Troy, NY	(5.5)
32	Lewiston, ID-WA	8.3	92	Anderson, SC	(0.4)	151	Columbus, GA-AL	(5.5)
33	Fresno, CA	8.2	92	Cedar Rapids, IA	(0.4)	151	Madison, WI	(5.5)
34	Victoria, TX	7.9	94	Mansfield, OH	(0.5)	151	New York-W. Plains NY-NJ M.D.	(5.5)
35	Nassau-Suffolk, NY M.D.	7.6	95	Gainesville, FL	(0.9)	155	Omaha-Council Bluffs, NE-IA	(5.6)
36	Merced, CA	7.4	96	Hartford, CT	(1.1)	155	Sebastian-Vero Beach, FL	(5.6)
37	Barnstable Town, MA	7.0	97	Beaumont-Port Arthur, TX	(1.3)	157	Utica-Rome, NY	(5.7)
37	Salinas, CA	7.0	98	Boise City-Nampa, ID	(1.4)	158	Battle Creek, MI	(5.9)
39	Kennewick-Pasco-Richland, WA	6.7	98	Pensacola, FL	(1.4)	159	Altoona, PA	(6.0)
40	Worcester, MA	6.6	100	Honolulu, HI	(1.5)	160	Johnson City, TN	(6.3)
41	Warner Robins, GA	6.3	101	Indianapolis, IN	(1.6)	160	Santa Rosa-Petaluma, CA	(6.3)
41	Yuma, AZ	6.3	102	Allentown, PA-NJ	(1.7)	160	Wichita Falls, TX	(6.3)
43	Logan, UT-ID	5.9	103	Michigan City-La Porte, IN	(1.8)	163	Athens-Clarke County, GA	(6.5)
44	Amarillo, TX	5.8	103	San Diego, CA	(1.8)	164	Corvallis, OR	(6.7)
44	Hinesville, GA	5.8	105	Fayetteville, AR-MO	(2.0)	164	Deltona-Daytona Beach, FL	(6.7)
44	Pittsfield, MA	5.8	106	Hickory, NC	(2.1)	164	Mount Vernon-Anacortes, WA	(6.7)
47	Cape Girardeau, MO-IL	5.7	107	Peabody, MA M.D.	(2.2)	167	Goldsboro, NC	(7.0)
48	Harrisonburg, VA	5.4	108	Camden, NJ M.D.	(2.3)	167	Reading, PA	(7.0)
49	Valdosta, GA	5.3	108	Palm Bay-Melbourne, FL	(2.3)	167	Tuscaloosa, AL	(7.0)
50	Buffalo-Niagara Falls, NY	5.2	110	Visalia-Porterville, CA	(2.4)	170	Dayton, OH	(7.2)
50	Kingsport, TN-VA	5.2	111	Bellingham, WA	(2.5)	170	West Palm Beach, FL M.D.	(7.2)
50	Wichita, KS	5.2	111	Knoxville, TN	(2.5)	172	Eugene-Springfield, OR	(7.3)
53	Palm Coast, FL	5.1	111	Sacramento, CA	(2.5)	172	Fort Worth-Arlington, TX M.D.	(7.3)
54	Lawrence, KS	4.9	114	Bismarck, ND	(2.6)	172	Wilmington, DE-MD-NJ M.D.	(7.3)
55	Bakersfield, CA	4.3	115	Syracuse, NY	(2.7)	172	York-Hanover, PA	(7.3)
56	Cambridge-Newton, MA M.D.	4.0	116	Bridgeport-Stamford, CT	(2.8)	176	Anchorage, AK	(7.5)
56	Charleston, WV	4.0	116	Houma, LA	(2.8)	176	Pittsburgh, PA	(7.5)
58	Corpus Christi, TX	3.9	118	Newark-Union, NJ-PA M.D.	(3.1)	178	Greensboro-High Point, NC	(7.7)
58	Idaho Falls, ID	3.9	119	Denver-Aurora, CO	(3.3)	179	Los Angeles (greater), CA	(7.8)
60	Ogden-Clearfield, UT	3.3	119	Santa Ana-Anaheim, CA M.D.	(3.3)	180	Cleveland, TN	(7.9)

Note: All listings are for Metropolitan Statistical Areas (M.S.A.s) except for those ending with "M.D." Listings with "M.D." are Metropolitan Divisions which are smaller parts of eleven large M.S.A.s. See explanatory note at beginning of metropolitan area section.

Rank Order - Metro Area (continued)

RANK	METROPOLITAN AREA	% CHANGE
180	Riverside-San Bernardino, CA	(7.9)
182	Manhattan, KS	(8.0)
182	Prescott, AZ	(8.0)
184	Washington (greater) DC-VA-MD-WV	(8.1)
185	Panama City-Lynn Haven, FL	(8.2)
186	Jacksonville, NC	(8.3)
187	Los Angeles County, CA M.D.	(8.4)
187	Missoula, MT	(8.4)
187	Philadelphia (greater) PA-NJ-MD-DE	(8.4)
187	Portland-Vancouver, OR-WA	(8.4)
187	Salisbury, MD	(8.4)
192	San Jose, CA	(8.6)
192	Toledo, OH	(8.6)
192	Washington, DC-VA-MD-WV M.D.	(8.6)
195	Spartanburg, SC	(8.7)
196	Gadsden, AL	(8.8)
197	Ames, IA	(8.9)
198	Columbus, OH	(9.1)
198	Madera, CA	(9.1)
200	Spokane, WA	(9.2)
201	Milwaukee, WI	(9.3)
201	Rockingham County, NH M.D.	(9.3)
203	Morristown, TN	(9.4)
203	Punta Gorda, FL	(9.4)
203	Tulsa, OK	(9.4)
206	Ocala, FL	(9.5)
207	Fort Lauderdale, FL M.D.	(9.9)
207	Philadelphia, PA M.D.	(9.9)
209	Birmingham-Hoover, AL	(10.0)
209	Cape Coral-Fort Myers, FL	(10.0)
209	Lincoln, NE	(10.0)
212	Dallas (greater), TX	(10.2)
212	Racine, WI	(10.2)
214	Stockton, CA	(10.3)
215	Naples-Marco Island, FL	(10.4)
215	Rochester, NY	(10.4)
215	San Francisco-S. Mateo, CA M.D.	(10.4)
218	Pine Bluff, AR	(10.5)
219	Winchester, VA-WV	(10.6)
220	Grand Junction, CO	(10.9)
220	Tampa-St Petersburg, FL	(10.9)
222	Flagstaff, AZ	(11.2)
222	Miami (greater), FL	(11.2)
224	San Francisco (greater), CA	(11.5)
225	Dallas-Plano-Irving, TX M.D.	(11.6)
225	Greeley, CO	(11.6)
227	Longview, TX	(11.7)
227	Roanoke, VA	(11.7)
227	Waco, TX	(11.7)
230	Midland, TX	(12.0)
230	New Orleans, LA	(12.0)
230	Oakland-Fremont, CA M.D.	(12.0)
233	Atlanta, GA	(12.2)
233	Blacksburg, VA	(12.2)
233	San Luis Obispo, CA	(12.2)
233	Vallejo-Fairfield, CA	(12.2)
237	Jackson, TN	(12.3)
238	Hagerstown-Martinsburg, MD-WV	(12.4)
239	Tyler, TX	(12.5)
240	Dalton, GA	(12.6)
241	Lancaster, PA	(13.2)
241	Pocatello, ID	(13.2)
243	Phoenix-Mesa-Scottsdale, AZ	(13.5)

RANK	METROPOLITAN AREA	% CHANGE
244	Texarkana, TX-Texarkana, AR	(13.6)
245	Dubuque, IA	(13.7)
246	Durham-Chapel Hill, NC	(13.9)
246	Savannah, GA	(13.9)
248	Miami-Dade County, FL M.D.	(14.0)
248	Ocean City, NJ	(14.0)
250	College Station-Bryan, TX	(14.1)
251	Tallahassee, FL	(14.3)
252	Ann Arbor, MI	(14.5)
252	Charleston-North Charleston, SC	(14.5)
254	Medford, OR	(14.7)
255	Yuba City, CA	(15.0)
256	Jacksonville, FL	(15.3)
256	Tucson, AZ	(15.3)
258	Winston-Salem, NC	(15.4)
259	Vineland, NJ	(15.5)
260	Nashville-Davidson, TN	(15.6)
260	Port St. Lucie, FL	(15.6)
262	Killeen-Temple-Fort Hood, TX	(15.8)
263	Richmond, VA	(16.3)
263	Sioux Falls, SD	(16.3)
265	Provo-Orem, UT	(16.5)
266	Orlando, FL	(16.8)
267	Binghamton, NY	(16.9)
268	San Antonio, TX	(17.7)
269	Casper, WY	(17.8)
269	Elkhart-Goshen, IN	(17.8)
271	Albuquerque, NM	(18.3)
272	Erie, PA	(18.8)
273	Macon, GA	(18.9)
274	Asheville, NC	(19.3)
275	Charlotte-Gastonia, NC-SC	(20.1)
276	Brownsville-Harlingen, TX	(20.9)
276	Elmira, NY	(20.9)
278	Sandusky, OH	(22.1)
279	Carson City, NV	(22.3)
280	Florence, SC	(23.0)
281	Fayetteville, NC	(23.8)
282	Rapid City, SD	(24.0)
283	Fond du Lac, WI	(24.2)
284	Florence-Muscle Shoals, AL	(25.0)
285	Longview, WA	(27.5)
286	Kokomo, IN	(28.4)
287	Lebanon, PA	(28.8)
288	Danville, VA	(30.8)
289	St. George, UT	(32.1)
290	Glens Falls, NY	(39.6)
291	Napa, CA	(53.1)
NA	Albany, GA**	NA
NA	Alexandria, LA**	NA
NA	Anderson, IN**	NA
NA	Anniston-Oxford, AL**	NA
NA	Auburn, AL**	NA
NA	Augusta, GA-SC**	NA
NA	Bay City, MI**	NA
NA	Boulder, CO**	NA
NA	Bowling Green, KY**	NA
NA	Brunswick, GA**	NA
NA	Burlington-South Burlington, VT**	NA
NA	Chattanooga, TN-GA**	NA
NA	Cincinnati-Middletown, OH-KY-IN**	NA
NA	Clarksville, TN-KY**	NA
NA	Cleveland-Elyria-Mentor, OH**	NA

RANK	METROPOLITAN AREA	% CHANGE
NA	Coeur d'Alene, ID**	NA
NA	Crestview-Fort Walton Beach, FL**	NA
NA	Danville, IL**	NA
NA	Decatur, AL**	NA
NA	Decatur, IL**	NA
NA	Des Moines-West Des Moines, IA**	NA
NA	Detroit (greater), MI**	NA
NA	Detroit-Livonia-Dearborn, MI M.D.**	NA
NA	Dothan, AL**	NA
NA	Duluth, MN-WI**	NA
NA	El Centro, CA**	NA
NA	Elizabethtown, KY**	NA
NA	Evansville, IN-KY**	NA
NA	Fargo, ND-MN**	NA
NA	Farmington, NM**	NA
NA	Flint, MI**	NA
NA	Gainesville, GA**	NA
NA	Grand Forks, ND-MN**	NA
NA	Grand Rapids-Wyoming, MI**	NA
NA	Gulfport-Biloxi, MS**	NA
NA	Hattiesburg, MS**	NA
NA	Holland-Grand Haven, MI**	NA
NA	Ithaca, NY**	NA
NA	Jackson, MI**	NA
NA	Jefferson City, MO**	NA
NA	Kalamazoo-Portage, MI**	NA
NA	Kansas City, MO-KS**	NA
NA	La Crosse, WI-MN**	NA
NA	Lake Charles, LA**	NA
NA	Lansing-East Lansing, MI**	NA
NA	Lawton, OK**	NA
NA	Lexington-Fayette, KY**	NA
NA	Little Rock, AR**	NA
NA	Louisville, KY-IN**	NA
NA	Manchester-Nashua, NH**	NA
NA	Mankato-North Mankato, MN**	NA
NA	Minneapolis-St. Paul, MN-WI**	NA
NA	Monroe, MI**	NA
NA	Morgantown, WV**	NA
NA	Muskegon-Norton Shores, MI**	NA
NA	New Haven-Milford, CT**	NA
NA	Niles-Benton Harbor, MI**	NA
NA	North Port-Bradenton-Sarasota, FL**	NA
NA	Oklahoma City, OK**	NA
NA	Owensboro, KY**	NA
NA	Pueblo, CO**	NA
NA	Raleigh-Cary, NC**	NA
NA	Rochester, MN**	NA
NA	Rocky Mount, NC**	NA
NA	Rome, GA**	NA
NA	Saginaw, MI**	NA
NA	Seattle-Bellevue-Everett, WA M.D.**	NA
NA	Seattle-Tacoma-Bellevue, WA**	NA
NA	Shreveport-Bossier City, LA**	NA
NA	South Bend-Mishawaka, IN-MI**	NA
NA	Springfield, MO**	NA
NA	St. Cloud, MN**	NA
NA	St. Louis, MO-IL**	NA
NA	Sumter, SC**	NA
NA	Tacoma, WA M.D.**	NA
NA	Warren-Farmington Hills, MI M.D.**	NA
NA	Wausau, WI**	NA
NA	Wilmington, NC**	NA

Source: CQ Press using reported data from the F.B.I. "Crime in the United States 2009"
*Violent crimes are offenses of murder, forcible rape, robbery, and aggravated assault.
**Not available.

8. Percent Change in Violent Crime Rate: 2005 to 2009
National Percent Change = 8.4% Decrease*

RANK	METROPOLITAN AREA	% CHANGE
41	Abilene, TX	16.9
16	Akron, OH	34.0
213	Albany-Schenectady-Troy, NY	(15.3)
6	Albany, GA	54.6
254	Albuquerque, NM	(22.2)
277	Alexandria, LA	(31.8)
234	Allentown, PA-NJ	(18.5)
83	Altoona, PA	5.1
107	Amarillo, TX	(0.2)
10	Ames, IA	39.4
54	Anchorage, AK	13.3
96	Anderson, IN	1.8
83	Anderson, SC	5.1
160	Ann Arbor, MI	(6.5)
NA	Anniston-Oxford, AL**	NA
92	Appleton, WI	3.5
187	Asheville, NC	(10.9)
12	Athens-Clarke County, GA	36.8
182	Atlanta, GA	(10.6)
91	Atlantic City, NJ	4.1
NA	Auburn, AL**	NA
80	Augusta, GA-SC	5.8
93	Austin-Round Rock, TX	2.9
50	Bakersfield, CA	13.9
208	Baltimore-Towson, MD	(13.7)
100	Bangor, ME	0.7
45	Barnstable Town, MA	14.6
126	Baton Rouge, LA	(3.0)
182	Battle Creek, MI	(10.6)
NA	Bay City, MI**	NA
119	Beaumont-Port Arthur, TX	(2.2)
135	Bellingham, WA	(4.1)
114	Bend, OR	(1.0)
127	Bethesda-Frederick, MD M.D.	(3.1)
80	Billings, MT	5.8
52	Binghamton, NY	13.7
NA	Birmingham-Hoover, AL**	NA
1	Bismarck, ND	88.0
95	Blacksburg, VA	2.2
7	Bloomington, IN	49.1
NA	Boise City-Nampa, ID**	NA
102	Boston (greater), MA-NH	0.5
120	Boston-Quincy, MA M.D.	(2.3)
NA	Boulder, CO**	NA
NA	Bowling Green, KY**	NA
83	Bremerton-Silverdale, WA	5.1
58	Bridgeport-Stamford, CT	11.0
274	Brownsville-Harlingen, TX	(30.3)
60	Brunswick, GA	10.1
107	Buffalo-Niagara Falls, NY	(0.2)
NA	Burlington-South Burlington, VT**	NA
185	Burlington, NC	(10.8)
40	Cambridge-Newton, MA M.D.	17.0
98	Camden, NJ M.D.	1.3
263	Cape Coral-Fort Myers, FL	(25.7)
NA	Cape Girardeau, MO-IL**	NA
283	Carson City, NV	(34.9)
164	Casper, WY	(7.3)
184	Cedar Rapids, IA	(10.7)
269	Charleston-North Charleston, SC	(27.0)
48	Charleston, WV	14.3
286	Charlotte-Gastonia, NC-SC	(36.9)
260	Charlottesville, VA	(25.2)
104	Chattanooga, TN-GA	0.1
55	Cheyenne, WY	12.9
38	Chico, CA	20.0
NA	Cincinnati-Middletown, OH-KY-IN**	NA
NA	Clarksville, TN-KY**	NA
NA	Cleveland-Elyria-Mentor, OH**	NA
NA	Cleveland, TN**	NA
78	Coeur d'Alene, ID	5.9
225	College Station-Bryan, TX	(16.4)
149	Colorado Springs, CO	(5.4)
140	Columbia, MO	(4.5)
86	Columbia, SC	4.8
31	Columbus, GA-AL	23.5
260	Columbus, IN	(25.2)
220	Columbus, OH	(16.1)
63	Corpus Christi, TX	9.1
162	Corvallis, OR	(6.7)
NA	Crestview-Fort Walton Beach, FL**	NA
13	Cumberland, MD-WV	35.6
262	Dallas (greater), TX	(25.4)
279	Dallas-Plano-Irving, TX M.D.	(32.2)
NA	Dalton, GA**	NA
NA	Danville, IL**	NA
258	Danville, VA	(23.8)
62	Dayton, OH	9.2
NA	Decatur, AL**	NA
NA	Decatur, IL**	NA
NA	Deltona-Daytona Beach, FL**	NA
252	Denver-Aurora, CO	(21.9)
NA	Des Moines-West Des Moines, IA**	NA
185	Detroit (greater), MI	(10.8)
NA	Detroit-Livonia-Dearborn, MI M.D.**	NA
NA	Dothan, AL**	NA
88	Dover, DE	4.5
141	Dubuque, IA	(4.7)
NA	Duluth, MN-WI**	NA
194	Durham-Chapel Hill, NC	(11.1)
132	Eau Claire, WI	(3.7)
146	Edison, NJ M.D.	(5.0)
NA	El Centro, CA**	NA
70	El Paso, TX	7.7
NA	Elizabethtown, KY**	NA
270	Elkhart-Goshen, IN	(27.4)
245	Elmira, NY	(20.6)
143	Erie, PA	(4.8)
33	Eugene-Springfield, OR	22.6
NA	Evansville, IN-KY**	NA
NA	Fargo, ND-MN**	NA
NA	Farmington, NM**	NA
89	Fayetteville, AR-MO	4.4
139	Fayetteville, NC	(4.3)
291	Flagstaff, AZ	(43.8)
NA	Flint, MI**	NA
NA	Florence-Muscle Shoals, AL**	NA
290	Florence, SC	(40.0)
23	Fond du Lac, WI	28.9
56	Fort Collins-Loveland, CO	12.1
165	Fort Lauderdale, FL M.D.	(7.4)
251	Fort Smith, AR-OK	(21.7)
69	Fort Wayne, IN	7.8
170	Fort Worth-Arlington, TX M.D.	(8.2)
243	Fresno, CA	(20.0)
213	Gadsden, AL	(15.3)
175	Gainesville, FL	(8.8)
265	Gainesville, GA	(26.2)
NA	Glens Falls, NY**	NA
106	Goldsboro, NC	0.0
NA	Grand Forks, ND-MN**	NA
59	Grand Junction, CO	10.6
NA	Grand Rapids-Wyoming, MI**	NA
64	Great Falls, MT	9.0
287	Greeley, CO	(37.7)
143	Green Bay, WI	(4.8)
110	Greensboro-High Point, NC	(0.3)
NA	Gulfport-Biloxi, MS**	NA
250	Hagerstown-Martinsburg, MD-WV	(21.5)
168	Harrisburg-Carlisle, PA	(8.0)
19	Harrisonburg, VA	30.1
107	Hartford, CT	(0.2)
NA	Hattiesburg, MS**	NA
130	Hickory, NC	(3.6)
27	Hinesville, GA	25.7
NA	Holland-Grand Haven, MI**	NA
115	Honolulu, HI	(1.1)
141	Hot Springs, AR	(4.7)
134	Houma, LA	(4.0)
113	Houston, TX	(0.8)
228	Huntsville, AL	(17.0)
11	Idaho Falls, ID	38.9
61	Indianapolis, IN	9.3
36	Iowa City, IA	20.7
NA	Ithaca, NY**	NA
155	Jacksonville, FL	(6.2)
NA	Jacksonville, NC**	NA
NA	Jackson, MI**	NA
70	Jackson, MS	7.7
271	Jackson, TN	(27.6)
191	Janesville, WI	(11.0)
171	Jefferson City, MO	(8.3)
245	Johnson City, TN	(20.6)
284	Jonesboro, AR	(35.4)
NA	Kalamazoo-Portage, MI**	NA
201	Kansas City, MO-KS	(12.8)
49	Kennewick-Pasco-Richland, WA	14.0
187	Killeen-Temple-Fort Hood, TX	(10.9)
216	Kingsport, TN-VA	(15.5)
252	Kingston, NY	(21.9)
94	Knoxville, TN	2.4
278	Kokomo, IN	(32.0)
NA	La Crosse, WI-MN**	NA
45	Lafayette, IN	14.6
34	Lafayette, LA	21.1
25	Lake Charles, LA	26.4
NA	Lake Havasu City-Kingman, AZ**	NA
150	Lakeland, FL	(5.6)
130	Lancaster, PA	(3.6)
NA	Lansing-East Lansing, MI**	NA

Note: All listings are for Metropolitan Statistical Areas (M.S.A.s) except for those ending with "M.D." Listings with "M.D." are Metropolitan Divisions which are smaller parts of eleven large M.S.A.s. See explanatory note at beginning of metropolitan area section.

Alpha Order - Metro Area (continued)

RANK	METROPOLITAN AREA	% CHANGE
47	Laredo, TX	14.5
129	Las Cruces, NM	(3.5)
37	Las Vegas-Paradise, NV	20.2
16	Lawrence, KS	34.0
NA	Lawton, OK**	NA
293	Lebanon, PA	(48.9)
30	Lewiston-Auburn, ME	24.1
65	Lewiston, ID-WA	8.9
NA	Lexington-Fayette, KY**	NA
78	Lima, OH	5.9
243	Lincoln, NE	(20.0)
NA	Little Rock, AR**	NA
44	Logan, UT-ID	14.9
215	Longview, TX	(15.4)
281	Longview, WA	(32.9)
222	Los Angeles County, CA M.D.	(16.3)
220	Los Angeles (greater), CA	(16.1)
NA	Louisville, KY-IN**	NA
157	Lubbock, TX	(6.3)
18	Lynchburg, VA	33.4
197	Macon, GA	(12.2)
204	Madera, CA	(13.1)
112	Madison, WI	(0.5)
9	Manchester-Nashua, NH	44.1
NA	Manhattan, KS**	NA
NA	Mankato-North Mankato, MN**	NA
67	Mansfield, OH	7.9
199	McAllen-Edinburg-Mission, TX	(12.3)
285	Medford, OR	(35.6)
137	Memphis, TN-MS-AR	(4.2)
77	Merced, CA	6.0
206	Miami (greater), FL	(13.3)
239	Miami-Dade County, FL M.D.	(19.4)
150	Michigan City-La Porte, IN	(5.6)
128	Midland, TX	(3.3)
67	Milwaukee, WI	7.9
NA	Minneapolis-St. Paul, MN-WI**	NA
248	Missoula, MT	(21.4)
2	Mobile, AL	82.5
210	Modesto, CA	(14.2)
NA	Monroe, MI**	NA
282	Montgomery, AL	(34.2)
14	Morgantown, WV	35.4
222	Morristown, TN	(16.3)
181	Mount Vernon-Anacortes, WA	(10.4)
21	Muncie, IN	29.8
NA	Muskegon-Norton Shores, MI**	NA
232	Napa, CA	(18.1)
264	Naples-Marco Island, FL	(25.9)
265	Nashville-Davidson, TN	(26.2)
179	Nassau-Suffolk, NY M.D.	(9.8)
NA	New Haven-Milford, CT**	NA
NA	New Orleans, LA**	NA
218	New York (greater), NY-NJ-PA	(15.8)
230	New York-W. Plains NY-NJ M.D.	(17.7)
191	Newark-Union, NJ-PA M.D.	(11.0)
NA	Niles-Benton Harbor, MI**	NA
NA	North Port-Bradenton-Sarasota, FL**	NA
26	Norwich-New London, CT	25.8
74	Oakland-Fremont, CA M.D.	7.2
238	Ocala, FL	(19.1)
176	Ocean City, NJ	(8.9)
15	Odessa, TX	34.2

RANK	METROPOLITAN AREA	% CHANGE
154	Ogden-Clearfield, UT	(6.1)
NA	Oklahoma City, OK**	NA
157	Olympia, WA	(6.3)
172	Omaha-Council Bluffs, NE-IA	(8.5)
227	Orlando, FL	(16.9)
32	Oshkosh-Neenah, WI	23.4
NA	Owensboro, KY**	NA
122	Oxnard-Thousand Oaks, CA	(2.6)
70	Palm Bay-Melbourne, FL	7.7
NA	Palm Coast, FL**	NA
176	Panama City-Lynn Haven, FL	(8.9)
57	Pascagoula, MS	11.3
NA	Peabody, MA M.D.**	NA
73	Pensacola, FL	7.3
169	Philadelphia (greater) PA-NJ-MD-DE	(8.1)
196	Philadelphia, PA M.D.	(11.9)
257	Phoenix-Mesa-Scottsdale, AZ	(23.3)
76	Pine Bluff, AR	6.2
145	Pittsburgh, PA	(4.9)
118	Pittsfield, MA	(1.7)
235	Pocatello, ID	(18.7)
255	Port St. Lucie, FL	(23.0)
231	Portland-Vancouver, OR-WA	(18.0)
132	Portland, ME	(3.7)
103	Poughkeepsie, NY	0.3
179	Prescott, AZ	(9.8)
NA	Providence-New Bedford, RI-MA**	NA
276	Provo-Orem, UT	(31.1)
34	Pueblo, CO	21.1
275	Punta Gorda, FL	(31.0)
24	Racine, WI	28.3
219	Raleigh-Cary, NC	(15.9)
121	Rapid City, SD	(2.5)
211	Reading, PA	(14.9)
8	Redding, CA	48.3
124	Reno-Sparks, NV	(2.7)
272	Richmond, VA	(27.8)
209	Riverside-San Bernardino, CA	(14.1)
273	Roanoke, VA	(29.0)
NA	Rochester, MN**	NA
97	Rochester, NY	1.5
111	Rockingham County, NH M.D.	(0.4)
20	Rocky Mount, NC	30.0
29	Rome, GA	24.4
187	Sacramento, CA	(10.9)
NA	Saginaw, MI**	NA
267	Salem, OR	(26.5)
42	Salinas, CA	16.8
163	Salisbury, MD	(7.1)
87	Salt Lake City, UT	4.7
116	San Angelo, TX	(1.4)
173	San Antonio, TX	(8.7)
178	San Diego, CA	(9.6)
98	San Francisco (greater), CA	1.3
167	San Francisco-S. Mateo, CA M.D.	(7.5)
173	San Jose, CA	(8.7)
197	San Luis Obispo, CA	(12.2)
222	Sandusky, OH	(16.3)
205	Santa Ana-Anaheim, CA M.D.	(13.2)
52	Santa Barbara-Santa Maria, CA	13.7
82	Santa Cruz-Watsonville, CA	5.3
288	Santa Fe, NM	(38.7)
239	Santa Rosa-Petaluma, CA	(19.4)

RANK	METROPOLITAN AREA	% CHANGE
267	Savannah, GA	(26.5)
235	Scranton--Wilkes-Barre, PA	(18.7)
159	Seattle-Bellevue-Everett, WA M.D.	(6.4)
147	Seattle-Tacoma-Bellevue, WA	(5.2)
137	Sebastian-Vero Beach, FL	(4.2)
22	Sheboygan, WI	29.1
100	Sherman-Denison, TX	0.7
NA	Shreveport-Bossier City, LA**	NA
202	Sioux City, IA-NE-SD	(12.9)
237	Sioux Falls, SD	(18.9)
NA	South Bend-Mishawaka, IN-MI**	NA
152	Spartanburg, SC	(5.9)
155	Spokane, WA	(6.2)
229	Springfield, MA	(17.6)
NA	Springfield, MO**	NA
245	Springfield, OH	(20.6)
43	State College, PA	15.9
187	Stockton, CA	(10.9)
NA	St. Cloud, MN**	NA
292	St. George, UT	(48.5)
4	St. Joseph, MO-KS	67.3
NA	St. Louis, MO-IL**	NA
NA	Sumter, SC**	NA
202	Syracuse, NY	(12.9)
124	Tacoma, WA M.D.	(2.7)
160	Tallahassee, FL	(6.5)
248	Tampa-St Petersburg, FL	(21.4)
191	Texarkana, TX-Texarkana, AR	(11.0)
165	Toledo, OH	(7.4)
90	Topeka, KS	4.2
217	Trenton-Ewing, NJ	(15.7)
280	Tucson, AZ	(32.4)
195	Tulsa, OK	(11.4)
NA	Tuscaloosa, AL**	NA
207	Tyler, TX	(13.5)
66	Utica-Rome, NY	8.0
122	Valdosta, GA	(2.6)
NA	Vallejo-Fairfield, CA**	NA
5	Victoria, TX	57.8
289	Vineland, NJ	(39.6)
259	Visalia-Porterville, CA	(24.4)
117	Waco, TX	(1.5)
50	Warner Robins, GA	13.9
NA	Warren-Farmington Hills, MI M.D.**	NA
226	Washington (greater) DC-VA-MD-WV	(16.5)
233	Washington, DC-VA-MD-WV M.D.	(18.4)
3	Waterloo-Cedar Falls, IA	74.7
NA	Wausau, WI**	NA
152	Wenatchee, WA	(5.9)
148	West Palm Beach, FL M.D.	(5.3)
28	Wheeling, WV-OH	25.2
256	Wichita Falls, TX	(23.1)
NA	Wichita, KS**	NA
104	Williamsport, PA	0.1
75	Wilmington, DE-MD-NJ M.D.	6.7
NA	Wilmington, NC**	NA
200	Winchester, VA-WV	(12.5)
135	Winston-Salem, NC	(4.1)
39	Worcester, MA	17.7
212	York-Hanover, PA	(15.1)
NA	Youngstown, OH-PA**	NA
242	Yuba City, CA	(19.5)
239	Yuma, AZ	(19.4)

Source: CQ Press using reported data from the F.B.I. "Crime in the United States 2009"
*Violent crimes are offenses of murder, forcible rape, robbery, and aggravated assault.
**Not available.

8. Percent Change in Violent Crime Rate: 2005 to 2009 (continued)
National Percent Change = 8.4% Decrease*

RANK	METROPOLITAN AREA	% CHANGE
1	Bismarck, ND	88.0
2	Mobile, AL	82.5
3	Waterloo-Cedar Falls, IA	74.7
4	St. Joseph, MO-KS	67.3
5	Victoria, TX	57.8
6	Albany, GA	54.6
7	Bloomington, IN	49.1
8	Redding, CA	48.3
9	Manchester-Nashua, NH	44.1
10	Ames, IA	39.4
11	Idaho Falls, ID	38.9
12	Athens-Clarke County, GA	36.8
13	Cumberland, MD-WV	35.6
14	Morgantown, WV	35.4
15	Odessa, TX	34.2
16	Akron, OH	34.0
16	Lawrence, KS	34.0
18	Lynchburg, VA	33.4
19	Harrisonburg, VA	30.1
20	Rocky Mount, NC	30.0
21	Muncie, IN	29.8
22	Sheboygan, WI	29.1
23	Fond du Lac, WI	28.9
24	Racine, WI	28.3
25	Lake Charles, LA	26.4
26	Norwich-New London, CT	25.8
27	Hinesville, GA	25.7
28	Wheeling, WV-OH	25.2
29	Rome, GA	24.4
30	Lewiston-Auburn, ME	24.1
31	Columbus, GA-AL	23.5
32	Oshkosh-Neenah, WI	23.4
33	Eugene-Springfield, OR	22.6
34	Lafayette, LA	21.1
34	Pueblo, CO	21.1
36	Iowa City, IA	20.7
37	Las Vegas-Paradise, NV	20.2
38	Chico, CA	20.0
39	Worcester, MA	17.7
40	Cambridge-Newton, MA M.D.	17.0
41	Abilene, TX	16.9
42	Salinas, CA	16.8
43	State College, PA	15.9
44	Logan, UT-ID	14.9
45	Barnstable Town, MA	14.6
45	Lafayette, IN	14.6
47	Laredo, TX	14.5
48	Charleston, WV	14.3
49	Kennewick-Pasco-Richland, WA	14.0
50	Bakersfield, CA	13.9
50	Warner Robins, GA	13.9
52	Binghamton, NY	13.7
52	Santa Barbara-Santa Maria, CA	13.7
54	Anchorage, AK	13.3
55	Cheyenne, WY	12.9
56	Fort Collins-Loveland, CO	12.1
57	Pascagoula, MS	11.3
58	Bridgeport-Stamford, CT	11.0
59	Grand Junction, CO	10.6
60	Brunswick, GA	10.1
61	Indianapolis, IN	9.3
62	Dayton, OH	9.2
63	Corpus Christi, TX	9.1
64	Great Falls, MT	9.0
65	Lewiston, ID-WA	8.9
66	Utica-Rome, NY	8.0
67	Mansfield, OH	7.9
67	Milwaukee, WI	7.9
69	Fort Wayne, IN	7.8
70	El Paso, TX	7.7
70	Jackson, MS	7.7
70	Palm Bay-Melbourne, FL	7.7
73	Pensacola, FL	7.3
74	Oakland-Fremont, CA M.D.	7.2
75	Wilmington, DE-MD-NJ M.D.	6.7
76	Pine Bluff, AR	6.2
77	Merced, CA	6.0
78	Coeur d'Alene, ID	5.9
78	Lima, OH	5.9
80	Augusta, GA-SC	5.8
80	Billings, MT	5.8
82	Santa Cruz-Watsonville, CA	5.3
83	Altoona, PA	5.1
83	Anderson, SC	5.1
83	Bremerton-Silverdale, WA	5.1
86	Columbia, SC	4.8
87	Salt Lake City, UT	4.7
88	Dover, DE	4.5
89	Fayetteville, AR-MO	4.4
90	Topeka, KS	4.2
91	Atlantic City, NJ	4.1
92	Appleton, WI	3.5
93	Austin-Round Rock, TX	2.9
94	Knoxville, TN	2.4
95	Blacksburg, VA	2.2
96	Anderson, IN	1.8
97	Rochester, NY	1.5
98	Camden, NJ M.D.	1.3
98	San Francisco (greater), CA	1.3
100	Bangor, ME	0.7
100	Sherman-Denison, TX	0.7
102	Boston (greater), MA-NH	0.5
103	Poughkeepsie, NY	0.3
104	Chattanooga, TN-GA	0.1
104	Williamsport, PA	0.1
106	Goldsboro, NC	0.0
107	Amarillo, TX	(0.2)
107	Buffalo-Niagara Falls, NY	(0.2)
107	Hartford, CT	(0.2)
110	Greensboro-High Point, NC	(0.3)
111	Rockingham County, NH M.D.	(0.4)
112	Madison, WI	(0.5)
113	Houston, TX	(0.8)
114	Bend, OR	(1.0)
115	Honolulu, HI	(1.1)
116	San Angelo, TX	(1.4)
117	Waco, TX	(1.5)
118	Pittsfield, MA	(1.7)
119	Beaumont-Port Arthur, TX	(2.2)
120	Boston-Quincy, MA M.D.	(2.3)
121	Rapid City, SD	(2.5)
122	Oxnard-Thousand Oaks, CA	(2.6)
122	Valdosta, GA	(2.6)
124	Reno-Sparks, NV	(2.7)
124	Tacoma, WA M.D.	(2.7)
126	Baton Rouge, LA	(3.0)
127	Bethesda-Frederick, MD M.D.	(3.1)
128	Midland, TX	(3.3)
129	Las Cruces, NM	(3.5)
130	Hickory, NC	(3.6)
130	Lancaster, PA	(3.6)
132	Eau Claire, WI	(3.7)
132	Portland, ME	(3.7)
134	Houma, LA	(4.0)
135	Bellingham, WA	(4.1)
135	Winston-Salem, NC	(4.1)
137	Memphis, TN-MS-AR	(4.2)
137	Sebastian-Vero Beach, FL	(4.2)
139	Fayetteville, NC	(4.3)
140	Columbia, MO	(4.5)
141	Dubuque, IA	(4.7)
141	Hot Springs, AR	(4.7)
143	Erie, PA	(4.8)
143	Green Bay, WI	(4.8)
145	Pittsburgh, PA	(4.9)
146	Edison, NJ M.D.	(5.0)
147	Seattle-Tacoma-Bellevue, WA	(5.2)
148	West Palm Beach, FL M.D.	(5.3)
149	Colorado Springs, CO	(5.4)
150	Lakeland, FL	(5.6)
150	Michigan City-La Porte, IN	(5.6)
152	Spartanburg, SC	(5.9)
152	Wenatchee, WA	(5.9)
154	Ogden-Clearfield, UT	(6.1)
155	Jacksonville, FL	(6.2)
155	Spokane, WA	(6.2)
157	Lubbock, TX	(6.3)
157	Olympia, WA	(6.3)
159	Seattle-Bellevue-Everett, WA M.D.	(6.4)
160	Ann Arbor, MI	(6.5)
160	Tallahassee, FL	(6.5)
162	Corvallis, OR	(6.7)
163	Salisbury, MD	(7.1)
164	Casper, WY	(7.3)
165	Fort Lauderdale, FL M.D.	(7.4)
165	Toledo, OH	(7.4)
167	San Francisco-S. Mateo, CA M.D.	(7.5)
168	Harrisburg-Carlisle, PA	(8.0)
169	Philadelphia (greater) PA-NJ-MD-DE	(8.1)
170	Fort Worth-Arlington, TX M.D.	(8.2)
171	Jefferson City, MO	(8.3)
172	Omaha-Council Bluffs, NE-IA	(8.5)
173	San Antonio, TX	(8.7)
173	San Jose, CA	(8.7)
175	Gainesville, FL	(8.8)
176	Ocean City, NJ	(8.9)
176	Panama City-Lynn Haven, FL	(8.9)
178	San Diego, CA	(9.6)
179	Nassau-Suffolk, NY M.D.	(9.8)
179	Prescott, AZ	(9.8)

Note: All listings are for Metropolitan Statistical Areas (M.S.A.s) except for those ending with "M.D." Listings with "M.D." are Metropolitan Divisions which are smaller parts of eleven large M.S.A.s. See explanatory note at beginning of metropolitan area section.

RANK	METROPOLITAN AREA	% CHANGE
181	Mount Vernon-Anacortes, WA	(10.4)
182	Atlanta, GA	(10.6)
182	Battle Creek, MI	(10.6)
184	Cedar Rapids, IA	(10.7)
185	Burlington, NC	(10.8)
185	Detroit (greater), MI	(10.8)
187	Asheville, NC	(10.9)
187	Killeen-Temple-Fort Hood, TX	(10.9)
187	Sacramento, CA	(10.9)
187	Stockton, CA	(10.9)
191	Janesville, WI	(11.0)
191	Newark-Union, NJ-PA M.D.	(11.0)
191	Texarkana, TX-Texarkana, AR	(11.0)
194	Durham-Chapel Hill, NC	(11.1)
195	Tulsa, OK	(11.4)
196	Philadelphia, PA M.D.	(11.9)
197	Macon, GA	(12.2)
197	San Luis Obispo, CA	(12.2)
199	McAllen-Edinburg-Mission, TX	(12.3)
200	Winchester, VA-WV	(12.5)
201	Kansas City, MO-KS	(12.8)
202	Sioux City, IA-NE-SD	(12.9)
202	Syracuse, NY	(12.9)
204	Madera, CA	(13.1)
205	Santa Ana-Anaheim, CA M.D.	(13.2)
206	Miami (greater), FL	(13.3)
207	Tyler, TX	(13.5)
208	Baltimore-Towson, MD	(13.7)
209	Riverside-San Bernardino, CA	(14.1)
210	Modesto, CA	(14.2)
211	Reading, PA	(14.9)
212	York-Hanover, PA	(15.1)
213	Albany-Schenectady-Troy, NY	(15.3)
213	Gadsden, AL	(15.3)
215	Longview, TX	(15.4)
216	Kingsport, TN-VA	(15.5)
217	Trenton-Ewing, NJ	(15.7)
218	New York (greater), NY-NJ-PA	(15.8)
219	Raleigh-Cary, NC	(15.9)
220	Columbus, OH	(16.1)
220	Los Angeles (greater), CA	(16.1)
222	Los Angeles County, CA M.D.	(16.3)
222	Morristown, TN	(16.3)
222	Sandusky, OH	(16.3)
225	College Station-Bryan, TX	(16.4)
226	Washington (greater) DC-VA-MD-WV	(16.5)
227	Orlando, FL	(16.9)
228	Huntsville, AL	(17.0)
229	Springfield, MA	(17.6)
230	New York-W. Plains NY-NJ M.D.	(17.7)
231	Portland-Vancouver, OR-WA	(18.0)
232	Napa, CA	(18.1)
233	Washington, DC-VA-MD-WV M.D.	(18.4)
234	Allentown, PA-NJ	(18.5)
235	Pocatello, ID	(18.7)
235	Scranton--Wilkes-Barre, PA	(18.7)
237	Sioux Falls, SD	(18.9)
238	Ocala, FL	(19.1)
239	Miami-Dade County, FL M.D.	(19.4)
239	Santa Rosa-Petaluma, CA	(19.4)
239	Yuma, AZ	(19.4)
242	Yuba City, CA	(19.5)
243	Fresno, CA	(20.0)

RANK	METROPOLITAN AREA	% CHANGE
243	Lincoln, NE	(20.0)
245	Elmira, NY	(20.6)
245	Johnson City, TN	(20.6)
245	Springfield, OH	(20.6)
248	Missoula, MT	(21.4)
248	Tampa-St Petersburg, FL	(21.4)
250	Hagerstown-Martinsburg, MD-WV	(21.5)
251	Fort Smith, AR-OK	(21.7)
252	Denver-Aurora, CO	(21.9)
252	Kingston, NY	(21.9)
254	Albuquerque, NM	(22.2)
255	Port St. Lucie, FL	(23.0)
256	Wichita Falls, TX	(23.1)
257	Phoenix-Mesa-Scottsdale, AZ	(23.3)
258	Danville, VA	(23.8)
259	Visalia-Porterville, CA	(24.4)
260	Charlottesville, VA	(25.2)
260	Columbus, IN	(25.2)
262	Dallas (greater), TX	(25.4)
263	Cape Coral-Fort Myers, FL	(25.7)
264	Naples-Marco Island, FL	(25.9)
265	Gainesville, GA	(26.2)
265	Nashville-Davidson, TN	(26.2)
267	Salem, OR	(26.5)
267	Savannah, GA	(26.5)
269	Charleston-North Charleston, SC	(27.0)
270	Elkhart-Goshen, IN	(27.4)
271	Jackson, TN	(27.6)
272	Richmond, VA	(27.8)
273	Roanoke, VA	(29.0)
274	Brownsville-Harlingen, TX	(30.3)
275	Punta Gorda, FL	(31.0)
276	Provo-Orem, UT	(31.1)
277	Alexandria, LA	(31.8)
278	Kokomo, IN	(32.0)
279	Dallas-Plano-Irving, TX M.D.	(32.2)
280	Tucson, AZ	(32.4)
281	Longview, WA	(32.9)
282	Montgomery, AL	(34.2)
283	Carson City, NV	(34.9)
284	Jonesboro, AR	(35.4)
285	Medford, OR	(35.6)
286	Charlotte-Gastonia, NC-SC	(36.9)
287	Greeley, CO	(37.7)
288	Santa Fe, NM	(38.7)
289	Vineland, NJ	(39.6)
290	Florence, SC	(40.0)
291	Flagstaff, AZ	(43.8)
292	St. George, UT	(48.5)
293	Lebanon, PA	(48.9)
NA	Anniston-Oxford, AL**	NA
NA	Auburn, AL**	NA
NA	Bay City, MI**	NA
NA	Birmingham-Hoover, AL**	NA
NA	Boise City-Nampa, ID**	NA
NA	Boulder, CO**	NA
NA	Bowling Green, KY**	NA
NA	Burlington-South Burlington, VT**	NA
NA	Cape Girardeau, MO-IL**	NA
NA	Cincinnati-Middletown, OH-KY-IN**	NA
NA	Clarksville, TN-KY**	NA
NA	Cleveland-Elyria-Mentor, OH**	NA
NA	Cleveland, TN**	NA

RANK	METROPOLITAN AREA	% CHANGE
NA	Crestview-Fort Walton Beach, FL**	NA
NA	Dalton, GA**	NA
NA	Danville, IL**	NA
NA	Decatur, AL**	NA
NA	Decatur, IL**	NA
NA	Deltona-Daytona Beach, FL**	NA
NA	Des Moines-West Des Moines, IA**	NA
NA	Detroit-Livonia-Dearborn, MI M.D.**	NA
NA	Dothan, AL**	NA
NA	Duluth, MN-WI**	NA
NA	El Centro, CA**	NA
NA	Elizabethtown, KY**	NA
NA	Evansville, IN-KY**	NA
NA	Fargo, ND-MN**	NA
NA	Farmington, NM**	NA
NA	Flint, MI**	NA
NA	Florence-Muscle Shoals, AL**	NA
NA	Glens Falls, NY**	NA
NA	Grand Forks, ND-MN**	NA
NA	Grand Rapids-Wyoming, MI**	NA
NA	Gulfport-Biloxi, MS**	NA
NA	Hattiesburg, MS**	NA
NA	Holland-Grand Haven, MI**	NA
NA	Ithaca, NY**	NA
NA	Jacksonville, NC**	NA
NA	Jackson, MI**	NA
NA	Kalamazoo-Portage, MI**	NA
NA	La Crosse, WI-MN**	NA
NA	Lake Havasu City-Kingman, AZ**	NA
NA	Lansing-East Lansing, MI**	NA
NA	Lawton, OK**	NA
NA	Lexington-Fayette, KY**	NA
NA	Little Rock, AR**	NA
NA	Louisville, KY-IN**	NA
NA	Manhattan, KS**	NA
NA	Mankato-North Mankato, MN**	NA
NA	Minneapolis-St. Paul, MN-WI**	NA
NA	Monroe, MI**	NA
NA	Muskegon-Norton Shores, MI**	NA
NA	New Haven-Milford, CT**	NA
NA	New Orleans, LA**	NA
NA	Niles-Benton Harbor, MI**	NA
NA	North Port-Bradenton-Sarasota, FL**	NA
NA	Oklahoma City, OK**	NA
NA	Owensboro, KY**	NA
NA	Palm Coast, FL**	NA
NA	Peabody, MA M.D.**	NA
NA	Providence-New Bedford, RI-MA**	NA
NA	Rochester, MN**	NA
NA	Saginaw, MI**	NA
NA	Shreveport-Bossier City, LA**	NA
NA	South Bend-Mishawaka, IN-MI**	NA
NA	Springfield, MO**	NA
NA	St. Cloud, MN**	NA
NA	St. Louis, MO-IL**	NA
NA	Sumter, SC**	NA
NA	Tuscaloosa, AL**	NA
NA	Vallejo-Fairfield, CA**	NA
NA	Warren-Farmington Hills, MI M.D.**	NA
NA	Wausau, WI**	NA
NA	Wichita, KS**	NA
NA	Wilmington, NC**	NA
NA	Youngstown, OH-PA**	NA

Source: CQ Press using reported data from the F.B.I. "Crime in the United States 2009"
*Violent crimes are offenses of murder, forcible rape, robbery, and aggravated assault.
**Not available.

9. Murders in 2009
National Total = 15,241 Murders*

RANK	METROPOLITAN AREA	MURDERS
222	Abilene, TX	7
103	Akron, OH	28
112	Albany-Schenectady-Troy, NY	24
202	Albany, GA	9
59	Albuquerque, NM	68
191	Alexandria, LA	10
112	Allentown, PA-NJ	24
279	Altoona, PA	3
167	Amarillo, TX	13
359	Ames, IA	0
154	Anchorage, AK	14
340	Anderson, IN	1
202	Anderson, SC	9
237	Ann Arbor, MI	6
237	Anniston-Oxford, AL	6
279	Appleton, WI	3
182	Asheville, NC	11
182	Athens-Clarke County, GA	11
11	Atlanta, GA	325
112	Atlantic City, NJ	24
202	Auburn, AL	9
79	Augusta, GA-SC	42
81	Austin-Round Rock, TX	41
50	Bakersfield, CA	75
15	Baltimore-Towson, MD	298
258	Bangor, ME	4
258	Barnstable Town, MA	4
35	Baton Rouge, LA	110
154	Battle Creek, MI	14
279	Bay City, MI	3
129	Beaumont-Port Arthur, TX	19
211	Bellingham, WA	8
311	Bend, OR	2
118	Bethesda-Frederick, MD M.D.	22
279	Billings, MT	3
138	Binghamton, NY	17
37	Birmingham-Hoover, AL	105
279	Bismarck, ND	3
211	Blacksburg, VA	8
279	Bloomington, IN	3
191	Boise City-Nampa, ID	10
31	Boston (greater), MA-NH	111
50	Boston-Quincy, MA M.D.	75
222	Boulder, CO	7
279	Bowling Green, KY	3
258	Bremerton-Silverdale, WA	4
133	Bridgeport-Stamford, CT	18
211	Brownsville-Harlingen, TX	8
144	Brunswick, GA	16
50	Buffalo-Niagara Falls, NY	75
340	Burlington-South Burlington, VT	1
258	Burlington, NC	4
133	Cambridge-Newton, MA M.D.	18
68	Camden, NJ M.D.	50
82	Cape Coral-Fort Myers, FL	40
311	Cape Girardeau, MO-IL	2
359	Carson City, NV	0
359	Casper, WY	0
340	Cedar Rapids, IA	1
87	Charleston-North Charleston, SC	36
104	Charleston, WV	26
41	Charlotte-Gastonia, NC-SC	98
340	Charlottesville, VA	1
112	Chattanooga, TN-GA	24
258	Cheyenne, WY	4
191	Chico, CA	10
42	Cincinnati-Middletown, OH-KY-IN	89
125	Clarksville, TN-KY	20
29	Cleveland-Elyria-Mentor, OH	122
279	Cleveland, TN	3
311	Coeur d'Alene, ID	2
247	College Station-Bryan, TX	5
121	Colorado Springs, CO	21
279	Columbia, MO	3
71	Columbia, SC	47
144	Columbus, GA-AL	16
359	Columbus, IN	0
38	Columbus, OH	103
149	Corpus Christi, TX	15
340	Corvallis, OR	1
247	Crestview-Fort Walton Beach, FL	5
311	Cumberland, MD-WV	2
13	Dallas (greater), TX	310
18	Dallas-Plano-Irving, TX M.D.	235
311	Dalton, GA	2
237	Danville, IL	6
202	Danville, VA	9
71	Dayton, OH	47
311	Decatur, AL	2
279	Decatur, IL	3
129	Deltona-Daytona Beach, FL	19
39	Denver-Aurora, CO	100
222	Des Moines-West Des Moines, IA	7
6	Detroit (greater), MI	447
8	Detroit-Livonia-Dearborn, MI M.D.	398
279	Dothan, AL	3
258	Dover, DE	4
311	Dubuque, IA	2
247	Duluth, MN-WI	5
100	Durham-Chapel Hill, NC	29
340	Eau Claire, WI	1
98	Edison, NJ M.D.	30
279	El Centro, CA	3
144	El Paso, TX	16
311	Elizabethtown, KY	2
211	Elkhart-Goshen, IN	8
258	Elmira, NY	4
191	Erie, PA	10
258	Eugene-Springfield, OR	4
222	Evansville, IN-KY	7
311	Fargo, ND-MN	2
279	Farmington, NM	3
211	Fayetteville, AR-MO	8
89	Fayetteville, NC	35
237	Flagstaff, AZ	6
77	Flint, MI	44
222	Florence-Muscle Shoals, AL	7
125	Florence, SC	20
311	Fond du Lac, WI	2
237	Fort Collins-Loveland, CO	6
49	Fort Lauderdale, FL M.D.	76
191	Fort Smith, AR-OK	10
118	Fort Wayne, IN	22
50	Fort Worth-Arlington, TX M.D.	75
56	Fresno, CA	69
279	Gadsden, AL	3
222	Gainesville, FL	7
247	Gainesville, GA	5
359	Glens Falls, NY	0
154	Goldsboro, NC	14
359	Grand Forks, ND-MN	0
311	Grand Junction, CO	2
167	Grand Rapids-Wyoming, MI	13
222	Great Falls, MT	7
222	Greeley, CO	7
247	Green Bay, WI	5
89	Greensboro-High Point, NC	35
175	Gulfport-Biloxi, MS	12
279	Hagerstown-Martinsburg, MD-WV	3
104	Harrisburg-Carlisle, PA	26
311	Harrisonburg, VA	2
74	Hartford, CT	46
191	Hattiesburg, MS	10
138	Hickory, NC	17
311	Hinesville, GA	2
258	Holland-Grand Haven, MI	4
154	Honolulu, HI	14
191	Hot Springs, AR	10
154	Houma, LA	14
5	Houston, TX	462
121	Huntsville, AL	21
311	Idaho Falls, ID	2
31	Indianapolis, IN	111
311	Iowa City, IA	2
279	Ithaca, NY	3
30	Jacksonville, FL	120
182	Jacksonville, NC	11
211	Jackson, MI	8
77	Jackson, MS	44
149	Jackson, TN	15
237	Janesville, WI	6
247	Jefferson City, MO	5
182	Johnson City, TN	11
279	Jonesboro, AR	3
175	Kalamazoo-Portage, MI	12
24	Kansas City, MO-KS	163
340	Kennewick-Pasco-Richland, WA	1
167	Killeen-Temple-Fort Hood, TX	13
191	Kingsport, TN-VA	10
340	Kingston, NY	1
95	Knoxville, TN	31
340	Kokomo, IN	1
340	La Crosse, WI-MN	1
359	Lafayette, IN	0
154	Lafayette, LA	14
129	Lake Charles, LA	19
211	Lake Havasu City-Kingman, AZ	8
111	Lakeland, FL	25
175	Lancaster, PA	12
175	Lansing-East Lansing, MI	12

Note: All listings are for Metropolitan Statistical Areas (M.S.A.s) except for those ending with "M.D." Listings with "M.D." are Metropolitan Divisions which are smaller parts of eleven large M.S.A.s. See explanatory note at beginning of metropolitan area section.

Alpha Order - Metro Area (continued)

RANK	METROPOLITAN AREA	MURDERS
138	Laredo, TX	17
222	Las Cruces, NM	7
27	Las Vegas-Paradise, NV	133
359	Lawrence, KS	0
202	Lawton, OK	9
211	Lebanon, PA	8
359	Lewiston-Auburn, ME	0
340	Lewiston, ID-WA	1
154	Lexington-Fayette, KY	14
237	Lima, OH	6
258	Lincoln, NE	4
65	Little Rock, AR	51
359	Logan, UT-ID	0
138	Longview, TX	17
340	Longview, WA	1
3	Los Angeles County, CA M.D.	699
2	Los Angeles (greater), CA	768
56	Louisville, KY-IN	69
154	Lubbock, TX	14
247	Lynchburg, VA	5
117	Macon, GA	23
279	Madera, CA	3
182	Madison, WI	11
237	Manchester-Nashua, NH	6
258	Manhattan, KS	4
340	Mankato-North Mankato, MN	1
279	Mansfield, OH	3
82	McAllen-Edinburg-Mission, TX	40
311	Medford, OR	2
25	Memphis, TN-MS-AR	157
104	Merced, CA	26
9	Miami (greater), FL	377
21	Miami-Dade County, FL M.D.	215
279	Michigan City-La Porte, IN	3
279	Midland, TX	3
47	Milwaukee, WI	81
63	Minneapolis-St. Paul, MN-WI	55
340	Missoula, MT	1
87	Mobile, AL	36
74	Modesto, CA	46
247	Monroe, MI	5
84	Montgomery, AL	39
311	Morgantown, WV	2
279	Morristown, TN	3
279	Mount Vernon-Anacortes, WA	3
237	Muncie, IN	6
237	Muskegon-Norton Shores, MI	6
340	Napa, CA	1
154	Naples-Marco Island, FL	14
35	Nashville-Davidson, TN	110
61	Nassau-Suffolk, NY M.D.	63
98	New Haven-Milford, CT	30
17	New Orleans, LA	252
1	New York (greater), NY-NJ-PA	778
4	New York-W. Plains NY-NJ M.D.	551
26	Newark-Union, NJ-PA M.D.	134
279	Niles-Benton Harbor, MI	3
79	North Port-Bradenton-Sarasota, FL	42
258	Norwich-New London, CT	4
20	Oakland-Fremont, CA M.D.	227
175	Ocala, FL	12
340	Ocean City, NJ	1
222	Odessa, TX	7

RANK	METROPOLITAN AREA	MURDERS
222	Ogden-Clearfield, UT	7
46	Oklahoma City, OK	83
247	Olympia, WA	5
93	Omaha-Council Bluffs, NE-IA	33
31	Orlando, FL	111
359	Oshkosh-Neenah, WI	0
311	Owensboro, KY	2
100	Oxnard-Thousand Oaks, CA	29
104	Palm Bay-Melbourne, FL	26
279	Palm Coast, FL	3
202	Panama City-Lynn Haven, FL	9
222	Pascagoula, MS	7
149	Peabody, MA M.D.	15
133	Pensacola, FL	18
7	Philadelphia (greater) PA-NJ-MD-DE	436
10	Philadelphia, PA M.D.	351
19	Phoenix-Mesa-Scottsdale, AZ	230
154	Pine Bluff, AR	14
31	Pittsburgh, PA	111
311	Pittsfield, MA	2
340	Pocatello, ID	1
138	Port St. Lucie, FL	17
70	Portland-Vancouver, OR-WA	48
167	Portland, ME	13
167	Poughkeepsie, NY	13
279	Prescott, AZ	3
71	Providence-New Bedford, RI-MA	47
258	Provo-Orem, UT	4
154	Pueblo, CO	14
279	Punta Gorda, FL	3
247	Racine, WI	5
104	Raleigh-Cary, NC	26
311	Rapid City, SD	2
144	Reading, PA	16
279	Redding, CA	3
133	Reno-Sparks, NV	18
55	Richmond, VA	72
22	Riverside-San Bernardino, CA	214
175	Roanoke, VA	12
340	Rochester, MN	1
85	Rochester, NY	37
279	Rockingham County, NH M.D.	3
182	Rocky Mount, NC	11
279	Rome, GA	3
44	Sacramento, CA	86
154	Saginaw, MI	14
222	Salem, OR	7
65	Salinas, CA	51
222	Salisbury, MD	7
121	Salt Lake City, UT	21
202	San Angelo, TX	9
28	San Antonio, TX	130
50	San Diego, CA	75
16	San Francisco (greater), CA	292
60	San Francisco-S. Mateo, CA M.D.	65
74	San Jose, CA	46
258	San Luis Obispo, CA	4
311	Sandusky, OH	2
56	Santa Ana-Anaheim, CA M.D.	69
182	Santa Barbara-Santa Maria, CA	11
191	Santa Cruz-Watsonville, CA	10
149	Santa Fe, NM	15
202	Santa Rosa-Petaluma, CA	9

RANK	METROPOLITAN AREA	MURDERS
95	Savannah, GA	31
104	Scranton--Wilkes-Barre, PA	26
62	Seattle-Bellevue-Everett, WA M.D.	60
42	Seattle-Tacoma-Bellevue, WA	89
222	Sebastian-Vero Beach, FL	7
311	Sheboygan, WI	2
258	Sherman-Denison, TX	4
85	Shreveport-Bossier City, LA	37
258	Sioux City, IA-NE-SD	4
340	Sioux Falls, SD	1
129	South Bend-Mishawaka, IN-MI	19
167	Spartanburg, SC	13
191	Spokane, WA	10
112	Springfield, MA	24
211	Springfield, MO	8
258	Springfield, OH	4
311	State College, PA	2
65	Stockton, CA	51
311	St. Cloud, MN	2
311	St. George, UT	2
258	St. Joseph, MO-KS	4
23	St. Louis, MO-IL	210
175	Sumter, SC	12
121	Syracuse, NY	21
100	Tacoma, WA M.D.	29
167	Tallahassee, FL	13
40	Tampa-St Petersburg, FL	99
149	Texarkana, TX-Texarkana, AR	15
89	Toledo, OH	35
125	Topeka, KS	20
138	Trenton-Ewing, NJ	17
63	Tucson, AZ	55
48	Tulsa, OK	80
154	Tuscaloosa, AL	14
247	Tyler, TX	5
211	Utica-Rome, NY	8
182	Valdosta, GA	11
125	Vallejo-Fairfield, CA	20
279	Victoria, TX	3
211	Vineland, NJ	8
95	Visalia-Porterville, CA	31
167	Waco, TX	13
258	Warner Robins, GA	4
69	Warren-Farmington Hills, MI M.D.	49
11	Washington (greater) DC-VA-MD-WV	325
14	Washington, DC-VA-MD-WV M.D.	303
311	Waterloo-Cedar Falls, IA	2
311	Wausau, WI	2
311	Wenatchee, WA	2
44	West Palm Beach, FL M.D.	86
258	Wheeling, WV-OH	4
182	Wichita Falls, TX	11
104	Wichita, KS	26
311	Williamsport, PA	2
89	Wilmington, DE-MD-NJ M.D.	35
202	Wilmington, NC	9
279	Winchester, VA-WV	3
118	Winston-Salem, NC	22
144	Worcester, MA	16
133	York-Hanover, PA	18
94	Youngstown, OH-PA	32
258	Yuba City, CA	4
191	Yuma, AZ	10

Source: Reported data from the F.B.I. "Crime in the United States 2009"
*Includes nonnegligent manslaughter.

9. Murders in 2009 (continued)
National Total = 15,241 Murders*

RANK	METROPOLITAN AREA	MURDERS
1	New York (greater), NY-NJ-PA	778
2	Los Angeles (greater), CA	768
3	Los Angeles County, CA M.D.	699
4	New York-W. Plains NY-NJ M.D.	551
5	Houston, TX	462
6	Detroit (greater), MI	447
7	Philadelphia (greater) PA-NJ-MD-DE	436
8	Detroit-Livonia-Dearborn, MI M.D.	398
9	Miami (greater), FL	377
10	Philadelphia, PA M.D.	351
11	Atlanta, GA	325
11	Washington (greater) DC-VA-MD-WV	325
13	Dallas (greater), TX	310
14	Washington, DC-VA-MD-WV M.D.	303
15	Baltimore-Towson, MD	298
16	San Francisco (greater), CA	292
17	New Orleans, LA	252
18	Dallas-Plano-Irving, TX M.D.	235
19	Phoenix-Mesa-Scottsdale, AZ	230
20	Oakland-Fremont, CA M.D.	227
21	Miami-Dade County, FL M.D.	215
22	Riverside-San Bernardino, CA	214
23	St. Louis, MO-IL	210
24	Kansas City, MO-KS	163
25	Memphis, TN-MS-AR	157
26	Newark-Union, NJ-PA M.D.	134
27	Las Vegas-Paradise, NV	133
28	San Antonio, TX	130
29	Cleveland-Elyria-Mentor, OH	122
30	Jacksonville, FL	120
31	Boston (greater), MA-NH	111
31	Indianapolis, IN	111
31	Orlando, FL	111
31	Pittsburgh, PA	111
35	Baton Rouge, LA	110
35	Nashville-Davidson, TN	110
37	Birmingham-Hoover, AL	105
38	Columbus, OH	103
39	Denver-Aurora, CO	100
40	Tampa-St Petersburg, FL	99
41	Charlotte-Gastonia, NC-SC	98
42	Cincinnati-Middletown, OH-KY-IN	89
42	Seattle-Tacoma-Bellevue, WA	89
44	Sacramento, CA	86
44	West Palm Beach, FL M.D.	86
46	Oklahoma City, OK	83
47	Milwaukee, WI	81
48	Tulsa, OK	80
49	Fort Lauderdale, FL M.D.	76
50	Bakersfield, CA	75
50	Boston-Quincy, MA M.D.	75
50	Buffalo-Niagara Falls, NY	75
50	Fort Worth-Arlington, TX M.D.	75
50	San Diego, CA	75
55	Richmond, VA	72
56	Fresno, CA	69
56	Louisville, KY-IN	69
56	Santa Ana-Anaheim, CA M.D.	69
59	Albuquerque, NM	68
60	San Francisco-S. Mateo, CA M.D.	65
61	Nassau-Suffolk, NY M.D.	63
62	Seattle-Bellevue-Everett, WA M.D.	60
63	Minneapolis-St. Paul, MN-WI	55
63	Tucson, AZ	55
65	Little Rock, AR	51
65	Salinas, CA	51
65	Stockton, CA	51
68	Camden, NJ M.D.	50
69	Warren-Farmington Hills, MI M.D.	49
70	Portland-Vancouver, OR-WA	48
71	Columbia, SC	47
71	Dayton, OH	47
71	Providence-New Bedford, RI-MA	47
74	Hartford, CT	46
74	Modesto, CA	46
74	San Jose, CA	46
77	Flint, MI	44
77	Jackson, MS	44
79	Augusta, GA-SC	42
79	North Port-Bradenton-Sarasota, FL	42
81	Austin-Round Rock, TX	41
82	Cape Coral-Fort Myers, FL	40
82	McAllen-Edinburg-Mission, TX	40
84	Montgomery, AL	39
85	Rochester, NY	37
85	Shreveport-Bossier City, LA	37
87	Charleston-North Charleston, SC	36
87	Mobile, AL	36
89	Fayetteville, NC	35
89	Greensboro-High Point, NC	35
89	Toledo, OH	35
89	Wilmington, DE-MD-NJ M.D.	35
93	Omaha-Council Bluffs, NE-IA	33
94	Youngstown, OH-PA	32
95	Knoxville, TN	31
95	Savannah, GA	31
95	Visalia-Porterville, CA	31
98	Edison, NJ M.D.	30
98	New Haven-Milford, CT	30
100	Durham-Chapel Hill, NC	29
100	Oxnard-Thousand Oaks, CA	29
100	Tacoma, WA M.D.	29
103	Akron, OH	28
104	Charleston, WV	26
104	Harrisburg-Carlisle, PA	26
104	Merced, CA	26
104	Palm Bay-Melbourne, FL	26
104	Raleigh-Cary, NC	26
104	Scranton--Wilkes-Barre, PA	26
104	Wichita, KS	26
111	Lakeland, FL	25
112	Albany-Schenectady-Troy, NY	24
112	Allentown, PA-NJ	24
112	Atlantic City, NJ	24
112	Chattanooga, TN-GA	24
112	Springfield, MA	24
117	Macon, GA	23
118	Bethesda-Frederick, MD M.D.	22
118	Fort Wayne, IN	22
118	Winston-Salem, NC	22
121	Colorado Springs, CO	21
121	Huntsville, AL	21
121	Salt Lake City, UT	21
121	Syracuse, NY	21
125	Clarksville, TN-KY	20
125	Florence, SC	20
125	Topeka, KS	20
125	Vallejo-Fairfield, CA	20
129	Beaumont-Port Arthur, TX	19
129	Deltona-Daytona Beach, FL	19
129	Lake Charles, LA	19
129	South Bend-Mishawaka, IN-MI	19
133	Bridgeport-Stamford, CT	18
133	Cambridge-Newton, MA M.D.	18
133	Pensacola, FL	18
133	Reno-Sparks, NV	18
133	York-Hanover, PA	18
138	Binghamton, NY	17
138	Hickory, NC	17
138	Laredo, TX	17
138	Longview, TX	17
138	Port St. Lucie, FL	17
138	Trenton-Ewing, NJ	17
144	Brunswick, GA	16
144	Columbus, GA-AL	16
144	El Paso, TX	16
144	Reading, PA	16
144	Worcester, MA	16
149	Corpus Christi, TX	15
149	Jackson, TN	15
149	Peabody, MA M.D.	15
149	Santa Fe, NM	15
149	Texarkana, TX-Texarkana, AR	15
154	Anchorage, AK	14
154	Battle Creek, MI	14
154	Goldsboro, NC	14
154	Honolulu, HI	14
154	Houma, LA	14
154	Lafayette, LA	14
154	Lexington-Fayette, KY	14
154	Lubbock, TX	14
154	Naples-Marco Island, FL	14
154	Pine Bluff, AR	14
154	Pueblo, CO	14
154	Saginaw, MI	14
154	Tuscaloosa, AL	14
167	Amarillo, TX	13
167	Grand Rapids-Wyoming, MI	13
167	Killeen-Temple-Fort Hood, TX	13
167	Portland, ME	13
167	Poughkeepsie, NY	13
167	Spartanburg, SC	13
167	Tallahassee, FL	13
167	Waco, TX	13
175	Gulfport-Biloxi, MS	12
175	Kalamazoo-Portage, MI	12
175	Lancaster, PA	12
175	Lansing-East Lansing, MI	12
175	Ocala, FL	12
175	Roanoke, VA	12

Note: All listings are for Metropolitan Statistical Areas (M.S.A.s) except for those ending with "M.D." Listings with "M.D." are Metropolitan Divisions which are smaller parts of eleven large M.S.A.s. See explanatory note at beginning of metropolitan area section.

RANK	METROPOLITAN AREA	MURDERS
175	Sumter, SC	12
182	Asheville, NC	11
182	Athens-Clarke County, GA	11
182	Jacksonville, NC	11
182	Johnson City, TN	11
182	Madison, WI	11
182	Rocky Mount, NC	11
182	Santa Barbara-Santa Maria, CA	11
182	Valdosta, GA	11
182	Wichita Falls, TX	11
191	Alexandria, LA	10
191	Boise City-Nampa, ID	10
191	Chico, CA	10
191	Erie, PA	10
191	Fort Smith, AR-OK	10
191	Hattiesburg, MS	10
191	Hot Springs, AR	10
191	Kingsport, TN-VA	10
191	Santa Cruz-Watsonville, CA	10
191	Spokane, WA	10
191	Yuma, AZ	10
202	Albany, GA	9
202	Anderson, SC	9
202	Auburn, AL	9
202	Danville, VA	9
202	Lawton, OK	9
202	Panama City-Lynn Haven, FL	9
202	San Angelo, TX	9
202	Santa Rosa-Petaluma, CA	9
202	Wilmington, NC	9
211	Bellingham, WA	8
211	Blacksburg, VA	8
211	Brownsville-Harlingen, TX	8
211	Elkhart-Goshen, IN	8
211	Fayetteville, AR-MO	8
211	Jackson, MI	8
211	Lake Havasu City-Kingman, AZ	8
211	Lebanon, PA	8
211	Springfield, MO	8
211	Utica-Rome, NY	8
211	Vineland, NJ	8
222	Abilene, TX	7
222	Boulder, CO	7
222	Des Moines-West Des Moines, IA	7
222	Evansville, IN-KY	7
222	Florence-Muscle Shoals, AL	7
222	Gainesville, FL	7
222	Great Falls, MT	7
222	Greeley, CO	7
222	Las Cruces, NM	7
222	Odessa, TX	7
222	Ogden-Clearfield, UT	7
222	Pascagoula, MS	7
222	Salem, OR	7
222	Salisbury, MD	7
222	Sebastian-Vero Beach, FL	7
237	Ann Arbor, MI	6
237	Anniston-Oxford, AL	6
237	Danville, IL	6
237	Flagstaff, AZ	6
237	Fort Collins-Loveland, CO	6
237	Janesville, WI	6
237	Lima, OH	6

RANK	METROPOLITAN AREA	MURDERS
237	Manchester-Nashua, NH	6
237	Muncie, IN	6
237	Muskegon-Norton Shores, MI	6
247	College Station-Bryan, TX	5
247	Crestview-Fort Walton Beach, FL	5
247	Duluth, MN-WI	5
247	Gainesville, GA	5
247	Green Bay, WI	5
247	Jefferson City, MO	5
247	Lynchburg, VA	5
247	Monroe, MI	5
247	Olympia, WA	5
247	Racine, WI	5
247	Tyler, TX	5
258	Bangor, ME	4
258	Barnstable Town, MA	4
258	Bremerton-Silverdale, WA	4
258	Burlington, NC	4
258	Cheyenne, WY	4
258	Dover, DE	4
258	Elmira, NY	4
258	Eugene-Springfield, OR	4
258	Holland-Grand Haven, MI	4
258	Lincoln, NE	4
258	Manhattan, KS	4
258	Norwich-New London, CT	4
258	Provo-Orem, UT	4
258	San Luis Obispo, CA	4
258	Sherman-Denison, TX	4
258	Sioux City, IA-NE-SD	4
258	Springfield, OH	4
258	St. Joseph, MO-KS	4
258	Warner Robins, GA	4
258	Wheeling, WV-OH	4
258	Yuba City, CA	4
279	Altoona, PA	3
279	Appleton, WI	3
279	Bay City, MI	3
279	Billings, MT	3
279	Bismarck, ND	3
279	Bloomington, IN	3
279	Bowling Green, KY	3
279	Cleveland, TN	3
279	Columbia, MO	3
279	Decatur, IL	3
279	Dothan, AL	3
279	El Centro, CA	3
279	Farmington, NM	3
279	Gadsden, AL	3
279	Hagerstown-Martinsburg, MD-WV	3
279	Ithaca, NY	3
279	Jonesboro, AR	3
279	Madera, CA	3
279	Mansfield, OH	3
279	Michigan City-La Porte, IN	3
279	Midland, TX	3
279	Morristown, TN	3
279	Mount Vernon-Anacortes, WA	3
279	Niles-Benton Harbor, MI	3
279	Palm Coast, FL	3
279	Prescott, AZ	3
279	Punta Gorda, FL	3
279	Redding, CA	3

RANK	METROPOLITAN AREA	MURDERS
279	Rockingham County, NH M.D.	3
279	Rome, GA	3
279	Victoria, TX	3
279	Winchester, VA-WV	3
311	Bend, OR	2
311	Cape Girardeau, MO-IL	2
311	Coeur d'Alene, ID	2
311	Cumberland, MD-WV	2
311	Dalton, GA	2
311	Decatur, AL	2
311	Dubuque, IA	2
311	Elizabethtown, KY	2
311	Fargo, ND-MN	2
311	Fond du Lac, WI	2
311	Grand Junction, CO	2
311	Harrisonburg, VA	2
311	Hinesville, GA	2
311	Idaho Falls, ID	2
311	Iowa City, IA	2
311	Medford, OR	2
311	Morgantown, WV	2
311	Owensboro, KY	2
311	Pittsfield, MA	2
311	Rapid City, SD	2
311	Sandusky, OH	2
311	Sheboygan, WI	2
311	State College, PA	2
311	St. Cloud, MN	2
311	St. George, UT	2
311	Waterloo-Cedar Falls, IA	2
311	Wausau, WI	2
311	Wenatchee, WA	2
311	Williamsport, PA	2
340	Anderson, IN	1
340	Burlington-South Burlington, VT	1
340	Cedar Rapids, IA	1
340	Charlottesville, VA	1
340	Corvallis, OR	1
340	Eau Claire, WI	1
340	Kennewick-Pasco-Richland, WA	1
340	Kingston, NY	1
340	Kokomo, IN	1
340	La Crosse, WI-MN	1
340	Lewiston, ID-WA	1
340	Longview, WA	1
340	Mankato-North Mankato, MN	1
340	Missoula, MT	1
340	Napa, CA	1
340	Ocean City, NJ	1
340	Pocatello, ID	1
340	Rochester, MN	1
340	Sioux Falls, SD	1
359	Ames, IA	0
359	Carson City, NV	0
359	Casper, WY	0
359	Columbus, IN	0
359	Glens Falls, NY	0
359	Grand Forks, ND-MN	0
359	Lafayette, IN	0
359	Lawrence, KS	0
359	Lewiston-Auburn, ME	0
359	Logan, UT-ID	0
359	Oshkosh-Neenah, WI	0

Source: Reported data from the F.B.I. "Crime in the United States 2009"
*Includes nonnegligent manslaughter.

10. Murder Rate in 2009
National Rate = 5.0 Murders per 100,000 Population*

RANK	METROPOLITAN AREA	RATE
152	Abilene, TX	4.4
163	Akron, OH	4.0
214	Albany-Schenectady-Troy, NY	2.8
105	Albany, GA	5.4
46	Albuquerque, NM	7.9
77	Alexandria, LA	6.5
208	Allentown, PA-NJ	2.9
244	Altoona, PA	2.4
110	Amarillo, TX	5.3
359	Ames, IA	0.0
141	Anchorage, AK	4.6
346	Anderson, IN	0.8
133	Anderson, SC	4.8
296	Ann Arbor, MI	1.7
110	Anniston-Oxford, AL	5.3
319	Appleton, WI	1.4
221	Asheville, NC	2.7
89	Athens-Clarke County, GA	5.8
88	Atlanta, GA	5.9
31	Atlantic City, NJ	8.8
75	Auburn, AL	6.6
49	Augusta, GA-SC	7.8
244	Austin-Round Rock, TX	2.4
26	Bakersfield, CA	9.2
11	Baltimore-Towson, MD	11.1
221	Bangor, ME	2.7
286	Barnstable Town, MA	1.8
4	Baton Rouge, LA	14.0
14	Battle Creek, MI	10.4
214	Bay City, MI	2.8
126	Beaumont-Port Arthur, TX	5.0
163	Bellingham, WA	4.0
330	Bend, OR	1.2
286	Bethesda-Frederick, MD M.D.	1.8
267	Billings, MT	2.0
62	Binghamton, NY	7.0
25	Birmingham-Hoover, AL	9.3
214	Bismarck, ND	2.8
126	Blacksburg, VA	5.0
306	Bloomington, IN	1.6
306	Boise City-Nampa, ID	1.6
244	Boston (greater), MA-NH	2.4
172	Boston-Quincy, MA M.D.	3.9
244	Boulder, CO	2.4
235	Bowling Green, KY	2.5
296	Bremerton-Silverdale, WA	1.7
267	Bridgeport-Stamford, CT	2.0
267	Brownsville-Harlingen, TX	2.0
3	Brunswick, GA	15.5
73	Buffalo-Niagara Falls, NY	6.7
352	Burlington-South Burlington, VT	0.5
221	Burlington, NC	2.7
330	Cambridge-Newton, MA M.D.	1.2
163	Camden, NJ M.D.	4.0
75	Cape Coral-Fort Myers, FL	6.6
262	Cape Girardeau, MO-IL	2.1
359	Carson City, NV	0.0
359	Casper, WY	0.0
356	Cedar Rapids, IA	0.4
102	Charleston-North Charleston, SC	5.5
37	Charleston, WV	8.6
97	Charlotte-Gastonia, NC-SC	5.6
352	Charlottesville, VA	0.5
141	Chattanooga, TN-GA	4.6
150	Cheyenne, WY	4.5
150	Chico, CA	4.5
160	Cincinnati-Middletown, OH-KY-IN	4.1
50	Clarksville, TN-KY	7.5
89	Cleveland-Elyria-Mentor, OH	5.8
229	Cleveland, TN	2.6
319	Coeur d'Alene, ID	1.4
244	College Station-Bryan, TX	2.4
196	Colorado Springs, CO	3.3
286	Columbia, MO	1.8
80	Columbia, SC	6.3
97	Columbus, GA-AL	5.6
359	Columbus, IN	0.0
93	Columbus, OH	5.7
181	Corpus Christi, TX	3.6
330	Corvallis, OR	1.2
214	Crestview-Fort Walton Beach, FL	2.8
267	Cumberland, MD-WV	2.0
133	Dallas (greater), TX	4.8
105	Dallas-Plano-Irving, TX M.D.	5.4
312	Dalton, GA	1.5
50	Danville, IL	7.5
39	Danville, VA	8.5
97	Dayton, OH	5.6
325	Decatur, AL	1.3
214	Decatur, IL	2.8
176	Deltona-Daytona Beach, FL	3.8
172	Denver-Aurora, CO	3.9
330	Des Moines-West Des Moines, IA	1.2
18	Detroit (greater), MI	10.1
2	Detroit-Livonia-Dearborn, MI M.D.	20.6
262	Dothan, AL	2.1
235	Dover, DE	2.5
259	Dubuque, IA	2.2
286	Duluth, MN-WI	1.8
89	Durham-Chapel Hill, NC	5.8
351	Eau Claire, WI	0.6
325	Edison, NJ M.D.	1.3
286	El Centro, CA	1.8
262	El Paso, TX	2.1
286	Elizabethtown, KY	1.8
163	Elkhart-Goshen, IN	4.0
141	Elmira, NY	4.6
181	Erie, PA	3.6
335	Eugene-Springfield, OR	1.1
267	Evansville, IN-KY	2.0
341	Fargo, ND-MN	1.0
244	Farmington, NM	2.4
296	Fayetteville, AR-MO	1.7
23	Fayetteville, NC	9.7
137	Flagstaff, AZ	4.7
16	Flint, MI	10.3
133	Florence-Muscle Shoals, AL	4.8
21	Florence, SC	9.9
267	Fond du Lac, WI	2.0
267	Fort Collins-Loveland, CO	2.0
155	Fort Lauderdale, FL M.D.	4.3
190	Fort Smith, AR-OK	3.4
110	Fort Wayne, IN	5.3
189	Fort Worth-Arlington, TX M.D.	3.5
50	Fresno, CA	7.5
208	Gadsden, AL	2.9
221	Gainesville, FL	2.7
229	Gainesville, GA	2.6
359	Glens Falls, NY	0.0
8	Goldsboro, NC	12.3
359	Grand Forks, ND-MN	0.0
319	Grand Junction, CO	1.4
296	Grand Rapids-Wyoming, MI	1.7
39	Great Falls, MT	8.5
221	Greeley, CO	2.7
306	Green Bay, WI	1.6
130	Greensboro-High Point, NC	4.9
121	Gulfport-Biloxi, MS	5.1
335	Hagerstown-Martinsburg, MD-WV	1.1
130	Harrisburg-Carlisle, PA	4.9
296	Harrisonburg, VA	1.7
141	Hartford, CT	4.6
62	Hattiesburg, MS	7.0
141	Hickory, NC	4.6
208	Hinesville, GA	2.9
312	Holland-Grand Haven, MI	1.5
312	Honolulu, HI	1.5
18	Hot Springs, AR	10.1
67	Houma, LA	6.9
46	Houston, TX	7.9
116	Huntsville, AL	5.2
306	Idaho Falls, ID	1.6
79	Indianapolis, IN	6.4
325	Iowa City, IA	1.3
205	Ithaca, NY	3.0
28	Jacksonville, FL	9.1
77	Jacksonville, NC	6.5
126	Jackson, MI	5.0
44	Jackson, MS	8.1
6	Jackson, TN	13.2
178	Janesville, WI	3.7
190	Jefferson City, MO	3.4
97	Johnson City, TN	5.6
235	Jonesboro, AR	2.5
178	Kalamazoo-Portage, MI	3.7
46	Kansas City, MO-KS	7.9
356	Kennewick-Pasco-Richland, WA	0.4
190	Killeen-Temple-Fort Hood, TX	3.4
196	Kingsport, TN-VA	3.3
352	Kingston, NY	0.5
152	Knoxville, TN	4.4
341	Kokomo, IN	1.0
346	La Crosse, WI-MN	0.8
359	Lafayette, IN	0.0
110	Lafayette, LA	5.3
22	Lake Charles, LA	9.8
163	Lake Havasu City-Kingman, AZ	4.0
155	Lakeland, FL	4.3
244	Lancaster, PA	2.4
229	Lansing-East Lansing, MI	2.6

Note: All listings are for Metropolitan Statistical Areas (M.S.A.s) except for those ending with "M.D." Listings with "M.D." are Metropolitan Divisions which are smaller parts of eleven large M.S.A.s. See explanatory note at beginning of metropolitan area section.

Alpha Order - Metro Area (continued)

RANK	METROPOLITAN AREA	RATE
62	Laredo, TX	7.0
190	Las Cruces, NM	3.4
62	Las Vegas-Paradise, NV	7.0
359	Lawrence, KS	0.0
45	Lawton, OK	8.0
83	Lebanon, PA	6.1
359	Lewiston-Auburn, ME	0.0
306	Lewiston, ID-WA	1.6
205	Lexington-Fayette, KY	3.0
93	Lima, OH	5.7
325	Lincoln, NE	1.3
56	Little Rock, AR	7.4
359	Logan, UT-ID	0.0
41	Longview, TX	8.2
341	Longview, WA	1.0
60	Los Angeles County, CA M.D.	7.1
85	Los Angeles (greater), CA	6.0
102	Louisville, KY-IN	5.5
121	Lubbock, TX	5.1
267	Lynchburg, VA	2.0
20	Macon, GA	10.0
267	Madera, CA	2.0
281	Madison, WI	1.9
312	Manchester-Nashua, NH	1.5
201	Manhattan, KS	3.2
335	Mankato-North Mankato, MN	1.1
244	Mansfield, OH	2.4
105	McAllen-Edinburg-Mission, TX	5.4
341	Medford, OR	1.0
9	Memphis, TN-MS-AR	12.1
14	Merced, CA	10.4
67	Miami (greater), FL	6.9
35	Miami-Dade County, FL M.D.	8.7
221	Michigan City-La Porte, IN	2.7
255	Midland, TX	2.3
116	Milwaukee, WI	5.2
296	Minneapolis-St. Paul, MN-WI	1.7
345	Missoula, MT	0.9
31	Mobile, AL	8.8
30	Modesto, CA	8.9
196	Monroe, MI	3.3
13	Montgomery, AL	10.5
296	Morgantown, WV	1.7
259	Morristown, TN	2.2
235	Mount Vernon-Anacortes, WA	2.5
116	Muncie, IN	5.2
190	Muskegon-Norton Shores, MI	3.4
348	Napa, CA	0.7
152	Naples-Marco Island, FL	4.4
67	Nashville-Davidson, TN	6.9
259	Nassau-Suffolk, NY M.D.	2.2
176	New Haven-Milford, CT	3.8
1	New Orleans, LA	21.4
160	New York (greater), NY-NJ-PA	4.1
137	New York-W. Plains NY-NJ M.D.	4.7
80	Newark-Union, NJ-PA M.D.	6.3
281	Niles-Benton Harbor, MI	1.9
83	North Port-Bradenton-Sarasota, FL	6.1
208	Norwich-New London, CT	2.9
28	Oakland-Fremont, CA M.D.	9.1
181	Ocala, FL	3.6
335	Ocean City, NJ	1.1
116	Odessa, TX	5.2

RANK	METROPOLITAN AREA	RATE
325	Ogden-Clearfield, UT	1.3
70	Oklahoma City, OK	6.8
267	Olympia, WA	2.0
172	Omaha-Council Bluffs, NE-IA	3.9
110	Orlando, FL	5.3
359	Oshkosh-Neenah, WI	0.0
286	Owensboro, KY	1.8
181	Oxnard-Thousand Oaks, CA	3.6
133	Palm Bay-Melbourne, FL	4.8
203	Palm Coast, FL	3.1
102	Panama City-Lynn Haven, FL	5.5
141	Pascagoula, MS	4.6
267	Peabody, MA M.D.	2.0
163	Pensacola, FL	4.0
58	Philadelphia (greater) PA-NJ-MD-DE	7.3
31	Philadelphia, PA M.D.	8.8
110	Phoenix-Mesa-Scottsdale, AZ	5.3
4	Pine Bluff, AR	14.0
137	Pittsburgh, PA	4.7
312	Pittsfield, MA	1.5
335	Pocatello, ID	1.1
160	Port St. Lucie, FL	4.1
262	Portland-Vancouver, OR-WA	2.1
235	Portland, ME	2.5
281	Poughkeepsie, NY	1.9
319	Prescott, AZ	1.4
208	Providence-New Bedford, RI-MA	2.9
348	Provo-Orem, UT	0.7
31	Pueblo, CO	8.8
267	Punta Gorda, FL	2.0
235	Racine, WI	2.5
255	Raleigh-Cary, NC	2.3
306	Rapid City, SD	1.6
172	Reading, PA	3.9
296	Redding, CA	1.7
155	Reno-Sparks, NV	4.3
89	Richmond, VA	5.8
121	Riverside-San Bernardino, CA	5.1
163	Roanoke, VA	4.0
352	Rochester, MN	0.5
181	Rochester, NY	3.6
348	Rockingham County, NH M.D.	0.7
50	Rocky Mount, NC	7.5
203	Rome, GA	3.1
163	Sacramento, CA	4.0
62	Saginaw, MI	7.0
286	Salem, OR	1.8
7	Salinas, CA	12.5
93	Salisbury, MD	5.7
281	Salt Lake City, UT	1.9
41	San Angelo, TX	8.2
80	San Antonio, TX	6.3
235	San Diego, CA	2.5
70	San Francisco (greater), CA	6.8
178	San Francisco-S. Mateo, CA M.D.	3.7
235	San Jose, CA	2.5
312	San Luis Obispo, CA	1.5
229	Sandusky, OH	2.6
255	Santa Ana-Anaheim, CA M.D.	2.3
221	Santa Barbara-Santa Maria, CA	2.7
163	Santa Cruz-Watsonville, CA	4.0
16	Santa Fe, NM	10.3
281	Santa Rosa-Petaluma, CA	1.9

RANK	METROPOLITAN AREA	RATE
26	Savannah, GA	9.2
137	Scranton--Wilkes-Barre, PA	4.7
255	Seattle-Bellevue-Everett, WA M.D.	2.3
229	Seattle-Tacoma-Bellevue, WA	2.6
116	Sebastian-Vero Beach, FL	5.2
296	Sheboygan, WI	1.7
196	Sherman-Denison, TX	3.3
24	Shreveport-Bossier City, LA	9.4
214	Sioux City, IA-NE-SD	2.8
356	Sioux Falls, SD	0.4
85	South Bend-Mishawaka, IN-MI	6.0
141	Spartanburg, SC	4.6
262	Spokane, WA	2.1
190	Springfield, MA	3.4
286	Springfield, MO	1.8
208	Springfield, OH	2.9
319	State College, PA	1.4
50	Stockton, CA	7.5
335	St. Cloud, MN	1.1
319	St. George, UT	1.4
201	St. Joseph, MO-KS	3.2
56	St. Louis, MO-IL	7.4
10	Sumter, SC	11.5
196	Syracuse, NY	3.3
181	Tacoma, WA M.D.	3.6
181	Tallahassee, FL	3.6
181	Tampa-St Petersburg, FL	3.6
12	Texarkana, TX-Texarkana, AR	11.0
105	Toledo, OH	5.4
35	Topeka, KS	8.7
141	Trenton-Ewing, NJ	4.6
105	Tucson, AZ	5.4
37	Tulsa, OK	8.6
73	Tuscaloosa, AL	6.7
244	Tyler, TX	2.4
221	Utica-Rome, NY	2.7
41	Valdosta, GA	8.2
130	Vallejo-Fairfield, CA	4.9
229	Victoria, TX	2.6
121	Vineland, NJ	5.1
59	Visalia-Porterville, CA	7.2
97	Waco, TX	5.6
205	Warner Robins, GA	3.0
267	Warren-Farmington Hills, MI M.D.	2.0
85	Washington (greater) DC-VA-MD-WV	6.0
60	Washington, DC-VA-MD-WV M.D.	7.1
330	Waterloo-Cedar Falls, IA	1.2
312	Wausau, WI	1.5
286	Wenatchee, WA	1.8
70	West Palm Beach, FL M.D.	6.8
214	Wheeling, WV-OH	2.8
50	Wichita Falls, TX	7.5
155	Wichita, KS	4.3
296	Williamsport, PA	1.7
126	Wilmington, DE-MD-NJ M.D.	5.0
235	Wilmington, NC	2.5
244	Winchester, VA-WV	2.4
141	Winston-Salem, NC	4.6
267	Worcester, MA	2.0
159	York-Hanover, PA	4.2
93	Youngstown, OH-PA	5.7
244	Yuba City, CA	2.4
121	Yuma, AZ	5.1

Source: Reported data from the F.B.I. "Crime in the United States 2009"

*Includes nonnegligent manslaughter.

10. Murder Rate in 2009 (continued)
National Rate = 5.0 Murders per 100,000 Population*

RANK	METROPOLITAN AREA	RATE
1	New Orleans, LA	21.4
2	Detroit-Livonia-Dearborn, MI M.D.	20.6
3	Brunswick, GA	15.5
4	Baton Rouge, LA	14.0
4	Pine Bluff, AR	14.0
6	Jackson, TN	13.2
7	Salinas, CA	12.5
8	Goldsboro, NC	12.3
9	Memphis, TN-MS-AR	12.1
10	Sumter, SC	11.5
11	Baltimore-Towson, MD	11.1
12	Texarkana, TX-Texarkana, AR	11.0
13	Montgomery, AL	10.5
14	Battle Creek, MI	10.4
14	Merced, CA	10.4
16	Flint, MI	10.3
16	Santa Fe, NM	10.3
18	Detroit (greater), MI	10.1
18	Hot Springs, AR	10.1
20	Macon, GA	10.0
21	Florence, SC	9.9
22	Lake Charles, LA	9.8
23	Fayetteville, NC	9.7
24	Shreveport-Bossier City, LA	9.4
25	Birmingham-Hoover, AL	9.3
26	Bakersfield, CA	9.2
26	Savannah, GA	9.2
28	Jacksonville, FL	9.1
28	Oakland-Fremont, CA M.D.	9.1
30	Modesto, CA	8.9
31	Atlantic City, NJ	8.8
31	Mobile, AL	8.8
31	Philadelphia, PA M.D.	8.8
31	Pueblo, CO	8.8
35	Miami-Dade County, FL M.D.	8.7
35	Topeka, KS	8.7
37	Charleston, WV	8.6
37	Tulsa, OK	8.6
39	Danville, VA	8.5
39	Great Falls, MT	8.5
41	Longview, TX	8.2
41	San Angelo, TX	8.2
41	Valdosta, GA	8.2
44	Jackson, MS	8.1
45	Lawton, OK	8.0
46	Albuquerque, NM	7.9
46	Houston, TX	7.9
46	Kansas City, MO-KS	7.9
49	Augusta, GA-SC	7.8
50	Clarksville, TN-KY	7.5
50	Danville, IL	7.5
50	Fresno, CA	7.5
50	Rocky Mount, NC	7.5
50	Stockton, CA	7.5
50	Wichita Falls, TX	7.5
56	Little Rock, AR	7.4
56	St. Louis, MO-IL	7.4
58	Philadelphia (greater) PA-NJ-MD-DE	7.3
59	Visalia-Porterville, CA	7.2
60	Los Angeles County, CA M.D.	7.1
60	Washington, DC-VA-MD-WV M.D.	7.1
62	Binghamton, NY	7.0
62	Hattiesburg, MS	7.0
62	Laredo, TX	7.0
62	Las Vegas-Paradise, NV	7.0
62	Saginaw, MI	7.0
67	Houma, LA	6.9
67	Miami (greater), FL	6.9
67	Nashville-Davidson, TN	6.9
70	Oklahoma City, OK	6.8
70	San Francisco (greater), CA	6.8
70	West Palm Beach, FL M.D.	6.8
73	Buffalo-Niagara Falls, NY	6.7
73	Tuscaloosa, AL	6.7
75	Auburn, AL	6.6
75	Cape Coral-Fort Myers, FL	6.6
77	Alexandria, LA	6.5
77	Jacksonville, NC	6.5
79	Indianapolis, IN	6.4
80	Columbia, SC	6.3
80	Newark-Union, NJ-PA M.D.	6.3
80	San Antonio, TX	6.3
83	Lebanon, PA	6.1
83	North Port-Bradenton-Sarasota, FL	6.1
85	Los Angeles (greater), CA	6.0
85	South Bend-Mishawaka, IN-MI	6.0
85	Washington (greater) DC-VA-MD-WV	6.0
88	Atlanta, GA	5.9
89	Athens-Clarke County, GA	5.8
89	Cleveland-Elyria-Mentor, OH	5.8
89	Durham-Chapel Hill, NC	5.8
89	Richmond, VA	5.8
93	Columbus, OH	5.7
93	Lima, OH	5.7
93	Salisbury, MD	5.7
93	Youngstown, OH-PA	5.7
97	Charlotte-Gastonia, NC-SC	5.6
97	Columbus, GA-AL	5.6
97	Dayton, OH	5.6
97	Johnson City, TN	5.6
97	Waco, TX	5.6
102	Charleston-North Charleston, SC	5.5
102	Louisville, KY-IN	5.5
102	Panama City-Lynn Haven, FL	5.5
105	Albany, GA	5.4
105	Dallas-Plano-Irving, TX M.D.	5.4
105	McAllen-Edinburg-Mission, TX	5.4
105	Toledo, OH	5.4
105	Tucson, AZ	5.4
110	Amarillo, TX	5.3
110	Anniston-Oxford, AL	5.3
110	Fort Wayne, IN	5.3
110	Lafayette, LA	5.3
110	Orlando, FL	5.3
110	Phoenix-Mesa-Scottsdale, AZ	5.3
116	Huntsville, AL	5.2
116	Milwaukee, WI	5.2
116	Muncie, IN	5.2
116	Odessa, TX	5.2
116	Sebastian-Vero Beach, FL	5.2
121	Gulfport-Biloxi, MS	5.1
121	Lubbock, TX	5.1
121	Riverside-San Bernardino, CA	5.1
121	Vineland, NJ	5.1
121	Yuma, AZ	5.1
126	Beaumont-Port Arthur, TX	5.0
126	Blacksburg, VA	5.0
126	Jackson, MI	5.0
126	Wilmington, DE-MD-NJ M.D.	5.0
130	Greensboro-High Point, NC	4.9
130	Harrisburg-Carlisle, PA	4.9
130	Vallejo-Fairfield, CA	4.9
133	Anderson, SC	4.8
133	Dallas (greater), TX	4.8
133	Florence-Muscle Shoals, AL	4.8
133	Palm Bay-Melbourne, FL	4.8
137	Flagstaff, AZ	4.7
137	New York-W. Plains NY-NJ M.D.	4.7
137	Pittsburgh, PA	4.7
137	Scranton--Wilkes-Barre, PA	4.7
141	Anchorage, AK	4.6
141	Chattanooga, TN-GA	4.6
141	Elmira, NY	4.6
141	Hartford, CT	4.6
141	Hickory, NC	4.6
141	Pascagoula, MS	4.6
141	Spartanburg, SC	4.6
141	Trenton-Ewing, NJ	4.6
141	Winston-Salem, NC	4.6
150	Cheyenne, WY	4.5
150	Chico, CA	4.5
152	Abilene, TX	4.4
152	Knoxville, TN	4.4
152	Naples-Marco Island, FL	4.4
155	Fort Lauderdale, FL M.D.	4.3
155	Lakeland, FL	4.3
155	Reno-Sparks, NV	4.3
155	Wichita, KS	4.3
159	York-Hanover, PA	4.2
160	Cincinnati-Middletown, OH-KY-IN	4.1
160	New York (greater), NY-NJ-PA	4.1
160	Port St. Lucie, FL	4.1
163	Akron, OH	4.0
163	Bellingham, WA	4.0
163	Camden, NJ M.D.	4.0
163	Elkhart-Goshen, IN	4.0
163	Lake Havasu City-Kingman, AZ	4.0
163	Pensacola, FL	4.0
163	Roanoke, VA	4.0
163	Sacramento, CA	4.0
163	Santa Cruz-Watsonville, CA	4.0
172	Boston-Quincy, MA M.D.	3.9
172	Denver-Aurora, CO	3.9
172	Omaha-Council Bluffs, NE-IA	3.9
172	Reading, PA	3.9
176	Deltona-Daytona Beach, FL	3.8
176	New Haven-Milford, CT	3.8
178	Janesville, WI	3.7
178	Kalamazoo-Portage, MI	3.7
178	San Francisco-S. Mateo, CA M.D.	3.7

Note: All listings are for Metropolitan Statistical Areas (M.S.A.s) except for those ending with "M.D." Listings with "M.D." are Metropolitan Divisions which are smaller parts of eleven large M.S.A.s. See explanatory note at beginning of metropolitan area section.

RANK	METROPOLITAN AREA	RATE
181	Corpus Christi, TX	3.6
181	Erie, PA	3.6
181	Ocala, FL	3.6
181	Oxnard-Thousand Oaks, CA	3.6
181	Rochester, NY	3.6
181	Tacoma, WA M.D.	3.6
181	Tallahassee, FL	3.6
181	Tampa-St Petersburg, FL	3.6
189	Fort Worth-Arlington, TX M.D.	3.5
190	Fort Smith, AR-OK	3.4
190	Jefferson City, MO	3.4
190	Killeen-Temple-Fort Hood, TX	3.4
190	Las Cruces, NM	3.4
190	Muskegon-Norton Shores, MI	3.4
190	Springfield, MA	3.4
196	Colorado Springs, CO	3.3
196	Kingsport, TN-VA	3.3
196	Monroe, MI	3.3
196	Sherman-Denison, TX	3.3
196	Syracuse, NY	3.3
201	Manhattan, KS	3.2
201	St. Joseph, MO-KS	3.2
203	Palm Coast, FL	3.1
203	Rome, GA	3.1
205	Ithaca, NY	3.0
205	Lexington-Fayette, KY	3.0
205	Warner Robins, GA	3.0
208	Allentown, PA-NJ	2.9
208	Gadsden, AL	2.9
208	Hinesville, GA	2.9
208	Norwich-New London, CT	2.9
208	Providence-New Bedford, RI-MA	2.9
208	Springfield, OH	2.9
214	Albany-Schenectady-Troy, NY	2.8
214	Bay City, MI	2.8
214	Bismarck, ND	2.8
214	Crestview-Fort Walton Beach, FL	2.8
214	Decatur, IL	2.8
214	Sioux City, IA-NE-SD	2.8
214	Wheeling, WV-OH	2.8
221	Asheville, NC	2.7
221	Bangor, ME	2.7
221	Burlington, NC	2.7
221	Gainesville, FL	2.7
221	Greeley, CO	2.7
221	Michigan City-La Porte, IN	2.7
221	Santa Barbara-Santa Maria, CA	2.7
221	Utica-Rome, NY	2.7
229	Cleveland, TN	2.6
229	Gainesville, GA	2.6
229	Lansing-East Lansing, MI	2.6
229	Sandusky, OH	2.6
229	Seattle-Tacoma-Bellevue, WA	2.6
229	Victoria, TX	2.6
235	Bowling Green, KY	2.5
235	Dover, DE	2.5
235	Jonesboro, AR	2.5
235	Mount Vernon-Anacortes, WA	2.5
235	Portland, ME	2.5
235	Racine, WI	2.5
235	San Diego, CA	2.5
235	San Jose, CA	2.5
235	Wilmington, NC	2.5
244	Altoona, PA	2.4
244	Austin-Round Rock, TX	2.4
244	Boston (greater), MA-NH	2.4
244	Boulder, CO	2.4
244	College Station-Bryan, TX	2.4
244	Farmington, NM	2.4
244	Lancaster, PA	2.4
244	Mansfield, OH	2.4
244	Tyler, TX	2.4
244	Winchester, VA-WV	2.4
244	Yuba City, CA	2.4
255	Midland, TX	2.3
255	Raleigh-Cary, NC	2.3
255	Santa Ana-Anaheim, CA M.D.	2.3
255	Seattle-Bellevue-Everett, WA M.D.	2.3
259	Dubuque, IA	2.2
259	Morristown, TN	2.2
259	Nassau-Suffolk, NY M.D.	2.2
262	Cape Girardeau, MO-IL	2.1
262	Dothan, AL	2.1
262	El Paso, TX	2.1
262	Portland-Vancouver, OR-WA	2.1
262	Spokane, WA	2.1
267	Billings, MT	2.0
267	Bridgeport-Stamford, CT	2.0
267	Brownsville-Harlingen, TX	2.0
267	Cumberland, MD-WV	2.0
267	Evansville, IN-KY	2.0
267	Fond du Lac, WI	2.0
267	Fort Collins-Loveland, CO	2.0
267	Lynchburg, VA	2.0
267	Madera, CA	2.0
267	Olympia, WA	2.0
267	Peabody, MA M.D.	2.0
267	Punta Gorda, FL	2.0
267	Warren-Farmington Hills, MI M.D.	2.0
267	Worcester, MA	2.0
281	Madison, WI	1.9
281	Niles-Benton Harbor, MI	1.9
281	Poughkeepsie, NY	1.9
281	Salt Lake City, UT	1.9
281	Santa Rosa-Petaluma, CA	1.9
286	Barnstable Town, MA	1.8
286	Bethesda-Frederick, MD M.D.	1.8
286	Columbia, MO	1.8
286	Duluth, MN-WI	1.8
286	El Centro, CA	1.8
286	Elizabethtown, KY	1.8
286	Owensboro, KY	1.8
286	Salem, OR	1.8
286	Springfield, MO	1.8
286	Wenatchee, WA	1.8
296	Ann Arbor, MI	1.7
296	Bremerton-Silverdale, WA	1.7
296	Fayetteville, AR-MO	1.7
296	Grand Rapids-Wyoming, MI	1.7
296	Harrisonburg, VA	1.7
296	Minneapolis-St. Paul, MN-WI	1.7
296	Morgantown, WV	1.7
296	Redding, CA	1.7
296	Sheboygan, WI	1.7
296	Williamsport, PA	1.7
306	Bloomington, IN	1.6
306	Boise City-Nampa, ID	1.6
306	Green Bay, WI	1.6
306	Idaho Falls, ID	1.6
306	Lewiston, ID-WA	1.6
306	Rapid City, SD	1.6
312	Dalton, GA	1.5
312	Holland-Grand Haven, MI	1.5
312	Honolulu, HI	1.5
312	Manchester-Nashua, NH	1.5
312	Pittsfield, MA	1.5
312	San Luis Obispo, CA	1.5
312	Wausau, WI	1.5
319	Appleton, WI	1.4
319	Coeur d'Alene, ID	1.4
319	Grand Junction, CO	1.4
319	Prescott, AZ	1.4
319	State College, PA	1.4
319	St. George, UT	1.4
325	Decatur, AL	1.3
325	Edison, NJ M.D.	1.3
325	Iowa City, IA	1.3
325	Lincoln, NE	1.3
325	Ogden-Clearfield, UT	1.3
330	Bend, OR	1.2
330	Cambridge-Newton, MA M.D.	1.2
330	Corvallis, OR	1.2
330	Des Moines-West Des Moines, IA	1.2
330	Waterloo-Cedar Falls, IA	1.2
335	Eugene-Springfield, OR	1.1
335	Hagerstown-Martinsburg, MD-WV	1.1
335	Mankato-North Mankato, MN	1.1
335	Ocean City, NJ	1.1
335	Pocatello, ID	1.1
335	St. Cloud, MN	1.1
341	Fargo, ND-MN	1.0
341	Kokomo, IN	1.0
341	Longview, WA	1.0
341	Medford, OR	1.0
345	Missoula, MT	0.9
346	Anderson, IN	0.8
346	La Crosse, WI-MN	0.8
348	Napa, CA	0.7
348	Provo-Orem, UT	0.7
348	Rockingham County, NH M.D.	0.7
351	Eau Claire, WI	0.6
352	Burlington-South Burlington, VT	0.5
352	Charlottesville, VA	0.5
352	Kingston, NY	0.5
352	Rochester, MN	0.5
356	Cedar Rapids, IA	0.4
356	Kennewick-Pasco-Richland, WA	0.4
356	Sioux Falls, SD	0.4
359	Ames, IA	0.0
359	Carson City, NV	0.0
359	Casper, WY	0.0
359	Columbus, IN	0.0
359	Glens Falls, NY	0.0
359	Grand Forks, ND-MN	0.0
359	Lafayette, IN	0.0
359	Lawrence, KS	0.0
359	Lewiston-Auburn, ME	0.0
359	Logan, UT-ID	0.0
359	Oshkosh-Neenah, WI	0.0

Source: Reported data from the F.B.I. "Crime in the United States 2009"
*Includes nonnegligent manslaughter.

11. Percent Change in Murder Rate: 2008 to 2009
National Percent Change = 8.1% Decrease*

RANK	METROPOLITAN AREA	% CHANGE
105	Abilene, TX	0.0
71	Akron, OH	17.6
99	Albany-Schenectady-Troy, NY	3.7
NA	Albany, GA**	NA
98	Albuquerque, NM	3.9
NA	Alexandria, LA**	NA
100	Allentown, PA-NJ	3.6
208	Altoona, PA	(25.0)
165	Amarillo, TX	(13.1)
294	Ames, IA	(100.0)
46	Anchorage, AK	39.4
NA	Anderson, IN**	NA
263	Anderson, SC	(51.5)
249	Ann Arbor, MI	(45.2)
NA	Anniston-Oxford, AL**	NA
29	Appleton, WI	55.6
64	Asheville, NC	22.7
13	Athens-Clarke County, GA	123.1
191	Atlanta, GA	(20.3)
78	Atlantic City, NJ	14.3
40	Auburn, AL	46.7
102	Augusta, GA-SC	1.3
66	Austin-Round Rock, TX	20.0
56	Bakersfield, CA	29.6
134	Baltimore-Towson, MD	(1.8)
16	Bangor, ME	107.7
18	Barnstable Town, MA	100.0
95	Baton Rouge, LA	4.5
9	Battle Creek, MI	181.1
NA	Bay City, MI**	NA
96	Beaumont-Port Arthur, TX	4.2
3	Bellingham, WA	300.0
NA	Bend, OR***	NA
174	Bethesda-Frederick, MD M.D.	(14.3)
105	Billings, MT	0.0
1	Binghamton, NY	775.0
153	Birmingham-Hoover, AL	(9.7)
38	Bismarck, ND	47.4
54	Blacksburg, VA	31.6
216	Bloomington, IN	(27.3)
18	Boise City-Nampa, ID	100.0
146	Boston (greater), MA-NH	(7.7)
168	Boston-Quincy, MA M.D.	(13.3)
NA	Boulder, CO**	NA
NA	Bowling Green, KY**	NA
186	Bremerton-Silverdale, WA	(19.0)
254	Bridgeport-Stamford, CT	(48.7)
240	Brownsville-Harlingen, TX	(39.4)
NA	Brunswick, GA**	NA
26	Buffalo-Niagara Falls, NY	71.8
NA	Burlington-South Burlington, VT**	NA
105	Burlington, NC	0.0
66	Cambridge-Newton, MA M.D.	20.0
236	Camden, NJ M.D.	(36.5)
167	Cape Coral-Fort Myers, FL	(13.2)
262	Cape Girardeau, MO-IL	(51.2)
105	Carson City, NV	0.0
294	Casper, WY	(100.0)
289	Cedar Rapids, IA	(80.0)
214	Charleston-North Charleston, SC	(26.7)
22	Charleston, WV	87.0
221	Charlotte-Gastonia, NC-SC	(30.9)
293	Charlottesville, VA	(89.1)
182	Chattanooga, TN-GA	(17.9)
52	Cheyenne, WY	32.4
44	Chico, CA	40.6
NA	Cincinnati-Middletown, OH-KY-IN**	NA
NA	Clarksville, TN-KY**	NA
NA	Cleveland-Elyria-Mentor, OH**	NA
137	Cleveland, TN	(3.7)
NA	Coeur d'Alene, ID**	NA
258	College Station-Bryan, TX	(51.0)
231	Colorado Springs, CO	(34.0)
272	Columbia, MO	(58.1)
76	Columbia, SC	14.5
269	Columbus, GA-AL	(54.8)
294	Columbus, IN	(100.0)
181	Columbus, OH	(17.4)
218	Corpus Christi, TX	(29.4)
105	Corvallis, OR	0.0
NA	Crestview-Fort Walton Beach, FL**	NA
277	Cumberland, MD-WV	(60.8)
164	Dallas (greater), TX	(12.7)
160	Dallas-Plano-Irving, TX M.D.	(11.5)
15	Dalton, GA	114.3
NA	Danville, IL**	NA
224	Danville, VA	(31.5)
88	Dayton, OH	7.7
284	Decatur, AL	(67.5)
NA	Decatur, IL**	NA
60	Deltona-Daytona Beach, FL	26.7
65	Denver-Aurora, CO	21.9
NA	Des Moines-West Des Moines, IA**	NA
NA	Detroit (greater), MI**	NA
NA	Detroit-Livonia-Dearborn, MI M.D.**	NA
208	Dothan, AL	(25.0)
258	Dover, DE	(51.0)
NA	Dubuque, IA***	NA
66	Duluth, MN-WI	20.0
212	Durham-Chapel Hill, NC	(25.6)
268	Eau Claire, WI	(53.8)
86	Edison, NJ M.D.	8.3
281	El Centro, CA	(63.3)
187	El Paso, TX	(19.2)
NA	Elizabethtown, KY**	NA
105	Elkhart-Goshen, IN	0.0
105	Elmira, NY	0.0
81	Erie, PA	12.5
265	Eugene-Springfield, OR	(52.2)
NA	Evansville, IN-KY**	NA
NA	Fargo, ND-MN***	NA
280	Farmington, NM	(63.1)
142	Fayetteville, AR-MO	(5.6)
175	Fayetteville, NC	(14.9)
17	Flagstaff, AZ	104.3
NA	Flint, MI**	NA
78	Florence-Muscle Shoals, AL	14.3
154	Florence, SC	(10.0)
18	Fond du Lac, WI	100.0
71	Fort Collins-Loveland, CO	17.6
155	Fort Lauderdale, FL M.D.	(10.4)
42	Fort Smith, AR-OK	41.7
165	Fort Wayne, IN	(13.1)
192	Fort Worth-Arlington, TX M.D.	(20.5)
96	Fresno, CA	4.2
242	Gadsden, AL	(39.6)
73	Gainesville, FL	17.4
NA	Gainesville, GA**	NA
294	Glens Falls, NY	(100.0)
59	Goldsboro, NC	26.8
294	Grand Forks, ND-MN	(100.0)
287	Grand Junction, CO	(71.4)
NA	Grand Rapids-Wyoming, MI**	NA
6	Great Falls, MT	254.2
81	Greeley, CO	12.5
12	Green Bay, WI	128.6
201	Greensboro-High Point, NC	(23.4)
NA	Gulfport-Biloxi, MS**	NA
265	Hagerstown-Martinsburg, MD-WV	(52.2)
49	Harrisburg-Carlisle, PA	36.1
105	Harrisonburg, VA	0.0
85	Hartford, CT	9.5
NA	Hattiesburg, MS**	NA
244	Hickory, NC	(42.5)
274	Hinesville, GA	(58.6)
NA	Holland-Grand Haven, MI**	NA
208	Honolulu, HI	(25.0)
11	Hot Springs, AR	146.3
58	Houma, LA	27.8
102	Houston, TX	1.3
86	Huntsville, AL	8.3
105	Idaho Falls, ID	0.0
170	Indianapolis, IN	(13.5)
288	Iowa City, IA	(75.9)
32	Ithaca, NY	50.0
144	Jacksonville, FL	(6.2)
135	Jacksonville, NC	(3.0)
NA	Jackson, MI**	NA
245	Jackson, MS	(42.6)
32	Jackson, TN	50.0
37	Janesville, WI	48.0
NA	Jefferson City, MO**	NA
5	Johnson City, TN	273.3
273	Jonesboro, AR	(58.3)
NA	Kalamazoo-Portage, MI**	NA
NA	Kansas City, MO-KS**	NA
270	Kennewick-Pasco-Richland, WA	(55.6)
194	Killeen-Temple-Fort Hood, TX	(20.9)
239	Kingsport, TN-VA	(37.7)
291	Kingston, NY	(84.8)
204	Knoxville, TN	(24.1)
282	Kokomo, IN	(66.7)
105	La Crosse, WI-MN	0.0
294	Lafayette, IN	(100.0)
148	Lafayette, LA	(8.6)
NA	Lake Charles, LA**	NA
105	Lake Havasu City-Kingman, AZ	0.0
247	Lakeland, FL	(43.4)
27	Lancaster, PA	71.4
NA	Lansing-East Lansing, MI**	NA

Note: All listings are for Metropolitan Statistical Areas (M.S.A.s) except for those ending with "M.D." Listings with "M.D." are Metropolitan Divisions which are smaller parts of eleven large M.S.A.s. See explanatory note at beginning of metropolitan area section.

RANK	METROPOLITAN AREA	% CHANGE
31	Laredo, TX	52.2
205	Las Cruces, NM	(24.4)
139	Las Vegas-Paradise, NV	(4.1)
294	Lawrence, KS	(100.0)
NA	Lawton, OK**	NA
4	Lebanon, PA	281.3
294	Lewiston-Auburn, ME	(100.0)
285	Lewiston, ID-WA	(68.0)
NA	Lexington-Fayette, KY**	NA
7	Lima, OH	200.0
233	Lincoln, NE	(35.0)
NA	Little Rock, AR**	NA
294	Logan, UT-ID	(100.0)
83	Longview, TX	12.3
256	Longview, WA	(50.0)
169	Los Angeles County, CA M.D.	(13.4)
161	Los Angeles (greater), CA	(11.8)
NA	Louisville, KY-IN**	NA
30	Lubbock, TX	54.5
240	Lynchburg, VA	(39.4)
105	Macon, GA	0.0
286	Madera, CA	(70.1)
203	Madison, WI	(24.0)
NA	Manchester-Nashua, NH**	NA
135	Manhattan, KS	(3.0)
NA	Mankato-North Mankato, MN***	NA
105	Mansfield, OH	0.0
199	McAllen-Edinburg-Mission, TX	(22.9)
105	Medford, OR	0.0
138	Memphis, TN-MS-AR	(4.0)
63	Merced, CA	23.8
150	Miami (greater), FL	(9.2)
151	Miami-Dade County, FL M.D.	(9.4)
243	Michigan City-La Porte, IN	(41.3)
213	Midland, TX	(25.8)
92	Milwaukee, WI	6.1
238	Minneapolis-St. Paul, MN-WI	(37.0)
267	Missoula, MT	(52.6)
248	Mobile, AL	(45.0)
36	Modesto, CA	48.3
NA	Monroe, MI**	NA
48	Montgomery, AL	38.2
NA	Morgantown, WV**	NA
105	Morristown, TN	0.0
283	Mount Vernon-Anacortes, WA	(67.1)
2	Muncie, IN	477.8
NA	Muskegon-Norton Shores, MI**	NA
163	Napa, CA	(12.5)
23	Naples-Marco Island, FL	76.0
91	Nashville-Davidson, TN	6.2
162	Nassau-Suffolk, NY M.D.	(12.0)
NA	New Haven-Milford, CT**	NA
141	New Orleans, LA	(4.5)
149	New York (greater), NY-NJ-PA	(8.9)
159	New York-W. Plains NY-NJ M.D.	(11.3)
133	Newark-Union, NJ-PA M.D.	(1.6)
NA	Niles-Benton Harbor, MI**	NA
NA	North Port-Bradenton-Sarasota, FL**	NA
222	Norwich-New London, CT	(31.0)
104	Oakland-Fremont, CA M.D.	1.1
251	Ocala, FL	(46.3)
NA	Ocean City, NJ***	NA
225	Odessa, TX	(31.6)

RANK	METROPOLITAN AREA	% CHANGE
202	Ogden-Clearfield, UT	(23.5)
NA	Oklahoma City, OK**	NA
61	Olympia, WA	25.0
233	Omaha-Council Bluffs, NE-IA	(35.0)
228	Orlando, FL	(32.9)
294	Oshkosh-Neenah, WI	(100.0)
NA	Owensboro, KY**	NA
146	Oxnard-Thousand Oaks, CA	(7.7)
74	Palm Bay-Melbourne, FL	17.1
NA	Palm Coast, FL***	NA
182	Panama City-Lynn Haven, FL	(17.9)
46	Pascagoula, MS	39.4
105	Peabody, MA M.D.	0.0
206	Pensacola, FL	(24.5)
189	Philadelphia (greater) PA-NJ-MD-DE	(19.8)
171	Philadelphia, PA M.D.	(13.7)
188	Phoenix-Mesa-Scottsdale, AZ	(19.7)
227	Pine Bluff, AR	(32.7)
152	Pittsburgh, PA	(9.6)
105	Pittsfield, MA	0.0
105	Pocatello, ID	0.0
57	Port St. Lucie, FL	28.1
94	Portland-Vancouver, OR-WA	5.0
70	Portland, ME	19.0
219	Poughkeepsie, NY	(29.6)
197	Prescott, AZ	(22.2)
84	Providence-New Bedford, RI-MA	11.5
75	Provo-Orem, UT	16.7
NA	Pueblo, CO**	NA
105	Punta Gorda, FL	0.0
258	Racine, WI	(51.0)
261	Raleigh-Cary, NC	(51.1)
263	Rapid City, SD	(51.5)
105	Reading, PA	0.0
198	Redding, CA	(22.7)
69	Reno-Sparks, NV	19.4
145	Richmond, VA	(6.5)
101	Riverside-San Bernardino, CA	2.0
232	Roanoke, VA	(34.4)
290	Rochester, MN	(81.5)
208	Rochester, NY	(25.0)
105	Rockingham County, NH M.D.	0.0
NA	Rocky Mount, NC**	NA
NA	Rome, GA**	NA
206	Sacramento, CA	(24.5)
NA	Saginaw, MI**	NA
271	Salem, OR	(56.1)
45	Salinas, CA	40.4
175	Salisbury, MD	(14.9)
105	Salt Lake City, UT	0.0
35	San Angelo, TX	49.1
184	San Antonio, TX	(18.2)
179	San Diego, CA	(16.7)
177	San Francisco (greater), CA	(16.0)
252	San Francisco-S. Mateo, CA M.D.	(46.4)
172	San Jose, CA	(13.8)
105	San Luis Obispo, CA	0.0
105	Sandusky, OH	0.0
140	Santa Ana-Anaheim, CA M.D.	(4.2)
199	Santa Barbara-Santa Maria, CA	(22.9)
61	Santa Cruz-Watsonville, CA	25.0
77	Santa Fe, NM	14.4
215	Santa Rosa-Petaluma, CA	(26.9)

RANK	METROPOLITAN AREA	% CHANGE
80	Savannah, GA	13.6
90	Scranton--Wilkes-Barre, PA	6.8
NA	Seattle-Bellevue-Everett, WA M.D.**	NA
NA	Seattle-Tacoma-Bellevue, WA**	NA
25	Sebastian-Vero Beach, FL	73.3
NA	Sheboygan, WI***	NA
53	Sherman-Denison, TX	32.0
132	Shreveport-Bossier City, LA	(1.1)
229	Sioux City, IA-NE-SD	(33.3)
292	Sioux Falls, SD	(86.7)
NA	South Bend-Mishawaka, IN-MI**	NA
226	Spartanburg, SC	(32.4)
255	Spokane, WA	(48.8)
55	Springfield, MA	30.8
NA	Springfield, MO**	NA
275	Springfield, OH	(59.2)
NA	State College, PA***	NA
39	Stockton, CA	47.1
14	St. Cloud, MN	120.0
105	St. George, UT	0.0
50	St. Joseph, MO-KS	33.3
158	St. Louis, MO-IL	(10.8)
NA	Sumter, SC**	NA
223	Syracuse, NY	(31.3)
NA	Tacoma, WA M.D.**	NA
178	Tallahassee, FL	(16.3)
235	Tampa-St Petersburg, FL	(35.7)
8	Texarkana, TX-Texarkana, AR	197.3
24	Toledo, OH	74.2
21	Topeka, KS	97.7
220	Trenton-Ewing, NJ	(30.3)
246	Tucson, AZ	(43.2)
89	Tulsa, OK	7.5
185	Tuscaloosa, AL	(18.3)
279	Tyler, TX	(62.5)
105	Utica-Rome, NY	0.0
10	Valdosta, GA	164.5
180	Vallejo-Fairfield, CA	(16.9)
41	Victoria, TX	44.4
253	Vineland, NJ	(46.9)
217	Visalia-Porterville, CA	(28.7)
172	Waco, TX	(13.8)
256	Warner Robins, GA	(50.0)
NA	Warren-Farmington Hills, MI M.D.**	NA
190	Washington (greater) DC-VA-MD-WV	(20.0)
195	Washington, DC-VA-MD-WV M.D.	(21.1)
229	Waterloo-Cedar Falls, IA	(33.3)
NA	Wausau, WI**	NA
278	Wenatchee, WA	(60.9)
156	West Palm Beach, FL M.D.	(10.5)
50	Wheeling, WV-OH	33.3
28	Wichita Falls, TX	59.6
196	Wichita, KS	(21.8)
105	Williamsport, PA	0.0
237	Wilmington, DE-MD-NJ M.D.	(36.7)
250	Wilmington, NC	(45.7)
32	Winchester, VA-WV	50.0
143	Winston-Salem, NC	(6.1)
93	Worcester, MA	5.3
157	York-Hanover, PA	(10.6)
193	Youngstown, OH-PA	(20.8)
276	Yuba City, CA	(60.0)
42	Yuma, AZ	41.7

Source: CQ Press using reported data from the F.B.I. "Crime in the United States 2009"
*Includes nonnegligent manslaughter. **Not available. ***These metro areas had murder rates of 0 in 2008 but had at least one murder in 2009. Calculating percent increase from zero results in an infinite number. This is shown as "NA."

11. Percent Change in Murder Rate: 2008 to 2009 (continued)
National Percent Change = 8.1% Decrease*

RANK	METROPOLITAN AREA	% CHANGE	RANK	METROPOLITAN AREA	% CHANGE	RANK	METROPOLITAN AREA	% CHANGE
1	Binghamton, NY	775.0	61	Olympia, WA	25.0	105	Pittsfield, MA	0.0
2	Muncie, IN	477.8	61	Santa Cruz-Watsonville, CA	25.0	105	Pocatello, ID	0.0
3	Bellingham, WA	300.0	63	Merced, CA	23.8	105	Punta Gorda, FL	0.0
4	Lebanon, PA	281.3	64	Asheville, NC	22.7	105	Reading, PA	0.0
5	Johnson City, TN	273.3	65	Denver-Aurora, CO	21.9	105	Rockingham County, NH M.D.	0.0
6	Great Falls, MT	254.2	66	Austin-Round Rock, TX	20.0	105	Salt Lake City, UT	0.0
7	Lima, OH	200.0	66	Cambridge-Newton, MA M.D.	20.0	105	San Luis Obispo, CA	0.0
8	Texarkana, TX-Texarkana, AR	197.3	66	Duluth, MN-WI	20.0	105	Sandusky, OH	0.0
9	Battle Creek, MI	181.1	69	Reno-Sparks, NV	19.4	105	St. George, UT	0.0
10	Valdosta, GA	164.5	70	Portland, ME	19.0	105	Utica-Rome, NY	0.0
11	Hot Springs, AR	146.3	71	Akron, OH	17.6	105	Williamsport, PA	0.0
12	Green Bay, WI	128.6	71	Fort Collins-Loveland, CO	17.6	132	Shreveport-Bossier City, LA	(1.1)
13	Athens-Clarke County, GA	123.1	73	Gainesville, FL	17.4	133	Newark-Union, NJ-PA M.D.	(1.6)
14	St. Cloud, MN	120.0	74	Palm Bay-Melbourne, FL	17.1	134	Baltimore-Towson, MD	(1.8)
15	Dalton, GA	114.3	75	Provo-Orem, UT	16.7	135	Jacksonville, NC	(3.0)
16	Bangor, ME	107.7	76	Columbia, SC	14.5	135	Manhattan, KS	(3.0)
17	Flagstaff, AZ	104.3	77	Santa Fe, NM	14.4	137	Cleveland, TN	(3.7)
18	Barnstable Town, MA	100.0	78	Atlantic City, NJ	14.3	138	Memphis, TN-MS-AR	(4.0)
18	Boise City-Nampa, ID	100.0	78	Florence-Muscle Shoals, AL	14.3	139	Las Vegas-Paradise, NV	(4.1)
18	Fond du Lac, WI	100.0	80	Savannah, GA	13.6	140	Santa Ana-Anaheim, CA M.D.	(4.2)
21	Topeka, KS	97.7	81	Erie, PA	12.5	141	New Orleans, LA	(4.5)
22	Charleston, WV	87.0	81	Greeley, CO	12.5	142	Fayetteville, AR-MO	(5.6)
23	Naples-Marco Island, FL	76.0	83	Longview, TX	12.3	143	Winston-Salem, NC	(6.1)
24	Toledo, OH	74.2	84	Providence-New Bedford, RI-MA	11.5	144	Jacksonville, FL	(6.2)
25	Sebastian-Vero Beach, FL	73.3	85	Hartford, CT	9.5	145	Richmond, VA	(6.5)
26	Buffalo-Niagara Falls, NY	71.8	86	Edison, NJ M.D.	8.3	146	Boston (greater), MA-NH	(7.7)
27	Lancaster, PA	71.4	86	Huntsville, AL	8.3	146	Oxnard-Thousand Oaks, CA	(7.7)
28	Wichita Falls, TX	59.6	88	Dayton, OH	7.7	148	Lafayette, LA	(8.6)
29	Appleton, WI	55.6	89	Tulsa, OK	7.5	149	New York (greater), NY-NJ-PA	(8.9)
30	Lubbock, TX	54.5	90	Scranton--Wilkes-Barre, PA	6.8	150	Miami (greater), FL	(9.2)
31	Laredo, TX	52.2	91	Nashville-Davidson, TN	6.2	151	Miami-Dade County, FL M.D.	(9.4)
32	Ithaca, NY	50.0	92	Milwaukee, WI	6.1	152	Pittsburgh, PA	(9.6)
32	Jackson, TN	50.0	93	Worcester, MA	5.3	153	Birmingham-Hoover, AL	(9.7)
32	Winchester, VA-WV	50.0	94	Portland-Vancouver, OR-WA	5.0	154	Florence, SC	(10.0)
35	San Angelo, TX	49.1	95	Baton Rouge, LA	4.5	155	Fort Lauderdale, FL M.D.	(10.4)
36	Modesto, CA	48.3	96	Beaumont-Port Arthur, TX	4.2	156	West Palm Beach, FL M.D.	(10.5)
37	Janesville, WI	48.0	96	Fresno, CA	4.2	157	York-Hanover, PA	(10.6)
38	Bismarck, ND	47.4	98	Albuquerque, NM	3.9	158	St. Louis, MO-IL	(10.8)
39	Stockton, CA	47.1	99	Albany-Schenectady-Troy, NY	3.7	159	New York-W. Plains NY-NJ M.D.	(11.3)
40	Auburn, AL	46.7	100	Allentown, PA-NJ	3.6	160	Dallas-Plano-Irving, TX M.D.	(11.5)
41	Victoria, TX	44.4	101	Riverside-San Bernardino, CA	2.0	161	Los Angeles (greater), CA	(11.8)
42	Fort Smith, AR-OK	41.7	102	Augusta, GA-SC	1.3	162	Nassau-Suffolk, NY M.D.	(12.0)
42	Yuma, AZ	41.7	102	Houston, TX	1.3	163	Napa, CA	(12.5)
44	Chico, CA	40.6	104	Oakland-Fremont, CA M.D.	1.1	164	Dallas (greater), TX	(12.7)
45	Salinas, CA	40.4	105	Abilene, TX	0.0	165	Amarillo, TX	(13.1)
46	Anchorage, AK	39.4	105	Billings, MT	0.0	165	Fort Wayne, IN	(13.1)
46	Pascagoula, MS	39.4	105	Burlington, NC	0.0	167	Cape Coral-Fort Myers, FL	(13.2)
48	Montgomery, AL	38.2	105	Carson City, NV	0.0	168	Boston-Quincy, MA M.D.	(13.3)
49	Harrisburg-Carlisle, PA	36.1	105	Corvallis, OR	0.0	169	Los Angeles County, CA M.D.	(13.4)
50	St. Joseph, MO-KS	33.3	105	Elkhart-Goshen, IN	0.0	170	Indianapolis, IN	(13.5)
50	Wheeling, WV-OH	33.3	105	Elmira, NY	0.0	171	Philadelphia, PA M.D.	(13.7)
52	Cheyenne, WY	32.4	105	Harrisonburg, VA	0.0	172	San Jose, CA	(13.8)
53	Sherman-Denison, TX	32.0	105	Idaho Falls, ID	0.0	172	Waco, TX	(13.8)
54	Blacksburg, VA	31.6	105	La Crosse, WI-MN	0.0	174	Bethesda-Frederick, MD M.D.	(14.3)
55	Springfield, MA	30.8	105	Lake Havasu City-Kingman, AZ	0.0	175	Fayetteville, NC	(14.9)
56	Bakersfield, CA	29.6	105	Macon, GA	0.0	175	Salisbury, MD	(14.9)
57	Port St. Lucie, FL	28.1	105	Mansfield, OH	0.0	177	San Francisco (greater), CA	(16.0)
58	Houma, LA	27.8	105	Medford, OR	0.0	178	Tallahassee, FL	(16.3)
59	Goldsboro, NC	26.8	105	Morristown, TN	0.0	179	San Diego, CA	(16.7)
60	Deltona-Daytona Beach, FL	26.7	105	Peabody, MA M.D.	0.0	180	Vallejo-Fairfield, CA	(16.9)

Note: All listings are for Metropolitan Statistical Areas (M.S.A.s) except for those ending with "M.D." Listings with "M.D." are Metropolitan Divisions which are smaller parts of eleven large M.S.A.s. See explanatory note at beginning of metropolitan area section.

Rank Order - Metro Area (continued)

RANK	METROPOLITAN AREA	% CHANGE
181	Columbus, OH	(17.4)
182	Chattanooga, TN-GA	(17.9)
182	Panama City-Lynn Haven, FL	(17.9)
184	San Antonio, TX	(18.2)
185	Tuscaloosa, AL	(18.3)
186	Bremerton-Silverdale, WA	(19.0)
187	El Paso, TX	(19.2)
188	Phoenix-Mesa-Scottsdale, AZ	(19.7)
189	Philadelphia (greater) PA-NJ-MD-DE	(19.8)
190	Washington (greater) DC-VA-MD-WV	(20.0)
191	Atlanta, GA	(20.3)
192	Fort Worth-Arlington, TX M.D.	(20.5)
193	Youngstown, OH-PA	(20.8)
194	Killeen-Temple-Fort Hood, TX	(20.9)
195	Washington, DC-VA-MD-WV M.D.	(21.1)
196	Wichita, KS	(21.8)
197	Prescott, AZ	(22.2)
198	Redding, CA	(22.7)
199	McAllen-Edinburg-Mission, TX	(22.9)
199	Santa Barbara-Santa Maria, CA	(22.9)
201	Greensboro-High Point, NC	(23.4)
202	Ogden-Clearfield, UT	(23.5)
203	Madison, WI	(24.0)
204	Knoxville, TN	(24.1)
205	Las Cruces, NM	(24.4)
206	Pensacola, FL	(24.5)
206	Sacramento, CA	(24.5)
208	Altoona, PA	(25.0)
208	Dothan, AL	(25.0)
208	Honolulu, HI	(25.0)
208	Rochester, NY	(25.0)
212	Durham-Chapel Hill, NC	(25.6)
213	Midland, TX	(25.8)
214	Charleston-North Charleston, SC	(26.7)
215	Santa Rosa-Petaluma, CA	(26.9)
216	Bloomington, IN	(27.3)
217	Visalia-Porterville, CA	(28.7)
218	Corpus Christi, TX	(29.4)
219	Poughkeepsie, NY	(29.6)
220	Trenton-Ewing, NJ	(30.3)
221	Charlotte-Gastonia, NC-SC	(30.9)
222	Norwich-New London, CT	(31.0)
223	Syracuse, NY	(31.3)
224	Danville, VA	(31.5)
225	Odessa, TX	(31.6)
226	Spartanburg, SC	(32.4)
227	Pine Bluff, AR	(32.7)
228	Orlando, FL	(32.9)
229	Sioux City, IA-NE-SD	(33.3)
229	Waterloo-Cedar Falls, IA	(33.3)
231	Colorado Springs, CO	(34.0)
232	Roanoke, VA	(34.4)
233	Lincoln, NE	(35.0)
233	Omaha-Council Bluffs, NE-IA	(35.0)
235	Tampa-St Petersburg, FL	(35.7)
236	Camden, NJ M.D.	(36.5)
237	Wilmington, DE-MD-NJ M.D.	(36.7)
238	Minneapolis-St. Paul, MN-WI	(37.0)
239	Kingsport, TN-VA	(37.7)
240	Brownsville-Harlingen, TX	(39.4)
240	Lynchburg, VA	(39.4)
242	Gadsden, AL	(39.6)
243	Michigan City-La Porte, IN	(41.3)

RANK	METROPOLITAN AREA	% CHANGE
244	Hickory, NC	(42.5)
245	Jackson, MS	(42.6)
246	Tucson, AZ	(43.2)
247	Lakeland, FL	(43.4)
248	Mobile, AL	(45.0)
249	Ann Arbor, MI	(45.2)
250	Wilmington, NC	(45.7)
251	Ocala, FL	(46.3)
252	San Francisco-S. Mateo, CA M.D.	(46.4)
253	Vineland, NJ	(46.9)
254	Bridgeport-Stamford, CT	(48.7)
255	Spokane, WA	(48.8)
256	Longview, WA	(50.0)
256	Warner Robins, GA	(50.0)
258	College Station-Bryan, TX	(51.0)
258	Dover, DE	(51.0)
258	Racine, WI	(51.0)
261	Raleigh-Cary, NC	(51.1)
262	Cape Girardeau, MO-IL	(51.2)
263	Anderson, SC	(51.5)
263	Rapid City, SD	(51.5)
265	Eugene-Springfield, OR	(52.2)
265	Hagerstown-Martinsburg, MD-WV	(52.2)
267	Missoula, MT	(52.6)
268	Eau Claire, WI	(53.8)
269	Columbus, GA-AL	(54.8)
270	Kennewick-Pasco-Richland, WA	(55.6)
271	Salem, OR	(56.1)
272	Columbia, MO	(58.1)
273	Jonesboro, AR	(58.3)
274	Hinesville, GA	(58.6)
275	Springfield, OH	(59.2)
276	Yuba City, CA	(60.0)
277	Cumberland, MD-WV	(60.8)
278	Wenatchee, WA	(60.9)
279	Tyler, TX	(62.5)
280	Farmington, NM	(63.1)
281	El Centro, CA	(63.3)
282	Kokomo, IN	(66.7)
283	Mount Vernon-Anacortes, WA	(67.1)
284	Decatur, AL	(67.5)
285	Lewiston, ID-WA	(68.0)
286	Madera, CA	(70.1)
287	Grand Junction, CO	(71.4)
288	Iowa City, IA	(75.9)
289	Cedar Rapids, IA	(80.0)
290	Rochester, MN	(81.5)
291	Kingston, NY	(84.8)
292	Sioux Falls, SD	(86.7)
293	Charlottesville, VA	(89.1)
294	Ames, IA	(100.0)
294	Casper, WY	(100.0)
294	Columbus, IN	(100.0)
294	Glens Falls, NY	(100.0)
294	Grand Forks, ND-MN	(100.0)
294	Lafayette, IN	(100.0)
294	Lawrence, KS	(100.0)
294	Lewiston-Auburn, ME	(100.0)
294	Logan, UT-ID	(100.0)
294	Oshkosh-Neenah, WI	(100.0)
NA	Albany, GA**	NA
NA	Alexandria, LA**	NA
NA	Anderson, IN**	NA

RANK	METROPOLITAN AREA	% CHANGE
NA	Anniston-Oxford, AL**	NA
NA	Bay City, MI**	NA
NA	Bend, OR***	NA
NA	Boulder, CO**	NA
NA	Bowling Green, KY**	NA
NA	Brunswick, GA**	NA
NA	Burlington-South Burlington, VT**	NA
NA	Cincinnati-Middletown, OH-KY-IN**	NA
NA	Clarksville, TN-KY**	NA
NA	Cleveland-Elyria-Mentor, OH**	NA
NA	Coeur d'Alene, ID**	NA
NA	Crestview-Fort Walton Beach, FL**	NA
NA	Danville, IL**	NA
NA	Decatur, IL**	NA
NA	Des Moines-West Des Moines, IA**	NA
NA	Detroit (greater), MI**	NA
NA	Detroit-Livonia-Dearborn, MI M.D.**	NA
NA	Dubuque, IA***	NA
NA	Elizabethtown, KY**	NA
NA	Evansville, IN-KY**	NA
NA	Fargo, ND-MN***	NA
NA	Flint, MI**	NA
NA	Gainesville, GA**	NA
NA	Grand Rapids-Wyoming, MI**	NA
NA	Gulfport-Biloxi, MS**	NA
NA	Hattiesburg, MS**	NA
NA	Holland-Grand Haven, MI**	NA
NA	Jackson, MI**	NA
NA	Jefferson City, MO**	NA
NA	Kalamazoo-Portage, MI**	NA
NA	Kansas City, MO-KS**	NA
NA	Lake Charles, LA**	NA
NA	Lansing-East Lansing, MI**	NA
NA	Lawton, OK**	NA
NA	Lexington-Fayette, KY**	NA
NA	Little Rock, AR**	NA
NA	Louisville, KY-IN**	NA
NA	Manchester-Nashua, NH**	NA
NA	Mankato-North Mankato, MN***	NA
NA	Monroe, MI**	NA
NA	Morgantown, WV**	NA
NA	Muskegon-Norton Shores, MI**	NA
NA	New Haven-Milford, CT**	NA
NA	Niles-Benton Harbor, MI**	NA
NA	North Port-Bradenton-Sarasota, FL**	NA
NA	Ocean City, NJ***	NA
NA	Oklahoma City, OK**	NA
NA	Owensboro, KY**	NA
NA	Palm Coast, FL***	NA
NA	Pueblo, CO**	NA
NA	Rocky Mount, NC**	NA
NA	Rome, GA**	NA
NA	Saginaw, MI**	NA
NA	Seattle-Bellevue-Everett, WA M.D.**	NA
NA	Seattle-Tacoma-Bellevue, WA**	NA
NA	Sheboygan, WI***	NA
NA	South Bend-Mishawaka, IN-MI**	NA
NA	Springfield, MO**	NA
NA	State College, PA***	NA
NA	Sumter, SC**	NA
NA	Tacoma, WA M.D.**	NA
NA	Warren-Farmington Hills, MI M.D.**	NA
NA	Wausau, WI**	NA

Source: CQ Press using reported data from the F.B.I. "Crime in the United States 2009"

*Includes nonnegligent manslaughter. **Not available. ***These metro areas had murder rates of 0 in 2008 but had at least one murder in 2009. Calculating percent increase from zero results in an infinite number. This is shown as "NA."

12. Percent Change in Murder Rate: 2005 to 2009
National Percent Change = 12.1% Decrease*

RANK	METROPOLITAN AREA	% CHANGE
107	Abilene, TX	2.3
201	Akron, OH	(25.9)
133	Albany-Schenectady-Troy, NY	(6.7)
86	Albany, GA	12.5
166	Albuquerque, NM	(15.1)
158	Alexandria, LA	(13.3)
211	Allentown, PA-NJ	(29.3)
269	Altoona, PA	(56.4)
82	Amarillo, TX	15.2
108	Ames, IA	0.0
171	Anchorage, AK	(16.4)
278	Anderson, IN	(65.2)
255	Anderson, SC	(47.3)
210	Ann Arbor, MI	(29.2)
NA	Anniston-Oxford, AL**	NA
39	Appleton, WI	55.6
197	Asheville, NC	(25.0)
19	Athens-Clarke County, GA	107.1
160	Atlanta, GA	(14.5)
43	Atlantic City, NJ	49.2
56	Auburn, AL	34.7
40	Augusta, GA-SC	52.9
172	Austin-Round Rock, TX	(17.2)
116	Bakersfield, CA	(1.1)
152	Baltimore-Towson, MD	(12.6)
NA	Bangor, ME***	NA
55	Barnstable Town, MA	38.5
78	Baton Rouge, LA	17.6
18	Battle Creek, MI	108.0
NA	Bay City, MI**	NA
229	Beaumont-Port Arthur, TX	(35.1)
46	Bellingham, WA	48.1
272	Bend, OR	(58.6)
127	Bethesda-Frederick, MD M.D.	(5.3)
244	Billings, MT	(41.2)
17	Binghamton, NY	118.8
NA	Birmingham-Hoover, AL**	NA
NA	Bismarck, ND***	NA
6	Blacksburg, VA	284.6
131	Bloomington, IN	(5.9)
NA	Boise City-Nampa, ID**	NA
146	Boston (greater), MA-NH	(11.1)
192	Boston-Quincy, MA M.D.	(23.5)
NA	Boulder, CO**	NA
NA	Bowling Green, KY**	NA
247	Bremerton-Silverdale, WA	(41.4)
251	Bridgeport-Stamford, CT	(42.9)
244	Brownsville-Harlingen, TX	(41.2)
3	Brunswick, GA	416.7
79	Buffalo-Niagara Falls, NY	17.5
NA	Burlington-South Burlington, VT**	NA
263	Burlington, NC	(52.6)
57	Cambridge-Newton, MA M.D.	33.3
106	Camden, NJ M.D.	2.6
99	Cape Coral-Fort Myers, FL	4.8
NA	Cape Girardeau, MO-IL**	NA
291	Carson City, NV	(100.0)
291	Casper, WY	(100.0)
108	Cedar Rapids, IA	0.0
179	Charleston-North Charleston, SC	(19.1)

RANK	METROPOLITAN AREA	% CHANGE
62	Charleston, WV	32.3
209	Charlotte-Gastonia, NC-SC	(29.1)
287	Charlottesville, VA	(84.8)
200	Chattanooga, TN-GA	(25.8)
188	Cheyenne, WY	(22.4)
124	Chico, CA	(4.3)
NA	Cincinnati-Middletown, OH-KY-IN**	NA
NA	Clarksville, TN-KY**	NA
NA	Cleveland-Elyria-Mentor, OH**	NA
NA	Cleveland, TN**	NA
277	Coeur d'Alene, ID	(65.0)
256	College Station-Bryan, TX	(48.9)
84	Colorado Springs, CO	13.8
282	Columbia, MO	(69.5)
147	Columbia, SC	(11.3)
240	Columbus, GA-AL	(40.4)
108	Columbus, IN	0.0
159	Columbus, OH	(13.6)
69	Corpus Christi, TX	24.1
108	Corvallis, OR	0.0
NA	Crestview-Fort Walton Beach, FL**	NA
21	Cumberland, MD-WV	100.0
212	Dallas (greater), TX	(29.4)
202	Dallas-Plano-Irving, TX M.D.	(26.0)
NA	Dalton, GA**	NA
NA	Danville, IL**	NA
164	Danville, VA	(15.0)
81	Dayton, OH	16.7
108	Decatur, AL	0.0
NA	Decatur, IL**	NA
NA	Deltona-Daytona Beach, FL**	NA
186	Denver-Aurora, CO	(22.0)
NA	Des Moines-West Des Moines, IA**	NA
104	Detroit (greater), MI	3.1
NA	Detroit-Livonia-Dearborn, MI M.D.**	NA
285	Dothan, AL	(71.2)
144	Dover, DE	(10.7)
21	Dubuque, IA	100.0
NA	Duluth, MN-WI**	NA
252	Durham-Chapel Hill, NC	(44.8)
108	Eau Claire, WI	0.0
77	Edison, NJ M.D.	18.2
NA	El Centro, CA***	NA
167	El Paso, TX	(16.0)
NA	Elizabethtown, KY**	NA
64	Elkhart-Goshen, IN	29.0
100	Elmira, NY	4.5
65	Erie, PA	28.6
266	Eugene-Springfield, OR	(54.2)
NA	Evansville, IN-KY**	NA
232	Fargo, ND-MN	(37.5)
197	Farmington, NM	(25.0)
237	Fayetteville, AR-MO	(39.3)
43	Fayetteville, NC	49.2
2	Flagstaff, AZ	487.5
NA	Flint, MI**	NA
NA	Florence-Muscle Shoals, AL**	NA
70	Florence, SC	23.8
NA	Fond du Lac, WI***	NA
88	Fort Collins-Loveland, CO	11.1

RANK	METROPOLITAN AREA	% CHANGE
71	Fort Lauderdale, FL M.D.	22.9
177	Fort Smith, AR-OK	(19.0)
184	Fort Wayne, IN	(20.9)
232	Fort Worth-Arlington, TX M.D.	(37.5)
162	Fresno, CA	(14.8)
270	Gadsden, AL	(56.7)
136	Gainesville, FL	(6.9)
206	Gainesville, GA	(27.8)
NA	Glens Falls, NY**	NA
93	Goldsboro, NC	9.8
291	Grand Forks, ND-MN	(100.0)
NA	Grand Junction, CO***	NA
NA	Grand Rapids-Wyoming, MI**	NA
8	Great Falls, MT	240.0
154	Greeley, CO	(12.9)
264	Green Bay, WI	(52.9)
234	Greensboro-High Point, NC	(38.8)
NA	Gulfport-Biloxi, MS**	NA
274	Hagerstown-Martinsburg, MD-WV	(60.7)
61	Harrisburg-Carlisle, PA	32.4
129	Harrisonburg, VA	(5.6)
87	Hartford, CT	12.2
NA	Hattiesburg, MS**	NA
156	Hickory, NC	(13.2)
13	Hinesville, GA	123.1
NA	Holland-Grand Haven, MI**	NA
148	Honolulu, HI	(11.8)
80	Hot Springs, AR	17.4
67	Houma, LA	25.5
156	Houston, TX	(13.2)
243	Huntsville, AL	(40.9)
NA	Idaho Falls, ID***	NA
161	Indianapolis, IN	(14.7)
32	Iowa City, IA	85.7
NA	Ithaca, NY**	NA
94	Jacksonville, FL	9.6
NA	Jacksonville, NC**	NA
NA	Jackson, MI**	NA
193	Jackson, MS	(23.6)
33	Jackson, TN	83.3
48	Janesville, WI	48.0
267	Jefferson City, MO	(55.8)
98	Johnson City, TN	5.7
54	Jonesboro, AR	38.9
NA	Kalamazoo-Portage, MI**	NA
181	Kansas City, MO-KS	(19.4)
289	Kennewick-Pasco-Richland, WA	(87.5)
195	Killeen-Temple-Fort Hood, TX	(24.4)
191	Kingsport, TN-VA	(23.3)
281	Kingston, NY	(68.8)
203	Knoxville, TN	(26.7)
290	Kokomo, IN	(91.5)
108	La Crosse, WI-MN	0.0
291	Lafayette, IN	(100.0)
176	Lafayette, LA	(18.5)
38	Lake Charles, LA	58.1
NA	Lake Havasu City-Kingman, AZ**	NA
71	Lakeland, FL	22.9
21	Lancaster, PA	100.0
NA	Lansing-East Lansing, MI**	NA

Note: All listings are for Metropolitan Statistical Areas (M.S.A.s) except for those ending with "M.D." Listings with "M.D." are Metropolitan Divisions which are smaller parts of eleven large M.S.A.s. See explanatory note at beginning of metropolitan area section.

RANK	METROPOLITAN AREA	% CHANGE
219	Laredo, TX	(32.0)
177	Las Cruces, NM	(19.0)
219	Las Vegas-Paradise, NV	(32.0)
291	Lawrence, KS	(100.0)
NA	Lawton, OK**	NA
1	Lebanon, PA	662.5
291	Lewiston-Auburn, ME	(100.0)
261	Lewiston, ID-WA	(51.5)
NA	Lexington-Fayette, KY**	NA
76	Lima, OH	21.3
137	Lincoln, NE	(7.1)
NA	Little Rock, AR**	NA
291	Logan, UT-ID	(100.0)
135	Longview, TX	(6.8)
280	Longview, WA	(67.7)
223	Los Angeles County, CA M.D.	(33.6)
218	Los Angeles (greater), CA	(31.8)
NA	Louisville, KY-IN**	NA
122	Lubbock, TX	(3.8)
262	Lynchburg, VA	(52.4)
167	Macon, GA	(16.0)
286	Madera, CA	(71.8)
4	Madison, WI	375.0
148	Manchester-Nashua, NH	(11.8)
NA	Manhattan, KS**	NA
NA	Mankato-North Mankato, MN**	NA
42	Mansfield, OH	50.0
118	McAllen-Edinburg-Mission, TX	(1.8)
276	Medford, OR	(61.5)
154	Memphis, TN-MS-AR	(12.9)
85	Merced, CA	13.0
67	Miami (greater), FL	25.5
75	Miami-Dade County, FL M.D.	22.5
271	Michigan City-La Porte, IN	(57.1)
11	Midland, TX	187.5
238	Milwaukee, WI	(39.5)
NA	Minneapolis-St. Paul, MN-WI**	NA
284	Missoula, MT	(70.0)
208	Mobile, AL	(29.0)
45	Modesto, CA	48.3
NA	Monroe, MI**	NA
83	Montgomery, AL	14.1
129	Morgantown, WV	(5.6)
50	Morristown, TN	46.7
138	Mount Vernon-Anacortes, WA	(7.4)
10	Muncie, IN	205.9
NA	Muskegon-Norton Shores, MI**	NA
151	Napa, CA	(12.5)
50	Naples-Marco Island, FL	46.7
162	Nashville-Davidson, TN	(14.8)
92	Nassau-Suffolk, NY M.D.	10.0
NA	New Haven-Milford, CT**	NA
NA	New Orleans, LA**	NA
174	New York (greater), NY-NJ-PA	(18.0)
173	New York-W. Plains NY-NJ M.D.	(17.5)
214	Newark-Union, NJ-PA M.D.	(30.0)
NA	Niles-Benton Harbor, MI**	NA
NA	North Port-Bradenton-Sarasota, FL**	NA
19	Norwich-New London, CT	107.1
94	Oakland-Fremont, CA M.D.	9.6
221	Ocala, FL	(33.3)
253	Ocean City, NJ	(45.0)
89	Odessa, TX	10.6
228	Ogden-Clearfield, UT	(35.0)
NA	Oklahoma City, OK**	NA
14	Olympia, WA	122.2
125	Omaha-Council Bluffs, NE-IA	(4.9)
119	Orlando, FL	(1.9)
291	Oshkosh-Neenah, WI	(100.0)
NA	Owensboro, KY**	NA
143	Oxnard-Thousand Oaks, CA	(10.0)
53	Palm Bay-Melbourne, FL	41.2
NA	Palm Coast, FL**	NA
16	Panama City-Lynn Haven, FL	120.0
238	Pascagoula, MS	(39.5)
NA	Peabody, MA M.D.**	NA
46	Pensacola, FL	48.1
182	Philadelphia (greater) PA-NJ-MD-DE	(20.7)
196	Philadelphia, PA M.D.	(24.8)
231	Phoenix-Mesa-Scottsdale, AZ	(36.9)
207	Pine Bluff, AR	(28.6)
120	Pittsburgh, PA	(2.1)
226	Pittsfield, MA	(34.8)
140	Pocatello, ID	(8.3)
96	Port St. Lucie, FL	7.9
180	Portland-Vancouver, OR-WA	(19.2)
34	Portland, ME	78.6
126	Poughkeepsie, NY	(5.0)
214	Prescott, AZ	(30.0)
NA	Providence-New Bedford, RI-MA**	NA
248	Provo-Orem, UT	(41.7)
103	Pueblo, CO	3.5
36	Punta Gorda, FL	66.7
282	Racine, WI	(69.5)
216	Raleigh-Cary, NC	(30.3)
230	Rapid City, SD	(36.0)
224	Reading, PA	(33.9)
189	Redding, CA	(22.7)
71	Reno-Sparks, NV	22.9
258	Richmond, VA	(50.4)
217	Riverside-San Bernardino, CA	(31.1)
244	Roanoke, VA	(41.2)
NA	Rochester, MN***	NA
235	Rochester, NY	(39.0)
248	Rockingham County, NH M.D.	(41.7)
185	Rocky Mount, NC	(21.1)
49	Rome, GA	47.6
225	Sacramento, CA	(34.4)
NA	Saginaw, MI**	NA
221	Salem, OR	(33.3)
7	Salinas, CA	267.6
60	Salisbury, MD	32.6
242	Salt Lake City, UT	(40.6)
15	San Angelo, TX	121.6
90	San Antonio, TX	10.5
194	San Diego, CA	(24.2)
164	San Francisco (greater), CA	(15.0)
260	San Francisco-S. Mateo, CA M.D.	(51.3)
108	San Jose, CA	0.0
132	San Luis Obispo, CA	(6.3)
21	Sandusky, OH	100.0
139	Santa Ana-Anaheim, CA M.D.	(8.0)
74	Santa Barbara-Santa Maria, CA	22.7
21	Santa Cruz-Watsonville, CA	100.0
12	Santa Fe, NM	139.5
35	Santa Rosa-Petaluma, CA	72.7
144	Savannah, GA	(10.7)
41	Scranton--Wilkes-Barre, PA	51.6
182	Seattle-Bellevue-Everett, WA M.D.	(20.7)
169	Seattle-Tacoma-Bellevue, WA	(16.1)
9	Sebastian-Vero Beach, FL	225.0
NA	Sheboygan, WI***	NA
63	Sherman-Denison, TX	32.0
150	Shreveport-Bossier City, LA	(12.1)
21	Sioux City, IA-NE-SD	100.0
288	Sioux Falls, SD	(86.2)
NA	South Bend-Mishawaka, IN-MI**	NA
268	Spartanburg, SC	(56.2)
248	Spokane, WA	(41.7)
204	Springfield, MA	(27.7)
NA	Springfield, MO**	NA
265	Springfield, OH	(54.0)
21	State College, PA	100.0
153	Stockton, CA	(12.8)
274	St. Cloud, MN	(60.7)
187	St. George, UT	(22.2)
57	St. Joseph, MO-KS	33.3
117	St. Louis, MO-IL	(1.3)
NA	Sumter, SC**	NA
104	Syracuse, NY	3.1
121	Tacoma, WA M.D.	(2.7)
235	Tallahassee, FL	(39.0)
170	Tampa-St Petersburg, FL	(16.3)
31	Texarkana, TX-Texarkana, AR	86.4
91	Toledo, OH	10.2
29	Topeka, KS	97.7
259	Trenton-Ewing, NJ	(50.5)
227	Tucson, AZ	(34.9)
97	Tulsa, OK	6.2
NA	Tuscaloosa, AL**	NA
272	Tyler, TX	(58.6)
175	Utica-Rome, NY	(18.2)
102	Valdosta, GA	3.8
NA	Vallejo-Fairfield, CA**	NA
199	Victoria, TX	(25.7)
122	Vineland, NJ	(3.8)
254	Visalia-Porterville, CA	(46.3)
141	Waco, TX	(9.7)
30	Warner Robins, GA	87.5
NA	Warren-Farmington Hills, MI M.D.**	NA
204	Washington (greater) DC-VA-MD-WV	(27.7)
213	Washington, DC-VA-MD-WV M.D.	(29.7)
21	Waterloo-Cedar Falls, IA	100.0
NA	Wausau, WI**	NA
127	Wenatchee, WA	(5.3)
66	West Palm Beach, FL M.D.	25.9
5	Wheeling, WV-OH	300.0
52	Wichita Falls, TX	41.5
NA	Wichita, KS**	NA
257	Williamsport, PA	(50.0)
101	Wilmington, DE-MD-NJ M.D.	4.2
241	Wilmington, NC	(40.5)
57	Winchester, VA-WV	33.3
142	Winston-Salem, NC	(9.8)
36	Worcester, MA	66.7
133	York-Hanover, PA	(6.7)
NA	Youngstown, OH-PA**	NA
279	Yuba City, CA	(66.7)
189	Yuma, AZ	(22.7)

Source: CQ Press using reported data from the F.B.I. "Crime in the United States 2009"

*Includes nonnegligent manslaughter. **Not available. ***These metro areas had murder rates of 0 in 2005 but had at least one murder in 2009. Calculating percent increase from zero results in an infinite number. This is shown as "NA."

12. Percent Change in Murder Rate: 2005 to 2009 (continued)
National Percent Change = 12.1% Decrease*

RANK	METROPOLITAN AREA	% CHANGE
1	Lebanon, PA	662.5
2	Flagstaff, AZ	487.5
3	Brunswick, GA	416.7
4	Madison, WI	375.0
5	Wheeling, WV-OH	300.0
6	Blacksburg, VA	284.6
7	Salinas, CA	267.6
8	Great Falls, MT	240.0
9	Sebastian-Vero Beach, FL	225.0
10	Muncie, IN	205.9
11	Midland, TX	187.5
12	Santa Fe, NM	139.5
13	Hinesville, GA	123.1
14	Olympia, WA	122.2
15	San Angelo, TX	121.6
16	Panama City-Lynn Haven, FL	120.0
17	Binghamton, NY	118.8
18	Battle Creek, MI	108.0
19	Athens-Clarke County, GA	107.1
19	Norwich-New London, CT	107.1
21	Cumberland, MD-WV	100.0
21	Dubuque, IA	100.0
21	Lancaster, PA	100.0
21	Sandusky, OH	100.0
21	Santa Cruz-Watsonville, CA	100.0
21	Sioux City, IA-NE-SD	100.0
21	State College, PA	100.0
21	Waterloo-Cedar Falls, IA	100.0
29	Topeka, KS	97.7
30	Warner Robins, GA	87.5
31	Texarkana, TX-Texarkana, AR	86.4
32	Iowa City, IA	85.7
33	Jackson, TN	83.3
34	Portland, ME	78.6
35	Santa Rosa-Petaluma, CA	72.7
36	Punta Gorda, FL	66.7
36	Worcester, MA	66.7
38	Lake Charles, LA	58.1
39	Appleton, WI	55.6
40	Augusta, GA-SC	52.9
41	Scranton--Wilkes-Barre, PA	51.6
42	Mansfield, OH	50.0
43	Atlantic City, NJ	49.2
43	Fayetteville, NC	49.2
45	Modesto, CA	48.3
46	Bellingham, WA	48.1
46	Pensacola, FL	48.1
48	Janesville, WI	48.0
49	Rome, GA	47.6
50	Morristown, TN	46.7
50	Naples-Marco Island, FL	46.7
52	Wichita Falls, TX	41.5
53	Palm Bay-Melbourne, FL	41.2
54	Jonesboro, AR	38.9
55	Barnstable Town, MA	38.5
56	Auburn, AL	34.7
57	Cambridge-Newton, MA M.D.	33.3
57	St. Joseph, MO-KS	33.3
57	Winchester, VA-WV	33.3
60	Salisbury, MD	32.6
61	Harrisburg-Carlisle, PA	32.4
62	Charleston, WV	32.3
63	Sherman-Denison, TX	32.0
64	Elkhart-Goshen, IN	29.0
65	Erie, PA	28.6
66	West Palm Beach, FL M.D.	25.9
67	Houma, LA	25.5
67	Miami (greater), FL	25.5
69	Corpus Christi, TX	24.1
70	Florence, SC	23.8
71	Fort Lauderdale, FL M.D.	22.9
71	Lakeland, FL	22.9
71	Reno-Sparks, NV	22.9
74	Santa Barbara-Santa Maria, CA	22.7
75	Miami-Dade County, FL M.D.	22.5
76	Lima, OH	21.3
77	Edison, NJ M.D.	18.2
78	Baton Rouge, LA	17.6
79	Buffalo-Niagara Falls, NY	17.5
80	Hot Springs, AR	17.4
81	Dayton, OH	16.7
82	Amarillo, TX	15.2
83	Montgomery, AL	14.1
84	Colorado Springs, CO	13.8
85	Merced, CA	13.0
86	Albany, GA	12.5
87	Hartford, CT	12.2
88	Fort Collins-Loveland, CO	11.1
89	Odessa, TX	10.6
90	San Antonio, TX	10.5
91	Toledo, OH	10.2
92	Nassau-Suffolk, NY M.D.	10.0
93	Goldsboro, NC	9.8
94	Jacksonville, FL	9.6
94	Oakland-Fremont, CA M.D.	9.6
96	Port St. Lucie, FL	7.9
97	Tulsa, OK	6.2
98	Johnson City, TN	5.7
99	Cape Coral-Fort Myers, FL	4.8
100	Elmira, NY	4.5
101	Wilmington, DE-MD-NJ M.D.	4.2
102	Valdosta, GA	3.8
103	Pueblo, CO	3.5
104	Detroit (greater), MI	3.1
104	Syracuse, NY	3.1
106	Camden, NJ M.D.	2.6
107	Abilene, TX	2.3
108	Ames, IA	0.0
108	Cedar Rapids, IA	0.0
108	Columbus, IN	0.0
108	Corvallis, OR	0.0
108	Decatur, AL	0.0
108	Eau Claire, WI	0.0
108	La Crosse, WI-MN	0.0
108	San Jose, CA	0.0
116	Bakersfield, CA	(1.1)
117	St. Louis, MO-IL	(1.3)
118	McAllen-Edinburg-Mission, TX	(1.8)
119	Orlando, FL	(1.9)
120	Pittsburgh, PA	(2.1)
121	Tacoma, WA M.D.	(2.7)
122	Lubbock, TX	(3.8)
122	Vineland, NJ	(3.8)
124	Chico, CA	(4.3)
125	Omaha-Council Bluffs, NE-IA	(4.9)
126	Poughkeepsie, NY	(5.0)
127	Bethesda-Frederick, MD M.D.	(5.3)
127	Wenatchee, WA	(5.3)
129	Harrisonburg, VA	(5.6)
129	Morgantown, WV	(5.6)
131	Bloomington, IN	(5.9)
132	San Luis Obispo, CA	(6.3)
133	Albany-Schenectady-Troy, NY	(6.7)
133	York-Hanover, PA	(6.7)
135	Longview, TX	(6.8)
136	Gainesville, FL	(6.9)
137	Lincoln, NE	(7.1)
138	Mount Vernon-Anacortes, WA	(7.4)
139	Santa Ana-Anaheim, CA M.D.	(8.0)
140	Pocatello, ID	(8.3)
141	Waco, TX	(9.7)
142	Winston-Salem, NC	(9.8)
143	Oxnard-Thousand Oaks, CA	(10.0)
144	Dover, DE	(10.7)
144	Savannah, GA	(10.7)
146	Boston (greater), MA-NH	(11.1)
147	Columbia, SC	(11.3)
148	Honolulu, HI	(11.8)
148	Manchester-Nashua, NH	(11.8)
150	Shreveport-Bossier City, LA	(12.1)
151	Napa, CA	(12.5)
152	Baltimore-Towson, MD	(12.6)
153	Stockton, CA	(12.8)
154	Greeley, CO	(12.9)
154	Memphis, TN-MS-AR	(12.9)
156	Hickory, NC	(13.2)
156	Houston, TX	(13.2)
158	Alexandria, LA	(13.3)
159	Columbus, OH	(13.6)
160	Atlanta, GA	(14.5)
161	Indianapolis, IN	(14.7)
162	Fresno, CA	(14.8)
162	Nashville-Davidson, TN	(14.8)
164	Danville, VA	(15.0)
164	San Francisco (greater), CA	(15.0)
166	Albuquerque, NM	(15.1)
167	El Paso, TX	(16.0)
167	Macon, GA	(16.0)
169	Seattle-Tacoma-Bellevue, WA	(16.1)
170	Tampa-St Petersburg, FL	(16.3)
171	Anchorage, AK	(16.4)
172	Austin-Round Rock, TX	(17.2)
173	New York-W. Plains NY-NJ M.D.	(17.5)
174	New York (greater), NY-NJ-PA	(18.0)
175	Utica-Rome, NY	(18.2)
176	Lafayette, LA	(18.5)
177	Fort Smith, AR-OK	(19.0)
177	Las Cruces, NM	(19.0)
179	Charleston-North Charleston, SC	(19.1)
180	Portland-Vancouver, OR-WA	(19.2)

Note: All listings are for Metropolitan Statistical Areas (M.S.A.s) except for those ending with "M.D." Listings with "M.D." are Metropolitan Divisions which are smaller parts of eleven large M.S.A.s. See explanatory note at beginning of metropolitan area section.

RANK	METROPOLITAN AREA	% CHANGE
181	Kansas City, MO-KS	(19.4)
182	Philadelphia (greater) PA-NJ-MD-DE	(20.7)
182	Seattle-Bellevue-Everett, WA M.D.	(20.7)
184	Fort Wayne, IN	(20.9)
185	Rocky Mount, NC	(21.1)
186	Denver-Aurora, CO	(22.0)
187	St. George, UT	(22.2)
188	Cheyenne, WY	(22.4)
189	Redding, CA	(22.7)
189	Yuma, AZ	(22.7)
191	Kingsport, TN-VA	(23.3)
192	Boston-Quincy, MA M.D.	(23.5)
193	Jackson, MS	(23.6)
194	San Diego, CA	(24.2)
195	Killeen-Temple-Fort Hood, TX	(24.4)
196	Philadelphia, PA M.D.	(24.8)
197	Asheville, NC	(25.0)
197	Farmington, NM	(25.0)
199	Victoria, TX	(25.7)
200	Chattanooga, TN-GA	(25.8)
201	Akron, OH	(25.9)
202	Dallas-Plano-Irving, TX M.D.	(26.0)
203	Knoxville, TN	(26.7)
204	Springfield, MA	(27.7)
204	Washington (greater) DC-VA-MD-WV	(27.7)
206	Gainesville, GA	(27.8)
207	Pine Bluff, AR	(28.6)
208	Mobile, AL	(29.0)
209	Charlotte-Gastonia, NC-SC	(29.1)
210	Ann Arbor, MI	(29.2)
211	Allentown, PA-NJ	(29.3)
212	Dallas (greater), TX	(29.4)
213	Washington, DC-VA-MD-WV M.D.	(29.7)
214	Newark-Union, NJ-PA M.D.	(30.0)
214	Prescott, AZ	(30.0)
216	Raleigh-Cary, NC	(30.3)
217	Riverside-San Bernardino, CA	(31.1)
218	Los Angeles (greater), CA	(31.8)
219	Laredo, TX	(32.0)
219	Las Vegas-Paradise, NV	(32.0)
221	Ocala, FL	(33.3)
221	Salem, OR	(33.3)
223	Los Angeles County, CA M.D.	(33.6)
224	Reading, PA	(33.9)
225	Sacramento, CA	(34.4)
226	Pittsfield, MA	(34.8)
227	Tucson, AZ	(34.9)
228	Ogden-Clearfield, UT	(35.0)
229	Beaumont-Port Arthur, TX	(35.1)
230	Rapid City, SD	(36.0)
231	Phoenix-Mesa-Scottsdale, AZ	(36.9)
232	Fargo, ND-MN	(37.5)
232	Fort Worth-Arlington, TX M.D.	(37.5)
234	Greensboro-High Point, NC	(38.8)
235	Rochester, NY	(39.0)
235	Tallahassee, FL	(39.0)
237	Fayetteville, AR-MO	(39.3)
238	Milwaukee, WI	(39.5)
238	Pascagoula, MS	(39.5)
240	Columbus, GA-AL	(40.4)
241	Wilmington, NC	(40.5)
242	Salt Lake City, UT	(40.6)
243	Huntsville, AL	(40.9)

RANK	METROPOLITAN AREA	% CHANGE
244	Billings, MT	(41.2)
244	Brownsville-Harlingen, TX	(41.2)
244	Roanoke, VA	(41.2)
247	Bremerton-Silverdale, WA	(41.4)
248	Provo-Orem, UT	(41.7)
248	Rockingham County, NH M.D.	(41.7)
248	Spokane, WA	(41.7)
251	Bridgeport-Stamford, CT	(42.9)
252	Durham-Chapel Hill, NC	(44.8)
253	Ocean City, NJ	(45.0)
254	Visalia-Porterville, CA	(46.3)
255	Anderson, SC	(47.3)
256	College Station-Bryan, TX	(48.9)
257	Williamsport, PA	(50.0)
258	Richmond, VA	(50.4)
259	Trenton-Ewing, NJ	(50.5)
260	San Francisco-S. Mateo, CA M.D.	(51.3)
261	Lewiston, ID-WA	(51.5)
262	Lynchburg, VA	(52.4)
263	Burlington, NC	(52.6)
264	Green Bay, WI	(52.9)
265	Springfield, OH	(54.0)
266	Eugene-Springfield, OR	(54.2)
267	Jefferson City, MO	(55.8)
268	Spartanburg, SC	(56.2)
269	Altoona, PA	(56.4)
270	Gadsden, AL	(56.7)
271	Michigan City-La Porte, IN	(57.1)
272	Bend, OR	(58.6)
272	Tyler, TX	(58.6)
274	Hagerstown-Martinsburg, MD-WV	(60.7)
274	St. Cloud, MN	(60.7)
276	Medford, OR	(61.5)
277	Coeur d'Alene, ID	(65.0)
278	Anderson, IN	(65.2)
279	Yuba City, CA	(66.7)
280	Longview, WA	(67.7)
281	Kingston, NY	(68.8)
282	Columbia, MO	(69.5)
282	Racine, WI	(69.5)
284	Missoula, MT	(70.0)
285	Dothan, AL	(71.2)
286	Madera, CA	(71.8)
287	Charlottesville, VA	(84.8)
288	Sioux Falls, SD	(86.2)
289	Kennewick-Pasco-Richland, WA	(87.5)
290	Kokomo, IN	(91.5)
291	Carson City, NV	(100.0)
291	Casper, WY	(100.0)
291	Grand Forks, ND-MN	(100.0)
291	Lafayette, IN	(100.0)
291	Lawrence, KS	(100.0)
291	Lewiston-Auburn, ME	(100.0)
291	Logan, UT-ID	(100.0)
291	Oshkosh-Neenah, WI	(100.0)
NA	Anniston-Oxford, AL**	NA
NA	Bangor, ME***	NA
NA	Bay City, MI**	NA
NA	Birmingham-Hoover, AL**	NA
NA	Bismarck, ND***	NA
NA	Boise City-Nampa, ID**	NA
NA	Boulder, CO**	NA
NA	Bowling Green, KY**	NA

RANK	METROPOLITAN AREA	% CHANGE
NA	Burlington-South Burlington, VT**	NA
NA	Cape Girardeau, MO-IL**	NA
NA	Cincinnati-Middletown, OH-KY-IN**	NA
NA	Clarksville, TN-KY**	NA
NA	Cleveland-Elyria-Mentor, OH**	NA
NA	Cleveland, TN**	NA
NA	Crestview-Fort Walton Beach, FL**	NA
NA	Dalton, GA**	NA
NA	Danville, IL**	NA
NA	Decatur, IL**	NA
NA	Deltona-Daytona Beach, FL**	NA
NA	Des Moines-West Des Moines, IA**	NA
NA	Detroit-Livonia-Dearborn, MI M.D.**	NA
NA	Duluth, MN-WI**	NA
NA	El Centro, CA***	NA
NA	Elizabethtown, KY**	NA
NA	Evansville, IN-KY**	NA
NA	Flint, MI**	NA
NA	Florence-Muscle Shoals, AL**	NA
NA	Fond du Lac, WI***	NA
NA	Glens Falls, NY**	NA
NA	Grand Junction, CO***	NA
NA	Grand Rapids-Wyoming, MI**	NA
NA	Gulfport-Biloxi, MS**	NA
NA	Hattiesburg, MS**	NA
NA	Holland-Grand Haven, MI**	NA
NA	Idaho Falls, ID***	NA
NA	Ithaca, NY**	NA
NA	Jacksonville, NC**	NA
NA	Jackson, MI**	NA
NA	Kalamazoo-Portage, MI**	NA
NA	Lake Havasu City-Kingman, AZ**	NA
NA	Lansing-East Lansing, MI**	NA
NA	Lawton, OK**	NA
NA	Lexington-Fayette, KY**	NA
NA	Little Rock, AR**	NA
NA	Louisville, KY-IN**	NA
NA	Manhattan, KS**	NA
NA	Mankato-North Mankato, MN**	NA
NA	Minneapolis-St. Paul, MN-WI**	NA
NA	Monroe, MI**	NA
NA	Muskegon-Norton Shores, MI**	NA
NA	New Haven-Milford, CT**	NA
NA	New Orleans, LA**	NA
NA	Niles-Benton Harbor, MI**	NA
NA	North Port-Bradenton-Sarasota, FL**	NA
NA	Oklahoma City, OK**	NA
NA	Owensboro, KY**	NA
NA	Palm Coast, FL**	NA
NA	Peabody, MA M.D.**	NA
NA	Providence-New Bedford, RI-MA**	NA
NA	Rochester, MN***	NA
NA	Saginaw, MI**	NA
NA	Sheboygan, WI***	NA
NA	South Bend-Mishawaka, IN-MI**	NA
NA	Springfield, MO**	NA
NA	Sumter, SC**	NA
NA	Tuscaloosa, AL**	NA
NA	Vallejo-Fairfield, CA**	NA
NA	Warren-Farmington Hills, MI M.D.**	NA
NA	Wausau, WI**	NA
NA	Wichita, KS**	NA
NA	Youngstown, OH-PA**	NA

Source: CQ Press using reported data from the F.B.I. "Crime in the United States 2009"
*Includes nonnegligent manslaughter. **Not available. ***These metro areas had murder rates of 0 in 2005 but had at least one murder in 2009. Calculating percent increase from zero results in an infinite number. This is shown as "NA."

13. Rapes in 2009
National Total = 88,097 Rapes*

RANK	METROPOLITAN AREA	RAPES
135	Abilene, TX	134
67	Akron, OH	311
114	Albany-Schenectady-Troy, NY	162
221	Albany, GA	66
52	Albuquerque, NM	421
279	Alexandria, LA	41
109	Allentown, PA-NJ	165
284	Altoona, PA	39
168	Amarillo, TX	108
313	Ames, IA	32
71	Anchorage, AK	289
289	Anderson, IN	38
214	Anderson, SC	68
118	Ann Arbor, MI	158
231	Anniston-Oxford, AL	63
289	Appleton, WI	38
183	Asheville, NC	92
251	Athens-Clarke County, GA	54
12	Atlanta, GA	1,170
236	Atlantic City, NJ	60
247	Auburn, AL	55
90	Augusta, GA-SC	212
47	Austin-Round Rock, TX	455
93	Bakersfield, CA	205
40	Baltimore-Towson, MD	552
336	Bangor, ME	21
205	Barnstable Town, MA	76
117	Baton Rouge, LA	160
189	Battle Creek, MI	87
210	Bay City, MI	73
109	Beaumont-Port Arthur, TX	165
205	Bellingham, WA	76
289	Bend, OR	38
112	Bethesda-Frederick, MD M.D.	163
306	Billings, MT	34
271	Binghamton, NY	46
50	Birmingham-Hoover, AL	433
300	Bismarck, ND	36
226	Blacksburg, VA	65
240	Bloomington, IN	58
89	Boise City-Nampa, ID	215
17	Boston (greater), MA-NH	996
41	Boston-Quincy, MA M.D.	538
218	Boulder, CO	67
240	Bowling Green, KY	58
106	Bremerton-Silverdale, WA	169
119	Bridgeport-Stamford, CT	154
181	Brownsville-Harlingen, TX	95
295	Brunswick, GA	37
74	Buffalo-Niagara Falls, NY	260
240	Burlington-South Burlington, VT	58
267	Burlington, NC	48
83	Cambridge-Newton, MA M.D.	229
92	Camden, NJ M.D.	210
151	Cape Coral-Fort Myers, FL	121
322	Cape Girardeau, MO-IL	28
357	Carson City, NV	1
327	Casper, WY	26
221	Cedar Rapids, IA	66
86	Charleston-North Charleston, SC	218
214	Charleston, WV	68
44	Charlotte-Gastonia, NC-SC	498
214	Charlottesville, VA	68
140	Chattanooga, TN-GA	130
281	Cheyenne, WY	40
189	Chico, CA	87
32	Cincinnati-Middletown, OH-KY-IN	720
178	Clarksville, TN-KY	97
32	Cleveland-Elyria-Mentor, OH	720
322	Cleveland, TN	28
197	Coeur d'Alene, ID	82
184	College Station-Bryan, TX	91
52	Colorado Springs, CO	421
289	Columbia, MO	38
72	Columbia, SC	288
221	Columbus, GA-AL	66
356	Columbus, IN	7
21	Columbus, OH	832
75	Corpus Christi, TX	252
348	Corvallis, OR	15
236	Crestview-Fort Walton Beach, FL	60
319	Cumberland, MD-WV	29
3	Dallas (greater), TX	1,944
11	Dallas-Plano-Irving, TX M.D.	1,178
313	Dalton, GA	32
NA	Danville, IL**	NA
351	Danville, VA	13
65	Dayton, OH	313
304	Decatur, AL	35
NA	Decatur, IL**	NA
132	Deltona-Daytona Beach, FL	138
10	Denver-Aurora, CO	1,225
80	Des Moines-West Des Moines, IA	236
8	Detroit (greater), MI	1,412
35	Detroit-Livonia-Dearborn, MI M.D.	676
272	Dothan, AL	45
199	Dover, DE	81
340	Dubuque, IA	18
NA	Duluth, MN-WI**	NA
154	Durham-Chapel Hill, NC	120
284	Eau Claire, WI	39
93	Edison, NJ M.D.	205
340	El Centro, CA	18
82	El Paso, TX	231
331	Elizabethtown, KY	25
247	Elkhart-Goshen, IN	55
351	Elmira, NY	13
151	Erie, PA	121
161	Eugene-Springfield, OR	114
174	Evansville, IN-KY	102
NA	Fargo, ND-MN**	NA
130	Farmington, NM	141
76	Fayetteville, AR-MO	245
147	Fayetteville, NC	123
233	Flagstaff, AZ	62
81	Flint, MI	235
306	Florence-Muscle Shoals, AL	34
199	Florence, SC	81
319	Fond du Lac, WI	29
126	Fort Collins-Loveland, CO	143
49	Fort Lauderdale, FL M.D.	439
165	Fort Smith, AR-OK	110
177	Fort Wayne, IN	98
25	Fort Worth-Arlington, TX M.D.	766
103	Fresno, CA	178
245	Gadsden, AL	57
122	Gainesville, FL	149
284	Gainesville, GA	39
348	Glens Falls, NY	15
353	Goldsboro, NC	12
NA	Grand Forks, ND-MN**	NA
209	Grand Junction, CO	74
59	Grand Rapids-Wyoming, MI	351
346	Great Falls, MT	16
210	Greeley, CO	73
173	Green Bay, WI	103
121	Greensboro-High Point, NC	151
254	Gulfport-Biloxi, MS	53
262	Hagerstown-Martinsburg, MD-WV	50
107	Harrisburg-Carlisle, PA	168
324	Harrisonburg, VA	27
97	Hartford, CT	193
239	Hattiesburg, MS	59
240	Hickory, NC	58
306	Hinesville, GA	34
145	Holland-Grand Haven, MI	124
77	Honolulu, HI	243
277	Hot Springs, AR	42
247	Houma, LA	55
6	Houston, TX	1,715
141	Huntsville, AL	128
272	Idaho Falls, ID	45
38	Indianapolis, IN	570
262	Iowa City, IA	50
353	Ithaca, NY	12
63	Jacksonville, FL	331
179	Jacksonville, NC	96
172	Jackson, MI	105
86	Jackson, MS	218
304	Jackson, TN	35
281	Janesville, WI	40
316	Jefferson City, MO	30
281	Johnson City, TN	40
267	Jonesboro, AR	48
95	Kalamazoo-Portage, MI	201
34	Kansas City, MO-KS	700
168	Kennewick-Pasco-Richland, WA	108
116	Killeen-Temple-Fort Hood, TX	161
179	Kingsport, TN-VA	96
324	Kingston, NY	27
79	Knoxville, TN	238
334	Kokomo, IN	23
NA	La Crosse, WI-MN**	NA
272	Lafayette, IN	45
187	Lafayette, LA	89
137	Lake Charles, LA	132
306	Lake Havasu City-Kingman, AZ	34
99	Lakeland, FL	186
184	Lancaster, PA	91
88	Lansing-East Lansing, MI	217

Note: All listings are for Metropolitan Statistical Areas (M.S.A.s) except for those ending with "M.D." Listings with "M.D." are Metropolitan Divisions which are smaller parts of eleven large M.S.A.s. See explanatory note at beginning of metropolitan area section.

Alpha Order - Metro Area (continued)

RANK	METROPOLITAN AREA	RAPES
204	Laredo, TX	77
218	Las Cruces, NM	67
23	Las Vegas-Paradise, NV	810
221	Lawrence, KS	66
191	Lawton, OK	86
348	Lebanon, PA	15
295	Lewiston-Auburn, ME	37
339	Lewiston, ID-WA	19
128	Lexington-Fayette, KY	142
208	Lima, OH	75
134	Lincoln, NE	137
57	Little Rock, AR	365
316	Logan, UT-ID	30
193	Longview, TX	85
246	Longview, WA	56
2	Los Angeles County, CA M.D.	2,114
1	Los Angeles (greater), CA	2,570
58	Louisville, KY-IN	361
156	Lubbock, TX	118
228	Lynchburg, VA	64
258	Macon, GA	51
300	Madera, CA	36
191	Madison, WI	86
151	Manchester-Nashua, NH	121
214	Manhattan, KS	68
NA	Mankato-North Mankato, MN**	NA
275	Mansfield, OH	44
90	McAllen-Edinburg-Mission, TX	212
247	Medford, OR	55
39	Memphis, TN-MS-AR	553
203	Merced, CA	78
9	Miami (greater), FL	1,404
37	Miami-Dade County, FL M.D.	577
324	Michigan City-La Porte, IN	27
255	Midland, TX	52
68	Milwaukee, WI	302
NA	Minneapolis-St. Paul, MN-WI**	NA
289	Missoula, MT	38
228	Mobile, AL	64
150	Modesto, CA	122
197	Monroe, MI	82
141	Montgomery, AL	128
336	Morgantown, WV	21
295	Morristown, TN	37
258	Mount Vernon-Anacortes, WA	51
251	Muncie, IN	54
193	Muskegon-Norton Shores, MI	85
306	Napa, CA	34
258	Naples-Marco Island, FL	51
42	Nashville-Davidson, TN	518
102	Nassau-Suffolk, NY M.D.	181
126	New Haven-Milford, CT	143
73	New Orleans, LA	282
5	New York (greater), NY-NJ-PA	1,773
15	New York-W. Plains NY-NJ M.D.	1,094
70	Newark-Union, NJ-PA M.D.	293
160	Niles-Benton Harbor, MI	115
101	North Port-Bradenton-Sarasota, FL	182
240	Norwich-New London, CT	58
26	Oakland-Fremont, CA M.D.	753
111	Ocala, FL	164
327	Ocean City, NJ	26
300	Odessa, TX	36

RANK	METROPOLITAN AREA	RAPES
128	Ogden-Clearfield, UT	142
43	Oklahoma City, OK	501
176	Olympia, WA	99
62	Omaha-Council Bluffs, NE-IA	332
31	Orlando, FL	731
331	Oshkosh-Neenah, WI	25
277	Owensboro, KY	42
158	Oxnard-Thousand Oaks, CA	116
105	Palm Bay-Melbourne, FL	174
335	Palm Coast, FL	22
195	Panama City-Lynn Haven, FL	83
233	Pascagoula, MS	62
135	Peabody, MA M.D.	134
85	Pensacola, FL	226
4	Philadelphia (greater) PA-NJ-MD-DE	1,911
7	Philadelphia, PA M.D.	1,523
13	Phoenix-Mesa-Scottsdale, AZ	1,110
228	Pine Bluff, AR	64
51	Pittsburgh, PA	432
255	Pittsfield, MA	52
306	Pocatello, ID	34
161	Port St. Lucie, FL	114
22	Portland-Vancouver, OR-WA	821
132	Portland, ME	138
195	Poughkeepsie, NY	83
295	Prescott, AZ	37
48	Providence-New Bedford, RI-MA	449
166	Provo-Orem, UT	109
315	Pueblo, CO	31
340	Punta Gorda, FL	18
279	Racine, WI	41
97	Raleigh-Cary, NC	193
139	Rapid City, SD	131
251	Reading, PA	54
164	Redding, CA	111
141	Reno-Sparks, NV	128
95	Richmond, VA	201
18	Riverside-San Bernardino, CA	928
218	Roanoke, VA	67
NA	Rochester, MN**	NA
78	Rochester, NY	240
181	Rockingham County, NH M.D.	95
262	Rocky Mount, NC	50
327	Rome, GA	26
36	Sacramento, CA	627
184	Saginaw, MI	91
145	Salem, OR	124
144	Salinas, CA	125
284	Salisbury, MD	39
45	Salt Lake City, UT	481
201	San Angelo, TX	79
20	San Antonio, TX	869
27	San Diego, CA	746
14	San Francisco (greater), CA	1,098
61	San Francisco-S. Mateo, CA M.D.	345
55	San Jose, CA	396
187	San Luis Obispo, CA	89
343	Sandusky, OH	17
46	Santa Ana-Anaheim, CA M.D.	456
147	Santa Barbara-Santa Maria, CA	123
201	Santa Cruz-Watsonville, CA	79
289	Santa Fe, NM	38
112	Santa Rosa-Petaluma, CA	163

RANK	METROPOLITAN AREA	RAPES
205	Savannah, GA	76
154	Scranton--Wilkes-Barre, PA	120
29	Seattle-Bellevue-Everett, WA M.D.	743
16	Seattle-Tacoma-Bellevue, WA	1,090
346	Sebastian-Vero Beach, FL	16
327	Sheboygan, WI	26
355	Sherman-Denison, TX	10
NA	Shreveport-Bossier City, LA**	NA
306	Sioux City, IA-NE-SD	34
122	Sioux Falls, SD	149
166	South Bend-Mishawaka, IN-MI	109
175	Spartanburg, SC	101
158	Spokane, WA	116
66	Springfield, MA	312
119	Springfield, MO	154
265	Springfield, OH	49
331	State College, PA	25
124	Stockton, CA	148
NA	St. Cloud, MN**	NA
316	St. George, UT	30
343	St. Joseph, MO-KS	17
NA	St. Louis, MO-IL**	NA
343	Sumter, SC	17
131	Syracuse, NY	140
60	Tacoma, WA M.D.	347
108	Tallahassee, FL	167
24	Tampa-St Petersburg, FL	806
210	Texarkana, TX-Texarkana, AR	73
84	Toledo, OH	228
226	Topeka, KS	65
231	Trenton-Ewing, NJ	63
69	Tucson, AZ	301
54	Tulsa, OK	416
236	Tuscaloosa, AL	60
171	Tyler, TX	106
235	Utica-Rome, NY	61
255	Valdosta, GA	52
163	Vallejo-Fairfield, CA	112
221	Victoria, TX	66
319	Vineland, NJ	29
137	Visalia-Porterville, CA	132
147	Waco, TX	123
336	Warner Robins, GA	21
30	Warren-Farmington Hills, MI M.D.	736
19	Washington (greater) DC-VA-MD-WV	908
28	Washington, DC-VA-MD-WV M.D.	745
213	Waterloo-Cedar Falls, IA	70
284	Wausau, WI	39
300	Wenatchee, WA	36
56	West Palm Beach, FL M.D.	388
267	Wheeling, WV-OH	48
265	Wichita Falls, TX	49
64	Wichita, KS	318
276	Williamsport, PA	43
103	Wilmington, DE-MD-NJ M.D.	178
168	Wilmington, NC	108
258	Winchester, VA-WV	51
114	Winston-Salem, NC	162
100	Worcester, MA	185
156	York-Hanover, PA	118
125	Youngstown, OH-PA	145
267	Yuba City, CA	48
295	Yuma, AZ	37

Source: Reported data from the F.B.I. "Crime in the United States 2009"
*Forcible rape is the carnal knowledge of a female forcibly and against her will. Assaults or attempts to commit rape by force or threat of force are included. However, statutory rape without force and other sex offenses are excluded. **Not available

13. Rapes in 2009 (continued)
National Total = 88,097 Rapes*

RANK	METROPOLITAN AREA	RAPES	RANK	METROPOLITAN AREA	RAPES	RANK	METROPOLITAN AREA	RAPES
1	Los Angeles (greater), CA	2,570	61	San Francisco-S. Mateo, CA M.D.	345	121	Greensboro-High Point, NC	151
2	Los Angeles County, CA M.D.	2,114	62	Omaha-Council Bluffs, NE-IA	332	122	Gainesville, FL	149
3	Dallas (greater), TX	1,944	63	Jacksonville, FL	331	122	Sioux Falls, SD	149
4	Philadelphia (greater) PA-NJ-MD-DE	1,911	64	Wichita, KS	318	124	Stockton, CA	148
5	New York (greater), NY-NJ-PA	1,773	65	Dayton, OH	313	125	Youngstown, OH-PA	145
6	Houston, TX	1,715	66	Springfield, MA	312	126	Fort Collins-Loveland, CO	143
7	Philadelphia, PA M.D.	1,523	67	Akron, OH	311	126	New Haven-Milford, CT	143
8	Detroit (greater), MI	1,412	68	Milwaukee, WI	302	128	Lexington-Fayette, KY	142
9	Miami (greater), FL	1,404	69	Tucson, AZ	301	128	Ogden-Clearfield, UT	142
10	Denver-Aurora, CO	1,225	70	Newark-Union, NJ-PA M.D.	293	130	Farmington, NM	141
11	Dallas-Plano-Irving, TX M.D.	1,178	71	Anchorage, AK	289	131	Syracuse, NY	140
12	Atlanta, GA	1,170	72	Columbia, SC	288	132	Deltona-Daytona Beach, FL	138
13	Phoenix-Mesa-Scottsdale, AZ	1,110	73	New Orleans, LA	282	132	Portland, ME	138
14	San Francisco (greater), CA	1,098	74	Buffalo-Niagara Falls, NY	260	134	Lincoln, NE	137
15	New York-W. Plains NY-NJ M.D.	1,094	75	Corpus Christi, TX	252	135	Abilene, TX	134
16	Seattle-Tacoma-Bellevue, WA	1,090	76	Fayetteville, AR-MO	245	135	Peabody, MA M.D.	134
17	Boston (greater), MA-NH	996	77	Honolulu, HI	243	137	Lake Charles, LA	132
18	Riverside-San Bernardino, CA	928	78	Rochester, NY	240	137	Visalia-Porterville, CA	132
19	Washington (greater) DC-VA-MD-WV	908	79	Knoxville, TN	238	139	Rapid City, SD	131
20	San Antonio, TX	869	80	Des Moines-West Des Moines, IA	236	140	Chattanooga, TN-GA	130
21	Columbus, OH	832	81	Flint, MI	235	141	Huntsville, AL	128
22	Portland-Vancouver, OR-WA	821	82	El Paso, TX	231	141	Montgomery, AL	128
23	Las Vegas-Paradise, NV	810	83	Cambridge-Newton, MA M.D.	229	141	Reno-Sparks, NV	128
24	Tampa-St Petersburg, FL	806	84	Toledo, OH	228	144	Salinas, CA	125
25	Fort Worth-Arlington, TX M.D.	766	85	Pensacola, FL	226	145	Holland-Grand Haven, MI	124
26	Oakland-Fremont, CA M.D.	753	86	Charleston-North Charleston, SC	218	145	Salem, OR	124
27	San Diego, CA	746	86	Jackson, MS	218	147	Fayetteville, NC	123
28	Washington, DC-VA-MD-WV M.D.	745	88	Lansing-East Lansing, MI	217	147	Santa Barbara-Santa Maria, CA	123
29	Seattle-Bellevue-Everett, WA M.D.	743	89	Boise City-Nampa, ID	215	147	Waco, TX	123
30	Warren-Farmington Hills, MI M.D.	736	90	Augusta, GA-SC	212	150	Modesto, CA	122
31	Orlando, FL	731	90	McAllen-Edinburg-Mission, TX	212	151	Cape Coral-Fort Myers, FL	121
32	Cincinnati-Middletown, OH-KY-IN	720	92	Camden, NJ M.D.	210	151	Erie, PA	121
32	Cleveland-Elyria-Mentor, OH	720	93	Bakersfield, CA	205	151	Manchester-Nashua, NH	121
34	Kansas City, MO-KS	700	93	Edison, NJ M.D.	205	154	Durham-Chapel Hill, NC	120
35	Detroit-Livonia-Dearborn, MI M.D.	676	95	Kalamazoo-Portage, MI	201	154	Scranton--Wilkes-Barre, PA	120
36	Sacramento, CA	627	95	Richmond, VA	201	156	Lubbock, TX	118
37	Miami-Dade County, FL M.D.	577	97	Hartford, CT	193	156	York-Hanover, PA	118
38	Indianapolis, IN	570	97	Raleigh-Cary, NC	193	158	Oxnard-Thousand Oaks, CA	116
39	Memphis, TN-MS-AR	553	99	Lakeland, FL	186	158	Spokane, WA	116
40	Baltimore-Towson, MD	552	100	Worcester, MA	185	160	Niles-Benton Harbor, MI	115
41	Boston-Quincy, MA M.D.	538	101	North Port-Bradenton-Sarasota, FL	182	161	Eugene-Springfield, OR	114
42	Nashville-Davidson, TN	518	102	Nassau-Suffolk, NY M.D.	181	161	Port St. Lucie, FL	114
43	Oklahoma City, OK	501	103	Fresno, CA	178	163	Vallejo-Fairfield, CA	112
44	Charlotte-Gastonia, NC-SC	498	103	Wilmington, DE-MD-NJ M.D.	178	164	Redding, CA	111
45	Salt Lake City, UT	481	105	Palm Bay-Melbourne, FL	174	165	Fort Smith, AR-OK	110
46	Santa Ana-Anaheim, CA M.D.	456	106	Bremerton-Silverdale, WA	169	166	Provo-Orem, UT	109
47	Austin-Round Rock, TX	455	107	Harrisburg-Carlisle, PA	168	166	South Bend-Mishawaka, IN-MI	109
48	Providence-New Bedford, RI-MA	449	108	Tallahassee, FL	167	168	Amarillo, TX	108
49	Fort Lauderdale, FL M.D.	439	109	Allentown, PA-NJ	165	168	Kennewick-Pasco-Richland, WA	108
50	Birmingham-Hoover, AL	433	109	Beaumont-Port Arthur, TX	165	168	Wilmington, NC	108
51	Pittsburgh, PA	432	111	Ocala, FL	164	171	Tyler, TX	106
52	Albuquerque, NM	421	112	Bethesda-Frederick, MD M.D.	163	172	Jackson, MI	105
52	Colorado Springs, CO	421	112	Santa Rosa-Petaluma, CA	163	173	Green Bay, WI	103
54	Tulsa, OK	416	114	Albany-Schenectady-Troy, NY	162	174	Evansville, IN-KY	102
55	San Jose, CA	396	114	Winston-Salem, NC	162	175	Spartanburg, SC	101
56	West Palm Beach, FL M.D.	388	116	Killeen-Temple-Fort Hood, TX	161	176	Olympia, WA	99
57	Little Rock, AR	365	117	Baton Rouge, LA	160	177	Fort Wayne, IN	98
58	Louisville, KY-IN	361	118	Ann Arbor, MI	158	178	Clarksville, TN-KY	97
59	Grand Rapids-Wyoming, MI	351	119	Bridgeport-Stamford, CT	154	179	Jacksonville, NC	96
60	Tacoma, WA M.D.	347	119	Springfield, MO	154	179	Kingsport, TN-VA	96

Note: All listings are for Metropolitan Statistical Areas (M.S.A.s) except for those ending with "M.D." Listings with "M.D." are Metropolitan Divisions which are smaller parts of eleven large M.S.A.s. See explanatory note at beginning of metropolitan area section.

Rank Order - Metro Area (continued)

RANK	METROPOLITAN AREA	RAPES
181	Brownsville-Harlingen, TX	95
181	Rockingham County, NH M.D.	95
183	Asheville, NC	92
184	College Station-Bryan, TX	91
184	Lancaster, PA	91
184	Saginaw, MI	91
187	Lafayette, LA	89
187	San Luis Obispo, CA	89
189	Battle Creek, MI	87
189	Chico, CA	87
191	Lawton, OK	86
191	Madison, WI	86
193	Longview, TX	85
193	Muskegon-Norton Shores, MI	85
195	Panama City-Lynn Haven, FL	83
195	Poughkeepsie, NY	83
197	Coeur d'Alene, ID	82
197	Monroe, MI	82
199	Dover, DE	81
199	Florence, SC	81
201	San Angelo, TX	79
201	Santa Cruz-Watsonville, CA	79
203	Merced, CA	78
204	Laredo, TX	77
205	Barnstable Town, MA	76
205	Bellingham, WA	76
205	Savannah, GA	76
208	Lima, OH	75
209	Grand Junction, CO	74
210	Bay City, MI	73
210	Greeley, CO	73
210	Texarkana, TX-Texarkana, AR	73
213	Waterloo-Cedar Falls, IA	70
214	Anderson, SC	68
214	Charleston, WV	68
214	Charlottesville, VA	68
214	Manhattan, KS	68
218	Boulder, CO	67
218	Las Cruces, NM	67
218	Roanoke, VA	67
221	Albany, GA	66
221	Cedar Rapids, IA	66
221	Columbus, GA-AL	66
221	Lawrence, KS	66
221	Victoria, TX	66
226	Blacksburg, VA	65
226	Topeka, KS	65
228	Lynchburg, VA	64
228	Mobile, AL	64
228	Pine Bluff, AR	64
231	Anniston-Oxford, AL	63
231	Trenton-Ewing, NJ	63
233	Flagstaff, AZ	62
233	Pascagoula, MS	62
235	Utica-Rome, NY	61
236	Atlantic City, NJ	60
236	Crestview-Fort Walton Beach, FL	60
236	Tuscaloosa, AL	60
239	Hattiesburg, MS	59
240	Bloomington, IN	58
240	Bowling Green, KY	58
240	Burlington-South Burlington, VT	58
240	Hickory, NC	58

RANK	METROPOLITAN AREA	RAPES
240	Norwich-New London, CT	58
245	Gadsden, AL	57
246	Longview, WA	56
247	Auburn, AL	55
247	Elkhart-Goshen, IN	55
247	Houma, LA	55
247	Medford, OR	55
251	Athens-Clarke County, GA	54
251	Muncie, IN	54
251	Reading, PA	54
254	Gulfport-Biloxi, MS	53
255	Midland, TX	52
255	Pittsfield, MA	52
255	Valdosta, GA	52
258	Macon, GA	51
258	Mount Vernon-Anacortes, WA	51
258	Naples-Marco Island, FL	51
258	Winchester, VA-WV	51
262	Hagerstown-Martinsburg, MD-WV	50
262	Iowa City, IA	50
262	Rocky Mount, NC	50
265	Springfield, OH	49
265	Wichita Falls, TX	49
267	Burlington, NC	48
267	Jonesboro, AR	48
267	Wheeling, WV-OH	48
267	Yuba City, CA	48
271	Binghamton, NY	46
272	Dothan, AL	45
272	Idaho Falls, ID	45
272	Lafayette, IN	45
275	Mansfield, OH	44
276	Williamsport, PA	43
277	Hot Springs, AR	42
277	Owensboro, KY	42
279	Alexandria, LA	41
279	Racine, WI	41
281	Cheyenne, WY	40
281	Janesville, WI	40
281	Johnson City, TN	40
284	Altoona, PA	39
284	Eau Claire, WI	39
284	Gainesville, GA	39
284	Salisbury, MD	39
284	Wausau, WI	39
289	Anderson, IN	38
289	Appleton, WI	38
289	Bend, OR	38
289	Columbia, MO	38
289	Missoula, MT	38
289	Santa Fe, NM	38
295	Brunswick, GA	37
295	Lewiston-Auburn, ME	37
295	Morristown, TN	37
295	Prescott, AZ	37
295	Yuma, AZ	37
300	Bismarck, ND	36
300	Madera, CA	36
300	Odessa, TX	36
300	Wenatchee, WA	36
304	Decatur, AL	35
304	Jackson, TN	35
306	Billings, MT	34

RANK	METROPOLITAN AREA	RAPES
306	Florence-Muscle Shoals, AL	34
306	Hinesville, GA	34
306	Lake Havasu City-Kingman, AZ	34
306	Napa, CA	34
306	Pocatello, ID	34
306	Sioux City, IA-NE-SD	34
313	Ames, IA	32
313	Dalton, GA	32
315	Pueblo, CO	31
316	Jefferson City, MO	30
316	Logan, UT-ID	30
316	St. George, UT	30
319	Cumberland, MD-WV	29
319	Fond du Lac, WI	29
319	Vineland, NJ	29
322	Cape Girardeau, MO-IL	28
322	Cleveland, TN	28
324	Harrisonburg, VA	27
324	Kingston, NY	27
324	Michigan City-La Porte, IN	27
327	Casper, WY	26
327	Ocean City, NJ	26
327	Rome, GA	26
327	Sheboygan, WI	26
331	Elizabethtown, KY	25
331	Oshkosh-Neenah, WI	25
331	State College, PA	25
334	Kokomo, IN	23
335	Palm Coast, FL	22
336	Bangor, ME	21
336	Morgantown, WV	21
336	Warner Robins, GA	21
339	Lewiston, ID-WA	19
340	Dubuque, IA	18
340	El Centro, CA	18
340	Punta Gorda, FL	18
343	Sandusky, OH	17
343	St. Joseph, MO-KS	17
343	Sumter, SC	17
346	Great Falls, MT	16
346	Sebastian-Vero Beach, FL	16
348	Corvallis, OR	15
348	Glens Falls, NY	15
348	Lebanon, PA	15
351	Danville, VA	13
351	Elmira, NY	13
353	Goldsboro, NC	12
353	Ithaca, NY	12
355	Sherman-Denison, TX	10
356	Columbus, IN	7
357	Carson City, NV	1
NA	Danville, IL**	NA
NA	Decatur, IL**	NA
NA	Duluth, MN-WI**	NA
NA	Fargo, ND-MN**	NA
NA	Grand Forks, ND-MN**	NA
NA	La Crosse, WI-MN**	NA
NA	Mankato-North Mankato, MN**	NA
NA	Minneapolis-St. Paul, MN-WI**	NA
NA	Rochester, MN**	NA
NA	Shreveport-Bossier City, LA**	NA
NA	St. Cloud, MN**	NA
NA	St. Louis, MO-IL**	NA

Source: Reported data from the F.B.I. "Crime in the United States 2009"

*Forcible rape is the carnal knowledge of a female forcibly and against her will. Assaults or attempts to commit rape by force or threat of force are included. However, statutory rape without force and other sex offenses are excluded. **Not available

14. Rape Rate in 2009
National Rate = 28.7 Rapes per 100,000 Population*

RANK	METROPOLITAN AREA	RATE
4	Abilene, TX	83.9
62	Akron, OH	44.4
303	Albany-Schenectady-Troy, NY	18.9
89	Albany, GA	40.0
43	Albuquerque, NM	48.8
218	Alexandria, LA	26.5
291	Allentown, PA-NJ	20.2
167	Altoona, PA	31.2
63	Amarillo, TX	43.9
107	Ames, IA	36.6
3	Anchorage, AK	94.7
190	Anderson, IN	28.9
107	Anderson, SC	36.6
56	Ann Arbor, MI	45.3
25	Anniston-Oxford, AL	55.2
317	Appleton, WI	17.1
269	Asheville, NC	22.2
197	Athens-Clarke County, GA	28.3
282	Atlanta, GA	21.3
275	Atlantic City, NJ	22.0
84	Auburn, AL	40.5
92	Augusta, GA-SC	39.4
217	Austin-Round Rock, TX	26.7
230	Bakersfield, CA	25.2
287	Baltimore-Towson, MD	20.5
337	Bangor, ME	14.1
133	Barnstable Town, MA	33.9
290	Baton Rouge, LA	20.3
14	Battle Creek, MI	64.4
10	Bay City, MI	68.4
64	Beaumont-Port Arthur, TX	43.7
101	Bellingham, WA	37.8
251	Bend, OR	23.2
339	Bethesda-Frederick, MD M.D.	13.6
269	Billings, MT	22.2
305	Binghamton, NY	18.8
98	Birmingham-Hoover, AL	38.3
137	Bismarck, ND	33.7
83	Blacksburg, VA	40.7
162	Bloomington, IN	31.3
118	Boise City-Nampa, ID	35.0
278	Boston (greater), MA-NH	21.7
200	Boston-Quincy, MA M.D.	28.1
263	Boulder, CO	22.6
45	Bowling Green, KY	48.4
9	Bremerton-Silverdale, WA	69.8
314	Bridgeport-Stamford, CT	17.5
243	Brownsville-Harlingen, TX	23.8
112	Brunswick, GA	35.7
251	Buffalo-Niagara Falls, NY	23.2
202	Burlington-South Burlington, VT	27.7
155	Burlington, NC	31.9
331	Cambridge-Newton, MA M.D.	15.2
322	Camden, NJ M.D.	16.7
294	Cape Coral-Fort Myers, FL	19.9
179	Cape Girardeau, MO-IL	29.9
357	Carson City, NV	1.8
123	Casper, WY	34.7
222	Cedar Rapids, IA	25.7
144	Charleston-North Charleston, SC	33.0
267	Charleston, WV	22.4
195	Charlotte-Gastonia, NC-SC	28.4
126	Charlottesville, VA	34.4
233	Chattanooga, TN-GA	24.8
58	Cheyenne, WY	44.8
94	Chico, CA	39.3
142	Cincinnati-Middletown, OH-KY-IN	33.1
107	Clarksville, TN-KY	36.6
126	Cleveland-Elyria-Mentor, OH	34.4
236	Cleveland, TN	24.7
20	Coeur d'Alene, ID	58.4
66	College Station-Bryan, TX	43.3
12	Colorado Springs, CO	67.0
259	Columbia, MO	22.8
96	Columbia, SC	38.8
258	Columbus, GA-AL	22.9
353	Columbus, IN	9.2
53	Columbus, OH	46.3
19	Corpus Christi, TX	60.4
309	Corvallis, OR	18.3
138	Crestview-Fort Walton Beach, FL	33.5
184	Cumberland, MD-WV	29.3
177	Dallas (greater), TX	30.1
209	Dallas-Plano-Irving, TX M.D.	27.2
245	Dalton, GA	23.7
NA	Danville, IL**	NA
342	Danville, VA	12.3
102	Dayton, OH	37.4
256	Decatur, AL	23.1
NA	Decatur, IL**	NA
204	Deltona-Daytona Beach, FL	27.6
47	Denver-Aurora, CO	48.0
76	Des Moines-West Des Moines, IA	41.8
151	Detroit (greater), MI	32.1
118	Detroit-Livonia-Dearborn, MI M.D.	35.0
159	Dothan, AL	31.5
37	Dover, DE	50.9
299	Dubuque, IA	19.4
NA	Duluth, MN-WI**	NA
240	Durham-Chapel Hill, NC	24.1
238	Eau Claire, WI	24.4
354	Edison, NJ M.D.	8.8
349	El Centro, CA	10.8
168	El Paso, TX	30.8
271	Elizabethtown, KY	22.1
207	Elkhart-Goshen, IN	27.3
334	Elmira, NY	14.9
66	Erie, PA	43.3
146	Eugene-Springfield, OR	32.7
189	Evansville, IN-KY	29.0
NA	Fargo, ND-MN**	NA
1	Farmington, NM	113.9
31	Fayetteville, AR-MO	53.5
129	Fayetteville, NC	34.3
46	Flagstaff, AZ	48.3
26	Flint, MI	55.1
249	Florence-Muscle Shoals, AL	23.5
87	Florence, SC	40.2
188	Fond du Lac, WI	29.1
47	Fort Collins-Loveland, CO	48.0
231	Fort Lauderdale, FL M.D.	25.1
102	Fort Smith, AR-OK	37.4
245	Fort Wayne, IN	23.7
110	Fort Worth-Arlington, TX M.D.	36.1
299	Fresno, CA	19.4
28	Gadsden, AL	54.9
21	Gainesville, FL	57.5
286	Gainesville, GA	20.6
347	Glens Falls, NY	11.6
350	Goldsboro, NC	10.5
NA	Grand Forks, ND-MN**	NA
38	Grand Junction, CO	50.5
57	Grand Rapids-Wyoming, MI	45.1
295	Great Falls, MT	19.5
198	Greeley, CO	28.2
135	Green Bay, WI	33.8
283	Greensboro-High Point, NC	21.2
261	Gulfport-Biloxi, MS	22.7
306	Hagerstown-Martinsburg, MD-WV	18.5
160	Harrisburg-Carlisle, PA	31.4
264	Harrisonburg, VA	22.5
302	Hartford, CT	19.2
79	Hattiesburg, MS	41.3
326	Hickory, NC	15.9
41	Hinesville, GA	49.0
50	Holland-Grand Haven, MI	47.4
215	Honolulu, HI	26.8
72	Hot Springs, AR	42.5
210	Houma, LA	27.1
184	Houston, TX	29.3
157	Huntsville, AL	31.7
111	Idaho Falls, ID	36.0
146	Indianapolis, IN	32.7
142	Iowa City, IA	33.1
346	Ithaca, NY	11.8
232	Jacksonville, FL	25.0
23	Jacksonville, NC	57.1
13	Jackson, MI	65.8
87	Jackson, MS	40.2
168	Jackson, TN	30.8
233	Janesville, WI	24.8
288	Jefferson City, MO	20.4
291	Johnson City, TN	20.2
85	Jonesboro, AR	40.4
17	Kalamazoo-Portage, MI	62.2
131	Kansas City, MO-KS	34.0
61	Kennewick-Pasco-Richland, WA	44.5
76	Killeen-Temple-Fort Hood, TX	41.8
162	Kingsport, TN-VA	31.3
335	Kingston, NY	14.8
133	Knoxville, TN	33.9
251	Kokomo, IN	23.2
NA	La Crosse, WI-MN**	NA
256	Lafayette, IN	23.1
135	Lafayette, LA	33.8
11	Lake Charles, LA	68.0
317	Lake Havasu City-Kingman, AZ	17.1
157	Lakeland, FL	31.7
311	Lancaster, PA	17.9
49	Lansing-East Lansing, MI	47.9

Note: All listings are for Metropolitan Statistical Areas (M.S.A.s) except for those ending with "M.D." Listings with "M.D." are Metropolitan Divisions which are smaller parts of eleven large M.S.A.s. See explanatory note at beginning of metropolitan area section.

RANK	METROPOLITAN AREA	RATE
156	Laredo, TX	31.8
149	Las Cruces, NM	32.6
72	Las Vegas-Paradise, NV	42.5
24	Lawrence, KS	56.6
5	Lawton, OK	76.7
348	Lebanon, PA	11.5
124	Lewiston-Auburn, ME	34.6
162	Lewiston, ID-WA	31.3
176	Lexington-Fayette, KY	30.2
8	Lima, OH	71.4
54	Lincoln, NE	45.7
33	Little Rock, AR	53.3
247	Logan, UT-ID	23.6
80	Longview, TX	41.2
29	Longview, WA	54.5
281	Los Angeles County, CA M.D.	21.4
293	Los Angeles (greater), CA	20.0
191	Louisville, KY-IN	28.7
68	Lubbock, TX	43.2
222	Lynchburg, VA	25.7
271	Macon, GA	22.1
241	Madera, CA	23.9
332	Madison, WI	15.1
179	Manchester-Nashua, NH	29.9
27	Manhattan, KS	55.0
NA	Mankato-North Mankato, MN**	NA
115	Mansfield, OH	35.2
195	McAllen-Edinburg-Mission, TX	28.4
210	Medford, OR	27.1
71	Memphis, TN-MS-AR	42.6
162	Merced, CA	31.3
226	Miami (greater), FL	25.5
251	Miami-Dade County, FL M.D.	23.2
239	Michigan City-La Porte, IN	24.3
90	Midland, TX	39.6
299	Milwaukee, WI	19.4
NA	Minneapolis-St. Paul, MN-WI**	NA
118	Missoula, MT	35.0
328	Mobile, AL	15.7
247	Modesto, CA	23.6
30	Monroe, MI	53.6
124	Montgomery, AL	34.6
313	Morgantown, WV	17.6
214	Morristown, TN	26.9
74	Mount Vernon-Anacortes, WA	42.3
51	Muncie, IN	47.2
43	Muskegon-Norton Shores, MI	48.8
227	Napa, CA	25.4
326	Naples-Marco Island, FL	15.9
146	Nashville-Davidson, TN	32.7
356	Nassau-Suffolk, NY M.D.	6.3
310	New Haven-Milford, CT	18.0
241	New Orleans, LA	23.9
351	New York (greater), NY-NJ-PA	9.3
351	New York-W. Plains NY-NJ M.D.	9.3
338	Newark-Union, NJ-PA M.D.	13.8
6	Niles-Benton Harbor, MI	72.6
219	North Port-Bradenton-Sarasota, FL	26.3
76	Norwich-New London, CT	41.8
178	Oakland-Fremont, CA M.D.	30.0
42	Ocala, FL	48.9
207	Ocean City, NJ	27.3
212	Odessa, TX	27.0

RANK	METROPOLITAN AREA	RATE
219	Ogden-Clearfield, UT	26.3
81	Oklahoma City, OK	40.9
92	Olympia, WA	39.4
95	Omaha-Council Bluffs, NE-IA	39.2
118	Orlando, FL	35.0
330	Oshkosh-Neenah, WI	15.4
104	Owensboro, KY	37.1
336	Oxnard-Thousand Oaks, CA	14.5
150	Palm Bay-Melbourne, FL	32.3
259	Palm Coast, FL	22.8
38	Panama City-Lynn Haven, FL	50.5
85	Pascagoula, MS	40.4
311	Peabody, MA M.D.	17.9
40	Pensacola, FL	49.8
153	Philadelphia (greater) PA-NJ-MD-DE	32.0
100	Philadelphia, PA M.D.	38.0
227	Phoenix-Mesa-Scottsdale, AZ	25.4
15	Pine Bluff, AR	63.8
307	Pittsburgh, PA	18.4
90	Pittsfield, MA	39.6
98	Pocatello, ID	38.3
202	Port St. Lucie, FL	27.7
106	Portland-Vancouver, OR-WA	36.7
215	Portland, ME	26.8
343	Poughkeepsie, NY	12.2
321	Prescott, AZ	16.9
201	Providence-New Bedford, RI-MA	27.9
295	Provo-Orem, UT	19.5
295	Pueblo, CO	19.5
344	Punta Gorda, FL	12.0
288	Racine, WI	20.4
317	Raleigh-Cary, NC	17.1
2	Rapid City, SD	105.7
341	Reading, PA	13.2
18	Redding, CA	61.2
171	Reno-Sparks, NV	30.6
325	Richmond, VA	16.1
271	Riverside-San Bernardino, CA	22.1
268	Roanoke, VA	22.3
NA	Rochester, MN**	NA
251	Rochester, NY	23.2
264	Rockingham County, NH M.D.	22.5
131	Rocky Mount, NC	34.0
212	Rome, GA	27.0
184	Sacramento, CA	29.3
54	Saginaw, MI	45.7
162	Salem, OR	31.3
170	Salinas, CA	30.7
153	Salisbury, MD	32.0
69	Salt Lake City, UT	42.7
7	San Angelo, TX	71.8
75	San Antonio, TX	41.9
233	San Diego, CA	24.8
222	San Francisco (greater), CA	25.7
295	San Francisco-S. Mateo, CA M.D.	19.5
278	San Jose, CA	21.7
139	San Luis Obispo, CA	33.4
271	Sandusky, OH	22.1
332	Santa Ana-Anaheim, CA M.D.	15.1
174	Santa Barbara-Santa Maria, CA	30.4
160	Santa Cruz-Watsonville, CA	31.4
221	Santa Fe, NM	26.0
118	Santa Rosa-Petaluma, CA	35.0

RANK	METROPOLITAN AREA	RATE
264	Savannah, GA	22.5
276	Scranton--Wilkes-Barre, PA	21.8
193	Seattle-Bellevue-Everett, WA M.D.	28.6
151	Seattle-Tacoma-Bellevue, WA	32.1
344	Sebastian-Vero Beach, FL	12.0
261	Sheboygan, WI	22.7
355	Sherman-Denison, TX	8.3
NA	Shreveport-Bossier City, LA**	NA
243	Sioux City, IA-NE-SD	23.8
16	Sioux Falls, SD	62.3
126	South Bend-Mishawaka, IN-MI	34.4
114	Spartanburg, SC	35.4
236	Spokane, WA	24.7
60	Springfield, MA	44.7
113	Springfield, MO	35.6
116	Springfield, OH	35.1
317	State College, PA	17.1
278	Stockton, CA	21.7
NA	St. Cloud, MN**	NA
284	St. George, UT	20.9
340	St. Joseph, MO-KS	13.4
NA	St. Louis, MO-IL**	NA
324	Sumter, SC	16.2
276	Syracuse, NY	21.8
65	Tacoma, WA M.D.	43.4
52	Tallahassee, FL	46.6
184	Tampa-St Petersburg, FL	29.3
31	Texarkana, TX-Texarkana, AR	53.5
116	Toledo, OH	35.1
198	Topeka, KS	28.2
316	Trenton-Ewing, NJ	17.2
183	Tucson, AZ	29.5
58	Tulsa, OK	44.8
191	Tuscaloosa, AL	28.7
36	Tyler, TX	51.8
285	Utica-Rome, NY	20.8
97	Valdosta, GA	38.7
205	Vallejo-Fairfield, CA	27.5
21	Victoria, TX	57.5
307	Vineland, NJ	18.4
171	Visalia-Porterville, CA	30.6
34	Waco, TX	52.9
329	Warner Robins, GA	15.5
181	Warren-Farmington Hills, MI M.D.	29.7
322	Washington (greater) DC-VA-MD-WV	16.7
314	Washington, DC-VA-MD-WV M.D.	17.5
69	Waterloo-Cedar Falls, IA	42.7
181	Wausau, WI	29.7
145	Wenatchee, WA	32.8
171	West Palm Beach, FL M.D.	30.6
140	Wheeling, WV-OH	33.3
140	Wichita Falls, TX	33.3
35	Wichita, KS	52.3
105	Williamsport, PA	36.9
227	Wilmington, DE-MD-NJ M.D.	25.4
175	Wilmington, NC	30.3
82	Winchester, VA-WV	40.8
130	Winston-Salem, NC	34.2
250	Worcester, MA	23.3
206	York-Hanover, PA	27.4
222	Youngstown, OH-PA	25.7
193	Yuba City, CA	28.6
303	Yuma, AZ	18.9

Source: Reported data from the F.B.I. "Crime in the United States 2009"

*Forcible rape is the carnal knowledge of a female forcibly and against her will. Assaults or attempts to commit rape by force or threat of force are included. However, statutory rape without force and other sex offenses are excluded. **Not available

14. Rape Rate in 2009 (continued)
National Rate = 28.7 Rapes per 100,000 Population*

RANK	METROPOLITAN AREA	RATE
1	Farmington, NM	113.9
2	Rapid City, SD	105.7
3	Anchorage, AK	94.7
4	Abilene, TX	83.9
5	Lawton, OK	76.7
6	Niles-Benton Harbor, MI	72.6
7	San Angelo, TX	71.8
8	Lima, OH	71.4
9	Bremerton-Silverdale, WA	69.8
10	Bay City, MI	68.4
11	Lake Charles, LA	68.0
12	Colorado Springs, CO	67.0
13	Jackson, MI	65.8
14	Battle Creek, MI	64.4
15	Pine Bluff, AR	63.8
16	Sioux Falls, SD	62.3
17	Kalamazoo-Portage, MI	62.2
18	Redding, CA	61.2
19	Corpus Christi, TX	60.4
20	Coeur d'Alene, ID	58.4
21	Gainesville, FL	57.5
21	Victoria, TX	57.5
23	Jacksonville, NC	57.1
24	Lawrence, KS	56.6
25	Anniston-Oxford, AL	55.2
26	Flint, MI	55.1
27	Manhattan, KS	55.0
28	Gadsden, AL	54.9
29	Longview, WA	54.5
30	Monroe, MI	53.6
31	Fayetteville, AR-MO	53.5
31	Texarkana, TX-Texarkana, AR	53.5
33	Little Rock, AR	53.3
34	Waco, TX	52.9
35	Wichita, KS	52.3
36	Tyler, TX	51.8
37	Dover, DE	50.9
38	Grand Junction, CO	50.5
38	Panama City-Lynn Haven, FL	50.5
40	Pensacola, FL	49.8
41	Hinesville, GA	49.0
42	Ocala, FL	48.9
43	Albuquerque, NM	48.8
43	Muskegon-Norton Shores, MI	48.8
45	Bowling Green, KY	48.4
46	Flagstaff, AZ	48.3
47	Denver-Aurora, CO	48.0
47	Fort Collins-Loveland, CO	48.0
49	Lansing-East Lansing, MI	47.9
50	Holland-Grand Haven, MI	47.4
51	Muncie, IN	47.2
52	Tallahassee, FL	46.6
53	Columbus, OH	46.3
54	Lincoln, NE	45.7
54	Saginaw, MI	45.7
56	Ann Arbor, MI	45.3
57	Grand Rapids-Wyoming, MI	45.1
58	Cheyenne, WY	44.8
58	Tulsa, OK	44.8
60	Springfield, MA	44.7
61	Kennewick-Pasco-Richland, WA	44.5
62	Akron, OH	44.4
63	Amarillo, TX	43.9
64	Beaumont-Port Arthur, TX	43.7
65	Tacoma, WA M.D.	43.4
66	College Station-Bryan, TX	43.3
66	Erie, PA	43.3
68	Lubbock, TX	43.2
69	Salt Lake City, UT	42.7
69	Waterloo-Cedar Falls, IA	42.7
71	Memphis, TN-MS-AR	42.6
72	Hot Springs, AR	42.5
72	Las Vegas-Paradise, NV	42.5
74	Mount Vernon-Anacortes, WA	42.3
75	San Antonio, TX	41.9
76	Des Moines-West Des Moines, IA	41.8
76	Killeen-Temple-Fort Hood, TX	41.8
76	Norwich-New London, CT	41.8
79	Hattiesburg, MS	41.3
80	Longview, TX	41.2
81	Oklahoma City, OK	40.9
82	Winchester, VA-WV	40.8
83	Blacksburg, VA	40.7
84	Auburn, AL	40.5
85	Jonesboro, AR	40.4
85	Pascagoula, MS	40.4
87	Florence, SC	40.2
87	Jackson, MS	40.2
89	Albany, GA	40.0
90	Midland, TX	39.6
90	Pittsfield, MA	39.6
92	Augusta, GA-SC	39.4
92	Olympia, WA	39.4
94	Chico, CA	39.3
95	Omaha-Council Bluffs, NE-IA	39.2
96	Columbia, SC	38.8
97	Valdosta, GA	38.7
98	Birmingham-Hoover, AL	38.3
98	Pocatello, ID	38.3
100	Philadelphia, PA M.D.	38.0
101	Bellingham, WA	37.8
102	Dayton, OH	37.4
102	Fort Smith, AR-OK	37.4
104	Owensboro, KY	37.1
105	Williamsport, PA	36.9
106	Portland-Vancouver, OR-WA	36.7
107	Ames, IA	36.6
107	Anderson, SC	36.6
107	Clarksville, TN-KY	36.6
110	Fort Worth-Arlington, TX M.D.	36.1
111	Idaho Falls, ID	36.0
112	Brunswick, GA	35.7
113	Springfield, MO	35.6
114	Spartanburg, SC	35.4
115	Mansfield, OH	35.2
116	Springfield, OH	35.1
116	Toledo, OH	35.1
118	Boise City-Nampa, ID	35.0
118	Detroit-Livonia-Dearborn, MI M.D.	35.0
118	Missoula, MT	35.0
118	Orlando, FL	35.0
118	Santa Rosa-Petaluma, CA	35.0
123	Casper, WY	34.7
124	Lewiston-Auburn, ME	34.6
124	Montgomery, AL	34.6
126	Charlottesville, VA	34.4
126	Cleveland-Elyria-Mentor, OH	34.4
126	South Bend-Mishawaka, IN-MI	34.4
129	Fayetteville, NC	34.3
130	Winston-Salem, NC	34.2
131	Kansas City, MO-KS	34.0
131	Rocky Mount, NC	34.0
133	Barnstable Town, MA	33.9
133	Knoxville, TN	33.9
135	Green Bay, WI	33.8
135	Lafayette, LA	33.8
137	Bismarck, ND	33.7
138	Crestview-Fort Walton Beach, FL	33.5
139	San Luis Obispo, CA	33.4
140	Wheeling, WV-OH	33.3
140	Wichita Falls, TX	33.3
142	Cincinnati-Middletown, OH-KY-IN	33.1
142	Iowa City, IA	33.1
144	Charleston-North Charleston, SC	33.0
145	Wenatchee, WA	32.8
146	Eugene-Springfield, OR	32.7
146	Indianapolis, IN	32.7
146	Nashville-Davidson, TN	32.7
149	Las Cruces, NM	32.6
150	Palm Bay-Melbourne, FL	32.3
151	Detroit (greater), MI	32.1
151	Seattle-Tacoma-Bellevue, WA	32.1
153	Philadelphia (greater) PA-NJ-MD-DE	32.0
153	Salisbury, MD	32.0
155	Burlington, NC	31.9
156	Laredo, TX	31.8
157	Huntsville, AL	31.7
157	Lakeland, FL	31.7
159	Dothan, AL	31.5
160	Harrisburg-Carlisle, PA	31.4
160	Santa Cruz-Watsonville, CA	31.4
162	Bloomington, IN	31.3
162	Kingsport, TN-VA	31.3
162	Lewiston, ID-WA	31.3
162	Merced, CA	31.3
162	Salem, OR	31.3
167	Altoona, PA	31.2
168	El Paso, TX	30.8
168	Jackson, TN	30.8
170	Salinas, CA	30.7
171	Reno-Sparks, NV	30.6
171	Visalia-Porterville, CA	30.6
171	West Palm Beach, FL M.D.	30.6
174	Santa Barbara-Santa Maria, CA	30.4
175	Wilmington, NC	30.3
176	Lexington-Fayette, KY	30.2
177	Dallas (greater), TX	30.1
178	Oakland-Fremont, CA M.D.	30.0
179	Cape Girardeau, MO-IL	29.9
179	Manchester-Nashua, NH	29.9

Note: All listings are for Metropolitan Statistical Areas (M.S.A.s) except for those ending with "M.D." Listings with "M.D." are Metropolitan Divisions which are smaller parts of eleven large M.S.A.s. See explanatory note at beginning of metropolitan area section.

RANK	METROPOLITAN AREA	RATE
181	Warren-Farmington Hills, MI M.D.	29.7
181	Wausau, WI	29.7
183	Tucson, AZ	29.5
184	Cumberland, MD-WV	29.3
184	Houston, TX	29.3
184	Sacramento, CA	29.3
184	Tampa-St Petersburg, FL	29.3
188	Fond du Lac, WI	29.1
189	Evansville, IN-KY	29.0
190	Anderson, IN	28.9
191	Louisville, KY-IN	28.7
191	Tuscaloosa, AL	28.7
193	Seattle-Bellevue-Everett, WA M.D.	28.6
193	Yuba City, CA	28.6
195	Charlotte-Gastonia, NC-SC	28.4
195	McAllen-Edinburg-Mission, TX	28.4
197	Athens-Clarke County, GA	28.3
198	Greeley, CO	28.2
198	Topeka, KS	28.2
200	Boston-Quincy, MA M.D.	28.1
201	Providence-New Bedford, RI-MA	27.9
202	Burlington-South Burlington, VT	27.7
202	Port St. Lucie, FL	27.7
204	Deltona-Daytona Beach, FL	27.6
205	Vallejo-Fairfield, CA	27.5
206	York-Hanover, PA	27.4
207	Elkhart-Goshen, IN	27.3
207	Ocean City, NJ	27.3
209	Dallas-Plano-Irving, TX M.D.	27.2
210	Houma, LA	27.1
210	Medford, OR	27.1
212	Odessa, TX	27.0
212	Rome, GA	27.0
214	Morristown, TN	26.9
215	Honolulu, HI	26.8
215	Portland, ME	26.8
217	Austin-Round Rock, TX	26.7
218	Alexandria, LA	26.5
219	North Port-Bradenton-Sarasota, FL	26.3
219	Ogden-Clearfield, UT	26.3
221	Santa Fe, NM	26.0
222	Cedar Rapids, IA	25.7
222	Lynchburg, VA	25.7
222	San Francisco (greater), CA	25.7
222	Youngstown, OH-PA	25.7
226	Miami (greater), FL	25.5
227	Napa, CA	25.4
227	Phoenix-Mesa-Scottsdale, AZ	25.4
227	Wilmington, DE-MD-NJ M.D.	25.4
230	Bakersfield, CA	25.2
231	Fort Lauderdale, FL M.D.	25.1
232	Jacksonville, FL	25.0
233	Chattanooga, TN-GA	24.8
233	Janesville, WI	24.8
233	San Diego, CA	24.8
236	Cleveland, TN	24.7
236	Spokane, WA	24.7
238	Eau Claire, WI	24.4
239	Michigan City-La Porte, IN	24.3
240	Durham-Chapel Hill, NC	24.1
241	Madera, CA	23.9
241	New Orleans, LA	23.9
243	Brownsville-Harlingen, TX	23.8
243	Sioux City, IA-NE-SD	23.8
245	Dalton, GA	23.7
245	Fort Wayne, IN	23.7
247	Logan, UT-ID	23.6
247	Modesto, CA	23.6
249	Florence-Muscle Shoals, AL	23.5
250	Worcester, MA	23.3
251	Bend, OR	23.2
251	Buffalo-Niagara Falls, NY	23.2
251	Kokomo, IN	23.2
251	Miami-Dade County, FL M.D.	23.2
251	Rochester, NY	23.2
256	Decatur, AL	23.1
256	Lafayette, IN	23.1
258	Columbus, GA-AL	22.9
259	Columbia, MO	22.8
259	Palm Coast, FL	22.8
261	Gulfport-Biloxi, MS	22.7
261	Sheboygan, WI	22.7
263	Boulder, CO	22.6
264	Harrisonburg, VA	22.5
264	Rockingham County, NH M.D.	22.5
264	Savannah, GA	22.5
267	Charleston, WV	22.4
268	Roanoke, VA	22.3
269	Asheville, NC	22.2
269	Billings, MT	22.2
271	Elizabethtown, KY	22.1
271	Macon, GA	22.1
271	Riverside-San Bernardino, CA	22.1
271	Sandusky, OH	22.1
275	Atlantic City, NJ	22.0
276	Scranton--Wilkes-Barre, PA	21.8
276	Syracuse, NY	21.8
278	Boston (greater), MA-NH	21.7
278	San Jose, CA	21.7
278	Stockton, CA	21.7
281	Los Angeles County, CA M.D.	21.4
282	Atlanta, GA	21.3
283	Greensboro-High Point, NC	21.2
284	St. George, UT	20.9
285	Utica-Rome, NY	20.8
286	Gainesville, GA	20.6
287	Baltimore-Towson, MD	20.5
288	Jefferson City, MO	20.4
288	Racine, WI	20.4
290	Baton Rouge, LA	20.3
291	Allentown, PA-NJ	20.2
291	Johnson City, TN	20.2
293	Los Angeles (greater), CA	20.0
294	Cape Coral-Fort Myers, FL	19.9
295	Great Falls, MT	19.5
295	Provo-Orem, UT	19.5
295	Pueblo, CO	19.5
295	San Francisco-S. Mateo, CA M.D.	19.5
299	Dubuque, IA	19.4
299	Fresno, CA	19.4
299	Milwaukee, WI	19.4
302	Hartford, CT	19.2
303	Albany-Schenectady-Troy, NY	18.9
303	Yuma, AZ	18.9
305	Binghamton, NY	18.8
306	Hagerstown-Martinsburg, MD-WV	18.5
307	Pittsburgh, PA	18.4
307	Vineland, NJ	18.4
309	Corvallis, OR	18.3
310	New Haven-Milford, CT	18.0
311	Lancaster, PA	17.9
311	Peabody, MA M.D.	17.9
313	Morgantown, WV	17.6
314	Bridgeport-Stamford, CT	17.5
314	Washington, DC-VA-MD-WV M.D.	17.5
316	Trenton-Ewing, NJ	17.2
317	Appleton, WI	17.1
317	Lake Havasu City-Kingman, AZ	17.1
317	Raleigh-Cary, NC	17.1
317	State College, PA	17.1
321	Prescott, AZ	16.9
322	Camden, NJ M.D.	16.7
322	Washington (greater) DC-VA-MD-WV	16.7
324	Sumter, SC	16.2
325	Richmond, VA	16.1
326	Hickory, NC	15.9
326	Naples-Marco Island, FL	15.9
328	Mobile, AL	15.7
329	Warner Robins, GA	15.5
330	Oshkosh-Neenah, WI	15.4
331	Cambridge-Newton, MA M.D.	15.2
332	Madison, WI	15.1
332	Santa Ana-Anaheim, CA M.D.	15.1
334	Elmira, NY	14.9
335	Kingston, NY	14.8
336	Oxnard-Thousand Oaks, CA	14.5
337	Bangor, ME	14.1
338	Newark-Union, NJ-PA M.D.	13.8
339	Bethesda-Frederick, MD M.D.	13.6
340	St. Joseph, MO-KS	13.4
341	Reading, PA	13.2
342	Danville, VA	12.3
343	Poughkeepsie, NY	12.2
344	Punta Gorda, FL	12.0
344	Sebastian-Vero Beach, FL	12.0
346	Ithaca, NY	11.8
347	Glens Falls, NY	11.6
348	Lebanon, PA	11.5
349	El Centro, CA	10.8
350	Goldsboro, NC	10.5
351	New York (greater), NY-NJ-PA	9.3
351	New York-W. Plains NY-NJ M.D.	9.3
353	Columbus, IN	9.2
354	Edison, NJ M.D.	8.8
355	Sherman-Denison, TX	8.3
356	Nassau-Suffolk, NY M.D.	6.3
357	Carson City, NV	1.8
NA	Danville, IL**	NA
NA	Decatur, IL**	NA
NA	Duluth, MN-WI**	NA
NA	Fargo, ND-MN**	NA
NA	Grand Forks, ND-MN**	NA
NA	La Crosse, WI-MN**	NA
NA	Mankato-North Mankato, MN**	NA
NA	Minneapolis-St. Paul, MN-WI**	NA
NA	Rochester, MN**	NA
NA	Shreveport-Bossier City, LA**	NA
NA	St. Cloud, MN**	NA
NA	St. Louis, MO-IL**	NA

Source: Reported data from the F.B.I. "Crime in the United States 2009"

*Forcible rape is the carnal knowledge of a female forcibly and against her will. Assaults or attempts to commit rape by force or threat of force are included. However, statutory rape without force and other sex offenses are excluded. **Not available

15. Percent Change in Rape Rate: 2008 to 2009
National Percent Change = 3.5% Decrease*

RANK	METROPOLITAN AREA	% CHANGE
15	Abilene, TX	40.5
66	Akron, OH	10.2
186	Albany-Schenectady-Troy, NY	(10.0)
NA	Albany, GA**	NA
252	Albuquerque, NM	(20.7)
NA	Alexandria, LA**	NA
24	Allentown, PA-NJ	30.3
25	Altoona, PA	30.0
249	Amarillo, TX	(20.0)
239	Ames, IA	(17.6)
75	Anchorage, AK	7.6
NA	Anderson, IN**	NA
41	Anderson, SC	21.6
36	Ann Arbor, MI	24.1
NA	Anniston-Oxford, AL**	NA
171	Appleton, WI	(8.1)
144	Asheville, NC	(4.3)
231	Athens-Clarke County, GA	(16.3)
75	Atlanta, GA	7.6
195	Atlantic City, NJ	(10.9)
236	Auburn, AL	(17.2)
236	Augusta, GA-SC	(17.2)
167	Austin-Round Rock, TX	(7.3)
209	Bakersfield, CA	(13.1)
101	Baltimore-Towson, MD	2.0
10	Bangor, ME	50.0
153	Barnstable Town, MA	(5.3)
128	Baton Rouge, LA	(2.4)
240	Battle Creek, MI	(17.8)
NA	Bay City, MI**	NA
129	Beaumont-Port Arthur, TX	(2.5)
79	Bellingham, WA	6.2
287	Bend, OR	(30.1)
107	Bethesda-Frederick, MD M.D.	0.0
295	Billings, MT	(37.8)
297	Binghamton, NY	(45.7)
175	Birmingham-Hoover, AL	(8.8)
263	Bismarck, ND	(23.4)
64	Blacksburg, VA	10.6
38	Bloomington, IN	22.7
177	Boise City-Nampa, ID	(9.1)
145	Boston (greater), MA-NH	(4.4)
106	Boston-Quincy, MA M.D.	0.4
NA	Boulder, CO**	NA
NA	Bowling Green, KY**	NA
225	Bremerton-Silverdale, WA	(15.0)
55	Bridgeport-Stamford, CT	13.6
285	Brownsville-Harlingen, TX	(29.6)
NA	Brunswick, GA**	NA
176	Buffalo-Niagara Falls, NY	(9.0)
NA	Burlington-South Burlington, VT**	NA
14	Burlington, NC	42.4
181	Cambridge-Newton, MA M.D.	(9.5)
280	Camden, NJ M.D.	(28.9)
264	Cape Coral-Fort Myers, FL	(23.5)
48	Cape Girardeau, MO-IL	16.3
NA	Carson City, NV***	NA
283	Casper, WY	(29.3)
20	Cedar Rapids, IA	33.9
243	Charleston-North Charleston, SC	(18.5)
218	Charleston, WV	(13.8)
166	Charlotte-Gastonia, NC-SC	(7.2)
56	Charlottesville, VA	13.5
117	Chattanooga, TN-GA	(1.2)
19	Cheyenne, WY	35.8
156	Chico, CA	(6.2)
NA	Cincinnati-Middletown, OH-KY-IN**	NA
NA	Clarksville, TN-KY**	NA
NA	Cleveland-Elyria-Mentor, OH**	NA
262	Cleveland, TN	(23.3)
NA	Coeur d'Alene, ID**	NA
253	College Station-Bryan, TX	(21.1)
110	Colorado Springs, CO	(0.1)
17	Columbia, MO	39.0
49	Columbia, SC	15.8
278	Columbus, GA-AL	(28.2)
18	Columbus, IN	37.3
182	Columbus, OH	(9.6)
94	Corpus Christi, TX	3.4
269	Corvallis, OR	(25.0)
NA	Crestview-Fort Walton Beach, FL**	NA
51	Cumberland, MD-WV	15.4
135	Dallas (greater), TX	(2.9)
135	Dallas-Plano-Irving, TX M.D.	(2.9)
37	Dalton, GA	23.4
NA	Danville, IL**	NA
290	Danville, VA	(32.0)
162	Dayton, OH	(7.0)
212	Decatur, AL	(13.5)
NA	Decatur, IL**	NA
223	Deltona-Daytona Beach, FL	(14.6)
59	Denver-Aurora, CO	12.4
NA	Des Moines-West Des Moines, IA**	NA
NA	Detroit (greater), MI**	NA
NA	Detroit-Livonia-Dearborn, MI M.D.**	NA
240	Dothan, AL	(17.8)
245	Dover, DE	(19.3)
288	Dubuque, IA	(30.7)
NA	Duluth, MN-WI**	NA
89	Durham-Chapel Hill, NC	5.2
29	Eau Claire, WI	29.1
115	Edison, NJ M.D.	(1.1)
247	El Centro, CA	(19.4)
73	El Paso, TX	7.7
NA	Elizabethtown, KY**	NA
253	Elkhart-Goshen, IN	(21.1)
275	Elmira, NY	(27.3)
143	Erie, PA	(4.2)
96	Eugene-Springfield, OR	2.8
NA	Evansville, IN-KY**	NA
NA	Fargo, ND-MN**	NA
159	Farmington, NM	(6.5)
131	Fayetteville, AR-MO	(2.6)
71	Fayetteville, NC	8.5
258	Flagstaff, AZ	(22.7)
NA	Flint, MI**	NA
286	Florence-Muscle Shoals, AL	(29.9)
191	Florence, SC	(10.5)
266	Fond du Lac, WI	(24.0)
72	Fort Collins-Loveland, CO	7.9
223	Fort Lauderdale, FL M.D.	(14.6)
289	Fort Smith, AR-OK	(31.8)
257	Fort Wayne, IN	(22.5)
132	Fort Worth-Arlington, TX M.D.	(2.7)
99	Fresno, CA	2.6
45	Gadsden, AL	18.3
65	Gainesville, FL	10.4
NA	Gainesville, GA**	NA
300	Glens Falls, NY	(62.5)
3	Goldsboro, NC	98.1
NA	Grand Forks, ND-MN**	NA
212	Grand Junction, CO	(13.5)
NA	Grand Rapids-Wyoming, MI**	NA
12	Great Falls, MT	45.5
152	Greeley, CO	(5.1)
139	Green Bay, WI	(3.4)
264	Greensboro-High Point, NC	(23.5)
NA	Gulfport-Biloxi, MS**	NA
11	Hagerstown-Martinsburg, MD-WV	49.2
100	Harrisburg-Carlisle, PA	2.3
31	Harrisonburg, VA	27.1
169	Hartford, CT	(7.7)
NA	Hattiesburg, MS**	NA
205	Hickory, NC	(12.2)
4	Hinesville, GA	75.0
NA	Holland-Grand Haven, MI**	NA
44	Honolulu, HI	19.6
154	Hot Springs, AR	(6.0)
83	Houma, LA	5.9
150	Houston, TX	(4.9)
149	Huntsville, AL	(4.8)
220	Idaho Falls, ID	(14.3)
157	Indianapolis, IN	(6.3)
161	Iowa City, IA	(6.8)
222	Ithaca, NY	(14.5)
212	Jacksonville, FL	(13.5)
8	Jacksonville, NC	56.9
NA	Jackson, MI**	NA
111	Jackson, MS	(0.2)
234	Jackson, TN	(17.0)
280	Janesville, WI	(28.9)
NA	Jefferson City, MO**	NA
194	Johnson City, TN	(10.6)
226	Jonesboro, AR	(15.3)
NA	Kalamazoo-Portage, MI**	NA
NA	Kansas City, MO-KS**	NA
67	Kennewick-Pasco-Richland, WA	9.9
80	Killeen-Temple-Fort Hood, TX	6.1
245	Kingsport, TN-VA	(19.3)
298	Kingston, NY	(47.1)
107	Knoxville, TN	0.0
141	Kokomo, IN	(3.7)
NA	La Crosse, WI-MN**	NA
69	Lafayette, IN	9.0
268	Lafayette, LA	(24.9)
NA	Lake Charles, LA**	NA
291	Lake Havasu City-Kingman, AZ	(33.2)
62	Lakeland, FL	11.2
270	Lancaster, PA	(25.1)
NA	Lansing-East Lansing, MI**	NA

Note: All listings are for Metropolitan Statistical Areas (M.S.A.s) except for those ending with "M.D." Listings with "M.D." are Metropolitan Divisions which are smaller parts of eleven large M.S.A.s. See explanatory note at beginning of metropolitan area section.

RANK	METROPOLITAN AREA	% CHANGE
168	Laredo, TX	(7.6)
151	Las Cruces, NM	(5.0)
183	Las Vegas-Paradise, NV	(9.8)
21	Lawrence, KS	33.5
NA	Lawton, OK**	NA
284	Lebanon, PA	(29.4)
98	Lewiston-Auburn, ME	2.7
7	Lewiston, ID-WA	57.3
NA	Lexington-Fayette, KY**	NA
195	Lima, OH	(10.9)
57	Lincoln, NE	13.4
NA	Little Rock, AR**	NA
242	Logan, UT-ID	(18.1)
209	Longview, TX	(13.1)
296	Longview, WA	(41.1)
132	Los Angeles County, CA M.D.	(2.7)
113	Los Angeles (greater), CA	(1.0)
NA	Louisville, KY-IN**	NA
73	Lubbock, TX	7.7
255	Lynchburg, VA	(21.4)
259	Macon, GA	(23.0)
140	Madera, CA	(3.6)
267	Madison, WI	(24.1)
NA	Manchester-Nashua, NH**	NA
104	Manhattan, KS	1.1
NA	Mankato-North Mankato, MN**	NA
186	Mansfield, OH	(10.0)
47	McAllen-Edinburg-Mission, TX	17.8
274	Medford, OR	(26.2)
86	Memphis, TN-MS-AR	5.4
61	Merced, CA	11.4
216	Miami (greater), FL	(13.6)
248	Miami-Dade County, FL M.D.	(19.7)
148	Michigan City-La Porte, IN	(4.7)
279	Midland, TX	(28.6)
145	Milwaukee, WI	(4.4)
NA	Minneapolis-St. Paul, MN-WI**	NA
43	Missoula, MT	21.1
124	Mobile, AL	(1.9)
216	Modesto, CA	(13.6)
NA	Monroe, MI**	NA
29	Montgomery, AL	29.1
NA	Morgantown, WV**	NA
208	Morristown, TN	(12.9)
107	Mount Vernon-Anacortes, WA	0.0
16	Muncie, IN	39.2
NA	Muskegon-Norton Shores, MI**	NA
211	Napa, CA	(13.3)
177	Naples-Marco Island, FL	(9.1)
171	Nashville-Davidson, TN	(8.1)
120	Nassau-Suffolk, NY M.D.	(1.6)
NA	New Haven-Milford, CT**	NA
95	New Orleans, LA	3.0
142	New York (greater), NY-NJ-PA	(4.1)
162	New York-W. Plains NY-NJ M.D.	(7.0)
103	Newark-Union, NJ-PA M.D.	1.5
NA	Niles-Benton Harbor, MI**	NA
NA	North Port-Bradenton-Sarasota, FL**	NA
80	Norwich-New London, CT	6.1
135	Oakland-Fremont, CA M.D.	(2.9)
127	Ocala, FL	(2.2)
229	Ocean City, NJ	(16.0)
1	Odessa, TX	771.0

RANK	METROPOLITAN AREA	% CHANGE
203	Ogden-Clearfield, UT	(12.0)
NA	Oklahoma City, OK**	NA
70	Olympia, WA	8.8
84	Omaha-Council Bluffs, NE-IA	5.7
183	Orlando, FL	(9.8)
191	Oshkosh-Neenah, WI	(10.5)
NA	Owensboro, KY**	NA
159	Oxnard-Thousand Oaks, CA	(6.5)
138	Palm Bay-Melbourne, FL	(3.0)
9	Palm Coast, FL	53.0
202	Panama City-Lynn Haven, FL	(11.9)
105	Pascagoula, MS	1.0
169	Peabody, MA M.D.	(7.7)
32	Pensacola, FL	26.7
121	Philadelphia (greater) PA-NJ-MD-DE	(1.8)
92	Philadelphia, PA M.D.	4.1
91	Phoenix-Mesa-Scottsdale, AZ	4.5
272	Pine Bluff, AR	(25.3)
190	Pittsburgh, PA	(10.2)
291	Pittsfield, MA	(33.2)
271	Pocatello, ID	(25.2)
126	Port St. Lucie, FL	(2.1)
112	Portland-Vancouver, OR-WA	(0.8)
244	Portland, ME	(19.0)
277	Poughkeepsie, NY	(27.8)
206	Prescott, AZ	(12.4)
121	Providence-New Bedford, RI-MA	(1.8)
261	Provo-Orem, UT	(23.2)
NA	Pueblo, CO**	NA
39	Punta Gorda, FL	22.4
6	Racine, WI	59.4
228	Raleigh-Cary, NC	(15.8)
199	Rapid City, SD	(11.4)
238	Reading, PA	(17.5)
233	Redding, CA	(16.8)
191	Reno-Sparks, NV	(10.5)
276	Richmond, VA	(27.5)
164	Riverside-San Bernardino, CA	(7.1)
260	Roanoke, VA	(23.1)
NA	Rochester, MN**	NA
68	Rochester, NY	9.4
221	Rockingham County, NH M.D.	(14.4)
NA	Rocky Mount, NC**	NA
NA	Rome, GA**	NA
86	Sacramento, CA	5.4
NA	Saginaw, MI**	NA
42	Salem, OR	21.3
33	Salinas, CA	25.8
119	Salisbury, MD	(1.5)
75	Salt Lake City, UT	7.6
58	San Angelo, TX	12.7
22	San Antonio, TX	32.2
207	San Diego, CA	(12.7)
132	San Francisco (greater), CA	(2.7)
129	San Francisco-S. Mateo, CA M.D.	(2.5)
88	San Jose, CA	5.3
235	San Luis Obispo, CA	(17.1)
23	Sandusky, OH	30.8
85	Santa Ana-Anaheim, CA M.D.	5.6
188	Santa Barbara-Santa Maria, CA	(10.1)
102	Santa Cruz-Watsonville, CA	1.9
294	Santa Fe, NM	(34.2)
60	Santa Rosa-Petaluma, CA	11.8

RANK	METROPOLITAN AREA	% CHANGE
27	Savannah, GA	29.3
96	Scranton--Wilkes-Barre, PA	2.8
NA	Seattle-Bellevue-Everett, WA M.D.**	NA
NA	Seattle-Tacoma-Bellevue, WA**	NA
299	Sebastian-Vero Beach, FL	(59.2)
5	Sheboygan, WI	62.1
293	Sherman-Denison, TX	(33.6)
NA	Shreveport-Bossier City, LA**	NA
273	Sioux City, IA-NE-SD	(26.1)
115	Sioux Falls, SD	(1.1)
NA	South Bend-Mishawaka, IN-MI**	NA
250	Spartanburg, SC	(20.3)
231	Spokane, WA	(16.3)
125	Springfield, MA	(2.0)
NA	Springfield, MO**	NA
26	Springfield, OH	29.5
35	State College, PA	24.8
212	Stockton, CA	(13.5)
NA	St. Cloud, MN**	NA
164	St. George, UT	(7.1)
256	St. Joseph, MO-KS	(21.6)
NA	St. Louis, MO-IL**	NA
NA	Sumter, SC**	NA
219	Syracuse, NY	(14.2)
NA	Tacoma, WA M.D.**	NA
185	Tallahassee, FL	(9.9)
227	Tampa-St Petersburg, FL	(15.6)
13	Texarkana, TX-Texarkana, AR	44.2
49	Toledo, OH	15.8
54	Topeka, KS	13.7
53	Trenton-Ewing, NJ	14.7
200	Tucson, AZ	(11.7)
89	Tulsa, OK	5.2
197	Tuscaloosa, AL	(11.1)
28	Tyler, TX	29.2
93	Utica-Rome, NY	3.5
46	Valdosta, GA	18.0
174	Vallejo-Fairfield, CA	(8.6)
78	Victoria, TX	7.5
52	Vineland, NJ	15.0
34	Visalia-Porterville, CA	25.4
251	Waco, TX	(20.5)
155	Warner Robins, GA	(6.1)
NA	Warren-Farmington Hills, MI M.D.**	NA
179	Washington (greater) DC-VA-MD-WV	(9.2)
198	Washington, DC-VA-MD-WV M.D.	(11.2)
82	Waterloo-Cedar Falls, IA	6.0
NA	Wausau, WI**	NA
282	Wenatchee, WA	(29.0)
118	West Palm Beach, FL M.D.	(1.3)
121	Wheeling, WV-OH	(1.8)
204	Wichita Falls, TX	(12.1)
179	Wichita, KS	(9.2)
2	Williamsport, PA	152.7
157	Wilmington, DE-MD-NJ M.D.	(6.3)
200	Wilmington, NC	(11.7)
230	Winchester, VA-WV	(16.2)
147	Winston-Salem, NC	(4.5)
63	Worcester, MA	11.0
40	York-Hanover, PA	21.8
173	Youngstown, OH-PA	(8.2)
188	Yuba City, CA	(10.1)
113	Yuma, AZ	(1.0)

Source: CQ Press using reported data from the F.B.I. "Crime in the United States 2009"

*Forcible rape is the carnal knowledge of a female forcibly and against her will. **Not available. ***Carson City had a rape rate of 0 in 2008 but had 1 rape in 2009. Calculating percent increase from zero results in an infinite number. This is shown as "NA."

15. Percent Change in Rape Rate: 2008 to 2009 (continued)
National Percent Change = 3.5% Decrease*

RANK	METROPOLITAN AREA	% CHANGE
1	Odessa, TX	771.0
2	Williamsport, PA	152.7
3	Goldsboro, NC	98.1
4	Hinesville, GA	75.0
5	Sheboygan, WI	62.1
6	Racine, WI	59.4
7	Lewiston, ID-WA	57.3
8	Jacksonville, NC	56.9
9	Palm Coast, FL	53.0
10	Bangor, ME	50.0
11	Hagerstown-Martinsburg, MD-WV	49.2
12	Great Falls, MT	45.5
13	Texarkana, TX-Texarkana, AR	44.2
14	Burlington, NC	42.4
15	Abilene, TX	40.5
16	Muncie, IN	39.2
17	Columbia, MO	39.0
18	Columbus, IN	37.3
19	Cheyenne, WY	35.8
20	Cedar Rapids, IA	33.9
21	Lawrence, KS	33.5
22	San Antonio, TX	32.2
23	Sandusky, OH	30.8
24	Allentown, PA-NJ	30.3
25	Altoona, PA	30.0
26	Springfield, OH	29.5
27	Savannah, GA	29.3
28	Tyler, TX	29.2
29	Eau Claire, WI	29.1
29	Montgomery, AL	29.1
31	Harrisonburg, VA	27.1
32	Pensacola, FL	26.7
33	Salinas, CA	25.8
34	Visalia-Porterville, CA	25.4
35	State College, PA	24.8
36	Ann Arbor, MI	24.1
37	Dalton, GA	23.4
38	Bloomington, IN	22.7
39	Punta Gorda, FL	22.4
40	York-Hanover, PA	21.8
41	Anderson, SC	21.6
42	Salem, OR	21.3
43	Missoula, MT	21.1
44	Honolulu, HI	19.6
45	Gadsden, AL	18.3
46	Valdosta, GA	18.0
47	McAllen-Edinburg-Mission, TX	17.8
48	Cape Girardeau, MO-IL	16.3
49	Columbia, SC	15.8
49	Toledo, OH	15.8
51	Cumberland, MD-WV	15.4
52	Vineland, NJ	15.0
53	Trenton-Ewing, NJ	14.7
54	Topeka, KS	13.7
55	Bridgeport-Stamford, CT	13.6
56	Charlottesville, VA	13.5
57	Lincoln, NE	13.4
58	San Angelo, TX	12.7
59	Denver-Aurora, CO	12.4
60	Santa Rosa-Petaluma, CA	11.8
61	Merced, CA	11.4
62	Lakeland, FL	11.2
63	Worcester, MA	11.0
64	Blacksburg, VA	10.6
65	Gainesville, FL	10.4
66	Akron, OH	10.2
67	Kennewick-Pasco-Richland, WA	9.9
68	Rochester, NY	9.4
69	Lafayette, IN	9.0
70	Olympia, WA	8.8
71	Fayetteville, NC	8.5
72	Fort Collins-Loveland, CO	7.9
73	El Paso, TX	7.7
73	Lubbock, TX	7.7
75	Anchorage, AK	7.6
75	Atlanta, GA	7.6
75	Salt Lake City, UT	7.6
78	Victoria, TX	7.5
79	Bellingham, WA	6.2
80	Killeen-Temple-Fort Hood, TX	6.1
80	Norwich-New London, CT	6.1
82	Waterloo-Cedar Falls, IA	6.0
83	Houma, LA	5.9
84	Omaha-Council Bluffs, NE-IA	5.7
85	Santa Ana-Anaheim, CA M.D.	5.6
86	Memphis, TN-MS-AR	5.4
86	Sacramento, CA	5.4
88	San Jose, CA	5.3
89	Durham-Chapel Hill, NC	5.2
89	Tulsa, OK	5.2
91	Phoenix-Mesa-Scottsdale, AZ	4.5
92	Philadelphia, PA M.D.	4.1
93	Utica-Rome, NY	3.5
94	Corpus Christi, TX	3.4
95	New Orleans, LA	3.0
96	Eugene-Springfield, OR	2.8
96	Scranton--Wilkes-Barre, PA	2.8
98	Lewiston-Auburn, ME	2.7
99	Fresno, CA	2.6
100	Harrisburg-Carlisle, PA	2.3
101	Baltimore-Towson, MD	2.0
102	Santa Cruz-Watsonville, CA	1.9
103	Newark-Union, NJ-PA M.D.	1.5
104	Manhattan, KS	1.1
105	Pascagoula, MS	1.0
106	Boston-Quincy, MA M.D.	0.4
107	Bethesda-Frederick, MD M.D.	0.0
107	Knoxville, TN	0.0
107	Mount Vernon-Anacortes, WA	0.0
110	Colorado Springs, CO	(0.1)
111	Jackson, MS	(0.2)
112	Portland-Vancouver, OR-WA	(0.8)
113	Los Angeles (greater), CA	(1.0)
113	Yuma, AZ	(1.0)
115	Edison, NJ M.D.	(1.1)
115	Sioux Falls, SD	(1.1)
117	Chattanooga, TN-GA	(1.2)
118	West Palm Beach, FL M.D.	(1.3)
119	Salisbury, MD	(1.5)
120	Nassau-Suffolk, NY M.D.	(1.6)
121	Philadelphia (greater) PA-NJ-MD-DE	(1.8)
121	Providence-New Bedford, RI-MA	(1.8)
121	Wheeling, WV-OH	(1.8)
124	Mobile, AL	(1.9)
125	Springfield, MA	(2.0)
126	Port St. Lucie, FL	(2.1)
127	Ocala, FL	(2.2)
128	Baton Rouge, LA	(2.4)
129	Beaumont-Port Arthur, TX	(2.5)
129	San Francisco-S. Mateo, CA M.D.	(2.5)
131	Fayetteville, AR-MO	(2.6)
132	Fort Worth-Arlington, TX M.D.	(2.7)
132	Los Angeles County, CA M.D.	(2.7)
132	San Francisco (greater), CA	(2.7)
135	Dallas (greater), TX	(2.9)
135	Dallas-Plano-Irving, TX M.D.	(2.9)
135	Oakland-Fremont, CA M.D.	(2.9)
138	Palm Bay-Melbourne, FL	(3.0)
139	Green Bay, WI	(3.4)
140	Madera, CA	(3.6)
141	Kokomo, IN	(3.7)
142	New York (greater), NY-NJ-PA	(4.1)
143	Erie, PA	(4.2)
144	Asheville, NC	(4.3)
145	Boston (greater), MA-NH	(4.4)
145	Milwaukee, WI	(4.4)
147	Winston-Salem, NC	(4.5)
148	Michigan City-La Porte, IN	(4.7)
149	Huntsville, AL	(4.8)
150	Houston, TX	(4.9)
151	Las Cruces, NM	(5.0)
152	Greeley, CO	(5.1)
153	Barnstable Town, MA	(5.3)
154	Hot Springs, AR	(6.0)
155	Warner Robins, GA	(6.1)
156	Chico, CA	(6.2)
157	Indianapolis, IN	(6.3)
157	Wilmington, DE-MD-NJ M.D.	(6.3)
159	Farmington, NM	(6.5)
159	Oxnard-Thousand Oaks, CA	(6.5)
161	Iowa City, IA	(6.8)
162	Dayton, OH	(7.0)
162	New York-W. Plains NY-NJ M.D.	(7.0)
164	Riverside-San Bernardino, CA	(7.1)
164	St. George, UT	(7.1)
166	Charlotte-Gastonia, NC-SC	(7.2)
167	Austin-Round Rock, TX	(7.3)
168	Laredo, TX	(7.6)
169	Hartford, CT	(7.7)
169	Peabody, MA M.D.	(7.7)
171	Appleton, WI	(8.1)
171	Nashville-Davidson, TN	(8.1)
173	Youngstown, OH-PA	(8.2)
174	Vallejo-Fairfield, CA	(8.6)
175	Birmingham-Hoover, AL	(8.8)
176	Buffalo-Niagara Falls, NY	(9.0)
177	Boise City-Nampa, ID	(9.1)
177	Naples-Marco Island, FL	(9.1)
179	Washington (greater) DC-VA-MD-WV	(9.2)
179	Wichita, KS	(9.2)

Note: All listings are for Metropolitan Statistical Areas (M.S.A.s) except for those ending with "M.D." Listings with "M.D." are Metropolitan Divisions which are smaller parts of eleven large M.S.A.s. See explanatory note at beginning of metropolitan area section.

RANK	METROPOLITAN AREA	% CHANGE
181	Cambridge-Newton, MA M.D.	(9.5)
182	Columbus, OH	(9.6)
183	Las Vegas-Paradise, NV	(9.8)
183	Orlando, FL	(9.8)
185	Tallahassee, FL	(9.9)
186	Albany-Schenectady-Troy, NY	(10.0)
186	Mansfield, OH	(10.0)
188	Santa Barbara-Santa Maria, CA	(10.1)
188	Yuba City, CA	(10.1)
190	Pittsburgh, PA	(10.2)
191	Florence, SC	(10.5)
191	Oshkosh-Neenah, WI	(10.5)
191	Reno-Sparks, NV	(10.5)
194	Johnson City, TN	(10.6)
195	Atlantic City, NJ	(10.9)
195	Lima, OH	(10.9)
197	Tuscaloosa, AL	(11.1)
198	Washington, DC-VA-MD-WV M.D.	(11.2)
199	Rapid City, SD	(11.4)
200	Tucson, AZ	(11.7)
200	Wilmington, NC	(11.7)
202	Panama City-Lynn Haven, FL	(11.9)
203	Ogden-Clearfield, UT	(12.0)
204	Wichita Falls, TX	(12.1)
205	Hickory, NC	(12.2)
206	Prescott, AZ	(12.4)
207	San Diego, CA	(12.7)
208	Morristown, TN	(12.9)
209	Bakersfield, CA	(13.1)
209	Longview, TX	(13.1)
211	Napa, CA	(13.3)
212	Decatur, AL	(13.5)
212	Grand Junction, CO	(13.5)
212	Jacksonville, FL	(13.5)
212	Stockton, CA	(13.5)
216	Miami (greater), FL	(13.6)
216	Modesto, CA	(13.6)
218	Charleston, WV	(13.8)
219	Syracuse, NY	(14.2)
220	Idaho Falls, ID	(14.3)
221	Rockingham County, NH M.D.	(14.4)
222	Ithaca, NY	(14.5)
223	Deltona-Daytona Beach, FL	(14.6)
223	Fort Lauderdale, FL M.D.	(14.6)
225	Bremerton-Silverdale, WA	(15.0)
226	Jonesboro, AR	(15.3)
227	Tampa-St Petersburg, FL	(15.6)
228	Raleigh-Cary, NC	(15.8)
229	Ocean City, NJ	(16.0)
230	Winchester, VA-WV	(16.2)
231	Athens-Clarke County, GA	(16.3)
231	Spokane, WA	(16.3)
233	Redding, CA	(16.8)
234	Jackson, TN	(17.0)
235	San Luis Obispo, CA	(17.1)
236	Auburn, AL	(17.2)
236	Augusta, GA-SC	(17.2)
238	Reading, PA	(17.5)
239	Ames, IA	(17.6)
240	Battle Creek, MI	(17.8)
240	Dothan, AL	(17.8)
242	Logan, UT-ID	(18.1)
243	Charleston-North Charleston, SC	(18.5)

RANK	METROPOLITAN AREA	% CHANGE
244	Portland, ME	(19.0)
245	Dover, DE	(19.3)
245	Kingsport, TN-VA	(19.3)
247	El Centro, CA	(19.4)
248	Miami-Dade County, FL M.D.	(19.7)
249	Amarillo, TX	(20.0)
250	Spartanburg, SC	(20.3)
251	Waco, TX	(20.5)
252	Albuquerque, NM	(20.7)
253	College Station-Bryan, TX	(21.1)
253	Elkhart-Goshen, IN	(21.1)
255	Lynchburg, VA	(21.4)
256	St. Joseph, MO-KS	(21.6)
257	Fort Wayne, IN	(22.5)
258	Flagstaff, AZ	(22.7)
259	Macon, GA	(23.0)
260	Roanoke, VA	(23.1)
261	Provo-Orem, UT	(23.2)
262	Cleveland, TN	(23.3)
263	Bismarck, ND	(23.4)
264	Cape Coral-Fort Myers, FL	(23.5)
264	Greensboro-High Point, NC	(23.5)
266	Fond du Lac, WI	(24.0)
267	Madison, WI	(24.1)
268	Lafayette, LA	(24.9)
269	Corvallis, OR	(25.0)
270	Lancaster, PA	(25.1)
271	Pocatello, ID	(25.2)
272	Pine Bluff, AR	(25.3)
273	Sioux City, IA-NE-SD	(26.1)
274	Medford, OR	(26.2)
275	Elmira, NY	(27.3)
276	Richmond, VA	(27.5)
277	Poughkeepsie, NY	(27.8)
278	Columbus, GA-AL	(28.2)
279	Midland, TX	(28.6)
280	Camden, NJ M.D.	(28.9)
280	Janesville, WI	(28.9)
282	Wenatchee, WA	(29.0)
283	Casper, WY	(29.3)
284	Lebanon, PA	(29.4)
285	Brownsville-Harlingen, TX	(29.6)
286	Florence-Muscle Shoals, AL	(29.9)
287	Bend, OR	(30.1)
288	Dubuque, IA	(30.7)
289	Fort Smith, AR-OK	(31.8)
290	Danville, VA	(32.0)
291	Lake Havasu City-Kingman, AZ	(33.2)
291	Pittsfield, MA	(33.2)
293	Sherman-Denison, TX	(33.6)
294	Santa Fe, NM	(34.2)
295	Billings, MT	(37.8)
296	Longview, WA	(41.1)
297	Binghamton, NY	(45.7)
298	Kingston, NY	(47.1)
299	Sebastian-Vero Beach, FL	(59.2)
300	Glens Falls, NY	(62.5)
NA	Albany, GA**	NA
NA	Alexandria, LA**	NA
NA	Anderson, IN**	NA
NA	Anniston-Oxford, AL**	NA
NA	Bay City, MI**	NA
NA	Boulder, CO**	NA

RANK	METROPOLITAN AREA	% CHANGE
NA	Bowling Green, KY**	NA
NA	Brunswick, GA**	NA
NA	Burlington-South Burlington, VT**	NA
NA	Carson City, NV***	NA
NA	Cincinnati-Middletown, OH-KY-IN**	NA
NA	Clarksville, TN-KY**	NA
NA	Cleveland-Elyria-Mentor, OH**	NA
NA	Coeur d'Alene, ID**	NA
NA	Crestview-Fort Walton Beach, FL**	NA
NA	Danville, IL**	NA
NA	Decatur, IL**	NA
NA	Des Moines-West Des Moines, IA**	NA
NA	Detroit (greater), MI**	NA
NA	Detroit-Livonia-Dearborn, MI M.D.**	NA
NA	Duluth, MN-WI**	NA
NA	Elizabethtown, KY**	NA
NA	Evansville, IN-KY**	NA
NA	Fargo, ND-MN**	NA
NA	Flint, MI**	NA
NA	Gainesville, GA**	NA
NA	Grand Forks, ND-MN**	NA
NA	Grand Rapids-Wyoming, MI**	NA
NA	Gulfport-Biloxi, MS**	NA
NA	Hattiesburg, MS**	NA
NA	Holland-Grand Haven, MI**	NA
NA	Jackson, MI**	NA
NA	Jefferson City, MO**	NA
NA	Kalamazoo-Portage, MI**	NA
NA	Kansas City, MO-KS**	NA
NA	La Crosse, WI-MN**	NA
NA	Lake Charles, LA**	NA
NA	Lansing-East Lansing, MI**	NA
NA	Lawton, OK**	NA
NA	Lexington-Fayette, KY**	NA
NA	Little Rock, AR**	NA
NA	Louisville, KY-IN**	NA
NA	Manchester-Nashua, NH**	NA
NA	Mankato-North Mankato, MN**	NA
NA	Minneapolis-St. Paul, MN-WI**	NA
NA	Monroe, MI**	NA
NA	Morgantown, WV**	NA
NA	Muskegon-Norton Shores, MI**	NA
NA	New Haven-Milford, CT**	NA
NA	Niles-Benton Harbor, MI**	NA
NA	North Port-Bradenton-Sarasota, FL**	NA
NA	Oklahoma City, OK**	NA
NA	Owensboro, KY**	NA
NA	Pueblo, CO**	NA
NA	Rochester, MN**	NA
NA	Rocky Mount, NC**	NA
NA	Rome, GA**	NA
NA	Saginaw, MI**	NA
NA	Seattle-Bellevue-Everett, WA M.D.**	NA
NA	Seattle-Tacoma-Bellevue, WA**	NA
NA	Shreveport-Bossier City, LA**	NA
NA	South Bend-Mishawaka, IN-MI**	NA
NA	Springfield, MO**	NA
NA	St. Cloud, MN**	NA
NA	St. Louis, MO-IL**	NA
NA	Sumter, SC**	NA
NA	Tacoma, WA M.D.**	NA
NA	Warren-Farmington Hills, MI M.D.**	NA
NA	Wausau, WI**	NA

Source: CQ Press using reported data from the F.B.I. "Crime in the United States 2009"

*Forcible rape is the carnal knowledge of a female forcibly and against her will. **Not available. ***Carson City had a rape rate of 0 in 2008 but had 1 rape in 2009. Calculating percent increase from zero results in an infinite number. This is shown as "NA."

16. Percent Change in Rape Rate: 2005 to 2009
National Percent Change = 9.8% Decrease*

RANK	METROPOLITAN AREA	% CHANGE
13	Abilene, TX	64.8
132	Akron, OH	(6.1)
247	Albany-Schenectady-Troy, NY	(28.9)
27	Albany, GA	31.1
82	Albuquerque, NM	2.5
239	Alexandria, LA	(26.4)
64	Allentown, PA-NJ	6.9
111	Altoona, PA	(2.8)
56	Amarillo, TX	9.8
101	Ames, IA	(1.6)
39	Anchorage, AK	21.1
11	Anderson, IN	72.0
126	Anderson, SC	(5.4)
66	Ann Arbor, MI	6.1
NA	Anniston-Oxford, AL**	NA
115	Appleton, WI	(3.4)
58	Asheville, NC	9.4
57	Athens-Clarke County, GA	9.7
117	Atlanta, GA	(4.1)
252	Atlantic City, NJ	(29.5)
45	Auburn, AL	14.4
182	Augusta, GA-SC	(17.2)
226	Austin-Round Rock, TX	(23.7)
140	Bakersfield, CA	(9.0)
90	Baltimore-Towson, MD	0.0
23	Bangor, ME	39.6
72	Barnstable Town, MA	4.6
264	Baton Rouge, LA	(33.2)
168	Battle Creek, MI	(14.6)
NA	Bay City, MI**	NA
114	Beaumont-Port Arthur, TX	(3.3)
117	Bellingham, WA	(4.1)
279	Bend, OR	(40.4)
179	Bethesda-Frederick, MD M.D.	(16.6)
236	Billings, MT	(24.7)
174	Binghamton, NY	(16.1)
NA	Birmingham-Hoover, AL**	NA
10	Bismarck, ND	74.6
31	Blacksburg, VA	24.5
107	Bloomington, IN	(1.9)
NA	Boise City-Nampa, ID**	NA
109	Boston (greater), MA-NH	(2.3)
110	Boston-Quincy, MA M.D.	(2.4)
NA	Boulder, CO**	NA
NA	Bowling Green, KY**	NA
203	Bremerton-Silverdale, WA	(19.9)
54	Bridgeport-Stamford, CT	11.5
271	Brownsville-Harlingen, TX	(37.0)
90	Brunswick, GA	0.0
209	Buffalo-Niagara Falls, NY	(21.1)
NA	Burlington-South Burlington, VT**	NA
18	Burlington, NC	49.8
65	Cambridge-Newton, MA M.D.	6.3
205	Camden, NJ M.D.	(20.5)
285	Cape Coral-Fort Myers, FL	(44.1)
NA	Cape Girardeau, MO-IL**	NA
290	Carson City, NV	(48.6)
1	Casper, WY	243.6
113	Cedar Rapids, IA	(3.0)
261	Charleston-North Charleston, SC	(32.9)
35	Charleston, WV	23.1
233	Charlotte-Gastonia, NC-SC	(24.1)
197	Charlottesville, VA	(19.1)
262	Chattanooga, TN-GA	(33.0)
21	Cheyenne, WY	42.2
164	Chico, CA	(14.0)
NA	Cincinnati-Middletown, OH-KY-IN**	NA
NA	Clarksville, TN-KY**	NA
NA	Cleveland-Elyria-Mentor, OH**	NA
NA	Cleveland, TN**	NA
55	Coeur d'Alene, ID	11.0
214	College Station-Bryan, TX	(21.3)
33	Colorado Springs, CO	23.4
41	Columbia, MO	20.0
127	Columbia, SC	(5.8)
12	Columbus, GA-AL	68.4
259	Columbus, IN	(32.4)
121	Columbus, OH	(4.3)
154	Corpus Christi, TX	(12.1)
69	Corvallis, OR	5.2
NA	Crestview-Fort Walton Beach, FL**	NA
143	Cumberland, MD-WV	(9.8)
152	Dallas (greater), TX	(12.0)
166	Dallas-Plano-Irving, TX M.D.	(14.5)
NA	Dalton, GA**	NA
NA	Danville, IL**	NA
288	Danville, VA	(46.1)
171	Dayton, OH	(15.0)
37	Decatur, AL	22.2
NA	Decatur, IL**	NA
NA	Deltona-Daytona Beach, FL**	NA
70	Denver-Aurora, CO	5.0
NA	Des Moines-West Des Moines, IA**	NA
194	Detroit (greater), MI	(18.5)
NA	Detroit-Livonia-Dearborn, MI M.D.**	NA
282	Dothan, AL	(42.1)
104	Dover, DE	(1.7)
200	Dubuque, IA	(19.5)
NA	Duluth, MN-WI**	NA
160	Durham-Chapel Hill, NC	(13.0)
4	Eau Claire, WI	134.6
181	Edison, NJ M.D.	(17.0)
295	El Centro, CA	(55.2)
266	El Paso, TX	(33.8)
NA	Elizabethtown, KY**	NA
155	Elkhart-Goshen, IN	(12.2)
293	Elmira, NY	(52.1)
72	Erie, PA	4.6
74	Eugene-Springfield, OR	4.5
NA	Evansville, IN-KY**	NA
NA	Fargo, ND-MN**	NA
38	Farmington, NM	21.4
117	Fayetteville, AR-MO	(4.1)
26	Fayetteville, NC	34.5
198	Flagstaff, AZ	(19.4)
NA	Flint, MI**	NA
NA	Florence-Muscle Shoals, AL**	NA
210	Florence, SC	(21.2)
2	Fond du Lac, WI	219.8
208	Fort Collins-Loveland, CO	(20.7)
179	Fort Lauderdale, FL M.D.	(16.6)
229	Fort Smith, AR-OK	(24.0)
147	Fort Wayne, IN	(10.6)
136	Fort Worth-Arlington, TX M.D.	(7.9)
265	Fresno, CA	(33.6)
52	Gadsden, AL	11.8
206	Gainesville, FL	(20.6)
257	Gainesville, GA	(30.4)
NA	Glens Falls, NY**	NA
16	Goldsboro, NC	52.2
NA	Grand Forks, ND-MN**	NA
3	Grand Junction, CO	150.0
NA	Grand Rapids-Wyoming, MI**	NA
217	Great Falls, MT	(21.4)
176	Greeley, CO	(16.3)
42	Green Bay, WI	19.4
117	Greensboro-High Point, NC	(4.1)
NA	Gulfport-Biloxi, MS**	NA
6	Hagerstown-Martinsburg, MD-WV	107.9
151	Harrisburg-Carlisle, PA	(11.8)
84	Harrisonburg, VA	1.8
71	Hartford, CT	4.9
NA	Hattiesburg, MS**	NA
242	Hickory, NC	(27.1)
9	Hinesville, GA	82.8
NA	Holland-Grand Haven, MI**	NA
78	Honolulu, HI	3.9
229	Hot Springs, AR	(24.0)
222	Houma, LA	(23.0)
189	Houston, TX	(18.2)
174	Huntsville, AL	(16.1)
134	Idaho Falls, ID	(7.2)
185	Indianapolis, IN	(17.6)
210	Iowa City, IA	(21.2)
NA	Ithaca, NY**	NA
97	Jacksonville, FL	(0.4)
NA	Jacksonville, NC**	NA
NA	Jackson, MI**	NA
176	Jackson, MS	(16.3)
292	Jackson, TN	(50.3)
267	Janesville, WI	(36.1)
163	Jefferson City, MO	(13.9)
121	Johnson City, TN	(4.3)
159	Jonesboro, AR	(12.6)
NA	Kalamazoo-Portage, MI**	NA
158	Kansas City, MO-KS	(12.4)
22	Kennewick-Pasco-Richland, WA	40.8
166	Killeen-Temple-Fort Hood, TX	(14.5)
227	Kingsport, TN-VA	(23.8)
299	Kingston, NY	(59.2)
47	Knoxville, TN	14.1
244	Kokomo, IN	(28.4)
NA	La Crosse, WI-MN**	NA
224	Lafayette, IN	(23.3)
268	Lafayette, LA	(36.3)
50	Lake Charles, LA	12.4
NA	Lake Havasu City-Kingman, AZ**	NA
168	Lakeland, FL	(14.6)
81	Lancaster, PA	2.9
NA	Lansing-East Lansing, MI**	NA

Note: All listings are for Metropolitan Statistical Areas (M.S.A.s) except for those ending with "M.D." Listings with "M.D." are Metropolitan Divisions which are smaller parts of eleven large M.S.A.s. See explanatory note at beginning of metropolitan area section.

RANK	METROPOLITAN AREA	% CHANGE
90	Laredo, TX	0.0
298	Las Cruces, NM	(59.0)
89	Las Vegas-Paradise, NV	0.2
8	Lawrence, KS	94.5
NA	Lawton, OK**	NA
296	Lebanon, PA	(55.3)
32	Lewiston-Auburn, ME	24.0
30	Lewiston, ID-WA	25.2
NA	Lexington-Fayette, KY**	NA
250	Lima, OH	(29.3)
90	Lincoln, NE	0.0
NA	Little Rock, AR**	NA
214	Logan, UT-ID	(21.3)
173	Longview, TX	(15.2)
200	Longview, WA	(19.5)
144	Los Angeles County, CA M.D.	(10.1)
135	Los Angeles (greater), CA	(7.8)
NA	Louisville, KY-IN**	NA
142	Lubbock, TX	(9.4)
46	Lynchburg, VA	14.2
260	Macon, GA	(32.6)
233	Madera, CA	(24.1)
277	Madison, WI	(40.3)
101	Manchester-Nashua, NH	(1.6)
NA	Manhattan, KS**	NA
NA	Mankato-North Mankato, MN**	NA
150	Mansfield, OH	(11.6)
189	McAllen-Edinburg-Mission, TX	(18.2)
195	Medford, OR	(18.6)
129	Memphis, TN-MS-AR	(6.0)
140	Merced, CA	(9.0)
221	Miami (greater), FL	(22.3)
243	Miami-Dade County, FL M.D.	(28.0)
63	Michigan City-La Porte, IN	7.0
274	Midland, TX	(39.4)
125	Milwaukee, WI	(4.9)
NA	Minneapolis-St. Paul, MN-WI**	NA
269	Missoula, MT	(36.4)
277	Mobile, AL	(40.3)
138	Modesto, CA	(8.2)
NA	Monroe, MI**	NA
210	Montgomery, AL	(21.2)
245	Morgantown, WV	(28.5)
48	Morristown, TN	13.0
206	Mount Vernon-Anacortes, WA	(20.6)
249	Muncie, IN	(29.2)
NA	Muskegon-Norton Shores, MI**	NA
128	Napa, CA	(5.9)
291	Naples-Marco Island, FL	(49.2)
241	Nashville-Davidson, TN	(27.0)
170	Nassau-Suffolk, NY M.D.	(14.9)
NA	New Haven-Milford, CT**	NA
NA	New Orleans, LA**	NA
254	New York (greater), NY-NJ-PA	(30.1)
272	New York-W. Plains NY-NJ M.D.	(38.4)
108	Newark-Union, NJ-PA M.D.	(2.1)
NA	Niles-Benton Harbor, MI**	NA
NA	North Port-Bradenton-Sarasota, FL**	NA
224	Norwich-New London, CT	(23.3)
88	Oakland-Fremont, CA M.D.	0.7
129	Ocala, FL	(6.0)
7	Ocean City, NJ	96.4
5	Odessa, TX	126.9

RANK	METROPOLITAN AREA	% CHANGE
214	Ogden-Clearfield, UT	(21.3)
NA	Oklahoma City, OK**	NA
24	Olympia, WA	38.2
116	Omaha-Council Bluffs, NE-IA	(3.9)
184	Orlando, FL	(17.5)
152	Oshkosh-Neenah, WI	(12.0)
NA	Owensboro, KY**	NA
204	Oxnard-Thousand Oaks, CA	(20.3)
210	Palm Bay-Melbourne, FL	(21.2)
NA	Palm Coast, FL**	NA
157	Panama City-Lynn Haven, FL	(12.3)
165	Pascagoula, MS	(14.2)
NA	Peabody, MA M.D.**	NA
43	Pensacola, FL	19.1
98	Philadelphia (greater) PA-NJ-MD-DE	(0.6)
68	Philadelphia, PA M.D.	5.8
229	Phoenix-Mesa-Scottsdale, AZ	(24.0)
28	Pine Bluff, AR	28.6
101	Pittsburgh, PA	(1.6)
124	Pittsfield, MA	(4.8)
229	Pocatello, ID	(24.0)
60	Port St. Lucie, FL	8.6
171	Portland-Vancouver, OR-WA	(15.0)
129	Portland, ME	(6.0)
289	Poughkeepsie, NY	(47.0)
235	Prescott, AZ	(24.2)
NA	Providence-New Bedford, RI-MA**	NA
273	Provo-Orem, UT	(39.3)
33	Pueblo, CO	23.4
297	Punta Gorda, FL	(56.2)
112	Racine, WI	(2.9)
189	Raleigh-Cary, NC	(18.2)
44	Rapid City, SD	16.8
275	Reading, PA	(39.7)
137	Redding, CA	(8.0)
258	Reno-Sparks, NV	(30.9)
246	Richmond, VA	(28.8)
219	Riverside-San Bernardino, CA	(21.9)
253	Roanoke, VA	(29.9)
NA	Rochester, MN**	NA
74	Rochester, NY	4.5
262	Rockingham County, NH M.D.	(33.0)
36	Rocky Mount, NC	22.7
15	Rome, GA	53.4
62	Sacramento, CA	7.7
NA	Saginaw, MI**	NA
98	Salem, OR	(0.6)
61	Salinas, CA	8.5
90	Salisbury, MD	0.0
133	Salt Lake City, UT	(6.2)
29	San Angelo, TX	28.4
95	San Antonio, TX	(0.2)
144	San Diego, CA	(10.1)
123	San Francisco (greater), CA	(4.5)
161	San Francisco-S. Mateo, CA M.D.	(13.7)
139	San Jose, CA	(8.4)
49	San Luis Obispo, CA	12.5
58	Sandusky, OH	9.4
79	Santa Ana-Anaheim, CA M.D.	3.4
79	Santa Barbara-Santa Maria, CA	3.4
250	Santa Cruz-Watsonville, CA	(29.3)
287	Santa Fe, NM	(45.5)
104	Santa Rosa-Petaluma, CA	(1.7)

RANK	METROPOLITAN AREA	% CHANGE
240	Savannah, GA	(26.7)
270	Scranton--Wilkes-Barre, PA	(36.6)
223	Seattle-Bellevue-Everett, WA M.D.	(23.1)
183	Seattle-Tacoma-Bellevue, WA	(17.3)
294	Sebastian-Vero Beach, FL	(53.8)
146	Sheboygan, WI	(10.3)
255	Sherman-Denison, TX	(30.3)
NA	Shreveport-Bossier City, LA**	NA
276	Sioux City, IA-NE-SD	(39.9)
202	Sioux Falls, SD	(19.8)
NA	South Bend-Mishawaka, IN-MI**	NA
53	Spartanburg, SC	11.7
188	Spokane, WA	(17.9)
86	Springfield, MA	1.4
NA	Springfield, MO**	NA
281	Springfield, OH	(41.8)
40	State College, PA	20.4
218	Stockton, CA	(21.7)
NA	St. Cloud, MN**	NA
155	St. George, UT	(12.2)
280	St. Joseph, MO-KS	(41.0)
NA	St. Louis, MO-IL**	NA
NA	Sumter, SC**	NA
162	Syracuse, NY	(13.8)
100	Tacoma, WA M.D.	(1.1)
238	Tallahassee, FL	(25.8)
248	Tampa-St Petersburg, FL	(29.1)
25	Texarkana, TX-Texarkana, AR	35.8
96	Toledo, OH	(0.3)
176	Topeka, KS	(16.3)
50	Trenton-Ewing, NJ	12.4
283	Tucson, AZ	(42.2)
106	Tulsa, OK	(1.8)
NA	Tuscaloosa, AL**	NA
148	Tyler, TX	(10.8)
237	Utica-Rome, NY	(24.9)
85	Valdosta, GA	1.6
NA	Vallejo-Fairfield, CA**	NA
14	Victoria, TX	54.2
286	Vineland, NJ	(45.4)
67	Visalia-Porterville, CA	5.9
87	Waco, TX	1.3
77	Warner Robins, GA	4.0
NA	Warren-Farmington Hills, MI M.D.**	NA
186	Washington (greater) DC-VA-MD-WV	(17.7)
189	Washington, DC-VA-MD-WV M.D.	(18.2)
83	Waterloo-Cedar Falls, IA	2.2
NA	Wausau, WI**	NA
219	Wenatchee, WA	(21.9)
196	West Palm Beach, FL M.D.	(19.0)
20	Wheeling, WV-OH	42.3
76	Wichita Falls, TX	4.4
NA	Wichita, KS**	NA
17	Williamsport, PA	51.2
198	Wilmington, DE-MD-NJ M.D.	(19.4)
255	Wilmington, NC	(30.3)
19	Winchester, VA-WV	45.7
149	Winston-Salem, NC	(11.2)
283	Worcester, MA	(42.2)
228	York-Hanover, PA	(23.9)
NA	Youngstown, OH-PA**	NA
187	Yuba City, CA	(17.8)
189	Yuma, AZ	(18.2)

Source: CQ Press using reported data from the F.B.I. "Crime in the United States 2009"
*Forcible rape is the carnal knowledge of a female forcibly and against her will. Assaults or attempts to commit rape by force or threat of force are included. However, statutory rape without force and other sex offenses are excluded. **Not available

16. Percent Change in Rape Rate: 2005 to 2009 (continued)
National Percent Change = 9.8% Decrease*

RANK	METROPOLITAN AREA	% CHANGE
1	Casper, WY	243.6
2	Fond du Lac, WI	219.8
3	Grand Junction, CO	150.0
4	Eau Claire, WI	134.6
5	Odessa, TX	126.9
6	Hagerstown-Martinsburg, MD-WV	107.9
7	Ocean City, NJ	96.4
8	Lawrence, KS	94.5
9	Hinesville, GA	82.8
10	Bismarck, ND	74.6
11	Anderson, IN	72.0
12	Columbus, GA-AL	68.4
13	Abilene, TX	64.8
14	Victoria, TX	54.2
15	Rome, GA	53.4
16	Goldsboro, NC	52.2
17	Williamsport, PA	51.2
18	Burlington, NC	49.8
19	Winchester, VA-WV	45.7
20	Wheeling, WV-OH	42.3
21	Cheyenne, WY	42.2
22	Kennewick-Pasco-Richland, WA	40.8
23	Bangor, ME	39.6
24	Olympia, WA	38.2
25	Texarkana, TX-Texarkana, AR	35.8
26	Fayetteville, NC	34.5
27	Albany, GA	31.1
28	Pine Bluff, AR	28.6
29	San Angelo, TX	28.4
30	Lewiston, ID-WA	25.2
31	Blacksburg, VA	24.5
32	Lewiston-Auburn, ME	24.0
33	Colorado Springs, CO	23.4
33	Pueblo, CO	23.4
35	Charleston, WV	23.1
36	Rocky Mount, NC	22.7
37	Decatur, AL	22.2
38	Farmington, NM	21.4
39	Anchorage, AK	21.1
40	State College, PA	20.4
41	Columbia, MO	20.0
42	Green Bay, WI	19.4
43	Pensacola, FL	19.1
44	Rapid City, SD	16.8
45	Auburn, AL	14.4
46	Lynchburg, VA	14.2
47	Knoxville, TN	14.1
48	Morristown, TN	13.0
49	San Luis Obispo, CA	12.5
50	Lake Charles, LA	12.4
50	Trenton-Ewing, NJ	12.4
52	Gadsden, AL	11.8
53	Spartanburg, SC	11.7
54	Bridgeport-Stamford, CT	11.5
55	Coeur d'Alene, ID	11.0
56	Amarillo, TX	9.8
57	Athens-Clarke County, GA	9.7
58	Asheville, NC	9.4
58	Sandusky, OH	9.4
60	Port St. Lucie, FL	8.6

RANK	METROPOLITAN AREA	% CHANGE
61	Salinas, CA	8.5
62	Sacramento, CA	7.7
63	Michigan City-La Porte, IN	7.0
64	Allentown, PA-NJ	6.9
65	Cambridge-Newton, MA M.D.	6.3
66	Ann Arbor, MI	6.1
67	Visalia-Porterville, CA	5.9
68	Philadelphia, PA M.D.	5.8
69	Corvallis, OR	5.2
70	Denver-Aurora, CO	5.0
71	Hartford, CT	4.9
72	Barnstable Town, MA	4.6
72	Erie, PA	4.6
74	Eugene-Springfield, OR	4.5
74	Rochester, NY	4.5
76	Wichita Falls, TX	4.4
77	Warner Robins, GA	4.0
78	Honolulu, HI	3.9
79	Santa Ana-Anaheim, CA M.D.	3.4
79	Santa Barbara-Santa Maria, CA	3.4
81	Lancaster, PA	2.9
82	Albuquerque, NM	2.5
83	Waterloo-Cedar Falls, IA	2.2
84	Harrisonburg, VA	1.8
85	Valdosta, GA	1.6
86	Springfield, MA	1.4
87	Waco, TX	1.3
88	Oakland-Fremont, CA M.D.	0.7
89	Las Vegas-Paradise, NV	0.2
90	Baltimore-Towson, MD	0.0
90	Brunswick, GA	0.0
90	Laredo, TX	0.0
90	Lincoln, NE	0.0
90	Salisbury, MD	0.0
95	San Antonio, TX	(0.2)
96	Toledo, OH	(0.3)
97	Jacksonville, FL	(0.4)
98	Philadelphia (greater) PA-NJ-MD-DE	(0.6)
98	Salem, OR	(0.6)
100	Tacoma, WA M.D.	(1.1)
101	Ames, IA	(1.6)
101	Manchester-Nashua, NH	(1.6)
101	Pittsburgh, PA	(1.6)
104	Dover, DE	(1.7)
104	Santa Rosa-Petaluma, CA	(1.7)
106	Tulsa, OK	(1.8)
107	Bloomington, IN	(1.9)
108	Newark-Union, NJ-PA M.D.	(2.1)
109	Boston (greater), MA-NH	(2.3)
110	Boston-Quincy, MA M.D.	(2.4)
111	Altoona, PA	(2.8)
112	Racine, WI	(2.9)
113	Cedar Rapids, IA	(3.0)
114	Beaumont-Port Arthur, TX	(3.3)
115	Appleton, WI	(3.4)
116	Omaha-Council Bluffs, NE-IA	(3.9)
117	Atlanta, GA	(4.1)
117	Bellingham, WA	(4.1)
117	Fayetteville, AR-MO	(4.1)
117	Greensboro-High Point, NC	(4.1)

RANK	METROPOLITAN AREA	% CHANGE
121	Columbus, OH	(4.3)
121	Johnson City, TN	(4.3)
123	San Francisco (greater), CA	(4.5)
124	Pittsfield, MA	(4.8)
125	Milwaukee, WI	(4.9)
126	Anderson, SC	(5.4)
127	Columbia, SC	(5.8)
128	Napa, CA	(5.9)
129	Memphis, TN-MS-AR	(6.0)
129	Ocala, FL	(6.0)
129	Portland, ME	(6.0)
132	Akron, OH	(6.1)
133	Salt Lake City, UT	(6.2)
134	Idaho Falls, ID	(7.2)
135	Los Angeles (greater), CA	(7.8)
136	Fort Worth-Arlington, TX M.D.	(7.9)
137	Redding, CA	(8.0)
138	Modesto, CA	(8.2)
139	San Jose, CA	(8.4)
140	Bakersfield, CA	(9.0)
140	Merced, CA	(9.0)
142	Lubbock, TX	(9.4)
143	Cumberland, MD-WV	(9.8)
144	Los Angeles County, CA M.D.	(10.1)
144	San Diego, CA	(10.1)
146	Sheboygan, WI	(10.3)
147	Fort Wayne, IN	(10.6)
148	Tyler, TX	(10.8)
149	Winston-Salem, NC	(11.2)
150	Mansfield, OH	(11.6)
151	Harrisburg-Carlisle, PA	(11.8)
152	Dallas (greater), TX	(12.0)
152	Oshkosh-Neenah, WI	(12.0)
154	Corpus Christi, TX	(12.1)
155	Elkhart-Goshen, IN	(12.2)
155	St. George, UT	(12.2)
157	Panama City-Lynn Haven, FL	(12.3)
158	Kansas City, MO-KS	(12.4)
159	Jonesboro, AR	(12.6)
160	Durham-Chapel Hill, NC	(13.0)
161	San Francisco-S. Mateo, CA M.D.	(13.7)
162	Syracuse, NY	(13.8)
163	Jefferson City, MO	(13.9)
164	Chico, CA	(14.0)
165	Pascagoula, MS	(14.2)
166	Dallas-Plano-Irving, TX M.D.	(14.5)
166	Killeen-Temple-Fort Hood, TX	(14.5)
168	Battle Creek, MI	(14.6)
168	Lakeland, FL	(14.6)
170	Nassau-Suffolk, NY M.D.	(14.9)
171	Dayton, OH	(15.0)
171	Portland-Vancouver, OR-WA	(15.0)
173	Longview, TX	(15.2)
174	Binghamton, NY	(16.1)
174	Huntsville, AL	(16.1)
176	Greeley, CO	(16.3)
176	Jackson, MS	(16.3)
176	Topeka, KS	(16.3)
179	Bethesda-Frederick, MD M.D.	(16.6)
179	Fort Lauderdale, FL M.D.	(16.6)

Note: All listings are for Metropolitan Statistical Areas (M.S.A.s) except for those ending with "M.D." Listings with "M.D." are Metropolitan Divisions which are smaller parts of eleven large M.S.A.s. See explanatory note at beginning of metropolitan area section.

RANK	METROPOLITAN AREA	% CHANGE
181	Edison, NJ M.D.	(17.0)
182	Augusta, GA-SC	(17.2)
183	Seattle-Tacoma-Bellevue, WA	(17.3)
184	Orlando, FL	(17.5)
185	Indianapolis, IN	(17.6)
186	Washington (greater) DC-VA-MD-WV	(17.7)
187	Yuba City, CA	(17.8)
188	Spokane, WA	(17.9)
189	Houston, TX	(18.2)
189	McAllen-Edinburg-Mission, TX	(18.2)
189	Raleigh-Cary, NC	(18.2)
189	Washington, DC-VA-MD-WV M.D.	(18.2)
189	Yuma, AZ	(18.2)
194	Detroit (greater), MI	(18.5)
195	Medford, OR	(18.6)
196	West Palm Beach, FL M.D.	(19.0)
197	Charlottesville, VA	(19.1)
198	Flagstaff, AZ	(19.4)
198	Wilmington, DE-MD-NJ M.D.	(19.4)
200	Dubuque, IA	(19.5)
200	Longview, WA	(19.5)
202	Sioux Falls, SD	(19.8)
203	Bremerton-Silverdale, WA	(19.9)
204	Oxnard-Thousand Oaks, CA	(20.3)
205	Camden, NJ M.D.	(20.5)
206	Gainesville, FL	(20.6)
206	Mount Vernon-Anacortes, WA	(20.6)
208	Fort Collins-Loveland, CO	(20.7)
209	Buffalo-Niagara Falls, NY	(21.1)
210	Florence, SC	(21.2)
210	Iowa City, IA	(21.2)
210	Montgomery, AL	(21.2)
210	Palm Bay-Melbourne, FL	(21.2)
214	College Station-Bryan, TX	(21.3)
214	Logan, UT-ID	(21.3)
214	Ogden-Clearfield, UT	(21.3)
217	Great Falls, MT	(21.4)
218	Stockton, CA	(21.7)
219	Riverside-San Bernardino, CA	(21.9)
219	Wenatchee, WA	(21.9)
221	Miami (greater), FL	(22.3)
222	Houma, LA	(23.0)
223	Seattle-Bellevue-Everett, WA M.D.	(23.1)
224	Lafayette, IN	(23.3)
224	Norwich-New London, CT	(23.3)
226	Austin-Round Rock, TX	(23.7)
227	Kingsport, TN-VA	(23.8)
228	York-Hanover, PA	(23.9)
229	Fort Smith, AR-OK	(24.0)
229	Hot Springs, AR	(24.0)
229	Phoenix-Mesa-Scottsdale, AZ	(24.0)
229	Pocatello, ID	(24.0)
233	Charlotte-Gastonia, NC-SC	(24.1)
233	Madera, CA	(24.1)
235	Prescott, AZ	(24.2)
236	Billings, MT	(24.7)
237	Utica-Rome, NY	(24.9)
238	Tallahassee, FL	(25.8)
239	Alexandria, LA	(26.4)
240	Savannah, GA	(26.7)
241	Nashville-Davidson, TN	(27.0)
242	Hickory, NC	(27.1)
243	Miami-Dade County, FL M.D.	(28.0)

RANK	METROPOLITAN AREA	% CHANGE
244	Kokomo, IN	(28.4)
245	Morgantown, WV	(28.5)
246	Richmond, VA	(28.8)
247	Albany-Schenectady-Troy, NY	(28.9)
248	Tampa-St Petersburg, FL	(29.1)
249	Muncie, IN	(29.2)
250	Lima, OH	(29.3)
250	Santa Cruz-Watsonville, CA	(29.3)
252	Atlantic City, NJ	(29.5)
253	Roanoke, VA	(29.9)
254	New York (greater), NY-NJ-PA	(30.1)
255	Sherman-Denison, TX	(30.3)
255	Wilmington, NC	(30.3)
257	Gainesville, GA	(30.4)
258	Reno-Sparks, NV	(30.9)
259	Columbus, IN	(32.4)
260	Macon, GA	(32.6)
261	Charleston-North Charleston, SC	(32.9)
262	Chattanooga, TN-GA	(33.0)
262	Rockingham County, NH M.D.	(33.0)
264	Baton Rouge, LA	(33.2)
265	Fresno, CA	(33.6)
266	El Paso, TX	(33.8)
267	Janesville, WI	(36.1)
268	Lafayette, LA	(36.3)
269	Missoula, MT	(36.4)
270	Scranton--Wilkes-Barre, PA	(36.6)
271	Brownsville-Harlingen, TX	(37.0)
272	New York-W. Plains NY-NJ M.D.	(38.4)
273	Provo-Orem, UT	(39.3)
274	Midland, TX	(39.4)
275	Reading, PA	(39.7)
276	Sioux City, IA-NE-SD	(39.9)
277	Madison, WI	(40.3)
277	Mobile, AL	(40.3)
279	Bend, OR	(40.4)
280	St. Joseph, MO-KS	(41.0)
281	Springfield, OH	(41.8)
282	Dothan, AL	(42.1)
283	Tucson, AZ	(42.2)
283	Worcester, MA	(42.2)
285	Cape Coral-Fort Myers, FL	(44.1)
286	Vineland, NJ	(45.4)
287	Santa Fe, NM	(45.5)
288	Danville, VA	(46.1)
289	Poughkeepsie, NY	(47.0)
290	Carson City, NV	(48.6)
291	Naples-Marco Island, FL	(49.2)
292	Jackson, TN	(50.3)
293	Elmira, NY	(52.1)
294	Sebastian-Vero Beach, FL	(53.8)
295	El Centro, CA	(55.2)
296	Lebanon, PA	(55.3)
297	Punta Gorda, FL	(56.2)
298	Las Cruces, NM	(59.0)
299	Kingston, NY	(59.2)
NA	Anniston-Oxford, AL**	NA
NA	Bay City, MI**	NA
NA	Birmingham-Hoover, AL**	NA
NA	Boise City-Nampa, ID**	NA
NA	Boulder, CO**	NA
NA	Bowling Green, KY**	NA
NA	Burlington-South Burlington, VT**	NA

RANK	METROPOLITAN AREA	% CHANGE
NA	Cape Girardeau, MO-IL**	NA
NA	Cincinnati-Middletown, OH-KY-IN**	NA
NA	Clarksville, TN-KY**	NA
NA	Cleveland-Elyria-Mentor, OH**	NA
NA	Cleveland, TN**	NA
NA	Crestview-Fort Walton Beach, FL**	NA
NA	Dalton, GA**	NA
NA	Danville, IL**	NA
NA	Decatur, IL**	NA
NA	Deltona-Daytona Beach, FL**	NA
NA	Des Moines-West Des Moines, IA**	NA
NA	Detroit-Livonia-Dearborn, MI M.D.**	NA
NA	Duluth, MN-WI**	NA
NA	Elizabethtown, KY**	NA
NA	Evansville, IN-KY**	NA
NA	Fargo, ND-MN**	NA
NA	Flint, MI**	NA
NA	Florence-Muscle Shoals, AL**	NA
NA	Glens Falls, NY**	NA
NA	Grand Forks, ND-MN**	NA
NA	Grand Rapids-Wyoming, MI**	NA
NA	Gulfport-Biloxi, MS**	NA
NA	Hattiesburg, MS**	NA
NA	Holland-Grand Haven, MI**	NA
NA	Ithaca, NY**	NA
NA	Jacksonville, NC**	NA
NA	Jackson, MI**	NA
NA	Kalamazoo-Portage, MI**	NA
NA	La Crosse, WI-MN**	NA
NA	Lake Havasu City-Kingman, AZ**	NA
NA	Lansing-East Lansing, MI**	NA
NA	Lawton, OK**	NA
NA	Lexington-Fayette, KY**	NA
NA	Little Rock, AR**	NA
NA	Louisville, KY-IN**	NA
NA	Manhattan, KS**	NA
NA	Mankato-North Mankato, MN**	NA
NA	Minneapolis-St. Paul, MN-WI**	NA
NA	Monroe, MI**	NA
NA	Muskegon-Norton Shores, MI**	NA
NA	New Haven-Milford, CT**	NA
NA	New Orleans, LA**	NA
NA	Niles-Benton Harbor, MI**	NA
NA	North Port-Bradenton-Sarasota, FL**	NA
NA	Oklahoma City, OK**	NA
NA	Owensboro, KY**	NA
NA	Palm Coast, FL**	NA
NA	Peabody, MA M.D.**	NA
NA	Providence-New Bedford, RI-MA**	NA
NA	Rochester, MN**	NA
NA	Saginaw, MI**	NA
NA	Shreveport-Bossier City, LA**	NA
NA	South Bend-Mishawaka, IN-MI**	NA
NA	Springfield, MO**	NA
NA	St. Cloud, MN**	NA
NA	St. Louis, MO-IL**	NA
NA	Sumter, SC**	NA
NA	Tuscaloosa, AL**	NA
NA	Vallejo-Fairfield, CA**	NA
NA	Warren-Farmington Hills, MI M.D.**	NA
NA	Wausau, WI**	NA
NA	Wichita, KS**	NA
NA	Youngstown, OH-PA**	NA

Source: CQ Press using reported data from the F.B.I. "Crime in the United States 2009"

*Forcible rape is the carnal knowledge of a female forcibly and against her will. Assaults or attempts to commit rape by force or threat of force are included. However, statutory rape without force and other sex offenses are excluded. **Not available

17. Robberies in 2009
National Total = 408,217 Robberies*

RANK	METROPOLITAN AREA	ROBBERY
228	Abilene, TX	146
95	Akron, OH	916
96	Albany-Schenectady-Troy, NY	885
180	Albany, GA	251
75	Albuquerque, NM	1,267
193	Alexandria, LA	206
102	Allentown, PA-NJ	798
305	Altoona, PA	58
151	Amarillo, TX	358
357	Ames, IA	20
132	Anchorage, AK	543
290	Anderson, IN	78
205	Anderson, SC	185
188	Ann Arbor, MI	223
210	Anniston-Oxford, AL	172
350	Appleton, WI	29
176	Asheville, NC	262
209	Athens-Clarke County, GA	174
12	Atlanta, GA	9,678
121	Atlantic City, NJ	625
226	Auburn, AL	148
90	Augusta, GA-SC	1,012
59	Austin-Round Rock, TX	1,670
73	Bakersfield, CA	1,331
19	Baltimore-Towson, MD	6,492
308	Bangor, ME	56
232	Barnstable Town, MA	139
62	Baton Rouge, LA	1,589
215	Battle Creek, MI	169
305	Bay City, MI	58
119	Beaumont-Port Arthur, TX	639
274	Bellingham, WA	90
346	Bend, OR	32
77	Bethesda-Frederick, MD M.D.	1,241
291	Billings, MT	76
269	Binghamton, NY	93
52	Birmingham-Hoover, AL	2,186
365	Bismarck, ND	13
313	Blacksburg, VA	53
269	Bloomington, IN	93
239	Boise City-Nampa, ID	127
23	Boston (greater), MA-NH	5,113
38	Boston-Quincy, MA M.D.	3,532
244	Boulder, CO	117
292	Bowling Green, KY	73
255	Bremerton-Silverdale, WA	107
82	Bridgeport-Stamford, CT	1,181
164	Brownsville-Harlingen, TX	297
225	Brunswick, GA	152
54	Buffalo-Niagara Falls, NY	2,155
336	Burlington-South Burlington, VT	39
218	Burlington, NC	163
93	Cambridge-Newton, MA M.D.	945
60	Camden, NJ M.D.	1,662
105	Cape Coral-Fort Myers, FL	725
308	Cape Girardeau, MO-IL	56
353	Carson City, NV	26
362	Casper, WY	16
242	Cedar Rapids, IA	121
87	Charleston-North Charleston, SC	1,058
182	Charleston, WV	243
42	Charlotte-Gastonia, NC-SC	3,115
241	Charlottesville, VA	124
120	Chattanooga, TN-GA	635
349	Cheyenne, WY	30
203	Chico, CA	187
36	Cincinnati-Middletown, OH-KY-IN	3,580
201	Clarksville, TN-KY	190
25	Cleveland-Elyria-Mentor, OH	4,791
315	Cleveland, TN	50
317	Coeur d'Alene, ID	48
211	College Station-Bryan, TX	171
129	Colorado Springs, CO	561
208	Columbia, MO	175
88	Columbia, SC	1,042
112	Columbus, GA-AL	686
352	Columbus, IN	27
33	Columbus, OH	3,960
139	Corpus Christi, TX	508
354	Corvallis, OR	25
233	Crestview-Fort Walton Beach, FL	138
321	Cumberland, MD-WV	47
10	Dallas (greater), TX	10,361
15	Dallas-Plano-Irving, TX M.D.	7,727
337	Dalton, GA	38
247	Danville, IL	115
269	Danville, VA	93
80	Dayton, OH	1,228
283	Decatur, AL	86
222	Decatur, IL	157
109	Deltona-Daytona Beach, FL	702
53	Denver-Aurora, CO	2,173
166	Des Moines-West Des Moines, IA	294
14	Detroit (greater), MI	8,559
17	Detroit-Livonia-Dearborn, MI M.D.	7,048
206	Dothan, AL	183
202	Dover, DE	189
360	Dubuque, IA	17
219	Duluth, MN-WI	162
97	Durham-Chapel Hill, NC	875
356	Eau Claire, WI	21
71	Edison, NJ M.D.	1,399
262	El Centro, CA	99
138	El Paso, TX	511
337	Elizabethtown, KY	38
224	Elkhart-Goshen, IN	155
350	Elmira, NY	29
221	Erie, PA	161
171	Eugene-Springfield, OR	271
199	Evansville, IN-KY	195
325	Fargo, ND-MN	45
325	Farmington, NM	45
259	Fayetteville, AR-MO	102
113	Fayetteville, NC	674
303	Flagstaff, AZ	61
99	Flint, MI	846
274	Florence-Muscle Shoals, AL	90
167	Florence, SC	292
368	Fond du Lac, WI	7
255	Fort Collins-Loveland, CO	107
40	Fort Lauderdale, FL M.D.	3,374
213	Fort Smith, AR-OK	170
137	Fort Wayne, IN	512
48	Fort Worth-Arlington, TX M.D.	2,634
69	Fresno, CA	1,453
250	Gadsden, AL	113
149	Gainesville, FL	377
298	Gainesville, GA	68
367	Glens Falls, NY	11
235	Goldsboro, NC	132
345	Grand Forks, ND-MN	33
294	Grand Junction, CO	70
103	Grand Rapids-Wyoming, MI	796
334	Great Falls, MT	41
273	Greeley, CO	92
266	Green Bay, WI	96
72	Greensboro-High Point, NC	1,377
173	Gulfport-Biloxi, MS	269
226	Hagerstown-Martinsburg, MD-WV	148
106	Harrisburg-Carlisle, PA	711
341	Harrisonburg, VA	35
83	Hartford, CT	1,145
285	Hattiesburg, MS	84
183	Hickory, NC	242
267	Hinesville, GA	95
327	Holland-Grand Haven, MI	44
98	Honolulu, HI	869
230	Hot Springs, AR	141
180	Houma, LA	251
5	Houston, TX	16,180
130	Huntsville, AL	551
358	Idaho Falls, ID	18
30	Indianapolis, IN	4,163
296	Iowa City, IA	69
342	Ithaca, NY	34
46	Jacksonville, FL	2,729
262	Jacksonville, NC	99
255	Jackson, MI	107
85	Jackson, MS	1,092
200	Jackson, TN	194
254	Janesville, WI	108
301	Jefferson City, MO	65
276	Johnson City, TN	89
286	Jonesboro, AR	83
165	Kalamazoo-Portage, MI	296
44	Kansas City, MO-KS	3,004
260	Kennewick-Pasco-Richland, WA	100
163	Killeen-Temple-Fort Hood, TX	306
238	Kingsport, TN-VA	128
264	Kingston, NY	98
94	Knoxville, TN	929
328	Kokomo, IN	43
337	La Crosse, WI-MN	38
279	Lafayette, IN	87
148	Lafayette, LA	391
171	Lake Charles, LA	271
296	Lake Havasu City-Kingman, AZ	69
123	Lakeland, FL	604
153	Lancaster, PA	348
150	Lansing-East Lansing, MI	364

Note: All listings are for Metropolitan Statistical Areas (M.S.A.s) except for those ending with "M.D." Listings with "M.D." are Metropolitan Divisions which are smaller parts of eleven large M.S.A.s. See explanatory note at beginning of metropolitan area section.

Alpha Order - Metro Area (continued)

RANK	METROPOLITAN AREA	ROBBERY
162	Laredo, TX	310
248	Las Cruces, NM	114
22	Las Vegas-Paradise, NV	5,399
279	Lawrence, KS	87
207	Lawton, OK	182
328	Lebanon, PA	43
305	Lewiston-Auburn, ME	58
366	Lewiston, ID-WA	12
115	Lexington-Fayette, KY	658
216	Lima, OH	167
195	Lincoln, NE	199
78	Little Rock, AR	1,240
369	Logan, UT-ID	2
179	Longview, TX	252
335	Longview, WA	40
3	Los Angeles County, CA M.D.	24,528
2	Los Angeles (greater), CA	27,456
56	Louisville, KY-IN	1,879
156	Lubbock, TX	325
251	Lynchburg, VA	111
146	Macon, GA	406
219	Madera, CA	162
141	Madison, WI	469
184	Manchester-Nashua, NH	237
317	Manhattan, KS	48
362	Mankato-North Mankato, MN	16
288	Mansfield, OH	81
111	McAllen-Edinburg-Mission, TX	691
342	Medford, OR	34
26	Memphis, TN-MS-AR	4,575
169	Merced, CA	276
7	Miami (greater), FL	13,095
16	Miami-Dade County, FL M.D.	7,054
276	Michigan City-La Porte, IN	89
276	Midland, TX	89
39	Milwaukee, WI	3,470
41	Minneapolis-St. Paul, MN-WI	3,250
342	Missoula, MT	34
81	Mobile, AL	1,211
108	Modesto, CA	706
310	Monroe, MI	54
135	Montgomery, AL	535
313	Morgantown, WV	53
287	Morristown, TN	82
310	Mount Vernon-Anacortes, WA	54
234	Muncie, IN	134
197	Muskegon-Norton Shores, MI	196
269	Napa, CA	93
195	Naples-Marco Island, FL	199
50	Nashville-Davidson, TN	2,460
51	Nassau-Suffolk, NY M.D.	2,257
70	New Haven-Milford, CT	1,423
57	New Orleans, LA	1,808
1	New York (greater), NY-NJ-PA	30,270
4	New York-W. Plains NY-NJ M.D.	22,590
32	Newark-Union, NJ-PA M.D.	4,024
265	Niles-Benton Harbor, MI	97
92	North Port-Bradenton-Sarasota, FL	947
237	Norwich-New London, CT	129
18	Oakland-Fremont, CA M.D.	6,948
175	Ocala, FL	266
294	Ocean City, NJ	70
192	Odessa, TX	216
194	Ogden-Clearfield, UT	200
66	Oklahoma City, OK	1,528
252	Olympia, WA	110
89	Omaha-Council Bluffs, NE-IA	1,035
37	Orlando, FL	3,538
321	Oshkosh-Neenah, WI	47
332	Owensboro, KY	42
104	Oxnard-Thousand Oaks, CA	757
124	Palm Bay-Melbourne, FL	598
317	Palm Coast, FL	48
213	Panama City-Lynn Haven, FL	170
242	Pascagoula, MS	121
131	Peabody, MA M.D.	549
116	Pensacola, FL	657
6	Philadelphia (greater) PA-NJ-MD-DE	14,055
9	Philadelphia, PA M.D.	10,924
20	Phoenix-Mesa-Scottsdale, AZ	6,086
191	Pine Bluff, AR	218
49	Pittsburgh, PA	2,567
340	Pittsfield, MA	36
364	Pocatello, ID	14
147	Port St. Lucie, FL	394
55	Portland-Vancouver, OR-WA	1,895
185	Portland, ME	231
122	Poughkeepsie, NY	607
316	Prescott, AZ	49
63	Providence-New Bedford, RI-MA	1,587
284	Provo-Orem, UT	85
211	Pueblo, CO	171
302	Punta Gorda, FL	62
174	Racine, WI	267
84	Raleigh-Cary, NC	1,127
332	Rapid City, SD	42
143	Reading, PA	461
236	Redding, CA	130
135	Reno-Sparks, NV	535
61	Richmond, VA	1,639
21	Riverside-San Bernardino, CA	5,675
187	Roanoke, VA	225
303	Rochester, MN	61
86	Rochester, NY	1,083
279	Rockingham County, NH M.D.	87
157	Rocky Mount, NC	323
267	Rome, GA	95
34	Sacramento, CA	3,680
155	Saginaw, MI	327
203	Salem, OR	187
116	Salinas, CA	657
170	Salisbury, MD	274
91	Salt Lake City, UT	968
324	San Angelo, TX	46
43	San Antonio, TX	3,032
31	San Diego, CA	4,033
8	San Francisco (greater), CA	11,305
27	San Francisco-S. Mateo, CA M.D.	4,357
65	San Jose, CA	1,553
258	San Luis Obispo, CA	106
321	Sandusky, OH	47
45	Santa Ana-Anaheim, CA M.D.	2,928
176	Santa Barbara-Santa Maria, CA	262
190	Santa Cruz-Watsonville, CA	222
245	Santa Fe, NM	116
158	Santa Rosa-Petaluma, CA	318
106	Savannah, GA	711
160	Scranton--Wilkes-Barre, PA	316
35	Seattle-Bellevue-Everett, WA M.D.	3,626
24	Seattle-Tacoma-Bellevue, WA	4,863
289	Sebastian-Vero Beach, FL	80
346	Sheboygan, WI	32
299	Sherman-Denison, TX	67
128	Shreveport-Bossier City, LA	570
328	Sioux City, IA-NE-SD	43
317	Sioux Falls, SD	48
144	South Bend-Mishawaka, IN-MI	455
152	Spartanburg, SC	352
133	Spokane, WA	538
100	Springfield, MA	825
154	Springfield, MO	339
188	Springfield, OH	223
354	State College, PA	25
58	Stockton, CA	1,759
328	St. Cloud, MN	43
358	St. George, UT	18
248	St. Joseph, MO-KS	114
29	St. Louis, MO-IL	4,182
231	Sumter, SC	140
133	Syracuse, NY	538
79	Tacoma, WA M.D.	1,237
124	Tallahassee, FL	598
28	Tampa-St Petersburg, FL	4,290
186	Texarkana, TX-Texarkana, AR	227
74	Toledo, OH	1,326
158	Topeka, KS	318
110	Trenton-Ewing, NJ	699
64	Tucson, AZ	1,559
76	Tulsa, OK	1,248
168	Tuscaloosa, AL	283
245	Tyler, TX	116
197	Utica-Rome, NY	196
229	Valdosta, GA	143
101	Vallejo-Fairfield, CA	810
279	Victoria, TX	87
161	Vineland, NJ	311
140	Visalia-Porterville, CA	488
178	Waco, TX	260
240	Warner Robins, GA	125
67	Warren-Farmington Hills, MI M.D.	1,511
11	Washington (greater) DC-VA-MD-WV	10,331
13	Washington, DC-VA-MD-WV M.D.	9,090
223	Waterloo-Cedar Falls, IA	156
360	Wausau, WI	17
348	Wenatchee, WA	31
47	West Palm Beach, FL M.D.	2,667
310	Wheeling, WV-OH	54
217	Wichita Falls, TX	165
127	Wichita, KS	578
293	Williamsport, PA	72
68	Wilmington, DE-MD-NJ M.D.	1,469
145	Wilmington, NC	415
300	Winchester, VA-WV	66
114	Winston-Salem, NC	660
124	Worcester, MA	598
142	York-Hanover, PA	464
118	Youngstown, OH-PA	656
260	Yuba City, CA	100
253	Yuma, AZ	109

Source: Reported data from the F.B.I. "Crime in the United States 2009"
*Robbery is the taking of anything of value by force or threat of force. Attempts are included.

17. Robberies in 2009 (continued)
National Total = 408,217 Robberies*

RANK	METROPOLITAN AREA	ROBBERY
1	New York (greater), NY-NJ-PA	30,270
2	Los Angeles (greater), CA	27,456
3	Los Angeles County, CA M.D.	24,528
4	New York-W. Plains NY-NJ M.D.	22,590
5	Houston, TX	16,180
6	Philadelphia (greater) PA-NJ-MD-DE	14,055
7	Miami (greater), FL	13,095
8	San Francisco (greater), CA	11,305
9	Philadelphia, PA M.D.	10,924
10	Dallas (greater), TX	10,361
11	Washington (greater) DC-VA-MD-WV	10,331
12	Atlanta, GA	9,678
13	Washington, DC-VA-MD-WV M.D.	9,090
14	Detroit (greater), MI	8,559
15	Dallas-Plano-Irving, TX M.D.	7,727
16	Miami-Dade County, FL M.D.	7,054
17	Detroit-Livonia-Dearborn, MI M.D.	7,048
18	Oakland-Fremont, CA M.D.	6,948
19	Baltimore-Towson, MD	6,492
20	Phoenix-Mesa-Scottsdale, AZ	6,086
21	Riverside-San Bernardino, CA	5,675
22	Las Vegas-Paradise, NV	5,399
23	Boston (greater), MA-NH	5,113
24	Seattle-Tacoma-Bellevue, WA	4,863
25	Cleveland-Elyria-Mentor, OH	4,791
26	Memphis, TN-MS-AR	4,575
27	San Francisco-S. Mateo, CA M.D.	4,357
28	Tampa-St Petersburg, FL	4,290
29	St. Louis, MO-IL	4,182
30	Indianapolis, IN	4,163
31	San Diego, CA	4,033
32	Newark-Union, NJ-PA M.D.	4,024
33	Columbus, OH	3,960
34	Sacramento, CA	3,680
35	Seattle-Bellevue-Everett, WA M.D.	3,626
36	Cincinnati-Middletown, OH-KY-IN	3,580
37	Orlando, FL	3,538
38	Boston-Quincy, MA M.D.	3,532
39	Milwaukee, WI	3,470
40	Fort Lauderdale, FL M.D.	3,374
41	Minneapolis-St. Paul, MN-WI	3,250
42	Charlotte-Gastonia, NC-SC	3,115
43	San Antonio, TX	3,032
44	Kansas City, MO-KS	3,004
45	Santa Ana-Anaheim, CA M.D.	2,928
46	Jacksonville, FL	2,729
47	West Palm Beach, FL M.D.	2,667
48	Fort Worth-Arlington, TX M.D.	2,634
49	Pittsburgh, PA	2,567
50	Nashville-Davidson, TN	2,460
51	Nassau-Suffolk, NY M.D.	2,257
52	Birmingham-Hoover, AL	2,186
53	Denver-Aurora, CO	2,173
54	Buffalo-Niagara Falls, NY	2,155
55	Portland-Vancouver, OR-WA	1,895
56	Louisville, KY-IN	1,879
57	New Orleans, LA	1,808
58	Stockton, CA	1,759
59	Austin-Round Rock, TX	1,670
60	Camden, NJ M.D.	1,662
61	Richmond, VA	1,639
62	Baton Rouge, LA	1,589
63	Providence-New Bedford, RI-MA	1,587
64	Tucson, AZ	1,559
65	San Jose, CA	1,553
66	Oklahoma City, OK	1,528
67	Warren-Farmington Hills, MI M.D.	1,511
68	Wilmington, DE-MD-NJ M.D.	1,469
69	Fresno, CA	1,453
70	New Haven-Milford, CT	1,423
71	Edison, NJ M.D.	1,399
72	Greensboro-High Point, NC	1,377
73	Bakersfield, CA	1,331
74	Toledo, OH	1,326
75	Albuquerque, NM	1,267
76	Tulsa, OK	1,248
77	Bethesda-Frederick, MD M.D.	1,241
78	Little Rock, AR	1,240
79	Tacoma, WA M.D.	1,237
80	Dayton, OH	1,228
81	Mobile, AL	1,211
82	Bridgeport-Stamford, CT	1,181
83	Hartford, CT	1,145
84	Raleigh-Cary, NC	1,127
85	Jackson, MS	1,092
86	Rochester, NY	1,083
87	Charleston-North Charleston, SC	1,058
88	Columbia, SC	1,042
89	Omaha-Council Bluffs, NE-IA	1,035
90	Augusta, GA-SC	1,012
91	Salt Lake City, UT	968
92	North Port-Bradenton-Sarasota, FL	947
93	Cambridge-Newton, MA M.D.	945
94	Knoxville, TN	929
95	Akron, OH	916
96	Albany-Schenectady-Troy, NY	885
97	Durham-Chapel Hill, NC	875
98	Honolulu, HI	869
99	Flint, MI	846
100	Springfield, MA	825
101	Vallejo-Fairfield, CA	810
102	Allentown, PA-NJ	798
103	Grand Rapids-Wyoming, MI	796
104	Oxnard-Thousand Oaks, CA	757
105	Cape Coral-Fort Myers, FL	725
106	Harrisburg-Carlisle, PA	711
106	Savannah, GA	711
108	Modesto, CA	706
109	Deltona-Daytona Beach, FL	702
110	Trenton-Ewing, NJ	699
111	McAllen-Edinburg-Mission, TX	691
112	Columbus, GA-AL	686
113	Fayetteville, NC	674
114	Winston-Salem, NC	660
115	Lexington-Fayette, KY	658
116	Pensacola, FL	657
116	Salinas, CA	657
118	Youngstown, OH-PA	656
119	Beaumont-Port Arthur, TX	639
120	Chattanooga, TN-GA	635
121	Atlantic City, NJ	625
122	Poughkeepsie, NY	607
123	Lakeland, FL	604
124	Palm Bay-Melbourne, FL	598
124	Tallahassee, FL	598
124	Worcester, MA	598
127	Wichita, KS	578
128	Shreveport-Bossier City, LA	570
129	Colorado Springs, CO	561
130	Huntsville, AL	551
131	Peabody, MA M.D.	549
132	Anchorage, AK	543
133	Spokane, WA	538
133	Syracuse, NY	538
135	Montgomery, AL	535
135	Reno-Sparks, NV	535
137	Fort Wayne, IN	512
138	El Paso, TX	511
139	Corpus Christi, TX	508
140	Visalia-Porterville, CA	488
141	Madison, WI	469
142	York-Hanover, PA	464
143	Reading, PA	461
144	South Bend-Mishawaka, IN-MI	455
145	Wilmington, NC	415
146	Macon, GA	406
147	Port St. Lucie, FL	394
148	Lafayette, LA	391
149	Gainesville, FL	377
150	Lansing-East Lansing, MI	364
151	Amarillo, TX	358
152	Spartanburg, SC	352
153	Lancaster, PA	348
154	Springfield, MO	339
155	Saginaw, MI	327
156	Lubbock, TX	325
157	Rocky Mount, NC	323
158	Santa Rosa-Petaluma, CA	318
158	Topeka, KS	318
160	Scranton--Wilkes-Barre, PA	316
161	Vineland, NJ	311
162	Laredo, TX	310
163	Killeen-Temple-Fort Hood, TX	306
164	Brownsville-Harlingen, TX	297
165	Kalamazoo-Portage, MI	296
166	Des Moines-West Des Moines, IA	294
167	Florence, SC	292
168	Tuscaloosa, AL	283
169	Merced, CA	276
170	Salisbury, MD	274
171	Eugene-Springfield, OR	271
171	Lake Charles, LA	271
173	Gulfport-Biloxi, MS	269
174	Racine, WI	267
175	Ocala, FL	266
176	Asheville, NC	262
176	Santa Barbara-Santa Maria, CA	262
178	Waco, TX	260
179	Longview, TX	252
180	Albany, GA	251

Note: All listings are for Metropolitan Statistical Areas (M.S.A.s) except for those ending with "M.D." Listings with "M.D." are Metropolitan Divisions which are smaller parts of eleven large M.S.A.s. See explanatory note at beginning of metropolitan area section.

RANK	METROPOLITAN AREA	ROBBERY
180	Houma, LA	251
182	Charleston, WV	243
183	Hickory, NC	242
184	Manchester-Nashua, NH	237
185	Portland, ME	231
186	Texarkana, TX-Texarkana, AR	227
187	Roanoke, VA	225
188	Ann Arbor, MI	223
188	Springfield, OH	223
190	Santa Cruz-Watsonville, CA	222
191	Pine Bluff, AR	218
192	Odessa, TX	216
193	Alexandria, LA	206
194	Ogden-Clearfield, UT	200
195	Lincoln, NE	199
195	Naples-Marco Island, FL	199
197	Muskegon-Norton Shores, MI	196
197	Utica-Rome, NY	196
199	Evansville, IN-KY	195
200	Jackson, TN	194
201	Clarksville, TN-KY	190
202	Dover, DE	189
203	Chico, CA	187
203	Salem, OR	187
205	Anderson, SC	185
206	Dothan, AL	183
207	Lawton, OK	182
208	Columbia, MO	175
209	Athens-Clarke County, GA	174
210	Anniston-Oxford, AL	172
211	College Station-Bryan, TX	171
211	Pueblo, CO	171
213	Fort Smith, AR-OK	170
213	Panama City-Lynn Haven, FL	170
215	Battle Creek, MI	169
216	Lima, OH	167
217	Wichita Falls, TX	165
218	Burlington, NC	163
219	Duluth, MN-WI	162
219	Madera, CA	162
221	Erie, PA	161
222	Decatur, IL	157
223	Waterloo-Cedar Falls, IA	156
224	Elkhart-Goshen, IN	155
225	Brunswick, GA	152
226	Auburn, AL	148
226	Hagerstown-Martinsburg, MD-WV	148
228	Abilene, TX	146
229	Valdosta, GA	143
230	Hot Springs, AR	141
231	Sumter, SC	140
232	Barnstable Town, MA	139
233	Crestview-Fort Walton Beach, FL	138
234	Muncie, IN	134
235	Goldsboro, NC	132
236	Redding, CA	130
237	Norwich-New London, CT	129
238	Kingsport, TN-VA	128
239	Boise City-Nampa, ID	127
240	Warner Robins, GA	125
241	Charlottesville, VA	124
242	Cedar Rapids, IA	121
242	Pascagoula, MS	121

RANK	METROPOLITAN AREA	ROBBERY
244	Boulder, CO	117
245	Santa Fe, NM	116
245	Tyler, TX	116
247	Danville, IL	115
248	Las Cruces, NM	114
248	St. Joseph, MO-KS	114
250	Gadsden, AL	113
251	Lynchburg, VA	111
252	Olympia, WA	110
253	Yuma, AZ	109
254	Janesville, WI	108
255	Bremerton-Silverdale, WA	107
255	Fort Collins-Loveland, CO	107
255	Jackson, MI	107
258	San Luis Obispo, CA	106
259	Fayetteville, AR-MO	102
260	Kennewick-Pasco-Richland, WA	100
260	Yuba City, CA	100
262	El Centro, CA	99
262	Jacksonville, NC	99
264	Kingston, NY	98
265	Niles-Benton Harbor, MI	97
266	Green Bay, WI	96
267	Hinesville, GA	95
267	Rome, GA	95
269	Binghamton, NY	93
269	Bloomington, IN	93
269	Danville, VA	93
269	Napa, CA	93
273	Greeley, CO	92
274	Bellingham, WA	90
274	Florence-Muscle Shoals, AL	90
276	Johnson City, TN	89
276	Michigan City-La Porte, IN	89
276	Midland, TX	89
279	Lafayette, IN	87
279	Lawrence, KS	87
279	Rockingham County, NH M.D.	87
279	Victoria, TX	87
283	Decatur, AL	86
284	Provo-Orem, UT	85
285	Hattiesburg, MS	84
286	Jonesboro, AR	83
287	Morristown, TN	82
288	Mansfield, OH	81
289	Sebastian-Vero Beach, FL	80
290	Anderson, IN	78
291	Billings, MT	76
292	Bowling Green, KY	73
293	Williamsport, PA	72
294	Grand Junction, CO	70
294	Ocean City, NJ	70
296	Iowa City, IA	69
296	Lake Havasu City-Kingman, AZ	69
298	Gainesville, GA	68
299	Sherman-Denison, TX	67
300	Winchester, VA-WV	66
301	Jefferson City, MO	65
302	Punta Gorda, FL	62
303	Flagstaff, AZ	61
303	Rochester, MN	61
305	Altoona, PA	58
305	Bay City, MI	58

RANK	METROPOLITAN AREA	ROBBERY
305	Lewiston-Auburn, ME	58
308	Bangor, ME	56
308	Cape Girardeau, MO-IL	56
310	Monroe, MI	54
310	Mount Vernon-Anacortes, WA	54
310	Wheeling, WV-OH	54
313	Blacksburg, VA	53
313	Morgantown, WV	53
315	Cleveland, TN	50
316	Prescott, AZ	49
317	Coeur d'Alene, ID	48
317	Manhattan, KS	48
317	Palm Coast, FL	48
317	Sioux Falls, SD	48
321	Cumberland, MD-WV	47
321	Oshkosh-Neenah, WI	47
321	Sandusky, OH	47
324	San Angelo, TX	46
325	Fargo, ND-MN	45
325	Farmington, NM	45
327	Holland-Grand Haven, MI	44
328	Kokomo, IN	43
328	Lebanon, PA	43
328	Sioux City, IA-NE-SD	43
328	St. Cloud, MN	43
332	Owensboro, KY	42
332	Rapid City, SD	42
334	Great Falls, MT	41
335	Longview, WA	40
336	Burlington-South Burlington, VT	39
337	Dalton, GA	38
337	Elizabethtown, KY	38
337	La Crosse, WI-MN	38
340	Pittsfield, MA	36
341	Harrisonburg, VA	35
342	Ithaca, NY	34
342	Medford, OR	34
342	Missoula, MT	34
345	Grand Forks, ND-MN	33
346	Bend, OR	32
346	Sheboygan, WI	32
348	Wenatchee, WA	31
349	Cheyenne, WY	30
350	Appleton, WI	29
350	Elmira, NY	29
352	Columbus, IN	27
353	Carson City, NV	26
354	Corvallis, OR	25
354	State College, PA	25
356	Eau Claire, WI	21
357	Ames, IA	20
358	Idaho Falls, ID	18
358	St. George, UT	18
360	Dubuque, IA	17
360	Wausau, WI	17
362	Casper, WY	16
362	Mankato-North Mankato, MN	16
364	Pocatello, ID	14
365	Bismarck, ND	13
366	Lewiston, ID-WA	12
367	Glens Falls, NY	11
368	Fond du Lac, WI	7
369	Logan, UT-ID	2

Source: Reported data from the F.B.I. "Crime in the United States 2009"

*Robbery is the taking of anything of value by force or threat of force. Attempts are included.

18. Robbery Rate in 2009
National Rate = 133.0 Robberies per 100,000 Population*

RANK	METROPOLITAN AREA	RATE
189	Abilene, TX	91.5
125	Akron, OH	130.7
170	Albany-Schenectady-Troy, NY	103.3
80	Albany, GA	152.0
85	Albuquerque, NM	147.0
120	Alexandria, LA	132.9
179	Allentown, PA-NJ	97.6
287	Altoona, PA	46.4
91	Amarillo, TX	145.5
342	Ames, IA	22.9
52	Anchorage, AK	177.9
257	Anderson, IN	59.3
174	Anderson, SC	99.6
239	Ann Arbor, MI	64.0
81	Anniston-Oxford, AL	150.7
362	Appleton, WI	13.1
240	Asheville, NC	63.4
191	Athens-Clarke County, GA	91.1
54	Atlanta, GA	176.1
18	Atlantic City, NJ	229.3
159	Auburn, AL	109.1
46	Augusta, GA-SC	188.2
178	Austin-Round Rock, TX	97.9
65	Bakersfield, CA	163.4
13	Baltimore-Towson, MD	241.1
310	Bangor, ME	37.6
245	Barnstable Town, MA	62.0
32	Baton Rouge, LA	201.7
129	Battle Creek, MI	125.1
272	Bay City, MI	54.3
60	Beaumont-Port Arthur, TX	169.1
292	Bellingham, WA	44.7
352	Bend, OR	19.6
168	Bethesda-Frederick, MD M.D.	103.9
280	Billings, MT	49.5
309	Binghamton, NY	38.1
38	Birmingham-Hoover, AL	193.3
366	Bismarck, ND	12.2
327	Blacksburg, VA	33.2
277	Bloomington, IN	50.2
348	Boise City-Nampa, ID	20.7
155	Boston (greater), MA-NH	111.5
48	Boston-Quincy, MA M.D.	184.7
306	Boulder, CO	39.5
249	Bowling Green, KY	61.0
296	Bremerton-Silverdale, WA	44.2
115	Bridgeport-Stamford, CT	134.5
221	Brownsville-Harlingen, TX	74.3
86	Brunswick, GA	146.8
41	Buffalo-Niagara Falls, NY	192.6
353	Burlington-South Burlington, VT	18.6
161	Burlington, NC	108.5
241	Cambridge-Newton, MA M.D.	62.8
123	Camden, NJ M.D.	132.2
139	Cape Coral-Fort Myers, FL	119.4
252	Cape Girardeau, MO-IL	59.8
281	Carson City, NV	47.7
347	Casper, WY	21.4
286	Cedar Rapids, IA	47.1
70	Charleston-North Charleston, SC	160.4
207	Charleston, WV	79.9
53	Charlotte-Gastonia, NC-SC	177.8
241	Charlottesville, VA	62.8
138	Chattanooga, TN-GA	121.2
324	Cheyenne, WY	33.6
201	Chico, CA	84.4
63	Cincinnati-Middletown, OH-KY-IN	164.4
224	Clarksville, TN-KY	71.6
19	Cleveland-Elyria-Mentor, OH	228.9
298	Cleveland, TN	44.1
321	Coeur d'Alene, ID	34.2
204	College Station-Bryan, TX	81.3
194	Colorado Springs, CO	89.3
166	Columbia, MO	105.1
101	Columbia, SC	140.5
15	Columbus, GA-AL	238.5
317	Columbus, IN	35.6
22	Columbus, OH	220.3
137	Corpus Christi, TX	121.8
333	Corvallis, OR	30.4
215	Crestview-Fort Walton Beach, FL	77.1
284	Cumberland, MD-WV	47.4
69	Dallas (greater), TX	160.6
51	Dallas-Plano-Irving, TX M.D.	178.4
339	Dalton, GA	28.1
97	Danville, IL	143.7
196	Danville, VA	88.0
87	Dayton, OH	146.6
265	Decatur, AL	56.9
88	Decatur, IL	146.4
102	Deltona-Daytona Beach, FL	140.4
198	Denver-Aurora, CO	85.2
276	Des Moines-West Des Moines, IA	52.1
37	Detroit (greater), MI	194.3
1	Detroit-Livonia-Dearborn, MI M.D.	365.1
126	Dothan, AL	128.2
141	Dover, DE	118.7
354	Dubuque, IA	18.3
258	Duluth, MN-WI	58.9
56	Durham-Chapel Hill, NC	175.6
362	Eau Claire, WI	13.1
252	Edison, NJ M.D.	59.8
254	El Centro, CA	59.6
230	El Paso, TX	68.1
324	Elizabethtown, KY	33.6
216	Elkhart-Goshen, IN	77.0
327	Elmira, NY	33.2
263	Erie, PA	57.6
214	Eugene-Springfield, OR	77.8
270	Evansville, IN-KY	55.4
344	Fargo, ND-MN	22.6
314	Farmington, NM	36.3
346	Fayetteville, AR-MO	22.3
47	Fayetteville, NC	187.8
283	Flagstaff, AZ	47.5
35	Flint, MI	198.5
243	Florence-Muscle Shoals, AL	62.3
93	Florence, SC	144.8
368	Fond du Lac, WI	7.0
315	Fort Collins-Loveland, CO	35.9
39	Fort Lauderdale, FL M.D.	192.9
262	Fort Smith, AR-OK	57.8
132	Fort Wayne, IN	123.6
131	Fort Worth-Arlington, TX M.D.	124.3
74	Fresno, CA	158.2
160	Gadsden, AL	108.9
92	Gainesville, FL	145.4
315	Gainesville, GA	35.9
367	Glens Falls, NY	8.5
146	Goldsboro, NC	115.9
323	Grand Forks, ND-MN	33.7
281	Grand Junction, CO	47.7
172	Grand Rapids-Wyoming, MI	102.4
278	Great Falls, MT	49.9
318	Greeley, CO	35.5
331	Green Bay, WI	31.5
39	Greensboro-High Point, NC	192.9
147	Gulfport-Biloxi, MS	115.1
271	Hagerstown-Martinsburg, MD-WV	54.9
120	Harrisburg-Carlisle, PA	132.9
335	Harrisonburg, VA	29.2
149	Hartford, CT	113.6
260	Hattiesburg, MS	58.8
236	Hickory, NC	66.1
109	Hinesville, GA	136.8
357	Holland-Grand Haven, MI	16.8
182	Honolulu, HI	95.8
100	Hot Springs, AR	142.5
133	Houma, LA	123.5
7	Houston, TX	276.2
112	Huntsville, AL	136.5
361	Idaho Falls, ID	14.4
14	Indianapolis, IN	239.0
288	Iowa City, IA	45.6
326	Ithaca, NY	33.5
30	Jacksonville, FL	206.0
258	Jacksonville, NC	58.9
233	Jackson, MI	67.0
33	Jackson, MS	201.4
58	Jackson, TN	170.8
232	Janesville, WI	67.1
296	Jefferson City, MO	44.2
289	Johnson City, TN	44.9
226	Jonesboro, AR	69.8
189	Kalamazoo-Portage, MI	91.5
90	Kansas City, MO-KS	145.8
304	Kennewick-Pasco-Richland, WA	41.2
208	Killeen-Temple-Fort Hood, TX	79.5
301	Kingsport, TN-VA	41.8
274	Kingston, NY	53.8
122	Knoxville, TN	132.3
300	Kokomo, IN	43.3
337	La Crosse, WI-MN	28.7
292	Lafayette, IN	44.7
83	Lafayette, LA	148.6
104	Lake Charles, LA	139.6
320	Lake Havasu City-Kingman, AZ	34.7
171	Lakeland, FL	102.9
228	Lancaster, PA	68.6
205	Lansing-East Lansing, MI	80.4

Note: All listings are for Metropolitan Statistical Areas (M.S.A.s) except for those ending with "M.D." Listings with "M.D." are Metropolitan Divisions which are smaller parts of eleven large M.S.A.s. See explanatory note at beginning of metropolitan area section.

Alpha Order - Metro Area (continued)

RANK	METROPOLITAN AREA	RATE
127	Laredo, TX	127.9
269	Las Cruces, NM	55.5
5	Las Vegas-Paradise, NV	283.6
220	Lawrence, KS	74.6
66	Lawton, OK	162.3
329	Lebanon, PA	33.0
273	Lewiston-Auburn, ME	54.2
351	Lewiston, ID-WA	19.8
103	Lexington-Fayette, KY	139.7
72	Lima, OH	158.9
235	Lincoln, NE	66.5
49	Little Rock, AR	180.9
369	Logan, UT-ID	1.6
135	Longview, TX	122.2
307	Longview, WA	38.9
11	Los Angeles County, CA M.D.	248.7
26	Los Angeles (greater), CA	213.1
82	Louisville, KY-IN	149.6
140	Lubbock, TX	118.9
294	Lynchburg, VA	44.6
55	Macon, GA	175.9
164	Madera, CA	107.4
203	Madison, WI	82.6
261	Manchester-Nashua, NH	58.6
308	Manhattan, KS	38.8
355	Mankato-North Mankato, MN	17.1
237	Mansfield, OH	64.8
187	McAllen-Edinburg-Mission, TX	92.5
358	Medford, OR	16.7
2	Memphis, TN-MS-AR	352.2
157	Merced, CA	110.7
16	Miami (greater), FL	238.0
4	Miami-Dade County, FL M.D.	284.2
206	Michigan City-La Porte, IN	80.1
231	Midland, TX	67.8
21	Milwaukee, WI	223.3
175	Minneapolis-St. Paul, MN-WI	99.5
332	Missoula, MT	31.3
3	Mobile, AL	296.2
109	Modesto, CA	136.8
319	Monroe, MI	35.3
95	Montgomery, AL	144.7
295	Morgantown, WV	44.3
256	Morristown, TN	59.5
290	Mount Vernon-Anacortes, WA	44.8
143	Muncie, IN	117.1
152	Muskegon-Norton Shores, MI	112.6
227	Napa, CA	69.4
244	Naples-Marco Island, FL	62.2
76	Nashville-Davidson, TN	155.2
212	Nassau-Suffolk, NY M.D.	78.5
50	New Haven-Milford, CT	179.1
78	New Orleans, LA	153.3
73	New York (greater), NY-NJ-PA	158.7
42	New York-W. Plains NY-NJ M.D.	192.5
44	Newark-Union, NJ-PA M.D.	189.6
247	Niles-Benton Harbor, MI	61.2
111	North Port-Bradenton-Sarasota, FL	136.6
186	Norwich-New London, CT	93.1
6	Oakland-Fremont, CA M.D.	277.1
210	Ocala, FL	79.3
222	Ocean City, NJ	73.6
67	Odessa, TX	161.9

RANK	METROPOLITAN AREA	RATE
312	Ogden-Clearfield, UT	37.1
130	Oklahoma City, OK	124.6
299	Olympia, WA	43.8
136	Omaha-Council Bluffs, NE-IA	122.1
59	Orlando, FL	169.5
336	Oshkosh-Neenah, WI	28.9
312	Owensboro, KY	37.1
185	Oxnard-Thousand Oaks, CA	94.7
156	Palm Bay-Melbourne, FL	111.0
279	Palm Coast, FL	49.7
169	Panama City-Lynn Haven, FL	103.5
211	Pascagoula, MS	78.9
223	Peabody, MA M.D.	73.5
95	Pensacola, FL	144.7
17	Philadelphia (greater) PA-NJ-MD-DE	235.4
8	Philadelphia, PA M.D.	272.3
105	Phoenix-Mesa-Scottsdale, AZ	139.5
24	Pine Bluff, AR	217.3
158	Pittsburgh, PA	109.3
341	Pittsfield, MA	27.4
359	Pocatello, ID	15.8
181	Port St. Lucie, FL	95.9
200	Portland-Vancouver, OR-WA	84.6
290	Portland, ME	44.8
193	Poughkeepsie, NY	89.5
345	Prescott, AZ	22.4
176	Providence-New Bedford, RI-MA	98.8
360	Provo-Orem, UT	15.2
163	Pueblo, CO	107.7
303	Punta Gorda, FL	41.4
119	Racine, WI	133.1
173	Raleigh-Cary, NC	99.9
322	Rapid City, SD	33.9
150	Reading, PA	113.0
224	Redding, CA	71.6
127	Reno-Sparks, NV	127.9
124	Richmond, VA	131.6
114	Riverside-San Bernardino, CA	134.9
219	Roanoke, VA	74.9
330	Rochester, MN	32.9
167	Rochester, NY	104.8
349	Rockingham County, NH M.D.	20.6
23	Rocky Mount, NC	219.8
176	Rome, GA	98.8
57	Sacramento, CA	172.0
63	Saginaw, MI	164.4
285	Salem, OR	47.2
68	Salinas, CA	161.3
20	Salisbury, MD	224.6
197	Salt Lake City, UT	85.9
301	San Angelo, TX	41.8
89	San Antonio, TX	146.3
117	San Diego, CA	134.0
9	San Francisco (greater), CA	264.4
12	San Francisco-S. Mateo, CA M.D.	246.4
198	San Jose, CA	85.2
305	San Luis Obispo, CA	39.8
249	Sandusky, OH	61.0
180	Santa Ana-Anaheim, CA M.D.	97.0
237	Santa Barbara-Santa Maria, CA	64.8
195	Santa Cruz-Watsonville, CA	88.1
208	Santa Fe, NM	79.5
229	Santa Rosa-Petaluma, CA	68.3

RANK	METROPOLITAN AREA	RATE
27	Savannah, GA	210.4
264	Scranton--Wilkes-Barre, PA	57.5
105	Seattle-Bellevue-Everett, WA M.D.	139.5
99	Seattle-Tacoma-Bellevue, WA	143.1
251	Sebastian-Vero Beach, FL	60.0
340	Sheboygan, WI	27.9
267	Sherman-Denison, TX	55.9
93	Shreveport-Bossier City, LA	144.8
334	Sioux City, IA-NE-SD	30.0
350	Sioux Falls, SD	20.1
98	South Bend-Mishawaka, IN-MI	143.5
134	Spartanburg, SC	123.3
148	Spokane, WA	114.3
142	Springfield, MA	118.2
213	Springfield, MO	78.3
71	Springfield, OH	159.6
355	State College, PA	17.1
10	Stockton, CA	257.6
343	St. Cloud, MN	22.7
365	St. George, UT	12.6
192	St. Joseph, MO-KS	90.0
84	St. Louis, MO-IL	147.8
118	Sumter, SC	133.7
202	Syracuse, NY	83.7
77	Tacoma, WA M.D.	154.6
61	Tallahassee, FL	166.9
75	Tampa-St Petersburg, FL	155.9
62	Texarkana, TX-Texarkana, AR	166.4
31	Toledo, OH	204.0
108	Topeka, KS	138.0
43	Trenton-Ewing, NJ	190.9
79	Tucson, AZ	152.8
115	Tulsa, OK	134.5
113	Tuscaloosa, AL	135.2
266	Tyler, TX	56.7
234	Utica-Rome, NY	66.9
165	Valdosta, GA	106.4
34	Vallejo-Fairfield, CA	198.9
217	Victoria, TX	75.8
36	Vineland, NJ	196.9
150	Visalia-Porterville, CA	113.0
154	Waco, TX	111.9
188	Warner Robins, GA	92.4
248	Warren-Farmington Hills, MI M.D.	61.1
45	Washington (greater) DC-VA-MD-WV	189.5
25	Washington, DC-VA-MD-WV M.D.	213.5
183	Waterloo-Cedar Falls, IA	95.1
364	Wausau, WI	12.9
338	Wenatchee, WA	28.2
28	West Palm Beach, FL M.D.	210.1
311	Wheeling, WV-OH	37.4
153	Wichita Falls, TX	112.2
183	Wichita, KS	95.1
246	Williamsport, PA	61.7
29	Wilmington, DE-MD-NJ M.D.	209.2
144	Wilmington, NC	116.4
275	Winchester, VA-WV	52.8
107	Winston-Salem, NC	139.2
218	Worcester, MA	75.2
162	York-Hanover, PA	107.8
144	Youngstown, OH-PA	116.4
254	Yuba City, CA	59.6
268	Yuma, AZ	55.6

Source: Reported data from the F.B.I. "Crime in the United States 2009"

*Robbery is the taking of anything of value by force or threat of force. Attempts are included.

18. Robbery Rate in 2009 (continued)
National Rate = 133.0 Robberies per 100,000 Population*

RANK	METROPOLITAN AREA	RATE
1	Detroit-Livonia-Dearborn, MI M.D.	365.1
2	Memphis, TN-MS-AR	352.2
3	Mobile, AL	296.2
4	Miami-Dade County, FL M.D.	284.2
5	Las Vegas-Paradise, NV	283.6
6	Oakland-Fremont, CA M.D.	277.1
7	Houston, TX	276.2
8	Philadelphia, PA M.D.	272.3
9	San Francisco (greater), CA	264.4
10	Stockton, CA	257.6
11	Los Angeles County, CA M.D.	248.7
12	San Francisco-S. Mateo, CA M.D.	246.4
13	Baltimore-Towson, MD	241.1
14	Indianapolis, IN	239.0
15	Columbus, GA-AL	238.5
16	Miami (greater), FL	238.0
17	Philadelphia (greater) PA-NJ-MD-DE	235.4
18	Atlantic City, NJ	229.3
19	Cleveland-Elyria-Mentor, OH	228.9
20	Salisbury, MD	224.6
21	Milwaukee, WI	223.3
22	Columbus, OH	220.3
23	Rocky Mount, NC	219.8
24	Pine Bluff, AR	217.3
25	Washington, DC-VA-MD-WV M.D.	213.5
26	Los Angeles (greater), CA	213.1
27	Savannah, GA	210.4
28	West Palm Beach, FL M.D.	210.1
29	Wilmington, DE-MD-NJ M.D.	209.2
30	Jacksonville, FL	206.0
31	Toledo, OH	204.0
32	Baton Rouge, LA	201.7
33	Jackson, MS	201.4
34	Vallejo-Fairfield, CA	198.9
35	Flint, MI	198.5
36	Vineland, NJ	196.9
37	Detroit (greater), MI	194.3
38	Birmingham-Hoover, AL	193.3
39	Fort Lauderdale, FL M.D.	192.9
39	Greensboro-High Point, NC	192.9
41	Buffalo-Niagara Falls, NY	192.6
42	New York-W. Plains NY-NJ M.D.	192.5
43	Trenton-Ewing, NJ	190.9
44	Newark-Union, NJ-PA M.D.	189.6
45	Washington (greater) DC-VA-MD-WV	189.5
46	Augusta, GA-SC	188.2
47	Fayetteville, NC	187.8
48	Boston-Quincy, MA M.D.	184.7
49	Little Rock, AR	180.9
50	New Haven-Milford, CT	179.1
51	Dallas-Plano-Irving, TX M.D.	178.4
52	Anchorage, AK	177.9
53	Charlotte-Gastonia, NC-SC	177.8
54	Atlanta, GA	176.1
55	Macon, GA	175.9
56	Durham-Chapel Hill, NC	175.6
57	Sacramento, CA	172.0
58	Jackson, TN	170.8
59	Orlando, FL	169.5
60	Beaumont-Port Arthur, TX	169.1
61	Tallahassee, FL	166.9
62	Texarkana, TX-Texarkana, AR	166.4
63	Cincinnati-Middletown, OH-KY-IN	164.4
63	Saginaw, MI	164.4
65	Bakersfield, CA	163.4
66	Lawton, OK	162.3
67	Odessa, TX	161.9
68	Salinas, CA	161.3
69	Dallas (greater), TX	160.6
70	Charleston-North Charleston, SC	160.4
71	Springfield, OH	159.6
72	Lima, OH	158.9
73	New York (greater), NY-NJ-PA	158.7
74	Fresno, CA	158.2
75	Tampa-St Petersburg, FL	155.9
76	Nashville-Davidson, TN	155.2
77	Tacoma, WA M.D.	154.6
78	New Orleans, LA	153.3
79	Tucson, AZ	152.8
80	Albany, GA	152.0
81	Anniston-Oxford, AL	150.7
82	Louisville, KY-IN	149.6
83	Lafayette, LA	148.6
84	St. Louis, MO-IL	147.8
85	Albuquerque, NM	147.0
86	Brunswick, GA	146.8
87	Dayton, OH	146.6
88	Decatur, IL	146.4
89	San Antonio, TX	146.3
90	Kansas City, MO-KS	145.8
91	Amarillo, TX	145.5
92	Gainesville, FL	145.4
93	Florence, SC	144.8
93	Shreveport-Bossier City, LA	144.8
95	Montgomery, AL	144.7
95	Pensacola, FL	144.7
97	Danville, IL	143.7
98	South Bend-Mishawaka, IN-MI	143.5
99	Seattle-Tacoma-Bellevue, WA	143.1
100	Hot Springs, AR	142.5
101	Columbia, SC	140.5
102	Deltona-Daytona Beach, FL	140.4
103	Lexington-Fayette, KY	139.7
104	Lake Charles, LA	139.6
105	Phoenix-Mesa-Scottsdale, AZ	139.5
105	Seattle-Bellevue-Everett, WA M.D.	139.5
107	Winston-Salem, NC	139.2
108	Topeka, KS	138.0
109	Hinesville, GA	136.8
109	Modesto, CA	136.8
111	North Port-Bradenton-Sarasota, FL	136.6
112	Huntsville, AL	136.5
113	Tuscaloosa, AL	135.2
114	Riverside-San Bernardino, CA	134.9
115	Bridgeport-Stamford, CT	134.5
115	Tulsa, OK	134.5
117	San Diego, CA	134.0
118	Sumter, SC	133.7
119	Racine, WI	133.1
120	Alexandria, LA	132.9
120	Harrisburg-Carlisle, PA	132.9
122	Knoxville, TN	132.3
123	Camden, NJ M.D.	132.2
124	Richmond, VA	131.6
125	Akron, OH	130.7
126	Dothan, AL	128.2
127	Laredo, TX	127.9
127	Reno-Sparks, NV	127.9
129	Battle Creek, MI	125.1
130	Oklahoma City, OK	124.6
131	Fort Worth-Arlington, TX M.D.	124.3
132	Fort Wayne, IN	123.6
133	Houma, LA	123.5
134	Spartanburg, SC	123.3
135	Longview, TX	122.2
136	Omaha-Council Bluffs, NE-IA	122.1
137	Corpus Christi, TX	121.8
138	Chattanooga, TN-GA	121.2
139	Cape Coral-Fort Myers, FL	119.4
140	Lubbock, TX	118.9
141	Dover, DE	118.7
142	Springfield, MA	118.2
143	Muncie, IN	117.1
144	Wilmington, NC	116.4
144	Youngstown, OH-PA	116.4
146	Goldsboro, NC	115.9
147	Gulfport-Biloxi, MS	115.1
148	Spokane, WA	114.3
149	Hartford, CT	113.6
150	Reading, PA	113.0
150	Visalia-Porterville, CA	113.0
152	Muskegon-Norton Shores, MI	112.6
153	Wichita Falls, TX	112.2
154	Waco, TX	111.9
155	Boston (greater), MA-NH	111.5
156	Palm Bay-Melbourne, FL	111.0
157	Merced, CA	110.7
158	Pittsburgh, PA	109.3
159	Auburn, AL	109.1
160	Gadsden, AL	108.9
161	Burlington, NC	108.5
162	York-Hanover, PA	107.8
163	Pueblo, CO	107.7
164	Madera, CA	107.4
165	Valdosta, GA	106.4
166	Columbia, MO	105.1
167	Rochester, NY	104.8
168	Bethesda-Frederick, MD M.D.	103.9
169	Panama City-Lynn Haven, FL	103.5
170	Albany-Schenectady-Troy, NY	103.3
171	Lakeland, FL	102.9
172	Grand Rapids-Wyoming, MI	102.4
173	Raleigh-Cary, NC	99.9
174	Anderson, SC	99.6
175	Minneapolis-St. Paul, MN-WI	99.5
176	Providence-New Bedford, RI-MA	98.8
176	Rome, GA	98.8
178	Austin-Round Rock, TX	97.9
179	Allentown, PA-NJ	97.6
180	Santa Ana-Anaheim, CA M.D.	97.0

Note: All listings are for Metropolitan Statistical Areas (M.S.A.s) except for those ending with "M.D." Listings with "M.D." are Metropolitan Divisions which are smaller parts of eleven large M.S.A.s. See explanatory note at beginning of metropolitan area section.

Rank Order - Metro Area (continued)

RANK	METROPOLITAN AREA	RATE
181	Port St. Lucie, FL	95.9
182	Honolulu, HI	95.8
183	Waterloo-Cedar Falls, IA	95.1
183	Wichita, KS	95.1
185	Oxnard-Thousand Oaks, CA	94.7
186	Norwich-New London, CT	93.1
187	McAllen-Edinburg-Mission, TX	92.5
188	Warner Robins, GA	92.4
189	Abilene, TX	91.5
189	Kalamazoo-Portage, MI	91.5
191	Athens-Clarke County, GA	91.1
192	St. Joseph, MO-KS	90.0
193	Poughkeepsie, NY	89.5
194	Colorado Springs, CO	89.3
195	Santa Cruz-Watsonville, CA	88.1
196	Danville, VA	88.0
197	Salt Lake City, UT	85.9
198	Denver-Aurora, CO	85.2
198	San Jose, CA	85.2
200	Portland-Vancouver, OR-WA	84.6
201	Chico, CA	84.4
202	Syracuse, NY	83.7
203	Madison, WI	82.6
204	College Station-Bryan, TX	81.3
205	Lansing-East Lansing, MI	80.4
206	Michigan City-La Porte, IN	80.1
207	Charleston, WV	79.9
208	Killeen-Temple-Fort Hood, TX	79.5
208	Santa Fe, NM	79.5
210	Ocala, FL	79.3
211	Pascagoula, MS	78.9
212	Nassau-Suffolk, NY M.D.	78.5
213	Springfield, MO	78.3
214	Eugene-Springfield, OR	77.8
215	Crestview-Fort Walton Beach, FL	77.1
216	Elkhart-Goshen, IN	77.0
217	Victoria, TX	75.8
218	Worcester, MA	75.2
219	Roanoke, VA	74.9
220	Lawrence, KS	74.6
221	Brownsville-Harlingen, TX	74.3
222	Ocean City, NJ	73.6
223	Peabody, MA M.D.	73.5
224	Clarksville, TN-KY	71.6
224	Redding, CA	71.6
226	Jonesboro, AR	69.8
227	Napa, CA	69.4
228	Lancaster, PA	68.6
229	Santa Rosa-Petaluma, CA	68.3
230	El Paso, TX	68.1
231	Midland, TX	67.8
232	Janesville, WI	67.1
233	Jackson, MI	67.0
234	Utica-Rome, NY	66.9
235	Lincoln, NE	66.5
236	Hickory, NC	66.1
237	Mansfield, OH	64.8
237	Santa Barbara-Santa Maria, CA	64.8
239	Ann Arbor, MI	64.0
240	Asheville, NC	63.4
241	Cambridge-Newton, MA M.D.	62.8
241	Charlottesville, VA	62.8
243	Florence-Muscle Shoals, AL	62.3

RANK	METROPOLITAN AREA	RATE
244	Naples-Marco Island, FL	62.2
245	Barnstable Town, MA	62.0
246	Williamsport, PA	61.7
247	Niles-Benton Harbor, MI	61.2
248	Warren-Farmington Hills, MI M.D.	61.1
249	Bowling Green, KY	61.0
249	Sandusky, OH	61.0
251	Sebastian-Vero Beach, FL	60.0
252	Cape Girardeau, MO-IL	59.8
252	Edison, NJ M.D.	59.8
254	El Centro, CA	59.6
254	Yuba City, CA	59.6
256	Morristown, TN	59.5
257	Anderson, IN	59.3
258	Duluth, MN-WI	58.9
258	Jacksonville, NC	58.9
260	Hattiesburg, MS	58.8
261	Manchester-Nashua, NH	58.6
262	Fort Smith, AR-OK	57.8
263	Erie, PA	57.6
264	Scranton--Wilkes-Barre, PA	57.5
265	Decatur, AL	56.9
266	Tyler, TX	56.7
267	Sherman-Denison, TX	55.9
268	Yuma, AZ	55.6
269	Las Cruces, NM	55.5
270	Evansville, IN-KY	55.4
271	Hagerstown-Martinsburg, MD-WV	54.9
272	Bay City, MI	54.3
273	Lewiston-Auburn, ME	54.2
274	Kingston, NY	53.8
275	Winchester, VA-WV	52.8
276	Des Moines-West Des Moines, IA	52.1
277	Bloomington, IN	50.2
278	Great Falls, MT	49.9
279	Palm Coast, FL	49.7
280	Billings, MT	49.5
281	Carson City, NV	47.7
281	Grand Junction, CO	47.7
283	Flagstaff, AZ	47.5
284	Cumberland, MD-WV	47.4
285	Salem, OR	47.2
286	Cedar Rapids, IA	47.1
287	Altoona, PA	46.4
288	Iowa City, IA	45.6
289	Johnson City, TN	44.9
290	Mount Vernon-Anacortes, WA	44.8
290	Portland, ME	44.8
292	Bellingham, WA	44.7
292	Lafayette, IN	44.7
294	Lynchburg, VA	44.6
295	Morgantown, WV	44.3
296	Bremerton-Silverdale, WA	44.2
296	Jefferson City, MO	44.2
298	Cleveland, TN	44.1
299	Olympia, WA	43.8
300	Kokomo, IN	43.3
301	Kingsport, TN-VA	41.8
301	San Angelo, TX	41.8
303	Punta Gorda, FL	41.4
304	Kennewick-Pasco-Richland, WA	41.2
305	San Luis Obispo, CA	39.8
306	Boulder, CO	39.5

RANK	METROPOLITAN AREA	RATE
307	Longview, WA	38.9
308	Manhattan, KS	38.8
309	Binghamton, NY	38.1
310	Bangor, ME	37.6
311	Wheeling, WV-OH	37.4
312	Ogden-Clearfield, UT	37.1
312	Owensboro, KY	37.1
314	Farmington, NM	36.3
315	Fort Collins-Loveland, CO	35.9
315	Gainesville, GA	35.9
317	Columbus, IN	35.6
318	Greeley, CO	35.5
319	Monroe, MI	35.3
320	Lake Havasu City-Kingman, AZ	34.7
321	Coeur d'Alene, ID	34.2
322	Rapid City, SD	33.9
323	Grand Forks, ND-MN	33.7
324	Cheyenne, WY	33.6
324	Elizabethtown, KY	33.6
326	Ithaca, NY	33.5
327	Blacksburg, VA	33.2
327	Elmira, NY	33.2
329	Lebanon, PA	33.0
330	Rochester, MN	32.9
331	Green Bay, WI	31.5
332	Missoula, MT	31.3
333	Corvallis, OR	30.4
334	Sioux City, IA-NE-SD	30.0
335	Harrisonburg, VA	29.2
336	Oshkosh-Neenah, WI	28.9
337	La Crosse, WI-MN	28.7
338	Wenatchee, WA	28.2
339	Dalton, GA	28.1
340	Sheboygan, WI	27.9
341	Pittsfield, MA	27.4
342	Ames, IA	22.9
343	St. Cloud, MN	22.7
344	Fargo, ND-MN	22.6
345	Prescott, AZ	22.4
346	Fayetteville, AR-MO	22.3
347	Casper, WY	21.4
348	Boise City-Nampa, ID	20.7
349	Rockingham County, NH M.D.	20.6
350	Sioux Falls, SD	20.1
351	Lewiston, ID-WA	19.8
352	Bend, OR	19.6
353	Burlington-South Burlington, VT	18.6
354	Dubuque, IA	18.3
355	Mankato-North Mankato, MN	17.1
355	State College, PA	17.1
357	Holland-Grand Haven, MI	16.8
358	Medford, OR	16.7
359	Pocatello, ID	15.8
360	Provo-Orem, UT	15.2
361	Idaho Falls, ID	14.4
362	Appleton, WI	13.1
362	Eau Claire, WI	13.1
364	Wausau, WI	12.9
365	St. George, UT	12.6
366	Bismarck, ND	12.2
367	Glens Falls, NY	8.5
368	Fond du Lac, WI	7.0
369	Logan, UT-ID	1.6

Source: Reported data from the F.B.I. "Crime in the United States 2009"

*Robbery is the taking of anything of value by force or threat of force. Attempts are included.

19. Percent Change in Robbery Rate: 2008 to 2009
National Percent Change = 8.8% Decrease*

RANK	METROPOLITAN AREA	% CHANGE
273	Abilene, TX	(22.5)
158	Akron, OH	(7.3)
159	Albany-Schenectady-Troy, NY	(7.4)
NA	Albany, GA**	NA
267	Albuquerque, NM	(21.9)
NA	Alexandria, LA**	NA
140	Allentown, PA-NJ	(5.5)
305	Altoona, PA	(36.3)
67	Amarillo, TX	8.0
3	Ames, IA	95.7
118	Anchorage, AK	(2.8)
NA	Anderson, IN**	NA
195	Anderson, SC	(10.8)
281	Ann Arbor, MI	(24.3)
NA	Anniston-Oxford, AL**	NA
35	Appleton, WI	20.2
290	Asheville, NC	(27.8)
299	Athens-Clarke County, GA	(31.3)
257	Atlanta, GA	(19.4)
40	Atlantic City, NJ	18.3
263	Auburn, AL	(20.8)
111	Augusta, GA-SC	(1.5)
79	Austin-Round Rock, TX	4.3
88	Bakersfield, CA	1.9
189	Baltimore-Towson, MD	(10.2)
10	Bangor, ME	46.9
11	Barnstable Town, MA	45.9
59	Baton Rouge, LA	10.7
71	Battle Creek, MI	6.5
NA	Bay City, MI**	NA
75	Beaumont-Port Arthur, TX	6.0
97	Bellingham, WA	1.1
304	Bend, OR	(34.9)
184	Bethesda-Frederick, MD M.D.	(9.7)
19	Billings, MT	36.4
294	Binghamton, NY	(28.5)
262	Birmingham-Hoover, AL	(20.5)
180	Bismarck, ND	(9.0)
26	Blacksburg, VA	24.8
14	Bloomington, IN	40.6
117	Boise City-Nampa, ID	(2.4)
94	Boston (greater), MA-NH	1.3
107	Boston-Quincy, MA M.D.	(1.0)
NA	Boulder, CO**	NA
NA	Bowling Green, KY**	NA
145	Bremerton-Silverdale, WA	(6.4)
110	Bridgeport-Stamford, CT	(1.4)
175	Brownsville-Harlingen, TX	(8.8)
NA	Brunswick, GA**	NA
65	Buffalo-Niagara Falls, NY	8.1
NA	Burlington-South Burlington, VT**	NA
137	Burlington, NC	(5.2)
92	Cambridge-Newton, MA M.D.	1.5
162	Camden, NJ M.D.	(7.8)
156	Cape Coral-Fort Myers, FL	(6.9)
235	Cape Girardeau, MO-IL	(15.2)
68	Carson City, NV	7.9
286	Casper, WY	(25.4)
236	Cedar Rapids, IA	(15.3)
274	Charleston-North Charleston, SC	(23.2)
69	Charleston, WV	7.8
267	Charlotte-Gastonia, NC-SC	(21.9)
113	Charlottesville, VA	(1.6)
90	Chattanooga, TN-GA	1.8
111	Cheyenne, WY	(1.5)
62	Chico, CA	9.8
NA	Cincinnati-Middletown, OH-KY-IN**	NA
NA	Clarksville, TN-KY**	NA
NA	Cleveland-Elyria-Mentor, OH**	NA
172	Cleveland, TN	(8.5)
NA	Coeur d'Alene, ID**	NA
114	College Station-Bryan, TX	(2.2)
100	Colorado Springs, CO	0.7
51	Columbia, MO	13.5
202	Columbia, SC	(12.2)
133	Columbus, GA-AL	(4.7)
4	Columbus, IN	91.4
150	Columbus, OH	(6.6)
144	Corpus Christi, TX	(6.0)
27	Corvallis, OR	24.6
NA	Crestview-Fort Walton Beach, FL**	NA
50	Cumberland, MD-WV	13.9
216	Dallas (greater), TX	(13.5)
222	Dallas-Plano-Irving, TX M.D.	(14.1)
297	Dalton, GA	(29.8)
NA	Danville, IL**	NA
291	Danville, VA	(27.9)
167	Dayton, OH	(8.2)
305	Decatur, AL	(36.3)
NA	Decatur, IL**	NA
122	Deltona-Daytona Beach, FL	(3.3)
137	Denver-Aurora, CO	(5.2)
NA	Des Moines-West Des Moines, IA**	NA
NA	Detroit (greater), MI**	NA
NA	Detroit-Livonia-Dearborn, MI M.D.**	NA
247	Dothan, AL	(16.8)
134	Dover, DE	(5.0)
302	Dubuque, IA	(32.0)
145	Duluth, MN-WI	(6.4)
280	Durham-Chapel Hill, NC	(24.1)
184	Eau Claire, WI	(9.7)
153	Edison, NJ M.D.	(6.7)
274	El Centro, CA	(23.2)
116	El Paso, TX	(2.3)
NA	Elizabethtown, KY**	NA
283	Elkhart-Goshen, IN	(24.7)
265	Elmira, NY	(21.3)
311	Erie, PA	(55.4)
195	Eugene-Springfield, OR	(10.8)
NA	Evansville, IN-KY**	NA
30	Fargo, ND-MN	22.2
175	Farmington, NM	(8.8)
83	Fayetteville, AR-MO	2.8
288	Fayetteville, NC	(26.6)
238	Flagstaff, AZ	(15.5)
NA	Flint, MI**	NA
296	Florence-Muscle Shoals, AL	(29.6)
226	Florence, SC	(14.4)
298	Fond du Lac, WI	(30.7)
6	Fort Collins-Loveland, CO	54.1
243	Fort Lauderdale, FL M.D.	(16.3)
30	Fort Smith, AR-OK	22.2
94	Fort Wayne, IN	1.3
199	Fort Worth-Arlington, TX M.D.	(11.8)
55	Fresno, CA	11.9
293	Gadsden, AL	(28.3)
81	Gainesville, FL	3.8
NA	Gainesville, GA**	NA
234	Glens Falls, NY	(15.0)
250	Goldsboro, NC	(17.0)
2	Grand Forks, ND-MN	105.5
8	Grand Junction, CO	47.2
NA	Grand Rapids-Wyoming, MI**	NA
21	Great Falls, MT	32.4
150	Greeley, CO	(6.6)
230	Green Bay, WI	(14.6)
175	Greensboro-High Point, NC	(8.8)
NA	Gulfport-Biloxi, MS**	NA
255	Hagerstown-Martinsburg, MD-WV	(18.5)
120	Harrisburg-Carlisle, PA	(3.1)
29	Harrisonburg, VA	23.2
153	Hartford, CT	(6.7)
NA	Hattiesburg, MS**	NA
186	Hickory, NC	(9.9)
20	Hinesville, GA	35.8
NA	Holland-Grand Haven, MI**	NA
145	Honolulu, HI	(6.4)
42	Hot Springs, AR	17.6
12	Houma, LA	45.0
65	Houston, TX	8.1
80	Huntsville, AL	4.0
43	Idaho Falls, ID	17.1
131	Indianapolis, IN	(4.4)
191	Iowa City, IA	(10.4)
119	Ithaca, NY	(2.9)
253	Jacksonville, FL	(17.9)
303	Jacksonville, NC	(32.1)
NA	Jackson, MI**	NA
90	Jackson, MS	1.8
285	Jackson, TN	(25.3)
141	Janesville, WI	(5.6)
NA	Jefferson City, MO**	NA
41	Johnson City, TN	18.2
238	Jonesboro, AR	(15.5)
NA	Kalamazoo-Portage, MI**	NA
NA	Kansas City, MO-KS**	NA
183	Kennewick-Pasco-Richland, WA	(9.6)
271	Killeen-Temple-Fort Hood, TX	(22.1)
76	Kingsport, TN-VA	5.8
17	Kingston, NY	38.3
88	Knoxville, TN	1.9
308	Kokomo, IN	(36.6)
125	La Crosse, WI-MN	(3.4)
24	Lafayette, IN	27.4
165	Lafayette, LA	(7.9)
NA	Lake Charles, LA**	NA
73	Lake Havasu City-Kingman, AZ	6.4
240	Lakeland, FL	(15.7)
120	Lancaster, PA	(3.1)
NA	Lansing-East Lansing, MI**	NA

Note: All listings are for Metropolitan Statistical Areas (M.S.A.s) except for those ending with "M.D." Listings with "M.D." are Metropolitan Divisions which are smaller parts of eleven large M.S.A.s. See explanatory note at beginning of metropolitan area section.

Alpha Order - Metro Area (continued)

RANK	METROPOLITAN AREA	% CHANGE
139	Laredo, TX	(5.3)
38	Las Cruces, NM	18.8
162	Las Vegas-Paradise, NV	(7.8)
63	Lawrence, KS	9.1
NA	Lawton, OK**	NA
291	Lebanon, PA	(27.9)
34	Lewiston-Auburn, ME	20.4
64	Lewiston, ID-WA	8.2
NA	Lexington-Fayette, KY**	NA
200	Lima, OH	(11.9)
181	Lincoln, NE	(9.4)
NA	Little Rock, AR**	NA
102	Logan, UT-ID	0.0
201	Longview, TX	(12.1)
305	Longview, WA	(36.3)
167	Los Angeles County, CA M.D.	(8.2)
162	Los Angeles (greater), CA	(7.8)
NA	Louisville, KY-IN**	NA
85	Lubbock, TX	2.7
231	Lynchburg, VA	(14.7)
209	Macon, GA	(12.7)
216	Madera, CA	(13.5)
87	Madison, WI	2.1
NA	Manchester-Nashua, NH**	NA
204	Manhattan, KS	(12.4)
53	Mankato-North Mankato, MN	12.5
237	Mansfield, OH	(15.4)
97	McAllen-Edinburg-Mission, TX	1.1
310	Medford, OR	(50.4)
219	Memphis, TN-MS-AR	(13.8)
82	Merced, CA	3.2
220	Miami (greater), FL	(14.0)
241	Miami-Dade County, FL M.D.	(16.2)
172	Michigan City-La Porte, IN	(8.5)
215	Midland, TX	(13.3)
136	Milwaukee, WI	(5.1)
233	Minneapolis-St. Paul, MN-WI	(14.9)
15	Missoula, MT	39.7
96	Mobile, AL	1.2
209	Modesto, CA	(12.7)
NA	Monroe, MI**	NA
122	Montgomery, AL	(3.3)
NA	Morgantown, WV**	NA
77	Morristown, TN	5.1
126	Mount Vernon-Anacortes, WA	(3.7)
5	Muncie, IN	58.5
NA	Muskegon-Norton Shores, MI**	NA
22	Napa, CA	31.7
232	Naples-Marco Island, FL	(14.8)
247	Nashville-Davidson, TN	(16.8)
70	Nassau-Suffolk, NY M.D.	7.7
NA	New Haven-Milford, CT**	NA
251	New Orleans, LA	(17.1)
212	New York (greater), NY-NJ-PA	(13.1)
244	New York-W. Plains NY-NJ M.D.	(16.5)
126	Newark-Union, NJ-PA M.D.	(3.7)
NA	Niles-Benton Harbor, MI**	NA
NA	North Port-Bradenton-Sarasota, FL**	NA
9	Norwich-New London, CT	47.1
228	Oakland-Fremont, CA M.D.	(14.5)
241	Ocala, FL	(16.2)
149	Ocean City, NJ	(6.5)
1	Odessa, TX	140.6
252	Ogden-Clearfield, UT	(17.6)
NA	Oklahoma City, OK**	NA
134	Olympia, WA	(5.0)
114	Omaha-Council Bluffs, NE-IA	(2.2)
295	Orlando, FL	(29.2)
54	Oshkosh-Neenah, WI	12.0
NA	Owensboro, KY**	NA
207	Oxnard-Thousand Oaks, CA	(12.6)
188	Palm Bay-Melbourne, FL	(10.0)
249	Palm Coast, FL	(16.9)
108	Panama City-Lynn Haven, FL	(1.3)
159	Pascagoula, MS	(7.4)
48	Peabody, MA M.D.	14.0
174	Pensacola, FL	(8.6)
166	Philadelphia (greater) PA-NJ-MD-DE	(8.0)
167	Philadelphia, PA M.D.	(8.2)
260	Phoenix-Mesa-Scottsdale, AZ	(20.4)
244	Pine Bluff, AR	(16.5)
181	Pittsburgh, PA	(9.4)
22	Pittsfield, MA	31.7
213	Pocatello, ID	(13.2)
278	Port St. Lucie, FL	(23.8)
143	Portland-Vancouver, OR-WA	(5.9)
48	Portland, ME	14.0
78	Poughkeepsie, NY	4.8
74	Prescott, AZ	6.2
101	Providence-New Bedford, RI-MA	0.5
47	Provo-Orem, UT	15.2
NA	Pueblo, CO**	NA
205	Punta Gorda, FL	(12.5)
265	Racine, WI	(21.3)
282	Raleigh-Cary, NC	(24.6)
276	Rapid City, SD	(23.6)
254	Reading, PA	(18.2)
28	Redding, CA	24.3
246	Reno-Sparks, NV	(16.7)
224	Richmond, VA	(14.2)
194	Riverside-San Bernardino, CA	(10.7)
207	Roanoke, VA	(12.6)
209	Rochester, MN	(12.7)
257	Rochester, NY	(19.4)
58	Rockingham County, NH M.D.	10.8
NA	Rocky Mount, NC**	NA
NA	Rome, GA**	NA
122	Sacramento, CA	(3.3)
NA	Saginaw, MI**	NA
220	Salem, OR	(14.0)
56	Salinas, CA	11.6
45	Salisbury, MD	16.7
153	Salt Lake City, UT	(6.7)
300	San Angelo, TX	(31.4)
128	San Antonio, TX	(3.9)
106	San Diego, CA	(0.7)
226	San Francisco (greater), CA	(14.4)
225	San Francisco-S. Mateo, CA M.D.	(14.3)
197	San Jose, CA	(11.1)
150	San Luis Obispo, CA	(6.6)
260	Sandusky, OH	(20.4)
130	Santa Ana-Anaheim, CA M.D.	(4.1)
192	Santa Barbara-Santa Maria, CA	(10.6)
259	Santa Cruz-Watsonville, CA	(20.2)
32	Santa Fe, NM	20.6
46	Santa Rosa-Petaluma, CA	15.4
267	Savannah, GA	(21.9)
85	Scranton--Wilkes-Barre, PA	2.7
NA	Seattle-Bellevue-Everett, WA M.D.**	NA
NA	Seattle-Tacoma-Bellevue, WA**	NA
270	Sebastian-Vero Beach, FL	(22.0)
61	Sheboygan, WI	10.3
13	Sherman-Denison, TX	42.2
171	Shreveport-Bossier City, LA	(8.3)
284	Sioux City, IA-NE-SD	(24.8)
102	Sioux Falls, SD	0.0
NA	South Bend-Mishawaka, IN-MI**	NA
256	Spartanburg, SC	(18.9)
141	Spokane, WA	(5.6)
92	Springfield, MA	1.5
NA	Springfield, MO**	NA
7	Springfield, OH	53.0
128	State College, PA	(3.9)
213	Stockton, CA	(13.2)
300	St. Cloud, MN	(31.4)
309	St. George, UT	(44.0)
37	St. Joseph, MO-KS	19.2
108	St. Louis, MO-IL	(1.3)
NA	Sumter, SC**	NA
99	Syracuse, NY	1.0
NA	Tacoma, WA M.D.**	NA
287	Tallahassee, FL	(26.2)
198	Tampa-St Petersburg, FL	(11.7)
18	Texarkana, TX-Texarkana, AR	37.6
192	Toledo, OH	(10.6)
57	Topeka, KS	11.2
131	Trenton-Ewing, NJ	(4.4)
222	Tucson, AZ	(14.1)
104	Tulsa, OK	(0.4)
186	Tuscaloosa, AL	(9.9)
289	Tyler, TX	(27.6)
218	Utica-Rome, NY	(13.7)
228	Valdosta, GA	(14.5)
190	Vallejo-Fairfield, CA	(10.3)
39	Victoria, TX	18.4
202	Vineland, NJ	(12.2)
83	Visalia-Porterville, CA	2.8
205	Waco, TX	(12.5)
52	Warner Robins, GA	12.8
NA	Warren-Farmington Hills, MI M.D.**	NA
159	Washington (greater) DC-VA-MD-WV	(7.4)
157	Washington, DC-VA-MD-WV M.D.	(7.0)
25	Waterloo-Cedar Falls, IA	26.5
NA	Wausau, WI**	NA
16	Wenatchee, WA	38.9
145	West Palm Beach, FL M.D.	(6.4)
278	Wheeling, WV-OH	(23.8)
272	Wichita Falls, TX	(22.2)
60	Wichita, KS	10.6
36	Williamsport, PA	19.6
179	Wilmington, DE-MD-NJ M.D.	(8.9)
175	Wilmington, NC	(8.8)
33	Winchester, VA-WV	20.5
264	Winston-Salem, NC	(21.2)
71	Worcester, MA	6.5
167	York-Hanover, PA	(8.2)
104	Youngstown, OH-PA	(0.4)
276	Yuba City, CA	(23.6)
44	Yuma, AZ	16.8

Source: CQ Press using reported data from the F.B.I. "Crime in the United States 2009"
*Robbery is the taking of anything of value by force or threat of force. Attempts are included.
**Not available.

19. Percent Change in Robbery Rate: 2008 to 2009 (continued)
National Percent Change = 8.8% Decrease*

RANK	METROPOLITAN AREA	% CHANGE
1	Odessa, TX	140.6
2	Grand Forks, ND-MN	105.5
3	Ames, IA	95.7
4	Columbus, IN	91.4
5	Muncie, IN	58.5
6	Fort Collins-Loveland, CO	54.1
7	Springfield, OH	53.0
8	Grand Junction, CO	47.2
9	Norwich-New London, CT	47.1
10	Bangor, ME	46.9
11	Barnstable Town, MA	45.9
12	Houma, LA	45.0
13	Sherman-Denison, TX	42.2
14	Bloomington, IN	40.6
15	Missoula, MT	39.7
16	Wenatchee, WA	38.9
17	Kingston, NY	38.3
18	Texarkana, TX-Texarkana, AR	37.6
19	Billings, MT	36.4
20	Hinesville, GA	35.8
21	Great Falls, MT	32.4
22	Napa, CA	31.7
22	Pittsfield, MA	31.7
24	Lafayette, IN	27.4
25	Waterloo-Cedar Falls, IA	26.5
26	Blacksburg, VA	24.8
27	Corvallis, OR	24.6
28	Redding, CA	24.3
29	Harrisonburg, VA	23.2
30	Fargo, ND-MN	22.2
30	Fort Smith, AR-OK	22.2
32	Santa Fe, NM	20.6
33	Winchester, VA-WV	20.5
34	Lewiston-Auburn, ME	20.4
35	Appleton, WI	20.2
36	Williamsport, PA	19.6
37	St. Joseph, MO-KS	19.2
38	Las Cruces, NM	18.8
39	Victoria, TX	18.4
40	Atlantic City, NJ	18.3
41	Johnson City, TN	18.2
42	Hot Springs, AR	17.6
43	Idaho Falls, ID	17.1
44	Yuma, AZ	16.8
45	Salisbury, MD	16.7
46	Santa Rosa-Petaluma, CA	15.4
47	Provo-Orem, UT	15.2
48	Peabody, MA M.D.	14.0
48	Portland, ME	14.0
50	Cumberland, MD-WV	13.9
51	Columbia, MO	13.5
52	Warner Robins, GA	12.8
53	Mankato-North Mankato, MN	12.5
54	Oshkosh-Neenah, WI	12.0
55	Fresno, CA	11.9
56	Salinas, CA	11.6
57	Topeka, KS	11.2
58	Rockingham County, NH M.D.	10.8
59	Baton Rouge, LA	10.7
60	Wichita, KS	10.6
61	Sheboygan, WI	10.3
62	Chico, CA	9.8
63	Lawrence, KS	9.1
64	Lewiston, ID-WA	8.2
65	Buffalo-Niagara Falls, NY	8.1
65	Houston, TX	8.1
67	Amarillo, TX	8.0
68	Carson City, NV	7.9
69	Charleston, WV	7.8
70	Nassau-Suffolk, NY M.D.	7.7
71	Battle Creek, MI	6.5
71	Worcester, MA	6.5
73	Lake Havasu City-Kingman, AZ	6.4
74	Prescott, AZ	6.2
75	Beaumont-Port Arthur, TX	6.0
76	Kingsport, TN-VA	5.8
77	Morristown, TN	5.1
78	Poughkeepsie, NY	4.8
79	Austin-Round Rock, TX	4.3
80	Huntsville, AL	4.0
81	Gainesville, FL	3.8
82	Merced, CA	3.2
83	Fayetteville, AR-MO	2.8
83	Visalia-Porterville, CA	2.8
85	Lubbock, TX	2.7
85	Scranton--Wilkes-Barre, PA	2.7
87	Madison, WI	2.1
88	Bakersfield, CA	1.9
88	Knoxville, TN	1.9
90	Chattanooga, TN-GA	1.8
90	Jackson, MS	1.8
92	Cambridge-Newton, MA M.D.	1.5
92	Springfield, MA	1.5
94	Boston (greater), MA-NH	1.3
94	Fort Wayne, IN	1.3
96	Mobile, AL	1.2
97	Bellingham, WA	1.1
97	McAllen-Edinburg-Mission, TX	1.1
99	Syracuse, NY	1.0
100	Colorado Springs, CO	0.7
101	Providence-New Bedford, RI-MA	0.5
102	Logan, UT-ID	0.0
102	Sioux Falls, SD	0.0
104	Tulsa, OK	(0.4)
104	Youngstown, OH-PA	(0.4)
106	San Diego, CA	(0.7)
107	Boston-Quincy, MA M.D.	(1.0)
108	Panama City-Lynn Haven, FL	(1.3)
108	St. Louis, MO-IL	(1.3)
110	Bridgeport-Stamford, CT	(1.4)
111	Augusta, GA-SC	(1.5)
111	Cheyenne, WY	(1.5)
113	Charlottesville, VA	(1.6)
114	College Station-Bryan, TX	(2.2)
114	Omaha-Council Bluffs, NE-IA	(2.2)
116	El Paso, TX	(2.3)
117	Boise City-Nampa, ID	(2.4)
118	Anchorage, AK	(2.8)
119	Ithaca, NY	(2.9)
120	Harrisburg-Carlisle, PA	(3.1)
120	Lancaster, PA	(3.1)
122	Deltona-Daytona Beach, FL	(3.3)
122	Montgomery, AL	(3.3)
122	Sacramento, CA	(3.3)
125	La Crosse, WI-MN	(3.4)
126	Mount Vernon-Anacortes, WA	(3.7)
126	Newark-Union, NJ-PA M.D.	(3.7)
128	San Antonio, TX	(3.9)
128	State College, PA	(3.9)
130	Santa Ana-Anaheim, CA M.D.	(4.1)
131	Indianapolis, IN	(4.4)
131	Trenton-Ewing, NJ	(4.4)
133	Columbus, GA-AL	(4.7)
134	Dover, DE	(5.0)
134	Olympia, WA	(5.0)
136	Milwaukee, WI	(5.1)
137	Burlington, NC	(5.2)
137	Denver-Aurora, CO	(5.2)
139	Laredo, TX	(5.3)
140	Allentown, PA-NJ	(5.5)
141	Janesville, WI	(5.6)
141	Spokane, WA	(5.6)
143	Portland-Vancouver, OR-WA	(5.9)
144	Corpus Christi, TX	(6.0)
145	Bremerton-Silverdale, WA	(6.4)
145	Duluth, MN-WI	(6.4)
145	Honolulu, HI	(6.4)
145	West Palm Beach, FL M.D.	(6.4)
149	Ocean City, NJ	(6.5)
150	Columbus, OH	(6.6)
150	Greeley, CO	(6.6)
150	San Luis Obispo, CA	(6.6)
153	Edison, NJ M.D.	(6.7)
153	Hartford, CT	(6.7)
153	Salt Lake City, UT	(6.7)
156	Cape Coral-Fort Myers, FL	(6.9)
157	Washington, DC-VA-MD-WV M.D.	(7.0)
158	Akron, OH	(7.3)
159	Albany-Schenectady-Troy, NY	(7.4)
159	Pascagoula, MS	(7.4)
159	Washington (greater) DC-VA-MD-WV	(7.4)
162	Camden, NJ M.D.	(7.8)
162	Las Vegas-Paradise, NV	(7.8)
162	Los Angeles (greater), CA	(7.8)
165	Lafayette, LA	(7.9)
166	Philadelphia (greater) PA-NJ-MD-DE	(8.0)
167	Dayton, OH	(8.2)
167	Los Angeles County, CA M.D.	(8.2)
167	Philadelphia, PA M.D.	(8.2)
167	York-Hanover, PA	(8.2)
171	Shreveport-Bossier City, LA	(8.3)
172	Cleveland, TN	(8.5)
172	Michigan City-La Porte, IN	(8.5)
174	Pensacola, FL	(8.6)
175	Brownsville-Harlingen, TX	(8.8)
175	Farmington, NM	(8.8)
175	Greensboro-High Point, NC	(8.8)
175	Wilmington, NC	(8.8)
179	Wilmington, DE-MD-NJ M.D.	(8.9)
180	Bismarck, ND	(9.0)

Note: All listings are for Metropolitan Statistical Areas (M.S.A.s) except for those ending with "M.D." Listings with "M.D." are Metropolitan Divisions which are smaller parts of eleven large M.S.A.s. See explanatory note at beginning of metropolitan area section.

RANK	METROPOLITAN AREA	% CHANGE
181	Lincoln, NE	(9.4)
181	Pittsburgh, PA	(9.4)
183	Kennewick-Pasco-Richland, WA	(9.6)
184	Bethesda-Frederick, MD M.D.	(9.7)
184	Eau Claire, WI	(9.7)
186	Hickory, NC	(9.9)
186	Tuscaloosa, AL	(9.9)
188	Palm Bay-Melbourne, FL	(10.0)
189	Baltimore-Towson, MD	(10.2)
190	Vallejo-Fairfield, CA	(10.3)
191	Iowa City, IA	(10.4)
192	Santa Barbara-Santa Maria, CA	(10.6)
192	Toledo, OH	(10.6)
194	Riverside-San Bernardino, CA	(10.7)
195	Anderson, SC	(10.8)
195	Eugene-Springfield, OR	(10.8)
197	San Jose, CA	(11.1)
198	Tampa-St Petersburg, FL	(11.7)
199	Fort Worth-Arlington, TX M.D.	(11.8)
200	Lima, OH	(11.9)
201	Longview, TX	(12.1)
202	Columbia, SC	(12.2)
202	Vineland, NJ	(12.2)
204	Manhattan, KS	(12.4)
205	Punta Gorda, FL	(12.5)
205	Waco, TX	(12.5)
207	Oxnard-Thousand Oaks, CA	(12.6)
207	Roanoke, VA	(12.6)
209	Macon, GA	(12.7)
209	Modesto, CA	(12.7)
209	Rochester, MN	(12.7)
212	New York (greater), NY-NJ-PA	(13.1)
213	Pocatello, ID	(13.2)
213	Stockton, CA	(13.2)
215	Midland, TX	(13.3)
216	Dallas (greater), TX	(13.5)
216	Madera, CA	(13.5)
218	Utica-Rome, NY	(13.7)
219	Memphis, TN-MS-AR	(13.8)
220	Miami (greater), FL	(14.0)
220	Salem, OR	(14.0)
222	Dallas-Plano-Irving, TX M.D.	(14.1)
222	Tucson, AZ	(14.1)
224	Richmond, VA	(14.2)
225	San Francisco-S. Mateo, CA M.D.	(14.3)
226	Florence, SC	(14.4)
226	San Francisco (greater), CA	(14.4)
228	Oakland-Fremont, CA M.D.	(14.5)
228	Valdosta, GA	(14.5)
230	Green Bay, WI	(14.6)
231	Lynchburg, VA	(14.7)
232	Naples-Marco Island, FL	(14.8)
233	Minneapolis-St. Paul, MN-WI	(14.9)
234	Glens Falls, NY	(15.0)
235	Cape Girardeau, MO-IL	(15.2)
236	Cedar Rapids, IA	(15.3)
237	Mansfield, OH	(15.4)
238	Flagstaff, AZ	(15.5)
238	Jonesboro, AR	(15.5)
240	Lakeland, FL	(15.7)
241	Miami-Dade County, FL M.D.	(16.2)
241	Ocala, FL	(16.2)
243	Fort Lauderdale, FL M.D.	(16.3)
244	New York-W. Plains NY-NJ M.D.	(16.5)
244	Pine Bluff, AR	(16.5)
246	Reno-Sparks, NV	(16.7)
247	Dothan, AL	(16.8)
247	Nashville-Davidson, TN	(16.8)
249	Palm Coast, FL	(16.9)
250	Goldsboro, NC	(17.0)
251	New Orleans, LA	(17.1)
252	Ogden-Clearfield, UT	(17.6)
253	Jacksonville, FL	(17.9)
254	Reading, PA	(18.2)
255	Hagerstown-Martinsburg, MD-WV	(18.5)
256	Spartanburg, SC	(18.9)
257	Atlanta, GA	(19.4)
257	Rochester, NY	(19.4)
259	Santa Cruz-Watsonville, CA	(20.2)
260	Phoenix-Mesa-Scottsdale, AZ	(20.4)
260	Sandusky, OH	(20.4)
262	Birmingham-Hoover, AL	(20.5)
263	Auburn, AL	(20.8)
264	Winston-Salem, NC	(21.2)
265	Elmira, NY	(21.3)
265	Racine, WI	(21.3)
267	Albuquerque, NM	(21.9)
267	Charlotte-Gastonia, NC-SC	(21.9)
267	Savannah, GA	(21.9)
270	Sebastian-Vero Beach, FL	(22.0)
271	Killeen-Temple-Fort Hood, TX	(22.1)
272	Wichita Falls, TX	(22.2)
273	Abilene, TX	(22.5)
274	Charleston-North Charleston, SC	(23.2)
274	El Centro, CA	(23.2)
276	Rapid City, SD	(23.6)
276	Yuba City, CA	(23.6)
278	Port St. Lucie, FL	(23.8)
278	Wheeling, WV-OH	(23.8)
280	Durham-Chapel Hill, NC	(24.1)
281	Ann Arbor, MI	(24.3)
282	Raleigh-Cary, NC	(24.6)
283	Elkhart-Goshen, IN	(24.7)
284	Sioux City, IA-NE-SD	(24.8)
285	Jackson, TN	(25.3)
286	Casper, WY	(25.4)
287	Tallahassee, FL	(26.2)
288	Fayetteville, NC	(26.6)
289	Tyler, TX	(27.6)
290	Asheville, NC	(27.8)
291	Danville, VA	(27.9)
291	Lebanon, PA	(27.9)
293	Gadsden, AL	(28.3)
294	Binghamton, NY	(28.5)
295	Orlando, FL	(29.2)
296	Florence-Muscle Shoals, AL	(29.6)
297	Dalton, GA	(29.8)
298	Fond du Lac, WI	(30.7)
299	Athens-Clarke County, GA	(31.3)
300	San Angelo, TX	(31.4)
300	St. Cloud, MN	(31.4)
302	Dubuque, IA	(32.0)
303	Jacksonville, NC	(32.1)
304	Bend, OR	(34.9)
305	Altoona, PA	(36.3)
305	Decatur, AL	(36.3)
305	Longview, WA	(36.3)
308	Kokomo, IN	(36.6)
309	St. George, UT	(44.0)
310	Medford, OR	(50.4)
311	Erie, PA	(55.4)
NA	Albany, GA**	NA
NA	Alexandria, LA**	NA
NA	Anderson, IN**	NA
NA	Anniston-Oxford, AL**	NA
NA	Bay City, MI**	NA
NA	Boulder, CO**	NA
NA	Bowling Green, KY**	NA
NA	Brunswick, GA**	NA
NA	Burlington-South Burlington, VT**	NA
NA	Cincinnati-Middletown, OH-KY-IN**	NA
NA	Clarksville, TN-KY**	NA
NA	Cleveland-Elyria-Mentor, OH**	NA
NA	Coeur d'Alene, ID**	NA
NA	Crestview-Fort Walton Beach, FL**	NA
NA	Danville, IL**	NA
NA	Decatur, IL**	NA
NA	Des Moines-West Des Moines, IA**	NA
NA	Detroit (greater), MI**	NA
NA	Detroit-Livonia-Dearborn, MI M.D.**	NA
NA	Elizabethtown, KY**	NA
NA	Evansville, IN-KY**	NA
NA	Flint, MI**	NA
NA	Gainesville, GA**	NA
NA	Grand Rapids-Wyoming, MI**	NA
NA	Gulfport-Biloxi, MS**	NA
NA	Hattiesburg, MS**	NA
NA	Holland-Grand Haven, MI**	NA
NA	Jackson, MI**	NA
NA	Jefferson City, MO**	NA
NA	Kalamazoo-Portage, MI**	NA
NA	Kansas City, MO-KS**	NA
NA	Lake Charles, LA**	NA
NA	Lansing-East Lansing, MI**	NA
NA	Lawton, OK**	NA
NA	Lexington-Fayette, KY**	NA
NA	Little Rock, AR**	NA
NA	Louisville, KY-IN**	NA
NA	Manchester-Nashua, NH**	NA
NA	Monroe, MI**	NA
NA	Morgantown, WV**	NA
NA	Muskegon-Norton Shores, MI**	NA
NA	New Haven-Milford, CT**	NA
NA	Niles-Benton Harbor, MI**	NA
NA	North Port-Bradenton-Sarasota, FL**	NA
NA	Oklahoma City, OK**	NA
NA	Owensboro, KY**	NA
NA	Pueblo, CO**	NA
NA	Rocky Mount, NC**	NA
NA	Rome, GA**	NA
NA	Saginaw, MI**	NA
NA	Seattle-Bellevue-Everett, WA M.D.**	NA
NA	Seattle-Tacoma-Bellevue, WA**	NA
NA	South Bend-Mishawaka, IN-MI**	NA
NA	Springfield, MO**	NA
NA	Sumter, SC**	NA
NA	Tacoma, WA M.D.**	NA
NA	Warren-Farmington Hills, MI M.D.**	NA
NA	Wausau, WI**	NA

Source: CQ Press using reported data from the F.B.I. "Crime in the United States 2009"
*Robbery is the taking of anything of value by force or threat of force. Attempts are included.
**Not available.

20. Percent Change in Robbery Rate: 2005 to 2009
National Percent Change = 5.6% Decrease*

RANK	METROPOLITAN AREA	% CHANGE
192	Abilene, TX	(5.5)
86	Akron, OH	12.1
180	Albany-Schenectady-Troy, NY	(3.5)
104	Albany, GA	9.1
239	Albuquerque, NM	(13.0)
75	Alexandria, LA	16.0
226	Allentown, PA-NJ	(9.9)
298	Altoona, PA	(38.3)
161	Amarillo, TX	(0.8)
147	Ames, IA	2.7
44	Anchorage, AK	30.7
149	Anderson, IN	2.4
102	Anderson, SC	9.5
266	Ann Arbor, MI	(20.4)
NA	Anniston-Oxford, AL**	NA
39	Appleton, WI	33.7
273	Asheville, NC	(22.5)
121	Athens-Clarke County, GA	6.3
228	Atlanta, GA	(10.1)
99	Atlantic City, NJ	9.9
79	Auburn, AL	15.2
55	Augusta, GA-SC	24.1
154	Austin-Round Rock, TX	1.3
49	Bakersfield, CA	27.0
221	Baltimore-Towson, MD	(9.4)
15	Bangor, ME	69.4
7	Barnstable Town, MA	102.0
135	Baton Rouge, LA	4.5
59	Battle Creek, MI	21.8
NA	Bay City, MI**	NA
74	Beaumont-Port Arthur, TX	17.5
156	Bellingham, WA	(0.4)
269	Bend, OR	(21.6)
191	Bethesda-Frederick, MD M.D.	(5.1)
38	Billings, MT	33.8
179	Binghamton, NY	(3.1)
NA	Birmingham-Hoover, AL**	NA
107	Bismarck, ND	8.9
183	Blacksburg, VA	(4.0)
61	Bloomington, IN	21.3
NA	Boise City-Nampa, ID**	NA
199	Boston (greater), MA-NH	(6.3)
187	Boston-Quincy, MA M.D.	(4.6)
NA	Boulder, CO**	NA
NA	Bowling Green, KY**	NA
227	Bremerton-Silverdale, WA	(10.0)
77	Bridgeport-Stamford, CT	15.4
116	Brownsville-Harlingen, TX	7.5
58	Brunswick, GA	22.2
168	Buffalo-Niagara Falls, NY	(2.0)
NA	Burlington-South Burlington, VT**	NA
67	Burlington, NC	18.4
221	Cambridge-Newton, MA M.D.	(9.4)
126	Camden, NJ M.D.	5.8
278	Cape Coral-Fort Myers, FL	(23.7)
NA	Cape Girardeau, MO-IL**	NA
149	Carson City, NV	2.4
209	Casper, WY	(7.4)
210	Cedar Rapids, IA	(7.5)
265	Charleston-North Charleston, SC	(20.2)
53	Charleston, WV	24.8
299	Charlotte-Gastonia, NC-SC	(40.9)
80	Charlottesville, VA	14.2
91	Chattanooga, TN-GA	11.0
44	Cheyenne, WY	30.7
105	Chico, CA	9.0
NA	Cincinnati-Middletown, OH-KY-IN**	NA
NA	Clarksville, TN-KY**	NA
NA	Cleveland-Elyria-Mentor, OH**	NA
NA	Cleveland, TN**	NA
20	Coeur d'Alene, ID	59.1
117	College Station-Bryan, TX	7.3
101	Colorado Springs, CO	9.8
51	Columbia, MO	25.3
159	Columbia, SC	(0.6)
37	Columbus, GA-AL	34.6
34	Columbus, IN	37.5
244	Columbus, OH	(14.1)
195	Corpus Christi, TX	(5.9)
121	Corvallis, OR	6.3
NA	Crestview-Fort Walton Beach, FL**	NA
10	Cumberland, MD-WV	85.2
260	Dallas (greater), TX	(17.7)
267	Dallas-Plano-Irving, TX M.D.	(20.5)
NA	Dalton, GA**	NA
NA	Danville, IL**	NA
207	Danville, VA	(7.2)
134	Dayton, OH	5.0
118	Decatur, AL	7.0
NA	Decatur, IL**	NA
NA	Deltona-Daytona Beach, FL**	NA
288	Denver-Aurora, CO	(30.7)
NA	Des Moines-West Des Moines, IA**	NA
223	Detroit (greater), MI	(9.5)
NA	Detroit-Livonia-Dearborn, MI M.D.**	NA
164	Dothan, AL	(1.5)
14	Dover, DE	72.5
17	Dubuque, IA	67.9
NA	Duluth, MN-WI**	NA
170	Durham-Chapel Hill, NC	(2.2)
292	Eau Claire, WI	(32.8)
160	Edison, NJ M.D.	(0.7)
259	El Centro, CA	(17.6)
141	El Paso, TX	3.5
NA	Elizabethtown, KY**	NA
248	Elkhart-Goshen, IN	(14.6)
295	Elmira, NY	(34.9)
294	Erie, PA	(34.0)
34	Eugene-Springfield, OR	37.5
NA	Evansville, IN-KY**	NA
6	Fargo, ND-MN	105.5
190	Farmington, NM	(5.0)
170	Fayetteville, AR-MO	(2.2)
152	Fayetteville, NC	2.0
263	Flagstaff, AZ	(18.5)
NA	Flint, MI**	NA
NA	Florence-Muscle Shoals, AL**	NA
296	Florence, SC	(35.0)
297	Fond du Lac, WI	(36.9)
70	Fort Collins-Loveland, CO	18.1
147	Fort Lauderdale, FL M.D.	2.7
95	Fort Smith, AR-OK	10.5
65	Fort Wayne, IN	19.3
216	Fort Worth-Arlington, TX M.D.	(8.8)
244	Fresno, CA	(14.1)
293	Gadsden, AL	(33.8)
62	Gainesville, FL	21.0
207	Gainesville, GA	(7.2)
NA	Glens Falls, NY**	NA
212	Goldsboro, NC	(7.8)
1	Grand Forks, ND-MN	195.6
22	Grand Junction, CO	50.0
NA	Grand Rapids-Wyoming, MI**	NA
19	Great Falls, MT	61.0
236	Greeley, CO	(12.3)
50	Green Bay, WI	26.5
90	Greensboro-High Point, NC	11.1
NA	Gulfport-Biloxi, MS**	NA
249	Hagerstown-Martinsburg, MD-WV	(15.0)
218	Harrisburg-Carlisle, PA	(8.9)
240	Harrisonburg, VA	(13.4)
243	Hartford, CT	(13.8)
NA	Hattiesburg, MS**	NA
98	Hickory, NC	10.2
32	Hinesville, GA	38.0
NA	Holland-Grand Haven, MI**	NA
141	Honolulu, HI	3.5
48	Hot Springs, AR	27.5
13	Houma, LA	73.2
158	Houston, TX	(0.5)
277	Huntsville, AL	(23.4)
52	Idaho Falls, ID	25.2
111	Indianapolis, IN	8.2
28	Iowa City, IA	39.9
NA	Ithaca, NY**	NA
151	Jacksonville, FL	2.3
NA	Jacksonville, NC**	NA
NA	Jackson, MI**	NA
30	Jackson, MS	38.8
168	Jackson, TN	(2.0)
201	Janesville, WI	(6.5)
77	Jefferson City, MO	15.4
203	Johnson City, TN	(6.7)
285	Jonesboro, AR	(27.9)
NA	Kalamazoo-Portage, MI**	NA
215	Kansas City, MO-KS	(8.1)
99	Kennewick-Pasco-Richland, WA	9.9
258	Killeen-Temple-Fort Hood, TX	(17.0)
234	Kingsport, TN-VA	(11.1)
219	Kingston, NY	(9.3)
68	Knoxville, TN	18.3
301	Kokomo, IN	(44.9)
47	La Crosse, WI-MN	28.1
229	Lafayette, IN	(10.4)
21	Lafayette, LA	57.9
94	Lake Charles, LA	10.6
NA	Lake Havasu City-Kingman, AZ**	NA
141	Lakeland, FL	3.5
130	Lancaster, PA	5.4
NA	Lansing-East Lansing, MI**	NA

Note: All listings are for Metropolitan Statistical Areas (M.S.A.s) except for those ending with "M.D." Listings with "M.D." are Metropolitan Divisions which are smaller parts of eleven large M.S.A.s. See explanatory note at beginning of metropolitan area section.

RANK	METROPOLITAN AREA	% CHANGE
84	Laredo, TX	12.8
242	Las Cruces, NM	(13.6)
66	Las Vegas-Paradise, NV	18.9
9	Lawrence, KS	87.4
NA	Lawton, OK**	NA
304	Lebanon, PA	(54.3)
42	Lewiston-Auburn, ME	32.2
114	Lewiston, ID-WA	7.6
NA	Lexington-Fayette, KY**	NA
85	Lima, OH	12.5
261	Lincoln, NE	(18.3)
NA	Little Rock, AR**	NA
306	Logan, UT-ID	(74.2)
25	Longview, TX	44.8
290	Longview, WA	(31.0)
204	Los Angeles County, CA M.D.	(6.8)
194	Los Angeles (greater), CA	(5.8)
NA	Louisville, KY-IN**	NA
181	Lubbock, TX	(3.6)
166	Lynchburg, VA	(1.8)
126	Macon, GA	5.8
41	Madera, CA	32.9
125	Madison, WI	5.9
73	Manchester-Nashua, NH	17.7
NA	Manhattan, KS**	NA
NA	Mankato-North Mankato, MN**	NA
286	Mansfield, OH	(28.4)
64	McAllen-Edinburg-Mission, TX	20.0
305	Medford, OR	(57.1)
224	Memphis, TN-MS-AR	(9.6)
123	Merced, CA	6.0
162	Miami (greater), FL	(1.2)
206	Miami-Dade County, FL M.D.	(7.0)
177	Michigan City-La Porte, IN	(2.9)
24	Midland, TX	48.0
141	Milwaukee, WI	3.5
NA	Minneapolis-St. Paul, MN-WI**	NA
270	Missoula, MT	(21.8)
16	Mobile, AL	68.6
141	Modesto, CA	3.5
NA	Monroe, MI**	NA
302	Montgomery, AL	(45.2)
188	Morgantown, WV	(4.7)
56	Morristown, TN	23.2
178	Mount Vernon-Anacortes, WA	(3.0)
8	Muncie, IN	95.2
NA	Muskegon-Norton Shores, MI**	NA
5	Napa, CA	110.3
241	Naples-Marco Island, FL	(13.5)
274	Nashville-Davidson, TN	(22.7)
198	Nassau-Suffolk, NY M.D.	(6.2)
NA	New Haven-Milford, CT**	NA
NA	New Orleans, LA**	NA
271	New York (greater), NY-NJ-PA	(21.9)
281	New York-W. Plains NY-NJ M.D.	(26.1)
213	Newark-Union, NJ-PA M.D.	(7.9)
NA	Niles-Benton Harbor, MI**	NA
NA	North Port-Bradenton-Sarasota, FL**	NA
156	Norwich-New London, CT	(0.4)
103	Oakland-Fremont, CA M.D.	9.3
195	Ocala, FL	(5.9)
173	Ocean City, NJ	(2.3)
2	Odessa, TX	169.4

RANK	METROPOLITAN AREA	% CHANGE
219	Ogden-Clearfield, UT	(9.3)
NA	Oklahoma City, OK**	NA
163	Olympia, WA	(1.4)
63	Omaha-Council Bluffs, NE-IA	20.4
262	Orlando, FL	(18.4)
4	Oshkosh-Neenah, WI	120.6
NA	Owensboro, KY**	NA
136	Oxnard-Thousand Oaks, CA	4.3
70	Palm Bay-Melbourne, FL	18.1
NA	Palm Coast, FL**	NA
152	Panama City-Lynn Haven, FL	2.0
137	Pascagoula, MS	4.2
NA	Peabody, MA M.D.**	NA
36	Pensacola, FL	35.0
204	Philadelphia (greater) PA-NJ-MD-DE	(6.8)
235	Philadelphia, PA M.D.	(11.2)
247	Phoenix-Mesa-Scottsdale, AZ	(14.3)
133	Pine Bluff, AR	5.1
225	Pittsburgh, PA	(9.7)
287	Pittsfield, MA	(30.5)
23	Pocatello, ID	49.1
231	Port St. Lucie, FL	(10.5)
213	Portland-Vancouver, OR-WA	(7.9)
57	Portland, ME	22.7
131	Poughkeepsie, NY	5.3
132	Prescott, AZ	5.2
NA	Providence-New Bedford, RI-MA**	NA
54	Provo-Orem, UT	24.6
174	Pueblo, CO	(2.4)
138	Punta Gorda, FL	4.0
176	Racine, WI	(2.7)
233	Raleigh-Cary, NC	(10.9)
186	Rapid City, SD	(4.5)
210	Reading, PA	(7.5)
40	Redding, CA	33.6
193	Reno-Sparks, NV	(5.6)
279	Richmond, VA	(23.9)
202	Riverside-San Bernardino, CA	(6.6)
257	Roanoke, VA	(16.9)
275	Rochester, MN	(22.8)
253	Rochester, NY	(15.5)
120	Rockingham County, NH M.D.	6.7
43	Rocky Mount, NC	32.1
91	Rome, GA	11.0
184	Sacramento, CA	(4.1)
NA	Saginaw, MI**	NA
255	Salem, OR	(15.9)
68	Salinas, CA	18.3
110	Salisbury, MD	8.6
81	Salt Lake City, UT	13.8
86	San Angelo, TX	12.1
76	San Antonio, TX	15.6
155	San Diego, CA	0.4
113	San Francisco (greater), CA	7.8
128	San Francisco-S. Mateo, CA M.D.	5.7
89	San Jose, CA	11.4
82	San Luis Obispo, CA	13.4
252	Sandusky, OH	(15.4)
123	Santa Ana-Anaheim, CA M.D.	6.0
138	Santa Barbara-Santa Maria, CA	4.0
185	Santa Cruz-Watsonville, CA	(4.2)
32	Santa Fe, NM	38.0
88	Santa Rosa-Petaluma, CA	11.8

RANK	METROPOLITAN AREA	% CHANGE
253	Savannah, GA	(15.5)
264	Scranton--Wilkes-Barre, PA	(20.1)
95	Seattle-Bellevue-Everett, WA M.D.	10.5
109	Seattle-Tacoma-Bellevue, WA	8.8
229	Sebastian-Vero Beach, FL	(10.4)
3	Sheboygan, WI	165.7
46	Sherman-Denison, TX	29.1
282	Shreveport-Bossier City, LA	(26.6)
276	Sioux City, IA-NE-SD	(22.9)
300	Sioux Falls, SD	(44.5)
NA	South Bend-Mishawaka, IN-MI**	NA
112	Spartanburg, SC	7.9
29	Spokane, WA	39.4
272	Springfield, MA	(22.3)
NA	Springfield, MO**	NA
280	Springfield, OH	(24.6)
27	State College, PA	41.3
182	Stockton, CA	(3.7)
93	St. Cloud, MN	10.7
95	St. George, UT	10.5
18	St. Joseph, MO-KS	65.4
200	St. Louis, MO-IL	(6.4)
NA	Sumter, SC**	NA
268	Syracuse, NY	(20.9)
140	Tacoma, WA M.D.	3.8
114	Tallahassee, FL	7.6
141	Tampa-St Petersburg, FL	3.5
12	Texarkana, TX-Texarkana, AR	80.7
189	Toledo, OH	(4.9)
83	Topeka, KS	13.0
288	Trenton-Ewing, NJ	(30.7)
283	Tucson, AZ	(27.0)
175	Tulsa, OK	(2.5)
NA	Tuscaloosa, AL**	NA
303	Tyler, TX	(46.8)
118	Utica-Rome, NY	7.0
237	Valdosta, GA	(12.4)
NA	Vallejo-Fairfield, CA**	NA
30	Victoria, TX	38.8
284	Vineland, NJ	(27.4)
166	Visalia-Porterville, CA	(1.8)
238	Waco, TX	(12.8)
197	Warner Robins, GA	(6.0)
NA	Warren-Farmington Hills, MI M.D.**	NA
250	Washington (greater) DC-VA-MD-WV	(15.1)
256	Washington, DC-VA-MD-WV M.D.	(16.5)
11	Waterloo-Cedar Falls, IA	81.8
NA	Wausau, WI**	NA
129	Wenatchee, WA	5.6
107	West Palm Beach, FL M.D.	8.9
59	Wheeling, WV-OH	21.8
291	Wichita Falls, TX	(31.5)
NA	Wichita, KS**	NA
170	Williamsport, PA	(2.2)
70	Wilmington, DE-MD-NJ M.D.	18.1
231	Wilmington, NC	(10.5)
26	Winchester, VA-WV	43.5
216	Winston-Salem, NC	(8.8)
165	Worcester, MA	(1.6)
105	York-Hanover, PA	9.0
NA	Youngstown, OH-PA**	NA
250	Yuba City, CA	(15.1)
246	Yuma, AZ	(14.2)

Source: CQ Press using reported data from the F.B.I. "Crime in the United States 2009"
*Robbery is the taking of anything of value by force or threat of force. Attempts are included.
**Not available.

20. Percent Change in Robbery Rate: 2005 to 2009 (continued)
National Percent Change = 5.6% Decrease*

RANK	METROPOLITAN AREA	% CHANGE
1	Grand Forks, ND-MN	195.6
2	Odessa, TX	169.4
3	Sheboygan, WI	165.7
4	Oshkosh-Neenah, WI	120.6
5	Napa, CA	110.3
6	Fargo, ND-MN	105.5
7	Barnstable Town, MA	102.0
8	Muncie, IN	95.2
9	Lawrence, KS	87.4
10	Cumberland, MD-WV	85.2
11	Waterloo-Cedar Falls, IA	81.8
12	Texarkana, TX-Texarkana, AR	80.7
13	Houma, LA	73.2
14	Dover, DE	72.5
15	Bangor, ME	69.4
16	Mobile, AL	68.6
17	Dubuque, IA	67.9
18	St. Joseph, MO-KS	65.4
19	Great Falls, MT	61.0
20	Coeur d'Alene, ID	59.1
21	Lafayette, LA	57.9
22	Grand Junction, CO	50.0
23	Pocatello, ID	49.1
24	Midland, TX	48.0
25	Longview, TX	44.8
26	Winchester, VA-WV	43.5
27	State College, PA	41.3
28	Iowa City, IA	39.9
29	Spokane, WA	39.4
30	Jackson, MS	38.8
30	Victoria, TX	38.8
32	Hinesville, GA	38.0
32	Santa Fe, NM	38.0
34	Columbus, IN	37.5
34	Eugene-Springfield, OR	37.5
36	Pensacola, FL	35.0
37	Columbus, GA-AL	34.6
38	Billings, MT	33.8
39	Appleton, WI	33.7
40	Redding, CA	33.6
41	Madera, CA	32.9
42	Lewiston-Auburn, ME	32.2
43	Rocky Mount, NC	32.1
44	Anchorage, AK	30.7
44	Cheyenne, WY	30.7
46	Sherman-Denison, TX	29.1
47	La Crosse, WI-MN	28.1
48	Hot Springs, AR	27.5
49	Bakersfield, CA	27.0
50	Green Bay, WI	26.5
51	Columbia, MO	25.3
52	Idaho Falls, ID	25.2
53	Charleston, WV	24.8
54	Provo-Orem, UT	24.6
55	Augusta, GA-SC	24.1
56	Morristown, TN	23.2
57	Portland, ME	22.7
58	Brunswick, GA	22.2
59	Battle Creek, MI	21.8
59	Wheeling, WV-OH	21.8
61	Bloomington, IN	21.3
62	Gainesville, FL	21.0
63	Omaha-Council Bluffs, NE-IA	20.4
64	McAllen-Edinburg-Mission, TX	20.0
65	Fort Wayne, IN	19.3
66	Las Vegas-Paradise, NV	18.9
67	Burlington, NC	18.4
68	Knoxville, TN	18.3
68	Salinas, CA	18.3
70	Fort Collins-Loveland, CO	18.1
70	Palm Bay-Melbourne, FL	18.1
70	Wilmington, DE-MD-NJ M.D.	18.1
73	Manchester-Nashua, NH	17.7
74	Beaumont-Port Arthur, TX	17.5
75	Alexandria, LA	16.0
76	San Antonio, TX	15.6
77	Bridgeport-Stamford, CT	15.4
77	Jefferson City, MO	15.4
79	Auburn, AL	15.2
80	Charlottesville, VA	14.2
81	Salt Lake City, UT	13.8
82	San Luis Obispo, CA	13.4
83	Topeka, KS	13.0
84	Laredo, TX	12.8
85	Lima, OH	12.5
86	Akron, OH	12.1
86	San Angelo, TX	12.1
88	Santa Rosa-Petaluma, CA	11.8
89	San Jose, CA	11.4
90	Greensboro-High Point, NC	11.1
91	Chattanooga, TN-GA	11.0
91	Rome, GA	11.0
93	St. Cloud, MN	10.7
94	Lake Charles, LA	10.6
95	Fort Smith, AR-OK	10.5
95	Seattle-Bellevue-Everett, WA M.D.	10.5
95	St. George, UT	10.5
98	Hickory, NC	10.2
99	Atlantic City, NJ	9.9
99	Kennewick-Pasco-Richland, WA	9.9
101	Colorado Springs, CO	9.8
102	Anderson, SC	9.5
103	Oakland-Fremont, CA M.D.	9.3
104	Albany, GA	9.1
105	Chico, CA	9.0
105	York-Hanover, PA	9.0
107	Bismarck, ND	8.9
107	West Palm Beach, FL M.D.	8.9
109	Seattle-Tacoma-Bellevue, WA	8.8
110	Salisbury, MD	8.6
111	Indianapolis, IN	8.2
112	Spartanburg, SC	7.9
113	San Francisco (greater), CA	7.8
114	Lewiston, ID-WA	7.6
114	Tallahassee, FL	7.6
116	Brownsville-Harlingen, TX	7.5
117	College Station-Bryan, TX	7.3
118	Decatur, AL	7.0
118	Utica-Rome, NY	7.0
120	Rockingham County, NH M.D.	6.7
121	Athens-Clarke County, GA	6.3
121	Corvallis, OR	6.3
123	Merced, CA	6.0
123	Santa Ana-Anaheim, CA M.D.	6.0
125	Madison, WI	5.9
126	Camden, NJ M.D.	5.8
126	Macon, GA	5.8
128	San Francisco-S. Mateo, CA M.D.	5.7
129	Wenatchee, WA	5.6
130	Lancaster, PA	5.4
131	Poughkeepsie, NY	5.3
132	Prescott, AZ	5.2
133	Pine Bluff, AR	5.1
134	Dayton, OH	5.0
135	Baton Rouge, LA	4.5
136	Oxnard-Thousand Oaks, CA	4.3
137	Pascagoula, MS	4.2
138	Punta Gorda, FL	4.0
138	Santa Barbara-Santa Maria, CA	4.0
140	Tacoma, WA M.D.	3.8
141	El Paso, TX	3.5
141	Honolulu, HI	3.5
141	Lakeland, FL	3.5
141	Milwaukee, WI	3.5
141	Modesto, CA	3.5
141	Tampa-St Petersburg, FL	3.5
147	Ames, IA	2.7
147	Fort Lauderdale, FL M.D.	2.7
149	Anderson, IN	2.4
149	Carson City, NV	2.4
151	Jacksonville, FL	2.3
152	Fayetteville, NC	2.0
152	Panama City-Lynn Haven, FL	2.0
154	Austin-Round Rock, TX	1.3
155	San Diego, CA	0.4
156	Bellingham, WA	(0.4)
156	Norwich-New London, CT	(0.4)
158	Houston, TX	(0.5)
159	Columbia, SC	(0.6)
160	Edison, NJ M.D.	(0.7)
161	Amarillo, TX	(0.8)
162	Miami (greater), FL	(1.2)
163	Olympia, WA	(1.4)
164	Dothan, AL	(1.5)
165	Worcester, MA	(1.6)
166	Lynchburg, VA	(1.8)
166	Visalia-Porterville, CA	(1.8)
168	Buffalo-Niagara Falls, NY	(2.0)
168	Jackson, TN	(2.0)
170	Durham-Chapel Hill, NC	(2.2)
170	Fayetteville, AR-MO	(2.2)
170	Williamsport, PA	(2.2)
173	Ocean City, NJ	(2.3)
174	Pueblo, CO	(2.4)
175	Tulsa, OK	(2.5)
176	Racine, WI	(2.7)
177	Michigan City-La Porte, IN	(2.9)
178	Mount Vernon-Anacortes, WA	(3.0)
179	Binghamton, NY	(3.1)
180	Albany-Schenectady-Troy, NY	(3.5)

Note: All listings are for Metropolitan Statistical Areas (M.S.A.s) except for those ending with "M.D." Listings with "M.D." are Metropolitan Divisions which are smaller parts of eleven large M.S.A.s. See explanatory note at beginning of metropolitan area section.

Rank Order - Metro Area (continued)

RANK	METROPOLITAN AREA	% CHANGE
181	Lubbock, TX	(3.6)
182	Stockton, CA	(3.7)
183	Blacksburg, VA	(4.0)
184	Sacramento, CA	(4.1)
185	Santa Cruz-Watsonville, CA	(4.2)
186	Rapid City, SD	(4.5)
187	Boston-Quincy, MA M.D.	(4.6)
188	Morgantown, WV	(4.7)
189	Toledo, OH	(4.9)
190	Farmington, NM	(5.0)
191	Bethesda-Frederick, MD M.D.	(5.1)
192	Abilene, TX	(5.5)
193	Reno-Sparks, NV	(5.6)
194	Los Angeles (greater), CA	(5.8)
195	Corpus Christi, TX	(5.9)
195	Ocala, FL	(5.9)
197	Warner Robins, GA	(6.0)
198	Nassau-Suffolk, NY M.D.	(6.2)
199	Boston (greater), MA-NH	(6.3)
200	St. Louis, MO-IL	(6.4)
201	Janesville, WI	(6.5)
202	Riverside-San Bernardino, CA	(6.6)
203	Johnson City, TN	(6.7)
204	Los Angeles County, CA M.D.	(6.8)
204	Philadelphia (greater) PA-NJ-MD-DE	(6.8)
206	Miami-Dade County, FL M.D.	(7.0)
207	Danville, VA	(7.2)
207	Gainesville, GA	(7.2)
209	Casper, WY	(7.4)
210	Cedar Rapids, IA	(7.5)
210	Reading, PA	(7.5)
212	Goldsboro, NC	(7.8)
213	Newark-Union, NJ-PA M.D.	(7.9)
213	Portland-Vancouver, OR-WA	(7.9)
215	Kansas City, MO-KS	(8.1)
216	Fort Worth-Arlington, TX M.D.	(8.8)
216	Winston-Salem, NC	(8.8)
218	Harrisburg-Carlisle, PA	(8.9)
219	Kingston, NY	(9.3)
219	Ogden-Clearfield, UT	(9.3)
221	Baltimore-Towson, MD	(9.4)
221	Cambridge-Newton, MA M.D.	(9.4)
223	Detroit (greater), MI	(9.5)
224	Memphis, TN-MS-AR	(9.6)
225	Pittsburgh, PA	(9.7)
226	Allentown, PA-NJ	(9.9)
227	Bremerton-Silverdale, WA	(10.0)
228	Atlanta, GA	(10.1)
229	Lafayette, IN	(10.4)
229	Sebastian-Vero Beach, FL	(10.4)
231	Port St. Lucie, FL	(10.5)
231	Wilmington, NC	(10.5)
233	Raleigh-Cary, NC	(10.9)
234	Kingsport, TN-VA	(11.1)
235	Philadelphia, PA M.D.	(11.2)
236	Greeley, CO	(12.3)
237	Valdosta, GA	(12.4)
238	Waco, TX	(12.8)
239	Albuquerque, NM	(13.0)
240	Harrisonburg, VA	(13.4)
241	Naples-Marco Island, FL	(13.5)
242	Las Cruces, NM	(13.6)
243	Hartford, CT	(13.8)

RANK	METROPOLITAN AREA	% CHANGE
244	Columbus, OH	(14.1)
244	Fresno, CA	(14.1)
246	Yuma, AZ	(14.2)
247	Phoenix-Mesa-Scottsdale, AZ	(14.3)
248	Elkhart-Goshen, IN	(14.6)
249	Hagerstown-Martinsburg, MD-WV	(15.0)
250	Washington (greater) DC-VA-MD-WV	(15.1)
250	Yuba City, CA	(15.1)
252	Sandusky, OH	(15.4)
253	Rochester, NY	(15.5)
253	Savannah, GA	(15.5)
255	Salem, OR	(15.9)
256	Washington, DC-VA-MD-WV M.D.	(16.5)
257	Roanoke, VA	(16.9)
258	Killeen-Temple-Fort Hood, TX	(17.0)
259	El Centro, CA	(17.6)
260	Dallas (greater), TX	(17.7)
261	Lincoln, NE	(18.3)
262	Orlando, FL	(18.4)
263	Flagstaff, AZ	(18.5)
264	Scranton--Wilkes-Barre, PA	(20.1)
265	Charleston-North Charleston, SC	(20.2)
266	Ann Arbor, MI	(20.4)
267	Dallas-Plano-Irving, TX M.D.	(20.5)
268	Syracuse, NY	(20.9)
269	Bend, OR	(21.6)
270	Missoula, MT	(21.8)
271	New York (greater), NY-NJ-PA	(21.9)
272	Springfield, MA	(22.3)
273	Asheville, NC	(22.5)
274	Nashville-Davidson, TN	(22.7)
275	Rochester, MN	(22.8)
276	Sioux City, IA-NE-SD	(22.9)
277	Huntsville, AL	(23.4)
278	Cape Coral-Fort Myers, FL	(23.7)
279	Richmond, VA	(23.9)
280	Springfield, OH	(24.6)
281	New York-W. Plains NY-NJ M.D.	(26.1)
282	Shreveport-Bossier City, LA	(26.6)
283	Tucson, AZ	(27.0)
284	Vineland, NJ	(27.4)
285	Jonesboro, AR	(27.9)
286	Mansfield, OH	(28.4)
287	Pittsfield, MA	(30.5)
288	Denver-Aurora, CO	(30.7)
288	Trenton-Ewing, NJ	(30.7)
290	Longview, WA	(31.0)
291	Wichita Falls, TX	(31.5)
292	Eau Claire, WI	(32.8)
293	Gadsden, AL	(33.8)
294	Erie, PA	(34.0)
295	Elmira, NY	(34.9)
296	Florence, SC	(35.0)
297	Fond du Lac, WI	(36.9)
298	Altoona, PA	(38.3)
299	Charlotte-Gastonia, NC-SC	(40.9)
300	Sioux Falls, SD	(44.5)
301	Kokomo, IN	(44.9)
302	Montgomery, AL	(45.2)
303	Tyler, TX	(46.8)
304	Lebanon, PA	(54.3)
305	Medford, OR	(57.1)
306	Logan, UT-ID	(74.2)

RANK	METROPOLITAN AREA	% CHANGE
NA	Anniston-Oxford, AL**	NA
NA	Bay City, MI**	NA
NA	Birmingham-Hoover, AL**	NA
NA	Boise City-Nampa, ID**	NA
NA	Boulder, CO**	NA
NA	Bowling Green, KY**	NA
NA	Burlington-South Burlington, VT**	NA
NA	Cape Girardeau, MO-IL**	NA
NA	Cincinnati-Middletown, OH-KY-IN**	NA
NA	Clarksville, TN-KY**	NA
NA	Cleveland-Elyria-Mentor, OH**	NA
NA	Cleveland, TN**	NA
NA	Crestview-Fort Walton Beach, FL**	NA
NA	Dalton, GA**	NA
NA	Danville, IL**	NA
NA	Decatur, IL**	NA
NA	Deltona-Daytona Beach, FL**	NA
NA	Des Moines-West Des Moines, IA**	NA
NA	Detroit-Livonia-Dearborn, MI M.D.**	NA
NA	Duluth, MN-WI**	NA
NA	Elizabethtown, KY**	NA
NA	Evansville, IN-KY**	NA
NA	Flint, MI**	NA
NA	Florence-Muscle Shoals, AL**	NA
NA	Glens Falls, NY**	NA
NA	Grand Rapids-Wyoming, MI**	NA
NA	Gulfport-Biloxi, MS**	NA
NA	Hattiesburg, MS**	NA
NA	Holland-Grand Haven, MI**	NA
NA	Ithaca, NY**	NA
NA	Jacksonville, NC**	NA
NA	Jackson, MI**	NA
NA	Kalamazoo-Portage, MI**	NA
NA	Lake Havasu City-Kingman, AZ**	NA
NA	Lansing-East Lansing, MI**	NA
NA	Lawton, OK**	NA
NA	Lexington-Fayette, KY**	NA
NA	Little Rock, AR**	NA
NA	Louisville, KY-IN**	NA
NA	Manhattan, KS**	NA
NA	Mankato-North Mankato, MN**	NA
NA	Minneapolis-St. Paul, MN-WI**	NA
NA	Monroe, MI**	NA
NA	Muskegon-Norton Shores, MI**	NA
NA	New Haven-Milford, CT**	NA
NA	New Orleans, LA**	NA
NA	Niles-Benton Harbor, MI**	NA
NA	North Port-Bradenton-Sarasota, FL**	NA
NA	Oklahoma City, OK**	NA
NA	Owensboro, KY**	NA
NA	Palm Coast, FL**	NA
NA	Peabody, MA M.D.**	NA
NA	Providence-New Bedford, RI-MA**	NA
NA	Saginaw, MI**	NA
NA	South Bend-Mishawaka, IN-MI**	NA
NA	Springfield, MO**	NA
NA	Sumter, SC**	NA
NA	Tuscaloosa, AL**	NA
NA	Vallejo-Fairfield, CA**	NA
NA	Warren-Farmington Hills, MI M.D.**	NA
NA	Wausau, WI**	NA
NA	Wichita, KS**	NA
NA	Youngstown, OH-PA**	NA

Source: CQ Press using reported data from the F.B.I. "Crime in the United States 2009"
*Robbery is the taking of anything of value by force or threat of force. Attempts are included.
**Not available.

21. Aggravated Assaults in 2009
National Total = 806,843 Aggravated Assaults*

RANK	METROPOLITAN AREA	ASSAULTS
231	Abilene, TX	454
128	Akron, OH	1,248
108	Albany-Schenectady-Troy, NY	1,584
194	Albany, GA	631
52	Albuquerque, NM	3,869
170	Alexandria, LA	782
147	Allentown, PA-NJ	1,005
297	Altoona, PA	249
132	Amarillo, TX	1,182
321	Ames, IA	176
103	Anchorage, AK	1,760
353	Anderson, IN	87
153	Anderson, SC	952
173	Ann Arbor, MI	735
204	Anniston-Oxford, AL	588
320	Appleton, WI	186
205	Asheville, NC	583
222	Athens-Clarke County, GA	493
11	Atlanta, GA	12,988
172	Atlantic City, NJ	756
NA	Auburn, AL**	NA
152	Augusta, GA-SC	966
51	Austin-Round Rock, TX	3,908
61	Bakersfield, CA	3,281
14	Baltimore-Towson, MD	12,114
360	Bangor, ME	43
165	Barnstable Town, MA	825
57	Baton Rouge, LA	3,634
187	Battle Creek, MI	657
312	Bay City, MI	203
131	Beaumont-Port Arthur, TX	1,198
294	Bellingham, WA	269
292	Bend, OR	274
112	Bethesda-Frederick, MD M.D.	1,529
299	Billings, MT	242
267	Binghamton, NY	325
60	Birmingham-Hoover, AL	3,321
323	Bismarck, ND	169
318	Blacksburg, VA	193
255	Bloomington, IN	358
141	Boise City-Nampa, ID	1,088
13	Boston (greater), MA-NH	12,137
32	Boston-Quincy, MA M.D.	6,923
217	Boulder, CO	528
335	Bowling Green, KY	127
168	Bremerton-Silverdale, WA	789
118	Bridgeport-Stamford, CT	1,439
154	Brownsville-Harlingen, TX	937
201	Brunswick, GA	596
62	Buffalo-Niagara Falls, NY	3,269
301	Burlington-South Burlington, VT	234
228	Burlington, NC	462
66	Cambridge-Newton, MA M.D.	3,029
77	Camden, NJ M.D.	2,552
105	Cape Coral-Fort Myers, FL	1,675
290	Cape Girardeau, MO-IL	277
327	Carson City, NV	153
339	Casper, WY	121
261	Cedar Rapids, IA	343
72	Charleston-North Charleston, SC	2,754
148	Charleston, WV	993
39	Charlotte-Gastonia, NC-SC	5,544
302	Charlottesville, VA	233
82	Chattanooga, TN-GA	2,301
349	Cheyenne, WY	106
191	Chico, CA	648
65	Cincinnati-Middletown, OH-KY-IN	3,055
162	Clarksville, TN-KY	860
59	Cleveland-Elyria-Mentor, OH	3,340
189	Cleveland, TN	654
258	Coeur d'Alene, ID	350
196	College Station-Bryan, TX	627
99	Colorado Springs, CO	1,834
231	Columbia, MO	454
46	Columbia, SC	4,266
175	Columbus, GA-AL	732
359	Columbus, IN	48
102	Columbus, OH	1,763
91	Corpus Christi, TX	1,964
358	Corvallis, OR	62
267	Crestview-Fort Walton Beach, FL	325
249	Cumberland, MD-WV	377
9	Dallas (greater), TX	13,880
26	Dallas-Plano-Irving, TX M.D.	8,215
269	Dalton, GA	324
284	Danville, IL	299
341	Danville, VA	120
130	Dayton, OH	1,205
NA	Decatur, AL**	NA
229	Decatur, IL	459
94	Deltona-Daytona Beach, FL	1,903
40	Denver-Aurora, CO	5,350
146	Des Moines-West Des Moines, IA	1,017
7	Detroit (greater), MI	18,511
9	Detroit-Livonia-Dearborn, MI M.D.	13,880
NA	Dothan, AL**	NA
174	Dover, DE	733
271	Dubuque, IA	323
246	Duluth, MN-WI	385
132	Durham-Chapel Hill, NC	1,182
332	Eau Claire, WI	132
84	Edison, NJ M.D.	2,197
NA	El Centro, CA**	NA
78	El Paso, TX	2,545
291	Elizabethtown, KY	276
361	Elkhart-Goshen, IN	42
343	Elmira, NY	115
240	Erie, PA	402
186	Eugene-Springfield, OR	668
219	Evansville, IN-KY	523
287	Fargo, ND-MN	291
176	Farmington, NM	730
142	Fayetteville, AR-MO	1,045
135	Fayetteville, NC	1,166
285	Flagstaff, AZ	296
85	Flint, MI	2,163
283	Florence-Muscle Shoals, AL	301
136	Florence, SC	1,165
336	Fond du Lac, WI	124
210	Fort Collins-Loveland, CO	551
37	Fort Lauderdale, FL M.D.	5,673
151	Fort Smith, AR-OK	980
244	Fort Wayne, IN	388
38	Fort Worth-Arlington, TX M.D.	5,665
67	Fresno, CA	2,994
316	Gadsden, AL	194
114	Gainesville, FL	1,519
304	Gainesville, GA	230
345	Glens Falls, NY	111
256	Goldsboro, NC	357
330	Grand Forks, ND-MN	139
286	Grand Junction, CO	294
100	Grand Rapids-Wyoming, MI	1,794
325	Great Falls, MT	166
212	Greeley, CO	539
250	Green Bay, WI	373
96	Greensboro-High Point, NC	1,858
303	Gulfport-Biloxi, MS	231
236	Hagerstown-Martinsburg, MD-WV	440
166	Harrisburg-Carlisle, PA	821
341	Harrisonburg, VA	120
109	Hartford, CT	1,581
346	Hattiesburg, MS	109
184	Hickory, NC	682
316	Hinesville, GA	194
288	Holland-Grand Haven, MI	282
121	Honolulu, HI	1,411
237	Hot Springs, AR	432
206	Houma, LA	576
5	Houston, TX	23,052
154	Huntsville, AL	937
281	Idaho Falls, ID	303
34	Indianapolis, IN	6,094
272	Iowa City, IA	321
NA	Ithaca, NY**	NA
35	Jacksonville, FL	6,038
257	Jacksonville, NC	355
230	Jackson, MI	458
171	Jackson, MS	766
207	Jackson, TN	569
298	Janesville, WI	244
252	Jefferson City, MO	362
212	Johnson City, TN	539
265	Jonesboro, AR	331
157	Kalamazoo-Portage, MI	908
30	Kansas City, MO-KS	7,177
233	Kennewick-Pasco-Richland, WA	450
164	Killeen-Temple-Fort Hood, TX	828
156	Kingsport, TN-VA	924
273	Kingston, NY	319
83	Knoxville, TN	2,273
332	Kokomo, IN	132
319	La Crosse, WI-MN	188
262	Lafayette, IN	339
113	Lafayette, LA	1,526
145	Lake Charles, LA	1,030
260	Lake Havasu City-Kingman, AZ	345
93	Lakeland, FL	1,919
242	Lancaster, PA	391
127	Lansing-East Lansing, MI	1,256

Note: All listings are for Metropolitan Statistical Areas (M.S.A.s) except for those ending with "M.D." Listings with "M.D." are Metropolitan Divisions which are smaller parts of eleven large M.S.A.s. See explanatory note at beginning of metropolitan area section.

RANK	METROPOLITAN AREA	ASSAULTS
149	Laredo, TX	991
188	Las Cruces, NM	655
23	Las Vegas-Paradise, NV	9,097
264	Lawrence, KS	332
161	Lawton, OK	865
326	Lebanon, PA	155
355	Lewiston-Auburn, ME	67
357	Lewiston, ID-WA	65
126	Lexington-Fayette, KY	1,259
277	Lima, OH	310
162	Lincoln, NE	860
55	Little Rock, AR	3,754
356	Logan, UT-ID	66
167	Longview, TX	802
339	Longview, WA	121
4	Los Angeles County, CA M.D.	27,406
3	Los Angeles (greater), CA	31,382
81	Louisville, KY-IN	2,344
96	Lubbock, TX	1,858
223	Lynchburg, VA	491
214	Macon, GA	536
224	Madera, CA	484
176	Madison, WI	730
216	Manchester-Nashua, NH	532
279	Manhattan, KS	308
352	Mankato-North Mankato, MN	88
343	Mansfield, OH	115
86	McAllen-Edinburg-Mission, TX	2,093
280	Medford, OR	305
22	Memphis, TN-MS-AR	9,613
124	Merced, CA	1,278
6	Miami (greater), FL	22,527
15	Miami-Dade County, FL M.D.	11,951
351	Michigan City-La Porte, IN	94
269	Midland, TX	324
54	Milwaukee, WI	3,826
41	Minneapolis-St. Paul, MN-WI	5,150
313	Missoula, MT	201
107	Mobile, AL	1,652
98	Modesto, CA	1,847
314	Monroe, MI	199
185	Montgomery, AL	672
263	Morgantown, WV	335
253	Morristown, TN	361
338	Mount Vernon-Anacortes, WA	123
300	Muncie, IN	240
234	Muskegon-Norton Shores, MI	447
295	Napa, CA	265
169	Naples-Marco Island, FL	786
29	Nashville-Davidson, TN	7,362
73	Nassau-Suffolk, NY M.D.	2,728
89	New Haven-Milford, CT	1,976
47	New Orleans, LA	4,116
1	New York (greater), NY-NJ-PA	40,021
2	New York-W. Plains NY-NJ M.D.	31,444
56	Newark-Union, NJ-PA M.D.	3,652
239	Niles-Benton Harbor, MI	417
69	North Port-Bradenton-Sarasota, FL	2,882
245	Norwich-New London, CT	387
28	Oakland-Fremont, CA M.D.	7,518
117	Ocala, FL	1,469
323	Ocean City, NJ	169
192	Odessa, TX	635

RANK	METROPOLITAN AREA	ASSAULTS
215	Ogden-Clearfield, UT	533
NA	Oklahoma City, OK**	NA
240	Olympia, WA	402
92	Omaha-Council Bluffs, NE-IA	1,939
20	Orlando, FL	9,873
274	Oshkosh-Neenah, WI	311
354	Owensboro, KY	71
139	Oxnard-Thousand Oaks, CA	1,119
70	Palm Bay-Melbourne, FL	2,819
307	Palm Coast, FL	223
178	Panama City-Lynn Haven, FL	728
306	Pascagoula, MS	226
95	Peabody, MA M.D.	1,874
87	Pensacola, FL	2,067
8	Philadelphia (greater) PA-NJ-MD-DE	17,962
12	Philadelphia, PA M.D.	12,652
21	Phoenix-Mesa-Scottsdale, AZ	9,748
209	Pine Bluff, AR	556
42	Pittsburgh, PA	4,943
226	Pittsfield, MA	466
322	Pocatello, ID	170
134	Port St. Lucie, FL	1,176
64	Portland-Vancouver, OR-WA	3,248
274	Portland, ME	311
137	Poughkeepsie, NY	1,162
199	Prescott, AZ	608
50	Providence-New Bedford, RI-MA	3,937
305	Provo-Orem, UT	229
181	Pueblo, CO	713
243	Punta Gorda, FL	389
289	Racine, WI	278
101	Raleigh-Cary, NC	1,792
311	Rapid City, SD	211
179	Reading, PA	723
144	Redding, CA	1,036
116	Reno-Sparks, NV	1,485
104	Richmond, VA	1,740
18	Riverside-San Bernardino, CA	10,599
202	Roanoke, VA	595
315	Rochester, MN	197
106	Rochester, NY	1,662
274	Rockingham County, NH M.D.	311
200	Rocky Mount, NC	602
282	Rome, GA	302
33	Sacramento, CA	6,487
120	Saginaw, MI	1,420
197	Salem, OR	616
123	Salinas, CA	1,285
182	Salisbury, MD	707
80	Salt Lake City, UT	2,449
293	San Angelo, TX	272
36	San Antonio, TX	5,700
27	San Diego, CA	7,921
16	San Francisco (greater), CA	11,377
53	San Francisco-S. Mateo, CA M.D.	3,859
63	San Jose, CA	3,264
221	San Luis Obispo, CA	495
336	Sandusky, OH	124
49	Santa Ana-Anaheim, CA M.D.	3,976
115	Santa Barbara-Santa Maria, CA	1,501
158	Santa Cruz-Watsonville, CA	904
227	Santa Fe, NM	463
119	Santa Rosa-Petaluma, CA	1,427

RANK	METROPOLITAN AREA	ASSAULTS
195	Savannah, GA	630
150	Scranton--Wilkes-Barre, PA	982
45	Seattle-Bellevue-Everett, WA M.D.	4,404
31	Seattle-Tacoma-Bellevue, WA	7,019
259	Sebastian-Vero Beach, FL	347
350	Sheboygan, WI	99
296	Sherman-Denison, TX	259
NA	Shreveport-Bossier City, LA**	NA
266	Sioux City, IA-NE-SD	326
278	Sioux Falls, SD	309
203	South Bend-Mishawaka, IN-MI	593
124	Spartanburg, SC	1,278
140	Spokane, WA	1,111
78	Springfield, MA	2,545
122	Springfield, MO	1,332
309	Springfield, OH	213
334	State College, PA	131
58	Stockton, CA	3,573
308	St. Cloud, MN	214
331	St. George, UT	134
248	St. Joseph, MO-KS	383
25	St. Louis, MO-IL	8,410
218	Sumter, SC	526
129	Syracuse, NY	1,226
75	Tacoma, WA M.D.	2,615
90	Tallahassee, FL	1,970
17	Tampa-St Petersburg, FL	11,005
180	Texarkana, TX-Texarkana, AR	714
88	Toledo, OH	2,034
208	Topeka, KS	557
159	Trenton-Ewing, NJ	898
76	Tucson, AZ	2,566
48	Tulsa, OK	4,024
192	Tuscaloosa, AL	635
190	Tyler, TX	652
211	Utica-Rome, NY	547
247	Valdosta, GA	384
138	Vallejo-Fairfield, CA	1,122
225	Victoria, TX	483
220	Vineland, NJ	511
110	Visalia-Porterville, CA	1,579
160	Waco, TX	867
254	Warner Robins, GA	359
44	Warren-Farmington Hills, MI M.D.	4,631
19	Washington (greater) DC-VA-MD-WV	10,378
24	Washington, DC-VA-MD-WV M.D.	8,849
183	Waterloo-Cedar Falls, IA	694
328	Wausau, WI	148
329	Wenatchee, WA	146
43	West Palm Beach, FL M.D.	4,903
309	Wheeling, WV-OH	213
251	Wichita Falls, TX	367
68	Wichita, KS	2,983
346	Williamsport, PA	109
71	Wilmington, DE-MD-NJ M.D.	2,758
NA	Wilmington, NC**	NA
348	Winchester, VA-WV	107
111	Winston-Salem, NC	1,577
74	Worcester, MA	2,705
238	York-Hanover, PA	418
143	Youngstown, OH-PA	1,037
235	Yuba City, CA	443
198	Yuma, AZ	615

Source: Reported data from the F.B.I. "Crime in the United States 2009"
*Aggravated assault is an attack for the purpose of inflicting severe bodily injury.
**Not available.

21. Aggravated Assaults in 2009 (continued)
National Total = 806,843 Aggravated Assaults*

RANK	METROPOLITAN AREA	ASSAULTS
1	New York (greater), NY-NJ-PA	40,021
2	New York-W. Plains NY-NJ M.D.	31,444
3	Los Angeles (greater), CA	31,382
4	Los Angeles County, CA M.D.	27,406
5	Houston, TX	23,052
6	Miami (greater), FL	22,527
7	Detroit (greater), MI	18,511
8	Philadelphia (greater) PA-NJ-MD-DE	17,962
9	Dallas (greater), TX	13,880
9	Detroit-Livonia-Dearborn, MI M.D.	13,880
11	Atlanta, GA	12,988
12	Philadelphia, PA M.D.	12,652
13	Boston (greater), MA-NH	12,137
14	Baltimore-Towson, MD	12,114
15	Miami-Dade County, FL M.D.	11,951
16	San Francisco (greater), CA	11,377
17	Tampa-St Petersburg, FL	11,005
18	Riverside-San Bernardino, CA	10,599
19	Washington (greater) DC-VA-MD-WV	10,378
20	Orlando, FL	9,873
21	Phoenix-Mesa-Scottsdale, AZ	9,748
22	Memphis, TN-MS-AR	9,613
23	Las Vegas-Paradise, NV	9,097
24	Washington, DC-VA-MD-WV M.D.	8,849
25	St. Louis, MO-IL	8,410
26	Dallas-Plano-Irving, TX M.D.	8,215
27	San Diego, CA	7,921
28	Oakland-Fremont, CA M.D.	7,518
29	Nashville-Davidson, TN	7,362
30	Kansas City, MO-KS	7,177
31	Seattle-Tacoma-Bellevue, WA	7,019
32	Boston-Quincy, MA M.D.	6,923
33	Sacramento, CA	6,487
34	Indianapolis, IN	6,094
35	Jacksonville, FL	6,038
36	San Antonio, TX	5,700
37	Fort Lauderdale, FL M.D.	5,673
38	Fort Worth-Arlington, TX M.D.	5,665
39	Charlotte-Gastonia, NC-SC	5,544
40	Denver-Aurora, CO	5,350
41	Minneapolis-St. Paul, MN-WI	5,150
42	Pittsburgh, PA	4,943
43	West Palm Beach, FL M.D.	4,903
44	Warren-Farmington Hills, MI M.D.	4,631
45	Seattle-Bellevue-Everett, WA M.D.	4,404
46	Columbia, SC	4,266
47	New Orleans, LA	4,116
48	Tulsa, OK	4,024
49	Santa Ana-Anaheim, CA M.D.	3,976
50	Providence-New Bedford, RI-MA	3,937
51	Austin-Round Rock, TX	3,908
52	Albuquerque, NM	3,869
53	San Francisco-S. Mateo, CA M.D.	3,859
54	Milwaukee, WI	3,826
55	Little Rock, AR	3,754
56	Newark-Union, NJ-PA M.D.	3,652
57	Baton Rouge, LA	3,634
58	Stockton, CA	3,573
59	Cleveland-Elyria-Mentor, OH	3,340
60	Birmingham-Hoover, AL	3,321
61	Bakersfield, CA	3,281
62	Buffalo-Niagara Falls, NY	3,269
63	San Jose, CA	3,264
64	Portland-Vancouver, OR-WA	3,248
65	Cincinnati-Middletown, OH-KY-IN	3,055
66	Cambridge-Newton, MA M.D.	3,029
67	Fresno, CA	2,994
68	Wichita, KS	2,983
69	North Port-Bradenton-Sarasota, FL	2,882
70	Palm Bay-Melbourne, FL	2,819
71	Wilmington, DE-MD-NJ M.D.	2,758
72	Charleston-North Charleston, SC	2,754
73	Nassau-Suffolk, NY M.D.	2,728
74	Worcester, MA	2,705
75	Tacoma, WA M.D.	2,615
76	Tucson, AZ	2,566
77	Camden, NJ M.D.	2,552
78	El Paso, TX	2,545
78	Springfield, MA	2,545
80	Salt Lake City, UT	2,449
81	Louisville, KY-IN	2,344
82	Chattanooga, TN-GA	2,301
83	Knoxville, TN	2,273
84	Edison, NJ M.D.	2,197
85	Flint, MI	2,163
86	McAllen-Edinburg-Mission, TX	2,093
87	Pensacola, FL	2,067
88	Toledo, OH	2,034
89	New Haven-Milford, CT	1,976
90	Tallahassee, FL	1,970
91	Corpus Christi, TX	1,964
92	Omaha-Council Bluffs, NE-IA	1,939
93	Lakeland, FL	1,919
94	Deltona-Daytona Beach, FL	1,903
95	Peabody, MA M.D.	1,874
96	Greensboro-High Point, NC	1,858
96	Lubbock, TX	1,858
98	Modesto, CA	1,847
99	Colorado Springs, CO	1,834
100	Grand Rapids-Wyoming, MI	1,794
101	Raleigh-Cary, NC	1,792
102	Columbus, OH	1,763
103	Anchorage, AK	1,760
104	Richmond, VA	1,740
105	Cape Coral-Fort Myers, FL	1,675
106	Rochester, NY	1,662
107	Mobile, AL	1,652
108	Albany-Schenectady-Troy, NY	1,584
109	Hartford, CT	1,581
110	Visalia-Porterville, CA	1,579
111	Winston-Salem, NC	1,577
112	Bethesda-Frederick, MD M.D.	1,529
113	Lafayette, LA	1,526
114	Gainesville, FL	1,519
115	Santa Barbara-Santa Maria, CA	1,501
116	Reno-Sparks, NV	1,485
117	Ocala, FL	1,469
118	Bridgeport-Stamford, CT	1,439
119	Santa Rosa-Petaluma, CA	1,427
120	Saginaw, MI	1,420
121	Honolulu, HI	1,411
122	Springfield, MO	1,332
123	Salinas, CA	1,285
124	Merced, CA	1,278
124	Spartanburg, SC	1,278
126	Lexington-Fayette, KY	1,259
127	Lansing-East Lansing, MI	1,256
128	Akron, OH	1,248
129	Syracuse, NY	1,226
130	Dayton, OH	1,205
131	Beaumont-Port Arthur, TX	1,198
132	Amarillo, TX	1,182
132	Durham-Chapel Hill, NC	1,182
134	Port St. Lucie, FL	1,176
135	Fayetteville, NC	1,166
136	Florence, SC	1,165
137	Poughkeepsie, NY	1,162
138	Vallejo-Fairfield, CA	1,122
139	Oxnard-Thousand Oaks, CA	1,119
140	Spokane, WA	1,111
141	Boise City-Nampa, ID	1,088
142	Fayetteville, AR-MO	1,045
143	Youngstown, OH-PA	1,037
144	Redding, CA	1,036
145	Lake Charles, LA	1,030
146	Des Moines-West Des Moines, IA	1,017
147	Allentown, PA-NJ	1,005
148	Charleston, WV	993
149	Laredo, TX	991
150	Scranton--Wilkes-Barre, PA	982
151	Fort Smith, AR-OK	980
152	Augusta, GA-SC	966
153	Anderson, SC	952
154	Brownsville-Harlingen, TX	937
154	Huntsville, AL	937
156	Kingsport, TN-VA	924
157	Kalamazoo-Portage, MI	908
158	Santa Cruz-Watsonville, CA	904
159	Trenton-Ewing, NJ	898
160	Waco, TX	867
161	Lawton, OK	865
162	Clarksville, TN-KY	860
162	Lincoln, NE	860
164	Killeen-Temple-Fort Hood, TX	828
165	Barnstable Town, MA	825
166	Harrisburg-Carlisle, PA	821
167	Longview, TX	802
168	Bremerton-Silverdale, WA	789
169	Naples-Marco Island, FL	786
170	Alexandria, LA	782
171	Jackson, MS	766
172	Atlantic City, NJ	756
173	Ann Arbor, MI	735
174	Dover, DE	733
175	Columbus, GA-AL	732
176	Farmington, NM	730
176	Madison, WI	730
178	Panama City-Lynn Haven, FL	728
179	Reading, PA	723
180	Texarkana, TX-Texarkana, AR	714

Note: All listings are for Metropolitan Statistical Areas (M.S.A.s) except for those ending with "M.D." Listings with "M.D." are Metropolitan Divisions which are smaller parts of eleven large M.S.A.s. See explanatory note at beginning of metropolitan area section.

RANK	METROPOLITAN AREA	ASSAULTS
181	Pueblo, CO	713
182	Salisbury, MD	707
183	Waterloo-Cedar Falls, IA	694
184	Hickory, NC	682
185	Montgomery, AL	672
186	Eugene-Springfield, OR	668
187	Battle Creek, MI	657
188	Las Cruces, NM	655
189	Cleveland, TN	654
190	Tyler, TX	652
191	Chico, CA	648
192	Odessa, TX	635
192	Tuscaloosa, AL	635
194	Albany, GA	631
195	Savannah, GA	630
196	College Station-Bryan, TX	627
197	Salem, OR	616
198	Yuma, AZ	615
199	Prescott, AZ	608
200	Rocky Mount, NC	602
201	Brunswick, GA	596
202	Roanoke, VA	595
203	South Bend-Mishawaka, IN-MI	593
204	Anniston-Oxford, AL	588
205	Asheville, NC	583
206	Houma, LA	576
207	Jackson, TN	569
208	Topeka, KS	557
209	Pine Bluff, AR	556
210	Fort Collins-Loveland, CO	551
211	Utica-Rome, NY	547
212	Greeley, CO	539
212	Johnson City, TN	539
214	Macon, GA	536
215	Ogden-Clearfield, UT	533
216	Manchester-Nashua, NH	532
217	Boulder, CO	528
218	Sumter, SC	526
219	Evansville, IN-KY	523
220	Vineland, NJ	511
221	San Luis Obispo, CA	495
222	Athens-Clarke County, GA	493
223	Lynchburg, VA	491
224	Madera, CA	484
225	Victoria, TX	483
226	Pittsfield, MA	466
227	Santa Fe, NM	463
228	Burlington, NC	462
229	Decatur, IL	459
230	Jackson, MI	458
231	Abilene, TX	454
231	Columbia, MO	454
233	Kennewick-Pasco-Richland, WA	450
234	Muskegon-Norton Shores, MI	447
235	Yuba City, CA	443
236	Hagerstown-Martinsburg, MD-WV	440
237	Hot Springs, AR	432
238	York-Hanover, PA	418
239	Niles-Benton Harbor, MI	417
240	Erie, PA	402
240	Olympia, WA	402
242	Lancaster, PA	391
243	Punta Gorda, FL	389

RANK	METROPOLITAN AREA	ASSAULTS
244	Fort Wayne, IN	388
245	Norwich-New London, CT	387
246	Duluth, MN-WI	385
247	Valdosta, GA	384
248	St. Joseph, MO-KS	383
249	Cumberland, MD-WV	377
250	Green Bay, WI	373
251	Wichita Falls, TX	367
252	Jefferson City, MO	362
253	Morristown, TN	361
254	Warner Robins, GA	359
255	Bloomington, IN	358
256	Goldsboro, NC	357
257	Jacksonville, NC	355
258	Coeur d'Alene, ID	350
259	Sebastian-Vero Beach, FL	347
260	Lake Havasu City-Kingman, AZ	345
261	Cedar Rapids, IA	343
262	Lafayette, IN	339
263	Morgantown, WV	335
264	Lawrence, KS	332
265	Jonesboro, AR	331
266	Sioux City, IA-NE-SD	326
267	Binghamton, NY	325
267	Crestview-Fort Walton Beach, FL	325
269	Dalton, GA	324
269	Midland, TX	324
271	Dubuque, IA	323
272	Iowa City, IA	321
273	Kingston, NY	319
274	Oshkosh-Neenah, WI	311
274	Portland, ME	311
274	Rockingham County, NH M.D.	311
277	Lima, OH	310
278	Sioux Falls, SD	309
279	Manhattan, KS	308
280	Medford, OR	305
281	Idaho Falls, ID	303
282	Rome, GA	302
283	Florence-Muscle Shoals, AL	301
284	Danville, IL	299
285	Flagstaff, AZ	296
286	Grand Junction, CO	294
287	Fargo, ND-MN	291
288	Holland-Grand Haven, MI	282
289	Racine, WI	278
290	Cape Girardeau, MO-IL	277
291	Elizabethtown, KY	276
292	Bend, OR	274
293	San Angelo, TX	272
294	Bellingham, WA	269
295	Napa, CA	265
296	Sherman-Denison, TX	259
297	Altoona, PA	249
298	Janesville, WI	244
299	Billings, MT	242
300	Muncie, IN	240
301	Burlington-South Burlington, VT	234
302	Charlottesville, VA	233
303	Gulfport-Biloxi, MS	231
304	Gainesville, GA	230
305	Provo-Orem, UT	229
306	Pascagoula, MS	226

RANK	METROPOLITAN AREA	ASSAULTS
307	Palm Coast, FL	223
308	St. Cloud, MN	214
309	Springfield, OH	213
309	Wheeling, WV-OH	213
311	Rapid City, SD	211
312	Bay City, MI	203
313	Missoula, MT	201
314	Monroe, MI	199
315	Rochester, MN	197
316	Gadsden, AL	194
316	Hinesville, GA	194
318	Blacksburg, VA	193
319	La Crosse, WI-MN	188
320	Appleton, WI	186
321	Ames, IA	176
322	Pocatello, ID	170
323	Bismarck, ND	169
323	Ocean City, NJ	169
325	Great Falls, MT	166
326	Lebanon, PA	155
327	Carson City, NV	153
328	Wausau, WI	148
329	Wenatchee, WA	146
330	Grand Forks, ND-MN	139
331	St. George, UT	134
332	Eau Claire, WI	132
332	Kokomo, IN	132
334	State College, PA	131
335	Bowling Green, KY	127
336	Fond du Lac, WI	124
336	Sandusky, OH	124
338	Mount Vernon-Anacortes, WA	123
339	Casper, WY	121
339	Longview, WA	121
341	Danville, VA	120
341	Harrisonburg, VA	120
343	Elmira, NY	115
343	Mansfield, OH	115
345	Glens Falls, NY	111
346	Hattiesburg, MS	109
346	Williamsport, PA	109
348	Winchester, VA-WV	107
349	Cheyenne, WY	106
350	Sheboygan, WI	99
351	Michigan City-La Porte, IN	94
352	Mankato-North Mankato, MN	88
353	Anderson, IN	87
354	Owensboro, KY	71
355	Lewiston-Auburn, ME	67
356	Logan, UT-ID	66
357	Lewiston, ID-WA	65
358	Corvallis, OR	62
359	Columbus, IN	48
360	Bangor, ME	43
361	Elkhart-Goshen, IN	42
NA	Auburn, AL**	NA
NA	Decatur, AL**	NA
NA	Dothan, AL**	NA
NA	El Centro, CA**	NA
NA	Ithaca, NY**	NA
NA	Oklahoma City, OK**	NA
NA	Shreveport-Bossier City, LA**	NA
NA	Wilmington, NC**	NA

Source: Reported data from the F.B.I. "Crime in the United States 2009"

*Aggravated assault is an attack for the purpose of inflicting severe bodily injury.

**Not available.

22. Aggravated Assault Rate in 2009
National Rate = 262.8 Aggravated Assaults per 100,000 Population*

RANK	METROPOLITAN AREA	RATE
134	Abilene, TX	284.4
254	Akron, OH	178.0
244	Albany-Schenectady-Troy, NY	184.9
68	Albany, GA	382.0
45	Albuquerque, NM	448.7
27	Alexandria, LA	504.5
313	Allentown, PA-NJ	122.9
222	Altoona, PA	199.1
33	Amarillo, TX	480.4
219	Ames, IA	201.4
12	Anchorage, AK	576.5
353	Anderson, IN	66.1
24	Anderson, SC	512.4
208	Ann Arbor, MI	210.8
23	Anniston-Oxford, AL	515.1
347	Appleton, WI	83.9
294	Asheville, NC	141.0
165	Athens-Clarke County, GA	258.0
188	Atlanta, GA	236.4
146	Atlantic City, NJ	277.3
NA	Auburn, AL**	NA
250	Augusta, GA-SC	179.6
196	Austin-Round Rock, TX	229.1
62	Bakersfield, CA	402.8
43	Baltimore-Towson, MD	449.8
360	Bangor, ME	28.9
74	Barnstable Town, MA	367.8
39	Baton Rouge, LA	461.3
31	Battle Creek, MI	486.4
232	Bay City, MI	190.1
104	Beaumont-Port Arthur, TX	316.9
300	Bellingham, WA	133.7
265	Bend, OR	167.4
311	Bethesda-Frederick, MD M.D.	128.0
275	Billings, MT	157.7
302	Binghamton, NY	133.0
125	Birmingham-Hoover, AL	293.7
274	Bismarck, ND	158.0
316	Blacksburg, VA	120.8
226	Bloomington, IN	193.3
256	Boise City-Nampa, ID	177.2
157	Boston (greater), MA-NH	264.6
77	Boston-Quincy, MA M.D.	362.0
253	Boulder, CO	178.3
328	Bowling Green, KY	106.1
93	Bremerton-Silverdale, WA	326.0
266	Bridgeport-Stamford, CT	163.9
190	Brownsville-Harlingen, TX	234.3
13	Brunswick, GA	575.7
127	Buffalo-Niagara Falls, NY	292.1
324	Burlington-South Burlington, VT	111.9
113	Burlington, NC	307.5
219	Cambridge-Newton, MA M.D.	201.4
217	Camden, NJ M.D.	203.0
147	Cape Coral-Fort Myers, FL	275.8
123	Cape Girardeau, MO-IL	295.6
136	Carson City, NV	280.9
268	Casper, WY	161.6
301	Cedar Rapids, IA	133.4
56	Charleston-North Charleston, SC	417.5
92	Charleston, WV	326.7
105	Charlotte-Gastonia, NC-SC	316.4
319	Charlottesville, VA	118.0
48	Chattanooga, TN-GA	439.3
318	Cheyenne, WY	118.6
126	Chico, CA	292.6
295	Cincinnati-Middletown, OH-KY-IN	140.3
97	Clarksville, TN-KY	324.2
272	Cleveland-Elyria-Mentor, OH	159.6
11	Cleveland, TN	576.7
172	Coeur d'Alene, ID	249.3
121	College Station-Bryan, TX	298.2
128	Colorado Springs, CO	292.0
150	Columbia, MO	272.7
14	Columbia, SC	575.2
167	Columbus, GA-AL	254.5
354	Columbus, IN	63.2
333	Columbus, OH	98.1
37	Corpus Christi, TX	470.8
351	Corvallis, OR	75.5
248	Crestview-Fort Walton Beach, FL	181.5
70	Cumberland, MD-WV	380.3
204	Dallas (greater), TX	215.2
233	Dallas-Plano-Irving, TX M.D.	189.7
186	Dalton, GA	239.8
71	Danville, IL	373.7
321	Danville, VA	113.5
289	Dayton, OH	143.8
NA	Decatur, AL**	NA
52	Decatur, IL	428.0
69	Deltona-Daytona Beach, FL	380.7
211	Denver-Aurora, CO	209.7
249	Des Moines-West Des Moines, IA	180.2
55	Detroit (greater), MI	420.3
3	Detroit-Livonia-Dearborn, MI M.D.	719.0
NA	Dothan, AL**	NA
40	Dover, DE	460.4
85	Dubuque, IA	347.4
296	Duluth, MN-WI	140.1
187	Durham-Chapel Hill, NC	237.2
348	Eau Claire, WI	82.6
337	Edison, NJ M.D.	93.9
NA	El Centro, CA**	NA
87	El Paso, TX	339.4
182	Elizabethtown, KY	244.3
361	Elkhart-Goshen, IN	20.9
307	Elmira, NY	131.5
290	Erie, PA	143.7
227	Eugene-Springfield, OR	191.7
284	Evansville, IN-KY	148.7
287	Fargo, ND-MN	146.0
6	Farmington, NM	589.6
198	Fayetteville, AR-MO	228.3
95	Fayetteville, NC	324.8
195	Flagstaff, AZ	230.4
26	Flint, MI	507.5
213	Florence-Muscle Shoals, AL	208.3
10	Florence, SC	577.6
312	Fond du Lac, WI	124.5
245	Fort Collins-Loveland, CO	184.8
96	Fort Lauderdale, FL M.D.	324.3
88	Fort Smith, AR-OK	333.0
338	Fort Wayne, IN	93.7
154	Fort Worth-Arlington, TX M.D.	267.3
94	Fresno, CA	325.9
235	Gadsden, AL	187.0
7	Gainesville, FL	585.9
315	Gainesville, GA	121.3
344	Glens Falls, NY	85.9
109	Goldsboro, NC	313.5
291	Grand Forks, ND-MN	142.1
221	Grand Junction, CO	200.5
194	Grand Rapids-Wyoming, MI	230.7
218	Great Falls, MT	202.0
214	Greeley, CO	208.1
314	Green Bay, WI	122.3
162	Greensboro-High Point, NC	260.3
331	Gulfport-Biloxi, MS	98.9
267	Hagerstown-Martinsburg, MD-WV	163.1
280	Harrisburg-Carlisle, PA	153.5
330	Harrisonburg, VA	100.0
277	Hartford, CT	156.9
350	Hattiesburg, MS	76.3
239	Hickory, NC	186.4
140	Hinesville, GA	279.3
325	Holland-Grand Haven, MI	107.7
278	Honolulu, HI	155.5
50	Hot Springs, AR	436.7
135	Houma, LA	283.5
64	Houston, TX	393.4
192	Huntsville, AL	232.1
184	Idaho Falls, ID	242.3
82	Indianapolis, IN	349.8
206	Iowa City, IA	212.2
NA	Ithaca, NY**	NA
41	Jacksonville, FL	455.7
207	Jacksonville, NC	211.2
130	Jackson, MI	286.8
293	Jackson, MS	141.3
29	Jackson, TN	500.8
282	Janesville, WI	151.5
177	Jefferson City, MO	246.2
151	Johnson City, TN	272.1
142	Jonesboro, AR	278.3
137	Kalamazoo-Portage, MI	280.8
84	Kansas City, MO-KS	348.3
242	Kennewick-Pasco-Richland, WA	185.3
205	Killeen-Temple-Fort Hood, TX	215.0
118	Kingsport, TN-VA	301.6
258	Kingston, NY	175.2
98	Knoxville, TN	323.8
302	Kokomo, IN	133.0
292	La Crosse, WI-MN	142.0
259	Lafayette, IN	174.0
8	Lafayette, LA	580.1
19	Lake Charles, LA	530.7
260	Lake Havasu City-Kingman, AZ	173.3
90	Lakeland, FL	326.9
349	Lancaster, PA	77.1
145	Lansing-East Lansing, MI	277.4

Note: All listings are for Metropolitan Statistical Areas (M.S.A.s) except for those ending with "M.D." Listings with "M.D." are Metropolitan Divisions which are smaller parts of eleven large M.S.A.s. See explanatory note at beginning of metropolitan area section.

RANK	METROPOLITAN AREA	RATE
60	Laredo, TX	408.8
101	Las Cruces, NM	319.0
34	Las Vegas-Paradise, NV	477.8
133	Lawrence, KS	284.7
1	Lawton, OK	771.3
317	Lebanon, PA	119.0
356	Lewiston-Auburn, ME	62.6
326	Lewiston, ID-WA	107.2
153	Lexington-Fayette, KY	267.4
124	Lima, OH	294.9
129	Lincoln, NE	287.2
18	Little Rock, AR	547.7
358	Logan, UT-ID	51.9
66	Longview, TX	388.9
320	Longview, WA	117.7
143	Los Angeles County, CA M.D.	277.8
183	Los Angeles (greater), CA	243.6
237	Louisville, KY-IN	186.6
5	Lubbock, TX	679.9
225	Lynchburg, VA	197.4
191	Macon, GA	232.3
100	Madera, CA	320.8
310	Madison, WI	128.5
306	Manchester-Nashua, NH	131.6
173	Manhattan, KS	249.2
336	Mankato-North Mankato, MN	94.2
341	Mansfield, OH	92.0
138	McAllen-Edinburg-Mission, TX	280.3
283	Medford, OR	150.2
2	Memphis, TN-MS-AR	740.0
24	Merced, CA	512.4
59	Miami (greater), FL	409.5
32	Miami-Dade County, FL M.D.	481.4
346	Michigan City-La Porte, IN	84.6
176	Midland, TX	246.8
177	Milwaukee, WI	246.2
276	Minneapolis-St. Paul, MN-WI	157.6
243	Missoula, MT	185.1
61	Mobile, AL	404.1
79	Modesto, CA	357.8
308	Monroe, MI	130.0
247	Montgomery, AL	181.7
139	Morgantown, WV	280.1
161	Morristown, TN	262.0
329	Mount Vernon-Anacortes, WA	102.1
211	Muncie, IN	209.7
166	Muskegon-Norton Shores, MI	256.8
224	Napa, CA	197.8
179	Naples-Marco Island, FL	245.6
38	Nashville-Davidson, TN	464.6
335	Nassau-Suffolk, NY M.D.	94.9
174	New Haven-Milford, CT	248.6
83	New Orleans, LA	349.0
210	New York (greater), NY-NJ-PA	209.8
152	New York-W. Plains NY-NJ M.D.	267.9
261	Newark-Union, NJ-PA M.D.	172.0
159	Niles-Benton Harbor, MI	263.1
57	North Port-Bradenton-Sarasota, FL	415.8
141	Norwich-New London, CT	279.2
120	Oakland-Fremont, CA M.D.	299.9
49	Ocala, FL	438.0
255	Ocean City, NJ	177.7
35	Odessa, TX	476.0

RANK	METROPOLITAN AREA	RATE
332	Ogden-Clearfield, UT	98.8
NA	Oklahoma City, OK**	NA
271	Olympia, WA	160.1
197	Omaha-Council Bluffs, NE-IA	228.7
36	Orlando, FL	473.0
229	Oshkosh-Neenah, WI	191.3
355	Owensboro, KY	62.7
297	Oxnard-Thousand Oaks, CA	139.9
20	Palm Bay-Melbourne, FL	523.3
193	Palm Coast, FL	230.8
47	Panama City-Lynn Haven, FL	443.0
286	Pascagoula, MS	147.3
170	Peabody, MA M.D.	250.8
42	Pensacola, FL	455.4
119	Philadelphia (greater) PA-NJ-MD-DE	300.9
106	Philadelphia, PA M.D.	315.4
200	Phoenix-Mesa-Scottsdale, AZ	223.4
16	Pine Bluff, AR	554.1
209	Pittsburgh, PA	210.4
81	Pittsfield, MA	354.9
228	Pocatello, ID	191.6
131	Port St. Lucie, FL	286.2
288	Portland-Vancouver, OR-WA	145.0
357	Portland, ME	60.3
262	Poughkeepsie, NY	171.4
143	Prescott, AZ	277.8
181	Providence-New Bedford, RI-MA	245.0
359	Provo-Orem, UT	40.9
44	Pueblo, CO	449.1
164	Punta Gorda, FL	260.0
299	Racine, WI	138.6
273	Raleigh-Cary, NC	158.9
263	Rapid City, SD	170.3
256	Reading, PA	177.2
15	Redding, CA	570.8
80	Reno-Sparks, NV	355.1
298	Richmond, VA	139.7
168	Riverside-San Bernardino, CA	251.9
223	Roanoke, VA	198.1
327	Rochester, MN	106.2
270	Rochester, NY	160.9
352	Rockingham County, NH M.D.	73.6
58	Rocky Mount, NC	409.6
108	Rome, GA	314.1
116	Sacramento, CA	303.2
4	Saginaw, MI	713.8
278	Salem, OR	155.5
106	Salinas, CA	315.4
9	Salisbury, MD	579.5
202	Salt Lake City, UT	217.3
175	San Angelo, TX	247.0
149	San Antonio, TX	275.1
159	San Diego, CA	263.1
155	San Francisco (greater), CA	266.1
201	San Francisco-S. Mateo, CA M.D.	218.2
251	San Jose, CA	179.1
241	San Luis Obispo, CA	185.8
269	Sandusky, OH	161.0
305	Santa Ana-Anaheim, CA M.D.	131.7
73	Santa Barbara-Santa Maria, CA	371.0
78	Santa Cruz-Watsonville, CA	358.8
103	Santa Fe, NM	317.2
114	Santa Rosa-Petaluma, CA	306.3

RANK	METROPOLITAN AREA	RATE
239	Savannah, GA	186.4
252	Scranton--Wilkes-Barre, PA	178.7
264	Seattle-Bellevue-Everett, WA M.D.	169.5
216	Seattle-Tacoma-Bellevue, WA	206.5
163	Sebastian-Vero Beach, FL	260.1
343	Sheboygan, WI	86.3
203	Sherman-Denison, TX	216.1
NA	Shreveport-Bossier City, LA**	NA
199	Sioux City, IA-NE-SD	227.8
309	Sioux Falls, SD	129.2
235	South Bend-Mishawaka, IN-MI	187.0
46	Spartanburg, SC	447.8
189	Spokane, WA	236.1
76	Springfield, MA	364.8
112	Springfield, MO	307.6
281	Springfield, OH	152.4
342	State College, PA	89.6
20	Stockton, CA	523.3
322	St. Cloud, MN	112.9
339	St. George, UT	93.5
117	St. Joseph, MO-KS	302.4
122	St. Louis, MO-IL	297.2
28	Sumter, SC	502.5
230	Syracuse, NY	190.7
90	Tacoma, WA M.D.	326.9
17	Tallahassee, FL	549.7
63	Tampa-St Petersburg, FL	400.0
20	Texarkana, TX-Texarkana, AR	523.3
111	Toledo, OH	312.9
185	Topeka, KS	241.7
180	Trenton-Ewing, NJ	245.2
169	Tucson, AZ	251.5
51	Tulsa, OK	433.6
115	Tuscaloosa, AL	303.5
102	Tyler, TX	318.7
237	Utica-Rome, NY	186.6
132	Valdosta, GA	285.8
148	Vallejo-Fairfield, CA	275.5
54	Victoria, TX	421.0
99	Vineland, NJ	323.5
75	Visalia-Porterville, CA	365.8
72	Waco, TX	373.2
156	Warner Robins, GA	265.4
234	Warren-Farmington Hills, MI M.D.	187.2
231	Washington (greater) DC-VA-MD-WV	190.3
215	Washington, DC-VA-MD-WV M.D.	207.8
53	Waterloo-Cedar Falls, IA	423.1
323	Wausau, WI	112.6
304	Wenatchee, WA	132.9
67	West Palm Beach, FL M.D.	386.3
285	Wheeling, WV-OH	147.6
171	Wichita Falls, TX	249.6
30	Wichita, KS	490.6
339	Williamsport, PA	93.5
65	Wilmington, DE-MD-NJ M.D.	392.8
NA	Wilmington, NC**	NA
345	Winchester, VA-WV	85.5
89	Winston-Salem, NC	332.6
86	Worcester, MA	340.1
334	York-Hanover, PA	97.1
246	Youngstown, OH-PA	184.0
158	Yuba City, CA	263.9
109	Yuma, AZ	313.5

Source: Reported data from the F.B.I. "Crime in the United States 2009"
*Aggravated assault is an attack for the purpose of inflicting severe bodily injury.
**Not available.

22. Aggravated Assault Rate in 2009 (continued)
National Rate = 262.8 Aggravated Assaults per 100,000 Population*

RANK	METROPOLITAN AREA	RATE
1	Lawton, OK	771.3
2	Memphis, TN-MS-AR	740.0
3	Detroit-Livonia-Dearborn, MI M.D.	719.0
4	Saginaw, MI	713.8
5	Lubbock, TX	679.9
6	Farmington, NM	589.6
7	Gainesville, FL	585.9
8	Lafayette, LA	580.1
9	Salisbury, MD	579.5
10	Florence, SC	577.6
11	Cleveland, TN	576.7
12	Anchorage, AK	576.5
13	Brunswick, GA	575.7
14	Columbia, SC	575.2
15	Redding, CA	570.8
16	Pine Bluff, AR	554.1
17	Tallahassee, FL	549.7
18	Little Rock, AR	547.7
19	Lake Charles, LA	530.7
20	Palm Bay-Melbourne, FL	523.3
20	Stockton, CA	523.3
20	Texarkana, TX-Texarkana, AR	523.3
23	Anniston-Oxford, AL	515.1
24	Anderson, SC	512.4
24	Merced, CA	512.4
26	Flint, MI	507.5
27	Alexandria, LA	504.5
28	Sumter, SC	502.5
29	Jackson, TN	500.8
30	Wichita, KS	490.6
31	Battle Creek, MI	486.4
32	Miami-Dade County, FL M.D.	481.4
33	Amarillo, TX	480.4
34	Las Vegas-Paradise, NV	477.8
35	Odessa, TX	476.0
36	Orlando, FL	473.0
37	Corpus Christi, TX	470.8
38	Nashville-Davidson, TN	464.6
39	Baton Rouge, LA	461.3
40	Dover, DE	460.4
41	Jacksonville, FL	455.7
42	Pensacola, FL	455.4
43	Baltimore-Towson, MD	449.8
44	Pueblo, CO	449.1
45	Albuquerque, NM	448.7
46	Spartanburg, SC	447.8
47	Panama City-Lynn Haven, FL	443.0
48	Chattanooga, TN-GA	439.3
49	Ocala, FL	438.0
50	Hot Springs, AR	436.7
51	Tulsa, OK	433.6
52	Decatur, IL	428.0
53	Waterloo-Cedar Falls, IA	423.1
54	Victoria, TX	421.0
55	Detroit (greater), MI	420.3
56	Charleston-North Charleston, SC	417.5
57	North Port-Bradenton-Sarasota, FL	415.8
58	Rocky Mount, NC	409.6
59	Miami (greater), FL	409.5
60	Laredo, TX	408.8
61	Mobile, AL	404.1
62	Bakersfield, CA	402.8
63	Tampa-St Petersburg, FL	400.0
64	Houston, TX	393.4
65	Wilmington, DE-MD-NJ M.D.	392.8
66	Longview, TX	388.9
67	West Palm Beach, FL M.D.	386.3
68	Albany, GA	382.0
69	Deltona-Daytona Beach, FL	380.7
70	Cumberland, MD-WV	380.3
71	Danville, IL	373.7
72	Waco, TX	373.2
73	Santa Barbara-Santa Maria, CA	371.0
74	Barnstable Town, MA	367.8
75	Visalia-Porterville, CA	365.8
76	Springfield, MA	364.8
77	Boston-Quincy, MA M.D.	362.0
78	Santa Cruz-Watsonville, CA	358.8
79	Modesto, CA	357.8
80	Reno-Sparks, NV	355.1
81	Pittsfield, MA	354.9
82	Indianapolis, IN	349.8
83	New Orleans, LA	349.0
84	Kansas City, MO-KS	348.3
85	Dubuque, IA	347.4
86	Worcester, MA	340.1
87	El Paso, TX	339.4
88	Fort Smith, AR-OK	333.0
89	Winston-Salem, NC	332.6
90	Lakeland, FL	326.9
90	Tacoma, WA M.D.	326.9
92	Charleston, WV	326.7
93	Bremerton-Silverdale, WA	326.0
94	Fresno, CA	325.9
95	Fayetteville, NC	324.8
96	Fort Lauderdale, FL M.D.	324.3
97	Clarksville, TN-KY	324.2
98	Knoxville, TN	323.8
99	Vineland, NJ	323.5
100	Madera, CA	320.8
101	Las Cruces, NM	319.0
102	Tyler, TX	318.7
103	Santa Fe, NM	317.2
104	Beaumont-Port Arthur, TX	316.9
105	Charlotte-Gastonia, NC-SC	316.4
106	Philadelphia, PA M.D.	315.4
106	Salinas, CA	315.4
108	Rome, GA	314.1
109	Goldsboro, NC	313.5
109	Yuma, AZ	313.5
111	Toledo, OH	312.9
112	Springfield, MO	307.6
113	Burlington, NC	307.5
114	Santa Rosa-Petaluma, CA	306.3
115	Tuscaloosa, AL	303.5
116	Sacramento, CA	303.2
117	St. Joseph, MO-KS	302.4
118	Kingsport, TN-VA	301.6
119	Philadelphia (greater) PA-NJ-MD-DE	300.9
120	Oakland-Fremont, CA M.D.	299.9
121	College Station-Bryan, TX	298.2
122	St. Louis, MO-IL	297.2
123	Cape Girardeau, MO-IL	295.6
124	Lima, OH	294.9
125	Birmingham-Hoover, AL	293.7
126	Chico, CA	292.6
127	Buffalo-Niagara Falls, NY	292.1
128	Colorado Springs, CO	292.0
129	Lincoln, NE	287.2
130	Jackson, MI	286.8
131	Port St. Lucie, FL	286.2
132	Valdosta, GA	285.8
133	Lawrence, KS	284.7
134	Abilene, TX	284.4
135	Houma, LA	283.5
136	Carson City, NV	280.9
137	Kalamazoo-Portage, MI	280.8
138	McAllen-Edinburg-Mission, TX	280.3
139	Morgantown, WV	280.1
140	Hinesville, GA	279.3
141	Norwich-New London, CT	279.2
142	Jonesboro, AR	278.3
143	Los Angeles County, CA M.D.	277.8
143	Prescott, AZ	277.8
145	Lansing-East Lansing, MI	277.4
146	Atlantic City, NJ	277.3
147	Cape Coral-Fort Myers, FL	275.8
148	Vallejo-Fairfield, CA	275.5
149	San Antonio, TX	275.1
150	Columbia, MO	272.7
151	Johnson City, TN	272.1
152	New York-W. Plains NY-NJ M.D.	267.9
153	Lexington-Fayette, KY	267.4
154	Fort Worth-Arlington, TX M.D.	267.3
155	San Francisco (greater), CA	266.1
156	Warner Robins, GA	265.4
157	Boston (greater), MA-NH	264.6
158	Yuba City, CA	263.9
159	Niles-Benton Harbor, MI	263.1
159	San Diego, CA	263.1
161	Morristown, TN	262.0
162	Greensboro-High Point, NC	260.3
163	Sebastian-Vero Beach, FL	260.1
164	Punta Gorda, FL	260.0
165	Athens-Clarke County, GA	258.0
166	Muskegon-Norton Shores, MI	256.8
167	Columbus, GA-AL	254.5
168	Riverside-San Bernardino, CA	251.9
169	Tucson, AZ	251.5
170	Peabody, MA M.D.	250.8
171	Wichita Falls, TX	249.6
172	Coeur d'Alene, ID	249.3
173	Manhattan, KS	249.2
174	New Haven-Milford, CT	248.6
175	San Angelo, TX	247.0
176	Midland, TX	246.8
177	Jefferson City, MO	246.2
177	Milwaukee, WI	246.2
179	Naples-Marco Island, FL	245.6
180	Trenton-Ewing, NJ	245.2

Note: All listings are for Metropolitan Statistical Areas (M.S.A.s) except for those ending with "M.D." Listings with "M.D." are Metropolitan Divisions which are smaller parts of eleven large M.S.A.s. See explanatory note at beginning of metropolitan area section.

Rank Order - Metro Area (continued)

RANK	METROPOLITAN AREA	RATE
181	Providence-New Bedford, RI-MA	245.0
182	Elizabethtown, KY	244.3
183	Los Angeles (greater), CA	243.6
184	Idaho Falls, ID	242.3
185	Topeka, KS	241.7
186	Dalton, GA	239.8
187	Durham-Chapel Hill, NC	237.2
188	Atlanta, GA	236.4
189	Spokane, WA	236.1
190	Brownsville-Harlingen, TX	234.3
191	Macon, GA	232.3
192	Huntsville, AL	232.1
193	Palm Coast, FL	230.8
194	Grand Rapids-Wyoming, MI	230.7
195	Flagstaff, AZ	230.4
196	Austin-Round Rock, TX	229.1
197	Omaha-Council Bluffs, NE-IA	228.7
198	Fayetteville, AR-MO	228.3
199	Sioux City, IA-NE-SD	227.8
200	Phoenix-Mesa-Scottsdale, AZ	223.4
201	San Francisco-S. Mateo, CA M.D.	218.2
202	Salt Lake City, UT	217.3
203	Sherman-Denison, TX	216.1
204	Dallas (greater), TX	215.2
205	Killeen-Temple-Fort Hood, TX	215.0
206	Iowa City, IA	212.2
207	Jacksonville, NC	211.2
208	Ann Arbor, MI	210.8
209	Pittsburgh, PA	210.4
210	New York (greater), NY-NJ-PA	209.8
211	Denver-Aurora, CO	209.7
211	Muncie, IN	209.7
213	Florence-Muscle Shoals, AL	208.3
214	Greeley, CO	208.1
215	Washington, DC-VA-MD-WV M.D.	207.8
216	Seattle-Tacoma-Bellevue, WA	206.5
217	Camden, NJ M.D.	203.0
218	Great Falls, MT	202.0
219	Ames, IA	201.4
219	Cambridge-Newton, MA M.D.	201.4
221	Grand Junction, CO	200.5
222	Altoona, PA	199.1
223	Roanoke, VA	198.1
224	Napa, CA	197.8
225	Lynchburg, VA	197.4
226	Bloomington, IN	193.3
227	Eugene-Springfield, OR	191.7
228	Pocatello, ID	191.6
229	Oshkosh-Neenah, WI	191.3
230	Syracuse, NY	190.7
231	Washington (greater) DC-VA-MD-WV	190.3
232	Bay City, MI	190.1
233	Dallas-Plano-Irving, TX M.D.	189.7
234	Warren-Farmington Hills, MI M.D.	187.2
235	Gadsden, AL	187.0
235	South Bend-Mishawaka, IN-MI	187.0
237	Louisville, KY-IN	186.6
237	Utica-Rome, NY	186.6
239	Hickory, NC	186.4
239	Savannah, GA	186.4
241	San Luis Obispo, CA	185.8
242	Kennewick-Pasco-Richland, WA	185.3
243	Missoula, MT	185.1

RANK	METROPOLITAN AREA	RATE
244	Albany-Schenectady-Troy, NY	184.9
245	Fort Collins-Loveland, CO	184.8
246	Youngstown, OH-PA	184.0
247	Montgomery, AL	181.7
248	Crestview-Fort Walton Beach, FL	181.5
249	Des Moines-West Des Moines, IA	180.2
250	Augusta, GA-SC	179.6
251	San Jose, CA	179.1
252	Scranton--Wilkes-Barre, PA	178.7
253	Boulder, CO	178.3
254	Akron, OH	178.0
255	Ocean City, NJ	177.7
256	Boise City-Nampa, ID	177.2
256	Reading, PA	177.2
258	Kingston, NY	175.2
259	Lafayette, IN	174.0
260	Lake Havasu City-Kingman, AZ	173.3
261	Newark-Union, NJ-PA M.D.	172.0
262	Poughkeepsie, NY	171.4
263	Rapid City, SD	170.3
264	Seattle-Bellevue-Everett, WA M.D.	169.5
265	Bend, OR	167.4
266	Bridgeport-Stamford, CT	163.9
267	Hagerstown-Martinsburg, MD-WV	163.1
268	Casper, WY	161.6
269	Sandusky, OH	161.0
270	Rochester, NY	160.9
271	Olympia, WA	160.1
272	Cleveland-Elyria-Mentor, OH	159.6
273	Raleigh-Cary, NC	158.9
274	Bismarck, ND	158.0
275	Billings, MT	157.7
276	Minneapolis-St. Paul, MN-WI	157.6
277	Hartford, CT	156.9
278	Honolulu, HI	155.5
278	Salem, OR	155.5
280	Harrisburg-Carlisle, PA	153.5
281	Springfield, OH	152.4
282	Janesville, WI	151.5
283	Medford, OR	150.2
284	Evansville, IN-KY	148.7
285	Wheeling, WV-OH	147.6
286	Pascagoula, MS	147.3
287	Fargo, ND-MN	146.0
288	Portland-Vancouver, OR-WA	145.0
289	Dayton, OH	143.8
290	Erie, PA	143.7
291	Grand Forks, ND-MN	142.1
292	La Crosse, WI-MN	142.0
293	Jackson, MS	141.3
294	Asheville, NC	141.0
295	Cincinnati-Middletown, OH-KY-IN	140.3
296	Duluth, MN-WI	140.1
297	Oxnard-Thousand Oaks, CA	139.9
298	Richmond, VA	139.7
299	Racine, WI	138.6
300	Bellingham, WA	133.7
301	Cedar Rapids, IA	133.4
302	Binghamton, NY	133.0
302	Kokomo, IN	133.0
304	Wenatchee, WA	132.9
305	Santa Ana-Anaheim, CA M.D.	131.7
306	Manchester-Nashua, NH	131.6

RANK	METROPOLITAN AREA	RATE
307	Elmira, NY	131.5
308	Monroe, MI	130.0
309	Sioux Falls, SD	129.2
310	Madison, WI	128.5
311	Bethesda-Frederick, MD M.D.	128.0
312	Fond du Lac, WI	124.5
313	Allentown, PA-NJ	122.9
314	Green Bay, WI	122.3
315	Gainesville, GA	121.3
316	Blacksburg, VA	120.8
317	Lebanon, PA	119.0
318	Cheyenne, WY	118.6
319	Charlottesville, VA	118.0
320	Longview, WA	117.7
321	Danville, VA	113.5
322	St. Cloud, MN	112.9
323	Wausau, WI	112.6
324	Burlington-South Burlington, VT	111.9
325	Holland-Grand Haven, MI	107.7
326	Lewiston, ID-WA	107.2
327	Rochester, MN	106.2
328	Bowling Green, KY	106.1
329	Mount Vernon-Anacortes, WA	102.1
330	Harrisonburg, VA	100.0
331	Gulfport-Biloxi, MS	98.9
332	Ogden-Clearfield, UT	98.8
333	Columbus, OH	98.1
334	York-Hanover, PA	97.1
335	Nassau-Suffolk, NY M.D.	94.9
336	Mankato-North Mankato, MN	94.2
337	Edison, NJ M.D.	93.9
338	Fort Wayne, IN	93.7
339	St. George, UT	93.5
339	Williamsport, PA	93.5
341	Mansfield, OH	92.0
342	State College, PA	89.6
343	Sheboygan, WI	86.3
344	Glens Falls, NY	85.9
345	Winchester, VA-WV	85.5
346	Michigan City-La Porte, IN	84.6
347	Appleton, WI	83.9
348	Eau Claire, WI	82.6
349	Lancaster, PA	77.1
350	Hattiesburg, MS	76.3
351	Corvallis, OR	75.5
352	Rockingham County, NH M.D.	73.6
353	Anderson, IN	66.1
354	Columbus, IN	63.2
355	Owensboro, KY	62.7
356	Lewiston-Auburn, ME	62.6
357	Portland, ME	60.3
358	Logan, UT-ID	51.9
359	Provo-Orem, UT	40.9
360	Bangor, ME	28.9
361	Elkhart-Goshen, IN	20.9
NA	Auburn, AL**	NA
NA	Decatur, AL**	NA
NA	Dothan, AL**	NA
NA	El Centro, CA**	NA
NA	Ithaca, NY**	NA
NA	Oklahoma City, OK**	NA
NA	Shreveport-Bossier City, LA**	NA
NA	Wilmington, NC**	NA

Source: Reported data from the F.B.I. "Crime in the United States 2009"
*Aggravated assault is an attack for the purpose of inflicting severe bodily injury.
**Not available.

23. Percent Change in Aggravated Assault Rate: 2008 to 2009
National Percent Change = 5.0% Decrease*

RANK	METROPOLITAN AREA	% CHANGE
57	Abilene, TX	6.3
38	Akron, OH	9.6
137	Albany-Schenectady-Troy, NY	(3.9)
NA	Albany, GA**	NA
271	Albuquerque, NM	(17.1)
NA	Alexandria, LA**	NA
129	Allentown, PA-NJ	(2.6)
94	Altoona, PA	1.2
43	Amarillo, TX	8.6
220	Ames, IA	(10.3)
232	Anchorage, AK	(11.1)
NA	Anderson, IN**	NA
92	Anderson, SC	1.6
266	Ann Arbor, MI	(16.5)
NA	Anniston-Oxford, AL**	NA
117	Appleton, WI	(1.3)
273	Asheville, NC	(17.4)
49	Athens-Clarke County, GA	7.3
173	Atlanta, GA	(7.4)
52	Atlantic City, NJ	6.7
NA	Auburn, AL**	NA
NA	Augusta, GA-SC**	NA
74	Austin-Round Rock, TX	3.8
60	Bakersfield, CA	6.1
126	Baltimore-Towson, MD	(2.5)
291	Bangor, ME	(27.2)
77	Barnstable Town, MA	3.4
24	Baton Rouge, LA	13.6
186	Battle Creek, MI	(8.2)
NA	Bay City, MI**	NA
146	Beaumont-Port Arthur, TX	(4.7)
178	Bellingham, WA	(7.8)
5	Bend, OR	42.0
102	Bethesda-Frederick, MD M.D.	0.2
154	Billings, MT	(5.3)
220	Binghamton, NY	(10.3)
118	Birmingham-Hoover, AL	(1.7)
79	Bismarck, ND	3.3
284	Blacksburg, VA	(24.6)
7	Bloomington, IN	36.2
105	Boise City-Nampa, ID	(0.1)
89	Boston (greater), MA-NH	2.0
79	Boston-Quincy, MA M.D.	3.3
NA	Boulder, CO**	NA
NA	Bowling Green, KY**	NA
123	Bremerton-Silverdale, WA	(2.1)
142	Bridgeport-Stamford, CT	(4.3)
281	Brownsville-Harlingen, TX	(23.0)
NA	Brunswick, GA**	NA
75	Buffalo-Niagara Falls, NY	3.7
NA	Burlington-South Burlington, VT**	NA
175	Burlington, NC	(7.6)
62	Cambridge-Newton, MA M.D.	5.9
59	Camden, NJ M.D.	6.2
217	Cape Coral-Fort Myers, FL	(10.2)
33	Cape Girardeau, MO-IL	11.0
288	Carson City, NV	(26.3)
247	Casper, WY	(13.0)
88	Cedar Rapids, IA	2.2
213	Charleston-North Charleston, SC	(10.0)
76	Charleston, WV	3.5
276	Charlotte-Gastonia, NC-SC	(19.9)
77	Charlottesville, VA	3.4
NA	Chattanooga, TN-GA**	NA
260	Cheyenne, WY	(15.2)
26	Chico, CA	13.1
NA	Cincinnati-Middletown, OH-KY-IN**	NA
NA	Clarksville, TN-KY**	NA
NA	Cleveland-Elyria-Mentor, OH**	NA
172	Cleveland, TN	(7.1)
NA	Coeur d'Alene, ID**	NA
261	College Station-Bryan, TX	(15.3)
158	Colorado Springs, CO	(5.7)
13	Columbia, MO	25.8
64	Columbia, SC	4.9
116	Columbus, GA-AL	(1.2)
151	Columbus, IN	(5.1)
252	Columbus, OH	(13.7)
49	Corpus Christi, TX	7.3
224	Corvallis, OR	(10.4)
NA	Crestview-Fort Walton Beach, FL**	NA
110	Cumberland, MD-WV	(0.6)
192	Dallas (greater), TX	(8.5)
226	Dallas-Plano-Irving, TX M.D.	(10.5)
246	Dalton, GA	(12.9)
NA	Danville, IL**	NA
296	Danville, VA	(32.8)
168	Dayton, OH	(6.6)
NA	Decatur, AL**	NA
NA	Decatur, IL**	NA
175	Deltona-Daytona Beach, FL	(7.6)
162	Denver-Aurora, CO	(5.9)
NA	Des Moines-West Des Moines, IA**	NA
NA	Detroit (greater), MI**	NA
NA	Detroit-Livonia-Dearborn, MI M.D.**	NA
NA	Dothan, AL**	NA
133	Dover, DE	(3.2)
236	Dubuque, IA	(11.8)
72	Duluth, MN-WI	3.9
160	Durham-Chapel Hill, NC	(5.8)
14	Eau Claire, WI	25.0
118	Edison, NJ M.D.	(1.7)
NA	El Centro, CA**	NA
98	El Paso, TX	0.9
NA	Elizabethtown, KY**	NA
11	Elkhart-Goshen, IN	26.7
277	Elmira, NY	(20.5)
28	Erie, PA	12.2
170	Eugene-Springfield, OR	(6.9)
NA	Evansville, IN-KY**	NA
36	Fargo, ND-MN	10.4
NA	Farmington, NM**	NA
125	Fayetteville, AR-MO	(2.4)
286	Fayetteville, NC	(24.7)
190	Flagstaff, AZ	(8.4)
NA	Flint, MI**	NA
283	Florence-Muscle Shoals, AL	(23.6)
287	Florence, SC	(25.7)
284	Fond du Lac, WI	(24.6)
184	Fort Collins-Loveland, CO	(8.1)
151	Fort Lauderdale, FL M.D.	(5.1)
139	Fort Smith, AR-OK	(4.0)
3	Fort Wayne, IN	44.2
155	Fort Worth-Arlington, TX M.D.	(5.5)
51	Fresno, CA	7.0
94	Gadsden, AL	1.2
132	Gainesville, FL	(3.0)
NA	Gainesville, GA**	NA
298	Glens Falls, NY	(35.4)
155	Goldsboro, NC	(5.5)
193	Grand Forks, ND-MN	(8.6)
269	Grand Junction, CO	(16.9)
NA	Grand Rapids-Wyoming, MI**	NA
104	Great Falls, MT	0.0
251	Greeley, CO	(13.5)
135	Green Bay, WI	(3.7)
147	Greensboro-High Point, NC	(4.9)
NA	Gulfport-Biloxi, MS**	NA
252	Hagerstown-Martinsburg, MD-WV	(13.7)
82	Harrisburg-Carlisle, PA	2.8
124	Harrisonburg, VA	(2.2)
70	Hartford, CT	4.0
NA	Hattiesburg, MS**	NA
70	Hickory, NC	4.0
197	Hinesville, GA	(8.8)
NA	Holland-Grand Haven, MI**	NA
113	Honolulu, HI	(1.1)
227	Hot Springs, AR	(10.7)
265	Houma, LA	(16.0)
107	Houston, TX	(0.3)
179	Huntsville, AL	(7.9)
53	Idaho Falls, ID	6.6
97	Indianapolis, IN	1.1
46	Iowa City, IA	7.8
NA	Ithaca, NY**	NA
258	Jacksonville, FL	(14.2)
211	Jacksonville, NC	(9.9)
NA	Jackson, MI**	NA
207	Jackson, MS	(9.4)
174	Jackson, TN	(7.5)
41	Janesville, WI	9.0
NA	Jefferson City, MO**	NA
224	Johnson City, TN	(10.4)
37	Jonesboro, AR	10.0
NA	Kalamazoo-Portage, MI**	NA
NA	Kansas City, MO-KS**	NA
34	Kennewick-Pasco-Richland, WA	10.8
267	Killeen-Temple-Fort Hood, TX	(16.6)
39	Kingsport, TN-VA	9.4
143	Kingston, NY	(4.4)
140	Knoxville, TN	(4.1)
293	Kokomo, IN	(28.0)
228	La Crosse, WI-MN	(10.8)
126	Lafayette, IN	(2.5)
45	Lafayette, LA	8.3
NA	Lake Charles, LA**	NA
62	Lake Havasu City-Kingman, AZ	5.9
121	Lakeland, FL	(1.9)
275	Lancaster, PA	(18.9)
NA	Lansing-East Lansing, MI**	NA

Note: All listings are for Metropolitan Statistical Areas (M.S.A.s) except for those ending with "M.D." Listings with "M.D." are Metropolitan Divisions which are smaller parts of eleven large M.S.A.s. See explanatory note at beginning of metropolitan area section.

Alpha Order - Metro Area (continued)

RANK	METROPOLITAN AREA	% CHANGE
144	Laredo, TX	(4.5)
184	Las Cruces, NM	(8.1)
105	Las Vegas-Paradise, NV	(0.1)
98	Lawrence, KS	0.9
NA	Lawton, OK**	NA
295	Lebanon, PA	(31.9)
210	Lewiston-Auburn, ME	(9.7)
85	Lewiston, ID-WA	2.5
NA	Lexington-Fayette, KY**	NA
91	Lima, OH	1.7
245	Lincoln, NE	(12.8)
NA	Little Rock, AR**	NA
10	Logan, UT-ID	27.2
236	Longview, TX	(11.8)
256	Longview, WA	(14.0)
197	Los Angeles County, CA M.D.	(8.8)
186	Los Angeles (greater), CA	(8.2)
NA	Louisville, KY-IN**	NA
107	Lubbock, TX	(0.3)
4	Lynchburg, VA	42.8
282	Macon, GA	(23.2)
169	Madera, CA	(6.7)
171	Madison, WI	(7.0)
NA	Manchester-Nashua, NH**	NA
203	Manhattan, KS	(9.2)
68	Mankato-North Mankato, MN	4.3
19	Mansfield, OH	18.9
20	McAllen-Edinburg-Mission, TX	18.0
144	Medford, OR	(4.5)
111	Memphis, TN-MS-AR	(0.8)
46	Merced, CA	7.8
206	Miami (greater), FL	(9.3)
241	Miami-Dade County, FL M.D.	(12.4)
40	Michigan City-La Porte, IN	9.2
181	Midland, TX	(8.0)
250	Milwaukee, WI	(13.4)
179	Minneapolis-St. Paul, MN-WI	(7.9)
268	Missoula, MT	(16.7)
1	Mobile, AL	164.5
103	Modesto, CA	0.1
NA	Monroe, MI**	NA
22	Montgomery, AL	17.1
NA	Morgantown, WV**	NA
236	Morristown, TN	(11.8)
166	Mount Vernon-Anacortes, WA	(6.4)
195	Muncie, IN	(8.7)
NA	Muskegon-Norton Shores, MI**	NA
299	Napa, CA	(63.6)
216	Naples-Marco Island, FL	(10.1)
264	Nashville-Davidson, TN	(15.9)
43	Nassau-Suffolk, NY M.D.	8.6
NA	New Haven-Milford, CT**	NA
231	New Orleans, LA	(10.9)
72	New York (greater), NY-NJ-PA	3.9
66	New York-W. Plains NY-NJ M.D.	4.7
131	Newark-Union, NJ-PA M.D.	(2.9)
NA	Niles-Benton Harbor, MI**	NA
NA	North Port-Bradenton-Sarasota, FL**	NA
23	Norwich-New London, CT	16.4
228	Oakland-Fremont, CA M.D.	(10.8)
190	Ocala, FL	(8.4)
270	Ocean City, NJ	(17.0)
177	Odessa, TX	(7.7)

RANK	METROPOLITAN AREA	% CHANGE
17	Ogden-Clearfield, UT	20.9
NA	Oklahoma City, OK**	NA
195	Olympia, WA	(8.7)
189	Omaha-Council Bluffs, NE-IA	(8.3)
234	Orlando, FL	(11.5)
12	Oshkosh-Neenah, WI	26.5
NA	Owensboro, KY**	NA
100	Oxnard-Thousand Oaks, CA	0.4
109	Palm Bay-Melbourne, FL	(0.5)
54	Palm Coast, FL	6.5
201	Panama City-Lynn Haven, FL	(9.1)
15	Pascagoula, MS	24.9
160	Peabody, MA M.D.	(5.8)
113	Pensacola, FL	(1.1)
203	Philadelphia (greater) PA-NJ-MD-DE	(9.2)
244	Philadelphia, PA M.D.	(12.6)
220	Phoenix-Mesa-Scottsdale, AZ	(10.3)
147	Pine Bluff, AR	(4.9)
165	Pittsburgh, PA	(6.2)
31	Pittsfield, MA	11.4
220	Pocatello, ID	(10.3)
257	Port St. Lucie, FL	(14.1)
235	Portland-Vancouver, OR-WA	(11.7)
101	Portland, ME	0.3
158	Poughkeepsie, NY	(5.7)
193	Prescott, AZ	(8.6)
89	Providence-New Bedford, RI-MA	2.0
279	Provo-Orem, UT	(21.8)
NA	Pueblo, CO**	NA
213	Punta Gorda, FL	(10.0)
118	Racine, WI	(1.7)
NA	Raleigh-Cary, NC**	NA
294	Rapid City, SD	(29.8)
82	Reading, PA	2.8
35	Redding, CA	10.5
86	Reno-Sparks, NV	2.4
272	Richmond, VA	(17.2)
167	Riverside-San Bernardino, CA	(6.5)
203	Roanoke, VA	(9.2)
NA	Rochester, MN**	NA
157	Rochester, NY	(5.6)
240	Rockingham County, NH M.D.	(12.3)
NA	Rocky Mount, NC**	NA
NA	Rome, GA**	NA
126	Sacramento, CA	(2.5)
NA	Saginaw, MI**	NA
130	Salem, OR	(2.7)
86	Salinas, CA	2.4
263	Salisbury, MD	(15.8)
93	Salt Lake City, UT	1.3
69	San Angelo, TX	4.2
292	San Antonio, TX	(27.4)
113	San Diego, CA	(1.1)
200	San Francisco (greater), CA	(9.0)
151	San Francisco-S. Mateo, CA M.D.	(5.1)
199	San Jose, CA	(8.9)
241	San Luis Obispo, CA	(12.4)
290	Sandusky, OH	(27.0)
135	Santa Ana-Anaheim, CA M.D.	(3.7)
16	Santa Barbara-Santa Maria, CA	23.4
94	Santa Cruz-Watsonville, CA	1.2
29	Santa Fe, NM	11.6
233	Santa Rosa-Petaluma, CA	(11.4)

RANK	METROPOLITAN AREA	% CHANGE
181	Savannah, GA	(8.0)
112	Scranton--Wilkes-Barre, PA	(0.9)
NA	Seattle-Bellevue-Everett, WA M.D.**	NA
NA	Seattle-Tacoma-Bellevue, WA**	NA
64	Sebastian-Vero Beach, FL	4.9
8	Sheboygan, WI	35.5
141	Sherman-Denison, TX	(4.2)
NA	Shreveport-Bossier City, LA**	NA
25	Sioux City, IA-NE-SD	13.5
280	Sioux Falls, SD	(22.7)
NA	South Bend-Mishawaka, IN-MI**	NA
137	Spartanburg, SC	(3.9)
207	Spokane, WA	(9.4)
164	Springfield, MA	(6.0)
NA	Springfield, MO**	NA
6	Springfield, OH	41.2
2	State College, PA	48.3
201	Stockton, CA	(9.1)
228	St. Cloud, MN	(10.8)
297	St. George, UT	(34.5)
21	St. Joseph, MO-KS	17.4
259	St. Louis, MO-IL	(14.5)
NA	Sumter, SC**	NA
122	Syracuse, NY	(2.0)
NA	Tacoma, WA M.D.**	NA
217	Tallahassee, FL	(10.2)
211	Tampa-St Petersburg, FL	(9.9)
289	Texarkana, TX-Texarkana, AR	(26.5)
217	Toledo, OH	(10.2)
42	Topeka, KS	8.7
9	Trenton-Ewing, NJ	34.1
262	Tucson, AZ	(15.5)
249	Tulsa, OK	(13.3)
147	Tuscaloosa, AL	(4.9)
247	Tyler, TX	(13.0)
134	Utica-Rome, NY	(3.5)
32	Valdosta, GA	11.3
252	Vallejo-Fairfield, CA	(13.7)
61	Victoria, TX	6.0
274	Vineland, NJ	(17.8)
147	Visalia-Porterville, CA	(4.9)
213	Waco, TX	(10.0)
55	Warner Robins, GA	6.4
NA	Warren-Farmington Hills, MI M.D.**	NA
186	Washington (greater) DC-VA-MD-WV	(8.2)
209	Washington, DC-VA-MD-WV M.D.	(9.5)
18	Waterloo-Cedar Falls, IA	20.8
NA	Wausau, WI**	NA
29	Wenatchee, WA	11.6
181	West Palm Beach, FL M.D.	(8.0)
27	Wheeling, WV-OH	12.3
84	Wichita Falls, TX	2.7
55	Wichita, KS	6.4
48	Williamsport, PA	7.7
162	Wilmington, DE-MD-NJ M.D.	(5.9)
NA	Wilmington, NC**	NA
278	Winchester, VA-WV	(21.3)
255	Winston-Salem, NC	(13.9)
57	Worcester, MA	6.3
239	York-Hanover, PA	(12.0)
81	Youngstown, OH-PA	3.1
241	Yuba City, CA	(12.4)
66	Yuma, AZ	4.7

Source: CQ Press using reported data from the F.B.I. "Crime in the United States 2009"
*Aggravated assault is an attack for the purpose of inflicting severe bodily injury.
**Not available.

23. Percent Change in Aggravated Assault Rate: 2008 to 2009 (continued)
National Percent Change = 5.0% Decrease*

RANK	METROPOLITAN AREA	% CHANGE	RANK	METROPOLITAN AREA	% CHANGE	RANK	METROPOLITAN AREA	% CHANGE
1	Mobile, AL	164.5	61	Victoria, TX	6.0	121	Lakeland, FL	(1.9)
2	State College, PA	48.3	62	Cambridge-Newton, MA M.D.	5.9	122	Syracuse, NY	(2.0)
3	Fort Wayne, IN	44.2	62	Lake Havasu City-Kingman, AZ	5.9	123	Bremerton-Silverdale, WA	(2.1)
4	Lynchburg, VA	42.8	64	Columbia, SC	4.9	124	Harrisonburg, VA	(2.2)
5	Bend, OR	42.0	64	Sebastian-Vero Beach, FL	4.9	125	Fayetteville, AR-MO	(2.4)
6	Springfield, OH	41.2	66	New York-W. Plains NY-NJ M.D.	4.7	126	Baltimore-Towson, MD	(2.5)
7	Bloomington, IN	36.2	66	Yuma, AZ	4.7	126	Lafayette, IN	(2.5)
8	Sheboygan, WI	35.5	68	Mankato-North Mankato, MN	4.3	126	Sacramento, CA	(2.5)
9	Trenton-Ewing, NJ	34.1	69	San Angelo, TX	4.2	129	Allentown, PA-NJ	(2.6)
10	Logan, UT-ID	27.2	70	Hartford, CT	4.0	130	Salem, OR	(2.7)
11	Elkhart-Goshen, IN	26.7	70	Hickory, NC	4.0	131	Newark-Union, NJ-PA M.D.	(2.9)
12	Oshkosh-Neenah, WI	26.5	72	Duluth, MN-WI	3.9	132	Gainesville, FL	(3.0)
13	Columbia, MO	25.8	72	New York (greater), NY-NJ-PA	3.9	133	Dover, DE	(3.2)
14	Eau Claire, WI	25.0	74	Austin-Round Rock, TX	3.8	134	Utica-Rome, NY	(3.5)
15	Pascagoula, MS	24.9	75	Buffalo-Niagara Falls, NY	3.7	135	Green Bay, WI	(3.7)
16	Santa Barbara-Santa Maria, CA	23.4	76	Charleston, WV	3.5	135	Santa Ana-Anaheim, CA M.D.	(3.7)
17	Ogden-Clearfield, UT	20.9	77	Barnstable Town, MA	3.4	137	Albany-Schenectady-Troy, NY	(3.9)
18	Waterloo-Cedar Falls, IA	20.8	77	Charlottesville, VA	3.4	137	Spartanburg, SC	(3.9)
19	Mansfield, OH	18.9	79	Bismarck, ND	3.3	139	Fort Smith, AR-OK	(4.0)
20	McAllen-Edinburg-Mission, TX	18.0	79	Boston-Quincy, MA M.D.	3.3	140	Knoxville, TN	(4.1)
21	St. Joseph, MO-KS	17.4	81	Youngstown, OH-PA	3.1	141	Sherman-Denison, TX	(4.2)
22	Montgomery, AL	17.1	82	Harrisburg-Carlisle, PA	2.8	142	Bridgeport-Stamford, CT	(4.3)
23	Norwich-New London, CT	16.4	82	Reading, PA	2.8	143	Kingston, NY	(4.4)
24	Baton Rouge, LA	13.6	84	Wichita Falls, TX	2.7	144	Laredo, TX	(4.5)
25	Sioux City, IA-NE-SD	13.5	85	Lewiston, ID-WA	2.5	144	Medford, OR	(4.5)
26	Chico, CA	13.1	86	Reno-Sparks, NV	2.4	146	Beaumont-Port Arthur, TX	(4.7)
27	Wheeling, WV-OH	12.3	86	Salinas, CA	2.4	147	Greensboro-High Point, NC	(4.9)
28	Erie, PA	12.2	88	Cedar Rapids, IA	2.2	147	Pine Bluff, AR	(4.9)
29	Santa Fe, NM	11.6	89	Boston (greater), MA-NH	2.0	147	Tuscaloosa, AL	(4.9)
29	Wenatchee, WA	11.6	89	Providence-New Bedford, RI-MA	2.0	147	Visalia-Porterville, CA	(4.9)
31	Pittsfield, MA	11.4	91	Lima, OH	1.7	151	Columbus, IN	(5.1)
32	Valdosta, GA	11.3	92	Anderson, SC	1.6	151	Fort Lauderdale, FL M.D.	(5.1)
33	Cape Girardeau, MO-IL	11.0	93	Salt Lake City, UT	1.3	151	San Francisco-S. Mateo, CA M.D.	(5.1)
34	Kennewick-Pasco-Richland, WA	10.8	94	Altoona, PA	1.2	154	Billings, MT	(5.3)
35	Redding, CA	10.5	94	Gadsden, AL	1.2	155	Fort Worth-Arlington, TX M.D.	(5.5)
36	Fargo, ND-MN	10.4	94	Santa Cruz-Watsonville, CA	1.2	155	Goldsboro, NC	(5.5)
37	Jonesboro, AR	10.0	97	Indianapolis, IN	1.1	157	Rochester, NY	(5.6)
38	Akron, OH	9.6	98	El Paso, TX	0.9	158	Colorado Springs, CO	(5.7)
39	Kingsport, TN-VA	9.4	98	Lawrence, KS	0.9	158	Poughkeepsie, NY	(5.7)
40	Michigan City-La Porte, IN	9.2	100	Oxnard-Thousand Oaks, CA	0.4	160	Durham-Chapel Hill, NC	(5.8)
41	Janesville, WI	9.0	101	Portland, ME	0.3	160	Peabody, MA M.D.	(5.8)
42	Topeka, KS	8.7	102	Bethesda-Frederick, MD M.D.	0.2	162	Denver-Aurora, CO	(5.9)
43	Amarillo, TX	8.6	103	Modesto, CA	0.1	162	Wilmington, DE-MD-NJ M.D.	(5.9)
43	Nassau-Suffolk, NY M.D.	8.6	104	Great Falls, MT	0.0	164	Springfield, MA	(6.0)
45	Lafayette, LA	8.3	105	Boise City-Nampa, ID	(0.1)	165	Pittsburgh, PA	(6.2)
46	Iowa City, IA	7.8	105	Las Vegas-Paradise, NV	(0.1)	166	Mount Vernon-Anacortes, WA	(6.4)
46	Merced, CA	7.8	107	Houston, TX	(0.3)	167	Riverside-San Bernardino, CA	(6.5)
48	Williamsport, PA	7.7	107	Lubbock, TX	(0.3)	168	Dayton, OH	(6.6)
49	Athens-Clarke County, GA	7.3	109	Palm Bay-Melbourne, FL	(0.5)	169	Madera, CA	(6.7)
49	Corpus Christi, TX	7.3	110	Cumberland, MD-WV	(0.6)	170	Eugene-Springfield, OR	(6.9)
51	Fresno, CA	7.0	111	Memphis, TN-MS-AR	(0.8)	171	Madison, WI	(7.0)
52	Atlantic City, NJ	6.7	112	Scranton--Wilkes-Barre, PA	(0.9)	172	Cleveland, TN	(7.1)
53	Idaho Falls, ID	6.6	113	Honolulu, HI	(1.1)	173	Atlanta, GA	(7.4)
54	Palm Coast, FL	6.5	113	Pensacola, FL	(1.1)	174	Jackson, TN	(7.5)
55	Warner Robins, GA	6.4	113	San Diego, CA	(1.1)	175	Burlington, NC	(7.6)
55	Wichita, KS	6.4	116	Columbus, GA-AL	(1.2)	175	Deltona-Daytona Beach, FL	(7.6)
57	Abilene, TX	6.3	117	Appleton, WI	(1.3)	177	Odessa, TX	(7.7)
57	Worcester, MA	6.3	118	Birmingham-Hoover, AL	(1.7)	178	Bellingham, WA	(7.8)
59	Camden, NJ M.D.	6.2	118	Edison, NJ M.D.	(1.7)	179	Huntsville, AL	(7.9)
60	Bakersfield, CA	6.1	118	Racine, WI	(1.7)	179	Minneapolis-St. Paul, MN-WI	(7.9)

Note: All listings are for Metropolitan Statistical Areas (M.S.A.s) except for those ending with "M.D." Listings with "M.D." are Metropolitan Divisions which are smaller parts of eleven large M.S.A.s. See explanatory note at beginning of metropolitan area section.

Rank Order - Metro Area (continued)

RANK	METROPOLITAN AREA	% CHANGE
181	Midland, TX	(8.0)
181	Savannah, GA	(8.0)
181	West Palm Beach, FL M.D.	(8.0)
184	Fort Collins-Loveland, CO	(8.1)
184	Las Cruces, NM	(8.1)
186	Battle Creek, MI	(8.2)
186	Los Angeles (greater), CA	(8.2)
186	Washington (greater) DC-VA-MD-WV	(8.2)
189	Omaha-Council Bluffs, NE-IA	(8.3)
190	Flagstaff, AZ	(8.4)
190	Ocala, FL	(8.4)
192	Dallas (greater), TX	(8.5)
193	Grand Forks, ND-MN	(8.6)
193	Prescott, AZ	(8.6)
195	Muncie, IN	(8.7)
195	Olympia, WA	(8.7)
197	Hinesville, GA	(8.8)
197	Los Angeles County, CA M.D.	(8.8)
199	San Jose, CA	(8.9)
200	San Francisco (greater), CA	(9.0)
201	Panama City-Lynn Haven, FL	(9.1)
201	Stockton, CA	(9.1)
203	Manhattan, KS	(9.2)
203	Philadelphia (greater) PA-NJ-MD-DE	(9.2)
203	Roanoke, VA	(9.2)
206	Miami (greater), FL	(9.3)
207	Jackson, MS	(9.4)
207	Spokane, WA	(9.4)
209	Washington, DC-VA-MD-WV M.D.	(9.5)
210	Lewiston-Auburn, ME	(9.7)
211	Jacksonville, NC	(9.9)
211	Tampa-St Petersburg, FL	(9.9)
213	Charleston-North Charleston, SC	(10.0)
213	Punta Gorda, FL	(10.0)
213	Waco, TX	(10.0)
216	Naples-Marco Island, FL	(10.1)
217	Cape Coral-Fort Myers, FL	(10.2)
217	Tallahassee, FL	(10.2)
217	Toledo, OH	(10.2)
220	Ames, IA	(10.3)
220	Binghamton, NY	(10.3)
220	Phoenix-Mesa-Scottsdale, AZ	(10.3)
220	Pocatello, ID	(10.3)
224	Corvallis, OR	(10.4)
224	Johnson City, TN	(10.4)
226	Dallas-Plano-Irving, TX M.D.	(10.5)
227	Hot Springs, AR	(10.7)
228	La Crosse, WI-MN	(10.8)
228	Oakland-Fremont, CA M.D.	(10.8)
228	St. Cloud, MN	(10.8)
231	New Orleans, LA	(10.9)
232	Anchorage, AK	(11.1)
233	Santa Rosa-Petaluma, CA	(11.4)
234	Orlando, FL	(11.5)
235	Portland-Vancouver, OR-WA	(11.7)
236	Dubuque, IA	(11.8)
236	Longview, TX	(11.8)
236	Morristown, TN	(11.8)
239	York-Hanover, PA	(12.0)
240	Rockingham County, NH M.D.	(12.3)
241	Miami-Dade County, FL M.D.	(12.4)
241	San Luis Obispo, CA	(12.4)
241	Yuba City, CA	(12.4)
244	Philadelphia, PA M.D.	(12.6)
245	Lincoln, NE	(12.8)
246	Dalton, GA	(12.9)
247	Casper, WY	(13.0)
247	Tyler, TX	(13.0)
249	Tulsa, OK	(13.3)
250	Milwaukee, WI	(13.4)
251	Greeley, CO	(13.5)
252	Columbus, OH	(13.7)
252	Hagerstown-Martinsburg, MD-WV	(13.7)
252	Vallejo-Fairfield, CA	(13.7)
255	Winston-Salem, NC	(13.9)
256	Longview, WA	(14.0)
257	Port St. Lucie, FL	(14.1)
258	Jacksonville, FL	(14.2)
259	St. Louis, MO-IL	(14.5)
260	Cheyenne, WY	(15.2)
261	College Station-Bryan, TX	(15.3)
262	Tucson, AZ	(15.5)
263	Salisbury, MD	(15.8)
264	Nashville-Davidson, TN	(15.9)
265	Houma, LA	(16.0)
266	Ann Arbor, MI	(16.5)
267	Killeen-Temple-Fort Hood, TX	(16.6)
268	Missoula, MT	(16.7)
269	Grand Junction, CO	(16.9)
270	Ocean City, NJ	(17.0)
271	Albuquerque, NM	(17.1)
272	Richmond, VA	(17.2)
273	Asheville, NC	(17.4)
274	Vineland, NJ	(17.8)
275	Lancaster, PA	(18.9)
276	Charlotte-Gastonia, NC-SC	(19.9)
277	Elmira, NY	(20.5)
278	Winchester, VA-WV	(21.3)
279	Provo-Orem, UT	(21.8)
280	Sioux Falls, SD	(22.7)
281	Brownsville-Harlingen, TX	(23.0)
282	Macon, GA	(23.2)
283	Florence-Muscle Shoals, AL	(23.6)
284	Blacksburg, VA	(24.6)
284	Fond du Lac, WI	(24.6)
286	Fayetteville, NC	(24.7)
287	Florence, SC	(25.7)
288	Carson City, NV	(26.3)
289	Texarkana, TX-Texarkana, AR	(26.5)
290	Sandusky, OH	(27.0)
291	Bangor, ME	(27.2)
292	San Antonio, TX	(27.4)
293	Kokomo, IN	(28.0)
294	Rapid City, SD	(29.8)
295	Lebanon, PA	(31.9)
296	Danville, VA	(32.8)
297	St. George, UT	(34.5)
298	Glens Falls, NY	(35.4)
299	Napa, CA	(63.6)
NA	Albany, GA**	NA
NA	Alexandria, LA**	NA
NA	Anderson, IN**	NA
NA	Anniston-Oxford, AL**	NA
NA	Auburn, AL**	NA
NA	Augusta, GA-SC**	NA
NA	Bay City, MI**	NA
NA	Boulder, CO**	NA
NA	Bowling Green, KY**	NA
NA	Brunswick, GA**	NA
NA	Burlington-South Burlington, VT**	NA
NA	Chattanooga, TN-GA**	NA
NA	Cincinnati-Middletown, OH-KY-IN**	NA
NA	Clarksville, TN-KY**	NA
NA	Cleveland-Elyria-Mentor, OH**	NA
NA	Coeur d'Alene, ID**	NA
NA	Crestview-Fort Walton Beach, FL**	NA
NA	Danville, IL**	NA
NA	Decatur, AL**	NA
NA	Decatur, IL**	NA
NA	Des Moines-West Des Moines, IA**	NA
NA	Detroit (greater), MI**	NA
NA	Detroit-Livonia-Dearborn, MI M.D.**	NA
NA	Dothan, AL**	NA
NA	El Centro, CA**	NA
NA	Elizabethtown, KY**	NA
NA	Evansville, IN-KY**	NA
NA	Farmington, NM**	NA
NA	Flint, MI**	NA
NA	Gainesville, GA**	NA
NA	Grand Rapids-Wyoming, MI**	NA
NA	Gulfport-Biloxi, MS**	NA
NA	Hattiesburg, MS**	NA
NA	Holland-Grand Haven, MI**	NA
NA	Ithaca, NY**	NA
NA	Jackson, MI**	NA
NA	Jefferson City, MO**	NA
NA	Kalamazoo-Portage, MI**	NA
NA	Kansas City, MO-KS**	NA
NA	Lake Charles, LA**	NA
NA	Lansing-East Lansing, MI**	NA
NA	Lawton, OK**	NA
NA	Lexington-Fayette, KY**	NA
NA	Little Rock, AR**	NA
NA	Louisville, KY-IN**	NA
NA	Manchester-Nashua, NH**	NA
NA	Monroe, MI**	NA
NA	Morgantown, WV**	NA
NA	Muskegon-Norton Shores, MI**	NA
NA	New Haven-Milford, CT**	NA
NA	Niles-Benton Harbor, MI**	NA
NA	North Port-Bradenton-Sarasota, FL**	NA
NA	Oklahoma City, OK**	NA
NA	Owensboro, KY**	NA
NA	Pueblo, CO**	NA
NA	Raleigh-Cary, NC**	NA
NA	Rochester, MN**	NA
NA	Rocky Mount, NC**	NA
NA	Rome, GA**	NA
NA	Saginaw, MI**	NA
NA	Seattle-Bellevue-Everett, WA M.D.**	NA
NA	Seattle-Tacoma-Bellevue, WA**	NA
NA	Shreveport-Bossier City, LA**	NA
NA	South Bend-Mishawaka, IN-MI**	NA
NA	Springfield, MO**	NA
NA	Sumter, SC**	NA
NA	Tacoma, WA M.D.**	NA
NA	Warren-Farmington Hills, MI M.D.**	NA
NA	Wausau, WI**	NA
NA	Wilmington, NC**	NA

Source: CQ Press using reported data from the F.B.I. "Crime in the United States 2009"
*Aggravated assault is an attack for the purpose of inflicting severe bodily injury.
**Not available.

24. Percent Change in Aggravated Assault Rate: 2005 to 2009
National Percent Change = 9.6% Decrease*

RANK	METROPOLITAN AREA	% CHANGE
54	Abilene, TX	16.0
9	Akron, OH	83.3
224	Albany-Schenectady-Troy, NY	(19.3)
5	Albany, GA	90.7
258	Albuquerque, NM	(26.8)
286	Alexandria, LA	(38.8)
256	Allentown, PA-NJ	(26.6)
30	Altoona, PA	30.4
116	Amarillo, TX	(0.9)
16	Ames, IA	57.8
77	Anchorage, AK	8.0
180	Anderson, IN	(12.3)
84	Anderson, SC	6.2
126	Ann Arbor, MI	(3.7)
NA	Anniston-Oxford, AL**	NA
105	Appleton, WI	1.0
144	Asheville, NC	(6.9)
17	Athens-Clarke County, GA	55.6
177	Atlanta, GA	(11.5)
96	Atlantic City, NJ	2.6
NA	Auburn, AL**	NA
129	Augusta, GA-SC	(4.5)
76	Austin-Round Rock, TX	8.3
71	Bakersfield, CA	11.5
204	Baltimore-Towson, MD	(16.4)
292	Bangor, ME	(42.7)
80	Barnstable Town, MA	7.7
132	Baton Rouge, LA	(4.7)
208	Battle Creek, MI	(16.7)
NA	Bay City, MI**	NA
159	Beaumont-Port Arthur, TX	(9.5)
139	Bellingham, WA	(6.1)
64	Bend, OR	14.0
114	Bethesda-Frederick, MD M.D.	0.2
85	Billings, MT	6.0
42	Binghamton, NY	22.9
NA	Birmingham-Hoover, AL**	NA
4	Bismarck, ND	99.0
132	Blacksburg, VA	(4.7)
12	Bloomington, IN	75.2
NA	Boise City-Nampa, ID**	NA
91	Boston (greater), MA-NH	4.1
116	Boston-Quincy, MA M.D.	(0.9)
NA	Boulder, CO**	NA
NA	Bowling Green, KY**	NA
56	Bremerton-Silverdale, WA	15.8
75	Bridgeport-Stamford, CT	8.8
281	Brownsville-Harlingen, TX	(36.6)
87	Brunswick, GA	5.8
93	Buffalo-Niagara Falls, NY	2.9
NA	Burlington-South Burlington, VT**	NA
233	Burlington, NC	(20.4)
32	Cambridge-Newton, MA M.D.	29.7
112	Camden, NJ M.D.	0.7
253	Cape Coral-Fort Myers, FL	(25.4)
NA	Cape Girardeau, MO-IL**	NA
285	Carson City, NV	(38.2)
219	Casper, WY	(18.8)
187	Cedar Rapids, IA	(13.1)
265	Charleston-North Charleston, SC	(28.8)
73	Charleston, WV	11.1
279	Charlotte-Gastonia, NC-SC	(35.6)
282	Charlottesville, VA	(37.1)
113	Chattanooga, TN-GA	0.6
94	Cheyenne, WY	2.8
28	Chico, CA	31.2
NA	Cincinnati-Middletown, OH-KY-IN**	NA
NA	Clarksville, TN-KY**	NA
NA	Cleveland-Elyria-Mentor, OH**	NA
NA	Cleveland, TN**	NA
104	Coeur d'Alene, ID	1.3
229	College Station-Bryan, TX	(20.0)
192	Colorado Springs, CO	(13.9)
183	Columbia, MO	(12.8)
81	Columbia, SC	7.3
61	Columbus, GA-AL	14.7
289	Columbus, IN	(39.8)
248	Columbus, OH	(24.6)
52	Corpus Christi, TX	17.5
188	Corvallis, OR	(13.3)
NA	Crestview-Fort Walton Beach, FL**	NA
23	Cumberland, MD-WV	36.1
271	Dallas (greater), TX	(31.6)
290	Dallas-Plano-Irving, TX M.D.	(42.1)
NA	Dalton, GA**	NA
NA	Danville, IL**	NA
270	Danville, VA	(30.8)
40	Dayton, OH	23.2
NA	Decatur, AL**	NA
NA	Decatur, IL**	NA
NA	Deltona-Daytona Beach, FL**	NA
239	Denver-Aurora, CO	(22.5)
NA	Des Moines-West Des Moines, IA**	NA
172	Detroit (greater), MI	(11.0)
NA	Detroit-Livonia-Dearborn, MI M.D.**	NA
NA	Dothan, AL**	NA
128	Dover, DE	(4.4)
139	Dubuque, IA	(6.1)
NA	Duluth, MN-WI**	NA
201	Durham-Chapel Hill, NC	(15.3)
186	Eau Claire, WI	(13.0)
142	Edison, NJ M.D.	(6.6)
NA	El Centro, CA**	NA
58	El Paso, TX	15.4
NA	Elizabethtown, KY**	NA
299	Elkhart-Goshen, IN	(60.9)
161	Elmira, NY	(9.6)
72	Erie, PA	11.4
43	Eugene-Springfield, OR	21.9
NA	Evansville, IN-KY**	NA
3	Fargo, ND-MN	109.5
NA	Farmington, NM**	NA
78	Fayetteville, AR-MO	7.9
174	Fayetteville, NC	(11.2)
297	Flagstaff, AZ	(50.9)
NA	Flint, MI**	NA
NA	Florence-Muscle Shoals, AL**	NA
291	Florence, SC	(42.5)
51	Fond du Lac, WI	17.6
39	Fort Collins-Loveland, CO	24.4
179	Fort Lauderdale, FL M.D.	(12.1)
250	Fort Smith, AR-OK	(25.2)
99	Fort Wayne, IN	2.1
147	Fort Worth-Arlington, TX M.D.	(7.4)
237	Fresno, CA	(21.8)
136	Gadsden, AL	(5.2)
183	Gainesville, FL	(12.8)
266	Gainesville, GA	(29.6)
NA	Glens Falls, NY**	NA
102	Goldsboro, NC	1.7
22	Grand Forks, ND-MN	37.0
153	Grand Junction, CO	(8.6)
NA	Grand Rapids-Wyoming, MI**	NA
101	Great Falls, MT	1.8
292	Greeley, CO	(42.7)
192	Green Bay, WI	(13.9)
138	Greensboro-High Point, NC	(6.0)
NA	Gulfport-Biloxi, MS**	NA
263	Hagerstown-Martinsburg, MD-WV	(27.9)
145	Harrisburg-Carlisle, PA	(7.3)
13	Harrisonburg, VA	66.1
70	Hartford, CT	11.6
NA	Hattiesburg, MS**	NA
135	Hickory, NC	(5.0)
64	Hinesville, GA	14.0
NA	Holland-Grand Haven, MI**	NA
129	Honolulu, HI	(4.5)
167	Hot Springs, AR	(10.3)
217	Houma, LA	(18.3)
110	Houston, TX	0.8
178	Huntsville, AL	(12.0)
21	Idaho Falls, ID	49.9
63	Indianapolis, IN	14.2
35	Iowa City, IA	27.3
NA	Ithaca, NY**	NA
166	Jacksonville, FL	(10.2)
NA	Jacksonville, NC**	NA
NA	Jackson, MI**	NA
175	Jackson, MS	(11.3)
274	Jackson, TN	(32.8)
152	Janesville, WI	(8.0)
164	Jefferson City, MO	(9.8)
246	Johnson City, TN	(23.8)
288	Jonesboro, AR	(39.5)
NA	Kalamazoo-Portage, MI**	NA
196	Kansas City, MO-KS	(14.5)
69	Kennewick-Pasco-Richland, WA	11.8
145	Killeen-Temple-Fort Hood, TX	(7.3)
198	Kingsport, TN-VA	(15.0)
220	Kingston, NY	(18.9)
124	Knoxville, TN	(3.5)
240	Kokomo, IN	(22.6)
25	La Crosse, WI-MN	35.0
24	Lafayette, IN	35.1
45	Lafayette, LA	20.7
26	Lake Charles, LA	33.0
NA	Lake Havasu City-Kingman, AZ**	NA
148	Lakeland, FL	(7.5)
185	Lancaster, PA	(12.9)
NA	Lansing-East Lansing, MI**	NA

Note: All listings are for Metropolitan Statistical Areas (M.S.A.s) except for those ending with "M.D." Listings with "M.D." are Metropolitan Divisions which are smaller parts of eleven large M.S.A.s. See explanatory note at beginning of metropolitan area section.

Alpha Order - Metro Area (continued)

RANK	METROPOLITAN AREA	% CHANGE
50	Laredo, TX	17.8
60	Las Cruces, NM	15.0
37	Las Vegas-Paradise, NV	24.5
48	Lawrence, KS	18.9
NA	Lawton, OK**	NA
296	Lebanon, PA	(49.0)
37	Lewiston-Auburn, ME	24.5
82	Lewiston, ID-WA	7.0
NA	Lexington-Fayette, KY**	NA
55	Lima, OH	15.9
242	Lincoln, NE	(22.9)
NA	Little Rock, AR**	NA
11	Logan, UT-ID	78.4
251	Longview, TX	(25.3)
284	Longview, WA	(37.6)
243	Los Angeles County, CA M.D.	(23.2)
245	Los Angeles (greater), CA	(23.6)
NA	Louisville, KY-IN**	NA
142	Lubbock, TX	(6.6)
20	Lynchburg, VA	51.7
229	Macon, GA	(20.0)
233	Madera, CA	(20.4)
99	Madison, WI	2.1
10	Manchester-Nashua, NH	83.0
NA	Manhattan, KS**	NA
NA	Mankato-North Mankato, MN**	NA
6	Mansfield, OH	90.1
222	McAllen-Edinburg-Mission, TX	(19.1)
278	Medford, OR	(34.2)
119	Memphis, TN-MS-AR	(1.1)
82	Merced, CA	7.0
221	Miami (greater), FL	(19.0)
251	Miami-Dade County, FL M.D.	(25.3)
148	Michigan City-La Porte, IN	(7.5)
127	Midland, TX	(3.9)
57	Milwaukee, WI	15.5
NA	Minneapolis-St. Paul, MN-WI**	NA
209	Missoula, MT	(17.0)
1	Mobile, AL	121.3
235	Modesto, CA	(20.5)
NA	Monroe, MI**	NA
257	Montgomery, AL	(26.7)
18	Morgantown, WV	54.8
247	Morristown, TN	(24.1)
154	Mount Vernon-Anacortes, WA	(8.8)
34	Muncie, IN	28.0
NA	Muskegon-Norton Shores, MI**	NA
276	Napa, CA	(33.5)
259	Naples-Marco Island, FL	(27.0)
260	Nashville-Davidson, TN	(27.5)
181	Nassau-Suffolk, NY M.D.	(12.6)
NA	New Haven-Milford, CT**	NA
NA	New Orleans, LA**	NA
161	New York (greater), NY-NJ-PA	(9.6)
157	New York-W. Plains NY-NJ M.D.	(9.1)
195	Newark-Union, NJ-PA M.D.	(14.0)
NA	Niles-Benton Harbor, MI**	NA
NA	North Port-Bradenton-Sarasota, FL**	NA
19	Norwich-New London, CT	53.4
86	Oakland-Fremont, CA M.D.	5.9
238	Ocala, FL	(22.1)
215	Ocean City, NJ	(17.7)
67	Odessa, TX	12.6

RANK	METROPOLITAN AREA	% CHANGE
107	Ogden-Clearfield, UT	0.9
NA	Oklahoma City, OK**	NA
197	Olympia, WA	(14.8)
226	Omaha-Council Bluffs, NE-IA	(19.5)
204	Orlando, FL	(16.4)
47	Oshkosh-Neenah, WI	19.9
NA	Owensboro, KY**	NA
129	Oxnard-Thousand Oaks, CA	(4.5)
78	Palm Bay-Melbourne, FL	7.9
NA	Palm Coast, FL**	NA
175	Panama City-Lynn Haven, FL	(11.3)
31	Pascagoula, MS	30.1
NA	Peabody, MA M.D.**	NA
115	Pensacola, FL	(0.5)
159	Philadelphia (greater) PA-NJ-MD-DE	(9.5)
191	Philadelphia, PA M.D.	(13.8)
261	Phoenix-Mesa-Scottsdale, AZ	(27.6)
87	Pine Bluff, AR	5.8
121	Pittsburgh, PA	(2.5)
97	Pittsfield, MA	2.2
236	Pocatello, ID	(20.7)
264	Port St. Lucie, FL	(28.7)
244	Portland-Vancouver, OR-WA	(23.5)
213	Portland, ME	(17.6)
90	Poughkeepsie, NY	4.3
161	Prescott, AZ	(9.6)
NA	Providence-New Bedford, RI-MA**	NA
283	Provo-Orem, UT	(37.3)
33	Pueblo, CO	28.8
275	Punta Gorda, FL	(33.0)
2	Racine, WI	118.3
217	Raleigh-Cary, NC	(18.3)
171	Rapid City, SD	(10.9)
203	Reading, PA	(16.2)
15	Redding, CA	61.7
102	Reno-Sparks, NV	1.7
267	Richmond, VA	(29.7)
206	Riverside-San Bernardino, CA	(16.5)
272	Roanoke, VA	(32.4)
95	Rochester, MN	2.7
49	Rochester, NY	18.2
58	Rockingham County, NH M.D.	15.4
29	Rocky Mount, NC	31.1
36	Rome, GA	27.0
200	Sacramento, CA	(15.2)
NA	Saginaw, MI**	NA
273	Salem, OR	(32.6)
66	Salinas, CA	13.8
181	Salisbury, MD	(12.6)
89	Salt Lake City, UT	4.4
169	San Angelo, TX	(10.8)
223	San Antonio, TX	(19.2)
190	San Diego, CA	(13.7)
123	San Francisco (greater), CA	(3.4)
212	San Francisco-S. Mateo, CA M.D.	(17.4)
202	San Jose, CA	(16.1)
224	San Luis Obispo, CA	(19.3)
229	Sandusky, OH	(20.0)
249	Santa Ana-Anaheim, CA M.D.	(24.7)
53	Santa Barbara-Santa Maria, CA	16.5
68	Santa Cruz-Watsonville, CA	12.3
295	Santa Fe, NM	(46.9)
254	Santa Rosa-Petaluma, CA	(25.8)

RANK	METROPOLITAN AREA	% CHANGE
280	Savannah, GA	(36.4)
206	Scranton--Wilkes-Barre, PA	(16.5)
192	Seattle-Bellevue-Everett, WA M.D.	(13.9)
172	Seattle-Tacoma-Bellevue, WA	(11.0)
107	Sebastian-Vero Beach, FL	0.9
46	Sheboygan, WI	20.5
124	Sherman-Denison, TX	(3.5)
NA	Shreveport-Bossier City, LA**	NA
150	Sioux City, IA-NE-SD	(7.7)
168	Sioux Falls, SD	(10.7)
NA	South Bend-Mishawaka, IN-MI**	NA
157	Spartanburg, SC	(9.1)
213	Spokane, WA	(17.6)
215	Springfield, MA	(17.7)
NA	Springfield, MO**	NA
141	Springfield, OH	(6.3)
74	State College, PA	10.6
189	Stockton, CA	(13.6)
134	St. Cloud, MN	(4.9)
298	St. George, UT	(55.9)
8	St. Joseph, MO-KS	83.5
210	St. Louis, MO-IL	(17.3)
NA	Sumter, SC**	NA
155	Syracuse, NY	(8.9)
137	Tacoma, WA M.D.	(5.7)
151	Tallahassee, FL	(7.8)
262	Tampa-St Petersburg, FL	(27.7)
255	Texarkana, TX-Texarkana, AR	(26.3)
165	Toledo, OH	(9.9)
110	Topeka, KS	0.8
105	Trenton-Ewing, NJ	1.0
277	Tucson, AZ	(34.0)
198	Tulsa, OK	(15.0)
NA	Tuscaloosa, AL**	NA
120	Tyler, TX	(2.3)
62	Utica-Rome, NY	14.4
107	Valdosta, GA	0.9
NA	Vallejo-Fairfield, CA**	NA
14	Victoria, TX	63.4
294	Vineland, NJ	(45.1)
269	Visalia-Porterville, CA	(30.4)
97	Waco, TX	2.2
40	Warner Robins, GA	23.2
NA	Warren-Farmington Hills, MI M.D.**	NA
210	Washington (greater) DC-VA-MD-WV	(17.3)
228	Washington, DC-VA-MD-WV M.D.	(19.9)
7	Waterloo-Cedar Falls, IA	86.4
NA	Wausau, WI**	NA
122	Wenatchee, WA	(3.3)
169	West Palm Beach, FL M.D.	(10.8)
44	Wheeling, WV-OH	21.3
241	Wichita Falls, TX	(22.7)
NA	Wichita, KS**	NA
156	Williamsport, PA	(9.0)
92	Wilmington, DE-MD-NJ M.D.	3.6
NA	Wilmington, NC**	NA
287	Winchester, VA-WV	(39.3)
118	Winston-Salem, NC	(1.0)
27	Worcester, MA	32.6
268	York-Hanover, PA	(30.2)
NA	Youngstown, OH-PA**	NA
227	Yuba City, CA	(19.6)
232	Yuma, AZ	(20.3)

Source: CQ Press using reported data from the F.B.I. "Crime in the United States 2009"
*Aggravated assault is an attack for the purpose of inflicting severe bodily injury.
**Not available.

24. Percent Change in Aggravated Assault Rate: 2005 to 2009 (continued)

National Percent Change = 9.6% Decrease*

RANK	METROPOLITAN AREA	% CHANGE
1	Mobile, AL	121.3
2	Racine, WI	118.3
3	Fargo, ND-MN	109.5
4	Bismarck, ND	99.0
5	Albany, GA	90.7
6	Mansfield, OH	90.1
7	Waterloo-Cedar Falls, IA	86.4
8	St. Joseph, MO-KS	83.5
9	Akron, OH	83.3
10	Manchester-Nashua, NH	83.0
11	Logan, UT-ID	78.4
12	Bloomington, IN	75.2
13	Harrisonburg, VA	66.1
14	Victoria, TX	63.4
15	Redding, CA	61.7
16	Ames, IA	57.8
17	Athens-Clarke County, GA	55.6
18	Morgantown, WV	54.8
19	Norwich-New London, CT	53.4
20	Lynchburg, VA	51.7
21	Idaho Falls, ID	49.9
22	Grand Forks, ND-MN	37.0
23	Cumberland, MD-WV	36.1
24	Lafayette, IN	35.1
25	La Crosse, WI-MN	35.0
26	Lake Charles, LA	33.0
27	Worcester, MA	32.6
28	Chico, CA	31.2
29	Rocky Mount, NC	31.1
30	Altoona, PA	30.4
31	Pascagoula, MS	30.1
32	Cambridge-Newton, MA M.D.	29.7
33	Pueblo, CO	28.8
34	Muncie, IN	28.0
35	Iowa City, IA	27.3
36	Rome, GA	27.0
37	Las Vegas-Paradise, NV	24.5
37	Lewiston-Auburn, ME	24.5
39	Fort Collins-Loveland, CO	24.4
40	Dayton, OH	23.2
40	Warner Robins, GA	23.2
42	Binghamton, NY	22.9
43	Eugene-Springfield, OR	21.9
44	Wheeling, WV-OH	21.3
45	Lafayette, LA	20.7
46	Sheboygan, WI	20.5
47	Oshkosh-Neenah, WI	19.9
48	Lawrence, KS	18.9
49	Rochester, NY	18.2
50	Laredo, TX	17.8
51	Fond du Lac, WI	17.6
52	Corpus Christi, TX	17.5
53	Santa Barbara-Santa Maria, CA	16.5
54	Abilene, TX	16.0
55	Lima, OH	15.9
56	Bremerton-Silverdale, WA	15.8
57	Milwaukee, WI	15.5
58	El Paso, TX	15.4
58	Rockingham County, NH M.D.	15.4
60	Las Cruces, NM	15.0
61	Columbus, GA-AL	14.7
62	Utica-Rome, NY	14.4
63	Indianapolis, IN	14.2
64	Bend, OR	14.0
64	Hinesville, GA	14.0
66	Salinas, CA	13.8
67	Odessa, TX	12.6
68	Santa Cruz-Watsonville, CA	12.3
69	Kennewick-Pasco-Richland, WA	11.8
70	Hartford, CT	11.6
71	Bakersfield, CA	11.5
72	Erie, PA	11.4
73	Charleston, WV	11.1
74	State College, PA	10.6
75	Bridgeport-Stamford, CT	8.8
76	Austin-Round Rock, TX	8.3
77	Anchorage, AK	8.0
78	Fayetteville, AR-MO	7.9
78	Palm Bay-Melbourne, FL	7.9
80	Barnstable Town, MA	7.7
81	Columbia, SC	7.3
82	Lewiston, ID-WA	7.0
82	Merced, CA	7.0
84	Anderson, SC	6.2
85	Billings, MT	6.0
86	Oakland-Fremont, CA M.D.	5.9
87	Brunswick, GA	5.8
87	Pine Bluff, AR	5.8
89	Salt Lake City, UT	4.4
90	Poughkeepsie, NY	4.3
91	Boston (greater), MA-NH	4.1
92	Wilmington, DE-MD-NJ M.D.	3.6
93	Buffalo-Niagara Falls, NY	2.9
94	Cheyenne, WY	2.8
95	Rochester, MN	2.7
96	Atlantic City, NJ	2.6
97	Pittsfield, MA	2.2
97	Waco, TX	2.2
99	Fort Wayne, IN	2.1
99	Madison, WI	2.1
101	Great Falls, MT	1.8
102	Goldsboro, NC	1.7
102	Reno-Sparks, NV	1.7
104	Coeur d'Alene, ID	1.3
105	Appleton, WI	1.0
105	Trenton-Ewing, NJ	1.0
107	Ogden-Clearfield, UT	0.9
107	Sebastian-Vero Beach, FL	0.9
107	Valdosta, GA	0.9
110	Houston, TX	0.8
110	Topeka, KS	0.8
112	Camden, NJ M.D.	0.7
113	Chattanooga, TN-GA	0.6
114	Bethesda-Frederick, MD M.D.	0.2
115	Pensacola, FL	(0.5)
116	Amarillo, TX	(0.9)
116	Boston-Quincy, MA M.D.	(0.9)
118	Winston-Salem, NC	(1.0)
119	Memphis, TN-MS-AR	(1.1)
120	Tyler, TX	(2.3)
121	Pittsburgh, PA	(2.5)
122	Wenatchee, WA	(3.3)
123	San Francisco (greater), CA	(3.4)
124	Knoxville, TN	(3.5)
124	Sherman-Denison, TX	(3.5)
126	Ann Arbor, MI	(3.7)
127	Midland, TX	(3.9)
128	Dover, DE	(4.4)
129	Augusta, GA-SC	(4.5)
129	Honolulu, HI	(4.5)
129	Oxnard-Thousand Oaks, CA	(4.5)
132	Baton Rouge, LA	(4.7)
132	Blacksburg, VA	(4.7)
134	St. Cloud, MN	(4.9)
135	Hickory, NC	(5.0)
136	Gadsden, AL	(5.2)
137	Tacoma, WA M.D.	(5.7)
138	Greensboro-High Point, NC	(6.0)
139	Bellingham, WA	(6.1)
139	Dubuque, IA	(6.1)
141	Springfield, OH	(6.3)
142	Edison, NJ M.D.	(6.6)
142	Lubbock, TX	(6.6)
144	Asheville, NC	(6.9)
145	Harrisburg-Carlisle, PA	(7.3)
145	Killeen-Temple-Fort Hood, TX	(7.3)
147	Fort Worth-Arlington, TX M.D.	(7.4)
148	Lakeland, FL	(7.5)
148	Michigan City-La Porte, IN	(7.5)
150	Sioux City, IA-NE-SD	(7.7)
151	Tallahassee, FL	(7.8)
152	Janesville, WI	(8.0)
153	Grand Junction, CO	(8.6)
154	Mount Vernon-Anacortes, WA	(8.8)
155	Syracuse, NY	(8.9)
156	Williamsport, PA	(9.0)
157	New York-W. Plains NY-NJ M.D.	(9.1)
157	Spartanburg, SC	(9.1)
159	Beaumont-Port Arthur, TX	(9.5)
159	Philadelphia (greater) PA-NJ-MD-DE	(9.5)
161	Elmira, NY	(9.6)
161	New York (greater), NY-NJ-PA	(9.6)
161	Prescott, AZ	(9.6)
164	Jefferson City, MO	(9.8)
165	Toledo, OH	(9.9)
166	Jacksonville, FL	(10.2)
167	Hot Springs, AR	(10.3)
168	Sioux Falls, SD	(10.7)
169	San Angelo, TX	(10.8)
169	West Palm Beach, FL M.D.	(10.8)
171	Rapid City, SD	(10.9)
172	Detroit (greater), MI	(11.0)
172	Seattle-Tacoma-Bellevue, WA	(11.0)
174	Fayetteville, NC	(11.2)
175	Jackson, MS	(11.3)
175	Panama City-Lynn Haven, FL	(11.3)
177	Atlanta, GA	(11.5)
178	Huntsville, AL	(12.0)
179	Fort Lauderdale, FL M.D.	(12.1)
180	Anderson, IN	(12.3)

Note: All listings are for Metropolitan Statistical Areas (M.S.A.s) except for those ending with "M.D." Listings with "M.D." are Metropolitan Divisions which are smaller parts of eleven large M.S.A.s. See explanatory note at beginning of metropolitan area section.

RANK	METROPOLITAN AREA	% CHANGE
181	Nassau-Suffolk, NY M.D.	(12.6)
181	Salisbury, MD	(12.6)
183	Columbia, MO	(12.8)
183	Gainesville, FL	(12.8)
185	Lancaster, PA	(12.9)
186	Eau Claire, WI	(13.0)
187	Cedar Rapids, IA	(13.1)
188	Corvallis, OR	(13.3)
189	Stockton, CA	(13.6)
190	San Diego, CA	(13.7)
191	Philadelphia, PA M.D.	(13.8)
192	Colorado Springs, CO	(13.9)
192	Green Bay, WI	(13.9)
192	Seattle-Bellevue-Everett, WA M.D.	(13.9)
195	Newark-Union, NJ-PA M.D.	(14.0)
196	Kansas City, MO-KS	(14.5)
197	Olympia, WA	(14.8)
198	Kingsport, TN-VA	(15.0)
198	Tulsa, OK	(15.0)
200	Sacramento, CA	(15.2)
201	Durham-Chapel Hill, NC	(15.3)
202	San Jose, CA	(16.1)
203	Reading, PA	(16.2)
204	Baltimore-Towson, MD	(16.4)
204	Orlando, FL	(16.4)
206	Riverside-San Bernardino, CA	(16.5)
206	Scranton--Wilkes-Barre, PA	(16.5)
208	Battle Creek, MI	(16.7)
209	Missoula, MT	(17.0)
210	St. Louis, MO-IL	(17.3)
210	Washington (greater) DC-VA-MD-WV	(17.3)
212	San Francisco-S. Mateo, CA M.D.	(17.4)
213	Portland, ME	(17.6)
213	Spokane, WA	(17.6)
215	Ocean City, NJ	(17.7)
215	Springfield, MA	(17.7)
217	Houma, LA	(18.3)
217	Raleigh-Cary, NC	(18.3)
219	Casper, WY	(18.8)
220	Kingston, NY	(18.9)
221	Miami (greater), FL	(19.0)
222	McAllen-Edinburg-Mission, TX	(19.1)
223	San Antonio, TX	(19.2)
224	Albany-Schenectady-Troy, NY	(19.3)
224	San Luis Obispo, CA	(19.3)
226	Omaha-Council Bluffs, NE-IA	(19.5)
227	Yuba City, CA	(19.6)
228	Washington, DC-VA-MD-WV M.D.	(19.9)
229	College Station-Bryan, TX	(20.0)
229	Macon, GA	(20.0)
229	Sandusky, OH	(20.0)
232	Yuma, AZ	(20.3)
233	Burlington, NC	(20.4)
233	Madera, CA	(20.4)
235	Modesto, CA	(20.5)
236	Pocatello, ID	(20.7)
237	Fresno, CA	(21.8)
238	Ocala, FL	(22.1)
239	Denver-Aurora, CO	(22.5)
240	Kokomo, IN	(22.6)
241	Wichita Falls, TX	(22.7)
242	Lincoln, NE	(22.9)
243	Los Angeles County, CA M.D.	(23.2)

RANK	METROPOLITAN AREA	% CHANGE
244	Portland-Vancouver, OR-WA	(23.5)
245	Los Angeles (greater), CA	(23.6)
246	Johnson City, TN	(23.8)
247	Morristown, TN	(24.1)
248	Columbus, OH	(24.6)
249	Santa Ana-Anaheim, CA M.D.	(24.7)
250	Fort Smith, AR-OK	(25.2)
251	Longview, TX	(25.3)
251	Miami-Dade County, FL M.D.	(25.3)
253	Cape Coral-Fort Myers, FL	(25.4)
254	Santa Rosa-Petaluma, CA	(25.8)
255	Texarkana, TX-Texarkana, AR	(26.3)
256	Allentown, PA-NJ	(26.6)
257	Montgomery, AL	(26.7)
258	Albuquerque, NM	(26.8)
259	Naples-Marco Island, FL	(27.0)
260	Nashville-Davidson, TN	(27.5)
261	Phoenix-Mesa-Scottsdale, AZ	(27.6)
262	Tampa-St Petersburg, FL	(27.7)
263	Hagerstown-Martinsburg, MD-WV	(27.9)
264	Port St. Lucie, FL	(28.7)
265	Charleston-North Charleston, SC	(28.8)
266	Gainesville, GA	(29.6)
267	Richmond, VA	(29.7)
268	York-Hanover, PA	(30.2)
269	Visalia-Porterville, CA	(30.4)
270	Danville, VA	(30.8)
271	Dallas (greater), TX	(31.6)
272	Roanoke, VA	(32.4)
273	Salem, OR	(32.6)
274	Jackson, TN	(32.8)
275	Punta Gorda, FL	(33.0)
276	Napa, CA	(33.5)
277	Tucson, AZ	(34.0)
278	Medford, OR	(34.2)
279	Charlotte-Gastonia, NC-SC	(35.6)
280	Savannah, GA	(36.4)
281	Brownsville-Harlingen, TX	(36.6)
282	Charlottesville, VA	(37.1)
283	Provo-Orem, UT	(37.3)
284	Longview, WA	(37.6)
285	Carson City, NV	(38.2)
286	Alexandria, LA	(38.8)
287	Winchester, VA-WV	(39.3)
288	Jonesboro, AR	(39.5)
289	Columbus, IN	(39.8)
290	Dallas-Plano-Irving, TX M.D.	(42.1)
291	Florence, SC	(42.5)
292	Bangor, ME	(42.7)
292	Greeley, CO	(42.7)
294	Vineland, NJ	(45.1)
295	Santa Fe, NM	(46.9)
296	Lebanon, PA	(49.0)
297	Flagstaff, AZ	(50.9)
298	St. George, UT	(55.9)
299	Elkhart-Goshen, IN	(60.9)
NA	Anniston-Oxford, AL**	NA
NA	Auburn, AL**	NA
NA	Bay City, MI**	NA
NA	Birmingham-Hoover, AL**	NA
NA	Boise City-Nampa, ID**	NA
NA	Boulder, CO**	NA
NA	Bowling Green, KY**	NA

RANK	METROPOLITAN AREA	% CHANGE
NA	Burlington-South Burlington, VT**	NA
NA	Cape Girardeau, MO-IL**	NA
NA	Cincinnati-Middletown, OH-KY-IN**	NA
NA	Clarksville, TN-KY**	NA
NA	Cleveland-Elyria-Mentor, OH**	NA
NA	Cleveland, TN**	NA
NA	Crestview-Fort Walton Beach, FL**	NA
NA	Dalton, GA**	NA
NA	Danville, IL**	NA
NA	Decatur, AL**	NA
NA	Decatur, IL**	NA
NA	Deltona-Daytona Beach, FL**	NA
NA	Des Moines-West Des Moines, IA**	NA
NA	Detroit-Livonia-Dearborn, MI M.D.**	NA
NA	Dothan, AL**	NA
NA	Duluth, MN-WI**	NA
NA	El Centro, CA**	NA
NA	Elizabethtown, KY**	NA
NA	Evansville, IN-KY**	NA
NA	Farmington, NM**	NA
NA	Flint, MI**	NA
NA	Florence-Muscle Shoals, AL**	NA
NA	Glens Falls, NY**	NA
NA	Grand Rapids-Wyoming, MI**	NA
NA	Gulfport-Biloxi, MS**	NA
NA	Hattiesburg, MS**	NA
NA	Holland-Grand Haven, MI**	NA
NA	Ithaca, NY**	NA
NA	Jacksonville, NC**	NA
NA	Jackson, MI**	NA
NA	Kalamazoo-Portage, MI**	NA
NA	Lake Havasu City-Kingman, AZ**	NA
NA	Lansing-East Lansing, MI**	NA
NA	Lawton, OK**	NA
NA	Lexington-Fayette, KY**	NA
NA	Little Rock, AR**	NA
NA	Louisville, KY-IN**	NA
NA	Manhattan, KS**	NA
NA	Mankato-North Mankato, MN**	NA
NA	Minneapolis-St. Paul, MN-WI**	NA
NA	Monroe, MI**	NA
NA	Muskegon-Norton Shores, MI**	NA
NA	New Haven-Milford, CT**	NA
NA	New Orleans, LA**	NA
NA	Niles-Benton Harbor, MI**	NA
NA	North Port-Bradenton-Sarasota, FL**	NA
NA	Oklahoma City, OK**	NA
NA	Owensboro, KY**	NA
NA	Palm Coast, FL**	NA
NA	Peabody, MA M.D.**	NA
NA	Providence-New Bedford, RI-MA**	NA
NA	Saginaw, MI**	NA
NA	Shreveport-Bossier City, LA**	NA
NA	South Bend-Mishawaka, IN-MI**	NA
NA	Springfield, MO**	NA
NA	Sumter, SC**	NA
NA	Tuscaloosa, AL**	NA
NA	Vallejo-Fairfield, CA**	NA
NA	Warren-Farmington Hills, MI M.D.**	NA
NA	Wausau, WI**	NA
NA	Wichita, KS**	NA
NA	Wilmington, NC**	NA
NA	Youngstown, OH-PA**	NA

Source: CQ Press using reported data from the F.B.I. "Crime in the United States 2009"
*Aggravated assault is an attack for the purpose of inflicting severe bodily injury.
**Not available.

25. Property Crimes in 2009
National Total = 9,320,971 Property Crimes*

RANK	METROPOLITAN AREA	CRIMES
231	Abilene, TX	5,607
89	Akron, OH	22,909
94	Albany-Schenectady-Troy, NY	21,873
198	Albany, GA	7,140
62	Albuquerque, NM	37,368
200	Alexandria, LA	7,078
106	Allentown, PA-NJ	19,065
340	Altoona, PA	2,368
148	Amarillo, TX	11,864
346	Ames, IA	2,280
155	Anchorage, AK	11,210
264	Anderson, IN	4,649
190	Anderson, SC	7,856
174	Ann Arbor, MI	9,348
235	Anniston-Oxford, AL	5,466
276	Appleton, WI	4,447
164	Asheville, NC	10,164
192	Athens-Clarke County, GA	7,671
8	Atlanta, GA	194,529
175	Atlantic City, NJ	9,298
NA	Auburn, AL**	NA
87	Augusta, GA-SC	24,987
36	Austin-Round Rock, TX	68,644
72	Bakersfield, CA	31,445
26	Baltimore-Towson, MD	88,764
254	Bangor, ME	5,027
201	Barnstable Town, MA	7,006
70	Baton Rouge, LA	33,701
238	Battle Creek, MI	5,343
336	Bay City, MI	2,595
125	Beaumont-Port Arthur, TX	14,918
202	Bellingham, WA	6,989
284	Bend, OR	4,089
82	Bethesda-Frederick, MD M.D.	28,016
227	Billings, MT	5,662
213	Binghamton, NY	6,166
53	Birmingham-Hoover, AL	51,286
348	Bismarck, ND	2,239
283	Blacksburg, VA	4,142
237	Bloomington, IN	5,383
144	Boise City-Nampa, ID	12,208
23	Boston (greater), MA-NH	98,609
56	Boston-Quincy, MA M.D.	46,053
199	Boulder, CO	7,134
288	Bowling Green, KY	3,922
214	Bremerton-Silverdale, WA	6,156
114	Bridgeport-Stamford, CT	17,241
105	Brownsville-Harlingen, TX	19,074
258	Brunswick, GA	4,819
68	Buffalo-Niagara Falls, NY	33,998
207	Burlington-South Burlington, VT	6,417
222	Burlington, NC	5,802
81	Cambridge-Newton, MA M.D.	28,315
73	Camden, NJ M.D.	30,916
111	Cape Coral-Fort Myers, FL	17,940
317	Cape Girardeau, MO-IL	3,016
359	Carson City, NV	1,151
319	Casper, WY	2,954
195	Cedar Rapids, IA	7,226
NA	Charleston-North Charleston, SC**	NA
166	Charleston, WV	9,660
37	Charlotte-Gastonia, NC-SC	68,374
247	Charlottesville, VA	5,185
91	Chattanooga, TN-GA	22,502
324	Cheyenne, WY	2,884
209	Chico, CA	6,338
32	Cincinnati-Middletown, OH-KY-IN	71,996
189	Clarksville, TN-KY	7,981
44	Cleveland-Elyria-Mentor, OH	59,408
304	Cleveland, TN	3,385
295	Coeur d'Alene, ID	3,713
177	College Station-Bryan, TX	9,158
112	Colorado Springs, CO	17,809
245	Columbia, MO	5,248
76	Columbia, SC	29,611
113	Columbus, GA-AL	17,709
335	Columbus, IN	2,612
31	Columbus, OH	77,126
99	Corpus Christi, TX	20,873
344	Corvallis, OR	2,292
248	Crestview-Fort Walton Beach, FL	5,176
330	Cumberland, MD-WV	2,756
3	Dallas (greater), TX	252,361
9	Dallas-Plano-Irving, TX M.D.	165,377
289	Dalton, GA	3,900
313	Danville, IL	3,155
321	Danville, VA	2,936
79	Dayton, OH	28,562
259	Decatur, AL	4,817
296	Decatur, IL	3,669
109	Deltona-Daytona Beach, FL	18,359
33	Denver-Aurora, CO	71,361
122	Des Moines-West Des Moines, IA	15,592
15	Detroit (greater), MI	135,260
30	Detroit-Livonia-Dearborn, MI M.D.	83,282
NA	Dothan, AL**	NA
228	Dover, DE	5,658
351	Dubuque, IA	2,182
173	Duluth, MN-WI	9,365
103	Durham-Chapel Hill, NC	19,994
310	Eau Claire, WI	3,249
58	Edison, NJ M.D.	43,410
NA	El Centro, CA**	NA
92	El Paso, TX	21,909
353	Elizabethtown, KY	2,054
238	Elkhart-Goshen, IN	5,343
354	Elmira, NY	1,962
204	Erie, PA	6,663
131	Eugene-Springfield, OR	14,238
169	Evansville, IN-KY	9,606
249	Fargo, ND-MN	5,111
316	Farmington, NM	3,032
154	Fayetteville, AR-MO	11,376
100	Fayetteville, NC	20,655
278	Flagstaff, AZ	4,396
116	Flint, MI	16,252
275	Florence-Muscle Shoals, AL	4,455
162	Florence, SC	10,312
358	Fond du Lac, WI	1,773
187	Fort Collins-Loveland, CO	8,266
35	Fort Lauderdale, FL M.D.	69,568
172	Fort Smith, AR-OK	9,398
149	Fort Wayne, IN	11,577
28	Fort Worth-Arlington, TX M.D.	86,984
65	Fresno, CA	35,152
294	Gadsden, AL	3,734
157	Gainesville, FL	11,105
272	Gainesville, GA	4,515
352	Glens Falls, NY	2,073
255	Goldsboro, NC	5,001
343	Grand Forks, ND-MN	2,298
273	Grand Junction, CO	4,511
95	Grand Rapids-Wyoming, MI	21,771
331	Great Falls, MT	2,702
215	Greeley, CO	6,104
220	Green Bay, WI	5,921
74	Greensboro-High Point, NC	30,807
163	Gulfport-Biloxi, MS	10,207
217	Hagerstown-Martinsburg, MD-WV	6,078
151	Harrisburg-Carlisle, PA	11,474
357	Harrisonburg, VA	1,823
83	Hartford, CT	27,761
NA	Hattiesburg, MS**	NA
141	Hickory, NC	12,262
334	Hinesville, GA	2,657
269	Holland-Grand Haven, MI	4,568
71	Honolulu, HI	33,375
211	Hot Springs, AR	6,206
206	Houma, LA	6,648
6	Houston, TX	241,437
129	Huntsville, AL	14,572
332	Idaho Falls, ID	2,691
39	Indianapolis, IN	66,672
323	Iowa City, IA	2,901
341	Ithaca, NY	2,358
45	Jacksonville, FL	57,086
216	Jacksonville, NC	6,079
281	Jackson, MI	4,154
97	Jackson, MS	21,030
225	Jackson, TN	5,693
267	Janesville, WI	4,606
309	Jefferson City, MO	3,250
232	Johnson City, TN	5,551
268	Jonesboro, AR	4,569
152	Kalamazoo-Portage, MI	11,462
NA	Kansas City, MO-KS**	NA
218	Kennewick-Pasco-Richland, WA	6,012
145	Killeen-Temple-Fort Hood, TX	12,103
161	Kingsport, TN-VA	10,384
302	Kingston, NY	3,440
88	Knoxville, TN	24,783
307	Kokomo, IN	3,314
306	La Crosse, WI-MN	3,362
233	Lafayette, IN	5,536
146	Lafayette, LA	11,979
179	Lake Charles, LA	9,073
203	Lake Havasu City-Kingman, AZ	6,747
93	Lakeland, FL	21,882
165	Lancaster, PA	9,932
147	Lansing-East Lansing, MI	11,892

Note: All listings are for Metropolitan Statistical Areas (M.S.A.s) except for those ending with "M.D." Listings with "M.D." are Metropolitan Divisions which are smaller parts of eleven large M.S.A.s. See explanatory note at beginning of metropolitan area section.

Alpha Order - Metro Area (continued)

RANK	METROPOLITAN AREA	CRIMES
133	Laredo, TX	14,116
205	Las Cruces, NM	6,660
42	Las Vegas-Paradise, NV	61,525
251	Lawrence, KS	5,081
242	Lawton, OK	5,322
350	Lebanon, PA	2,198
337	Lewiston-Auburn, ME	2,502
356	Lewiston, ID-WA	1,833
118	Lexington-Fayette, KY	15,971
274	Lima, OH	4,506
159	Lincoln, NE	10,645
64	Little Rock, AR	36,186
355	Logan, UT-ID	1,924
167	Longview, TX	9,631
291	Longview, WA	3,893
5	Los Angeles County, CA M.D.	241,960
2	Los Angeles (greater), CA	302,654
60	Louisville, KY-IN	41,798
130	Lubbock, TX	14,456
263	Lynchburg, VA	4,687
153	Macon, GA	11,404
312	Madera, CA	3,170
126	Madison, WI	14,903
176	Manchester-Nashua, NH	9,200
328	Manhattan, KS	2,763
329	Mankato-North Mankato, MN	2,758
257	Mansfield, OH	4,929
63	McAllen-Edinburg-Mission, TX	37,311
253	Medford, OR	5,065
40	Memphis, TN-MS-AR	65,884
185	Merced, CA	8,310
4	Miami (greater), FL	244,389
16	Miami-Dade County, FL M.D.	122,854
286	Michigan City-La Porte, IN	4,045
270	Midland, TX	4,559
47	Milwaukee, WI	56,378
24	Minneapolis-St. Paul, MN-WI	97,445
327	Missoula, MT	2,765
102	Mobile, AL	20,066
96	Modesto, CA	21,577
297	Monroe, MI	3,656
123	Montgomery, AL	15,513
325	Morgantown, WV	2,831
277	Morristown, TN	4,442
234	Mount Vernon-Anacortes, WA	5,469
305	Muncie, IN	3,363
194	Muskegon-Norton Shores, MI	7,258
314	Napa, CA	3,116
221	Naples-Marco Island, FL	5,861
50	Nashville-Davidson, TN	53,143
54	Nassau-Suffolk, NY M.D.	49,052
85	New Haven-Milford, CT	25,974
NA	New Orleans, LA**	NA
1	New York (greater), NY-NJ-PA	333,906
7	New York-W. Plains NY-NJ M.D.	199,549
59	Newark-Union, NJ-PA M.D.	41,895
260	Niles-Benton Harbor, MI	4,788
84	North Port-Bradenton-Sarasota, FL	27,159
299	Norwich-New London, CT	3,578
27	Oakland-Fremont, CA M.D.	87,413
183	Ocala, FL	8,480
280	Ocean City, NJ	4,244
226	Odessa, TX	5,663
128	Ogden-Clearfield, UT	14,639
48	Oklahoma City, OK	54,709
193	Olympia, WA	7,452
80	Omaha-Council Bluffs, NE-IA	28,519
29	Orlando, FL	83,452
290	Oshkosh-Neenah, WI	3,895
311	Owensboro, KY	3,186
124	Oxnard-Thousand Oaks, CA	15,329
110	Palm Bay-Melbourne, FL	17,975
345	Palm Coast, FL	2,291
197	Panama City-Lynn Haven, FL	7,164
243	Pascagoula, MS	5,307
117	Peabody, MA M.D.	16,109
127	Pensacola, FL	14,731
10	Philadelphia (greater) PA-NJ-MD-DE	157,469
21	Philadelphia, PA M.D.	103,673
11	Phoenix-Mesa-Scottsdale, AZ	157,161
250	Pine Bluff, AR	5,103
55	Pittsburgh, PA	47,997
322	Pittsfield, MA	2,928
339	Pocatello, ID	2,419
150	Port St. Lucie, FL	11,559
41	Portland-Vancouver, OR-WA	65,588
139	Portland, ME	12,546
135	Poughkeepsie, NY	13,279
271	Prescott, AZ	4,550
61	Providence-New Bedford, RI-MA	41,086
140	Provo-Orem, UT	12,273
261	Pueblo, CO	4,710
282	Punta Gorda, FL	4,151
230	Racine, WI	5,642
75	Raleigh-Cary, NC	29,720
301	Rapid City, SD	3,474
168	Reading, PA	9,607
265	Redding, CA	4,640
134	Reno-Sparks, NV	13,561
69	Richmond, VA	33,864
18	Riverside-San Bernardino, CA	119,210
184	Roanoke, VA	8,464
293	Rochester, MN	3,867
78	Rochester, NY	28,608
188	Rockingham County, NH M.D.	8,132
208	Rocky Mount, NC	6,365
315	Rome, GA	3,093
38	Sacramento, CA	68,361
212	Saginaw, MI	6,181
142	Salem, OR	12,257
156	Salinas, CA	11,204
256	Salisbury, MD	4,970
49	Salt Lake City, UT	53,441
266	San Angelo, TX	4,625
19	San Antonio, TX	113,628
34	San Diego, CA	69,738
13	San Francisco (greater), CA	143,999
46	San Francisco-S. Mateo, CA M.D.	56,586
57	San Jose, CA	43,862
219	San Luis Obispo, CA	5,977
342	Sandusky, OH	2,355
43	Santa Ana-Anaheim, CA M.D.	60,694
181	Santa Barbara-Santa Maria, CA	8,909
180	Santa Cruz-Watsonville, CA	9,059
224	Santa Fe, NM	5,751
171	Santa Rosa-Petaluma, CA	9,450
132	Savannah, GA	14,210
143	Scranton--Wilkes-Barre, PA	12,229
22	Seattle-Bellevue-Everett, WA M.D.	102,225
14	Seattle-Tacoma-Bellevue, WA	137,001
287	Sebastian-Vero Beach, FL	4,034
320	Sheboygan, WI	2,941
292	Sherman-Denison, TX	3,884
121	Shreveport-Bossier City, LA	15,645
300	Sioux City, IA-NE-SD	3,530
236	Sioux Falls, SD	5,392
137	South Bend-Mishawaka, IN-MI	12,974
158	Spartanburg, SC	10,871
101	Spokane, WA	20,070
104	Springfield, MA	19,930
107	Springfield, MO	19,056
228	Springfield, OH	5,658
333	State College, PA	2,677
77	Stockton, CA	28,772
279	St. Cloud, MN	4,374
338	St. George, UT	2,458
262	St. Joseph, MO-KS	4,702
25	St. Louis, MO-IL	89,656
303	Sumter, SC	3,433
119	Syracuse, NY	15,945
66	Tacoma, WA M.D.	34,776
138	Tallahassee, FL	12,872
20	Tampa-St Petersburg, FL	106,322
223	Texarkana, TX-Texarkana, AR	5,758
NA	Toledo, OH**	NA
178	Topeka, KS	9,096
191	Trenton-Ewing, NJ	7,701
NA	Tucson, AZ**	NA
67	Tulsa, OK	34,358
170	Tuscaloosa, AL	9,546
186	Tyler, TX	8,303
196	Utica-Rome, NY	7,187
252	Valdosta, GA	5,068
136	Vallejo-Fairfield, CA	13,270
240	Victoria, TX	5,337
244	Vineland, NJ	5,260
120	Visalia-Porterville, CA	15,681
160	Waco, TX	10,408
246	Warner Robins, GA	5,212
51	Warren-Farmington Hills, MI M.D.	51,978
12	Washington (greater) DC-VA-MD-WV	148,521
17	Washington, DC-VA-MD-WV M.D.	120,505
285	Waterloo-Cedar Falls, IA	4,055
347	Wausau, WI	2,247
308	Wenatchee, WA	3,288
52	West Palm Beach, FL M.D.	51,967
326	Wheeling, WV-OH	2,817
210	Wichita Falls, TX	6,316
86	Wichita, KS	25,048
349	Williamsport, PA	2,213
90	Wilmington, DE-MD-NJ M.D.	22,880
NA	Wilmington, NC**	NA
318	Winchester, VA-WV	2,994
98	Winston-Salem, NC	20,900
115	Worcester, MA	17,090
182	York-Hanover, PA	8,906
108	Youngstown, OH-PA	18,446
298	Yuba City, CA	3,617
241	Yuma, AZ	5,333

Source: Reported data from the F.B.I. "Crime in the United States 2009"
*Property crimes are offenses of burglary, larceny-theft, and motor vehicle theft. Attempts are included.
**Not available.

25. Property Crimes in 2009 (continued)
National Total = 9,320,971 Property Crimes*

RANK	METROPOLITAN AREA	CRIMES
1	New York (greater), NY-NJ-PA	333,906
2	Los Angeles (greater), CA	302,654
3	Dallas (greater), TX	252,361
4	Miami (greater), FL	244,389
5	Los Angeles County, CA M.D.	241,960
6	Houston, TX	241,437
7	New York-W. Plains NY-NJ M.D.	199,549
8	Atlanta, GA	194,529
9	Dallas-Plano-Irving, TX M.D.	165,377
10	Philadelphia (greater) PA-NJ-MD-DE	157,469
11	Phoenix-Mesa-Scottsdale, AZ	157,161
12	Washington (greater) DC-VA-MD-WV	148,521
13	San Francisco (greater), CA	143,999
14	Seattle-Tacoma-Bellevue, WA	137,001
15	Detroit (greater), MI	135,260
16	Miami-Dade County, FL M.D.	122,854
17	Washington, DC-VA-MD-WV M.D.	120,505
18	Riverside-San Bernardino, CA	119,210
19	San Antonio, TX	113,628
20	Tampa-St Petersburg, FL	106,322
21	Philadelphia, PA M.D.	103,673
22	Seattle-Bellevue-Everett, WA M.D.	102,225
23	Boston (greater), MA-NH	98,609
24	Minneapolis-St. Paul, MN-WI	97,445
25	St. Louis, MO-IL	89,656
26	Baltimore-Towson, MD	88,764
27	Oakland-Fremont, CA M.D.	87,413
28	Fort Worth-Arlington, TX M.D.	86,984
29	Orlando, FL	83,452
30	Detroit-Livonia-Dearborn, MI M.D.	83,282
31	Columbus, OH	77,126
32	Cincinnati-Middletown, OH-KY-IN	71,996
33	Denver-Aurora, CO	71,361
34	San Diego, CA	69,738
35	Fort Lauderdale, FL M.D.	69,568
36	Austin-Round Rock, TX	68,644
37	Charlotte-Gastonia, NC-SC	68,374
38	Sacramento, CA	68,361
39	Indianapolis, IN	66,672
40	Memphis, TN-MS-AR	65,884
41	Portland-Vancouver, OR-WA	65,588
42	Las Vegas-Paradise, NV	61,525
43	Santa Ana-Anaheim, CA M.D.	60,694
44	Cleveland-Elyria-Mentor, OH	59,408
45	Jacksonville, FL	57,086
46	San Francisco-S. Mateo, CA M.D.	56,586
47	Milwaukee, WI	56,378
48	Oklahoma City, OK	54,709
49	Salt Lake City, UT	53,441
50	Nashville-Davidson, TN	53,143
51	Warren-Farmington Hills, MI M.D.	51,978
52	West Palm Beach, FL M.D.	51,967
53	Birmingham-Hoover, AL	51,286
54	Nassau-Suffolk, NY M.D.	49,052
55	Pittsburgh, PA	47,997
56	Boston-Quincy, MA M.D.	46,053
57	San Jose, CA	43,862
58	Edison, NJ M.D.	43,410
59	Newark-Union, NJ-PA M.D.	41,895
60	Louisville, KY-IN	41,798
61	Providence-New Bedford, RI-MA	41,086
62	Albuquerque, NM	37,368
63	McAllen-Edinburg-Mission, TX	37,311
64	Little Rock, AR	36,186
65	Fresno, CA	35,152
66	Tacoma, WA M.D.	34,776
67	Tulsa, OK	34,358
68	Buffalo-Niagara Falls, NY	33,998
69	Richmond, VA	33,864
70	Baton Rouge, LA	33,701
71	Honolulu, HI	33,375
72	Bakersfield, CA	31,445
73	Camden, NJ M.D.	30,916
74	Greensboro-High Point, NC	30,807
75	Raleigh-Cary, NC	29,720
76	Columbia, SC	29,611
77	Stockton, CA	28,772
78	Rochester, NY	28,608
79	Dayton, OH	28,562
80	Omaha-Council Bluffs, NE-IA	28,519
81	Cambridge-Newton, MA M.D.	28,315
82	Bethesda-Frederick, MD M.D.	28,016
83	Hartford, CT	27,761
84	North Port-Bradenton-Sarasota, FL	27,159
85	New Haven-Milford, CT	25,974
86	Wichita, KS	25,048
87	Augusta, GA-SC	24,987
88	Knoxville, TN	24,783
89	Akron, OH	22,909
90	Wilmington, DE-MD-NJ M.D.	22,880
91	Chattanooga, TN-GA	22,502
92	El Paso, TX	21,909
93	Lakeland, FL	21,882
94	Albany-Schenectady-Troy, NY	21,873
95	Grand Rapids-Wyoming, MI	21,771
96	Modesto, CA	21,577
97	Jackson, MS	21,030
98	Winston-Salem, NC	20,900
99	Corpus Christi, TX	20,873
100	Fayetteville, NC	20,655
101	Spokane, WA	20,070
102	Mobile, AL	20,066
103	Durham-Chapel Hill, NC	19,994
104	Springfield, MA	19,930
105	Brownsville-Harlingen, TX	19,074
106	Allentown, PA-NJ	19,065
107	Springfield, MO	19,056
108	Youngstown, OH-PA	18,446
109	Deltona-Daytona Beach, FL	18,359
110	Palm Bay-Melbourne, FL	17,975
111	Cape Coral-Fort Myers, FL	17,940
112	Colorado Springs, CO	17,809
113	Columbus, GA-AL	17,709
114	Bridgeport-Stamford, CT	17,241
115	Worcester, MA	17,090
116	Flint, MI	16,252
117	Peabody, MA M.D.	16,109
118	Lexington-Fayette, KY	15,971
119	Syracuse, NY	15,945
120	Visalia-Porterville, CA	15,681
121	Shreveport-Bossier City, LA	15,645
122	Des Moines-West Des Moines, IA	15,592
123	Montgomery, AL	15,513
124	Oxnard-Thousand Oaks, CA	15,329
125	Beaumont-Port Arthur, TX	14,918
126	Madison, WI	14,903
127	Pensacola, FL	14,731
128	Ogden-Clearfield, UT	14,639
129	Huntsville, AL	14,572
130	Lubbock, TX	14,456
131	Eugene-Springfield, OR	14,238
132	Savannah, GA	14,210
133	Laredo, TX	14,116
134	Reno-Sparks, NV	13,561
135	Poughkeepsie, NY	13,279
136	Vallejo-Fairfield, CA	13,270
137	South Bend-Mishawaka, IN-MI	12,974
138	Tallahassee, FL	12,872
139	Portland, ME	12,546
140	Provo-Orem, UT	12,273
141	Hickory, NC	12,262
142	Salem, OR	12,257
143	Scranton--Wilkes-Barre, PA	12,229
144	Boise City-Nampa, ID	12,208
145	Killeen-Temple-Fort Hood, TX	12,103
146	Lafayette, LA	11,979
147	Lansing-East Lansing, MI	11,892
148	Amarillo, TX	11,864
149	Fort Wayne, IN	11,577
150	Port St. Lucie, FL	11,559
151	Harrisburg-Carlisle, PA	11,474
152	Kalamazoo-Portage, MI	11,462
153	Macon, GA	11,404
154	Fayetteville, AR-MO	11,376
155	Anchorage, AK	11,210
156	Salinas, CA	11,204
157	Gainesville, FL	11,105
158	Spartanburg, SC	10,871
159	Lincoln, NE	10,645
160	Waco, TX	10,408
161	Kingsport, TN-VA	10,384
162	Florence, SC	10,312
163	Gulfport-Biloxi, MS	10,207
164	Asheville, NC	10,164
165	Lancaster, PA	9,932
166	Charleston, WV	9,660
167	Longview, TX	9,631
168	Reading, PA	9,607
169	Evansville, IN-KY	9,606
170	Tuscaloosa, AL	9,546
171	Santa Rosa-Petaluma, CA	9,450
172	Fort Smith, AR-OK	9,398
173	Duluth, MN-WI	9,365
174	Ann Arbor, MI	9,348
175	Atlantic City, NJ	9,298
176	Manchester-Nashua, NH	9,200
177	College Station-Bryan, TX	9,158
178	Topeka, KS	9,096
179	Lake Charles, LA	9,073
180	Santa Cruz-Watsonville, CA	9,059

Note: All listings are for Metropolitan Statistical Areas (M.S.A.s) except for those ending with "M.D." Listings with "M.D." are Metropolitan Divisions which are smaller parts of eleven large M.S.A.s. See explanatory note at beginning of metropolitan area section.

RANK	METROPOLITAN AREA	CRIMES
181	Santa Barbara-Santa Maria, CA	8,909
182	York-Hanover, PA	8,906
183	Ocala, FL	8,480
184	Roanoke, VA	8,464
185	Merced, CA	8,310
186	Tyler, TX	8,303
187	Fort Collins-Loveland, CO	8,266
188	Rockingham County, NH M.D.	8,132
189	Clarksville, TN-KY	7,981
190	Anderson, SC	7,856
191	Trenton-Ewing, NJ	7,701
192	Athens-Clarke County, GA	7,671
193	Olympia, WA	7,452
194	Muskegon-Norton Shores, MI	7,258
195	Cedar Rapids, IA	7,226
196	Utica-Rome, NY	7,187
197	Panama City-Lynn Haven, FL	7,164
198	Albany, GA	7,140
199	Boulder, CO	7,134
200	Alexandria, LA	7,078
201	Barnstable Town, MA	7,006
202	Bellingham, WA	6,989
203	Lake Havasu City-Kingman, AZ	6,747
204	Erie, PA	6,663
205	Las Cruces, NM	6,660
206	Houma, LA	6,648
207	Burlington-South Burlington, VT	6,417
208	Rocky Mount, NC	6,365
209	Chico, CA	6,338
210	Wichita Falls, TX	6,316
211	Hot Springs, AR	6,206
212	Saginaw, MI	6,181
213	Binghamton, NY	6,166
214	Bremerton-Silverdale, WA	6,156
215	Greeley, CO	6,104
216	Jacksonville, NC	6,079
217	Hagerstown-Martinsburg, MD-WV	6,078
218	Kennewick-Pasco-Richland, WA	6,012
219	San Luis Obispo, CA	5,977
220	Green Bay, WI	5,921
221	Naples-Marco Island, FL	5,861
222	Burlington, NC	5,802
223	Texarkana, TX-Texarkana, AR	5,758
224	Santa Fe, NM	5,751
225	Jackson, TN	5,693
226	Odessa, TX	5,663
227	Billings, MT	5,662
228	Dover, DE	5,658
228	Springfield, OH	5,658
230	Racine, WI	5,642
231	Abilene, TX	5,607
232	Johnson City, TN	5,551
233	Lafayette, IN	5,536
234	Mount Vernon-Anacortes, WA	5,469
235	Anniston-Oxford, AL	5,466
236	Sioux Falls, SD	5,392
237	Bloomington, IN	5,383
238	Battle Creek, MI	5,343
238	Elkhart-Goshen, IN	5,343
240	Victoria, TX	5,337
241	Yuma, AZ	5,333
242	Lawton, OK	5,322
243	Pascagoula, MS	5,307

RANK	METROPOLITAN AREA	CRIMES
244	Vineland, NJ	5,260
245	Columbia, MO	5,248
246	Warner Robins, GA	5,212
247	Charlottesville, VA	5,185
248	Crestview-Fort Walton Beach, FL	5,176
249	Fargo, ND-MN	5,111
250	Pine Bluff, AR	5,103
251	Lawrence, KS	5,081
252	Valdosta, GA	5,068
253	Medford, OR	5,065
254	Bangor, ME	5,027
255	Goldsboro, NC	5,001
256	Salisbury, MD	4,970
257	Mansfield, OH	4,929
258	Brunswick, GA	4,819
259	Decatur, AL	4,817
260	Niles-Benton Harbor, MI	4,788
261	Pueblo, CO	4,710
262	St. Joseph, MO-KS	4,702
263	Lynchburg, VA	4,687
264	Anderson, IN	4,649
265	Redding, CA	4,640
266	San Angelo, TX	4,625
267	Janesville, WI	4,606
268	Jonesboro, AR	4,569
269	Holland-Grand Haven, MI	4,568
270	Midland, TX	4,559
271	Prescott, AZ	4,550
272	Gainesville, GA	4,515
273	Grand Junction, CO	4,511
274	Lima, OH	4,506
275	Florence-Muscle Shoals, AL	4,455
276	Appleton, WI	4,447
277	Morristown, TN	4,442
278	Flagstaff, AZ	4,396
279	St. Cloud, MN	4,374
280	Ocean City, NJ	4,244
281	Jackson, MI	4,154
282	Punta Gorda, FL	4,151
283	Blacksburg, VA	4,142
284	Bend, OR	4,089
285	Waterloo-Cedar Falls, IA	4,055
286	Michigan City-La Porte, IN	4,045
287	Sebastian-Vero Beach, FL	4,034
288	Bowling Green, KY	3,922
289	Dalton, GA	3,900
290	Oshkosh-Neenah, WI	3,895
291	Longview, WA	3,893
292	Sherman-Denison, TX	3,884
293	Rochester, MN	3,867
294	Gadsden, AL	3,734
295	Coeur d'Alene, ID	3,713
296	Decatur, IL	3,669
297	Monroe, MI	3,656
298	Yuba City, CA	3,617
299	Norwich-New London, CT	3,578
300	Sioux City, IA-NE-SD	3,530
301	Rapid City, SD	3,474
302	Kingston, NY	3,440
303	Sumter, SC	3,433
304	Cleveland, TN	3,385
305	Muncie, IN	3,363
306	La Crosse, WI-MN	3,362

RANK	METROPOLITAN AREA	CRIMES
307	Kokomo, IN	3,314
308	Wenatchee, WA	3,288
309	Jefferson City, MO	3,250
310	Eau Claire, WI	3,249
311	Owensboro, KY	3,186
312	Madera, CA	3,170
313	Danville, IL	3,155
314	Napa, CA	3,116
315	Rome, GA	3,093
316	Farmington, NM	3,032
317	Cape Girardeau, MO-IL	3,016
318	Winchester, VA-WV	2,994
319	Casper, WY	2,954
320	Sheboygan, WI	2,941
321	Danville, VA	2,936
322	Pittsfield, MA	2,928
323	Iowa City, IA	2,901
324	Cheyenne, WY	2,884
325	Morgantown, WV	2,831
326	Wheeling, WV-OH	2,817
327	Missoula, MT	2,765
328	Manhattan, KS	2,763
329	Mankato-North Mankato, MN	2,758
330	Cumberland, MD-WV	2,756
331	Great Falls, MT	2,702
332	Idaho Falls, ID	2,691
333	State College, PA	2,677
334	Hinesville, GA	2,657
335	Columbus, IN	2,612
336	Bay City, MI	2,595
337	Lewiston-Auburn, ME	2,502
338	St. George, UT	2,458
339	Pocatello, ID	2,419
340	Altoona, PA	2,368
341	Ithaca, NY	2,358
342	Sandusky, OH	2,355
343	Grand Forks, ND-MN	2,298
344	Corvallis, OR	2,292
345	Palm Coast, FL	2,291
346	Ames, IA	2,280
347	Wausau, WI	2,247
348	Bismarck, ND	2,239
349	Williamsport, PA	2,213
350	Lebanon, PA	2,198
351	Dubuque, IA	2,182
352	Glens Falls, NY	2,073
353	Elizabethtown, KY	2,054
354	Elmira, NY	1,962
355	Logan, UT-ID	1,924
356	Lewiston, ID-WA	1,833
357	Harrisonburg, VA	1,823
358	Fond du Lac, WI	1,773
359	Carson City, NV	1,151
NA	Auburn, AL**	NA
NA	Charleston-North Charleston, SC**	NA
NA	Dothan, AL**	NA
NA	El Centro, CA**	NA
NA	Hattiesburg, MS**	NA
NA	Kansas City, MO-KS**	NA
NA	New Orleans, LA**	NA
NA	Toledo, OH**	NA
NA	Tucson, AZ**	NA
NA	Wilmington, NC**	NA

Source: Reported data from the F.B.I. "Crime in the United States 2009"

*Property crimes are offenses of burglary, larceny-theft, and motor vehicle theft. Attempts are included.

**Not available.

26. Property Crime Rate in 2009
National Rate = 3,036.1 Property Crimes per 100,000 Population*

RANK	METROPOLITAN AREA	RATE
130	Abilene, TX	3,512.5
161	Akron, OH	3,268.4
258	Albany-Schenectady-Troy, NY	2,553.1
46	Albany, GA	4,322.9
44	Albuquerque, NM	4,334.1
27	Alexandria, LA	4,566.5
295	Allentown, PA-NJ	2,331.6
341	Altoona, PA	1,893.4
17	Amarillo, TX	4,822.0
249	Ames, IA	2,608.7
114	Anchorage, AK	3,672.0
128	Anderson, IN	3,534.7
58	Anderson, SC	4,228.3
241	Ann Arbor, MI	2,681.5
18	Anniston-Oxford, AL	4,788.2
329	Appleton, WI	2,006.7
272	Asheville, NC	2,457.7
77	Athens-Clarke County, GA	4,014.2
127	Atlanta, GA	3,540.5
138	Atlantic City, NJ	3,410.9
NA	Auburn, AL**	NA
26	Augusta, GA-SC	4,646.5
76	Austin-Round Rock, TX	4,024.8
97	Bakersfield, CA	3,860.6
155	Baltimore-Towson, MD	3,296.0
144	Bangor, ME	3,379.0
182	Barnstable Town, MA	3,123.5
55	Baton Rouge, LA	4,278.3
83	Battle Creek, MI	3,955.6
277	Bay City, MI	2,430.3
85	Beaumont-Port Arthur, TX	3,946.7
132	Bellingham, WA	3,473.7
264	Bend, OR	2,498.8
293	Bethesda-Frederick, MD M.D.	2,345.9
111	Billings, MT	3,690.0
263	Binghamton, NY	2,523.3
31	Birmingham-Hoover, AL	4,535.6
321	Bismarck, ND	2,093.5
251	Blacksburg, VA	2,593.5
205	Bloomington, IN	2,906.7
330	Boise City-Nampa, ID	1,988.2
314	Boston (greater), MA-NH	2,150.0
279	Boston-Quincy, MA M.D.	2,408.1
278	Boulder, CO	2,408.9
158	Bowling Green, KY	3,275.3
260	Bremerton-Silverdale, WA	2,543.5
332	Bridgeport-Stamford, CT	1,963.6
19	Brownsville-Harlingen, TX	4,769.0
24	Brunswick, GA	4,654.9
190	Buffalo-Niagara Falls, NY	3,038.0
188	Burlington-South Burlington, VT	3,067.4
96	Burlington, NC	3,861.5
344	Cambridge-Newton, MA M.D.	1,882.3
271	Camden, NJ M.D.	2,459.2
200	Cape Coral-Fort Myers, FL	2,954.5
172	Cape Girardeau, MO-IL	3,218.3
317	Carson City, NV	2,113.4
86	Casper, WY	3,946.2
220	Cedar Rapids, IA	2,810.4
NA	Charleston-North Charleston, SC**	NA
178	Charleston, WV	3,177.8
93	Charlotte-Gastonia, NC-SC	3,902.2
247	Charlottesville, VA	2,625.5
51	Chattanooga, TN-GA	4,296.0
170	Cheyenne, WY	3,227.6
208	Chico, CA	2,861.7
154	Cincinnati-Middletown, OH-KY-IN	3,305.4
194	Clarksville, TN-KY	3,008.3
212	Cleveland-Elyria-Mentor, OH	2,838.1
196	Cleveland, TN	2,984.8
243	Coeur d'Alene, ID	2,644.4
42	College Station-Bryan, TX	4,355.1
213	Colorado Springs, CO	2,835.5
180	Columbia, MO	3,152.6
80	Columbia, SC	3,992.7
2	Columbus, GA-AL	6,157.4
135	Columbus, IN	3,441.3
52	Columbus, OH	4,290.8
12	Corpus Christi, TX	5,003.1
226	Corvallis, OR	2,791.2
206	Crestview-Fort Walton Beach, FL	2,890.0
227	Cumberland, MD-WV	2,780.1
92	Dallas (greater), TX	3,912.7
103	Dallas-Plano-Irving, TX M.D.	3,819.3
207	Dalton, GA	2,886.7
88	Danville, IL	3,942.9
228	Danville, VA	2,777.1
139	Dayton, OH	3,408.9
177	Decatur, AL	3,184.6
137	Decatur, IL	3,421.6
113	Deltona-Daytona Beach, FL	3,672.8
224	Denver-Aurora, CO	2,797.5
232	Des Moines-West Des Moines, IA	2,762.5
187	Detroit (greater), MI	3,071.0
48	Detroit-Livonia-Dearborn, MI M.D.	4,314.3
NA	Dothan, AL**	NA
125	Dover, DE	3,553.6
292	Dubuque, IA	2,346.6
140	Duluth, MN-WI	3,406.7
78	Durham-Chapel Hill, NC	4,012.7
326	Eau Claire, WI	2,032.9
345	Edison, NJ M.D.	1,854.6
NA	El Centro, CA**	NA
204	El Paso, TX	2,921.4
348	Elizabethtown, KY	1,818.2
242	Elkhart-Goshen, IN	2,654.4
303	Elmira, NY	2,244.1
284	Erie, PA	2,382.1
71	Eugene-Springfield, OR	4,085.2
235	Evansville, IN-KY	2,731.4
255	Fargo, ND-MN	2,563.9
275	Farmington, NM	2,448.9
266	Fayetteville, AR-MO	2,484.8
4	Fayetteville, NC	5,753.7
136	Flagstaff, AZ	3,422.1
104	Flint, MI	3,813.4
185	Florence-Muscle Shoals, AL	3,082.7
8	Florence, SC	5,112.4
349	Fond du Lac, WI	1,779.5
230	Fort Collins-Loveland, CO	2,772.8
81	Fort Lauderdale, FL M.D.	3,976.5
176	Fort Smith, AR-OK	3,193.2
225	Fort Wayne, IN	2,795.4
68	Fort Worth-Arlington, TX M.D.	4,103.6
101	Fresno, CA	3,826.2
121	Gadsden, AL	3,598.7
54	Gainesville, FL	4,283.6
285	Gainesville, GA	2,380.8
357	Glens Falls, NY	1,604.0
38	Goldsboro, NC	4,391.1
291	Grand Forks, ND-MN	2,348.5
186	Grand Junction, CO	3,077.0
223	Grand Rapids-Wyoming, MI	2,800.0
156	Great Falls, MT	3,287.4
288	Greeley, CO	2,356.7
336	Green Bay, WI	1,941.0
47	Greensboro-High Point, NC	4,315.4
39	Gulfport-Biloxi, MS	4,369.1
302	Hagerstown-Martinsburg, MD-WV	2,253.0
316	Harrisburg-Carlisle, PA	2,144.9
358	Harrisonburg, VA	1,518.7
233	Hartford, CT	2,755.4
NA	Hattiesburg, MS**	NA
148	Hickory, NC	3,350.9
102	Hinesville, GA	3,825.4
351	Holland-Grand Haven, MI	1,745.3
112	Honolulu, HI	3,679.2
1	Hot Springs, AR	6,273.4
160	Houma, LA	3,272.0
66	Houston, TX	4,120.8
119	Huntsville, AL	3,610.0
313	Idaho Falls, ID	2,151.8
100	Indianapolis, IN	3,827.1
338	Iowa City, IA	1,917.6
297	Ithaca, NY	2,320.5
49	Jacksonville, FL	4,308.4
118	Jacksonville, NC	3,616.0
250	Jackson, MI	2,601.2
94	Jackson, MS	3,878.2
11	Jackson, TN	5,010.8
209	Janesville, WI	2,860.7
308	Jefferson City, MO	2,210.1
222	Johnson City, TN	2,802.5
99	Jonesboro, AR	3,841.7
126	Kalamazoo-Portage, MI	3,544.9
NA	Kansas City, MO-KS**	NA
268	Kennewick-Pasco-Richland, WA	2,475.9
181	Killeen-Temple-Fort Hood, TX	3,142.5
143	Kingsport, TN-VA	3,389.0
342	Kingston, NY	1,889.7
129	Knoxville, TN	3,530.2
149	Kokomo, IN	3,339.9
261	La Crosse, WI-MN	2,539.1
211	Lafayette, IN	2,841.2
29	Lafayette, LA	4,554.0
22	Lake Charles, LA	4,675.2
142	Lake Havasu City-Kingman, AZ	3,389.8
108	Lakeland, FL	3,727.4
334	Lancaster, PA	1,958.3
246	Lansing-East Lansing, MI	2,626.1

Note: All listings are for Metropolitan Statistical Areas (M.S.A.s) except for those ending with "M.D." Listings with "M.D." are Metropolitan Divisions which are smaller parts of eleven large M.S.A.s. See explanatory note at beginning of metropolitan area section.

Alpha Order - Metro Area (continued)

RANK	METROPOLITAN AREA	RATE
3	Laredo, TX	5,822.3
166	Las Cruces, NM	3,243.3
169	Las Vegas-Paradise, NV	3,231.5
41	Lawrence, KS	4,357.6
20	Lawton, OK	4,745.8
356	Lebanon, PA	1,687.5
294	Lewiston-Auburn, ME	2,338.2
192	Lewiston, ID-WA	3,022.9
141	Lexington-Fayette, KY	3,392.0
53	Lima, OH	4,286.9
124	Lincoln, NE	3,554.7
7	Little Rock, AR	5,279.6
359	Logan, UT-ID	1,513.6
23	Longview, TX	4,670.8
106	Longview, WA	3,786.4
273	Los Angeles County, CA M.D.	2,453.0
290	Los Angeles (greater), CA	2,349.5
153	Louisville, KY-IN	3,327.2
6	Lubbock, TX	5,289.6
343	Lynchburg, VA	1,884.6
15	Macon, GA	4,942.1
319	Madera, CA	2,101.3
248	Madison, WI	2,623.7
300	Manchester-Nashua, NH	2,275.5
305	Manhattan, KS	2,235.5
201	Mankato-North Mankato, MN	2,953.8
87	Mansfield, OH	3,944.6
13	McAllen-Edinburg-Mission, TX	4,996.3
265	Medford, OR	2,495.0
10	Memphis, TN-MS-AR	5,071.8
151	Merced, CA	3,331.6
35	Miami (greater), FL	4,442.5
14	Miami-Dade County, FL M.D.	4,949.0
115	Michigan City-La Porte, IN	3,639.1
133	Midland, TX	3,472.4
117	Milwaukee, WI	3,628.2
197	Minneapolis-St. Paul, MN-WI	2,982.8
259	Missoula, MT	2,546.4
16	Mobile, AL	4,908.3
64	Modesto, CA	4,180.0
283	Monroe, MI	2,388.4
63	Montgomery, AL	4,194.4
287	Morgantown, WV	2,367.4
171	Morristown, TN	3,223.7
30	Mount Vernon-Anacortes, WA	4,540.9
202	Muncie, IN	2,938.8
65	Muskegon-Norton Shores, MI	4,169.6
296	Napa, CA	2,325.4
347	Naples-Marco Island, FL	1,831.0
147	Nashville-Davidson, TN	3,353.5
354	Nassau-Suffolk, NY M.D.	1,706.2
161	New Haven-Milford, CT	3,268.4
NA	New Orleans, LA**	NA
350	New York (greater), NY-NJ-PA	1,750.5
355	New York-W. Plains NY-NJ M.D.	1,700.2
331	Newark-Union, NJ-PA M.D.	1,973.5
193	Niles-Benton Harbor, MI	3,020.8
91	North Port-Bradenton-Sarasota, FL	3,918.1
253	Norwich-New London, CT	2,581.3
131	Oakland-Fremont, CA M.D.	3,486.8
262	Ocala, FL	2,528.1
33	Ocean City, NJ	4,462.7
57	Odessa, TX	4,245.1
240	Ogden-Clearfield, UT	2,714.6
34	Oklahoma City, OK	4,461.1
198	Olympia, WA	2,967.4
146	Omaha-Council Bluffs, NE-IA	3,364.2
79	Orlando, FL	3,998.1
281	Oshkosh-Neenah, WI	2,395.5
217	Owensboro, KY	2,813.2
339	Oxnard-Thousand Oaks, CA	1,916.9
150	Palm Bay-Melbourne, FL	3,336.8
286	Palm Coast, FL	2,371.3
40	Panama City-Lynn Haven, FL	4,359.6
134	Pascagoula, MS	3,459.2
311	Peabody, MA M.D.	2,155.6
165	Pensacola, FL	3,245.5
244	Philadelphia (greater) PA-NJ-MD-DE	2,637.5
252	Philadelphia, PA M.D.	2,584.7
120	Phoenix-Mesa-Scottsdale, AZ	3,602.4
9	Pine Bluff, AR	5,085.8
325	Pittsburgh, PA	2,043.5
306	Pittsfield, MA	2,230.0
236	Pocatello, ID	2,726.0
218	Port St. Lucie, FL	2,812.8
203	Portland-Vancouver, OR-WA	2,929.0
276	Portland, ME	2,432.0
333	Poughkeepsie, NY	1,958.6
323	Prescott, AZ	2,078.6
256	Providence-New Bedford, RI-MA	2,556.6
310	Provo-Orem, UT	2,193.3
199	Pueblo, CO	2,966.9
229	Punta Gorda, FL	2,774.0
219	Racine, WI	2,812.4
245	Raleigh-Cary, NC	2,635.0
221	Rapid City, SD	2,803.8
289	Reading, PA	2,354.7
257	Redding, CA	2,556.3
167	Reno-Sparks, NV	3,242.4
238	Richmond, VA	2,719.1
214	Riverside-San Bernardino, CA	2,832.8
216	Roanoke, VA	2,818.1
322	Rochester, MN	2,084.8
231	Rochester, NY	2,769.6
337	Rockingham County, NH M.D.	1,924.7
45	Rocky Mount, NC	4,330.4
173	Rome, GA	3,217.0
175	Sacramento, CA	3,195.2
183	Saginaw, MI	3,106.9
184	Salem, OR	3,094.5
234	Salinas, CA	2,750.1
72	Salisbury, MD	4,073.6
21	Salt Lake City, UT	4,742.1
62	San Angelo, TX	4,200.6
5	San Antonio, TX	5,483.9
298	San Diego, CA	2,316.2
145	San Francisco (greater), CA	3,368.0
174	San Francisco-S. Mateo, CA M.D.	3,199.6
280	San Jose, CA	2,407.4
304	San Luis Obispo, CA	2,243.8
189	Sandusky, OH	3,057.9
328	Santa Ana-Anaheim, CA M.D.	2,011.1
309	Santa Barbara-Santa Maria, CA	2,201.9
122	Santa Cruz-Watsonville, CA	3,595.4
89	Santa Fe, NM	3,939.5
327	Santa Rosa-Petaluma, CA	2,028.6
61	Savannah, GA	4,205.3
307	Scranton--Wilkes-Barre, PA	2,225.9
90	Seattle-Bellevue-Everett, WA M.D.	3,933.4
75	Seattle-Tacoma-Bellevue, WA	4,030.8
191	Sebastian-Vero Beach, FL	3,023.5
254	Sheboygan, WI	2,564.0
168	Sherman-Denison, TX	3,241.2
82	Shreveport-Bossier City, LA	3,975.2
270	Sioux City, IA-NE-SD	2,466.3
301	Sioux Falls, SD	2,253.7
70	South Bend-Mishawaka, IN-MI	4,091.5
105	Spartanburg, SC	3,808.8
56	Spokane, WA	4,265.0
210	Springfield, MA	2,856.6
37	Springfield, MO	4,399.9
74	Springfield, OH	4,048.6
346	State College, PA	1,831.4
60	Stockton, CA	4,213.9
299	St. Cloud, MN	2,307.4
352	St. George, UT	1,715.6
109	St. Joseph, MO-KS	3,712.6
179	St. Louis, MO-IL	3,168.4
157	Sumter, SC	3,279.7
267	Syracuse, NY	2,480.0
43	Tacoma, WA M.D.	4,347.3
123	Tallahassee, FL	3,591.7
95	Tampa-St Petersburg, FL	3,864.9
59	Texarkana, TX-Texarkana, AR	4,220.1
NA	Toledo, OH**	NA
84	Topeka, KS	3,947.8
318	Trenton-Ewing, NJ	2,102.8
NA	Tucson, AZ**	NA
110	Tulsa, OK	3,701.9
28	Tuscaloosa, AL	4,561.9
73	Tyler, TX	4,058.5
274	Utica-Rome, NY	2,452.2
107	Valdosta, GA	3,771.5
164	Vallejo-Fairfield, CA	3,258.1
25	Victoria, TX	4,651.6
152	Vineland, NJ	3,329.9
116	Visalia-Porterville, CA	3,632.3
32	Waco, TX	4,480.0
98	Warner Robins, GA	3,853.7
320	Warren-Farmington Hills, MI M.D.	2,101.0
237	Washington (greater) DC-VA-MD-WV	2,724.1
215	Washington, DC-VA-MD-WV M.D.	2,830.1
269	Waterloo-Cedar Falls, IA	2,471.9
353	Wausau, WI	1,709.1
195	Wenatchee, WA	2,992.7
69	West Palm Beach, FL M.D.	4,094.0
335	Wheeling, WV-OH	1,951.6
50	Wichita Falls, TX	4,296.1
67	Wichita, KS	4,119.6
340	Williamsport, PA	1,897.8
163	Wilmington, DE-MD-NJ M.D.	3,258.6
NA	Wilmington, NC**	NA
282	Winchester, VA-WV	2,393.1
36	Winston-Salem, NC	4,407.8
315	Worcester, MA	2,148.8
324	York-Hanover, PA	2,068.3
159	Youngstown, OH-PA	3,272.3
312	Yuba City, CA	2,154.9
239	Yuma, AZ	2,718.2

Source: Reported data from the F.B.I. "Crime in the United States 2009"

*Property crimes are offenses of burglary, larceny-theft, and motor vehicle theft. Attempts are included.

**Not available.

26. Property Crime Rate in 2009 (continued)
National Rate = 3,036.1 Property Crimes per 100,000 Population*

RANK	METROPOLITAN AREA	RATE
1	Hot Springs, AR	6,273.4
2	Columbus, GA-AL	6,157.4
3	Laredo, TX	5,822.3
4	Fayetteville, NC	5,753.7
5	San Antonio, TX	5,483.9
6	Lubbock, TX	5,289.6
7	Little Rock, AR	5,279.6
8	Florence, SC	5,112.4
9	Pine Bluff, AR	5,085.8
10	Memphis, TN-MS-AR	5,071.8
11	Jackson, TN	5,010.8
12	Corpus Christi, TX	5,003.1
13	McAllen-Edinburg-Mission, TX	4,996.3
14	Miami-Dade County, FL M.D.	4,949.0
15	Macon, GA	4,942.1
16	Mobile, AL	4,908.3
17	Amarillo, TX	4,822.0
18	Anniston-Oxford, AL	4,788.2
19	Brownsville-Harlingen, TX	4,769.0
20	Lawton, OK	4,745.8
21	Salt Lake City, UT	4,742.1
22	Lake Charles, LA	4,675.2
23	Longview, TX	4,670.8
24	Brunswick, GA	4,654.9
25	Victoria, TX	4,651.6
26	Augusta, GA-SC	4,646.5
27	Alexandria, LA	4,566.5
28	Tuscaloosa, AL	4,561.9
29	Lafayette, LA	4,554.0
30	Mount Vernon-Anacortes, WA	4,540.9
31	Birmingham-Hoover, AL	4,535.6
32	Waco, TX	4,480.0
33	Ocean City, NJ	4,462.7
34	Oklahoma City, OK	4,461.1
35	Miami (greater), FL	4,442.5
36	Winston-Salem, NC	4,407.8
37	Springfield, MO	4,399.9
38	Goldsboro, NC	4,391.1
39	Gulfport-Biloxi, MS	4,369.1
40	Panama City-Lynn Haven, FL	4,359.6
41	Lawrence, KS	4,357.6
42	College Station-Bryan, TX	4,355.1
43	Tacoma, WA M.D.	4,347.3
44	Albuquerque, NM	4,334.1
45	Rocky Mount, NC	4,330.4
46	Albany, GA	4,322.9
47	Greensboro-High Point, NC	4,315.4
48	Detroit-Livonia-Dearborn, MI M.D.	4,314.3
49	Jacksonville, FL	4,308.4
50	Wichita Falls, TX	4,296.1
51	Chattanooga, TN-GA	4,296.0
52	Columbus, OH	4,290.8
53	Lima, OH	4,286.9
54	Gainesville, FL	4,283.6
55	Baton Rouge, LA	4,278.3
56	Spokane, WA	4,265.0
57	Odessa, TX	4,245.1
58	Anderson, SC	4,228.3
59	Texarkana, TX-Texarkana, AR	4,220.1
60	Stockton, CA	4,213.9
61	Savannah, GA	4,205.3
62	San Angelo, TX	4,200.6
63	Montgomery, AL	4,194.4
64	Modesto, CA	4,180.0
65	Muskegon-Norton Shores, MI	4,169.6
66	Houston, TX	4,120.8
67	Wichita, KS	4,119.6
68	Fort Worth-Arlington, TX M.D.	4,103.6
69	West Palm Beach, FL M.D.	4,094.0
70	South Bend-Mishawaka, IN-MI	4,091.5
71	Eugene-Springfield, OR	4,085.2
72	Salisbury, MD	4,073.6
73	Tyler, TX	4,058.5
74	Springfield, OH	4,048.6
75	Seattle-Tacoma-Bellevue, WA	4,030.8
76	Austin-Round Rock, TX	4,024.8
77	Athens-Clarke County, GA	4,014.2
78	Durham-Chapel Hill, NC	4,012.7
79	Orlando, FL	3,998.1
80	Columbia, SC	3,992.7
81	Fort Lauderdale, FL M.D.	3,976.5
82	Shreveport-Bossier City, LA	3,975.2
83	Battle Creek, MI	3,955.6
84	Topeka, KS	3,947.8
85	Beaumont-Port Arthur, TX	3,946.7
86	Casper, WY	3,946.2
87	Mansfield, OH	3,944.6
88	Danville, IL	3,942.9
89	Santa Fe, NM	3,939.5
90	Seattle-Bellevue-Everett, WA M.D.	3,933.4
91	North Port-Bradenton-Sarasota, FL	3,918.1
92	Dallas (greater), TX	3,912.7
93	Charlotte-Gastonia, NC-SC	3,902.2
94	Jackson, MS	3,878.2
95	Tampa-St Petersburg, FL	3,864.9
96	Burlington, NC	3,861.5
97	Bakersfield, CA	3,860.6
98	Warner Robins, GA	3,853.7
99	Jonesboro, AR	3,841.7
100	Indianapolis, IN	3,827.1
101	Fresno, CA	3,826.2
102	Hinesville, GA	3,825.4
103	Dallas-Plano-Irving, TX M.D.	3,819.3
104	Flint, MI	3,813.4
105	Spartanburg, SC	3,808.8
106	Longview, WA	3,786.4
107	Valdosta, GA	3,771.5
108	Lakeland, FL	3,727.4
109	St. Joseph, MO-KS	3,712.6
110	Tulsa, OK	3,701.9
111	Billings, MT	3,690.0
112	Honolulu, HI	3,679.2
113	Deltona-Daytona Beach, FL	3,672.8
114	Anchorage, AK	3,672.0
115	Michigan City-La Porte, IN	3,639.1
116	Visalia-Porterville, CA	3,632.3
117	Milwaukee, WI	3,628.2
118	Jacksonville, NC	3,616.0
119	Huntsville, AL	3,610.0
120	Phoenix-Mesa-Scottsdale, AZ	3,602.4
121	Gadsden, AL	3,598.7
122	Santa Cruz-Watsonville, CA	3,595.4
123	Tallahassee, FL	3,591.7
124	Lincoln, NE	3,554.7
125	Dover, DE	3,553.6
126	Kalamazoo-Portage, MI	3,544.9
127	Atlanta, GA	3,540.5
128	Anderson, IN	3,534.7
129	Knoxville, TN	3,530.2
130	Abilene, TX	3,512.5
131	Oakland-Fremont, CA M.D.	3,486.8
132	Bellingham, WA	3,473.7
133	Midland, TX	3,472.4
134	Pascagoula, MS	3,459.2
135	Columbus, IN	3,441.3
136	Flagstaff, AZ	3,422.1
137	Decatur, IL	3,421.6
138	Atlantic City, NJ	3,410.9
139	Dayton, OH	3,408.9
140	Duluth, MN-WI	3,406.7
141	Lexington-Fayette, KY	3,392.0
142	Lake Havasu City-Kingman, AZ	3,389.8
143	Kingsport, TN-VA	3,389.0
144	Bangor, ME	3,379.0
145	San Francisco (greater), CA	3,368.0
146	Omaha-Council Bluffs, NE-IA	3,364.2
147	Nashville-Davidson, TN	3,353.5
148	Hickory, NC	3,350.9
149	Kokomo, IN	3,339.9
150	Palm Bay-Melbourne, FL	3,336.8
151	Merced, CA	3,331.6
152	Vineland, NJ	3,329.9
153	Louisville, KY-IN	3,327.2
154	Cincinnati-Middletown, OH-KY-IN	3,305.4
155	Baltimore-Towson, MD	3,296.0
156	Great Falls, MT	3,287.4
157	Sumter, SC	3,279.7
158	Bowling Green, KY	3,275.3
159	Youngstown, OH-PA	3,272.3
160	Houma, LA	3,272.0
161	Akron, OH	3,268.4
161	New Haven-Milford, CT	3,268.4
163	Wilmington, DE-MD-NJ M.D.	3,258.6
164	Vallejo-Fairfield, CA	3,258.1
165	Pensacola, FL	3,245.5
166	Las Cruces, NM	3,243.3
167	Reno-Sparks, NV	3,242.4
168	Sherman-Denison, TX	3,241.2
169	Las Vegas-Paradise, NV	3,231.5
170	Cheyenne, WY	3,227.6
171	Morristown, TN	3,223.7
172	Cape Girardeau, MO-IL	3,218.3
173	Rome, GA	3,217.0
174	San Francisco-S. Mateo, CA M.D.	3,199.6
175	Sacramento, CA	3,195.2
176	Fort Smith, AR-OK	3,193.2
177	Decatur, AL	3,184.6
178	Charleston, WV	3,177.8
179	St. Louis, MO-IL	3,168.4
180	Columbia, MO	3,152.6

Note: All listings are for Metropolitan Statistical Areas (M.S.A.s) except for those ending with "M.D." Listings with "M.D." are Metropolitan Divisions which are smaller parts of eleven large M.S.A.s. See explanatory note at beginning of metropolitan area section.

Rank Order - Metro Area (continued)

RANK	METROPOLITAN AREA	RATE
181	Killeen-Temple-Fort Hood, TX	3,142.5
182	Barnstable Town, MA	3,123.5
183	Saginaw, MI	3,106.9
184	Salem, OR	3,094.5
185	Florence-Muscle Shoals, AL	3,082.7
186	Grand Junction, CO	3,077.0
187	Detroit (greater), MI	3,071.0
188	Burlington-South Burlington, VT	3,067.4
189	Sandusky, OH	3,057.9
190	Buffalo-Niagara Falls, NY	3,038.0
191	Sebastian-Vero Beach, FL	3,023.5
192	Lewiston, ID-WA	3,022.9
193	Niles-Benton Harbor, MI	3,020.8
194	Clarksville, TN-KY	3,008.3
195	Wenatchee, WA	2,992.7
196	Cleveland, TN	2,984.8
197	Minneapolis-St. Paul, MN-WI	2,982.8
198	Olympia, WA	2,967.4
199	Pueblo, CO	2,966.9
200	Cape Coral-Fort Myers, FL	2,954.5
201	Mankato-North Mankato, MN	2,953.8
202	Muncie, IN	2,938.8
203	Portland-Vancouver, OR-WA	2,929.0
204	El Paso, TX	2,921.4
205	Bloomington, IN	2,906.7
206	Crestview-Fort Walton Beach, FL	2,890.0
207	Dalton, GA	2,886.7
208	Chico, CA	2,861.7
209	Janesville, WI	2,860.7
210	Springfield, MA	2,856.6
211	Lafayette, IN	2,841.2
212	Cleveland-Elyria-Mentor, OH	2,838.1
213	Colorado Springs, CO	2,835.5
214	Riverside-San Bernardino, CA	2,832.8
215	Washington, DC-VA-MD-WV M.D.	2,830.1
216	Roanoke, VA	2,818.1
217	Owensboro, KY	2,813.2
218	Port St. Lucie, FL	2,812.8
219	Racine, WI	2,812.4
220	Cedar Rapids, IA	2,810.4
221	Rapid City, SD	2,803.8
222	Johnson City, TN	2,802.5
223	Grand Rapids-Wyoming, MI	2,800.0
224	Denver-Aurora, CO	2,797.5
225	Fort Wayne, IN	2,795.4
226	Corvallis, OR	2,791.2
227	Cumberland, MD-WV	2,780.1
228	Danville, VA	2,777.1
229	Punta Gorda, FL	2,774.0
230	Fort Collins-Loveland, CO	2,772.8
231	Rochester, NY	2,769.6
232	Des Moines-West Des Moines, IA	2,762.5
233	Hartford, CT	2,755.4
234	Salinas, CA	2,750.1
235	Evansville, IN-KY	2,731.4
236	Pocatello, ID	2,726.0
237	Washington (greater) DC-VA-MD-WV	2,724.1
238	Richmond, VA	2,719.1
239	Yuma, AZ	2,718.2
240	Ogden-Clearfield, UT	2,714.6
241	Ann Arbor, MI	2,681.5
242	Elkhart-Goshen, IN	2,654.4
243	Coeur d'Alene, ID	2,644.4

RANK	METROPOLITAN AREA	RATE
244	Philadelphia (greater) PA-NJ-MD-DE	2,637.5
245	Raleigh-Cary, NC	2,635.0
246	Lansing-East Lansing, MI	2,626.1
247	Charlottesville, VA	2,625.5
248	Madison, WI	2,623.7
249	Ames, IA	2,608.7
250	Jackson, MI	2,601.2
251	Blacksburg, VA	2,593.5
252	Philadelphia, PA M.D.	2,584.7
253	Norwich-New London, CT	2,581.3
254	Sheboygan, WI	2,564.0
255	Fargo, ND-MN	2,563.9
256	Providence-New Bedford, RI-MA	2,556.6
257	Redding, CA	2,556.3
258	Albany-Schenectady-Troy, NY	2,553.1
259	Missoula, MT	2,546.4
260	Bremerton-Silverdale, WA	2,543.5
261	La Crosse, WI-MN	2,539.1
262	Ocala, FL	2,528.1
263	Binghamton, NY	2,523.3
264	Bend, OR	2,498.8
265	Medford, OR	2,495.0
266	Fayetteville, AR-MO	2,484.8
267	Syracuse, NY	2,480.0
268	Kennewick-Pasco-Richland, WA	2,475.9
269	Waterloo-Cedar Falls, IA	2,471.9
270	Sioux City, IA-NE-SD	2,466.3
271	Camden, NJ M.D.	2,459.2
272	Asheville, NC	2,457.7
273	Los Angeles County, CA M.D.	2,453.0
274	Utica-Rome, NY	2,452.2
275	Farmington, NM	2,448.9
276	Portland, ME	2,432.0
277	Bay City, MI	2,430.3
278	Boulder, CO	2,408.9
279	Boston-Quincy, MA M.D.	2,408.1
280	San Jose, CA	2,407.4
281	Oshkosh-Neenah, WI	2,395.5
282	Winchester, VA-WV	2,393.1
283	Monroe, MI	2,388.4
284	Erie, PA	2,382.1
285	Gainesville, GA	2,380.8
286	Palm Coast, FL	2,371.3
287	Morgantown, WV	2,367.4
288	Greeley, CO	2,356.7
289	Reading, PA	2,354.7
290	Los Angeles (greater), CA	2,349.5
291	Grand Forks, ND-MN	2,348.5
292	Dubuque, IA	2,346.6
293	Bethesda-Frederick, MD M.D.	2,345.9
294	Lewiston-Auburn, ME	2,338.2
295	Allentown, PA-NJ	2,331.6
296	Napa, CA	2,325.4
297	Ithaca, NY	2,320.5
298	San Diego, CA	2,316.2
299	St. Cloud, MN	2,307.4
300	Manchester-Nashua, NH	2,275.5
301	Sioux Falls, SD	2,253.7
302	Hagerstown-Martinsburg, MD-WV	2,253.0
303	Elmira, NY	2,244.1
304	San Luis Obispo, CA	2,243.8
305	Manhattan, KS	2,235.5
306	Pittsfield, MA	2,230.0

RANK	METROPOLITAN AREA	RATE
307	Scranton--Wilkes-Barre, PA	2,225.9
308	Jefferson City, MO	2,210.1
309	Santa Barbara-Santa Maria, CA	2,201.9
310	Provo-Orem, UT	2,193.3
311	Peabody, MA M.D.	2,155.6
312	Yuba City, CA	2,154.9
313	Idaho Falls, ID	2,151.8
314	Boston (greater), MA-NH	2,150.0
315	Worcester, MA	2,148.8
316	Harrisburg-Carlisle, PA	2,144.9
317	Carson City, NV	2,113.4
318	Trenton-Ewing, NJ	2,102.8
319	Madera, CA	2,101.3
320	Warren-Farmington Hills, MI M.D.	2,101.0
321	Bismarck, ND	2,093.5
322	Rochester, MN	2,084.8
323	Prescott, AZ	2,078.6
324	York-Hanover, PA	2,068.3
325	Pittsburgh, PA	2,043.5
326	Eau Claire, WI	2,032.9
327	Santa Rosa-Petaluma, CA	2,028.6
328	Santa Ana-Anaheim, CA M.D.	2,011.1
329	Appleton, WI	2,006.7
330	Boise City-Nampa, ID	1,988.2
331	Newark-Union, NJ-PA M.D.	1,973.5
332	Bridgeport-Stamford, CT	1,963.6
333	Poughkeepsie, NY	1,958.6
334	Lancaster, PA	1,958.3
335	Wheeling, WV-OH	1,951.6
336	Green Bay, WI	1,941.0
337	Rockingham County, NH M.D.	1,924.7
338	Iowa City, IA	1,917.6
339	Oxnard-Thousand Oaks, CA	1,916.9
340	Williamsport, PA	1,897.8
341	Altoona, PA	1,893.4
342	Kingston, NY	1,889.7
343	Lynchburg, VA	1,884.6
344	Cambridge-Newton, MA M.D.	1,882.3
345	Edison, NJ M.D.	1,854.6
346	State College, PA	1,831.4
347	Naples-Marco Island, FL	1,831.0
348	Elizabethtown, KY	1,818.2
349	Fond du Lac, WI	1,779.5
350	New York (greater), NY-NJ-PA	1,750.5
351	Holland-Grand Haven, MI	1,745.3
352	St. George, UT	1,715.6
353	Wausau, WI	1,709.1
354	Nassau-Suffolk, NY M.D.	1,706.2
355	New York-W. Plains NY-NJ M.D.	1,700.2
356	Lebanon, PA	1,687.5
357	Glens Falls, NY	1,604.0
358	Harrisonburg, VA	1,518.7
359	Logan, UT-ID	1,513.6
NA	Auburn, AL**	NA
NA	Charleston-North Charleston, SC**	NA
NA	Dothan, AL**	NA
NA	El Centro, CA**	NA
NA	Hattiesburg, MS**	NA
NA	Kansas City, MO-KS**	NA
NA	New Orleans, LA**	NA
NA	Toledo, OH**	NA
NA	Tucson, AZ**	NA
NA	Wilmington, NC**	NA

Source: Reported data from the F.B.I. "Crime in the United States 2009"

*Property crimes are offenses of burglary, larceny-theft, and motor vehicle theft. Attempts are included.

**Not available.

27. Percent Change in Property Crime Rate: 2008 to 2009
National Percent Change = 5.5% Decrease*

RANK	METROPOLITAN AREA	% CHANGE
12	Abilene, TX	9.2
87	Akron, OH	(1.3)
80	Albany-Schenectady-Troy, NY	(0.8)
NA	Albany, GA**	NA
265	Albuquerque, NM	(11.7)
NA	Alexandria, LA**	NA
248	Allentown, PA-NJ	(10.2)
268	Altoona, PA	(10.9)
25	Amarillo, TX	5.9
111	Ames, IA	(2.9)
14	Anchorage, AK	8.7
NA	Anderson, IN**	NA
NA	Anderson, SC**	NA
90	Ann Arbor, MI	(1.4)
NA	Anniston-Oxford, AL**	NA
296	Appleton, WI	(20.5)
279	Asheville, NC	(14.3)
283	Athens-Clarke County, GA	(15.3)
261	Atlanta, GA	(11.4)
NA	Atlantic City, NJ**	NA
NA	Auburn, AL**	NA
124	Augusta, GA-SC	(3.9)
40	Austin-Round Rock, TX	3.1
106	Bakersfield, CA	(2.7)
205	Baltimore-Towson, MD	(7.7)
36	Bangor, ME	4.0
28	Barnstable Town, MA	4.9
NA	Baton Rouge, LA**	NA
189	Battle Creek, MI	(6.7)
NA	Bay City, MI**	NA
51	Beaumont-Port Arthur, TX	2.1
152	Bellingham, WA	(5.0)
286	Bend, OR	(15.6)
222	Bethesda-Frederick, MD M.D.	(8.5)
19	Billings, MT	7.6
236	Binghamton, NY	(9.6)
135	Birmingham-Hoover, AL	(4.3)
115	Bismarck, ND	(3.5)
146	Blacksburg, VA	(4.8)
11	Bloomington, IN	11.0
268	Boise City-Nampa, ID	(12.0)
150	Boston (greater), MA-NH	(4.9)
166	Boston-Quincy, MA M.D.	(5.5)
NA	Boulder, CO**	NA
NA	Bowling Green, KY**	NA
170	Bremerton-Silverdale, WA	(5.7)
170	Bridgeport-Stamford, CT	(5.7)
100	Brownsville-Harlingen, TX	(2.0)
NA	Brunswick, GA**	NA
102	Buffalo-Niagara Falls, NY	(2.3)
NA	Burlington-South Burlington, VT**	NA
138	Burlington, NC	(4.4)
220	Cambridge-Newton, MA M.D.	(8.3)
255	Camden, NJ M.D.	(10.7)
288	Cape Coral-Fort Myers, FL	(15.8)
170	Cape Girardeau, MO-IL	(5.7)
232	Carson City, NV	(9.3)
33	Casper, WY	4.2
158	Cedar Rapids, IA	(5.2)
NA	Charleston-North Charleston, SC**	NA
165	Charleston, WV	(5.4)
291	Charlotte-Gastonia, NC-SC	(16.3)
43	Charlottesville, VA	2.9
103	Chattanooga, TN-GA	(2.5)
239	Cheyenne, WY	(9.7)
170	Chico, CA	(5.7)
NA	Cincinnati-Middletown, OH-KY-IN**	NA
NA	Clarksville, TN-KY**	NA
NA	Cleveland-Elyria-Mentor, OH**	NA
246	Cleveland, TN	(10.1)
NA	Coeur d'Alene, ID**	NA
13	College Station-Bryan, TX	9.0
213	Colorado Springs, CO	(8.0)
115	Columbia, MO	(3.5)
73	Columbia, SC	0.0
42	Columbus, GA-AL	3.0
16	Columbus, IN	8.1
80	Columbus, OH	(0.8)
207	Corpus Christi, TX	(7.8)
4	Corvallis, OR	17.6
NA	Crestview-Fort Walton Beach, FL**	NA
50	Cumberland, MD-WV	2.3
121	Dallas (greater), TX	(3.7)
160	Dallas-Plano-Irving, TX M.D.	(5.3)
80	Dalton, GA	(0.8)
NA	Danville, IL**	NA
277	Danville, VA	(13.1)
112	Dayton, OH	(3.0)
290	Decatur, AL	(16.0)
NA	Decatur, IL**	NA
138	Deltona-Daytona Beach, FL	(4.4)
107	Denver-Aurora, CO	(2.8)
NA	Des Moines-West Des Moines, IA**	NA
NA	Detroit (greater), MI**	NA
NA	Detroit-Livonia-Dearborn, MI M.D.**	NA
NA	Dothan, AL**	NA
46	Dover, DE	2.7
87	Dubuque, IA	(1.3)
98	Duluth, MN-WI	(1.9)
168	Durham-Chapel Hill, NC	(5.6)
184	Eau Claire, WI	(6.2)
179	Edison, NJ M.D.	(6.1)
NA	El Centro, CA**	NA
179	El Paso, TX	(6.1)
NA	Elizabethtown, KY**	NA
299	Elkhart-Goshen, IN	(25.9)
207	Elmira, NY	(7.8)
115	Erie, PA	(3.5)
279	Eugene-Springfield, OR	(14.3)
NA	Evansville, IN-KY**	NA
NA	Fargo, ND-MN**	NA
57	Farmington, NM	1.6
63	Fayetteville, AR-MO	1.1
143	Fayetteville, NC	(4.5)
257	Flagstaff, AZ	(10.8)
NA	Flint, MI**	NA
285	Florence-Muscle Shoals, AL	(15.5)
152	Florence, SC	(5.0)
146	Fond du Lac, WI	(4.8)
76	Fort Collins-Loveland, CO	(0.4)
107	Fort Lauderdale, FL M.D.	(2.8)
8	Fort Smith, AR-OK	12.7
241	Fort Wayne, IN	(9.8)
77	Fort Worth-Arlington, TX M.D.	(0.6)
189	Fresno, CA	(6.7)
96	Gadsden, AL	(1.8)
64	Gainesville, FL	1.0
NA	Gainesville, GA**	NA
232	Glens Falls, NY	(9.3)
227	Goldsboro, NC	(8.9)
222	Grand Forks, ND-MN	(8.5)
44	Grand Junction, CO	2.8
NA	Grand Rapids-Wyoming, MI**	NA
278	Great Falls, MT	(13.4)
207	Greeley, CO	(7.8)
293	Green Bay, WI	(17.3)
198	Greensboro-High Point, NC	(7.2)
NA	Gulfport-Biloxi, MS**	NA
204	Hagerstown-Martinsburg, MD-WV	(7.6)
115	Harrisburg-Carlisle, PA	(3.5)
94	Harrisonburg, VA	(1.7)
124	Hartford, CT	(3.9)
NA	Hattiesburg, MS**	NA
124	Hickory, NC	(3.9)
98	Hinesville, GA	(1.9)
NA	Holland-Grand Haven, MI**	NA
28	Honolulu, HI	4.9
150	Hot Springs, AR	(4.9)
40	Houma, LA	3.1
16	Houston, TX	8.1
236	Huntsville, AL	(9.6)
203	Idaho Falls, ID	(7.5)
155	Indianapolis, IN	(5.1)
222	Iowa City, IA	(8.5)
60	Ithaca, NY	1.2
243	Jacksonville, FL	(9.9)
66	Jacksonville, NC	0.7
NA	Jackson, MI**	NA
51	Jackson, MS	2.1
138	Jackson, TN	(4.4)
289	Janesville, WI	(15.9)
NA	Jefferson City, MO**	NA
101	Johnson City, TN	(2.1)
135	Jonesboro, AR	(4.3)
NA	Kalamazoo-Portage, MI**	NA
NA	Kansas City, MO-KS**	NA
179	Kennewick-Pasco-Richland, WA	(6.1)
83	Killeen-Temple-Fort Hood, TX	(0.9)
93	Kingsport, TN-VA	(1.5)
21	Kingston, NY	7.3
158	Knoxville, TN	(5.2)
226	Kokomo, IN	(8.8)
112	La Crosse, WI-MN	(3.0)
67	Lafayette, IN	0.6
5	Lafayette, LA	14.8
NA	Lake Charles, LA**	NA
146	Lake Havasu City-Kingman, AZ	(4.8)
225	Lakeland, FL	(8.7)
195	Lancaster, PA	(6.9)
NA	Lansing-East Lansing, MI**	NA

Note: All listings are for Metropolitan Statistical Areas (M.S.A.s) except for those ending with "M.D." Listings with "M.D." are Metropolitan Divisions which are smaller parts of eleven large M.S.A.s. See explanatory note at beginning of metropolitan area section.

RANK	METROPOLITAN AREA	% CHANGE
176	Laredo, TX	(5.9)
57	Las Cruces, NM	1.6
267	Las Vegas-Paradise, NV	(11.9)
185	Lawrence, KS	(6.3)
NA	Lawton, OK**	NA
133	Lebanon, PA	(4.2)
60	Lewiston-Auburn, ME	1.2
20	Lewiston, ID-WA	7.5
NA	Lexington-Fayette, KY**	NA
198	Lima, OH	(7.2)
144	Lincoln, NE	(4.6)
NA	Little Rock, AR**	NA
207	Logan, UT-ID	(7.8)
49	Longview, TX	2.4
64	Longview, WA	1.0
189	Los Angeles County, CA M.D.	(6.7)
188	Los Angeles (greater), CA	(6.5)
NA	Louisville, KY-IN**	NA
35	Lubbock, TX	4.1
282	Lynchburg, VA	(14.8)
218	Macon, GA	(8.2)
124	Madera, CA	(3.9)
186	Madison, WI	(6.4)
NA	Manchester-Nashua, NH**	NA
292	Manhattan, KS	(16.9)
51	Mankato-North Mankato, MN	2.1
121	Mansfield, OH	(3.7)
15	McAllen-Edinburg-Mission, TX	8.2
177	Medford, OR	(6.0)
266	Memphis, TN-MS-AR	(11.8)
215	Merced, CA	(8.1)
189	Miami (greater), FL	(6.7)
252	Miami-Dade County, FL M.D.	(10.4)
245	Michigan City-La Porte, IN	(10.0)
22	Midland, TX	6.7
160	Milwaukee, WI	(5.3)
227	Minneapolis-St. Paul, MN-WI	(8.9)
275	Missoula, MT	(12.6)
69	Mobile, AL	0.4
193	Modesto, CA	(6.8)
NA	Monroe, MI**	NA
261	Montgomery, AL	(11.4)
NA	Morgantown, WV**	NA
254	Morristown, TN	(10.6)
69	Mount Vernon-Anacortes, WA	0.4
119	Muncie, IN	(3.6)
NA	Muskegon-Norton Shores, MI**	NA
152	Napa, CA	(5.0)
155	Naples-Marco Island, FL	(5.1)
200	Nashville-Davidson, TN	(7.3)
87	Nassau-Suffolk, NY M.D.	(1.3)
NA	New Haven-Milford, CT**	NA
NA	New Orleans, LA**	NA
177	New York (greater), NY-NJ-PA	(6.0)
175	New York-W. Plains NY-NJ M.D.	(5.8)
268	Newark-Union, NJ-PA M.D.	(12.0)
NA	Niles-Benton Harbor, MI**	NA
NA	North Port-Bradenton-Sarasota, FL**	NA
31	Norwich-New London, CT	4.5
215	Oakland-Fremont, CA M.D.	(8.1)
73	Ocala, FL	0.0
211	Ocean City, NJ	(7.9)
24	Odessa, TX	6.0
75	Ogden-Clearfield, UT	(0.1)
NA	Oklahoma City, OK**	NA
276	Olympia, WA	(12.8)
114	Omaha-Council Bluffs, NE-IA	(3.4)
253	Orlando, FL	(10.5)
94	Oshkosh-Neenah, WI	(1.7)
NA	Owensboro, KY**	NA
146	Oxnard-Thousand Oaks, CA	(4.8)
124	Palm Bay-Melbourne, FL	(3.9)
55	Palm Coast, FL	1.8
23	Panama City-Lynn Haven, FL	6.3
56	Pascagoula, MS	1.7
83	Peabody, MA M.D.	(0.9)
57	Pensacola, FL	1.6
264	Philadelphia (greater) PA-NJ-MD-DE	(11.6)
272	Philadelphia, PA M.D.	(12.2)
284	Phoenix-Mesa-Scottsdale, AZ	(15.4)
274	Pine Bluff, AR	(12.4)
160	Pittsburgh, PA	(5.3)
107	Pittsfield, MA	(2.8)
119	Pocatello, ID	(3.6)
243	Port St. Lucie, FL	(9.9)
248	Portland-Vancouver, OR-WA	(10.2)
72	Portland, ME	0.3
138	Poughkeepsie, NY	(4.4)
239	Prescott, AZ	(9.7)
218	Providence-New Bedford, RI-MA	(8.2)
179	Provo-Orem, UT	(6.1)
NA	Pueblo, CO**	NA
286	Punta Gorda, FL	(15.6)
251	Racine, WI	(10.3)
131	Raleigh-Cary, NC	(4.1)
48	Rapid City, SD	2.5
200	Reading, PA	(7.3)
211	Redding, CA	(7.9)
272	Reno-Sparks, NV	(12.2)
121	Richmond, VA	(3.7)
205	Riverside-San Bernardino, CA	(7.7)
90	Roanoke, VA	(1.4)
86	Rochester, MN	(1.2)
38	Rochester, NY	3.3
37	Rockingham County, NH M.D.	3.8
NA	Rocky Mount, NC**	NA
NA	Rome, GA**	NA
131	Sacramento, CA	(4.1)
NA	Saginaw, MI**	NA
248	Salem, OR	(10.2)
107	Salinas, CA	(2.8)
33	Salisbury, MD	4.2
69	Salt Lake City, UT	0.4
168	San Angelo, TX	(5.6)
202	San Antonio, TX	(7.4)
294	San Diego, CA	(18.1)
197	San Francisco (greater), CA	(7.1)
166	San Francisco-S. Mateo, CA M.D.	(5.5)
77	San Jose, CA	(0.6)
138	San Luis Obispo, CA	(4.4)
271	Sandusky, OH	(12.1)
160	Santa Ana-Anaheim, CA M.D.	(5.3)
170	Santa Barbara-Santa Maria, CA	(5.7)
7	Santa Cruz-Watsonville, CA	14.0
1	Santa Fe, NM	23.1
18	Santa Rosa-Petaluma, CA	7.9
130	Savannah, GA	(4.0)
124	Scranton--Wilkes-Barre, PA	(3.9)
NA	Seattle-Bellevue-Everett, WA M.D.**	NA
NA	Seattle-Tacoma-Bellevue, WA**	NA
186	Sebastian-Vero Beach, FL	(6.4)
196	Sheboygan, WI	(7.0)
10	Sherman-Denison, TX	11.3
85	Shreveport-Bossier City, LA	(1.0)
28	Sioux City, IA-NE-SD	4.9
6	Sioux Falls, SD	14.5
NA	South Bend-Mishawaka, IN-MI**	NA
259	Spartanburg, SC	(11.1)
9	Spokane, WA	11.9
103	Springfield, MA	(2.5)
NA	Springfield, MO**	NA
229	Springfield, OH	(9.0)
51	State College, PA	2.1
281	Stockton, CA	(14.4)
268	St. Cloud, MN	(12.0)
297	St. George, UT	(23.7)
68	St. Joseph, MO-KS	0.5
193	St. Louis, MO-IL	(6.8)
NA	Sumter, SC**	NA
39	Syracuse, NY	3.2
NA	Tacoma, WA M.D.**	NA
215	Tallahassee, FL	(8.1)
179	Tampa-St Petersburg, FL	(6.1)
26	Texarkana, TX-Texarkana, AR	5.8
NA	Toledo, OH**	NA
255	Topeka, KS	(10.7)
155	Trenton-Ewing, NJ	(5.1)
NA	Tucson, AZ**	NA
60	Tulsa, OK	1.2
96	Tuscaloosa, AL	(1.8)
2	Tyler, TX	18.8
44	Utica-Rome, NY	2.8
26	Valdosta, GA	5.8
246	Vallejo-Fairfield, CA	(10.1)
3	Victoria, TX	17.8
259	Vineland, NJ	(11.1)
220	Visalia-Porterville, CA	(8.3)
135	Waco, TX	(4.3)
261	Warner Robins, GA	(11.4)
NA	Warren-Farmington Hills, MI M.D.**	NA
231	Washington (greater) DC-VA-MD-WV	(9.2)
234	Washington, DC-VA-MD-WV M.D.	(9.4)
160	Waterloo-Cedar Falls, IA	(5.3)
NA	Wausau, WI**	NA
32	Wenatchee, WA	4.3
133	West Palm Beach, FL M.D.	(4.2)
103	Wheeling, WV-OH	(2.5)
295	Wichita Falls, TX	(18.7)
145	Wichita, KS	(4.7)
213	Williamsport, PA	(8.0)
241	Wilmington, DE-MD-NJ M.D.	(9.8)
NA	Wilmington, NC**	NA
234	Winchester, VA-WV	(9.4)
230	Winston-Salem, NC	(9.1)
47	Worcester, MA	2.6
236	York-Hanover, PA	(9.6)
79	Youngstown, OH-PA	(0.7)
298	Yuba City, CA	(25.6)
90	Yuma, AZ	(1.4)

Source: CQ Press using reported data from the F.B.I. "Crime in the United States 2009"
*Property crimes are offenses of burglary, larceny-theft, and motor vehicle theft. Attempts are included.
**Not available.

27. Percent Change in Property Crime Rate: 2008 to 2009 (continued)
National Percent Change = 5.5% Decrease*

RANK	METROPOLITAN AREA	% CHANGE
1	Santa Fe, NM	23.1
2	Tyler, TX	18.8
3	Victoria, TX	17.8
4	Corvallis, OR	17.6
5	Lafayette, LA	14.8
6	Sioux Falls, SD	14.5
7	Santa Cruz-Watsonville, CA	14.0
8	Fort Smith, AR-OK	12.7
9	Spokane, WA	11.9
10	Sherman-Denison, TX	11.3
11	Bloomington, IN	11.0
12	Abilene, TX	9.2
13	College Station-Bryan, TX	9.0
14	Anchorage, AK	8.7
15	McAllen-Edinburg-Mission, TX	8.2
16	Columbus, IN	8.1
16	Houston, TX	8.1
18	Santa Rosa-Petaluma, CA	7.9
19	Billings, MT	7.6
20	Lewiston, ID-WA	7.5
21	Kingston, NY	7.3
22	Midland, TX	6.7
23	Panama City-Lynn Haven, FL	6.3
24	Odessa, TX	6.0
25	Amarillo, TX	5.9
26	Texarkana, TX-Texarkana, AR	5.8
26	Valdosta, GA	5.8
28	Barnstable Town, MA	4.9
28	Honolulu, HI	4.9
28	Sioux City, IA-NE-SD	4.9
31	Norwich-New London, CT	4.5
32	Wenatchee, WA	4.3
33	Casper, WY	4.2
33	Salisbury, MD	4.2
35	Lubbock, TX	4.1
36	Bangor, ME	4.0
37	Rockingham County, NH M.D.	3.8
38	Rochester, NY	3.3
39	Syracuse, NY	3.2
40	Austin-Round Rock, TX	3.1
40	Houma, LA	3.1
42	Columbus, GA-AL	3.0
43	Charlottesville, VA	2.9
44	Grand Junction, CO	2.8
44	Utica-Rome, NY	2.8
46	Dover, DE	2.7
47	Worcester, MA	2.6
48	Rapid City, SD	2.5
49	Longview, TX	2.4
50	Cumberland, MD-WV	2.3
51	Beaumont-Port Arthur, TX	2.1
51	Jackson, MS	2.1
51	Mankato-North Mankato, MN	2.1
51	State College, PA	2.1
55	Palm Coast, FL	1.8
56	Pascagoula, MS	1.7
57	Farmington, NM	1.6
57	Las Cruces, NM	1.6
57	Pensacola, FL	1.6
60	Ithaca, NY	1.2
60	Lewiston-Auburn, ME	1.2
60	Tulsa, OK	1.2
63	Fayetteville, AR-MO	1.1
64	Gainesville, FL	1.0
64	Longview, WA	1.0
66	Jacksonville, NC	0.7
67	Lafayette, IN	0.6
68	St. Joseph, MO-KS	0.5
69	Mobile, AL	0.4
69	Mount Vernon-Anacortes, WA	0.4
69	Salt Lake City, UT	0.4
72	Portland, ME	0.3
73	Columbia, SC	0.0
73	Ocala, FL	0.0
75	Ogden-Clearfield, UT	(0.1)
76	Fort Collins-Loveland, CO	(0.4)
77	Fort Worth-Arlington, TX M.D.	(0.6)
77	San Jose, CA	(0.6)
79	Youngstown, OH-PA	(0.7)
80	Albany-Schenectady-Troy, NY	(0.8)
80	Columbus, OH	(0.8)
80	Dalton, GA	(0.8)
83	Killeen-Temple-Fort Hood, TX	(0.9)
83	Peabody, MA M.D.	(0.9)
85	Shreveport-Bossier City, LA	(1.0)
86	Rochester, MN	(1.2)
87	Akron, OH	(1.3)
87	Dubuque, IA	(1.3)
87	Nassau-Suffolk, NY M.D.	(1.3)
90	Ann Arbor, MI	(1.4)
90	Roanoke, VA	(1.4)
90	Yuma, AZ	(1.4)
93	Kingsport, TN-VA	(1.5)
94	Harrisonburg, VA	(1.7)
94	Oshkosh-Neenah, WI	(1.7)
96	Gadsden, AL	(1.8)
96	Tuscaloosa, AL	(1.8)
98	Duluth, MN-WI	(1.9)
98	Hinesville, GA	(1.9)
100	Brownsville-Harlingen, TX	(2.0)
101	Johnson City, TN	(2.1)
102	Buffalo-Niagara Falls, NY	(2.3)
103	Chattanooga, TN-GA	(2.5)
103	Springfield, MA	(2.5)
103	Wheeling, WV-OH	(2.5)
106	Bakersfield, CA	(2.7)
107	Denver-Aurora, CO	(2.8)
107	Fort Lauderdale, FL M.D.	(2.8)
107	Pittsfield, MA	(2.8)
107	Salinas, CA	(2.8)
111	Ames, IA	(2.9)
112	Dayton, OH	(3.0)
112	La Crosse, WI-MN	(3.0)
114	Omaha-Council Bluffs, NE-IA	(3.4)
115	Bismarck, ND	(3.5)
115	Columbia, MO	(3.5)
115	Erie, PA	(3.5)
115	Harrisburg-Carlisle, PA	(3.5)
119	Muncie, IN	(3.6)
119	Pocatello, ID	(3.6)
121	Dallas (greater), TX	(3.7)
121	Mansfield, OH	(3.7)
121	Richmond, VA	(3.7)
124	Augusta, GA-SC	(3.9)
124	Hartford, CT	(3.9)
124	Hickory, NC	(3.9)
124	Madera, CA	(3.9)
124	Palm Bay-Melbourne, FL	(3.9)
124	Scranton--Wilkes-Barre, PA	(3.9)
130	Savannah, GA	(4.0)
131	Raleigh-Cary, NC	(4.1)
131	Sacramento, CA	(4.1)
133	Lebanon, PA	(4.2)
133	West Palm Beach, FL M.D.	(4.2)
135	Birmingham-Hoover, AL	(4.3)
135	Jonesboro, AR	(4.3)
135	Waco, TX	(4.3)
138	Burlington, NC	(4.4)
138	Deltona-Daytona Beach, FL	(4.4)
138	Jackson, TN	(4.4)
138	Poughkeepsie, NY	(4.4)
138	San Luis Obispo, CA	(4.4)
143	Fayetteville, NC	(4.5)
144	Lincoln, NE	(4.6)
145	Wichita, KS	(4.7)
146	Blacksburg, VA	(4.8)
146	Fond du Lac, WI	(4.8)
146	Lake Havasu City-Kingman, AZ	(4.8)
146	Oxnard-Thousand Oaks, CA	(4.8)
150	Boston (greater), MA-NH	(4.9)
150	Hot Springs, AR	(4.9)
152	Bellingham, WA	(5.0)
152	Florence, SC	(5.0)
152	Napa, CA	(5.0)
155	Indianapolis, IN	(5.1)
155	Naples-Marco Island, FL	(5.1)
155	Trenton-Ewing, NJ	(5.1)
158	Cedar Rapids, IA	(5.2)
158	Knoxville, TN	(5.2)
160	Dallas-Plano-Irving, TX M.D.	(5.3)
160	Milwaukee, WI	(5.3)
160	Pittsburgh, PA	(5.3)
160	Santa Ana-Anaheim, CA M.D.	(5.3)
160	Waterloo-Cedar Falls, IA	(5.3)
165	Charleston, WV	(5.4)
166	Boston-Quincy, MA M.D.	(5.5)
166	San Francisco-S. Mateo, CA M.D.	(5.5)
168	Durham-Chapel Hill, NC	(5.6)
168	San Angelo, TX	(5.6)
170	Bremerton-Silverdale, WA	(5.7)
170	Bridgeport-Stamford, CT	(5.7)
170	Cape Girardeau, MO-IL	(5.7)
170	Chico, CA	(5.7)
170	Santa Barbara-Santa Maria, CA	(5.7)
175	New York-W. Plains NY-NJ M.D.	(5.8)
176	Laredo, TX	(5.9)
177	Medford, OR	(6.0)
177	New York (greater), NY-NJ-PA	(6.0)
179	Edison, NJ M.D.	(6.1)
179	El Paso, TX	(6.1)

Note: All listings are for Metropolitan Statistical Areas (M.S.A.s) except for those ending with "M.D." Listings with "M.D." are Metropolitan Divisions which are smaller parts of eleven large M.S.A.s. See explanatory note at beginning of metropolitan area section.

Rank Order - Metro Area (continued)

RANK	METROPOLITAN AREA	% CHANGE
179	Kennewick-Pasco-Richland, WA	(6.1)
179	Provo-Orem, UT	(6.1)
179	Tampa-St Petersburg, FL	(6.1)
184	Eau Claire, WI	(6.2)
185	Lawrence, KS	(6.3)
186	Madison, WI	(6.4)
186	Sebastian-Vero Beach, FL	(6.4)
188	Los Angeles (greater), CA	(6.5)
189	Battle Creek, MI	(6.7)
189	Fresno, CA	(6.7)
189	Los Angeles County, CA M.D.	(6.7)
189	Miami (greater), FL	(6.7)
193	Modesto, CA	(6.8)
193	St. Louis, MO-IL	(6.8)
195	Lancaster, PA	(6.9)
196	Sheboygan, WI	(7.0)
197	San Francisco (greater), CA	(7.1)
198	Greensboro-High Point, NC	(7.2)
198	Lima, OH	(7.2)
200	Nashville-Davidson, TN	(7.3)
200	Reading, PA	(7.3)
202	San Antonio, TX	(7.4)
203	Idaho Falls, ID	(7.5)
204	Hagerstown-Martinsburg, MD-WV	(7.6)
205	Baltimore-Towson, MD	(7.7)
205	Riverside-San Bernardino, CA	(7.7)
207	Corpus Christi, TX	(7.8)
207	Elmira, NY	(7.8)
207	Greeley, CO	(7.8)
207	Logan, UT-ID	(7.8)
211	Ocean City, NJ	(7.9)
211	Redding, CA	(7.9)
213	Colorado Springs, CO	(8.0)
213	Williamsport, PA	(8.0)
215	Merced, CA	(8.1)
215	Oakland-Fremont, CA M.D.	(8.1)
215	Tallahassee, FL	(8.1)
218	Macon, GA	(8.2)
218	Providence-New Bedford, RI-MA	(8.2)
220	Cambridge-Newton, MA M.D.	(8.3)
220	Visalia-Porterville, CA	(8.3)
222	Bethesda-Frederick, MD M.D.	(8.5)
222	Grand Forks, ND-MN	(8.5)
222	Iowa City, IA	(8.5)
225	Lakeland, FL	(8.7)
226	Kokomo, IN	(8.8)
227	Goldsboro, NC	(8.9)
227	Minneapolis-St. Paul, MN-WI	(8.9)
229	Springfield, OH	(9.0)
230	Winston-Salem, NC	(9.1)
231	Washington (greater) DC-VA-MD-WV	(9.2)
232	Carson City, NV	(9.3)
232	Glens Falls, NY	(9.3)
234	Washington, DC-VA-MD-WV M.D.	(9.4)
234	Winchester, VA-WV	(9.4)
236	Binghamton, NY	(9.6)
236	Huntsville, AL	(9.6)
236	York-Hanover, PA	(9.6)
239	Cheyenne, WY	(9.7)
239	Prescott, AZ	(9.7)
241	Fort Wayne, IN	(9.8)
241	Wilmington, DE-MD-NJ M.D.	(9.8)
243	Jacksonville, FL	(9.9)

RANK	METROPOLITAN AREA	% CHANGE
243	Port St. Lucie, FL	(9.9)
245	Michigan City-La Porte, IN	(10.0)
246	Cleveland, TN	(10.1)
246	Vallejo-Fairfield, CA	(10.1)
248	Allentown, PA-NJ	(10.2)
248	Portland-Vancouver, OR-WA	(10.2)
248	Salem, OR	(10.2)
251	Racine, WI	(10.3)
252	Miami-Dade County, FL M.D.	(10.4)
253	Orlando, FL	(10.5)
254	Morristown, TN	(10.6)
255	Camden, NJ M.D.	(10.7)
255	Topeka, KS	(10.7)
257	Flagstaff, AZ	(10.8)
258	Altoona, PA	(10.9)
259	Spartanburg, SC	(11.1)
259	Vineland, NJ	(11.1)
261	Atlanta, GA	(11.4)
261	Montgomery, AL	(11.4)
261	Warner Robins, GA	(11.4)
264	Philadelphia (greater) PA-NJ-MD-DE	(11.6)
265	Albuquerque, NM	(11.7)
266	Memphis, TN-MS-AR	(11.8)
267	Las Vegas-Paradise, NV	(11.9)
268	Boise City-Nampa, ID	(12.0)
268	Newark-Union, NJ-PA M.D.	(12.0)
268	St. Cloud, MN	(12.0)
271	Sandusky, OH	(12.1)
272	Philadelphia, PA M.D.	(12.2)
272	Reno-Sparks, NV	(12.2)
274	Pine Bluff, AR	(12.4)
275	Missoula, MT	(12.6)
276	Olympia, WA	(12.8)
277	Danville, VA	(13.1)
278	Great Falls, MT	(13.4)
279	Asheville, NC	(14.3)
279	Eugene-Springfield, OR	(14.3)
281	Stockton, CA	(14.4)
282	Lynchburg, VA	(14.8)
283	Athens-Clarke County, GA	(15.3)
284	Phoenix-Mesa-Scottsdale, AZ	(15.4)
285	Florence-Muscle Shoals, AL	(15.5)
286	Bend, OR	(15.6)
286	Punta Gorda, FL	(15.6)
288	Cape Coral-Fort Myers, FL	(15.8)
289	Janesville, WI	(15.9)
290	Decatur, AL	(16.0)
291	Charlotte-Gastonia, NC-SC	(16.3)
292	Manhattan, KS	(16.9)
293	Green Bay, WI	(17.3)
294	San Diego, CA	(18.1)
295	Wichita Falls, TX	(18.7)
296	Appleton, WI	(20.5)
297	St. George, UT	(23.7)
298	Yuba City, CA	(25.6)
299	Elkhart-Goshen, IN	(25.9)
NA	Albany, GA**	NA
NA	Alexandria, LA**	NA
NA	Anderson, IN**	NA
NA	Anderson, SC**	NA
NA	Anniston-Oxford, AL**	NA
NA	Atlantic City, NJ**	NA
NA	Auburn, AL**	NA

RANK	METROPOLITAN AREA	% CHANGE
NA	Baton Rouge, LA**	NA
NA	Bay City, MI**	NA
NA	Boulder, CO**	NA
NA	Bowling Green, KY**	NA
NA	Brunswick, GA**	NA
NA	Burlington-South Burlington, VT**	NA
NA	Charleston-North Charleston, SC**	NA
NA	Cincinnati-Middletown, OH-KY-IN**	NA
NA	Clarksville, TN-KY**	NA
NA	Cleveland-Elyria-Mentor, OH**	NA
NA	Coeur d'Alene, ID**	NA
NA	Crestview-Fort Walton Beach, FL**	NA
NA	Danville, IL**	NA
NA	Decatur, IL**	NA
NA	Des Moines-West Des Moines, IA**	NA
NA	Detroit (greater), MI**	NA
NA	Detroit-Livonia-Dearborn, MI M.D.**	NA
NA	Dothan, AL**	NA
NA	El Centro, CA**	NA
NA	Elizabethtown, KY**	NA
NA	Evansville, IN-KY**	NA
NA	Fargo, ND-MN**	NA
NA	Flint, MI**	NA
NA	Gainesville, GA**	NA
NA	Grand Rapids-Wyoming, MI**	NA
NA	Gulfport-Biloxi, MS**	NA
NA	Hattiesburg, MS**	NA
NA	Holland-Grand Haven, MI**	NA
NA	Jackson, MI**	NA
NA	Jefferson City, MO**	NA
NA	Kalamazoo-Portage, MI**	NA
NA	Kansas City, MO-KS**	NA
NA	Lake Charles, LA**	NA
NA	Lansing-East Lansing, MI**	NA
NA	Lawton, OK**	NA
NA	Lexington-Fayette, KY**	NA
NA	Little Rock, AR**	NA
NA	Louisville, KY-IN**	NA
NA	Manchester-Nashua, NH**	NA
NA	Monroe, MI**	NA
NA	Morgantown, WV**	NA
NA	Muskegon-Norton Shores, MI**	NA
NA	New Haven-Milford, CT**	NA
NA	New Orleans, LA**	NA
NA	Niles-Benton Harbor, MI**	NA
NA	North Port-Bradenton-Sarasota, FL**	NA
NA	Oklahoma City, OK**	NA
NA	Owensboro, KY**	NA
NA	Pueblo, CO**	NA
NA	Rocky Mount, NC**	NA
NA	Rome, GA**	NA
NA	Saginaw, MI**	NA
NA	Seattle-Bellevue-Everett, WA M.D.**	NA
NA	Seattle-Tacoma-Bellevue, WA**	NA
NA	South Bend-Mishawaka, IN-MI**	NA
NA	Springfield, MO**	NA
NA	Sumter, SC**	NA
NA	Tacoma, WA M.D.**	NA
NA	Toledo, OH**	NA
NA	Tucson, AZ**	NA
NA	Warren-Farmington Hills, MI M.D.**	NA
NA	Wausau, WI**	NA
NA	Wilmington, NC**	NA

Source: CQ Press using reported data from the F.B.I. "Crime in the United States 2009"
*Property crimes are offenses of burglary, larceny-theft, and motor vehicle theft. Attempts are included.
**Not available.

28. Percent Change in Property Crime Rate: 2005 to 2009
National Percent Change = 11.5% Decrease*

RANK	METROPOLITAN AREA	% CHANGE
129	Abilene, TX	(8.7)
151	Akron, OH	(10.8)
85	Albany-Schenectady-Troy, NY	(4.1)
23	Albany, GA	6.5
166	Albuquerque, NM	(11.8)
90	Alexandria, LA	(4.6)
128	Allentown, PA-NJ	(8.6)
247	Altoona, PA	(22.3)
140	Amarillo, TX	(9.9)
96	Ames, IA	(5.1)
187	Anchorage, AK	(14.1)
13	Anderson, IN	10.8
196	Anderson, SC	(15.3)
144	Ann Arbor, MI	(10.4)
NA	Anniston-Oxford, AL**	NA
106	Appleton, WI	(6.3)
256	Asheville, NC	(24.8)
83	Athens-Clarke County, GA	(3.8)
186	Atlanta, GA	(14.0)
191	Atlantic City, NJ	(14.6)
NA	Auburn, AL**	NA
39	Augusta, GA-SC	2.8
74	Austin-Round Rock, TX	(2.6)
202	Bakersfield, CA	(16.0)
93	Baltimore-Towson, MD	(4.9)
3	Bangor, ME	18.4
1	Barnstable Town, MA	33.3
133	Baton Rouge, LA	(9.4)
79	Battle Creek, MI	(3.5)
NA	Bay City, MI**	NA
170	Beaumont-Port Arthur, TX	(12.3)
282	Bellingham, WA	(33.4)
291	Bend, OR	(43.0)
45	Bethesda-Frederick, MD M.D.	1.9
227	Billings, MT	(19.8)
49	Binghamton, NY	0.9
NA	Birmingham-Hoover, AL**	NA
95	Bismarck, ND	(5.0)
77	Blacksburg, VA	(3.1)
18	Bloomington, IN	7.9
NA	Boise City-Nampa, ID**	NA
81	Boston (greater), MA-NH	(3.6)
146	Boston-Quincy, MA M.D.	(10.5)
NA	Boulder, CO**	NA
NA	Bowling Green, KY**	NA
164	Bremerton-Silverdale, WA	(11.6)
173	Bridgeport-Stamford, CT	(12.6)
96	Brownsville-Harlingen, TX	(5.1)
37	Brunswick, GA	3.1
51	Buffalo-Niagara Falls, NY	0.8
NA	Burlington-South Burlington, VT**	NA
78	Burlington, NC	(3.3)
64	Cambridge-Newton, MA M.D.	(1.1)
70	Camden, NJ M.D.	(2.4)
206	Cape Coral-Fort Myers, FL	(16.4)
NA	Cape Girardeau, MO-IL**	NA
198	Carson City, NV	(15.6)
216	Casper, WY	(17.4)
159	Cedar Rapids, IA	(11.4)
NA	Charleston-North Charleston, SC**	NA
248	Charleston, WV	(22.8)
253	Charlotte-Gastonia, NC-SC	(24.5)
67	Charlottesville, VA	(1.5)
111	Chattanooga, TN-GA	(7.1)
165	Cheyenne, WY	(11.7)
206	Chico, CA	(16.4)
NA	Cincinnati-Middletown, OH-KY-IN**	NA
NA	Clarksville, TN-KY**	NA
NA	Cleveland-Elyria-Mentor, OH**	NA
NA	Cleveland, TN**	NA
246	Coeur d'Alene, ID	(21.9)
99	College Station-Bryan, TX	(5.3)
278	Colorado Springs, CO	(30.9)
34	Columbia, MO	3.7
60	Columbia, SC	(0.6)
9	Columbus, GA-AL	12.6
176	Columbus, IN	(12.9)
157	Columbus, OH	(11.1)
232	Corpus Christi, TX	(20.5)
261	Corvallis, OR	(25.7)
NA	Crestview-Fort Walton Beach, FL**	NA
9	Cumberland, MD-WV	12.6
215	Dallas (greater), TX	(17.2)
224	Dallas-Plano-Irving, TX M.D.	(19.0)
NA	Dalton, GA**	NA
NA	Danville, IL**	NA
13	Danville, VA	10.8
138	Dayton, OH	(9.8)
171	Decatur, AL	(12.5)
NA	Decatur, IL**	NA
NA	Deltona-Daytona Beach, FL**	NA
288	Denver-Aurora, CO	(37.2)
NA	Des Moines-West Des Moines, IA**	NA
NA	Detroit (greater), MI**	NA
NA	Detroit-Livonia-Dearborn, MI M.D.**	NA
NA	Dothan, AL**	NA
5	Dover, DE	18.1
40	Dubuque, IA	2.6
NA	Duluth, MN-WI**	NA
150	Durham-Chapel Hill, NC	(10.7)
151	Eau Claire, WI	(10.8)
64	Edison, NJ M.D.	(1.1)
NA	El Centro, CA**	NA
102	El Paso, TX	(5.8)
NA	Elizabethtown, KY**	NA
272	Elkhart-Goshen, IN	(29.1)
250	Elmira, NY	(23.1)
4	Erie, PA	18.3
261	Eugene-Springfield, OR	(25.7)
NA	Evansville, IN-KY**	NA
6	Fargo, ND-MN	14.7
119	Farmington, NM	(7.6)
226	Fayetteville, AR-MO	(19.5)
35	Fayetteville, NC	3.5
269	Flagstaff, AZ	(28.2)
NA	Flint, MI**	NA
NA	Florence-Muscle Shoals, AL**	NA
151	Florence, SC	(10.8)
72	Fond du Lac, WI	(2.5)
121	Fort Collins-Loveland, CO	(7.8)
17	Fort Lauderdale, FL M.D.	8.9
108	Fort Smith, AR-OK	(6.5)
194	Fort Wayne, IN	(15.0)
185	Fort Worth-Arlington, TX M.D.	(13.7)
231	Fresno, CA	(20.3)
230	Gadsden, AL	(20.1)
32	Gainesville, FL	3.9
285	Gainesville, GA	(33.8)
NA	Glens Falls, NY**	NA
44	Goldsboro, NC	2.4
273	Grand Forks, ND-MN	(29.9)
258	Grand Junction, CO	(25.3)
NA	Grand Rapids-Wyoming, MI**	NA
273	Great Falls, MT	(29.9)
294	Greeley, CO	(46.8)
214	Green Bay, WI	(17.1)
108	Greensboro-High Point, NC	(6.5)
NA	Gulfport-Biloxi, MS**	NA
59	Hagerstown-Martinsburg, MD-WV	(0.5)
159	Harrisburg-Carlisle, PA	(11.4)
74	Harrisonburg, VA	(2.6)
188	Hartford, CT	(14.2)
NA	Hattiesburg, MS**	NA
118	Hickory, NC	(7.5)
56	Hinesville, GA	0.2
NA	Holland-Grand Haven, MI**	NA
237	Honolulu, HI	(21.1)
217	Hot Springs, AR	(17.5)
151	Houma, LA	(10.8)
70	Houston, TX	(2.4)
260	Huntsville, AL	(25.4)
218	Idaho Falls, ID	(17.9)
133	Indianapolis, IN	(9.4)
159	Iowa City, IA	(11.4)
NA	Ithaca, NY**	NA
88	Jacksonville, FL	(4.5)
NA	Jacksonville, NC**	NA
NA	Jackson, MI**	NA
51	Jackson, MS	0.8
148	Jackson, TN	(10.6)
242	Janesville, WI	(21.5)
209	Jefferson City, MO	(16.7)
258	Johnson City, TN	(25.3)
242	Jonesboro, AR	(21.5)
NA	Kalamazoo-Portage, MI**	NA
NA	Kansas City, MO-KS**	NA
283	Kennewick-Pasco-Richland, WA	(33.5)
191	Killeen-Temple-Fort Hood, TX	(14.6)
76	Kingsport, TN-VA	(2.9)
86	Kingston, NY	(4.3)
114	Knoxville, TN	(7.3)
234	Kokomo, IN	(20.7)
15	La Crosse, WI-MN	9.3
131	Lafayette, IN	(9.2)
20	Lafayette, LA	7.5
53	Lake Charles, LA	0.7
NA	Lake Havasu City-Kingman, AZ**	NA
125	Lakeland, FL	(8.4)
167	Lancaster, PA	(11.9)
NA	Lansing-East Lansing, MI**	NA

Note: All listings are for Metropolitan Statistical Areas (M.S.A.s) except for those ending with "M.D." Listings with "M.D." are Metropolitan Divisions which are smaller parts of eleven large M.S.A.s. See explanatory note at beginning of metropolitan area section.

RANK	METROPOLITAN AREA	% CHANGE
49	Laredo, TX	0.9
48	Las Cruces, NM	1.1
273	Las Vegas-Paradise, NV	(29.9)
19	Lawrence, KS	7.8
NA	Lawton, OK**	NA
232	Lebanon, PA	(20.5)
176	Lewiston-Auburn, ME	(12.9)
212	Lewiston, ID-WA	(16.9)
NA	Lexington-Fayette, KY**	NA
66	Lima, OH	(1.2)
266	Lincoln, NE	(27.3)
NA	Little Rock, AR**	NA
220	Logan, UT-ID	(18.4)
69	Longview, TX	(1.9)
289	Longview, WA	(37.8)
188	Los Angeles County, CA M.D.	(14.2)
193	Los Angeles (greater), CA	(14.7)
NA	Louisville, KY-IN**	NA
84	Lubbock, TX	(4.0)
103	Lynchburg, VA	(5.9)
229	Macon, GA	(20.0)
270	Madera, CA	(28.6)
120	Madison, WI	(7.7)
12	Manchester-Nashua, NH	11.8
NA	Manhattan, KS**	NA
NA	Mankato-North Mankato, MN**	NA
171	Mansfield, OH	(12.5)
93	McAllen-Edinburg-Mission, TX	(4.9)
287	Medford, OR	(35.8)
209	Memphis, TN-MS-AR	(16.7)
201	Merced, CA	(15.9)
67	Miami (greater), FL	(1.5)
103	Miami-Dade County, FL M.D.	(5.9)
103	Michigan City-La Porte, IN	(5.9)
54	Midland, TX	0.6
38	Milwaukee, WI	3.0
NA	Minneapolis-St. Paul, MN-WI**	NA
292	Missoula, MT	(44.0)
27	Mobile, AL	5.4
248	Modesto, CA	(22.8)
NA	Monroe, MI**	NA
174	Montgomery, AL	(12.8)
60	Morgantown, WV	(0.6)
98	Morristown, TN	(5.2)
290	Mount Vernon-Anacortes, WA	(39.2)
111	Muncie, IN	(7.1)
NA	Muskegon-Norton Shores, MI**	NA
99	Napa, CA	(5.3)
183	Naples-Marco Island, FL	(13.3)
222	Nashville-Davidson, TN	(18.9)
46	Nassau-Suffolk, NY M.D.	1.5
NA	New Haven-Milford, CT**	NA
NA	New Orleans, LA**	NA
159	New York (greater), NY-NJ-PA	(11.4)
184	New York-W. Plains NY-NJ M.D.	(13.6)
240	Newark-Union, NJ-PA M.D.	(21.4)
NA	Niles-Benton Harbor, MI**	NA
NA	North Port-Bradenton-Sarasota, FL**	NA
57	Norwich-New London, CT	0.1
196	Oakland-Fremont, CA M.D.	(15.3)
169	Ocala, FL	(12.2)
55	Ocean City, NJ	0.5
22	Odessa, TX	6.9

RANK	METROPOLITAN AREA	% CHANGE
181	Ogden-Clearfield, UT	(13.2)
NA	Oklahoma City, OK**	NA
239	Olympia, WA	(21.3)
225	Omaha-Council Bluffs, NE-IA	(19.4)
114	Orlando, FL	(7.3)
8	Oshkosh-Neenah, WI	12.9
NA	Owensboro, KY**	NA
123	Oxnard-Thousand Oaks, CA	(8.0)
31	Palm Bay-Melbourne, FL	4.0
NA	Palm Coast, FL**	NA
29	Panama City-Lynn Haven, FL	4.3
107	Pascagoula, MS	(6.4)
NA	Peabody, MA M.D.**	NA
43	Pensacola, FL	2.5
79	Philadelphia (greater) PA-NJ-MD-DE	(3.5)
101	Philadelphia, PA M.D.	(5.5)
279	Phoenix-Mesa-Scottsdale, AZ	(31.2)
121	Pine Bluff, AR	(7.8)
202	Pittsburgh, PA	(16.0)
7	Pittsfield, MA	13.2
168	Pocatello, ID	(12.1)
92	Port St. Lucie, FL	(4.7)
283	Portland-Vancouver, OR-WA	(33.5)
60	Portland, ME	(0.6)
30	Poughkeepsie, NY	4.2
277	Prescott, AZ	(30.4)
NA	Providence-New Bedford, RI-MA**	NA
271	Provo-Orem, UT	(28.7)
295	Pueblo, CO	(47.7)
140	Punta Gorda, FL	(9.9)
228	Racine, WI	(19.9)
136	Raleigh-Cary, NC	(9.7)
117	Rapid City, SD	(7.4)
206	Reading, PA	(16.4)
252	Redding, CA	(24.1)
236	Reno-Sparks, NV	(20.9)
NA	Richmond, VA**	NA
250	Riverside-San Bernardino, CA	(23.1)
190	Roanoke, VA	(14.5)
26	Rochester, MN	6.0
124	Rochester, NY	(8.2)
2	Rockingham County, NH M.D.	20.3
138	Rocky Mount, NC	(9.8)
286	Rome, GA	(34.9)
240	Sacramento, CA	(21.4)
NA	Saginaw, MI**	NA
280	Salem, OR	(32.8)
242	Salinas, CA	(21.5)
81	Salisbury, MD	(3.6)
142	Salt Lake City, UT	(10.3)
238	San Angelo, TX	(21.2)
40	San Antonio, TX	2.6
276	San Diego, CA	(30.0)
179	San Francisco (greater), CA	(13.1)
131	San Francisco-S. Mateo, CA M.D.	(9.2)
130	San Jose, CA	(9.1)
146	San Luis Obispo, CA	(10.5)
213	Sandusky, OH	(17.0)
202	Santa Ana-Anaheim, CA M.D.	(16.0)
126	Santa Barbara-Santa Maria, CA	(8.5)
163	Santa Cruz-Watsonville, CA	(11.5)
24	Santa Fe, NM	6.4
234	Santa Rosa-Petaluma, CA	(20.7)

RANK	METROPOLITAN AREA	% CHANGE
158	Savannah, GA	(11.2)
110	Scranton--Wilkes-Barre, PA	(6.6)
265	Seattle-Bellevue-Everett, WA M.D.	(26.6)
254	Seattle-Tacoma-Bellevue, WA	(24.6)
148	Sebastian-Vero Beach, FL	(10.6)
63	Sheboygan, WI	(0.7)
181	Sherman-Denison, TX	(13.2)
221	Shreveport-Bossier City, LA	(18.8)
200	Sioux City, IA-NE-SD	(15.7)
87	Sioux Falls, SD	(4.4)
NA	South Bend-Mishawaka, IN-MI**	NA
195	Spartanburg, SC	(15.2)
72	Spokane, WA	(2.5)
114	Springfield, MA	(7.3)
NA	Springfield, MO**	NA
281	Springfield, OH	(32.9)
126	State College, PA	(8.5)
254	Stockton, CA	(24.6)
136	St. Cloud, MN	(9.7)
267	St. George, UT	(27.7)
144	St. Joseph, MO-KS	(10.4)
178	St. Louis, MO-IL	(13.0)
NA	Sumter, SC**	NA
36	Syracuse, NY	3.2
219	Tacoma, WA M.D.	(18.2)
135	Tallahassee, FL	(9.5)
113	Tampa-St Petersburg, FL	(7.2)
58	Texarkana, TX-Texarkana, AR	(0.4)
NA	Toledo, OH**	NA
268	Topeka, KS	(27.8)
209	Trenton-Ewing, NJ	(16.7)
NA	Tucson, AZ**	NA
155	Tulsa, OK	(11.0)
NA	Tuscaloosa, AL**	NA
40	Tyler, TX	2.6
15	Utica-Rome, NY	9.3
242	Valdosta, GA	(21.5)
NA	Vallejo-Fairfield, CA**	NA
11	Victoria, TX	12.1
198	Vineland, NJ	(15.6)
NA	Visalia-Porterville, CA**	NA
222	Waco, TX	(18.9)
33	Warner Robins, GA	3.8
NA	Warren-Farmington Hills, MI M.D.**	NA
142	Washington (greater) DC-VA-MD-WV	(10.3)
174	Washington, DC-VA-MD-WV M.D.	(12.8)
179	Waterloo-Cedar Falls, IA	(13.1)
NA	Wausau, WI**	NA
264	Wenatchee, WA	(26.3)
90	West Palm Beach, FL M.D.	(4.6)
25	Wheeling, WV-OH	6.2
257	Wichita Falls, TX	(24.9)
NA	Wichita, KS**	NA
155	Williamsport, PA	(11.0)
28	Wilmington, DE-MD-NJ M.D.	4.6
NA	Wilmington, NC**	NA
88	Winchester, VA-WV	(4.5)
47	Winston-Salem, NC	1.3
21	Worcester, MA	7.2
205	York-Hanover, PA	(16.3)
NA	Youngstown, OH-PA**	NA
293	Yuba City, CA	(44.1)
263	Yuma, AZ	(26.0)

Source: CQ Press using reported data from the F.B.I. "Crime in the United States 2009"

*Property crimes are offenses of burglary, larceny-theft, and motor vehicle theft. Attempts are included.

**Not available.

28. Percent Change in Property Crime Rate: 2005 to 2009 (continued)
National Percent Change = 11.5% Decrease*

RANK	METROPOLITAN AREA	% CHANGE	RANK	METROPOLITAN AREA	% CHANGE	RANK	METROPOLITAN AREA	% CHANGE
1	Barnstable Town, MA	33.3	60	Morgantown, WV	(0.6)	121	Fort Collins-Loveland, CO	(7.8)
2	Rockingham County, NH M.D.	20.3	60	Portland, ME	(0.6)	121	Pine Bluff, AR	(7.8)
3	Bangor, ME	18.4	63	Sheboygan, WI	(0.7)	123	Oxnard-Thousand Oaks, CA	(8.0)
4	Erie, PA	18.3	64	Cambridge-Newton, MA M.D.	(1.1)	124	Rochester, NY	(8.2)
5	Dover, DE	18.1	64	Edison, NJ M.D.	(1.1)	125	Lakeland, FL	(8.4)
6	Fargo, ND-MN	14.7	66	Lima, OH	(1.2)	126	Santa Barbara-Santa Maria, CA	(8.5)
7	Pittsfield, MA	13.2	67	Charlottesville, VA	(1.5)	126	State College, PA	(8.5)
8	Oshkosh-Neenah, WI	12.9	67	Miami (greater), FL	(1.5)	128	Allentown, PA-NJ	(8.6)
9	Columbus, GA-AL	12.6	69	Longview, TX	(1.9)	129	Abilene, TX	(8.7)
9	Cumberland, MD-WV	12.6	70	Camden, NJ M.D.	(2.4)	130	San Jose, CA	(9.1)
11	Victoria, TX	12.1	70	Houston, TX	(2.4)	131	Lafayette, IN	(9.2)
12	Manchester-Nashua, NH	11.8	72	Fond du Lac, WI	(2.5)	131	San Francisco-S. Mateo, CA M.D.	(9.2)
13	Anderson, IN	10.8	72	Spokane, WA	(2.5)	133	Baton Rouge, LA	(9.4)
13	Danville, VA	10.8	74	Austin-Round Rock, TX	(2.6)	133	Indianapolis, IN	(9.4)
15	La Crosse, WI-MN	9.3	74	Harrisonburg, VA	(2.6)	135	Tallahassee, FL	(9.5)
15	Utica-Rome, NY	9.3	76	Kingsport, TN-VA	(2.9)	136	Raleigh-Cary, NC	(9.7)
17	Fort Lauderdale, FL M.D.	8.9	77	Blacksburg, VA	(3.1)	136	St. Cloud, MN	(9.7)
18	Bloomington, IN	7.9	78	Burlington, NC	(3.3)	138	Dayton, OH	(9.8)
19	Lawrence, KS	7.8	79	Battle Creek, MI	(3.5)	138	Rocky Mount, NC	(9.8)
20	Lafayette, LA	7.5	79	Philadelphia (greater) PA-NJ-MD-DE	(3.5)	140	Amarillo, TX	(9.9)
21	Worcester, MA	7.2	81	Boston (greater), MA-NH	(3.6)	140	Punta Gorda, FL	(9.9)
22	Odessa, TX	6.9	81	Salisbury, MD	(3.6)	142	Salt Lake City, UT	(10.3)
23	Albany, GA	6.5	83	Athens-Clarke County, GA	(3.8)	142	Washington (greater) DC-VA-MD-WV	(10.3)
24	Santa Fe, NM	6.4	84	Lubbock, TX	(4.0)	144	Ann Arbor, MI	(10.4)
25	Wheeling, WV-OH	6.2	85	Albany-Schenectady-Troy, NY	(4.1)	144	St. Joseph, MO-KS	(10.4)
26	Rochester, MN	6.0	86	Kingston, NY	(4.3)	146	Boston-Quincy, MA M.D.	(10.5)
27	Mobile, AL	5.4	87	Sioux Falls, SD	(4.4)	146	San Luis Obispo, CA	(10.5)
28	Wilmington, DE-MD-NJ M.D.	4.6	88	Jacksonville, FL	(4.5)	148	Jackson, TN	(10.6)
29	Panama City-Lynn Haven, FL	4.3	88	Winchester, VA-WV	(4.5)	148	Sebastian-Vero Beach, FL	(10.6)
30	Poughkeepsie, NY	4.2	90	Alexandria, LA	(4.6)	150	Durham-Chapel Hill, NC	(10.7)
31	Palm Bay-Melbourne, FL	4.0	90	West Palm Beach, FL M.D.	(4.6)	151	Akron, OH	(10.8)
32	Gainesville, FL	3.9	92	Port St. Lucie, FL	(4.7)	151	Eau Claire, WI	(10.8)
33	Warner Robins, GA	3.8	93	Baltimore-Towson, MD	(4.9)	151	Florence, SC	(10.8)
34	Columbia, MO	3.7	93	McAllen-Edinburg-Mission, TX	(4.9)	151	Houma, LA	(10.8)
35	Fayetteville, NC	3.5	95	Bismarck, ND	(5.0)	155	Tulsa, OK	(11.0)
36	Syracuse, NY	3.2	96	Ames, IA	(5.1)	155	Williamsport, PA	(11.0)
37	Brunswick, GA	3.1	96	Brownsville-Harlingen, TX	(5.1)	157	Columbus, OH	(11.1)
38	Milwaukee, WI	3.0	98	Morristown, TN	(5.2)	158	Savannah, GA	(11.2)
39	Augusta, GA-SC	2.8	99	College Station-Bryan, TX	(5.3)	159	Cedar Rapids, IA	(11.4)
40	Dubuque, IA	2.6	99	Napa, CA	(5.3)	159	Harrisburg-Carlisle, PA	(11.4)
40	San Antonio, TX	2.6	101	Philadelphia, PA M.D.	(5.5)	159	Iowa City, IA	(11.4)
40	Tyler, TX	2.6	102	El Paso, TX	(5.8)	159	New York (greater), NY-NJ-PA	(11.4)
43	Pensacola, FL	2.5	103	Lynchburg, VA	(5.9)	163	Santa Cruz-Watsonville, CA	(11.5)
44	Goldsboro, NC	2.4	103	Miami-Dade County, FL M.D.	(5.9)	164	Bremerton-Silverdale, WA	(11.6)
45	Bethesda-Frederick, MD M.D.	1.9	103	Michigan City-La Porte, IN	(5.9)	165	Cheyenne, WY	(11.7)
46	Nassau-Suffolk, NY M.D.	1.5	106	Appleton, WI	(6.3)	166	Albuquerque, NM	(11.8)
47	Winston-Salem, NC	1.3	107	Pascagoula, MS	(6.4)	167	Lancaster, PA	(11.9)
48	Las Cruces, NM	1.1	108	Fort Smith, AR-OK	(6.5)	168	Pocatello, ID	(12.1)
49	Binghamton, NY	0.9	108	Greensboro-High Point, NC	(6.5)	169	Ocala, FL	(12.2)
49	Laredo, TX	0.9	110	Scranton--Wilkes-Barre, PA	(6.6)	170	Beaumont-Port Arthur, TX	(12.3)
51	Buffalo-Niagara Falls, NY	0.8	111	Chattanooga, TN-GA	(7.1)	171	Decatur, AL	(12.5)
51	Jackson, MS	0.8	111	Muncie, IN	(7.1)	171	Mansfield, OH	(12.5)
53	Lake Charles, LA	0.7	113	Tampa-St Petersburg, FL	(7.2)	173	Bridgeport-Stamford, CT	(12.6)
54	Midland, TX	0.6	114	Knoxville, TN	(7.3)	174	Montgomery, AL	(12.8)
55	Ocean City, NJ	0.5	114	Orlando, FL	(7.3)	174	Washington, DC-VA-MD-WV M.D.	(12.8)
56	Hinesville, GA	0.2	114	Springfield, MA	(7.3)	176	Columbus, IN	(12.9)
57	Norwich-New London, CT	0.1	117	Rapid City, SD	(7.4)	176	Lewiston-Auburn, ME	(12.9)
58	Texarkana, TX-Texarkana, AR	(0.4)	118	Hickory, NC	(7.5)	178	St. Louis, MO-IL	(13.0)
59	Hagerstown-Martinsburg, MD-WV	(0.5)	119	Farmington, NM	(7.6)	179	San Francisco (greater), CA	(13.1)
60	Columbia, SC	(0.6)	120	Madison, WI	(7.7)	179	Waterloo-Cedar Falls, IA	(13.1)

Note: All listings are for Metropolitan Statistical Areas (M.S.A.s) except for those ending with "M.D." Listings with "M.D." are Metropolitan Divisions which are smaller parts of eleven large M.S.A.s. See explanatory note at beginning of metropolitan area section.

Rank Order - Metro Area (continued)

RANK	METROPOLITAN AREA	% CHANGE
181	Ogden-Clearfield, UT	(13.2)
181	Sherman-Denison, TX	(13.2)
183	Naples-Marco Island, FL	(13.3)
184	New York-W. Plains NY-NJ M.D.	(13.6)
185	Fort Worth-Arlington, TX M.D.	(13.7)
186	Atlanta, GA	(14.0)
187	Anchorage, AK	(14.1)
188	Hartford, CT	(14.2)
188	Los Angeles County, CA M.D.	(14.2)
190	Roanoke, VA	(14.5)
191	Atlantic City, NJ	(14.6)
191	Killeen-Temple-Fort Hood, TX	(14.6)
193	Los Angeles (greater), CA	(14.7)
194	Fort Wayne, IN	(15.0)
195	Spartanburg, SC	(15.2)
196	Anderson, SC	(15.3)
196	Oakland-Fremont, CA M.D.	(15.3)
198	Carson City, NV	(15.6)
198	Vineland, NJ	(15.6)
200	Sioux City, IA-NE-SD	(15.7)
201	Merced, CA	(15.9)
202	Bakersfield, CA	(16.0)
202	Pittsburgh, PA	(16.0)
202	Santa Ana-Anaheim, CA M.D.	(16.0)
205	York-Hanover, PA	(16.3)
206	Cape Coral-Fort Myers, FL	(16.4)
206	Chico, CA	(16.4)
206	Reading, PA	(16.4)
209	Jefferson City, MO	(16.7)
209	Memphis, TN-MS-AR	(16.7)
209	Trenton-Ewing, NJ	(16.7)
212	Lewiston, ID-WA	(16.9)
213	Sandusky, OH	(17.0)
214	Green Bay, WI	(17.1)
215	Dallas (greater), TX	(17.2)
216	Casper, WY	(17.4)
217	Hot Springs, AR	(17.5)
218	Idaho Falls, ID	(17.9)
219	Tacoma, WA M.D.	(18.2)
220	Logan, UT-ID	(18.4)
221	Shreveport-Bossier City, LA	(18.8)
222	Nashville-Davidson, TN	(18.9)
222	Waco, TX	(18.9)
224	Dallas-Plano-Irving, TX M.D.	(19.0)
225	Omaha-Council Bluffs, NE-IA	(19.4)
226	Fayetteville, AR-MO	(19.5)
227	Billings, MT	(19.8)
228	Racine, WI	(19.9)
229	Macon, GA	(20.0)
230	Gadsden, AL	(20.1)
231	Fresno, CA	(20.3)
232	Corpus Christi, TX	(20.5)
232	Lebanon, PA	(20.5)
234	Kokomo, IN	(20.7)
234	Santa Rosa-Petaluma, CA	(20.7)
236	Reno-Sparks, NV	(20.9)
237	Honolulu, HI	(21.1)
238	San Angelo, TX	(21.2)
239	Olympia, WA	(21.3)
240	Newark-Union, NJ-PA M.D.	(21.4)
240	Sacramento, CA	(21.4)
242	Janesville, WI	(21.5)
242	Jonesboro, AR	(21.5)

RANK	METROPOLITAN AREA	% CHANGE
242	Salinas, CA	(21.5)
242	Valdosta, GA	(21.5)
246	Coeur d'Alene, ID	(21.9)
247	Altoona, PA	(22.3)
248	Charleston, WV	(22.8)
248	Modesto, CA	(22.8)
250	Elmira, NY	(23.1)
250	Riverside-San Bernardino, CA	(23.1)
252	Redding, CA	(24.1)
253	Charlotte-Gastonia, NC-SC	(24.5)
254	Seattle-Tacoma-Bellevue, WA	(24.6)
254	Stockton, CA	(24.6)
256	Asheville, NC	(24.8)
257	Wichita Falls, TX	(24.9)
258	Grand Junction, CO	(25.3)
258	Johnson City, TN	(25.3)
260	Huntsville, AL	(25.4)
261	Corvallis, OR	(25.7)
261	Eugene-Springfield, OR	(25.7)
263	Yuma, AZ	(26.0)
264	Wenatchee, WA	(26.3)
265	Seattle-Bellevue-Everett, WA M.D.	(26.6)
266	Lincoln, NE	(27.3)
267	St. George, UT	(27.7)
268	Topeka, KS	(27.8)
269	Flagstaff, AZ	(28.2)
270	Madera, CA	(28.6)
271	Provo-Orem, UT	(28.7)
272	Elkhart-Goshen, IN	(29.1)
273	Grand Forks, ND-MN	(29.9)
273	Great Falls, MT	(29.9)
273	Las Vegas-Paradise, NV	(29.9)
276	San Diego, CA	(30.0)
277	Prescott, AZ	(30.4)
278	Colorado Springs, CO	(30.9)
279	Phoenix-Mesa-Scottsdale, AZ	(31.2)
280	Salem, OR	(32.8)
281	Springfield, OH	(32.9)
282	Bellingham, WA	(33.4)
283	Kennewick-Pasco-Richland, WA	(33.5)
283	Portland-Vancouver, OR-WA	(33.5)
285	Gainesville, GA	(33.8)
286	Rome, GA	(34.9)
287	Medford, OR	(35.8)
288	Denver-Aurora, CO	(37.2)
289	Longview, WA	(37.8)
290	Mount Vernon-Anacortes, WA	(39.2)
291	Bend, OR	(43.0)
292	Missoula, MT	(44.0)
293	Yuba City, CA	(44.1)
294	Greeley, CO	(46.8)
295	Pueblo, CO	(47.7)
NA	Anniston-Oxford, AL**	NA
NA	Auburn, AL**	NA
NA	Bay City, MI**	NA
NA	Birmingham-Hoover, AL**	NA
NA	Boise City-Nampa, ID**	NA
NA	Boulder, CO**	NA
NA	Bowling Green, KY**	NA
NA	Burlington-South Burlington, VT**	NA
NA	Cape Girardeau, MO-IL**	NA
NA	Charleston-North Charleston, SC**	NA
NA	Cincinnati-Middletown, OH-KY-IN**	NA

RANK	METROPOLITAN AREA	% CHANGE
NA	Clarksville, TN-KY**	NA
NA	Cleveland-Elyria-Mentor, OH**	NA
NA	Cleveland, TN**	NA
NA	Crestview-Fort Walton Beach, FL**	NA
NA	Dalton, GA**	NA
NA	Danville, IL**	NA
NA	Decatur, IL**	NA
NA	Deltona-Daytona Beach, FL**	NA
NA	Des Moines-West Des Moines, IA**	NA
NA	Detroit (greater), MI**	NA
NA	Detroit-Livonia-Dearborn, MI M.D.**	NA
NA	Dothan, AL**	NA
NA	Duluth, MN-WI**	NA
NA	El Centro, CA**	NA
NA	Elizabethtown, KY**	NA
NA	Evansville, IN-KY**	NA
NA	Flint, MI**	NA
NA	Florence-Muscle Shoals, AL**	NA
NA	Glens Falls, NY**	NA
NA	Grand Rapids-Wyoming, MI**	NA
NA	Gulfport-Biloxi, MS**	NA
NA	Hattiesburg, MS**	NA
NA	Holland-Grand Haven, MI**	NA
NA	Ithaca, NY**	NA
NA	Jacksonville, NC**	NA
NA	Jackson, MI**	NA
NA	Kalamazoo-Portage, MI**	NA
NA	Kansas City, MO-KS**	NA
NA	Lake Havasu City-Kingman, AZ**	NA
NA	Lansing-East Lansing, MI**	NA
NA	Lawton, OK**	NA
NA	Lexington-Fayette, KY**	NA
NA	Little Rock, AR**	NA
NA	Louisville, KY-IN**	NA
NA	Manhattan, KS**	NA
NA	Mankato-North Mankato, MN**	NA
NA	Minneapolis-St. Paul, MN-WI**	NA
NA	Monroe, MI**	NA
NA	Muskegon-Norton Shores, MI**	NA
NA	New Haven-Milford, CT**	NA
NA	New Orleans, LA**	NA
NA	Niles-Benton Harbor, MI**	NA
NA	North Port-Bradenton-Sarasota, FL**	NA
NA	Oklahoma City, OK**	NA
NA	Owensboro, KY**	NA
NA	Palm Coast, FL**	NA
NA	Peabody, MA M.D.**	NA
NA	Providence-New Bedford, RI-MA**	NA
NA	Richmond, VA**	NA
NA	Saginaw, MI**	NA
NA	South Bend-Mishawaka, IN-MI**	NA
NA	Springfield, MO**	NA
NA	Sumter, SC**	NA
NA	Toledo, OH**	NA
NA	Tucson, AZ**	NA
NA	Tuscaloosa, AL**	NA
NA	Vallejo-Fairfield, CA**	NA
NA	Visalia-Porterville, CA**	NA
NA	Warren-Farmington Hills, MI M.D.**	NA
NA	Wausau, WI**	NA
NA	Wichita, KS**	NA
NA	Wilmington, NC**	NA
NA	Youngstown, OH-PA**	NA

Source: CQ Press using reported data from the F.B.I. "Crime in the United States 2009"

*Property crimes are offenses of burglary, larceny-theft, and motor vehicle theft. Attempts are included.

**Not available.

29. Burglaries in 2009
National Total = 2,199,125 Burglaries*

RANK	METROPOLITAN AREA	BURGLARY
229	Abilene, TX	1,488
88	Akron, OH	6,095
117	Albany-Schenectady-Troy, NY	4,093
179	Albany, GA	2,176
61	Albuquerque, NM	9,260
189	Alexandria, LA	1,863
132	Allentown, PA-NJ	3,489
344	Altoona, PA	444
150	Amarillo, TX	2,801
347	Ames, IA	430
205	Anchorage, AK	1,724
260	Anderson, IN	1,147
182	Anderson, SC	2,120
168	Ann Arbor, MI	2,400
192	Anniston-Oxford, AL	1,832
319	Appleton, WI	628
142	Asheville, NC	3,081
171	Athens-Clarke County, GA	2,369
5	Atlanta, GA	54,190
196	Atlantic City, NJ	1,776
NA	Auburn, AL**	NA
84	Augusta, GA-SC	6,690
45	Austin-Round Rock, TX	13,403
59	Bakersfield, CA	9,413
30	Baltimore-Towson, MD	18,191
284	Bangor, ME	946
156	Barnstable Town, MA	2,704
63	Baton Rouge, LA	8,920
210	Battle Creek, MI	1,666
323	Bay City, MI	601
109	Beaumont-Port Arthur, TX	4,363
237	Bellingham, WA	1,400
305	Bend, OR	770
124	Bethesda-Frederick, MD M.D.	3,829
280	Billings, MT	956
285	Binghamton, NY	944
43	Birmingham-Hoover, AL	13,947
360	Bismarck, ND	308
289	Blacksburg, VA	901
224	Bloomington, IN	1,511
158	Boise City-Nampa, ID	2,645
26	Boston (greater), MA-NH	19,216
65	Boston-Quincy, MA M.D.	8,482
240	Boulder, CO	1,367
296	Bowling Green, KY	848
227	Bremerton-Silverdale, WA	1,499
136	Bridgeport-Stamford, CT	3,217
127	Brownsville-Harlingen, TX	3,736
247	Brunswick, GA	1,318
73	Buffalo-Niagara Falls, NY	7,608
259	Burlington-South Burlington, VT	1,148
215	Burlington, NC	1,621
90	Cambridge-Newton, MA M.D.	5,903
85	Camden, NJ M.D.	6,589
92	Cape Coral-Fort Myers, FL	5,858
328	Cape Girardeau, MO-IL	591
363	Carson City, NV	268
332	Casper, WY	562
207	Cedar Rapids, IA	1,696
NA	Charleston-North Charleston, SC**	NA
157	Charleston, WV	2,675
35	Charlotte-Gastonia, NC-SC	17,400
315	Charlottesville, VA	649
99	Chattanooga, TN-GA	5,356
356	Cheyenne, WY	334
201	Chico, CA	1,733
37	Cincinnati-Middletown, OH-KY-IN	17,088
155	Clarksville, TN-KY	2,731
33	Cleveland-Elyria-Mentor, OH	17,642
299	Cleveland, TN	818
291	Coeur d'Alene, ID	896
173	College Station-Bryan, TX	2,312
116	Colorado Springs, CO	4,124
283	Columbia, MO	948
77	Columbia, SC	7,119
105	Columbus, GA-AL	4,812
354	Columbus, IN	340
23	Columbus, OH	20,925
107	Corpus Christi, TX	4,402
351	Corvallis, OR	383
271	Crestview-Fort Walton Beach, FL	1,038
306	Cumberland, MD-WV	763
1	Dallas (greater), TX	63,689
8	Dallas-Plano-Irving, TX M.D.	41,805
301	Dalton, GA	803
266	Danville, IL	1,101
309	Danville, VA	725
72	Dayton, OH	7,659
257	Decatur, AL	1,178
226	Decatur, IL	1,503
104	Deltona-Daytona Beach, FL	4,858
44	Denver-Aurora, CO	13,642
141	Des Moines-West Des Moines, IA	3,084
9	Detroit (greater), MI	36,813
17	Detroit-Livonia-Dearborn, MI M.D.	25,879
NA	Dothan, AL**	NA
243	Dover, DE	1,354
325	Dubuque, IA	595
213	Duluth, MN-WI	1,635
87	Durham-Chapel Hill, NC	6,215
333	Eau Claire, WI	546
66	Edison, NJ M.D.	8,351
198	El Centro, CA	1,758
151	El Paso, TX	2,793
345	Elizabethtown, KY	443
245	Elkhart-Goshen, IN	1,340
350	Elmira, NY	384
200	Erie, PA	1,738
137	Eugene-Springfield, OR	3,211
191	Evansville, IN-KY	1,842
275	Fargo, ND-MN	1,012
312	Farmington, NM	701
160	Fayetteville, AR-MO	2,610
78	Fayetteville, NC	6,919
322	Flagstaff, AZ	605
93	Flint, MI	5,776
255	Florence-Muscle Shoals, AL	1,203
152	Florence, SC	2,782
364	Fond du Lac, WI	235
242	Fort Collins-Loveland, CO	1,356
39	Fort Lauderdale, FL M.D.	15,952
162	Fort Smith, AR-OK	2,549
153	Fort Wayne, IN	2,739
21	Fort Worth-Arlington, TX M.D.	21,884
70	Fresno, CA	7,912
294	Gadsden, AL	868
145	Gainesville, FL	2,979
256	Gainesville, GA	1,196
355	Glens Falls, NY	336
208	Goldsboro, NC	1,688
346	Grand Forks, ND-MN	438
298	Grand Junction, CO	823
98	Grand Rapids-Wyoming, MI	5,397
361	Great Falls, MT	299
248	Greeley, CO	1,307
254	Green Bay, WI	1,233
58	Greensboro-High Point, NC	9,447
146	Gulfport-Biloxi, MS	2,964
239	Hagerstown-Martinsburg, MD-WV	1,372
188	Harrisburg-Carlisle, PA	1,945
362	Harrisonburg, VA	298
103	Hartford, CT	5,044
279	Hattiesburg, MS	969
118	Hickory, NC	4,074
277	Hinesville, GA	1,001
273	Holland-Grand Haven, MI	1,022
89	Honolulu, HI	5,999
183	Hot Springs, AR	2,119
253	Houma, LA	1,239
3	Houston, TX	60,690
123	Huntsville, AL	3,841
339	Idaho Falls, ID	507
29	Indianapolis, IN	18,298
329	Iowa City, IA	587
353	Ithaca, NY	362
41	Jacksonville, FL	14,747
187	Jacksonville, NC	1,983
288	Jackson, MI	905
81	Jackson, MS	6,764
225	Jackson, TN	1,509
295	Janesville, WI	862
314	Jefferson City, MO	667
234	Johnson City, TN	1,443
194	Jonesboro, AR	1,825
140	Kalamazoo-Portage, MI	3,123
NA	Kansas City, MO-KS**	NA
263	Kennewick-Pasco-Richland, WA	1,134
134	Killeen-Temple-Fort Hood, TX	3,441
159	Kingsport, TN-VA	2,624
311	Kingston, NY	705
82	Knoxville, TN	6,724
308	Kokomo, IN	753
326	La Crosse, WI-MN	592
267	Lafayette, IN	1,083
167	Lafayette, LA	2,416
121	Lake Charles, LA	3,960
209	Lake Havasu City-Kingman, AZ	1,667
79	Lakeland, FL	6,842
203	Lancaster, PA	1,726
148	Lansing-East Lansing, MI	2,924

Note: All listings are for Metropolitan Statistical Areas (M.S.A.s) except for those ending with "M.D." Listings with "M.D." are Metropolitan Divisions which are smaller parts of eleven large M.S.A.s. See explanatory note at beginning of metropolitan area section.

Alpha Order - Metro Area (continued)

RANK	METROPOLITAN AREA	BURGLARY
178	Laredo, TX	2,282
218	Las Cruces, NM	1,579
36	Las Vegas-Paradise, NV	17,163
297	Lawrence, KS	845
217	Lawton, OK	1,602
348	Lebanon, PA	422
340	Lewiston-Auburn, ME	493
357	Lewiston, ID-WA	332
129	Lexington-Fayette, KY	3,643
238	Lima, OH	1,385
199	Lincoln, NE	1,739
52	Little Rock, AR	10,384
359	Logan, UT-ID	314
174	Longview, TX	2,307
299	Longview, WA	818
7	Los Angeles County, CA M.D.	50,558
2	Los Angeles (greater), CA	61,496
50	Louisville, KY-IN	10,733
111	Lubbock, TX	4,263
292	Lynchburg, VA	886
144	Macon, GA	3,024
258	Madera, CA	1,166
161	Madison, WI	2,553
212	Manchester-Nashua, NH	1,640
336	Manhattan, KS	536
342	Mankato-North Mankato, MN	475
228	Mansfield, OH	1,492
68	McAllen-Edinburg-Mission, TX	7,935
317	Medford, OR	638
25	Memphis, TN-MS-AR	19,408
172	Merced, CA	2,318
4	Miami (greater), FL	54,500
18	Miami-Dade County, FL M.D.	25,345
287	Michigan City-La Porte, IN	929
264	Midland, TX	1,116
60	Milwaukee, WI	9,391
31	Minneapolis-St. Paul, MN-WI	17,723
349	Missoula, MT	391
91	Mobile, AL	5,872
94	Modesto, CA	5,748
293	Monroe, MI	876
110	Montgomery, AL	4,294
313	Morgantown, WV	676
274	Morristown, TN	1,015
275	Mount Vernon-Anacortes, WA	1,012
303	Muncie, IN	783
233	Muskegon-Norton Shores, MI	1,455
310	Napa, CA	716
249	Naples-Marco Island, FL	1,287
47	Nashville-Davidson, TN	12,282
76	Nassau-Suffolk, NY M.D.	7,121
112	New Haven-Milford, CT	4,220
NA	New Orleans, LA**	NA
6	New York (greater), NY-NJ-PA	53,310
13	New York-W. Plains NY-NJ M.D.	28,901
62	Newark-Union, NJ-PA M.D.	8,937
278	Niles-Benton Harbor, MI	993
83	North Port-Bradenton-Sarasota, FL	6,706
320	Norwich-New London, CT	608
27	Oakland-Fremont, CA M.D.	18,839
169	Ocala, FL	2,384
270	Ocean City, NJ	1,045
216	Odessa, TX	1,611
170	Ogden-Clearfield, UT	2,371
40	Oklahoma City, OK	15,948
214	Olympia, WA	1,634
100	Omaha-Council Bluffs, NE-IA	5,233
20	Orlando, FL	22,784
304	Oshkosh-Neenah, WI	778
316	Owensboro, KY	648
147	Oxnard-Thousand Oaks, CA	2,954
115	Palm Bay-Melbourne, FL	4,137
326	Palm Coast, FL	592
204	Panama City-Lynn Haven, FL	1,725
190	Pascagoula, MS	1,845
131	Peabody, MA M.D.	3,550
126	Pensacola, FL	3,745
12	Philadelphia (greater) PA-NJ-MD-DE	30,014
28	Philadelphia, PA M.D.	18,328
10	Phoenix-Mesa-Scottsdale, AZ	36,192
184	Pine Bluff, AR	2,030
51	Pittsburgh, PA	10,469
281	Pittsfield, MA	953
358	Pocatello, ID	331
135	Port St. Lucie, FL	3,363
54	Portland-Vancouver, OR-WA	9,709
163	Portland, ME	2,548
185	Poughkeepsie, NY	2,005
262	Prescott, AZ	1,135
57	Providence-New Bedford, RI-MA	9,487
195	Provo-Orem, UT	1,777
219	Pueblo, CO	1,558
269	Punta Gorda, FL	1,068
230	Racine, WI	1,468
71	Raleigh-Cary, NC	7,826
335	Rapid City, SD	540
181	Reading, PA	2,153
232	Redding, CA	1,462
138	Reno-Sparks, NV	3,209
80	Richmond, VA	6,838
11	Riverside-San Bernardino, CA	32,847
222	Roanoke, VA	1,544
320	Rochester, MN	608
95	Rochester, NY	5,703
250	Rockingham County, NH M.D.	1,281
177	Rocky Mount, NC	2,285
302	Rome, GA	787
38	Sacramento, CA	16,421
165	Saginaw, MI	2,474
180	Salem, OR	2,163
139	Salinas, CA	3,151
221	Salisbury, MD	1,553
64	Salt Lake City, UT	8,800
265	San Angelo, TX	1,111
19	San Antonio, TX	23,603
42	San Diego, CA	14,522
15	San Francisco (greater), CA	28,386
56	San Francisco-S. Mateo, CA M.D.	9,547
74	San Jose, CA	7,539
235	San Luis Obispo, CA	1,433
334	Sandusky, OH	545
48	Santa Ana-Anaheim, CA M.D.	10,938
175	Santa Barbara-Santa Maria, CA	2,290
202	Santa Cruz-Watsonville, CA	1,732
143	Santa Fe, NM	3,041
186	Santa Rosa-Petaluma, CA	1,993
130	Savannah, GA	3,590
166	Scranton--Wilkes-Barre, PA	2,428
24	Seattle-Bellevue-Everett, WA M.D.	20,746
14	Seattle-Tacoma-Bellevue, WA	28,673
272	Sebastian-Vero Beach, FL	1,034
341	Sheboygan, WI	477
286	Sherman-Denison, TX	939
125	Shreveport-Bossier City, LA	3,826
307	Sioux City, IA-NE-SD	756
282	Sioux Falls, SD	949
133	South Bend-Mishawaka, IN-MI	3,461
153	Spartanburg, SC	2,739
119	Spokane, WA	4,071
101	Springfield, MA	5,143
128	Springfield, MO	3,697
220	Springfield, OH	1,556
352	State College, PA	382
75	Stockton, CA	7,521
331	St. Cloud, MN	574
337	St. George, UT	518
251	St. Joseph, MO-KS	1,251
34	St. Louis, MO-IL	17,541
252	Sumter, SC	1,250
122	Syracuse, NY	3,934
69	Tacoma, WA M.D.	7,927
106	Tallahassee, FL	4,806
16	Tampa-St Petersburg, FL	27,088
197	Texarkana, TX-Texarkana, AR	1,762
53	Toledo, OH	9,977
176	Topeka, KS	2,286
211	Trenton-Ewing, NJ	1,663
67	Tucson, AZ	7,998
55	Tulsa, OK	9,629
149	Tuscaloosa, AL	2,851
192	Tyler, TX	1,832
246	Utica-Rome, NY	1,336
241	Valdosta, GA	1,362
113	Vallejo-Fairfield, CA	4,168
244	Victoria, TX	1,344
236	Vineland, NJ	1,429
114	Visalia-Porterville, CA	4,139
164	Waco, TX	2,538
261	Warner Robins, GA	1,139
49	Warren-Farmington Hills, MI M.D.	10,934
22	Washington (greater) DC-VA-MD-WV	21,514
32	Washington, DC-VA-MD-WV M.D.	17,685
268	Waterloo-Cedar Falls, IA	1,077
338	Wausau, WI	515
324	Wenatchee, WA	599
46	West Palm Beach, FL M.D.	13,203
318	Wheeling, WV-OH	637
223	Wichita Falls, TX	1,539
97	Wichita, KS	5,450
343	Williamsport, PA	453
102	Wilmington, DE-MD-NJ M.D.	5,097
108	Wilmington, NC	4,378
330	Winchester, VA-WV	584
86	Winston-Salem, NC	6,521
120	Worcester, MA	3,987
231	York-Hanover, PA	1,467
96	Youngstown, OH-PA	5,678
290	Yuba City, CA	899
206	Yuma, AZ	1,706

Source: Reported data from the F.B.I. "Crime in the United States 2009"

*Burglary is the unlawful entry of a structure to commit a felony or theft. Attempts are included.

**Not available.

29. Burglaries in 2009 (continued)
National Total = 2,199,125 Burglaries*

RANK	METROPOLITAN AREA	BURGLARY
1	Dallas (greater), TX	63,689
2	Los Angeles (greater), CA	61,496
3	Houston, TX	60,690
4	Miami (greater), FL	54,500
5	Atlanta, GA	54,190
6	New York (greater), NY-NJ-PA	53,310
7	Los Angeles County, CA M.D.	50,558
8	Dallas-Plano-Irving, TX M.D.	41,805
9	Detroit (greater), MI	36,813
10	Phoenix-Mesa-Scottsdale, AZ	36,192
11	Riverside-San Bernardino, CA	32,847
12	Philadelphia (greater) PA-NJ-MD-DE	30,014
13	New York-W. Plains NY-NJ M.D.	28,901
14	Seattle-Tacoma-Bellevue, WA	28,673
15	San Francisco (greater), CA	28,386
16	Tampa-St Petersburg, FL	27,088
17	Detroit-Livonia-Dearborn, MI M.D.	25,879
18	Miami-Dade County, FL M.D.	25,345
19	San Antonio, TX	23,603
20	Orlando, FL	22,784
21	Fort Worth-Arlington, TX M.D.	21,884
22	Washington (greater) DC-VA-MD-WV	21,514
23	Columbus, OH	20,925
24	Seattle-Bellevue-Everett, WA M.D.	20,746
25	Memphis, TN-MS-AR	19,408
26	Boston (greater), MA-NH	19,216
27	Oakland-Fremont, CA M.D.	18,839
28	Philadelphia, PA M.D.	18,328
29	Indianapolis, IN	18,298
30	Baltimore-Towson, MD	18,191
31	Minneapolis-St. Paul, MN-WI	17,723
32	Washington, DC-VA-MD-WV M.D.	17,685
33	Cleveland-Elyria-Mentor, OH	17,642
34	St. Louis, MO-IL	17,541
35	Charlotte-Gastonia, NC-SC	17,400
36	Las Vegas-Paradise, NV	17,163
37	Cincinnati-Middletown, OH-KY-IN	17,088
38	Sacramento, CA	16,421
39	Fort Lauderdale, FL M.D.	15,952
40	Oklahoma City, OK	15,948
41	Jacksonville, FL	14,747
42	San Diego, CA	14,522
43	Birmingham-Hoover, AL	13,947
44	Denver-Aurora, CO	13,642
45	Austin-Round Rock, TX	13,403
46	West Palm Beach, FL M.D.	13,203
47	Nashville-Davidson, TN	12,282
48	Santa Ana-Anaheim, CA M.D.	10,938
49	Warren-Farmington Hills, MI M.D.	10,934
50	Louisville, KY-IN	10,733
51	Pittsburgh, PA	10,469
52	Little Rock, AR	10,384
53	Toledo, OH	9,977
54	Portland-Vancouver, OR-WA	9,709
55	Tulsa, OK	9,629
56	San Francisco-S. Mateo, CA M.D.	9,547
57	Providence-New Bedford, RI-MA	9,487
58	Greensboro-High Point, NC	9,447
59	Bakersfield, CA	9,413
60	Milwaukee, WI	9,391
61	Albuquerque, NM	9,260
62	Newark-Union, NJ-PA M.D.	8,937
63	Baton Rouge, LA	8,920
64	Salt Lake City, UT	8,800
65	Boston-Quincy, MA M.D.	8,482
66	Edison, NJ M.D.	8,351
67	Tucson, AZ	7,998
68	McAllen-Edinburg-Mission, TX	7,935
69	Tacoma, WA M.D.	7,927
70	Fresno, CA	7,912
71	Raleigh-Cary, NC	7,826
72	Dayton, OH	7,659
73	Buffalo-Niagara Falls, NY	7,608
74	San Jose, CA	7,539
75	Stockton, CA	7,521
76	Nassau-Suffolk, NY M.D.	7,121
77	Columbia, SC	7,119
78	Fayetteville, NC	6,919
79	Lakeland, FL	6,842
80	Richmond, VA	6,838
81	Jackson, MS	6,764
82	Knoxville, TN	6,724
83	North Port-Bradenton-Sarasota, FL	6,706
84	Augusta, GA-SC	6,690
85	Camden, NJ M.D.	6,589
86	Winston-Salem, NC	6,521
87	Durham-Chapel Hill, NC	6,215
88	Akron, OH	6,095
89	Honolulu, HI	5,999
90	Cambridge-Newton, MA M.D.	5,903
91	Mobile, AL	5,872
92	Cape Coral-Fort Myers, FL	5,858
93	Flint, MI	5,776
94	Modesto, CA	5,748
95	Rochester, NY	5,703
96	Youngstown, OH-PA	5,678
97	Wichita, KS	5,450
98	Grand Rapids-Wyoming, MI	5,397
99	Chattanooga, TN-GA	5,356
100	Omaha-Council Bluffs, NE-IA	5,233
101	Springfield, MA	5,143
102	Wilmington, DE-MD-NJ M.D.	5,097
103	Hartford, CT	5,044
104	Deltona-Daytona Beach, FL	4,858
105	Columbus, GA-AL	4,812
106	Tallahassee, FL	4,806
107	Corpus Christi, TX	4,402
108	Wilmington, NC	4,378
109	Beaumont-Port Arthur, TX	4,363
110	Montgomery, AL	4,294
111	Lubbock, TX	4,263
112	New Haven-Milford, CT	4,220
113	Vallejo-Fairfield, CA	4,168
114	Visalia-Porterville, CA	4,139
115	Palm Bay-Melbourne, FL	4,137
116	Colorado Springs, CO	4,124
117	Albany-Schenectady-Troy, NY	4,093
118	Hickory, NC	4,074
119	Spokane, WA	4,071
120	Worcester, MA	3,987
121	Lake Charles, LA	3,960
122	Syracuse, NY	3,934
123	Huntsville, AL	3,841
124	Bethesda-Frederick, MD M.D.	3,829
125	Shreveport-Bossier City, LA	3,826
126	Pensacola, FL	3,745
127	Brownsville-Harlingen, TX	3,736
128	Springfield, MO	3,697
129	Lexington-Fayette, KY	3,643
130	Savannah, GA	3,590
131	Peabody, MA M.D.	3,550
132	Allentown, PA-NJ	3,489
133	South Bend-Mishawaka, IN-MI	3,461
134	Killeen-Temple-Fort Hood, TX	3,441
135	Port St. Lucie, FL	3,363
136	Bridgeport-Stamford, CT	3,217
137	Eugene-Springfield, OR	3,211
138	Reno-Sparks, NV	3,209
139	Salinas, CA	3,151
140	Kalamazoo-Portage, MI	3,123
141	Des Moines-West Des Moines, IA	3,084
142	Asheville, NC	3,081
143	Santa Fe, NM	3,041
144	Macon, GA	3,024
145	Gainesville, FL	2,979
146	Gulfport-Biloxi, MS	2,964
147	Oxnard-Thousand Oaks, CA	2,954
148	Lansing-East Lansing, MI	2,924
149	Tuscaloosa, AL	2,851
150	Amarillo, TX	2,801
151	El Paso, TX	2,793
152	Florence, SC	2,782
153	Fort Wayne, IN	2,739
153	Spartanburg, SC	2,739
155	Clarksville, TN-KY	2,731
156	Barnstable Town, MA	2,704
157	Charleston, WV	2,675
158	Boise City-Nampa, ID	2,645
159	Kingsport, TN-VA	2,624
160	Fayetteville, AR-MO	2,610
161	Madison, WI	2,553
162	Fort Smith, AR-OK	2,549
163	Portland, ME	2,548
164	Waco, TX	2,538
165	Saginaw, MI	2,474
166	Scranton--Wilkes-Barre, PA	2,428
167	Lafayette, LA	2,416
168	Ann Arbor, MI	2,400
169	Ocala, FL	2,384
170	Ogden-Clearfield, UT	2,371
171	Athens-Clarke County, GA	2,369
172	Merced, CA	2,318
173	College Station-Bryan, TX	2,312
174	Longview, TX	2,307
175	Santa Barbara-Santa Maria, CA	2,290
176	Topeka, KS	2,286
177	Rocky Mount, NC	2,285
178	Laredo, TX	2,282
179	Albany, GA	2,176
180	Salem, OR	2,163

Note: All listings are for Metropolitan Statistical Areas (M.S.A.s) except for those ending with "M.D." Listings with "M.D." are Metropolitan Divisions which are smaller parts of eleven large M.S.A.s. See explanatory note at beginning of metropolitan area section.

RANK	METROPOLITAN AREA	BURGLARY
181	Reading, PA	2,153
182	Anderson, SC	2,120
183	Hot Springs, AR	2,119
184	Pine Bluff, AR	2,030
185	Poughkeepsie, NY	2,005
186	Santa Rosa-Petaluma, CA	1,993
187	Jacksonville, NC	1,983
188	Harrisburg-Carlisle, PA	1,945
189	Alexandria, LA	1,863
190	Pascagoula, MS	1,845
191	Evansville, IN-KY	1,842
192	Anniston-Oxford, AL	1,832
192	Tyler, TX	1,832
194	Jonesboro, AR	1,825
195	Provo-Orem, UT	1,777
196	Atlantic City, NJ	1,776
197	Texarkana, TX-Texarkana, AR	1,762
198	El Centro, CA	1,758
199	Lincoln, NE	1,739
200	Erie, PA	1,738
201	Chico, CA	1,733
202	Santa Cruz-Watsonville, CA	1,732
203	Lancaster, PA	1,726
204	Panama City-Lynn Haven, FL	1,725
205	Anchorage, AK	1,724
206	Yuma, AZ	1,706
207	Cedar Rapids, IA	1,696
208	Goldsboro, NC	1,688
209	Lake Havasu City-Kingman, AZ	1,667
210	Battle Creek, MI	1,666
211	Trenton-Ewing, NJ	1,663
212	Manchester-Nashua, NH	1,640
213	Duluth, MN-WI	1,635
214	Olympia, WA	1,634
215	Burlington, NC	1,621
216	Odessa, TX	1,611
217	Lawton, OK	1,602
218	Las Cruces, NM	1,579
219	Pueblo, CO	1,558
220	Springfield, OH	1,556
221	Salisbury, MD	1,553
222	Roanoke, VA	1,544
223	Wichita Falls, TX	1,539
224	Bloomington, IN	1,511
225	Jackson, TN	1,509
226	Decatur, IL	1,503
227	Bremerton-Silverdale, WA	1,499
228	Mansfield, OH	1,492
229	Abilene, TX	1,488
230	Racine, WI	1,468
231	York-Hanover, PA	1,467
232	Redding, CA	1,462
233	Muskegon-Norton Shores, MI	1,455
234	Johnson City, TN	1,443
235	San Luis Obispo, CA	1,433
236	Vineland, NJ	1,429
237	Bellingham, WA	1,400
238	Lima, OH	1,385
239	Hagerstown-Martinsburg, MD-WV	1,372
240	Boulder, CO	1,367
241	Valdosta, GA	1,362
242	Fort Collins-Loveland, CO	1,356
243	Dover, DE	1,354

RANK	METROPOLITAN AREA	BURGLARY
244	Victoria, TX	1,344
245	Elkhart-Goshen, IN	1,340
246	Utica-Rome, NY	1,336
247	Brunswick, GA	1,318
248	Greeley, CO	1,307
249	Naples-Marco Island, FL	1,287
250	Rockingham County, NH M.D.	1,281
251	St. Joseph, MO-KS	1,251
252	Sumter, SC	1,250
253	Houma, LA	1,239
254	Green Bay, WI	1,233
255	Florence-Muscle Shoals, AL	1,203
256	Gainesville, GA	1,196
257	Decatur, AL	1,178
258	Madera, CA	1,166
259	Burlington-South Burlington, VT	1,148
260	Anderson, IN	1,147
261	Warner Robins, GA	1,139
262	Prescott, AZ	1,135
263	Kennewick-Pasco-Richland, WA	1,134
264	Midland, TX	1,116
265	San Angelo, TX	1,111
266	Danville, IL	1,101
267	Lafayette, IN	1,083
268	Waterloo-Cedar Falls, IA	1,077
269	Punta Gorda, FL	1,068
270	Ocean City, NJ	1,045
271	Crestview-Fort Walton Beach, FL	1,038
272	Sebastian-Vero Beach, FL	1,034
273	Holland-Grand Haven, MI	1,022
274	Morristown, TN	1,015
275	Fargo, ND-MN	1,012
275	Mount Vernon-Anacortes, WA	1,012
277	Hinesville, GA	1,001
278	Niles-Benton Harbor, MI	993
279	Hattiesburg, MS	969
280	Billings, MT	956
281	Pittsfield, MA	953
282	Sioux Falls, SD	949
283	Columbia, MO	948
284	Bangor, ME	946
285	Binghamton, NY	944
286	Sherman-Denison, TX	939
287	Michigan City-La Porte, IN	929
288	Jackson, MI	905
289	Blacksburg, VA	901
290	Yuba City, CA	899
291	Coeur d'Alene, ID	896
292	Lynchburg, VA	886
293	Monroe, MI	876
294	Gadsden, AL	868
295	Janesville, WI	862
296	Bowling Green, KY	848
297	Lawrence, KS	845
298	Grand Junction, CO	823
299	Cleveland, TN	818
299	Longview, WA	818
301	Dalton, GA	803
302	Rome, GA	787
303	Muncie, IN	783
304	Oshkosh-Neenah, WI	778
305	Bend, OR	770
306	Cumberland, MD-WV	763

RANK	METROPOLITAN AREA	BURGLARY
307	Sioux City, IA-NE-SD	756
308	Kokomo, IN	753
309	Danville, VA	725
310	Napa, CA	716
311	Kingston, NY	705
312	Farmington, NM	701
313	Morgantown, WV	676
314	Jefferson City, MO	667
315	Charlottesville, VA	649
316	Owensboro, KY	648
317	Medford, OR	638
318	Wheeling, WV-OH	637
319	Appleton, WI	628
320	Norwich-New London, CT	608
320	Rochester, MN	608
322	Flagstaff, AZ	605
323	Bay City, MI	601
324	Wenatchee, WA	599
325	Dubuque, IA	595
326	La Crosse, WI-MN	592
326	Palm Coast, FL	592
328	Cape Girardeau, MO-IL	591
329	Iowa City, IA	587
330	Winchester, VA-WV	584
331	St. Cloud, MN	574
332	Casper, WY	562
333	Eau Claire, WI	546
334	Sandusky, OH	545
335	Rapid City, SD	540
336	Manhattan, KS	536
337	St. George, UT	518
338	Wausau, WI	515
339	Idaho Falls, ID	507
340	Lewiston-Auburn, ME	493
341	Sheboygan, WI	477
342	Mankato-North Mankato, MN	475
343	Williamsport, PA	453
344	Altoona, PA	444
345	Elizabethtown, KY	443
346	Grand Forks, ND-MN	438
347	Ames, IA	430
348	Lebanon, PA	422
349	Missoula, MT	391
350	Elmira, NY	384
351	Corvallis, OR	383
352	State College, PA	382
353	Ithaca, NY	362
354	Columbus, IN	340
355	Glens Falls, NY	336
356	Cheyenne, WY	334
357	Lewiston, ID-WA	332
358	Pocatello, ID	331
359	Logan, UT-ID	314
360	Bismarck, ND	308
361	Great Falls, MT	299
362	Harrisonburg, VA	298
363	Carson City, NV	268
364	Fond du Lac, WI	235
NA	Auburn, AL**	NA
NA	Charleston-North Charleston, SC**	NA
NA	Dothan, AL**	NA
NA	Kansas City, MO-KS**	NA
NA	New Orleans, LA**	NA

Source: Reported data from the F.B.I. "Crime in the United States 2009"
*Burglary is the unlawful entry of a structure to commit a felony or theft. Attempts are included.
**Not available.

30. Burglary Rate in 2009
National Rate = 716.3 Burglaries per 100,000 Population*

RANK	METROPOLITAN AREA	RATE
115	Abilene, TX	932.1
128	Akron, OH	869.6
277	Albany-Schenectady-Troy, NY	477.7
29	Albany, GA	1,317.5
74	Albuquerque, NM	1,074.0
47	Alexandria, LA	1,201.9
309	Allentown, PA-NJ	426.7
342	Altoona, PA	355.0
60	Amarillo, TX	1,138.4
274	Ames, IA	492.0
238	Anchorage, AK	564.7
127	Anderson, IN	872.1
58	Anderson, SC	1,141.0
193	Ann Arbor, MI	688.5
7	Anniston-Oxford, AL	1,604.8
356	Appleton, WI	283.4
177	Asheville, NC	745.0
40	Athens-Clarke County, GA	1,239.7
99	Atlanta, GA	986.3
207	Atlantic City, NJ	651.5
NA	Auburn, AL**	NA
38	Augusta, GA-SC	1,244.0
156	Austin-Round Rock, TX	785.9
55	Bakersfield, CA	1,155.7
199	Baltimore-Towson, MD	675.5
212	Bangor, ME	635.9
45	Barnstable Town, MA	1,205.5
61	Baton Rouge, LA	1,132.4
41	Battle Creek, MI	1,233.4
240	Bay City, MI	562.9
56	Beaumont-Port Arthur, TX	1,154.3
190	Bellingham, WA	695.8
281	Bend, OR	470.6
349	Bethesda-Frederick, MD M.D.	320.6
216	Billings, MT	623.0
328	Binghamton, NY	386.3
41	Birmingham-Hoover, AL	1,233.4
355	Bismarck, ND	288.0
239	Blacksburg, VA	564.2
152	Bloomington, IN	815.9
307	Boise City-Nampa, ID	430.8
311	Boston (greater), MA-NH	419.0
297	Boston-Quincy, MA M.D.	443.5
285	Boulder, CO	461.6
188	Bowling Green, KY	708.2
219	Bremerton-Silverdale, WA	619.4
333	Bridgeport-Stamford, CT	366.4
114	Brownsville-Harlingen, TX	934.1
33	Brunswick, GA	1,273.1
197	Buffalo-Niagara Falls, NY	679.8
245	Burlington-South Burlington, VT	548.8
73	Burlington, NC	1,078.9
321	Cambridge-Newton, MA M.D.	392.4
260	Camden, NJ M.D.	524.1
107	Cape Coral-Fort Myers, FL	964.7
214	Cape Girardeau, MO-IL	630.6
273	Carson City, NV	492.1
176	Casper, WY	750.8
204	Cedar Rapids, IA	659.6
NA	Charleston-North Charleston, SC**	NA
126	Charleston, WV	880.0
93	Charlotte-Gastonia, NC-SC	993.0
346	Charlottesville, VA	328.6
88	Chattanooga, TN-GA	1,022.6
329	Cheyenne, WY	373.8
160	Chico, CA	782.5
157	Cincinnati-Middletown, OH-KY-IN	784.5
86	Clarksville, TN-KY	1,029.4
139	Cleveland-Elyria-Mentor, OH	842.8
185	Cleveland, TN	721.3
211	Coeur d'Alene, ID	638.1
68	College Station-Bryan, TX	1,099.5
205	Colorado Springs, CO	656.6
233	Columbia, MO	569.5
108	Columbia, SC	959.9
6	Columbus, GA-AL	1,673.1
293	Columbus, IN	447.9
53	Columbus, OH	1,164.1
78	Corpus Christi, TX	1,055.1
284	Corvallis, OR	466.4
229	Crestview-Fort Walton Beach, FL	579.6
169	Cumberland, MD-WV	769.7
98	Dallas (greater), TX	987.5
106	Dallas-Plano-Irving, TX M.D.	965.5
226	Dalton, GA	594.4
20	Danville, IL	1,376.0
195	Danville, VA	685.8
119	Dayton, OH	914.1
163	Decatur, AL	778.8
18	Decatur, IL	1,401.6
103	Deltona-Daytona Beach, FL	971.9
255	Denver-Aurora, CO	534.8
247	Des Moines-West Des Moines, IA	546.4
145	Detroit (greater), MI	835.8
25	Detroit-Livonia-Dearborn, MI M.D.	1,340.6
NA	Dothan, AL**	NA
136	Dover, DE	850.4
210	Dubuque, IA	639.9
225	Duluth, MN-WI	594.8
37	Durham-Chapel Hill, NC	1,247.3
343	Eau Claire, WI	341.6
339	Edison, NJ M.D.	356.8
77	El Centro, CA	1,059.1
331	El Paso, TX	372.4
322	Elizabethtown, KY	392.1
200	Elkhart-Goshen, IN	665.7
302	Elmira, NY	439.2
217	Erie, PA	621.3
117	Eugene-Springfield, OR	921.3
261	Evansville, IN-KY	523.8
267	Fargo, ND-MN	507.7
235	Farmington, NM	566.2
232	Fayetteville, AR-MO	570.1
5	Fayetteville, NC	1,927.4
280	Flagstaff, AZ	471.0
23	Flint, MI	1,355.3
147	Florence-Muscle Shoals, AL	832.4
19	Florence, SC	1,379.2
364	Fond du Lac, WI	235.9
289	Fort Collins-Loveland, CO	454.9
120	Fort Lauderdale, FL M.D.	911.8
130	Fort Smith, AR-OK	866.1
202	Fort Wayne, IN	661.4
85	Fort Worth-Arlington, TX M.D.	1,032.4
132	Fresno, CA	861.2
143	Gadsden, AL	836.5
57	Gainesville, FL	1,149.1
213	Gainesville, GA	630.7
359	Glens Falls, NY	260.0
14	Goldsboro, NC	1,482.1
294	Grand Forks, ND-MN	447.6
241	Grand Junction, CO	561.4
191	Grand Rapids-Wyoming, MI	694.1
334	Great Falls, MT	363.8
268	Greeley, CO	504.6
317	Green Bay, WI	404.2
27	Greensboro-High Point, NC	1,323.3
35	Gulfport-Biloxi, MS	1,268.7
266	Hagerstown-Martinsburg, MD-WV	508.6
335	Harrisburg-Carlisle, PA	363.6
360	Harrisonburg, VA	248.3
271	Hartford, CT	500.6
198	Hattiesburg, MS	678.5
65	Hickory, NC	1,113.3
15	Hinesville, GA	1,441.2
324	Holland-Grand Haven, MI	390.5
203	Honolulu, HI	661.3
1	Hot Springs, AR	2,142.0
223	Houma, LA	609.8
84	Houston, TX	1,035.8
112	Huntsville, AL	951.5
316	Idaho Falls, ID	405.4
79	Indianapolis, IN	1,050.3
326	Iowa City, IA	388.0
340	Ithaca, NY	356.2
66	Jacksonville, FL	1,113.0
50	Jacksonville, NC	1,179.6
234	Jackson, MI	566.7
36	Jackson, MS	1,247.4
26	Jackson, TN	1,328.2
254	Janesville, WI	535.4
291	Jefferson City, MO	453.6
181	Johnson City, TN	728.5
11	Jonesboro, AR	1,534.5
105	Kalamazoo-Portage, MI	965.9
NA	Kansas City, MO-KS**	NA
282	Kennewick-Pasco-Richland, WA	467.0
125	Killeen-Temple-Fort Hood, TX	893.5
133	Kingsport, TN-VA	856.4
327	Kingston, NY	387.3
111	Knoxville, TN	957.8
174	Kokomo, IN	758.9
295	La Crosse, WI-MN	447.1
242	Lafayette, IN	555.8
118	Lafayette, LA	918.5
3	Lake Charles, LA	2,040.5
142	Lake Havasu City-Kingman, AZ	837.5
52	Lakeland, FL	1,165.5
345	Lancaster, PA	340.3
209	Lansing-East Lansing, MI	645.7

Note: All listings are for Metropolitan Statistical Areas (M.S.A.s) except for those ending with "M.D." Listings with "M.D." are Metropolitan Divisions which are smaller parts of eleven large M.S.A.s. See explanatory note at beginning of metropolitan area section.

RANK	METROPOLITAN AREA	RATE	RANK	METROPOLITAN AREA	RATE	RANK	METROPOLITAN AREA	RATE
113	Laredo, TX	941.2	301	Ogden-Clearfield, UT	439.7	76	Savannah, GA	1,062.4
170	Las Cruces, NM	768.9	31	Oklahoma City, OK	1,300.4	299	Scranton--Wilkes-Barre, PA	441.9
122	Las Vegas-Paradise, NV	901.4	208	Olympia, WA	650.7	154	Seattle-Bellevue-Everett, WA M.D.	798.3
184	Lawrence, KS	724.7	220	Omaha-Council Bluffs, NE-IA	617.3	138	Seattle-Tacoma-Bellevue, WA	843.6
17	Lawton, OK	1,428.5	71	Orlando, FL	1,091.6	164	Sebastian-Vero Beach, FL	775.0
348	Lebanon, PA	324.0	276	Oshkosh-Neenah, WI	478.5	312	Sheboygan, WI	415.8
286	Lewiston-Auburn, ME	460.7	231	Owensboro, KY	572.2	159	Sherman-Denison, TX	783.6
246	Lewiston, ID-WA	547.5	332	Oxnard-Thousand Oaks, CA	369.4	102	Shreveport-Bossier City, LA	972.1
166	Lexington-Fayette, KY	773.7	171	Palm Bay-Melbourne, FL	768.0	258	Sioux City, IA-NE-SD	528.2
28	Lima, OH	1,317.7	221	Palm Coast, FL	612.7	319	Sioux Falls, SD	396.7
228	Lincoln, NE	580.7	80	Panama City-Lynn Haven, FL	1,049.7	72	South Bend-Mishawaka, IN-MI	1,091.5
12	Little Rock, AR	1,515.1	46	Pascagoula, MS	1,202.6	109	Spartanburg, SC	959.6
362	Logan, UT-ID	247.0	279	Peabody, MA M.D.	475.0	131	Spokane, WA	865.1
62	Longview, TX	1,118.8	149	Pensacola, FL	825.1	178	Springfield, MA	737.2
155	Longview, WA	795.6	269	Philadelphia (greater) PA-NJ-MD-DE	502.7	135	Springfield, MO	853.6
264	Los Angeles County, CA M.D.	512.6	287	Philadelphia, PA M.D.	456.9	64	Springfield, OH	1,113.4
278	Los Angeles (greater), CA	477.4	148	Phoenix-Mesa-Scottsdale, AZ	829.6	358	State College, PA	261.3
134	Louisville, KY-IN	854.4	4	Pine Bluff, AR	2,023.1	67	Stockton, CA	1,101.5
8	Lubbock, TX	1,559.9	296	Pittsburgh, PA	445.7	353	St. Cloud, MN	302.8
340	Lynchburg, VA	356.2	183	Pittsfield, MA	725.8	337	St. George, UT	361.5
30	Macon, GA	1,310.5	330	Pocatello, ID	373.0	97	St. Joseph, MO-KS	987.8
168	Madera, CA	772.9	151	Port St. Lucie, FL	818.4	218	St. Louis, MO-IL	619.9
292	Madison, WI	449.5	306	Portland-Vancouver, OR-WA	433.6	48	Sumter, SC	1,194.2
315	Manchester-Nashua, NH	405.6	272	Portland, ME	493.9	222	Syracuse, NY	611.9
305	Manhattan, KS	433.7	354	Poughkeepsie, NY	295.7	95	Tacoma, WA M.D.	990.9
265	Mankato-North Mankato, MN	508.7	262	Prescott, AZ	518.5	24	Tallahassee, FL	1,341.0
49	Mansfield, OH	1,194.0	227	Providence-New Bedford, RI-MA	590.3	100	Tampa-St Petersburg, FL	984.7
75	McAllen-Edinburg-Mission, TX	1,062.6	350	Provo-Orem, UT	317.6	32	Texarkana, TX-Texarkana, AR	1,291.4
351	Medford, OR	314.3	101	Pueblo, CO	981.4	10	Toledo, OH	1,535.0
13	Memphis, TN-MS-AR	1,494.0	186	Punta Gorda, FL	713.7	94	Topeka, KS	992.2
116	Merced, CA	929.3	180	Racine, WI	731.8	290	Trenton-Ewing, NJ	454.1
96	Miami (greater), FL	990.7	192	Raleigh-Cary, NC	693.9	158	Tucson, AZ	784.0
89	Miami-Dade County, FL M.D.	1,021.0	304	Rapid City, SD	435.8	83	Tulsa, OK	1,037.5
145	Michigan City-La Porte, IN	835.8	259	Reading, PA	527.7	22	Tuscaloosa, AL	1,362.5
137	Midland, TX	850.0	153	Redding, CA	805.5	124	Tyler, TX	895.5
224	Milwaukee, WI	604.4	173	Reno-Sparks, NV	767.3	288	Utica-Rome, NY	455.8
250	Minneapolis-St. Paul, MN-WI	542.5	244	Richmond, VA	549.1	90	Valdosta, GA	1,013.6
338	Missoula, MT	360.1	162	Riverside-San Bernardino, CA	780.5	87	Vallejo-Fairfield, CA	1,023.3
16	Mobile, AL	1,436.3	263	Roanoke, VA	514.1	51	Victoria, TX	1,171.4
63	Modesto, CA	1,113.5	347	Rochester, MN	327.8	121	Vineland, NJ	904.6
230	Monroe, MI	572.3	243	Rochester, NY	552.1	110	Visalia-Porterville, CA	958.7
54	Montgomery, AL	1,161.0	352	Rockingham County, NH M.D.	303.2	70	Waco, TX	1,092.5
237	Morgantown, WV	565.3	9	Rocky Mount, NC	1,554.6	140	Warner Robins, GA	842.2
179	Morristown, TN	736.6	150	Rome, GA	818.6	298	Warren-Farmington Hills, MI M.D.	442.0
141	Mount Vernon-Anacortes, WA	840.3	172	Sacramento, CA	767.5	320	Washington (greater) DC-VA-MD-WV	394.6
196	Muncie, IN	684.2	39	Saginaw, MI	1,243.6	313	Washington, DC-VA-MD-WV M.D.	415.3
144	Muskegon-Norton Shores, MI	835.9	248	Salem, OR	546.1	206	Waterloo-Cedar Falls, IA	656.5
256	Napa, CA	534.3	167	Salinas, CA	773.4	323	Wausau, WI	391.7
318	Naples-Marco Island, FL	402.1	34	Salisbury, MD	1,272.9	249	Wenatchee, WA	545.2
164	Nashville-Davidson, TN	775.0	161	Salt Lake City, UT	780.9	82	West Palm Beach, FL M.D.	1,040.2
361	Nassau-Suffolk, NY M.D.	247.7	91	San Angelo, TX	1,009.0	300	Wheeling, WV-OH	441.3
257	New Haven-Milford, CT	531.0	59	San Antonio, TX	1,139.1	81	Wichita Falls, TX	1,046.8
NA	New Orleans, LA**	NA	275	San Diego, CA	482.3	123	Wichita, KS	896.4
357	New York (greater), NY-NJ-PA	279.5	201	San Francisco (greater), CA	663.9	325	Williamsport, PA	388.5
363	New York-W. Plains NY-NJ M.D.	246.2	251	San Francisco-S. Mateo, CA M.D.	539.8	182	Wilmington, DE-MD-NJ M.D.	725.9
310	Newark-Union, NJ-PA M.D.	421.0	314	San Jose, CA	413.8	43	Wilmington, NC	1,227.5
215	Niles-Benton Harbor, MI	626.5	252	San Luis Obispo, CA	537.9	283	Winchester, VA-WV	466.8
104	North Port-Bradenton-Sarasota, FL	967.4	189	Sandusky, OH	707.7	21	Winston-Salem, NC	1,375.3
303	Norwich-New London, CT	438.6	336	Santa Ana-Anaheim, CA M.D.	362.4	270	Worcester, MA	501.3
175	Oakland-Fremont, CA M.D.	751.5	236	Santa Barbara-Santa Maria, CA	566.0	344	York-Hanover, PA	340.7
187	Ocala, FL	710.7	194	Santa Cruz-Watsonville, CA	687.4	92	Youngstown, OH-PA	1,007.3
69	Ocean City, NJ	1,098.9	2	Santa Fe, NM	2,083.1	253	Yuba City, CA	535.6
44	Odessa, TX	1,207.6	308	Santa Rosa-Petaluma, CA	427.8	129	Yuma, AZ	869.5

Source: Reported data from the F.B.I. "Crime in the United States 2009"
*Burglary is the unlawful entry of a structure to commit a felony or theft. Attempts are included.
**Not available.

30. Burglary Rate in 2009 (continued)
National Rate = 716.3 Burglaries per 100,000 Population*

RANK	METROPOLITAN AREA	RATE
1	Hot Springs, AR	2,142.0
2	Santa Fe, NM	2,083.1
3	Lake Charles, LA	2,040.5
4	Pine Bluff, AR	2,023.1
5	Fayetteville, NC	1,927.4
6	Columbus, GA-AL	1,673.1
7	Anniston-Oxford, AL	1,604.8
8	Lubbock, TX	1,559.9
9	Rocky Mount, NC	1,554.6
10	Toledo, OH	1,535.0
11	Jonesboro, AR	1,534.5
12	Little Rock, AR	1,515.1
13	Memphis, TN-MS-AR	1,494.0
14	Goldsboro, NC	1,482.1
15	Hinesville, GA	1,441.2
16	Mobile, AL	1,436.3
17	Lawton, OK	1,428.5
18	Decatur, IL	1,401.6
19	Florence, SC	1,379.2
20	Danville, IL	1,376.0
21	Winston-Salem, NC	1,375.3
22	Tuscaloosa, AL	1,362.5
23	Flint, MI	1,355.3
24	Tallahassee, FL	1,341.0
25	Detroit-Livonia-Dearborn, MI M.D.	1,340.6
26	Jackson, TN	1,328.2
27	Greensboro-High Point, NC	1,323.3
28	Lima, OH	1,317.7
29	Albany, GA	1,317.5
30	Macon, GA	1,310.5
31	Oklahoma City, OK	1,300.4
32	Texarkana, TX-Texarkana, AR	1,291.4
33	Brunswick, GA	1,273.1
34	Salisbury, MD	1,272.9
35	Gulfport-Biloxi, MS	1,268.7
36	Jackson, MS	1,247.4
37	Durham-Chapel Hill, NC	1,247.3
38	Augusta, GA-SC	1,244.0
39	Saginaw, MI	1,243.6
40	Athens-Clarke County, GA	1,239.7
41	Battle Creek, MI	1,233.4
41	Birmingham-Hoover, AL	1,233.4
43	Wilmington, NC	1,227.5
44	Odessa, TX	1,207.6
45	Barnstable Town, MA	1,205.5
46	Pascagoula, MS	1,202.6
47	Alexandria, LA	1,201.9
48	Sumter, SC	1,194.2
49	Mansfield, OH	1,194.0
50	Jacksonville, NC	1,179.6
51	Victoria, TX	1,171.4
52	Lakeland, FL	1,165.5
53	Columbus, OH	1,164.1
54	Montgomery, AL	1,161.0
55	Bakersfield, CA	1,155.7
56	Beaumont-Port Arthur, TX	1,154.3
57	Gainesville, FL	1,149.1
58	Anderson, SC	1,141.0
59	San Antonio, TX	1,139.1
60	Amarillo, TX	1,138.4
61	Baton Rouge, LA	1,132.4
62	Longview, TX	1,118.8
63	Modesto, CA	1,113.5
64	Springfield, OH	1,113.4
65	Hickory, NC	1,113.3
66	Jacksonville, FL	1,113.0
67	Stockton, CA	1,101.5
68	College Station-Bryan, TX	1,099.5
69	Ocean City, NJ	1,098.9
70	Waco, TX	1,092.5
71	Orlando, FL	1,091.6
72	South Bend-Mishawaka, IN-MI	1,091.5
73	Burlington, NC	1,078.9
74	Albuquerque, NM	1,074.0
75	McAllen-Edinburg-Mission, TX	1,062.6
76	Savannah, GA	1,062.4
77	El Centro, CA	1,059.1
78	Corpus Christi, TX	1,055.1
79	Indianapolis, IN	1,050.3
80	Panama City-Lynn Haven, FL	1,049.7
81	Wichita Falls, TX	1,046.8
82	West Palm Beach, FL M.D.	1,040.2
83	Tulsa, OK	1,037.5
84	Houston, TX	1,035.8
85	Fort Worth-Arlington, TX M.D.	1,032.4
86	Clarksville, TN-KY	1,029.4
87	Vallejo-Fairfield, CA	1,023.3
88	Chattanooga, TN-GA	1,022.6
89	Miami-Dade County, FL M.D.	1,021.0
90	Valdosta, GA	1,013.6
91	San Angelo, TX	1,009.0
92	Youngstown, OH-PA	1,007.3
93	Charlotte-Gastonia, NC-SC	993.0
94	Topeka, KS	992.2
95	Tacoma, WA M.D.	990.9
96	Miami (greater), FL	990.7
97	St. Joseph, MO-KS	987.8
98	Dallas (greater), TX	987.5
99	Atlanta, GA	986.3
100	Tampa-St Petersburg, FL	984.7
101	Pueblo, CO	981.4
102	Shreveport-Bossier City, LA	972.1
103	Deltona-Daytona Beach, FL	971.9
104	North Port-Bradenton-Sarasota, FL	967.4
105	Kalamazoo-Portage, MI	965.9
106	Dallas-Plano-Irving, TX M.D.	965.5
107	Cape Coral-Fort Myers, FL	964.7
108	Columbia, SC	959.9
109	Spartanburg, SC	959.6
110	Visalia-Porterville, CA	958.7
111	Knoxville, TN	957.8
112	Huntsville, AL	951.5
113	Laredo, TX	941.2
114	Brownsville-Harlingen, TX	934.1
115	Abilene, TX	932.1
116	Merced, CA	929.3
117	Eugene-Springfield, OR	921.3
118	Lafayette, LA	918.5
119	Dayton, OH	914.1
120	Fort Lauderdale, FL M.D.	911.8
121	Vineland, NJ	904.6
122	Las Vegas-Paradise, NV	901.4
123	Wichita, KS	896.4
124	Tyler, TX	895.5
125	Killeen-Temple-Fort Hood, TX	893.5
126	Charleston, WV	880.0
127	Anderson, IN	872.1
128	Akron, OH	869.6
129	Yuma, AZ	869.5
130	Fort Smith, AR-OK	866.1
131	Spokane, WA	865.1
132	Fresno, CA	861.2
133	Kingsport, TN-VA	856.4
134	Louisville, KY-IN	854.4
135	Springfield, MO	853.6
136	Dover, DE	850.4
137	Midland, TX	850.0
138	Seattle-Tacoma-Bellevue, WA	843.6
139	Cleveland-Elyria-Mentor, OH	842.8
140	Warner Robins, GA	842.2
141	Mount Vernon-Anacortes, WA	840.3
142	Lake Havasu City-Kingman, AZ	837.5
143	Gadsden, AL	836.5
144	Muskegon-Norton Shores, MI	835.9
145	Detroit (greater), MI	835.8
145	Michigan City-La Porte, IN	835.8
147	Florence-Muscle Shoals, AL	832.4
148	Phoenix-Mesa-Scottsdale, AZ	829.6
149	Pensacola, FL	825.1
150	Rome, GA	818.6
151	Port St. Lucie, FL	818.4
152	Bloomington, IN	815.9
153	Redding, CA	805.5
154	Seattle-Bellevue-Everett, WA M.D.	798.3
155	Longview, WA	795.6
156	Austin-Round Rock, TX	785.9
157	Cincinnati-Middletown, OH-KY-IN	784.5
158	Tucson, AZ	784.0
159	Sherman-Denison, TX	783.6
160	Chico, CA	782.5
161	Salt Lake City, UT	780.9
162	Riverside-San Bernardino, CA	780.5
163	Decatur, AL	778.8
164	Nashville-Davidson, TN	775.0
164	Sebastian-Vero Beach, FL	775.0
166	Lexington-Fayette, KY	773.7
167	Salinas, CA	773.4
168	Madera, CA	772.9
169	Cumberland, MD-WV	769.7
170	Las Cruces, NM	768.9
171	Palm Bay-Melbourne, FL	768.0
172	Sacramento, CA	767.5
173	Reno-Sparks, NV	767.3
174	Kokomo, IN	758.9
175	Oakland-Fremont, CA M.D.	751.5
176	Casper, WY	750.8
177	Asheville, NC	745.0
178	Springfield, MA	737.2
179	Morristown, TN	736.6
180	Racine, WI	731.8

Note: All listings are for Metropolitan Statistical Areas (M.S.A.s) except for those ending with "M.D." Listings with "M.D." are Metropolitan Divisions which are smaller parts of eleven large M.S.A.s. See explanatory note at beginning of metropolitan area section.

RANK	METROPOLITAN AREA	RATE
181	Johnson City, TN	728.5
182	Wilmington, DE-MD-NJ M.D.	725.9
183	Pittsfield, MA	725.8
184	Lawrence, KS	724.7
185	Cleveland, TN	721.3
186	Punta Gorda, FL	713.7
187	Ocala, FL	710.7
188	Bowling Green, KY	708.2
189	Sandusky, OH	707.7
190	Bellingham, WA	695.8
191	Grand Rapids-Wyoming, MI	694.1
192	Raleigh-Cary, NC	693.9
193	Ann Arbor, MI	688.5
194	Santa Cruz-Watsonville, CA	687.4
195	Danville, VA	685.8
196	Muncie, IN	684.2
197	Buffalo-Niagara Falls, NY	679.8
198	Hattiesburg, MS	678.5
199	Baltimore-Towson, MD	675.5
200	Elkhart-Goshen, IN	665.7
201	San Francisco (greater), CA	663.9
202	Fort Wayne, IN	661.4
203	Honolulu, HI	661.3
204	Cedar Rapids, IA	659.6
205	Colorado Springs, CO	656.6
206	Waterloo-Cedar Falls, IA	656.5
207	Atlantic City, NJ	651.5
208	Olympia, WA	650.7
209	Lansing-East Lansing, MI	645.7
210	Dubuque, IA	639.9
211	Coeur d'Alene, ID	638.1
212	Bangor, ME	635.9
213	Gainesville, GA	630.7
214	Cape Girardeau, MO-IL	630.6
215	Niles-Benton Harbor, MI	626.5
216	Billings, MT	623.0
217	Erie, PA	621.3
218	St. Louis, MO-IL	619.9
219	Bremerton-Silverdale, WA	619.4
220	Omaha-Council Bluffs, NE-IA	617.3
221	Palm Coast, FL	612.7
222	Syracuse, NY	611.9
223	Houma, LA	609.8
224	Milwaukee, WI	604.4
225	Duluth, MN-WI	594.8
226	Dalton, GA	594.4
227	Providence-New Bedford, RI-MA	590.3
228	Lincoln, NE	580.7
229	Crestview-Fort Walton Beach, FL	579.6
230	Monroe, MI	572.3
231	Owensboro, KY	572.2
232	Fayetteville, AR-MO	570.1
233	Columbia, MO	569.5
234	Jackson, MI	566.7
235	Farmington, NM	566.2
236	Santa Barbara-Santa Maria, CA	566.0
237	Morgantown, WV	565.3
238	Anchorage, AK	564.7
239	Blacksburg, VA	564.2
240	Bay City, MI	562.9
241	Grand Junction, CO	561.4
242	Lafayette, IN	555.8
243	Rochester, NY	552.1
244	Richmond, VA	549.1
245	Burlington-South Burlington, VT	548.8
246	Lewiston, ID-WA	547.5
247	Des Moines-West Des Moines, IA	546.4
248	Salem, OR	546.1
249	Wenatchee, WA	545.2
250	Minneapolis-St. Paul, MN-WI	542.5
251	San Francisco-S. Mateo, CA M.D.	539.8
252	San Luis Obispo, CA	537.9
253	Yuba City, CA	535.6
254	Janesville, WI	535.4
255	Denver-Aurora, CO	534.8
256	Napa, CA	534.3
257	New Haven-Milford, CT	531.0
258	Sioux City, IA-NE-SD	528.2
259	Reading, PA	527.7
260	Camden, NJ M.D.	524.1
261	Evansville, IN-KY	523.8
262	Prescott, AZ	518.5
263	Roanoke, VA	514.1
264	Los Angeles County, CA M.D.	512.6
265	Mankato-North Mankato, MN	508.7
266	Hagerstown-Martinsburg, MD-WV	508.6
267	Fargo, ND-MN	507.7
268	Greeley, CO	504.6
269	Philadelphia (greater) PA-NJ-MD-DE	502.7
270	Worcester, MA	501.3
271	Hartford, CT	500.6
272	Portland, ME	493.9
273	Carson City, NV	492.1
274	Ames, IA	492.0
275	San Diego, CA	482.3
276	Oshkosh-Neenah, WI	478.5
277	Albany-Schenectady-Troy, NY	477.7
278	Los Angeles (greater), CA	477.4
279	Peabody, MA M.D.	475.0
280	Flagstaff, AZ	471.0
281	Bend, OR	470.6
282	Kennewick-Pasco-Richland, WA	467.0
283	Winchester, VA-WV	466.8
284	Corvallis, OR	466.4
285	Boulder, CO	461.6
286	Lewiston-Auburn, ME	460.7
287	Philadelphia, PA M.D.	456.9
288	Utica-Rome, NY	455.8
289	Fort Collins-Loveland, CO	454.9
290	Trenton-Ewing, NJ	454.1
291	Jefferson City, MO	453.6
292	Madison, WI	449.5
293	Columbus, IN	447.9
294	Grand Forks, ND-MN	447.6
295	La Crosse, WI-MN	447.1
296	Pittsburgh, PA	445.7
297	Boston-Quincy, MA M.D.	443.5
298	Warren-Farmington Hills, MI M.D.	442.0
299	Scranton--Wilkes-Barre, PA	441.9
300	Wheeling, WV-OH	441.3
301	Ogden-Clearfield, UT	439.7
302	Elmira, NY	439.2
303	Norwich-New London, CT	438.6
304	Rapid City, SD	435.8
305	Manhattan, KS	433.7
306	Portland-Vancouver, OR-WA	433.6
307	Boise City-Nampa, ID	430.8
308	Santa Rosa-Petaluma, CA	427.8
309	Allentown, PA-NJ	426.7
310	Newark-Union, NJ-PA M.D.	421.0
311	Boston (greater), MA-NH	419.0
312	Sheboygan, WI	415.8
313	Washington, DC-VA-MD-WV M.D.	415.3
314	San Jose, CA	413.8
315	Manchester-Nashua, NH	405.6
316	Idaho Falls, ID	405.4
317	Green Bay, WI	404.2
318	Naples-Marco Island, FL	402.1
319	Sioux Falls, SD	396.7
320	Washington (greater) DC-VA-MD-WV	394.6
321	Cambridge-Newton, MA M.D.	392.4
322	Elizabethtown, KY	392.1
323	Wausau, WI	391.7
324	Holland-Grand Haven, MI	390.5
325	Williamsport, PA	388.5
326	Iowa City, IA	388.0
327	Kingston, NY	387.3
328	Binghamton, NY	386.3
329	Cheyenne, WY	373.8
330	Pocatello, ID	373.0
331	El Paso, TX	372.4
332	Oxnard-Thousand Oaks, CA	369.4
333	Bridgeport-Stamford, CT	366.4
334	Great Falls, MT	363.8
335	Harrisburg-Carlisle, PA	363.6
336	Santa Ana-Anaheim, CA M.D.	362.4
337	St. George, UT	361.5
338	Missoula, MT	360.1
339	Edison, NJ M.D.	356.8
340	Ithaca, NY	356.2
340	Lynchburg, VA	356.2
342	Altoona, PA	355.0
343	Eau Claire, WI	341.6
344	York-Hanover, PA	340.7
345	Lancaster, PA	340.3
346	Charlottesville, VA	328.6
347	Rochester, MN	327.8
348	Lebanon, PA	324.0
349	Bethesda-Frederick, MD M.D.	320.6
350	Provo-Orem, UT	317.6
351	Medford, OR	314.3
352	Rockingham County, NH M.D.	303.2
353	St. Cloud, MN	302.8
354	Poughkeepsie, NY	295.7
355	Bismarck, ND	288.0
356	Appleton, WI	283.4
357	New York (greater), NY-NJ-PA	279.5
358	State College, PA	261.3
359	Glens Falls, NY	260.0
360	Harrisonburg, VA	248.3
361	Nassau-Suffolk, NY M.D.	247.7
362	Logan, UT-ID	247.0
363	New York-W. Plains NY-NJ M.D.	246.2
364	Fond du Lac, WI	235.9
NA	Auburn, AL**	NA
NA	Charleston-North Charleston, SC**	NA
NA	Dothan, AL**	NA
NA	Kansas City, MO-KS**	NA
NA	New Orleans, LA**	NA

Source: Reported data from the F.B.I. "Crime in the United States 2009"

*Burglary is the unlawful entry of a structure to commit a felony or theft. Attempts are included.

**Not available.

31. Percent Change in Burglary Rate: 2008 to 2009
National Percent Change = 2.2% Decrease*

RANK	METROPOLITAN AREA	% CHANGE
75	Abilene, TX	4.8
141	Akron, OH	(1.5)
198	Albany-Schenectady-Troy, NY	(6.5)
NA	Albany, GA**	NA
178	Albuquerque, NM	(5.2)
NA	Alexandria, LA**	NA
206	Allentown, PA-NJ	(7.0)
302	Altoona, PA	(31.5)
68	Amarillo, TX	5.9
282	Ames, IA	(15.7)
3	Anchorage, AK	33.2
NA	Anderson, IN**	NA
NA	Anderson, SC**	NA
75	Ann Arbor, MI	4.8
NA	Anniston-Oxford, AL**	NA
194	Appleton, WI	(6.1)
234	Asheville, NC	(9.3)
93	Athens-Clarke County, GA	2.4
226	Atlanta, GA	(8.4)
NA	Atlantic City, NJ**	NA
NA	Auburn, AL**	NA
69	Augusta, GA-SC	5.7
123	Austin-Round Rock, TX	(0.4)
110	Bakersfield, CA	0.5
189	Baltimore-Towson, MD	(5.8)
23	Bangor, ME	15.5
10	Barnstable Town, MA	23.7
88	Baton Rouge, LA	3.0
54	Battle Creek, MI	8.2
NA	Bay City, MI**	NA
172	Beaumont-Port Arthur, TX	(4.5)
196	Bellingham, WA	(6.2)
286	Bend, OR	(16.8)
285	Bethesda-Frederick, MD M.D.	(16.7)
13	Billings, MT	20.3
258	Binghamton, NY	(12.0)
142	Birmingham-Hoover, AL	(1.6)
184	Bismarck, ND	(5.5)
168	Blacksburg, VA	(4.0)
5	Bloomington, IN	31.9
254	Boise City-Nampa, ID	(11.7)
214	Boston (greater), MA-NH	(7.6)
225	Boston-Quincy, MA M.D.	(8.3)
NA	Boulder, CO**	NA
NA	Bowling Green, KY**	NA
259	Bremerton-Silverdale, WA	(12.2)
88	Bridgeport-Stamford, CT	3.0
239	Brownsville-Harlingen, TX	(9.8)
NA	Brunswick, GA**	NA
157	Buffalo-Niagara Falls, NY	(2.9)
NA	Burlington-South Burlington, VT**	NA
247	Burlington, NC	(10.3)
199	Cambridge-Newton, MA M.D.	(6.6)
229	Camden, NJ M.D.	(9.0)
190	Cape Coral-Fort Myers, FL	(5.9)
127	Cape Girardeau, MO-IL	(0.5)
221	Carson City, NV	(8.2)
41	Casper, WY	10.0
115	Cedar Rapids, IA	0.0
NA	Charleston-North Charleston, SC**	NA
16	Charleston, WV	18.8
286	Charlotte-Gastonia, NC-SC	(16.8)
188	Charlottesville, VA	(5.7)
115	Chattanooga, TN-GA	0.0
291	Cheyenne, WY	(20.2)
214	Chico, CA	(7.6)
NA	Cincinnati-Middletown, OH-KY-IN**	NA
NA	Clarksville, TN-KY**	NA
NA	Cleveland-Elyria-Mentor, OH**	NA
190	Cleveland, TN	(5.9)
NA	Coeur d'Alene, ID**	NA
43	College Station-Bryan, TX	9.8
182	Colorado Springs, CO	(5.3)
290	Columbia, MO	(18.7)
44	Columbia, SC	9.7
14	Columbus, GA-AL	19.6
1	Columbus, IN	53.6
135	Columbus, OH	(1.1)
246	Corpus Christi, TX	(10.1)
21	Corvallis, OR	16.0
NA	Crestview-Fort Walton Beach, FL**	NA
17	Cumberland, MD-WV	17.5
135	Dallas (greater), TX	(1.1)
178	Dallas-Plano-Irving, TX M.D.	(5.2)
132	Dalton, GA	(0.9)
NA	Danville, IL**	NA
170	Danville, VA	(4.2)
80	Dayton, OH	4.1
299	Decatur, AL	(24.0)
NA	Decatur, IL**	NA
171	Deltona-Daytona Beach, FL	(4.3)
217	Denver-Aurora, CO	(7.7)
NA	Des Moines-West Des Moines, IA**	NA
NA	Detroit (greater), MI**	NA
NA	Detroit-Livonia-Dearborn, MI M.D.**	NA
NA	Dothan, AL**	NA
25	Dover, DE	15.3
86	Dubuque, IA	3.2
59	Duluth, MN-WI	7.0
112	Durham-Chapel Hill, NC	0.2
289	Eau Claire, WI	(17.9)
177	Edison, NJ M.D.	(5.0)
250	El Centro, CA	(11.0)
107	El Paso, TX	1.0
NA	Elizabethtown, KY**	NA
300	Elkhart-Goshen, IN	(24.8)
265	Elmira, NY	(12.7)
129	Erie, PA	(0.6)
77	Eugene-Springfield, OR	4.6
NA	Evansville, IN-KY**	NA
NA	Fargo, ND-MN**	NA
304	Farmington, NM	(39.8)
183	Fayetteville, AR-MO	(5.4)
55	Fayetteville, NC	7.9
281	Flagstaff, AZ	(15.6)
NA	Flint, MI**	NA
268	Florence-Muscle Shoals, AL	(13.1)
73	Florence, SC	4.9
114	Fond du Lac, WI	0.1
204	Fort Collins-Loveland, CO	(6.9)
95	Fort Lauderdale, FL M.D.	2.0
21	Fort Smith, AR-OK	16.0
199	Fort Wayne, IN	(6.6)
55	Fort Worth-Arlington, TX M.D.	7.9
101	Fresno, CA	1.7
66	Gadsden, AL	6.1
87	Gainesville, FL	3.1
NA	Gainesville, GA**	NA
169	Glens Falls, NY	(4.1)
122	Goldsboro, NC	(0.3)
52	Grand Forks, ND-MN	8.4
174	Grand Junction, CO	(4.7)
NA	Grand Rapids-Wyoming, MI**	NA
232	Great Falls, MT	(9.2)
273	Greeley, CO	(13.6)
146	Green Bay, WI	(1.9)
221	Greensboro-High Point, NC	(8.2)
NA	Gulfport-Biloxi, MS**	NA
206	Hagerstown-Martinsburg, MD-WV	(7.0)
260	Harrisburg-Carlisle, PA	(12.3)
294	Harrisonburg, VA	(22.3)
72	Hartford, CT	5.0
NA	Hattiesburg, MS**	NA
33	Hickory, NC	12.7
35	Hinesville, GA	11.8
NA	Holland-Grand Haven, MI**	NA
190	Honolulu, HI	(5.9)
38	Hot Springs, AR	10.4
19	Houma, LA	16.5
51	Houston, TX	8.6
118	Huntsville, AL	(0.1)
280	Idaho Falls, ID	(15.4)
85	Indianapolis, IN	3.4
293	Iowa City, IA	(21.5)
275	Ithaca, NY	(14.7)
202	Jacksonville, FL	(6.7)
24	Jacksonville, NC	15.4
NA	Jackson, MI**	NA
58	Jackson, MS	7.6
105	Jackson, TN	1.2
268	Janesville, WI	(13.1)
NA	Jefferson City, MO**	NA
38	Johnson City, TN	10.4
147	Jonesboro, AR	(2.0)
NA	Kalamazoo-Portage, MI**	NA
NA	Kansas City, MO-KS**	NA
297	Kennewick-Pasco-Richland, WA	(23.1)
153	Killeen-Temple-Fort Hood, TX	(2.4)
80	Kingsport, TN-VA	4.1
271	Kingston, NY	(13.3)
147	Knoxville, TN	(2.0)
255	Kokomo, IN	(11.8)
44	La Crosse, WI-MN	9.7
218	Lafayette, IN	(7.8)
73	Lafayette, LA	4.9
NA	Lake Charles, LA**	NA
256	Lake Havasu City-Kingman, AZ	(11.9)
104	Lakeland, FL	1.4
239	Lancaster, PA	(9.8)
NA	Lansing-East Lansing, MI**	NA

Note: All listings are for Metropolitan Statistical Areas (M.S.A.s) except for those ending with "M.D." Listings with "M.D." are Metropolitan Divisions which are smaller parts of eleven large M.S.A.s. See explanatory note at beginning of metropolitan area section.

Alpha Order - Metro Area (continued)

RANK	METROPOLITAN AREA	% CHANGE
111	Laredo, TX	0.3
46	Las Cruces, NM	9.6
252	Las Vegas-Paradise, NV	(11.3)
272	Lawrence, KS	(13.4)
NA	Lawton, OK**	NA
70	Lebanon, PA	5.4
118	Lewiston-Auburn, ME	(0.1)
150	Lewiston, ID-WA	(2.1)
NA	Lexington-Fayette, KY**	NA
100	Lima, OH	1.8
118	Lincoln, NE	(0.1)
NA	Little Rock, AR**	NA
295	Logan, UT-ID	(22.7)
91	Longview, TX	2.5
42	Longview, WA	9.9
212	Los Angeles County, CA M.D.	(7.2)
206	Los Angeles (greater), CA	(7.0)
NA	Louisville, KY-IN**	NA
18	Lubbock, TX	16.9
102	Lynchburg, VA	1.5
137	Macon, GA	(1.2)
38	Madera, CA	10.4
296	Madison, WI	(22.8)
NA	Manchester-Nashua, NH**	NA
292	Manhattan, KS	(20.4)
15	Mankato-North Mankato, MN	19.0
67	Mansfield, OH	6.0
79	McAllen-Edinburg-Mission, TX	4.3
252	Medford, OR	(11.3)
237	Memphis, TN-MS-AR	(9.6)
95	Merced, CA	2.0
155	Miami (greater), FL	(2.7)
204	Miami-Dade County, FL M.D.	(6.9)
83	Michigan City-La Porte, IN	3.6
98	Midland, TX	1.9
129	Milwaukee, WI	(0.6)
190	Minneapolis-St. Paul, MN-WI	(5.9)
60	Missoula, MT	6.9
32	Mobile, AL	13.1
95	Modesto, CA	2.0
NA	Monroe, MI**	NA
239	Montgomery, AL	(9.8)
NA	Morgantown, WV**	NA
228	Morristown, TN	(8.9)
211	Mount Vernon-Anacortes, WA	(7.1)
27	Muncie, IN	15.0
NA	Muskegon-Norton Shores, MI**	NA
213	Napa, CA	(7.5)
178	Naples-Marco Island, FL	(5.2)
108	Nashville-Davidson, TN	0.8
161	Nassau-Suffolk, NY M.D.	(3.2)
NA	New Haven-Milford, CT**	NA
NA	New Orleans, LA**	NA
206	New York (greater), NY-NJ-PA	(7.0)
218	New York-W. Plains NY-NJ M.D.	(7.8)
231	Newark-Union, NJ-PA M.D.	(9.1)
NA	Niles-Benton Harbor, MI**	NA
NA	North Port-Bradenton-Sarasota, FL**	NA
249	Norwich-New London, CT	(10.9)
155	Oakland-Fremont, CA M.D.	(2.7)
132	Ocala, FL	(0.9)
49	Ocean City, NJ	8.8
4	Odessa, TX	32.2

RANK	METROPOLITAN AREA	% CHANGE
142	Ogden-Clearfield, UT	(1.6)
NA	Oklahoma City, OK**	NA
214	Olympia, WA	(7.6)
127	Omaha-Council Bluffs, NE-IA	(0.5)
244	Orlando, FL	(10.0)
173	Oshkosh-Neenah, WI	(4.6)
NA	Owensboro, KY**	NA
243	Oxnard-Thousand Oaks, CA	(9.9)
284	Palm Bay-Melbourne, FL	(16.4)
64	Palm Coast, FL	6.5
63	Panama City-Lynn Haven, FL	6.6
2	Pascagoula, MS	40.2
263	Peabody, MA M.D.	(12.6)
64	Pensacola, FL	6.5
256	Philadelphia (greater) PA-NJ-MD-DE	(11.9)
274	Philadelphia, PA M.D.	(13.7)
248	Phoenix-Mesa-Scottsdale, AZ	(10.5)
139	Pine Bluff, AR	(1.3)
106	Pittsburgh, PA	1.1
218	Pittsfield, MA	(7.8)
161	Pocatello, ID	(3.2)
163	Port St. Lucie, FL	(3.4)
263	Portland-Vancouver, OR-WA	(12.6)
70	Portland, ME	5.4
268	Poughkeepsie, NY	(13.1)
229	Prescott, AZ	(9.0)
151	Providence-New Bedford, RI-MA	(2.2)
232	Provo-Orem, UT	(9.2)
NA	Pueblo, CO**	NA
275	Punta Gorda, FL	(14.7)
267	Racine, WI	(12.9)
112	Raleigh-Cary, NC	0.2
221	Rapid City, SD	(8.2)
121	Reading, PA	(0.2)
102	Redding, CA	1.5
237	Reno-Sparks, NV	(9.6)
163	Richmond, VA	(3.4)
157	Riverside-San Bernardino, CA	(2.9)
144	Roanoke, VA	(1.7)
288	Rochester, MN	(17.5)
84	Rochester, NY	3.5
55	Rockingham County, NH M.D.	7.9
NA	Rocky Mount, NC**	NA
NA	Rome, GA**	NA
115	Sacramento, CA	0.0
NA	Saginaw, MI**	NA
239	Salem, OR	(9.8)
90	Salinas, CA	2.8
8	Salisbury, MD	25.6
47	Salt Lake City, UT	9.5
160	San Angelo, TX	(3.1)
176	San Antonio, TX	(4.9)
278	San Diego, CA	(15.1)
151	San Francisco (greater), CA	(2.2)
137	San Francisco-S. Mateo, CA M.D.	(1.2)
98	San Jose, CA	1.9
202	San Luis Obispo, CA	(6.7)
262	Sandusky, OH	(12.5)
194	Santa Ana-Anaheim, CA M.D.	(6.1)
34	Santa Barbara-Santa Maria, CA	12.0
52	Santa Cruz-Watsonville, CA	8.4
9	Santa Fe, NM	24.7
166	Santa Rosa-Petaluma, CA	(3.9)

RANK	METROPOLITAN AREA	% CHANGE
159	Savannah, GA	(3.0)
123	Scranton--Wilkes-Barre, PA	(0.4)
NA	Seattle-Bellevue-Everett, WA M.D.**	NA
NA	Seattle-Tacoma-Bellevue, WA**	NA
184	Sebastian-Vero Beach, FL	(5.5)
94	Sheboygan, WI	2.1
78	Sherman-Denison, TX	4.4
36	Shreveport-Bossier City, LA	11.2
29	Sioux City, IA-NE-SD	13.6
29	Sioux Falls, SD	13.6
NA	South Bend-Mishawaka, IN-MI**	NA
260	Spartanburg, SC	(12.3)
48	Spokane, WA	9.3
154	Springfield, MA	(2.6)
NA	Springfield, MO**	NA
7	Springfield, OH	28.2
297	State College, PA	(23.1)
147	Stockton, CA	(2.0)
206	St. Cloud, MN	(7.0)
301	St. George, UT	(24.9)
20	St. Joseph, MO-KS	16.3
236	St. Louis, MO-IL	(9.5)
NA	Sumter, SC**	NA
61	Syracuse, NY	6.8
NA	Tacoma, WA M.D.**	NA
109	Tallahassee, FL	0.7
184	Tampa-St Petersburg, FL	(5.5)
31	Texarkana, TX-Texarkana, AR	13.4
11	Toledo, OH	21.9
131	Topeka, KS	(0.8)
178	Trenton-Ewing, NJ	(5.2)
199	Tucson, AZ	(6.6)
145	Tulsa, OK	(1.8)
91	Tuscaloosa, AL	2.5
25	Tyler, TX	15.3
265	Utica-Rome, NY	(12.7)
12	Valdosta, GA	20.4
61	Vallejo-Fairfield, CA	6.8
37	Victoria, TX	10.9
187	Vineland, NJ	(5.6)
80	Visalia-Porterville, CA	4.1
244	Waco, TX	(10.0)
227	Warner Robins, GA	(8.8)
NA	Warren-Farmington Hills, MI M.D.**	NA
197	Washington (greater) DC-VA-MD-WV	(6.4)
166	Washington, DC-VA-MD-WV M.D.	(3.9)
140	Waterloo-Cedar Falls, IA	(1.4)
NA	Wausau, WI**	NA
28	Wenatchee, WA	14.0
123	West Palm Beach, FL M.D.	(0.4)
132	Wheeling, WV-OH	(0.9)
278	Wichita Falls, TX	(15.1)
123	Wichita, KS	(0.4)
282	Williamsport, PA	(15.7)
221	Wilmington, DE-MD-NJ M.D.	(8.2)
175	Wilmington, NC	(4.8)
277	Winchester, VA-WV	(14.9)
165	Winston-Salem, NC	(3.6)
234	Worcester, MA	(9.3)
251	York-Hanover, PA	(11.2)
49	Youngstown, OH-PA	8.8
303	Yuba City, CA	(32.4)
6	Yuma, AZ	28.6

Source: CQ Press using reported data from the F.B.I. "Crime in the United States 2009"
*Burglary is the unlawful entry of a structure to commit a felony or theft. Attempts are included.
**Not available.

31. Percent Change in Burglary Rate: 2008 to 2009 (continued)
National Percent Change = 2.2% Decrease*

RANK	METROPOLITAN AREA	% CHANGE
1	Columbus, IN	53.6
2	Pascagoula, MS	40.2
3	Anchorage, AK	33.2
4	Odessa, TX	32.2
5	Bloomington, IN	31.9
6	Yuma, AZ	28.6
7	Springfield, OH	28.2
8	Salisbury, MD	25.6
9	Santa Fe, NM	24.7
10	Barnstable Town, MA	23.7
11	Toledo, OH	21.9
12	Valdosta, GA	20.4
13	Billings, MT	20.3
14	Columbus, GA-AL	19.6
15	Mankato-North Mankato, MN	19.0
16	Charleston, WV	18.8
17	Cumberland, MD-WV	17.5
18	Lubbock, TX	16.9
19	Houma, LA	16.5
20	St. Joseph, MO-KS	16.3
21	Corvallis, OR	16.0
21	Fort Smith, AR-OK	16.0
23	Bangor, ME	15.5
24	Jacksonville, NC	15.4
25	Dover, DE	15.3
25	Tyler, TX	15.3
27	Muncie, IN	15.0
28	Wenatchee, WA	14.0
29	Sioux City, IA-NE-SD	13.6
29	Sioux Falls, SD	13.6
31	Texarkana, TX-Texarkana, AR	13.4
32	Mobile, AL	13.1
33	Hickory, NC	12.7
34	Santa Barbara-Santa Maria, CA	12.0
35	Hinesville, GA	11.8
36	Shreveport-Bossier City, LA	11.2
37	Victoria, TX	10.9
38	Hot Springs, AR	10.4
38	Johnson City, TN	10.4
38	Madera, CA	10.4
41	Casper, WY	10.0
42	Longview, WA	9.9
43	College Station-Bryan, TX	9.8
44	Columbia, SC	9.7
44	La Crosse, WI-MN	9.7
46	Las Cruces, NM	9.6
47	Salt Lake City, UT	9.5
48	Spokane, WA	9.3
49	Ocean City, NJ	8.8
49	Youngstown, OH-PA	8.8
51	Houston, TX	8.6
52	Grand Forks, ND-MN	8.4
52	Santa Cruz-Watsonville, CA	8.4
54	Battle Creek, MI	8.2
55	Fayetteville, NC	7.9
55	Fort Worth-Arlington, TX M.D.	7.9
55	Rockingham County, NH M.D.	7.9
58	Jackson, MS	7.6
59	Duluth, MN-WI	7.0
60	Missoula, MT	6.9
61	Syracuse, NY	6.8
61	Vallejo-Fairfield, CA	6.8
63	Panama City-Lynn Haven, FL	6.6
64	Palm Coast, FL	6.5
64	Pensacola, FL	6.5
66	Gadsden, AL	6.1
67	Mansfield, OH	6.0
68	Amarillo, TX	5.9
69	Augusta, GA-SC	5.7
70	Lebanon, PA	5.4
70	Portland, ME	5.4
72	Hartford, CT	5.0
73	Florence, SC	4.9
73	Lafayette, LA	4.9
75	Abilene, TX	4.8
75	Ann Arbor, MI	4.8
77	Eugene-Springfield, OR	4.6
78	Sherman-Denison, TX	4.4
79	McAllen-Edinburg-Mission, TX	4.3
80	Dayton, OH	4.1
80	Kingsport, TN-VA	4.1
80	Visalia-Porterville, CA	4.1
83	Michigan City-La Porte, IN	3.6
84	Rochester, NY	3.5
85	Indianapolis, IN	3.4
86	Dubuque, IA	3.2
87	Gainesville, FL	3.1
88	Baton Rouge, LA	3.0
88	Bridgeport-Stamford, CT	3.0
90	Salinas, CA	2.8
91	Longview, TX	2.5
91	Tuscaloosa, AL	2.5
93	Athens-Clarke County, GA	2.4
94	Sheboygan, WI	2.1
95	Fort Lauderdale, FL M.D.	2.0
95	Merced, CA	2.0
95	Modesto, CA	2.0
98	Midland, TX	1.9
98	San Jose, CA	1.9
100	Lima, OH	1.8
101	Fresno, CA	1.7
102	Lynchburg, VA	1.5
102	Redding, CA	1.5
104	Lakeland, FL	1.4
105	Jackson, TN	1.2
106	Pittsburgh, PA	1.1
107	El Paso, TX	1.0
108	Nashville-Davidson, TN	0.8
109	Tallahassee, FL	0.7
110	Bakersfield, CA	0.5
111	Laredo, TX	0.3
112	Durham-Chapel Hill, NC	0.2
112	Raleigh-Cary, NC	0.2
114	Fond du Lac, WI	0.1
115	Cedar Rapids, IA	0.0
115	Chattanooga, TN-GA	0.0
115	Sacramento, CA	0.0
118	Huntsville, AL	(0.1)
118	Lewiston-Auburn, ME	(0.1)
118	Lincoln, NE	(0.1)
121	Reading, PA	(0.2)
122	Goldsboro, NC	(0.3)
123	Austin-Round Rock, TX	(0.4)
123	Scranton--Wilkes-Barre, PA	(0.4)
123	West Palm Beach, FL M.D.	(0.4)
123	Wichita, KS	(0.4)
127	Cape Girardeau, MO-IL	(0.5)
127	Omaha-Council Bluffs, NE-IA	(0.5)
129	Erie, PA	(0.6)
129	Milwaukee, WI	(0.6)
131	Topeka, KS	(0.8)
132	Dalton, GA	(0.9)
132	Ocala, FL	(0.9)
132	Wheeling, WV-OH	(0.9)
135	Columbus, OH	(1.1)
135	Dallas (greater), TX	(1.1)
137	Macon, GA	(1.2)
137	San Francisco-S. Mateo, CA M.D.	(1.2)
139	Pine Bluff, AR	(1.3)
140	Waterloo-Cedar Falls, IA	(1.4)
141	Akron, OH	(1.5)
142	Birmingham-Hoover, AL	(1.6)
142	Ogden-Clearfield, UT	(1.6)
144	Roanoke, VA	(1.7)
145	Tulsa, OK	(1.8)
146	Green Bay, WI	(1.9)
147	Jonesboro, AR	(2.0)
147	Knoxville, TN	(2.0)
147	Stockton, CA	(2.0)
150	Lewiston, ID-WA	(2.1)
151	Providence-New Bedford, RI-MA	(2.2)
151	San Francisco (greater), CA	(2.2)
153	Killeen-Temple-Fort Hood, TX	(2.4)
154	Springfield, MA	(2.6)
155	Miami (greater), FL	(2.7)
155	Oakland-Fremont, CA M.D.	(2.7)
157	Buffalo-Niagara Falls, NY	(2.9)
157	Riverside-San Bernardino, CA	(2.9)
159	Savannah, GA	(3.0)
160	San Angelo, TX	(3.1)
161	Nassau-Suffolk, NY M.D.	(3.2)
161	Pocatello, ID	(3.2)
163	Port St. Lucie, FL	(3.4)
163	Richmond, VA	(3.4)
165	Winston-Salem, NC	(3.6)
166	Santa Rosa-Petaluma, CA	(3.9)
166	Washington, DC-VA-MD-WV M.D.	(3.9)
168	Blacksburg, VA	(4.0)
169	Glens Falls, NY	(4.1)
170	Danville, VA	(4.2)
171	Deltona-Daytona Beach, FL	(4.3)
172	Beaumont-Port Arthur, TX	(4.5)
173	Oshkosh-Neenah, WI	(4.6)
174	Grand Junction, CO	(4.7)
175	Wilmington, NC	(4.8)
176	San Antonio, TX	(4.9)
177	Edison, NJ M.D.	(5.0)
178	Albuquerque, NM	(5.2)
178	Dallas-Plano-Irving, TX M.D.	(5.2)
178	Naples-Marco Island, FL	(5.2)

Note: All listings are for Metropolitan Statistical Areas (M.S.A.s) except for those ending with "M.D." Listings with "M.D." are Metropolitan Divisions which are smaller parts of eleven large M.S.A.s. See explanatory note at beginning of metropolitan area section.

Rank Order - Metro Area (continued)

RANK	METROPOLITAN AREA	% CHANGE
178	Trenton-Ewing, NJ	(5.2)
182	Colorado Springs, CO	(5.3)
183	Fayetteville, AR-MO	(5.4)
184	Bismarck, ND	(5.5)
184	Sebastian-Vero Beach, FL	(5.5)
184	Tampa-St Petersburg, FL	(5.5)
187	Vineland, NJ	(5.6)
188	Charlottesville, VA	(5.7)
189	Baltimore-Towson, MD	(5.8)
190	Cape Coral-Fort Myers, FL	(5.9)
190	Cleveland, TN	(5.9)
190	Honolulu, HI	(5.9)
190	Minneapolis-St. Paul, MN-WI	(5.9)
194	Appleton, WI	(6.1)
194	Santa Ana-Anaheim, CA M.D.	(6.1)
196	Bellingham, WA	(6.2)
197	Washington (greater) DC-VA-MD-WV	(6.4)
198	Albany-Schenectady-Troy, NY	(6.5)
199	Cambridge-Newton, MA M.D.	(6.6)
199	Fort Wayne, IN	(6.6)
199	Tucson, AZ	(6.6)
202	Jacksonville, FL	(6.7)
202	San Luis Obispo, CA	(6.7)
204	Fort Collins-Loveland, CO	(6.9)
204	Miami-Dade County, FL M.D.	(6.9)
206	Allentown, PA-NJ	(7.0)
206	Hagerstown-Martinsburg, MD-WV	(7.0)
206	Los Angeles (greater), CA	(7.0)
206	New York (greater), NY-NJ-PA	(7.0)
206	St. Cloud, MN	(7.0)
211	Mount Vernon-Anacortes, WA	(7.1)
212	Los Angeles County, CA M.D.	(7.2)
213	Napa, CA	(7.5)
214	Boston (greater), MA-NH	(7.6)
214	Chico, CA	(7.6)
214	Olympia, WA	(7.6)
217	Denver-Aurora, CO	(7.7)
218	Lafayette, IN	(7.8)
218	New York-W. Plains NY-NJ M.D.	(7.8)
218	Pittsfield, MA	(7.8)
221	Carson City, NV	(8.2)
221	Greensboro-High Point, NC	(8.2)
221	Rapid City, SD	(8.2)
221	Wilmington, DE-MD-NJ M.D.	(8.2)
225	Boston-Quincy, MA M.D.	(8.3)
226	Atlanta, GA	(8.4)
227	Warner Robins, GA	(8.8)
228	Morristown, TN	(8.9)
229	Camden, NJ M.D.	(9.0)
229	Prescott, AZ	(9.0)
231	Newark-Union, NJ-PA M.D.	(9.1)
232	Great Falls, MT	(9.2)
232	Provo-Orem, UT	(9.2)
234	Asheville, NC	(9.3)
234	Worcester, MA	(9.3)
236	St. Louis, MO-IL	(9.5)
237	Memphis, TN-MS-AR	(9.6)
237	Reno-Sparks, NV	(9.6)
239	Brownsville-Harlingen, TX	(9.8)
239	Lancaster, PA	(9.8)
239	Montgomery, AL	(9.8)
239	Salem, OR	(9.8)
243	Oxnard-Thousand Oaks, CA	(9.9)

RANK	METROPOLITAN AREA	% CHANGE
244	Orlando, FL	(10.0)
244	Waco, TX	(10.0)
246	Corpus Christi, TX	(10.1)
247	Burlington, NC	(10.3)
248	Phoenix-Mesa-Scottsdale, AZ	(10.5)
249	Norwich-New London, CT	(10.9)
250	El Centro, CA	(11.0)
251	York-Hanover, PA	(11.2)
252	Las Vegas-Paradise, NV	(11.3)
252	Medford, OR	(11.3)
254	Boise City-Nampa, ID	(11.7)
255	Kokomo, IN	(11.8)
256	Lake Havasu City-Kingman, AZ	(11.9)
256	Philadelphia (greater) PA-NJ-MD-DE	(11.9)
258	Binghamton, NY	(12.0)
259	Bremerton-Silverdale, WA	(12.2)
260	Harrisburg-Carlisle, PA	(12.3)
260	Spartanburg, SC	(12.3)
262	Sandusky, OH	(12.5)
263	Peabody, MA M.D.	(12.6)
263	Portland-Vancouver, OR-WA	(12.6)
265	Elmira, NY	(12.7)
265	Utica-Rome, NY	(12.7)
267	Racine, WI	(12.9)
268	Florence-Muscle Shoals, AL	(13.1)
268	Janesville, WI	(13.1)
268	Poughkeepsie, NY	(13.1)
271	Kingston, NY	(13.3)
272	Lawrence, KS	(13.4)
273	Greeley, CO	(13.6)
274	Philadelphia, PA M.D.	(13.7)
275	Ithaca, NY	(14.7)
275	Punta Gorda, FL	(14.7)
277	Winchester, VA-WV	(14.9)
278	San Diego, CA	(15.1)
278	Wichita Falls, TX	(15.1)
280	Idaho Falls, ID	(15.4)
281	Flagstaff, AZ	(15.6)
282	Ames, IA	(15.7)
282	Williamsport, PA	(15.7)
284	Palm Bay-Melbourne, FL	(16.4)
285	Bethesda-Frederick, MD M.D.	(16.7)
286	Bend, OR	(16.8)
286	Charlotte-Gastonia, NC-SC	(16.8)
288	Rochester, MN	(17.5)
289	Eau Claire, WI	(17.9)
290	Columbia, MO	(18.7)
291	Cheyenne, WY	(20.2)
292	Manhattan, KS	(20.4)
293	Iowa City, IA	(21.5)
294	Harrisonburg, VA	(22.3)
295	Logan, UT-ID	(22.7)
296	Madison, WI	(22.8)
297	Kennewick-Pasco-Richland, WA	(23.1)
297	State College, PA	(23.1)
299	Decatur, AL	(24.0)
300	Elkhart-Goshen, IN	(24.8)
301	St. George, UT	(24.9)
302	Altoona, PA	(31.5)
303	Yuba City, CA	(32.4)
304	Farmington, NM	(39.8)
NA	Albany, GA**	NA
NA	Alexandria, LA**	NA

RANK	METROPOLITAN AREA	% CHANGE
NA	Anderson, IN**	NA
NA	Anderson, SC**	NA
NA	Anniston-Oxford, AL**	NA
NA	Atlantic City, NJ**	NA
NA	Auburn, AL**	NA
NA	Bay City, MI**	NA
NA	Boulder, CO**	NA
NA	Bowling Green, KY**	NA
NA	Brunswick, GA**	NA
NA	Burlington-South Burlington, VT**	NA
NA	Charleston-North Charleston, SC**	NA
NA	Cincinnati-Middletown, OH-KY-IN**	NA
NA	Clarksville, TN-KY**	NA
NA	Cleveland-Elyria-Mentor, OH**	NA
NA	Coeur d'Alene, ID**	NA
NA	Crestview-Fort Walton Beach, FL**	NA
NA	Danville, IL**	NA
NA	Decatur, IL**	NA
NA	Des Moines-West Des Moines, IA**	NA
NA	Detroit (greater), MI**	NA
NA	Detroit-Livonia-Dearborn, MI M.D.**	NA
NA	Dothan, AL**	NA
NA	Elizabethtown, KY**	NA
NA	Evansville, IN-KY**	NA
NA	Fargo, ND-MN**	NA
NA	Flint, MI**	NA
NA	Gainesville, GA**	NA
NA	Grand Rapids-Wyoming, MI**	NA
NA	Gulfport-Biloxi, MS**	NA
NA	Hattiesburg, MS**	NA
NA	Holland-Grand Haven, MI**	NA
NA	Jackson, MI**	NA
NA	Jefferson City, MO**	NA
NA	Kalamazoo-Portage, MI**	NA
NA	Kansas City, MO-KS**	NA
NA	Lake Charles, LA**	NA
NA	Lansing-East Lansing, MI**	NA
NA	Lawton, OK**	NA
NA	Lexington-Fayette, KY**	NA
NA	Little Rock, AR**	NA
NA	Louisville, KY-IN**	NA
NA	Manchester-Nashua, NH**	NA
NA	Monroe, MI**	NA
NA	Morgantown, WV**	NA
NA	Muskegon-Norton Shores, MI**	NA
NA	New Haven-Milford, CT**	NA
NA	New Orleans, LA**	NA
NA	Niles-Benton Harbor, MI**	NA
NA	North Port-Bradenton-Sarasota, FL**	NA
NA	Oklahoma City, OK**	NA
NA	Owensboro, KY**	NA
NA	Pueblo, CO**	NA
NA	Rocky Mount, NC**	NA
NA	Rome, GA**	NA
NA	Saginaw, MI**	NA
NA	Seattle-Bellevue-Everett, WA M.D.**	NA
NA	Seattle-Tacoma-Bellevue, WA**	NA
NA	South Bend-Mishawaka, IN-MI**	NA
NA	Springfield, MO**	NA
NA	Sumter, SC**	NA
NA	Tacoma, WA M.D.**	NA
NA	Warren-Farmington Hills, MI M.D.**	NA
NA	Wausau, WI**	NA

Source: CQ Press using reported data from the F.B.I. "Crime in the United States 2009"
*Burglary is the unlawful entry of a structure to commit a felony or theft. Attempts are included.
**Not available.

32. Percent Change in Burglary Rate: 2005 to 2009
National Percent Change = 1.5% Decrease*

RANK	METROPOLITAN AREA	% CHANGE
238	Abilene, TX	(15.1)
110	Akron, OH	1.8
205	Albany-Schenectady-Troy, NY	(10.4)
117	Albany, GA	0.8
135	Albuquerque, NM	(2.2)
161	Alexandria, LA	(5.4)
146	Allentown, PA-NJ	(3.4)
296	Altoona, PA	(40.7)
140	Amarillo, TX	(2.8)
293	Ames, IA	(37.4)
220	Anchorage, AK	(12.5)
17	Anderson, IN	34.6
149	Anderson, SC	(3.6)
115	Ann Arbor, MI	1.1
NA	Anniston-Oxford, AL**	NA
221	Appleton, WI	(12.6)
228	Asheville, NC	(13.4)
1	Athens-Clarke County, GA	66.8
84	Atlanta, GA	5.3
151	Atlantic City, NJ	(3.7)
NA	Auburn, AL**	NA
13	Augusta, GA-SC	37.5
120	Austin-Round Rock, TX	0.3
116	Bakersfield, CA	0.9
127	Baltimore-Towson, MD	(0.6)
34	Bangor, ME	21.2
8	Barnstable Town, MA	48.1
71	Baton Rouge, LA	8.8
7	Battle Creek, MI	49.8
NA	Bay City, MI**	NA
180	Beaumont-Port Arthur, TX	(7.2)
283	Bellingham, WA	(27.6)
298	Bend, OR	(42.3)
246	Bethesda-Frederick, MD M.D.	(16.4)
57	Billings, MT	13.6
64	Binghamton, NY	10.9
NA	Birmingham-Hoover, AL**	NA
103	Bismarck, ND	2.9
47	Blacksburg, VA	15.9
10	Bloomington, IN	41.2
NA	Boise City-Nampa, ID**	NA
200	Boston (greater), MA-NH	(10.0)
235	Boston-Quincy, MA M.D.	(14.9)
NA	Boulder, CO**	NA
NA	Bowling Green, KY**	NA
254	Bremerton-Silverdale, WA	(17.5)
154	Bridgeport-Stamford, CT	(4.4)
162	Brownsville-Harlingen, TX	(5.6)
32	Brunswick, GA	21.9
90	Buffalo-Niagara Falls, NY	4.0
NA	Burlington-South Burlington, VT**	NA
94	Burlington, NC	3.5
174	Cambridge-Newton, MA M.D.	(6.4)
102	Camden, NJ M.D.	3.0
88	Cape Coral-Fort Myers, FL	4.1
NA	Cape Girardeau, MO-IL**	NA
279	Carson City, NV	(26.2)
274	Casper, WY	(24.2)
52	Cedar Rapids, IA	14.9
NA	Charleston-North Charleston, SC**	NA
192	Charleston, WV	(9.0)
281	Charlotte-Gastonia, NC-SC	(26.6)
204	Charlottesville, VA	(10.3)
57	Chattanooga, TN-GA	13.6
236	Cheyenne, WY	(15.0)
276	Chico, CA	(24.9)
NA	Cincinnati-Middletown, OH-KY-IN**	NA
NA	Clarksville, TN-KY**	NA
NA	Cleveland-Elyria-Mentor, OH**	NA
NA	Cleveland, TN**	NA
197	Coeur d'Alene, ID	(9.7)
175	College Station-Bryan, TX	(6.5)
254	Colorado Springs, CO	(17.5)
86	Columbia, MO	4.8
37	Columbia, SC	19.4
9	Columbus, GA-AL	47.3
132	Columbus, IN	(1.9)
171	Columbus, OH	(6.3)
189	Corpus Christi, TX	(8.8)
202	Corvallis, OR	(10.1)
NA	Crestview-Fort Walton Beach, FL**	NA
14	Cumberland, MD-WV	35.8
168	Dallas (greater), TX	(6.1)
197	Dallas-Plano-Irving, TX M.D.	(9.7)
NA	Dalton, GA**	NA
NA	Danville, IL**	NA
5	Danville, VA	56.1
73	Dayton, OH	8.5
138	Decatur, AL	(2.4)
NA	Decatur, IL**	NA
NA	Deltona-Daytona Beach, FL**	NA
291	Denver-Aurora, CO	(33.9)
NA	Des Moines-West Des Moines, IA**	NA
56	Detroit (greater), MI	13.8
NA	Detroit-Livonia-Dearborn, MI M.D.**	NA
NA	Dothan, AL**	NA
6	Dover, DE	54.7
41	Dubuque, IA	18.1
NA	Duluth, MN-WI**	NA
76	Durham-Chapel Hill, NC	8.0
212	Eau Claire, WI	(11.0)
80	Edison, NJ M.D.	6.2
282	El Centro, CA	(26.7)
99	El Paso, TX	3.2
NA	Elizabethtown, KY**	NA
178	Elkhart-Goshen, IN	(7.1)
183	Elmira, NY	(7.8)
11	Erie, PA	40.4
226	Eugene-Springfield, OR	(13.1)
NA	Evansville, IN-KY**	NA
16	Fargo, ND-MN	34.9
177	Farmington, NM	(7.0)
62	Fayetteville, AR-MO	12.5
60	Fayetteville, NC	12.9
288	Flagstaff, AZ	(33.2)
NA	Flint, MI**	NA
NA	Florence-Muscle Shoals, AL**	NA
132	Florence, SC	(1.9)
164	Fond du Lac, WI	(5.7)
195	Fort Collins-Loveland, CO	(9.4)
30	Fort Lauderdale, FL M.D.	22.0
74	Fort Smith, AR-OK	8.2
147	Fort Wayne, IN	(3.5)
111	Fort Worth-Arlington, TX M.D.	1.7
129	Fresno, CA	(1.0)
185	Gadsden, AL	(8.1)
66	Gainesville, FL	10.2
181	Gainesville, GA	(7.5)
NA	Glens Falls, NY**	NA
20	Goldsboro, NC	28.7
185	Grand Forks, ND-MN	(8.1)
284	Grand Junction, CO	(27.9)
NA	Grand Rapids-Wyoming, MI**	NA
153	Great Falls, MT	(4.2)
302	Greeley, CO	(50.8)
178	Green Bay, WI	(7.1)
130	Greensboro-High Point, NC	(1.2)
NA	Gulfport-Biloxi, MS**	NA
46	Hagerstown-Martinsburg, MD-WV	16.0
246	Harrisburg-Carlisle, PA	(16.4)
261	Harrisonburg, VA	(19.5)
139	Hartford, CT	(2.6)
NA	Hattiesburg, MS**	NA
140	Hickory, NC	(2.8)
3	Hinesville, GA	58.7
NA	Holland-Grand Haven, MI**	NA
143	Honolulu, HI	(3.2)
65	Hot Springs, AR	10.5
241	Houma, LA	(15.5)
100	Houston, TX	3.1
233	Huntsville, AL	(14.7)
256	Idaho Falls, ID	(18.2)
49	Indianapolis, IN	15.7
203	Iowa City, IA	(10.2)
NA	Ithaca, NY**	NA
43	Jacksonville, FL	16.7
NA	Jacksonville, NC**	NA
NA	Jackson, MI**	NA
23	Jackson, MS	26.0
196	Jackson, TN	(9.6)
265	Janesville, WI	(21.4)
272	Jefferson City, MO	(23.9)
225	Johnson City, TN	(13.0)
242	Jonesboro, AR	(15.6)
NA	Kalamazoo-Portage, MI**	NA
NA	Kansas City, MO-KS**	NA
288	Kennewick-Pasco-Richland, WA	(33.2)
249	Killeen-Temple-Fort Hood, TX	(16.9)
39	Kingsport, TN-VA	18.9
30	Kingston, NY	22.0
92	Knoxville, TN	3.8
285	Kokomo, IN	(30.4)
15	La Crosse, WI-MN	35.4
218	Lafayette, IN	(12.3)
100	Lafayette, LA	3.1
18	Lake Charles, LA	32.3
NA	Lake Havasu City-Kingman, AZ**	NA
35	Lakeland, FL	20.9
262	Lancaster, PA	(20.1)
NA	Lansing-East Lansing, MI**	NA

Note: All listings are for Metropolitan Statistical Areas (M.S.A.s) except for those ending with "M.D." Listings with "M.D." are Metropolitan Divisions which are smaller parts of eleven large M.S.A.s. See explanatory note at beginning of metropolitan area section.

Alpha Order - Metro Area (continued)

RANK	METROPOLITAN AREA	% CHANGE
22	Laredo, TX	26.5
97	Las Cruces, NM	3.3
243	Las Vegas-Paradise, NV	(15.9)
82	Lawrence, KS	5.4
NA	Lawton, OK**	NA
240	Lebanon, PA	(15.4)
135	Lewiston-Auburn, ME	(2.2)
182	Lewiston, ID-WA	(7.6)
NA	Lexington-Fayette, KY**	NA
42	Lima, OH	17.6
269	Lincoln, NE	(22.2)
NA	Little Rock, AR**	NA
250	Logan, UT-ID	(17.2)
87	Longview, TX	4.7
299	Longview, WA	(47.0)
224	Los Angeles County, CA M.D.	(12.9)
232	Los Angeles (greater), CA	(14.0)
NA	Louisville, KY-IN**	NA
24	Lubbock, TX	25.7
109	Lynchburg, VA	1.9
160	Macon, GA	(5.3)
157	Madera, CA	(4.6)
131	Madison, WI	(1.6)
54	Manchester-Nashua, NH	14.8
NA	Manhattan, KS**	NA
NA	Mankato-North Mankato, MN**	NA
66	Mansfield, OH	10.2
88	McAllen-Edinburg-Mission, TX	4.1
301	Medford, OR	(50.3)
213	Memphis, TN-MS-AR	(11.1)
152	Merced, CA	(3.9)
85	Miami (greater), FL	4.9
149	Miami-Dade County, FL M.D.	(3.6)
2	Michigan City-La Porte, IN	65.6
44	Midland, TX	16.4
29	Milwaukee, WI	22.2
NA	Minneapolis-St. Paul, MN-WI**	NA
286	Missoula, MT	(31.4)
59	Mobile, AL	13.4
50	Modesto, CA	15.5
NA	Monroe, MI**	NA
207	Montgomery, AL	(10.8)
158	Morgantown, WV	(4.9)
51	Morristown, TN	15.0
295	Mount Vernon-Anacortes, WA	(40.6)
47	Muncie, IN	15.9
NA	Muskegon-Norton Shores, MI**	NA
70	Napa, CA	9.2
229	Naples-Marco Island, FL	(13.7)
123	Nashville-Davidson, TN	0.0
134	Nassau-Suffolk, NY M.D.	(2.0)
NA	New Haven-Milford, CT**	NA
NA	New Orleans, LA**	NA
216	New York (greater), NY-NJ-PA	(11.9)
257	New York-W. Plains NY-NJ M.D.	(18.6)
187	Newark-Union, NJ-PA M.D.	(8.5)
NA	Niles-Benton Harbor, MI**	NA
NA	North Port-Bradenton-Sarasota, FL**	NA
171	Norwich-New London, CT	(6.3)
199	Oakland-Fremont, CA M.D.	(9.9)
239	Ocala, FL	(15.3)
28	Ocean City, NJ	23.4
4	Odessa, TX	57.7

RANK	METROPOLITAN AREA	% CHANGE
207	Ogden-Clearfield, UT	(10.8)
NA	Oklahoma City, OK**	NA
252	Olympia, WA	(17.4)
184	Omaha-Council Bluffs, NE-IA	(7.9)
122	Orlando, FL	0.2
36	Oshkosh-Neenah, WI	19.5
NA	Owensboro, KY**	NA
265	Oxnard-Thousand Oaks, CA	(21.4)
169	Palm Bay-Melbourne, FL	(6.2)
NA	Palm Coast, FL**	NA
27	Panama City-Lynn Haven, FL	23.5
96	Pascagoula, MS	3.4
NA	Peabody, MA M.D.**	NA
69	Pensacola, FL	9.7
119	Philadelphia (greater) PA-NJ-MD-DE	0.6
123	Philadelphia, PA M.D.	0.0
258	Phoenix-Mesa-Scottsdale, AZ	(18.7)
126	Pine Bluff, AR	(0.5)
114	Pittsburgh, PA	1.2
20	Pittsfield, MA	28.7
292	Pocatello, ID	(34.8)
82	Port St. Lucie, FL	5.4
294	Portland-Vancouver, OR-WA	(39.3)
79	Portland, ME	6.9
142	Poughkeepsie, NY	(3.1)
271	Prescott, AZ	(22.4)
NA	Providence-New Bedford, RI-MA**	NA
297	Provo-Orem, UT	(41.9)
268	Pueblo, CO	(21.7)
154	Punta Gorda, FL	(4.4)
93	Racine, WI	3.7
210	Raleigh-Cary, NC	(10.9)
272	Rapid City, SD	(23.9)
233	Reading, PA	(14.7)
188	Redding, CA	(8.6)
166	Reno-Sparks, NV	(6.0)
207	Richmond, VA	(10.8)
189	Riverside-San Bernardino, CA	(8.8)
128	Roanoke, VA	(0.8)
214	Rochester, MN	(11.5)
108	Rochester, NY	2.4
38	Rockingham County, NH M.D.	19.2
75	Rocky Mount, NC	8.1
287	Rome, GA	(32.2)
244	Sacramento, CA	(16.0)
NA	Saginaw, MI**	NA
280	Salem, OR	(26.4)
52	Salinas, CA	14.9
60	Salisbury, MD	12.9
104	Salt Lake City, UT	2.8
215	San Angelo, TX	(11.6)
55	San Antonio, TX	14.2
260	San Diego, CA	(19.4)
223	San Francisco (greater), CA	(12.7)
252	San Francisco-S. Mateo, CA M.D.	(17.4)
227	San Jose, CA	(13.3)
169	San Luis Obispo, CA	(6.2)
166	Sandusky, OH	(6.0)
258	Santa Ana-Anaheim, CA M.D.	(18.7)
68	Santa Barbara-Santa Maria, CA	9.9
206	Santa Cruz-Watsonville, CA	(10.6)
45	Santa Fe, NM	16.3
231	Santa Rosa-Petaluma, CA	(13.8)

RANK	METROPOLITAN AREA	% CHANGE
90	Savannah, GA	4.0
175	Scranton--Wilkes-Barre, PA	(6.5)
218	Seattle-Bellevue-Everett, WA M.D.	(12.3)
216	Seattle-Tacoma-Bellevue, WA	(11.9)
125	Sebastian-Vero Beach, FL	(0.2)
19	Sheboygan, WI	30.1
221	Sherman-Denison, TX	(12.6)
194	Shreveport-Bossier City, LA	(9.3)
264	Sioux City, IA-NE-SD	(20.9)
162	Sioux Falls, SD	(5.6)
NA	South Bend-Mishawaka, IN-MI**	NA
189	Spartanburg, SC	(8.8)
145	Spokane, WA	(3.3)
165	Springfield, MA	(5.8)
NA	Springfield, MO**	NA
290	Springfield, OH	(33.3)
250	State College, PA	(17.2)
111	Stockton, CA	1.7
275	St. Cloud, MN	(24.7)
278	St. George, UT	(26.0)
26	St. Joseph, MO-KS	23.9
113	St. Louis, MO-IL	1.5
NA	Sumter, SC**	NA
62	Syracuse, NY	12.5
210	Tacoma, WA M.D.	(10.9)
78	Tallahassee, FL	7.4
97	Tampa-St Petersburg, FL	3.3
12	Texarkana, TX-Texarkana, AR	38.4
32	Toledo, OH	21.9
137	Topeka, KS	(2.3)
244	Trenton-Ewing, NJ	(16.0)
192	Tucson, AZ	(9.0)
147	Tulsa, OK	(3.5)
NA	Tuscaloosa, AL**	NA
236	Tyler, TX	(15.0)
158	Utica-Rome, NY	(4.9)
72	Valdosta, GA	8.6
NA	Vallejo-Fairfield, CA**	NA
40	Victoria, TX	18.6
105	Vineland, NJ	2.6
248	Visalia-Porterville, CA	(16.8)
270	Waco, TX	(22.3)
171	Warner Robins, GA	(6.3)
NA	Warren-Farmington Hills, MI M.D.**	NA
107	Washington (greater) DC-VA-MD-WV	2.5
77	Washington, DC-VA-MD-WV M.D.	7.8
156	Waterloo-Cedar Falls, IA	(4.5)
NA	Wausau, WI**	NA
277	Wenatchee, WA	(25.0)
94	West Palm Beach, FL M.D.	3.5
143	Wheeling, WV-OH	(3.2)
267	Wichita Falls, TX	(21.6)
NA	Wichita, KS**	NA
200	Williamsport, PA	(10.0)
120	Wilmington, DE-MD-NJ M.D.	0.3
263	Wilmington, NC	(20.3)
25	Winchester, VA-WV	24.3
117	Winston-Salem, NC	0.8
81	Worcester, MA	5.6
229	York-Hanover, PA	(13.7)
NA	Youngstown, OH-PA**	NA
300	Yuba City, CA	(47.4)
105	Yuma, AZ	2.6

Source: CQ Press using reported data from the F.B.I. "Crime in the United States 2009"

*Burglary is the unlawful entry of a structure to commit a felony or theft. Attempts are included.

**Not available.

32. Percent Change in Burglary Rate: 2005 to 2009 (continued)
National Percent Change = 1.5% Decrease*

RANK	METROPOLITAN AREA	% CHANGE
1	Athens-Clarke County, GA	66.8
2	Michigan City-La Porte, IN	65.6
3	Hinesville, GA	58.7
4	Odessa, TX	57.7
5	Danville, VA	56.1
6	Dover, DE	54.7
7	Battle Creek, MI	49.8
8	Barnstable Town, MA	48.1
9	Columbus, GA-AL	47.3
10	Bloomington, IN	41.2
11	Erie, PA	40.4
12	Texarkana, TX-Texarkana, AR	38.4
13	Augusta, GA-SC	37.5
14	Cumberland, MD-WV	35.8
15	La Crosse, WI-MN	35.4
16	Fargo, ND-MN	34.9
17	Anderson, IN	34.6
18	Lake Charles, LA	32.3
19	Sheboygan, WI	30.1
20	Goldsboro, NC	28.7
20	Pittsfield, MA	28.7
22	Laredo, TX	26.5
23	Jackson, MS	26.0
24	Lubbock, TX	25.7
25	Winchester, VA-WV	24.3
26	St. Joseph, MO-KS	23.9
27	Panama City-Lynn Haven, FL	23.5
28	Ocean City, NJ	23.4
29	Milwaukee, WI	22.2
30	Fort Lauderdale, FL M.D.	22.0
30	Kingston, NY	22.0
32	Brunswick, GA	21.9
32	Toledo, OH	21.9
34	Bangor, ME	21.2
35	Lakeland, FL	20.9
36	Oshkosh-Neenah, WI	19.5
37	Columbia, SC	19.4
38	Rockingham County, NH M.D.	19.2
39	Kingsport, TN-VA	18.9
40	Victoria, TX	18.6
41	Dubuque, IA	18.1
42	Lima, OH	17.6
43	Jacksonville, FL	16.7
44	Midland, TX	16.4
45	Santa Fe, NM	16.3
46	Hagerstown-Martinsburg, MD-WV	16.0
47	Blacksburg, VA	15.9
47	Muncie, IN	15.9
49	Indianapolis, IN	15.7
50	Modesto, CA	15.5
51	Morristown, TN	15.0
52	Cedar Rapids, IA	14.9
52	Salinas, CA	14.9
54	Manchester-Nashua, NH	14.8
55	San Antonio, TX	14.2
56	Detroit (greater), MI	13.8
57	Billings, MT	13.6
57	Chattanooga, TN-GA	13.6
59	Mobile, AL	13.4
60	Fayetteville, NC	12.9
60	Salisbury, MD	12.9
62	Fayetteville, AR-MO	12.5
62	Syracuse, NY	12.5
64	Binghamton, NY	10.9
65	Hot Springs, AR	10.5
66	Gainesville, FL	10.2
66	Mansfield, OH	10.2
68	Santa Barbara-Santa Maria, CA	9.9
69	Pensacola, FL	9.7
70	Napa, CA	9.2
71	Baton Rouge, LA	8.8
72	Valdosta, GA	8.6
73	Dayton, OH	8.5
74	Fort Smith, AR-OK	8.2
75	Rocky Mount, NC	8.1
76	Durham-Chapel Hill, NC	8.0
77	Washington, DC-VA-MD-WV M.D.	7.8
78	Tallahassee, FL	7.4
79	Portland, ME	6.9
80	Edison, NJ M.D.	6.2
81	Worcester, MA	5.6
82	Lawrence, KS	5.4
82	Port St. Lucie, FL	5.4
84	Atlanta, GA	5.3
85	Miami (greater), FL	4.9
86	Columbia, MO	4.8
87	Longview, TX	4.7
88	Cape Coral-Fort Myers, FL	4.1
88	McAllen-Edinburg-Mission, TX	4.1
90	Buffalo-Niagara Falls, NY	4.0
90	Savannah, GA	4.0
92	Knoxville, TN	3.8
93	Racine, WI	3.7
94	Burlington, NC	3.5
94	West Palm Beach, FL M.D.	3.5
96	Pascagoula, MS	3.4
97	Las Cruces, NM	3.3
97	Tampa-St Petersburg, FL	3.3
99	El Paso, TX	3.2
100	Houston, TX	3.1
100	Lafayette, LA	3.1
102	Camden, NJ M.D.	3.0
103	Bismarck, ND	2.9
104	Salt Lake City, UT	2.8
105	Vineland, NJ	2.6
105	Yuma, AZ	2.6
107	Washington (greater) DC-VA-MD-WV	2.5
108	Rochester, NY	2.4
109	Lynchburg, VA	1.9
110	Akron, OH	1.8
111	Fort Worth-Arlington, TX M.D.	1.7
111	Stockton, CA	1.7
113	St. Louis, MO-IL	1.5
114	Pittsburgh, PA	1.2
115	Ann Arbor, MI	1.1
116	Bakersfield, CA	0.9
117	Albany, GA	0.8
117	Winston-Salem, NC	0.8
119	Philadelphia (greater) PA-NJ-MD-DE	0.6
120	Austin-Round Rock, TX	0.3
120	Wilmington, DE-MD-NJ M.D.	0.3
122	Orlando, FL	0.2
123	Nashville-Davidson, TN	0.0
123	Philadelphia, PA M.D.	0.0
125	Sebastian-Vero Beach, FL	(0.2)
126	Pine Bluff, AR	(0.5)
127	Baltimore-Towson, MD	(0.6)
128	Roanoke, VA	(0.8)
129	Fresno, CA	(1.0)
130	Greensboro-High Point, NC	(1.2)
131	Madison, WI	(1.6)
132	Columbus, IN	(1.9)
132	Florence, SC	(1.9)
134	Nassau-Suffolk, NY M.D.	(2.0)
135	Albuquerque, NM	(2.2)
135	Lewiston-Auburn, ME	(2.2)
137	Topeka, KS	(2.3)
138	Decatur, AL	(2.4)
139	Hartford, CT	(2.6)
140	Amarillo, TX	(2.8)
140	Hickory, NC	(2.8)
142	Poughkeepsie, NY	(3.1)
143	Honolulu, HI	(3.2)
143	Wheeling, WV-OH	(3.2)
145	Spokane, WA	(3.3)
146	Allentown, PA-NJ	(3.4)
147	Fort Wayne, IN	(3.5)
147	Tulsa, OK	(3.5)
149	Anderson, SC	(3.6)
149	Miami-Dade County, FL M.D.	(3.6)
151	Atlantic City, NJ	(3.7)
152	Merced, CA	(3.9)
153	Great Falls, MT	(4.2)
154	Bridgeport-Stamford, CT	(4.4)
154	Punta Gorda, FL	(4.4)
156	Waterloo-Cedar Falls, IA	(4.5)
157	Madera, CA	(4.6)
158	Morgantown, WV	(4.9)
158	Utica-Rome, NY	(4.9)
160	Macon, GA	(5.3)
161	Alexandria, LA	(5.4)
162	Brownsville-Harlingen, TX	(5.6)
162	Sioux Falls, SD	(5.6)
164	Fond du Lac, WI	(5.7)
165	Springfield, MA	(5.8)
166	Reno-Sparks, NV	(6.0)
166	Sandusky, OH	(6.0)
168	Dallas (greater), TX	(6.1)
169	Palm Bay-Melbourne, FL	(6.2)
169	San Luis Obispo, CA	(6.2)
171	Columbus, OH	(6.3)
171	Norwich-New London, CT	(6.3)
171	Warner Robins, GA	(6.3)
174	Cambridge-Newton, MA M.D.	(6.4)
175	College Station-Bryan, TX	(6.5)
175	Scranton--Wilkes-Barre, PA	(6.5)
177	Farmington, NM	(7.0)
178	Elkhart-Goshen, IN	(7.1)
178	Green Bay, WI	(7.1)
180	Beaumont-Port Arthur, TX	(7.2)

Note: All listings are for Metropolitan Statistical Areas (M.S.A.s) except for those ending with "M.D." Listings with "M.D." are Metropolitan Divisions which are smaller parts of eleven large M.S.A.s. See explanatory note at beginning of metropolitan area section.

RANK	METROPOLITAN AREA	% CHANGE
181	Gainesville, GA	(7.5)
182	Lewiston, ID-WA	(7.6)
183	Elmira, NY	(7.8)
184	Omaha-Council Bluffs, NE-IA	(7.9)
185	Gadsden, AL	(8.1)
185	Grand Forks, ND-MN	(8.1)
187	Newark-Union, NJ-PA M.D.	(8.5)
188	Redding, CA	(8.6)
189	Corpus Christi, TX	(8.8)
189	Riverside-San Bernardino, CA	(8.8)
189	Spartanburg, SC	(8.8)
192	Charleston, WV	(9.0)
192	Tucson, AZ	(9.0)
194	Shreveport-Bossier City, LA	(9.3)
195	Fort Collins-Loveland, CO	(9.4)
196	Jackson, TN	(9.6)
197	Coeur d'Alene, ID	(9.7)
197	Dallas-Plano-Irving, TX M.D.	(9.7)
199	Oakland-Fremont, CA M.D.	(9.9)
200	Boston (greater), MA-NH	(10.0)
200	Williamsport, PA	(10.0)
202	Corvallis, OR	(10.1)
203	Iowa City, IA	(10.2)
204	Charlottesville, VA	(10.3)
205	Albany-Schenectady-Troy, NY	(10.4)
206	Santa Cruz-Watsonville, CA	(10.6)
207	Montgomery, AL	(10.8)
207	Ogden-Clearfield, UT	(10.8)
207	Richmond, VA	(10.8)
210	Raleigh-Cary, NC	(10.9)
210	Tacoma, WA M.D.	(10.9)
212	Eau Claire, WI	(11.0)
213	Memphis, TN-MS-AR	(11.1)
214	Rochester, MN	(11.5)
215	San Angelo, TX	(11.6)
216	New York (greater), NY-NJ-PA	(11.9)
216	Seattle-Tacoma-Bellevue, WA	(11.9)
218	Lafayette, IN	(12.3)
218	Seattle-Bellevue-Everett, WA M.D.	(12.3)
220	Anchorage, AK	(12.5)
221	Appleton, WI	(12.6)
221	Sherman-Denison, TX	(12.6)
223	San Francisco (greater), CA	(12.7)
224	Los Angeles County, CA M.D.	(12.9)
225	Johnson City, TN	(13.0)
226	Eugene-Springfield, OR	(13.1)
227	San Jose, CA	(13.3)
228	Asheville, NC	(13.4)
229	Naples-Marco Island, FL	(13.7)
229	York-Hanover, PA	(13.7)
231	Santa Rosa-Petaluma, CA	(13.8)
232	Los Angeles (greater), CA	(14.0)
233	Huntsville, AL	(14.7)
233	Reading, PA	(14.7)
235	Boston-Quincy, MA M.D.	(14.9)
236	Cheyenne, WY	(15.0)
236	Tyler, TX	(15.0)
238	Abilene, TX	(15.1)
239	Ocala, FL	(15.3)
240	Lebanon, PA	(15.4)
241	Houma, LA	(15.5)
242	Jonesboro, AR	(15.6)
243	Las Vegas-Paradise, NV	(15.9)
244	Sacramento, CA	(16.0)
244	Trenton-Ewing, NJ	(16.0)
246	Bethesda-Frederick, MD M.D.	(16.4)
246	Harrisburg-Carlisle, PA	(16.4)
248	Visalia-Porterville, CA	(16.8)
249	Killeen-Temple-Fort Hood, TX	(16.9)
250	Logan, UT-ID	(17.2)
250	State College, PA	(17.2)
252	Olympia, WA	(17.4)
252	San Francisco-S. Mateo, CA M.D.	(17.4)
254	Bremerton-Silverdale, WA	(17.5)
254	Colorado Springs, CO	(17.5)
256	Idaho Falls, ID	(18.2)
257	New York-W. Plains NY-NJ M.D.	(18.6)
258	Phoenix-Mesa-Scottsdale, AZ	(18.7)
258	Santa Ana-Anaheim, CA M.D.	(18.7)
260	San Diego, CA	(19.4)
261	Harrisonburg, VA	(19.5)
262	Lancaster, PA	(20.1)
263	Wilmington, NC	(20.3)
264	Sioux City, IA-NE-SD	(20.9)
265	Janesville, WI	(21.4)
265	Oxnard-Thousand Oaks, CA	(21.4)
267	Wichita Falls, TX	(21.6)
268	Pueblo, CO	(21.7)
269	Lincoln, NE	(22.2)
270	Waco, TX	(22.3)
271	Prescott, AZ	(22.4)
272	Jefferson City, MO	(23.9)
272	Rapid City, SD	(23.9)
274	Casper, WY	(24.2)
275	St. Cloud, MN	(24.7)
276	Chico, CA	(24.9)
277	Wenatchee, WA	(25.0)
278	St. George, UT	(26.0)
279	Carson City, NV	(26.2)
280	Salem, OR	(26.4)
281	Charlotte-Gastonia, NC-SC	(26.6)
282	El Centro, CA	(26.7)
283	Bellingham, WA	(27.6)
284	Grand Junction, CO	(27.9)
285	Kokomo, IN	(30.4)
286	Missoula, MT	(31.4)
287	Rome, GA	(32.2)
288	Flagstaff, AZ	(33.2)
288	Kennewick-Pasco-Richland, WA	(33.2)
290	Springfield, OH	(33.3)
291	Denver-Aurora, CO	(33.9)
292	Pocatello, ID	(34.8)
293	Ames, IA	(37.4)
294	Portland-Vancouver, OR-WA	(39.3)
295	Mount Vernon-Anacortes, WA	(40.6)
296	Altoona, PA	(40.7)
297	Provo-Orem, UT	(41.9)
298	Bend, OR	(42.3)
299	Longview, WA	(47.0)
300	Yuba City, CA	(47.4)
301	Medford, OR	(50.3)
302	Greeley, CO	(50.8)
NA	Anniston-Oxford, AL**	NA
NA	Auburn, AL**	NA
NA	Bay City, MI**	NA
NA	Birmingham-Hoover, AL**	NA
NA	Boise City-Nampa, ID**	NA
NA	Boulder, CO**	NA
NA	Bowling Green, KY**	NA
NA	Burlington-South Burlington, VT**	NA
NA	Cape Girardeau, MO-IL**	NA
NA	Charleston-North Charleston, SC**	NA
NA	Cincinnati-Middletown, OH-KY-IN**	NA
NA	Clarksville, TN-KY**	NA
NA	Cleveland-Elyria-Mentor, OH**	NA
NA	Cleveland, TN**	NA
NA	Crestview-Fort Walton Beach, FL**	NA
NA	Dalton, GA**	NA
NA	Danville, IL**	NA
NA	Decatur, IL**	NA
NA	Deltona-Daytona Beach, FL**	NA
NA	Des Moines-West Des Moines, IA**	NA
NA	Detroit-Livonia-Dearborn, MI M.D.**	NA
NA	Dothan, AL**	NA
NA	Duluth, MN-WI**	NA
NA	Elizabethtown, KY**	NA
NA	Evansville, IN-KY**	NA
NA	Flint, MI**	NA
NA	Florence-Muscle Shoals, AL**	NA
NA	Glens Falls, NY**	NA
NA	Grand Rapids-Wyoming, MI**	NA
NA	Gulfport-Biloxi, MS**	NA
NA	Hattiesburg, MS**	NA
NA	Holland-Grand Haven, MI**	NA
NA	Ithaca, NY**	NA
NA	Jacksonville, NC**	NA
NA	Jackson, MI**	NA
NA	Kalamazoo-Portage, MI**	NA
NA	Kansas City, MO-KS**	NA
NA	Lake Havasu City-Kingman, AZ**	NA
NA	Lansing-East Lansing, MI**	NA
NA	Lawton, OK**	NA
NA	Lexington-Fayette, KY**	NA
NA	Little Rock, AR**	NA
NA	Louisville, KY-IN**	NA
NA	Manhattan, KS**	NA
NA	Mankato-North Mankato, MN**	NA
NA	Minneapolis-St. Paul, MN-WI**	NA
NA	Monroe, MI**	NA
NA	Muskegon-Norton Shores, MI**	NA
NA	New Haven-Milford, CT**	NA
NA	New Orleans, LA**	NA
NA	Niles-Benton Harbor, MI**	NA
NA	North Port-Bradenton-Sarasota, FL**	NA
NA	Oklahoma City, OK**	NA
NA	Owensboro, KY**	NA
NA	Palm Coast, FL**	NA
NA	Peabody, MA M.D.**	NA
NA	Providence-New Bedford, RI-MA**	NA
NA	Saginaw, MI**	NA
NA	South Bend-Mishawaka, IN-MI**	NA
NA	Springfield, MO**	NA
NA	Sumter, SC**	NA
NA	Tuscaloosa, AL**	NA
NA	Vallejo-Fairfield, CA**	NA
NA	Warren-Farmington Hills, MI M.D.**	NA
NA	Wausau, WI**	NA
NA	Wichita, KS**	NA
NA	Youngstown, OH-PA**	NA

Source: CQ Press using reported data from the F.B.I. "Crime in the United States 2009"

*Burglary is the unlawful entry of a structure to commit a felony or theft. Attempts are included.

**Not available.

33. Larceny-Thefts in 2009
National Total = 6,327,230 Larceny-Thefts*

RANK	METROPOLITAN AREA	THEFTS	RANK	METROPOLITAN AREA	THEFTS	RANK	METROPOLITAN AREA	THEFTS
240	Abilene, TX	3,816	185	Charleston, WV	6,295	36	Fort Lauderdale, FL M.D.	48,487
98	Akron, OH	15,408	37	Charlotte-Gastonia, NC-SC	45,750	181	Fort Smith, AR-OK	6,423
91	Albany-Schenectady-Troy, NY	16,919	220	Charlottesville, VA	4,241	152	Fort Wayne, IN	8,289
211	Albany, GA	4,532	96	Chattanooga, TN-GA	15,614	27	Fort Worth-Arlington, TX M.D.	59,643
67	Albuquerque, NM	23,768	313	Cheyenne, WY	2,404	75	Fresno, CA	21,749
205	Alexandria, LA	4,905	243	Chico, CA	3,765	299	Gadsden, AL	2,660
100	Allentown, PA-NJ	14,517	30	Cincinnati-Middletown, OH-KY-IN	51,302	160	Gainesville, FL	7,415
345	Altoona, PA	1,812	206	Clarksville, TN-KY	4,857	285	Gainesville, GA	2,992
151	Amarillo, TX	8,307	51	Cleveland-Elyria-Mentor, OH	35,887	352	Glens Falls, NY	1,682
347	Ames, IA	1,786	316	Cleveland, TN	2,380	283	Goldsboro, NC	3,018
149	Anchorage, AK	8,570	302	Coeur d'Alene, ID	2,616	350	Grand Forks, ND-MN	1,750
271	Anderson, IN	3,220	176	College Station-Bryan, TX	6,493	262	Grand Junction, CO	3,392
202	Anderson, SC	5,084	111	Colorado Springs, CO	12,350	97	Grand Rapids-Wyoming, MI	15,434
182	Ann Arbor, MI	6,400	226	Columbia, MO	4,108	319	Great Falls, MT	2,270
264	Anniston-Oxford, AL	3,365	81	Columbia, SC	19,896	216	Greeley, CO	4,350
247	Appleton, WI	3,680	123	Columbus, GA-AL	11,136	212	Green Bay, WI	4,436
183	Asheville, NC	6,346	330	Columbus, IN	2,077	82	Greensboro-High Point, NC	19,791
204	Athens-Clarke County, GA	4,930	31	Columbus, OH	51,071	172	Gulfport-Biloxi, MS	6,730
8	Atlanta, GA	118,285	95	Corpus Christi, TX	15,713	218	Hagerstown-Martinsburg, MD-WV	4,325
168	Atlantic City, NJ	7,148	344	Corvallis, OR	1,822	143	Harrisburg-Carlisle, PA	9,091
232	Auburn, AL	3,929	234	Crestview-Fort Walton Beach, FL	3,876	363	Harrisonburg, VA	1,435
94	Augusta, GA-SC	15,891	341	Cumberland, MD-WV	1,927	78	Hartford, CT	20,281
29	Austin-Round Rock, TX	52,199	4	Dallas (greater), TX	165,125	NA	Hattiesburg, MS**	NA
89	Bakersfield, CA	17,034	11	Dallas-Plano-Irving, TX M.D.	105,482	159	Hickory, NC	7,520
26	Baltimore-Towson, MD	61,555	286	Dalton, GA	2,913	359	Hinesville, GA	1,520
230	Bangor, ME	3,954	340	Danville, IL	1,933	261	Holland-Grand Haven, MI	3,412
227	Barnstable Town, MA	4,088	328	Danville, VA	2,107	68	Honolulu, HI	23,647
71	Baton Rouge, LA	22,796	84	Dayton, OH	19,230	246	Hot Springs, AR	3,702
258	Battle Creek, MI	3,478	257	Decatur, AL	3,486	203	Houma, LA	5,018
342	Bay City, MI	1,887	336	Decatur, IL	1,989	5	Houston, TX	155,841
132	Beaumont-Port Arthur, TX	9,658	114	Deltona-Daytona Beach, FL	12,075	136	Huntsville, AL	9,537
195	Bellingham, WA	5,323	33	Denver-Aurora, CO	49,085	333	Idaho Falls, ID	2,029
275	Bend, OR	3,149	119	Des Moines-West Des Moines, IA	11,527	39	Indianapolis, IN	42,936
73	Bethesda-Frederick, MD M.D.	22,188	19	Detroit (greater), MI	75,888	324	Iowa City, IA	2,186
215	Billings, MT	4,387	44	Detroit-Livonia-Dearborn, MI M.D.	39,984	337	Ithaca, NY	1,962
200	Binghamton, NY	5,100	278	Dothan, AL	3,117	47	Jacksonville, FL	38,889
54	Birmingham-Hoover, AL	33,805	229	Dover, DE	4,055	236	Jacksonville, NC	3,849
348	Bismarck, ND	1,771	360	Dubuque, IA	1,493	282	Jackson, MI	3,046
280	Blacksburg, VA	3,114	166	Duluth, MN-WI	7,294	112	Jackson, MS	12,157
254	Bloomington, IN	3,582	107	Durham-Chapel Hill, NC	12,696	241	Jackson, TN	3,798
144	Boise City-Nampa, ID	9,068	305	Eau Claire, WI	2,575	255	Janesville, WI	3,564
21	Boston (greater), MA-NH	71,548	58	Edison, NJ M.D.	33,156	310	Jefferson City, MO	2,461
57	Boston-Quincy, MA M.D.	33,489	NA	El Centro, CA**	NA	235	Johnson City, TN	3,856
192	Boulder, CO	5,447	90	El Paso, TX	16,977	304	Jonesboro, AR	2,600
289	Bowling Green, KY	2,891	356	Elizabethtown, KY	1,556	155	Kalamazoo-Portage, MI	7,799
219	Bremerton-Silverdale, WA	4,309	248	Elkhart-Goshen, IN	3,657	35	Kansas City, MO-KS	48,714
113	Bridgeport-Stamford, CT	12,144	358	Elmira, NY	1,533	213	Kennewick-Pasco-Richland, WA	4,429
99	Brownsville-Harlingen, TX	14,544	207	Erie, PA	4,705	154	Killeen-Temple-Fort Hood, TX	8,230
267	Brunswick, GA	3,290	134	Eugene-Springfield, OR	9,574	165	Kingsport, TN-VA	7,299
66	Buffalo-Niagara Falls, NY	24,108	163	Evansville, IN-KY	7,365	301	Kingston, NY	2,618
199	Burlington-South Burlington, VT	5,102	244	Fargo, ND-MN	3,762	92	Knoxville, TN	16,623
233	Burlington, NC	3,906	331	Farmington, NM	2,072	309	Kokomo, IN	2,466
77	Cambridge-Newton, MA M.D.	20,431	153	Fayetteville, AR-MO	8,253	300	La Crosse, WI-MN	2,653
72	Camden, NJ M.D.	22,327	109	Fayetteville, NC	12,562	224	Lafayette, IN	4,154
126	Cape Coral-Fort Myers, FL	10,844	250	Flagstaff, AZ	3,651	145	Lafayette, LA	8,933
317	Cape Girardeau, MO-IL	2,356	139	Flint, MI	9,275	210	Lake Charles, LA	4,537
365	Carson City, NV	797	279	Florence-Muscle Shoals, AL	3,116	209	Lake Havasu City-Kingman, AZ	4,641
323	Casper, WY	2,232	171	Florence, SC	6,860	102	Lakeland, FL	13,914
197	Cedar Rapids, IA	5,202	361	Fond du Lac, WI	1,486	156	Lancaster, PA	7,773
88	Charleston-North Charleston, SC	17,103	175	Fort Collins-Loveland, CO	6,513	150	Lansing-East Lansing, MI	8,501

Note: All listings are for Metropolitan Statistical Areas (M.S.A.s) except for those ending with "M.D." Listings with "M.D." are Metropolitan Divisions which are smaller parts of eleven large M.S.A.s. See explanatory note at beginning of metropolitan area section.

Alpha Order - Metro Area (continued)

RANK	METROPOLITAN AREA	THEFTS
128	Laredo, TX	10,310
208	Las Cruces, NM	4,675
56	Las Vegas-Paradise, NV	33,570
228	Lawrence, KS	4,064
259	Lawton, OK	3,441
351	Lebanon, PA	1,701
339	Lewiston-Auburn, ME	1,936
364	Lewiston, ID-WA	1,406
118	Lexington-Fayette, KY	11,582
290	Lima, OH	2,875
148	Lincoln, NE	8,594
69	Little Rock, AR	23,413
357	Logan, UT-ID	1,537
178	Longview, TX	6,486
298	Longview, WA	2,686
7	Los Angeles County, CA M.D.	144,589
2	Los Angeles (greater), CA	188,100
60	Louisville, KY-IN	28,460
133	Lubbock, TX	9,583
256	Lynchburg, VA	3,525
161	Macon, GA	7,408
362	Madera, CA	1,484
116	Madison, WI	11,782
167	Manchester-Nashua, NH	7,183
326	Manhattan, KS	2,148
325	Mankato-North Mankato, MN	2,180
266	Mansfield, OH	3,341
62	McAllen-Edinburg-Mission, TX	26,750
221	Medford, OR	4,239
43	Memphis, TN-MS-AR	41,094
201	Merced, CA	5,089
3	Miami (greater), FL	169,207
16	Miami-Dade County, FL M.D.	85,359
288	Michigan City-La Porte, IN	2,899
269	Midland, TX	3,228
41	Milwaukee, WI	41,362
20	Minneapolis-St. Paul, MN-WI	73,085
322	Missoula, MT	2,235
108	Mobile, AL	12,598
110	Modesto, CA	12,428
307	Monroe, MI	2,568
130	Montgomery, AL	10,113
334	Morgantown, WV	2,023
270	Morristown, TN	3,223
222	Mount Vernon-Anacortes, WA	4,191
315	Muncie, IN	2,394
193	Muskegon-Norton Shores, MI	5,437
329	Napa, CA	2,091
217	Naples-Marco Island, FL	4,346
49	Nashville-Davidson, TN	37,855
48	Nassau-Suffolk, NY M.D.	38,712
83	New Haven-Milford, CT	19,329
63	New Orleans, LA	26,369
1	New York (greater), NY-NJ-PA	253,510
6	New York-W. Plains NY-NJ M.D.	155,404
64	Newark-Union, NJ-PA M.D.	26,238
251	Niles-Benton Harbor, MI	3,622
85	North Port-Bradenton-Sarasota, FL	19,190
293	Norwich-New London, CT	2,808
32	Oakland-Fremont, CA M.D.	49,314
190	Ocala, FL	5,724
277	Ocean City, NJ	3,118
245	Odessa, TX	3,724
120	Ogden-Clearfield, UT	11,512
55	Oklahoma City, OK	33,670
196	Olympia, WA	5,291
79	Omaha-Council Bluffs, NE-IA	20,272
28	Orlando, FL	54,647
284	Oshkosh-Neenah, WI	2,996
312	Owensboro, KY	2,409
122	Oxnard-Thousand Oaks, CA	11,221
106	Palm Bay-Melbourne, FL	12,873
355	Palm Coast, FL	1,589
198	Panama City-Lynn Haven, FL	5,108
274	Pascagoula, MS	3,158
124	Peabody, MA M.D.	11,111
129	Pensacola, FL	10,136
9	Philadelphia (greater) PA-NJ-MD-DE	114,431
18	Philadelphia, PA M.D.	76,050
12	Phoenix-Mesa-Scottsdale, AZ	102,745
303	Pine Bluff, AR	2,603
53	Pittsburgh, PA	34,935
343	Pittsfield, MA	1,877
335	Pocatello, ID	2,004
157	Port St. Lucie, FL	7,770
34	Portland-Vancouver, OR-WA	48,986
135	Portland, ME	9,573
127	Poughkeepsie, NY	10,841
273	Prescott, AZ	3,184
61	Providence-New Bedford, RI-MA	28,179
131	Provo-Orem, UT	9,943
297	Pueblo, CO	2,762
287	Punta Gorda, FL	2,906
231	Racine, WI	3,936
80	Raleigh-Cary, NC	20,115
295	Rapid City, SD	2,775
177	Reading, PA	6,488
292	Redding, CA	2,839
141	Reno-Sparks, NV	9,218
65	Richmond, VA	24,453
24	Riverside-San Bernardino, CA	67,830
180	Roanoke, VA	6,475
281	Rochester, MN	3,098
76	Rochester, NY	21,420
174	Rockingham County, NH M.D.	6,517
242	Rocky Mount, NC	3,775
327	Rome, GA	2,122
40	Sacramento, CA	41,868
263	Saginaw, MI	3,391
146	Salem, OR	8,818
186	Salinas, CA	6,245
268	Salisbury, MD	3,236
45	Salt Lake City, UT	39,524
265	San Angelo, TX	3,347
17	San Antonio, TX	83,138
42	San Diego, CA	41,278
14	San Francisco (greater), CA	88,827
46	San Francisco-S. Mateo, CA M.D.	39,513
59	San Jose, CA	28,838
223	San Luis Obispo, CA	4,169
349	Sandusky, OH	1,755
38	Santa Ana-Anaheim, CA M.D.	43,511
189	Santa Barbara-Santa Maria, CA	5,937
179	Santa Cruz-Watsonville, CA	6,480
311	Santa Fe, NM	2,416
173	Santa Rosa-Petaluma, CA	6,671
140	Savannah, GA	9,222
142	Scranton--Wilkes-Barre, PA	9,163
22	Seattle-Bellevue-Everett, WA M.D.	71,217
13	Seattle-Tacoma-Bellevue, WA	94,210
291	Sebastian-Vero Beach, FL	2,849
314	Sheboygan, WI	2,396
296	Sherman-Denison, TX	2,765
125	Shreveport-Bossier City, LA	10,856
306	Sioux City, IA-NE-SD	2,570
225	Sioux Falls, SD	4,110
147	South Bend-Mishawaka, IN-MI	8,814
164	Spartanburg, SC	7,341
103	Spokane, WA	13,739
105	Springfield, MA	13,181
101	Springfield, MO	14,275
239	Springfield, OH	3,826
321	State College, PA	2,246
87	Stockton, CA	17,260
249	St. Cloud, MN	3,656
345	St. George, UT	1,812
271	St. Joseph, MO-KS	3,220
25	St. Louis, MO-IL	63,245
338	Sumter, SC	1,943
121	Syracuse, NY	11,389
70	Tacoma, WA M.D.	22,993
158	Tallahassee, FL	7,559
23	Tampa-St Petersburg, FL	70,799
252	Texarkana, TX-Texarkana, AR	3,606
NA	Toledo, OH**	NA
184	Topeka, KS	6,300
194	Trenton-Ewing, NJ	5,404
NA	Tucson, AZ**	NA
74	Tulsa, OK	21,828
187	Tuscaloosa, AL	6,154
188	Tyler, TX	6,043
191	Utica-Rome, NY	5,696
260	Valdosta, GA	3,430
169	Vallejo-Fairfield, CA	7,018
238	Victoria, TX	3,831
253	Vineland, NJ	3,604
138	Visalia-Porterville, CA	9,326
162	Waco, TX	7,393
237	Warner Robins, GA	3,846
50	Warren-Farmington Hills, MI M.D.	35,904
10	Washington (greater) DC-VA-MD-WV	108,922
15	Washington, DC-VA-MD-WV M.D.	86,734
294	Waterloo-Cedar Falls, IA	2,776
354	Wausau, WI	1,670
308	Wenatchee, WA	2,535
52	West Palm Beach, FL M.D.	35,361
332	Wheeling, WV-OH	2,030
214	Wichita Falls, TX	4,421
86	Wichita, KS	17,632
353	Williamsport, PA	1,675
93	Wilmington, DE-MD-NJ M.D.	16,054
137	Wilmington, NC	9,336
320	Winchester, VA-WV	2,261
104	Winston-Salem, NC	13,187
115	Worcester, MA	11,866
170	York-Hanover, PA	6,987
117	Youngstown, OH-PA	11,628
318	Yuba City, CA	2,309
276	Yuma, AZ	3,128

Source: Reported data from the F.B.I. "Crime in the United States 2009"
*Larceny-theft is the unlawful taking of property. Attempts are included.
**Not available.

33. Larceny-Thefts in 2009 (continued)
National Total = 6,327,230 Larceny-Thefts*

RANK	METROPOLITAN AREA	THEFTS	RANK	METROPOLITAN AREA	THEFTS	RANK	METROPOLITAN AREA	THEFTS
1	New York (greater), NY-NJ-PA	253,510	61	Providence-New Bedford, RI-MA	28,179	121	Syracuse, NY	11,389
2	Los Angeles (greater), CA	188,100	62	McAllen-Edinburg-Mission, TX	26,750	122	Oxnard-Thousand Oaks, CA	11,221
3	Miami (greater), FL	169,207	63	New Orleans, LA	26,369	123	Columbus, GA-AL	11,136
4	Dallas (greater), TX	165,125	64	Newark-Union, NJ-PA M.D.	26,238	124	Peabody, MA M.D.	11,111
5	Houston, TX	155,841	65	Richmond, VA	24,453	125	Shreveport-Bossier City, LA	10,856
6	New York-W. Plains NY-NJ M.D.	155,404	66	Buffalo-Niagara Falls, NY	24,108	126	Cape Coral-Fort Myers, FL	10,844
7	Los Angeles County, CA M.D.	144,589	67	Albuquerque, NM	23,768	127	Poughkeepsie, NY	10,841
8	Atlanta, GA	118,285	68	Honolulu, HI	23,647	128	Laredo, TX	10,310
9	Philadelphia (greater) PA-NJ-MD-DE	114,431	69	Little Rock, AR	23,413	129	Pensacola, FL	10,136
10	Washington (greater) DC-VA-MD-WV	108,922	70	Tacoma, WA M.D.	22,993	130	Montgomery, AL	10,113
11	Dallas-Plano-Irving, TX M.D.	105,482	71	Baton Rouge, LA	22,796	131	Provo-Orem, UT	9,943
12	Phoenix-Mesa-Scottsdale, AZ	102,745	72	Camden, NJ M.D.	22,327	132	Beaumont-Port Arthur, TX	9,658
13	Seattle-Tacoma-Bellevue, WA	94,210	73	Bethesda-Frederick, MD M.D.	22,188	133	Lubbock, TX	9,583
14	San Francisco (greater), CA	88,827	74	Tulsa, OK	21,828	134	Eugene-Springfield, OR	9,574
15	Washington, DC-VA-MD-WV M.D.	86,734	75	Fresno, CA	21,749	135	Portland, ME	9,573
16	Miami-Dade County, FL M.D.	85,359	76	Rochester, NY	21,420	136	Huntsville, AL	9,537
17	San Antonio, TX	83,138	77	Cambridge-Newton, MA M.D.	20,431	137	Wilmington, NC	9,336
18	Philadelphia, PA M.D.	76,050	78	Hartford, CT	20,281	138	Visalia-Porterville, CA	9,326
19	Detroit (greater), MI	75,888	79	Omaha-Council Bluffs, NE-IA	20,272	139	Flint, MI	9,275
20	Minneapolis-St. Paul, MN-WI	73,085	80	Raleigh-Cary, NC	20,115	140	Savannah, GA	9,222
21	Boston (greater), MA-NH	71,548	81	Columbia, SC	19,896	141	Reno-Sparks, NV	9,218
22	Seattle-Bellevue-Everett, WA M.D.	71,217	82	Greensboro-High Point, NC	19,791	142	Scranton--Wilkes-Barre, PA	9,163
23	Tampa-St Petersburg, FL	70,799	83	New Haven-Milford, CT	19,329	143	Harrisburg-Carlisle, PA	9,091
24	Riverside-San Bernardino, CA	67,830	84	Dayton, OH	19,230	144	Boise City-Nampa, ID	9,068
25	St. Louis, MO-IL	63,245	85	North Port-Bradenton-Sarasota, FL	19,190	145	Lafayette, LA	8,933
26	Baltimore-Towson, MD	61,555	86	Wichita, KS	17,632	146	Salem, OR	8,818
27	Fort Worth-Arlington, TX M.D.	59,643	87	Stockton, CA	17,260	147	South Bend-Mishawaka, IN-MI	8,814
28	Orlando, FL	54,647	88	Charleston-North Charleston, SC	17,103	148	Lincoln, NE	8,594
29	Austin-Round Rock, TX	52,199	89	Bakersfield, CA	17,034	149	Anchorage, AK	8,570
30	Cincinnati-Middletown, OH-KY-IN	51,302	90	El Paso, TX	16,977	150	Lansing-East Lansing, MI	8,501
31	Columbus, OH	51,071	91	Albany-Schenectady-Troy, NY	16,919	151	Amarillo, TX	8,307
32	Oakland-Fremont, CA M.D.	49,314	92	Knoxville, TN	16,623	152	Fort Wayne, IN	8,289
33	Denver-Aurora, CO	49,085	93	Wilmington, DE-MD-NJ M.D.	16,054	153	Fayetteville, AR-MO	8,253
34	Portland-Vancouver, OR-WA	48,986	94	Augusta, GA-SC	15,891	154	Killeen-Temple-Fort Hood, TX	8,230
35	Kansas City, MO-KS	48,714	95	Corpus Christi, TX	15,713	155	Kalamazoo-Portage, MI	7,799
36	Fort Lauderdale, FL M.D.	48,487	96	Chattanooga, TN-GA	15,614	156	Lancaster, PA	7,773
37	Charlotte-Gastonia, NC-SC	45,750	97	Grand Rapids-Wyoming, MI	15,434	157	Port St. Lucie, FL	7,770
38	Santa Ana-Anaheim, CA M.D.	43,511	98	Akron, OH	15,408	158	Tallahassee, FL	7,559
39	Indianapolis, IN	42,936	99	Brownsville-Harlingen, TX	14,544	159	Hickory, NC	7,520
40	Sacramento, CA	41,868	100	Allentown, PA-NJ	14,517	160	Gainesville, FL	7,415
41	Milwaukee, WI	41,362	101	Springfield, MO	14,275	161	Macon, GA	7,408
42	San Diego, CA	41,278	102	Lakeland, FL	13,914	162	Waco, TX	7,393
43	Memphis, TN-MS-AR	41,094	103	Spokane, WA	13,739	163	Evansville, IN-KY	7,365
44	Detroit-Livonia-Dearborn, MI M.D.	39,984	104	Winston-Salem, NC	13,187	164	Spartanburg, SC	7,341
45	Salt Lake City, UT	39,524	105	Springfield, MA	13,181	165	Kingsport, TN-VA	7,299
46	San Francisco-S. Mateo, CA M.D.	39,513	106	Palm Bay-Melbourne, FL	12,873	166	Duluth, MN-WI	7,294
47	Jacksonville, FL	38,889	107	Durham-Chapel Hill, NC	12,696	167	Manchester-Nashua, NH	7,183
48	Nassau-Suffolk, NY M.D.	38,712	108	Mobile, AL	12,598	168	Atlantic City, NJ	7,148
49	Nashville-Davidson, TN	37,855	109	Fayetteville, NC	12,562	169	Vallejo-Fairfield, CA	7,018
50	Warren-Farmington Hills, MI M.D.	35,904	110	Modesto, CA	12,428	170	York-Hanover, PA	6,987
51	Cleveland-Elyria-Mentor, OH	35,887	111	Colorado Springs, CO	12,350	171	Florence, SC	6,860
52	West Palm Beach, FL M.D.	35,361	112	Jackson, MS	12,157	172	Gulfport-Biloxi, MS	6,730
53	Pittsburgh, PA	34,935	113	Bridgeport-Stamford, CT	12,144	173	Santa Rosa-Petaluma, CA	6,671
54	Birmingham-Hoover, AL	33,805	114	Deltona-Daytona Beach, FL	12,075	174	Rockingham County, NH M.D.	6,517
55	Oklahoma City, OK	33,670	115	Worcester, MA	11,866	175	Fort Collins-Loveland, CO	6,513
56	Las Vegas-Paradise, NV	33,570	116	Madison, WI	11,782	176	College Station-Bryan, TX	6,493
57	Boston-Quincy, MA M.D.	33,489	117	Youngstown, OH-PA	11,628	177	Reading, PA	6,488
58	Edison, NJ M.D.	33,156	118	Lexington-Fayette, KY	11,582	178	Longview, TX	6,486
59	San Jose, CA	28,838	119	Des Moines-West Des Moines, IA	11,527	179	Santa Cruz-Watsonville, CA	6,480
60	Louisville, KY-IN	28,460	120	Ogden-Clearfield, UT	11,512	180	Roanoke, VA	6,475

Note: All listings are for Metropolitan Statistical Areas (M.S.A.s) except for those ending with "M.D." Listings with "M.D." are Metropolitan Divisions which are smaller parts of eleven large M.S.A.s. See explanatory note at beginning of metropolitan area section.

Rank Order - Metro Area (continued)

RANK	METROPOLITAN AREA	THEFTS
181	Fort Smith, AR-OK	6,423
182	Ann Arbor, MI	6,400
183	Asheville, NC	6,346
184	Topeka, KS	6,300
185	Charleston, WV	6,295
186	Salinas, CA	6,245
187	Tuscaloosa, AL	6,154
188	Tyler, TX	6,043
189	Santa Barbara-Santa Maria, CA	5,937
190	Ocala, FL	5,724
191	Utica-Rome, NY	5,696
192	Boulder, CO	5,447
193	Muskegon-Norton Shores, MI	5,437
194	Trenton-Ewing, NJ	5,404
195	Bellingham, WA	5,323
196	Olympia, WA	5,291
197	Cedar Rapids, IA	5,202
198	Panama City-Lynn Haven, FL	5,108
199	Burlington-South Burlington, VT	5,102
200	Binghamton, NY	5,100
201	Merced, CA	5,089
202	Anderson, SC	5,084
203	Houma, LA	5,018
204	Athens-Clarke County, GA	4,930
205	Alexandria, LA	4,905
206	Clarksville, TN-KY	4,857
207	Erie, PA	4,705
208	Las Cruces, NM	4,675
209	Lake Havasu City-Kingman, AZ	4,641
210	Lake Charles, LA	4,537
211	Albany, GA	4,532
212	Green Bay, WI	4,436
213	Kennewick-Pasco-Richland, WA	4,429
214	Wichita Falls, TX	4,421
215	Billings, MT	4,387
216	Greeley, CO	4,350
217	Naples-Marco Island, FL	4,346
218	Hagerstown-Martinsburg, MD-WV	4,325
219	Bremerton-Silverdale, WA	4,309
220	Charlottesville, VA	4,241
221	Medford, OR	4,239
222	Mount Vernon-Anacortes, WA	4,191
223	San Luis Obispo, CA	4,169
224	Lafayette, IN	4,154
225	Sioux Falls, SD	4,110
226	Columbia, MO	4,108
227	Barnstable Town, MA	4,088
228	Lawrence, KS	4,064
229	Dover, DE	4,055
230	Bangor, ME	3,954
231	Racine, WI	3,936
232	Auburn, AL	3,929
233	Burlington, NC	3,906
234	Crestview-Fort Walton Beach, FL	3,876
235	Johnson City, TN	3,856
236	Jacksonville, NC	3,849
237	Warner Robins, GA	3,846
238	Victoria, TX	3,831
239	Springfield, OH	3,826
240	Abilene, TX	3,816
241	Jackson, TN	3,798
242	Rocky Mount, NC	3,775
243	Chico, CA	3,765

RANK	METROPOLITAN AREA	THEFTS
244	Fargo, ND-MN	3,762
245	Odessa, TX	3,724
246	Hot Springs, AR	3,702
247	Appleton, WI	3,680
248	Elkhart-Goshen, IN	3,657
249	St. Cloud, MN	3,656
250	Flagstaff, AZ	3,651
251	Niles-Benton Harbor, MI	3,622
252	Texarkana, TX-Texarkana, AR	3,606
253	Vineland, NJ	3,604
254	Bloomington, IN	3,582
255	Janesville, WI	3,564
256	Lynchburg, VA	3,525
257	Decatur, AL	3,486
258	Battle Creek, MI	3,478
259	Lawton, OK	3,441
260	Valdosta, GA	3,430
261	Holland-Grand Haven, MI	3,412
262	Grand Junction, CO	3,392
263	Saginaw, MI	3,391
264	Anniston-Oxford, AL	3,365
265	San Angelo, TX	3,347
266	Mansfield, OH	3,341
267	Brunswick, GA	3,290
268	Salisbury, MD	3,236
269	Midland, TX	3,228
270	Morristown, TN	3,223
271	Anderson, IN	3,220
271	St. Joseph, MO-KS	3,220
273	Prescott, AZ	3,184
274	Pascagoula, MS	3,158
275	Bend, OR	3,149
276	Yuma, AZ	3,128
277	Ocean City, NJ	3,118
278	Dothan, AL	3,117
279	Florence-Muscle Shoals, AL	3,116
280	Blacksburg, VA	3,114
281	Rochester, MN	3,098
282	Jackson, MI	3,046
283	Goldsboro, NC	3,018
284	Oshkosh-Neenah, WI	2,996
285	Gainesville, GA	2,992
286	Dalton, GA	2,913
287	Punta Gorda, FL	2,906
288	Michigan City-La Porte, IN	2,899
289	Bowling Green, KY	2,891
290	Lima, OH	2,875
291	Sebastian-Vero Beach, FL	2,849
292	Redding, CA	2,839
293	Norwich-New London, CT	2,808
294	Waterloo-Cedar Falls, IA	2,776
295	Rapid City, SD	2,775
296	Sherman-Denison, TX	2,765
297	Pueblo, CO	2,762
298	Longview, WA	2,686
299	Gadsden, AL	2,660
300	La Crosse, WI-MN	2,653
301	Kingston, NY	2,618
302	Coeur d'Alene, ID	2,616
303	Pine Bluff, AR	2,603
304	Jonesboro, AR	2,600
305	Eau Claire, WI	2,575
306	Sioux City, IA-NE-SD	2,570

RANK	METROPOLITAN AREA	THEFTS
307	Monroe, MI	2,568
308	Wenatchee, WA	2,535
309	Kokomo, IN	2,466
310	Jefferson City, MO	2,461
311	Santa Fe, NM	2,416
312	Owensboro, KY	2,409
313	Cheyenne, WY	2,404
314	Sheboygan, WI	2,396
315	Muncie, IN	2,394
316	Cleveland, TN	2,380
317	Cape Girardeau, MO-IL	2,356
318	Yuba City, CA	2,309
319	Great Falls, MT	2,270
320	Winchester, VA-WV	2,261
321	State College, PA	2,246
322	Missoula, MT	2,235
323	Casper, WY	2,232
324	Iowa City, IA	2,186
325	Mankato-North Mankato, MN	2,180
326	Manhattan, KS	2,148
327	Rome, GA	2,122
328	Danville, VA	2,107
329	Napa, CA	2,091
330	Columbus, IN	2,077
331	Farmington, NM	2,072
332	Wheeling, WV-OH	2,030
333	Idaho Falls, ID	2,029
334	Morgantown, WV	2,023
335	Pocatello, ID	2,004
336	Decatur, IL	1,989
337	Ithaca, NY	1,962
338	Sumter, SC	1,943
339	Lewiston-Auburn, ME	1,936
340	Danville, IL	1,933
341	Cumberland, MD-WV	1,927
342	Bay City, MI	1,887
343	Pittsfield, MA	1,877
344	Corvallis, OR	1,822
345	Altoona, PA	1,812
345	St. George, UT	1,812
347	Ames, IA	1,786
348	Bismarck, ND	1,771
349	Sandusky, OH	1,755
350	Grand Forks, ND-MN	1,750
351	Lebanon, PA	1,701
352	Glens Falls, NY	1,682
353	Williamsport, PA	1,675
354	Wausau, WI	1,670
355	Palm Coast, FL	1,589
356	Elizabethtown, KY	1,556
357	Logan, UT-ID	1,537
358	Elmira, NY	1,533
359	Hinesville, GA	1,520
360	Dubuque, IA	1,493
361	Fond du Lac, WI	1,486
362	Madera, CA	1,484
363	Harrisonburg, VA	1,435
364	Lewiston, ID-WA	1,406
365	Carson City, NV	797
NA	El Centro, CA**	NA
NA	Hattiesburg, MS**	NA
NA	Toledo, OH**	NA
NA	Tucson, AZ**	NA

Source: Reported data from the F.B.I. "Crime in the United States 2009"
*Larceny-theft is the unlawful taking of property. Attempts are included.
**Not available.

34. Larceny-Theft Rate in 2009
National Rate = 2,060.9 Larceny-Thefts per 100,000 Population*

RANK	METROPOLITAN AREA	RATE
133	Abilene, TX	2,390.5
177	Akron, OH	2,198.2
228	Albany-Schenectady-Troy, NY	1,974.8
72	Albany, GA	2,743.9
69	Albuquerque, NM	2,756.7
25	Alexandria, LA	3,164.5
274	Allentown, PA-NJ	1,775.4
337	Altoona, PA	1,448.8
17	Amarillo, TX	3,376.3
216	Ames, IA	2,043.5
58	Anchorage, AK	2,807.2
123	Anderson, IN	2,448.2
75	Anderson, SC	2,736.4
258	Ann Arbor, MI	1,835.9
42	Anniston-Oxford, AL	2,947.7
300	Appleton, WI	1,660.6
321	Asheville, NC	1,534.5
102	Athens-Clarke County, GA	2,579.9
191	Atlanta, GA	2,152.8
92	Atlantic City, NJ	2,622.2
47	Auburn, AL	2,895.1
40	Augusta, GA-SC	2,955.0
34	Austin-Round Rock, TX	3,060.6
203	Bakersfield, CA	2,091.3
157	Baltimore-Towson, MD	2,285.7
86	Bangor, ME	2,657.7
261	Barnstable Town, MA	1,822.5
48	Baton Rouge, LA	2,893.9
103	Battle Creek, MI	2,574.8
276	Bay City, MI	1,767.2
110	Beaumont-Port Arthur, TX	2,555.1
90	Bellingham, WA	2,645.7
242	Bend, OR	1,924.4
252	Bethesda-Frederick, MD M.D.	1,857.9
53	Billings, MT	2,859.0
206	Binghamton, NY	2,087.0
37	Birmingham-Hoover, AL	2,989.6
301	Bismarck, ND	1,655.9
234	Blacksburg, VA	1,949.8
239	Bloomington, IN	1,934.2
328	Boise City-Nampa, ID	1,476.8
318	Boston (greater), MA-NH	1,560.0
280	Boston-Quincy, MA M.D.	1,751.2
257	Boulder, CO	1,839.3
129	Bowling Green, KY	2,414.3
270	Bremerton-Silverdale, WA	1,780.4
348	Bridgeport-Stamford, CT	1,383.1
6	Brownsville-Harlingen, TX	3,636.4
24	Brunswick, GA	3,178.0
190	Buffalo-Niagara Falls, NY	2,154.2
124	Burlington-South Burlington, VT	2,438.8
99	Burlington, NC	2,599.6
352	Cambridge-Newton, MA M.D.	1,358.2
273	Camden, NJ M.D.	1,776.0
268	Cape Coral-Fort Myers, FL	1,785.9
116	Cape Girardeau, MO-IL	2,514.1
332	Carson City, NV	1,463.4
38	Casper, WY	2,981.7
221	Cedar Rapids, IA	2,023.2
101	Charleston-North Charleston, SC	2,592.5
211	Charleston, WV	2,070.8
96	Charlotte-Gastonia, NC-SC	2,611.0
192	Charlottesville, VA	2,147.5
39	Chattanooga, TN-GA	2,981.0
81	Cheyenne, WY	2,690.4
289	Chico, CA	1,700.0
142	Cincinnati-Middletown, OH-KY-IN	2,355.3
259	Clarksville, TN-KY	1,830.7
286	Cleveland-Elyria-Mentor, OH	1,714.4
200	Cleveland, TN	2,098.6
251	Coeur d'Alene, ID	1,863.1
30	College Station-Bryan, TX	3,087.8
230	Colorado Springs, CO	1,966.3
119	Columbia, MO	2,467.8
82	Columbia, SC	2,682.8
3	Columbus, GA-AL	3,872.0
75	Columbus, IN	2,736.4
56	Columbus, OH	2,841.3
4	Corpus Christi, TX	3,766.3
173	Corvallis, OR	2,218.8
185	Crestview-Fort Walton Beach, FL	2,164.1
236	Cumberland, MD-WV	1,943.9
109	Dallas (greater), TX	2,560.2
125	Dallas-Plano-Irving, TX M.D.	2,436.0
187	Dalton, GA	2,156.1
127	Danville, IL	2,415.7
226	Danville, VA	1,992.9
154	Dayton, OH	2,295.1
153	Decatur, AL	2,304.6
255	Decatur, IL	1,854.9
127	Deltona-Daytona Beach, FL	2,415.7
243	Denver-Aurora, CO	1,924.2
217	Des Moines-West Des Moines, IA	2,042.3
284	Detroit (greater), MI	1,723.0
210	Detroit-Livonia-Dearborn, MI M.D.	2,071.3
182	Dothan, AL	2,183.5
113	Dover, DE	2,546.8
308	Dubuque, IA	1,605.7
87	Duluth, MN-WI	2,653.3
112	Durham-Chapel Hill, NC	2,548.0
307	Eau Claire, WI	1,611.2
345	Edison, NJ M.D.	1,416.5
NA	El Centro, CA**	NA
163	El Paso, TX	2,263.7
349	Elizabethtown, KY	1,377.4
262	Elkhart-Goshen, IN	1,816.8
278	Elmira, NY	1,753.4
293	Erie, PA	1,682.1
70	Eugene-Springfield, OR	2,747.0
201	Evansville, IN-KY	2,094.2
249	Fargo, ND-MN	1,887.2
296	Farmington, NM	1,673.5
265	Fayetteville, AR-MO	1,802.7
10	Fayetteville, NC	3,499.3
55	Flagstaff, AZ	2,842.2
184	Flint, MI	2,176.3
187	Florence-Muscle Shoals, AL	2,156.1
15	Florence, SC	3,401.0
325	Fond du Lac, WI	1,491.5
181	Fort Collins-Loveland, CO	2,184.8
65	Fort Lauderdale, FL M.D.	2,771.5
183	Fort Smith, AR-OK	2,182.4
224	Fort Wayne, IN	2,001.5
57	Fort Worth-Arlington, TX M.D.	2,813.7
139	Fresno, CA	2,367.3
108	Gadsden, AL	2,563.6
52	Gainesville, FL	2,860.3
314	Gainesville, GA	1,577.7
359	Glens Falls, NY	1,301.5
89	Goldsboro, NC	2,649.9
267	Grand Forks, ND-MN	1,788.5
150	Grand Junction, CO	2,313.7
227	Grand Rapids-Wyoming, MI	1,985.0
67	Great Falls, MT	2,761.8
294	Greeley, CO	1,679.5
335	Green Bay, WI	1,454.2
63	Greensboro-High Point, NC	2,772.3
49	Gulfport-Biloxi, MS	2,880.8
309	Hagerstown-Martinsburg, MD-WV	1,603.2
290	Harrisburg-Carlisle, PA	1,699.4
364	Harrisonburg, VA	1,195.5
222	Hartford, CT	2,013.0
NA	Hattiesburg, MS**	NA
215	Hickory, NC	2,055.0
178	Hinesville, GA	2,188.4
358	Holland-Grand Haven, MI	1,303.6
98	Honolulu, HI	2,606.8
5	Hot Springs, AR	3,742.2
118	Houma, LA	2,469.7
85	Houston, TX	2,659.9
141	Huntsville, AL	2,362.6
305	Idaho Falls, ID	1,622.5
120	Indianapolis, IN	2,464.6
338	Iowa City, IA	1,445.0
240	Ithaca, NY	1,930.8
44	Jacksonville, FL	2,935.1
155	Jacksonville, NC	2,289.5
245	Jackson, MI	1,907.4
165	Jackson, MS	2,241.9
18	Jackson, TN	3,342.9
174	Janesville, WI	2,213.5
296	Jefferson City, MO	1,673.5
235	Johnson City, TN	1,946.8
180	Jonesboro, AR	2,186.1
130	Kalamazoo-Portage, MI	2,412.0
140	Kansas City, MO-KS	2,363.9
260	Kennewick-Pasco-Richland, WA	1,824.0
193	Killeen-Temple-Fort Hood, TX	2,136.9
136	Kingsport, TN-VA	2,382.2
340	Kingston, NY	1,438.1
138	Knoxville, TN	2,367.8
117	Kokomo, IN	2,485.3
223	La Crosse, WI-MN	2,003.7
196	Lafayette, IN	2,131.9
16	Lafayette, LA	3,396.0
146	Lake Charles, LA	2,337.9
148	Lake Havasu City-Kingman, AZ	2,331.7
137	Lakeland, FL	2,370.1
323	Lancaster, PA	1,532.6
250	Lansing-East Lansing, MI	1,877.3

Note: All listings are for Metropolitan Statistical Areas (M.S.A.s) except for those ending with "M.D." Listings with "M.D." are Metropolitan Divisions which are smaller parts of eleven large M.S.A.s. See explanatory note at beginning of metropolitan area section.

Alpha Order - Metro Area (continued)

RANK	METROPOLITAN AREA	RATE
1	Laredo, TX	4,252.5
161	Las Cruces, NM	2,276.6
277	Las Vegas-Paradise, NV	1,763.2
11	Lawrence, KS	3,485.4
33	Lawton, OK	3,068.4
357	Lebanon, PA	1,306.0
263	Lewiston-Auburn, ME	1,809.3
149	Lewiston, ID-WA	2,318.7
121	Lexington-Fayette, KY	2,459.8
77	Lima, OH	2,735.2
51	Lincoln, NE	2,869.8
14	Little Rock, AR	3,416.0
363	Logan, UT-ID	1,209.1
27	Longview, TX	3,145.5
95	Longview, WA	2,612.4
331	Los Angeles County, CA M.D.	1,465.9
333	Los Angeles (greater), CA	1,460.2
162	Louisville, KY-IN	2,265.5
9	Lubbock, TX	3,506.5
344	Lynchburg, VA	1,417.3
22	Macon, GA	3,210.4
365	Madera, CA	983.7
208	Madison, WI	2,074.2
272	Manchester-Nashua, NH	1,776.6
282	Manhattan, KS	1,737.9
147	Mankato-North Mankato, MN	2,334.7
83	Mansfield, OH	2,673.7
7	McAllen-Edinburg-Mission, TX	3,582.1
205	Medford, OR	2,088.1
26	Memphis, TN-MS-AR	3,163.4
218	Merced, CA	2,040.2
32	Miami (greater), FL	3,075.8
13	Miami-Dade County, FL M.D.	3,438.5
97	Michigan City-La Porte, IN	2,608.1
122	Midland, TX	2,458.6
84	Milwaukee, WI	2,661.9
167	Minneapolis-St. Paul, MN-WI	2,237.2
214	Missoula, MT	2,058.3
31	Mobile, AL	3,081.6
131	Modesto, CA	2,407.6
295	Monroe, MI	1,677.6
78	Montgomery, AL	2,734.4
292	Morgantown, WV	1,691.7
145	Morristown, TN	2,339.0
12	Mount Vernon-Anacortes, WA	3,479.8
202	Muncie, IN	2,092.0
28	Muskegon-Norton Shores, MI	3,123.4
317	Napa, CA	1,560.5
353	Naples-Marco Island, FL	1,357.7
135	Nashville-Davidson, TN	2,388.8
354	Nassau-Suffolk, NY M.D.	1,346.5
126	New Haven-Milford, CT	2,432.2
168	New Orleans, LA	2,236.2
355	New York (greater), NY-NJ-PA	1,329.0
356	New York-W. Plains NY-NJ M.D.	1,324.0
362	Newark-Union, NJ-PA M.D.	1,236.0
158	Niles-Benton Harbor, MI	2,285.2
66	North Port-Bradenton-Sarasota, FL	2,768.5
220	Norwich-New London, CT	2,025.8
229	Oakland-Fremont, CA M.D.	1,967.1
287	Ocala, FL	1,706.5
21	Ocean City, NJ	3,278.7
59	Odessa, TX	2,791.6
195	Ogden-Clearfield, UT	2,134.8
71	Oklahoma City, OK	2,745.5
199	Olympia, WA	2,106.9
132	Omaha-Council Bluffs, NE-IA	2,391.3
93	Orlando, FL	2,618.1
256	Oshkosh-Neenah, WI	1,842.6
197	Owensboro, KY	2,127.1
347	Oxnard-Thousand Oaks, CA	1,403.2
134	Palm Bay-Melbourne, FL	2,389.7
303	Palm Coast, FL	1,644.7
29	Panama City-Lynn Haven, FL	3,108.4
213	Pascagoula, MS	2,058.5
327	Peabody, MA M.D.	1,486.8
171	Pensacola, FL	2,233.1
244	Philadelphia (greater) PA-NJ-MD-DE	1,916.7
246	Philadelphia, PA M.D.	1,896.0
143	Phoenix-Mesa-Scottsdale, AZ	2,355.1
100	Pine Bluff, AR	2,594.2
326	Pittsburgh, PA	1,487.4
343	Pittsfield, MA	1,429.6
164	Pocatello, ID	2,258.4
247	Port St. Lucie, FL	1,890.8
179	Portland-Vancouver, OR-WA	2,187.6
254	Portland, ME	1,855.7
310	Poughkeepsie, NY	1,599.0
334	Prescott, AZ	1,454.6
278	Providence-New Bedford, RI-MA	1,753.4
271	Provo-Orem, UT	1,776.9
281	Pueblo, CO	1,739.8
238	Punta Gorda, FL	1,942.0
232	Racine, WI	1,962.0
269	Raleigh-Cary, NC	1,783.4
166	Rapid City, SD	2,239.7
312	Reading, PA	1,590.2
316	Redding, CA	1,564.1
176	Reno-Sparks, NV	2,204.0
231	Richmond, VA	1,963.5
306	Riverside-San Bernardino, CA	1,611.8
189	Roanoke, VA	2,155.9
298	Rochester, MN	1,670.2
209	Rochester, NY	2,073.7
319	Rockingham County, NH M.D.	1,542.5
107	Rocky Mount, NC	2,568.3
175	Rome, GA	2,207.1
233	Sacramento, CA	1,956.9
288	Saginaw, MI	1,704.5
172	Salem, OR	2,226.2
322	Salinas, CA	1,532.9
88	Salisbury, MD	2,652.4
8	Salt Lake City, UT	3,507.2
35	San Angelo, TX	3,039.9
2	San Antonio, TX	4,012.4
351	San Diego, CA	1,371.0
207	San Francisco (greater), CA	2,077.6
170	San Francisco-S. Mateo, CA M.D.	2,234.2
313	San Jose, CA	1,582.8
315	San Luis Obispo, CA	1,565.0
160	Sandusky, OH	2,278.8
339	Santa Ana-Anaheim, CA M.D.	1,441.8
330	Santa Barbara-Santa Maria, CA	1,467.3
106	Santa Cruz-Watsonville, CA	2,571.8
302	Santa Fe, NM	1,655.0
342	Santa Rosa-Petaluma, CA	1,432.1
80	Savannah, GA	2,729.1
299	Scranton--Wilkes-Barre, PA	1,667.8
73	Seattle-Bellevue-Everett, WA M.D.	2,740.3
64	Seattle-Tacoma-Bellevue, WA	2,771.8
194	Sebastian-Vero Beach, FL	2,135.4
204	Sheboygan, WI	2,088.8
151	Sherman-Denison, TX	2,307.4
68	Shreveport-Bossier City, LA	2,758.4
266	Sioux City, IA-NE-SD	1,795.5
285	Sioux Falls, SD	1,717.9
62	South Bend-Mishawaka, IN-MI	2,779.6
105	Spartanburg, SC	2,572.0
45	Spokane, WA	2,919.7
248	Springfield, MA	1,889.3
20	Springfield, MO	3,296.0
74	Springfield, OH	2,737.7
320	State College, PA	1,536.5
115	Stockton, CA	2,527.9
241	St. Cloud, MN	1,928.7
361	St. George, UT	1,264.7
114	St. Joseph, MO-KS	2,542.4
169	St. Louis, MO-IL	2,235.0
253	Sumter, SC	1,856.2
275	Syracuse, NY	1,771.4
50	Tacoma, WA M.D.	2,874.3
198	Tallahassee, FL	2,109.2
104	Tampa-St Petersburg, FL	2,573.6
91	Texarkana, TX-Texarkana, AR	2,642.9
NA	Toledo, OH**	NA
79	Topeka, KS	2,734.3
329	Trenton-Ewing, NJ	1,475.6
NA	Tucson, AZ**	NA
144	Tulsa, OK	2,351.9
43	Tuscaloosa, AL	2,940.9
41	Tyler, TX	2,953.8
237	Utica-Rome, NY	1,943.5
111	Valdosta, GA	2,552.6
283	Vallejo-Fairfield, CA	1,723.1
19	Victoria, TX	3,339.0
159	Vineland, NJ	2,281.5
186	Visalia-Porterville, CA	2,160.2
23	Waco, TX	3,182.2
54	Warner Robins, GA	2,843.7
336	Warren-Farmington Hills, MI M.D.	1,451.3
225	Washington (greater) DC-VA-MD-WV	1,997.8
219	Washington, DC-VA-MD-WV M.D.	2,037.0
291	Waterloo-Cedar Falls, IA	1,692.2
360	Wausau, WI	1,270.3
151	Wenatchee, WA	2,307.4
60	West Palm Beach, FL M.D.	2,785.8
346	Wheeling, WV-OH	1,406.4
36	Wichita Falls, TX	3,007.1
46	Wichita, KS	2,899.9
341	Williamsport, PA	1,436.5
156	Wilmington, DE-MD-NJ M.D.	2,286.4
94	Wilmington, NC	2,617.6
264	Winchester, VA-WV	1,807.2
61	Winston-Salem, NC	2,781.1
324	Worcester, MA	1,491.9
304	York-Hanover, PA	1,622.6
212	Youngstown, OH-PA	2,062.8
350	Yuba City, CA	1,375.6
311	Yuma, AZ	1,594.3

Source: Reported data from the F.B.I. "Crime in the United States 2009"
*Larceny-theft is the unlawful taking of property. Attempts are included.
**Not available.

34. Larceny-Theft Rate in 2009 (continued)
National Rate = 2,060.9 Larceny-Thefts per 100,000 Population*

RANK	METROPOLITAN AREA	RATE
1	Laredo, TX	4,252.5
2	San Antonio, TX	4,012.4
3	Columbus, GA-AL	3,872.0
4	Corpus Christi, TX	3,766.3
5	Hot Springs, AR	3,742.2
6	Brownsville-Harlingen, TX	3,636.4
7	McAllen-Edinburg-Mission, TX	3,582.1
8	Salt Lake City, UT	3,507.2
9	Lubbock, TX	3,506.5
10	Fayetteville, NC	3,499.3
11	Lawrence, KS	3,485.4
12	Mount Vernon-Anacortes, WA	3,479.8
13	Miami-Dade County, FL M.D.	3,438.5
14	Little Rock, AR	3,416.0
15	Florence, SC	3,401.0
16	Lafayette, LA	3,396.0
17	Amarillo, TX	3,376.3
18	Jackson, TN	3,342.9
19	Victoria, TX	3,339.0
20	Springfield, MO	3,296.0
21	Ocean City, NJ	3,278.7
22	Macon, GA	3,210.4
23	Waco, TX	3,182.2
24	Brunswick, GA	3,178.0
25	Alexandria, LA	3,164.5
26	Memphis, TN-MS-AR	3,163.4
27	Longview, TX	3,145.5
28	Muskegon-Norton Shores, MI	3,123.4
29	Panama City-Lynn Haven, FL	3,108.4
30	College Station-Bryan, TX	3,087.8
31	Mobile, AL	3,081.6
32	Miami (greater), FL	3,075.8
33	Lawton, OK	3,068.4
34	Austin-Round Rock, TX	3,060.6
35	San Angelo, TX	3,039.9
36	Wichita Falls, TX	3,007.1
37	Birmingham-Hoover, AL	2,989.6
38	Casper, WY	2,981.7
39	Chattanooga, TN-GA	2,981.0
40	Augusta, GA-SC	2,955.0
41	Tyler, TX	2,953.8
42	Anniston-Oxford, AL	2,947.7
43	Tuscaloosa, AL	2,940.9
44	Jacksonville, FL	2,935.1
45	Spokane, WA	2,919.7
46	Wichita, KS	2,899.9
47	Auburn, AL	2,895.1
48	Baton Rouge, LA	2,893.9
49	Gulfport-Biloxi, MS	2,880.8
50	Tacoma, WA M.D.	2,874.3
51	Lincoln, NE	2,869.8
52	Gainesville, FL	2,860.3
53	Billings, MT	2,859.0
54	Warner Robins, GA	2,843.7
55	Flagstaff, AZ	2,842.2
56	Columbus, OH	2,841.3
57	Fort Worth-Arlington, TX M.D.	2,813.7
58	Anchorage, AK	2,807.2
59	Odessa, TX	2,791.6
60	West Palm Beach, FL M.D.	2,785.8
61	Winston-Salem, NC	2,781.1
62	South Bend-Mishawaka, IN-MI	2,779.6
63	Greensboro-High Point, NC	2,772.3
64	Seattle-Tacoma-Bellevue, WA	2,771.8
65	Fort Lauderdale, FL M.D.	2,771.5
66	North Port-Bradenton-Sarasota, FL	2,768.5
67	Great Falls, MT	2,761.8
68	Shreveport-Bossier City, LA	2,758.4
69	Albuquerque, NM	2,756.7
70	Eugene-Springfield, OR	2,747.0
71	Oklahoma City, OK	2,745.5
72	Albany, GA	2,743.9
73	Seattle-Bellevue-Everett, WA M.D.	2,740.3
74	Springfield, OH	2,737.7
75	Anderson, SC	2,736.4
75	Columbus, IN	2,736.4
77	Lima, OH	2,735.2
78	Montgomery, AL	2,734.4
79	Topeka, KS	2,734.3
80	Savannah, GA	2,729.1
81	Cheyenne, WY	2,690.4
82	Columbia, SC	2,682.8
83	Mansfield, OH	2,673.7
84	Milwaukee, WI	2,661.9
85	Houston, TX	2,659.9
86	Bangor, ME	2,657.7
87	Duluth, MN-WI	2,653.3
88	Salisbury, MD	2,652.4
89	Goldsboro, NC	2,649.9
90	Bellingham, WA	2,645.7
91	Texarkana, TX-Texarkana, AR	2,642.9
92	Atlantic City, NJ	2,622.2
93	Orlando, FL	2,618.1
94	Wilmington, NC	2,617.6
95	Longview, WA	2,612.4
96	Charlotte-Gastonia, NC-SC	2,611.0
97	Michigan City-La Porte, IN	2,608.1
98	Honolulu, HI	2,606.8
99	Burlington, NC	2,599.6
100	Pine Bluff, AR	2,594.2
101	Charleston-North Charleston, SC	2,592.5
102	Athens-Clarke County, GA	2,579.9
103	Battle Creek, MI	2,574.8
104	Tampa-St Petersburg, FL	2,573.6
105	Spartanburg, SC	2,572.0
106	Santa Cruz-Watsonville, CA	2,571.8
107	Rocky Mount, NC	2,568.3
108	Gadsden, AL	2,563.6
109	Dallas (greater), TX	2,560.2
110	Beaumont-Port Arthur, TX	2,555.1
111	Valdosta, GA	2,552.6
112	Durham-Chapel Hill, NC	2,548.0
113	Dover, DE	2,546.8
114	St. Joseph, MO-KS	2,542.4
115	Stockton, CA	2,527.9
116	Cape Girardeau, MO-IL	2,514.1
117	Kokomo, IN	2,485.3
118	Houma, LA	2,469.7
119	Columbia, MO	2,467.8
120	Indianapolis, IN	2,464.6
121	Lexington-Fayette, KY	2,459.8
122	Midland, TX	2,458.6
123	Anderson, IN	2,448.2
124	Burlington-South Burlington, VT	2,438.8
125	Dallas-Plano-Irving, TX M.D.	2,436.0
126	New Haven-Milford, CT	2,432.2
127	Danville, IL	2,415.7
127	Deltona-Daytona Beach, FL	2,415.7
129	Bowling Green, KY	2,414.3
130	Kalamazoo-Portage, MI	2,412.0
131	Modesto, CA	2,407.6
132	Omaha-Council Bluffs, NE-IA	2,391.3
133	Abilene, TX	2,390.5
134	Palm Bay-Melbourne, FL	2,389.7
135	Nashville-Davidson, TN	2,388.8
136	Kingsport, TN-VA	2,382.2
137	Lakeland, FL	2,370.1
138	Knoxville, TN	2,367.8
139	Fresno, CA	2,367.3
140	Kansas City, MO-KS	2,363.9
141	Huntsville, AL	2,362.6
142	Cincinnati-Middletown, OH-KY-IN	2,355.3
143	Phoenix-Mesa-Scottsdale, AZ	2,355.1
144	Tulsa, OK	2,351.9
145	Morristown, TN	2,339.0
146	Lake Charles, LA	2,337.9
147	Mankato-North Mankato, MN	2,334.7
148	Lake Havasu City-Kingman, AZ	2,331.7
149	Lewiston, ID-WA	2,318.7
150	Grand Junction, CO	2,313.7
151	Sherman-Denison, TX	2,307.4
151	Wenatchee, WA	2,307.4
153	Decatur, AL	2,304.6
154	Dayton, OH	2,295.1
155	Jacksonville, NC	2,289.5
156	Wilmington, DE-MD-NJ M.D.	2,286.4
157	Baltimore-Towson, MD	2,285.7
158	Niles-Benton Harbor, MI	2,285.2
159	Vineland, NJ	2,281.5
160	Sandusky, OH	2,278.8
161	Las Cruces, NM	2,276.6
162	Louisville, KY-IN	2,265.5
163	El Paso, TX	2,263.7
164	Pocatello, ID	2,258.4
165	Jackson, MS	2,241.9
166	Rapid City, SD	2,239.7
167	Minneapolis-St. Paul, MN-WI	2,237.2
168	New Orleans, LA	2,236.2
169	St. Louis, MO-IL	2,235.0
170	San Francisco-S. Mateo, CA M.D.	2,234.2
171	Pensacola, FL	2,233.1
172	Salem, OR	2,226.2
173	Corvallis, OR	2,218.8
174	Janesville, WI	2,213.5
175	Rome, GA	2,207.1
176	Reno-Sparks, NV	2,204.0
177	Akron, OH	2,198.2
178	Hinesville, GA	2,188.4
179	Portland-Vancouver, OR-WA	2,187.6
180	Jonesboro, AR	2,186.1

Note: All listings are for Metropolitan Statistical Areas (M.S.A.s) except for those ending with "M.D." Listings with "M.D." are Metropolitan Divisions which are smaller parts of eleven large M.S.A.s. See explanatory note at beginning of metropolitan area section.

RANK	METROPOLITAN AREA	RATE
181	Fort Collins-Loveland, CO	2,184.8
182	Dothan, AL	2,183.5
183	Fort Smith, AR-OK	2,182.4
184	Flint, MI	2,176.3
185	Crestview-Fort Walton Beach, FL	2,164.1
186	Visalia-Porterville, CA	2,160.2
187	Dalton, GA	2,156.1
187	Florence-Muscle Shoals, AL	2,156.1
189	Roanoke, VA	2,155.9
190	Buffalo-Niagara Falls, NY	2,154.2
191	Atlanta, GA	2,152.8
192	Charlottesville, VA	2,147.5
193	Killeen-Temple-Fort Hood, TX	2,136.9
194	Sebastian-Vero Beach, FL	2,135.4
195	Ogden-Clearfield, UT	2,134.8
196	Lafayette, IN	2,131.9
197	Owensboro, KY	2,127.1
198	Tallahassee, FL	2,109.2
199	Olympia, WA	2,106.9
200	Cleveland, TN	2,098.6
201	Evansville, IN-KY	2,094.2
202	Muncie, IN	2,092.0
203	Bakersfield, CA	2,091.3
204	Sheboygan, WI	2,088.8
205	Medford, OR	2,088.1
206	Binghamton, NY	2,087.0
207	San Francisco (greater), CA	2,077.6
208	Madison, WI	2,074.2
209	Rochester, NY	2,073.7
210	Detroit-Livonia-Dearborn, MI M.D.	2,071.3
211	Charleston, WV	2,070.8
212	Youngstown, OH-PA	2,062.8
213	Pascagoula, MS	2,058.5
214	Missoula, MT	2,058.3
215	Hickory, NC	2,055.0
216	Ames, IA	2,043.5
217	Des Moines-West Des Moines, IA	2,042.3
218	Merced, CA	2,040.2
219	Washington, DC-VA-MD-WV M.D.	2,037.0
220	Norwich-New London, CT	2,025.8
221	Cedar Rapids, IA	2,023.2
222	Hartford, CT	2,013.0
223	La Crosse, WI-MN	2,003.7
224	Fort Wayne, IN	2,001.5
225	Washington (greater) DC-VA-MD-WV	1,997.8
226	Danville, VA	1,992.9
227	Grand Rapids-Wyoming, MI	1,985.0
228	Albany-Schenectady-Troy, NY	1,974.8
229	Oakland-Fremont, CA M.D.	1,967.1
230	Colorado Springs, CO	1,966.3
231	Richmond, VA	1,963.5
232	Racine, WI	1,962.0
233	Sacramento, CA	1,956.9
234	Blacksburg, VA	1,949.8
235	Johnson City, TN	1,946.8
236	Cumberland, MD-WV	1,943.9
237	Utica-Rome, NY	1,943.5
238	Punta Gorda, FL	1,942.0
239	Bloomington, IN	1,934.2
240	Ithaca, NY	1,930.8
241	St. Cloud, MN	1,928.7
242	Bend, OR	1,924.4
243	Denver-Aurora, CO	1,924.2
244	Philadelphia (greater) PA-NJ-MD-DE	1,916.7
245	Jackson, MI	1,907.4
246	Philadelphia, PA M.D.	1,896.0
247	Port St. Lucie, FL	1,890.8
248	Springfield, MA	1,889.3
249	Fargo, ND-MN	1,887.2
250	Lansing-East Lansing, MI	1,877.3
251	Coeur d'Alene, ID	1,863.1
252	Bethesda-Frederick, MD M.D.	1,857.9
253	Sumter, SC	1,856.2
254	Portland, ME	1,855.7
255	Decatur, IL	1,854.9
256	Oshkosh-Neenah, WI	1,842.6
257	Boulder, CO	1,839.3
258	Ann Arbor, MI	1,835.9
259	Clarksville, TN-KY	1,830.7
260	Kennewick-Pasco-Richland, WA	1,824.0
261	Barnstable Town, MA	1,822.5
262	Elkhart-Goshen, IN	1,816.8
263	Lewiston-Auburn, ME	1,809.3
264	Winchester, VA-WV	1,807.2
265	Fayetteville, AR-MO	1,802.7
266	Sioux City, IA-NE-SD	1,795.5
267	Grand Forks, ND-MN	1,788.5
268	Cape Coral-Fort Myers, FL	1,785.9
269	Raleigh-Cary, NC	1,783.4
270	Bremerton-Silverdale, WA	1,780.4
271	Provo-Orem, UT	1,776.9
272	Manchester-Nashua, NH	1,776.6
273	Camden, NJ M.D.	1,776.0
274	Allentown, PA-NJ	1,775.4
275	Syracuse, NY	1,771.4
276	Bay City, MI	1,767.2
277	Las Vegas-Paradise, NV	1,763.2
278	Elmira, NY	1,753.4
278	Providence-New Bedford, RI-MA	1,753.4
280	Boston-Quincy, MA M.D.	1,751.2
281	Pueblo, CO	1,739.8
282	Manhattan, KS	1,737.9
283	Vallejo-Fairfield, CA	1,723.1
284	Detroit (greater), MI	1,723.0
285	Sioux Falls, SD	1,717.9
286	Cleveland-Elyria-Mentor, OH	1,714.4
287	Ocala, FL	1,706.5
288	Saginaw, MI	1,704.5
289	Chico, CA	1,700.0
290	Harrisburg-Carlisle, PA	1,699.4
291	Waterloo-Cedar Falls, IA	1,692.2
292	Morgantown, WV	1,691.7
293	Erie, PA	1,682.1
294	Greeley, CO	1,679.5
295	Monroe, MI	1,677.6
296	Farmington, NM	1,673.5
296	Jefferson City, MO	1,673.5
298	Rochester, MN	1,670.2
299	Scranton--Wilkes-Barre, PA	1,667.8
300	Appleton, WI	1,660.6
301	Bismarck, ND	1,655.9
302	Santa Fe, NM	1,655.0
303	Palm Coast, FL	1,644.7
304	York-Hanover, PA	1,622.6
305	Idaho Falls, ID	1,622.5
306	Riverside-San Bernardino, CA	1,611.8
307	Eau Claire, WI	1,611.2
308	Dubuque, IA	1,605.7
309	Hagerstown-Martinsburg, MD-WV	1,603.2
310	Poughkeepsie, NY	1,599.0
311	Yuma, AZ	1,594.3
312	Reading, PA	1,590.2
313	San Jose, CA	1,582.8
314	Gainesville, GA	1,577.7
315	San Luis Obispo, CA	1,565.0
316	Redding, CA	1,564.1
317	Napa, CA	1,560.5
318	Boston (greater), MA-NH	1,560.0
319	Rockingham County, NH M.D.	1,542.5
320	State College, PA	1,536.5
321	Asheville, NC	1,534.5
322	Salinas, CA	1,532.9
323	Lancaster, PA	1,532.6
324	Worcester, MA	1,491.9
325	Fond du Lac, WI	1,491.5
326	Pittsburgh, PA	1,487.4
327	Peabody, MA M.D.	1,486.8
328	Boise City-Nampa, ID	1,476.8
329	Trenton-Ewing, NJ	1,475.6
330	Santa Barbara-Santa Maria, CA	1,467.3
331	Los Angeles County, CA M.D.	1,465.9
332	Carson City, NV	1,463.4
333	Los Angeles (greater), CA	1,460.2
334	Prescott, AZ	1,454.6
335	Green Bay, WI	1,454.2
336	Warren-Farmington Hills, MI M.D.	1,451.3
337	Altoona, PA	1,448.8
338	Iowa City, IA	1,445.0
339	Santa Ana-Anaheim, CA M.D.	1,441.8
340	Kingston, NY	1,438.1
341	Williamsport, PA	1,436.5
342	Santa Rosa-Petaluma, CA	1,432.1
343	Pittsfield, MA	1,429.6
344	Lynchburg, VA	1,417.3
345	Edison, NJ M.D.	1,416.5
346	Wheeling, WV-OH	1,406.4
347	Oxnard-Thousand Oaks, CA	1,403.2
348	Bridgeport-Stamford, CT	1,383.1
349	Elizabethtown, KY	1,377.4
350	Yuba City, CA	1,375.6
351	San Diego, CA	1,371.0
352	Cambridge-Newton, MA M.D.	1,358.2
353	Naples-Marco Island, FL	1,357.7
354	Nassau-Suffolk, NY M.D.	1,346.5
355	New York (greater), NY-NJ-PA	1,329.0
356	New York-W. Plains NY-NJ M.D.	1,324.0
357	Lebanon, PA	1,306.0
358	Holland-Grand Haven, MI	1,303.6
359	Glens Falls, NY	1,301.5
360	Wausau, WI	1,270.3
361	St. George, UT	1,264.7
362	Newark-Union, NJ-PA M.D.	1,236.0
363	Logan, UT-ID	1,209.1
364	Harrisonburg, VA	1,195.5
365	Madera, CA	983.7
NA	El Centro, CA**	NA
NA	Hattiesburg, MS**	NA
NA	Toledo, OH**	NA
NA	Tucson, AZ**	NA

Source: Reported data from the F.B.I. "Crime in the United States 2009"
*Larceny-theft is the unlawful taking of property. Attempts are included.
**Not available.

35. Percent Change in Larceny-Theft Rate: 2008 to 2009
National Percent Change = 4.8% Decrease*

RANK	METROPOLITAN AREA	% CHANGE
15	Abilene, TX	10.6
89	Akron, OH	(0.7)
69	Albany-Schenectady-Troy, NY	0.7
NA	Albany, GA**	NA
254	Albuquerque, NM	(10.7)
NA	Alexandria, LA**	NA
257	Allentown, PA-NJ	(10.9)
157	Altoona, PA	(4.5)
27	Amarillo, TX	7.2
51	Ames, IA	3.0
40	Anchorage, AK	4.5
NA	Anderson, IN**	NA
283	Anderson, SC	(14.0)
116	Ann Arbor, MI	(2.7)
NA	Anniston-Oxford, AL**	NA
306	Appleton, WI	(22.8)
292	Asheville, NC	(15.5)
302	Athens-Clarke County, GA	(20.2)
258	Atlanta, GA	(11.0)
67	Atlantic City, NJ	1.0
175	Auburn, AL	(5.4)
199	Augusta, GA-SC	(7.0)
35	Austin-Round Rock, TX	5.4
136	Bakersfield, CA	(3.5)
190	Baltimore-Towson, MD	(6.2)
55	Bangor, ME	2.4
144	Barnstable Town, MA	(4.2)
23	Baton Rouge, LA	8.0
274	Battle Creek, MI	(12.4)
NA	Bay City, MI**	NA
28	Beaumont-Port Arthur, TX	6.7
121	Bellingham, WA	(3.0)
284	Bend, OR	(14.1)
168	Bethesda-Frederick, MD M.D.	(5.0)
29	Billings, MT	6.3
232	Binghamton, NY	(9.0)
132	Birmingham-Hoover, AL	(3.4)
148	Bismarck, ND	(4.3)
126	Blacksburg, VA	(3.1)
39	Bloomington, IN	4.6
258	Boise City-Nampa, ID	(11.0)
137	Boston (greater), MA-NH	(3.6)
161	Boston-Quincy, MA M.D.	(4.6)
NA	Boulder, CO**	NA
NA	Bowling Green, KY**	NA
144	Bremerton-Silverdale, WA	(4.2)
204	Bridgeport-Stamford, CT	(7.1)
75	Brownsville-Harlingen, TX	0.0
NA	Brunswick, GA**	NA
92	Buffalo-Niagara Falls, NY	(0.9)
NA	Burlington-South Burlington, VT**	NA
107	Burlington, NC	(2.0)
225	Cambridge-Newton, MA M.D.	(8.6)
237	Camden, NJ M.D.	(9.2)
302	Cape Coral-Fort Myers, FL	(20.2)
206	Cape Girardeau, MO-IL	(7.3)
236	Carson City, NV	(9.1)
51	Casper, WY	3.0
168	Cedar Rapids, IA	(5.0)
171	Charleston-North Charleston, SC	(5.1)
269	Charleston, WV	(11.8)
280	Charlotte-Gastonia, NC-SC	(13.6)
37	Charlottesville, VA	5.1
102	Chattanooga, TN-GA	(1.6)
225	Cheyenne, WY	(8.6)
199	Chico, CA	(7.0)
NA	Cincinnati-Middletown, OH-KY-IN**	NA
NA	Clarksville, TN-KY**	NA
NA	Cleveland-Elyria-Mentor, OH**	NA
262	Cleveland, TN	(11.3)
NA	Coeur d'Alene, ID**	NA
17	College Station-Bryan, TX	10.0
237	Colorado Springs, CO	(9.2)
65	Columbia, MO	1.2
80	Columbia, SC	(0.4)
95	Columbus, GA-AL	(1.1)
71	Columbus, IN	0.6
57	Columbus, OH	2.2
196	Corpus Christi, TX	(6.9)
5	Corvallis, OR	20.6
NA	Crestview-Fort Walton Beach, FL**	NA
109	Cumberland, MD-WV	(2.2)
129	Dallas (greater), TX	(3.2)
143	Dallas-Plano-Irving, TX M.D.	(4.1)
76	Dalton, GA	(0.1)
NA	Danville, IL**	NA
288	Danville, VA	(14.8)
113	Dayton, OH	(2.6)
277	Decatur, AL	(12.9)
NA	Decatur, IL**	NA
167	Deltona-Daytona Beach, FL	(4.9)
83	Denver-Aurora, CO	(0.5)
NA	Des Moines-West Des Moines, IA**	NA
NA	Detroit (greater), MI**	NA
NA	Detroit-Livonia-Dearborn, MI M.D.**	NA
286	Dothan, AL	(14.2)
61	Dover, DE	2.0
121	Dubuque, IA	(3.0)
132	Duluth, MN-WI	(3.4)
195	Durham-Chapel Hill, NC	(6.7)
144	Eau Claire, WI	(4.2)
184	Edison, NJ M.D.	(5.8)
NA	El Centro, CA**	NA
111	El Paso, TX	(2.5)
NA	Elizabethtown, KY**	NA
308	Elkhart-Goshen, IN	(26.2)
199	Elmira, NY	(7.0)
141	Erie, PA	(3.8)
296	Eugene-Springfield, OR	(16.0)
NA	Evansville, IN-KY**	NA
90	Fargo, ND-MN	(0.8)
1	Farmington, NM	33.4
43	Fayetteville, AR-MO	3.9
232	Fayetteville, NC	(9.0)
249	Flagstaff, AZ	(10.4)
NA	Flint, MI**	NA
293	Florence-Muscle Shoals, AL	(15.6)
193	Florence, SC	(6.6)
155	Fond du Lac, WI	(4.4)
63	Fort Collins-Loveland, CO	1.4
111	Fort Lauderdale, FL M.D.	(2.5)
10	Fort Smith, AR-OK	14.5
223	Fort Wayne, IN	(8.5)
103	Fort Worth-Arlington, TX M.D.	(1.7)
227	Fresno, CA	(8.7)
140	Gadsden, AL	(3.7)
76	Gainesville, FL	(0.1)
NA	Gainesville, GA**	NA
261	Glens Falls, NY	(11.2)
247	Goldsboro, NC	(10.2)
255	Grand Forks, ND-MN	(10.8)
32	Grand Junction, CO	5.9
NA	Grand Rapids-Wyoming, MI**	NA
282	Great Falls, MT	(13.9)
193	Greeley, CO	(6.6)
304	Green Bay, WI	(20.6)
161	Greensboro-High Point, NC	(4.6)
NA	Gulfport-Biloxi, MS**	NA
196	Hagerstown-Martinsburg, MD-WV	(6.9)
83	Harrisburg-Carlisle, PA	(0.5)
34	Harrisonburg, VA	5.8
118	Hartford, CT	(2.8)
NA	Hattiesburg, MS**	NA
241	Hickory, NC	(9.5)
252	Hinesville, GA	(10.6)
NA	Holland-Grand Haven, MI**	NA
17	Honolulu, HI	10.0
275	Hot Springs, AR	(12.5)
64	Houma, LA	1.3
16	Houston, TX	10.2
267	Huntsville, AL	(11.7)
185	Idaho Falls, ID	(5.9)
148	Indianapolis, IN	(4.3)
144	Iowa City, IA	(4.2)
31	Ithaca, NY	6.0
227	Jacksonville, FL	(8.7)
121	Jacksonville, NC	(3.0)
NA	Jackson, MI**	NA
69	Jackson, MS	0.7
132	Jackson, TN	(3.4)
291	Janesville, WI	(15.4)
NA	Jefferson City, MO**	NA
181	Johnson City, TN	(5.6)
174	Jonesboro, AR	(5.3)
NA	Kalamazoo-Portage, MI**	NA
NA	Kansas City, MO-KS**	NA
87	Kennewick-Pasco-Richland, WA	(0.6)
68	Killeen-Temple-Fort Hood, TX	0.9
90	Kingsport, TN-VA	(0.8)
11	Kingston, NY	14.1
121	Knoxville, TN	(3.0)
199	Kokomo, IN	(7.0)
165	La Crosse, WI-MN	(4.8)
46	Lafayette, IN	3.6
4	Lafayette, LA	21.4
NA	Lake Charles, LA**	NA
87	Lake Havasu City-Kingman, AZ	(0.6)
252	Lakeland, FL	(10.6)
175	Lancaster, PA	(5.4)
NA	Lansing-East Lansing, MI**	NA

Note: All listings are for Metropolitan Statistical Areas (M.S.A.s) except for those ending with "M.D." Listings with "M.D." are Metropolitan Divisions which are smaller parts of eleven large M.S.A.s. See explanatory note at beginning of metropolitan area section.

RANK	METROPOLITAN AREA	% CHANGE
181	Laredo, TX	(5.6)
72	Las Cruces, NM	0.5
208	Las Vegas-Paradise, NV	(7.5)
137	Lawrence, KS	(3.6)
NA	Lawton, OK**	NA
178	Lebanon, PA	(5.5)
50	Lewiston-Auburn, ME	3.1
25	Lewiston, ID-WA	7.8
NA	Lexington-Fayette, KY**	NA
262	Lima, OH	(11.3)
168	Lincoln, NE	(5.0)
NA	Little Rock, AR**	NA
178	Logan, UT-ID	(5.5)
58	Longview, TX	2.1
126	Longview, WA	(3.1)
113	Los Angeles County, CA M.D.	(2.6)
118	Los Angeles (greater), CA	(2.8)
NA	Louisville, KY-IN**	NA
72	Lubbock, TX	0.5
298	Lynchburg, VA	(17.9)
227	Macon, GA	(8.7)
284	Madera, CA	(14.1)
83	Madison, WI	(0.5)
NA	Manchester-Nashua, NH**	NA
287	Manhattan, KS	(14.3)
83	Mankato-North Mankato, MN	(0.5)
192	Mansfield, OH	(6.4)
14	McAllen-Edinburg-Mission, TX	11.8
148	Medford, OR	(4.3)
264	Memphis, TN-MS-AR	(11.4)
247	Merced, CA	(10.2)
172	Miami (greater), FL	(5.2)
215	Miami-Dade County, FL M.D.	(8.2)
279	Michigan City-La Porte, IN	(13.2)
23	Midland, TX	8.0
118	Milwaukee, WI	(2.8)
230	Minneapolis-St. Paul, MN-WI	(8.8)
290	Missoula, MT	(15.2)
126	Mobile, AL	(3.1)
219	Modesto, CA	(8.4)
NA	Monroe, MI**	NA
272	Montgomery, AL	(12.2)
NA	Morgantown, WV**	NA
210	Morristown, TN	(7.8)
40	Mount Vernon-Anacortes, WA	4.5
223	Muncie, IN	(8.5)
NA	Muskegon-Norton Shores, MI**	NA
163	Napa, CA	(4.7)
130	Naples-Marco Island, FL	(3.3)
216	Nashville-Davidson, TN	(8.3)
79	Nassau-Suffolk, NY M.D.	(0.3)
NA	New Haven-Milford, CT**	NA
212	New Orleans, LA	(8.1)
157	New York (greater), NY-NJ-PA	(4.5)
148	New York-W. Plains NY-NJ M.D.	(4.3)
243	Newark-Union, NJ-PA M.D.	(9.7)
NA	Niles-Benton Harbor, MI**	NA
NA	North Port-Bradenton-Sarasota, FL**	NA
19	Norwich-New London, CT	9.4
208	Oakland-Fremont, CA M.D.	(7.5)
53	Ocala, FL	2.9
270	Ocean City, NJ	(12.0)
80	Odessa, TX	(0.4)

RANK	METROPOLITAN AREA	% CHANGE
74	Ogden-Clearfield, UT	0.2
NA	Oklahoma City, OK**	NA
295	Olympia, WA	(15.9)
105	Omaha-Council Bluffs, NE-IA	(1.8)
216	Orlando, FL	(8.3)
78	Oshkosh-Neenah, WI	(0.2)
NA	Owensboro, KY**	NA
108	Oxnard-Thousand Oaks, CA	(2.1)
49	Palm Bay-Melbourne, FL	3.2
58	Palm Coast, FL	2.1
26	Panama City-Lynn Haven, FL	7.4
196	Pascagoula, MS	(6.9)
38	Peabody, MA M.D.	5.0
66	Pensacola, FL	1.1
241	Philadelphia (greater) PA-NJ-MD-DE	(9.5)
244	Philadelphia, PA M.D.	(9.9)
276	Phoenix-Mesa-Scottsdale, AZ	(12.8)
300	Pine Bluff, AR	(19.6)
175	Pittsburgh, PA	(5.4)
62	Pittsfield, MA	1.7
137	Pocatello, ID	(3.6)
264	Port St. Lucie, FL	(11.4)
232	Portland-Vancouver, OR-WA	(9.0)
80	Portland, ME	(0.4)
105	Poughkeepsie, NY	(1.8)
232	Prescott, AZ	(9.0)
216	Providence-New Bedford, RI-MA	(8.3)
181	Provo-Orem, UT	(5.6)
NA	Pueblo, CO**	NA
293	Punta Gorda, FL	(15.6)
212	Racine, WI	(8.1)
163	Raleigh-Cary, NC	(4.7)
32	Rapid City, SD	5.9
207	Reading, PA	(7.4)
244	Redding, CA	(9.9)
266	Reno-Sparks, NV	(11.5)
113	Richmond, VA	(2.6)
219	Riverside-San Bernardino, CA	(8.4)
94	Roanoke, VA	(1.0)
30	Rochester, MN	6.2
36	Rochester, NY	5.3
43	Rockingham County, NH M.D.	3.9
NA	Rocky Mount, NC**	NA
NA	Rome, GA**	NA
148	Sacramento, CA	(4.3)
NA	Saginaw, MI**	NA
270	Salem, OR	(12.0)
165	Salinas, CA	(4.8)
97	Salisbury, MD	(1.3)
92	Salt Lake City, UT	(0.9)
148	San Angelo, TX	(4.3)
188	San Antonio, TX	(6.1)
281	San Diego, CA	(13.8)
188	San Francisco (greater), CA	(6.1)
148	San Francisco-S. Mateo, CA M.D.	(4.3)
98	San Jose, CA	(1.4)
157	San Luis Obispo, CA	(4.5)
260	Sandusky, OH	(11.1)
132	Santa Ana-Anaheim, CA M.D.	(3.4)
244	Santa Barbara-Santa Maria, CA	(9.9)
9	Santa Cruz-Watsonville, CA	14.8
6	Santa Fe, NM	20.3
12	Santa Rosa-Petaluma, CA	13.8

RANK	METROPOLITAN AREA	% CHANGE
141	Savannah, GA	(3.8)
157	Scranton--Wilkes-Barre, PA	(4.5)
NA	Seattle-Bellevue-Everett, WA M.D.**	NA
NA	Seattle-Tacoma-Bellevue, WA**	NA
199	Sebastian-Vero Beach, FL	(7.0)
212	Sheboygan, WI	(8.1)
13	Sherman-Denison, TX	13.5
109	Shreveport-Bossier City, LA	(2.2)
54	Sioux City, IA-NE-SD	2.5
7	Sioux Falls, SD	15.4
NA	South Bend-Mishawaka, IN-MI**	NA
219	Spartanburg, SC	(8.4)
8	Spokane, WA	15.1
99	Springfield, MA	(1.5)
NA	Springfield, MO**	NA
297	Springfield, OH	(16.5)
20	State College, PA	9.2
301	Stockton, CA	(19.7)
273	St. Cloud, MN	(12.3)
307	St. George, UT	(23.0)
130	St. Joseph, MO-KS	(3.3)
155	St. Louis, MO-IL	(4.4)
NA	Sumter, SC**	NA
46	Syracuse, NY	3.6
NA	Tacoma, WA M.D.**	NA
255	Tallahassee, FL	(10.8)
191	Tampa-St Petersburg, FL	(6.3)
58	Texarkana, TX-Texarkana, AR	2.1
NA	Toledo, OH**	NA
251	Topeka, KS	(10.5)
103	Trenton-Ewing, NJ	(1.7)
NA	Tucson, AZ**	NA
42	Tulsa, OK	4.2
99	Tuscaloosa, AL	(1.5)
3	Tyler, TX	21.7
21	Utica-Rome, NY	8.9
56	Valdosta, GA	2.3
289	Vallejo-Fairfield, CA	(15.0)
2	Victoria, TX	22.2
278	Vineland, NJ	(13.1)
239	Visalia-Porterville, CA	(9.4)
99	Waco, TX	(1.5)
267	Warner Robins, GA	(11.7)
NA	Warren-Farmington Hills, MI M.D.**	NA
205	Washington (greater) DC-VA-MD-WV	(7.2)
210	Washington, DC-VA-MD-WV M.D.	(7.8)
186	Waterloo-Cedar Falls, IA	(6.0)
NA	Wausau, WI**	NA
48	Wenatchee, WA	3.3
116	West Palm Beach, FL M.D.	(2.7)
95	Wheeling, WV-OH	(1.1)
299	Wichita Falls, TX	(18.0)
172	Wichita, KS	(5.2)
186	Williamsport, PA	(6.0)
219	Wilmington, DE-MD-NJ M.D.	(8.4)
43	Wilmington, NC	3.9
178	Winchester, VA-WV	(5.5)
249	Winston-Salem, NC	(10.4)
21	Worcester, MA	8.9
230	York-Hanover, PA	(8.8)
121	Youngstown, OH-PA	(3.0)
305	Yuba City, CA	(21.6)
239	Yuma, AZ	(9.4)

Source: CQ Press using reported data from the F.B.I. "Crime in the United States 2009"
*Larceny-theft is the unlawful taking of property. Attempts are included.
**Not available.

35. Percent Change in Larceny-Theft Rate: 2008 to 2009 (continued)
National Percent Change = 4.8% Decrease*

RANK	METROPOLITAN AREA	% CHANGE
1	Farmington, NM	33.4
2	Victoria, TX	22.2
3	Tyler, TX	21.7
4	Lafayette, LA	21.4
5	Corvallis, OR	20.6
6	Santa Fe, NM	20.3
7	Sioux Falls, SD	15.4
8	Spokane, WA	15.1
9	Santa Cruz-Watsonville, CA	14.8
10	Fort Smith, AR-OK	14.5
11	Kingston, NY	14.1
12	Santa Rosa-Petaluma, CA	13.8
13	Sherman-Denison, TX	13.5
14	McAllen-Edinburg-Mission, TX	11.8
15	Abilene, TX	10.6
16	Houston, TX	10.2
17	College Station-Bryan, TX	10.0
17	Honolulu, HI	10.0
19	Norwich-New London, CT	9.4
20	State College, PA	9.2
21	Utica-Rome, NY	8.9
21	Worcester, MA	8.9
23	Baton Rouge, LA	8.0
23	Midland, TX	8.0
25	Lewiston, ID-WA	7.8
26	Panama City-Lynn Haven, FL	7.4
27	Amarillo, TX	7.2
28	Beaumont-Port Arthur, TX	6.7
29	Billings, MT	6.3
30	Rochester, MN	6.2
31	Ithaca, NY	6.0
32	Grand Junction, CO	5.9
32	Rapid City, SD	5.9
34	Harrisonburg, VA	5.8
35	Austin-Round Rock, TX	5.4
36	Rochester, NY	5.3
37	Charlottesville, VA	5.1
38	Peabody, MA M.D.	5.0
39	Bloomington, IN	4.6
40	Anchorage, AK	4.5
40	Mount Vernon-Anacortes, WA	4.5
42	Tulsa, OK	4.2
43	Fayetteville, AR-MO	3.9
43	Rockingham County, NH M.D.	3.9
43	Wilmington, NC	3.9
46	Lafayette, IN	3.6
46	Syracuse, NY	3.6
48	Wenatchee, WA	3.3
49	Palm Bay-Melbourne, FL	3.2
50	Lewiston-Auburn, ME	3.1
51	Ames, IA	3.0
51	Casper, WY	3.0
53	Ocala, FL	2.9
54	Sioux City, IA-NE-SD	2.5
55	Bangor, ME	2.4
56	Valdosta, GA	2.3
57	Columbus, OH	2.2
58	Longview, TX	2.1
58	Palm Coast, FL	2.1
58	Texarkana, TX-Texarkana, AR	2.1
61	Dover, DE	2.0
62	Pittsfield, MA	1.7
63	Fort Collins-Loveland, CO	1.4
64	Houma, LA	1.3
65	Columbia, MO	1.2
66	Pensacola, FL	1.1
67	Atlantic City, NJ	1.0
68	Killeen-Temple-Fort Hood, TX	0.9
69	Albany-Schenectady-Troy, NY	0.7
69	Jackson, MS	0.7
71	Columbus, IN	0.6
72	Las Cruces, NM	0.5
72	Lubbock, TX	0.5
74	Ogden-Clearfield, UT	0.2
75	Brownsville-Harlingen, TX	0.0
76	Dalton, GA	(0.1)
76	Gainesville, FL	(0.1)
78	Oshkosh-Neenah, WI	(0.2)
79	Nassau-Suffolk, NY M.D.	(0.3)
80	Columbia, SC	(0.4)
80	Odessa, TX	(0.4)
80	Portland, ME	(0.4)
83	Denver-Aurora, CO	(0.5)
83	Harrisburg-Carlisle, PA	(0.5)
83	Madison, WI	(0.5)
83	Mankato-North Mankato, MN	(0.5)
87	Kennewick-Pasco-Richland, WA	(0.6)
87	Lake Havasu City-Kingman, AZ	(0.6)
89	Akron, OH	(0.7)
90	Fargo, ND-MN	(0.8)
90	Kingsport, TN-VA	(0.8)
92	Buffalo-Niagara Falls, NY	(0.9)
92	Salt Lake City, UT	(0.9)
94	Roanoke, VA	(1.0)
95	Columbus, GA-AL	(1.1)
95	Wheeling, WV-OH	(1.1)
97	Salisbury, MD	(1.3)
98	San Jose, CA	(1.4)
99	Springfield, MA	(1.5)
99	Tuscaloosa, AL	(1.5)
99	Waco, TX	(1.5)
102	Chattanooga, TN-GA	(1.6)
103	Fort Worth-Arlington, TX M.D.	(1.7)
103	Trenton-Ewing, NJ	(1.7)
105	Omaha-Council Bluffs, NE-IA	(1.8)
105	Poughkeepsie, NY	(1.8)
107	Burlington, NC	(2.0)
108	Oxnard-Thousand Oaks, CA	(2.1)
109	Cumberland, MD-WV	(2.2)
109	Shreveport-Bossier City, LA	(2.2)
111	El Paso, TX	(2.5)
111	Fort Lauderdale, FL M.D.	(2.5)
113	Dayton, OH	(2.6)
113	Los Angeles County, CA M.D.	(2.6)
113	Richmond, VA	(2.6)
116	Ann Arbor, MI	(2.7)
116	West Palm Beach, FL M.D.	(2.7)
118	Hartford, CT	(2.8)
118	Los Angeles (greater), CA	(2.8)
118	Milwaukee, WI	(2.8)
121	Bellingham, WA	(3.0)
121	Dubuque, IA	(3.0)
121	Jacksonville, NC	(3.0)
121	Knoxville, TN	(3.0)
121	Youngstown, OH-PA	(3.0)
126	Blacksburg, VA	(3.1)
126	Longview, WA	(3.1)
126	Mobile, AL	(3.1)
129	Dallas (greater), TX	(3.2)
130	Naples-Marco Island, FL	(3.3)
130	St. Joseph, MO-KS	(3.3)
132	Birmingham-Hoover, AL	(3.4)
132	Duluth, MN-WI	(3.4)
132	Jackson, TN	(3.4)
132	Santa Ana-Anaheim, CA M.D.	(3.4)
136	Bakersfield, CA	(3.5)
137	Boston (greater), MA-NH	(3.6)
137	Lawrence, KS	(3.6)
137	Pocatello, ID	(3.6)
140	Gadsden, AL	(3.7)
141	Erie, PA	(3.8)
141	Savannah, GA	(3.8)
143	Dallas-Plano-Irving, TX M.D.	(4.1)
144	Barnstable Town, MA	(4.2)
144	Bremerton-Silverdale, WA	(4.2)
144	Eau Claire, WI	(4.2)
144	Iowa City, IA	(4.2)
148	Bismarck, ND	(4.3)
148	Indianapolis, IN	(4.3)
148	Medford, OR	(4.3)
148	New York-W. Plains NY-NJ M.D.	(4.3)
148	Sacramento, CA	(4.3)
148	San Angelo, TX	(4.3)
148	San Francisco-S. Mateo, CA M.D.	(4.3)
155	Fond du Lac, WI	(4.4)
155	St. Louis, MO-IL	(4.4)
157	Altoona, PA	(4.5)
157	New York (greater), NY-NJ-PA	(4.5)
157	San Luis Obispo, CA	(4.5)
157	Scranton--Wilkes-Barre, PA	(4.5)
161	Boston-Quincy, MA M.D.	(4.6)
161	Greensboro-High Point, NC	(4.6)
163	Napa, CA	(4.7)
163	Raleigh-Cary, NC	(4.7)
165	La Crosse, WI-MN	(4.8)
165	Salinas, CA	(4.8)
167	Deltona-Daytona Beach, FL	(4.9)
168	Bethesda-Frederick, MD M.D.	(5.0)
168	Cedar Rapids, IA	(5.0)
168	Lincoln, NE	(5.0)
171	Charleston-North Charleston, SC	(5.1)
172	Miami (greater), FL	(5.2)
172	Wichita, KS	(5.2)
174	Jonesboro, AR	(5.3)
175	Auburn, AL	(5.4)
175	Lancaster, PA	(5.4)
175	Pittsburgh, PA	(5.4)
178	Lebanon, PA	(5.5)
178	Logan, UT-ID	(5.5)
178	Winchester, VA-WV	(5.5)

Note: All listings are for Metropolitan Statistical Areas (M.S.A.s) except for those ending with "M.D." Listings with "M.D." are Metropolitan Divisions which are smaller parts of eleven large M.S.A.s. See explanatory note at beginning of metropolitan area section.

RANK	METROPOLITAN AREA	% CHANGE
181	Johnson City, TN	(5.6)
181	Laredo, TX	(5.6)
181	Provo-Orem, UT	(5.6)
184	Edison, NJ M.D.	(5.8)
185	Idaho Falls, ID	(5.9)
186	Waterloo-Cedar Falls, IA	(6.0)
186	Williamsport, PA	(6.0)
188	San Antonio, TX	(6.1)
188	San Francisco (greater), CA	(6.1)
190	Baltimore-Towson, MD	(6.2)
191	Tampa-St Petersburg, FL	(6.3)
192	Mansfield, OH	(6.4)
193	Florence, SC	(6.6)
193	Greeley, CO	(6.6)
195	Durham-Chapel Hill, NC	(6.7)
196	Corpus Christi, TX	(6.9)
196	Hagerstown-Martinsburg, MD-WV	(6.9)
196	Pascagoula, MS	(6.9)
199	Augusta, GA-SC	(7.0)
199	Chico, CA	(7.0)
199	Elmira, NY	(7.0)
199	Kokomo, IN	(7.0)
199	Sebastian-Vero Beach, FL	(7.0)
204	Bridgeport-Stamford, CT	(7.1)
205	Washington (greater) DC-VA-MD-WV	(7.2)
206	Cape Girardeau, MO-IL	(7.3)
207	Reading, PA	(7.4)
208	Las Vegas-Paradise, NV	(7.5)
208	Oakland-Fremont, CA M.D.	(7.5)
210	Morristown, TN	(7.8)
210	Washington, DC-VA-MD-WV M.D.	(7.8)
212	New Orleans, LA	(8.1)
212	Racine, WI	(8.1)
212	Sheboygan, WI	(8.1)
215	Miami-Dade County, FL M.D.	(8.2)
216	Nashville-Davidson, TN	(8.3)
216	Orlando, FL	(8.3)
216	Providence-New Bedford, RI-MA	(8.3)
219	Modesto, CA	(8.4)
219	Riverside-San Bernardino, CA	(8.4)
219	Spartanburg, SC	(8.4)
219	Wilmington, DE-MD-NJ M.D.	(8.4)
223	Fort Wayne, IN	(8.5)
223	Muncie, IN	(8.5)
225	Cambridge-Newton, MA M.D.	(8.6)
225	Cheyenne, WY	(8.6)
227	Fresno, CA	(8.7)
227	Jacksonville, FL	(8.7)
227	Macon, GA	(8.7)
230	Minneapolis-St. Paul, MN-WI	(8.8)
230	York-Hanover, PA	(8.8)
232	Binghamton, NY	(9.0)
232	Fayetteville, NC	(9.0)
232	Portland-Vancouver, OR-WA	(9.0)
232	Prescott, AZ	(9.0)
236	Carson City, NV	(9.1)
237	Camden, NJ M.D.	(9.2)
237	Colorado Springs, CO	(9.2)
239	Visalia-Porterville, CA	(9.4)
239	Yuma, AZ	(9.4)
241	Hickory, NC	(9.5)
241	Philadelphia (greater) PA-NJ-MD-DE	(9.5)
243	Newark-Union, NJ-PA M.D.	(9.7)

RANK	METROPOLITAN AREA	% CHANGE
244	Philadelphia, PA M.D.	(9.9)
244	Redding, CA	(9.9)
244	Santa Barbara-Santa Maria, CA	(9.9)
247	Goldsboro, NC	(10.2)
247	Merced, CA	(10.2)
249	Flagstaff, AZ	(10.4)
249	Winston-Salem, NC	(10.4)
251	Topeka, KS	(10.5)
252	Hinesville, GA	(10.6)
252	Lakeland, FL	(10.6)
254	Albuquerque, NM	(10.7)
255	Grand Forks, ND-MN	(10.8)
255	Tallahassee, FL	(10.8)
257	Allentown, PA-NJ	(10.9)
258	Atlanta, GA	(11.0)
258	Boise City-Nampa, ID	(11.0)
260	Sandusky, OH	(11.1)
261	Glens Falls, NY	(11.2)
262	Cleveland, TN	(11.3)
262	Lima, OH	(11.3)
264	Memphis, TN-MS-AR	(11.4)
264	Port St. Lucie, FL	(11.4)
266	Reno-Sparks, NV	(11.5)
267	Huntsville, AL	(11.7)
267	Warner Robins, GA	(11.7)
269	Charleston, WV	(11.8)
270	Ocean City, NJ	(12.0)
270	Salem, OR	(12.0)
272	Montgomery, AL	(12.2)
273	St. Cloud, MN	(12.3)
274	Battle Creek, MI	(12.4)
275	Hot Springs, AR	(12.5)
276	Phoenix-Mesa-Scottsdale, AZ	(12.8)
277	Decatur, AL	(12.9)
278	Vineland, NJ	(13.1)
279	Michigan City-La Porte, IN	(13.2)
280	Charlotte-Gastonia, NC-SC	(13.6)
281	San Diego, CA	(13.8)
282	Great Falls, MT	(13.9)
283	Anderson, SC	(14.0)
284	Bend, OR	(14.1)
284	Madera, CA	(14.1)
286	Dothan, AL	(14.2)
287	Manhattan, KS	(14.3)
288	Danville, VA	(14.8)
289	Vallejo-Fairfield, CA	(15.0)
290	Missoula, MT	(15.2)
291	Janesville, WI	(15.4)
292	Asheville, NC	(15.5)
293	Florence-Muscle Shoals, AL	(15.6)
293	Punta Gorda, FL	(15.6)
295	Olympia, WA	(15.9)
296	Eugene-Springfield, OR	(16.0)
297	Springfield, OH	(16.5)
298	Lynchburg, VA	(17.9)
299	Wichita Falls, TX	(18.0)
300	Pine Bluff, AR	(19.6)
301	Stockton, CA	(19.7)
302	Athens-Clarke County, GA	(20.2)
302	Cape Coral-Fort Myers, FL	(20.2)
304	Green Bay, WI	(20.6)
305	Yuba City, CA	(21.6)
306	Appleton, WI	(22.8)

RANK	METROPOLITAN AREA	% CHANGE
307	St. George, UT	(23.0)
308	Elkhart-Goshen, IN	(26.2)
NA	Albany, GA**	NA
NA	Alexandria, LA**	NA
NA	Anderson, IN**	NA
NA	Anniston-Oxford, AL**	NA
NA	Bay City, MI**	NA
NA	Boulder, CO**	NA
NA	Bowling Green, KY**	NA
NA	Brunswick, GA**	NA
NA	Burlington-South Burlington, VT**	NA
NA	Cincinnati-Middletown, OH-KY-IN**	NA
NA	Clarksville, TN-KY**	NA
NA	Cleveland-Elyria-Mentor, OH**	NA
NA	Coeur d'Alene, ID**	NA
NA	Crestview-Fort Walton Beach, FL**	NA
NA	Danville, IL**	NA
NA	Decatur, IL**	NA
NA	Des Moines-West Des Moines, IA**	NA
NA	Detroit (greater), MI**	NA
NA	Detroit-Livonia-Dearborn, MI M.D.**	NA
NA	El Centro, CA**	NA
NA	Elizabethtown, KY**	NA
NA	Evansville, IN-KY**	NA
NA	Flint, MI**	NA
NA	Gainesville, GA**	NA
NA	Grand Rapids-Wyoming, MI**	NA
NA	Gulfport-Biloxi, MS**	NA
NA	Hattiesburg, MS**	NA
NA	Holland-Grand Haven, MI**	NA
NA	Jackson, MI**	NA
NA	Jefferson City, MO**	NA
NA	Kalamazoo-Portage, MI**	NA
NA	Kansas City, MO-KS**	NA
NA	Lake Charles, LA**	NA
NA	Lansing-East Lansing, MI**	NA
NA	Lawton, OK**	NA
NA	Lexington-Fayette, KY**	NA
NA	Little Rock, AR**	NA
NA	Louisville, KY-IN**	NA
NA	Manchester-Nashua, NH**	NA
NA	Monroe, MI**	NA
NA	Morgantown, WV**	NA
NA	Muskegon-Norton Shores, MI**	NA
NA	New Haven-Milford, CT**	NA
NA	Niles-Benton Harbor, MI**	NA
NA	North Port-Bradenton-Sarasota, FL**	NA
NA	Oklahoma City, OK**	NA
NA	Owensboro, KY**	NA
NA	Pueblo, CO**	NA
NA	Rocky Mount, NC**	NA
NA	Rome, GA**	NA
NA	Saginaw, MI**	NA
NA	Seattle-Bellevue-Everett, WA M.D.**	NA
NA	Seattle-Tacoma-Bellevue, WA**	NA
NA	South Bend-Mishawaka, IN-MI**	NA
NA	Springfield, MO**	NA
NA	Sumter, SC**	NA
NA	Tacoma, WA M.D.**	NA
NA	Toledo, OH**	NA
NA	Tucson, AZ**	NA
NA	Warren-Farmington Hills, MI M.D.**	NA
NA	Wausau, WI**	NA

Source: CQ Press using reported data from the F.B.I. "Crime in the United States 2009"
*Larceny-theft is the unlawful taking of property. Attempts are included.
**Not available.

36. Percent Change in Larceny-Theft Rate: 2005 to 2009
National Percent Change = 9.9% Decrease*

RANK	METROPOLITAN AREA	% CHANGE
103	Abilene, TX	(5.5)
173	Akron, OH	(12.2)
59	Albany-Schenectady-Troy, NY	0.1
22	Albany, GA	9.7
182	Albuquerque, NM	(13.0)
60	Alexandria, LA	(0.3)
140	Allentown, PA-NJ	(8.7)
204	Altoona, PA	(15.8)
142	Amarillo, TX	(8.9)
24	Ames, IA	8.5
160	Anchorage, AK	(10.7)
41	Anderson, IN	3.5
227	Anderson, SC	(18.3)
150	Ann Arbor, MI	(9.8)
NA	Anniston-Oxford, AL**	NA
101	Appleton, WI	(5.2)
272	Asheville, NC	(26.4)
226	Athens-Clarke County, GA	(18.2)
209	Atlanta, GA	(16.3)
212	Atlantic City, NJ	(16.7)
131	Auburn, AL	(7.7)
99	Augusta, GA-SC	(5.1)
74	Austin-Round Rock, TX	(1.6)
243	Bakersfield, CA	(21.1)
76	Baltimore-Towson, MD	(2.2)
3	Bangor, ME	18.8
1	Barnstable Town, MA	30.9
174	Baton Rouge, LA	(12.3)
203	Battle Creek, MI	(15.7)
NA	Bay City, MI**	NA
178	Beaumont-Port Arthur, TX	(12.6)
288	Bellingham, WA	(32.7)
300	Bend, OR	(40.2)
15	Bethesda-Frederick, MD M.D.	11.3
258	Billings, MT	(24.0)
66	Binghamton, NY	(0.7)
NA	Birmingham-Hoover, AL**	NA
89	Bismarck, ND	(4.1)
106	Blacksburg, VA	(5.6)
63	Bloomington, IN	(0.6)
NA	Boise City-Nampa, ID**	NA
33	Boston (greater), MA-NH	5.3
66	Boston-Quincy, MA M.D.	(0.7)
NA	Boulder, CO**	NA
NA	Bowling Green, KY**	NA
106	Bremerton-Silverdale, WA	(5.6)
174	Bridgeport-Stamford, CT	(12.3)
87	Brownsville-Harlingen, TX	(3.9)
68	Brunswick, GA	(1.0)
37	Buffalo-Niagara Falls, NY	4.1
NA	Burlington-South Burlington, VT**	NA
106	Burlington, NC	(5.6)
31	Cambridge-Newton, MA M.D.	5.5
61	Camden, NJ M.D.	(0.5)
219	Cape Coral-Fort Myers, FL	(17.2)
NA	Cape Girardeau, MO-IL**	NA
157	Carson City, NV	(10.6)
218	Casper, WY	(17.1)
215	Cedar Rapids, IA	(17.0)
186	Charleston-North Charleston, SC	(13.2)
264	Charleston, WV	(25.0)
224	Charlotte-Gastonia, NC-SC	(17.9)
50	Charlottesville, VA	1.2
154	Chattanooga, TN-GA	(10.2)
169	Cheyenne, WY	(12.1)
79	Chico, CA	(3.0)
NA	Cincinnati-Middletown, OH-KY-IN**	NA
NA	Clarksville, TN-KY**	NA
NA	Cleveland-Elyria-Mentor, OH**	NA
NA	Cleveland, TN**	NA
253	Coeur d'Alene, ID	(22.4)
90	College Station-Bryan, TX	(4.3)
290	Colorado Springs, CO	(32.9)
27	Columbia, MO	6.5
103	Columbia, SC	(5.5)
33	Columbus, GA-AL	5.3
222	Columbus, IN	(17.5)
115	Columbus, OH	(6.3)
253	Corpus Christi, TX	(22.4)
273	Corvallis, OR	(26.9)
NA	Crestview-Fort Walton Beach, FL**	NA
26	Cumberland, MD-WV	7.3
229	Dallas (greater), TX	(18.4)
238	Dallas-Plano-Irving, TX M.D.	(20.1)
NA	Dalton, GA**	NA
NA	Danville, IL**	NA
36	Danville, VA	4.4
137	Dayton, OH	(8.4)
181	Decatur, AL	(12.8)
NA	Decatur, IL**	NA
NA	Deltona-Daytona Beach, FL**	NA
285	Denver-Aurora, CO	(32.0)
NA	Des Moines-West Des Moines, IA**	NA
102	Detroit (greater), MI	(5.4)
NA	Detroit-Livonia-Dearborn, MI M.D.**	NA
246	Dothan, AL	(21.4)
9	Dover, DE	12.8
71	Dubuque, IA	(1.4)
NA	Duluth, MN-WI**	NA
206	Durham-Chapel Hill, NC	(16.1)
153	Eau Claire, WI	(10.1)
54	Edison, NJ M.D.	0.5
NA	El Centro, CA**	NA
84	El Paso, TX	(3.7)
NA	Elizabethtown, KY**	NA
293	Elkhart-Goshen, IN	(34.2)
271	Elmira, NY	(26.1)
7	Erie, PA	14.1
251	Eugene-Springfield, OR	(22.2)
NA	Evansville, IN-KY**	NA
12	Fargo, ND-MN	12.4
93	Farmington, NM	(4.6)
260	Fayetteville, AR-MO	(24.5)
58	Fayetteville, NC	0.3
270	Flagstaff, AZ	(26.0)
NA	Flint, MI**	NA
NA	Florence-Muscle Shoals, AL**	NA
184	Florence, SC	(13.1)
70	Fond du Lac, WI	(1.3)
82	Fort Collins-Loveland, CO	(3.4)
17	Fort Lauderdale, FL M.D.	10.8
148	Fort Smith, AR-OK	(9.4)
207	Fort Wayne, IN	(16.2)
196	Fort Worth-Arlington, TX M.D.	(15.0)
243	Fresno, CA	(21.1)
247	Gadsden, AL	(21.8)
39	Gainesville, FL	3.8
297	Gainesville, GA	(37.0)
NA	Glens Falls, NY**	NA
145	Goldsboro, NC	(9.1)
284	Grand Forks, ND-MN	(31.8)
255	Grand Junction, CO	(22.9)
NA	Grand Rapids-Wyoming, MI**	NA
286	Great Falls, MT	(32.1)
301	Greeley, CO	(43.3)
223	Green Bay, WI	(17.8)
110	Greensboro-High Point, NC	(5.7)
NA	Gulfport-Biloxi, MS**	NA
77	Hagerstown-Martinsburg, MD-WV	(2.8)
144	Harrisburg-Carlisle, PA	(9.0)
42	Harrisonburg, VA	2.9
182	Hartford, CT	(13.0)
NA	Hattiesburg, MS**	NA
118	Hickory, NC	(6.5)
239	Hinesville, GA	(20.2)
NA	Holland-Grand Haven, MI**	NA
234	Honolulu, HI	(19.4)
273	Hot Springs, AR	(26.9)
157	Houma, LA	(10.6)
54	Houston, TX	0.5
277	Huntsville, AL	(28.4)
215	Idaho Falls, ID	(17.0)
136	Indianapolis, IN	(8.2)
169	Iowa City, IA	(12.1)
NA	Ithaca, NY**	NA
95	Jacksonville, FL	(4.9)
NA	Jacksonville, NC**	NA
NA	Jackson, MI**	NA
110	Jackson, MS	(5.7)
120	Jackson, TN	(6.7)
242	Janesville, WI	(20.3)
178	Jefferson City, MO	(12.6)
276	Johnson City, TN	(28.1)
256	Jonesboro, AR	(23.5)
NA	Kalamazoo-Portage, MI**	NA
265	Kansas City, MO-KS	(25.4)
288	Kennewick-Pasco-Richland, WA	(32.7)
187	Killeen-Temple-Fort Hood, TX	(13.3)
113	Kingsport, TN-VA	(6.2)
133	Kingston, NY	(7.9)
113	Knoxville, TN	(6.2)
194	Kokomo, IN	(14.7)
32	La Crosse, WI-MN	5.4
128	Lafayette, IN	(7.4)
14	Lafayette, LA	11.9
209	Lake Charles, LA	(16.3)
NA	Lake Havasu City-Kingman, AZ**	NA
192	Lakeland, FL	(14.3)
135	Lancaster, PA	(8.1)
NA	Lansing-East Lansing, MI**	NA

Note: All listings are for Metropolitan Statistical Areas (M.S.A.s) except for those ending with "M.D." Listings with "M.D." are Metropolitan Divisions which are smaller parts of eleven large M.S.A.s. See explanatory note at beginning of metropolitan area section.

Alpha Order - Metro Area (continued)

RANK	METROPOLITAN AREA	% CHANGE
124	Laredo, TX	(7.2)
46	Las Cruces, NM	2.3
220	Las Vegas-Paradise, NV	(17.3)
22	Lawrence, KS	9.7
NA	Lawton, OK**	NA
225	Lebanon, PA	(18.1)
187	Lewiston-Auburn, ME	(13.3)
227	Lewiston, ID-WA	(18.3)
NA	Lexington-Fayette, KY**	NA
140	Lima, OH	(8.7)
275	Lincoln, NE	(27.9)
NA	Little Rock, AR**	NA
231	Logan, UT-ID	(19.0)
80	Longview, TX	(3.2)
293	Longview, WA	(34.2)
116	Los Angeles County, CA M.D.	(6.4)
112	Los Angeles (greater), CA	(6.0)
NA	Louisville, KY-IN**	NA
155	Lubbock, TX	(10.5)
118	Lynchburg, VA	(6.5)
247	Macon, GA	(21.8)
296	Madera, CA	(36.6)
120	Madison, WI	(6.7)
6	Manchester-Nashua, NH	14.4
NA	Manhattan, KS**	NA
NA	Mankato-North Mankato, MN**	NA
211	Mansfield, OH	(16.4)
130	McAllen-Edinburg-Mission, TX	(7.5)
282	Medford, OR	(30.5)
169	Memphis, TN-MS-AR	(12.1)
197	Merced, CA	(15.1)
46	Miami (greater), FL	2.3
71	Miami-Dade County, FL M.D.	(1.4)
199	Michigan City-La Porte, IN	(15.4)
86	Midland, TX	(3.8)
30	Milwaukee, WI	5.8
NA	Minneapolis-St. Paul, MN-WI**	NA
302	Missoula, MT	(45.5)
44	Mobile, AL	2.7
260	Modesto, CA	(24.5)
NA	Monroe, MI**	NA
184	Montgomery, AL	(13.1)
53	Morgantown, WV	0.6
88	Morristown, TN	(4.0)
298	Mount Vernon-Anacortes, WA	(37.1)
169	Muncie, IN	(12.1)
NA	Muskegon-Norton Shores, MI**	NA
139	Napa, CA	(8.5)
151	Naples-Marco Island, FL	(9.9)
239	Nashville-Davidson, TN	(20.2)
29	Nassau-Suffolk, NY M.D.	5.9
NA	New Haven-Milford, CT**	NA
NA	New Orleans, LA**	NA
106	New York (greater), NY-NJ-PA	(5.6)
133	New York-W. Plains NY-NJ M.D.	(7.9)
189	Newark-Union, NJ-PA M.D.	(13.5)
NA	Niles-Benton Harbor, MI**	NA
NA	North Port-Bradenton-Sarasota, FL**	NA
35	Norwich-New London, CT	5.1
162	Oakland-Fremont, CA M.D.	(11.1)
123	Ocala, FL	(7.0)
82	Ocean City, NJ	(3.4)
128	Odessa, TX	(7.4)

RANK	METROPOLITAN AREA	% CHANGE
167	Ogden-Clearfield, UT	(12.0)
NA	Oklahoma City, OK**	NA
236	Olympia, WA	(19.8)
215	Omaha-Council Bluffs, NE-IA	(17.0)
92	Orlando, FL	(4.4)
13	Oshkosh-Neenah, WI	12.3
NA	Owensboro, KY**	NA
43	Oxnard-Thousand Oaks, CA	2.8
19	Palm Bay-Melbourne, FL	10.4
NA	Palm Coast, FL**	NA
56	Panama City-Lynn Haven, FL	0.4
78	Pascagoula, MS	(2.9)
NA	Peabody, MA M.D.**	NA
40	Pensacola, FL	3.7
49	Philadelphia (greater) PA-NJ-MD-DE	1.5
56	Philadelphia, PA M.D.	0.4
259	Phoenix-Mesa-Scottsdale, AZ	(24.1)
195	Pine Bluff, AR	(14.8)
205	Pittsburgh, PA	(15.9)
16	Pittsfield, MA	11.1
116	Pocatello, ID	(6.4)
61	Port St. Lucie, FL	(0.5)
279	Portland-Vancouver, OR-WA	(29.4)
63	Portland, ME	(0.6)
25	Poughkeepsie, NY	8.4
282	Prescott, AZ	(30.5)
NA	Providence-New Bedford, RI-MA**	NA
263	Provo-Orem, UT	(24.7)
303	Pueblo, CO	(57.2)
146	Punta Gorda, FL	(9.2)
256	Racine, WI	(23.5)
132	Raleigh-Cary, NC	(7.8)
80	Rapid City, SD	(3.2)
164	Reading, PA	(11.6)
249	Redding, CA	(22.0)
231	Reno-Sparks, NV	(19.0)
243	Richmond, VA	(21.1)
239	Riverside-San Bernardino, CA	(20.2)
201	Roanoke, VA	(15.6)
11	Rochester, MN	12.6
99	Rochester, NY	(5.1)
2	Rockingham County, NH M.D.	22.9
221	Rocky Mount, NC	(17.4)
295	Rome, GA	(35.2)
167	Sacramento, CA	(12.0)
NA	Saginaw, MI**	NA
290	Salem, OR	(32.9)
287	Salinas, CA	(32.6)
137	Salisbury, MD	(8.4)
163	Salt Lake City, UT	(11.4)
252	San Angelo, TX	(22.3)
51	San Antonio, TX	0.8
265	San Diego, CA	(25.4)
103	San Francisco (greater), CA	(5.5)
44	San Francisco-S. Mateo, CA M.D.	2.7
126	San Jose, CA	(7.3)
149	San Luis Obispo, CA	(9.6)
231	Sandusky, OH	(19.0)
94	Santa Ana-Anaheim, CA M.D.	(4.8)
147	Santa Barbara-Santa Maria, CA	(9.3)
157	Santa Cruz-Watsonville, CA	(10.6)
68	Santa Fe, NM	(1.0)
236	Santa Rosa-Petaluma, CA	(19.8)

RANK	METROPOLITAN AREA	% CHANGE
191	Savannah, GA	(13.6)
95	Scranton--Wilkes-Barre, PA	(4.9)
214	Seattle-Bellevue-Everett, WA M.D.	(16.8)
199	Seattle-Tacoma-Bellevue, WA	(15.4)
160	Sebastian-Vero Beach, FL	(10.7)
84	Sheboygan, WI	(3.7)
165	Sherman-Denison, TX	(11.7)
235	Shreveport-Bossier City, LA	(19.5)
189	Sioux City, IA-NE-SD	(13.5)
75	Sioux Falls, SD	(2.0)
NA	South Bend-Mishawaka, IN-MI**	NA
212	Spartanburg, SC	(16.7)
48	Spokane, WA	1.8
52	Springfield, MA	0.7
NA	Springfield, MO**	NA
281	Springfield, OH	(30.4)
98	State College, PA	(5.0)
268	Stockton, CA	(25.8)
95	St. Cloud, MN	(4.9)
249	St. George, UT	(22.0)
198	St. Joseph, MO-KS	(15.2)
176	St. Louis, MO-IL	(12.4)
NA	Sumter, SC**	NA
28	Syracuse, NY	6.0
155	Tacoma, WA M.D.	(10.5)
177	Tallahassee, FL	(12.5)
122	Tampa-St Petersburg, FL	(6.8)
166	Texarkana, TX-Texarkana, AR	(11.8)
NA	Toledo, OH**	NA
290	Topeka, KS	(32.9)
178	Trenton-Ewing, NJ	(12.6)
NA	Tucson, AZ**	NA
126	Tulsa, OK	(7.3)
NA	Tuscaloosa, AL**	NA
20	Tyler, TX	10.1
5	Utica-Rome, NY	15.4
278	Valdosta, GA	(28.6)
NA	Vallejo-Fairfield, CA**	NA
9	Victoria, TX	12.8
230	Vineland, NJ	(18.8)
267	Visalia-Porterville, CA	(25.6)
192	Waco, TX	(14.3)
18	Warner Robins, GA	10.6
NA	Warren-Farmington Hills, MI M.D.**	NA
71	Washington (greater) DC-VA-MD-WV	(1.4)
90	Washington, DC-VA-MD-WV M.D.	(4.3)
201	Waterloo-Cedar Falls, IA	(15.6)
NA	Wausau, WI**	NA
268	Wenatchee, WA	(25.8)
63	West Palm Beach, FL M.D.	(0.6)
8	Wheeling, WV-OH	13.1
260	Wichita Falls, TX	(24.5)
NA	Wichita, KS**	NA
142	Williamsport, PA	(8.9)
20	Wilmington, DE-MD-NJ M.D.	10.1
151	Wilmington, NC	(9.9)
124	Winchester, VA-WV	(7.2)
38	Winston-Salem, NC	3.9
4	Worcester, MA	16.1
207	York-Hanover, PA	(16.2)
NA	Youngstown, OH-PA**	NA
299	Yuba City, CA	(39.3)
280	Yuma, AZ	(29.5)

Source: CQ Press using reported data from the F.B.I. "Crime in the United States 2009"
*Larceny-theft is the unlawful taking of property. Attempts are included.
**Not available.

36. Percent Change in Larceny-Theft Rate: 2005 to 2009 (continued)
National Percent Change = 9.9% Decrease*

RANK	METROPOLITAN AREA	% CHANGE
1	Barnstable Town, MA	30.9
2	Rockingham County, NH M.D.	22.9
3	Bangor, ME	18.8
4	Worcester, MA	16.1
5	Utica-Rome, NY	15.4
6	Manchester-Nashua, NH	14.4
7	Erie, PA	14.1
8	Wheeling, WV-OH	13.1
9	Dover, DE	12.8
9	Victoria, TX	12.8
11	Rochester, MN	12.6
12	Fargo, ND-MN	12.4
13	Oshkosh-Neenah, WI	12.3
14	Lafayette, LA	11.9
15	Bethesda-Frederick, MD M.D.	11.3
16	Pittsfield, MA	11.1
17	Fort Lauderdale, FL M.D.	10.8
18	Warner Robins, GA	10.6
19	Palm Bay-Melbourne, FL	10.4
20	Tyler, TX	10.1
20	Wilmington, DE-MD-NJ M.D.	10.1
22	Albany, GA	9.7
22	Lawrence, KS	9.7
24	Ames, IA	8.5
25	Poughkeepsie, NY	8.4
26	Cumberland, MD-WV	7.3
27	Columbia, MO	6.5
28	Syracuse, NY	6.0
29	Nassau-Suffolk, NY M.D.	5.9
30	Milwaukee, WI	5.8
31	Cambridge-Newton, MA M.D.	5.5
32	La Crosse, WI-MN	5.4
33	Boston (greater), MA-NH	5.3
33	Columbus, GA-AL	5.3
35	Norwich-New London, CT	5.1
36	Danville, VA	4.4
37	Buffalo-Niagara Falls, NY	4.1
38	Winston-Salem, NC	3.9
39	Gainesville, FL	3.8
40	Pensacola, FL	3.7
41	Anderson, IN	3.5
42	Harrisonburg, VA	2.9
43	Oxnard-Thousand Oaks, CA	2.8
44	Mobile, AL	2.7
44	San Francisco-S. Mateo, CA M.D.	2.7
46	Las Cruces, NM	2.3
46	Miami (greater), FL	2.3
48	Spokane, WA	1.8
49	Philadelphia (greater) PA-NJ-MD-DE	1.5
50	Charlottesville, VA	1.2
51	San Antonio, TX	0.8
52	Springfield, MA	0.7
53	Morgantown, WV	0.6
54	Edison, NJ M.D.	0.5
54	Houston, TX	0.5
56	Panama City-Lynn Haven, FL	0.4
56	Philadelphia, PA M.D.	0.4
58	Fayetteville, NC	0.3
59	Albany-Schenectady-Troy, NY	0.1
60	Alexandria, LA	(0.3)
61	Camden, NJ M.D.	(0.5)
61	Port St. Lucie, FL	(0.5)
63	Bloomington, IN	(0.6)
63	Portland, ME	(0.6)
63	West Palm Beach, FL M.D.	(0.6)
66	Binghamton, NY	(0.7)
66	Boston-Quincy, MA M.D.	(0.7)
68	Brunswick, GA	(1.0)
68	Santa Fe, NM	(1.0)
70	Fond du Lac, WI	(1.3)
71	Dubuque, IA	(1.4)
71	Miami-Dade County, FL M.D.	(1.4)
71	Washington (greater) DC-VA-MD-WV	(1.4)
74	Austin-Round Rock, TX	(1.6)
75	Sioux Falls, SD	(2.0)
76	Baltimore-Towson, MD	(2.2)
77	Hagerstown-Martinsburg, MD-WV	(2.8)
78	Pascagoula, MS	(2.9)
79	Chico, CA	(3.0)
80	Longview, TX	(3.2)
80	Rapid City, SD	(3.2)
82	Fort Collins-Loveland, CO	(3.4)
82	Ocean City, NJ	(3.4)
84	El Paso, TX	(3.7)
84	Sheboygan, WI	(3.7)
86	Midland, TX	(3.8)
87	Brownsville-Harlingen, TX	(3.9)
88	Morristown, TN	(4.0)
89	Bismarck, ND	(4.1)
90	College Station-Bryan, TX	(4.3)
90	Washington, DC-VA-MD-WV M.D.	(4.3)
92	Orlando, FL	(4.4)
93	Farmington, NM	(4.6)
94	Santa Ana-Anaheim, CA M.D.	(4.8)
95	Jacksonville, FL	(4.9)
95	Scranton--Wilkes-Barre, PA	(4.9)
95	St. Cloud, MN	(4.9)
98	State College, PA	(5.0)
99	Augusta, GA-SC	(5.1)
99	Rochester, NY	(5.1)
101	Appleton, WI	(5.2)
102	Detroit (greater), MI	(5.4)
103	Abilene, TX	(5.5)
103	Columbia, SC	(5.5)
103	San Francisco (greater), CA	(5.5)
106	Blacksburg, VA	(5.6)
106	Bremerton-Silverdale, WA	(5.6)
106	Burlington, NC	(5.6)
106	New York (greater), NY-NJ-PA	(5.6)
110	Greensboro-High Point, NC	(5.7)
110	Jackson, MS	(5.7)
112	Los Angeles (greater), CA	(6.0)
113	Kingsport, TN-VA	(6.2)
113	Knoxville, TN	(6.2)
115	Columbus, OH	(6.3)
116	Los Angeles County, CA M.D.	(6.4)
116	Pocatello, ID	(6.4)
118	Hickory, NC	(6.5)
118	Lynchburg, VA	(6.5)
120	Jackson, TN	(6.7)
120	Madison, WI	(6.7)
122	Tampa-St Petersburg, FL	(6.8)
123	Ocala, FL	(7.0)
124	Laredo, TX	(7.2)
124	Winchester, VA-WV	(7.2)
126	San Jose, CA	(7.3)
126	Tulsa, OK	(7.3)
128	Lafayette, IN	(7.4)
128	Odessa, TX	(7.4)
130	McAllen-Edinburg-Mission, TX	(7.5)
131	Auburn, AL	(7.7)
132	Raleigh-Cary, NC	(7.8)
133	Kingston, NY	(7.9)
133	New York-W. Plains NY-NJ M.D.	(7.9)
135	Lancaster, PA	(8.1)
136	Indianapolis, IN	(8.2)
137	Dayton, OH	(8.4)
137	Salisbury, MD	(8.4)
139	Napa, CA	(8.5)
140	Allentown, PA-NJ	(8.7)
140	Lima, OH	(8.7)
142	Amarillo, TX	(8.9)
142	Williamsport, PA	(8.9)
144	Harrisburg-Carlisle, PA	(9.0)
145	Goldsboro, NC	(9.1)
146	Punta Gorda, FL	(9.2)
147	Santa Barbara-Santa Maria, CA	(9.3)
148	Fort Smith, AR-OK	(9.4)
149	San Luis Obispo, CA	(9.6)
150	Ann Arbor, MI	(9.8)
151	Naples-Marco Island, FL	(9.9)
151	Wilmington, NC	(9.9)
153	Eau Claire, WI	(10.1)
154	Chattanooga, TN-GA	(10.2)
155	Lubbock, TX	(10.5)
155	Tacoma, WA M.D.	(10.5)
157	Carson City, NV	(10.6)
157	Houma, LA	(10.6)
157	Santa Cruz-Watsonville, CA	(10.6)
160	Anchorage, AK	(10.7)
160	Sebastian-Vero Beach, FL	(10.7)
162	Oakland-Fremont, CA M.D.	(11.1)
163	Salt Lake City, UT	(11.4)
164	Reading, PA	(11.6)
165	Sherman-Denison, TX	(11.7)
166	Texarkana, TX-Texarkana, AR	(11.8)
167	Ogden-Clearfield, UT	(12.0)
167	Sacramento, CA	(12.0)
169	Cheyenne, WY	(12.1)
169	Iowa City, IA	(12.1)
169	Memphis, TN-MS-AR	(12.1)
169	Muncie, IN	(12.1)
173	Akron, OH	(12.2)
174	Baton Rouge, LA	(12.3)
174	Bridgeport-Stamford, CT	(12.3)
176	St. Louis, MO-IL	(12.4)
177	Tallahassee, FL	(12.5)
178	Beaumont-Port Arthur, TX	(12.6)
178	Jefferson City, MO	(12.6)
178	Trenton-Ewing, NJ	(12.6)

Note: All listings are for Metropolitan Statistical Areas (M.S.A.s) except for those ending with "M.D." Listings with "M.D." are Metropolitan Divisions which are smaller parts of eleven large M.S.A.s. See explanatory note at beginning of metropolitan area section.

RANK	METROPOLITAN AREA	% CHANGE
181	Decatur, AL	(12.8)
182	Albuquerque, NM	(13.0)
182	Hartford, CT	(13.0)
184	Florence, SC	(13.1)
184	Montgomery, AL	(13.1)
186	Charleston-North Charleston, SC	(13.2)
187	Killeen-Temple-Fort Hood, TX	(13.3)
187	Lewiston-Auburn, ME	(13.3)
189	Newark-Union, NJ-PA M.D.	(13.5)
189	Sioux City, IA-NE-SD	(13.5)
191	Savannah, GA	(13.6)
192	Lakeland, FL	(14.3)
192	Waco, TX	(14.3)
194	Kokomo, IN	(14.7)
195	Pine Bluff, AR	(14.8)
196	Fort Worth-Arlington, TX M.D.	(15.0)
197	Merced, CA	(15.1)
198	St. Joseph, MO-KS	(15.2)
199	Michigan City-La Porte, IN	(15.4)
199	Seattle-Tacoma-Bellevue, WA	(15.4)
201	Roanoke, VA	(15.6)
201	Waterloo-Cedar Falls, IA	(15.6)
203	Battle Creek, MI	(15.7)
204	Altoona, PA	(15.8)
205	Pittsburgh, PA	(15.9)
206	Durham-Chapel Hill, NC	(16.1)
207	Fort Wayne, IN	(16.2)
207	York-Hanover, PA	(16.2)
209	Atlanta, GA	(16.3)
209	Lake Charles, LA	(16.3)
211	Mansfield, OH	(16.4)
212	Atlantic City, NJ	(16.7)
212	Spartanburg, SC	(16.7)
214	Seattle-Bellevue-Everett, WA M.D.	(16.8)
215	Cedar Rapids, IA	(17.0)
215	Idaho Falls, ID	(17.0)
215	Omaha-Council Bluffs, NE-IA	(17.0)
218	Casper, WY	(17.1)
219	Cape Coral-Fort Myers, FL	(17.2)
220	Las Vegas-Paradise, NV	(17.3)
221	Rocky Mount, NC	(17.4)
222	Columbus, IN	(17.5)
223	Green Bay, WI	(17.8)
224	Charlotte-Gastonia, NC-SC	(17.9)
225	Lebanon, PA	(18.1)
226	Athens-Clarke County, GA	(18.2)
227	Anderson, SC	(18.3)
227	Lewiston, ID-WA	(18.3)
229	Dallas (greater), TX	(18.4)
230	Vineland, NJ	(18.8)
231	Logan, UT-ID	(19.0)
231	Reno-Sparks, NV	(19.0)
231	Sandusky, OH	(19.0)
234	Honolulu, HI	(19.4)
235	Shreveport-Bossier City, LA	(19.5)
236	Olympia, WA	(19.8)
236	Santa Rosa-Petaluma, CA	(19.8)
238	Dallas-Plano-Irving, TX M.D.	(20.1)
239	Hinesville, GA	(20.2)
239	Nashville-Davidson, TN	(20.2)
239	Riverside-San Bernardino, CA	(20.2)
242	Janesville, WI	(20.3)
243	Bakersfield, CA	(21.1)

RANK	METROPOLITAN AREA	% CHANGE
243	Fresno, CA	(21.1)
243	Richmond, VA	(21.1)
246	Dothan, AL	(21.4)
247	Gadsden, AL	(21.8)
247	Macon, GA	(21.8)
249	Redding, CA	(22.0)
249	St. George, UT	(22.0)
251	Eugene-Springfield, OR	(22.2)
252	San Angelo, TX	(22.3)
253	Coeur d'Alene, ID	(22.4)
253	Corpus Christi, TX	(22.4)
255	Grand Junction, CO	(22.9)
256	Jonesboro, AR	(23.5)
256	Racine, WI	(23.5)
258	Billings, MT	(24.0)
259	Phoenix-Mesa-Scottsdale, AZ	(24.1)
260	Fayetteville, AR-MO	(24.5)
260	Modesto, CA	(24.5)
260	Wichita Falls, TX	(24.5)
263	Provo-Orem, UT	(24.7)
264	Charleston, WV	(25.0)
265	Kansas City, MO-KS	(25.4)
265	San Diego, CA	(25.4)
267	Visalia-Porterville, CA	(25.6)
268	Stockton, CA	(25.8)
268	Wenatchee, WA	(25.8)
270	Flagstaff, AZ	(26.0)
271	Elmira, NY	(26.1)
272	Asheville, NC	(26.4)
273	Corvallis, OR	(26.9)
273	Hot Springs, AR	(26.9)
275	Lincoln, NE	(27.9)
276	Johnson City, TN	(28.1)
277	Huntsville, AL	(28.4)
278	Valdosta, GA	(28.6)
279	Portland-Vancouver, OR-WA	(29.4)
280	Yuma, AZ	(29.5)
281	Springfield, OH	(30.4)
282	Medford, OR	(30.5)
282	Prescott, AZ	(30.5)
284	Grand Forks, ND-MN	(31.8)
285	Denver-Aurora, CO	(32.0)
286	Great Falls, MT	(32.1)
287	Salinas, CA	(32.6)
288	Bellingham, WA	(32.7)
288	Kennewick-Pasco-Richland, WA	(32.7)
290	Colorado Springs, CO	(32.9)
290	Salem, OR	(32.9)
290	Topeka, KS	(32.9)
293	Elkhart-Goshen, IN	(34.2)
293	Longview, WA	(34.2)
295	Rome, GA	(35.2)
296	Madera, CA	(36.6)
297	Gainesville, GA	(37.0)
298	Mount Vernon-Anacortes, WA	(37.1)
299	Yuba City, CA	(39.3)
300	Bend, OR	(40.2)
301	Greeley, CO	(43.3)
302	Missoula, MT	(45.5)
303	Pueblo, CO	(57.2)
NA	Anniston-Oxford, AL**	NA
NA	Bay City, MI**	NA
NA	Birmingham-Hoover, AL**	NA

RANK	METROPOLITAN AREA	% CHANGE
NA	Boise City-Nampa, ID**	NA
NA	Boulder, CO**	NA
NA	Bowling Green, KY**	NA
NA	Burlington-South Burlington, VT**	NA
NA	Cape Girardeau, MO-IL**	NA
NA	Cincinnati-Middletown, OH-KY-IN**	NA
NA	Clarksville, TN-KY**	NA
NA	Cleveland-Elyria-Mentor, OH**	NA
NA	Cleveland, TN**	NA
NA	Crestview-Fort Walton Beach, FL**	NA
NA	Dalton, GA**	NA
NA	Danville, IL**	NA
NA	Decatur, IL**	NA
NA	Deltona-Daytona Beach, FL**	NA
NA	Des Moines-West Des Moines, IA**	NA
NA	Detroit-Livonia-Dearborn, MI M.D.**	NA
NA	Duluth, MN-WI**	NA
NA	El Centro, CA**	NA
NA	Elizabethtown, KY**	NA
NA	Evansville, IN-KY**	NA
NA	Flint, MI**	NA
NA	Florence-Muscle Shoals, AL**	NA
NA	Glens Falls, NY**	NA
NA	Grand Rapids-Wyoming, MI**	NA
NA	Gulfport-Biloxi, MS**	NA
NA	Hattiesburg, MS**	NA
NA	Holland-Grand Haven, MI**	NA
NA	Ithaca, NY**	NA
NA	Jacksonville, NC**	NA
NA	Jackson, MI**	NA
NA	Kalamazoo-Portage, MI**	NA
NA	Lake Havasu City-Kingman, AZ**	NA
NA	Lansing-East Lansing, MI**	NA
NA	Lawton, OK**	NA
NA	Lexington-Fayette, KY**	NA
NA	Little Rock, AR**	NA
NA	Louisville, KY-IN**	NA
NA	Manhattan, KS**	NA
NA	Mankato-North Mankato, MN**	NA
NA	Minneapolis-St. Paul, MN-WI**	NA
NA	Monroe, MI**	NA
NA	Muskegon-Norton Shores, MI**	NA
NA	New Haven-Milford, CT**	NA
NA	New Orleans, LA**	NA
NA	Niles-Benton Harbor, MI**	NA
NA	North Port-Bradenton-Sarasota, FL**	NA
NA	Oklahoma City, OK**	NA
NA	Owensboro, KY**	NA
NA	Palm Coast, FL**	NA
NA	Peabody, MA M.D.**	NA
NA	Providence-New Bedford, RI-MA**	NA
NA	Saginaw, MI**	NA
NA	South Bend-Mishawaka, IN-MI**	NA
NA	Springfield, MO**	NA
NA	Sumter, SC**	NA
NA	Toledo, OH**	NA
NA	Tucson, AZ**	NA
NA	Tuscaloosa, AL**	NA
NA	Vallejo-Fairfield, CA**	NA
NA	Warren-Farmington Hills, MI M.D.**	NA
NA	Wausau, WI**	NA
NA	Wichita, KS**	NA
NA	Youngstown, OH-PA**	NA

Source: CQ Press using reported data from the F.B.I. "Crime in the United States 2009"
*Larceny-theft is the unlawful taking of property. Attempts are included.
**Not available.

37. Motor Vehicle Thefts in 2009
National Total = 794,616 Motor Vehicle Thefts*

RANK	METROPOLITAN AREA	THEFTS
235	Abilene, TX	303
109	Akron, OH	1,406
138	Albany-Schenectady-Troy, NY	861
191	Albany, GA	432
54	Albuquerque, NM	4,340
231	Alexandria, LA	310
127	Allentown, PA-NJ	1,059
334	Altoona, PA	112
147	Amarillo, TX	756
358	Ames, IA	64
135	Anchorage, AK	916
242	Anderson, IN	282
157	Anderson, SC	652
167	Ann Arbor, MI	548
248	Anniston-Oxford, AL	269
315	Appleton, WI	139
150	Asheville, NC	737
212	Athens-Clarke County, GA	372
8	Atlanta, GA	22,054
211	Atlantic City, NJ	374
NA	Auburn, AL**	NA
77	Augusta, GA-SC	2,406
66	Austin-Round Rock, TX	3,042
52	Bakersfield, CA	4,998
26	Baltimore-Towson, MD	9,018
326	Bangor, ME	127
269	Barnstable Town, MA	214
88	Baton Rouge, LA	1,985
278	Battle Creek, MI	199
337	Bay City, MI	107
137	Beaumont-Port Arthur, TX	897
249	Bellingham, WA	266
294	Bend, OR	170
87	Bethesda-Frederick, MD M.D.	1,999
228	Billings, MT	319
328	Binghamton, NY	122
60	Birmingham-Hoover, AL	3,534
300	Bismarck, ND	160
326	Blacksburg, VA	127
241	Bloomington, IN	290
177	Boise City-Nampa, ID	495
30	Boston (greater), MA-NH	7,845
55	Boston-Quincy, MA M.D.	4,082
227	Boulder, CO	320
286	Bowling Green, KY	183
217	Bremerton-Silverdale, WA	348
92	Bridgeport-Stamford, CT	1,880
143	Brownsville-Harlingen, TX	794
271	Brunswick, GA	211
79	Buffalo-Niagara Falls, NY	2,282
295	Burlington-South Burlington, VT	167
247	Burlington, NC	275
89	Cambridge-Newton, MA M.D.	1,981
86	Camden, NJ M.D.	2,000
114	Cape Coral-Fort Myers, FL	1,238
355	Cape Girardeau, MO-IL	69
347	Carson City, NV	86
300	Casper, WY	160
224	Cedar Rapids, IA	328
85	Charleston-North Charleston, SC	2,068
153	Charleston, WV	690
46	Charlotte-Gastonia, NC-SC	5,224
238	Charlottesville, VA	295
102	Chattanooga, TN-GA	1,532
311	Cheyenne, WY	146
141	Chico, CA	840
59	Cincinnati-Middletown, OH-KY-IN	3,606
201	Clarksville, TN-KY	393
40	Cleveland-Elyria-Mentor, OH	5,879
282	Cleveland, TN	187
277	Coeur d'Alene, ID	201
216	College Station-Bryan, TX	353
111	Colorado Springs, CO	1,335
280	Columbia, MO	192
72	Columbia, SC	2,596
95	Columbus, GA-AL	1,761
279	Columbus, IN	195
48	Columbus, OH	5,130
146	Corpus Christi, TX	758
346	Corvallis, OR	87
251	Crestview-Fort Walton Beach, FL	262
357	Cumberland, MD-WV	66
6	Dallas (greater), TX	23,547
13	Dallas-Plano-Irving, TX M.D.	18,090
284	Dalton, GA	184
330	Danville, IL	121
338	Danville, VA	104
97	Dayton, OH	1,673
307	Decatur, AL	153
290	Decatur, IL	177
108	Deltona-Daytona Beach, FL	1,426
28	Denver-Aurora, CO	8,634
128	Des Moines-West Des Moines, IA	981
7	Detroit (greater), MI	22,559
15	Detroit-Livonia-Dearborn, MI M.D.	17,419
265	Dothan, AL	223
255	Dover, DE	249
344	Dubuque, IA	94
188	Duluth, MN-WI	436
126	Durham-Chapel Hill, NC	1,083
323	Eau Claire, WI	128
91	Edison, NJ M.D.	1,903
133	El Centro, CA	940
82	El Paso, TX	2,139
360	Elizabethtown, KY	55
218	Elkhart-Goshen, IN	346
365	Elmira, NY	45
266	Erie, PA	220
105	Eugene-Springfield, OR	1,453
199	Evansville, IN-KY	399
220	Fargo, ND-MN	337
252	Farmington, NM	259
172	Fayetteville, AR-MO	513
119	Fayetteville, NC	1,174
314	Flagstaff, AZ	140
116	Flint, MI	1,201
317	Florence-Muscle Shoals, AL	136
155	Florence, SC	670
363	Fond du Lac, WI	52
200	Fort Collins-Loveland, CO	397
49	Fort Lauderdale, FL M.D.	5,129
194	Fort Smith, AR-OK	426
166	Fort Wayne, IN	549
43	Fort Worth-Arlington, TX M.D.	5,457
42	Fresno, CA	5,491
272	Gadsden, AL	206
151	Gainesville, FL	711
226	Gainesville, GA	327
360	Glens Falls, NY	55
238	Goldsboro, NC	295
335	Grand Forks, ND-MN	110
237	Grand Junction, CO	296
133	Grand Rapids-Wyoming, MI	940
320	Great Falls, MT	133
184	Greeley, CO	447
253	Green Bay, WI	252
101	Greensboro-High Point, NC	1,569
172	Gulfport-Biloxi, MS	513
208	Hagerstown-Martinsburg, MD-WV	381
187	Harrisburg-Carlisle, PA	438
345	Harrisonburg, VA	90
75	Hartford, CT	2,436
305	Hattiesburg, MS	154
156	Hickory, NC	668
317	Hinesville, GA	136
319	Holland-Grand Haven, MI	134
58	Honolulu, HI	3,729
207	Hot Springs, AR	385
202	Houma, LA	391
5	Houston, TX	24,906
117	Huntsville, AL	1,194
303	Idaho Falls, ID	155
44	Indianapolis, IN	5,438
323	Iowa City, IA	128
366	Ithaca, NY	34
61	Jacksonville, FL	3,450
256	Jacksonville, NC	247
275	Jackson, MI	203
83	Jackson, MS	2,109
206	Jackson, TN	386
288	Janesville, WI	180
328	Jefferson City, MO	122
253	Johnson City, TN	252
312	Jonesboro, AR	144
169	Kalamazoo-Portage, MI	540
31	Kansas City, MO-KS	7,527
183	Kennewick-Pasco-Richland, WA	449
191	Killeen-Temple-Fort Hood, TX	432
181	Kingsport, TN-VA	461
332	Kingston, NY	117
107	Knoxville, TN	1,436
342	Kokomo, IN	95
332	La Crosse, WI-MN	117
236	Lafayette, IN	299
160	Lafayette, LA	630
163	Lake Charles, LA	576
186	Lake Havasu City-Kingman, AZ	439
123	Lakeland, FL	1,126
189	Lancaster, PA	433
180	Lansing-East Lansing, MI	467

Note: All listings are for Metropolitan Statistical Areas (M.S.A.s) except for those ending with "M.D." Listings with "M.D." are Metropolitan Divisions which are smaller parts of eleven large M.S.A.s. See explanatory note at beginning of metropolitan area section.

RANK	METROPOLITAN AREA	THEFTS
103	Laredo, TX	1,524
198	Las Cruces, NM	406
22	Las Vegas-Paradise, NV	10,792
293	Lawrence, KS	172
243	Lawton, OK	279
352	Lebanon, PA	75
353	Lewiston-Auburn, ME	73
342	Lewiston, ID-WA	95
149	Lexington-Fayette, KY	746
257	Lima, OH	246
230	Lincoln, NE	312
78	Little Rock, AR	2,389
353	Logan, UT-ID	73
142	Longview, TX	838
205	Longview, WA	389
2	Los Angeles County, CA M.D.	46,813
1	Los Angeles (greater), CA	53,058
71	Louisville, KY-IN	2,605
162	Lubbock, TX	610
244	Lynchburg, VA	276
129	Macon, GA	972
171	Madera, CA	520
164	Madison, WI	568
209	Manchester-Nashua, NH	377
351	Manhattan, KS	79
339	Mankato-North Mankato, MN	103
341	Mansfield, OH	96
70	McAllen-Edinburg-Mission, TX	2,626
281	Medford, OR	188
45	Memphis, TN-MS-AR	5,382
136	Merced, CA	903
9	Miami (greater), FL	20,682
21	Miami-Dade County, FL M.D.	12,150
267	Michigan City-La Porte, IN	217
268	Midland, TX	215
41	Milwaukee, WI	5,625
37	Minneapolis-St. Paul, MN-WI	6,637
315	Missoula, MT	139
100	Mobile, AL	1,596
64	Modesto, CA	3,401
270	Monroe, MI	212
124	Montgomery, AL	1,106
321	Morgantown, WV	132
273	Morristown, TN	204
249	Mount Vernon-Anacortes, WA	266
283	Muncie, IN	186
214	Muskegon-Norton Shores, MI	366
232	Napa, CA	309
262	Naples-Marco Island, FL	228
68	Nashville-Davidson, TN	3,006
65	Nassau-Suffolk, NY M.D.	3,219
76	New Haven-Milford, CT	2,425
NA	New Orleans, LA**	NA
3	New York (greater), NY-NJ-PA	27,086
17	New York-W. Plains NY-NJ M.D.	15,244
36	Newark-Union, NJ-PA M.D.	6,720
292	Niles-Benton Harbor, MI	173
113	North Port-Bradenton-Sarasota, FL	1,263
297	Norwich-New London, CT	162
10	Oakland-Fremont, CA M.D.	19,260
212	Ocala, FL	372
350	Ocean City, NJ	81
224	Odessa, TX	328

RANK	METROPOLITAN AREA	THEFTS
147	Ogden-Clearfield, UT	756
51	Oklahoma City, OK	5,091
170	Olympia, WA	527
67	Omaha-Council Bluffs, NE-IA	3,014
39	Orlando, FL	6,021
330	Oshkosh-Neenah, WI	121
322	Owensboro, KY	129
120	Oxnard-Thousand Oaks, CA	1,154
131	Palm Bay-Melbourne, FL	965
335	Palm Coast, FL	110
223	Panama City-Lynn Haven, FL	331
234	Pascagoula, MS	304
106	Peabody, MA M.D.	1,448
139	Pensacola, FL	850
20	Philadelphia (greater) PA-NJ-MD-DE	13,024
25	Philadelphia, PA M.D.	9,295
12	Phoenix-Mesa-Scottsdale, AZ	18,224
179	Pine Bluff, AR	470
73	Pittsburgh, PA	2,593
340	Pittsfield, MA	98
349	Pocatello, ID	84
194	Port St. Lucie, FL	426
34	Portland-Vancouver, OR-WA	6,893
196	Portland, ME	425
189	Poughkeepsie, NY	433
260	Prescott, AZ	231
62	Providence-New Bedford, RI-MA	3,420
165	Provo-Orem, UT	553
203	Pueblo, CO	390
290	Punta Gorda, FL	177
259	Racine, WI	238
94	Raleigh-Cary, NC	1,779
302	Rapid City, SD	159
130	Reading, PA	966
219	Redding, CA	339
122	Reno-Sparks, NV	1,134
74	Richmond, VA	2,573
11	Riverside-San Bernardino, CA	18,533
185	Roanoke, VA	445
299	Rochester, MN	161
104	Rochester, NY	1,485
221	Rockingham County, NH M.D.	334
233	Rocky Mount, NC	305
284	Rome, GA	184
24	Sacramento, CA	10,072
229	Saginaw, MI	316
112	Salem, OR	1,276
93	Salinas, CA	1,808
287	Salisbury, MD	181
50	Salt Lake City, UT	5,117
295	San Angelo, TX	167
35	San Antonio, TX	6,887
19	San Diego, CA	13,938
4	San Francisco (greater), CA	26,786
32	San Francisco-S. Mateo, CA M.D.	7,526
33	San Jose, CA	7,485
210	San Luis Obispo, CA	375
360	Sandusky, OH	55
38	Santa Ana-Anaheim, CA M.D.	6,245
154	Santa Barbara-Santa Maria, CA	682
140	Santa Cruz-Watsonville, CA	847
240	Santa Fe, NM	294
145	Santa Rosa-Petaluma, CA	786

RANK	METROPOLITAN AREA	THEFTS
110	Savannah, GA	1,398
158	Scranton--Wilkes-Barre, PA	638
23	Seattle-Bellevue-Everett, WA M.D.	10,262
18	Seattle-Tacoma-Bellevue, WA	14,118
308	Sebastian-Vero Beach, FL	151
356	Sheboygan, WI	68
288	Sherman-Denison, TX	180
132	Shreveport-Bossier City, LA	963
273	Sioux City, IA-NE-SD	204
222	Sioux Falls, SD	333
152	South Bend-Mishawaka, IN-MI	699
144	Spartanburg, SC	791
80	Spokane, WA	2,260
99	Springfield, MA	1,606
125	Springfield, MO	1,084
244	Springfield, OH	276
364	State College, PA	49
56	Stockton, CA	3,991
312	St. Cloud, MN	144
323	St. George, UT	128
260	St. Joseph, MO-KS	231
27	St. Louis, MO-IL	8,870
258	Sumter, SC	240
161	Syracuse, NY	622
57	Tacoma, WA M.D.	3,856
175	Tallahassee, FL	507
29	Tampa-St Petersburg, FL	8,435
203	Texarkana, TX-Texarkana, AR	390
98	Toledo, OH	1,669
174	Topeka, KS	510
159	Trenton-Ewing, NJ	634
53	Tucson, AZ	4,872
69	Tulsa, OK	2,901
168	Tuscaloosa, AL	541
193	Tyler, TX	428
303	Utica-Rome, NY	155
244	Valdosta, GA	276
84	Vallejo-Fairfield, CA	2,084
297	Victoria, TX	162
263	Vineland, NJ	227
81	Visalia-Porterville, CA	2,216
178	Waco, TX	477
263	Warner Robins, GA	227
47	Warren-Farmington Hills, MI M.D.	5,140
14	Washington (greater) DC-VA-MD-WV	18,085
16	Washington, DC-VA-MD-WV M.D.	16,086
276	Waterloo-Cedar Falls, IA	202
359	Wausau, WI	62
305	Wenatchee, WA	154
63	West Palm Beach, FL M.D.	3,403
309	Wheeling, WV-OH	150
215	Wichita Falls, TX	356
90	Wichita, KS	1,966
348	Williamsport, PA	85
96	Wilmington, DE-MD-NJ M.D.	1,729
NA	Wilmington, NC**	NA
310	Winchester, VA-WV	149
118	Winston-Salem, NC	1,192
115	Worcester, MA	1,237
182	York-Hanover, PA	452
121	Youngstown, OH-PA	1,140
197	Yuba City, CA	409
176	Yuma, AZ	499

Source: Reported data from the F.B.I. "Crime in the United States 2009"

*Motor vehicle theft includes the theft or attempted theft of a self-propelled vehicle. Excludes motorboats, construction equipment, airplanes, and farming equipment. **Not available.

37. Motor Vehicle Thefts in 2009 (continued)
National Total = 794,616 Motor Vehicle Thefts*

RANK	METROPOLITAN AREA	THEFTS	RANK	METROPOLITAN AREA	THEFTS	RANK	METROPOLITAN AREA	THEFTS
1	Los Angeles (greater), CA	53,058	61	Jacksonville, FL	3,450	121	Youngstown, OH-PA	1,140
2	Los Angeles County, CA M.D.	46,813	62	Providence-New Bedford, RI-MA	3,420	122	Reno-Sparks, NV	1,134
3	New York (greater), NY-NJ-PA	27,086	63	West Palm Beach, FL M.D.	3,403	123	Lakeland, FL	1,126
4	San Francisco (greater), CA	26,786	64	Modesto, CA	3,401	124	Montgomery, AL	1,106
5	Houston, TX	24,906	65	Nassau-Suffolk, NY M.D.	3,219	125	Springfield, MO	1,084
6	Dallas (greater), TX	23,547	66	Austin-Round Rock, TX	3,042	126	Durham-Chapel Hill, NC	1,083
7	Detroit (greater), MI	22,559	67	Omaha-Council Bluffs, NE-IA	3,014	127	Allentown, PA-NJ	1,059
8	Atlanta, GA	22,054	68	Nashville-Davidson, TN	3,006	128	Des Moines-West Des Moines, IA	981
9	Miami (greater), FL	20,682	69	Tulsa, OK	2,901	129	Macon, GA	972
10	Oakland-Fremont, CA M.D.	19,260	70	McAllen-Edinburg-Mission, TX	2,626	130	Reading, PA	966
11	Riverside-San Bernardino, CA	18,533	71	Louisville, KY-IN	2,605	131	Palm Bay-Melbourne, FL	965
12	Phoenix-Mesa-Scottsdale, AZ	18,224	72	Columbia, SC	2,596	132	Shreveport-Bossier City, LA	963
13	Dallas-Plano-Irving, TX M.D.	18,090	73	Pittsburgh, PA	2,593	133	El Centro, CA	940
14	Washington (greater) DC-VA-MD-WV	18,085	74	Richmond, VA	2,573	133	Grand Rapids-Wyoming, MI	940
15	Detroit-Livonia-Dearborn, MI M.D.	17,419	75	Hartford, CT	2,436	135	Anchorage, AK	916
16	Washington, DC-VA-MD-WV M.D.	16,086	76	New Haven-Milford, CT	2,425	136	Merced, CA	903
17	New York-W. Plains NY-NJ M.D.	15,244	77	Augusta, GA-SC	2,406	137	Beaumont-Port Arthur, TX	897
18	Seattle-Tacoma-Bellevue, WA	14,118	78	Little Rock, AR	2,389	138	Albany-Schenectady-Troy, NY	861
19	San Diego, CA	13,938	79	Buffalo-Niagara Falls, NY	2,282	139	Pensacola, FL	850
20	Philadelphia (greater) PA-NJ-MD-DE	13,024	80	Spokane, WA	2,260	140	Santa Cruz-Watsonville, CA	847
21	Miami-Dade County, FL M.D.	12,150	81	Visalia-Porterville, CA	2,216	141	Chico, CA	840
22	Las Vegas-Paradise, NV	10,792	82	El Paso, TX	2,139	142	Longview, TX	838
23	Seattle-Bellevue-Everett, WA M.D.	10,262	83	Jackson, MS	2,109	143	Brownsville-Harlingen, TX	794
24	Sacramento, CA	10,072	84	Vallejo-Fairfield, CA	2,084	144	Spartanburg, SC	791
25	Philadelphia, PA M.D.	9,295	85	Charleston-North Charleston, SC	2,068	145	Santa Rosa-Petaluma, CA	786
26	Baltimore-Towson, MD	9,018	86	Camden, NJ M.D.	2,000	146	Corpus Christi, TX	758
27	St. Louis, MO-IL	8,870	87	Bethesda-Frederick, MD M.D.	1,999	147	Amarillo, TX	756
28	Denver-Aurora, CO	8,634	88	Baton Rouge, LA	1,985	147	Ogden-Clearfield, UT	756
29	Tampa-St Petersburg, FL	8,435	89	Cambridge-Newton, MA M.D.	1,981	149	Lexington-Fayette, KY	746
30	Boston (greater), MA-NH	7,845	90	Wichita, KS	1,966	150	Asheville, NC	737
31	Kansas City, MO-KS	7,527	91	Edison, NJ M.D.	1,903	151	Gainesville, FL	711
32	San Francisco-S. Mateo, CA M.D.	7,526	92	Bridgeport-Stamford, CT	1,880	152	South Bend-Mishawaka, IN-MI	699
33	San Jose, CA	7,485	93	Salinas, CA	1,808	153	Charleston, WV	690
34	Portland-Vancouver, OR-WA	6,893	94	Raleigh-Cary, NC	1,779	154	Santa Barbara-Santa Maria, CA	682
35	San Antonio, TX	6,887	95	Columbus, GA-AL	1,761	155	Florence, SC	670
36	Newark-Union, NJ-PA M.D.	6,720	96	Wilmington, DE-MD-NJ M.D.	1,729	156	Hickory, NC	668
37	Minneapolis-St. Paul, MN-WI	6,637	97	Dayton, OH	1,673	157	Anderson, SC	652
38	Santa Ana-Anaheim, CA M.D.	6,245	98	Toledo, OH	1,669	158	Scranton--Wilkes-Barre, PA	638
39	Orlando, FL	6,021	99	Springfield, MA	1,606	159	Trenton-Ewing, NJ	634
40	Cleveland-Elyria-Mentor, OH	5,879	100	Mobile, AL	1,596	160	Lafayette, LA	630
41	Milwaukee, WI	5,625	101	Greensboro-High Point, NC	1,569	161	Syracuse, NY	622
42	Fresno, CA	5,491	102	Chattanooga, TN-GA	1,532	162	Lubbock, TX	610
43	Fort Worth-Arlington, TX M.D.	5,457	103	Laredo, TX	1,524	163	Lake Charles, LA	576
44	Indianapolis, IN	5,438	104	Rochester, NY	1,485	164	Madison, WI	568
45	Memphis, TN-MS-AR	5,382	105	Eugene-Springfield, OR	1,453	165	Provo-Orem, UT	553
46	Charlotte-Gastonia, NC-SC	5,224	106	Peabody, MA M.D.	1,448	166	Fort Wayne, IN	549
47	Warren-Farmington Hills, MI M.D.	5,140	107	Knoxville, TN	1,436	167	Ann Arbor, MI	548
48	Columbus, OH	5,130	108	Deltona-Daytona Beach, FL	1,426	168	Tuscaloosa, AL	541
49	Fort Lauderdale, FL M.D.	5,129	109	Akron, OH	1,406	169	Kalamazoo-Portage, MI	540
50	Salt Lake City, UT	5,117	110	Savannah, GA	1,398	170	Olympia, WA	527
51	Oklahoma City, OK	5,091	111	Colorado Springs, CO	1,335	171	Madera, CA	520
52	Bakersfield, CA	4,998	112	Salem, OR	1,276	172	Fayetteville, AR-MO	513
53	Tucson, AZ	4,872	113	North Port-Bradenton-Sarasota, FL	1,263	172	Gulfport-Biloxi, MS	513
54	Albuquerque, NM	4,340	114	Cape Coral-Fort Myers, FL	1,238	174	Topeka, KS	510
55	Boston-Quincy, MA M.D.	4,082	115	Worcester, MA	1,237	175	Tallahassee, FL	507
56	Stockton, CA	3,991	116	Flint, MI	1,201	176	Yuma, AZ	499
57	Tacoma, WA M.D.	3,856	117	Huntsville, AL	1,194	177	Boise City-Nampa, ID	495
58	Honolulu, HI	3,729	118	Winston-Salem, NC	1,192	178	Waco, TX	477
59	Cincinnati-Middletown, OH-KY-IN	3,606	119	Fayetteville, NC	1,174	179	Pine Bluff, AR	470
60	Birmingham-Hoover, AL	3,534	120	Oxnard-Thousand Oaks, CA	1,154	180	Lansing-East Lansing, MI	467

Note: All listings are for Metropolitan Statistical Areas (M.S.A.s) except for those ending with "M.D." Listings with "M.D." are Metropolitan Divisions which are smaller parts of eleven large M.S.A.s. See explanatory note at beginning of metropolitan area section.

RANK	METROPOLITAN AREA	THEFTS
181	Kingsport, TN-VA	461
182	York-Hanover, PA	452
183	Kennewick-Pasco-Richland, WA	449
184	Greeley, CO	447
185	Roanoke, VA	445
186	Lake Havasu City-Kingman, AZ	439
187	Harrisburg-Carlisle, PA	438
188	Duluth, MN-WI	436
189	Lancaster, PA	433
189	Poughkeepsie, NY	433
191	Albany, GA	432
191	Killeen-Temple-Fort Hood, TX	432
193	Tyler, TX	428
194	Fort Smith, AR-OK	426
194	Port St. Lucie, FL	426
196	Portland, ME	425
197	Yuba City, CA	409
198	Las Cruces, NM	406
199	Evansville, IN-KY	399
200	Fort Collins-Loveland, CO	397
201	Clarksville, TN-KY	393
202	Houma, LA	391
203	Pueblo, CO	390
203	Texarkana, TX-Texarkana, AR	390
205	Longview, WA	389
206	Jackson, TN	386
207	Hot Springs, AR	385
208	Hagerstown-Martinsburg, MD-WV	381
209	Manchester-Nashua, NH	377
210	San Luis Obispo, CA	375
211	Atlantic City, NJ	374
212	Athens-Clarke County, GA	372
212	Ocala, FL	372
214	Muskegon-Norton Shores, MI	366
215	Wichita Falls, TX	356
216	College Station-Bryan, TX	353
217	Bremerton-Silverdale, WA	348
218	Elkhart-Goshen, IN	346
219	Redding, CA	339
220	Fargo, ND-MN	337
221	Rockingham County, NH M.D.	334
222	Sioux Falls, SD	333
223	Panama City-Lynn Haven, FL	331
224	Cedar Rapids, IA	328
224	Odessa, TX	328
226	Gainesville, GA	327
227	Boulder, CO	320
228	Billings, MT	319
229	Saginaw, MI	316
230	Lincoln, NE	312
231	Alexandria, LA	310
232	Napa, CA	309
233	Rocky Mount, NC	305
234	Pascagoula, MS	304
235	Abilene, TX	303
236	Lafayette, IN	299
237	Grand Junction, CO	296
238	Charlottesville, VA	295
238	Goldsboro, NC	295
240	Santa Fe, NM	294
241	Bloomington, IN	290
242	Anderson, IN	282
243	Lawton, OK	279

RANK	METROPOLITAN AREA	THEFTS
244	Lynchburg, VA	276
244	Springfield, OH	276
244	Valdosta, GA	276
247	Burlington, NC	275
248	Anniston-Oxford, AL	269
249	Bellingham, WA	266
249	Mount Vernon-Anacortes, WA	266
251	Crestview-Fort Walton Beach, FL	262
252	Farmington, NM	259
253	Green Bay, WI	252
253	Johnson City, TN	252
255	Dover, DE	249
256	Jacksonville, NC	247
257	Lima, OH	246
258	Sumter, SC	240
259	Racine, WI	238
260	Prescott, AZ	231
260	St. Joseph, MO-KS	231
262	Naples-Marco Island, FL	228
263	Vineland, NJ	227
263	Warner Robins, GA	227
265	Dothan, AL	223
266	Erie, PA	220
267	Michigan City-La Porte, IN	217
268	Midland, TX	215
269	Barnstable Town, MA	214
270	Monroe, MI	212
271	Brunswick, GA	211
272	Gadsden, AL	206
273	Morristown, TN	204
273	Sioux City, IA-NE-SD	204
275	Jackson, MI	203
276	Waterloo-Cedar Falls, IA	202
277	Coeur d'Alene, ID	201
278	Battle Creek, MI	199
279	Columbus, IN	195
280	Columbia, MO	192
281	Medford, OR	188
282	Cleveland, TN	187
283	Muncie, IN	186
284	Dalton, GA	184
284	Rome, GA	184
286	Bowling Green, KY	183
287	Salisbury, MD	181
288	Janesville, WI	180
288	Sherman-Denison, TX	180
290	Decatur, IL	177
290	Punta Gorda, FL	177
292	Niles-Benton Harbor, MI	173
293	Lawrence, KS	172
294	Bend, OR	170
295	Burlington-South Burlington, VT	167
295	San Angelo, TX	167
297	Norwich-New London, CT	162
297	Victoria, TX	162
299	Rochester, MN	161
300	Bismarck, ND	160
300	Casper, WY	160
302	Rapid City, SD	159
303	Idaho Falls, ID	155
303	Utica-Rome, NY	155
305	Hattiesburg, MS	154
305	Wenatchee, WA	154

RANK	METROPOLITAN AREA	THEFTS
307	Decatur, AL	153
308	Sebastian-Vero Beach, FL	151
309	Wheeling, WV-OH	150
310	Winchester, VA-WV	149
311	Cheyenne, WY	146
312	Jonesboro, AR	144
312	St. Cloud, MN	144
314	Flagstaff, AZ	140
315	Appleton, WI	139
315	Missoula, MT	139
317	Florence-Muscle Shoals, AL	136
317	Hinesville, GA	136
319	Holland-Grand Haven, MI	134
320	Great Falls, MT	133
321	Morgantown, WV	132
322	Owensboro, KY	129
323	Eau Claire, WI	128
323	Iowa City, IA	128
323	St. George, UT	128
326	Bangor, ME	127
326	Blacksburg, VA	127
328	Binghamton, NY	122
328	Jefferson City, MO	122
330	Danville, IL	121
330	Oshkosh-Neenah, WI	121
332	Kingston, NY	117
332	La Crosse, WI-MN	117
334	Altoona, PA	112
335	Grand Forks, ND-MN	110
335	Palm Coast, FL	110
337	Bay City, MI	107
338	Danville, VA	104
339	Mankato-North Mankato, MN	103
340	Pittsfield, MA	98
341	Mansfield, OH	96
342	Kokomo, IN	95
342	Lewiston, ID-WA	95
344	Dubuque, IA	94
345	Harrisonburg, VA	90
346	Corvallis, OR	87
347	Carson City, NV	86
348	Williamsport, PA	85
349	Pocatello, ID	84
350	Ocean City, NJ	81
351	Manhattan, KS	79
352	Lebanon, PA	75
353	Lewiston-Auburn, ME	73
353	Logan, UT-ID	73
355	Cape Girardeau, MO-IL	69
356	Sheboygan, WI	68
357	Cumberland, MD-WV	66
358	Ames, IA	64
359	Wausau, WI	62
360	Elizabethtown, KY	55
360	Glens Falls, NY	55
360	Sandusky, OH	55
363	Fond du Lac, WI	52
364	State College, PA	49
365	Elmira, NY	45
366	Ithaca, NY	34
NA	Auburn, AL**	NA
NA	New Orleans, LA**	NA
NA	Wilmington, NC**	NA

Source: Reported data from the F.B.I. "Crime in the United States 2009"

*Motor vehicle theft includes the theft or attempted theft of a self-propelled vehicle. Excludes motorboats, construction equipment, airplanes, and farming equipment. **Not available.

38. Motor Vehicle Theft Rate in 2009
National Rate = 258.8 Motor Vehicle Thefts per 100,000 Population*

RANK	METROPOLITAN AREA	RATE	RANK	METROPOLITAN AREA	RATE	RANK	METROPOLITAN AREA	RATE
179	Abilene, TX	189.8	127	Charleston, WV	227.0	86	Fort Lauderdale, FL M.D.	293.2
164	Akron, OH	200.6	83	Charlotte-Gastonia, NC-SC	298.1	240	Fort Smith, AR-OK	144.7
307	Albany-Schenectady-Troy, NY	100.5	231	Charlottesville, VA	149.4	259	Fort Wayne, IN	132.6
99	Albany, GA	261.6	87	Chattanooga, TN-GA	292.5	103	Fort Worth-Arlington, TX M.D.	257.4
15	Albuquerque, NM	503.4	209	Cheyenne, WY	163.4	8	Fresno, CA	597.7
165	Alexandria, LA	200.0	47	Chico, CA	379.3	167	Gadsden, AL	198.5
263	Allentown, PA-NJ	129.5	205	Cincinnati-Middletown, OH-KY-IN	165.6	96	Gainesville, FL	274.3
319	Altoona, PA	89.6	234	Clarksville, TN-KY	148.1	195	Gainesville, GA	172.4
78	Amarillo, TX	307.3	94	Cleveland-Elyria-Mentor, OH	280.9	364	Glens Falls, NY	42.6
344	Ames, IA	73.2	207	Cleveland, TN	164.9	101	Goldsboro, NC	259.0
81	Anchorage, AK	300.0	245	Coeur d'Alene, ID	143.2	283	Grand Forks, ND-MN	112.4
137	Anderson, IN	214.4	201	College Station-Bryan, TX	167.9	161	Grand Junction, CO	201.9
57	Anderson, SC	350.9	142	Colorado Springs, CO	212.6	272	Grand Rapids-Wyoming, MI	120.9
218	Ann Arbor, MI	157.2	278	Columbia, MO	115.3	211	Great Falls, MT	161.8
121	Anniston-Oxford, AL	235.6	58	Columbia, SC	350.0	194	Greeley, CO	172.6
353	Appleton, WI	62.7	7	Columbus, GA-AL	612.3	328	Green Bay, WI	82.6
191	Asheville, NC	178.2	104	Columbus, IN	256.9	133	Greensboro-High Point, NC	219.8
174	Athens-Clarke County, GA	194.7	90	Columbus, OH	285.4	134	Gulfport-Biloxi, MS	219.6
42	Atlanta, GA	401.4	188	Corpus Christi, TX	181.7	249	Hagerstown-Martinsburg, MD-WV	141.2
256	Atlantic City, NJ	137.2	297	Corvallis, OR	105.9	330	Harrisburg-Carlisle, PA	81.9
NA	Auburn, AL**	NA	239	Crestview-Fort Walton Beach, FL	146.3	340	Harrisonburg, VA	75.0
25	Augusta, GA-SC	447.4	349	Cumberland, MD-WV	66.6	117	Hartford, CT	241.8
190	Austin-Round Rock, TX	178.4	52	Dallas (greater), TX	365.1	296	Hattiesburg, MS	107.8
6	Bakersfield, CA	613.6	31	Dallas-Plano-Irving, TX M.D.	417.8	185	Hickory, NC	182.5
64	Baltimore-Towson, MD	334.9	257	Dalton, GA	136.2	172	Hinesville, GA	195.8
323	Bangor, ME	85.4	227	Danville, IL	151.2	360	Holland-Grand Haven, MI	51.2
314	Barnstable Town, MA	95.4	311	Danville, VA	98.4	39	Honolulu, HI	411.1
107	Baton Rouge, LA	252.0	166	Dayton, OH	199.7	45	Hot Springs, AR	389.2
237	Battle Creek, MI	147.3	305	Decatur, AL	101.2	176	Houma, LA	192.4
308	Bay City, MI	100.2	206	Decatur, IL	165.1	29	Houston, TX	425.1
119	Beaumont-Port Arthur, TX	237.3	91	Deltona-Daytona Beach, FL	285.3	85	Huntsville, AL	295.8
260	Bellingham, WA	132.2	62	Denver-Aurora, CO	338.5	269	Idaho Falls, ID	123.9
301	Bend, OR	103.9	192	Des Moines-West Des Moines, IA	173.8	76	Indianapolis, IN	312.2
203	Bethesda-Frederick, MD M.D.	167.4	13	Detroit (greater), MI	512.2	326	Iowa City, IA	84.6
147	Billings, MT	207.9	1	Detroit-Livonia-Dearborn, MI M.D.	902.4	365	Ithaca, NY	33.5
361	Binghamton, NY	49.9	222	Dothan, AL	156.2	100	Jacksonville, FL	260.4
75	Birmingham-Hoover, AL	312.5	221	Dover, DE	156.4	238	Jacksonville, NC	146.9
230	Bismarck, ND	149.6	306	Dubuque, IA	101.1	268	Jackson, MI	127.1
335	Blacksburg, VA	79.5	214	Duluth, MN-WI	158.6	46	Jackson, MS	388.9
220	Bloomington, IN	156.6	136	Durham-Chapel Hill, NC	217.4	61	Jackson, TN	339.7
332	Boise City-Nampa, ID	80.6	333	Eau Claire, WI	80.1	287	Janesville, WI	111.8
197	Boston (greater), MA-NH	171.0	331	Edison, NJ M.D.	81.3	327	Jefferson City, MO	83.0
140	Boston-Quincy, MA M.D.	213.4	11	El Centro, CA	566.3	267	Johnson City, TN	127.2
295	Boulder, CO	108.1	92	El Paso, TX	285.2	271	Jonesboro, AR	121.1
225	Bowling Green, KY	152.8	362	Elizabethtown, KY	48.7	204	Kalamazoo-Portage, MI	167.0
242	Bremerton-Silverdale, WA	143.8	196	Elkhart-Goshen, IN	171.9	51	Kansas City, MO-KS	365.3
138	Bridgeport-Stamford, CT	214.1	359	Elmira, NY	51.5	183	Kennewick-Pasco-Richland, WA	184.9
167	Brownsville-Harlingen, TX	198.5	337	Erie, PA	78.7	284	Killeen-Temple-Fort Hood, TX	112.2
158	Brunswick, GA	203.8	33	Eugene-Springfield, OR	416.9	228	Kingsport, TN-VA	150.5
156	Buffalo-Niagara Falls, NY	203.9	281	Evansville, IN-KY	113.5	350	Kingston, NY	64.3
334	Burlington-South Burlington, VT	79.8	198	Fargo, ND-MN	169.1	155	Knoxville, TN	204.5
184	Burlington, NC	183.0	145	Farmington, NM	209.2	313	Kokomo, IN	95.7
261	Cambridge-Newton, MA M.D.	131.7	285	Fayetteville, AR-MO	112.1	321	La Crosse, WI-MN	88.4
212	Camden, NJ M.D.	159.1	68	Fayetteville, NC	327.0	224	Lafayette, IN	153.5
156	Cape Coral-Fort Myers, FL	203.9	294	Flagstaff, AZ	109.0	118	Lafayette, LA	239.5
343	Cape Girardeau, MO-IL	73.6	93	Flint, MI	281.8	84	Lake Charles, LA	296.8
216	Carson City, NV	157.9	316	Florence-Muscle Shoals, AL	94.1	131	Lake Havasu City-Kingman, AZ	220.6
139	Casper, WY	213.7	66	Florence, SC	332.2	177	Lakeland, FL	191.8
266	Cedar Rapids, IA	127.6	358	Fond du Lac, WI	52.2	323	Lancaster, PA	85.4
72	Charleston-North Charleston, SC	313.5	258	Fort Collins-Loveland, CO	133.2	304	Lansing-East Lansing, MI	103.1

Note: All listings are for Metropolitan Statistical Areas (M.S.A.s) except for those ending with "M.D." Listings with "M.D." are Metropolitan Divisions which are smaller parts of eleven large M.S.A.s. See explanatory note at beginning of metropolitan area section.

RANK	METROPOLITAN AREA	RATE
4	Laredo, TX	628.6
170	Las Cruces, NM	197.7
10	Las Vegas-Paradise, NV	566.8
236	Lawrence, KS	147.5
110	Lawton, OK	248.8
355	Lebanon, PA	57.6
348	Lewiston-Auburn, ME	68.2
219	Lewiston, ID-WA	156.7
215	Lexington-Fayette, KY	158.4
122	Lima, OH	234.0
300	Lincoln, NE	104.2
59	Little Rock, AR	348.6
356	Logan, UT-ID	57.4
41	Longview, TX	406.4
48	Longview, WA	378.3
20	Los Angeles County, CA M.D.	474.6
38	Los Angeles (greater), CA	411.9
150	Louisville, KY-IN	207.4
128	Lubbock, TX	223.2
288	Lynchburg, VA	111.0
30	Macon, GA	421.2
60	Madera, CA	344.7
309	Madison, WI	100.0
317	Manchester-Nashua, NH	93.2
351	Manhattan, KS	63.9
292	Mankato-North Mankato, MN	110.3
338	Mansfield, OH	76.8
56	McAllen-Edinburg-Mission, TX	351.6
318	Medford, OR	92.6
36	Memphis, TN-MS-AR	414.3
53	Merced, CA	362.0
50	Miami (greater), FL	376.0
16	Miami-Dade County, FL M.D.	489.4
173	Michigan City-La Porte, IN	195.2
208	Midland, TX	163.8
53	Milwaukee, WI	362.0
159	Minneapolis-St. Paul, MN-WI	203.2
265	Missoula, MT	128.0
44	Mobile, AL	390.4
3	Modesto, CA	658.9
255	Monroe, MI	138.5
82	Montgomery, AL	299.0
290	Morgantown, WV	110.4
235	Morristown, TN	148.0
130	Mount Vernon-Anacortes, WA	220.9
210	Muncie, IN	162.5
143	Muskegon-Norton Shores, MI	210.3
124	Napa, CA	230.6
347	Naples-Marco Island, FL	71.2
180	Nashville-Davidson, TN	189.7
286	Nassau-Suffolk, NY M.D.	112.0
80	New Haven-Milford, CT	305.1
NA	New Orleans, LA**	NA
247	New York (greater), NY-NJ-PA	142.0
262	New York-W. Plains NY-NJ M.D.	129.9
71	Newark-Union, NJ-PA M.D.	316.6
293	Niles-Benton Harbor, MI	109.1
187	North Port-Bradenton-Sarasota, FL	182.2
276	Norwich-New London, CT	116.9
2	Oakland-Fremont, CA M.D.	768.3
289	Ocala, FL	110.9
325	Ocean City, NJ	85.2
112	Odessa, TX	245.9

RANK	METROPOLITAN AREA	RATE
252	Ogden-Clearfield, UT	140.2
35	Oklahoma City, OK	415.1
144	Olympia, WA	209.8
55	Omaha-Council Bluffs, NE-IA	355.5
88	Orlando, FL	288.5
342	Oshkosh-Neenah, WI	74.4
279	Owensboro, KY	113.9
241	Oxnard-Thousand Oaks, CA	144.3
189	Palm Bay-Melbourne, FL	179.1
279	Palm Coast, FL	113.9
162	Panama City-Lynn Haven, FL	201.4
169	Pascagoula, MS	198.2
175	Peabody, MA M.D.	193.8
181	Pensacola, FL	187.3
135	Philadelphia (greater) PA-NJ-MD-DE	218.1
123	Philadelphia, PA M.D.	231.7
32	Phoenix-Mesa-Scottsdale, AZ	417.7
22	Pine Bluff, AR	468.4
290	Pittsburgh, PA	110.4
341	Pittsfield, MA	74.6
315	Pocatello, ID	94.7
303	Port St. Lucie, FL	103.7
77	Portland-Vancouver, OR-WA	307.8
329	Portland, ME	82.4
351	Poughkeepsie, NY	63.9
298	Prescott, AZ	105.5
141	Providence-New Bedford, RI-MA	212.8
310	Provo-Orem, UT	98.8
113	Pueblo, CO	245.7
275	Punta Gorda, FL	118.3
274	Racine, WI	118.6
217	Raleigh-Cary, NC	157.7
264	Rapid City, SD	128.3
120	Reading, PA	236.8
182	Redding, CA	186.8
97	Reno-Sparks, NV	271.1
152	Richmond, VA	206.6
27	Riverside-San Bernardino, CA	440.4
233	Roanoke, VA	148.2
322	Rochester, MN	86.8
242	Rochester, NY	143.8
336	Rockingham County, NH M.D.	79.1
149	Rocky Mount, NC	207.5
178	Rome, GA	191.4
21	Sacramento, CA	470.8
213	Saginaw, MI	158.8
70	Salem, OR	322.1
26	Salinas, CA	443.8
232	Salisbury, MD	148.4
24	Salt Lake City, UT	454.1
226	San Angelo, TX	151.7
65	San Antonio, TX	332.4
23	San Diego, CA	462.9
5	San Francisco (greater), CA	626.5
28	San Francisco-S. Mateo, CA M.D.	425.6
40	San Jose, CA	410.8
251	San Luis Obispo, CA	140.8
346	Sandusky, OH	71.4
151	Santa Ana-Anaheim, CA M.D.	206.9
200	Santa Barbara-Santa Maria, CA	168.6
63	Santa Cruz-Watsonville, CA	336.2
162	Santa Fe, NM	201.4
199	Santa Rosa-Petaluma, CA	168.7

RANK	METROPOLITAN AREA	RATE
37	Savannah, GA	413.7
277	Scranton--Wilkes-Barre, PA	116.1
43	Seattle-Bellevue-Everett, WA M.D.	394.9
34	Seattle-Tacoma-Bellevue, WA	415.4
282	Sebastian-Vero Beach, FL	113.2
354	Sheboygan, WI	59.3
229	Sherman-Denison, TX	150.2
114	Shreveport-Bossier City, LA	244.7
246	Sioux City, IA-NE-SD	142.5
254	Sioux Falls, SD	139.2
132	South Bend-Mishawaka, IN-MI	220.4
95	Spartanburg, SC	277.1
18	Spokane, WA	480.3
125	Springfield, MA	230.2
109	Springfield, MO	250.3
171	Springfield, OH	197.5
365	State College, PA	33.5
9	Stockton, CA	584.5
339	St. Cloud, MN	76.0
320	St. George, UT	89.3
186	St. Joseph, MO-KS	182.4
72	St. Louis, MO-IL	313.5
126	Sumter, SC	229.3
312	Syracuse, NY	96.7
17	Tacoma, WA M.D.	482.0
248	Tallahassee, FL	141.5
79	Tampa-St Petersburg, FL	306.6
89	Texarkana, TX-Texarkana, AR	285.8
105	Toledo, OH	256.8
129	Topeka, KS	221.3
193	Trenton-Ewing, NJ	173.1
19	Tucson, AZ	477.5
74	Tulsa, OK	312.6
102	Tuscaloosa, AL	258.5
145	Tyler, TX	209.2
357	Utica-Rome, NY	52.9
153	Valdosta, GA	205.4
14	Vallejo-Fairfield, CA	511.7
249	Victoria, TX	141.2
244	Vineland, NJ	143.7
12	Visalia-Porterville, CA	513.3
154	Waco, TX	205.3
202	Warner Robins, GA	167.8
148	Warren-Farmington Hills, MI M.D.	207.8
67	Washington (greater) DC-VA-MD-WV	331.7
49	Washington, DC-VA-MD-WV M.D.	377.8
270	Waterloo-Cedar Falls, IA	123.1
363	Wausau, WI	47.2
252	Wenatchee, WA	140.2
98	West Palm Beach, FL M.D.	268.1
301	Wheeling, WV-OH	103.9
116	Wichita Falls, TX	242.1
69	Wichita, KS	323.3
345	Williamsport, PA	72.9
111	Wilmington, DE-MD-NJ M.D.	246.2
NA	Wilmington, NC**	NA
273	Winchester, VA-WV	119.1
108	Winston-Salem, NC	251.4
223	Worcester, MA	155.5
299	York-Hanover, PA	105.0
160	Youngstown, OH-PA	202.2
115	Yuba City, CA	243.7
106	Yuma, AZ	254.3

Source: Reported data from the F.B.I. "Crime in the United States 2009"
*Motor vehicle theft includes the theft or attempted theft of a self-propelled vehicle. Excludes motorboats, construction equipment, airplanes, and farming equipment. **Not available.

38. Motor Vehicle Theft Rate in 2009 (continued)
National Rate = 258.8 Motor Vehicle Thefts per 100,000 Population*

RANK	METROPOLITAN AREA	RATE
1	Detroit-Livonia-Dearborn, MI M.D.	902.4
2	Oakland-Fremont, CA M.D.	768.3
3	Modesto, CA	658.9
4	Laredo, TX	628.6
5	San Francisco (greater), CA	626.5
6	Bakersfield, CA	613.6
7	Columbus, GA-AL	612.3
8	Fresno, CA	597.7
9	Stockton, CA	584.5
10	Las Vegas-Paradise, NV	566.8
11	El Centro, CA	566.3
12	Visalia-Porterville, CA	513.3
13	Detroit (greater), MI	512.2
14	Vallejo-Fairfield, CA	511.7
15	Albuquerque, NM	503.4
16	Miami-Dade County, FL M.D.	489.4
17	Tacoma, WA M.D.	482.0
18	Spokane, WA	480.3
19	Tucson, AZ	477.5
20	Los Angeles County, CA M.D.	474.6
21	Sacramento, CA	470.8
22	Pine Bluff, AR	468.4
23	San Diego, CA	462.9
24	Salt Lake City, UT	454.1
25	Augusta, GA-SC	447.4
26	Salinas, CA	443.8
27	Riverside-San Bernardino, CA	440.4
28	San Francisco-S. Mateo, CA M.D.	425.6
29	Houston, TX	425.1
30	Macon, GA	421.2
31	Dallas-Plano-Irving, TX M.D.	417.8
32	Phoenix-Mesa-Scottsdale, AZ	417.7
33	Eugene-Springfield, OR	416.9
34	Seattle-Tacoma-Bellevue, WA	415.4
35	Oklahoma City, OK	415.1
36	Memphis, TN-MS-AR	414.3
37	Savannah, GA	413.7
38	Los Angeles (greater), CA	411.9
39	Honolulu, HI	411.1
40	San Jose, CA	410.8
41	Longview, TX	406.4
42	Atlanta, GA	401.4
43	Seattle-Bellevue-Everett, WA M.D.	394.9
44	Mobile, AL	390.4
45	Hot Springs, AR	389.2
46	Jackson, MS	388.9
47	Chico, CA	379.3
48	Longview, WA	378.3
49	Washington, DC-VA-MD-WV M.D.	377.8
50	Miami (greater), FL	376.0
51	Kansas City, MO-KS	365.3
52	Dallas (greater), TX	365.1
53	Merced, CA	362.0
53	Milwaukee, WI	362.0
55	Omaha-Council Bluffs, NE-IA	355.5
56	McAllen-Edinburg-Mission, TX	351.6
57	Anderson, SC	350.9
58	Columbia, SC	350.0
59	Little Rock, AR	348.6
60	Madera, CA	344.7
61	Jackson, TN	339.7
62	Denver-Aurora, CO	338.5
63	Santa Cruz-Watsonville, CA	336.2
64	Baltimore-Towson, MD	334.9
65	San Antonio, TX	332.4
66	Florence, SC	332.2
67	Washington (greater) DC-VA-MD-WV	331.7
68	Fayetteville, NC	327.0
69	Wichita, KS	323.3
70	Salem, OR	322.1
71	Newark-Union, NJ-PA M.D.	316.6
72	Charleston-North Charleston, SC	313.5
72	St. Louis, MO-IL	313.5
74	Tulsa, OK	312.6
75	Birmingham-Hoover, AL	312.5
76	Indianapolis, IN	312.2
77	Portland-Vancouver, OR-WA	307.8
78	Amarillo, TX	307.3
79	Tampa-St Petersburg, FL	306.6
80	New Haven-Milford, CT	305.1
81	Anchorage, AK	300.0
82	Montgomery, AL	299.0
83	Charlotte-Gastonia, NC-SC	298.1
84	Lake Charles, LA	296.8
85	Huntsville, AL	295.8
86	Fort Lauderdale, FL M.D.	293.2
87	Chattanooga, TN-GA	292.5
88	Orlando, FL	288.5
89	Texarkana, TX-Texarkana, AR	285.8
90	Columbus, OH	285.4
91	Deltona-Daytona Beach, FL	285.3
92	El Paso, TX	285.2
93	Flint, MI	281.8
94	Cleveland-Elyria-Mentor, OH	280.9
95	Spartanburg, SC	277.1
96	Gainesville, FL	274.3
97	Reno-Sparks, NV	271.1
98	West Palm Beach, FL M.D.	268.1
99	Albany, GA	261.6
100	Jacksonville, FL	260.4
101	Goldsboro, NC	259.0
102	Tuscaloosa, AL	258.5
103	Fort Worth-Arlington, TX M.D.	257.4
104	Columbus, IN	256.9
105	Toledo, OH	256.8
106	Yuma, AZ	254.3
107	Baton Rouge, LA	252.0
108	Winston-Salem, NC	251.4
109	Springfield, MO	250.3
110	Lawton, OK	248.8
111	Wilmington, DE-MD-NJ M.D.	246.2
112	Odessa, TX	245.9
113	Pueblo, CO	245.7
114	Shreveport-Bossier City, LA	244.7
115	Yuba City, CA	243.7
116	Wichita Falls, TX	242.1
117	Hartford, CT	241.8
118	Lafayette, LA	239.5
119	Beaumont-Port Arthur, TX	237.3
120	Reading, PA	236.8
121	Anniston-Oxford, AL	235.6
122	Lima, OH	234.0
123	Philadelphia, PA M.D.	231.7
124	Napa, CA	230.6
125	Springfield, MA	230.2
126	Sumter, SC	229.3
127	Charleston, WV	227.0
128	Lubbock, TX	223.2
129	Topeka, KS	221.3
130	Mount Vernon-Anacortes, WA	220.9
131	Lake Havasu City-Kingman, AZ	220.6
132	South Bend-Mishawaka, IN-MI	220.4
133	Greensboro-High Point, NC	219.8
134	Gulfport-Biloxi, MS	219.6
135	Philadelphia (greater) PA-NJ-MD-DE	218.1
136	Durham-Chapel Hill, NC	217.4
137	Anderson, IN	214.4
138	Bridgeport-Stamford, CT	214.1
139	Casper, WY	213.7
140	Boston-Quincy, MA M.D.	213.4
141	Providence-New Bedford, RI-MA	212.8
142	Colorado Springs, CO	212.6
143	Muskegon-Norton Shores, MI	210.3
144	Olympia, WA	209.8
145	Farmington, NM	209.2
145	Tyler, TX	209.2
147	Billings, MT	207.9
148	Warren-Farmington Hills, MI M.D.	207.8
149	Rocky Mount, NC	207.5
150	Louisville, KY-IN	207.4
151	Santa Ana-Anaheim, CA M.D.	206.9
152	Richmond, VA	206.6
153	Valdosta, GA	205.4
154	Waco, TX	205.3
155	Knoxville, TN	204.5
156	Buffalo-Niagara Falls, NY	203.9
156	Cape Coral-Fort Myers, FL	203.9
158	Brunswick, GA	203.8
159	Minneapolis-St. Paul, MN-WI	203.2
160	Youngstown, OH-PA	202.2
161	Grand Junction, CO	201.9
162	Panama City-Lynn Haven, FL	201.4
162	Santa Fe, NM	201.4
164	Akron, OH	200.6
165	Alexandria, LA	200.0
166	Dayton, OH	199.7
167	Brownsville-Harlingen, TX	198.5
167	Gadsden, AL	198.5
169	Pascagoula, MS	198.2
170	Las Cruces, NM	197.7
171	Springfield, OH	197.5
172	Hinesville, GA	195.8
173	Michigan City-La Porte, IN	195.2
174	Athens-Clarke County, GA	194.7
175	Peabody, MA M.D.	193.8
176	Houma, LA	192.4
177	Lakeland, FL	191.8
178	Rome, GA	191.4
179	Abilene, TX	189.8
180	Nashville-Davidson, TN	189.7

Note: All listings are for Metropolitan Statistical Areas (M.S.A.s) except for those ending with "M.D." Listings with "M.D." are Metropolitan Divisions which are smaller parts of eleven large M.S.A.s. See explanatory note at beginning of metropolitan area section.

Rank Order - Metro Area (continued)

RANK	METROPOLITAN AREA	RATE
181	Pensacola, FL	187.3
182	Redding, CA	186.8
183	Kennewick-Pasco-Richland, WA	184.9
184	Burlington, NC	183.0
185	Hickory, NC	182.5
186	St. Joseph, MO-KS	182.4
187	North Port-Bradenton-Sarasota, FL	182.2
188	Corpus Christi, TX	181.7
189	Palm Bay-Melbourne, FL	179.1
190	Austin-Round Rock, TX	178.4
191	Asheville, NC	178.2
192	Des Moines-West Des Moines, IA	173.8
193	Trenton-Ewing, NJ	173.1
194	Greeley, CO	172.6
195	Gainesville, GA	172.4
196	Elkhart-Goshen, IN	171.9
197	Boston (greater), MA-NH	171.0
198	Fargo, ND-MN	169.1
199	Santa Rosa-Petaluma, CA	168.7
200	Santa Barbara-Santa Maria, CA	168.6
201	College Station-Bryan, TX	167.9
202	Warner Robins, GA	167.8
203	Bethesda-Frederick, MD M.D.	167.4
204	Kalamazoo-Portage, MI	167.0
205	Cincinnati-Middletown, OH-KY-IN	165.6
206	Decatur, IL	165.1
207	Cleveland, TN	164.9
208	Midland, TX	163.8
209	Cheyenne, WY	163.4
210	Muncie, IN	162.5
211	Great Falls, MT	161.8
212	Camden, NJ M.D.	159.1
213	Saginaw, MI	158.8
214	Duluth, MN-WI	158.6
215	Lexington-Fayette, KY	158.4
216	Carson City, NV	157.9
217	Raleigh-Cary, NC	157.7
218	Ann Arbor, MI	157.2
219	Lewiston, ID-WA	156.7
220	Bloomington, IN	156.6
221	Dover, DE	156.4
222	Dothan, AL	156.2
223	Worcester, MA	155.5
224	Lafayette, IN	153.5
225	Bowling Green, KY	152.8
226	San Angelo, TX	151.7
227	Danville, IL	151.2
228	Kingsport, TN-VA	150.5
229	Sherman-Denison, TX	150.2
230	Bismarck, ND	149.6
231	Charlottesville, VA	149.4
232	Salisbury, MD	148.4
233	Roanoke, VA	148.2
234	Clarksville, TN-KY	148.1
235	Morristown, TN	148.0
236	Lawrence, KS	147.5
237	Battle Creek, MI	147.3
238	Jacksonville, NC	146.9
239	Crestview-Fort Walton Beach, FL	146.3
240	Fort Smith, AR-OK	144.7
241	Oxnard-Thousand Oaks, CA	144.3
242	Bremerton-Silverdale, WA	143.8
242	Rochester, NY	143.8
244	Vineland, NJ	143.7
245	Coeur d'Alene, ID	143.2
246	Sioux City, IA-NE-SD	142.5
247	New York (greater), NY-NJ-PA	142.0
248	Tallahassee, FL	141.5
249	Hagerstown-Martinsburg, MD-WV	141.2
249	Victoria, TX	141.2
251	San Luis Obispo, CA	140.8
252	Ogden-Clearfield, UT	140.2
252	Wenatchee, WA	140.2
254	Sioux Falls, SD	139.2
255	Monroe, MI	138.5
256	Atlantic City, NJ	137.2
257	Dalton, GA	136.2
258	Fort Collins-Loveland, CO	133.2
259	Fort Wayne, IN	132.6
260	Bellingham, WA	132.2
261	Cambridge-Newton, MA M.D.	131.7
262	New York-W. Plains NY-NJ M.D.	129.9
263	Allentown, PA-NJ	129.5
264	Rapid City, SD	128.3
265	Missoula, MT	128.0
266	Cedar Rapids, IA	127.6
267	Johnson City, TN	127.2
268	Jackson, MI	127.1
269	Idaho Falls, ID	123.9
270	Waterloo-Cedar Falls, IA	123.1
271	Jonesboro, AR	121.1
272	Grand Rapids-Wyoming, MI	120.9
273	Winchester, VA-WV	119.1
274	Racine, WI	118.6
275	Punta Gorda, FL	118.3
276	Norwich-New London, CT	116.9
277	Scranton--Wilkes-Barre, PA	116.1
278	Columbia, MO	115.3
279	Owensboro, KY	113.9
279	Palm Coast, FL	113.9
281	Evansville, IN-KY	113.5
282	Sebastian-Vero Beach, FL	113.2
283	Grand Forks, ND-MN	112.4
284	Killeen-Temple-Fort Hood, TX	112.2
285	Fayetteville, AR-MO	112.1
286	Nassau-Suffolk, NY M.D.	112.0
287	Janesville, WI	111.8
288	Lynchburg, VA	111.0
289	Ocala, FL	110.9
290	Morgantown, WV	110.4
290	Pittsburgh, PA	110.4
292	Mankato-North Mankato, MN	110.3
293	Niles-Benton Harbor, MI	109.1
294	Flagstaff, AZ	109.0
295	Boulder, CO	108.1
296	Hattiesburg, MS	107.8
297	Corvallis, OR	105.9
298	Prescott, AZ	105.5
299	York-Hanover, PA	105.0
300	Lincoln, NE	104.2
301	Bend, OR	103.9
301	Wheeling, WV-OH	103.9
303	Port St. Lucie, FL	103.7
304	Lansing-East Lansing, MI	103.1
305	Decatur, AL	101.2
306	Dubuque, IA	101.1
307	Albany-Schenectady-Troy, NY	100.5
308	Bay City, MI	100.2
309	Madison, WI	100.0
310	Provo-Orem, UT	98.8
311	Danville, VA	98.4
312	Syracuse, NY	96.7
313	Kokomo, IN	95.7
314	Barnstable Town, MA	95.4
315	Pocatello, ID	94.7
316	Florence-Muscle Shoals, AL	94.1
317	Manchester-Nashua, NH	93.2
318	Medford, OR	92.6
319	Altoona, PA	89.6
320	St. George, UT	89.3
321	La Crosse, WI-MN	88.4
322	Rochester, MN	86.8
323	Bangor, ME	85.4
323	Lancaster, PA	85.4
325	Ocean City, NJ	85.2
326	Iowa City, IA	84.6
327	Jefferson City, MO	83.0
328	Green Bay, WI	82.6
329	Portland, ME	82.4
330	Harrisburg-Carlisle, PA	81.9
331	Edison, NJ M.D.	81.3
332	Boise City-Nampa, ID	80.6
333	Eau Claire, WI	80.1
334	Burlington-South Burlington, VT	79.8
335	Blacksburg, VA	79.5
336	Rockingham County, NH M.D.	79.1
337	Erie, PA	78.7
338	Mansfield, OH	76.8
339	St. Cloud, MN	76.0
340	Harrisonburg, VA	75.0
341	Pittsfield, MA	74.6
342	Oshkosh-Neenah, WI	74.4
343	Cape Girardeau, MO-IL	73.6
344	Ames, IA	73.2
345	Williamsport, PA	72.9
346	Sandusky, OH	71.4
347	Naples-Marco Island, FL	71.2
348	Lewiston-Auburn, ME	68.2
349	Cumberland, MD-WV	66.6
350	Kingston, NY	64.3
351	Manhattan, KS	63.9
351	Poughkeepsie, NY	63.9
353	Appleton, WI	62.7
354	Sheboygan, WI	59.3
355	Lebanon, PA	57.6
356	Logan, UT-ID	57.4
357	Utica-Rome, NY	52.9
358	Fond du Lac, WI	52.2
359	Elmira, NY	51.5
360	Holland-Grand Haven, MI	51.2
361	Binghamton, NY	49.9
362	Elizabethtown, KY	48.7
363	Wausau, WI	47.2
364	Glens Falls, NY	42.6
365	Ithaca, NY	33.5
365	State College, PA	33.5
NA	Auburn, AL**	NA
NA	New Orleans, LA**	NA
NA	Wilmington, NC**	NA

Source: Reported data from the F.B.I. "Crime in the United States 2009"
*Motor vehicle theft includes the theft or attempted theft of a self-propelled vehicle. Excludes motorboats, construction equipment, airplanes, and farming equipment. **Not available.

39. Percent Change in Motor Vehicle Theft Rate: 2008 to 2009
National Percent Change = 17.8% Decrease*

RANK	METROPOLITAN AREA	% CHANGE
13	Abilene, TX	14.5
77	Akron, OH	(7.4)
47	Albany-Schenectady-Troy, NY	(2.0)
NA	Albany, GA**	NA
250	Albuquerque, NM	(26.8)
NA	Alexandria, LA**	NA
110	Allentown, PA-NJ	(10.8)
35	Altoona, PA	0.9
72	Amarillo, TX	(6.8)
301	Ames, IA	(38.0)
15	Anchorage, AK	11.8
NA	Anderson, IN**	NA
298	Anderson, SC	(35.6)
106	Ann Arbor, MI	(10.4)
NA	Anniston-Oxford, AL**	NA
130	Appleton, WI	(13.3)
223	Asheville, NC	(22.9)
293	Athens-Clarke County, GA	(34.1)
193	Atlanta, GA	(19.7)
177	Atlantic City, NJ	(17.8)
NA	Auburn, AL**	NA
75	Augusta, GA-SC	(7.3)
149	Austin-Round Rock, TX	(15.5)
65	Bakersfield, CA	(5.7)
197	Baltimore-Towson, MD	(20.2)
181	Bangor, ME	(18.1)
70	Barnstable Town, MA	(6.2)
NA	Baton Rouge, LA**	NA
82	Battle Creek, MI	(8.6)
NA	Bay City, MI**	NA
86	Beaumont-Port Arthur, TX	(8.8)
274	Bellingham, WA	(30.5)
286	Bend, OR	(33.2)
241	Bethesda-Frederick, MD M.D.	(25.3)
67	Billings, MT	(6.1)
148	Binghamton, NY	(15.4)
196	Birmingham-Hoover, AL	(20.0)
15	Bismarck, ND	11.8
297	Blacksburg, VA	(35.3)
27	Bloomington, IN	4.0
264	Boise City-Nampa, ID	(28.8)
86	Boston (greater), MA-NH	(8.8)
75	Boston-Quincy, MA M.D.	(7.3)
NA	Boulder, CO**	NA
NA	Bowling Green, KY**	NA
18	Bremerton-Silverdale, WA	9.1
102	Bridgeport-Stamford, CT	(10.0)
31	Brownsville-Harlingen, TX	2.4
NA	Brunswick, GA**	NA
135	Buffalo-Niagara Falls, NY	(14.0)
NA	Burlington-South Burlington, VT**	NA
43	Burlington, NC	(0.7)
110	Cambridge-Newton, MA M.D.	(10.8)
262	Camden, NJ M.D.	(28.7)
174	Cape Coral-Fort Myers, FL	(17.4)
20	Cape Girardeau, MO-IL	7.6
136	Carson City, NV	(14.2)
30	Casper, WY	3.0
253	Cedar Rapids, IA	(27.3)
246	Charleston-North Charleston, SC	(26.3)
161	Charleston, WV	(16.5)
287	Charlotte-Gastonia, NC-SC	(33.3)
71	Charlottesville, VA	(6.3)
166	Chattanooga, TN-GA	(17.0)
38	Cheyenne, WY	(0.2)
24	Chico, CA	5.9
NA	Cincinnati-Middletown, OH-KY-IN**	NA
NA	Clarksville, TN-KY**	NA
NA	Cleveland-Elyria-Mentor, OH**	NA
114	Cleveland, TN	(11.2)
NA	Coeur d'Alene, ID**	NA
92	College Station-Bryan, TX	(9.3)
59	Colorado Springs, CO	(5.0)
94	Columbia, MO	(9.4)
176	Columbia, SC	(17.7)
81	Columbus, GA-AL	(8.1)
2	Columbus, IN	49.5
219	Columbus, OH	(22.3)
126	Corpus Christi, TX	(12.3)
184	Corvallis, OR	(19.0)
NA	Crestview-Fort Walton Beach, FL**	NA
115	Cumberland, MD-WV	(11.3)
129	Dallas (greater), TX	(13.2)
123	Dallas-Plano-Irving, TX M.D.	(11.9)
118	Dalton, GA	(11.5)
NA	Danville, IL**	NA
272	Danville, VA	(30.3)
261	Dayton, OH	(28.5)
178	Decatur, AL	(17.9)
NA	Decatur, IL**	NA
44	Deltona-Daytona Beach, FL	(0.9)
74	Denver-Aurora, CO	(7.1)
NA	Des Moines-West Des Moines, IA**	NA
NA	Detroit (greater), MI**	NA
NA	Detroit-Livonia-Dearborn, MI M.D.**	NA
224	Dothan, AL	(23.1)
277	Dover, DE	(31.0)
48	Dubuque, IA	(2.1)
60	Duluth, MN-WI	(5.1)
213	Durham-Chapel Hill, NC	(21.7)
10	Eau Claire, WI	15.8
153	Edison, NJ M.D.	(15.9)
143	El Centro, CA	(14.7)
280	El Paso, TX	(31.9)
NA	Elizabethtown, KY**	NA
253	Elkhart-Goshen, IN	(27.3)
11	Elmira, NY	15.7
183	Erie, PA	(18.8)
281	Eugene-Springfield, OR	(32.2)
NA	Evansville, IN-KY**	NA
29	Fargo, ND-MN	3.4
49	Farmington, NM	(2.4)
79	Fayetteville, AR-MO	(7.7)
153	Fayetteville, NC	(15.9)
33	Flagstaff, AZ	1.1
NA	Flint, MI**	NA
273	Florence-Muscle Shoals, AL	(30.4)
220	Florence, SC	(22.5)
259	Fond du Lac, WI	(28.0)
56	Fort Collins-Loveland, CO	(4.5)
170	Fort Lauderdale, FL M.D.	(17.2)
197	Fort Smith, AR-OK	(20.2)
296	Fort Wayne, IN	(34.6)
173	Fort Worth-Arlington, TX M.D.	(17.3)
99	Fresno, CA	(9.9)
80	Gadsden, AL	(7.9)
25	Gainesville, FL	4.1
NA	Gainesville, GA**	NA
4	Glens Falls, NY	34.4
282	Goldsboro, NC	(32.3)
237	Grand Forks, ND-MN	(24.7)
82	Grand Junction, CO	(8.6)
NA	Grand Rapids-Wyoming, MI**	NA
133	Great Falls, MT	(13.7)
38	Greeley, CO	(0.2)
186	Green Bay, WI	(19.2)
257	Greensboro-High Point, NC	(27.8)
NA	Gulfport-Biloxi, MS**	NA
161	Hagerstown-Martinsburg, MD-WV	(16.5)
174	Harrisburg-Carlisle, PA	(17.4)
210	Harrisonburg, VA	(21.5)
230	Hartford, CT	(24.1)
NA	Hattiesburg, MS**	NA
186	Hickory, NC	(19.2)
7	Hinesville, GA	20.6
NA	Holland-Grand Haven, MI**	NA
62	Honolulu, HI	(5.4)
32	Hot Springs, AR	2.2
95	Houma, LA	(9.5)
54	Houston, TX	(4.1)
186	Huntsville, AL	(19.2)
36	Idaho Falls, ID	0.3
268	Indianapolis, IN	(29.6)
97	Iowa City, IA	(9.8)
302	Ithaca, NY	(38.1)
275	Jacksonville, FL	(30.7)
268	Jacksonville, NC	(29.6)
NA	Jackson, MI**	NA
64	Jackson, MS	(5.6)
256	Jackson, TN	(27.7)
294	Janesville, WI	(34.3)
NA	Jefferson City, MO**	NA
108	Johnson City, TN	(10.5)
127	Jonesboro, AR	(12.8)
NA	Kalamazoo-Portage, MI**	NA
NA	Kansas City, MO-KS**	NA
62	Kennewick-Pasco-Richland, WA	(5.4)
191	Killeen-Temple-Fort Hood, TX	(19.5)
270	Kingsport, TN-VA	(29.7)
8	Kingston, NY	19.5
285	Knoxville, TN	(32.9)
233	Kokomo, IN	(24.3)
153	La Crosse, WI-MN	(15.9)
73	Lafayette, IN	(7.0)
178	Lafayette, LA	(17.9)
NA	Lake Charles, LA**	NA
158	Lake Havasu City-Kingman, AZ	(16.1)
283	Lakeland, FL	(32.4)
184	Lancaster, PA	(19.0)
NA	Lansing-East Lansing, MI**	NA

Note: All listings are for Metropolitan Statistical Areas (M.S.A.s) except for those ending with "M.D." Listings with "M.D." are Metropolitan Divisions which are smaller parts of eleven large M.S.A.s. See explanatory note at beginning of metropolitan area section.

RANK	METROPOLITAN AREA	% CHANGE
144	Laredo, TX	(15.2)
121	Las Cruces, NM	(11.7)
230	Las Vegas-Paradise, NV	(24.1)
233	Lawrence, KS	(24.3)
NA	Lawton, OK**	NA
197	Lebanon, PA	(20.2)
262	Lewiston-Auburn, ME	(28.7)
1	Lewiston, ID-WA	57.3
NA	Lexington-Fayette, KY**	NA
51	Lima, OH	(2.7)
150	Lincoln, NE	(15.6)
NA	Little Rock, AR**	NA
3	Logan, UT-ID	35.4
25	Longview, TX	4.1
11	Longview, WA	15.7
170	Los Angeles County, CA M.D.	(17.2)
168	Los Angeles (greater), CA	(17.1)
NA	Louisville, KY-IN**	NA
125	Lubbock, TX	(12.1)
182	Lynchburg, VA	(18.4)
214	Macon, GA	(21.8)
33	Madera, CA	1.1
247	Madison, WI	(26.5)
NA	Manchester-Nashua, NH**	NA
307	Manhattan, KS	(46.6)
82	Mankato-North Mankato, MN	(8.6)
279	Mansfield, OH	(31.7)
106	McAllen-Edinburg-Mission, TX	(10.4)
208	Medford, OR	(21.3)
208	Memphis, TN-MS-AR	(21.3)
178	Merced, CA	(17.9)
237	Miami (greater), FL	(24.7)
257	Miami-Dade County, FL M.D.	(27.8)
166	Michigan City-La Porte, IN	(17.0)
14	Midland, TX	13.2
239	Milwaukee, WI	(24.8)
161	Minneapolis-St. Paul, MN-WI	(16.5)
139	Missoula, MT	(14.3)
113	Mobile, AL	(11.1)
133	Modesto, CA	(13.7)
NA	Monroe, MI**	NA
91	Montgomery, AL	(9.2)
NA	Morgantown, WV**	NA
306	Morristown, TN	(42.7)
226	Mount Vernon-Anacortes, WA	(23.6)
51	Muncie, IN	(2.7)
NA	Muskegon-Norton Shores, MI**	NA
37	Napa, CA	(0.1)
265	Naples-Marco Island, FL	(28.9)
218	Nashville-Davidson, TN	(22.2)
89	Nassau-Suffolk, NY M.D.	(9.0)
NA	New Haven-Milford, CT**	NA
NA	New Orleans, LA**	NA
168	New York (greater), NY-NJ-PA	(17.1)
157	New York-W. Plains NY-NJ M.D.	(16.0)
222	Newark-Union, NJ-PA M.D.	(22.8)
NA	Niles-Benton Harbor, MI**	NA
NA	North Port-Bradenton-Sarasota, FL**	NA
67	Norwich-New London, CT	(6.1)
136	Oakland-Fremont, CA M.D.	(14.2)
255	Ocala, FL	(27.4)
207	Ocean City, NJ	(21.2)
141	Odessa, TX	(14.5)

RANK	METROPOLITAN AREA	% CHANGE
41	Ogden-Clearfield, UT	(0.4)
NA	Oklahoma City, OK**	NA
19	Olympia, WA	8.2
161	Omaha-Council Bluffs, NE-IA	(16.5)
260	Orlando, FL	(28.3)
153	Oshkosh-Neenah, WI	(15.9)
NA	Owensboro, KY**	NA
144	Oxnard-Thousand Oaks, CA	(15.2)
230	Palm Bay-Melbourne, FL	(24.1)
205	Palm Coast, FL	(21.0)
89	Panama City-Lynn Haven, FL	(9.0)
305	Pascagoula, MS	(40.4)
99	Peabody, MA M.D.	(9.9)
119	Pensacola, FL	(11.6)
243	Philadelphia (greater) PA-NJ-MD-DE	(25.7)
241	Philadelphia, PA M.D.	(25.3)
290	Phoenix-Mesa-Scottsdale, AZ	(33.6)
119	Pine Bluff, AR	(11.6)
229	Pittsburgh, PA	(23.7)
245	Pittsfield, MA	(26.0)
61	Pocatello, ID	(5.3)
243	Port St. Lucie, FL	(25.7)
144	Portland-Vancouver, OR-WA	(15.2)
116	Portland, ME	(11.4)
195	Poughkeepsie, NY	(19.9)
203	Prescott, AZ	(20.9)
201	Providence-New Bedford, RI-MA	(20.5)
57	Provo-Orem, UT	(4.6)
NA	Pueblo, CO**	NA
202	Punta Gorda, FL	(20.7)
240	Racine, WI	(25.1)
136	Raleigh-Cary, NC	(14.2)
123	Rapid City, SD	(11.9)
189	Reading, PA	(19.4)
235	Redding, CA	(24.4)
225	Reno-Sparks, NV	(23.4)
132	Richmond, VA	(13.6)
128	Riverside-San Bernardino, CA	(13.0)
67	Roanoke, VA	(6.1)
303	Rochester, MN	(38.3)
194	Rochester, NY	(19.8)
102	Rockingham County, NH M.D.	(10.0)
NA	Rocky Mount, NC**	NA
NA	Rome, GA**	NA
97	Sacramento, CA	(9.8)
NA	Saginaw, MI**	NA
28	Salem, OR	3.7
58	Salinas, CA	(4.8)
267	Salisbury, MD	(29.3)
53	Salt Lake City, UT	(3.9)
292	San Angelo, TX	(34.0)
250	San Antonio, TX	(26.8)
277	San Diego, CA	(31.0)
142	San Francisco (greater), CA	(14.6)
151	San Francisco-S. Mateo, CA M.D.	(15.7)
38	San Jose, CA	(0.2)
21	San Luis Obispo, CA	7.3
295	Sandusky, OH	(34.5)
151	Santa Ana-Anaheim, CA M.D.	(15.7)
160	Santa Barbara-Santa Maria, CA	(16.4)
6	Santa Cruz-Watsonville, CA	20.8
5	Santa Fe, NM	30.3
55	Santa Rosa-Petaluma, CA	(4.3)

RANK	METROPOLITAN AREA	% CHANGE
78	Savannah, GA	(7.6)
85	Scranton--Wilkes-Barre, PA	(8.7)
NA	Seattle-Bellevue-Everett, WA M.D.**	NA
NA	Seattle-Tacoma-Bellevue, WA**	NA
46	Sebastian-Vero Beach, FL	(1.2)
226	Sheboygan, WI	(23.6)
9	Sherman-Denison, TX	17.5
226	Shreveport-Bossier City, LA	(23.6)
23	Sioux City, IA-NE-SD	6.1
22	Sioux Falls, SD	7.2
NA	South Bend-Mishawaka, IN-MI**	NA
252	Spartanburg, SC	(26.9)
42	Spokane, WA	(0.6)
99	Springfield, MA	(9.9)
NA	Springfield, MO**	NA
291	Springfield, OH	(33.9)
271	State College, PA	(30.2)
105	Stockton, CA	(10.2)
203	St. Cloud, MN	(20.9)
266	St. George, UT	(29.1)
147	St. Joseph, MO-KS	(15.3)
170	St. Louis, MO-IL	(17.2)
NA	Sumter, SC**	NA
197	Syracuse, NY	(20.2)
NA	Tacoma, WA M.D.**	NA
289	Tallahassee, FL	(33.4)
66	Tampa-St Petersburg, FL	(5.8)
17	Texarkana, TX-Texarkana, AR	9.4
92	Toledo, OH	(9.3)
304	Topeka, KS	(39.3)
248	Trenton-Ewing, NJ	(26.6)
299	Tucson, AZ	(36.3)
88	Tulsa, OK	(8.9)
216	Tuscaloosa, AL	(22.1)
44	Tyler, TX	(0.9)
284	Utica-Rome, NY	(32.6)
104	Valdosta, GA	(10.1)
191	Vallejo-Fairfield, CA	(19.5)
112	Victoria, TX	(11.0)
121	Vineland, NJ	(11.7)
210	Visalia-Porterville, CA	(21.5)
131	Waco, TX	(13.4)
189	Warner Robins, GA	(19.4)
NA	Warren-Farmington Hills, MI M.D.**	NA
216	Washington (greater) DC-VA-MD-WV	(22.1)
212	Washington, DC-VA-MD-WV M.D.	(21.6)
139	Waterloo-Cedar Falls, IA	(14.3)
NA	Wausau, WI**	NA
109	Wenatchee, WA	(10.7)
249	West Palm Beach, FL M.D.	(26.7)
221	Wheeling, WV-OH	(22.6)
300	Wichita Falls, TX	(37.4)
116	Wichita, KS	(11.4)
50	Williamsport, PA	(2.5)
235	Wilmington, DE-MD-NJ M.D.	(24.4)
NA	Wilmington, NC**	NA
287	Winchester, VA-WV	(33.3)
215	Winston-Salem, NC	(21.9)
96	Worcester, MA	(9.6)
161	York-Hanover, PA	(16.5)
159	Youngstown, OH-PA	(16.3)
275	Yuba City, CA	(30.7)
206	Yuma, AZ	(21.1)

Source: CQ Press using reported data from the F.B.I. "Crime in the United States 2009"
*Motor vehicle theft includes the theft or attempted theft of a self-propelled vehicle. Excludes motorboats, construction equipment, airplanes, and farming equipment. **Not available.

39. Percent Change in Motor Vehicle Theft Rate: 2008 to 2009 (continued)
National Percent Change = 17.8% Decrease*

RANK	METROPOLITAN AREA	% CHANGE
1	Lewiston, ID-WA	57.3
2	Columbus, IN	49.5
3	Logan, UT-ID	35.4
4	Glens Falls, NY	34.4
5	Santa Fe, NM	30.3
6	Santa Cruz-Watsonville, CA	20.8
7	Hinesville, GA	20.6
8	Kingston, NY	19.5
9	Sherman-Denison, TX	17.5
10	Eau Claire, WI	15.8
11	Elmira, NY	15.7
11	Longview, WA	15.7
13	Abilene, TX	14.5
14	Midland, TX	13.2
15	Anchorage, AK	11.8
15	Bismarck, ND	11.8
17	Texarkana, TX-Texarkana, AR	9.4
18	Bremerton-Silverdale, WA	9.1
19	Olympia, WA	8.2
20	Cape Girardeau, MO-IL	7.6
21	San Luis Obispo, CA	7.3
22	Sioux Falls, SD	7.2
23	Sioux City, IA-NE-SD	6.1
24	Chico, CA	5.9
25	Gainesville, FL	4.1
25	Longview, TX	4.1
27	Bloomington, IN	4.0
28	Salem, OR	3.7
29	Fargo, ND-MN	3.4
30	Casper, WY	3.0
31	Brownsville-Harlingen, TX	2.4
32	Hot Springs, AR	2.2
33	Flagstaff, AZ	1.1
33	Madera, CA	1.1
35	Altoona, PA	0.9
36	Idaho Falls, ID	0.3
37	Napa, CA	(0.1)
38	Cheyenne, WY	(0.2)
38	Greeley, CO	(0.2)
38	San Jose, CA	(0.2)
41	Ogden-Clearfield, UT	(0.4)
42	Spokane, WA	(0.6)
43	Burlington, NC	(0.7)
44	Deltona-Daytona Beach, FL	(0.9)
44	Tyler, TX	(0.9)
46	Sebastian-Vero Beach, FL	(1.2)
47	Albany-Schenectady-Troy, NY	(2.0)
48	Dubuque, IA	(2.1)
49	Farmington, NM	(2.4)
50	Williamsport, PA	(2.5)
51	Lima, OH	(2.7)
51	Muncie, IN	(2.7)
53	Salt Lake City, UT	(3.9)
54	Houston, TX	(4.1)
55	Santa Rosa-Petaluma, CA	(4.3)
56	Fort Collins-Loveland, CO	(4.5)
57	Provo-Orem, UT	(4.6)
58	Salinas, CA	(4.8)
59	Colorado Springs, CO	(5.0)
60	Duluth, MN-WI	(5.1)
61	Pocatello, ID	(5.3)
62	Honolulu, HI	(5.4)
62	Kennewick-Pasco-Richland, WA	(5.4)
64	Jackson, MS	(5.6)
65	Bakersfield, CA	(5.7)
66	Tampa-St Petersburg, FL	(5.8)
67	Billings, MT	(6.1)
67	Norwich-New London, CT	(6.1)
67	Roanoke, VA	(6.1)
70	Barnstable Town, MA	(6.2)
71	Charlottesville, VA	(6.3)
72	Amarillo, TX	(6.8)
73	Lafayette, IN	(7.0)
74	Denver-Aurora, CO	(7.1)
75	Augusta, GA-SC	(7.3)
75	Boston-Quincy, MA M.D.	(7.3)
77	Akron, OH	(7.4)
78	Savannah, GA	(7.6)
79	Fayetteville, AR-MO	(7.7)
80	Gadsden, AL	(7.9)
81	Columbus, GA-AL	(8.1)
82	Battle Creek, MI	(8.6)
82	Grand Junction, CO	(8.6)
82	Mankato-North Mankato, MN	(8.6)
85	Scranton--Wilkes-Barre, PA	(8.7)
86	Beaumont-Port Arthur, TX	(8.8)
86	Boston (greater), MA-NH	(8.8)
88	Tulsa, OK	(8.9)
89	Nassau-Suffolk, NY M.D.	(9.0)
89	Panama City-Lynn Haven, FL	(9.0)
91	Montgomery, AL	(9.2)
92	College Station-Bryan, TX	(9.3)
92	Toledo, OH	(9.3)
94	Columbia, MO	(9.4)
95	Houma, LA	(9.5)
96	Worcester, MA	(9.6)
97	Iowa City, IA	(9.8)
97	Sacramento, CA	(9.8)
99	Fresno, CA	(9.9)
99	Peabody, MA M.D.	(9.9)
99	Springfield, MA	(9.9)
102	Bridgeport-Stamford, CT	(10.0)
102	Rockingham County, NH M.D.	(10.0)
104	Valdosta, GA	(10.1)
105	Stockton, CA	(10.2)
106	Ann Arbor, MI	(10.4)
106	McAllen-Edinburg-Mission, TX	(10.4)
108	Johnson City, TN	(10.5)
109	Wenatchee, WA	(10.7)
110	Allentown, PA-NJ	(10.8)
110	Cambridge-Newton, MA M.D.	(10.8)
112	Victoria, TX	(11.0)
113	Mobile, AL	(11.1)
114	Cleveland, TN	(11.2)
115	Cumberland, MD-WV	(11.3)
116	Portland, ME	(11.4)
116	Wichita, KS	(11.4)
118	Dalton, GA	(11.5)
119	Pensacola, FL	(11.6)
119	Pine Bluff, AR	(11.6)
121	Las Cruces, NM	(11.7)
121	Vineland, NJ	(11.7)
123	Dallas-Plano-Irving, TX M.D.	(11.9)
123	Rapid City, SD	(11.9)
125	Lubbock, TX	(12.1)
126	Corpus Christi, TX	(12.3)
127	Jonesboro, AR	(12.8)
128	Riverside-San Bernardino, CA	(13.0)
129	Dallas (greater), TX	(13.2)
130	Appleton, WI	(13.3)
131	Waco, TX	(13.4)
132	Richmond, VA	(13.6)
133	Great Falls, MT	(13.7)
133	Modesto, CA	(13.7)
135	Buffalo-Niagara Falls, NY	(14.0)
136	Carson City, NV	(14.2)
136	Oakland-Fremont, CA M.D.	(14.2)
136	Raleigh-Cary, NC	(14.2)
139	Missoula, MT	(14.3)
139	Waterloo-Cedar Falls, IA	(14.3)
141	Odessa, TX	(14.5)
142	San Francisco (greater), CA	(14.6)
143	El Centro, CA	(14.7)
144	Laredo, TX	(15.2)
144	Oxnard-Thousand Oaks, CA	(15.2)
144	Portland-Vancouver, OR-WA	(15.2)
147	St. Joseph, MO-KS	(15.3)
148	Binghamton, NY	(15.4)
149	Austin-Round Rock, TX	(15.5)
150	Lincoln, NE	(15.6)
151	San Francisco-S. Mateo, CA M.D.	(15.7)
151	Santa Ana-Anaheim, CA M.D.	(15.7)
153	Edison, NJ M.D.	(15.9)
153	Fayetteville, NC	(15.9)
153	La Crosse, WI-MN	(15.9)
153	Oshkosh-Neenah, WI	(15.9)
157	New York-W. Plains NY-NJ M.D.	(16.0)
158	Lake Havasu City-Kingman, AZ	(16.1)
159	Youngstown, OH-PA	(16.3)
160	Santa Barbara-Santa Maria, CA	(16.4)
161	Charleston, WV	(16.5)
161	Hagerstown-Martinsburg, MD-WV	(16.5)
161	Minneapolis-St. Paul, MN-WI	(16.5)
161	Omaha-Council Bluffs, NE-IA	(16.5)
161	York-Hanover, PA	(16.5)
166	Chattanooga, TN-GA	(17.0)
166	Michigan City-La Porte, IN	(17.0)
168	Los Angeles (greater), CA	(17.1)
168	New York (greater), NY-NJ-PA	(17.1)
170	Fort Lauderdale, FL M.D.	(17.2)
170	Los Angeles County, CA M.D.	(17.2)
170	St. Louis, MO-IL	(17.2)
173	Fort Worth-Arlington, TX M.D.	(17.3)
174	Cape Coral-Fort Myers, FL	(17.4)
174	Harrisburg-Carlisle, PA	(17.4)
176	Columbia, SC	(17.7)
177	Atlantic City, NJ	(17.8)
178	Decatur, AL	(17.9)
178	Lafayette, LA	(17.9)
178	Merced, CA	(17.9)

Note: All listings are for Metropolitan Statistical Areas (M.S.A.s) except for those ending with "M.D." Listings with "M.D." are Metropolitan Divisions which are smaller parts of eleven large M.S.A.s. See explanatory note at beginning of metropolitan area section.

RANK	METROPOLITAN AREA	% CHANGE
181	Bangor, ME	(18.1)
182	Lynchburg, VA	(18.4)
183	Erie, PA	(18.8)
184	Corvallis, OR	(19.0)
184	Lancaster, PA	(19.0)
186	Green Bay, WI	(19.2)
186	Hickory, NC	(19.2)
186	Huntsville, AL	(19.2)
189	Reading, PA	(19.4)
189	Warner Robins, GA	(19.4)
191	Killeen-Temple-Fort Hood, TX	(19.5)
191	Vallejo-Fairfield, CA	(19.5)
193	Atlanta, GA	(19.7)
194	Rochester, NY	(19.8)
195	Poughkeepsie, NY	(19.9)
196	Birmingham-Hoover, AL	(20.0)
197	Baltimore-Towson, MD	(20.2)
197	Fort Smith, AR-OK	(20.2)
197	Lebanon, PA	(20.2)
197	Syracuse, NY	(20.2)
201	Providence-New Bedford, RI-MA	(20.5)
202	Punta Gorda, FL	(20.7)
203	Prescott, AZ	(20.9)
203	St. Cloud, MN	(20.9)
205	Palm Coast, FL	(21.0)
206	Yuma, AZ	(21.1)
207	Ocean City, NJ	(21.2)
208	Medford, OR	(21.3)
208	Memphis, TN-MS-AR	(21.3)
210	Harrisonburg, VA	(21.5)
210	Visalia-Porterville, CA	(21.5)
212	Washington, DC-VA-MD-WV M.D.	(21.6)
213	Durham-Chapel Hill, NC	(21.7)
214	Macon, GA	(21.8)
215	Winston-Salem, NC	(21.9)
216	Tuscaloosa, AL	(22.1)
216	Washington (greater) DC-VA-MD-WV	(22.1)
218	Nashville-Davidson, TN	(22.2)
219	Columbus, OH	(22.3)
220	Florence, SC	(22.5)
221	Wheeling, WV-OH	(22.6)
222	Newark-Union, NJ-PA M.D.	(22.8)
223	Asheville, NC	(22.9)
224	Dothan, AL	(23.1)
225	Reno-Sparks, NV	(23.4)
226	Mount Vernon-Anacortes, WA	(23.6)
226	Sheboygan, WI	(23.6)
226	Shreveport-Bossier City, LA	(23.6)
229	Pittsburgh, PA	(23.7)
230	Hartford, CT	(24.1)
230	Las Vegas-Paradise, NV	(24.1)
230	Palm Bay-Melbourne, FL	(24.1)
233	Kokomo, IN	(24.3)
233	Lawrence, KS	(24.3)
235	Redding, CA	(24.4)
235	Wilmington, DE-MD-NJ M.D.	(24.4)
237	Grand Forks, ND-MN	(24.7)
237	Miami (greater), FL	(24.7)
239	Milwaukee, WI	(24.8)
240	Racine, WI	(25.1)
241	Bethesda-Frederick, MD M.D.	(25.3)
241	Philadelphia, PA M.D.	(25.3)
243	Philadelphia (greater) PA-NJ-MD-DE	(25.7)
243	Port St. Lucie, FL	(25.7)
245	Pittsfield, MA	(26.0)
246	Charleston-North Charleston, SC	(26.3)
247	Madison, WI	(26.5)
248	Trenton-Ewing, NJ	(26.6)
249	West Palm Beach, FL M.D.	(26.7)
250	Albuquerque, NM	(26.8)
250	San Antonio, TX	(26.8)
252	Spartanburg, SC	(26.9)
253	Cedar Rapids, IA	(27.3)
253	Elkhart-Goshen, IN	(27.3)
255	Ocala, FL	(27.4)
256	Jackson, TN	(27.7)
257	Greensboro-High Point, NC	(27.8)
257	Miami-Dade County, FL M.D.	(27.8)
259	Fond du Lac, WI	(28.0)
260	Orlando, FL	(28.3)
261	Dayton, OH	(28.5)
262	Camden, NJ M.D.	(28.7)
262	Lewiston-Auburn, ME	(28.7)
264	Boise City-Nampa, ID	(28.8)
265	Naples-Marco Island, FL	(28.9)
266	St. George, UT	(29.1)
267	Salisbury, MD	(29.3)
268	Indianapolis, IN	(29.6)
268	Jacksonville, NC	(29.6)
270	Kingsport, TN-VA	(29.7)
271	State College, PA	(30.2)
272	Danville, VA	(30.3)
273	Florence-Muscle Shoals, AL	(30.4)
274	Bellingham, WA	(30.5)
275	Jacksonville, FL	(30.7)
275	Yuba City, CA	(30.7)
277	Dover, DE	(31.0)
277	San Diego, CA	(31.0)
279	Mansfield, OH	(31.7)
280	El Paso, TX	(31.9)
281	Eugene-Springfield, OR	(32.2)
282	Goldsboro, NC	(32.3)
283	Lakeland, FL	(32.4)
284	Utica-Rome, NY	(32.6)
285	Knoxville, TN	(32.9)
286	Bend, OR	(33.2)
287	Charlotte-Gastonia, NC-SC	(33.3)
287	Winchester, VA-WV	(33.3)
289	Tallahassee, FL	(33.4)
290	Phoenix-Mesa-Scottsdale, AZ	(33.6)
291	Springfield, OH	(33.9)
292	San Angelo, TX	(34.0)
293	Athens-Clarke County, GA	(34.1)
294	Janesville, WI	(34.3)
295	Sandusky, OH	(34.5)
296	Fort Wayne, IN	(34.6)
297	Blacksburg, VA	(35.3)
298	Anderson, SC	(35.6)
299	Tucson, AZ	(36.3)
300	Wichita Falls, TX	(37.4)
301	Ames, IA	(38.0)
302	Ithaca, NY	(38.1)
303	Rochester, MN	(38.3)
304	Topeka, KS	(39.3)
305	Pascagoula, MS	(40.4)
306	Morristown, TN	(42.7)
307	Manhattan, KS	(46.6)
NA	Albany, GA**	NA
NA	Alexandria, LA**	NA
NA	Anderson, IN**	NA
NA	Anniston-Oxford, AL**	NA
NA	Auburn, AL**	NA
NA	Baton Rouge, LA**	NA
NA	Bay City, MI**	NA
NA	Boulder, CO**	NA
NA	Bowling Green, KY**	NA
NA	Brunswick, GA**	NA
NA	Burlington-South Burlington, VT**	NA
NA	Cincinnati-Middletown, OH-KY-IN**	NA
NA	Clarksville, TN-KY**	NA
NA	Cleveland-Elyria-Mentor, OH**	NA
NA	Coeur d'Alene, ID**	NA
NA	Crestview-Fort Walton Beach, FL**	NA
NA	Danville, IL**	NA
NA	Decatur, IL**	NA
NA	Des Moines-West Des Moines, IA**	NA
NA	Detroit (greater), MI**	NA
NA	Detroit-Livonia-Dearborn, MI M.D.**	NA
NA	Elizabethtown, KY**	NA
NA	Evansville, IN-KY**	NA
NA	Flint, MI**	NA
NA	Gainesville, GA**	NA
NA	Grand Rapids-Wyoming, MI**	NA
NA	Gulfport-Biloxi, MS**	NA
NA	Hattiesburg, MS**	NA
NA	Holland-Grand Haven, MI**	NA
NA	Jackson, MI**	NA
NA	Jefferson City, MO**	NA
NA	Kalamazoo-Portage, MI**	NA
NA	Kansas City, MO-KS**	NA
NA	Lake Charles, LA**	NA
NA	Lansing-East Lansing, MI**	NA
NA	Lawton, OK**	NA
NA	Lexington-Fayette, KY**	NA
NA	Little Rock, AR**	NA
NA	Louisville, KY-IN**	NA
NA	Manchester-Nashua, NH**	NA
NA	Monroe, MI**	NA
NA	Morgantown, WV**	NA
NA	Muskegon-Norton Shores, MI**	NA
NA	New Haven-Milford, CT**	NA
NA	New Orleans, LA**	NA
NA	Niles-Benton Harbor, MI**	NA
NA	North Port-Bradenton-Sarasota, FL**	NA
NA	Oklahoma City, OK**	NA
NA	Owensboro, KY**	NA
NA	Pueblo, CO**	NA
NA	Rocky Mount, NC**	NA
NA	Rome, GA**	NA
NA	Saginaw, MI**	NA
NA	Seattle-Bellevue-Everett, WA M.D.**	NA
NA	Seattle-Tacoma-Bellevue, WA**	NA
NA	South Bend-Mishawaka, IN-MI**	NA
NA	Springfield, MO**	NA
NA	Sumter, SC**	NA
NA	Tacoma, WA M.D.**	NA
NA	Warren-Farmington Hills, MI M.D.**	NA
NA	Wausau, WI**	NA
NA	Wilmington, NC**	NA

Source: CQ Press using reported data from the F.B.I. "Crime in the United States 2009"
*Motor vehicle theft includes the theft or attempted theft of a self-propelled vehicle. Excludes motorboats, construction equipment, airplanes, and farming equipment. **Not available.

40. Percent Change in Motor Vehicle Theft Rate: 2005 to 2009
National Percent Change = 37.9% Decrease*

RANK	METROPOLITAN AREA	% CHANGE
42	Abilene, TX	(12.9)
146	Akron, OH	(33.9)
164	Albany-Schenectady-Troy, NY	(36.0)
11	Albany, GA	5.4
81	Albuquerque, NM	(22.2)
212	Alexandria, LA	(41.4)
78	Allentown, PA-NJ	(22.1)
86	Altoona, PA	(23.7)
157	Amarillo, TX	(35.0)
35	Ames, IA	(10.5)
182	Anchorage, AK	(38.5)
4	Anderson, IN	21.3
90	Anderson, SC	(24.1)
220	Ann Arbor, MI	(43.0)
NA	Anniston-Oxford, AL**	NA
25	Appleton, WI	(6.7)
232	Asheville, NC	(44.7)
118	Athens-Clarke County, GA	(29.2)
146	Atlanta, GA	(33.9)
70	Atlantic City, NJ	(20.2)
NA	Auburn, AL**	NA
36	Augusta, GA-SC	(10.7)
98	Austin-Round Rock, TX	(25.9)
82	Bakersfield, CA	(23.0)
97	Baltimore-Towson, MD	(25.7)
30	Bangor, ME	(8.0)
128	Barnstable Town, MA	(30.5)
149	Baton Rouge, LA	(34.2)
140	Battle Creek, MI	(33.0)
NA	Bay City, MI**	NA
109	Beaumont-Port Arthur, TX	(27.9)
289	Bellingham, WA	(59.5)
301	Bend, OR	(70.2)
140	Bethesda-Frederick, MD M.D.	(33.0)
116	Billings, MT	(29.0)
15	Binghamton, NY	(2.0)
NA	Birmingham-Hoover, AL**	NA
88	Bismarck, ND	(23.8)
161	Blacksburg, VA	(35.9)
29	Bloomington, IN	(7.4)
NA	Boise City-Nampa, ID**	NA
196	Boston (greater), MA-NH	(39.6)
247	Boston-Quincy, MA M.D.	(47.5)
NA	Boulder, CO**	NA
NA	Bowling Green, KY**	NA
200	Bremerton-Silverdale, WA	(40.5)
93	Bridgeport-Stamford, CT	(25.1)
76	Brownsville-Harlingen, TX	(21.7)
75	Brunswick, GA	(21.6)
120	Buffalo-Niagara Falls, NY	(29.7)
NA	Burlington-South Burlington, VT**	NA
28	Burlington, NC	(7.3)
142	Cambridge-Newton, MA M.D.	(33.2)
119	Camden, NJ M.D.	(29.4)
283	Cape Coral-Fort Myers, FL	(54.6)
NA	Cape Girardeau, MO-IL**	NA
72	Carson City, NV	(20.5)
7	Casper, WY	13.2
62	Cedar Rapids, IA	(19.6)
178	Charleston-North Charleston, SC	(38.1)
207	Charleston, WV	(40.9)
275	Charlotte-Gastonia, NC-SC	(53.1)
47	Charlottesville, VA	(15.6)
105	Chattanooga, TN-GA	(27.2)
12	Cheyenne, WY	4.6
195	Chico, CA	(39.5)
NA	Cincinnati-Middletown, OH-KY-IN**	NA
NA	Clarksville, TN-KY**	NA
NA	Cleveland-Elyria-Mentor, OH**	NA
NA	Cleveland, TN**	NA
256	Coeur d'Alene, ID	(48.7)
43	College Station-Bryan, TX	(14.0)
228	Colorado Springs, CO	(44.1)
159	Columbia, MO	(35.4)
23	Columbia, SC	(6.1)
24	Columbus, GA-AL	(6.5)
1	Columbus, IN	43.9
253	Columbus, OH	(48.4)
160	Corpus Christi, TX	(35.7)
246	Corvallis, OR	(47.4)
NA	Crestview-Fort Walton Beach, FL**	NA
101	Cumberland, MD-WV	(26.5)
136	Dallas (greater), TX	(32.5)
123	Dallas-Plano-Irving, TX M.D.	(29.9)
NA	Dalton, GA**	NA
NA	Danville, IL**	NA
177	Danville, VA	(38.0)
276	Dayton, OH	(53.4)
259	Decatur, AL	(49.0)
NA	Decatur, IL**	NA
NA	Deltona-Daytona Beach, FL**	NA
288	Denver-Aurora, CO	(58.6)
NA	Des Moines-West Des Moines, IA**	NA
NA	Detroit (greater), MI**	NA
NA	Detroit-Livonia-Dearborn, MI M.D.**	NA
107	Dothan, AL	(27.5)
78	Dover, DE	(22.1)
41	Dubuque, IA	(12.8)
NA	Duluth, MN-WI**	NA
104	Durham-Chapel Hill, NC	(27.1)
82	Eau Claire, WI	(23.0)
176	Edison, NJ M.D.	(37.5)
55	El Centro, CA	(18.6)
105	El Paso, TX	(27.2)
NA	Elizabethtown, KY**	NA
157	Elkhart-Goshen, IN	(35.0)
107	Elmira, NY	(27.5)
59	Erie, PA	(19.4)
280	Eugene-Springfield, OR	(54.2)
NA	Evansville, IN-KY**	NA
22	Fargo, ND-MN	(5.7)
102	Farmington, NM	(26.9)
215	Fayetteville, AR-MO	(42.0)
34	Fayetteville, NC	(10.2)
263	Flagstaff, AZ	(49.7)
NA	Flint, MI**	NA
NA	Florence-Muscle Shoals, AL**	NA
64	Florence, SC	(19.7)
53	Fond du Lac, WI	(17.8)
234	Fort Collins-Loveland, CO	(44.9)
103	Fort Lauderdale, FL M.D.	(27.0)
127	Fort Smith, AR-OK	(30.3)
184	Fort Wayne, IN	(38.7)
199	Fort Worth-Arlington, TX M.D.	(40.1)
161	Fresno, CA	(35.9)
170	Gadsden, AL	(36.6)
45	Gainesville, FL	(15.0)
287	Gainesville, GA	(58.0)
NA	Glens Falls, NY**	NA
5	Goldsboro, NC	17.0
278	Grand Forks, ND-MN	(53.5)
198	Grand Junction, CO	(40.0)
NA	Grand Rapids-Wyoming, MI**	NA
148	Great Falls, MT	(34.1)
293	Greeley, CO	(61.3)
197	Green Bay, WI	(39.9)
154	Greensboro-High Point, NC	(34.8)
NA	Gulfport-Biloxi, MS**	NA
59	Hagerstown-Martinsburg, MD-WV	(19.4)
131	Harrisburg-Carlisle, PA	(31.3)
46	Harrisonburg, VA	(15.3)
173	Hartford, CT	(37.2)
NA	Hattiesburg, MS**	NA
149	Hickory, NC	(34.2)
5	Hinesville, GA	17.0
NA	Holland-Grand Haven, MI**	NA
236	Honolulu, HI	(45.1)
112	Hot Springs, AR	(28.4)
13	Houma, LA	4.1
94	Houston, TX	(25.5)
124	Huntsville, AL	(30.1)
110	Idaho Falls, ID	(28.0)
264	Indianapolis, IN	(50.6)
19	Iowa City, IA	(4.3)
NA	Ithaca, NY**	NA
233	Jacksonville, FL	(44.8)
NA	Jacksonville, NC**	NA
NA	Jackson, MI**	NA
58	Jackson, MS	(19.0)
187	Jackson, TN	(38.9)
187	Janesville, WI	(38.9)
217	Jefferson City, MO	(42.4)
187	Johnson City, TN	(38.9)
230	Jonesboro, AR	(44.6)
NA	Kalamazoo-Portage, MI**	NA
227	Kansas City, MO-KS	(43.9)
213	Kennewick-Pasco-Richland, WA	(41.7)
62	Killeen-Temple-Fort Hood, TX	(19.6)
149	Kingsport, TN-VA	(34.2)
137	Kingston, NY	(32.7)
220	Knoxville, TN	(43.0)
276	Kokomo, IN	(53.4)
20	La Crosse, WI-MN	(4.7)
71	Lafayette, IN	(20.4)
86	Lafayette, LA	(23.7)
18	Lake Charles, LA	(3.4)
NA	Lake Havasu City-Kingman, AZ**	NA
226	Lakeland, FL	(43.6)
152	Lancaster, PA	(34.3)
NA	Lansing-East Lansing, MI**	NA

Note: All listings are for Metropolitan Statistical Areas (M.S.A.s) except for those ending with "M.D." Listings with "M.D." are Metropolitan Divisions which are smaller parts of eleven large M.S.A.s. See explanatory note at beginning of metropolitan area section.

Alpha Order - Metro Area (continued)

RANK	METROPOLITAN AREA	% CHANGE
2	Laredo, TX	42.1
51	Las Cruces, NM	(16.6)
290	Las Vegas-Paradise, NV	(59.8)
50	Lawrence, KS	(16.4)
NA	Lawton, OK**	NA
291	Lebanon, PA	(60.5)
239	Lewiston-Auburn, ME	(45.7)
92	Lewiston, ID-WA	(24.9)
NA	Lexington-Fayette, KY**	NA
8	Lima, OH	6.5
164	Lincoln, NE	(36.0)
NA	Little Rock, AR**	NA
37	Logan, UT-ID	(11.0)
31	Longview, TX	(8.7)
179	Longview, WA	(38.3)
139	Los Angeles County, CA M.D.	(32.8)
164	Los Angeles (greater), CA	(36.0)
NA	Louisville, KY-IN**	NA
167	Lubbock, TX	(36.2)
59	Lynchburg, VA	(19.4)
191	Macon, GA	(39.0)
205	Madera, CA	(40.7)
184	Madison, WI	(38.7)
114	Manchester-Nashua, NH	(28.5)
NA	Manhattan, KS**	NA
NA	Mankato-North Mankato, MN**	NA
299	Mansfield, OH	(66.2)
17	McAllen-Edinburg-Mission, TX	(2.6)
297	Medford, OR	(62.8)
256	Memphis, TN-MS-AR	(48.7)
187	Merced, CA	(38.9)
137	Miami (greater), FL	(32.7)
132	Miami-Dade County, FL M.D.	(31.5)
121	Michigan City-La Porte, IN	(29.8)
16	Midland, TX	(2.3)
117	Milwaukee, WI	(29.1)
NA	Minneapolis-St. Paul, MN-WI**	NA
249	Missoula, MT	(48.0)
14	Mobile, AL	0.6
249	Modesto, CA	(48.0)
NA	Monroe, MI**	NA
52	Montgomery, AL	(17.0)
10	Morgantown, WV	5.6
281	Morristown, TN	(54.3)
286	Mount Vernon-Anacortes, WA	(57.6)
48	Muncie, IN	(16.0)
NA	Muskegon-Norton Shores, MI**	NA
39	Napa, CA	(11.7)
258	Naples-Marco Island, FL	(48.8)
253	Nashville-Davidson, TN	(48.4)
110	Nassau-Suffolk, NY M.D.	(28.0)
NA	New Haven-Milford, CT**	NA
NA	New Orleans, LA**	NA
225	New York (greater), NY-NJ-PA	(43.3)
220	New York-W. Plains NY-NJ M.D.	(43.0)
260	Newark-Union, NJ-PA M.D.	(49.1)
NA	Niles-Benton Harbor, MI**	NA
NA	North Port-Bradenton-Sarasota, FL**	NA
168	Norwich-New London, CT	(36.5)
112	Oakland-Fremont, CA M.D.	(28.4)
240	Ocala, FL	(46.1)
228	Ocean City, NJ	(44.1)
3	Odessa, TX	30.2

RANK	METROPOLITAN AREA	% CHANGE
143	Ogden-Clearfield, UT	(33.3)
NA	Oklahoma City, OK**	NA
211	Olympia, WA	(41.3)
224	Omaha-Council Bluffs, NE-IA	(43.2)
200	Orlando, FL	(40.5)
26	Oshkosh-Neenah, WI	(7.1)
NA	Owensboro, KY**	NA
213	Oxnard-Thousand Oaks, CA	(41.7)
65	Palm Bay-Melbourne, FL	(19.9)
NA	Palm Coast, FL**	NA
44	Panama City-Lynn Haven, FL	(14.4)
272	Pascagoula, MS	(52.2)
NA	Peabody, MA M.D.**	NA
115	Pensacola, FL	(28.6)
172	Philadelphia (greater) PA-NJ-MD-DE	(36.9)
200	Philadelphia, PA M.D.	(40.5)
295	Phoenix-Mesa-Scottsdale, AZ	(62.4)
8	Pine Bluff, AR	6.5
268	Pittsburgh, PA	(51.0)
173	Pittsfield, MA	(37.2)
67	Pocatello, ID	(20.0)
294	Port St. Lucie, FL	(62.2)
251	Portland-Vancouver, OR-WA	(48.1)
126	Portland, ME	(30.2)
161	Poughkeepsie, NY	(35.9)
274	Prescott, AZ	(52.9)
NA	Providence-New Bedford, RI-MA**	NA
218	Provo-Orem, UT	(42.6)
134	Pueblo, CO	(31.6)
192	Punta Gorda, FL	(39.1)
265	Racine, WI	(50.7)
85	Raleigh-Cary, NC	(23.4)
32	Rapid City, SD	(9.7)
203	Reading, PA	(40.6)
292	Redding, CA	(61.0)
271	Reno-Sparks, NV	(51.9)
NA	Richmond, VA**	NA
237	Riverside-San Bernardino, CA	(45.5)
144	Roanoke, VA	(33.7)
84	Rochester, MN	(23.3)
269	Rochester, NY	(51.2)
40	Rockingham County, NH M.D.	(11.9)
57	Rocky Mount, NC	(18.9)
215	Rome, GA	(42.0)
261	Sacramento, CA	(49.2)
NA	Saginaw, MI**	NA
205	Salem, OR	(40.7)
69	Salinas, CA	(20.1)
99	Salisbury, MD	(26.1)
67	Salt Lake City, UT	(20.0)
234	San Angelo, TX	(44.9)
33	San Antonio, TX	(10.0)
242	San Diego, CA	(46.9)
135	San Francisco (greater), CA	(31.8)
183	San Francisco-S. Mateo, CA M.D.	(38.6)
38	San Jose, CA	(11.4)
129	San Luis Obispo, CA	(31.1)
193	Sandusky, OH	(39.3)
273	Santa Ana-Anaheim, CA M.D.	(52.4)
184	Santa Barbara-Santa Maria, CA	(38.7)
65	Santa Cruz-Watsonville, CA	(19.9)
48	Santa Fe, NM	(16.0)
193	Santa Rosa-Petaluma, CA	(39.3)

RANK	METROPOLITAN AREA	% CHANGE
95	Savannah, GA	(25.6)
99	Scranton--Wilkes-Barre, PA	(26.1)
298	Seattle-Bellevue-Everett, WA M.D.	(65.8)
296	Seattle-Tacoma-Bellevue, WA	(62.7)
245	Sebastian-Vero Beach, FL	(47.2)
168	Sheboygan, WI	(36.5)
144	Sherman-Denison, TX	(33.7)
181	Shreveport-Bossier City, LA	(38.4)
77	Sioux City, IA-NE-SD	(22.0)
89	Sioux Falls, SD	(24.0)
NA	South Bend-Mishawaka, IN-MI**	NA
73	Spartanburg, SC	(21.1)
74	Spokane, WA	(21.4)
237	Springfield, MA	(45.5)
NA	Springfield, MO**	NA
279	Springfield, OH	(53.6)
266	State College, PA	(50.9)
241	Stockton, CA	(46.7)
179	St. Cloud, MN	(38.3)
300	St. George, UT	(66.3)
248	St. Joseph, MO-KS	(47.9)
155	St. Louis, MO-IL	(34.9)
NA	Sumter, SC**	NA
252	Syracuse, NY	(48.3)
270	Tacoma, WA M.D.	(51.3)
282	Tallahassee, FL	(54.4)
132	Tampa-St Petersburg, FL	(31.5)
26	Texarkana, TX-Texarkana, AR	(7.1)
266	Toledo, OH	(50.9)
210	Topeka, KS	(41.2)
208	Trenton-Ewing, NJ	(41.1)
244	Tucson, AZ	(47.0)
223	Tulsa, OK	(43.1)
NA	Tuscaloosa, AL**	NA
21	Tyler, TX	(5.0)
152	Utica-Rome, NY	(34.3)
121	Valdosta, GA	(29.8)
NA	Vallejo-Fairfield, CA**	NA
124	Victoria, TX	(30.1)
219	Vineland, NJ	(42.7)
NA	Visalia-Porterville, CA**	NA
261	Waco, TX	(49.2)
130	Warner Robins, GA	(31.2)
NA	Warren-Farmington Hills, MI M.D.**	NA
242	Washington (greater) DC-VA-MD-WV	(46.9)
253	Washington, DC-VA-MD-WV M.D.	(48.4)
54	Waterloo-Cedar Falls, IA	(18.3)
NA	Wausau, WI**	NA
173	Wenatchee, WA	(37.2)
230	West Palm Beach, FL M.D.	(44.6)
91	Wheeling, WV-OH	(24.5)
203	Wichita Falls, TX	(40.6)
NA	Wichita, KS**	NA
208	Williamsport, PA	(41.1)
78	Wilmington, DE-MD-NJ M.D.	(22.1)
NA	Wilmington, NC**	NA
155	Winchester, VA-WV	(34.9)
56	Winston-Salem, NC	(18.7)
170	Worcester, MA	(36.6)
95	York-Hanover, PA	(25.6)
NA	Youngstown, OH-PA**	NA
285	Yuba City, CA	(57.4)
284	Yuma, AZ	(54.7)

Source: CQ Press using reported data from the F.B.I. "Crime in the United States 2009"
*Motor vehicle theft includes the theft or attempted theft of a self-propelled vehicle. Excludes motorboats, construction equipment, airplanes, and farming equipment. **Not available.

40. Percent Change in Motor Vehicle Theft Rate: 2005 to 2009 (continued)
National Percent Change = 37.9% Decrease*

RANK	METROPOLITAN AREA	% CHANGE
1	Columbus, IN	43.9
2	Laredo, TX	42.1
3	Odessa, TX	30.2
4	Anderson, IN	21.3
5	Goldsboro, NC	17.0
5	Hinesville, GA	17.0
7	Casper, WY	13.2
8	Lima, OH	6.5
8	Pine Bluff, AR	6.5
10	Morgantown, WV	5.6
11	Albany, GA	5.4
12	Cheyenne, WY	4.6
13	Houma, LA	4.1
14	Mobile, AL	0.6
15	Binghamton, NY	(2.0)
16	Midland, TX	(2.3)
17	McAllen-Edinburg-Mission, TX	(2.6)
18	Lake Charles, LA	(3.4)
19	Iowa City, IA	(4.3)
20	La Crosse, WI-MN	(4.7)
21	Tyler, TX	(5.0)
22	Fargo, ND-MN	(5.7)
23	Columbia, SC	(6.1)
24	Columbus, GA-AL	(6.5)
25	Appleton, WI	(6.7)
26	Oshkosh-Neenah, WI	(7.1)
26	Texarkana, TX-Texarkana, AR	(7.1)
28	Burlington, NC	(7.3)
29	Bloomington, IN	(7.4)
30	Bangor, ME	(8.0)
31	Longview, TX	(8.7)
32	Rapid City, SD	(9.7)
33	San Antonio, TX	(10.0)
34	Fayetteville, NC	(10.2)
35	Ames, IA	(10.5)
36	Augusta, GA-SC	(10.7)
37	Logan, UT-ID	(11.0)
38	San Jose, CA	(11.4)
39	Napa, CA	(11.7)
40	Rockingham County, NH M.D.	(11.9)
41	Dubuque, IA	(12.8)
42	Abilene, TX	(12.9)
43	College Station-Bryan, TX	(14.0)
44	Panama City-Lynn Haven, FL	(14.4)
45	Gainesville, FL	(15.0)
46	Harrisonburg, VA	(15.3)
47	Charlottesville, VA	(15.6)
48	Muncie, IN	(16.0)
48	Santa Fe, NM	(16.0)
50	Lawrence, KS	(16.4)
51	Las Cruces, NM	(16.6)
52	Montgomery, AL	(17.0)
53	Fond du Lac, WI	(17.8)
54	Waterloo-Cedar Falls, IA	(18.3)
55	El Centro, CA	(18.6)
56	Winston-Salem, NC	(18.7)
57	Rocky Mount, NC	(18.9)
58	Jackson, MS	(19.0)
59	Erie, PA	(19.4)
59	Hagerstown-Martinsburg, MD-WV	(19.4)
59	Lynchburg, VA	(19.4)
62	Cedar Rapids, IA	(19.6)
62	Killeen-Temple-Fort Hood, TX	(19.6)
64	Florence, SC	(19.7)
65	Palm Bay-Melbourne, FL	(19.9)
65	Santa Cruz-Watsonville, CA	(19.9)
67	Pocatello, ID	(20.0)
67	Salt Lake City, UT	(20.0)
69	Salinas, CA	(20.1)
70	Atlantic City, NJ	(20.2)
71	Lafayette, IN	(20.4)
72	Carson City, NV	(20.5)
73	Spartanburg, SC	(21.1)
74	Spokane, WA	(21.4)
75	Brunswick, GA	(21.6)
76	Brownsville-Harlingen, TX	(21.7)
77	Sioux City, IA-NE-SD	(22.0)
78	Allentown, PA-NJ	(22.1)
78	Dover, DE	(22.1)
78	Wilmington, DE-MD-NJ M.D.	(22.1)
81	Albuquerque, NM	(22.2)
82	Bakersfield, CA	(23.0)
82	Eau Claire, WI	(23.0)
84	Rochester, MN	(23.3)
85	Raleigh-Cary, NC	(23.4)
86	Altoona, PA	(23.7)
86	Lafayette, LA	(23.7)
88	Bismarck, ND	(23.8)
89	Sioux Falls, SD	(24.0)
90	Anderson, SC	(24.1)
91	Wheeling, WV-OH	(24.5)
92	Lewiston, ID-WA	(24.9)
93	Bridgeport-Stamford, CT	(25.1)
94	Houston, TX	(25.5)
95	Savannah, GA	(25.6)
95	York-Hanover, PA	(25.6)
97	Baltimore-Towson, MD	(25.7)
98	Austin-Round Rock, TX	(25.9)
99	Salisbury, MD	(26.1)
99	Scranton--Wilkes-Barre, PA	(26.1)
101	Cumberland, MD-WV	(26.5)
102	Farmington, NM	(26.9)
103	Fort Lauderdale, FL M.D.	(27.0)
104	Durham-Chapel Hill, NC	(27.1)
105	Chattanooga, TN-GA	(27.2)
105	El Paso, TX	(27.2)
107	Dothan, AL	(27.5)
107	Elmira, NY	(27.5)
109	Beaumont-Port Arthur, TX	(27.9)
110	Idaho Falls, ID	(28.0)
110	Nassau-Suffolk, NY M.D.	(28.0)
112	Hot Springs, AR	(28.4)
112	Oakland-Fremont, CA M.D.	(28.4)
114	Manchester-Nashua, NH	(28.5)
115	Pensacola, FL	(28.6)
116	Billings, MT	(29.0)
117	Milwaukee, WI	(29.1)
118	Athens-Clarke County, GA	(29.2)
119	Camden, NJ M.D.	(29.4)
120	Buffalo-Niagara Falls, NY	(29.7)
121	Michigan City-La Porte, IN	(29.8)
121	Valdosta, GA	(29.8)
123	Dallas-Plano-Irving, TX M.D.	(29.9)
124	Huntsville, AL	(30.1)
124	Victoria, TX	(30.1)
126	Portland, ME	(30.2)
127	Fort Smith, AR-OK	(30.3)
128	Barnstable Town, MA	(30.5)
129	San Luis Obispo, CA	(31.1)
130	Warner Robins, GA	(31.2)
131	Harrisburg-Carlisle, PA	(31.3)
132	Miami-Dade County, FL M.D.	(31.5)
132	Tampa-St Petersburg, FL	(31.5)
134	Pueblo, CO	(31.6)
135	San Francisco (greater), CA	(31.8)
136	Dallas (greater), TX	(32.5)
137	Kingston, NY	(32.7)
137	Miami (greater), FL	(32.7)
139	Los Angeles County, CA M.D.	(32.8)
140	Battle Creek, MI	(33.0)
140	Bethesda-Frederick, MD M.D.	(33.0)
142	Cambridge-Newton, MA M.D.	(33.2)
143	Ogden-Clearfield, UT	(33.3)
144	Roanoke, VA	(33.7)
144	Sherman-Denison, TX	(33.7)
146	Akron, OH	(33.9)
146	Atlanta, GA	(33.9)
148	Great Falls, MT	(34.1)
149	Baton Rouge, LA	(34.2)
149	Hickory, NC	(34.2)
149	Kingsport, TN-VA	(34.2)
152	Lancaster, PA	(34.3)
152	Utica-Rome, NY	(34.3)
154	Greensboro-High Point, NC	(34.8)
155	St. Louis, MO-IL	(34.9)
155	Winchester, VA-WV	(34.9)
157	Amarillo, TX	(35.0)
157	Elkhart-Goshen, IN	(35.0)
159	Columbia, MO	(35.4)
160	Corpus Christi, TX	(35.7)
161	Blacksburg, VA	(35.9)
161	Fresno, CA	(35.9)
161	Poughkeepsie, NY	(35.9)
164	Albany-Schenectady-Troy, NY	(36.0)
164	Lincoln, NE	(36.0)
164	Los Angeles (greater), CA	(36.0)
167	Lubbock, TX	(36.2)
168	Norwich-New London, CT	(36.5)
168	Sheboygan, WI	(36.5)
170	Gadsden, AL	(36.6)
170	Worcester, MA	(36.6)
172	Philadelphia (greater) PA-NJ-MD-DE	(36.9)
173	Hartford, CT	(37.2)
173	Pittsfield, MA	(37.2)
173	Wenatchee, WA	(37.2)
176	Edison, NJ M.D.	(37.5)
177	Danville, VA	(38.0)
178	Charleston-North Charleston, SC	(38.1)
179	Longview, WA	(38.3)
179	St. Cloud, MN	(38.3)

Note: All listings are for Metropolitan Statistical Areas (M.S.A.s) except for those ending with "M.D." Listings with "M.D." are Metropolitan Divisions which are smaller parts of eleven large M.S.A.s. See explanatory note at beginning of metropolitan area section.

Rank Order - Metro Area (continued)

RANK	METROPOLITAN AREA	% CHANGE
181	Shreveport-Bossier City, LA	(38.4)
182	Anchorage, AK	(38.5)
183	San Francisco-S. Mateo, CA M.D.	(38.6)
184	Fort Wayne, IN	(38.7)
184	Madison, WI	(38.7)
184	Santa Barbara-Santa Maria, CA	(38.7)
187	Jackson, TN	(38.9)
187	Janesville, WI	(38.9)
187	Johnson City, TN	(38.9)
187	Merced, CA	(38.9)
191	Macon, GA	(39.0)
192	Punta Gorda, FL	(39.1)
193	Sandusky, OH	(39.3)
193	Santa Rosa-Petaluma, CA	(39.3)
195	Chico, CA	(39.5)
196	Boston (greater), MA-NH	(39.6)
197	Green Bay, WI	(39.9)
198	Grand Junction, CO	(40.0)
199	Fort Worth-Arlington, TX M.D.	(40.1)
200	Bremerton-Silverdale, WA	(40.5)
200	Orlando, FL	(40.5)
200	Philadelphia, PA M.D.	(40.5)
203	Reading, PA	(40.6)
203	Wichita Falls, TX	(40.6)
205	Madera, CA	(40.7)
205	Salem, OR	(40.7)
207	Charleston, WV	(40.9)
208	Trenton-Ewing, NJ	(41.1)
208	Williamsport, PA	(41.1)
210	Topeka, KS	(41.2)
211	Olympia, WA	(41.3)
212	Alexandria, LA	(41.4)
213	Kennewick-Pasco-Richland, WA	(41.7)
213	Oxnard-Thousand Oaks, CA	(41.7)
215	Fayetteville, AR-MO	(42.0)
215	Rome, GA	(42.0)
217	Jefferson City, MO	(42.4)
218	Provo-Orem, UT	(42.6)
219	Vineland, NJ	(42.7)
220	Ann Arbor, MI	(43.0)
220	Knoxville, TN	(43.0)
220	New York-W. Plains NY-NJ M.D.	(43.0)
223	Tulsa, OK	(43.1)
224	Omaha-Council Bluffs, NE-IA	(43.2)
225	New York (greater), NY-NJ-PA	(43.3)
226	Lakeland, FL	(43.6)
227	Kansas City, MO-KS	(43.9)
228	Colorado Springs, CO	(44.1)
228	Ocean City, NJ	(44.1)
230	Jonesboro, AR	(44.6)
230	West Palm Beach, FL M.D.	(44.6)
232	Asheville, NC	(44.7)
233	Jacksonville, FL	(44.8)
234	Fort Collins-Loveland, CO	(44.9)
234	San Angelo, TX	(44.9)
236	Honolulu, HI	(45.1)
237	Riverside-San Bernardino, CA	(45.5)
237	Springfield, MA	(45.5)
239	Lewiston-Auburn, ME	(45.7)
240	Ocala, FL	(46.1)
241	Stockton, CA	(46.7)
242	San Diego, CA	(46.9)
242	Washington (greater) DC-VA-MD-WV	(46.9)
244	Tucson, AZ	(47.0)
245	Sebastian-Vero Beach, FL	(47.2)
246	Corvallis, OR	(47.4)
247	Boston-Quincy, MA M.D.	(47.5)
248	St. Joseph, MO-KS	(47.9)
249	Missoula, MT	(48.0)
249	Modesto, CA	(48.0)
251	Portland-Vancouver, OR-WA	(48.1)
252	Syracuse, NY	(48.3)
253	Columbus, OH	(48.4)
253	Nashville-Davidson, TN	(48.4)
253	Washington, DC-VA-MD-WV M.D.	(48.4)
256	Coeur d'Alene, ID	(48.7)
256	Memphis, TN-MS-AR	(48.7)
258	Naples-Marco Island, FL	(48.8)
259	Decatur, AL	(49.0)
260	Newark-Union, NJ-PA M.D.	(49.1)
261	Sacramento, CA	(49.2)
261	Waco, TX	(49.2)
263	Flagstaff, AZ	(49.7)
264	Indianapolis, IN	(50.6)
265	Racine, WI	(50.7)
266	State College, PA	(50.9)
266	Toledo, OH	(50.9)
268	Pittsburgh, PA	(51.0)
269	Rochester, NY	(51.2)
270	Tacoma, WA M.D.	(51.3)
271	Reno-Sparks, NV	(51.9)
272	Pascagoula, MS	(52.2)
273	Santa Ana-Anaheim, CA M.D.	(52.4)
274	Prescott, AZ	(52.9)
275	Charlotte-Gastonia, NC-SC	(53.1)
276	Dayton, OH	(53.4)
276	Kokomo, IN	(53.4)
278	Grand Forks, ND-MN	(53.5)
279	Springfield, OH	(53.6)
280	Eugene-Springfield, OR	(54.2)
281	Morristown, TN	(54.3)
282	Tallahassee, FL	(54.4)
283	Cape Coral-Fort Myers, FL	(54.6)
284	Yuma, AZ	(54.7)
285	Yuba City, CA	(57.4)
286	Mount Vernon-Anacortes, WA	(57.6)
287	Gainesville, GA	(58.0)
288	Denver-Aurora, CO	(58.6)
289	Bellingham, WA	(59.5)
290	Las Vegas-Paradise, NV	(59.8)
291	Lebanon, PA	(60.5)
292	Redding, CA	(61.0)
293	Greeley, CO	(61.3)
294	Port St. Lucie, FL	(62.2)
295	Phoenix-Mesa-Scottsdale, AZ	(62.4)
296	Seattle-Tacoma-Bellevue, WA	(62.7)
297	Medford, OR	(62.8)
298	Seattle-Bellevue-Everett, WA M.D.	(65.8)
299	Mansfield, OH	(66.2)
300	St. George, UT	(66.3)
301	Bend, OR	(70.2)
NA	Anniston-Oxford, AL**	NA
NA	Auburn, AL**	NA
NA	Bay City, MI**	NA
NA	Birmingham-Hoover, AL**	NA
NA	Boise City-Nampa, ID**	NA
NA	Boulder, CO**	NA
NA	Bowling Green, KY**	NA
NA	Burlington-South Burlington, VT**	NA
NA	Cape Girardeau, MO-IL**	NA
NA	Cincinnati-Middletown, OH-KY-IN**	NA
NA	Clarksville, TN-KY**	NA
NA	Cleveland-Elyria-Mentor, OH**	NA
NA	Cleveland, TN**	NA
NA	Crestview-Fort Walton Beach, FL**	NA
NA	Dalton, GA**	NA
NA	Danville, IL**	NA
NA	Decatur, IL**	NA
NA	Deltona-Daytona Beach, FL**	NA
NA	Des Moines-West Des Moines, IA**	NA
NA	Detroit (greater), MI**	NA
NA	Detroit-Livonia-Dearborn, MI M.D.**	NA
NA	Duluth, MN-WI**	NA
NA	Elizabethtown, KY**	NA
NA	Evansville, IN-KY**	NA
NA	Flint, MI**	NA
NA	Florence-Muscle Shoals, AL**	NA
NA	Glens Falls, NY**	NA
NA	Grand Rapids-Wyoming, MI**	NA
NA	Gulfport-Biloxi, MS**	NA
NA	Hattiesburg, MS**	NA
NA	Holland-Grand Haven, MI**	NA
NA	Ithaca, NY**	NA
NA	Jacksonville, NC**	NA
NA	Jackson, MI**	NA
NA	Kalamazoo-Portage, MI**	NA
NA	Lake Havasu City-Kingman, AZ**	NA
NA	Lansing-East Lansing, MI**	NA
NA	Lawton, OK**	NA
NA	Lexington-Fayette, KY**	NA
NA	Little Rock, AR**	NA
NA	Louisville, KY-IN**	NA
NA	Manhattan, KS**	NA
NA	Mankato-North Mankato, MN**	NA
NA	Minneapolis-St. Paul, MN-WI**	NA
NA	Monroe, MI**	NA
NA	Muskegon-Norton Shores, MI**	NA
NA	New Haven-Milford, CT**	NA
NA	New Orleans, LA**	NA
NA	Niles-Benton Harbor, MI**	NA
NA	North Port-Bradenton-Sarasota, FL**	NA
NA	Oklahoma City, OK**	NA
NA	Owensboro, KY**	NA
NA	Palm Coast, FL**	NA
NA	Peabody, MA M.D.**	NA
NA	Providence-New Bedford, RI-MA**	NA
NA	Richmond, VA**	NA
NA	Saginaw, MI**	NA
NA	South Bend-Mishawaka, IN-MI**	NA
NA	Springfield, MO**	NA
NA	Sumter, SC**	NA
NA	Tuscaloosa, AL**	NA
NA	Vallejo-Fairfield, CA**	NA
NA	Visalia-Porterville, CA**	NA
NA	Warren-Farmington Hills, MI M.D.**	NA
NA	Wausau, WI**	NA
NA	Wichita, KS**	NA
NA	Wilmington, NC**	NA
NA	Youngstown, OH-PA**	NA

Source: CQ Press using reported data from the F.B.I. "Crime in the United States 2009"
*Motor vehicle theft includes the theft or attempted theft of a self-propelled vehicle. Excludes motorboats, construction equipment, airplanes, and farming equipment. **Not available.

II. City Crime Statistics
(for Cities with Populations of 75,000 and Larger)

Please note the following for Tables 41 through 84 and 88 through 90:

- All listings are for cities of 75,000 or more in population that reported data to the F.B.I. for 2009.

41. Crimes in 2009
National Total = 10,639,369 Crimes*

RANK	CITY	CRIMES
189	Abilene, TX	5,488
85	Akron, OH	12,401
184	Albany, GA	5,600
192	Albany, NY	5,271
28	Albuquerque, NM	33,222
279	Alexandria, VA	3,583
369	Alhambra, CA	2,122
168	Allentown, PA	6,019
390	Allen, TX	1,613
84	Amarillo, TX	12,619
357	Amherst, NY	2,259
112	Anaheim, CA	9,177
83	Anchorage, AK	12,804
301	Ann Arbor, MI	3,220
283	Antioch, CA	3,550
42	Arlington, TX	22,846
316	Arvada, CO	2,886
164	Athens-Clarke, GA	6,116
17	Atlanta, GA	40,708
92	Aurora, CO	11,561
NA	Aurora, IL**	NA
13	Austin, TX	52,050
214	Avondale, AZ	4,740
55	Bakersfield, CA	17,704
377	Baldwin Park, CA	1,956
22	Baltimore, MD	38,827
58	Baton Rouge, LA	16,479
139	Beaumont, TX	7,333
383	Beaverton, OR	1,781
248	Bellevue, WA	4,112
223	Bellingham, WA	4,512
363	Bend, OR	2,186
146	Berkeley, CA	7,082
209	Billings, MT	4,856
46	Birmingham, AL	20,971
NA	Bloomington, MN**	NA
296	Boca Raton, FL	3,304
159	Boise, ID	6,295
35	Boston, MA	26,941
311	Boulder, CO	3,021
392	Brick Twnshp, NJ	1,506
143	Bridgeport, CT	7,142
232	Brockton, MA	4,401
360	Broken Arrow, OK	2,197
103	Brownsville, TX	10,232
358	Buena Park, CA	2,229
53	Buffalo, NY	18,401
314	Burbank, CA	2,916
274	Cambridge, MA	3,646
175	Camden, NJ	5,815
385	Canton Twnshp, MI	1,644
204	Canton, OH	4,924
220	Cape Coral, FL	4,565
362	Carlsbad, CA	2,195
238	Carrollton, TX	4,311
321	Carson, CA	2,831
367	Cary, NC	2,137
172	Cedar Rapids, IA	5,991
391	Centennial, CO	1,549
128	Chandler, AZ	8,198
219	Charleston, SC	4,586
15	Charlotte, NC	44,158
74	Chattanooga, TN	14,641
325	Cheektowaga, NY	2,780
122	Chesapeake, VA	8,562
NA	Chicago, IL**	NA
329	Chico, CA	2,662
353	Chino, CA	2,291
169	Chula Vista, CA	6,010
40	Cincinnati, OH	24,333
255	Citrus Heights, CA	4,042
373	Clarkstown, NY	1,990
191	Clarksville, TN	5,356
182	Clearwater, FL	5,644
31	Cleveland, OH	30,118
380	Clifton, NJ	1,890
335	Clinton Twnshp, MI	2,580
293	Clovis, CA	3,430
291	College Station, TX	3,437
352	Colonie, NY	2,345
57	Colorado Springs, CO	16,691
231	Columbia, MO	4,407
117	Columbia, SC	9,027
61	Columbus, GA	15,837
12	Columbus, OH	54,153
225	Compton, CA	4,508
241	Concord, CA	4,267
298	Coral Springs, FL	3,256
257	Corona, CA	4,024
52	Corpus Christi, TX	18,477
275	Costa Mesa, CA	3,625
360	Cranston, RI	2,197
5	Dallas, TX	81,585
372	Daly City, CA	1,993
384	Danbury, CT	1,666
173	Davenport, IA	5,894
239	Davie, FL	4,306
99	Dayton, OH	10,491
218	Dearborn, MI	4,594
NA	Decatur, IL**	NA
281	Denton, TX	3,577
39	Denver, CO	24,372
107	Des Moines, IA	9,755
8	Detroit, MI	68,446
258	Downey, CA	4,019
NA	Duluth, MN**	NA
81	Durham, NC	13,354
347	Edison Twnshp, NJ	2,456
382	Edmond, OK	1,849
310	El Cajon, CA	3,070
285	El Monte, CA	3,526
45	El Paso, TX	21,358
NA	Elgin, IL**	NA
155	Elizabeth, NJ	6,401
254	Elk Grove, CA	4,051
289	Erie, PA	3,490
224	Escondido, CA	4,509
115	Eugene, OR	9,097
176	Evansville, IN	5,808
135	Everett, WA	7,558
272	Fairfield, CA	3,683
233	Fall River, MA	4,398
289	Fargo, ND	3,490
388	Farmington Hills, MI	1,628
300	Fayetteville, AR	3,233
72	Fayetteville, NC	14,774
205	Federal Way, WA	4,902
120	Flint, MI	8,641
193	Fontana, CA	5,250
197	Fort Collins, CO	5,121
89	Fort Lauderdale, FL	11,855
179	Fort Smith, AR	5,704
102	Fort Wayne, IN	10,255
19	Fort Worth, TX	40,116
190	Fremont, CA	5,468
41	Fresno, CA	23,963
364	Frisco, TX	2,166
236	Fullerton, CA	4,350
136	Gainesville, FL	7,540
264	Garden Grove, CA	3,847
108	Garland, TX	9,706
251	Gary, IN	4,069
212	Gilbert, AZ	4,765
79	Glendale, AZ	13,636
253	Glendale, CA	4,057
125	Grand Prairie, TX	8,472
100	Grand Rapids, MI	10,439
328	Greece, NY	2,710
282	Greeley, CO	3,571
302	Green Bay, WI	3,215
56	Greensboro, NC	17,243
234	Gresham, OR	4,370
379	Hamilton Twnshp, NJ	1,898
226	Hammond, IN	4,495
181	Hampton, VA	5,680
133	Hartford, CT	7,792
323	Hawthorne, CA	2,804
196	Hayward, CA	5,146
177	Henderson, NV	5,783
375	Hesperia, CA	1,963
114	Hialeah, FL	9,138
171	High Point, NC	6,004
370	Hillsboro, OR	2,033
137	Hollywood, FL	7,537
26	Honolulu, HI	35,912
2	Houston, TX	146,526
203	Huntington Beach, CA	4,948
97	Huntsville, AL	10,954
131	Independence, MO	7,914
11	Indianapolis, IN	57,179
299	Indio, CA	3,249
251	Inglewood, CA	4,069
306	Irvine, CA	3,149
116	Irving, TX	9,031
14	Jacksonville, FL	48,553
320	Jacksonville, NC	2,839
73	Jackson, MS	14,697
134	Jersey City, NJ	7,775
NA	Joliet, IL**	NA
119	Kansas City, KS	8,682
29	Kansas City, MO	32,998
297	Kenosha, WI	3,287
237	Kent, WA	4,327
161	Killeen, TX	6,263
78	Knoxville, TN	13,787
121	Lafayette, LA	8,566
396	Lake Forest, CA	1,073
187	Lakeland, FL	5,517
346	Lakewood, CA	2,483
148	Lakewood, CO	7,003
227	Lancaster, CA	4,483
199	Lansing, MI	5,082
70	Laredo, TX	15,019
202	Las Cruces, NM	5,055
9	Las Vegas, NV	60,707
211	Lawrence, KS	4,814
167	Lawton, OK	6,020
354	Lee's Summit, MO	2,285
265	Lewisville, TX	3,816
88	Lexington, KY	11,884
94	Lincoln, NE	11,172
51	Little Rock, AR	18,623
381	Livermore, CA	1,888
349	Livonia, MI	2,408
63	Long Beach, CA	15,804
327	Longmont, CO	2,718

RANK	CITY	CRIMES
162	Longview, TX	6,206
3	Los Angeles, CA	118,310
30	Louisville, KY	30,676
69	Lubbock, TX	15,089
270	Lynn, MA	3,703
132	Macon, GA	7,822
118	Madison, WI	8,737
243	Manchester, NH	4,251
127	McAllen, TX	8,368
278	McKinney, TX	3,584
207	Melbourne, FL	4,886
10	Memphis, TN	59,250
279	Merced, CA	3,583
54	Mesa, AZ	18,079
141	Mesquite, TX	7,273
110	Miami Beach, FL	9,345
140	Miami Gardens, FL	7,300
37	Miami, FL	25,761
235	Midland, TX	4,351
16	Milwaukee, WI	41,375
44	Minneapolis, MN	22,101
247	Miramar, FL	4,115
395	Mission Viejo, CA	1,259
393	Missouri City, TX	1,423
59	Mobile, AL	16,117
91	Modesto, CA	11,688
87	Montgomery, AL	11,936
150	Moreno Valley, CA	6,879
185	Murfreesboro, TN	5,548
389	Murrieta, CA	1,627
355	Nampa, ID	2,270
NA	Naperville, IL**	NA
332	Nashua, NH	2,619
25	Nashville, TN	36,115
229	New Bedford, MA	4,419
111	New Haven, CT	9,226
66	New Orleans, LA	15,554
1	New York, NY	188,357
93	Newark, NJ	11,419
351	Newport Beach, CA	2,364
397	Newton, MA	1,065
75	Norfolk, VA	14,482
262	Norman, OK	3,945
144	North Charleston, SC	7,133
129	North Las Vegas, NV	8,183
333	Norwalk, CA	2,607
359	Norwalk, CT	2,211
34	Oakland, CA	26,966
213	Oceanside, CA	4,744
206	Odessa, TX	4,896
394	O'Fallon, MO	1,388
228	Ogden, UT	4,431
20	Oklahoma City, OK	39,145
318	Olathe, KS	2,873
47	Omaha, NE	20,654
174	Ontario, CA	5,878
324	Orange, CA	2,785
337	Orem, UT	2,570
49	Orlando, FL	20,171
210	Overland Park, KS	4,815
208	Oxnard, CA	4,858
312	Palm Bay, FL	2,958
230	Palmdale, CA	4,416
216	Pasadena, CA	4,641
158	Pasadena, TX	6,316
195	Paterson, NJ	5,154
368	Pearland, TX	2,136
180	Pembroke Pines, FL	5,686

RANK	CITY	CRIMES
194	Peoria, AZ	5,193
NA	Peoria, IL**	NA
6	Philadelphia, PA	75,051
7	Phoenix, AZ	74,347
71	Pittsburgh, PA	14,862
126	Plano, TX	8,457
259	Plantation, FL	4,010
198	Pomona, CA	5,102
166	Pompano Beach, FL	6,095
260	Port St. Lucie, FL	3,973
32	Portland, OR	29,600
157	Portsmouth, VA	6,350
113	Providence, RI	9,172
309	Provo, UT	3,086
240	Pueblo, CO	4,289
366	Quincy, MA	2,143
261	Racine, WI	3,969
62	Raleigh, NC	15,818
398	Ramapo, NY	732
250	Rancho Cucamon., CA	4,107
222	Reading, PA	4,554
273	Redding, CA	3,667
101	Reno, NV	10,283
294	Rialto, CA	3,404
266	Richardson, TX	3,805
186	Richmond, CA	5,535
105	Richmond, VA	9,980
371	Rio Rancho, NM	2,007
96	Riverside, CA	11,125
183	Roanoke, VA	5,614
NA	Rochester, MN**	NA
82	Rochester, NY	13,033
98	Rockford, IL	10,667
245	Roseville, CA	4,192
341	Roswell, GA	2,512
315	Round Rock, TX	2,900
38	Sacramento, CA	25,166
152	Salem, OR	6,789
165	Salinas, CA	6,099
64	Salt Lake City, UT	15,779
217	San Angelo, TX	4,615
4	San Antonio, TX	99,495
95	San Bernardino, CA	11,153
23	San Diego, CA	38,177
18	San Francisco, CA	40,466
36	San Jose, CA	26,194
263	San Leandro, CA	3,854
386	San Marcos, CA	1,642
342	San Mateo, CA	2,510
305	Sandy Springs, GA	3,164
276	Sandy, UT	3,623
123	Santa Ana, CA	8,524
295	Santa Barbara, CA	3,313
303	Santa Clara, CA	3,196
287	Santa Clarita, CA	3,494
338	Santa Maria, CA	2,561
269	Santa Monica, CA	3,747
200	Santa Rosa, CA	5,068
90	Savannah, GA	11,782
142	Scottsdale, AZ	7,208
21	Seattle, WA	38,951
86	Shreveport, LA	12,201
365	Simi Valley, CA	2,152
304	Sioux City, IA	3,175
201	Sioux Falls, SD	5,063
356	Somerville, MA	2,267
149	South Bend, IN	6,882
307	South Gate, CA	3,137

RANK	CITY	CRIMES
288	Southfield, MI	3,491
286	Sparks, NV	3,504
284	Spokane Valley, WA	3,527
76	Spokane, WA	14,436
NA	Springfield, IL**	NA
109	Springfield, MA	9,447
68	Springfield, MO	15,209
343	Stamford, CT	2,496
322	Sterling Heights, MI	2,825
50	Stockton, CA	19,130
387	St. George, UT	1,632
244	St. Joseph, MO	4,235
24	St. Louis, MO	36,948
80	St. Paul, MN	13,568
48	St. Petersburg, FL	20,532
345	Suffolk, VA	2,489
374	Sugar Land, TX	1,967
313	Sunnyvale, CA	2,938
242	Sunrise, FL	4,255
339	Surprise, AZ	2,516
145	Syracuse, NY	7,122
60	Tacoma, WA	15,921
104	Tallahassee, FL	10,085
65	Tampa, FL	15,557
343	Temecula, CA	2,496
106	Tempe, AZ	9,908
246	Thornton, CO	4,128
378	Thousand Oaks, CA	1,956
NA	Toledo, OH**	NA
336	Toms River Twnshp, NJ	2,578
138	Topeka, KS	7,417
308	Torrance, CA	3,133
330	Tracy, CA	2,660
268	Trenton, NJ	3,778
376	Troy, MI	1,959
NA	Tucson, AZ**	NA
33	Tulsa, OK	27,515
188	Tuscaloosa, AL	5,500
156	Tyler, TX	6,360
331	Upper Darby Twnshp, PA	2,653
350	Vacaville, CA	2,396
154	Vallejo, CA	6,476
153	Vancouver, WA	6,600
292	Ventura, CA	3,436
215	Victorville, CA	4,722
77	Virginia Beach, VA	14,269
177	Visalia, CA	5,783
326	Vista, CA	2,728
130	Waco, TX	7,993
221	Warren, MI	4,563
319	Warwick, RI	2,846
27	Washington, DC	34,593
169	Waterbury, CT	6,010
277	West Covina, CA	3,597
267	West Jordan, UT	3,782
160	West Palm Beach, FL	6,270
151	West Valley, UT	6,827
317	Westland, MI	2,876
334	Westminster, CA	2,596
271	Westminster, CO	3,686
348	Whittier, CA	2,442
163	Wichita Falls, TX	6,138
43	Wichita, KS	22,842
147	Wilmington, NC	7,050
67	Winston-Salem, NC	15,527
339	Woodbridge Twnshp, NJ	2,516
124	Worcester, MA	8,481
249	Yonkers, NY	4,110
256	Yuma, AZ	4,041

Source: CQ Press using reported data from the F.B.I. "Crime in the United States 2009"

*Includes murder, rape, robbery, aggravated assault, burglary, larceny-theft, and motor vehicle theft.

**Not available.

41. Crimes in 2009 (continued)
National Total = 10,639,369 Crimes*

RANK	CITY	CRIMES
1	New York, NY	188,357
2	Houston, TX	146,526
3	Los Angeles, CA	118,310
4	San Antonio, TX	99,495
5	Dallas, TX	81,585
6	Philadelphia, PA	75,051
7	Phoenix, AZ	74,347
8	Detroit, MI	68,446
9	Las Vegas, NV	60,707
10	Memphis, TN	59,250
11	Indianapolis, IN	57,179
12	Columbus, OH	54,153
13	Austin, TX	52,050
14	Jacksonville, FL	48,553
15	Charlotte, NC	44,158
16	Milwaukee, WI	41,375
17	Atlanta, GA	40,708
18	San Francisco, CA	40,466
19	Fort Worth, TX	40,116
20	Oklahoma City, OK	39,145
21	Seattle, WA	38,951
22	Baltimore, MD	38,827
23	San Diego, CA	38,177
24	St. Louis, MO	36,948
25	Nashville, TN	36,115
26	Honolulu, HI	35,912
27	Washington, DC	34,593
28	Albuquerque, NM	33,222
29	Kansas City, MO	32,998
30	Louisville, KY	30,676
31	Cleveland, OH	30,118
32	Portland, OR	29,600
33	Tulsa, OK	27,515
34	Oakland, CA	26,966
35	Boston, MA	26,941
36	San Jose, CA	26,194
37	Miami, FL	25,761
38	Sacramento, CA	25,166
39	Denver, CO	24,372
40	Cincinnati, OH	24,333
41	Fresno, CA	23,963
42	Arlington, TX	22,846
43	Wichita, KS	22,842
44	Minneapolis, MN	22,101
45	El Paso, TX	21,358
46	Birmingham, AL	20,971
47	Omaha, NE	20,654
48	St. Petersburg, FL	20,532
49	Orlando, FL	20,171
50	Stockton, CA	19,130
51	Little Rock, AR	18,623
52	Corpus Christi, TX	18,477
53	Buffalo, NY	18,401
54	Mesa, AZ	18,079
55	Bakersfield, CA	17,704
56	Greensboro, NC	17,243
57	Colorado Springs, CO	16,691
58	Baton Rouge, LA	16,479
59	Mobile, AL	16,117
60	Tacoma, WA	15,921
61	Columbus, GA	15,837
62	Raleigh, NC	15,818
63	Long Beach, CA	15,804
64	Salt Lake City, UT	15,779
65	Tampa, FL	15,557
66	New Orleans, LA	15,554
67	Winston-Salem, NC	15,527
68	Springfield, MO	15,209
69	Lubbock, TX	15,089
70	Laredo, TX	15,019
71	Pittsburgh, PA	14,862
72	Fayetteville, NC	14,774
73	Jackson, MS	14,697
74	Chattanooga, TN	14,641
75	Norfolk, VA	14,482
76	Spokane, WA	14,436
77	Virginia Beach, VA	14,269
78	Knoxville, TN	13,787
79	Glendale, AZ	13,636
80	St. Paul, MN	13,568
81	Durham, NC	13,354
82	Rochester, NY	13,033
83	Anchorage, AK	12,804
84	Amarillo, TX	12,619
85	Akron, OH	12,401
86	Shreveport, LA	12,201
87	Montgomery, AL	11,936
88	Lexington, KY	11,884
89	Fort Lauderdale, FL	11,855
90	Savannah, GA	11,782
91	Modesto, CA	11,688
92	Aurora, CO	11,561
93	Newark, NJ	11,419
94	Lincoln, NE	11,172
95	San Bernardino, CA	11,153
96	Riverside, CA	11,125
97	Huntsville, AL	10,954
98	Rockford, IL	10,667
99	Dayton, OH	10,491
100	Grand Rapids, MI	10,439
101	Reno, NV	10,283
102	Fort Wayne, IN	10,255
103	Brownsville, TX	10,232
104	Tallahassee, FL	10,085
105	Richmond, VA	9,980
106	Tempe, AZ	9,908
107	Des Moines, IA	9,755
108	Garland, TX	9,706
109	Springfield, MA	9,447
110	Miami Beach, FL	9,345
111	New Haven, CT	9,226
112	Anaheim, CA	9,177
113	Providence, RI	9,172
114	Hialeah, FL	9,138
115	Eugene, OR	9,097
116	Irving, TX	9,031
117	Columbia, SC	9,027
118	Madison, WI	8,737
119	Kansas City, KS	8,682
120	Flint, MI	8,641
121	Lafayette, LA	8,566
122	Chesapeake, VA	8,562
123	Santa Ana, CA	8,524
124	Worcester, MA	8,481
125	Grand Prairie, TX	8,472
126	Plano, TX	8,457
127	McAllen, TX	8,368
128	Chandler, AZ	8,198
129	North Las Vegas, NV	8,183
130	Waco, TX	7,993
131	Independence, MO	7,914
132	Macon, GA	7,822
133	Hartford, CT	7,792
134	Jersey City, NJ	7,775
135	Everett, WA	7,558
136	Gainesville, FL	7,540
137	Hollywood, FL	7,537
138	Topeka, KS	7,417
139	Beaumont, TX	7,333
140	Miami Gardens, FL	7,300
141	Mesquite, TX	7,273
142	Scottsdale, AZ	7,208
143	Bridgeport, CT	7,142
144	North Charleston, SC	7,133
145	Syracuse, NY	7,122
146	Berkeley, CA	7,082
147	Wilmington, NC	7,050
148	Lakewood, CO	7,003
149	South Bend, IN	6,882
150	Moreno Valley, CA	6,879
151	West Valley, UT	6,827
152	Salem, OR	6,789
153	Vancouver, WA	6,600
154	Vallejo, CA	6,476
155	Elizabeth, NJ	6,401
156	Tyler, TX	6,360
157	Portsmouth, VA	6,350
158	Pasadena, TX	6,316
159	Boise, ID	6,295
160	West Palm Beach, FL	6,270
161	Killeen, TX	6,263
162	Longview, TX	6,206
163	Wichita Falls, TX	6,138
164	Athens-Clarke, GA	6,116
165	Salinas, CA	6,099
166	Pompano Beach, FL	6,095
167	Lawton, OK	6,020
168	Allentown, PA	6,019
169	Chula Vista, CA	6,010
169	Waterbury, CT	6,010
171	High Point, NC	6,004
172	Cedar Rapids, IA	5,991
173	Davenport, IA	5,894
174	Ontario, CA	5,878
175	Camden, NJ	5,815
176	Evansville, IN	5,808
177	Henderson, NV	5,783
177	Visalia, CA	5,783
179	Fort Smith, AR	5,704
180	Pembroke Pines, FL	5,686
181	Hampton, VA	5,680
182	Clearwater, FL	5,644
183	Roanoke, VA	5,614
184	Albany, GA	5,600
185	Murfreesboro, TN	5,548
186	Richmond, CA	5,535
187	Lakeland, FL	5,517
188	Tuscaloosa, AL	5,500
189	Abilene, TX	5,488
190	Fremont, CA	5,468
191	Clarksville, TN	5,356
192	Albany, NY	5,271
193	Fontana, CA	5,250
194	Peoria, AZ	5,193
195	Paterson, NJ	5,154
196	Hayward, CA	5,146
197	Fort Collins, CO	5,121
198	Pomona, CA	5,102
199	Lansing, MI	5,082
200	Santa Rosa, CA	5,068
201	Sioux Falls, SD	5,063
202	Las Cruces, NM	5,055
203	Huntington Beach, CA	4,948
204	Canton, OH	4,924
205	Federal Way, WA	4,902
206	Odessa, TX	4,896

RANK	CITY	CRIMES	RANK	CITY	CRIMES	RANK	CITY	CRIMES
207	Melbourne, FL	4,886	275	Costa Mesa, CA	3,625	343	Stamford, CT	2,496
208	Oxnard, CA	4,858	276	Sandy, UT	3,623	343	Temecula, CA	2,496
209	Billings, MT	4,856	277	West Covina, CA	3,597	345	Suffolk, VA	2,489
210	Overland Park, KS	4,815	278	McKinney, TX	3,584	346	Lakewood, CA	2,483
211	Lawrence, KS	4,814	279	Alexandria, VA	3,583	347	Edison Twnshp, NJ	2,456
212	Gilbert, AZ	4,765	279	Merced, CA	3,583	348	Whittier, CA	2,442
213	Oceanside, CA	4,744	281	Denton, TX	3,577	349	Livonia, MI	2,408
214	Avondale, AZ	4,740	282	Greeley, CO	3,571	350	Vacaville, CA	2,396
215	Victorville, CA	4,722	283	Antioch, CA	3,550	351	Newport Beach, CA	2,364
216	Pasadena, CA	4,641	284	Spokane Valley, WA	3,527	352	Colonie, NY	2,345
217	San Angelo, TX	4,615	285	El Monte, CA	3,526	353	Chino, CA	2,291
218	Dearborn, MI	4,594	286	Sparks, NV	3,504	354	Lee's Summit, MO	2,285
219	Charleston, SC	4,586	287	Santa Clarita, CA	3,494	355	Nampa, ID	2,270
220	Cape Coral, FL	4,565	288	Southfield, MI	3,491	356	Somerville, MA	2,267
221	Warren, MI	4,563	289	Erie, PA	3,490	357	Amherst, NY	2,259
222	Reading, PA	4,554	289	Fargo, ND	3,490	358	Buena Park, CA	2,229
223	Bellingham, WA	4,512	291	College Station, TX	3,437	359	Norwalk, CT	2,211
224	Escondido, CA	4,509	292	Ventura, CA	3,436	360	Broken Arrow, OK	2,197
225	Compton, CA	4,508	293	Clovis, CA	3,430	360	Cranston, RI	2,197
226	Hammond, IN	4,495	294	Rialto, CA	3,404	362	Carlsbad, CA	2,195
227	Lancaster, CA	4,483	295	Santa Barbara, CA	3,313	363	Bend, OR	2,186
228	Ogden, UT	4,431	296	Boca Raton, FL	3,304	364	Frisco, TX	2,166
229	New Bedford, MA	4,419	297	Kenosha, WI	3,287	365	Simi Valley, CA	2,152
230	Palmdale, CA	4,416	298	Coral Springs, FL	3,256	366	Quincy, MA	2,143
231	Columbia, MO	4,407	299	Indio, CA	3,249	367	Cary, NC	2,137
232	Brockton, MA	4,401	300	Fayetteville, AR	3,233	368	Pearland, TX	2,136
233	Fall River, MA	4,398	301	Ann Arbor, MI	3,220	369	Alhambra, CA	2,122
234	Gresham, OR	4,370	302	Green Bay, WI	3,215	370	Hillsboro, OR	2,033
235	Midland, TX	4,351	303	Santa Clara, CA	3,196	371	Rio Rancho, NM	2,007
236	Fullerton, CA	4,350	304	Sioux City, IA	3,175	372	Daly City, CA	1,993
237	Kent, WA	4,327	305	Sandy Springs, GA	3,164	373	Clarkstown, NY	1,990
238	Carrollton, TX	4,311	306	Irvine, CA	3,149	374	Sugar Land, TX	1,967
239	Davie, FL	4,306	307	South Gate, CA	3,137	375	Hesperia, CA	1,963
240	Pueblo, CO	4,289	308	Torrance, CA	3,133	376	Troy, MI	1,959
241	Concord, CA	4,267	309	Provo, UT	3,086	377	Baldwin Park, CA	1,956
242	Sunrise, FL	4,255	310	El Cajon, CA	3,070	378	Thousand Oaks, CA	1,956
243	Manchester, NH	4,251	311	Boulder, CO	3,021	379	Hamilton Twnshp, NJ	1,898
244	St. Joseph, MO	4,235	312	Palm Bay, FL	2,958	380	Clifton, NJ	1,890
245	Roseville, CA	4,192	313	Sunnyvale, CA	2,938	381	Livermore, CA	1,888
246	Thornton, CO	4,128	314	Burbank, CA	2,916	382	Edmond, OK	1,849
247	Miramar, FL	4,115	315	Round Rock, TX	2,900	383	Beaverton, OR	1,781
248	Bellevue, WA	4,112	316	Arvada, CO	2,886	384	Danbury, CT	1,666
249	Yonkers, NY	4,110	317	Westland, MI	2,876	385	Canton Twnshp, MI	1,644
250	Rancho Cucamon., CA	4,107	318	Olathe, KS	2,873	386	San Marcos, CA	1,642
251	Gary, IN	4,069	319	Warwick, RI	2,846	387	St. George, UT	1,632
251	Inglewood, CA	4,069	320	Jacksonville, NC	2,839	388	Farmington Hills, MI	1,628
253	Glendale, CA	4,057	321	Carson, CA	2,831	389	Murrieta, CA	1,627
254	Elk Grove, CA	4,051	322	Sterling Heights, MI	2,825	390	Allen, TX	1,613
255	Citrus Heights, CA	4,042	323	Hawthorne, CA	2,804	391	Centennial, CO	1,549
256	Yuma, AZ	4,041	324	Orange, CA	2,785	392	Brick Twnshp, NJ	1,506
257	Corona, CA	4,024	325	Cheektowaga, NY	2,780	393	Missouri City, TX	1,423
258	Downey, CA	4,019	326	Vista, CA	2,728	394	O'Fallon, MO	1,388
259	Plantation, FL	4,010	327	Longmont, CO	2,718	395	Mission Viejo, CA	1,259
260	Port St. Lucie, FL	3,973	328	Greece, NY	2,710	396	Lake Forest, CA	1,073
261	Racine, WI	3,969	329	Chico, CA	2,662	397	Newton, MA	1,065
262	Norman, OK	3,945	330	Tracy, CA	2,660	398	Ramapo, NY	732
263	San Leandro, CA	3,854	331	Upper Darby Twnshp, PA	2,653	NA	Aurora, IL**	NA
264	Garden Grove, CA	3,847	332	Nashua, NH	2,619	NA	Bloomington, MN**	NA
265	Lewisville, TX	3,816	333	Norwalk, CA	2,607	NA	Chicago, IL**	NA
266	Richardson, TX	3,805	334	Westminster, CA	2,596	NA	Decatur, IL**	NA
267	West Jordan, UT	3,782	335	Clinton Twnshp, MI	2,580	NA	Duluth, MN**	NA
268	Trenton, NJ	3,778	336	Toms River Twnshp, NJ	2,578	NA	Elgin, IL**	NA
269	Santa Monica, CA	3,747	337	Orem, UT	2,570	NA	Joliet, IL**	NA
270	Lynn, MA	3,703	338	Santa Maria, CA	2,561	NA	Naperville, IL**	NA
271	Westminster, CO	3,686	339	Surprise, AZ	2,516	NA	Peoria, IL**	NA
272	Fairfield, CA	3,683	339	Woodbridge Twnshp, NJ	2,516	NA	Rochester, MN**	NA
273	Redding, CA	3,667	341	Roswell, GA	2,512	NA	Springfield, IL**	NA
274	Cambridge, MA	3,646	342	San Mateo, CA	2,510	NA	Toledo, OH**	NA
						NA	Tucson, AZ**	NA

Source: CQ Press using reported data from the F.B.I. "Crime in the United States 2009"
*Includes murder, rape, robbery, aggravated assault, burglary, larceny-theft, and motor vehicle theft.
**Not available.

42. Crime Rate in 2009
National Rate = 3,465.5 Crimes per 100,000 Population*

RANK	CITY	RATE
163	Abilene, TX	4,708.4
88	Akron, OH	6,005.4
24	Albany, GA	7,394.3
108	Albany, NY	5,640.8
73	Albuquerque, NM	6,260.8
346	Alexandria, VA	2,451.7
345	Alhambra, CA	2,468.7
111	Allentown, PA	5,608.1
386	Allen, TX	1,856.1
50	Amarillo, TX	6,685.0
376	Amherst, NY	2,046.2
317	Anaheim, CA	2,731.5
175	Anchorage, AK	4,519.6
308	Ann Arbor, MI	2,815.5
247	Antioch, CA	3,506.4
85	Arlington, TX	6,026.3
325	Arvada, CO	2,673.6
128	Athens-Clarke, GA	5,339.6
26	Atlanta, GA	7,362.6
239	Aurora, CO	3,568.1
NA	Aurora, IL**	NA
45	Austin, TX	6,768.8
129	Avondale, AZ	5,339.5
125	Bakersfield, CA	5,350.3
340	Baldwin Park, CA	2,522.6
83	Baltimore, MD	6,078.5
25	Baton Rouge, LA	7,383.5
53	Beaumont, TX	6,652.0
385	Beaverton, OR	1,910.5
266	Bellevue, WA	3,288.2
109	Bellingham, WA	5,622.9
319	Bend, OR	2,713.8
37	Berkeley, CA	6,998.7
171	Billings, MT	4,606.0
5	Birmingham, AL	9,223.2
NA	Bloomington, MN**	NA
215	Boca Raton, FL	3,843.8
285	Boise, ID	3,049.4
186	Boston, MA	4,315.9
287	Boulder, CO	3,019.9
384	Brick Twnshp, NJ	1,914.4
133	Bridgeport, CT	5,249.6
173	Brockton, MA	4,562.0
356	Broken Arrow, OK	2,327.0
104	Brownsville, TX	5,700.6
309	Buena Park, CA	2,802.9
40	Buffalo, NY	6,849.3
307	Burbank, CA	2,824.3
241	Cambridge, MA	3,544.4
26	Camden, NJ	7,362.6
382	Canton Twnshp, MI	1,989.5
69	Canton, OH	6,305.9
311	Cape Coral, FL	2,777.7
361	Carlsbad, CA	2,228.8
257	Carrollton, TX	3,383.0
284	Carson, CA	3,056.1
390	Cary, NC	1,597.7
168	Cedar Rapids, IA	4,652.2
392	Centennial, CO	1,558.6
275	Chandler, AZ	3,201.2
200	Charleston, SC	4,034.1
105	Charlotte, NC	5,678.0
12	Chattanooga, TN	8,485.8
238	Cheektowaga, NY	3,574.6
219	Chesapeake, VA	3,835.0
NA	Chicago, IL**	NA
280	Chico, CA	3,142.0
321	Chino, CA	2,707.2
326	Chula Vista, CA	2,673.0
28	Cincinnati, OH	7,294.8
156	Citrus Heights, CA	4,792.9
341	Clarkstown, NY	2,522.2
182	Clarksville, TN	4,402.4
123	Clearwater, FL	5,355.7
36	Cleveland, OH	7,016.6
349	Clifton, NJ	2,419.2
324	Clinton Twnshp, MI	2,688.7
236	Clovis, CA	3,601.8
207	College Station, TX	3,993.2
292	Colonie, NY	3,006.3
194	Colorado Springs, CO	4,155.9
189	Columbia, MO	4,295.8
33	Columbia, SC	7,058.7
10	Columbus, GA	8,504.3
31	Columbus, OH	7,131.1
154	Compton, CA	4,802.3
243	Concord, CA	3,525.2
334	Coral Springs, FL	2,591.2
331	Corona, CA	2,639.8
63	Corpus Christi, TX	6,426.6
265	Costa Mesa, CA	3,291.0
316	Cranston, RI	2,738.6
67	Dallas, TX	6,323.1
383	Daly City, CA	1,967.7
371	Danbury, CT	2,089.6
97	Davenport, IA	5,828.9
159	Davie, FL	4,776.6
39	Dayton, OH	6,858.4
121	Dearborn, MI	5,385.4
NA	Decatur, IL**	NA
303	Denton, TX	2,877.5
203	Denver, CO	4,030.6
147	Des Moines, IA	4,957.0
19	Detroit, MI	7,534.4
222	Downey, CA	3,735.2
NA	Duluth, MN**	NA
95	Durham, NC	5,870.1
344	Edison Twnshp, NJ	2,471.9
359	Edmond, OK	2,285.8
263	El Cajon, CA	3,320.1
302	El Monte, CA	2,880.1
249	El Paso, TX	3,451.5
NA	Elgin, IL**	NA
140	Elizabeth, NJ	5,124.5
301	Elk Grove, CA	2,881.7
260	Erie, PA	3,361.0
268	Escondido, CA	3,280.9
86	Eugene, OR	6,009.3
141	Evansville, IN	5,016.8
18	Everett, WA	7,678.5
244	Fairfield, CA	3,525.1
157	Fall River, MA	4,785.6
225	Fargo, ND	3,719.5
373	Farmington Hills, MI	2,083.4
187	Fayetteville, AR	4,303.8
11	Fayetteville, NC	8,491.0
98	Federal Way, WA	5,820.5
17	Flint, MI	7,738.9
313	Fontana, CA	2,758.8
228	Fort Collins, CO	3,697.8
59	Fort Lauderdale, FL	6,480.2
49	Fort Smith, AR	6,696.8
196	Fort Wayne, IN	4,076.2
114	Fort Worth, TX	5,545.1
323	Fremont, CA	2,697.4
145	Fresno, CA	4,978.1
380	Frisco, TX	2,001.0
267	Fullerton, CA	3,283.6
58	Gainesville, FL	6,541.4
358	Garden Grove, CA	2,319.7
179	Garland, TX	4,434.6
190	Gary, IN	4,273.3
374	Gilbert, AZ	2,055.7
126	Glendale, AZ	5,345.8
375	Glendale, CA	2,055.4
138	Grand Prairie, TX	5,141.8
119	Grand Rapids, MI	5,411.6
299	Greece, NY	2,905.4
218	Greeley, CO	3,836.9
277	Green Bay, WI	3,188.3
42	Greensboro, NC	6,810.3
191	Gresham, OR	4,265.0
370	Hamilton Twnshp, NJ	2,097.4
93	Hammond, IN	5,907.9
212	Hampton, VA	3,892.2
71	Hartford, CT	6,281.4
262	Hawthorne, CA	3,325.7
234	Hayward, CA	3,618.2
366	Henderson, NV	2,208.2
367	Hesperia, CA	2,208.0
184	Hialeah, FL	4,374.9
99	High Point, NC	5,791.2
369	Hillsboro, OR	2,105.4
131	Hollywood, FL	5,322.9
208	Honolulu, HI	3,958.9
62	Houston, TX	6,444.2
338	Huntington Beach, CA	2,564.9
79	Huntsville, AL	6,133.2
60	Independence, MO	6,477.6
34	Indianapolis, IN	7,029.0
233	Indio, CA	3,631.8
235	Inglewood, CA	3,610.1
394	Irvine, CA	1,460.1
178	Irving, TX	4,460.9
90	Jacksonville, FL	5,993.7
230	Jacksonville, NC	3,662.8
9	Jackson, MS	8,505.3
273	Jersey City, NJ	3,228.0
NA	Joliet, IL**	NA
81	Kansas City, KS	6,109.7
43	Kansas City, MO	6,808.1
259	Kenosha, WI	3,365.9
139	Kent, WA	5,129.0
137	Killeen, TX	5,190.2
23	Knoxville, TN	7,418.3
20	Lafayette, LA	7,522.7
395	Lake Forest, CA	1,421.0
96	Lakeland, FL	5,849.1
278	Lakewood, CA	3,169.8
144	Lakewood, CO	4,980.2
291	Lancaster, CA	3,013.9
177	Lansing, MI	4,481.8
54	Laredo, TX	6,617.9
122	Las Cruces, NM	5,376.3
181	Las Vegas, NV	4,407.7
133	Lawrence, KS	5,249.6
48	Lawton, OK	6,701.2
329	Lee's Summit, MO	2,663.4
231	Lewisville, TX	3,648.1
205	Lexington, KY	4,009.4
183	Lincoln, NE	4,390.9
3	Little Rock, AR	9,791.0
354	Livermore, CA	2,333.3
327	Livonia, MI	2,668.7
253	Long Beach, CA	3,406.3
281	Longmont, CO	3,102.4

RANK	CITY	RATE
16	Longview, TX	7,990.9
283	Los Angeles, CA	3,074.0
150	Louisville, KY	4,859.5
44	Lubbock, TX	6,769.9
199	Lynn, MA	4,062.6
13	Macon, GA	8,474.6
224	Madison, WI	3,726.4
209	Manchester, NH	3,911.8
68	McAllen, TX	6,310.8
320	McKinney, TX	2,712.2
72	Melbourne, FL	6,275.8
6	Memphis, TN	8,877.5
174	Merced, CA	4,553.1
216	Mesa, AZ	3,839.8
118	Mesquite, TX	5,470.8
1	Miami Beach, FL	11,090.7
55	Miami Gardens, FL	6,615.6
78	Miami, FL	6,145.2
201	Midland, TX	4,031.2
41	Milwaukee, WI	6,842.5
101	Minneapolis, MN	5,776.3
221	Miramar, FL	3,797.0
396	Mission Viejo, CA	1,331.5
387	Missouri City, TX	1,835.1
56	Mobile, AL	6,547.1
103	Modesto, CA	5,716.1
94	Montgomery, AL	5,885.1
248	Moreno Valley, CA	3,489.9
135	Murfreesboro, TN	5,238.4
393	Murrieta, CA	1,546.0
322	Nampa, ID	2,706.4
NA	Naperville, IL**	NA
286	Nashua, NH	3,025.9
92	Nashville, TN	5,918.8
160	New Bedford, MA	4,771.1
21	New Haven, CT	7,460.8
170	New Orleans, LA	4,623.3
360	New York, NY	2,242.1
195	Newark, NJ	4,089.9
295	Newport Beach, CA	2,958.3
397	Newton, MA	1,261.4
76	Norfolk, VA	6,160.0
232	Norman, OK	3,647.6
22	North Charleston, SC	7,431.6
245	North Las Vegas, NV	3,517.6
339	Norwalk, CA	2,535.8
330	Norwalk, CT	2,657.5
51	Oakland, CA	6,665.6
310	Oceanside, CA	2,781.1
149	Odessa, TX	4,907.3
389	O'Fallon, MO	1,723.6
130	Ogden, UT	5,337.5
35	Oklahoma City, OK	7,028.6
355	Olathe, KS	2,329.7
164	Omaha, NE	4,661.9
256	Ontario, CA	3,393.5
379	Orange, CA	2,030.9
315	Orem, UT	2,740.3
8	Orlando, FL	8,579.4
312	Overland Park, KS	2,772.2
333	Oxnard, CA	2,592.9
305	Palm Bay, FL	2,858.7
289	Palmdale, CA	3,016.9
274	Pasadena, CA	3,221.5
188	Pasadena, TX	4,297.7
240	Paterson, NJ	3,555.9
350	Pearland, TX	2,412.8
210	Pembroke Pines, FL	3,907.5

RANK	CITY	RATE
279	Peoria, AZ	3,159.4
NA	Peoria, IL**	NA
151	Philadelphia, PA	4,849.5
165	Phoenix, AZ	4,654.3
161	Pittsburgh, PA	4,759.9
282	Plano, TX	3,100.7
155	Plantation, FL	4,799.9
261	Pomona, CA	3,329.9
91	Pompano Beach, FL	5,984.9
348	Port St. Lucie, FL	2,421.5
132	Portland, OR	5,277.2
70	Portsmouth, VA	6,289.0
127	Providence, RI	5,343.0
336	Provo, UT	2,583.0
197	Pueblo, CO	4,074.2
364	Quincy, MA	2,218.9
153	Racine, WI	4,826.6
211	Raleigh, NC	3,896.0
398	Ramapo, NY	955.5
357	Rancho Cucamon., CA	2,324.6
106	Reading, PA	5,662.9
204	Redding, CA	4,019.0
167	Reno, NV	4,652.7
250	Rialto, CA	3,425.0
227	Richardson, TX	3,705.9
120	Richmond, CA	5,396.5
148	Richmond, VA	4,910.6
351	Rio Rancho, NM	2,406.0
226	Riverside, CA	3,709.9
84	Roanoke, VA	6,029.4
NA	Rochester, MN**	NA
66	Rochester, NY	6,341.0
46	Rockford, IL	6,753.7
237	Roseville, CA	3,587.6
306	Roswell, GA	2,842.6
332	Round Rock, TX	2,623.7
124	Sacramento, CA	5,351.0
185	Salem, OR	4,370.7
193	Salinas, CA	4,245.4
7	Salt Lake City, UT	8,731.0
142	San Angelo, TX	5,001.7
29	San Antonio, TX	7,241.6
112	San Bernardino, CA	5,585.4
300	San Diego, CA	2,903.7
143	San Francisco, CA	4,997.3
314	San Jose, CA	2,745.7
146	San Leandro, CA	4,961.6
381	San Marcos, CA	1,996.2
318	San Mateo, CA	2,722.1
217	Sandy Springs, GA	3,838.2
223	Sandy, UT	3,733.9
342	Santa Ana, CA	2,513.0
213	Santa Barbara, CA	3,865.1
304	Santa Clara, CA	2,876.5
377	Santa Clarita, CA	2,041.9
296	Santa Maria, CA	2,930.8
192	Santa Monica, CA	4,256.1
272	Santa Rosa, CA	3,237.5
116	Savannah, GA	5,539.0
290	Scottsdale, AZ	3,014.4
61	Seattle, WA	6,464.6
80	Shreveport, LA	6,111.8
388	Simi Valley, CA	1,770.6
214	Sioux City, IA	3,845.1
276	Sioux Falls, SD	3,190.9
288	Somerville, MA	3,018.2
52	South Bend, IN	6,660.5
270	South Gate, CA	3,245.7

RANK	CITY	RATE
169	Southfield, MI	4,650.1
220	Sparks, NV	3,832.8
198	Spokane Valley, WA	4,065.4
32	Spokane, WA	7,113.7
NA	Springfield, IL**	NA
77	Springfield, MA	6,153.1
4	Springfield, MO	9,708.3
372	Stamford, CT	2,088.6
365	Sterling Heights, MI	2,216.7
57	Stockton, CA	6,546.6
368	St. George, UT	2,164.7
115	St. Joseph, MO	5,540.6
2	St. Louis, MO	10,401.8
152	St. Paul, MN	4,842.4
14	St. Petersburg, FL	8,382.7
297	Suffolk, VA	2,930.7
353	Sugar Land, TX	2,378.6
362	Sunnyvale, CA	2,223.3
158	Sunrise, FL	4,784.3
352	Surprise, AZ	2,403.2
136	Syracuse, NY	5,190.7
15	Tacoma, WA	8,058.9
100	Tallahassee, FL	5,789.9
176	Tampa, FL	4,506.2
343	Temecula, CA	2,473.2
113	Tempe, AZ	5,582.4
246	Thornton, CO	3,515.7
391	Thousand Oaks, CA	1,580.8
NA	Toledo, OH**	NA
328	Toms River Twnshp, NJ	2,668.4
87	Topeka, KS	6,008.1
363	Torrance, CA	2,220.3
271	Tracy, CA	3,243.2
172	Trenton, NJ	4,573.4
347	Troy, MI	2,443.2
NA	Tucson, AZ**	NA
30	Tulsa, OK	7,149.5
89	Tuscaloosa, AL	5,998.6
64	Tyler, TX	6,406.2
255	Upper Darby Twnshp, PA	3,397.4
335	Vacaville, CA	2,589.2
107	Vallejo, CA	5,658.7
206	Vancouver, WA	3,996.4
264	Ventura, CA	3,303.9
202	Victorville, CA	4,030.7
269	Virginia Beach, VA	3,271.4
166	Visalia, CA	4,653.8
293	Vista, CA	2,989.5
65	Waco, TX	6,389.4
252	Warren, MI	3,418.4
258	Warwick, RI	3,368.5
102	Washington, DC	5,768.8
110	Waterbury, CT	5,616.5
254	West Covina, CA	3,398.3
242	West Jordan, UT	3,530.9
74	West Palm Beach, FL	6,222.5
117	West Valley, UT	5,484.8
229	Westland, MI	3,680.1
298	Westminster, CA	2,915.0
251	Westminster, CO	3,422.3
294	Whittier, CA	2,974.6
82	Wichita Falls, TX	6,084.2
75	Wichita, KS	6,213.2
38	Wilmington, NC	6,950.1
47	Winston-Salem, NC	6,722.3
337	Woodbridge Twnshp, NJ	2,567.0
162	Worcester, MA	4,752.0
378	Yonkers, NY	2,032.7
180	Yuma, AZ	4,419.6

Source: CQ Press using reported data from the F.B.I. "Crime in the United States 2009"

*Includes murder, rape, robbery, aggravated assault, burglary, larceny-theft, and motor vehicle theft.

**Not available.

42. Crime Rate in 2009 (continued)
National Rate = 3,465.5 Crimes per 100,000 Population*

RANK	CITY	RATE
1	Miami Beach, FL	11,090.7
2	St. Louis, MO	10,401.8
3	Little Rock, AR	9,791.0
4	Springfield, MO	9,708.3
5	Birmingham, AL	9,223.2
6	Memphis, TN	8,877.5
7	Salt Lake City, UT	8,731.0
8	Orlando, FL	8,579.4
9	Jackson, MS	8,505.3
10	Columbus, GA	8,504.3
11	Fayetteville, NC	8,491.0
12	Chattanooga, TN	8,485.8
13	Macon, GA	8,474.6
14	St. Petersburg, FL	8,382.7
15	Tacoma, WA	8,058.9
16	Longview, TX	7,990.9
17	Flint, MI	7,738.9
18	Everett, WA	7,678.5
19	Detroit, MI	7,534.4
20	Lafayette, LA	7,522.7
21	New Haven, CT	7,460.8
22	North Charleston, SC	7,431.6
23	Knoxville, TN	7,418.3
24	Albany, GA	7,394.3
25	Baton Rouge, LA	7,383.5
26	Atlanta, GA	7,362.6
26	Camden, NJ	7,362.6
28	Cincinnati, OH	7,294.8
29	San Antonio, TX	7,241.6
30	Tulsa, OK	7,149.5
31	Columbus, OH	7,131.1
32	Spokane, WA	7,113.7
33	Columbia, SC	7,058.7
34	Indianapolis, IN	7,029.0
35	Oklahoma City, OK	7,028.6
36	Cleveland, OH	7,016.6
37	Berkeley, CA	6,998.7
38	Wilmington, NC	6,950.1
39	Dayton, OH	6,858.4
40	Buffalo, NY	6,849.3
41	Milwaukee, WI	6,842.5
42	Greensboro, NC	6,810.3
43	Kansas City, MO	6,808.1
44	Lubbock, TX	6,769.9
45	Austin, TX	6,768.8
46	Rockford, IL	6,753.7
47	Winston-Salem, NC	6,722.3
48	Lawton, OK	6,701.2
49	Fort Smith, AR	6,696.8
50	Amarillo, TX	6,685.0
51	Oakland, CA	6,665.6
52	South Bend, IN	6,660.5
53	Beaumont, TX	6,652.0
54	Laredo, TX	6,617.9
55	Miami Gardens, FL	6,615.6
56	Mobile, AL	6,547.1
57	Stockton, CA	6,546.6
58	Gainesville, FL	6,541.4
59	Fort Lauderdale, FL	6,480.2
60	Independence, MO	6,477.6
61	Seattle, WA	6,464.6
62	Houston, TX	6,444.2
63	Corpus Christi, TX	6,426.6
64	Tyler, TX	6,406.2
65	Waco, TX	6,389.4
66	Rochester, NY	6,341.0
67	Dallas, TX	6,323.1
68	McAllen, TX	6,310.8
69	Canton, OH	6,305.9
70	Portsmouth, VA	6,289.0
71	Hartford, CT	6,281.4
72	Melbourne, FL	6,275.8
73	Albuquerque, NM	6,260.8
74	West Palm Beach, FL	6,222.5
75	Wichita, KS	6,213.2
76	Norfolk, VA	6,160.0
77	Springfield, MA	6,153.1
78	Miami, FL	6,145.2
79	Huntsville, AL	6,133.2
80	Shreveport, LA	6,111.8
81	Kansas City, KS	6,109.7
82	Wichita Falls, TX	6,084.2
83	Baltimore, MD	6,078.5
84	Roanoke, VA	6,029.4
85	Arlington, TX	6,026.3
86	Eugene, OR	6,009.3
87	Topeka, KS	6,008.1
88	Akron, OH	6,005.4
89	Tuscaloosa, AL	5,998.6
90	Jacksonville, FL	5,993.7
91	Pompano Beach, FL	5,984.9
92	Nashville, TN	5,918.8
93	Hammond, IN	5,907.9
94	Montgomery, AL	5,885.1
95	Durham, NC	5,870.1
96	Lakeland, FL	5,849.1
97	Davenport, IA	5,828.9
98	Federal Way, WA	5,820.5
99	High Point, NC	5,791.2
100	Tallahassee, FL	5,789.9
101	Minneapolis, MN	5,776.3
102	Washington, DC	5,768.8
103	Modesto, CA	5,716.1
104	Brownsville, TX	5,700.6
105	Charlotte, NC	5,678.0
106	Reading, PA	5,662.9
107	Vallejo, CA	5,658.7
108	Albany, NY	5,640.8
109	Bellingham, WA	5,622.9
110	Waterbury, CT	5,616.5
111	Allentown, PA	5,608.1
112	San Bernardino, CA	5,585.4
113	Tempe, AZ	5,582.4
114	Fort Worth, TX	5,545.1
115	St. Joseph, MO	5,540.6
116	Savannah, GA	5,539.0
117	West Valley, UT	5,484.8
118	Mesquite, TX	5,470.8
119	Grand Rapids, MI	5,411.6
120	Richmond, CA	5,396.5
121	Dearborn, MI	5,385.4
122	Las Cruces, NM	5,376.3
123	Clearwater, FL	5,355.7
124	Sacramento, CA	5,351.0
125	Bakersfield, CA	5,350.3
126	Glendale, AZ	5,345.8
127	Providence, RI	5,343.0
128	Athens-Clarke, GA	5,339.6
129	Avondale, AZ	5,339.5
130	Ogden, UT	5,337.5
131	Hollywood, FL	5,322.9
132	Portland, OR	5,277.2
133	Bridgeport, CT	5,249.6
133	Lawrence, KS	5,249.6
135	Murfreesboro, TN	5,238.4
136	Syracuse, NY	5,190.7
137	Killeen, TX	5,190.2
138	Grand Prairie, TX	5,141.8
139	Kent, WA	5,129.0
140	Elizabeth, NJ	5,124.5
141	Evansville, IN	5,016.8
142	San Angelo, TX	5,001.7
143	San Francisco, CA	4,997.3
144	Lakewood, CO	4,980.2
145	Fresno, CA	4,978.1
146	San Leandro, CA	4,961.6
147	Des Moines, IA	4,957.0
148	Richmond, VA	4,910.6
149	Odessa, TX	4,907.3
150	Louisville, KY	4,859.5
151	Philadelphia, PA	4,849.5
152	St. Paul, MN	4,842.4
153	Racine, WI	4,826.6
154	Compton, CA	4,802.3
155	Plantation, FL	4,799.9
156	Citrus Heights, CA	4,792.9
157	Fall River, MA	4,785.6
158	Sunrise, FL	4,784.3
159	Davie, FL	4,776.6
160	New Bedford, MA	4,771.1
161	Pittsburgh, PA	4,759.9
162	Worcester, MA	4,752.0
163	Abilene, TX	4,708.4
164	Omaha, NE	4,661.9
165	Phoenix, AZ	4,654.3
166	Visalia, CA	4,653.8
167	Reno, NV	4,652.7
168	Cedar Rapids, IA	4,652.2
169	Southfield, MI	4,650.1
170	New Orleans, LA	4,623.3
171	Billings, MT	4,606.0
172	Trenton, NJ	4,573.4
173	Brockton, MA	4,562.0
174	Merced, CA	4,553.1
175	Anchorage, AK	4,519.6
176	Tampa, FL	4,506.2
177	Lansing, MI	4,481.8
178	Irving, TX	4,460.9
179	Garland, TX	4,434.6
180	Yuma, AZ	4,419.6
181	Las Vegas, NV	4,407.7
182	Clarksville, TN	4,402.4
183	Lincoln, NE	4,390.9
184	Hialeah, FL	4,374.9
185	Salem, OR	4,370.7
186	Boston, MA	4,315.9
187	Fayetteville, AR	4,303.8
188	Pasadena, TX	4,297.7
189	Columbia, MO	4,295.8
190	Gary, IN	4,273.3
191	Gresham, OR	4,265.0
192	Santa Monica, CA	4,256.1
193	Salinas, CA	4,245.4
194	Colorado Springs, CO	4,155.9
195	Newark, NJ	4,089.9
196	Fort Wayne, IN	4,076.2
197	Pueblo, CO	4,074.2
198	Spokane Valley, WA	4,065.4
199	Lynn, MA	4,062.6
200	Charleston, SC	4,034.1
201	Midland, TX	4,031.2
202	Victorville, CA	4,030.7
203	Denver, CO	4,030.6
204	Redding, CA	4,019.0
205	Lexington, KY	4,009.4
206	Vancouver, WA	3,996.4

RANK	CITY	RATE
207	College Station, TX	3,993.2
208	Honolulu, HI	3,958.9
209	Manchester, NH	3,911.8
210	Pembroke Pines, FL	3,907.5
211	Raleigh, NC	3,896.0
212	Hampton, VA	3,892.2
213	Santa Barbara, CA	3,865.1
214	Sioux City, IA	3,845.1
215	Boca Raton, FL	3,843.8
216	Mesa, AZ	3,839.8
217	Sandy Springs, GA	3,838.2
218	Greeley, CO	3,836.9
219	Chesapeake, VA	3,835.0
220	Sparks, NV	3,832.8
221	Miramar, FL	3,797.0
222	Downey, CA	3,735.2
223	Sandy, UT	3,733.9
224	Madison, WI	3,726.4
225	Fargo, ND	3,719.5
226	Riverside, CA	3,709.9
227	Richardson, TX	3,705.9
228	Fort Collins, CO	3,697.8
229	Westland, MI	3,680.1
230	Jacksonville, NC	3,662.8
231	Lewisville, TX	3,648.1
232	Norman, OK	3,647.6
233	Indio, CA	3,631.8
234	Hayward, CA	3,618.2
235	Inglewood, CA	3,610.1
236	Clovis, CA	3,601.8
237	Roseville, CA	3,587.6
238	Cheektowaga, NY	3,574.6
239	Aurora, CO	3,568.1
240	Paterson, NJ	3,555.9
241	Cambridge, MA	3,544.4
242	West Jordan, UT	3,530.9
243	Concord, CA	3,525.2
244	Fairfield, CA	3,525.1
245	North Las Vegas, NV	3,517.6
246	Thornton, CO	3,515.7
247	Antioch, CA	3,506.4
248	Moreno Valley, CA	3,489.9
249	El Paso, TX	3,451.5
250	Rialto, CA	3,425.0
251	Westminster, CO	3,422.3
252	Warren, MI	3,418.4
253	Long Beach, CA	3,406.3
254	West Covina, CA	3,398.3
255	Upper Darby Twnshp, PA	3,397.4
256	Ontario, CA	3,393.5
257	Carrollton, TX	3,383.0
258	Warwick, RI	3,368.5
259	Kenosha, WI	3,365.9
260	Erie, PA	3,361.0
261	Pomona, CA	3,329.9
262	Hawthorne, CA	3,325.7
263	El Cajon, CA	3,320.1
264	Ventura, CA	3,303.9
265	Costa Mesa, CA	3,291.0
266	Bellevue, WA	3,288.2
267	Fullerton, CA	3,283.6
268	Escondido, CA	3,280.9
269	Virginia Beach, VA	3,271.4
270	South Gate, CA	3,245.7
271	Tracy, CA	3,243.2
272	Santa Rosa, CA	3,237.5
273	Jersey City, NJ	3,228.0
274	Pasadena, CA	3,221.5
275	Chandler, AZ	3,201.2
276	Sioux Falls, SD	3,190.9
277	Green Bay, WI	3,188.3
278	Lakewood, CA	3,169.8
279	Peoria, AZ	3,159.4
280	Chico, CA	3,142.0
281	Longmont, CO	3,102.4
282	Plano, TX	3,100.7
283	Los Angeles, CA	3,074.0
284	Carson, CA	3,056.1
285	Boise, ID	3,049.4
286	Nashua, NH	3,025.9
287	Boulder, CO	3,019.9
288	Somerville, MA	3,018.2
289	Palmdale, CA	3,016.9
290	Scottsdale, AZ	3,014.4
291	Lancaster, CA	3,013.9
292	Colonie, NY	3,006.3
293	Vista, CA	2,989.5
294	Whittier, CA	2,974.6
295	Newport Beach, CA	2,958.3
296	Santa Maria, CA	2,930.8
297	Suffolk, VA	2,930.7
298	Westminster, CA	2,915.0
299	Greece, NY	2,905.4
300	San Diego, CA	2,903.7
301	Elk Grove, CA	2,881.7
302	El Monte, CA	2,880.1
303	Denton, TX	2,877.5
304	Santa Clara, CA	2,876.5
305	Palm Bay, FL	2,858.7
306	Roswell, GA	2,842.6
307	Burbank, CA	2,824.3
308	Ann Arbor, MI	2,815.5
309	Buena Park, CA	2,802.9
310	Oceanside, CA	2,781.1
311	Cape Coral, FL	2,777.7
312	Overland Park, KS	2,772.2
313	Fontana, CA	2,758.8
314	San Jose, CA	2,745.7
315	Orem, UT	2,740.3
316	Cranston, RI	2,738.6
317	Anaheim, CA	2,731.5
318	San Mateo, CA	2,722.1
319	Bend, OR	2,713.8
320	McKinney, TX	2,712.2
321	Chino, CA	2,707.2
322	Nampa, ID	2,706.4
323	Fremont, CA	2,697.4
324	Clinton Twnshp, MI	2,688.7
325	Arvada, CO	2,673.6
326	Chula Vista, CA	2,673.0
327	Livonia, MI	2,668.7
328	Toms River Twnshp, NJ	2,668.4
329	Lee's Summit, MO	2,663.4
330	Norwalk, CT	2,657.5
331	Corona, CA	2,639.8
332	Round Rock, TX	2,623.7
333	Oxnard, CA	2,592.9
334	Coral Springs, FL	2,591.2
335	Vacaville, CA	2,589.2
336	Provo, UT	2,583.0
337	Woodbridge Twnshp, NJ	2,567.0
338	Huntington Beach, CA	2,564.9
339	Norwalk, CA	2,535.8
340	Baldwin Park, CA	2,522.6
341	Clarkstown, NY	2,522.2
342	Santa Ana, CA	2,513.0
343	Temecula, CA	2,473.2
344	Edison Twnshp, NJ	2,471.9
345	Alhambra, CA	2,468.7
346	Alexandria, VA	2,451.7
347	Troy, MI	2,443.2
348	Port St. Lucie, FL	2,421.5
349	Clifton, NJ	2,419.2
350	Pearland, TX	2,412.8
351	Rio Rancho, NM	2,406.0
352	Surprise, AZ	2,403.2
353	Sugar Land, TX	2,378.6
354	Livermore, CA	2,333.3
355	Olathe, KS	2,329.7
356	Broken Arrow, OK	2,327.0
357	Rancho Cucamon., CA	2,324.6
358	Garden Grove, CA	2,319.7
359	Edmond, OK	2,285.8
360	New York, NY	2,242.1
361	Carlsbad, CA	2,228.8
362	Sunnyvale, CA	2,223.3
363	Torrance, CA	2,220.3
364	Quincy, MA	2,218.9
365	Sterling Heights, MI	2,216.7
366	Henderson, NV	2,208.2
367	Hesperia, CA	2,208.0
368	St. George, UT	2,164.7
369	Hillsboro, OR	2,105.4
370	Hamilton Twnshp, NJ	2,097.4
371	Danbury, CT	2,089.6
372	Stamford, CT	2,088.6
373	Farmington Hills, MI	2,083.4
374	Gilbert, AZ	2,055.7
375	Glendale, CA	2,055.4
376	Amherst, NY	2,046.2
377	Santa Clarita, CA	2,041.9
378	Yonkers, NY	2,032.7
379	Orange, CA	2,030.9
380	Frisco, TX	2,001.0
381	San Marcos, CA	1,996.2
382	Canton Twnshp, MI	1,989.5
383	Daly City, CA	1,967.7
384	Brick Twnshp, NJ	1,914.4
385	Beaverton, OR	1,910.5
386	Allen, TX	1,856.1
387	Missouri City, TX	1,835.1
388	Simi Valley, CA	1,770.6
389	O'Fallon, MO	1,723.6
390	Cary, NC	1,597.7
391	Thousand Oaks, CA	1,580.8
392	Centennial, CO	1,558.6
393	Murrieta, CA	1,546.0
394	Irvine, CA	1,460.1
395	Lake Forest, CA	1,421.0
396	Mission Viejo, CA	1,331.5
397	Newton, MA	1,261.4
398	Ramapo, NY	955.5
NA	Aurora, IL**	NA
NA	Bloomington, MN**	NA
NA	Chicago, IL**	NA
NA	Decatur, IL**	NA
NA	Duluth, MN**	NA
NA	Elgin, IL**	NA
NA	Joliet, IL**	NA
NA	Naperville, IL**	NA
NA	Peoria, IL**	NA
NA	Rochester, MN**	NA
NA	Springfield, IL**	NA
NA	Toledo, OH**	NA
NA	Tucson, AZ**	NA

Source: CQ Press using reported data from the F.B.I. "Crime in the United States 2009"

*Includes murder, rape, robbery, aggravated assault, burglary, larceny-theft, and motor vehicle theft.

**Not available.

43. Percent Change in Crime Rate: 2008 to 2009

National Percent Change = 5.5% Decrease*

RANK	CITY	% CHANGE
32	Abilene, TX	6.3
112	Akron, OH	(1.6)
NA	Albany, GA**	NA
129	Albany, NY	(2.3)
275	Albuquerque, NM	(10.0)
224	Alexandria, VA	(7.0)
267	Alhambra, CA	(9.5)
220	Allentown, PA	(6.8)
93	Allen, TX	(0.3)
29	Amarillo, TX	6.5
68	Amherst, NY	1.6
188	Anaheim, CA	(5.5)
26	Anchorage, AK	6.7
NA	Ann Arbor, MI**	NA
182	Antioch, CA	(5.2)
72	Arlington, TX	1.1
123	Arvada, CO	(2.1)
316	Athens-Clarke, GA	(12.8)
338	Atlanta, GA	(15.4)
250	Aurora, CO	(8.1)
NA	Aurora, IL**	NA
45	Austin, TX	4.7
304	Avondale, AZ	(11.6)
167	Bakersfield, CA	(4.3)
141	Baldwin Park, CA	(2.8)
181	Baltimore, MD	(5.1)
14	Baton Rouge, LA	10.5
126	Beaumont, TX	(2.2)
366	Beaverton, OR	(22.5)
271	Bellevue, WA	(9.7)
131	Bellingham, WA	(2.4)
361	Bend, OR	(20.3)
188	Berkeley, CA	(5.5)
44	Billings, MT	4.9
268	Birmingham, AL	(9.6)
NA	Bloomington, MN**	NA
208	Boca Raton, FL	(6.1)
154	Boise, ID	(3.6)
279	Boston, MA	(10.4)
265	Boulder, CO	(9.4)
318	Brick Twnshp, NJ	(13.0)
253	Bridgeport, CT	(8.4)
NA	Brockton, MA**	NA
259	Broken Arrow, OK	(8.9)
215	Brownsville, TX	(6.4)
231	Buena Park, CA	(7.3)
151	Buffalo, NY	(3.5)
240	Burbank, CA	(7.8)
72	Cambridge, MA	1.1
342	Camden, NJ	(16.1)
NA	Canton Twnshp, MI**	NA
352	Canton, OH	(18.0)
346	Cape Coral, FL	(16.3)
341	Carlsbad, CA	(15.8)
83	Carrollton, TX	0.5
247	Carson, CA	(7.9)
354	Cary, NC	(18.3)
238	Cedar Rapids, IA	(7.7)
254	Centennial, CO	(8.5)
240	Chandler, AZ	(7.8)
340	Charleston, SC	(15.6)
360	Charlotte, NC	(20.2)
106	Chattanooga, TN	(1.2)
92	Cheektowaga, NY	(0.2)
24	Chesapeake, VA	8.1
NA	Chicago, IL**	NA
310	Chico, CA	(12.1)
261	Chino, CA	(9.0)
355	Chula Vista, CA	(18.7)
101	Cincinnati, OH	(0.8)
116	Citrus Heights, CA	(1.7)
34	Clarkstown, NY	5.8
185	Clarksville, TN	(5.4)
138	Clearwater, FL	(2.7)
138	Cleveland, OH	(2.7)
303	Clifton, NJ	(11.5)
NA	Clinton Twnshp, MI**	NA
76	Clovis, CA	0.7
85	College Station, TX	0.4
97	Colonie, NY	(0.5)
318	Colorado Springs, CO	(13.0)
91	Columbia, MO	(0.1)
10	Columbia, SC	12.1
88	Columbus, GA	0.2
102	Columbus, OH	(0.9)
282	Compton, CA	(10.5)
315	Concord, CA	(12.7)
87	Coral Springs, FL	0.3
237	Corona, CA	(7.6)
234	Corpus Christi, TX	(7.4)
154	Costa Mesa, CA	(3.6)
194	Cranston, RI	(5.6)
234	Dallas, TX	(7.4)
334	Daly City, CA	(15.0)
161	Danbury, CT	(3.9)
305	Davenport, IA	(11.7)
6	Davie, FL	13.1
179	Dayton, OH	(5.0)
NA	Dearborn, MI**	NA
NA	Decatur, IL**	NA
209	Denton, TX	(6.2)
38	Denver, CO	5.4
NA	Des Moines, IA**	NA
NA	Detroit, MI**	NA
257	Downey, CA	(8.8)
NA	Duluth, MN**	NA
188	Durham, NC	(5.5)
67	Edison Twnshp, NJ	2.0
129	Edmond, OK	(2.3)
365	El Cajon, CA	(21.1)
63	El Monte, CA	2.2
209	El Paso, TX	(6.2)
NA	Elgin, IL**	NA
222	Elizabeth, NJ	(6.9)
188	Elk Grove, CA	(5.5)
349	Erie, PA	(16.9)
198	Escondido, CA	(5.7)
312	Eugene, OR	(12.5)
112	Evansville, IN	(1.6)
222	Everett, WA	(6.9)
357	Fairfield, CA	(19.1)
205	Fall River, MA	(5.9)
19	Fargo, ND	8.7
NA	Farmington Hills, MI**	NA
58	Fayetteville, AR	3.0
158	Fayetteville, NC	(3.7)
70	Federal Way, WA	1.3
NA	Flint, MI**	NA
126	Fontana, CA	(2.2)
133	Fort Collins, CO	(2.6)
112	Fort Lauderdale, FL	(1.6)
34	Fort Smith, AR	5.8
248	Fort Wayne, IN	(8.0)
133	Fort Worth, TX	(2.6)
102	Fremont, CA	(0.9)
173	Fresno, CA	(4.7)
368	Frisco, TX	(25.1)
166	Fullerton, CA	(4.2)
34	Gainesville, FL	5.8
325	Garden Grove, CA	(13.8)
143	Garland, TX	(3.0)
356	Gary, IN	(18.8)
311	Gilbert, AZ	(12.4)
226	Glendale, AZ	(7.1)
261	Glendale, CA	(9.0)
57	Grand Prairie, TX	3.1
NA	Grand Rapids, MI**	NA
12	Greece, NY	11.3
277	Greeley, CO	(10.3)
296	Green Bay, WI	(11.2)
185	Greensboro, NC	(5.4)
118	Gresham, OR	(1.8)
240	Hamilton Twnshp, NJ	(7.8)
112	Hammond, IN	(1.6)
69	Hampton, VA	1.4
99	Hartford, CT	(0.6)
154	Hawthorne, CA	(3.6)
194	Hayward, CA	(5.6)
291	Henderson, NV	(10.8)
349	Hesperia, CA	(16.9)
348	Hialeah, FL	(16.6)
321	High Point, NC	(13.2)
369	Hillsboro, OR	(26.4)
171	Hollywood, FL	(4.6)
49	Honolulu, HI	4.4
30	Houston, TX	6.4
40	Huntington Beach, CA	5.1
287	Huntsville, AL	(10.7)
358	Independence, MO	(19.8)
154	Indianapolis, IN	(3.6)
74	Indio, CA	1.0
76	Inglewood, CA	0.7
254	Irvine, CA	(8.5)
158	Irving, TX	(3.7)
293	Jacksonville, FL	(10.9)
120	Jacksonville, NC	(2.0)
71	Jackson, MS	1.2
359	Jersey City, NJ	(19.9)
NA	Joliet, IL**	NA
NA	Kansas City, KS**	NA
294	Kansas City, MO	(11.0)
89	Kenosha, WI	0.0
342	Kent, WA	(16.1)
27	Killeen, TX	6.6
148	Knoxville, TN	(3.4)
30	Lafayette, LA	6.4
47	Lake Forest, CA	4.5
209	Lakeland, FL	(6.2)
63	Lakewood, CA	2.2
51	Lakewood, CO	4.2
367	Lancaster, CA	(22.6)
NA	Lansing, MI**	NA
206	Laredo, TX	(6.0)
76	Las Cruces, NM	0.7
277	Las Vegas, NV	(10.3)
194	Lawrence, KS	(5.6)
3	Lawton, OK	16.8
206	Lee's Summit, MO	(6.0)
40	Lewisville, TX	5.1
NA	Lexington, KY**	NA
151	Lincoln, NE	(3.5)
NA	Little Rock, AR**	NA
284	Livermore, CA	(10.6)
NA	Livonia, MI**	NA
111	Long Beach, CA	(1.5)
NA	Longmont, CO**	NA

RANK	CITY	% CHANGE
47	Longview, TX	4.5
226	Los Angeles, CA	(7.1)
NA	Louisville, KY**	NA
55	Lubbock, TX	3.5
169	Lynn, MA	(4.5)
264	Macon, GA	(9.2)
201	Madison, WI	(5.8)
39	Manchester, NH	5.2
97	McAllen, TX	(0.5)
5	McKinney, TX	14.1
209	Melbourne, FL	(6.2)
287	Memphis, TN	(10.7)
308	Merced, CA	(12.0)
301	Mesa, AZ	(11.4)
16	Mesquite, TX	9.6
76	Miami Beach, FL	0.7
218	Miami Gardens, FL	(6.6)
201	Miami, FL	(5.8)
21	Midland, TX	8.4
209	Milwaukee, WI	(6.2)
332	Minneapolis, MN	(14.8)
94	Miramar, FL	(0.4)
151	Mission Viejo, CA	(3.5)
58	Missouri City, TX	3.0
18	Mobile, AL	9.2
169	Modesto, CA	(4.5)
279	Montgomery, AL	(10.4)
226	Moreno Valley, CA	(7.1)
37	Murfreesboro, TN	5.6
66	Murrieta, CA	2.1
336	Nampa, ID	(15.3)
NA	Naperville, IL**	NA
NA	Nashua, NH**	NA
312	Nashville, TN	(12.5)
163	New Bedford, MA	(4.0)
NA	New Haven, CT**	NA
370	New Orleans, LA	(26.7)
198	New York, NY	(5.7)
240	Newark, NJ	(7.8)
82	Newport Beach, CA	0.6
329	Newton, MA	(14.5)
60	Norfolk, VA	2.4
11	Norman, OK	11.6
331	North Charleston, SC	(14.7)
295	North Las Vegas, NV	(11.1)
307	Norwalk, CA	(11.8)
176	Norwalk, CT	(4.8)
259	Oakland, CA	(8.9)
183	Oceanside, CA	(5.3)
56	Odessa, TX	3.2
333	O'Fallon, MO	(14.9)
143	Ogden, UT	(3.0)
61	Oklahoma City, OK	2.3
NA	Olathe, KS**	NA
177	Omaha, NE	(4.9)
240	Ontario, CA	(7.8)
339	Orange, CA	(15.5)
133	Orem, UT	(2.6)
344	Orlando, FL	(16.2)
21	Overland Park, KS	8.4
188	Oxnard, CA	(5.5)
118	Palm Bay, FL	(1.8)
268	Palmdale, CA	(9.6)
143	Pasadena, CA	(3.0)
8	Pasadena, TX	12.9
327	Paterson, NJ	(14.0)
42	Pearland, TX	5.0
251	Pembroke Pines, FL	(8.2)
336	Peoria, AZ	(15.3)
NA	Peoria, IL**	NA
344	Philadelphia, PA	(16.2)
363	Phoenix, AZ	(20.8)
240	Pittsburgh, PA	(7.8)
198	Plano, TX	(5.7)
284	Plantation, FL	(10.6)
346	Pomona, CA	(16.3)
305	Pompano Beach, FL	(11.7)
296	Port St. Lucie, FL	(11.2)
287	Portland, OR	(10.7)
83	Portsmouth, VA	0.5
287	Providence, RI	(10.7)
146	Provo, UT	(3.1)
NA	Pueblo, CO**	NA
177	Quincy, MA	(4.9)
298	Racine, WI	(11.3)
123	Raleigh, NC	(2.1)
273	Ramapo, NY	(9.9)
131	Rancho Cucamon., CA	(2.4)
272	Reading, PA	(9.8)
163	Redding, CA	(4.0)
268	Reno, NV	(9.6)
2	Rialto, CA	22.1
63	Richardson, TX	2.2
265	Richmond, CA	(9.4)
76	Richmond, VA	0.7
335	Rio Rancho, NM	(15.2)
328	Riverside, CA	(14.4)
179	Roanoke, VA	(5.0)
NA	Rochester, MN**	NA
146	Rochester, NY	(3.1)
308	Rockford, IL	(12.0)
254	Roseville, CA	(8.5)
194	Roswell, GA	(5.6)
171	Round Rock, TX	(4.6)
248	Sacramento, CA	(8.0)
321	Salem, OR	(13.2)
163	Salinas, CA	(4.0)
279	Salt Lake City, UT	(10.4)
214	San Angelo, TX	(6.3)
257	San Antonio, TX	(8.8)
138	San Bernardino, CA	(2.7)
362	San Diego, CA	(20.4)
231	San Francisco, CA	(7.3)
89	San Jose, CA	0.0
316	San Leandro, CA	(12.8)
282	San Marcos, CA	(10.5)
201	San Mateo, CA	(5.8)
173	Sandy Springs, GA	(4.7)
231	Sandy, UT	(7.3)
120	Santa Ana, CA	(2.0)
15	Santa Barbara, CA	10.4
126	Santa Clara, CA	(2.2)
106	Santa Clarita, CA	(1.2)
364	Santa Maria, CA	(20.9)
23	Santa Monica, CA	8.3
6	Santa Rosa, CA	13.1
218	Savannah, GA	(6.6)
324	Scottsdale, AZ	(13.5)
27	Seattle, WA	6.6
123	Shreveport, LA	(2.1)
100	Simi Valley, CA	(0.7)
45	Sioux City, IA	4.7
13	Sioux Falls, SD	11.0
330	Somerville, MA	(14.6)
301	South Bend, IN	(11.4)
216	South Gate, CA	(6.5)
NA	Southfield, MI**	NA
312	Sparks, NV	(12.5)
201	Spokane Valley, WA	(5.8)
4	Spokane, WA	15.8
NA	Springfield, IL**	NA
75	Springfield, MA	0.8
148	Springfield, MO	(3.4)
116	Stamford, CT	(1.7)
NA	Sterling Heights, MI**	NA
326	Stockton, CA	(13.9)
371	St. George, UT	(29.0)
33	St. Joseph, MO	6.1
120	St. Louis, MO	(2.0)
133	St. Paul, MN	(2.6)
20	St. Petersburg, FL	8.6
94	Suffolk, VA	(0.4)
51	Sugar Land, TX	4.2
42	Sunnyvale, CA	5.0
106	Sunrise, FL	(1.2)
261	Surprise, AZ	(9.0)
173	Syracuse, NY	(4.7)
224	Tacoma, WA	(7.0)
275	Tallahassee, FL	(10.0)
351	Tampa, FL	(17.8)
188	Temecula, CA	(5.5)
298	Tempe, AZ	(11.3)
109	Thornton, CO	(1.3)
61	Thousand Oaks, CA	2.3
NA	Toledo, OH**	NA
161	Toms River Twnshp, NJ	(3.9)
226	Topeka, KS	(7.1)
220	Torrance, CA	(6.8)
141	Tracy, CA	(2.8)
54	Trenton, NJ	3.6
NA	Troy, MI**	NA
NA	Tucson, AZ**	NA
104	Tulsa, OK	(1.1)
240	Tuscaloosa, AL	(7.8)
1	Tyler, TX	22.7
238	Upper Darby Twnshp, PA	(7.7)
104	Vacaville, CA	(1.1)
148	Vallejo, CA	(3.4)
183	Vancouver, WA	(5.3)
230	Ventura, CA	(7.2)
185	Victorville, CA	(5.4)
53	Virginia Beach, VA	4.0
298	Visalia, CA	(11.3)
284	Vista, CA	(10.6)
216	Waco, TX	(6.5)
NA	Warren, MI**	NA
76	Warwick, RI	0.7
236	Washington, DC	(7.5)
94	Waterbury, CT	(0.4)
318	West Covina, CA	(13.0)
17	West Jordan, UT	9.4
252	West Palm Beach, FL	(8.3)
158	West Valley, UT	(3.7)
NA	Westland, MI**	NA
273	Westminster, CA	(9.9)
167	Westminster, CO	(4.3)
110	Whittier, CA	(1.4)
353	Wichita Falls, TX	(18.2)
133	Wichita, KS	(2.6)
9	Wilmington, NC	12.7
291	Winston-Salem, NC	(10.8)
321	Woodbridge Twnshp, NJ	(13.2)
50	Worcester, MA	4.3
85	Yonkers, NY	0.4
25	Yuma, AZ	7.4

Source: CQ Press using reported data from the F.B.I. "Crime in the United States 2009"
*Includes murder, rape, robbery, aggravated assault, burglary, larceny-theft, and motor vehicle theft.
**Not available.

43. Percent Change in Crime Rate: 2008 to 2009 (continued)
National Percent Change = 5.5% Decrease*

RANK	CITY	% CHANGE
1	Tyler, TX	22.7
2	Rialto, CA	22.1
3	Lawton, OK	16.8
4	Spokane, WA	15.8
5	McKinney, TX	14.1
6	Davie, FL	13.1
6	Santa Rosa, CA	13.1
8	Pasadena, TX	12.9
9	Wilmington, NC	12.7
10	Columbia, SC	12.1
11	Norman, OK	11.6
12	Greece, NY	11.3
13	Sioux Falls, SD	11.0
14	Baton Rouge, LA	10.5
15	Santa Barbara, CA	10.4
16	Mesquite, TX	9.6
17	West Jordan, UT	9.4
18	Mobile, AL	9.2
19	Fargo, ND	8.7
20	St. Petersburg, FL	8.6
21	Midland, TX	8.4
21	Overland Park, KS	8.4
23	Santa Monica, CA	8.3
24	Chesapeake, VA	8.1
25	Yuma, AZ	7.4
26	Anchorage, AK	6.7
27	Killeen, TX	6.6
27	Seattle, WA	6.6
29	Amarillo, TX	6.5
30	Houston, TX	6.4
30	Lafayette, LA	6.4
32	Abilene, TX	6.3
33	St. Joseph, MO	6.1
34	Clarkstown, NY	5.8
34	Fort Smith, AR	5.8
34	Gainesville, FL	5.8
37	Murfreesboro, TN	5.6
38	Denver, CO	5.4
39	Manchester, NH	5.2
40	Huntington Beach, CA	5.1
40	Lewisville, TX	5.1
42	Pearland, TX	5.0
42	Sunnyvale, CA	5.0
44	Billings, MT	4.9
45	Austin, TX	4.7
45	Sioux City, IA	4.7
47	Lake Forest, CA	4.5
47	Longview, TX	4.5
49	Honolulu, HI	4.4
50	Worcester, MA	4.3
51	Lakewood, CO	4.2
51	Sugar Land, TX	4.2
53	Virginia Beach, VA	4.0
54	Trenton, NJ	3.6
55	Lubbock, TX	3.5
56	Odessa, TX	3.2
57	Grand Prairie, TX	3.1
58	Fayetteville, AR	3.0
58	Missouri City, TX	3.0
60	Norfolk, VA	2.4
61	Oklahoma City, OK	2.3
61	Thousand Oaks, CA	2.3
63	El Monte, CA	2.2
63	Lakewood, CA	2.2
63	Richardson, TX	2.2
66	Murrieta, CA	2.1
67	Edison Twnshp, NJ	2.0
68	Amherst, NY	1.6

RANK	CITY	% CHANGE
69	Hampton, VA	1.4
70	Federal Way, WA	1.3
71	Jackson, MS	1.2
72	Arlington, TX	1.1
72	Cambridge, MA	1.1
74	Indio, CA	1.0
75	Springfield, MA	0.8
76	Clovis, CA	0.7
76	Inglewood, CA	0.7
76	Las Cruces, NM	0.7
76	Miami Beach, FL	0.7
76	Richmond, VA	0.7
76	Warwick, RI	0.7
82	Newport Beach, CA	0.6
83	Carrollton, TX	0.5
83	Portsmouth, VA	0.5
85	College Station, TX	0.4
85	Yonkers, NY	0.4
87	Coral Springs, FL	0.3
88	Columbus, GA	0.2
89	Kenosha, WI	0.0
89	San Jose, CA	0.0
91	Columbia, MO	(0.1)
92	Cheektowaga, NY	(0.2)
93	Allen, TX	(0.3)
94	Miramar, FL	(0.4)
94	Suffolk, VA	(0.4)
94	Waterbury, CT	(0.4)
97	Colonie, NY	(0.5)
97	McAllen, TX	(0.5)
99	Hartford, CT	(0.6)
100	Simi Valley, CA	(0.7)
101	Cincinnati, OH	(0.8)
102	Columbus, OH	(0.9)
102	Fremont, CA	(0.9)
104	Tulsa, OK	(1.1)
104	Vacaville, CA	(1.1)
106	Chattanooga, TN	(1.2)
106	Santa Clarita, CA	(1.2)
106	Sunrise, FL	(1.2)
109	Thornton, CO	(1.3)
110	Whittier, CA	(1.4)
111	Long Beach, CA	(1.5)
112	Akron, OH	(1.6)
112	Evansville, IN	(1.6)
112	Fort Lauderdale, FL	(1.6)
112	Hammond, IN	(1.6)
116	Citrus Heights, CA	(1.7)
116	Stamford, CT	(1.7)
118	Gresham, OR	(1.8)
118	Palm Bay, FL	(1.8)
120	Jacksonville, NC	(2.0)
120	Santa Ana, CA	(2.0)
120	St. Louis, MO	(2.0)
123	Arvada, CO	(2.1)
123	Raleigh, NC	(2.1)
123	Shreveport, LA	(2.1)
126	Beaumont, TX	(2.2)
126	Fontana, CA	(2.2)
126	Santa Clara, CA	(2.2)
129	Albany, NY	(2.3)
129	Edmond, OK	(2.3)
131	Bellingham, WA	(2.4)
131	Rancho Cucamon., CA	(2.4)
133	Fort Collins, CO	(2.6)
133	Fort Worth, TX	(2.6)
133	Orem, UT	(2.6)
133	St. Paul, MN	(2.6)
133	Wichita, KS	(2.6)

RANK	CITY	% CHANGE
138	Clearwater, FL	(2.7)
138	Cleveland, OH	(2.7)
138	San Bernardino, CA	(2.7)
141	Baldwin Park, CA	(2.8)
141	Tracy, CA	(2.8)
143	Garland, TX	(3.0)
143	Ogden, UT	(3.0)
143	Pasadena, CA	(3.0)
146	Provo, UT	(3.1)
146	Rochester, NY	(3.1)
148	Knoxville, TN	(3.4)
148	Springfield, MO	(3.4)
148	Vallejo, CA	(3.4)
151	Buffalo, NY	(3.5)
151	Lincoln, NE	(3.5)
151	Mission Viejo, CA	(3.5)
154	Boise, ID	(3.6)
154	Costa Mesa, CA	(3.6)
154	Hawthorne, CA	(3.6)
154	Indianapolis, IN	(3.6)
158	Fayetteville, NC	(3.7)
158	Irving, TX	(3.7)
158	West Valley, UT	(3.7)
161	Danbury, CT	(3.9)
161	Toms River Twnshp, NJ	(3.9)
163	New Bedford, MA	(4.0)
163	Redding, CA	(4.0)
163	Salinas, CA	(4.0)
166	Fullerton, CA	(4.2)
167	Bakersfield, CA	(4.3)
167	Westminster, CO	(4.3)
169	Lynn, MA	(4.5)
169	Modesto, CA	(4.5)
171	Hollywood, FL	(4.6)
171	Round Rock, TX	(4.6)
173	Fresno, CA	(4.7)
173	Sandy Springs, GA	(4.7)
173	Syracuse, NY	(4.7)
176	Norwalk, CT	(4.8)
177	Omaha, NE	(4.9)
177	Quincy, MA	(4.9)
179	Dayton, OH	(5.0)
179	Roanoke, VA	(5.0)
181	Baltimore, MD	(5.1)
182	Antioch, CA	(5.2)
183	Oceanside, CA	(5.3)
183	Vancouver, WA	(5.3)
185	Clarksville, TN	(5.4)
185	Greensboro, NC	(5.4)
185	Victorville, CA	(5.4)
188	Anaheim, CA	(5.5)
188	Berkeley, CA	(5.5)
188	Durham, NC	(5.5)
188	Elk Grove, CA	(5.5)
188	Oxnard, CA	(5.5)
188	Temecula, CA	(5.5)
194	Cranston, RI	(5.6)
194	Hayward, CA	(5.6)
194	Lawrence, KS	(5.6)
194	Roswell, GA	(5.6)
198	Escondido, CA	(5.7)
198	New York, NY	(5.7)
198	Plano, TX	(5.7)
201	Madison, WI	(5.8)
201	Miami, FL	(5.8)
201	San Mateo, CA	(5.8)
201	Spokane Valley, WA	(5.8)
205	Fall River, MA	(5.9)
206	Laredo, TX	(6.0)

RANK	CITY	% CHANGE
206	Lee's Summit, MO	(6.0)
208	Boca Raton, FL	(6.1)
209	Denton, TX	(6.2)
209	El Paso, TX	(6.2)
209	Lakeland, FL	(6.2)
209	Melbourne, FL	(6.2)
209	Milwaukee, WI	(6.2)
214	San Angelo, TX	(6.3)
215	Brownsville, TX	(6.4)
216	South Gate, CA	(6.5)
216	Waco, TX	(6.5)
218	Miami Gardens, FL	(6.6)
218	Savannah, GA	(6.6)
220	Allentown, PA	(6.8)
220	Torrance, CA	(6.8)
222	Elizabeth, NJ	(6.9)
222	Everett, WA	(6.9)
224	Alexandria, VA	(7.0)
224	Tacoma, WA	(7.0)
226	Glendale, AZ	(7.1)
226	Los Angeles, CA	(7.1)
226	Moreno Valley, CA	(7.1)
226	Topeka, KS	(7.1)
230	Ventura, CA	(7.2)
231	Buena Park, CA	(7.3)
231	San Francisco, CA	(7.3)
231	Sandy, UT	(7.3)
234	Corpus Christi, TX	(7.4)
234	Dallas, TX	(7.4)
236	Washington, DC	(7.5)
237	Corona, CA	(7.6)
238	Cedar Rapids, IA	(7.7)
238	Upper Darby Twnshp, PA	(7.7)
240	Burbank, CA	(7.8)
240	Chandler, AZ	(7.8)
240	Hamilton Twnshp, NJ	(7.8)
240	Newark, NJ	(7.8)
240	Ontario, CA	(7.8)
240	Pittsburgh, PA	(7.8)
240	Tuscaloosa, AL	(7.8)
247	Carson, CA	(7.9)
248	Fort Wayne, IN	(8.0)
248	Sacramento, CA	(8.0)
250	Aurora, CO	(8.1)
251	Pembroke Pines, FL	(8.2)
252	West Palm Beach, FL	(8.3)
253	Bridgeport, CT	(8.4)
254	Centennial, CO	(8.5)
254	Irvine, CA	(8.5)
254	Roseville, CA	(8.5)
257	Downey, CA	(8.8)
257	San Antonio, TX	(8.8)
259	Broken Arrow, OK	(8.9)
259	Oakland, CA	(8.9)
261	Chino, CA	(9.0)
261	Glendale, CA	(9.0)
261	Surprise, AZ	(9.0)
264	Macon, GA	(9.2)
265	Boulder, CO	(9.4)
265	Richmond, CA	(9.4)
267	Alhambra, CA	(9.5)
268	Birmingham, AL	(9.6)
268	Palmdale, CA	(9.6)
268	Reno, NV	(9.6)
271	Bellevue, WA	(9.7)
272	Reading, PA	(9.8)
273	Ramapo, NY	(9.9)
273	Westminster, CA	(9.9)

RANK	CITY	% CHANGE
275	Albuquerque, NM	(10.0)
275	Tallahassee, FL	(10.0)
277	Greeley, CO	(10.3)
277	Las Vegas, NV	(10.3)
279	Boston, MA	(10.4)
279	Montgomery, AL	(10.4)
279	Salt Lake City, UT	(10.4)
282	Compton, CA	(10.5)
282	San Marcos, CA	(10.5)
284	Livermore, CA	(10.6)
284	Plantation, FL	(10.6)
284	Vista, CA	(10.6)
287	Huntsville, AL	(10.7)
287	Memphis, TN	(10.7)
287	Portland, OR	(10.7)
287	Providence, RI	(10.7)
291	Henderson, NV	(10.8)
291	Winston-Salem, NC	(10.8)
293	Jacksonville, FL	(10.9)
294	Kansas City, MO	(11.0)
295	North Las Vegas, NV	(11.1)
296	Green Bay, WI	(11.2)
296	Port St. Lucie, FL	(11.2)
298	Racine, WI	(11.3)
298	Tempe, AZ	(11.3)
298	Visalia, CA	(11.3)
301	Mesa, AZ	(11.4)
301	South Bend, IN	(11.4)
303	Clifton, NJ	(11.5)
304	Avondale, AZ	(11.6)
305	Davenport, IA	(11.7)
305	Pompano Beach, FL	(11.7)
307	Norwalk, CA	(11.8)
308	Merced, CA	(12.0)
308	Rockford, IL	(12.0)
310	Chico, CA	(12.1)
311	Gilbert, AZ	(12.4)
312	Eugene, OR	(12.5)
312	Nashville, TN	(12.5)
312	Sparks, NV	(12.5)
315	Concord, CA	(12.7)
316	Athens-Clarke, GA	(12.8)
316	San Leandro, CA	(12.8)
318	Brick Twnshp, NJ	(13.0)
318	Colorado Springs, CO	(13.0)
318	West Covina, CA	(13.0)
321	High Point, NC	(13.2)
321	Salem, OR	(13.2)
321	Woodbridge Twnshp, NJ	(13.2)
324	Scottsdale, AZ	(13.5)
325	Garden Grove, CA	(13.8)
326	Stockton, CA	(13.9)
327	Paterson, NJ	(14.0)
328	Riverside, CA	(14.4)
329	Newton, MA	(14.5)
330	Somerville, MA	(14.6)
331	North Charleston, SC	(14.7)
332	Minneapolis, MN	(14.8)
333	O'Fallon, MO	(14.9)
334	Daly City, CA	(15.0)
335	Rio Rancho, NM	(15.2)
336	Nampa, ID	(15.3)
336	Peoria, AZ	(15.3)
338	Atlanta, GA	(15.4)
339	Orange, CA	(15.5)
340	Charleston, SC	(15.6)
341	Carlsbad, CA	(15.8)
342	Camden, NJ	(16.1)

RANK	CITY	% CHANGE
342	Kent, WA	(16.1)
344	Orlando, FL	(16.2)
344	Philadelphia, PA	(16.2)
346	Cape Coral, FL	(16.3)
346	Pomona, CA	(16.3)
348	Hialeah, FL	(16.6)
349	Erie, PA	(16.9)
349	Hesperia, CA	(16.9)
351	Tampa, FL	(17.8)
352	Canton, OH	(18.0)
353	Wichita Falls, TX	(18.2)
354	Cary, NC	(18.3)
355	Chula Vista, CA	(18.7)
356	Gary, IN	(18.8)
357	Fairfield, CA	(19.1)
358	Independence, MO	(19.8)
359	Jersey City, NJ	(19.9)
360	Charlotte, NC	(20.2)
361	Bend, OR	(20.3)
362	San Diego, CA	(20.4)
363	Phoenix, AZ	(20.8)
364	Santa Maria, CA	(20.9)
365	El Cajon, CA	(21.1)
366	Beaverton, OR	(22.5)
367	Lancaster, CA	(22.6)
368	Frisco, TX	(25.1)
369	Hillsboro, OR	(26.4)
370	New Orleans, LA	(26.7)
371	St. George, UT	(29.0)
NA	Albany, GA**	NA
NA	Ann Arbor, MI**	NA
NA	Aurora, IL**	NA
NA	Bloomington, MN**	NA
NA	Brockton, MA**	NA
NA	Canton Twnshp, MI**	NA
NA	Chicago, IL**	NA
NA	Clinton Twnshp, MI**	NA
NA	Dearborn, MI**	NA
NA	Decatur, IL**	NA
NA	Des Moines, IA**	NA
NA	Detroit, MI**	NA
NA	Duluth, MN**	NA
NA	Elgin, IL**	NA
NA	Farmington Hills, MI**	NA
NA	Flint, MI**	NA
NA	Grand Rapids, MI**	NA
NA	Joliet, IL**	NA
NA	Kansas City, KS**	NA
NA	Lansing, MI**	NA
NA	Lexington, KY**	NA
NA	Little Rock, AR**	NA
NA	Livonia, MI**	NA
NA	Longmont, CO**	NA
NA	Louisville, KY**	NA
NA	Naperville, IL**	NA
NA	Nashua, NH**	NA
NA	New Haven, CT**	NA
NA	Olathe, KS**	NA
NA	Peoria, IL**	NA
NA	Pueblo, CO**	NA
NA	Rochester, MN**	NA
NA	Southfield, MI**	NA
NA	Springfield, IL**	NA
NA	Sterling Heights, MI**	NA
NA	Toledo, OH**	NA
NA	Troy, MI**	NA
NA	Tucson, AZ**	NA
NA	Warren, MI**	NA
NA	Westland, MI**	NA

Source: CQ Press using reported data from the F.B.I. "Crime in the United States 2009"

*Includes murder, rape, robbery, aggravated assault, burglary, larceny-theft, and motor vehicle theft.

**Not available.

44. Percent Change in Crime Rate: 2005 to 2009
National Percent Change = 11.2% Decrease*

RANK	CITY	% CHANGE
150	Abilene, TX	(9.6)
97	Akron, OH	(4.2)
47	Albany, GA	5.2
179	Albany, NY	(13.6)
167	Albuquerque, NM	(12.0)
198	Alexandria, VA	(15.9)
290	Alhambra, CA	(25.3)
150	Allentown, PA	(9.6)
252	Allen, TX	(20.8)
136	Amarillo, TX	(8.2)
19	Amherst, NY	12.8
216	Anaheim, CA	(17.5)
118	Anchorage, AK	(6.8)
NA	Ann Arbor, MI**	NA
55	Antioch, CA	2.6
88	Arlington, TX	(3.3)
336	Arvada, CO	(31.7)
103	Athens-Clarke, GA	(5.1)
221	Atlanta, GA	(17.9)
350	Aurora, CO	(36.2)
NA	Aurora, IL**	NA
52	Austin, TX	4.1
NA	Avondale, AZ**	NA
194	Bakersfield, CA	(15.7)
227	Baldwin Park, CA	(18.4)
169	Baltimore, MD	(12.4)
84	Baton Rouge, LA	(2.9)
240	Beaumont, TX	(19.7)
360	Beaverton, OR	(49.0)
238	Bellevue, WA	(19.4)
308	Bellingham, WA	(27.6)
359	Bend, OR	(47.4)
203	Berkeley, CA	(16.3)
255	Billings, MT	(21.2)
88	Birmingham, AL	(3.3)
NA	Bloomington, MN**	NA
74	Boca Raton, FL	(0.5)
310	Boise, ID	(27.8)
288	Boston, MA	(25.1)
301	Boulder, CO	(26.5)
30	Brick Twnshp, NJ	9.1
186	Bridgeport, CT	(14.7)
NA	Brockton, MA**	NA
169	Broken Arrow, OK	(12.4)
61	Brownsville, TX	1.4
69	Buena Park, CA	0.3
115	Buffalo, NY	(6.1)
80	Burbank, CA	(1.9)
116	Cambridge, MA	(6.3)
77	Camden, NJ	(1.5)
NA	Canton Twnshp, MI**	NA
287	Canton, OH	(25.0)
186	Cape Coral, FL	(14.7)
288	Carlsbad, CA	(25.1)
130	Carrollton, TX	(7.7)
105	Carson, CA	(5.4)
261	Cary, NC	(21.5)
201	Cedar Rapids, IA	(16.2)
329	Centennial, CO	(30.7)
233	Chandler, AZ	(19.0)
291	Charleston, SC	(25.5)
323	Charlotte, NC	(29.5)
128	Chattanooga, TN	(7.5)
43	Cheektowaga, NY	6.1
120	Chesapeake, VA	(7.0)
NA	Chicago, IL**	NA
283	Chico, CA	(24.1)
284	Chino, CA	(24.6)
343	Chula Vista, CA	(34.5)
168	Cincinnati, OH	(12.3)
NA	Citrus Heights, CA**	NA
NA	Clarkstown, NY**	NA
87	Clarksville, TN	(3.2)
82	Clearwater, FL	(2.0)
133	Cleveland, OH	(7.9)
110	Clifton, NJ	(5.8)
NA	Clinton Twnshp, MI**	NA
177	Clovis, CA	(13.1)
117	College Station, TX	(6.5)
270	Colonie, NY	(22.2)
306	Colorado Springs, CO	(27.3)
29	Columbia, MO	9.5
125	Columbia, SC	(7.4)
17	Columbus, GA	13.2
179	Columbus, OH	(13.6)
38	Compton, CA	7.0
344	Concord, CA	(34.7)
9	Coral Springs, FL	18.7
233	Corona, CA	(19.0)
211	Corpus Christi, TX	(17.2)
165	Costa Mesa, CA	(11.8)
62	Cranston, RI	1.2
291	Dallas, TX	(25.5)
228	Daly City, CA	(18.5)
96	Danbury, CT	(4.0)
335	Davenport, IA	(31.5)
12	Davie, FL	16.6
191	Dayton, OH	(15.4)
NA	Dearborn, MI**	NA
NA	Decatur, IL**	NA
347	Denton, TX	(35.9)
356	Denver, CO	(40.7)
NA	Des Moines, IA**	NA
NA	Detroit, MI**	NA
51	Downey, CA	4.2
NA	Duluth, MN**	NA
158	Durham, NC	(10.9)
130	Edison Twnshp, NJ	(7.7)
214	Edmond, OK	(17.3)
333	El Cajon, CA	(31.2)
194	El Monte, CA	(15.7)
118	El Paso, TX	(6.8)
NA	Elgin, IL**	NA
27	Elizabeth, NJ	10.1
NA	Elk Grove, CA**	NA
48	Erie, PA	4.8
246	Escondido, CA	(20.2)
190	Eugene, OR	(15.1)
146	Evansville, IN	(8.9)
134	Everett, WA	(8.1)
304	Fairfield, CA	(26.9)
NA	Fall River, MA**	NA
1	Fargo, ND	38.6
NA	Farmington Hills, MI**	NA
183	Fayetteville, AR	(14.4)
129	Fayetteville, NC	(7.6)
296	Federal Way, WA	(25.9)
NA	Flint, MI**	NA
72	Fontana, CA	(0.2)
83	Fort Collins, CO	(2.4)
182	Fort Lauderdale, FL	(14.3)
171	Fort Smith, AR	(12.5)
263	Fort Wayne, IN	(21.6)
214	Fort Worth, TX	(17.3)
54	Fremont, CA	3.2
267	Fresno, CA	(22.1)
361	Frisco, TX	(51.5)
160	Fullerton, CA	(11.3)
5	Gainesville, FL	24.6
294	Garden Grove, CA	(25.6)
25	Garland, TX	10.5
320	Gary, IN	(29.1)
316	Gilbert, AZ	(28.6)
110	Glendale, AZ	(5.8)
68	Glendale, CA	0.6
125	Grand Prairie, TX	(7.4)
NA	Grand Rapids, MI**	NA
2	Greece, NY	33.9
358	Greeley, CO	(45.3)
107	Green Bay, WI	(5.5)
78	Greensboro, NC	(1.7)
323	Gresham, OR	(29.5)
58	Hamilton Twnshp, NJ	1.9
152	Hammond, IN	(9.8)
93	Hampton, VA	(3.7)
315	Hartford, CT	(28.3)
42	Hawthorne, CA	6.3
200	Hayward, CA	(16.1)
307	Henderson, NV	(27.5)
309	Hesperia, CA	(27.7)
75	Hialeah, FL	(0.7)
209	High Point, NC	(16.8)
362	Hillsboro, OR	(54.2)
33	Hollywood, FL	8.2
243	Honolulu, HI	(20.0)
144	Houston, TX	(8.7)
26	Huntington Beach, CA	10.4
250	Huntsville, AL	(20.5)
237	Independence, MO	(19.3)
86	Indianapolis, IN	(3.1)
314	Indio, CA	(28.2)
64	Inglewood, CA	1.0
272	Irvine, CA	(22.4)
194	Irving, TX	(15.7)
100	Jacksonville, FL	(4.9)
NA	Jacksonville, NC**	NA
13	Jackson, MS	16.0
345	Jersey City, NJ	(34.8)
NA	Joliet, IL**	NA
285	Kansas City, KS	(24.9)
298	Kansas City, MO	(26.3)
67	Kenosha, WI	0.8
348	Kent, WA	(36.0)
278	Killeen, TX	(23.3)
49	Knoxville, TN	4.4
14	Lafayette, LA	15.1
65	Lake Forest, CA	0.9
92	Lakeland, FL	(3.6)
224	Lakewood, CA	(18.1)
251	Lakewood, CO	(20.7)
339	Lancaster, CA	(33.6)
NA	Lansing, MI**	NA
63	Laredo, TX	1.1
80	Las Cruces, NM	(1.9)
254	Las Vegas, NV	(21.0)
15	Lawrence, KS	14.4
22	Lawton, OK	11.8
158	Lee's Summit, MO	(10.9)
209	Lewisville, TX	(16.8)
NA	Lexington, KY**	NA
295	Lincoln, NE	(25.8)
NA	Little Rock, AR**	NA
59	Livermore, CA	1.8
NA	Livonia, MI**	NA
88	Long Beach, CA	(3.3)
NA	Longmont, CO**	NA

RANK	CITY	% CHANGE	RANK	CITY	% CHANGE	RANK	CITY	% CHANGE
44	Longview, TX	6.0	331	Peoria, AZ	(31.0)	NA	Southfield, MI**	NA
246	Los Angeles, CA	(20.2)	NA	Peoria, IL**	NA	157	Sparks, NV	(10.6)
NA	Louisville, KY**	NA	174	Philadelphia, PA	(12.9)	253	Spokane Valley, WA	(20.9)
99	Lubbock, TX	(4.7)	342	Phoenix, AZ	(34.4)	39	Spokane, WA	6.7
148	Lynn, MA	(9.3)	211	Pittsburgh, PA	(17.2)	NA	Springfield, IL**	NA
217	Macon, GA	(17.6)	219	Plano, TX	(17.7)	224	Springfield, MA	(18.1)
95	Madison, WI	(3.8)	21	Plantation, FL	12.4	32	Springfield, MO	8.3
20	Manchester, NH	12.7	248	Pomona, CA	(20.4)	138	Stamford, CT	(8.3)
153	McAllen, TX	(10.0)	222	Pompano Beach, FL	(18.0)	NA	Sterling Heights, MI**	NA
40	McKinney, TX	6.6	79	Port St. Lucie, FL	(1.8)	243	Stockton, CA	(20.0)
24	Melbourne, FL	11.4	334	Portland, OR	(31.3)	348	St. George, UT	(36.0)
178	Memphis, TN	(13.2)	49	Portsmouth, VA	4.4	136	St. Joseph, MO	(8.2)
328	Merced, CA	(30.2)	138	Providence, RI	(8.3)	274	St. Louis, MO	(22.7)
341	Mesa, AZ	(34.1)	279	Provo, UT	(23.6)	204	St. Paul, MN	(16.4)
8	Mesquite, TX	19.4	357	Pueblo, CO	(44.2)	45	St. Petersburg, FL	5.4
31	Miami Beach, FL	8.7	18	Quincy, MA	13.0	318	Suffolk, VA	(29.0)
241	Miami Gardens, FL	(19.8)	261	Racine, WI	(21.5)	141	Sugar Land, TX	(8.4)
233	Miami, FL	(19.0)	160	Raleigh, NC	(11.3)	76	Sunnyvale, CA	(1.0)
93	Midland, TX	(3.7)	103	Ramapo, NY	(5.1)	4	Sunrise, FL	25.1
53	Milwaukee, WI	3.4	264	Rancho Cucamon., CA	(21.7)	273	Surprise, AZ	(22.5)
267	Minneapolis, MN	(22.1)	282	Reading, PA	(24.0)	130	Syracuse, NY	(7.7)
40	Miramar, FL	6.6	276	Redding, CA	(23.0)	189	Tacoma, WA	(14.9)
110	Mission Viejo, CA	(5.8)	281	Reno, NV	(23.8)	145	Tallahassee, FL	(8.8)
184	Missouri City, TX	(14.6)	243	Rialto, CA	(20.0)	355	Tampa, FL	(40.6)
45	Mobile, AL	5.4	70	Richardson, TX	0.0	339	Temecula, CA	(33.6)
211	Modesto, CA	(17.2)	248	Richmond, CA	(20.4)	332	Tempe, AZ	(31.1)
230	Montgomery, AL	(18.7)	351	Richmond, VA	(37.3)	325	Thornton, CO	(29.9)
207	Moreno Valley, CA	(16.7)	108	Rio Rancho, NM	(5.6)	60	Thousand Oaks, CA	1.6
125	Murfreesboro, TN	(7.4)	326	Riverside, CA	(30.0)	NA	Toledo, OH**	NA
354	Murrieta, CA	(40.1)	270	Roanoke, VA	(22.2)	3	Toms River Twnshp, NJ	27.3
NA	Nampa, ID**	NA	NA	Rochester, MN**	NA	318	Topeka, KS	(29.0)
NA	Naperville, IL**	NA	184	Rochester, NY	(14.6)	162	Torrance, CA	(11.6)
7	Nashua, NH	19.8	NA	Rockford, IL**	NA	305	Tracy, CA	(27.2)
299	Nashville, TN	(26.4)	303	Roseville, CA	(26.8)	277	Trenton, NJ	(23.1)
34	New Bedford, MA	8.0	71	Roswell, GA	(0.1)	NA	Troy, MI**	NA
NA	New Haven, CT**	NA	113	Round Rock, TX	(5.9)	NA	Tucson, AZ**	NA
NA	New Orleans, LA**	NA	266	Sacramento, CA	(21.9)	141	Tulsa, OK	(8.4)
201	New York, NY	(16.2)	338	Salem, OR	(33.4)	172	Tuscaloosa, AL	(12.6)
297	Newark, NJ	(26.0)	232	Salinas, CA	(18.9)	28	Tyler, TX	10.0
147	Newport Beach, CA	(9.1)	114	Salt Lake City, UT	(6.0)	10	Upper Darby Twnshp, PA	17.8
176	Newton, MA	(13.0)	265	San Angelo, TX	(21.8)	162	Vacaville, CA	(11.6)
73	Norfolk, VA	(0.3)	56	San Antonio, TX	2.3	NA	Vallejo, CA**	NA
35	Norman, OK	7.7	231	San Bernardino, CA	(18.8)	302	Vancouver, WA	(26.7)
312	North Charleston, SC	(27.9)	327	San Diego, CA	(30.1)	219	Ventura, CA	(17.7)
346	North Las Vegas, NV	(35.4)	120	San Francisco, CA	(7.0)	313	Victorville, CA	(28.0)
217	Norwalk, CA	(17.6)	105	San Jose, CA	(5.4)	65	Virginia Beach, VA	0.9
267	Norwalk, CT	(22.1)	173	San Leandro, CA	(12.8)	351	Visalia, CA	(37.3)
120	Oakland, CA	(7.0)	299	San Marcos, CA	(26.4)	257	Vista, CA	(21.3)
322	Oceanside, CA	(29.4)	260	San Mateo, CA	(21.4)	257	Waco, TX	(21.3)
37	Odessa, TX	7.4	NA	Sandy Springs, GA**	NA	NA	Warren, MI**	NA
353	O'Fallon, MO	(38.3)	57	Sandy, UT	2.1	36	Warwick, RI	7.5
228	Ogden, UT	(18.5)	316	Santa Ana, CA	(28.6)	91	Washington, DC	(3.5)
242	Oklahoma City, OK	(19.9)	85	Santa Barbara, CA	(3.0)	108	Waterbury, CT	(5.6)
NA	Olathe, KS**	NA	206	Santa Clara, CA	(16.6)	193	West Covina, CA	(15.5)
255	Omaha, NE	(21.2)	174	Santa Clarita, CA	(12.9)	NA	West Jordan, UT**	NA
280	Ontario, CA	(23.7)	204	Santa Maria, CA	(16.4)	310	West Palm Beach, FL	(27.8)
285	Orange, CA	(24.9)	120	Santa Monica, CA	(7.0)	199	West Valley, UT	(16.0)
321	Orem, UT	(29.2)	191	Santa Rosa, CA	(15.4)	NA	Westland, MI**	NA
224	Orlando, FL	(18.1)	149	Savannah, GA	(9.4)	222	Westminster, CA	(18.0)
156	Overland Park, KS	(10.4)	194	Scottsdale, AZ	(15.7)	337	Westminster, CO	(33.0)
134	Oxnard, CA	(8.1)	257	Seattle, WA	(21.3)	164	Whittier, CA	(11.7)
330	Palm Bay, FL	(30.8)	239	Shreveport, LA	(19.6)	291	Wichita Falls, TX	(25.5)
275	Palmdale, CA	(22.8)	188	Simi Valley, CA	(14.8)	NA	Wichita, KS**	NA
153	Pasadena, CA	(10.0)	233	Sioux City, IA	(19.0)	155	Wilmington, NC	(10.3)
16	Pasadena, TX	13.6	124	Sioux Falls, SD	(7.3)	100	Winston-Salem, NC	(4.9)
143	Paterson, NJ	(8.5)	11	Somerville, MA	17.6	207	Woodbridge Twnshp, NJ	(16.7)
166	Pearland, TX	(11.9)	98	South Bend, IN	(4.6)	23	Worcester, MA	11.7
6	Pembroke Pines, FL	24.3	100	South Gate, CA	(4.9)	138	Yonkers, NY	(8.3)
						181	Yuma, AZ	(14.0)

Source: CQ Press using reported data from the F.B.I. "Crime in the United States 2009"
*Includes murder, rape, robbery, aggravated assault, burglary, larceny-theft, and motor vehicle theft.
**Not available.

44. Percent Change in Crime Rate: 2005 to 2009 (continued)
National Percent Change = 11.2% Decrease*

RANK	CITY	% CHANGE
1	Fargo, ND	38.6
2	Greece, NY	33.9
3	Toms River Twnshp, NJ	27.3
4	Sunrise, FL	25.1
5	Gainesville, FL	24.6
6	Pembroke Pines, FL	24.3
7	Nashua, NH	19.8
8	Mesquite, TX	19.4
9	Coral Springs, FL	18.7
10	Upper Darby Twnshp, PA	17.8
11	Somerville, MA	17.6
12	Davie, FL	16.6
13	Jackson, MS	16.0
14	Lafayette, LA	15.1
15	Lawrence, KS	14.4
16	Pasadena, TX	13.6
17	Columbus, GA	13.2
18	Quincy, MA	13.0
19	Amherst, NY	12.8
20	Manchester, NH	12.7
21	Plantation, FL	12.4
22	Lawton, OK	11.8
23	Worcester, MA	11.7
24	Melbourne, FL	11.4
25	Garland, TX	10.5
26	Huntington Beach, CA	10.4
27	Elizabeth, NJ	10.1
28	Tyler, TX	10.0
29	Columbia, MO	9.5
30	Brick Twnshp, NJ	9.1
31	Miami Beach, FL	8.7
32	Springfield, MO	8.3
33	Hollywood, FL	8.2
34	New Bedford, MA	8.0
35	Norman, OK	7.7
36	Warwick, RI	7.5
37	Odessa, TX	7.4
38	Compton, CA	7.0
39	Spokane, WA	6.7
40	McKinney, TX	6.6
40	Miramar, FL	6.6
42	Hawthorne, CA	6.3
43	Cheektowaga, NY	6.1
44	Longview, TX	6.0
45	Mobile, AL	5.4
45	St. Petersburg, FL	5.4
47	Albany, GA	5.2
48	Erie, PA	4.8
49	Knoxville, TN	4.4
49	Portsmouth, VA	4.4
51	Downey, CA	4.2
52	Austin, TX	4.1
53	Milwaukee, WI	3.4
54	Fremont, CA	3.2
55	Antioch, CA	2.6
56	San Antonio, TX	2.3
57	Sandy, UT	2.1
58	Hamilton Twnshp, NJ	1.9
59	Livermore, CA	1.8
60	Thousand Oaks, CA	1.6
61	Brownsville, TX	1.4
62	Cranston, RI	1.2
63	Laredo, TX	1.1
64	Inglewood, CA	1.0
65	Lake Forest, CA	0.9
65	Virginia Beach, VA	0.9
67	Kenosha, WI	0.8
68	Glendale, CA	0.6
69	Buena Park, CA	0.3
70	Richardson, TX	0.0
71	Roswell, GA	(0.1)
72	Fontana, CA	(0.2)
73	Norfolk, VA	(0.3)
74	Boca Raton, FL	(0.5)
75	Hialeah, FL	(0.7)
76	Sunnyvale, CA	(1.0)
77	Camden, NJ	(1.5)
78	Greensboro, NC	(1.7)
79	Port St. Lucie, FL	(1.8)
80	Burbank, CA	(1.9)
80	Las Cruces, NM	(1.9)
82	Clearwater, FL	(2.0)
83	Fort Collins, CO	(2.4)
84	Baton Rouge, LA	(2.9)
85	Santa Barbara, CA	(3.0)
86	Indianapolis, IN	(3.1)
87	Clarksville, TN	(3.2)
88	Arlington, TX	(3.3)
88	Birmingham, AL	(3.3)
88	Long Beach, CA	(3.3)
91	Washington, DC	(3.5)
92	Lakeland, FL	(3.6)
93	Hampton, VA	(3.7)
93	Midland, TX	(3.7)
95	Madison, WI	(3.8)
96	Danbury, CT	(4.0)
97	Akron, OH	(4.2)
98	South Bend, IN	(4.6)
99	Lubbock, TX	(4.7)
100	Jacksonville, FL	(4.9)
100	South Gate, CA	(4.9)
100	Winston-Salem, NC	(4.9)
103	Athens-Clarke, GA	(5.1)
103	Ramapo, NY	(5.1)
105	Carson, CA	(5.4)
105	San Jose, CA	(5.4)
107	Green Bay, WI	(5.5)
108	Rio Rancho, NM	(5.6)
108	Waterbury, CT	(5.6)
110	Clifton, NJ	(5.8)
110	Glendale, AZ	(5.8)
110	Mission Viejo, CA	(5.8)
113	Round Rock, TX	(5.9)
114	Salt Lake City, UT	(6.0)
115	Buffalo, NY	(6.1)
116	Cambridge, MA	(6.3)
117	College Station, TX	(6.5)
118	Anchorage, AK	(6.8)
118	El Paso, TX	(6.8)
120	Chesapeake, VA	(7.0)
120	Oakland, CA	(7.0)
120	San Francisco, CA	(7.0)
120	Santa Monica, CA	(7.0)
124	Sioux Falls, SD	(7.3)
125	Columbia, SC	(7.4)
125	Grand Prairie, TX	(7.4)
125	Murfreesboro, TN	(7.4)
128	Chattanooga, TN	(7.5)
129	Fayetteville, NC	(7.6)
130	Carrollton, TX	(7.7)
130	Edison Twnshp, NJ	(7.7)
130	Syracuse, NY	(7.7)
133	Cleveland, OH	(7.9)
134	Everett, WA	(8.1)
134	Oxnard, CA	(8.1)
136	Amarillo, TX	(8.2)
136	St. Joseph, MO	(8.2)
138	Providence, RI	(8.3)
138	Stamford, CT	(8.3)
138	Yonkers, NY	(8.3)
141	Sugar Land, TX	(8.4)
141	Tulsa, OK	(8.4)
143	Paterson, NJ	(8.5)
144	Houston, TX	(8.7)
145	Tallahassee, FL	(8.8)
146	Evansville, IN	(8.9)
147	Newport Beach, CA	(9.1)
148	Lynn, MA	(9.3)
149	Savannah, GA	(9.4)
150	Abilene, TX	(9.6)
150	Allentown, PA	(9.6)
152	Hammond, IN	(9.8)
153	McAllen, TX	(10.0)
153	Pasadena, CA	(10.0)
155	Wilmington, NC	(10.3)
156	Overland Park, KS	(10.4)
157	Sparks, NV	(10.6)
158	Durham, NC	(10.9)
158	Lee's Summit, MO	(10.9)
160	Fullerton, CA	(11.3)
160	Raleigh, NC	(11.3)
162	Torrance, CA	(11.6)
162	Vacaville, CA	(11.6)
164	Whittier, CA	(11.7)
165	Costa Mesa, CA	(11.8)
166	Pearland, TX	(11.9)
167	Albuquerque, NM	(12.0)
168	Cincinnati, OH	(12.3)
169	Baltimore, MD	(12.4)
169	Broken Arrow, OK	(12.4)
171	Fort Smith, AR	(12.5)
172	Tuscaloosa, AL	(12.6)
173	San Leandro, CA	(12.8)
174	Philadelphia, PA	(12.9)
174	Santa Clarita, CA	(12.9)
176	Newton, MA	(13.0)
177	Clovis, CA	(13.1)
178	Memphis, TN	(13.2)
179	Albany, NY	(13.6)
179	Columbus, OH	(13.6)
181	Yuma, AZ	(14.0)
182	Fort Lauderdale, FL	(14.3)
183	Fayetteville, AR	(14.4)
184	Missouri City, TX	(14.6)
184	Rochester, NY	(14.6)
186	Bridgeport, CT	(14.7)
186	Cape Coral, FL	(14.7)
188	Simi Valley, CA	(14.8)
189	Tacoma, WA	(14.9)
190	Eugene, OR	(15.1)
191	Dayton, OH	(15.4)
191	Santa Rosa, CA	(15.4)
193	West Covina, CA	(15.5)
194	Bakersfield, CA	(15.7)
194	El Monte, CA	(15.7)
194	Irving, TX	(15.7)
194	Scottsdale, AZ	(15.7)
198	Alexandria, VA	(15.9)
199	West Valley, UT	(16.0)
200	Hayward, CA	(16.1)
201	Cedar Rapids, IA	(16.2)
201	New York, NY	(16.2)
203	Berkeley, CA	(16.3)
204	Santa Maria, CA	(16.4)
204	St. Paul, MN	(16.4)
206	Santa Clara, CA	(16.6)

RANK	CITY	% CHANGE
207	Moreno Valley, CA	(16.7)
207	Woodbridge Twnshp, NJ	(16.7)
209	High Point, NC	(16.8)
209	Lewisville, TX	(16.8)
211	Corpus Christi, TX	(17.2)
211	Modesto, CA	(17.2)
211	Pittsburgh, PA	(17.2)
214	Edmond, OK	(17.3)
214	Fort Worth, TX	(17.3)
216	Anaheim, CA	(17.5)
217	Macon, GA	(17.6)
217	Norwalk, CA	(17.6)
219	Plano, TX	(17.7)
219	Ventura, CA	(17.7)
221	Atlanta, GA	(17.9)
222	Pompano Beach, FL	(18.0)
222	Westminster, CA	(18.0)
224	Lakewood, CA	(18.1)
224	Orlando, FL	(18.1)
224	Springfield, MA	(18.1)
227	Baldwin Park, CA	(18.4)
228	Daly City, CA	(18.5)
228	Ogden, UT	(18.5)
230	Montgomery, AL	(18.7)
231	San Bernardino, CA	(18.8)
232	Salinas, CA	(18.9)
233	Chandler, AZ	(19.0)
233	Corona, CA	(19.0)
233	Miami, FL	(19.0)
233	Sioux City, IA	(19.0)
237	Independence, MO	(19.3)
238	Bellevue, WA	(19.4)
239	Shreveport, LA	(19.6)
240	Beaumont, TX	(19.7)
241	Miami Gardens, FL	(19.8)
242	Oklahoma City, OK	(19.9)
243	Honolulu, HI	(20.0)
243	Rialto, CA	(20.0)
243	Stockton, CA	(20.0)
246	Escondido, CA	(20.2)
246	Los Angeles, CA	(20.2)
248	Pomona, CA	(20.4)
248	Richmond, CA	(20.4)
250	Huntsville, AL	(20.5)
251	Lakewood, CO	(20.7)
252	Allen, TX	(20.8)
253	Spokane Valley, WA	(20.9)
254	Las Vegas, NV	(21.0)
255	Billings, MT	(21.2)
255	Omaha, NE	(21.2)
257	Seattle, WA	(21.3)
257	Vista, CA	(21.3)
257	Waco, TX	(21.3)
260	San Mateo, CA	(21.4)
261	Cary, NC	(21.5)
261	Racine, WI	(21.5)
263	Fort Wayne, IN	(21.6)
264	Rancho Cucamon., CA	(21.7)
265	San Angelo, TX	(21.8)
266	Sacramento, CA	(21.9)
267	Fresno, CA	(22.1)
267	Minneapolis, MN	(22.1)
267	Norwalk, CT	(22.1)
270	Colonie, NY	(22.2)
270	Roanoke, VA	(22.2)
272	Irvine, CA	(22.4)
273	Surprise, AZ	(22.5)
274	St. Louis, MO	(22.7)
275	Palmdale, CA	(22.8)
276	Redding, CA	(23.0)
277	Trenton, NJ	(23.1)
278	Killeen, TX	(23.3)
279	Provo, UT	(23.6)
280	Ontario, CA	(23.7)
281	Reno, NV	(23.8)
282	Reading, PA	(24.0)
283	Chico, CA	(24.1)
284	Chino, CA	(24.6)
285	Kansas City, KS	(24.9)
285	Orange, CA	(24.9)
287	Canton, OH	(25.0)
288	Boston, MA	(25.1)
288	Carlsbad, CA	(25.1)
290	Alhambra, CA	(25.3)
291	Charleston, SC	(25.5)
291	Dallas, TX	(25.5)
291	Wichita Falls, TX	(25.5)
294	Garden Grove, CA	(25.6)
295	Lincoln, NE	(25.8)
296	Federal Way, WA	(25.9)
297	Newark, NJ	(26.0)
298	Kansas City, MO	(26.3)
299	Nashville, TN	(26.4)
299	San Marcos, CA	(26.4)
301	Boulder, CO	(26.5)
302	Vancouver, WA	(26.7)
303	Roseville, CA	(26.8)
304	Fairfield, CA	(26.9)
305	Tracy, CA	(27.2)
306	Colorado Springs, CO	(27.3)
307	Henderson, NV	(27.5)
308	Bellingham, WA	(27.6)
309	Hesperia, CA	(27.7)
310	Boise, ID	(27.8)
310	West Palm Beach, FL	(27.8)
312	North Charleston, SC	(27.9)
313	Victorville, CA	(28.0)
314	Indio, CA	(28.2)
315	Hartford, CT	(28.3)
316	Gilbert, AZ	(28.6)
316	Santa Ana, CA	(28.6)
318	Suffolk, VA	(29.0)
318	Topeka, KS	(29.0)
320	Gary, IN	(29.1)
321	Orem, UT	(29.2)
322	Oceanside, CA	(29.4)
323	Charlotte, NC	(29.5)
323	Gresham, OR	(29.5)
325	Thornton, CO	(29.9)
326	Riverside, CA	(30.0)
327	San Diego, CA	(30.1)
328	Merced, CA	(30.2)
329	Centennial, CO	(30.7)
330	Palm Bay, FL	(30.8)
331	Peoria, AZ	(31.0)
332	Tempe, AZ	(31.1)
333	El Cajon, CA	(31.2)
334	Portland, OR	(31.3)
335	Davenport, IA	(31.5)
336	Arvada, CO	(31.7)
337	Westminster, CO	(33.0)
338	Salem, OR	(33.4)
339	Lancaster, CA	(33.6)
339	Temecula, CA	(33.6)
341	Mesa, AZ	(34.1)
342	Phoenix, AZ	(34.4)
343	Chula Vista, CA	(34.5)
344	Concord, CA	(34.7)
345	Jersey City, NJ	(34.8)
346	North Las Vegas, NV	(35.4)
347	Denton, TX	(35.9)
348	Kent, WA	(36.0)
348	St. George, UT	(36.0)
350	Aurora, CO	(36.2)
351	Richmond, VA	(37.3)
351	Visalia, CA	(37.3)
353	O'Fallon, MO	(38.3)
354	Murrieta, CA	(40.1)
355	Tampa, FL	(40.6)
356	Denver, CO	(40.7)
357	Pueblo, CO	(44.2)
358	Greeley, CO	(45.3)
359	Bend, OR	(47.4)
360	Beaverton, OR	(49.0)
361	Frisco, TX	(51.5)
362	Hillsboro, OR	(54.2)
NA	Ann Arbor, MI**	NA
NA	Aurora, IL**	NA
NA	Avondale, AZ**	NA
NA	Bloomington, MN**	NA
NA	Brockton, MA**	NA
NA	Canton Twnshp, MI**	NA
NA	Chicago, IL**	NA
NA	Citrus Heights, CA**	NA
NA	Clarkstown, NY**	NA
NA	Clinton Twnshp, MI**	NA
NA	Dearborn, MI**	NA
NA	Decatur, IL**	NA
NA	Des Moines, IA**	NA
NA	Detroit, MI**	NA
NA	Duluth, MN**	NA
NA	Elgin, IL**	NA
NA	Elk Grove, CA**	NA
NA	Fall River, MA**	NA
NA	Farmington Hills, MI**	NA
NA	Flint, MI**	NA
NA	Grand Rapids, MI**	NA
NA	Jacksonville, NC**	NA
NA	Joliet, IL**	NA
NA	Lansing, MI**	NA
NA	Lexington, KY**	NA
NA	Little Rock, AR**	NA
NA	Livonia, MI**	NA
NA	Longmont, CO**	NA
NA	Louisville, KY**	NA
NA	Nampa, ID**	NA
NA	Naperville, IL**	NA
NA	New Haven, CT**	NA
NA	New Orleans, LA**	NA
NA	Olathe, KS**	NA
NA	Peoria, IL**	NA
NA	Rochester, MN**	NA
NA	Rockford, IL**	NA
NA	Sandy Springs, GA**	NA
NA	Southfield, MI**	NA
NA	Springfield, IL**	NA
NA	Sterling Heights, MI**	NA
NA	Toledo, OH**	NA
NA	Troy, MI**	NA
NA	Tucson, AZ**	NA
NA	Vallejo, CA**	NA
NA	Warren, MI**	NA
NA	West Jordan, UT**	NA
NA	Westland, MI**	NA
NA	Wichita, KS**	NA

Source: CQ Press using reported data from the F.B.I. "Crime in the United States 2009"

*Includes murder, rape, robbery, aggravated assault, burglary, larceny-theft, and motor vehicle theft.

**Not available.

45. Violent Crimes in 2009
National Total = 1,318,398 Violent Crimes*

RANK	CITY	CRIMES
198	Abilene, TX	658
78	Akron, OH	1,916
162	Albany, GA	812
135	Albany, NY	1,007
33	Albuquerque, NM	4,082
308	Alexandria, VA	287
323	Alhambra, CA	248
172	Allentown, PA	749
396	Allen, TX	78
94	Amarillo, TX	1,580
373	Amherst, NY	129
116	Anaheim, CA	1,184
59	Anchorage, AK	2,488
313	Ann Arbor, MI	270
151	Antioch, CA	897
62	Arlington, TX	2,330
341	Arvada, CO	190
236	Athens-Clarke, GA	472
19	Atlanta, GA	6,359
99	Aurora, CO	1,524
NA	Aurora, IL**	NA
34	Austin, TX	4,024
281	Avondale, AZ	351
66	Bakersfield, CA	2,099
304	Baldwin Park, CA	295
10	Baltimore, MD	9,664
51	Baton Rouge, LA	2,823
136	Beaumont, TX	1,002
342	Beaverton, OR	189
357	Bellevue, WA	162
347	Bellingham, WA	171
364	Bend, OR	150
203	Berkeley, CA	615
319	Billings, MT	259
53	Birmingham, AL	2,812
NA	Bloomington, MN**	NA
333	Boca Raton, FL	217
216	Boise, ID	538
21	Boston, MA	6,192
325	Boulder, CO	245
377	Brick Twnshp, NJ	124
98	Bridgeport, CT	1,527
115	Brockton, MA	1,194
344	Broken Arrow, OK	180
243	Brownsville, TX	454
324	Buena Park, CA	247
36	Buffalo, NY	3,920
321	Burbank, CA	253
230	Cambridge, MA	497
80	Camden, NJ	1,880
369	Canton Twnshp, MI	138
195	Canton, OH	683
289	Cape Coral, FL	332
308	Carlsbad, CA	287
322	Carrollton, TX	250
228	Carson, CA	500
370	Cary, NC	132
265	Cedar Rapids, IA	403
365	Centennial, CO	148
178	Chandler, AZ	740
209	Charleston, SC	595
25	Charlotte, NC	5,625
81	Chattanooga, TN	1,792
336	Cheektowaga, NY	210
158	Chesapeake, VA	831
NA	Chicago, IL**	NA
296	Chico, CA	310
349	Chino, CA	169

RANK	CITY	CRIMES
175	Chula Vista, CA	747
35	Cincinnati, OH	3,976
261	Citrus Heights, CA	415
392	Clarkstown, NY	92
163	Clarksville, TN	805
144	Clearwater, FL	924
22	Cleveland, OH	5,990
338	Clifton, NJ	197
310	Clinton Twnshp, MI	277
367	Clovis, CA	141
348	College Station, TX	170
399	Colonie, NY	61
73	Colorado Springs, CO	1,968
227	Columbia, MO	501
106	Columbia, SC	1,338
123	Columbus, GA	1,153
26	Columbus, OH	5,340
103	Compton, CA	1,457
267	Concord, CA	397
286	Coral Springs, FL	338
334	Corona, CA	214
60	Corpus Christi, TX	2,365
299	Costa Mesa, CA	304
380	Cranston, RI	120
8	Dallas, TX	10,221
328	Daly City, CA	240
371	Danbury, CT	130
179	Davenport, IA	739
250	Davie, FL	437
95	Dayton, OH	1,542
285	Dearborn, MI	339
NA	Decatur, IL**	NA
298	Denton, TX	306
41	Denver, CO	3,493
132	Des Moines, IA	1,067
5	Detroit, MI	17,868
247	Downey, CA	444
NA	Duluth, MN**	NA
93	Durham, NC	1,591
317	Edison Twnshp, NJ	264
394	Edmond, OK	87
241	El Cajon, CA	461
183	El Monte, CA	716
50	El Paso, TX	2,830
NA	Elgin, IL**	NA
109	Elizabeth, NJ	1,288
206	Elk Grove, CA	608
236	Erie, PA	472
202	Escondido, CA	629
238	Eugene, OR	470
252	Evansville, IN	432
205	Everett, WA	610
250	Fairfield, CA	437
130	Fall River, MA	1,086
300	Fargo, ND	303
386	Farmington Hills, MI	108
291	Fayetteville, AR	325
112	Fayetteville, NC	1,268
276	Federal Way, WA	369
63	Flint, MI	2,244
156	Fontana, CA	859
218	Fort Collins, CO	535
101	Fort Lauderdale, FL	1,481
185	Fort Smith, AR	712
154	Fort Wayne, IN	876
31	Fort Worth, TX	4,232
231	Fremont, CA	490
49	Fresno, CA	2,933
387	Frisco, TX	108

RANK	CITY	CRIMES
221	Fullerton, CA	526
121	Gainesville, FL	1,156
215	Garden Grove, CA	541
206	Garland, TX	608
197	Gary, IN	661
340	Gilbert, AZ	194
124	Glendale, AZ	1,147
301	Glendale, CA	302
223	Grand Prairie, TX	524
91	Grand Rapids, MI	1,604
389	Greece, NY	98
248	Greeley, CO	441
235	Green Bay, WI	473
76	Greensboro, NC	1,940
272	Gresham, OR	382
337	Hamilton Twnshp, NJ	205
176	Hammond, IN	741
243	Hampton, VA	454
92	Hartford, CT	1,603
190	Hawthorne, CA	700
176	Hayward, CA	741
204	Henderson, NV	612
306	Hesperia, CA	290
143	Hialeah, FL	925
196	High Point, NC	678
366	Hillsboro, OR	147
192	Hollywood, FL	696
58	Honolulu, HI	2,537
2	Houston, TX	25,593
273	Huntington Beach, CA	377
120	Huntsville, AL	1,164
172	Independence, MO	749
9	Indianapolis, IN	9,760
253	Indio, CA	428
133	Inglewood, CA	1,039
362	Irvine, CA	153
208	Irving, TX	604
17	Jacksonville, FL	6,772
327	Jacksonville, NC	241
100	Jackson, MS	1,515
82	Jersey City, NJ	1,791
NA	Joliet, IL**	NA
142	Kansas City, KS	940
20	Kansas City, MO	6,303
313	Kenosha, WI	270
226	Kent, WA	507
171	Killeen, TX	750
74	Knoxville, TN	1,966
127	Lafayette, LA	1,115
385	Lake Forest, CA	109
233	Lakeland, FL	487
279	Lakewood, CA	366
193	Lakewood, CO	689
139	Lancaster, CA	976
113	Lansing, MI	1,200
108	Laredo, TX	1,294
239	Las Cruces, NM	464
6	Las Vegas, NV	13,039
258	Lawrence, KS	424
128	Lawton, OK	1,098
388	Lee's Summit, MO	106
338	Lewisville, TX	197
85	Lexington, KY	1,760
119	Lincoln, NE	1,165
54	Little Rock, AR	2,795
359	Livermore, CA	161
345	Livonia, MI	176
46	Long Beach, CA	3,161
290	Longmont, CO	330

RANK	CITY	CRIMES
186	Longview, TX	708
3	Los Angeles, CA	24,070
38	Louisville, KY	3,769
67	Lubbock, TX	2,079
159	Lynn, MA	819
189	Macon, GA	704
157	Madison, WI	853
217	Manchester, NH	537
282	McAllen, TX	348
325	McKinney, TX	245
148	Melbourne, FL	906
7	Memphis, TN	12,055
181	Merced, CA	733
71	Mesa, AZ	2,000
219	Mesquite, TX	534
148	Miami Beach, FL	906
131	Miami Gardens, FL	1,069
28	Miami, FL	4,983
256	Midland, TX	426
18	Milwaukee, WI	6,584
30	Minneapolis, MN	4,242
223	Miramar, FL	524
390	Mission Viejo, CA	95
378	Missouri City, TX	123
72	Mobile, AL	1,994
104	Modesto, CA	1,419
155	Montgomery, AL	871
146	Moreno Valley, CA	921
191	Murfreesboro, TN	697
381	Murrieta, CA	118
311	Nampa, ID	274
NA	Naperville, IL**	NA
345	Nashua, NH	176
15	Nashville, TN	6,959
116	New Bedford, MA	1,184
64	New Haven, CT	2,183
55	New Orleans, LA	2,614
1	New York, NY	46,357
56	Newark, NJ	2,597
376	Newport Beach, CA	125
391	Newton, MA	94
95	Norfolk, VA	1,542
357	Norman, OK	162
138	North Charleston, SC	993
88	North Las Vegas, NV	1,668
242	Norwalk, CA	456
257	Norwalk, CT	425
16	Oakland, CA	6,793
172	Oceanside, CA	749
165	Odessa, TX	787
397	O'Fallon, MO	65
269	Ogden, UT	391
27	Oklahoma City, OK	5,181
317	Olathe, KS	264
61	Omaha, NE	2,363
182	Ontario, CA	732
360	Orange, CA	160
400	Orem, UT	50
52	Orlando, FL	2,814
297	Overland Park, KS	308
168	Oxnard, CA	771
220	Palm Bay, FL	532
160	Palmdale, CA	818
234	Pasadena, CA	483
188	Pasadena, TX	706
107	Paterson, NJ	1,318
372	Pearland, TX	130
302	Pembroke Pines, FL	300

RANK	CITY	CRIMES
293	Peoria, AZ	321
NA	Peoria, IL**	NA
4	Philadelphia, PA	19,163
11	Phoenix, AZ	8,730
48	Pittsburgh, PA	3,087
239	Plano, TX	464
275	Plantation, FL	372
140	Pomona, CA	968
134	Pompano Beach, FL	1,029
259	Port St. Lucie, FL	421
47	Portland, OR	3,105
187	Portsmouth, VA	707
118	Providence, RI	1,182
352	Provo, UT	167
151	Pueblo, CO	897
271	Quincy, MA	384
246	Racine, WI	448
70	Raleigh, NC	2,001
398	Ramapo, NY	63
283	Rancho Cucamon., CA	342
170	Reading, PA	766
194	Redding, CA	688
102	Reno, NV	1,473
214	Rialto, CA	542
331	Richardson, TX	230
129	Richmond, CA	1,095
90	Richmond, VA	1,631
330	Rio Rancho, NM	233
97	Riverside, CA	1,535
201	Roanoke, VA	639
NA	Rochester, MN**	NA
69	Rochester, NY	2,042
68	Rockford, IL	2,061
292	Roseville, CA	323
355	Roswell, GA	163
374	Round Rock, TX	128
32	Sacramento, CA	4,165
210	Salem, OR	576
125	Salinas, CA	1,133
110	Salt Lake City, UT	1,276
277	San Angelo, TX	368
12	San Antonio, TX	7,844
79	San Bernardino, CA	1,908
24	San Diego, CA	5,931
23	San Francisco, CA	5,957
42	San Jose, CA	3,439
263	San Leandro, CA	409
332	San Marcos, CA	226
286	San Mateo, CA	338
342	Sandy Springs, GA	189
352	Sandy, UT	167
87	Santa Ana, CA	1,726
253	Santa Barbara, CA	428
351	Santa Clara, CA	168
255	Santa Clarita, CA	427
180	Santa Maria, CA	735
268	Santa Monica, CA	393
164	Santa Rosa, CA	803
126	Savannah, GA	1,128
262	Scottsdale, AZ	410
37	Seattle, WA	3,861
84	Shreveport, LA	1,776
361	Simi Valley, CA	155
283	Sioux City, IA	342
243	Sioux Falls, SD	454
295	Somerville, MA	312
169	South Bend, IN	769
212	South Gate, CA	566

RANK	CITY	CRIMES
263	Southfield, MI	409
266	Sparks, NV	399
315	Spokane Valley, WA	265
111	Spokane, WA	1,270
NA	Springfield, IL**	NA
77	Springfield, MA	1,929
114	Springfield, MO	1,197
280	Stamford, CT	353
334	Sterling Heights, MI	214
39	Stockton, CA	3,703
393	St. George, UT	92
248	St. Joseph, MO	441
14	St. Louis, MO	7,353
65	St. Paul, MN	2,137
43	St. Petersburg, FL	3,334
307	Suffolk, VA	289
382	Sugar Land, TX	113
349	Sunnyvale, CA	169
305	Sunrise, FL	292
383	Surprise, AZ	111
105	Syracuse, NY	1,343
75	Tacoma, WA	1,944
89	Tallahassee, FL	1,647
56	Tampa, FL	2,597
375	Temecula, CA	126
145	Tempe, AZ	922
303	Thornton, CO	296
355	Thousand Oaks, CA	163
44	Toledo, OH	3,251
384	Toms River Twnshp, NJ	111
184	Topeka, KS	715
319	Torrance, CA	259
362	Tracy, CA	153
122	Trenton, NJ	1,154
395	Troy, MI	79
40	Tucson, AZ	3,560
29	Tulsa, OK	4,295
260	Tuscaloosa, AL	418
222	Tyler, TX	525
229	Upper Darby Twnshp, PA	499
311	Vacaville, CA	274
137	Vallejo, CA	998
199	Vancouver, WA	656
277	Ventura, CA	368
166	Victorville, CA	783
147	Virginia Beach, VA	910
200	Visalia, CA	648
231	Vista, CA	490
153	Waco, TX	883
167	Warren, MI	778
379	Warwick, RI	121
13	Washington, DC	7,586
274	Waterbury, CT	375
294	West Covina, CA	315
354	West Jordan, UT	165
150	West Palm Beach, FL	905
213	West Valley, UT	564
270	Westland, MI	387
315	Westminster, CA	265
328	Westminster, CO	240
288	Whittier, CA	337
225	Wichita Falls, TX	520
45	Wichita, KS	3,245
161	Wilmington, NC	814
86	Winston-Salem, NC	1,739
368	Woodbridge Twnshp, NJ	139
83	Worcester, MA	1,790
141	Yonkers, NY	965
211	Yuma, AZ	570

Source: Reported data from the F.B.I. "Crime in the United States 2009"

*Violent crimes are offenses of murder, forcible rape, robbery, and aggravated assault.

**Not available.

45. Violent Crimes in 2009 (continued)
National Total = 1,318,398 Violent Crimes*

RANK	CITY	CRIMES
1	New York, NY	46,357
2	Houston, TX	25,593
3	Los Angeles, CA	24,070
4	Philadelphia, PA	19,163
5	Detroit, MI	17,868
6	Las Vegas, NV	13,039
7	Memphis, TN	12,055
8	Dallas, TX	10,221
9	Indianapolis, IN	9,760
10	Baltimore, MD	9,664
11	Phoenix, AZ	8,730
12	San Antonio, TX	7,844
13	Washington, DC	7,586
14	St. Louis, MO	7,353
15	Nashville, TN	6,959
16	Oakland, CA	6,793
17	Jacksonville, FL	6,772
18	Milwaukee, WI	6,584
19	Atlanta, GA	6,359
20	Kansas City, MO	6,303
21	Boston, MA	6,192
22	Cleveland, OH	5,990
23	San Francisco, CA	5,957
24	San Diego, CA	5,931
25	Charlotte, NC	5,625
26	Columbus, OH	5,340
27	Oklahoma City, OK	5,181
28	Miami, FL	4,983
29	Tulsa, OK	4,295
30	Minneapolis, MN	4,242
31	Fort Worth, TX	4,232
32	Sacramento, CA	4,165
33	Albuquerque, NM	4,082
34	Austin, TX	4,024
35	Cincinnati, OH	3,976
36	Buffalo, NY	3,920
37	Seattle, WA	3,861
38	Louisville, KY	3,769
39	Stockton, CA	3,703
40	Tucson, AZ	3,560
41	Denver, CO	3,493
42	San Jose, CA	3,439
43	St. Petersburg, FL	3,334
44	Toledo, OH	3,251
45	Wichita, KS	3,245
46	Long Beach, CA	3,161
47	Portland, OR	3,105
48	Pittsburgh, PA	3,087
49	Fresno, CA	2,933
50	El Paso, TX	2,830
51	Baton Rouge, LA	2,823
52	Orlando, FL	2,814
53	Birmingham, AL	2,812
54	Little Rock, AR	2,795
55	New Orleans, LA	2,614
56	Newark, NJ	2,597
56	Tampa, FL	2,597
58	Honolulu, HI	2,537
59	Anchorage, AK	2,488
60	Corpus Christi, TX	2,365
61	Omaha, NE	2,363
62	Arlington, TX	2,330
63	Flint, MI	2,244
64	New Haven, CT	2,183
65	St. Paul, MN	2,137
66	Bakersfield, CA	2,099
67	Lubbock, TX	2,079
68	Rockford, IL	2,061
69	Rochester, NY	2,042
70	Raleigh, NC	2,001
71	Mesa, AZ	2,000
72	Mobile, AL	1,994
73	Colorado Springs, CO	1,968
74	Knoxville, TN	1,966
75	Tacoma, WA	1,944
76	Greensboro, NC	1,940
77	Springfield, MA	1,929
78	Akron, OH	1,916
79	San Bernardino, CA	1,908
80	Camden, NJ	1,880
81	Chattanooga, TN	1,792
82	Jersey City, NJ	1,791
83	Worcester, MA	1,790
84	Shreveport, LA	1,776
85	Lexington, KY	1,760
86	Winston-Salem, NC	1,739
87	Santa Ana, CA	1,726
88	North Las Vegas, NV	1,668
89	Tallahassee, FL	1,647
90	Richmond, VA	1,631
91	Grand Rapids, MI	1,604
92	Hartford, CT	1,603
93	Durham, NC	1,591
94	Amarillo, TX	1,580
95	Dayton, OH	1,542
95	Norfolk, VA	1,542
97	Riverside, CA	1,535
98	Bridgeport, CT	1,527
99	Aurora, CO	1,524
100	Jackson, MS	1,515
101	Fort Lauderdale, FL	1,481
102	Reno, NV	1,473
103	Compton, CA	1,457
104	Modesto, CA	1,419
105	Syracuse, NY	1,343
106	Columbia, SC	1,338
107	Paterson, NJ	1,318
108	Laredo, TX	1,294
109	Elizabeth, NJ	1,288
110	Salt Lake City, UT	1,276
111	Spokane, WA	1,270
112	Fayetteville, NC	1,268
113	Lansing, MI	1,200
114	Springfield, MO	1,197
115	Brockton, MA	1,194
116	Anaheim, CA	1,184
116	New Bedford, MA	1,184
118	Providence, RI	1,182
119	Lincoln, NE	1,165
120	Huntsville, AL	1,164
121	Gainesville, FL	1,156
122	Trenton, NJ	1,154
123	Columbus, GA	1,153
124	Glendale, AZ	1,147
125	Salinas, CA	1,133
126	Savannah, GA	1,128
127	Lafayette, LA	1,115
128	Lawton, OK	1,098
129	Richmond, CA	1,095
130	Fall River, MA	1,086
131	Miami Gardens, FL	1,069
132	Des Moines, IA	1,067
133	Inglewood, CA	1,039
134	Pompano Beach, FL	1,029
135	Albany, NY	1,007
136	Beaumont, TX	1,002
137	Vallejo, CA	998
138	North Charleston, SC	993
139	Lancaster, CA	976
140	Pomona, CA	968
141	Yonkers, NY	965
142	Kansas City, KS	940
143	Hialeah, FL	925
144	Clearwater, FL	924
145	Tempe, AZ	922
146	Moreno Valley, CA	921
147	Virginia Beach, VA	910
148	Melbourne, FL	906
148	Miami Beach, FL	906
150	West Palm Beach, FL	905
151	Antioch, CA	897
151	Pueblo, CO	897
153	Waco, TX	883
154	Fort Wayne, IN	876
155	Montgomery, AL	871
156	Fontana, CA	859
157	Madison, WI	853
158	Chesapeake, VA	831
159	Lynn, MA	819
160	Palmdale, CA	818
161	Wilmington, NC	814
162	Albany, GA	812
163	Clarksville, TN	805
164	Santa Rosa, CA	803
165	Odessa, TX	787
166	Victorville, CA	783
167	Warren, MI	778
168	Oxnard, CA	771
169	South Bend, IN	769
170	Reading, PA	766
171	Killeen, TX	750
172	Allentown, PA	749
172	Independence, MO	749
172	Oceanside, CA	749
175	Chula Vista, CA	747
176	Hammond, IN	741
176	Hayward, CA	741
178	Chandler, AZ	740
179	Davenport, IA	739
180	Santa Maria, CA	735
181	Merced, CA	733
182	Ontario, CA	732
183	El Monte, CA	716
184	Topeka, KS	715
185	Fort Smith, AR	712
186	Longview, TX	708
187	Portsmouth, VA	707
188	Pasadena, TX	706
189	Macon, GA	704
190	Hawthorne, CA	700
191	Murfreesboro, TN	697
192	Hollywood, FL	696
193	Lakewood, CO	689
194	Redding, CA	688
195	Canton, OH	683
196	High Point, NC	678
197	Gary, IN	661
198	Abilene, TX	658
199	Vancouver, WA	656
200	Visalia, CA	648
201	Roanoke, VA	639
202	Escondido, CA	629
203	Berkeley, CA	615
204	Henderson, NV	612
205	Everett, WA	610
206	Elk Grove, CA	608

RANK	CITY	CRIMES
206	Garland, TX	608
208	Irving, TX	604
209	Charleston, SC	595
210	Salem, OR	576
211	Yuma, AZ	570
212	South Gate, CA	566
213	West Valley, UT	564
214	Rialto, CA	542
215	Garden Grove, CA	541
216	Boise, ID	538
217	Manchester, NH	537
218	Fort Collins, CO	535
219	Mesquite, TX	534
220	Palm Bay, FL	532
221	Fullerton, CA	526
222	Tyler, TX	525
223	Grand Prairie, TX	524
223	Miramar, FL	524
225	Wichita Falls, TX	520
226	Kent, WA	507
227	Columbia, MO	501
228	Carson, CA	500
229	Upper Darby Twnshp, PA	499
230	Cambridge, MA	497
231	Fremont, CA	490
231	Vista, CA	490
233	Lakeland, FL	487
234	Pasadena, CA	483
235	Green Bay, WI	473
236	Athens-Clarke, GA	472
236	Erie, PA	472
238	Eugene, OR	470
239	Las Cruces, NM	464
239	Plano, TX	464
241	El Cajon, CA	461
242	Norwalk, CA	456
243	Brownsville, TX	454
243	Hampton, VA	454
243	Sioux Falls, SD	454
246	Racine, WI	448
247	Downey, CA	444
248	Greeley, CO	441
248	St. Joseph, MO	441
250	Davie, FL	437
250	Fairfield, CA	437
252	Evansville, IN	432
253	Indio, CA	428
253	Santa Barbara, CA	428
255	Santa Clarita, CA	427
256	Midland, TX	426
257	Norwalk, CT	425
258	Lawrence, KS	424
259	Port St. Lucie, FL	421
260	Tuscaloosa, AL	418
261	Citrus Heights, CA	415
262	Scottsdale, AZ	410
263	San Leandro, CA	409
263	Southfield, MI	409
265	Cedar Rapids, IA	403
266	Sparks, NV	399
267	Concord, CA	397
268	Santa Monica, CA	393
269	Ogden, UT	391
270	Westland, MI	387
271	Quincy, MA	384
272	Gresham, OR	382
273	Huntington Beach, CA	377
274	Waterbury, CT	375
275	Plantation, FL	372
276	Federal Way, WA	369
277	San Angelo, TX	368
277	Ventura, CA	368
279	Lakewood, CA	366
280	Stamford, CT	353
281	Avondale, AZ	351
282	McAllen, TX	348
283	Rancho Cucamon., CA	342
283	Sioux City, IA	342
285	Dearborn, MI	339
286	Coral Springs, FL	338
286	San Mateo, CA	338
288	Whittier, CA	337
289	Cape Coral, FL	332
290	Longmont, CO	330
291	Fayetteville, AR	325
292	Roseville, CA	323
293	Peoria, AZ	321
294	West Covina, CA	315
295	Somerville, MA	312
296	Chico, CA	310
297	Overland Park, KS	308
298	Denton, TX	306
299	Costa Mesa, CA	304
300	Fargo, ND	303
301	Glendale, CA	302
302	Pembroke Pines, FL	300
303	Thornton, CO	296
304	Baldwin Park, CA	295
305	Sunrise, FL	292
306	Hesperia, CA	290
307	Suffolk, VA	289
308	Alexandria, VA	287
308	Carlsbad, CA	287
310	Clinton Twnshp, MI	277
311	Nampa, ID	274
311	Vacaville, CA	274
313	Ann Arbor, MI	270
313	Kenosha, WI	270
315	Spokane Valley, WA	265
315	Westminster, CA	265
317	Edison Twnshp, NJ	264
317	Olathe, KS	264
319	Billings, MT	259
319	Torrance, CA	259
321	Burbank, CA	253
322	Carrollton, TX	250
323	Alhambra, CA	248
324	Buena Park, CA	247
325	Boulder, CO	245
325	McKinney, TX	245
327	Jacksonville, NC	241
328	Daly City, CA	240
328	Westminster, CO	240
330	Rio Rancho, NM	233
331	Richardson, TX	230
332	San Marcos, CA	226
333	Boca Raton, FL	217
334	Corona, CA	214
334	Sterling Heights, MI	214
336	Cheektowaga, NY	210
337	Hamilton Twnshp, NJ	205
338	Clifton, NJ	197
338	Lewisville, TX	197
340	Gilbert, AZ	194
341	Arvada, CO	190
342	Beaverton, OR	189
342	Sandy Springs, GA	189
344	Broken Arrow, OK	180
345	Livonia, MI	176
345	Nashua, NH	176
347	Bellingham, WA	171
348	College Station, TX	170
349	Chino, CA	169
349	Sunnyvale, CA	169
351	Santa Clara, CA	168
352	Provo, UT	167
352	Sandy, UT	167
354	West Jordan, UT	165
355	Roswell, GA	163
355	Thousand Oaks, CA	163
357	Bellevue, WA	162
357	Norman, OK	162
359	Livermore, CA	161
360	Orange, CA	160
361	Simi Valley, CA	155
362	Irvine, CA	153
362	Tracy, CA	153
364	Bend, OR	150
365	Centennial, CO	148
366	Hillsboro, OR	147
367	Clovis, CA	141
368	Woodbridge Twnshp, NJ	139
369	Canton Twnshp, MI	138
370	Cary, NC	132
371	Danbury, CT	130
372	Pearland, TX	130
373	Amherst, NY	129
374	Round Rock, TX	128
375	Temecula, CA	126
376	Newport Beach, CA	125
377	Brick Twnshp, NJ	124
378	Missouri City, TX	123
379	Warwick, RI	121
380	Cranston, RI	120
381	Murrieta, CA	118
382	Sugar Land, TX	113
383	Surprise, AZ	111
384	Toms River Twnshp, NJ	111
385	Lake Forest, CA	109
386	Farmington Hills, MI	108
387	Frisco, TX	108
388	Lee's Summit, MO	106
389	Greece, NY	98
390	Mission Viejo, CA	95
391	Newton, MA	94
392	Clarkstown, NY	92
393	St. George, UT	92
394	Edmond, OK	87
395	Troy, MI	79
396	Allen, TX	78
397	O'Fallon, MO	65
398	Ramapo, NY	63
399	Colonie, NY	61
400	Orem, UT	50
NA	Aurora, IL**	NA
NA	Bloomington, MN**	NA
NA	Chicago, IL**	NA
NA	Decatur, IL**	NA
NA	Duluth, MN**	NA
NA	Elgin, IL**	NA
NA	Joliet, IL**	NA
NA	Naperville, IL**	NA
NA	Peoria, IL**	NA
NA	Rochester, MN**	NA
NA	Springfield, IL**	NA

Source: Reported data from the F.B.I. "Crime in the United States 2009"

*Violent crimes are offenses of murder, forcible rape, robbery, and aggravated assault.

**Not available.

46. Violent Crime Rate in 2009
National Rate = 429.4 Violent Crimes per 100,000 Population*

RANK	CITY	RATE
165	Abilene, TX	564.5
71	Akron, OH	927.9
43	Albany, GA	1,072.2
41	Albany, NY	1,077.6
103	Albuquerque, NM	769.3
333	Alexandria, VA	196.4
291	Alhambra, CA	288.5
123	Allentown, PA	697.9
394	Allen, TX	89.8
89	Amarillo, TX	837.0
380	Amherst, NY	116.8
264	Anaheim, CA	352.4
82	Anchorage, AK	878.2
317	Ann Arbor, MI	236.1
79	Antioch, CA	886.0
149	Arlington, TX	614.6
347	Arvada, CO	176.0
241	Athens-Clarke, GA	412.1
33	Atlanta, GA	1,150.1
211	Aurora, CO	470.4
NA	Aurora, IL**	NA
181	Austin, TX	523.3
250	Avondale, AZ	395.4
141	Bakersfield, CA	634.3
253	Baldwin Park, CA	380.5
9	Baltimore, MD	1,512.9
21	Baton Rouge, LA	1,264.9
75	Beaumont, TX	909.0
328	Beaverton, OR	202.7
374	Bellevue, WA	129.5
324	Bellingham, WA	213.1
342	Bend, OR	186.2
152	Berkeley, CA	607.8
312	Billings, MT	245.7
25	Birmingham, AL	1,236.7
NA	Bloomington, MN**	NA
307	Boca Raton, FL	252.5
304	Boise, ID	260.6
56	Boston, MA	992.0
314	Boulder, CO	244.9
355	Brick Twnshp, NJ	157.6
36	Bridgeport, CT	1,122.4
24	Brockton, MA	1,237.7
339	Broken Arrow, OK	190.6
306	Brownsville, TX	252.9
280	Buena Park, CA	310.6
11	Buffalo, NY	1,459.1
313	Burbank, CA	245.0
205	Cambridge, MA	483.2
1	Camden, NJ	2,380.3
352	Canton Twnshp, MI	167.0
85	Canton, OH	874.7
329	Cape Coral, FL	202.0
288	Carlsbad, CA	291.4
334	Carrollton, TX	196.2
174	Carson, CA	539.8
392	Cary, NC	98.7
277	Cedar Rapids, IA	312.9
363	Centennial, CO	148.9
289	Chandler, AZ	289.0
180	Charleston, SC	523.4
116	Charlotte, NC	723.3
48	Chattanooga, TN	1,038.6
300	Cheektowaga, NY	270.0
257	Chesapeake, VA	372.2
NA	Chicago, IL**	NA
260	Chico, CA	365.9
330	Chino, CA	199.7
269	Chula Vista, CA	332.2
29	Cincinnati, OH	1,192.0
198	Citrus Heights, CA	492.1
382	Clarkstown, NY	116.6
131	Clarksville, TN	661.7
83	Clearwater, FL	876.8
13	Cleveland, OH	1,395.5
308	Clifton, NJ	252.2
290	Clinton Twnshp, MI	288.7
364	Clovis, CA	148.1
332	College Station, TX	197.5
398	Colonie, NY	78.2
200	Colorado Springs, CO	490.0
202	Columbia, MO	488.4
47	Columbia, SC	1,046.3
148	Columbus, GA	619.1
120	Columbus, OH	703.2
8	Compton, CA	1,552.1
271	Concord, CA	328.0
301	Coral Springs, FL	269.0
369	Corona, CA	140.4
94	Corpus Christi, TX	822.6
298	Costa Mesa, CA	276.0
362	Cranston, RI	149.6
99	Dallas, TX	792.2
316	Daly City, CA	237.0
353	Danbury, CT	163.1
114	Davenport, IA	730.8
203	Davie, FL	484.8
52	Dayton, OH	1,008.1
247	Dearborn, MI	397.4
NA	Decatur, IL**	NA
311	Denton, TX	246.2
161	Denver, CO	577.7
173	Des Moines, IA	542.2
4	Detroit, MI	1,966.9
240	Downey, CA	412.6
NA	Duluth, MN**	NA
122	Durham, NC	699.4
302	Edison Twnshp, NJ	265.7
387	Edmond, OK	107.6
193	El Cajon, CA	498.6
158	El Monte, CA	584.8
218	El Paso, TX	457.3
NA	Elgin, IL**	NA
50	Elizabeth, NJ	1,031.1
233	Elk Grove, CA	432.5
220	Erie, PA	454.6
217	Escondido, CA	457.7
281	Eugene, OR	310.5
255	Evansville, IN	373.2
147	Everett, WA	619.7
237	Fairfield, CA	418.3
31	Fall River, MA	1,181.7
275	Fargo, ND	322.9
371	Farmington Hills, MI	138.2
232	Fayetteville, AR	432.6
115	Fayetteville, NC	728.8
230	Federal Way, WA	438.1
3	Flint, MI	2,009.7
222	Fontana, CA	451.4
252	Fort Collins, CO	386.3
96	Fort Lauderdale, FL	809.5
91	Fort Smith, AR	835.9
266	Fort Wayne, IN	348.2
157	Fort Worth, TX	585.0
315	Fremont, CA	241.7
151	Fresno, CA	609.3
391	Frisco, TX	99.8
249	Fullerton, CA	397.0
53	Gainesville, FL	1,002.9
273	Garden Grove, CA	326.2
295	Garland, TX	277.8
124	Gary, IN	694.2
395	Gilbert, AZ	83.7
224	Glendale, AZ	449.7
358	Glendale, CA	153.0
276	Grand Prairie, TX	318.0
92	Grand Rapids, MI	831.5
389	Greece, NY	105.1
209	Greeley, CO	473.8
212	Green Bay, WI	469.1
104	Greensboro, NC	766.2
256	Gresham, OR	372.8
320	Hamilton Twnshp, NJ	226.5
61	Hammond, IN	973.9
278	Hampton, VA	311.1
17	Hartford, CT	1,292.2
93	Hawthorne, CA	830.2
183	Hayward, CA	521.0
318	Henderson, NV	233.7
273	Hesperia, CA	326.2
228	Hialeah, FL	442.9
136	High Point, NC	654.0
359	Hillsboro, OR	152.2
199	Hollywood, FL	491.5
293	Honolulu, HI	279.7
35	Houston, TX	1,125.6
335	Huntington Beach, CA	195.4
137	Huntsville, AL	651.7
150	Independence, MO	613.1
27	Indianapolis, IN	1,199.8
207	Indio, CA	478.4
72	Inglewood, CA	921.8
399	Irvine, CA	70.9
283	Irving, TX	298.3
90	Jacksonville, FL	836.0
279	Jacksonville, NC	310.9
84	Jackson, MS	876.7
112	Jersey City, NJ	743.6
NA	Joliet, IL**	NA
132	Kansas City, KS	661.5
16	Kansas City, MO	1,300.4
296	Kenosha, WI	276.5
153	Kent, WA	601.0
146	Killeen, TX	621.5
46	Knoxville, TN	1,057.8
59	Lafayette, LA	979.2
366	Lake Forest, CA	144.4
185	Lakeland, FL	516.3
213	Lakewood, CA	467.2
200	Lakewood, CO	490.0
134	Lancaster, CA	656.2
45	Lansing, MI	1,058.3
164	Laredo, TX	570.2
196	Las Cruces, NM	493.5
65	Las Vegas, NV	946.7
215	Lawrence, KS	462.4
26	Lawton, OK	1,222.2
378	Lee's Summit, MO	123.6
340	Lewisville, TX	188.3
155	Lexington, KY	593.8
216	Lincoln, NE	457.9
10	Little Rock, AR	1,469.5
331	Livermore, CA	199.0
337	Livonia, MI	195.1
128	Long Beach, CA	681.3
254	Longmont, CO	376.7

RANK	CITY	RATE
73	Longview, TX	911.6
144	Los Angeles, CA	625.4
154	Louisville, KY	597.1
67	Lubbock, TX	932.8
76	Lynn, MA	898.5
106	Macon, GA	762.7
261	Madison, WI	363.8
195	Manchester, NH	494.2
303	McAllen, TX	262.4
343	McKinney, TX	185.4
32	Melbourne, FL	1,163.7
5	Memphis, TN	1,806.2
68	Merced, CA	931.5
235	Mesa, AZ	424.8
244	Mesquite, TX	401.7
42	Miami Beach, FL	1,075.2
62	Miami Gardens, FL	968.8
30	Miami, FL	1,188.7
251	Midland, TX	394.7
40	Milwaukee, WI	1,088.9
39	Minneapolis, MN	1,108.7
204	Miramar, FL	483.5
390	Mission Viejo, CA	100.5
354	Missouri City, TX	158.6
95	Mobile, AL	810.0
125	Modesto, CA	694.0
234	Montgomery, AL	429.4
213	Moreno Valley, CA	467.2
133	Murfreesboro, TN	658.1
385	Murrieta, CA	112.1
272	Nampa, ID	326.7
NA	Naperville, IL**	NA
327	Nashua, NH	203.3
34	Nashville, TN	1,140.5
18	New Bedford, MA	1,278.3
6	New Haven, CT	1,765.3
102	New Orleans, LA	777.0
168	New York, NY	551.8
70	Newark, NJ	930.1
356	Newport Beach, CA	156.4
386	Newton, MA	111.3
135	Norfolk, VA	655.9
361	Norman, OK	149.8
49	North Charleston, SC	1,034.6
117	North Las Vegas, NV	717.0
227	Norwalk, CA	443.5
190	Norwalk, CT	510.8
7	Oakland, CA	1,679.1
229	Oceanside, CA	439.1
100	Odessa, TX	788.8
397	O'Fallon, MO	80.7
210	Ogden, UT	471.0
69	Oklahoma City, OK	930.3
323	Olathe, KS	214.1
176	Omaha, NE	533.4
236	Ontario, CA	422.6
381	Orange, CA	116.7
400	Orem, UT	53.3
28	Orlando, FL	1,196.9
346	Overland Park, KS	177.3
242	Oxnard, CA	411.5
187	Palm Bay, FL	514.1
166	Palmdale, CA	558.8
268	Pasadena, CA	335.3
206	Pasadena, TX	480.4
74	Paterson, NJ	909.3
365	Pearland, TX	146.8
326	Pembroke Pines, FL	206.2

Source: Reported data from the F.B.I. "Crime in the United States 2009"
*Violent crimes are offenses of murder, forcible rape, robbery, and aggravated assault.
**Not available.

RANK	CITY	RATE
336	Peoria, AZ	195.3
NA	Peoria, IL**	NA
23	Philadelphia, PA	1,238.2
169	Phoenix, AZ	546.5
57	Pittsburgh, PA	988.7
350	Plano, TX	170.1
226	Plantation, FL	445.3
142	Pomona, CA	631.8
51	Pompano Beach, FL	1,010.4
305	Port St. Lucie, FL	256.6
167	Portland, OR	553.6
121	Portsmouth, VA	700.2
126	Providence, RI	688.6
370	Provo, UT	139.8
87	Pueblo, CO	852.1
246	Quincy, MA	397.6
171	Racine, WI	544.8
197	Raleigh, NC	492.9
396	Ramapo, NY	82.2
338	Rancho Cucamon., CA	193.6
64	Reading, PA	952.5
108	Redding, CA	754.0
130	Reno, NV	666.5
170	Rialto, CA	545.3
321	Richardson, TX	224.0
44	Richmond, CA	1,067.6
97	Richmond, VA	802.5
294	Rio Rancho, NM	279.3
189	Riverside, CA	511.9
127	Roanoke, VA	686.3
NA	Rochester, MN**	NA
55	Rochester, NY	993.5
15	Rockford, IL	1,304.9
297	Roseville, CA	276.4
344	Roswell, GA	184.4
383	Round Rock, TX	115.8
80	Sacramento, CA	885.6
258	Salem, OR	370.8
101	Salinas, CA	788.7
118	Salt Lake City, UT	706.0
245	San Angelo, TX	398.8
163	San Antonio, TX	570.9
63	San Bernardino, CA	955.5
223	San Diego, CA	451.1
113	San Francisco, CA	735.7
262	San Jose, CA	360.5
179	San Leandro, CA	526.5
299	San Marcos, CA	274.7
259	San Mateo, CA	366.6
319	Sandy Springs, GA	229.3
348	Sandy, UT	172.1
191	Santa Ana, CA	508.9
192	Santa Barbara, CA	499.3
360	Santa Clara, CA	151.2
310	Santa Clarita, CA	249.5
88	Santa Maria, CA	841.1
225	Santa Monica, CA	446.4
188	Santa Rosa, CA	513.0
177	Savannah, GA	530.3
349	Scottsdale, AZ	171.5
139	Seattle, WA	640.8
78	Shreveport, LA	889.7
376	Simi Valley, CA	127.5
239	Sioux City, IA	414.2
292	Sioux Falls, SD	286.1
238	Somerville, MA	415.4
111	South Bend, IN	744.2
156	South Gate, CA	585.6

RANK	CITY	RATE
171	Southfield, MI	544.8
231	Sparks, NV	436.4
282	Spokane Valley, WA	305.5
143	Spokane, WA	625.8
NA	Springfield, IL**	NA
22	Springfield, MA	1,256.4
105	Springfield, MO	764.1
287	Stamford, CT	295.4
351	Sterling Heights, MI	167.9
19	Stockton, CA	1,267.2
379	St. George, UT	122.0
162	St. Joseph, MO	577.0
2	St. Louis, MO	2,070.1
106	St. Paul, MN	762.7
14	St. Petersburg, FL	1,361.2
267	Suffolk, VA	340.3
372	Sugar Land, TX	136.6
375	Sunnyvale, CA	127.9
270	Sunrise, FL	328.3
388	Surprise, AZ	106.0
60	Syracuse, NY	978.8
58	Tacoma, WA	984.0
66	Tallahassee, FL	945.6
110	Tampa, FL	752.2
377	Temecula, CA	124.8
184	Tempe, AZ	519.5
309	Thornton, CO	252.1
373	Thousand Oaks, CA	131.7
37	Toledo, OH	1,116.9
384	Toms River Twnshp, NJ	114.9
160	Topeka, KS	579.2
345	Torrance, CA	183.5
341	Tracy, CA	186.5
12	Trenton, NJ	1,396.9
393	Troy, MI	98.5
138	Tucson, AZ	649.7
38	Tulsa, OK	1,116.0
219	Tuscaloosa, AL	455.9
178	Tyler, TX	528.8
140	Upper Darby Twnshp, PA	639.0
286	Vacaville, CA	296.1
86	Vallejo, CA	872.0
248	Vancouver, WA	397.2
263	Ventura, CA	353.9
129	Victorville, CA	668.4
325	Virginia Beach, VA	208.6
182	Visalia, CA	521.5
175	Vista, CA	537.0
119	Waco, TX	705.8
159	Warren, MI	582.8
367	Warwick, RI	143.2
20	Washington, DC	1,265.1
265	Waterbury, CT	350.4
284	West Covina, CA	297.6
357	West Jordan, UT	154.0
77	West Palm Beach, FL	898.1
221	West Valley, UT	453.1
194	Westland, MI	495.2
284	Westminster, CA	297.6
322	Westminster, CO	222.8
243	Whittier, CA	410.5
186	Wichita Falls, TX	515.4
81	Wichita, KS	882.7
97	Wilmington, NC	802.5
109	Winston-Salem, NC	752.9
368	Woodbridge Twnshp, NJ	141.8
53	Worcester, MA	1,002.9
208	Yonkers, NY	477.3
145	Yuma, AZ	623.4

46. Violent Crime Rate in 2009 (continued)
National Rate = 429.4 Violent Crimes per 100,000 Population*

RANK	CITY	RATE
1	Camden, NJ	2,380.3
2	St. Louis, MO	2,070.1
3	Flint, MI	2,009.7
4	Detroit, MI	1,966.9
5	Memphis, TN	1,806.2
6	New Haven, CT	1,765.3
7	Oakland, CA	1,679.1
8	Compton, CA	1,552.1
9	Baltimore, MD	1,512.9
10	Little Rock, AR	1,469.5
11	Buffalo, NY	1,459.1
12	Trenton, NJ	1,396.9
13	Cleveland, OH	1,395.5
14	St. Petersburg, FL	1,361.2
15	Rockford, IL	1,304.9
16	Kansas City, MO	1,300.4
17	Hartford, CT	1,292.2
18	New Bedford, MA	1,278.3
19	Stockton, CA	1,267.2
20	Washington, DC	1,265.1
21	Baton Rouge, LA	1,264.9
22	Springfield, MA	1,256.4
23	Philadelphia, PA	1,238.2
24	Brockton, MA	1,237.7
25	Birmingham, AL	1,236.7
26	Lawton, OK	1,222.2
27	Indianapolis, IN	1,199.8
28	Orlando, FL	1,196.9
29	Cincinnati, OH	1,192.0
30	Miami, FL	1,188.7
31	Fall River, MA	1,181.7
32	Melbourne, FL	1,163.7
33	Atlanta, GA	1,150.1
34	Nashville, TN	1,140.5
35	Houston, TX	1,125.6
36	Bridgeport, CT	1,122.4
37	Toledo, OH	1,116.9
38	Tulsa, OK	1,116.0
39	Minneapolis, MN	1,108.7
40	Milwaukee, WI	1,088.9
41	Albany, NY	1,077.6
42	Miami Beach, FL	1,075.2
43	Albany, GA	1,072.2
44	Richmond, CA	1,067.6
45	Lansing, MI	1,058.3
46	Knoxville, TN	1,057.8
47	Columbia, SC	1,046.3
48	Chattanooga, TN	1,038.6
49	North Charleston, SC	1,034.6
50	Elizabeth, NJ	1,031.1
51	Pompano Beach, FL	1,010.4
52	Dayton, OH	1,008.1
53	Gainesville, FL	1,002.9
53	Worcester, MA	1,002.9
55	Rochester, NY	993.5
56	Boston, MA	992.0
57	Pittsburgh, PA	988.7
58	Tacoma, WA	984.0
59	Lafayette, LA	979.2
60	Syracuse, NY	978.8
61	Hammond, IN	973.9
62	Miami Gardens, FL	968.8
63	San Bernardino, CA	955.5
64	Reading, PA	952.5
65	Las Vegas, NV	946.7
66	Tallahassee, FL	945.6
67	Lubbock, TX	932.8
68	Merced, CA	931.5
69	Oklahoma City, OK	930.3
70	Newark, NJ	930.1
71	Akron, OH	927.9
72	Inglewood, CA	921.8
73	Longview, TX	911.6
74	Paterson, NJ	909.3
75	Beaumont, TX	909.0
76	Lynn, MA	898.5
77	West Palm Beach, FL	898.1
78	Shreveport, LA	889.7
79	Antioch, CA	886.0
80	Sacramento, CA	885.6
81	Wichita, KS	882.7
82	Anchorage, AK	878.2
83	Clearwater, FL	876.8
84	Jackson, MS	876.7
85	Canton, OH	874.7
86	Vallejo, CA	872.0
87	Pueblo, CO	852.1
88	Santa Maria, CA	841.1
89	Amarillo, TX	837.0
90	Jacksonville, FL	836.0
91	Fort Smith, AR	835.9
92	Grand Rapids, MI	831.5
93	Hawthorne, CA	830.2
94	Corpus Christi, TX	822.6
95	Mobile, AL	810.0
96	Fort Lauderdale, FL	809.5
97	Richmond, VA	802.5
97	Wilmington, NC	802.5
99	Dallas, TX	792.2
100	Odessa, TX	788.8
101	Salinas, CA	788.7
102	New Orleans, LA	777.0
103	Albuquerque, NM	769.3
104	Greensboro, NC	766.2
105	Springfield, MO	764.1
106	Macon, GA	762.7
106	St. Paul, MN	762.7
108	Redding, CA	754.0
109	Winston-Salem, NC	752.9
110	Tampa, FL	752.2
111	South Bend, IN	744.2
112	Jersey City, NJ	743.6
113	San Francisco, CA	735.7
114	Davenport, IA	730.8
115	Fayetteville, NC	728.8
116	Charlotte, NC	723.3
117	North Las Vegas, NV	717.0
118	Salt Lake City, UT	706.0
119	Waco, TX	705.8
120	Columbus, OH	703.2
121	Portsmouth, VA	700.2
122	Durham, NC	699.4
123	Allentown, PA	697.9
124	Gary, IN	694.2
125	Modesto, CA	694.0
126	Providence, RI	688.6
127	Roanoke, VA	686.3
128	Long Beach, CA	681.3
129	Victorville, CA	668.4
130	Reno, NV	666.5
131	Clarksville, TN	661.7
132	Kansas City, KS	661.5
133	Murfreesboro, TN	658.1
134	Lancaster, CA	656.2
135	Norfolk, VA	655.9
136	High Point, NC	654.0
137	Huntsville, AL	651.7
138	Tucson, AZ	649.7
139	Seattle, WA	640.8
140	Upper Darby Twnshp, PA	639.0
141	Bakersfield, CA	634.3
142	Pomona, CA	631.8
143	Spokane, WA	625.8
144	Los Angeles, CA	625.4
145	Yuma, AZ	623.4
146	Killeen, TX	621.5
147	Everett, WA	619.7
148	Columbus, GA	619.1
149	Arlington, TX	614.6
150	Independence, MO	613.1
151	Fresno, CA	609.3
152	Berkeley, CA	607.8
153	Kent, WA	601.0
154	Louisville, KY	597.1
155	Lexington, KY	593.8
156	South Gate, CA	585.6
157	Fort Worth, TX	585.0
158	El Monte, CA	584.8
159	Warren, MI	582.8
160	Topeka, KS	579.2
161	Denver, CO	577.7
162	St. Joseph, MO	577.0
163	San Antonio, TX	570.9
164	Laredo, TX	570.2
165	Abilene, TX	564.5
166	Palmdale, CA	558.8
167	Portland, OR	553.6
168	New York, NY	551.8
169	Phoenix, AZ	546.5
170	Rialto, CA	545.3
171	Racine, WI	544.8
171	Southfield, MI	544.8
173	Des Moines, IA	542.2
174	Carson, CA	539.8
175	Vista, CA	537.0
176	Omaha, NE	533.4
177	Savannah, GA	530.3
178	Tyler, TX	528.8
179	San Leandro, CA	526.5
180	Charleston, SC	523.4
181	Austin, TX	523.3
182	Visalia, CA	521.5
183	Hayward, CA	521.0
184	Tempe, AZ	519.5
185	Lakeland, FL	516.3
186	Wichita Falls, TX	515.4
187	Palm Bay, FL	514.1
188	Santa Rosa, CA	513.0
189	Riverside, CA	511.9
190	Norwalk, CT	510.8
191	Santa Ana, CA	508.9
192	Santa Barbara, CA	499.3
193	El Cajon, CA	498.6
194	Westland, MI	495.2
195	Manchester, NH	494.2
196	Las Cruces, NM	493.5
197	Raleigh, NC	492.9
198	Citrus Heights, CA	492.1
199	Hollywood, FL	491.5
200	Colorado Springs, CO	490.0
200	Lakewood, CO	490.0
202	Columbia, MO	488.4
203	Davie, FL	484.8
204	Miramar, FL	483.5
205	Cambridge, MA	483.2
206	Pasadena, TX	480.4

RANK	CITY	RATE
207	Indio, CA	478.4
208	Yonkers, NY	477.3
209	Greeley, CO	473.8
210	Ogden, UT	471.0
211	Aurora, CO	470.4
212	Green Bay, WI	469.1
213	Lakewood, CA	467.2
213	Moreno Valley, CA	467.2
215	Lawrence, KS	462.4
216	Lincoln, NE	457.9
217	Escondido, CA	457.7
218	El Paso, TX	457.3
219	Tuscaloosa, AL	455.9
220	Erie, PA	454.6
221	West Valley, UT	453.1
222	Fontana, CA	451.4
223	San Diego, CA	451.1
224	Glendale, AZ	449.7
225	Santa Monica, CA	446.4
226	Plantation, FL	445.3
227	Norwalk, CA	443.5
228	Hialeah, FL	442.9
229	Oceanside, CA	439.1
230	Federal Way, WA	438.1
231	Sparks, NV	436.4
232	Fayetteville, AR	432.6
233	Elk Grove, CA	432.5
234	Montgomery, AL	429.4
235	Mesa, AZ	424.8
236	Ontario, CA	422.6
237	Fairfield, CA	418.3
238	Somerville, MA	415.4
239	Sioux City, IA	414.2
240	Downey, CA	412.6
241	Athens-Clarke, GA	412.1
242	Oxnard, CA	411.5
243	Whittier, CA	410.5
244	Mesquite, TX	401.7
245	San Angelo, TX	398.8
246	Quincy, MA	397.6
247	Dearborn, MI	397.4
248	Vancouver, WA	397.2
249	Fullerton, CA	397.0
250	Avondale, AZ	395.4
251	Midland, TX	394.7
252	Fort Collins, CO	386.3
253	Baldwin Park, CA	380.5
254	Longmont, CO	376.7
255	Evansville, IN	373.2
256	Gresham, OR	372.8
257	Chesapeake, VA	372.2
258	Salem, OR	370.8
259	San Mateo, CA	366.6
260	Chico, CA	365.9
261	Madison, WI	363.8
262	San Jose, CA	360.5
263	Ventura, CA	353.9
264	Anaheim, CA	352.4
265	Waterbury, CT	350.4
266	Fort Wayne, IN	348.2
267	Suffolk, VA	340.3
268	Pasadena, CA	335.3
269	Chula Vista, CA	332.2
270	Sunrise, FL	328.3
271	Concord, CA	328.0
272	Nampa, ID	326.7
273	Garden Grove, CA	326.2
273	Hesperia, CA	326.2

RANK	CITY	RATE
275	Fargo, ND	322.9
276	Grand Prairie, TX	318.0
277	Cedar Rapids, IA	312.9
278	Hampton, VA	311.1
279	Jacksonville, NC	310.9
280	Buena Park, CA	310.6
281	Eugene, OR	310.5
282	Spokane Valley, WA	305.5
283	Irving, TX	298.3
284	West Covina, CA	297.6
284	Westminster, CA	297.6
286	Vacaville, CA	296.1
287	Stamford, CT	295.4
288	Carlsbad, CA	291.4
289	Chandler, AZ	289.0
290	Clinton Twnshp, MI	288.7
291	Alhambra, CA	288.5
292	Sioux Falls, SD	286.1
293	Honolulu, HI	279.7
294	Rio Rancho, NM	279.3
295	Garland, TX	277.8
296	Kenosha, WI	276.5
297	Roseville, CA	276.4
298	Costa Mesa, CA	276.0
299	San Marcos, CA	274.7
300	Cheektowaga, NY	270.0
301	Coral Springs, FL	269.0
302	Edison Twnshp, NJ	265.7
303	McAllen, TX	262.4
304	Boise, ID	260.6
305	Port St. Lucie, FL	256.6
306	Brownsville, TX	252.9
307	Boca Raton, FL	252.5
308	Clifton, NJ	252.2
309	Thornton, CO	252.1
310	Santa Clarita, CA	249.5
311	Denton, TX	246.2
312	Billings, MT	245.7
313	Burbank, CA	245.0
314	Boulder, CO	244.9
315	Fremont, CA	241.7
316	Daly City, CA	237.0
317	Ann Arbor, MI	236.1
318	Henderson, NV	233.7
319	Sandy Springs, GA	229.3
320	Hamilton Twnshp, NJ	226.5
321	Richardson, TX	224.0
322	Westminster, CO	222.8
323	Olathe, KS	214.1
324	Bellingham, WA	213.1
325	Virginia Beach, VA	208.6
326	Pembroke Pines, FL	206.2
327	Nashua, NH	203.3
328	Beaverton, OR	202.7
329	Cape Coral, FL	202.0
330	Chino, CA	199.7
331	Livermore, CA	199.0
332	College Station, TX	197.5
333	Alexandria, VA	196.4
334	Carrollton, TX	196.2
335	Huntington Beach, CA	195.4
336	Peoria, AZ	195.3
337	Livonia, MI	195.1
338	Rancho Cucamon., CA	193.6
339	Broken Arrow, OK	190.6
340	Lewisville, TX	188.3
341	Tracy, CA	186.5
342	Bend, OR	186.2

RANK	CITY	RATE
343	McKinney, TX	185.4
344	Roswell, GA	184.4
345	Torrance, CA	183.5
346	Overland Park, KS	177.3
347	Arvada, CO	176.0
348	Sandy, UT	172.1
349	Scottsdale, AZ	171.5
350	Plano, TX	170.1
351	Sterling Heights, MI	167.9
352	Canton Twnshp, MI	167.0
353	Danbury, CT	163.1
354	Missouri City, TX	158.6
355	Brick Twnshp, NJ	157.6
356	Newport Beach, CA	156.4
357	West Jordan, UT	154.0
358	Glendale, CA	153.0
359	Hillsboro, OR	152.2
360	Santa Clara, CA	151.2
361	Norman, OK	149.8
362	Cranston, RI	149.6
363	Centennial, CO	148.9
364	Clovis, CA	148.1
365	Pearland, TX	146.8
366	Lake Forest, CA	144.4
367	Warwick, RI	143.2
368	Woodbridge Twnshp, NJ	141.8
369	Corona, CA	140.4
370	Provo, UT	139.8
371	Farmington Hills, MI	138.2
372	Sugar Land, TX	136.6
373	Thousand Oaks, CA	131.7
374	Bellevue, WA	129.5
375	Sunnyvale, CA	127.9
376	Simi Valley, CA	127.5
377	Temecula, CA	124.8
378	Lee's Summit, MO	123.6
379	St. George, UT	122.0
380	Amherst, NY	116.8
381	Orange, CA	116.7
382	Clarkstown, NY	116.6
383	Round Rock, TX	115.8
384	Toms River Twnshp, NJ	114.9
385	Murrieta, CA	112.1
386	Newton, MA	111.3
387	Edmond, OK	107.6
388	Surprise, AZ	106.0
389	Greece, NY	105.1
390	Mission Viejo, CA	100.5
391	Frisco, TX	99.8
392	Cary, NC	98.7
393	Troy, MI	98.5
394	Allen, TX	89.8
395	Gilbert, AZ	83.7
396	Ramapo, NY	82.2
397	O'Fallon, MO	80.7
398	Colonie, NY	78.2
399	Irvine, CA	70.9
400	Orem, UT	53.3
NA	Aurora, IL**	NA
NA	Bloomington, MN**	NA
NA	Chicago, IL**	NA
NA	Decatur, IL**	NA
NA	Duluth, MN**	NA
NA	Elgin, IL**	NA
NA	Joliet, IL**	NA
NA	Naperville, IL**	NA
NA	Peoria, IL**	NA
NA	Rochester, MN**	NA
NA	Springfield, IL**	NA

Source: Reported data from the F.B.I. "Crime in the United States 2009"

*Violent crimes are offenses of murder, forcible rape, robbery, and aggravated assault.

**Not available.

47. Percent Change in Violent Crime Rate: 2008 to 2009
National Percent Change = 6.1% Decrease*

RANK	CITY	% CHANGE
90	Abilene, TX	1.3
92	Akron, OH	1.2
NA	Albany, GA**	NA
127	Albany, NY	(1.8)
282	Albuquerque, NM	(14.0)
288	Alexandria, VA	(14.6)
239	Alhambra, CA	(9.7)
201	Allentown, PA	(6.9)
26	Allen, TX	13.2
59	Amarillo, TX	6.6
223	Amherst, NY	(8.6)
245	Anaheim, CA	(10.4)
204	Anchorage, AK	(7.1)
NA	Ann Arbor, MI**	NA
83	Antioch, CA	2.0
82	Arlington, TX	2.1
267	Arvada, CO	(12.5)
266	Athens-Clarke, GA	(12.2)
316	Atlanta, GA	(17.2)
221	Aurora, CO	(8.3)
NA	Aurora, IL**	NA
99	Austin, TX	0.2
360	Avondale, AZ	(26.1)
106	Bakersfield, CA	(0.4)
32	Baldwin Park, CA	11.2
156	Baltimore, MD	(4.8)
58	Baton Rouge, LA	6.7
134	Beaumont, TX	(2.3)
189	Beaverton, OR	(6.5)
168	Bellevue, WA	(5.6)
207	Bellingham, WA	(7.2)
69	Bend, OR	4.4
170	Berkeley, CA	(5.7)
198	Billings, MT	(6.8)
276	Birmingham, AL	(13.1)
NA	Bloomington, MN**	NA
86	Boca Raton, FL	1.8
146	Boise, ID	(3.6)
242	Boston, MA	(10.2)
24	Boulder, CO	13.8
13	Brick Twnshp, NJ	17.4
192	Bridgeport, CT	(6.6)
NA	Brockton, MA**	NA
214	Broken Arrow, OK	(7.7)
369	Brownsville, TX	(29.4)
172	Buena Park, CA	(5.8)
60	Buffalo, NY	6.1
49	Burbank, CA	8.1
11	Cambridge, MA	18.3
83	Camden, NJ	2.0
NA	Canton Twnshp, MI**	NA
136	Canton, OH	(2.4)
231	Cape Coral, FL	(9.1)
6	Carlsbad, CA	25.4
308	Carrollton, TX	(15.9)
251	Carson, CA	(11.0)
19	Cary, NC	15.6
254	Cedar Rapids, IA	(11.3)
12	Centennial, CO	17.6
225	Chandler, AZ	(8.7)
362	Charleston, SC	(27.0)
348	Charlotte, NC	(22.4)
160	Chattanooga, TN	(4.9)
87	Cheektowaga, NY	1.7
297	Chesapeake, VA	(15.2)
NA	Chicago, IL**	NA
92	Chico, CA	1.2
296	Chino, CA	(15.1)
248	Chula Vista, CA	(10.8)
170	Cincinnati, OH	(5.7)
113	Citrus Heights, CA	(0.9)
246	Clarkstown, NY	(10.7)
305	Clarksville, TN	(15.7)
204	Clearwater, FL	(7.1)
134	Cleveland, OH	(2.3)
113	Clifton, NJ	(0.9)
NA	Clinton Twnshp, MI**	NA
180	Clovis, CA	(6.1)
372	College Station, TX	(34.0)
25	Colonie, NY	13.3
207	Colorado Springs, CO	(7.2)
5	Columbia, MO	25.9
8	Columbia, SC	21.7
237	Columbus, GA	(9.5)
233	Columbus, OH	(9.2)
304	Compton, CA	(15.6)
201	Concord, CA	(6.9)
46	Coral Springs, FL	8.8
354	Corona, CA	(24.0)
62	Corpus Christi, TX	5.9
284	Costa Mesa, CA	(14.1)
264	Cranston, RI	(12.0)
261	Dallas, TX	(11.5)
307	Daly City, CA	(15.8)
10	Danbury, CT	19.3
227	Davenport, IA	(8.8)
34	Davie, FL	11.1
203	Dayton, OH	(7.0)
NA	Dearborn, MI**	NA
NA	Decatur, IL**	NA
315	Denton, TX	(17.0)
85	Denver, CO	1.9
NA	Des Moines, IA**	NA
NA	Detroit, MI**	NA
117	Downey, CA	(1.0)
NA	Duluth, MN**	NA
287	Durham, NC	(14.5)
27	Edison Twnshp, NJ	13.1
56	Edmond, OK	7.0
273	El Cajon, CA	(12.9)
240	El Monte, CA	(10.0)
113	El Paso, TX	(0.9)
NA	Elgin, IL**	NA
22	Elizabeth, NJ	14.5
225	Elk Grove, CA	(8.7)
361	Erie, PA	(26.9)
40	Escondido, CA	10.2
174	Eugene, OR	(5.9)
192	Evansville, IN	(6.6)
67	Everett, WA	4.6
332	Fairfield, CA	(19.6)
123	Fall River, MA	(1.4)
42	Fargo, ND	9.9
NA	Farmington Hills, MI**	NA
152	Fayetteville, AR	(4.2)
350	Fayetteville, NC	(22.9)
21	Federal Way, WA	15.0
NA	Flint, MI**	NA
125	Fontana, CA	(1.6)
154	Fort Collins, CO	(4.5)
230	Fort Lauderdale, FL	(9.0)
52	Fort Smith, AR	7.5
54	Fort Wayne, IN	7.2
248	Fort Worth, TX	(10.8)
302	Fremont, CA	(15.5)
71	Fresno, CA	4.2
186	Frisco, TX	(6.4)
4	Fullerton, CA	28.6
47	Gainesville, FL	8.6
254	Garden Grove, CA	(11.3)
344	Garland, TX	(21.3)
358	Gary, IN	(25.4)
349	Gilbert, AZ	(22.5)
277	Glendale, AZ	(13.2)
282	Glendale, CA	(14.0)
163	Grand Prairie, TX	(5.1)
NA	Grand Rapids, MI**	NA
359	Greece, NY	(25.5)
308	Greeley, CO	(15.9)
177	Green Bay, WI	(6.0)
258	Greensboro, NC	(11.4)
354	Gresham, OR	(24.0)
17	Hamilton Twnshp, NJ	16.2
35	Hammond, IN	11.0
148	Hampton, VA	(3.8)
55	Hartford, CT	7.1
177	Hawthorne, CA	(6.0)
301	Hayward, CA	(15.4)
27	Henderson, NV	13.1
80	Hesperia, CA	2.4
333	Hialeah, FL	(19.9)
198	High Point, NC	(6.8)
258	Hillsboro, OR	(11.4)
280	Hollywood, FL	(13.3)
124	Honolulu, HI	(1.5)
87	Houston, TX	1.7
138	Huntington Beach, CA	(2.7)
216	Huntsville, AL	(7.8)
323	Independence, MO	(17.9)
106	Indianapolis, IN	(0.4)
43	Indio, CA	9.8
60	Inglewood, CA	6.1
20	Irvine, CA	15.1
316	Irving, TX	(17.2)
310	Jacksonville, FL	(16.1)
322	Jacksonville, NC	(17.6)
210	Jackson, MS	(7.3)
343	Jersey City, NJ	(21.2)
NA	Joliet, IL**	NA
NA	Kansas City, KS**	NA
186	Kansas City, MO	(6.4)
345	Kenosha, WI	(21.8)
177	Kent, WA	(6.0)
327	Killeen, TX	(18.6)
130	Knoxville, TN	(2.0)
271	Lafayette, LA	(12.7)
94	Lake Forest, CA	1.1
236	Lakeland, FL	(9.4)
109	Lakewood, CA	(0.7)
165	Lakewood, CO	(5.3)
329	Lancaster, CA	(18.9)
NA	Lansing, MI**	NA
186	Laredo, TX	(6.4)
212	Las Cruces, NM	(7.5)
148	Las Vegas, NV	(3.8)
81	Lawrence, KS	2.2
31	Lawton, OK	11.7
145	Lee's Summit, MO	(3.4)
328	Lewisville, TX	(18.8)
NA	Lexington, KY**	NA
241	Lincoln, NE	(10.1)
NA	Little Rock, AR**	NA
254	Livermore, CA	(11.3)
NA	Livonia, MI**	NA
98	Long Beach, CA	0.8
NA	Longmont, CO**	NA

RANK	CITY	% CHANGE
269	Longview, TX	(12.6)
235	Los Angeles, CA	(9.3)
NA	Louisville, KY**	NA
136	Lubbock, TX	(2.4)
111	Lynn, MA	(0.8)
334	Macon, GA	(20.1)
168	Madison, WI	(5.6)
73	Manchester, NH	4.1
218	McAllen, TX	(8.0)
264	McKinney, TX	(12.0)
207	Melbourne, FL	(7.2)
183	Memphis, TN	(6.2)
9	Merced, CA	19.6
297	Mesa, AZ	(15.2)
48	Mesquite, TX	8.3
233	Miami Beach, FL	(9.2)
150	Miami Gardens, FL	(4.0)
250	Miami, FL	(10.9)
122	Midland, TX	(1.3)
246	Milwaukee, WI	(10.7)
269	Minneapolis, MN	(12.6)
117	Miramar, FL	(1.0)
172	Mission Viejo, CA	(5.8)
366	Missouri City, TX	(27.7)
1	Mobile, AL	68.9
111	Modesto, CA	(0.8)
108	Montgomery, AL	(0.6)
302	Moreno Valley, CA	(15.5)
68	Murfreesboro, TN	4.5
3	Murrieta, CA	33.1
117	Nampa, ID	(1.0)
NA	Naperville, IL**	NA
NA	Nashua, NH**	NA
325	Nashville, TN	(18.3)
127	New Bedford, MA	(1.8)
NA	New Haven, CT**	NA
351	New Orleans, LA	(23.8)
160	New York, NY	(4.9)
132	Newark, NJ	(2.2)
319	Newport Beach, CA	(17.3)
340	Newton, MA	(20.8)
341	Norfolk, VA	(21.0)
142	Norman, OK	(3.1)
371	North Charleston, SC	(30.2)
94	North Las Vegas, NV	1.1
262	Norwalk, CA	(11.6)
78	Norwalk, CT	2.8
289	Oakland, CA	(14.7)
217	Oceanside, CA	(7.9)
23	Odessa, TX	14.1
146	O'Fallon, MO	(3.6)
87	Ogden, UT	1.7
156	Oklahoma City, OK	(4.8)
NA	Olathe, KS**	NA
263	Omaha, NE	(11.9)
319	Ontario, CA	(17.3)
368	Orange, CA	(28.4)
352	Orem, UT	(23.9)
367	Orlando, FL	(28.2)
102	Overland Park, KS	(0.1)
180	Oxnard, CA	(6.1)
140	Palm Bay, FL	(2.9)
220	Palmdale, CA	(8.1)
347	Pasadena, CA	(22.0)
44	Pasadena, TX	9.6
231	Paterson, NJ	(9.1)
27	Pearland, TX	13.1
356	Pembroke Pines, FL	(24.7)
180	Peoria, AZ	(6.1)
NA	Peoria, IL**	NA
284	Philadelphia, PA	(14.1)
316	Phoenix, AZ	(17.2)
227	Pittsburgh, PA	(8.8)
357	Plano, TX	(24.9)
73	Plantation, FL	4.1
314	Pomona, CA	(16.4)
293	Pompano Beach, FL	(14.9)
62	Port St. Lucie, FL	5.9
252	Portland, OR	(11.1)
113	Portsmouth, VA	(0.9)
90	Providence, RI	1.3
237	Provo, UT	(9.5)
NA	Pueblo, CO**	NA
45	Quincy, MA	8.9
321	Racine, WI	(17.4)
289	Raleigh, NC	(14.7)
337	Ramapo, NY	(20.5)
281	Rancho Cucamon., CA	(13.6)
254	Reading, PA	(11.3)
50	Redding, CA	7.9
160	Reno, NV	(4.9)
139	Rialto, CA	(2.8)
311	Richardson, TX	(16.2)
109	Richmond, CA	(0.7)
97	Richmond, VA	0.9
154	Rio Rancho, NM	(4.5)
335	Riverside, CA	(20.3)
299	Roanoke, VA	(15.3)
NA	Rochester, MN**	NA
258	Rochester, NY	(11.4)
204	Rockford, IL	(7.1)
151	Roseville, CA	(4.1)
194	Roswell, GA	(6.7)
211	Round Rock, TX	(7.4)
253	Sacramento, CA	(11.2)
104	Salem, OR	(0.3)
51	Salinas, CA	7.8
242	Salt Lake City, UT	(10.2)
129	San Angelo, TX	(1.9)
337	San Antonio, TX	(20.5)
213	San Bernardino, CA	(7.6)
163	San Diego, CA	(5.1)
273	San Francisco, CA	(12.9)
189	San Jose, CA	(6.5)
337	San Leandro, CA	(20.5)
66	San Marcos, CA	5.3
194	San Mateo, CA	(6.7)
289	Sandy Springs, GA	(14.7)
65	Sandy, UT	5.6
99	Santa Ana, CA	0.2
273	Santa Barbara, CA	(12.9)
364	Santa Clara, CA	(27.5)
78	Santa Clarita, CA	2.8
14	Santa Maria, CA	17.3
363	Santa Monica, CA	(27.1)
64	Santa Rosa, CA	5.8
271	Savannah, GA	(12.7)
143	Scottsdale, AZ	(3.2)
32	Seattle, WA	11.2
189	Shreveport, LA	(6.5)
299	Simi Valley, CA	(15.3)
69	Sioux City, IA	4.4
294	Sioux Falls, SD	(15.0)
94	Somerville, MA	1.1
174	South Bend, IN	(5.9)
156	South Gate, CA	(4.8)
NA	Southfield, MI**	NA
166	Sparks, NV	(5.4)
143	Spokane Valley, WA	(3.2)
194	Spokane, WA	(6.7)
NA	Springfield, IL**	NA
101	Springfield, MA	0.1
35	Springfield, MO	11.0
242	Stamford, CT	(10.2)
NA	Sterling Heights, MI**	NA
284	Stockton, CA	(14.1)
373	St. George, UT	(43.6)
7	St. Joseph, MO	24.8
102	St. Louis, MO	(0.1)
152	St. Paul, MN	(4.2)
126	St. Petersburg, FL	(1.7)
222	Suffolk, VA	(8.4)
330	Sugar Land, TX	(19.1)
229	Sunnyvale, CA	(8.9)
370	Sunrise, FL	(29.7)
198	Surprise, AZ	(6.8)
117	Syracuse, NY	(1.0)
140	Tacoma, WA	(2.9)
313	Tallahassee, FL	(16.3)
292	Tampa, FL	(14.8)
326	Temecula, CA	(18.4)
56	Tempe, AZ	7.0
346	Thornton, CO	(21.9)
39	Thousand Oaks, CA	10.4
131	Toledo, OH	(2.1)
104	Toms River Twnshp, NJ	(0.3)
16	Topeka, KS	16.6
294	Torrance, CA	(15.0)
15	Tracy, CA	17.2
18	Trenton, NJ	16.0
NA	Troy, MI**	NA
331	Tucson, AZ	(19.2)
277	Tulsa, OK	(13.2)
267	Tuscaloosa, AL	(12.5)
341	Tyler, TX	(21.0)
117	Upper Darby Twnshp, PA	(1.0)
184	Vacaville, CA	(6.3)
223	Vallejo, CA	(8.6)
53	Vancouver, WA	7.4
214	Ventura, CA	(7.7)
30	Victorville, CA	11.9
277	Virginia Beach, VA	(13.2)
174	Visalia, CA	(5.9)
156	Vista, CA	(4.8)
305	Waco, TX	(15.7)
NA	Warren, MI**	NA
2	Warwick, RI	45.5
218	Washington, DC	(8.0)
132	Waterbury, CT	(2.2)
335	West Covina, CA	(20.3)
352	West Jordan, UT	(23.9)
194	West Palm Beach, FL	(6.7)
167	West Valley, UT	(5.5)
NA	Westland, MI**	NA
35	Westminster, CA	11.0
311	Westminster, CO	(16.2)
38	Whittier, CA	10.6
184	Wichita Falls, TX	(6.3)
76	Wichita, KS	3.6
73	Wilmington, NC	4.1
324	Winston-Salem, NC	(18.0)
364	Woodbridge Twnshp, NJ	(27.5)
77	Worcester, MA	3.4
71	Yonkers, NY	4.2
41	Yuma, AZ	10.1

Source: CQ Press using reported data from the F.B.I. "Crime in the United States 2009"
*Violent crimes are offenses of murder, forcible rape, robbery, and aggravated assault.
**Not available.

47. Percent Change in Violent Crime Rate: 2008 to 2009 (continued)
National Percent Change = 6.1% Decrease*

RANK	CITY	% CHANGE
1	Mobile, AL	68.9
2	Warwick, RI	45.5
3	Murrieta, CA	33.1
4	Fullerton, CA	28.6
5	Columbia, MO	25.9
6	Carlsbad, CA	25.4
7	St. Joseph, MO	24.8
8	Columbia, SC	21.7
9	Merced, CA	19.6
10	Danbury, CT	19.3
11	Cambridge, MA	18.3
12	Centennial, CO	17.6
13	Brick Twnshp, NJ	17.4
14	Santa Maria, CA	17.3
15	Tracy, CA	17.2
16	Topeka, KS	16.6
17	Hamilton Twnshp, NJ	16.2
18	Trenton, NJ	16.0
19	Cary, NC	15.6
20	Irvine, CA	15.1
21	Federal Way, WA	15.0
22	Elizabeth, NJ	14.5
23	Odessa, TX	14.1
24	Boulder, CO	13.8
25	Colonie, NY	13.3
26	Allen, TX	13.2
27	Edison Twnshp, NJ	13.1
27	Henderson, NV	13.1
27	Pearland, TX	13.1
30	Victorville, CA	11.9
31	Lawton, OK	11.7
32	Baldwin Park, CA	11.2
32	Seattle, WA	11.2
34	Davie, FL	11.1
35	Hammond, IN	11.0
35	Springfield, MO	11.0
35	Westminster, CA	11.0
38	Whittier, CA	10.6
39	Thousand Oaks, CA	10.4
40	Escondido, CA	10.2
41	Yuma, AZ	10.1
42	Fargo, ND	9.9
43	Indio, CA	9.8
44	Pasadena, TX	9.6
45	Quincy, MA	8.9
46	Coral Springs, FL	8.8
47	Gainesville, FL	8.6
48	Mesquite, TX	8.3
49	Burbank, CA	8.1
50	Redding, CA	7.9
51	Salinas, CA	7.8
52	Fort Smith, AR	7.5
53	Vancouver, WA	7.4
54	Fort Wayne, IN	7.2
55	Hartford, CT	7.1
56	Edmond, OK	7.0
56	Tempe, AZ	7.0
58	Baton Rouge, LA	6.7
59	Amarillo, TX	6.6
60	Buffalo, NY	6.1
60	Inglewood, CA	6.1
62	Corpus Christi, TX	5.9
62	Port St. Lucie, FL	5.9
64	Santa Rosa, CA	5.8
65	Sandy, UT	5.6
66	San Marcos, CA	5.3
67	Everett, WA	4.6
68	Murfreesboro, TN	4.5
69	Bend, OR	4.4
69	Sioux City, IA	4.4
71	Fresno, CA	4.2
71	Yonkers, NY	4.2
73	Manchester, NH	4.1
73	Plantation, FL	4.1
73	Wilmington, NC	4.1
76	Wichita, KS	3.6
77	Worcester, MA	3.4
78	Norwalk, CT	2.8
78	Santa Clarita, CA	2.8
80	Hesperia, CA	2.4
81	Lawrence, KS	2.2
82	Arlington, TX	2.1
83	Antioch, CA	2.0
83	Camden, NJ	2.0
85	Denver, CO	1.9
86	Boca Raton, FL	1.8
87	Cheektowaga, NY	1.7
87	Houston, TX	1.7
87	Ogden, UT	1.7
90	Abilene, TX	1.3
90	Providence, RI	1.3
92	Akron, OH	1.2
92	Chico, CA	1.2
94	Lake Forest, CA	1.1
94	North Las Vegas, NV	1.1
94	Somerville, MA	1.1
97	Richmond, VA	0.9
98	Long Beach, CA	0.8
99	Austin, TX	0.2
99	Santa Ana, CA	0.2
101	Springfield, MA	0.1
102	Overland Park, KS	(0.1)
102	St. Louis, MO	(0.1)
104	Salem, OR	(0.3)
104	Toms River Twnshp, NJ	(0.3)
106	Bakersfield, CA	(0.4)
106	Indianapolis, IN	(0.4)
108	Montgomery, AL	(0.6)
109	Lakewood, CA	(0.7)
109	Richmond, CA	(0.7)
111	Lynn, MA	(0.8)
111	Modesto, CA	(0.8)
113	Citrus Heights, CA	(0.9)
113	Clifton, NJ	(0.9)
113	El Paso, TX	(0.9)
113	Portsmouth, VA	(0.9)
117	Downey, CA	(1.0)
117	Miramar, FL	(1.0)
117	Nampa, ID	(1.0)
117	Syracuse, NY	(1.0)
117	Upper Darby Twnshp, PA	(1.0)
122	Midland, TX	(1.3)
123	Fall River, MA	(1.4)
124	Honolulu, HI	(1.5)
125	Fontana, CA	(1.6)
126	St. Petersburg, FL	(1.7)
127	Albany, NY	(1.8)
127	New Bedford, MA	(1.8)
129	San Angelo, TX	(1.9)
130	Knoxville, TN	(2.0)
131	Toledo, OH	(2.1)
132	Newark, NJ	(2.2)
132	Waterbury, CT	(2.2)
134	Beaumont, TX	(2.3)
134	Cleveland, OH	(2.3)
136	Canton, OH	(2.4)
136	Lubbock, TX	(2.4)
138	Huntington Beach, CA	(2.7)
139	Rialto, CA	(2.8)
140	Palm Bay, FL	(2.9)
140	Tacoma, WA	(2.9)
142	Norman, OK	(3.1)
143	Scottsdale, AZ	(3.2)
143	Spokane Valley, WA	(3.2)
145	Lee's Summit, MO	(3.4)
146	Boise, ID	(3.6)
146	O'Fallon, MO	(3.6)
148	Hampton, VA	(3.8)
148	Las Vegas, NV	(3.8)
150	Miami Gardens, FL	(4.0)
151	Roseville, CA	(4.1)
152	Fayetteville, AR	(4.2)
152	St. Paul, MN	(4.2)
154	Fort Collins, CO	(4.5)
154	Rio Rancho, NM	(4.5)
156	Baltimore, MD	(4.8)
156	Oklahoma City, OK	(4.8)
156	South Gate, CA	(4.8)
156	Vista, CA	(4.8)
160	Chattanooga, TN	(4.9)
160	New York, NY	(4.9)
160	Reno, NV	(4.9)
163	Grand Prairie, TX	(5.1)
163	San Diego, CA	(5.1)
165	Lakewood, CO	(5.3)
166	Sparks, NV	(5.4)
167	West Valley, UT	(5.5)
168	Bellevue, WA	(5.6)
168	Madison, WI	(5.6)
170	Berkeley, CA	(5.7)
170	Cincinnati, OH	(5.7)
172	Buena Park, CA	(5.8)
172	Mission Viejo, CA	(5.8)
174	Eugene, OR	(5.9)
174	South Bend, IN	(5.9)
174	Visalia, CA	(5.9)
177	Green Bay, WI	(6.0)
177	Hawthorne, CA	(6.0)
177	Kent, WA	(6.0)
180	Clovis, CA	(6.1)
180	Oxnard, CA	(6.1)
180	Peoria, AZ	(6.1)
183	Memphis, TN	(6.2)
184	Vacaville, CA	(6.3)
184	Wichita Falls, TX	(6.3)
186	Frisco, TX	(6.4)
186	Kansas City, MO	(6.4)
186	Laredo, TX	(6.4)
189	Beaverton, OR	(6.5)
189	San Jose, CA	(6.5)
189	Shreveport, LA	(6.5)
192	Bridgeport, CT	(6.6)
192	Evansville, IN	(6.6)
194	Roswell, GA	(6.7)
194	San Mateo, CA	(6.7)
194	Spokane, WA	(6.7)
194	West Palm Beach, FL	(6.7)
198	Billings, MT	(6.8)
198	High Point, NC	(6.8)
198	Surprise, AZ	(6.8)
201	Allentown, PA	(6.9)
201	Concord, CA	(6.9)
203	Dayton, OH	(7.0)
204	Anchorage, AK	(7.1)
204	Clearwater, FL	(7.1)
204	Rockford, IL	(7.1)

RANK	CITY	% CHANGE
207	Bellingham, WA	(7.2)
207	Colorado Springs, CO	(7.2)
207	Melbourne, FL	(7.2)
210	Jackson, MS	(7.3)
211	Round Rock, TX	(7.4)
212	Las Cruces, NM	(7.5)
213	San Bernardino, CA	(7.6)
214	Broken Arrow, OK	(7.7)
214	Ventura, CA	(7.7)
216	Huntsville, AL	(7.8)
217	Oceanside, CA	(7.9)
218	McAllen, TX	(8.0)
218	Washington, DC	(8.0)
220	Palmdale, CA	(8.1)
221	Aurora, CO	(8.3)
222	Suffolk, VA	(8.4)
223	Amherst, NY	(8.6)
223	Vallejo, CA	(8.6)
225	Chandler, AZ	(8.7)
225	Elk Grove, CA	(8.7)
227	Davenport, IA	(8.8)
227	Pittsburgh, PA	(8.8)
229	Sunnyvale, CA	(8.9)
230	Fort Lauderdale, FL	(9.0)
231	Cape Coral, FL	(9.1)
231	Paterson, NJ	(9.1)
233	Columbus, OH	(9.2)
233	Miami Beach, FL	(9.2)
235	Los Angeles, CA	(9.3)
236	Lakeland, FL	(9.4)
237	Columbus, GA	(9.5)
237	Provo, UT	(9.5)
239	Alhambra, CA	(9.7)
240	El Monte, CA	(10.0)
241	Lincoln, NE	(10.1)
242	Boston, MA	(10.2)
242	Salt Lake City, UT	(10.2)
242	Stamford, CT	(10.2)
245	Anaheim, CA	(10.4)
246	Clarkstown, NY	(10.7)
246	Milwaukee, WI	(10.7)
248	Chula Vista, CA	(10.8)
248	Fort Worth, TX	(10.8)
250	Miami, FL	(10.9)
251	Carson, CA	(11.0)
252	Portland, OR	(11.1)
253	Sacramento, CA	(11.2)
254	Cedar Rapids, IA	(11.3)
254	Garden Grove, CA	(11.3)
254	Livermore, CA	(11.3)
254	Reading, PA	(11.3)
258	Greensboro, NC	(11.4)
258	Hillsboro, OR	(11.4)
258	Rochester, NY	(11.4)
261	Dallas, TX	(11.5)
262	Norwalk, CA	(11.6)
263	Omaha, NE	(11.9)
264	Cranston, RI	(12.0)
264	McKinney, TX	(12.0)
266	Athens-Clarke, GA	(12.2)
267	Arvada, CO	(12.5)
267	Tuscaloosa, AL	(12.5)
269	Longview, TX	(12.6)
269	Minneapolis, MN	(12.6)
271	Lafayette, LA	(12.7)
271	Savannah, GA	(12.7)
273	El Cajon, CA	(12.9)
273	San Francisco, CA	(12.9)
273	Santa Barbara, CA	(12.9)
276	Birmingham, AL	(13.1)
277	Glendale, AZ	(13.2)
277	Tulsa, OK	(13.2)
277	Virginia Beach, VA	(13.2)
280	Hollywood, FL	(13.3)
281	Rancho Cucamon., CA	(13.6)
282	Albuquerque, NM	(14.0)
282	Glendale, CA	(14.0)
284	Costa Mesa, CA	(14.1)
284	Philadelphia, PA	(14.1)
284	Stockton, CA	(14.1)
287	Durham, NC	(14.5)
288	Alexandria, VA	(14.6)
289	Oakland, CA	(14.7)
289	Raleigh, NC	(14.7)
289	Sandy Springs, GA	(14.7)
292	Tampa, FL	(14.8)
293	Pompano Beach, FL	(14.9)
294	Sioux Falls, SD	(15.0)
294	Torrance, CA	(15.0)
296	Chino, CA	(15.1)
297	Chesapeake, VA	(15.2)
297	Mesa, AZ	(15.2)
299	Roanoke, VA	(15.3)
299	Simi Valley, CA	(15.3)
301	Hayward, CA	(15.4)
302	Fremont, CA	(15.5)
302	Moreno Valley, CA	(15.5)
304	Compton, CA	(15.6)
305	Clarksville, TN	(15.7)
305	Waco, TX	(15.7)
307	Daly City, CA	(15.8)
308	Carrollton, TX	(15.9)
308	Greeley, CO	(15.9)
310	Jacksonville, FL	(16.1)
311	Richardson, TX	(16.2)
311	Westminster, CO	(16.2)
313	Tallahassee, FL	(16.3)
314	Pomona, CA	(16.4)
315	Denton, TX	(17.0)
316	Atlanta, GA	(17.2)
316	Irving, TX	(17.2)
316	Phoenix, AZ	(17.2)
319	Newport Beach, CA	(17.3)
319	Ontario, CA	(17.3)
321	Racine, WI	(17.4)
322	Jacksonville, NC	(17.6)
323	Independence, MO	(17.9)
324	Winston-Salem, NC	(18.0)
325	Nashville, TN	(18.3)
326	Temecula, CA	(18.4)
327	Killeen, TX	(18.6)
328	Lewisville, TX	(18.8)
329	Lancaster, CA	(18.9)
330	Sugar Land, TX	(19.1)
331	Tucson, AZ	(19.2)
332	Fairfield, CA	(19.6)
333	Hialeah, FL	(19.9)
334	Macon, GA	(20.1)
335	Riverside, CA	(20.3)
335	West Covina, CA	(20.3)
337	Ramapo, NY	(20.5)
337	San Antonio, TX	(20.5)
337	San Leandro, CA	(20.5)
340	Newton, MA	(20.8)
341	Norfolk, VA	(21.0)
341	Tyler, TX	(21.0)
343	Jersey City, NJ	(21.2)
344	Garland, TX	(21.3)
345	Kenosha, WI	(21.8)
346	Thornton, CO	(21.9)
347	Pasadena, CA	(22.0)
348	Charlotte, NC	(22.4)
349	Gilbert, AZ	(22.5)
350	Fayetteville, NC	(22.9)
351	New Orleans, LA	(23.8)
352	Orem, UT	(23.9)
352	West Jordan, UT	(23.9)
354	Corona, CA	(24.0)
354	Gresham, OR	(24.0)
356	Pembroke Pines, FL	(24.7)
357	Plano, TX	(24.9)
358	Gary, IN	(25.4)
359	Greece, NY	(25.5)
360	Avondale, AZ	(26.1)
361	Erie, PA	(26.9)
362	Charleston, SC	(27.0)
363	Santa Monica, CA	(27.1)
364	Santa Clara, CA	(27.5)
364	Woodbridge Twnshp, NJ	(27.5)
366	Missouri City, TX	(27.7)
367	Orlando, FL	(28.2)
368	Orange, CA	(28.4)
369	Brownsville, TX	(29.4)
370	Sunrise, FL	(29.7)
371	North Charleston, SC	(30.2)
372	College Station, TX	(34.0)
373	St. George, UT	(43.6)
NA	Albany, GA**	NA
NA	Ann Arbor, MI**	NA
NA	Aurora, IL**	NA
NA	Bloomington, MN**	NA
NA	Brockton, MA**	NA
NA	Canton Twnshp, MI**	NA
NA	Chicago, IL**	NA
NA	Clinton Twnshp, MI**	NA
NA	Dearborn, MI**	NA
NA	Decatur, IL**	NA
NA	Des Moines, IA**	NA
NA	Detroit, MI**	NA
NA	Duluth, MN**	NA
NA	Elgin, IL**	NA
NA	Farmington Hills, MI**	NA
NA	Flint, MI**	NA
NA	Grand Rapids, MI**	NA
NA	Joliet, IL**	NA
NA	Kansas City, KS**	NA
NA	Lansing, MI**	NA
NA	Lexington, KY**	NA
NA	Little Rock, AR**	NA
NA	Livonia, MI**	NA
NA	Longmont, CO**	NA
NA	Louisville, KY**	NA
NA	Naperville, IL**	NA
NA	Nashua, NH**	NA
NA	New Haven, CT**	NA
NA	Olathe, KS**	NA
NA	Peoria, IL**	NA
NA	Pueblo, CO**	NA
NA	Rochester, MN**	NA
NA	Southfield, MI**	NA
NA	Springfield, IL**	NA
NA	Sterling Heights, MI**	NA
NA	Troy, MI**	NA
NA	Warren, MI**	NA
NA	Westland, MI**	NA

Source: CQ Press using reported data from the F.B.I. "Crime in the United States 2009"
*Violent crimes are offenses of murder, forcible rape, robbery, and aggravated assault.
**Not available.

48. Percent Change in Violent Crime Rate: 2005 to 2009
National Percent Change = 8.4% Decrease*

RANK	CITY	% CHANGE
52	Abilene, TX	14.4
13	Akron, OH	55.7
8	Albany, GA	62.8
262	Albany, NY	(20.2)
257	Albuquerque, NM	(19.2)
355	Alexandria, VA	(44.7)
267	Alhambra, CA	(20.4)
213	Allentown, PA	(13.5)
53	Allen, TX	14.2
119	Amarillo, TX	0.1
26	Amherst, NY	27.4
307	Anaheim, CA	(26.7)
40	Anchorage, AK	19.4
NA	Ann Arbor, MI**	NA
8	Antioch, CA	62.8
151	Arlington, TX	(5.2)
160	Arvada, CO	(6.6)
34	Athens-Clarke, GA	22.0
332	Atlanta, GA	(31.3)
295	Aurora, CO	(24.2)
NA	Aurora, IL**	NA
77	Austin, TX	6.9
NA	Avondale, AZ**	NA
79	Bakersfield, CA	6.3
222	Baldwin Park, CA	(14.4)
215	Baltimore, MD	(13.8)
84	Baton Rouge, LA	5.2
175	Beaumont, TX	(8.2)
188	Beaverton, OR	(10.0)
196	Bellevue, WA	(10.8)
182	Bellingham, WA	(9.4)
194	Bend, OR	(10.7)
71	Berkeley, CA	9.0
37	Billings, MT	19.7
231	Birmingham, AL	(15.9)
NA	Bloomington, MN**	NA
235	Boca Raton, FL	(16.4)
336	Boise, ID	(32.1)
297	Boston, MA	(24.7)
81	Boulder, CO	6.0
2	Brick Twnshp, NJ	181.9
92	Bridgeport, CT	4.3
NA	Brockton, MA**	NA
215	Broken Arrow, OK	(13.8)
362	Brownsville, TX	(54.1)
255	Buena Park, CA	(18.9)
86	Buffalo, NY	5.0
91	Burbank, CA	4.4
128	Cambridge, MA	(1.7)
55	Camden, NJ	13.5
NA	Canton Twnshp, MI**	NA
88	Canton, OH	4.7
309	Cape Coral, FL	(26.8)
103	Carlsbad, CA	2.0
276	Carrollton, TX	(21.7)
273	Carson, CA	(21.2)
288	Cary, NC	(23.6)
171	Cedar Rapids, IA	(7.9)
333	Centennial, CO	(31.7)
256	Chandler, AZ	(19.0)
354	Charleston, SC	(44.5)
347	Charlotte, NC	(38.3)
164	Chattanooga, TN	(7.3)
169	Cheektowaga, NY	(7.6)
314	Chesapeake, VA	(27.4)
NA	Chicago, IL**	NA
102	Chico, CA	2.2
313	Chino, CA	(27.2)
305	Chula Vista, CA	(26.1)
114	Cincinnati, OH	0.6
NA	Citrus Heights, CA**	NA
NA	Clarkstown, NY**	NA
242	Clarksville, TN	(17.3)
130	Clearwater, FL	(1.9)
122	Cleveland, OH	(0.2)
38	Clifton, NJ	19.6
NA	Clinton Twnshp, MI**	NA
254	Clovis, CA	(18.7)
329	College Station, TX	(29.7)
284	Colonie, NY	(22.7)
100	Colorado Springs, CO	2.4
167	Columbia, MO	(7.5)
155	Columbia, SC	(5.9)
44	Columbus, GA	17.3
232	Columbus, OH	(16.0)
209	Compton, CA	(13.1)
257	Concord, CA	(19.2)
11	Coral Springs, FL	57.6
344	Corona, CA	(36.0)
49	Corpus Christi, TX	14.8
115	Costa Mesa, CA	0.3
196	Cranston, RI	(10.8)
345	Dallas, TX	(36.8)
233	Daly City, CA	(16.1)
120	Danbury, CT	(0.1)
356	Davenport, IA	(45.5)
18	Davie, FL	37.4
82	Dayton, OH	5.4
NA	Dearborn, MI**	NA
NA	Decatur, IL**	NA
341	Denton, TX	(34.9)
314	Denver, CO	(27.4)
NA	Des Moines, IA**	NA
NA	Detroit, MI**	NA
101	Downey, CA	2.3
NA	Duluth, MN**	NA
131	Durham, NC	(2.9)
46	Edison Twnshp, NJ	15.4
323	Edmond, OK	(28.6)
180	El Cajon, CA	(8.9)
110	El Monte, CA	1.1
83	El Paso, TX	5.3
NA	Elgin, IL**	NA
12	Elizabeth, NJ	56.6
NA	Elk Grove, CA**	NA
115	Erie, PA	0.3
186	Escondido, CA	(9.8)
19	Eugene, OR	36.8
173	Evansville, IN	(8.0)
57	Everett, WA	12.4
303	Fairfield, CA	(25.2)
NA	Fall River, MA**	NA
1	Fargo, ND	183.7
NA	Farmington Hills, MI**	NA
191	Fayetteville, AR	(10.4)
259	Fayetteville, NC	(19.5)
50	Federal Way, WA	14.7
NA	Flint, MI**	NA
128	Fontana, CA	(1.7)
56	Fort Collins, CO	12.5
182	Fort Lauderdale, FL	(9.4)
261	Fort Smith, AR	(20.1)
87	Fort Wayne, IN	4.9
177	Fort Worth, TX	(8.5)
153	Fremont, CA	(5.5)
317	Fresno, CA	(28.0)
223	Frisco, TX	(14.5)
19	Fullerton, CA	36.8
50	Gainesville, FL	14.7
306	Garden Grove, CA	(26.2)
159	Garland, TX	(6.4)
137	Gary, IN	(3.2)
345	Gilbert, AZ	(36.8)
278	Glendale, AZ	(22.3)
201	Glendale, CA	(11.4)
111	Grand Prairie, TX	1.0
NA	Grand Rapids, MI**	NA
14	Greece, NY	48.4
307	Greeley, CO	(26.7)
141	Green Bay, WI	(3.7)
163	Greensboro, NC	(7.1)
317	Gresham, OR	(28.0)
36	Hamilton Twnshp, NJ	20.2
68	Hammond, IN	10.0
282	Hampton, VA	(22.6)
59	Hartford, CT	12.1
16	Hawthorne, CA	38.7
47	Hayward, CA	15.2
30	Henderson, NV	25.8
74	Hesperia, CA	8.0
296	Hialeah, FL	(24.6)
117	High Point, NC	0.2
282	Hillsboro, OR	(22.6)
156	Hollywood, FL	(6.0)
127	Honolulu, HI	(1.1)
143	Houston, TX	(4.0)
246	Huntington Beach, CA	(17.6)
203	Huntsville, AL	(11.8)
215	Independence, MO	(13.8)
35	Indianapolis, IN	20.8
103	Indio, CA	2.0
108	Inglewood, CA	1.2
229	Irvine, CA	(15.7)
342	Irving, TX	(35.2)
112	Jacksonville, FL	0.7
NA	Jacksonville, NC**	NA
24	Jackson, MS	29.1
352	Jersey City, NJ	(43.2)
NA	Joliet, IL**	NA
243	Kansas City, KS	(17.5)
198	Kansas City, MO	(10.9)
88	Kenosha, WI	4.7
93	Kent, WA	3.8
292	Killeen, TX	(24.0)
67	Knoxville, TN	10.2
64	Lafayette, LA	10.8
167	Lake Forest, CA	(7.5)
78	Lakeland, FL	6.7
98	Lakewood, CA	2.8
90	Lakewood, CO	4.6
319	Lancaster, CA	(28.2)
NA	Lansing, MI**	NA
60	Laredo, TX	11.7
223	Las Cruces, NM	(14.5)
27	Las Vegas, NV	27.3
17	Lawrence, KS	37.6
10	Lawton, OK	62.3
310	Lee's Summit, MO	(26.9)
221	Lewisville, TX	(14.3)
NA	Lexington, KY**	NA
262	Lincoln, NE	(20.2)
NA	Little Rock, AR**	NA
64	Livermore, CA	10.8
NA	Livonia, MI**	NA
142	Long Beach, CA	(3.8)
NA	Longmont, CO**	NA

RANK	CITY	% CHANGE
243	Longview, TX	(17.5)
289	Los Angeles, CA	(23.8)
NA	Louisville, KY**	NA
199	Lubbock, TX	(11.3)
302	Lynn, MA	(25.1)
179	Macon, GA	(8.8)
143	Madison, WI	(4.0)
5	Manchester, NH	76.8
287	McAllen, TX	(23.5)
310	McKinney, TX	(26.9)
21	Melbourne, FL	31.1
131	Memphis, TN	(2.9)
41	Merced, CA	18.8
229	Mesa, AZ	(15.7)
120	Mesquite, TX	(0.1)
237	Miami Beach, FL	(16.5)
359	Miami Gardens, FL	(47.8)
299	Miami, FL	(24.8)
140	Midland, TX	(3.5)
79	Milwaukee, WI	6.3
289	Minneapolis, MN	(23.8)
96	Miramar, FL	3.2
202	Mission Viejo, CA	(11.5)
343	Missouri City, TX	(35.7)
6	Mobile, AL	73.7
69	Modesto, CA	9.8
357	Montgomery, AL	(47.1)
95	Moreno Valley, CA	3.3
226	Murfreesboro, TN	(15.4)
331	Murrieta, CA	(31.1)
NA	Nampa, ID**	NA
NA	Naperville, IL**	NA
70	Nashua, NH	9.2
326	Nashville, TN	(29.2)
45	New Bedford, MA	17.0
NA	New Haven, CT**	NA
NA	New Orleans, LA**	NA
248	New York, NY	(18.0)
164	Newark, NJ	(7.3)
96	Newport Beach, CA	3.2
251	Newton, MA	(18.4)
219	Norfolk, VA	(14.0)
337	Norman, OK	(33.5)
349	North Charleston, SC	(40.0)
211	North Las Vegas, NV	(13.2)
112	Norwalk, CA	0.7
15	Norwalk, CT	40.3
42	Oakland, CA	18.2
297	Oceanside, CA	(24.7)
29	Odessa, TX	26.2
170	O'Fallon, MO	(7.7)
122	Ogden, UT	(0.2)
71	Oklahoma City, OK	9.0
NA	Olathe, KS**	NA
153	Omaha, NE	(5.5)
237	Ontario, CA	(16.5)
330	Orange, CA	(30.1)
300	Orem, UT	(24.9)
339	Orlando, FL	(33.8)
351	Overland Park, KS	(41.4)
176	Oxnard, CA	(8.4)
137	Palm Bay, FL	(3.2)
326	Palmdale, CA	(29.2)
348	Pasadena, CA	(39.4)
61	Pasadena, TX	11.4
148	Paterson, NJ	(4.8)
181	Pearland, TX	(9.1)
190	Pembroke Pines, FL	(10.3)
166	Peoria, AZ	(7.4)
NA	Peoria, IL**	NA
228	Philadelphia, PA	(15.6)
301	Phoenix, AZ	(25.0)
139	Pittsburgh, PA	(3.4)
350	Plano, TX	(41.1)
7	Plantation, FL	72.3
260	Pomona, CA	(19.9)
338	Pompano Beach, FL	(33.6)
73	Port St. Lucie, FL	8.2
281	Portland, OR	(22.5)
276	Portsmouth, VA	(21.7)
108	Providence, RI	1.2
271	Provo, UT	(20.9)
22	Pueblo, CO	30.5
84	Quincy, MA	5.2
58	Racine, WI	12.2
262	Raleigh, NC	(20.2)
135	Ramapo, NY	(3.0)
237	Rancho Cucamon., CA	(16.5)
247	Reading, PA	(17.7)
33	Redding, CA	22.2
189	Reno, NV	(10.1)
335	Rialto, CA	(32.0)
212	Richardson, TX	(13.4)
158	Richmond, CA	(6.3)
340	Richmond, VA	(34.3)
220	Rio Rancho, NM	(14.1)
291	Riverside, CA	(23.9)
319	Roanoke, VA	(28.2)
NA	Rochester, MN**	NA
76	Rochester, NY	7.1
NA	Rockford, IL**	NA
269	Roseville, CA	(20.6)
66	Roswell, GA	10.4
262	Round Rock, TX	(20.2)
285	Sacramento, CA	(23.1)
278	Salem, OR	(22.3)
53	Salinas, CA	14.2
107	Salt Lake City, UT	1.6
146	San Angelo, TX	(4.2)
191	San Antonio, TX	(10.4)
292	San Bernardino, CA	(24.0)
209	San Diego, CA	(13.1)
171	San Francisco, CA	(7.9)
156	San Jose, CA	(6.0)
186	San Leandro, CA	(9.8)
266	San Marcos, CA	(20.3)
235	San Mateo, CA	(16.4)
NA	Sandy Springs, GA**	NA
125	Sandy, UT	(0.6)
148	Santa Ana, CA	(4.8)
275	Santa Barbara, CA	(21.6)
240	Santa Clara, CA	(16.7)
32	Santa Clarita, CA	23.2
43	Santa Maria, CA	18.0
322	Santa Monica, CA	(28.4)
278	Santa Rosa, CA	(22.3)
252	Savannah, GA	(18.5)
226	Scottsdale, AZ	(15.4)
184	Seattle, WA	(9.7)
274	Shreveport, LA	(21.3)
199	Simi Valley, CA	(11.3)
207	Sioux City, IA	(13.0)
241	Sioux Falls, SD	(16.8)
38	Somerville, MA	19.6
125	South Bend, IN	(0.6)
61	South Gate, CA	11.4
NA	Southfield, MI**	NA
105	Sparks, NV	1.9
292	Spokane Valley, WA	(24.0)
61	Spokane, WA	11.4
NA	Springfield, IL**	NA
326	Springfield, MA	(29.2)
23	Springfield, MO	30.1
117	Stamford, CT	0.2
NA	Sterling Heights, MI**	NA
225	Stockton, CA	(15.0)
364	St. George, UT	(66.3)
3	St. Joseph, MO	95.5
218	St. Louis, MO	(13.9)
207	St. Paul, MN	(13.0)
204	St. Petersburg, FL	(11.9)
353	Suffolk, VA	(43.3)
206	Sugar Land, TX	(12.5)
324	Sunnyvale, CA	(28.9)
268	Sunrise, FL	(20.5)
270	Surprise, AZ	(20.8)
194	Syracuse, NY	(10.7)
131	Tacoma, WA	(2.9)
173	Tallahassee, FL	(8.0)
358	Tampa, FL	(47.4)
363	Temecula, CA	(61.7)
253	Tempe, AZ	(18.6)
325	Thornton, CO	(29.1)
147	Thousand Oaks, CA	(4.7)
177	Toledo, OH	(8.5)
249	Toms River Twnshp, NJ	(18.3)
93	Topeka, KS	3.8
243	Torrance, CA	(17.5)
136	Tracy, CA	(3.1)
272	Trenton, NJ	(21.1)
NA	Troy, MI**	NA
334	Tucson, AZ	(31.9)
214	Tulsa, OK	(13.7)
312	Tuscaloosa, AL	(27.0)
233	Tyler, TX	(16.1)
4	Upper Darby Twnshp, PA	84.1
75	Vacaville, CA	7.3
NA	Vallejo, CA**	NA
124	Vancouver, WA	(0.3)
31	Ventura, CA	24.8
25	Victorville, CA	28.0
249	Virginia Beach, VA	(18.3)
360	Visalia, CA	(47.9)
160	Vista, CA	(6.6)
152	Waco, TX	(5.3)
NA	Warren, MI**	NA
99	Warwick, RI	2.5
184	Washington, DC	(9.7)
205	Waterbury, CT	(12.3)
162	West Covina, CA	(7.0)
NA	West Jordan, UT**	NA
321	West Palm Beach, FL	(28.3)
106	West Valley, UT	1.7
NA	Westland, MI**	NA
286	Westminster, CA	(23.3)
304	Westminster, CO	(25.6)
48	Whittier, CA	15.1
316	Wichita Falls, TX	(27.9)
NA	Wichita, KS**	NA
145	Wilmington, NC	(4.1)
193	Winston-Salem, NC	(10.6)
361	Woodbridge Twnshp, NJ	(52.7)
28	Worcester, MA	26.6
131	Yonkers, NY	(2.9)
150	Yuma, AZ	(4.9)

Source: CQ Press using reported data from the F.B.I. "Crime in the United States 2009"

*Violent crimes are offenses of murder, forcible rape, robbery, and aggravated assault.

**Not available.

48. Percent Change in Violent Crime Rate: 2005 to 2009 (continued)
National Percent Change = 8.4% Decrease*

RANK	CITY	% CHANGE
1	Fargo, ND	183.7
2	Brick Twnshp, NJ	181.9
3	St. Joseph, MO	95.5
4	Upper Darby Twnshp, PA	84.1
5	Manchester, NH	76.8
6	Mobile, AL	73.7
7	Plantation, FL	72.3
8	Albany, GA	62.8
8	Antioch, CA	62.8
10	Lawton, OK	62.3
11	Coral Springs, FL	57.6
12	Elizabeth, NJ	56.6
13	Akron, OH	55.7
14	Greece, NY	48.4
15	Norwalk, CT	40.3
16	Hawthorne, CA	38.7
17	Lawrence, KS	37.6
18	Davie, FL	37.4
19	Eugene, OR	36.8
19	Fullerton, CA	36.8
21	Melbourne, FL	31.1
22	Pueblo, CO	30.5
23	Springfield, MO	30.1
24	Jackson, MS	29.1
25	Victorville, CA	28.0
26	Amherst, NY	27.4
27	Las Vegas, NV	27.3
28	Worcester, MA	26.6
29	Odessa, TX	26.2
30	Henderson, NV	25.8
31	Ventura, CA	24.8
32	Santa Clarita, CA	23.2
33	Redding, CA	22.2
34	Athens-Clarke, GA	22.0
35	Indianapolis, IN	20.8
36	Hamilton Twnshp, NJ	20.2
37	Billings, MT	19.7
38	Clifton, NJ	19.6
38	Somerville, MA	19.6
40	Anchorage, AK	19.4
41	Merced, CA	18.8
42	Oakland, CA	18.2
43	Santa Maria, CA	18.0
44	Columbus, GA	17.3
45	New Bedford, MA	17.0
46	Edison Twnshp, NJ	15.4
47	Hayward, CA	15.2
48	Whittier, CA	15.1
49	Corpus Christi, TX	14.8
50	Federal Way, WA	14.7
50	Gainesville, FL	14.7
52	Abilene, TX	14.4
53	Allen, TX	14.2
53	Salinas, CA	14.2
55	Camden, NJ	13.5
56	Fort Collins, CO	12.5
57	Everett, WA	12.4
58	Racine, WI	12.2
59	Hartford, CT	12.1
60	Laredo, TX	11.7
61	Pasadena, TX	11.4
61	South Gate, CA	11.4
61	Spokane, WA	11.4
64	Lafayette, LA	10.8
64	Livermore, CA	10.8
66	Roswell, GA	10.4
67	Knoxville, TN	10.2
68	Hammond, IN	10.0
69	Modesto, CA	9.8
70	Nashua, NH	9.2
71	Berkeley, CA	9.0
71	Oklahoma City, OK	9.0
73	Port St. Lucie, FL	8.2
74	Hesperia, CA	8.0
75	Vacaville, CA	7.3
76	Rochester, NY	7.1
77	Austin, TX	6.9
78	Lakeland, FL	6.7
79	Bakersfield, CA	6.3
79	Milwaukee, WI	6.3
81	Boulder, CO	6.0
82	Dayton, OH	5.4
83	El Paso, TX	5.3
84	Baton Rouge, LA	5.2
84	Quincy, MA	5.2
86	Buffalo, NY	5.0
87	Fort Wayne, IN	4.9
88	Canton, OH	4.7
88	Kenosha, WI	4.7
90	Lakewood, CO	4.6
91	Burbank, CA	4.4
92	Bridgeport, CT	4.3
93	Kent, WA	3.8
93	Topeka, KS	3.8
95	Moreno Valley, CA	3.3
96	Miramar, FL	3.2
96	Newport Beach, CA	3.2
98	Lakewood, CA	2.8
99	Warwick, RI	2.5
100	Colorado Springs, CO	2.4
101	Downey, CA	2.3
102	Chico, CA	2.2
103	Carlsbad, CA	2.0
103	Indio, CA	2.0
105	Sparks, NV	1.9
106	West Valley, UT	1.7
107	Salt Lake City, UT	1.6
108	Inglewood, CA	1.2
108	Providence, RI	1.2
110	El Monte, CA	1.1
111	Grand Prairie, TX	1.0
112	Jacksonville, FL	0.7
112	Norwalk, CA	0.7
114	Cincinnati, OH	0.6
115	Costa Mesa, CA	0.3
115	Erie, PA	0.3
117	High Point, NC	0.2
117	Stamford, CT	0.2
119	Amarillo, TX	0.1
120	Danbury, CT	(0.1)
120	Mesquite, TX	(0.1)
122	Cleveland, OH	(0.2)
122	Ogden, UT	(0.2)
124	Vancouver, WA	(0.3)
125	Sandy, UT	(0.6)
125	South Bend, IN	(0.6)
127	Honolulu, HI	(1.1)
128	Cambridge, MA	(1.7)
128	Fontana, CA	(1.7)
130	Clearwater, FL	(1.9)
131	Durham, NC	(2.9)
131	Memphis, TN	(2.9)
131	Tacoma, WA	(2.9)
131	Yonkers, NY	(2.9)
135	Ramapo, NY	(3.0)
136	Tracy, CA	(3.1)
137	Gary, IN	(3.2)
137	Palm Bay, FL	(3.2)
139	Pittsburgh, PA	(3.4)
140	Midland, TX	(3.5)
141	Green Bay, WI	(3.7)
142	Long Beach, CA	(3.8)
143	Houston, TX	(4.0)
143	Madison, WI	(4.0)
145	Wilmington, NC	(4.1)
146	San Angelo, TX	(4.2)
147	Thousand Oaks, CA	(4.7)
148	Paterson, NJ	(4.8)
148	Santa Ana, CA	(4.8)
150	Yuma, AZ	(4.9)
151	Arlington, TX	(5.2)
152	Waco, TX	(5.3)
153	Fremont, CA	(5.5)
153	Omaha, NE	(5.5)
155	Columbia, SC	(5.9)
156	Hollywood, FL	(6.0)
156	San Jose, CA	(6.0)
158	Richmond, CA	(6.3)
159	Garland, TX	(6.4)
160	Arvada, CO	(6.6)
160	Vista, CA	(6.6)
162	West Covina, CA	(7.0)
163	Greensboro, NC	(7.1)
164	Chattanooga, TN	(7.3)
164	Newark, NJ	(7.3)
166	Peoria, AZ	(7.4)
167	Columbia, MO	(7.5)
167	Lake Forest, CA	(7.5)
169	Cheektowaga, NY	(7.6)
170	O'Fallon, MO	(7.7)
171	Cedar Rapids, IA	(7.9)
171	San Francisco, CA	(7.9)
173	Evansville, IN	(8.0)
173	Tallahassee, FL	(8.0)
175	Beaumont, TX	(8.2)
176	Oxnard, CA	(8.4)
177	Fort Worth, TX	(8.5)
177	Toledo, OH	(8.5)
179	Macon, GA	(8.8)
180	El Cajon, CA	(8.9)
181	Pearland, TX	(9.1)
182	Bellingham, WA	(9.4)
182	Fort Lauderdale, FL	(9.4)
184	Seattle, WA	(9.7)
184	Washington, DC	(9.7)
186	Escondido, CA	(9.8)
186	San Leandro, CA	(9.8)
188	Beaverton, OR	(10.0)
189	Reno, NV	(10.1)
190	Pembroke Pines, FL	(10.3)
191	Fayetteville, AR	(10.4)
191	San Antonio, TX	(10.4)
193	Winston-Salem, NC	(10.6)
194	Bend, OR	(10.7)
194	Syracuse, NY	(10.7)
196	Bellevue, WA	(10.8)
196	Cranston, RI	(10.8)
198	Kansas City, MO	(10.9)
199	Lubbock, TX	(11.3)
199	Simi Valley, CA	(11.3)
201	Glendale, CA	(11.4)
202	Mission Viejo, CA	(11.5)
203	Huntsville, AL	(11.8)
204	St. Petersburg, FL	(11.9)
205	Waterbury, CT	(12.3)
206	Sugar Land, TX	(12.5)

RANK	CITY	% CHANGE
207	Sioux City, IA	(13.0)
207	St. Paul, MN	(13.0)
209	Compton, CA	(13.1)
209	San Diego, CA	(13.1)
211	North Las Vegas, NV	(13.2)
212	Richardson, TX	(13.4)
213	Allentown, PA	(13.5)
214	Tulsa, OK	(13.7)
215	Baltimore, MD	(13.8)
215	Broken Arrow, OK	(13.8)
215	Independence, MO	(13.8)
218	St. Louis, MO	(13.9)
219	Norfolk, VA	(14.0)
220	Rio Rancho, NM	(14.1)
221	Lewisville, TX	(14.3)
222	Baldwin Park, CA	(14.4)
223	Frisco, TX	(14.5)
223	Las Cruces, NM	(14.5)
225	Stockton, CA	(15.0)
226	Murfreesboro, TN	(15.4)
226	Scottsdale, AZ	(15.4)
228	Philadelphia, PA	(15.6)
229	Irvine, CA	(15.7)
229	Mesa, AZ	(15.7)
231	Birmingham, AL	(15.9)
232	Columbus, OH	(16.0)
233	Daly City, CA	(16.1)
233	Tyler, TX	(16.1)
235	Boca Raton, FL	(16.4)
235	San Mateo, CA	(16.4)
237	Miami Beach, FL	(16.5)
237	Ontario, CA	(16.5)
237	Rancho Cucamon., CA	(16.5)
240	Santa Clara, CA	(16.7)
241	Sioux Falls, SD	(16.8)
242	Clarksville, TN	(17.3)
243	Kansas City, KS	(17.5)
243	Longview, TX	(17.5)
243	Torrance, CA	(17.5)
246	Huntington Beach, CA	(17.6)
247	Reading, PA	(17.7)
248	New York, NY	(18.0)
249	Toms River Twnshp, NJ	(18.3)
249	Virginia Beach, VA	(18.3)
251	Newton, MA	(18.4)
252	Savannah, GA	(18.5)
253	Tempe, AZ	(18.6)
254	Clovis, CA	(18.7)
255	Buena Park, CA	(18.9)
256	Chandler, AZ	(19.0)
257	Albuquerque, NM	(19.2)
257	Concord, CA	(19.2)
259	Fayetteville, NC	(19.5)
260	Pomona, CA	(19.9)
261	Fort Smith, AR	(20.1)
262	Albany, NY	(20.2)
262	Lincoln, NE	(20.2)
262	Raleigh, NC	(20.2)
262	Round Rock, TX	(20.2)
266	San Marcos, CA	(20.3)
267	Alhambra, CA	(20.4)
268	Sunrise, FL	(20.5)
269	Roseville, CA	(20.6)
270	Surprise, AZ	(20.8)
271	Provo, UT	(20.9)
272	Trenton, NJ	(21.1)
273	Carson, CA	(21.2)
274	Shreveport, LA	(21.3)
275	Santa Barbara, CA	(21.6)
276	Carrollton, TX	(21.7)
276	Portsmouth, VA	(21.7)
278	Glendale, AZ	(22.3)
278	Salem, OR	(22.3)
278	Santa Rosa, CA	(22.3)
281	Portland, OR	(22.5)
282	Hampton, VA	(22.6)
282	Hillsboro, OR	(22.6)
284	Colonie, NY	(22.7)
285	Sacramento, CA	(23.1)
286	Westminster, CA	(23.3)
287	McAllen, TX	(23.5)
288	Cary, NC	(23.6)
289	Los Angeles, CA	(23.8)
289	Minneapolis, MN	(23.8)
291	Riverside, CA	(23.9)
292	Killeen, TX	(24.0)
292	San Bernardino, CA	(24.0)
292	Spokane Valley, WA	(24.0)
295	Aurora, CO	(24.2)
296	Hialeah, FL	(24.6)
297	Boston, MA	(24.7)
297	Oceanside, CA	(24.7)
299	Miami, FL	(24.8)
300	Orem, UT	(24.9)
301	Phoenix, AZ	(25.0)
302	Lynn, MA	(25.1)
303	Fairfield, CA	(25.2)
304	Westminster, CO	(25.6)
305	Chula Vista, CA	(26.1)
306	Garden Grove, CA	(26.2)
307	Anaheim, CA	(26.7)
307	Greeley, CO	(26.7)
309	Cape Coral, FL	(26.8)
310	Lee's Summit, MO	(26.9)
310	McKinney, TX	(26.9)
312	Tuscaloosa, AL	(27.0)
313	Chino, CA	(27.2)
314	Chesapeake, VA	(27.4)
314	Denver, CO	(27.4)
316	Wichita Falls, TX	(27.9)
317	Fresno, CA	(28.0)
317	Gresham, OR	(28.0)
319	Lancaster, CA	(28.2)
319	Roanoke, VA	(28.2)
321	West Palm Beach, FL	(28.3)
322	Santa Monica, CA	(28.4)
323	Edmond, OK	(28.6)
324	Sunnyvale, CA	(28.9)
325	Thornton, CO	(29.1)
326	Nashville, TN	(29.2)
326	Palmdale, CA	(29.2)
326	Springfield, MA	(29.2)
329	College Station, TX	(29.7)
330	Orange, CA	(30.1)
331	Murrieta, CA	(31.1)
332	Atlanta, GA	(31.3)
333	Centennial, CO	(31.7)
334	Tucson, AZ	(31.9)
335	Rialto, CA	(32.0)
336	Boise, ID	(32.1)
337	Norman, OK	(33.5)
338	Pompano Beach, FL	(33.6)
339	Orlando, FL	(33.8)
340	Richmond, VA	(34.3)
341	Denton, TX	(34.9)
342	Irving, TX	(35.2)
343	Missouri City, TX	(35.7)
344	Corona, CA	(36.0)
345	Dallas, TX	(36.8)
345	Gilbert, AZ	(36.8)
347	Charlotte, NC	(38.3)
348	Pasadena, CA	(39.4)
349	North Charleston, SC	(40.0)
350	Plano, TX	(41.1)
351	Overland Park, KS	(41.4)
352	Jersey City, NJ	(43.2)
353	Suffolk, VA	(43.3)
354	Charleston, SC	(44.5)
355	Alexandria, VA	(44.7)
356	Davenport, IA	(45.5)
357	Montgomery, AL	(47.1)
358	Tampa, FL	(47.4)
359	Miami Gardens, FL	(47.8)
360	Visalia, CA	(47.9)
361	Woodbridge Twnshp, NJ	(52.7)
362	Brownsville, TX	(54.1)
363	Temecula, CA	(61.7)
364	St. George, UT	(66.3)
NA	Ann Arbor, MI**	NA
NA	Aurora, IL**	NA
NA	Avondale, AZ**	NA
NA	Bloomington, MN**	NA
NA	Brockton, MA**	NA
NA	Canton Twnshp, MI**	NA
NA	Chicago, IL**	NA
NA	Citrus Heights, CA**	NA
NA	Clarkstown, NY**	NA
NA	Clinton Twnshp, MI**	NA
NA	Dearborn, MI**	NA
NA	Decatur, IL**	NA
NA	Des Moines, IA**	NA
NA	Detroit, MI**	NA
NA	Duluth, MN**	NA
NA	Elgin, IL**	NA
NA	Elk Grove, CA**	NA
NA	Fall River, MA**	NA
NA	Farmington Hills, MI**	NA
NA	Flint, MI**	NA
NA	Grand Rapids, MI**	NA
NA	Jacksonville, NC**	NA
NA	Joliet, IL**	NA
NA	Lansing, MI**	NA
NA	Lexington, KY**	NA
NA	Little Rock, AR**	NA
NA	Livonia, MI**	NA
NA	Longmont, CO**	NA
NA	Louisville, KY**	NA
NA	Nampa, ID**	NA
NA	Naperville, IL**	NA
NA	New Haven, CT**	NA
NA	New Orleans, LA**	NA
NA	Olathe, KS**	NA
NA	Peoria, IL**	NA
NA	Rochester, MN**	NA
NA	Rockford, IL**	NA
NA	Sandy Springs, GA**	NA
NA	Southfield, MI**	NA
NA	Springfield, IL**	NA
NA	Sterling Heights, MI**	NA
NA	Troy, MI**	NA
NA	Vallejo, CA**	NA
NA	Warren, MI**	NA
NA	West Jordan, UT**	NA
NA	Westland, MI**	NA
NA	Wichita, KS**	NA

Source: CQ Press using reported data from the F.B.I. "Crime in the United States 2009"
*Violent crimes are offenses of murder, forcible rape, robbery, and aggravated assault.
**Not available.

49. Murders in 2009
National Total = 15,241 Murders*

RANK	CITY	MURDERS
173	Abilene, TX	7
86	Akron, OH	20
161	Albany, GA	8
150	Albany, NY	9
34	Albuquerque, NM	56
199	Alexandria, VA	5
386	Alhambra, CA	0
114	Allentown, PA	13
295	Allen, TX	2
141	Amarillo, TX	10
339	Amherst, NY	1
150	Anaheim, CA	9
109	Anchorage, AK	14
339	Ann Arbor, MI	1
199	Antioch, CA	5
126	Arlington, TX	12
295	Arvada, CO	2
141	Athens-Clarke, GA	10
22	Atlanta, GA	80
78	Aurora, CO	22
199	Aurora, IL	5
78	Austin, TX	22
199	Avondale, AZ	5
70	Bakersfield, CA	27
229	Baldwin Park, CA	4
7	Baltimore, MD	238
25	Baton Rouge, LA	75
199	Beaumont, TX	5
295	Beaverton, OR	2
295	Bellevue, WA	2
295	Bellingham, WA	2
386	Bend, OR	0
185	Berkeley, CA	6
295	Billings, MT	2
28	Birmingham, AL	65
295	Bloomington, MN	2
295	Boca Raton, FL	2
173	Boise, ID	7
36	Boston, MA	50
199	Boulder, CO	5
339	Brick Twnshp, NJ	1
126	Bridgeport, CT	12
150	Brockton, MA	9
295	Broken Arrow, OK	2
229	Brownsville, TX	4
295	Buena Park, CA	2
31	Buffalo, NY	60
339	Burbank, CA	1
295	Cambridge, MA	2
53	Camden, NJ	34
339	Canton Twnshp, MI	1
114	Canton, OH	13
260	Cape Coral, FL	3
199	Carlsbad, CA	5
229	Carrollton, TX	4
199	Carson, CA	5
386	Cary, NC	0
339	Cedar Rapids, IA	1
339	Centennial, CO	1
199	Chandler, AZ	5
150	Charleston, SC	9
33	Charlotte, NC	58
96	Chattanooga, TN	17
386	Cheektowaga, NY	0
126	Chesapeake, VA	12
2	Chicago, IL	458
260	Chico, CA	3
339	Chino, CA	1
229	Chula Vista, CA	4
35	Cincinnati, OH	55
386	Citrus Heights, CA	0
339	Clarkstown, NY	1
102	Clarksville, TN	16
260	Clearwater, FL	3
20	Cleveland, OH	86
386	Clifton, NJ	0
339	Clinton Twnshp, MI	1
339	Clovis, CA	1
260	College Station, TX	3
386	Colonie, NY	0
105	Colorado Springs, CO	15
260	Columbia, MO	3
114	Columbia, SC	13
114	Columbus, GA	13
21	Columbus, OH	83
49	Compton, CA	36
295	Concord, CA	2
295	Coral Springs, FL	2
161	Corona, CA	8
126	Corpus Christi, TX	12
339	Costa Mesa, CA	1
295	Cranston, RI	2
9	Dallas, TX	166
339	Daly City, CA	1
295	Danbury, CT	2
260	Davenport, IA	3
229	Davie, FL	4
44	Dayton, OH	39
260	Dearborn, MI	3
260	Decatur, IL	3
295	Denton, TX	2
44	Denver, CO	39
185	Des Moines, IA	6
3	Detroit, MI	365
229	Downey, CA	4
260	Duluth, MN	3
82	Durham, NC	21
339	Edison Twnshp, NJ	1
295	Edmond, OK	2
295	El Cajon, CA	2
260	El Monte, CA	3
126	El Paso, TX	12
260	Elgin, IL	3
199	Elizabeth, NJ	5
229	Elk Grove, CA	4
229	Erie, PA	4
229	Escondido, CA	4
339	Eugene, OR	1
260	Evansville, IN	3
295	Everett, WA	2
185	Fairfield, CA	6
229	Fall River, MA	4
295	Fargo, ND	2
339	Farmington Hills, MI	1
295	Fayetteville, AR	2
82	Fayetteville, NC	21
199	Federal Way, WA	5
49	Flint, MI	36
185	Fontana, CA	6
295	Fort Collins, CO	2
114	Fort Lauderdale, FL	13
260	Fort Smith, AR	3
90	Fort Wayne, IN	18
40	Fort Worth, TX	44
295	Fremont, CA	2
41	Fresno, CA	42
295	Frisco, TX	2
295	Fullerton, CA	2
260	Gainesville, FL	3
185	Garden Grove, CA	6
173	Garland, TX	7
37	Gary, IN	49
229	Gilbert, AZ	4
90	Glendale, AZ	18
260	Glendale, CA	3
173	Grand Prairie, TX	7
150	Grand Rapids, MI	9
339	Greece, NY	1
260	Greeley, CO	3
339	Green Bay, WI	1
74	Greensboro, NC	24
386	Gresham, OR	0
386	Hamilton Twnshp, NJ	0
135	Hammond, IN	11
135	Hampton, VA	11
55	Hartford, CT	33
229	Hawthorne, CA	4
173	Hayward, CA	7
229	Henderson, NV	4
260	Hesperia, CA	3
161	Hialeah, FL	8
260	High Point, NC	3
229	Hillsboro, OR	4
173	Hollywood, FL	7
109	Honolulu, HI	14
6	Houston, TX	287
339	Huntington Beach, CA	1
114	Huntsville, AL	13
260	Independence, MO	3
16	Indianapolis, IN	100
199	Indio, CA	5
70	Inglewood, CA	27
260	Irvine, CA	3
229	Irving, TX	4
18	Jacksonville, FL	99
161	Jacksonville, NC	8
47	Jackson, MS	37
66	Jersey City, NJ	28
126	Joliet, IL	12
51	Kansas City, KS	35
16	Kansas City, MO	100
229	Kenosha, WI	4
339	Kent, WA	1
199	Killeen, TX	5
78	Knoxville, TN	22
173	Lafayette, LA	7
386	Lake Forest, CA	0
199	Lakeland, FL	5
339	Lakewood, CA	1
199	Lakewood, CO	5
141	Lancaster, CA	10
135	Lansing, MI	11
96	Laredo, TX	17
229	Las Cruces, NM	4
14	Las Vegas, NV	111
386	Lawrence, KS	0
150	Lawton, OK	9
339	Lee's Summit, MO	1
260	Lewisville, TX	3
114	Lexington, KY	13
229	Lincoln, NE	4
58	Little Rock, AR	32
260	Livermore, CA	3
260	Livonia, MI	3
43	Long Beach, CA	40
339	Longmont, CO	1

RANK	CITY	MURDERS
135	Longview, TX	11
4	Los Angeles, CA	312
30	Louisville, KY	62
114	Lubbock, TX	13
229	Lynn, MA	4
90	Macon, GA	18
229	Madison, WI	4
295	Manchester, NH	2
229	McAllen, TX	4
386	McKinney, TX	0
185	Melbourne, FL	6
12	Memphis, TN	132
173	Merced, CA	7
109	Mesa, AZ	14
199	Mesquite, TX	5
173	Miami Beach, FL	7
74	Miami Gardens, FL	24
32	Miami, FL	59
260	Midland, TX	3
26	Milwaukee, WI	72
90	Minneapolis, MN	18
173	Miramar, FL	7
386	Mission Viejo, CA	0
339	Missouri City, TX	1
74	Mobile, AL	24
82	Modesto, CA	21
60	Montgomery, AL	31
185	Moreno Valley, CA	6
199	Murfreesboro, TN	5
386	Murrieta, CA	0
386	Nampa, ID	0
386	Naperville, IL	0
339	Nashua, NH	1
24	Nashville, TN	77
150	New Bedford, MA	9
126	New Haven, CT	12
8	New Orleans, LA	174
1	New York, NY	471
22	Newark, NJ	80
386	Newport Beach, CA	0
339	Newton, MA	1
53	Norfolk, VA	34
386	Norman, OK	0
141	North Charleston, SC	10
96	North Las Vegas, NV	17
114	Norwalk, CA	13
339	Norwalk, CT	1
15	Oakland, CA	104
229	Oceanside, CA	4
199	Odessa, TX	5
339	O'Fallon, MO	1
229	Ogden, UT	4
28	Oklahoma City, OK	65
386	Olathe, KS	0
62	Omaha, NE	30
199	Ontario, CA	5
295	Orange, CA	2
339	Orem, UT	1
66	Orlando, FL	28
260	Overland Park, KS	3
114	Oxnard, CA	13
199	Palm Bay, FL	5
161	Palmdale, CA	8
199	Pasadena, CA	5
161	Pasadena, TX	8
105	Paterson, NJ	15
339	Pearland, TX	1
229	Pembroke Pines, FL	4

RANK	CITY	MURDERS
161	Peoria, AZ	8
102	Peoria, IL	16
5	Philadelphia, PA	302
13	Phoenix, AZ	122
44	Pittsburgh, PA	39
229	Plano, TX	4
260	Plantation, FL	3
96	Pomona, CA	17
161	Pompano Beach, FL	8
339	Port St. Lucie, FL	1
88	Portland, OR	19
96	Portsmouth, VA	17
77	Providence, RI	23
339	Provo, UT	1
114	Pueblo, CO	13
199	Quincy, MA	5
260	Racine, WI	3
109	Raleigh, NC	14
339	Ramapo, NY	1
339	Rancho Cucamon., CA	1
126	Reading, PA	12
295	Redding, CA	2
150	Reno, NV	9
185	Rialto, CA	6
386	Richardson, TX	0
38	Richmond, CA	47
47	Richmond, VA	37
339	Rio Rancho, NM	1
105	Riverside, CA	15
150	Roanoke, VA	9
339	Rochester, MN	1
66	Rochester, NY	28
82	Rockford, IL	21
295	Roseville, CA	2
199	Roswell, GA	5
339	Round Rock, TX	1
62	Sacramento, CA	30
199	Salem, OR	5
65	Salinas, CA	29
260	Salt Lake City, UT	3
161	San Angelo, TX	8
18	San Antonio, TX	99
58	San Bernardino, CA	32
42	San Diego, CA	41
39	San Francisco, CA	45
66	San Jose, CA	28
295	San Leandro, CA	2
295	San Marcos, CA	2
295	San Mateo, CA	2
229	Sandy Springs, GA	4
295	Sandy, UT	2
72	Santa Ana, CA	25
260	Santa Barbara, CA	3
185	Santa Clara, CA	6
199	Santa Clarita, CA	5
199	Santa Maria, CA	5
260	Santa Monica, CA	3
295	Santa Rosa, CA	2
62	Savannah, GA	30
141	Scottsdale, AZ	10
78	Seattle, WA	22
60	Shreveport, LA	31
295	Simi Valley, CA	2
260	Sioux City, IA	3
339	Sioux Falls, SD	1
260	Somerville, MA	3
109	South Bend, IN	14
141	South Gate, CA	10

Source: Reported data from the F.B.I. "Crime in the United States 2009"
*Includes nonnegligent manslaughter.

RANK	CITY	MURDERS
295	Southfield, MI	2
199	Sparks, NV	5
339	Spokane Valley, WA	1
173	Spokane, WA	7
126	Springfield, IL	12
102	Springfield, MA	16
185	Springfield, MO	6
295	Stamford, CT	2
295	Sterling Heights, MI	2
55	Stockton, CA	33
386	St. George, UT	0
260	St. Joseph, MO	3
10	St. Louis, MO	143
114	St. Paul, MN	13
135	St. Petersburg, FL	11
185	Suffolk, VA	6
386	Sugar Land, TX	0
339	Sunnyvale, CA	1
229	Sunrise, FL	4
339	Surprise, AZ	1
90	Syracuse, NY	18
161	Tacoma, WA	8
185	Tallahassee, FL	6
86	Tampa, FL	20
339	Temecula, CA	1
295	Tempe, AZ	2
339	Thornton, CO	1
295	Thousand Oaks, CA	2
55	Toledo, OH	33
295	Toms River Twnshp, NJ	2
141	Topeka, KS	10
339	Torrance, CA	1
199	Tracy, CA	5
96	Trenton, NJ	17
386	Troy, MI	0
51	Tucson, AZ	35
27	Tulsa, OK	68
199	Tuscaloosa, AL	5
260	Tyler, TX	3
339	Upper Darby Twnshp, PA	1
339	Vacaville, CA	1
141	Vallejo, CA	10
185	Vancouver, WA	6
199	Ventura, CA	5
141	Victorville, CA	10
90	Virginia Beach, VA	18
150	Visalia, CA	9
386	Vista, CA	0
150	Waco, TX	9
229	Warren, MI	4
386	Warwick, RI	0
10	Washington, DC	143
185	Waterbury, CT	6
161	West Covina, CA	8
229	West Jordan, UT	4
88	West Palm Beach, FL	19
229	West Valley, UT	4
295	Westland, MI	2
386	Westminster, CA	0
295	Westminster, CO	2
260	Whittier, CA	3
135	Wichita Falls, TX	11
72	Wichita, KS	25
229	Wilmington, NC	4
105	Winston-Salem, NC	15
339	Woodbridge Twnshp, NJ	1
173	Worcester, MA	7
161	Yonkers, NY	8
295	Yuma, AZ	2

49. Murders in 2009 (continued)
National Total = 15,241 Murders*

RANK	CITY	MURDERS
1	New York, NY	471
2	Chicago, IL	458
3	Detroit, MI	365
4	Los Angeles, CA	312
5	Philadelphia, PA	302
6	Houston, TX	287
7	Baltimore, MD	238
8	New Orleans, LA	174
9	Dallas, TX	166
10	St. Louis, MO	143
10	Washington, DC	143
12	Memphis, TN	132
13	Phoenix, AZ	122
14	Las Vegas, NV	111
15	Oakland, CA	104
16	Indianapolis, IN	100
16	Kansas City, MO	100
18	Jacksonville, FL	99
18	San Antonio, TX	99
20	Cleveland, OH	86
21	Columbus, OH	83
22	Atlanta, GA	80
22	Newark, NJ	80
24	Nashville, TN	77
25	Baton Rouge, LA	75
26	Milwaukee, WI	72
27	Tulsa, OK	68
28	Birmingham, AL	65
28	Oklahoma City, OK	65
30	Louisville, KY	62
31	Buffalo, NY	60
32	Miami, FL	59
33	Charlotte, NC	58
34	Albuquerque, NM	56
35	Cincinnati, OH	55
36	Boston, MA	50
37	Gary, IN	49
38	Richmond, CA	47
39	San Francisco, CA	45
40	Fort Worth, TX	44
41	Fresno, CA	42
42	San Diego, CA	41
43	Long Beach, CA	40
44	Dayton, OH	39
44	Denver, CO	39
44	Pittsburgh, PA	39
47	Jackson, MS	37
47	Richmond, VA	37
49	Compton, CA	36
49	Flint, MI	36
51	Kansas City, KS	35
51	Tucson, AZ	35
53	Camden, NJ	34
53	Norfolk, VA	34
55	Hartford, CT	33
55	Stockton, CA	33
55	Toledo, OH	33
58	Little Rock, AR	32
58	San Bernardino, CA	32
60	Montgomery, AL	31
60	Shreveport, LA	31
62	Omaha, NE	30
62	Sacramento, CA	30
62	Savannah, GA	30
65	Salinas, CA	29
66	Jersey City, NJ	28
66	Orlando, FL	28
66	Rochester, NY	28
66	San Jose, CA	28
70	Bakersfield, CA	27
70	Inglewood, CA	27
72	Santa Ana, CA	25
72	Wichita, KS	25
74	Greensboro, NC	24
74	Miami Gardens, FL	24
74	Mobile, AL	24
77	Providence, RI	23
78	Aurora, CO	22
78	Austin, TX	22
78	Knoxville, TN	22
78	Seattle, WA	22
82	Durham, NC	21
82	Fayetteville, NC	21
82	Modesto, CA	21
82	Rockford, IL	21
86	Akron, OH	20
86	Tampa, FL	20
88	Portland, OR	19
88	West Palm Beach, FL	19
90	Fort Wayne, IN	18
90	Glendale, AZ	18
90	Macon, GA	18
90	Minneapolis, MN	18
90	Syracuse, NY	18
90	Virginia Beach, VA	18
96	Chattanooga, TN	17
96	Laredo, TX	17
96	North Las Vegas, NV	17
96	Pomona, CA	17
96	Portsmouth, VA	17
96	Trenton, NJ	17
102	Clarksville, TN	16
102	Peoria, IL	16
102	Springfield, MA	16
105	Colorado Springs, CO	15
105	Paterson, NJ	15
105	Riverside, CA	15
105	Winston-Salem, NC	15
109	Anchorage, AK	14
109	Honolulu, HI	14
109	Mesa, AZ	14
109	Raleigh, NC	14
109	South Bend, IN	14
114	Allentown, PA	13
114	Canton, OH	13
114	Columbia, SC	13
114	Columbus, GA	13
114	Fort Lauderdale, FL	13
114	Huntsville, AL	13
114	Lexington, KY	13
114	Lubbock, TX	13
114	Norwalk, CA	13
114	Oxnard, CA	13
114	Pueblo, CO	13
114	St. Paul, MN	13
126	Arlington, TX	12
126	Bridgeport, CT	12
126	Chesapeake, VA	12
126	Corpus Christi, TX	12
126	El Paso, TX	12
126	Joliet, IL	12
126	New Haven, CT	12
126	Reading, PA	12
126	Springfield, IL	12
135	Hammond, IN	11
135	Hampton, VA	11
135	Lansing, MI	11
135	Longview, TX	11
135	St. Petersburg, FL	11
135	Wichita Falls, TX	11
141	Amarillo, TX	10
141	Athens-Clarke, GA	10
141	Lancaster, CA	10
141	North Charleston, SC	10
141	Scottsdale, AZ	10
141	South Gate, CA	10
141	Topeka, KS	10
141	Vallejo, CA	10
141	Victorville, CA	10
150	Albany, NY	9
150	Anaheim, CA	9
150	Brockton, MA	9
150	Charleston, SC	9
150	Grand Rapids, MI	9
150	Lawton, OK	9
150	New Bedford, MA	9
150	Reno, NV	9
150	Roanoke, VA	9
150	Visalia, CA	9
150	Waco, TX	9
161	Albany, GA	8
161	Corona, CA	8
161	Hialeah, FL	8
161	Jacksonville, NC	8
161	Palmdale, CA	8
161	Pasadena, TX	8
161	Peoria, AZ	8
161	Pompano Beach, FL	8
161	San Angelo, TX	8
161	Tacoma, WA	8
161	West Covina, CA	8
161	Yonkers, NY	8
173	Abilene, TX	7
173	Boise, ID	7
173	Garland, TX	7
173	Grand Prairie, TX	7
173	Hayward, CA	7
173	Hollywood, FL	7
173	Lafayette, LA	7
173	Merced, CA	7
173	Miami Beach, FL	7
173	Miramar, FL	7
173	Spokane, WA	7
173	Worcester, MA	7
185	Berkeley, CA	6
185	Des Moines, IA	6
185	Fairfield, CA	6
185	Fontana, CA	6
185	Garden Grove, CA	6
185	Melbourne, FL	6
185	Moreno Valley, CA	6
185	Rialto, CA	6
185	Santa Clara, CA	6
185	Springfield, MO	6
185	Suffolk, VA	6
185	Tallahassee, FL	6
185	Vancouver, WA	6
185	Waterbury, CT	6
199	Alexandria, VA	5
199	Antioch, CA	5
199	Aurora, IL	5
199	Avondale, AZ	5
199	Beaumont, TX	5
199	Boulder, CO	5
199	Carlsbad, CA	5
199	Carson, CA	5

RANK	CITY	MURDERS
199	Chandler, AZ	5
199	Elizabeth, NJ	5
199	Federal Way, WA	5
199	Indio, CA	5
199	Killeen, TX	5
199	Lakeland, FL	5
199	Lakewood, CO	5
199	Mesquite, TX	5
199	Murfreesboro, TN	5
199	Odessa, TX	5
199	Ontario, CA	5
199	Palm Bay, FL	5
199	Pasadena, CA	5
199	Quincy, MA	5
199	Roswell, GA	5
199	Salem, OR	5
199	Santa Clarita, CA	5
199	Santa Maria, CA	5
199	Sparks, NV	5
199	Tracy, CA	5
199	Tuscaloosa, AL	5
199	Ventura, CA	5
229	Baldwin Park, CA	4
229	Brownsville, TX	4
229	Carrollton, TX	4
229	Chula Vista, CA	4
229	Davie, FL	4
229	Downey, CA	4
229	Elk Grove, CA	4
229	Erie, PA	4
229	Escondido, CA	4
229	Fall River, MA	4
229	Gilbert, AZ	4
229	Hawthorne, CA	4
229	Henderson, NV	4
229	Hillsboro, OR	4
229	Irving, TX	4
229	Kenosha, WI	4
229	Las Cruces, NM	4
229	Lincoln, NE	4
229	Lynn, MA	4
229	Madison, WI	4
229	McAllen, TX	4
229	Oceanside, CA	4
229	Ogden, UT	4
229	Pembroke Pines, FL	4
229	Plano, TX	4
229	Sandy Springs, GA	4
229	Sunrise, FL	4
229	Warren, MI	4
229	West Jordan, UT	4
229	West Valley, UT	4
229	Wilmington, NC	4
260	Cape Coral, FL	3
260	Chico, CA	3
260	Clearwater, FL	3
260	College Station, TX	3
260	Columbia, MO	3
260	Davenport, IA	3
260	Dearborn, MI	3
260	Decatur, IL	3
260	Duluth, MN	3
260	El Monte, CA	3
260	Elgin, IL	3
260	Evansville, IN	3
260	Fort Smith, AR	3
260	Gainesville, FL	3
260	Glendale, CA	3

RANK	CITY	MURDERS
260	Greeley, CO	3
260	Hesperia, CA	3
260	High Point, NC	3
260	Independence, MO	3
260	Irvine, CA	3
260	Lewisville, TX	3
260	Livermore, CA	3
260	Livonia, MI	3
260	Midland, TX	3
260	Overland Park, KS	3
260	Plantation, FL	3
260	Racine, WI	3
260	Salt Lake City, UT	3
260	Santa Barbara, CA	3
260	Santa Monica, CA	3
260	Sioux City, IA	3
260	Somerville, MA	3
260	St. Joseph, MO	3
260	Tyler, TX	3
260	Whittier, CA	3
295	Allen, TX	2
295	Arvada, CO	2
295	Beaverton, OR	2
295	Bellevue, WA	2
295	Bellingham, WA	2
295	Billings, MT	2
295	Bloomington, MN	2
295	Boca Raton, FL	2
295	Broken Arrow, OK	2
295	Buena Park, CA	2
295	Cambridge, MA	2
295	Concord, CA	2
295	Coral Springs, FL	2
295	Cranston, RI	2
295	Danbury, CT	2
295	Denton, TX	2
295	Edmond, OK	2
295	El Cajon, CA	2
295	Everett, WA	2
295	Fargo, ND	2
295	Fayetteville, AR	2
295	Fort Collins, CO	2
295	Fremont, CA	2
295	Frisco, TX	2
295	Fullerton, CA	2
295	Manchester, NH	2
295	Orange, CA	2
295	Redding, CA	2
295	Roseville, CA	2
295	San Leandro, CA	2
295	San Marcos, CA	2
295	San Mateo, CA	2
295	Sandy, UT	2
295	Santa Rosa, CA	2
295	Simi Valley, CA	2
295	Southfield, MI	2
295	Stamford, CT	2
295	Sterling Heights, MI	2
295	Tempe, AZ	2
295	Thousand Oaks, CA	2
295	Toms River Twnshp, NJ	2
295	Westland, MI	2
295	Westminster, CO	2
295	Yuma, AZ	2
339	Amherst, NY	1
339	Ann Arbor, MI	1
339	Brick Twnshp, NJ	1
339	Burbank, CA	1

RANK	CITY	MURDERS
339	Canton Twnshp, MI	1
339	Cedar Rapids, IA	1
339	Centennial, CO	1
339	Chino, CA	1
339	Clarkstown, NY	1
339	Clinton Twnshp, MI	1
339	Clovis, CA	1
339	Costa Mesa, CA	1
339	Daly City, CA	1
339	Edison Twnshp, NJ	1
339	Eugene, OR	1
339	Farmington Hills, MI	1
339	Greece, NY	1
339	Green Bay, WI	1
339	Huntington Beach, CA	1
339	Kent, WA	1
339	Lakewood, CA	1
339	Lee's Summit, MO	1
339	Longmont, CO	1
339	Missouri City, TX	1
339	Nashua, NH	1
339	Newton, MA	1
339	Norwalk, CT	1
339	O'Fallon, MO	1
339	Orem, UT	1
339	Pearland, TX	1
339	Port St. Lucie, FL	1
339	Provo, UT	1
339	Ramapo, NY	1
339	Rancho Cucamon., CA	1
339	Rio Rancho, NM	1
339	Rochester, MN	1
339	Round Rock, TX	1
339	Sioux Falls, SD	1
339	Spokane Valley, WA	1
339	Sunnyvale, CA	1
339	Surprise, AZ	1
339	Temecula, CA	1
339	Thornton, CO	1
339	Torrance, CA	1
339	Upper Darby Twnshp, PA	1
339	Vacaville, CA	1
339	Woodbridge Twnshp, NJ	1
386	Alhambra, CA	0
386	Bend, OR	0
386	Cary, NC	0
386	Cheektowaga, NY	0
386	Citrus Heights, CA	0
386	Clifton, NJ	0
386	Colonie, NY	0
386	Gresham, OR	0
386	Hamilton Twnshp, NJ	0
386	Lake Forest, CA	0
386	Lawrence, KS	0
386	McKinney, TX	0
386	Mission Viejo, CA	0
386	Murrieta, CA	0
386	Nampa, ID	0
386	Naperville, IL	0
386	Newport Beach, CA	0
386	Norman, OK	0
386	Olathe, KS	0
386	Richardson, TX	0
386	St. George, UT	0
386	Sugar Land, TX	0
386	Troy, MI	0
386	Vista, CA	0
386	Warwick, RI	0
386	Westminster, CA	0

Source: Reported data from the F.B.I. "Crime in the United States 2009"
*Includes nonnegligent manslaughter.

50. Murder Rate in 2009
National Rate = 5.0 Murders per 100,000 Population*

RANK	CITY	RATE
144	Abilene, TX	6.0
87	Akron, OH	9.7
74	Albany, GA	10.6
93	Albany, NY	9.6
74	Albuquerque, NM	10.6
235	Alexandria, VA	3.4
386	Alhambra, CA	0.0
62	Allentown, PA	12.1
289	Allen, TX	2.3
165	Amarillo, TX	5.3
372	Amherst, NY	0.9
272	Anaheim, CA	2.7
174	Anchorage, AK	4.9
372	Ann Arbor, MI	0.9
174	Antioch, CA	4.9
244	Arlington, TX	3.2
305	Arvada, CO	1.9
99	Athens-Clarke, GA	8.7
41	Atlanta, GA	14.5
132	Aurora, CO	6.8
259	Aurora, IL	2.9
259	Austin, TX	2.9
153	Avondale, AZ	5.6
106	Bakersfield, CA	8.2
167	Baldwin Park, CA	5.2
8	Baltimore, MD	37.3
9	Baton Rouge, LA	33.6
188	Beaumont, TX	4.5
297	Beaverton, OR	2.1
321	Bellevue, WA	1.6
280	Bellingham, WA	2.5
386	Bend, OR	0.0
146	Berkeley, CA	5.9
305	Billings, MT	1.9
12	Birmingham, AL	28.6
280	Bloomington, MN	2.5
289	Boca Raton, FL	2.3
235	Boise, ID	3.4
110	Boston, MA	8.0
171	Boulder, CO	5.0
336	Brick Twnshp, NJ	1.3
98	Bridgeport, CT	8.8
95	Brockton, MA	9.3
297	Broken Arrow, OK	2.1
292	Brownsville, TX	2.2
280	Buena Park, CA	2.5
19	Buffalo, NY	22.3
361	Burbank, CA	1.0
305	Cambridge, MA	1.9
4	Camden, NJ	43.0
344	Canton Twnshp, MI	1.2
34	Canton, OH	16.6
310	Cape Coral, FL	1.8
170	Carlsbad, CA	5.1
250	Carrollton, TX	3.1
161	Carson, CA	5.4
386	Cary, NC	0.0
377	Cedar Rapids, IA	0.8
361	Centennial, CO	1.0
302	Chandler, AZ	2.0
111	Charleston, SC	7.9
117	Charlotte, NC	7.5
85	Chattanooga, TN	9.9
386	Cheektowaga, NY	0.0
161	Chesapeake, VA	5.4
36	Chicago, IL	16.1
229	Chico, CA	3.5
344	Chino, CA	1.2

RANK	CITY	RATE
310	Chula Vista, CA	1.8
35	Cincinnati, OH	16.5
386	Citrus Heights, CA	0.0
336	Clarkstown, NY	1.3
52	Clarksville, TN	13.2
268	Clearwater, FL	2.8
25	Cleveland, OH	20.0
386	Clifton, NJ	0.0
361	Clinton Twnshp, MI	1.0
354	Clovis, CA	1.1
229	College Station, TX	3.5
386	Colonie, NY	0.0
216	Colorado Springs, CO	3.7
259	Columbia, MO	2.9
82	Columbia, SC	10.2
130	Columbus, GA	7.0
72	Columbus, OH	10.9
7	Compton, CA	38.4
314	Concord, CA	1.7
321	Coral Springs, FL	1.6
167	Corona, CA	5.2
196	Corpus Christi, TX	4.2
372	Costa Mesa, CA	0.9
280	Cranston, RI	2.5
54	Dallas, TX	12.9
361	Daly City, CA	1.0
280	Danbury, CT	2.5
252	Davenport, IA	3.0
191	Davie, FL	4.4
15	Dayton, OH	25.5
229	Dearborn, MI	3.5
204	Decatur, IL	4.0
321	Denton, TX	1.6
138	Denver, CO	6.4
252	Des Moines, IA	3.0
6	Detroit, MI	40.2
216	Downey, CA	3.7
222	Duluth, MN	3.6
96	Durham, NC	9.2
361	Edison Twnshp, NJ	1.0
280	Edmond, OK	2.5
292	El Cajon, CA	2.2
280	El Monte, CA	2.5
305	El Paso, TX	1.9
268	Elgin, IL	2.8
204	Elizabeth, NJ	4.0
268	Elk Grove, CA	2.8
209	Erie, PA	3.9
259	Escondido, CA	2.9
380	Eugene, OR	0.7
276	Evansville, IN	2.6
302	Everett, WA	2.0
150	Fairfield, CA	5.7
191	Fall River, MA	4.4
297	Fargo, ND	2.1
336	Farmington Hills, MI	1.3
272	Fayetteville, AR	2.7
62	Fayetteville, NC	12.1
146	Federal Way, WA	5.9
10	Flint, MI	32.2
244	Fontana, CA	3.2
334	Fort Collins, CO	1.4
127	Fort Lauderdale, FL	7.1
229	Fort Smith, AR	3.5
123	Fort Wayne, IN	7.2
141	Fort Worth, TX	6.1
361	Fremont, CA	1.0
99	Fresno, CA	8.7
310	Frisco, TX	1.8

RANK	CITY	RATE
328	Fullerton, CA	1.5
276	Gainesville, FL	2.6
222	Garden Grove, CA	3.6
244	Garland, TX	3.2
2	Gary, IN	51.5
314	Gilbert, AZ	1.7
127	Glendale, AZ	7.1
328	Glendale, CA	1.5
196	Grand Prairie, TX	4.2
183	Grand Rapids, MI	4.7
354	Greece, NY	1.1
244	Greeley, CO	3.2
361	Green Bay, WI	1.0
94	Greensboro, NC	9.5
386	Gresham, OR	0.0
386	Hamilton Twnshp, NJ	0.0
41	Hammond, IN	14.5
117	Hampton, VA	7.5
13	Hartford, CT	26.6
183	Hawthorne, CA	4.7
174	Hayward, CA	4.9
328	Henderson, NV	1.5
235	Hesperia, CA	3.4
213	Hialeah, FL	3.8
259	High Point, NC	2.9
199	Hillsboro, OR	4.1
174	Hollywood, FL	4.9
328	Honolulu, HI	1.5
55	Houston, TX	12.6
385	Huntington Beach, CA	0.5
121	Huntsville, AL	7.3
280	Independence, MO	2.5
59	Indianapolis, IN	12.3
153	Indio, CA	5.6
17	Inglewood, CA	24.0
334	Irvine, CA	1.4
302	Irving, TX	2.0
61	Jacksonville, FL	12.2
78	Jacksonville, NC	10.3
21	Jackson, MS	21.4
68	Jersey City, NJ	11.6
111	Joliet, IL	7.9
16	Kansas City, KS	24.6
22	Kansas City, MO	20.6
199	Kenosha, WI	4.1
344	Kent, WA	1.2
199	Killeen, TX	4.1
66	Knoxville, TN	11.8
141	Lafayette, LA	6.1
386	Lake Forest, CA	0.0
165	Lakeland, FL	5.3
336	Lakewood, CA	1.3
222	Lakewood, CO	3.6
135	Lancaster, CA	6.7
87	Lansing, MI	9.7
117	Laredo, TX	7.5
195	Las Cruces, NM	4.3
107	Las Vegas, NV	8.1
386	Lawrence, KS	0.0
84	Lawton, OK	10.0
344	Lee's Summit, MO	1.2
259	Lewisville, TX	2.9
191	Lexington, KY	4.4
321	Lincoln, NE	1.6
32	Little Rock, AR	16.8
216	Livermore, CA	3.7
243	Livonia, MI	3.3
103	Long Beach, CA	8.6
354	Longmont, CO	1.1

RANK	CITY	RATE
44	Longview, TX	14.2
107	Los Angeles, CA	8.1
86	Louisville, KY	9.8
148	Lubbock, TX	5.8
191	Lynn, MA	4.4
27	Macon, GA	19.5
314	Madison, WI	1.7
310	Manchester, NH	1.8
252	McAllen, TX	3.0
386	McKinney, TX	0.0
114	Melbourne, FL	7.7
26	Memphis, TN	19.8
97	Merced, CA	8.9
252	Mesa, AZ	3.0
213	Mesquite, TX	3.8
105	Miami Beach, FL	8.3
20	Miami Gardens, FL	21.7
45	Miami, FL	14.1
268	Midland, TX	2.8
64	Milwaukee, WI	11.9
183	Minneapolis, MN	4.7
136	Miramar, FL	6.5
386	Mission Viejo, CA	0.0
336	Missouri City, TX	1.3
87	Mobile, AL	9.7
78	Modesto, CA	10.3
39	Montgomery, AL	15.3
252	Moreno Valley, CA	3.0
183	Murfreesboro, TN	4.7
386	Murrieta, CA	0.0
386	Nampa, ID	0.0
386	Naperville, IL	0.0
344	Nashua, NH	1.2
55	Nashville, TN	12.6
87	New Bedford, MA	9.7
87	New Haven, CT	9.7
1	New Orleans, LA	51.7
153	New York, NY	5.6
11	Newark, NJ	28.7
386	Newport Beach, CA	0.0
344	Newton, MA	1.2
41	Norfolk, VA	14.5
386	Norman, OK	0.0
76	North Charleston, SC	10.4
121	North Las Vegas, NV	7.3
55	Norwalk, CA	12.6
344	Norwalk, CT	1.2
14	Oakland, CA	25.7
289	Oceanside, CA	2.3
171	Odessa, TX	5.0
344	O'Fallon, MO	1.2
180	Ogden, UT	4.8
67	Oklahoma City, OK	11.7
386	Olathe, KS	0.0
132	Omaha, NE	6.8
259	Ontario, CA	2.9
328	Orange, CA	1.5
354	Orem, UT	1.1
64	Orlando, FL	11.9
314	Overland Park, KS	1.7
131	Oxnard, CA	6.9
180	Palm Bay, FL	4.8
158	Palmdale, CA	5.5
229	Pasadena, CA	3.5
161	Pasadena, TX	5.4
78	Paterson, NJ	10.3
354	Pearland, TX	1.1
272	Pembroke Pines, FL	2.7

RANK	CITY	RATE
174	Peoria, AZ	4.9
47	Peoria, IL	14.0
27	Philadelphia, PA	19.5
115	Phoenix, AZ	7.6
58	Pittsburgh, PA	12.5
328	Plano, TX	1.5
222	Plantation, FL	3.6
71	Pomona, CA	11.1
111	Pompano Beach, FL	7.9
382	Port St. Lucie, FL	0.6
235	Portland, OR	3.4
32	Portsmouth, VA	16.8
50	Providence, RI	13.4
377	Provo, UT	0.8
59	Pueblo, CO	12.3
167	Quincy, MA	5.2
222	Racine, WI	3.6
235	Raleigh, NC	3.4
336	Ramapo, NY	1.3
382	Rancho Cucamon., CA	0.6
40	Reading, PA	14.9
292	Redding, CA	2.2
199	Reno, NV	4.1
144	Rialto, CA	6.0
386	Richardson, TX	0.0
3	Richmond, CA	45.8
30	Richmond, VA	18.2
344	Rio Rancho, NM	1.2
171	Riverside, CA	5.0
87	Roanoke, VA	9.7
361	Rochester, MN	1.0
48	Rochester, NY	13.6
51	Rockford, IL	13.3
314	Roseville, CA	1.7
150	Roswell, GA	5.7
372	Round Rock, TX	0.9
138	Sacramento, CA	6.4
244	Salem, OR	3.2
24	Salinas, CA	20.2
314	Salt Lake City, UT	1.7
99	San Angelo, TX	8.7
123	San Antonio, TX	7.2
37	San Bernardino, CA	16.0
250	San Diego, CA	3.1
153	San Francisco, CA	5.6
259	San Jose, CA	2.9
276	San Leandro, CA	2.6
288	San Marcos, CA	2.4
292	San Mateo, CA	2.2
174	Sandy Springs, GA	4.9
297	Sandy, UT	2.1
120	Santa Ana, CA	7.4
229	Santa Barbara, CA	3.5
161	Santa Clara, CA	5.4
259	Santa Clarita, CA	2.9
150	Santa Maria, CA	5.7
235	Santa Monica, CA	3.4
336	Santa Rosa, CA	1.3
45	Savannah, GA	14.1
196	Scottsdale, AZ	4.2
216	Seattle, WA	3.7
38	Shreveport, LA	15.5
321	Simi Valley, CA	1.6
222	Sioux City, IA	3.6
382	Sioux Falls, SD	0.6
204	Somerville, MA	4.0
49	South Bend, IN	13.5
78	South Gate, CA	10.3

RANK	CITY	RATE
272	Southfield, MI	2.7
158	Sparks, NV	5.5
344	Spokane Valley, WA	1.2
235	Spokane, WA	3.4
82	Springfield, IL	10.2
76	Springfield, MA	10.4
213	Springfield, MO	3.8
314	Stamford, CT	1.7
321	Sterling Heights, MI	1.6
69	Stockton, CA	11.3
386	St. George, UT	0.0
209	St. Joseph, MO	3.9
5	St. Louis, MO	40.3
187	St. Paul, MN	4.6
188	St. Petersburg, FL	4.5
127	Suffolk, VA	7.1
386	Sugar Land, TX	0.0
377	Sunnyvale, CA	0.8
188	Sunrise, FL	4.5
361	Surprise, AZ	1.0
53	Syracuse, NY	13.1
204	Tacoma, WA	4.0
235	Tallahassee, FL	3.4
148	Tampa, FL	5.8
361	Temecula, CA	1.0
354	Tempe, AZ	1.1
372	Thornton, CO	0.9
321	Thousand Oaks, CA	1.6
69	Toledo, OH	11.3
297	Toms River Twnshp, NJ	2.1
107	Topeka, KS	8.1
380	Torrance, CA	0.7
141	Tracy, CA	6.1
22	Trenton, NJ	20.6
386	Troy, MI	0.0
138	Tucson, AZ	6.4
31	Tulsa, OK	17.7
158	Tuscaloosa, AL	5.5
252	Tyler, TX	3.0
336	Upper Darby Twnshp, PA	1.3
354	Vacaville, CA	1.1
99	Vallejo, CA	8.7
222	Vancouver, WA	3.6
180	Ventura, CA	4.8
104	Victorville, CA	8.5
199	Virginia Beach, VA	4.1
123	Visalia, CA	7.2
386	Vista, CA	0.0
123	Waco, TX	7.2
252	Warren, MI	3.0
386	Warwick, RI	0.0
18	Washington, DC	23.8
153	Waterbury, CT	5.6
115	West Covina, CA	7.6
216	West Jordan, UT	3.7
29	West Palm Beach, FL	18.9
244	West Valley, UT	3.2
276	Westland, MI	2.6
386	Westminster, CA	0.0
305	Westminster, CO	1.9
216	Whittier, CA	3.7
72	Wichita Falls, TX	10.9
132	Wichita, KS	6.8
209	Wilmington, NC	3.9
136	Winston-Salem, NC	6.5
361	Woodbridge Twnshp, NJ	1.0
209	Worcester, MA	3.9
204	Yonkers, NY	4.0
292	Yuma, AZ	2.2

Source: CQ Press using reported data from the F.B.I. "Crime in the United States 2009"
*Includes nonnegligent manslaughter.

50. Murder Rate in 2009 (continued)
National Rate = 5.0 Murders per 100,000 Population*

RANK	CITY	RATE
1	New Orleans, LA	51.7
2	Gary, IN	51.5
3	Richmond, CA	45.8
4	Camden, NJ	43.0
5	St. Louis, MO	40.3
6	Detroit, MI	40.2
7	Compton, CA	38.4
8	Baltimore, MD	37.3
9	Baton Rouge, LA	33.6
10	Flint, MI	32.2
11	Newark, NJ	28.7
12	Birmingham, AL	28.6
13	Hartford, CT	26.6
14	Oakland, CA	25.7
15	Dayton, OH	25.5
16	Kansas City, KS	24.6
17	Inglewood, CA	24.0
18	Washington, DC	23.8
19	Buffalo, NY	22.3
20	Miami Gardens, FL	21.7
21	Jackson, MS	21.4
22	Kansas City, MO	20.6
22	Trenton, NJ	20.6
24	Salinas, CA	20.2
25	Cleveland, OH	20.0
26	Memphis, TN	19.8
27	Macon, GA	19.5
27	Philadelphia, PA	19.5
29	West Palm Beach, FL	18.9
30	Richmond, VA	18.2
31	Tulsa, OK	17.7
32	Little Rock, AR	16.8
32	Portsmouth, VA	16.8
34	Canton, OH	16.6
35	Cincinnati, OH	16.5
36	Chicago, IL	16.1
37	San Bernardino, CA	16.0
38	Shreveport, LA	15.5
39	Montgomery, AL	15.3
40	Reading, PA	14.9
41	Atlanta, GA	14.5
41	Hammond, IN	14.5
41	Norfolk, VA	14.5
44	Longview, TX	14.2
45	Miami, FL	14.1
45	Savannah, GA	14.1
47	Peoria, IL	14.0
48	Rochester, NY	13.6
49	South Bend, IN	13.5
50	Providence, RI	13.4
51	Rockford, IL	13.3
52	Clarksville, TN	13.2
53	Syracuse, NY	13.1
54	Dallas, TX	12.9
55	Houston, TX	12.6
55	Nashville, TN	12.6
55	Norwalk, CA	12.6
58	Pittsburgh, PA	12.5
59	Indianapolis, IN	12.3
59	Pueblo, CO	12.3
61	Jacksonville, FL	12.2
62	Allentown, PA	12.1
62	Fayetteville, NC	12.1
64	Milwaukee, WI	11.9
64	Orlando, FL	11.9
66	Knoxville, TN	11.8
67	Oklahoma City, OK	11.7
68	Jersey City, NJ	11.6

RANK	CITY	RATE
69	Stockton, CA	11.3
69	Toledo, OH	11.3
71	Pomona, CA	11.1
72	Columbus, OH	10.9
72	Wichita Falls, TX	10.9
74	Albany, GA	10.6
74	Albuquerque, NM	10.6
76	North Charleston, SC	10.4
76	Springfield, MA	10.4
78	Jacksonville, NC	10.3
78	Modesto, CA	10.3
78	Paterson, NJ	10.3
78	South Gate, CA	10.3
82	Columbia, SC	10.2
82	Springfield, IL	10.2
84	Lawton, OK	10.0
85	Chattanooga, TN	9.9
86	Louisville, KY	9.8
87	Akron, OH	9.7
87	Lansing, MI	9.7
87	Mobile, AL	9.7
87	New Bedford, MA	9.7
87	New Haven, CT	9.7
87	Roanoke, VA	9.7
93	Albany, NY	9.6
94	Greensboro, NC	9.5
95	Brockton, MA	9.3
96	Durham, NC	9.2
97	Merced, CA	8.9
98	Bridgeport, CT	8.8
99	Athens-Clarke, GA	8.7
99	Fresno, CA	8.7
99	San Angelo, TX	8.7
99	Vallejo, CA	8.7
103	Long Beach, CA	8.6
104	Victorville, CA	8.5
105	Miami Beach, FL	8.3
106	Bakersfield, CA	8.2
107	Las Vegas, NV	8.1
107	Los Angeles, CA	8.1
107	Topeka, KS	8.1
110	Boston, MA	8.0
111	Charleston, SC	7.9
111	Joliet, IL	7.9
111	Pompano Beach, FL	7.9
114	Melbourne, FL	7.7
115	Phoenix, AZ	7.6
115	West Covina, CA	7.6
117	Charlotte, NC	7.5
117	Hampton, VA	7.5
117	Laredo, TX	7.5
120	Santa Ana, CA	7.4
121	Huntsville, AL	7.3
121	North Las Vegas, NV	7.3
123	Fort Wayne, IN	7.2
123	San Antonio, TX	7.2
123	Visalia, CA	7.2
123	Waco, TX	7.2
127	Fort Lauderdale, FL	7.1
127	Glendale, AZ	7.1
127	Suffolk, VA	7.1
130	Columbus, GA	7.0
131	Oxnard, CA	6.9
132	Aurora, CO	6.8
132	Omaha, NE	6.8
132	Wichita, KS	6.8
135	Lancaster, CA	6.7
136	Miramar, FL	6.5
136	Winston-Salem, NC	6.5

RANK	CITY	RATE
138	Denver, CO	6.4
138	Sacramento, CA	6.4
138	Tucson, AZ	6.4
141	Fort Worth, TX	6.1
141	Lafayette, LA	6.1
141	Tracy, CA	6.1
144	Abilene, TX	6.0
144	Rialto, CA	6.0
146	Berkeley, CA	5.9
146	Federal Way, WA	5.9
148	Lubbock, TX	5.8
148	Tampa, FL	5.8
150	Fairfield, CA	5.7
150	Roswell, GA	5.7
150	Santa Maria, CA	5.7
153	Avondale, AZ	5.6
153	Indio, CA	5.6
153	New York, NY	5.6
153	San Francisco, CA	5.6
153	Waterbury, CT	5.6
158	Palmdale, CA	5.5
158	Sparks, NV	5.5
158	Tuscaloosa, AL	5.5
161	Carson, CA	5.4
161	Chesapeake, VA	5.4
161	Pasadena, TX	5.4
161	Santa Clara, CA	5.4
165	Amarillo, TX	5.3
165	Lakeland, FL	5.3
167	Baldwin Park, CA	5.2
167	Corona, CA	5.2
167	Quincy, MA	5.2
170	Carlsbad, CA	5.1
171	Boulder, CO	5.0
171	Odessa, TX	5.0
171	Riverside, CA	5.0
174	Anchorage, AK	4.9
174	Antioch, CA	4.9
174	Hayward, CA	4.9
174	Hollywood, FL	4.9
174	Peoria, AZ	4.9
174	Sandy Springs, GA	4.9
180	Ogden, UT	4.8
180	Palm Bay, FL	4.8
180	Ventura, CA	4.8
183	Grand Rapids, MI	4.7
183	Hawthorne, CA	4.7
183	Minneapolis, MN	4.7
183	Murfreesboro, TN	4.7
187	St. Paul, MN	4.6
188	Beaumont, TX	4.5
188	St. Petersburg, FL	4.5
188	Sunrise, FL	4.5
191	Davie, FL	4.4
191	Fall River, MA	4.4
191	Lexington, KY	4.4
191	Lynn, MA	4.4
195	Las Cruces, NM	4.3
196	Corpus Christi, TX	4.2
196	Grand Prairie, TX	4.2
196	Scottsdale, AZ	4.2
199	Hillsboro, OR	4.1
199	Kenosha, WI	4.1
199	Killeen, TX	4.1
199	Reno, NV	4.1
199	Virginia Beach, VA	4.1
204	Decatur, IL	4.0
204	Elizabeth, NJ	4.0
204	Somerville, MA	4.0

RANK	CITY	RATE
204	Tacoma, WA	4.0
204	Yonkers, NY	4.0
209	Erie, PA	3.9
209	St. Joseph, MO	3.9
209	Wilmington, NC	3.9
209	Worcester, MA	3.9
213	Hialeah, FL	3.8
213	Mesquite, TX	3.8
213	Springfield, MO	3.8
216	Colorado Springs, CO	3.7
216	Downey, CA	3.7
216	Livermore, CA	3.7
216	Seattle, WA	3.7
216	West Jordan, UT	3.7
216	Whittier, CA	3.7
222	Duluth, MN	3.6
222	Garden Grove, CA	3.6
222	Lakewood, CO	3.6
222	Plantation, FL	3.6
222	Racine, WI	3.6
222	Sioux City, IA	3.6
222	Vancouver, WA	3.6
229	Chico, CA	3.5
229	College Station, TX	3.5
229	Dearborn, MI	3.5
229	Fort Smith, AR	3.5
229	Pasadena, CA	3.5
229	Santa Barbara, CA	3.5
235	Alexandria, VA	3.4
235	Boise, ID	3.4
235	Hesperia, CA	3.4
235	Portland, OR	3.4
235	Raleigh, NC	3.4
235	Santa Monica, CA	3.4
235	Spokane, WA	3.4
235	Tallahassee, FL	3.4
243	Livonia, MI	3.3
244	Arlington, TX	3.2
244	Fontana, CA	3.2
244	Garland, TX	3.2
244	Greeley, CO	3.2
244	Salem, OR	3.2
244	West Valley, UT	3.2
250	Carrollton, TX	3.1
250	San Diego, CA	3.1
252	Davenport, IA	3.0
252	Des Moines, IA	3.0
252	McAllen, TX	3.0
252	Mesa, AZ	3.0
252	Moreno Valley, CA	3.0
252	Tyler, TX	3.0
252	Warren, MI	3.0
259	Aurora, IL	2.9
259	Austin, TX	2.9
259	Columbia, MO	2.9
259	Escondido, CA	2.9
259	High Point, NC	2.9
259	Lewisville, TX	2.9
259	Ontario, CA	2.9
259	San Jose, CA	2.9
259	Santa Clarita, CA	2.9
268	Clearwater, FL	2.8
268	Elgin, IL	2.8
268	Elk Grove, CA	2.8
268	Midland, TX	2.8
272	Anaheim, CA	2.7
272	Fayetteville, AR	2.7
272	Pembroke Pines, FL	2.7

RANK	CITY	RATE
272	Southfield, MI	2.7
276	Evansville, IN	2.6
276	Gainesville, FL	2.6
276	San Leandro, CA	2.6
276	Westland, MI	2.6
280	Bellingham, WA	2.5
280	Bloomington, MN	2.5
280	Buena Park, CA	2.5
280	Cranston, RI	2.5
280	Danbury, CT	2.5
280	Edmond, OK	2.5
280	El Monte, CA	2.5
280	Independence, MO	2.5
288	San Marcos, CA	2.4
289	Allen, TX	2.3
289	Boca Raton, FL	2.3
289	Oceanside, CA	2.3
292	Brownsville, TX	2.2
292	El Cajon, CA	2.2
292	Redding, CA	2.2
292	San Mateo, CA	2.2
292	Yuma, AZ	2.2
297	Beaverton, OR	2.1
297	Broken Arrow, OK	2.1
297	Fargo, ND	2.1
297	Sandy, UT	2.1
297	Toms River Twnshp, NJ	2.1
302	Chandler, AZ	2.0
302	Everett, WA	2.0
302	Irving, TX	2.0
305	Arvada, CO	1.9
305	Billings, MT	1.9
305	Cambridge, MA	1.9
305	El Paso, TX	1.9
305	Westminster, CO	1.9
310	Cape Coral, FL	1.8
310	Chula Vista, CA	1.8
310	Frisco, TX	1.8
310	Manchester, NH	1.8
314	Concord, CA	1.7
314	Gilbert, AZ	1.7
314	Madison, WI	1.7
314	Overland Park, KS	1.7
314	Roseville, CA	1.7
314	Salt Lake City, UT	1.7
314	Stamford, CT	1.7
321	Bellevue, WA	1.6
321	Coral Springs, FL	1.6
321	Denton, TX	1.6
321	Lincoln, NE	1.6
321	Simi Valley, CA	1.6
321	Sterling Heights, MI	1.6
321	Thousand Oaks, CA	1.6
328	Fullerton, CA	1.5
328	Glendale, CA	1.5
328	Henderson, NV	1.5
328	Honolulu, HI	1.5
328	Orange, CA	1.5
328	Plano, TX	1.5
334	Fort Collins, CO	1.4
334	Irvine, CA	1.4
336	Brick Twnshp, NJ	1.3
336	Clarkstown, NY	1.3
336	Farmington Hills, MI	1.3
336	Lakewood, CA	1.3
336	Missouri City, TX	1.3
336	Ramapo, NY	1.3
336	Santa Rosa, CA	1.3

RANK	CITY	RATE
336	Upper Darby Twnshp, PA	1.3
344	Canton Twnshp, MI	1.2
344	Chino, CA	1.2
344	Kent, WA	1.2
344	Lee's Summit, MO	1.2
344	Nashua, NH	1.2
344	Newton, MA	1.2
344	Norwalk, CT	1.2
344	O'Fallon, MO	1.2
344	Rio Rancho, NM	1.2
344	Spokane Valley, WA	1.2
354	Clovis, CA	1.1
354	Greece, NY	1.1
354	Longmont, CO	1.1
354	Orem, UT	1.1
354	Pearland, TX	1.1
354	Tempe, AZ	1.1
354	Vacaville, CA	1.1
361	Burbank, CA	1.0
361	Centennial, CO	1.0
361	Clinton Twnshp, MI	1.0
361	Daly City, CA	1.0
361	Edison Twnshp, NJ	1.0
361	Fremont, CA	1.0
361	Green Bay, WI	1.0
361	Rochester, MN	1.0
361	Surprise, AZ	1.0
361	Temecula, CA	1.0
361	Woodbridge Twnshp, NJ	1.0
372	Amherst, NY	0.9
372	Ann Arbor, MI	0.9
372	Costa Mesa, CA	0.9
372	Round Rock, TX	0.9
372	Thornton, CO	0.9
377	Cedar Rapids, IA	0.8
377	Provo, UT	0.8
377	Sunnyvale, CA	0.8
380	Eugene, OR	0.7
380	Torrance, CA	0.7
382	Port St. Lucie, FL	0.6
382	Rancho Cucamon., CA	0.6
382	Sioux Falls, SD	0.6
385	Huntington Beach, CA	0.5
386	Alhambra, CA	0.0
386	Bend, OR	0.0
386	Cary, NC	0.0
386	Cheektowaga, NY	0.0
386	Citrus Heights, CA	0.0
386	Clifton, NJ	0.0
386	Colonie, NY	0.0
386	Gresham, OR	0.0
386	Hamilton Twnshp, NJ	0.0
386	Lake Forest, CA	0.0
386	Lawrence, KS	0.0
386	McKinney, TX	0.0
386	Mission Viejo, CA	0.0
386	Murrieta, CA	0.0
386	Nampa, ID	0.0
386	Naperville, IL	0.0
386	Newport Beach, CA	0.0
386	Norman, OK	0.0
386	Olathe, KS	0.0
386	Richardson, TX	0.0
386	St. George, UT	0.0
386	Sugar Land, TX	0.0
386	Troy, MI	0.0
386	Vista, CA	0.0
386	Warwick, RI	0.0
386	Westminster, CA	0.0

Source: CQ Press using reported data from the F.B.I. "Crime in the United States 2009"

*Includes nonnegligent manslaughter.

51. Percent Change in Murder Rate: 2008 to 2009
National Percent Change = 8.1% Decrease*

RANK	CITY	% CHANGE
114	Abilene, TX	0.0
89	Akron, OH	18.3
NA	Albany, GA**	NA
114	Albany, NY	0.0
64	Albuquerque, NM	47.2
52	Alexandria, VA	61.9
343	Alhambra, CA	(100.0)
207	Allentown, PA	(18.8)
43	Allen, TX	91.7
221	Amarillo, TX	(23.2)
NA	Amherst, NY***	NA
205	Anaheim, CA	(18.2)
70	Anchorage, AK	36.1
NA	Ann Arbor, MI**	NA
263	Antioch, CA	(38.0)
291	Arlington, TX	(47.5)
26	Arvada, CO	111.1
4	Athens-Clarke, GA	383.3
233	Atlanta, GA	(26.4)
85	Aurora, CO	19.3
14	Aurora, IL	163.6
172	Austin, TX	(6.5)
319	Avondale, AZ	(60.3)
105	Bakersfield, CA	6.5
298	Baldwin Park, CA	(49.5)
111	Baltimore, MD	1.1
98	Baton Rouge, LA	13.9
243	Beaumont, TX	(29.7)
NA	Beaverton, OR***	NA
NA	Bellevue, WA***	NA
114	Bellingham, WA	0.0
114	Bend, OR	0.0
229	Berkeley, CA	(25.3)
114	Billings, MT	0.0
212	Birmingham, AL	(20.3)
28	Bloomington, MN	108.3
43	Boca Raton, FL	91.7
1	Boise, ID	580.0
216	Boston, MA	(22.3)
NA	Boulder, CO***	NA
NA	Brick Twnshp, NJ***	NA
267	Bridgeport, CT	(40.1)
NA	Brockton, MA**	NA
309	Broken Arrow, OK	(51.2)
168	Brownsville, TX	(4.3)
114	Buena Park, CA	0.0
51	Buffalo, NY	62.8
289	Burbank, CA	(47.4)
171	Cambridge, MA	(5.0)
265	Camden, NJ	(39.4)
NA	Canton Twnshp, MI**	NA
53	Canton, OH	61.2
317	Cape Coral, FL	(58.1)
15	Carlsbad, CA	155.0
164	Carrollton, TX	(3.1)
261	Carson, CA	(37.2)
343	Cary, NC	(100.0)
324	Cedar Rapids, IA	(66.7)
114	Centennial, CO	0.0
203	Chandler, AZ	(16.7)
260	Charleston, SC	(36.8)
249	Charlotte, NC	(31.2)
200	Chattanooga, TN	(15.4)
114	Cheektowaga, NY	0.0
114	Chesapeake, VA	0.0
183	Chicago, IL	(10.6)
65	Chico, CA	45.8
299	Chino, CA	(50.0)
252	Chula Vista, CA	(33.3)
223	Cincinnati, OH	(24.7)
343	Citrus Heights, CA	(100.0)
NA	Clarkstown, NY***	NA
13	Clarksville, TN	169.4
334	Clearwater, FL	(73.3)
197	Cleveland, OH	(14.9)
343	Clifton, NJ	(100.0)
NA	Clinton Twnshp, MI**	NA
292	Clovis, CA	(47.6)
7	College Station, TX	191.7
114	Colonie, NY	0.0
275	Colorado Springs, CO	(41.3)
270	Columbia, MO	(40.8)
160	Columbia, SC	(1.9)
315	Columbus, GA	(56.5)
225	Columbus, OH	(24.8)
77	Compton, CA	29.7
323	Concord, CA	(66.0)
299	Coral Springs, FL	(50.0)
29	Corona, CA	100.0
257	Corpus Christi, TX	(36.4)
114	Costa Mesa, CA	0.0
41	Cranston, RI	92.3
163	Dallas, TX	(3.0)
114	Daly City, CA	0.0
41	Danbury, CT	92.3
307	Davenport, IA	(50.8)
29	Davie, FL	100.0
106	Dayton, OH	6.3
NA	Dearborn, MI**	NA
NA	Decatur, IL**	NA
NA	Denton, TX***	NA
169	Denver, CO	(4.5)
NA	Des Moines, IA**	NA
NA	Detroit, MI**	NA
75	Downey, CA	32.1
60	Duluth, MN	50.0
196	Durham, NC	(14.8)
114	Edison Twnshp, NJ	0.0
NA	Edmond, OK***	NA
29	El Cajon, CA	100.0
337	El Monte, CA	(74.5)
250	El Paso, TX	(32.1)
63	Elgin, IL	47.4
322	Elizabeth, NJ	(61.5)
NA	Elk Grove, CA***	NA
276	Erie, PA	(41.8)
114	Escondido, CA	0.0
286	Eugene, OR	(46.2)
266	Evansville, IN	(39.5)
29	Everett, WA	100.0
87	Fairfield, CA	18.7
73	Fall River, MA	33.3
NA	Fargo, ND***	NA
NA	Farmington Hills, MI**	NA
40	Fayetteville, AR	92.9
180	Fayetteville, NC	(9.7)
261	Federal Way, WA	(37.2)
NA	Flint, MI**	NA
297	Fontana, CA	(49.2)
173	Fort Collins, CO	(6.7)
270	Fort Lauderdale, FL	(40.8)
65	Fort Smith, AR	45.8
240	Fort Wayne, IN	(28.0)
191	Fort Worth, TX	(12.9)
114	Fremont, CA	0.0
109	Fresno, CA	3.6
46	Frisco, TX	80.0
114	Fullerton, CA	0.0
114	Gainesville, FL	0.0
29	Garden Grove, CA	100.0
245	Garland, TX	(30.4)
113	Gary, IN	0.6
NA	Gilbert, AZ***	NA
103	Glendale, AZ	7.6
114	Glendale, CA	0.0
162	Grand Prairie, TX	(2.3)
NA	Grand Rapids, MI**	NA
114	Greece, NY	0.0
234	Greeley, CO	(27.3)
299	Green Bay, WI	(50.0)
157	Greensboro, NC	(1.0)
343	Gresham, OR	(100.0)
343	Hamilton Twnshp, NJ	(100.0)
194	Hammond, IN	(14.7)
69	Hampton, VA	36.4
104	Hartford, CT	6.8
114	Hawthorne, CA	0.0
161	Hayward, CA	(2.0)
226	Henderson, NV	(25.0)
114	Hesperia, CA	0.0
114	Hialeah, FL	0.0
333	High Point, NC	(73.1)
NA	Hillsboro, OR***	NA
287	Hollywood, FL	(46.7)
226	Honolulu, HI	(25.0)
166	Houston, TX	(3.8)
330	Huntington Beach, CA	(68.8)
244	Huntsville, AL	(29.8)
331	Independence, MO	(69.5)
190	Indianapolis, IN	(12.8)
16	Indio, CA	154.5
27	Inglewood, CA	108.7
10	Irvine, CA	180.0
279	Irving, TX	(42.9)
194	Jacksonville, FL	(14.7)
56	Jacksonville, NC	56.1
269	Jackson, MS	(40.7)
100	Jersey City, NJ	12.6
22	Joliet, IL	139.4
NA	Kansas City, KS**	NA
210	Kansas City, MO	(19.2)
74	Kenosha, WI	32.3
299	Kent, WA	(50.0)
312	Killeen, TX	(52.3)
217	Knoxville, TN	(22.4)
247	Lafayette, LA	(30.7)
343	Lake Forest, CA	(100.0)
308	Lakeland, FL	(50.9)
295	Lakewood, CA	(48.0)
3	Lakewood, CO	414.3
159	Lancaster, CA	(1.5)
NA	Lansing, MI**	NA
48	Laredo, TX	66.7
114	Las Cruces, NM	0.0
179	Las Vegas, NV	(9.0)
343	Lawrence, KS	(100.0)
59	Lawton, OK	51.5
299	Lee's Summit, MO	(50.0)
8	Lewisville, TX	190.0
NA	Lexington, KY**	NA
114	Lincoln, NE	0.0
NA	Little Rock, AR**	NA
6	Livermore, CA	208.3
NA	Livonia, MI**	NA
114	Long Beach, CA	0.0
NA	Longmont, CO**	NA

RANK	CITY	% CHANGE
81	Longview, TX	22.4
208	Los Angeles, CA	(19.0)
NA	Louisville, KY**	NA
54	Lubbock, TX	61.1
255	Lynn, MA	(34.3)
170	Macon, GA	(4.9)
320	Madison, WI	(60.5)
114	Manchester, NH	0.0
315	McAllen, TX	(56.5)
343	McKinney, TX	(100.0)
230	Melbourne, FL	(26.0)
165	Memphis, TN	(3.4)
257	Merced, CA	(36.4)
193	Mesa, AZ	(14.3)
50	Mesquite, TX	65.2
93	Miami Beach, FL	15.3
101	Miami Gardens, FL	12.4
167	Miami, FL	(4.1)
232	Midland, TX	(26.3)
112	Milwaukee, WI	0.8
311	Minneapolis, MN	(52.0)
67	Miramar, FL	44.4
114	Mission Viejo, CA	0.0
338	Missouri City, TX	(75.0)
277	Mobile, AL	(41.9)
88	Modesto, CA	18.4
71	Montgomery, AL	35.4
273	Moreno Valley, CA	(41.2)
212	Murfreesboro, TN	(20.3)
343	Murrieta, CA	(100.0)
114	Nampa, ID	0.0
343	Naperville, IL	(100.0)
NA	Nashua, NH**	NA
114	Nashville, TN	0.0
23	New Bedford, MA	120.5
NA	New Haven, CT**	NA
206	New Orleans, LA	(18.7)
185	New York, NY	(11.1)
84	Newark, NJ	20.1
114	Newport Beach, CA	0.0
NA	Newton, MA***	NA
82	Norfolk, VA	21.8
343	Norman, OK	(100.0)
248	North Charleston, SC	(31.1)
58	North Las Vegas, NV	52.1
24	Norwalk, CA	117.2
299	Norwalk, CT	(50.0)
181	Oakland, CA	(10.1)
215	Oceanside, CA	(20.7)
246	Odessa, TX	(30.6)
328	O'Fallon, MO	(68.4)
114	Ogden, UT	0.0
99	Oklahoma City, OK	13.6
NA	Olathe, KS**	NA
251	Omaha, NE	(32.7)
114	Ontario, CA	0.0
25	Orange, CA	114.3
292	Orem, UT	(47.6)
257	Orlando, FL	(36.4)
9	Overland Park, KS	183.3
177	Oxnard, CA	(8.0)
80	Palm Bay, FL	23.1
55	Palmdale, CA	57.1
48	Pasadena, CA	66.7
240	Pasadena, TX	(28.0)
187	Paterson, NJ	(12.0)
178	Pearland, TX	(8.3)
78	Pembroke Pines, FL	28.6

RANK	CITY	% CHANGE
175	Peoria, AZ	(7.5)
NA	Peoria, IL**	NA
198	Philadelphia, PA	(15.2)
236	Phoenix, AZ	(27.6)
285	Pittsburgh, PA	(46.1)
278	Plano, TX	(42.3)
226	Plantation, FL	(25.0)
199	Pomona, CA	(15.3)
182	Pompano Beach, FL	(10.2)
328	Port St. Lucie, FL	(68.4)
237	Portland, OR	(27.7)
97	Portsmouth, VA	14.3
45	Providence, RI	91.4
NA	Provo, UT***	NA
NA	Pueblo, CO**	NA
19	Quincy, MA	147.6
332	Racine, WI	(70.5)
321	Raleigh, NC	(60.9)
114	Ramapo, NY	0.0
282	Rancho Cucamon., CA	(45.5)
83	Reading, PA	20.2
252	Redding, CA	(33.3)
268	Reno, NV	(40.6)
284	Rialto, CA	(45.9)
343	Richardson, TX	(100.0)
47	Richmond, CA	72.2
91	Richmond, VA	17.4
176	Rio Rancho, NM	(7.7)
214	Riverside, CA	(20.6)
210	Roanoke, VA	(19.2)
338	Rochester, MN	(75.0)
254	Rochester, NY	(33.7)
108	Rockford, IL	4.7
NA	Roseville, CA***	NA
2	Roswell, GA	418.2
NA	Round Rock, TX***	NA
264	Sacramento, CA	(39.0)
283	Salem, OR	(45.8)
92	Salinas, CA	16.1
335	Salt Lake City, UT	(74.2)
76	San Angelo, TX	31.8
202	San Antonio, TX	(16.3)
114	San Bernardino, CA	0.0
239	San Diego, CA	(27.9)
313	San Francisco, CA	(54.5)
188	San Jose, CA	(12.1)
29	San Leandro, CA	100.0
29	San Marcos, CA	100.0
29	San Mateo, CA	100.0
NA	Sandy Springs, GA***	NA
NA	Sandy, UT***	NA
201	Santa Ana, CA	(15.9)
57	Santa Barbara, CA	52.2
60	Santa Clara, CA	50.0
21	Santa Clarita, CA	141.7
281	Santa Maria, CA	(45.2)
231	Santa Monica, CA	(26.1)
338	Santa Rosa, CA	(75.0)
96	Savannah, GA	14.6
29	Scottsdale, AZ	100.0
219	Seattle, WA	(22.9)
94	Shreveport, LA	14.8
310	Simi Valley, CA	(51.5)
272	Sioux City, IA	(41.0)
341	Sioux Falls, SD	(81.3)
62	Somerville, MA	48.1
174	South Bend, IN	(6.9)
18	South Gate, CA	151.2

RANK	CITY	% CHANGE
NA	Southfield, MI**	NA
NA	Sparks, NV***	NA
114	Spokane Valley, WA	0.0
294	Spokane, WA	(47.7)
NA	Springfield, IL**	NA
102	Springfield, MA	11.8
256	Springfield, MO	(34.5)
318	Stamford, CT	(59.5)
NA	Sterling Heights, MI**	NA
68	Stockton, CA	37.8
343	St. George, UT	(100.0)
114	St. Joseph, MO	0.0
192	St. Louis, MO	(14.1)
242	St. Paul, MN	(29.2)
280	St. Petersburg, FL	(45.1)
89	Suffolk, VA	18.3
114	Sugar Land, TX	0.0
287	Sunnyvale, CA	(46.7)
5	Sunrise, FL	309.1
NA	Surprise, AZ***	NA
223	Syracuse, NY	(24.7)
289	Tacoma, WA	(47.4)
237	Tallahassee, FL	(27.7)
235	Tampa, FL	(27.5)
324	Temecula, CA	(66.7)
327	Tempe, AZ	(67.6)
336	Thornton, CO	(74.3)
114	Thousand Oaks, CA	0.0
39	Toledo, OH	98.2
114	Toms River Twnshp, NJ	0.0
158	Topeka, KS	(1.2)
299	Torrance, CA	(50.0)
NA	Tracy, CA***	NA
184	Trenton, NJ	(10.8)
NA	Troy, MI**	NA
295	Tucson, AZ	(48.0)
72	Tulsa, OK	35.1
314	Tuscaloosa, AL	(54.9)
273	Tyler, TX	(41.2)
342	Upper Darby Twnshp, PA	(85.4)
114	Vacaville, CA	0.0
220	Vallejo, CA	(23.0)
NA	Vancouver, WA***	NA
17	Ventura, CA	152.6
20	Victorville, CA	142.9
79	Virginia Beach, VA	28.1
189	Visalia, CA	(12.2)
343	Vista, CA	(100.0)
209	Waco, TX	(19.1)
NA	Warren, MI**	NA
114	Warwick, RI	0.0
222	Washington, DC	(24.2)
86	Waterbury, CT	19.1
12	West Covina, CA	171.4
NA	West Jordan, UT***	NA
107	West Palm Beach, FL	5.6
29	West Valley, UT	100.0
NA	Westland, MI**	NA
343	Westminster, CA	(100.0)
114	Westminster, CO	0.0
110	Whittier, CA	2.8
11	Wichita Falls, TX	179.5
204	Wichita, KS	(18.1)
326	Wilmington, NC	(67.2)
218	Winston-Salem, NC	(22.6)
114	Woodbridge Twnshp, NJ	0.0
95	Worcester, MA	14.7
185	Yonkers, NY	(11.1)
299	Yuma, AZ	(50.0)

Source: CQ Press using reported data from the F.B.I. "Crime in the United States 2009"
*Includes nonnegligent manslaughter. **Not available. ***These cities had murder rates of 0 in 2008 but had at least one murder in 2009. Calculating percent increase from zero results in an infinite number. These are shown as "NA."

51. Percent Change in Murder Rate: 2008 to 2009 (continued)
National Percent Change = 8.1% Decrease*

RANK	CITY	% CHANGE
1	Boise, ID	580.0
2	Roswell, GA	418.2
3	Lakewood, CO	414.3
4	Athens-Clarke, GA	383.3
5	Sunrise, FL	309.1
6	Livermore, CA	208.3
7	College Station, TX	191.7
8	Lewisville, TX	190.0
9	Overland Park, KS	183.3
10	Irvine, CA	180.0
11	Wichita Falls, TX	179.5
12	West Covina, CA	171.4
13	Clarksville, TN	169.4
14	Aurora, IL	163.6
15	Carlsbad, CA	155.0
16	Indio, CA	154.5
17	Ventura, CA	152.6
18	South Gate, CA	151.2
19	Quincy, MA	147.6
20	Victorville, CA	142.9
21	Santa Clarita, CA	141.7
22	Joliet, IL	139.4
23	New Bedford, MA	120.5
24	Norwalk, CA	117.2
25	Orange, CA	114.3
26	Arvada, CO	111.1
27	Inglewood, CA	108.7
28	Bloomington, MN	108.3
29	Corona, CA	100.0
29	Davie, FL	100.0
29	El Cajon, CA	100.0
29	Everett, WA	100.0
29	Garden Grove, CA	100.0
29	San Leandro, CA	100.0
29	San Marcos, CA	100.0
29	San Mateo, CA	100.0
29	Scottsdale, AZ	100.0
29	West Valley, UT	100.0
39	Toledo, OH	98.2
40	Fayetteville, AR	92.9
41	Cranston, RI	92.3
41	Danbury, CT	92.3
43	Allen, TX	91.7
43	Boca Raton, FL	91.7
45	Providence, RI	91.4
46	Frisco, TX	80.0
47	Richmond, CA	72.2
48	Laredo, TX	66.7
48	Pasadena, CA	66.7
50	Mesquite, TX	65.2
51	Buffalo, NY	62.8
52	Alexandria, VA	61.9
53	Canton, OH	61.2
54	Lubbock, TX	61.1
55	Palmdale, CA	57.1
56	Jacksonville, NC	56.1
57	Santa Barbara, CA	52.2
58	North Las Vegas, NV	52.1
59	Lawton, OK	51.5
60	Duluth, MN	50.0
60	Santa Clara, CA	50.0
62	Somerville, MA	48.1
63	Elgin, IL	47.4
64	Albuquerque, NM	47.2
65	Chico, CA	45.8
65	Fort Smith, AR	45.8
67	Miramar, FL	44.4
68	Stockton, CA	37.8
69	Hampton, VA	36.4
70	Anchorage, AK	36.1
71	Montgomery, AL	35.4
72	Tulsa, OK	35.1
73	Fall River, MA	33.3
74	Kenosha, WI	32.3
75	Downey, CA	32.1
76	San Angelo, TX	31.8
77	Compton, CA	29.7
78	Pembroke Pines, FL	28.6
79	Virginia Beach, VA	28.1
80	Palm Bay, FL	23.1
81	Longview, TX	22.4
82	Norfolk, VA	21.8
83	Reading, PA	20.2
84	Newark, NJ	20.1
85	Aurora, CO	19.3
86	Waterbury, CT	19.1
87	Fairfield, CA	18.7
88	Modesto, CA	18.4
89	Akron, OH	18.3
89	Suffolk, VA	18.3
91	Richmond, VA	17.4
92	Salinas, CA	16.1
93	Miami Beach, FL	15.3
94	Shreveport, LA	14.8
95	Worcester, MA	14.7
96	Savannah, GA	14.6
97	Portsmouth, VA	14.3
98	Baton Rouge, LA	13.9
99	Oklahoma City, OK	13.6
100	Jersey City, NJ	12.6
101	Miami Gardens, FL	12.4
102	Springfield, MA	11.8
103	Glendale, AZ	7.6
104	Hartford, CT	6.8
105	Bakersfield, CA	6.5
106	Dayton, OH	6.3
107	West Palm Beach, FL	5.6
108	Rockford, IL	4.7
109	Fresno, CA	3.6
110	Whittier, CA	2.8
111	Baltimore, MD	1.1
112	Milwaukee, WI	0.8
113	Gary, IN	0.6
114	Abilene, TX	0.0
114	Albany, NY	0.0
114	Bellingham, WA	0.0
114	Bend, OR	0.0
114	Billings, MT	0.0
114	Buena Park, CA	0.0
114	Centennial, CO	0.0
114	Cheektowaga, NY	0.0
114	Chesapeake, VA	0.0
114	Colonie, NY	0.0
114	Costa Mesa, CA	0.0
114	Daly City, CA	0.0
114	Edison Twnshp, NJ	0.0
114	Escondido, CA	0.0
114	Fremont, CA	0.0
114	Fullerton, CA	0.0
114	Gainesville, FL	0.0
114	Glendale, CA	0.0
114	Greece, NY	0.0
114	Hawthorne, CA	0.0
114	Hesperia, CA	0.0
114	Hialeah, FL	0.0
114	Las Cruces, NM	0.0
114	Lincoln, NE	0.0
114	Long Beach, CA	0.0
114	Manchester, NH	0.0
114	Mission Viejo, CA	0.0
114	Nampa, ID	0.0
114	Nashville, TN	0.0
114	Newport Beach, CA	0.0
114	Ogden, UT	0.0
114	Ontario, CA	0.0
114	Ramapo, NY	0.0
114	San Bernardino, CA	0.0
114	Spokane Valley, WA	0.0
114	St. Joseph, MO	0.0
114	Sugar Land, TX	0.0
114	Thousand Oaks, CA	0.0
114	Toms River Twnshp, NJ	0.0
114	Vacaville, CA	0.0
114	Warwick, RI	0.0
114	Westminster, CO	0.0
114	Woodbridge Twnshp, NJ	0.0
157	Greensboro, NC	(1.0)
158	Topeka, KS	(1.2)
159	Lancaster, CA	(1.5)
160	Columbia, SC	(1.9)
161	Hayward, CA	(2.0)
162	Grand Prairie, TX	(2.3)
163	Dallas, TX	(3.0)
164	Carrollton, TX	(3.1)
165	Memphis, TN	(3.4)
166	Houston, TX	(3.8)
167	Miami, FL	(4.1)
168	Brownsville, TX	(4.3)
169	Denver, CO	(4.5)
170	Macon, GA	(4.9)
171	Cambridge, MA	(5.0)
172	Austin, TX	(6.5)
173	Fort Collins, CO	(6.7)
174	South Bend, IN	(6.9)
175	Peoria, AZ	(7.5)
176	Rio Rancho, NM	(7.7)
177	Oxnard, CA	(8.0)
178	Pearland, TX	(8.3)
179	Las Vegas, NV	(9.0)
180	Fayetteville, NC	(9.7)
181	Oakland, CA	(10.1)
182	Pompano Beach, FL	(10.2)
183	Chicago, IL	(10.6)
184	Trenton, NJ	(10.8)
185	New York, NY	(11.1)
185	Yonkers, NY	(11.1)
187	Paterson, NJ	(12.0)
188	San Jose, CA	(12.1)
189	Visalia, CA	(12.2)
190	Indianapolis, IN	(12.8)
191	Fort Worth, TX	(12.9)
192	St. Louis, MO	(14.1)
193	Mesa, AZ	(14.3)
194	Hammond, IN	(14.7)
194	Jacksonville, FL	(14.7)
196	Durham, NC	(14.8)
197	Cleveland, OH	(14.9)
198	Philadelphia, PA	(15.2)
199	Pomona, CA	(15.3)
200	Chattanooga, TN	(15.4)
201	Santa Ana, CA	(15.9)
202	San Antonio, TX	(16.3)
203	Chandler, AZ	(16.7)
204	Wichita, KS	(18.1)
205	Anaheim, CA	(18.2)
206	New Orleans, LA	(18.7)

RANK	CITY	% CHANGE
207	Allentown, PA	(18.8)
208	Los Angeles, CA	(19.0)
209	Waco, TX	(19.1)
210	Kansas City, MO	(19.2)
210	Roanoke, VA	(19.2)
212	Birmingham, AL	(20.3)
212	Murfreesboro, TN	(20.3)
214	Riverside, CA	(20.6)
215	Oceanside, CA	(20.7)
216	Boston, MA	(22.3)
217	Knoxville, TN	(22.4)
218	Winston-Salem, NC	(22.6)
219	Seattle, WA	(22.9)
220	Vallejo, CA	(23.0)
221	Amarillo, TX	(23.2)
222	Washington, DC	(24.2)
223	Cincinnati, OH	(24.7)
223	Syracuse, NY	(24.7)
225	Columbus, OH	(24.8)
226	Henderson, NV	(25.0)
226	Honolulu, HI	(25.0)
226	Plantation, FL	(25.0)
229	Berkeley, CA	(25.3)
230	Melbourne, FL	(26.0)
231	Santa Monica, CA	(26.1)
232	Midland, TX	(26.3)
233	Atlanta, GA	(26.4)
234	Greeley, CO	(27.3)
235	Tampa, FL	(27.5)
236	Phoenix, AZ	(27.6)
237	Portland, OR	(27.7)
237	Tallahassee, FL	(27.7)
239	San Diego, CA	(27.9)
240	Fort Wayne, IN	(28.0)
240	Pasadena, TX	(28.0)
242	St. Paul, MN	(29.2)
243	Beaumont, TX	(29.7)
244	Huntsville, AL	(29.8)
245	Garland, TX	(30.4)
246	Odessa, TX	(30.6)
247	Lafayette, LA	(30.7)
248	North Charleston, SC	(31.1)
249	Charlotte, NC	(31.2)
250	El Paso, TX	(32.1)
251	Omaha, NE	(32.7)
252	Chula Vista, CA	(33.3)
252	Redding, CA	(33.3)
254	Rochester, NY	(33.7)
255	Lynn, MA	(34.3)
256	Springfield, MO	(34.5)
257	Corpus Christi, TX	(36.4)
257	Merced, CA	(36.4)
257	Orlando, FL	(36.4)
260	Charleston, SC	(36.8)
261	Carson, CA	(37.2)
261	Federal Way, WA	(37.2)
263	Antioch, CA	(38.0)
264	Sacramento, CA	(39.0)
265	Camden, NJ	(39.4)
266	Evansville, IN	(39.5)
267	Bridgeport, CT	(40.1)
268	Reno, NV	(40.6)
269	Jackson, MS	(40.7)
270	Columbia, MO	(40.8)
270	Fort Lauderdale, FL	(40.8)
272	Sioux City, IA	(41.0)
273	Moreno Valley, CA	(41.2)
273	Tyler, TX	(41.2)

RANK	CITY	% CHANGE
275	Colorado Springs, CO	(41.3)
276	Erie, PA	(41.8)
277	Mobile, AL	(41.9)
278	Plano, TX	(42.3)
279	Irving, TX	(42.9)
280	St. Petersburg, FL	(45.1)
281	Santa Maria, CA	(45.2)
282	Rancho Cucamon., CA	(45.5)
283	Salem, OR	(45.8)
284	Rialto, CA	(45.9)
285	Pittsburgh, PA	(46.1)
286	Eugene, OR	(46.2)
287	Hollywood, FL	(46.7)
287	Sunnyvale, CA	(46.7)
289	Burbank, CA	(47.4)
289	Tacoma, WA	(47.4)
291	Arlington, TX	(47.5)
292	Clovis, CA	(47.6)
292	Orem, UT	(47.6)
294	Spokane, WA	(47.7)
295	Lakewood, CA	(48.0)
295	Tucson, AZ	(48.0)
297	Fontana, CA	(49.2)
298	Baldwin Park, CA	(49.5)
299	Chino, CA	(50.0)
299	Coral Springs, FL	(50.0)
299	Green Bay, WI	(50.0)
299	Kent, WA	(50.0)
299	Lee's Summit, MO	(50.0)
299	Norwalk, CT	(50.0)
299	Torrance, CA	(50.0)
299	Yuma, AZ	(50.0)
307	Davenport, IA	(50.8)
308	Lakeland, FL	(50.9)
309	Broken Arrow, OK	(51.2)
310	Simi Valley, CA	(51.5)
311	Minneapolis, MN	(52.0)
312	Killeen, TX	(52.3)
313	San Francisco, CA	(54.5)
314	Tuscaloosa, AL	(54.9)
315	Columbus, GA	(56.5)
315	McAllen, TX	(56.5)
317	Cape Coral, FL	(58.1)
318	Stamford, CT	(59.5)
319	Avondale, AZ	(60.3)
320	Madison, WI	(60.5)
321	Raleigh, NC	(60.9)
322	Elizabeth, NJ	(61.5)
323	Concord, CA	(66.0)
324	Cedar Rapids, IA	(66.7)
324	Temecula, CA	(66.7)
326	Wilmington, NC	(67.2)
327	Tempe, AZ	(67.6)
328	O'Fallon, MO	(68.4)
328	Port St. Lucie, FL	(68.4)
330	Huntington Beach, CA	(68.8)
331	Independence, MO	(69.5)
332	Racine, WI	(70.5)
333	High Point, NC	(73.1)
334	Clearwater, FL	(73.3)
335	Salt Lake City, UT	(74.2)
336	Thornton, CO	(74.3)
337	El Monte, CA	(74.5)
338	Missouri City, TX	(75.0)
338	Rochester, MN	(75.0)
338	Santa Rosa, CA	(75.0)
341	Sioux Falls, SD	(81.3)
342	Upper Darby Twnshp, PA	(85.4)

RANK	CITY	% CHANGE
343	Alhambra, CA	(100.0)
343	Cary, NC	(100.0)
343	Citrus Heights, CA	(100.0)
343	Clifton, NJ	(100.0)
343	Gresham, OR	(100.0)
343	Hamilton Twnshp, NJ	(100.0)
343	Lake Forest, CA	(100.0)
343	Lawrence, KS	(100.0)
343	McKinney, TX	(100.0)
343	Murrieta, CA	(100.0)
343	Naperville, IL	(100.0)
343	Norman, OK	(100.0)
343	Richardson, TX	(100.0)
343	St. George, UT	(100.0)
343	Vista, CA	(100.0)
343	Westminster, CA	(100.0)
NA	Albany, GA**	NA
NA	Amherst, NY***	NA
NA	Ann Arbor, MI**	NA
NA	Beaverton, OR***	NA
NA	Bellevue, WA***	NA
NA	Boulder, CO***	NA
NA	Brick Twnshp, NJ***	NA
NA	Brockton, MA**	NA
NA	Canton Twnshp, MI**	NA
NA	Clarkstown, NY***	NA
NA	Clinton Twnshp, MI**	NA
NA	Dearborn, MI**	NA
NA	Decatur, IL**	NA
NA	Denton, TX***	NA
NA	Des Moines, IA**	NA
NA	Detroit, MI**	NA
NA	Edmond, OK***	NA
NA	Elk Grove, CA***	NA
NA	Fargo, ND***	NA
NA	Farmington Hills, MI**	NA
NA	Flint, MI**	NA
NA	Gilbert, AZ***	NA
NA	Grand Rapids, MI**	NA
NA	Hillsboro, OR***	NA
NA	Kansas City, KS**	NA
NA	Lansing, MI**	NA
NA	Lexington, KY**	NA
NA	Little Rock, AR**	NA
NA	Livonia, MI**	NA
NA	Longmont, CO**	NA
NA	Louisville, KY**	NA
NA	Nashua, NH**	NA
NA	New Haven, CT**	NA
NA	Newton, MA***	NA
NA	Olathe, KS**	NA
NA	Peoria, IL**	NA
NA	Provo, UT***	NA
NA	Pueblo, CO**	NA
NA	Roseville, CA***	NA
NA	Round Rock, TX***	NA
NA	Sandy Springs, GA***	NA
NA	Sandy, UT***	NA
NA	Southfield, MI**	NA
NA	Sparks, NV***	NA
NA	Springfield, IL**	NA
NA	Sterling Heights, MI**	NA
NA	Surprise, AZ***	NA
NA	Tracy, CA***	NA
NA	Troy, MI**	NA
NA	Vancouver, WA***	NA
NA	Warren, MI**	NA
NA	West Jordan, UT***	NA
NA	Westland, MI**	NA

Source: CQ Press using reported data from the F.B.I. "Crime in the United States 2009"

*Includes nonnegligent manslaughter. **Not available. ***These cities had murder rates of 0 in 2008 but had at least one murder in 2009. Calculating percent increase from zero results in an infinite number. These are shown as "NA."

52. Percent Change in Murder Rate: 2005 to 2009
National Percent Change = 12.1% Decrease*

RANK	CITY	% CHANGE
56	Abilene, TX	39.5
195	Akron, OH	(23.6)
99	Albany, GA	3.9
81	Albany, NY	12.9
130	Albuquerque, NM	(1.9)
49	Alexandria, VA	47.8
335	Alhambra, CA	(100.0)
240	Allentown, PA	(38.3)
NA	Allen, TX***	NA
130	Amarillo, TX	(1.9)
107	Amherst, NY	0.0
149	Anaheim, CA	(10.0)
165	Anchorage, AK	(15.5)
NA	Ann Arbor, MI**	NA
281	Antioch, CA	(50.0)
287	Arlington, TX	(51.5)
107	Arvada, CO	0.0
34	Athens-Clarke, GA	85.1
215	Atlanta, GA	(30.6)
213	Aurora, CO	(28.4)
314	Aurora, IL	(65.5)
196	Austin, TX	(23.7)
NA	Avondale, AZ**	NA
207	Bakersfield, CA	(26.8)
174	Baldwin Park, CA	(17.5)
151	Baltimore, MD	(11.2)
45	Baton Rouge, LA	54.1
290	Beaumont, TX	(53.1)
37	Beaverton, OR	75.0
138	Bellevue, WA	(5.9)
244	Bellingham, WA	(39.0)
335	Bend, OR	(100.0)
22	Berkeley, CA	103.4
309	Billings, MT	(62.7)
229	Birmingham, AL	(35.4)
NA	Bloomington, MN**	NA
NA	Boca Raton, FL***	NA
62	Boise, ID	30.8
239	Boston, MA	(38.0)
NA	Boulder, CO***	NA
NA	Brick Twnshp, NJ***	NA
228	Bridgeport, CT	(35.3)
154	Brockton, MA	(12.3)
NA	Broken Arrow, OK***	NA
143	Brownsville, TX	(8.3)
107	Buena Park, CA	0.0
83	Buffalo, NY	12.6
315	Burbank, CA	(65.5)
234	Cambridge, MA	(36.7)
98	Camden, NJ	4.4
NA	Canton Twnshp, MI**	NA
6	Canton, OH	232.0
289	Cape Coral, FL	(52.6)
17	Carlsbad, CA	131.8
204	Carrollton, TX	(26.2)
208	Carson, CA	(27.0)
107	Cary, NC	0.0
107	Cedar Rapids, IA	0.0
317	Centennial, CO	(66.7)
259	Chandler, AZ	(42.9)
167	Charleston, SC	(16.0)
250	Charlotte, NC	(40.5)
219	Chattanooga, TN	(32.7)
107	Cheektowaga, NY	0.0
166	Chesapeake, VA	(15.6)
100	Chicago, IL	3.2
170	Chico, CA	(16.7)
294	Chino, CA	(53.8)

RANK	CITY	% CHANGE
201	Chula Vista, CA	(25.0)
226	Cincinnati, OH	(34.3)
NA	Citrus Heights, CA**	NA
NA	Clarkstown, NY**	NA
8	Clarksville, TN	193.3
313	Clearwater, FL	(65.4)
168	Cleveland, OH	(16.0)
335	Clifton, NJ	(100.0)
NA	Clinton Twnshp, MI**	NA
325	Clovis, CA	(77.1)
63	College Station, TX	29.6
107	Colonie, NY	0.0
75	Colorado Springs, CO	15.6
311	Columbia, MO	(62.8)
178	Columbia, SC	(19.7)
248	Columbus, GA	(40.2)
188	Columbus, OH	(22.1)
258	Compton, CA	(42.8)
20	Concord, CA	112.5
NA	Coral Springs, FL***	NA
28	Corona, CA	92.6
47	Corpus Christi, TX	50.0
317	Costa Mesa, CA	(66.7)
NA	Cranston, RI***	NA
184	Dallas, TX	(21.3)
281	Daly City, CA	(50.0)
29	Danbury, CT	92.3
302	Davenport, IA	(57.7)
35	Davie, FL	83.3
66	Dayton, OH	27.5
NA	Dearborn, MI**	NA
NA	Decatur, IL**	NA
320	Denton, TX	(68.0)
245	Denver, CO	(39.0)
NA	Des Moines, IA**	NA
NA	Detroit, MI**	NA
253	Downey, CA	(41.3)
NA	Duluth, MN**	NA
271	Durham, NC	(46.2)
NA	Edison Twnshp, NJ***	NA
36	Edmond, OK	78.6
97	El Cajon, CA	4.8
199	El Monte, CA	(24.2)
173	El Paso, TX	(17.4)
NA	Elgin, IL**	NA
322	Elizabeth, NJ	(70.6)
NA	Elk Grove, CA**	NA
220	Erie, PA	(32.8)
27	Escondido, CA	93.3
330	Eugene, OR	(80.0)
306	Evansville, IN	(61.8)
230	Everett, WA	(35.5)
224	Fairfield, CA	(33.7)
NA	Fall River, MA**	NA
135	Fargo, ND	(4.5)
NA	Farmington Hills, MI**	NA
157	Fayetteville, AR	(12.9)
88	Fayetteville, NC	10.0
176	Federal Way, WA	(19.2)
NA	Flint, MI**	NA
278	Fontana, CA	(49.2)
155	Fort Collins, CO	(12.5)
181	Fort Lauderdale, FL	(20.2)
257	Fort Smith, AR	(42.6)
233	Fort Wayne, IN	(36.3)
238	Fort Worth, TX	(37.8)
24	Fremont, CA	100.0
175	Fresno, CA	(17.9)
84	Frisco, TX	12.5

RANK	CITY	% CHANGE
NA	Fullerton, CA***	NA
255	Gainesville, FL	(42.2)
107	Garden Grove, CA	0.0
107	Garland, TX	0.0
152	Gary, IN	(11.2)
NA	Gilbert, AZ***	NA
147	Glendale, AZ	(9.0)
333	Glendale, CA	(84.0)
223	Grand Prairie, TX	(33.3)
NA	Grand Rapids, MI**	NA
273	Greece, NY	(47.6)
57	Greeley, CO	39.1
329	Green Bay, WI	(79.6)
203	Greensboro, NC	(25.2)
335	Gresham, OR	(100.0)
335	Hamilton Twnshp, NJ	(100.0)
64	Hammond, IN	29.5
105	Hampton, VA	1.4
60	Hartford, CT	33.0
304	Hawthorne, CA	(59.1)
194	Hayward, CA	(23.4)
305	Henderson, NV	(61.5)
236	Hesperia, CA	(37.0)
89	Hialeah, FL	8.6
316	High Point, NC	(65.9)
39	Hillsboro, OR	70.8
70	Hollywood, FL	19.5
153	Honolulu, HI	(11.8)
192	Houston, TX	(22.7)
107	Huntington Beach, CA	0.0
265	Huntsville, AL	(45.1)
293	Independence, MO	(53.7)
145	Indianapolis, IN	(8.9)
249	Indio, CA	(40.4)
91	Inglewood, CA	7.1
67	Irvine, CA	27.3
24	Irving, TX	100.0
92	Jacksonville, FL	7.0
NA	Jacksonville, NC***	NA
104	Jackson, MS	1.4
209	Jersey City, NJ	(27.0)
140	Joliet, IL	(7.1)
134	Kansas City, KS	(3.2)
206	Kansas City, MO	(26.7)
65	Kenosha, WI	28.1
317	Kent, WA	(66.7)
280	Killeen, TX	(49.4)
163	Knoxville, TN	(15.1)
161	Lafayette, LA	(14.1)
335	Lake Forest, CA	(100.0)
179	Lakeland, FL	(19.7)
NA	Lakewood, CA***	NA
101	Lakewood, CO	2.9
270	Lancaster, CA	(45.5)
NA	Lansing, MI**	NA
159	Laredo, TX	(13.8)
216	Las Cruces, NM	(30.6)
212	Las Vegas, NV	(28.3)
335	Lawrence, KS	(100.0)
50	Lawton, OK	47.1
141	Lee's Summit, MO	(7.7)
61	Lewisville, TX	31.8
NA	Lexington, KY**	NA
138	Lincoln, NE	(5.9)
NA	Little Rock, AR**	NA
9	Livermore, CA	184.6
NA	Livonia, MI**	NA
133	Long Beach, CA	(2.3)
NA	Longmont, CO**	NA

RANK	CITY	% CHANGE
59	Longview, TX	35.2
231	Los Angeles, CA	(35.7)
NA	Louisville, KY**	NA
86	Lubbock, TX	11.5
185	Lynn, MA	(21.4)
136	Macon, GA	(4.9)
31	Madison, WI	88.9
281	Manchester, NH	(50.0)
294	McAllen, TX	(53.8)
335	McKinney, TX	(100.0)
2	Melbourne, FL	492.3
132	Memphis, TN	(2.0)
227	Merced, CA	(35.0)
290	Mesa, AZ	(53.1)
211	Mesquite, TX	(28.3)
13	Miami Beach, FL	151.5
23	Miami Gardens, FL	102.8
103	Miami, FL	1.4
10	Midland, TX	180.0
256	Milwaukee, WI	(42.2)
308	Minneapolis, MN	(62.4)
18	Miramar, FL	124.1
335	Mission Viejo, CA	(100.0)
300	Missouri City, TX	(56.7)
217	Mobile, AL	(30.7)
11	Modesto, CA	171.1
93	Montgomery, AL	7.0
297	Moreno Valley, CA	(54.5)
26	Murfreesboro, TN	95.8
335	Murrieta, CA	(100.0)
NA	Nampa, ID**	NA
335	Naperville, IL	(100.0)
276	Nashua, NH	(47.8)
205	Nashville, TN	(26.3)
79	New Bedford, MA	14.1
NA	New Haven, CT**	NA
NA	New Orleans, LA**	NA
164	New York, NY	(15.2)
171	Newark, NJ	(16.8)
335	Newport Beach, CA	(100.0)
107	Newton, MA	0.0
251	Norfolk, VA	(40.8)
107	Norman, OK	0.0
177	North Charleston, SC	(19.4)
247	North Las Vegas, NV	(40.2)
68	Norwalk, CA	23.5
334	Norwalk, CT	(85.5)
87	Oakland, CA	10.8
267	Oceanside, CA	(45.2)
44	Odessa, TX	56.3
180	O'Fallon, MO	(20.0)
190	Ogden, UT	(22.6)
77	Oklahoma City, OK	14.7
NA	Olathe, KS**	NA
148	Omaha, NE	(9.3)
303	Ontario, CA	(58.6)
107	Orange, CA	0.0
NA	Orem, UT***	NA
80	Orlando, FL	13.3
55	Overland Park, KS	41.7
222	Oxnard, CA	(33.0)
19	Palm Bay, FL	118.2
288	Palmdale, CA	(51.8)
162	Pasadena, CA	(14.6)
42	Pasadena, TX	58.8
187	Paterson, NJ	(22.0)
254	Pearland, TX	(42.1)
218	Pembroke Pines, FL	(30.8)

RANK	CITY	% CHANGE
1	Peoria, AZ	600.0
82	Peoria, IL	12.9
197	Philadelphia, PA	(23.8)
279	Phoenix, AZ	(49.3)
225	Pittsburgh, PA	(34.2)
33	Plano, TX	87.5
186	Plantation, FL	(21.7)
172	Pomona, CA	(17.2)
53	Pompano Beach, FL	43.6
201	Port St. Lucie, FL	(25.0)
142	Portland, OR	(8.1)
193	Portsmouth, VA	(22.9)
72	Providence, RI	18.6
323	Provo, UT	(72.4)
128	Pueblo, CO	(0.8)
16	Quincy, MA	136.4
332	Racine, WI	(81.9)
262	Raleigh, NC	(43.3)
NA	Ramapo, NY***	NA
281	Rancho Cucamon., CA	(50.0)
266	Reading, PA	(45.2)
107	Redding, CA	0.0
96	Reno, NV	5.1
269	Rialto, CA	(45.5)
335	Richardson, TX	(100.0)
73	Richmond, CA	18.0
301	Richmond, VA	(57.7)
324	Rio Rancho, NM	(75.0)
50	Riverside, CA	47.1
261	Roanoke, VA	(43.3)
NA	Rochester, MN***	NA
268	Rochester, NY	(45.4)
90	Rockford, IL	7.3
NA	Roseville, CA***	NA
NA	Roswell, GA***	NA
NA	Round Rock, TX***	NA
263	Sacramento, CA	(43.9)
41	Salem, OR	60.0
4	Salinas, CA	329.8
321	Salt Lake City, UT	(68.5)
12	San Angelo, TX	163.6
95	San Antonio, TX	5.9
264	San Bernardino, CA	(44.8)
189	San Diego, CA	(22.5)
299	San Francisco, CA	(56.3)
107	San Jose, CA	0.0
277	San Leandro, CA	(48.0)
NA	San Marcos, CA***	NA
281	San Mateo, CA	(50.0)
NA	Sandy Springs, GA**	NA
30	Sandy, UT	90.9
46	Santa Ana, CA	51.0
NA	Santa Barbara, CA***	NA
84	Santa Clara, CA	12.5
40	Santa Clarita, CA	61.1
43	Santa Maria, CA	58.3
200	Santa Monica, CA	(24.4)
107	Santa Rosa, CA	0.0
106	Savannah, GA	0.7
14	Scottsdale, AZ	147.1
160	Seattle, WA	(14.0)
183	Shreveport, LA	(20.9)
NA	Simi Valley, CA***	NA
47	Sioux City, IA	50.0
328	Sioux Falls, SD	(79.3)
7	Somerville, MA	207.7
71	South Bend, IN	19.5
38	South Gate, CA	71.7

RANK	CITY	% CHANGE
NA	Southfield, MI**	NA
143	Sparks, NV	(8.3)
107	Spokane Valley, WA	0.0
275	Spokane, WA	(47.7)
15	Springfield, IL	137.2
156	Springfield, MA	(12.6)
76	Springfield, MO	15.2
20	Stamford, CT	112.5
NA	Sterling Heights, MI**	NA
191	Stockton, CA	(22.6)
335	St. George, UT	(100.0)
52	St. Joseph, MO	44.4
94	St. Louis, MO	6.3
272	St. Paul, MN	(46.5)
307	St. Petersburg, FL	(61.9)
243	Suffolk, VA	(38.8)
335	Sugar Land, TX	(100.0)
312	Sunnyvale, CA	(65.2)
5	Sunrise, FL	309.1
237	Surprise, AZ	(37.5)
129	Syracuse, NY	(1.5)
241	Tacoma, WA	(38.5)
246	Tallahassee, FL	(39.3)
137	Tampa, FL	(4.9)
327	Temecula, CA	(79.2)
296	Tempe, AZ	(54.2)
149	Thornton, CO	(10.0)
107	Thousand Oaks, CA	0.0
69	Toledo, OH	22.8
107	Toms River Twnshp, NJ	0.0
54	Topeka, KS	42.1
107	Torrance, CA	0.0
NA	Tracy, CA***	NA
260	Trenton, NJ	(43.1)
NA	Troy, MI**	NA
241	Tucson, AZ	(38.5)
74	Tulsa, OK	18.0
235	Tuscaloosa, AL	(36.8)
297	Tyler, TX	(54.5)
326	Upper Darby Twnshp, PA	(79.0)
273	Vacaville, CA	(47.6)
NA	Vallejo, CA**	NA
214	Vancouver, WA	(29.4)
3	Ventura, CA	380.0
252	Victorville, CA	(41.0)
145	Virginia Beach, VA	(8.9)
198	Visalia, CA	(24.2)
335	Vista, CA	(100.0)
210	Waco, TX	(28.0)
NA	Warren, MI**	NA
335	Warwick, RI	(100.0)
221	Washington, DC	(32.8)
102	Waterbury, CT	1.8
58	West Covina, CA	38.2
NA	West Jordan, UT**	NA
169	West Palm Beach, FL	(16.4)
310	West Valley, UT	(62.8)
NA	Westland, MI**	NA
335	Westminster, CA	(100.0)
107	Westminster, CO	0.0
232	Whittier, CA	(36.2)
32	Wichita Falls, TX	87.9
NA	Wichita, KS**	NA
292	Wilmington, NC	(53.6)
182	Winston-Salem, NC	(20.7)
281	Woodbridge Twnshp, NJ	(50.0)
77	Worcester, MA	14.7
158	Yonkers, NY	(13.0)
331	Yuma, AZ	(81.0)

Source: CQ Press using reported data from the F.B.I. "Crime in the United States 2009"
*Includes nonnegligent manslaughter. **Not available. ***These cities had murder rates of 0 in 2005 but had at least one murder in 2009. Calculating percent increase from zero results in an infinite number. These are shown as "NA."

52. Percent Change in Murder Rate: 2005 to 2009 (continued)
National Percent Change = 12.1% Decrease*

RANK	CITY	% CHANGE
1	Peoria, AZ	600.0
2	Melbourne, FL	492.3
3	Ventura, CA	380.0
4	Salinas, CA	329.8
5	Sunrise, FL	309.1
6	Canton, OH	232.0
7	Somerville, MA	207.7
8	Clarksville, TN	193.3
9	Livermore, CA	184.6
10	Midland, TX	180.0
11	Modesto, CA	171.1
12	San Angelo, TX	163.6
13	Miami Beach, FL	151.5
14	Scottsdale, AZ	147.1
15	Springfield, IL	137.2
16	Quincy, MA	136.4
17	Carlsbad, CA	131.8
18	Miramar, FL	124.1
19	Palm Bay, FL	118.2
20	Concord, CA	112.5
20	Stamford, CT	112.5
22	Berkeley, CA	103.4
23	Miami Gardens, FL	102.8
24	Fremont, CA	100.0
24	Irving, TX	100.0
26	Murfreesboro, TN	95.8
27	Escondido, CA	93.3
28	Corona, CA	92.6
29	Danbury, CT	92.3
30	Sandy, UT	90.9
31	Madison, WI	88.9
32	Wichita Falls, TX	87.9
33	Plano, TX	87.5
34	Athens-Clarke, GA	85.1
35	Davie, FL	83.3
36	Edmond, OK	78.6
37	Beaverton, OR	75.0
38	South Gate, CA	71.7
39	Hillsboro, OR	70.8
40	Santa Clarita, CA	61.1
41	Salem, OR	60.0
42	Pasadena, TX	58.8
43	Santa Maria, CA	58.3
44	Odessa, TX	56.3
45	Baton Rouge, LA	54.1
46	Santa Ana, CA	51.0
47	Corpus Christi, TX	50.0
47	Sioux City, IA	50.0
49	Alexandria, VA	47.8
50	Lawton, OK	47.1
50	Riverside, CA	47.1
52	St. Joseph, MO	44.4
53	Pompano Beach, FL	43.6
54	Topeka, KS	42.1
55	Overland Park, KS	41.7
56	Abilene, TX	39.5
57	Greeley, CO	39.1
58	West Covina, CA	38.2
59	Longview, TX	35.2
60	Hartford, CT	33.0
61	Lewisville, TX	31.8
62	Boise, ID	30.8
63	College Station, TX	29.6
64	Hammond, IN	29.5
65	Kenosha, WI	28.1
66	Dayton, OH	27.5
67	Irvine, CA	27.3
68	Norwalk, CA	23.5
69	Toledo, OH	22.8
70	Hollywood, FL	19.5
71	South Bend, IN	19.5
72	Providence, RI	18.6
73	Richmond, CA	18.0
74	Tulsa, OK	18.0
75	Colorado Springs, CO	15.6
76	Springfield, MO	15.2
77	Oklahoma City, OK	14.7
77	Worcester, MA	14.7
79	New Bedford, MA	14.1
80	Orlando, FL	13.3
81	Albany, NY	12.9
82	Peoria, IL	12.9
83	Buffalo, NY	12.6
84	Frisco, TX	12.5
84	Santa Clara, CA	12.5
86	Lubbock, TX	11.5
87	Oakland, CA	10.8
88	Fayetteville, NC	10.0
89	Hialeah, FL	8.6
90	Rockford, IL	7.3
91	Inglewood, CA	7.1
92	Jacksonville, FL	7.0
93	Montgomery, AL	7.0
94	St. Louis, MO	6.3
95	San Antonio, TX	5.9
96	Reno, NV	5.1
97	El Cajon, CA	4.8
98	Camden, NJ	4.4
99	Albany, GA	3.9
100	Chicago, IL	3.2
101	Lakewood, CO	2.9
102	Waterbury, CT	1.8
103	Miami, FL	1.4
104	Jackson, MS	1.4
105	Hampton, VA	1.4
106	Savannah, GA	0.7
107	Amherst, NY	0.0
107	Arvada, CO	0.0
107	Buena Park, CA	0.0
107	Cary, NC	0.0
107	Cedar Rapids, IA	0.0
107	Cheektowaga, NY	0.0
107	Colonie, NY	0.0
107	Garden Grove, CA	0.0
107	Garland, TX	0.0
107	Huntington Beach, CA	0.0
107	Newton, MA	0.0
107	Norman, OK	0.0
107	Orange, CA	0.0
107	Redding, CA	0.0
107	San Jose, CA	0.0
107	Santa Rosa, CA	0.0
107	Spokane Valley, WA	0.0
107	Thousand Oaks, CA	0.0
107	Toms River Twnshp, NJ	0.0
107	Torrance, CA	0.0
107	Westminster, CO	0.0
128	Pueblo, CO	(0.8)
129	Syracuse, NY	(1.5)
130	Albuquerque, NM	(1.9)
130	Amarillo, TX	(1.9)
132	Memphis, TN	(2.0)
133	Long Beach, CA	(2.3)
134	Kansas City, KS	(3.2)
135	Fargo, ND	(4.5)
136	Macon, GA	(4.9)
137	Tampa, FL	(4.9)
138	Bellevue, WA	(5.9)
138	Lincoln, NE	(5.9)
140	Joliet, IL	(7.1)
141	Lee's Summit, MO	(7.7)
142	Portland, OR	(8.1)
143	Brownsville, TX	(8.3)
143	Sparks, NV	(8.3)
145	Indianapolis, IN	(8.9)
145	Virginia Beach, VA	(8.9)
147	Glendale, AZ	(9.0)
148	Omaha, NE	(9.3)
149	Anaheim, CA	(10.0)
149	Thornton, CO	(10.0)
151	Baltimore, MD	(11.2)
152	Gary, IN	(11.2)
153	Honolulu, HI	(11.8)
154	Brockton, MA	(12.3)
155	Fort Collins, CO	(12.5)
156	Springfield, MA	(12.6)
157	Fayetteville, AR	(12.9)
158	Yonkers, NY	(13.0)
159	Laredo, TX	(13.8)
160	Seattle, WA	(14.0)
161	Lafayette, LA	(14.1)
162	Pasadena, CA	(14.6)
163	Knoxville, TN	(15.1)
164	New York, NY	(15.2)
165	Anchorage, AK	(15.5)
166	Chesapeake, VA	(15.6)
167	Charleston, SC	(16.0)
168	Cleveland, OH	(16.0)
169	West Palm Beach, FL	(16.4)
170	Chico, CA	(16.7)
171	Newark, NJ	(16.8)
172	Pomona, CA	(17.2)
173	El Paso, TX	(17.4)
174	Baldwin Park, CA	(17.5)
175	Fresno, CA	(17.9)
176	Federal Way, WA	(19.2)
177	North Charleston, SC	(19.4)
178	Columbia, SC	(19.7)
179	Lakeland, FL	(19.7)
180	O'Fallon, MO	(20.0)
181	Fort Lauderdale, FL	(20.2)
182	Winston-Salem, NC	(20.7)
183	Shreveport, LA	(20.9)
184	Dallas, TX	(21.3)
185	Lynn, MA	(21.4)
186	Plantation, FL	(21.7)
187	Paterson, NJ	(22.0)
188	Columbus, OH	(22.1)
189	San Diego, CA	(22.5)
190	Ogden, UT	(22.6)
191	Stockton, CA	(22.6)
192	Houston, TX	(22.7)
193	Portsmouth, VA	(22.9)
194	Hayward, CA	(23.4)
195	Akron, OH	(23.6)
196	Austin, TX	(23.7)
197	Philadelphia, PA	(23.8)
198	Visalia, CA	(24.2)
199	El Monte, CA	(24.2)
200	Santa Monica, CA	(24.4)
201	Chula Vista, CA	(25.0)
201	Port St. Lucie, FL	(25.0)
203	Greensboro, NC	(25.2)
204	Carrollton, TX	(26.2)
205	Nashville, TN	(26.3)
206	Kansas City, MO	(26.7)

RANK	CITY	% CHANGE
207	Bakersfield, CA	(26.8)
208	Carson, CA	(27.0)
209	Jersey City, NJ	(27.0)
210	Waco, TX	(28.0)
211	Mesquite, TX	(28.3)
212	Las Vegas, NV	(28.3)
213	Aurora, CO	(28.4)
214	Vancouver, WA	(29.4)
215	Atlanta, GA	(30.6)
216	Las Cruces, NM	(30.6)
217	Mobile, AL	(30.7)
218	Pembroke Pines, FL	(30.8)
219	Chattanooga, TN	(32.7)
220	Erie, PA	(32.8)
221	Washington, DC	(32.8)
222	Oxnard, CA	(33.0)
223	Grand Prairie, TX	(33.3)
224	Fairfield, CA	(33.7)
225	Pittsburgh, PA	(34.2)
226	Cincinnati, OH	(34.3)
227	Merced, CA	(35.0)
228	Bridgeport, CT	(35.3)
229	Birmingham, AL	(35.4)
230	Everett, WA	(35.5)
231	Los Angeles, CA	(35.7)
232	Whittier, CA	(36.2)
233	Fort Wayne, IN	(36.3)
234	Cambridge, MA	(36.7)
235	Tuscaloosa, AL	(36.8)
236	Hesperia, CA	(37.0)
237	Surprise, AZ	(37.5)
238	Fort Worth, TX	(37.8)
239	Boston, MA	(38.0)
240	Allentown, PA	(38.3)
241	Tacoma, WA	(38.5)
241	Tucson, AZ	(38.5)
243	Suffolk, VA	(38.8)
244	Bellingham, WA	(39.0)
245	Denver, CO	(39.0)
246	Tallahassee, FL	(39.3)
247	North Las Vegas, NV	(40.2)
248	Columbus, GA	(40.2)
249	Indio, CA	(40.4)
250	Charlotte, NC	(40.5)
251	Norfolk, VA	(40.8)
252	Victorville, CA	(41.0)
253	Downey, CA	(41.3)
254	Pearland, TX	(42.1)
255	Gainesville, FL	(42.2)
256	Milwaukee, WI	(42.2)
257	Fort Smith, AR	(42.6)
258	Compton, CA	(42.8)
259	Chandler, AZ	(42.9)
260	Trenton, NJ	(43.1)
261	Roanoke, VA	(43.3)
262	Raleigh, NC	(43.3)
263	Sacramento, CA	(43.9)
264	San Bernardino, CA	(44.8)
265	Huntsville, AL	(45.1)
266	Reading, PA	(45.2)
267	Oceanside, CA	(45.2)
268	Rochester, NY	(45.4)
269	Rialto, CA	(45.5)
270	Lancaster, CA	(45.5)
271	Durham, NC	(46.2)
272	St. Paul, MN	(46.5)
273	Greece, NY	(47.6)
273	Vacaville, CA	(47.6)
275	Spokane, WA	(47.7)
276	Nashua, NH	(47.8)
277	San Leandro, CA	(48.0)
278	Fontana, CA	(49.2)
279	Phoenix, AZ	(49.3)
280	Killeen, TX	(49.4)
281	Antioch, CA	(50.0)
281	Daly City, CA	(50.0)
281	Manchester, NH	(50.0)
281	Rancho Cucamon., CA	(50.0)
281	San Mateo, CA	(50.0)
281	Woodbridge Twnshp, NJ	(50.0)
287	Arlington, TX	(51.5)
288	Palmdale, CA	(51.8)
289	Cape Coral, FL	(52.6)
290	Beaumont, TX	(53.1)
290	Mesa, AZ	(53.1)
292	Wilmington, NC	(53.6)
293	Independence, MO	(53.7)
294	Chino, CA	(53.8)
294	McAllen, TX	(53.8)
296	Tempe, AZ	(54.2)
297	Moreno Valley, CA	(54.5)
297	Tyler, TX	(54.5)
299	San Francisco, CA	(56.3)
300	Missouri City, TX	(56.7)
301	Richmond, VA	(57.7)
302	Davenport, IA	(57.7)
303	Ontario, CA	(58.6)
304	Hawthorne, CA	(59.1)
305	Henderson, NV	(61.5)
306	Evansville, IN	(61.8)
307	St. Petersburg, FL	(61.9)
308	Minneapolis, MN	(62.4)
309	Billings, MT	(62.7)
310	West Valley, UT	(62.8)
311	Columbia, MO	(62.8)
312	Sunnyvale, CA	(65.2)
313	Clearwater, FL	(65.4)
314	Aurora, IL	(65.5)
315	Burbank, CA	(65.5)
316	High Point, NC	(65.9)
317	Centennial, CO	(66.7)
317	Costa Mesa, CA	(66.7)
317	Kent, WA	(66.7)
320	Denton, TX	(68.0)
321	Salt Lake City, UT	(68.5)
322	Elizabeth, NJ	(70.6)
323	Provo, UT	(72.4)
324	Rio Rancho, NM	(75.0)
325	Clovis, CA	(77.1)
326	Upper Darby Twnshp, PA	(79.0)
327	Temecula, CA	(79.2)
328	Sioux Falls, SD	(79.3)
329	Green Bay, WI	(79.6)
330	Eugene, OR	(80.0)
331	Yuma, AZ	(81.0)
332	Racine, WI	(81.9)
333	Glendale, CA	(84.0)
334	Norwalk, CT	(85.5)
335	Alhambra, CA	(100.0)
335	Bend, OR	(100.0)
335	Clifton, NJ	(100.0)
335	Gresham, OR	(100.0)
335	Hamilton Twnshp, NJ	(100.0)
335	Lake Forest, CA	(100.0)
335	Lawrence, KS	(100.0)
335	McKinney, TX	(100.0)
335	Mission Viejo, CA	(100.0)
335	Murrieta, CA	(100.0)
335	Naperville, IL	(100.0)
335	Newport Beach, CA	(100.0)
335	Richardson, TX	(100.0)
335	St. George, UT	(100.0)
335	Sugar Land, TX	(100.0)
335	Vista, CA	(100.0)
335	Warwick, RI	(100.0)
335	Westminster, CA	(100.0)
NA	Allen, TX***	NA
NA	Ann Arbor, MI**	NA
NA	Avondale, AZ**	NA
NA	Bloomington, MN**	NA
NA	Boca Raton, FL***	NA
NA	Boulder, CO***	NA
NA	Brick Twnshp, NJ***	NA
NA	Broken Arrow, OK***	NA
NA	Canton Twnshp, MI**	NA
NA	Citrus Heights, CA**	NA
NA	Clarkstown, NY**	NA
NA	Clinton Twnshp, MI**	NA
NA	Coral Springs, FL***	NA
NA	Cranston, RI***	NA
NA	Dearborn, MI**	NA
NA	Decatur, IL**	NA
NA	Des Moines, IA**	NA
NA	Detroit, MI**	NA
NA	Duluth, MN**	NA
NA	Edison Twnshp, NJ***	NA
NA	Elgin, IL**	NA
NA	Elk Grove, CA**	NA
NA	Fall River, MA**	NA
NA	Farmington Hills, MI**	NA
NA	Flint, MI**	NA
NA	Fullerton, CA***	NA
NA	Gilbert, AZ***	NA
NA	Grand Rapids, MI**	NA
NA	Jacksonville, NC***	NA
NA	Lakewood, CA***	NA
NA	Lansing, MI**	NA
NA	Lexington, KY**	NA
NA	Little Rock, AR**	NA
NA	Livonia, MI**	NA
NA	Longmont, CO**	NA
NA	Louisville, KY**	NA
NA	Nampa, ID**	NA
NA	New Haven, CT**	NA
NA	New Orleans, LA**	NA
NA	Olathe, KS**	NA
NA	Orem, UT***	NA
NA	Ramapo, NY***	NA
NA	Rochester, MN***	NA
NA	Roseville, CA***	NA
NA	Roswell, GA***	NA
NA	Round Rock, TX***	NA
NA	San Marcos, CA***	NA
NA	Sandy Springs, GA**	NA
NA	Santa Barbara, CA***	NA
NA	Simi Valley, CA***	NA
NA	Southfield, MI**	NA
NA	Sterling Heights, MI**	NA
NA	Tracy, CA***	NA
NA	Troy, MI**	NA
NA	Vallejo, CA**	NA
NA	Warren, MI**	NA
NA	West Jordan, UT**	NA
NA	Westland, MI**	NA
NA	Wichita, KS**	NA

Source: CQ Press using reported data from the F.B.I. "Crime in the United States 2009"
*Includes nonnegligent manslaughter. **Not available. ***These cities had murder rates of 0 in 2005 but had at least one murder in 2009. Calculating percent increase from zero results in an infinite number. These are shown as "NA."

53. Rapes in 2009
National Total = 88,097 Rapes*

RANK	CITY	RAPES
69	Abilene, TX	114
43	Akron, OH	189
177	Albany, GA	47
167	Albany, NY	49
18	Albuquerque, NM	326
367	Alexandria, VA	12
344	Alhambra, CA	15
111	Allentown, PA	72
353	Allen, TX	14
78	Amarillo, TX	99
386	Amherst, NY	7
111	Anaheim, CA	72
23	Anchorage, AK	282
249	Ann Arbor, MI	29
209	Antioch, CA	40
52	Arlington, TX	152
245	Arvada, CO	30
200	Athens-Clarke, GA	42
57	Atlanta, GA	135
37	Aurora, CO	216
NA	Aurora, IL**	NA
26	Austin, TX	265
294	Avondale, AZ	23
167	Bakersfield, CA	49
382	Baldwin Park, CA	9
50	Baltimore, MD	158
146	Baton Rouge, LA	55
108	Beaumont, TX	73
294	Beaverton, OR	23
280	Bellevue, WA	25
216	Bellingham, WA	37
353	Bend, OR	14
266	Berkeley, CA	27
255	Billings, MT	28
41	Birmingham, AL	198
NA	Bloomington, MN**	NA
287	Boca Raton, FL	24
116	Boise, ID	70
25	Boston, MA	269
234	Boulder, CO	32
385	Brick Twnshp, NJ	8
139	Bridgeport, CT	58
154	Brockton, MA	53
249	Broken Arrow, OK	29
272	Brownsville, TX	26
367	Buena Park, CA	12
56	Buffalo, NY	141
301	Burbank, CA	22
306	Cambridge, MA	21
135	Camden, NJ	60
306	Canton Twnshp, MI	21
122	Canton, OH	67
333	Cape Coral, FL	16
272	Carlsbad, CA	26
333	Carrollton, TX	16
353	Carson, CA	14
367	Cary, NC	12
197	Cedar Rapids, IA	43
306	Centennial, CO	21
183	Chandler, AZ	46
239	Charleston, SC	31
21	Charlotte, NC	303
154	Chattanooga, TN	53
344	Cheektowaga, NY	15
200	Chesapeake, VA	42
NA	Chicago, IL**	NA
200	Chico, CA	42
344	Chino, CA	15

RANK	CITY	RAPES
167	Chula Vista, CA	49
34	Cincinnati, OH	235
272	Citrus Heights, CA	26
397	Clarkstown, NY	3
146	Clarksville, TN	55
197	Clearwater, FL	43
13	Cleveland, OH	373
376	Clifton, NJ	10
287	Clinton Twnshp, MI	24
294	Clovis, CA	23
197	College Station, TX	43
400	Colonie, NY	1
15	Colorado Springs, CO	344
234	Columbia, MO	32
120	Columbia, SC	68
177	Columbus, GA	47
7	Columbus, OH	574
219	Compton, CA	36
320	Concord, CA	19
391	Coral Springs, FL	4
367	Corona, CA	12
38	Corpus Christi, TX	212
266	Costa Mesa, CA	27
311	Cranston, RI	20
9	Dallas, TX	485
326	Daly City, CA	18
280	Danbury, CT	25
177	Davenport, IA	47
306	Davie, FL	21
86	Dayton, OH	91
333	Dearborn, MI	16
NA	Decatur, IL**	NA
113	Denton, TX	71
16	Denver, CO	343
51	Des Moines, IA	153
17	Detroit, MI	335
326	Downey, CA	18
NA	Duluth, MN**	NA
131	Durham, NC	63
391	Edison Twnshp, NJ	4
333	Edmond, OK	16
249	El Cajon, CA	29
353	El Monte, CA	14
44	El Paso, TX	182
NA	Elgin, IL**	NA
192	Elizabeth, NJ	44
344	Elk Grove, CA	15
96	Erie, PA	83
200	Escondido, CA	42
108	Eugene, OR	73
135	Evansville, IN	60
159	Everett, WA	51
294	Fairfield, CA	23
183	Fall River, MA	46
151	Fargo, ND	54
376	Farmington Hills, MI	10
174	Fayetteville, AR	48
84	Fayetteville, NC	94
159	Federal Way, WA	51
86	Flint, MI	91
183	Fontana, CA	46
90	Fort Collins, CO	87
142	Fort Lauderdale, FL	56
132	Fort Smith, AR	62
105	Fort Wayne, IN	75
14	Fort Worth, TX	370
227	Fremont, CA	34
92	Fresno, CA	86
344	Frisco, TX	15

RANK	CITY	RAPES
192	Fullerton, CA	44
83	Gainesville, FL	95
227	Garden Grove, CA	34
151	Garland, TX	54
177	Gary, IN	47
301	Gilbert, AZ	22
151	Glendale, AZ	54
344	Glendale, CA	15
158	Grand Prairie, TX	52
102	Grand Rapids, MI	78
364	Greece, NY	13
209	Greeley, CO	40
124	Green Bay, WI	66
104	Greensboro, NC	76
216	Gresham, OR	37
376	Hamilton Twnshp, NJ	10
245	Hammond, IN	30
266	Hampton, VA	27
167	Hartford, CT	49
227	Hawthorne, CA	34
249	Hayward, CA	29
142	Henderson, NV	56
294	Hesperia, CA	23
234	Hialeah, FL	32
231	High Point, NC	33
239	Hillsboro, OR	31
209	Hollywood, FL	40
33	Honolulu, HI	243
4	Houston, TX	823
245	Huntington Beach, CA	30
88	Huntsville, AL	89
159	Independence, MO	51
10	Indianapolis, IN	460
255	Indio, CA	28
234	Inglewood, CA	32
255	Irvine, CA	28
227	Irving, TX	34
36	Jacksonville, FL	218
215	Jacksonville, NC	38
61	Jackson, MS	124
167	Jersey City, NJ	49
NA	Joliet, IL**	NA
100	Kansas City, KS	80
24	Kansas City, MO	276
219	Kenosha, WI	36
97	Kent, WA	82
119	Killeen, TX	69
54	Knoxville, TN	147
183	Lafayette, LA	46
397	Lake Forest, CA	3
231	Lakeland, FL	33
311	Lakewood, CA	20
94	Lakewood, CO	84
135	Lancaster, CA	60
88	Lansing, MI	89
108	Laredo, TX	73
294	Las Cruces, NM	23
5	Las Vegas, NV	698
140	Lawrence, KS	57
99	Lawton, OK	81
333	Lee's Summit, MO	16
306	Lewisville, TX	21
74	Lexington, KY	107
60	Lincoln, NE	126
47	Little Rock, AR	171
272	Livermore, CA	26
333	Livonia, MI	16
59	Long Beach, CA	131
333	Longmont, CO	16

RANK	CITY	RAPES
255	Longview, TX	28
1	Los Angeles, CA	903
35	Louisville, KY	230
85	Lubbock, TX	93
239	Lynn, MA	31
255	Macon, GA	28
255	Madison, WI	28
113	Manchester, NH	71
311	McAllen, TX	20
177	McKinney, TX	47
287	Melbourne, FL	24
12	Memphis, TN	382
266	Merced, CA	27
63	Mesa, AZ	123
330	Mesquite, TX	17
207	Miami Beach, FL	41
255	Miami Gardens, FL	28
128	Miami, FL	65
159	Midland, TX	51
39	Milwaukee, WI	204
11	Minneapolis, MN	413
223	Miramar, FL	35
390	Mission Viejo, CA	5
344	Missouri City, TX	15
216	Mobile, AL	37
146	Modesto, CA	55
93	Montgomery, AL	85
245	Moreno Valley, CA	30
183	Murfreesboro, TN	46
330	Murrieta, CA	17
213	Nampa, ID	39
NA	Naperville, IL**	NA
280	Nashua, NH	25
27	Nashville, TN	262
124	New Bedford, MA	66
138	New Haven, CT	59
80	New Orleans, LA	98
3	New York, NY	832
120	Newark, NJ	68
391	Newport Beach, CA	4
382	Newton, MA	9
75	Norfolk, VA	102
192	Norman, OK	44
146	North Charleston, SC	55
159	North Las Vegas, NV	51
333	Norwalk, CA	16
376	Norwalk, CT	10
18	Oakland, CA	326
132	Oceanside, CA	62
219	Odessa, TX	36
397	O'Fallon, MO	3
239	Ogden, UT	31
22	Oklahoma City, OK	294
174	Olathe, KS	48
42	Omaha, NE	192
167	Ontario, CA	49
373	Orange, CA	11
353	Orem, UT	14
65	Orlando, FL	117
255	Overland Park, KS	28
287	Oxnard, CA	24
272	Palm Bay, FL	26
207	Palmdale, CA	41
280	Pasadena, CA	25
142	Pasadena, TX	56
255	Paterson, NJ	28
311	Pearland, TX	20
376	Pembroke Pines, FL	10

RANK	CITY	RAPES
154	Peoria, AZ	53
NA	Peoria, IL**	NA
2	Philadelphia, PA	896
8	Phoenix, AZ	522
67	Pittsburgh, PA	116
191	Plano, TX	45
364	Plantation, FL	13
183	Pomona, CA	46
140	Pompano Beach, FL	57
159	Port St. Lucie, FL	51
31	Portland, OR	252
311	Portsmouth, VA	20
165	Providence, RI	50
223	Provo, UT	35
239	Pueblo, CO	31
311	Quincy, MA	20
223	Racine, WI	35
78	Raleigh, NC	99
391	Ramapo, NY	4
311	Rancho Cucamon., CA	20
301	Reading, PA	22
130	Redding, CA	64
94	Reno, NV	84
255	Rialto, CA	28
367	Richardson, TX	12
192	Richmond, CA	44
223	Richmond, VA	35
287	Rio Rancho, NM	24
80	Riverside, CA	98
272	Roanoke, VA	26
NA	Rochester, MN**	NA
82	Rochester, NY	97
70	Rockford, IL	112
353	Roseville, CA	14
373	Roswell, GA	11
294	Round Rock, TX	23
45	Sacramento, CA	179
113	Salem, OR	71
177	Salinas, CA	47
77	Salt Lake City, UT	100
128	San Angelo, TX	65
6	San Antonio, TX	628
134	San Bernardino, CA	61
20	San Diego, CA	318
45	San Francisco, CA	179
28	San Jose, CA	258
301	San Leandro, CA	22
333	San Marcos, CA	16
333	San Mateo, CA	16
320	Sandy Springs, GA	19
301	Sandy, UT	22
103	Santa Ana, CA	77
249	Santa Barbara, CA	29
311	Santa Clara, CA	20
311	Santa Clarita, CA	20
200	Santa Maria, CA	42
353	Santa Monica, CA	14
105	Santa Rosa, CA	75
183	Savannah, GA	46
320	Scottsdale, AZ	19
75	Seattle, WA	102
61	Shreveport, LA	124
376	Simi Valley, CA	10
280	Sioux City, IA	25
58	Sioux Falls, SD	133
386	Somerville, MA	7
142	South Bend, IN	56
320	South Gate, CA	19

RANK	CITY	RAPES
234	Southfield, MI	32
209	Sparks, NV	40
320	Spokane Valley, WA	19
105	Spokane, WA	75
NA	Springfield, IL**	NA
67	Springfield, MA	116
70	Springfield, MO	112
239	Stamford, CT	31
266	Sterling Heights, MI	27
97	Stockton, CA	82
364	St. George, UT	13
367	St. Joseph, MO	12
32	St. Louis, MO	250
48	St. Paul, MN	165
70	St. Petersburg, FL	112
231	Suffolk, VA	33
389	Sugar Land, TX	6
373	Sunnyvale, CA	11
353	Sunrise, FL	14
382	Surprise, AZ	9
116	Syracuse, NY	70
55	Tacoma, WA	143
64	Tallahassee, FL	120
100	Tampa, FL	80
353	Temecula, CA	14
124	Tempe, AZ	66
124	Thornton, CO	66
320	Thousand Oaks, CA	19
48	Toledo, OH	165
391	Toms River Twnshp, NJ	4
192	Topeka, KS	44
280	Torrance, CA	25
391	Tracy, CA	4
272	Trenton, NJ	26
330	Troy, MI	17
39	Tucson, AZ	204
29	Tulsa, OK	254
255	Tuscaloosa, AL	28
146	Tyler, TX	55
326	Upper Darby Twnshp, PA	18
344	Vacaville, CA	15
200	Vallejo, CA	42
65	Vancouver, WA	117
326	Ventura, CA	18
174	Victorville, CA	48
116	Virginia Beach, VA	70
154	Visalia, CA	53
249	Vista, CA	29
167	Waco, TX	49
122	Warren, MI	67
272	Warwick, RI	26
53	Washington, DC	150
344	Waterbury, CT	15
353	West Covina, CA	14
287	West Jordan, UT	24
200	West Palm Beach, FL	42
90	West Valley, UT	87
213	Westland, MI	39
353	Westminster, CA	14
266	Westminster, CO	27
333	Whittier, CA	16
183	Wichita Falls, TX	46
29	Wichita, KS	254
165	Wilmington, NC	50
73	Winston-Salem, NC	110
386	Woodbridge Twnshp, NJ	7
280	Worcester, MA	25
219	Yonkers, NY	36
287	Yuma, AZ	24

Source: Reported data from the F.B.I. "Crime in the United States 2009"

*Forcible rape is the carnal knowledge of a female forcibly and against her will. Assaults or attempts to commit rape by force or threat of force are included. However, statutory rape without force and other sex offenses are excluded. **Not available

53. Rapes in 2009 (continued)
National Total = 88,097 Rapes*

RANK	CITY	RAPES
1	Los Angeles, CA	903
2	Philadelphia, PA	896
3	New York, NY	832
4	Houston, TX	823
5	Las Vegas, NV	698
6	San Antonio, TX	628
7	Columbus, OH	574
8	Phoenix, AZ	522
9	Dallas, TX	485
10	Indianapolis, IN	460
11	Minneapolis, MN	413
12	Memphis, TN	382
13	Cleveland, OH	373
14	Fort Worth, TX	370
15	Colorado Springs, CO	344
16	Denver, CO	343
17	Detroit, MI	335
18	Albuquerque, NM	326
18	Oakland, CA	326
20	San Diego, CA	318
21	Charlotte, NC	303
22	Oklahoma City, OK	294
23	Anchorage, AK	282
24	Kansas City, MO	276
25	Boston, MA	269
26	Austin, TX	265
27	Nashville, TN	262
28	San Jose, CA	258
29	Tulsa, OK	254
29	Wichita, KS	254
31	Portland, OR	252
32	St. Louis, MO	250
33	Honolulu, HI	243
34	Cincinnati, OH	235
35	Louisville, KY	230
36	Jacksonville, FL	218
37	Aurora, CO	216
38	Corpus Christi, TX	212
39	Milwaukee, WI	204
39	Tucson, AZ	204
41	Birmingham, AL	198
42	Omaha, NE	192
43	Akron, OH	189
44	El Paso, TX	182
45	Sacramento, CA	179
45	San Francisco, CA	179
47	Little Rock, AR	171
48	St. Paul, MN	165
48	Toledo, OH	165
50	Baltimore, MD	158
51	Des Moines, IA	153
52	Arlington, TX	152
53	Washington, DC	150
54	Knoxville, TN	147
55	Tacoma, WA	143
56	Buffalo, NY	141
57	Atlanta, GA	135
58	Sioux Falls, SD	133
59	Long Beach, CA	131
60	Lincoln, NE	126
61	Jackson, MS	124
61	Shreveport, LA	124
63	Mesa, AZ	123
64	Tallahassee, FL	120
65	Orlando, FL	117
65	Vancouver, WA	117
67	Pittsburgh, PA	116
67	Springfield, MA	116
69	Abilene, TX	114
70	Rockford, IL	112
70	Springfield, MO	112
70	St. Petersburg, FL	112
73	Winston-Salem, NC	110
74	Lexington, KY	107
75	Norfolk, VA	102
75	Seattle, WA	102
77	Salt Lake City, UT	100
78	Amarillo, TX	99
78	Raleigh, NC	99
80	New Orleans, LA	98
80	Riverside, CA	98
82	Rochester, NY	97
83	Gainesville, FL	95
84	Fayetteville, NC	94
85	Lubbock, TX	93
86	Dayton, OH	91
86	Flint, MI	91
88	Huntsville, AL	89
88	Lansing, MI	89
90	Fort Collins, CO	87
90	West Valley, UT	87
92	Fresno, CA	86
93	Montgomery, AL	85
94	Lakewood, CO	84
94	Reno, NV	84
96	Erie, PA	83
97	Kent, WA	82
97	Stockton, CA	82
99	Lawton, OK	81
100	Kansas City, KS	80
100	Tampa, FL	80
102	Grand Rapids, MI	78
103	Santa Ana, CA	77
104	Greensboro, NC	76
105	Fort Wayne, IN	75
105	Santa Rosa, CA	75
105	Spokane, WA	75
108	Beaumont, TX	73
108	Eugene, OR	73
108	Laredo, TX	73
111	Allentown, PA	72
111	Anaheim, CA	72
113	Denton, TX	71
113	Manchester, NH	71
113	Salem, OR	71
116	Boise, ID	70
116	Syracuse, NY	70
116	Virginia Beach, VA	70
119	Killeen, TX	69
120	Columbia, SC	68
120	Newark, NJ	68
122	Canton, OH	67
122	Warren, MI	67
124	Green Bay, WI	66
124	New Bedford, MA	66
124	Tempe, AZ	66
124	Thornton, CO	66
128	Miami, FL	65
128	San Angelo, TX	65
130	Redding, CA	64
131	Durham, NC	63
132	Fort Smith, AR	62
132	Oceanside, CA	62
134	San Bernardino, CA	61
135	Camden, NJ	60
135	Evansville, IN	60
135	Lancaster, CA	60
138	New Haven, CT	59
139	Bridgeport, CT	58
140	Lawrence, KS	57
140	Pompano Beach, FL	57
142	Fort Lauderdale, FL	56
142	Henderson, NV	56
142	Pasadena, TX	56
142	South Bend, IN	56
146	Baton Rouge, LA	55
146	Clarksville, TN	55
146	Modesto, CA	55
146	North Charleston, SC	55
146	Tyler, TX	55
151	Fargo, ND	54
151	Garland, TX	54
151	Glendale, AZ	54
154	Brockton, MA	53
154	Chattanooga, TN	53
154	Peoria, AZ	53
154	Visalia, CA	53
158	Grand Prairie, TX	52
159	Everett, WA	51
159	Federal Way, WA	51
159	Independence, MO	51
159	Midland, TX	51
159	North Las Vegas, NV	51
159	Port St. Lucie, FL	51
165	Providence, RI	50
165	Wilmington, NC	50
167	Albany, NY	49
167	Bakersfield, CA	49
167	Chula Vista, CA	49
167	Hartford, CT	49
167	Jersey City, NJ	49
167	Ontario, CA	49
167	Waco, TX	49
174	Fayetteville, AR	48
174	Olathe, KS	48
174	Victorville, CA	48
177	Albany, GA	47
177	Columbus, GA	47
177	Davenport, IA	47
177	Gary, IN	47
177	McKinney, TX	47
177	Salinas, CA	47
183	Chandler, AZ	46
183	Fall River, MA	46
183	Fontana, CA	46
183	Lafayette, LA	46
183	Murfreesboro, TN	46
183	Pomona, CA	46
183	Savannah, GA	46
183	Wichita Falls, TX	46
191	Plano, TX	45
192	Elizabeth, NJ	44
192	Fullerton, CA	44
192	Norman, OK	44
192	Richmond, CA	44
192	Topeka, KS	44
197	Cedar Rapids, IA	43
197	Clearwater, FL	43
197	College Station, TX	43
200	Athens-Clarke, GA	42
200	Chesapeake, VA	42
200	Chico, CA	42
200	Escondido, CA	42
200	Santa Maria, CA	42
200	Vallejo, CA	42
200	West Palm Beach, FL	42

RANK	CITY	RAPES
207	Miami Beach, FL	41
207	Palmdale, CA	41
209	Antioch, CA	40
209	Greeley, CO	40
209	Hollywood, FL	40
209	Sparks, NV	40
213	Nampa, ID	39
213	Westland, MI	39
215	Jacksonville, NC	38
216	Bellingham, WA	37
216	Gresham, OR	37
216	Mobile, AL	37
219	Compton, CA	36
219	Kenosha, WI	36
219	Odessa, TX	36
219	Yonkers, NY	36
223	Miramar, FL	35
223	Provo, UT	35
223	Racine, WI	35
223	Richmond, VA	35
227	Fremont, CA	34
227	Garden Grove, CA	34
227	Hawthorne, CA	34
227	Irving, TX	34
231	High Point, NC	33
231	Lakeland, FL	33
231	Suffolk, VA	33
234	Boulder, CO	32
234	Columbia, MO	32
234	Hialeah, FL	32
234	Inglewood, CA	32
234	Southfield, MI	32
239	Charleston, SC	31
239	Hillsboro, OR	31
239	Lynn, MA	31
239	Ogden, UT	31
239	Pueblo, CO	31
239	Stamford, CT	31
245	Arvada, CO	30
245	Hammond, IN	30
245	Huntington Beach, CA	30
245	Moreno Valley, CA	30
249	Ann Arbor, MI	29
249	Broken Arrow, OK	29
249	El Cajon, CA	29
249	Hayward, CA	29
249	Santa Barbara, CA	29
249	Vista, CA	29
255	Billings, MT	28
255	Indio, CA	28
255	Irvine, CA	28
255	Longview, TX	28
255	Macon, GA	28
255	Madison, WI	28
255	Miami Gardens, FL	28
255	Overland Park, KS	28
255	Paterson, NJ	28
255	Rialto, CA	28
255	Tuscaloosa, AL	28
266	Berkeley, CA	27
266	Costa Mesa, CA	27
266	Hampton, VA	27
266	Merced, CA	27
266	Sterling Heights, MI	27
266	Westminster, CO	27
272	Brownsville, TX	26
272	Carlsbad, CA	26
272	Citrus Heights, CA	26
272	Livermore, CA	26
272	Palm Bay, FL	26
272	Roanoke, VA	26
272	Trenton, NJ	26
272	Warwick, RI	26
280	Bellevue, WA	25
280	Danbury, CT	25
280	Nashua, NH	25
280	Pasadena, CA	25
280	Sioux City, IA	25
280	Torrance, CA	25
280	Worcester, MA	25
287	Boca Raton, FL	24
287	Clinton Twnshp, MI	24
287	Melbourne, FL	24
287	Oxnard, CA	24
287	Rio Rancho, NM	24
287	West Jordan, UT	24
287	Yuma, AZ	24
294	Avondale, AZ	23
294	Beaverton, OR	23
294	Clovis, CA	23
294	Fairfield, CA	23
294	Hesperia, CA	23
294	Las Cruces, NM	23
294	Round Rock, TX	23
301	Burbank, CA	22
301	Gilbert, AZ	22
301	Reading, PA	22
301	San Leandro, CA	22
301	Sandy, UT	22
306	Cambridge, MA	21
306	Canton Twnshp, MI	21
306	Centennial, CO	21
306	Davie, FL	21
306	Lewisville, TX	21
311	Cranston, RI	20
311	Lakewood, CA	20
311	McAllen, TX	20
311	Pearland, TX	20
311	Portsmouth, VA	20
311	Quincy, MA	20
311	Rancho Cucamon., CA	20
311	Santa Clara, CA	20
311	Santa Clarita, CA	20
320	Concord, CA	19
320	Sandy Springs, GA	19
320	Scottsdale, AZ	19
320	South Gate, CA	19
320	Spokane Valley, WA	19
320	Thousand Oaks, CA	19
326	Daly City, CA	18
326	Downey, CA	18
326	Upper Darby Twnshp, PA	18
326	Ventura, CA	18
330	Mesquite, TX	17
330	Murrieta, CA	17
330	Troy, MI	17
333	Cape Coral, FL	16
333	Carrollton, TX	16
333	Dearborn, MI	16
333	Edmond, OK	16
333	Lee's Summit, MO	16
333	Livonia, MI	16
333	Longmont, CO	16
333	Norwalk, CA	16
333	San Marcos, CA	16
333	San Mateo, CA	16
333	Whittier, CA	16
344	Alhambra, CA	15
344	Cheektowaga, NY	15
344	Chino, CA	15
344	Elk Grove, CA	15
344	Frisco, TX	15
344	Glendale, CA	15
344	Missouri City, TX	15
344	Vacaville, CA	15
344	Waterbury, CT	15
353	Allen, TX	14
353	Bend, OR	14
353	Carson, CA	14
353	El Monte, CA	14
353	Orem, UT	14
353	Roseville, CA	14
353	Santa Monica, CA	14
353	Sunrise, FL	14
353	Temecula, CA	14
353	West Covina, CA	14
353	Westminster, CA	14
364	Greece, NY	13
364	Plantation, FL	13
364	St. George, UT	13
367	Alexandria, VA	12
367	Buena Park, CA	12
367	Cary, NC	12
367	Corona, CA	12
367	Richardson, TX	12
367	St. Joseph, MO	12
373	Orange, CA	11
373	Roswell, GA	11
373	Sunnyvale, CA	11
376	Clifton, NJ	10
376	Farmington Hills, MI	10
376	Hamilton Twnshp, NJ	10
376	Norwalk, CT	10
376	Pembroke Pines, FL	10
376	Simi Valley, CA	10
382	Baldwin Park, CA	9
382	Newton, MA	9
382	Surprise, AZ	9
385	Brick Twnshp, NJ	8
386	Amherst, NY	7
386	Somerville, MA	7
386	Woodbridge Twnshp, NJ	7
389	Sugar Land, TX	6
390	Mission Viejo, CA	5
391	Coral Springs, FL	4
391	Edison Twnshp, NJ	4
391	Newport Beach, CA	4
391	Ramapo, NY	4
391	Toms River Twnshp, NJ	4
391	Tracy, CA	4
397	Clarkstown, NY	3
397	Lake Forest, CA	3
397	O'Fallon, MO	3
400	Colonie, NY	1
NA	Aurora, IL**	NA
NA	Bloomington, MN**	NA
NA	Chicago, IL**	NA
NA	Decatur, IL**	NA
NA	Duluth, MN**	NA
NA	Elgin, IL**	NA
NA	Joliet, IL**	NA
NA	Naperville, IL**	NA
NA	Peoria, IL**	NA
NA	Rochester, MN**	NA
NA	Springfield, IL**	NA

Source: Reported data from the F.B.I. "Crime in the United States 2009"
*Forcible rape is the carnal knowledge of a female forcibly and against her will. Assaults or attempts to commit rape by force or threat of force are included. However, statutory rape without force and other sex offenses are excluded. **Not available

54. Rape Rate in 2009
National Rate = 28.7 Rapes per 100,000 Population*

RANK	CITY	RATE
3	Abilene, TX	97.8
5	Akron, OH	91.5
47	Albany, GA	62.1
75	Albany, NY	52.4
49	Albuquerque, NM	61.4
380	Alexandria, VA	8.2
312	Alhambra, CA	17.5
38	Allentown, PA	67.1
326	Allen, TX	16.1
75	Amarillo, TX	52.4
389	Amherst, NY	6.3
276	Anaheim, CA	21.4
2	Anchorage, AK	99.5
240	Ann Arbor, MI	25.4
134	Antioch, CA	39.5
133	Arlington, TX	40.1
223	Arvada, CO	27.8
153	Athens-Clarke, GA	36.7
255	Atlanta, GA	24.4
39	Aurora, CO	66.7
NA	Aurora, IL**	NA
166	Austin, TX	34.5
236	Avondale, AZ	25.9
346	Bakersfield, CA	14.8
366	Baldwin Park, CA	11.6
249	Baltimore, MD	24.7
252	Baton Rouge, LA	24.6
40	Beaumont, TX	66.2
249	Beaverton, OR	24.7
290	Bellevue, WA	20.0
103	Bellingham, WA	46.1
313	Bend, OR	17.4
231	Berkeley, CA	26.7
232	Billings, MT	26.6
8	Birmingham, AL	87.1
NA	Bloomington, MN**	NA
221	Boca Raton, FL	27.9
169	Boise, ID	33.9
114	Boston, MA	43.1
182	Boulder, CO	32.0
372	Brick Twnshp, NJ	10.2
119	Bridgeport, CT	42.6
69	Brockton, MA	54.9
195	Broken Arrow, OK	30.7
347	Brownsville, TX	14.5
341	Buena Park, CA	15.1
74	Buffalo, NY	52.5
278	Burbank, CA	21.3
286	Cambridge, MA	20.4
20	Camden, NJ	76.0
240	Canton Twnshp, MI	25.4
10	Canton, OH	85.8
374	Cape Coral, FL	9.7
233	Carlsbad, CA	26.4
359	Carrollton, TX	12.6
341	Carson, CA	15.1
377	Cary, NC	9.0
172	Cedar Rapids, IA	33.4
282	Centennial, CO	21.1
304	Chandler, AZ	18.0
226	Charleston, SC	27.3
138	Charlotte, NC	39.0
195	Chattanooga, TN	30.7
296	Cheektowaga, NY	19.3
299	Chesapeake, VA	18.8
NA	Chicago, IL**	NA
88	Chico, CA	49.6
309	Chino, CA	17.7
274	Chula Vista, CA	21.8
31	Cincinnati, OH	70.5
192	Citrus Heights, CA	30.8
397	Clarkstown, NY	3.8
108	Clarksville, TN	45.2
127	Clearwater, FL	40.8
9	Cleveland, OH	86.9
355	Clifton, NJ	12.8
246	Clinton Twnshp, MI	25.0
258	Clovis, CA	24.2
84	College Station, TX	50.0
400	Colonie, NY	1.3
11	Colorado Springs, CO	85.7
190	Columbia, MO	31.2
72	Columbia, SC	53.2
243	Columbus, GA	25.2
21	Columbus, OH	75.6
141	Compton, CA	38.4
330	Concord, CA	15.7
399	Coral Springs, FL	3.2
383	Corona, CA	7.9
23	Corpus Christi, TX	73.7
253	Costa Mesa, CA	24.5
248	Cranston, RI	24.9
145	Dallas, TX	37.6
307	Daly City, CA	17.8
187	Danbury, CT	31.4
101	Davenport, IA	46.5
262	Davie, FL	23.3
52	Dayton, OH	59.5
299	Dearborn, MI	18.8
NA	Decatur, IL**	NA
59	Denton, TX	57.1
61	Denver, CO	56.7
19	Des Moines, IA	77.7
151	Detroit, MI	36.9
322	Downey, CA	16.7
NA	Duluth, MN**	NA
224	Durham, NC	27.7
395	Edison Twnshp, NJ	4.0
291	Edmond, OK	19.8
187	El Cajon, CA	31.4
367	El Monte, CA	11.4
206	El Paso, TX	29.4
NA	Elgin, IL**	NA
164	Elizabeth, NJ	35.2
370	Elk Grove, CA	10.7
16	Erie, PA	79.9
197	Escondido, CA	30.6
94	Eugene, OR	48.2
77	Evansville, IN	51.8
77	Everett, WA	51.8
271	Fairfield, CA	22.0
83	Fall River, MA	50.1
55	Fargo, ND	57.6
355	Farmington Hills, MI	12.8
44	Fayetteville, AR	63.9
71	Fayetteville, NC	54.0
50	Federal Way, WA	60.6
14	Flint, MI	81.5
258	Fontana, CA	24.2
45	Fort Collins, CO	62.8
197	Fort Lauderdale, FL	30.6
24	Fort Smith, AR	72.8
205	Fort Wayne, IN	29.8
79	Fort Worth, TX	51.1
320	Fremont, CA	16.8
306	Fresno, CA	17.9
350	Frisco, TX	13.9
173	Fullerton, CA	33.2
13	Gainesville, FL	82.4
285	Garden Grove, CA	20.5
249	Garland, TX	24.7
90	Gary, IN	49.4
375	Gilbert, AZ	9.5
279	Glendale, AZ	21.2
385	Glendale, CA	7.6
185	Grand Prairie, TX	31.6
129	Grand Rapids, MI	40.4
350	Greece, NY	13.9
115	Greeley, CO	43.0
42	Green Bay, WI	65.5
203	Greensboro, NC	30.0
158	Gresham, OR	36.1
369	Hamilton Twnshp, NJ	11.1
136	Hammond, IN	39.4
302	Hampton, VA	18.5
134	Hartford, CT	39.5
131	Hawthorne, CA	40.3
286	Hayward, CA	20.4
276	Henderson, NV	21.4
236	Hesperia, CA	25.9
339	Hialeah, FL	15.3
183	High Point, NC	31.8
180	Hillsboro, OR	32.1
216	Hollywood, FL	28.2
230	Honolulu, HI	26.8
157	Houston, TX	36.2
334	Huntington Beach, CA	15.6
86	Huntsville, AL	49.8
123	Independence, MO	41.7
63	Indianapolis, IN	56.5
189	Indio, CA	31.3
213	Inglewood, CA	28.4
354	Irvine, CA	13.0
320	Irving, TX	16.8
228	Jacksonville, FL	26.9
92	Jacksonville, NC	49.0
26	Jackson, MS	71.8
288	Jersey City, NJ	20.3
NA	Joliet, IL**	NA
64	Kansas City, KS	56.3
60	Kansas City, MO	56.9
151	Kenosha, WI	36.9
4	Kent, WA	97.2
57	Killeen, TX	57.2
17	Knoxville, TN	79.1
129	Lafayette, LA	40.4
395	Lake Forest, CA	4.0
165	Lakeland, FL	35.0
239	Lakewood, CA	25.5
51	Lakewood, CO	59.7
131	Lancaster, CA	40.3
18	Lansing, MI	78.5
178	Laredo, TX	32.2
253	Las Cruces, NM	24.5
81	Las Vegas, NV	50.7
46	Lawrence, KS	62.2
6	Lawton, OK	90.2
301	Lee's Summit, MO	18.6
289	Lewisville, TX	20.1
158	Lexington, KY	36.1
89	Lincoln, NE	49.5
7	Little Rock, AR	89.9
180	Livermore, CA	32.1
309	Livonia, MI	17.7
216	Long Beach, CA	28.2
303	Longmont, CO	18.3

RANK	CITY	RATE	RANK	CITY	RATE	RANK	CITY	RATE
158	Longview, TX	36.1	178	Peoria, AZ	32.2	119	Southfield, MI	42.6
261	Los Angeles, CA	23.5	NA	Peoria, IL**	NA	110	Sparks, NV	43.8
155	Louisville, KY	36.4	54	Philadelphia, PA	57.9	272	Spokane Valley, WA	21.9
123	Lubbock, TX	41.7	174	Phoenix, AZ	32.7	150	Spokane, WA	37.0
168	Lynn, MA	34.0	147	Pittsburgh, PA	37.2	NA	Springfield, IL**	NA
201	Macon, GA	30.3	323	Plano, TX	16.5	21	Springfield, MA	75.6
363	Madison, WI	11.9	334	Plantation, FL	15.6	27	Springfield, MO	71.5
43	Manchester, NH	65.3	203	Pomona, CA	30.0	236	Stamford, CT	25.9
341	McAllen, TX	15.1	66	Pompano Beach, FL	56.0	279	Sterling Heights, MI	21.2
162	McKinney, TX	35.6	191	Port St. Lucie, FL	31.1	219	Stockton, CA	28.1
192	Melbourne, FL	30.8	109	Portland, OR	44.9	317	St. George, UT	17.2
57	Memphis, TN	57.2	291	Portsmouth, VA	19.8	330	St. Joseph, MO	15.7
167	Merced, CA	34.3	209	Providence, RI	29.1	32	St. Louis, MO	70.4
235	Mesa, AZ	26.1	208	Provo, UT	29.3	53	St. Paul, MN	58.9
355	Mesquite, TX	12.8	206	Pueblo, CO	29.4	104	St. Petersburg, FL	45.7
93	Miami Beach, FL	48.7	284	Quincy, MA	20.7	139	Suffolk, VA	38.9
240	Miami Gardens, FL	25.4	119	Racine, WI	42.6	386	Sugar Land, TX	7.3
337	Miami, FL	15.5	255	Raleigh, NC	24.4	379	Sunnyvale, CA	8.3
99	Midland, TX	47.3	391	Ramapo, NY	5.2	330	Sunrise, FL	15.7
171	Milwaukee, WI	33.7	368	Rancho Cucamon., CA	11.3	378	Surprise, AZ	8.6
1	Minneapolis, MN	107.9	225	Reading, PA	27.4	80	Syracuse, NY	51.0
177	Miramar, FL	32.3	34	Redding, CA	70.1	25	Tacoma, WA	72.4
390	Mission Viejo, CA	5.3	144	Reno, NV	38.0	37	Tallahassee, FL	68.9
296	Missouri City, TX	19.3	216	Rialto, CA	28.2	263	Tampa, FL	23.2
344	Mobile, AL	15.0	364	Richardson, TX	11.7	350	Temecula, CA	13.9
228	Modesto, CA	26.9	116	Richmond, CA	42.9	147	Tempe, AZ	37.2
122	Montgomery, AL	41.9	317	Richmond, VA	17.2	65	Thornton, CO	56.2
340	Moreno Valley, CA	15.2	212	Rio Rancho, NM	28.8	338	Thousand Oaks, CA	15.4
111	Murfreesboro, TN	43.4	174	Riverside, CA	32.7	61	Toledo, OH	56.7
324	Murrieta, CA	16.2	221	Roanoke, VA	27.9	394	Toms River Twnshp, NJ	4.1
101	Nampa, ID	46.5	NA	Rochester, MN**	NA	162	Topeka, KS	35.6
NA	Naperville, IL**	NA	100	Rochester, NY	47.2	309	Torrance, CA	17.7
211	Nashua, NH	28.9	29	Rockford, IL	70.9	393	Tracy, CA	4.9
116	Nashville, TN	42.9	361	Roseville, CA	12.0	186	Trenton, NJ	31.5
28	New Bedford, MA	71.3	360	Roswell, GA	12.4	279	Troy, MI	21.2
97	New Haven, CT	47.7	283	Round Rock, TX	20.8	147	Tucson, AZ	37.2
209	New Orleans, LA	29.1	142	Sacramento, CA	38.1	41	Tulsa, OK	66.0
373	New York, NY	9.9	104	Salem, OR	45.7	199	Tuscaloosa, AL	30.5
255	Newark, NJ	24.4	174	Salinas, CA	32.7	67	Tyler, TX	55.4
392	Newport Beach, CA	5.0	68	Salt Lake City, UT	55.3	264	Upper Darby Twnshp, PA	23.1
370	Newton, MA	10.7	32	San Angelo, TX	70.4	324	Vacaville, CA	16.2
111	Norfolk, VA	43.4	104	San Antonio, TX	45.7	153	Vallejo, CA	36.7
128	Norman, OK	40.7	199	San Bernardino, CA	30.5	30	Vancouver, WA	70.8
56	North Charleston, SC	57.3	258	San Diego, CA	24.2	316	Ventura, CA	17.3
272	North Las Vegas, NV	21.9	270	San Francisco, CA	22.1	126	Victorville, CA	41.0
334	Norwalk, CA	15.6	227	San Jose, CA	27.0	328	Virginia Beach, VA	16.0
361	Norwalk, CT	12.0	214	San Leandro, CA	28.3	118	Visalia, CA	42.7
15	Oakland, CA	80.6	294	San Marcos, CA	19.5	183	Vista, CA	31.8
156	Oceanside, CA	36.3	313	San Mateo, CA	17.4	137	Waco, TX	39.2
158	Odessa, TX	36.1	265	Sandy Springs, GA	23.0	82	Warren, MI	50.2
398	O'Fallon, MO	3.7	266	Sandy, UT	22.7	192	Warwick, RI	30.8
146	Ogden, UT	37.3	266	Santa Ana, CA	22.7	246	Washington, DC	25.0
73	Oklahoma City, OK	52.8	170	Santa Barbara, CA	33.8	348	Waterbury, CT	14.0
139	Olathe, KS	38.9	304	Santa Clara, CA	18.0	353	West Covina, CA	13.2
113	Omaha, NE	43.3	364	Santa Clarita, CA	11.7	269	West Jordan, UT	22.4
214	Ontario, CA	28.3	95	Santa Maria, CA	48.1	123	West Palm Beach, FL	41.7
382	Orange, CA	8.0	329	Santa Monica, CA	15.9	35	West Valley, UT	69.9
345	Orem, UT	14.9	96	Santa Rosa, CA	47.9	85	Westland, MI	49.9
86	Orlando, FL	49.8	275	Savannah, GA	21.6	330	Westminster, CA	15.7
326	Overland Park, KS	16.1	383	Scottsdale, AZ	7.9	244	Westminster, CO	25.1
355	Oxnard, CA	12.8	319	Seattle, WA	16.9	294	Whittier, CA	19.5
244	Palm Bay, FL	25.1	47	Shreveport, LA	62.1	107	Wichita Falls, TX	45.6
220	Palmdale, CA	28.0	380	Simi Valley, CA	8.2	36	Wichita, KS	69.1
313	Pasadena, CA	17.4	201	Sioux City, IA	30.3	91	Wilmington, NC	49.3
142	Pasadena, TX	38.1	12	Sioux Falls, SD	83.8	98	Winston-Salem, NC	47.6
296	Paterson, NJ	19.3	376	Somerville, MA	9.3	387	Woodbridge Twnshp, NJ	7.1
268	Pearland, TX	22.6	70	South Bend, IN	54.2	348	Worcester, MA	14.0
388	Pembroke Pines, FL	6.9	293	South Gate, CA	19.7	307	Yonkers, NY	17.8
						234	Yuma, AZ	26.2

Source: CQ Press using reported data from the F.B.I. "Crime in the United States 2009"

*Forcible rape is the carnal knowledge of a female forcibly and against her will. Assaults or attempts to commit rape by force or threat of force are included. However, statutory rape without force and other sex offenses are excluded. **Not available

54. Rape Rate in 2009 (continued)
National Rate = 28.7 Rapes per 100,000 Population*

RANK	CITY	RATE
1	Minneapolis, MN	107.9
2	Anchorage, AK	99.5
3	Abilene, TX	97.8
4	Kent, WA	97.2
5	Akron, OH	91.5
6	Lawton, OK	90.2
7	Little Rock, AR	89.9
8	Birmingham, AL	87.1
9	Cleveland, OH	86.9
10	Canton, OH	85.8
11	Colorado Springs, CO	85.7
12	Sioux Falls, SD	83.8
13	Gainesville, FL	82.4
14	Flint, MI	81.5
15	Oakland, CA	80.6
16	Erie, PA	79.9
17	Knoxville, TN	79.1
18	Lansing, MI	78.5
19	Des Moines, IA	77.7
20	Camden, NJ	76.0
21	Columbus, OH	75.6
21	Springfield, MA	75.6
23	Corpus Christi, TX	73.7
24	Fort Smith, AR	72.8
25	Tacoma, WA	72.4
26	Jackson, MS	71.8
27	Springfield, MO	71.5
28	New Bedford, MA	71.3
29	Rockford, IL	70.9
30	Vancouver, WA	70.8
31	Cincinnati, OH	70.5
32	San Angelo, TX	70.4
32	St. Louis, MO	70.4
34	Redding, CA	70.1
35	West Valley, UT	69.9
36	Wichita, KS	69.1
37	Tallahassee, FL	68.9
38	Allentown, PA	67.1
39	Aurora, CO	66.7
40	Beaumont, TX	66.2
41	Tulsa, OK	66.0
42	Green Bay, WI	65.5
43	Manchester, NH	65.3
44	Fayetteville, AR	63.9
45	Fort Collins, CO	62.8
46	Lawrence, KS	62.2
47	Albany, GA	62.1
47	Shreveport, LA	62.1
49	Albuquerque, NM	61.4
50	Federal Way, WA	60.6
51	Lakewood, CO	59.7
52	Dayton, OH	59.5
53	St. Paul, MN	58.9
54	Philadelphia, PA	57.9
55	Fargo, ND	57.6
56	North Charleston, SC	57.3
57	Killeen, TX	57.2
57	Memphis, TN	57.2
59	Denton, TX	57.1
60	Kansas City, MO	56.9
61	Denver, CO	56.7
61	Toledo, OH	56.7
63	Indianapolis, IN	56.5
64	Kansas City, KS	56.3
65	Thornton, CO	56.2
66	Pompano Beach, FL	56.0
67	Tyler, TX	55.4
68	Salt Lake City, UT	55.3
69	Brockton, MA	54.9
70	South Bend, IN	54.2
71	Fayetteville, NC	54.0
72	Columbia, SC	53.2
73	Oklahoma City, OK	52.8
74	Buffalo, NY	52.5
75	Albany, NY	52.4
75	Amarillo, TX	52.4
77	Evansville, IN	51.8
77	Everett, WA	51.8
79	Fort Worth, TX	51.1
80	Syracuse, NY	51.0
81	Las Vegas, NV	50.7
82	Warren, MI	50.2
83	Fall River, MA	50.1
84	College Station, TX	50.0
85	Westland, MI	49.9
86	Huntsville, AL	49.8
86	Orlando, FL	49.8
88	Chico, CA	49.6
89	Lincoln, NE	49.5
90	Gary, IN	49.4
91	Wilmington, NC	49.3
92	Jacksonville, NC	49.0
93	Miami Beach, FL	48.7
94	Eugene, OR	48.2
95	Santa Maria, CA	48.1
96	Santa Rosa, CA	47.9
97	New Haven, CT	47.7
98	Winston-Salem, NC	47.6
99	Midland, TX	47.3
100	Rochester, NY	47.2
101	Davenport, IA	46.5
101	Nampa, ID	46.5
103	Bellingham, WA	46.1
104	Salem, OR	45.7
104	San Antonio, TX	45.7
104	St. Petersburg, FL	45.7
107	Wichita Falls, TX	45.6
108	Clarksville, TN	45.2
109	Portland, OR	44.9
110	Sparks, NV	43.8
111	Murfreesboro, TN	43.4
111	Norfolk, VA	43.4
113	Omaha, NE	43.3
114	Boston, MA	43.1
115	Greeley, CO	43.0
116	Nashville, TN	42.9
116	Richmond, CA	42.9
118	Visalia, CA	42.7
119	Bridgeport, CT	42.6
119	Racine, WI	42.6
119	Southfield, MI	42.6
122	Montgomery, AL	41.9
123	Independence, MO	41.7
123	Lubbock, TX	41.7
123	West Palm Beach, FL	41.7
126	Victorville, CA	41.0
127	Clearwater, FL	40.8
128	Norman, OK	40.7
129	Grand Rapids, MI	40.4
129	Lafayette, LA	40.4
131	Hawthorne, CA	40.3
131	Lancaster, CA	40.3
133	Arlington, TX	40.1
134	Antioch, CA	39.5
134	Hartford, CT	39.5
136	Hammond, IN	39.4
137	Waco, TX	39.2
138	Charlotte, NC	39.0
139	Olathe, KS	38.9
139	Suffolk, VA	38.9
141	Compton, CA	38.4
142	Pasadena, TX	38.1
142	Sacramento, CA	38.1
144	Reno, NV	38.0
145	Dallas, TX	37.6
146	Ogden, UT	37.3
147	Pittsburgh, PA	37.2
147	Tempe, AZ	37.2
147	Tucson, AZ	37.2
150	Spokane, WA	37.0
151	Detroit, MI	36.9
151	Kenosha, WI	36.9
153	Athens-Clarke, GA	36.7
153	Vallejo, CA	36.7
155	Louisville, KY	36.4
156	Oceanside, CA	36.3
157	Houston, TX	36.2
158	Gresham, OR	36.1
158	Lexington, KY	36.1
158	Longview, TX	36.1
158	Odessa, TX	36.1
162	McKinney, TX	35.6
162	Topeka, KS	35.6
164	Elizabeth, NJ	35.2
165	Lakeland, FL	35.0
166	Austin, TX	34.5
167	Merced, CA	34.3
168	Lynn, MA	34.0
169	Boise, ID	33.9
170	Santa Barbara, CA	33.8
171	Milwaukee, WI	33.7
172	Cedar Rapids, IA	33.4
173	Fullerton, CA	33.2
174	Phoenix, AZ	32.7
174	Riverside, CA	32.7
174	Salinas, CA	32.7
177	Miramar, FL	32.3
178	Laredo, TX	32.2
178	Peoria, AZ	32.2
180	Hillsboro, OR	32.1
180	Livermore, CA	32.1
182	Boulder, CO	32.0
183	High Point, NC	31.8
183	Vista, CA	31.8
185	Grand Prairie, TX	31.6
186	Trenton, NJ	31.5
187	Danbury, CT	31.4
187	El Cajon, CA	31.4
189	Indio, CA	31.3
190	Columbia, MO	31.2
191	Port St. Lucie, FL	31.1
192	Citrus Heights, CA	30.8
192	Melbourne, FL	30.8
192	Warwick, RI	30.8
195	Broken Arrow, OK	30.7
195	Chattanooga, TN	30.7
197	Escondido, CA	30.6
197	Fort Lauderdale, FL	30.6
199	San Bernardino, CA	30.5
199	Tuscaloosa, AL	30.5
201	Macon, GA	30.3
201	Sioux City, IA	30.3
203	Greensboro, NC	30.0
203	Pomona, CA	30.0
205	Fort Wayne, IN	29.8
206	El Paso, TX	29.4

RANK	CITY	RATE
206	Pueblo, CO	29.4
208	Provo, UT	29.3
209	New Orleans, LA	29.1
209	Providence, RI	29.1
211	Nashua, NH	28.9
212	Rio Rancho, NM	28.8
213	Inglewood, CA	28.4
214	Ontario, CA	28.3
214	San Leandro, CA	28.3
216	Hollywood, FL	28.2
216	Long Beach, CA	28.2
216	Rialto, CA	28.2
219	Stockton, CA	28.1
220	Palmdale, CA	28.0
221	Boca Raton, FL	27.9
221	Roanoke, VA	27.9
223	Arvada, CO	27.8
224	Durham, NC	27.7
225	Reading, PA	27.4
226	Charleston, SC	27.3
227	San Jose, CA	27.0
228	Jacksonville, FL	26.9
228	Modesto, CA	26.9
230	Honolulu, HI	26.8
231	Berkeley, CA	26.7
232	Billings, MT	26.6
233	Carlsbad, CA	26.4
234	Yuma, AZ	26.2
235	Mesa, AZ	26.1
236	Avondale, AZ	25.9
236	Hesperia, CA	25.9
236	Stamford, CT	25.9
239	Lakewood, CA	25.5
240	Ann Arbor, MI	25.4
240	Canton Twnshp, MI	25.4
240	Miami Gardens, FL	25.4
243	Columbus, GA	25.2
244	Palm Bay, FL	25.1
244	Westminster, CO	25.1
246	Clinton Twnshp, MI	25.0
246	Washington, DC	25.0
248	Cranston, RI	24.9
249	Baltimore, MD	24.7
249	Beaverton, OR	24.7
249	Garland, TX	24.7
252	Baton Rouge, LA	24.6
253	Costa Mesa, CA	24.5
253	Las Cruces, NM	24.5
255	Atlanta, GA	24.4
255	Newark, NJ	24.4
255	Raleigh, NC	24.4
258	Clovis, CA	24.2
258	Fontana, CA	24.2
258	San Diego, CA	24.2
261	Los Angeles, CA	23.5
262	Davie, FL	23.3
263	Tampa, FL	23.2
264	Upper Darby Twnshp, PA	23.1
265	Sandy Springs, GA	23.0
266	Sandy, UT	22.7
266	Santa Ana, CA	22.7
268	Pearland, TX	22.6
269	West Jordan, UT	22.4
270	San Francisco, CA	22.1
271	Fairfield, CA	22.0
272	North Las Vegas, NV	21.9
272	Spokane Valley, WA	21.9
274	Chula Vista, CA	21.8

RANK	CITY	RATE
275	Savannah, GA	21.6
276	Anaheim, CA	21.4
276	Henderson, NV	21.4
278	Burbank, CA	21.3
279	Glendale, AZ	21.2
279	Sterling Heights, MI	21.2
279	Troy, MI	21.2
282	Centennial, CO	21.1
283	Round Rock, TX	20.8
284	Quincy, MA	20.7
285	Garden Grove, CA	20.5
286	Cambridge, MA	20.4
286	Hayward, CA	20.4
288	Jersey City, NJ	20.3
289	Lewisville, TX	20.1
290	Bellevue, WA	20.0
291	Edmond, OK	19.8
291	Portsmouth, VA	19.8
293	South Gate, CA	19.7
294	San Marcos, CA	19.5
294	Whittier, CA	19.5
296	Cheektowaga, NY	19.3
296	Missouri City, TX	19.3
296	Paterson, NJ	19.3
299	Chesapeake, VA	18.8
299	Dearborn, MI	18.8
301	Lee's Summit, MO	18.6
302	Hampton, VA	18.5
303	Longmont, CO	18.3
304	Chandler, AZ	18.0
304	Santa Clara, CA	18.0
306	Fresno, CA	17.9
307	Daly City, CA	17.8
307	Yonkers, NY	17.8
309	Chino, CA	17.7
309	Livonia, MI	17.7
309	Torrance, CA	17.7
312	Alhambra, CA	17.5
313	Bend, OR	17.4
313	Pasadena, CA	17.4
313	San Mateo, CA	17.4
316	Ventura, CA	17.3
317	Richmond, VA	17.2
317	St. George, UT	17.2
319	Seattle, WA	16.9
320	Fremont, CA	16.8
320	Irving, TX	16.8
322	Downey, CA	16.7
323	Plano, TX	16.5
324	Murrieta, CA	16.2
324	Vacaville, CA	16.2
326	Allen, TX	16.1
326	Overland Park, KS	16.1
328	Virginia Beach, VA	16.0
329	Santa Monica, CA	15.9
330	Concord, CA	15.7
330	St. Joseph, MO	15.7
330	Sunrise, FL	15.7
330	Westminster, CA	15.7
334	Huntington Beach, CA	15.6
334	Norwalk, CA	15.6
334	Plantation, FL	15.6
337	Miami, FL	15.5
338	Thousand Oaks, CA	15.4
339	Hialeah, FL	15.3
340	Moreno Valley, CA	15.2
341	Buena Park, CA	15.1
341	Carson, CA	15.1

RANK	CITY	RATE
341	McAllen, TX	15.1
344	Mobile, AL	15.0
345	Orem, UT	14.9
346	Bakersfield, CA	14.8
347	Brownsville, TX	14.5
348	Waterbury, CT	14.0
348	Worcester, MA	14.0
350	Frisco, TX	13.9
350	Greece, NY	13.9
350	Temecula, CA	13.9
353	West Covina, CA	13.2
354	Irvine, CA	13.0
355	Clifton, NJ	12.8
355	Farmington Hills, MI	12.8
355	Mesquite, TX	12.8
355	Oxnard, CA	12.8
359	Carrollton, TX	12.6
360	Roswell, GA	12.4
361	Norwalk, CT	12.0
361	Roseville, CA	12.0
363	Madison, WI	11.9
364	Richardson, TX	11.7
364	Santa Clarita, CA	11.7
366	Baldwin Park, CA	11.6
367	El Monte, CA	11.4
368	Rancho Cucamon., CA	11.3
369	Hamilton Twnshp, NJ	11.1
370	Elk Grove, CA	10.7
370	Newton, MA	10.7
372	Brick Twnshp, NJ	10.2
373	New York, NY	9.9
374	Cape Coral, FL	9.7
375	Gilbert, AZ	9.5
376	Somerville, MA	9.3
377	Cary, NC	9.0
378	Surprise, AZ	8.6
379	Sunnyvale, CA	8.3
380	Alexandria, VA	8.2
380	Simi Valley, CA	8.2
382	Orange, CA	8.0
383	Corona, CA	7.9
383	Scottsdale, AZ	7.9
385	Glendale, CA	7.6
386	Sugar Land, TX	7.3
387	Woodbridge Twnshp, NJ	7.1
388	Pembroke Pines, FL	6.9
389	Amherst, NY	6.3
390	Mission Viejo, CA	5.3
391	Ramapo, NY	5.2
392	Newport Beach, CA	5.0
393	Tracy, CA	4.9
394	Toms River Twnshp, NJ	4.1
395	Edison Twnshp, NJ	4.0
395	Lake Forest, CA	4.0
397	Clarkstown, NY	3.8
398	O'Fallon, MO	3.7
399	Coral Springs, FL	3.2
400	Colonie, NY	1.3
NA	Aurora, IL**	NA
NA	Bloomington, MN**	NA
NA	Chicago, IL**	NA
NA	Decatur, IL**	NA
NA	Duluth, MN**	NA
NA	Elgin, IL**	NA
NA	Joliet, IL**	NA
NA	Naperville, IL**	NA
NA	Peoria, IL**	NA
NA	Rochester, MN**	NA
NA	Springfield, IL**	NA

Source: CQ Press using reported data from the F.B.I. "Crime in the United States 2009"

*Forcible rape is the carnal knowledge of a female forcibly and against her will. Assaults or attempts to commit rape by force or threat of force are included. However, statutory rape without force and other sex offenses are excluded. **Not available

55. Percent Change in Rape Rate: 2008 to 2009
National Percent Change = 3.5% Decrease*

RANK	CITY	% CHANGE
55	Abilene, TX	29.2
93	Akron, OH	13.4
NA	Albany, GA**	NA
149	Albany, NY	2.7
240	Albuquerque, NM	(12.4)
369	Alexandria, VA	(61.5)
11	Alhambra, CA	88.2
4	Allentown, PA	118.6
9	Allen, TX	91.7
275	Amarillo, TX	(19.4)
1	Amherst, NY	250.0
249	Anaheim, CA	(14.1)
134	Anchorage, AK	6.0
NA	Ann Arbor, MI**	NA
41	Antioch, CA	37.2
129	Arlington, TX	6.9
114	Arvada, CO	9.9
292	Athens-Clarke, GA	(22.6)
146	Atlanta, GA	3.4
99	Aurora, CO	12.3
NA	Aurora, IL**	NA
197	Austin, TX	(4.7)
3	Avondale, AZ	121.4
157	Bakersfield, CA	0.7
155	Baldwin Park, CA	0.9
90	Baltimore, MD	14.4
248	Baton Rouge, LA	(14.0)
192	Beaumont, TX	(3.6)
199	Beaverton, OR	(5.0)
307	Bellevue, WA	(25.7)
25	Bellingham, WA	57.9
354	Bend, OR	(45.8)
122	Berkeley, CA	8.1
318	Billings, MT	(31.4)
205	Birmingham, AL	(6.2)
NA	Bloomington, MN**	NA
26	Boca Raton, FL	57.6
252	Boise, ID	(14.8)
114	Boston, MA	9.9
305	Boulder, CO	(25.2)
5	Brick Twnshp, NJ	100.0
164	Bridgeport, CT	0.2
NA	Brockton, MA**	NA
13	Broken Arrow, OK	76.4
180	Brownsville, TX	(1.4)
166	Buena Park, CA	0.0
269	Buffalo, NY	(18.5)
54	Burbank, CA	29.9
32	Cambridge, MA	47.8
263	Camden, NJ	(17.3)
NA	Canton Twnshp, MI**	NA
147	Canton, OH	3.0
358	Cape Coral, FL	(48.9)
126	Carlsbad, CA	7.3
212	Carrollton, TX	(6.7)
310	Carson, CA	(26.0)
206	Cary, NC	(6.3)
61	Cedar Rapids, IA	24.6
31	Centennial, CO	48.6
270	Chandler, AZ	(18.6)
360	Charleston, SC	(49.2)
118	Charlotte, NC	8.9
259	Chattanooga, TN	(16.3)
258	Cheektowaga, NY	(16.1)
338	Chesapeake, VA	(36.1)
NA	Chicago, IL**	NA
48	Chico, CA	34.4
126	Chino, CA	7.3
238	Chula Vista, CA	(11.4)
246	Cincinnati, OH	(12.9)
53	Citrus Heights, CA	30.0
372	Clarkstown, NY	(66.7)
213	Clarksville, TN	(7.0)
97	Clearwater, FL	12.7
237	Cleveland, OH	(11.0)
106	Clifton, NJ	11.3
NA	Clinton Twnshp, MI**	NA
74	Clovis, CA	19.8
188	College Station, TX	(2.5)
166	Colonie, NY	0.0
191	Colorado Springs, CO	(3.2)
19	Columbia, MO	66.0
79	Columbia, SC	19.3
333	Columbus, GA	(34.9)
217	Columbus, OH	(7.6)
299	Compton, CA	(24.4)
23	Concord, CA	58.6
5	Coral Springs, FL	100.0
363	Corona, CA	(51.5)
113	Corpus Christi, TX	10.0
321	Costa Mesa, CA	(31.6)
62	Cranston, RI	24.5
193	Dallas, TX	(3.8)
315	Daly City, CA	(28.5)
18	Danbury, CT	67.0
164	Davenport, IA	0.2
289	Davie, FL	(22.1)
243	Dayton, OH	(12.6)
NA	Dearborn, MI**	NA
NA	Decatur, IL**	NA
183	Denton, TX	(1.9)
80	Denver, CO	19.1
NA	Des Moines, IA**	NA
NA	Detroit, MI**	NA
302	Downey, CA	(24.8)
NA	Duluth, MN**	NA
267	Durham, NC	(18.0)
329	Edison Twnshp, NJ	(33.3)
142	Edmond, OK	4.8
264	El Cajon, CA	(17.4)
365	El Monte, CA	(56.2)
176	El Paso, TX	(0.7)
NA	Elgin, IL**	NA
27	Elizabeth, NJ	57.1
323	Elk Grove, CA	(32.3)
201	Erie, PA	(5.7)
46	Escondido, CA	34.8
72	Eugene, OR	20.8
220	Evansville, IN	(7.8)
325	Everett, WA	(32.8)
266	Fairfield, CA	(17.6)
317	Fall River, MA	(30.0)
148	Fargo, ND	2.9
NA	Farmington Hills, MI**	NA
65	Fayetteville, AR	24.3
57	Fayetteville, NC	28.6
15	Federal Way, WA	71.2
NA	Flint, MI**	NA
209	Fontana, CA	(6.6)
91	Fort Collins, CO	13.8
296	Fort Lauderdale, FL	(23.3)
318	Fort Smith, AR	(31.4)
287	Fort Wayne, IN	(22.0)
150	Fort Worth, TX	2.4
226	Fremont, CA	(8.7)
131	Fresno, CA	6.5
221	Frisco, TX	(7.9)
69	Fullerton, CA	22.5
126	Gainesville, FL	7.3
17	Garden Grove, CA	69.4
328	Garland, TX	(33.2)
214	Gary, IN	(7.3)
277	Gilbert, AZ	(19.5)
265	Glendale, AZ	(17.5)
316	Glendale, CA	(29.0)
140	Grand Prairie, TX	5.0
NA	Grand Rapids, MI**	NA
22	Greece, NY	61.6
250	Greeley, CO	(14.2)
247	Green Bay, WI	(13.4)
318	Greensboro, NC	(31.4)
361	Gresham, OR	(49.4)
107	Hamilton Twnshp, NJ	11.0
270	Hammond, IN	(18.6)
337	Hampton, VA	(35.8)
275	Hartford, CT	(19.4)
10	Hawthorne, CA	89.2
362	Hayward, CA	(49.5)
344	Henderson, NV	(39.0)
44	Hesperia, CA	35.6
260	Hialeah, FL	(16.4)
120	High Point, NC	8.5
257	Hillsboro, OR	(15.7)
303	Hollywood, FL	(25.0)
76	Honolulu, HI	19.6
122	Houston, TX	8.1
227	Huntington Beach, CA	(8.8)
215	Huntsville, AL	(7.4)
274	Independence, MO	(19.2)
194	Indianapolis, IN	(3.9)
209	Indio, CA	(6.6)
125	Inglewood, CA	7.6
30	Irvine, CA	51.2
121	Irving, TX	8.4
262	Jacksonville, FL	(17.2)
58	Jacksonville, NC	27.9
219	Jackson, MS	(7.7)
166	Jersey City, NJ	0.0
NA	Joliet, IL**	NA
NA	Kansas City, KS**	NA
145	Kansas City, MO	3.6
234	Kenosha, WI	(10.4)
181	Kent, WA	(1.7)
158	Killeen, TX	0.5
143	Knoxville, TN	4.2
342	Lafayette, LA	(37.1)
367	Lake Forest, CA	(57.0)
229	Lakeland, FL	(9.8)
28	Lakewood, CA	54.5
189	Lakewood, CO	(2.9)
189	Lancaster, CA	(2.9)
NA	Lansing, MI**	NA
222	Laredo, TX	(8.0)
345	Las Cruces, NM	(39.1)
203	Las Vegas, NV	(5.9)
39	Lawrence, KS	41.7
137	Lawton, OK	5.7
2	Lee's Summit, MO	162.0
273	Lewisville, TX	(19.0)
NA	Lexington, KY**	NA
112	Lincoln, NE	10.2
NA	Little Rock, AR**	NA
36	Livermore, CA	43.3
NA	Livonia, MI**	NA
116	Long Beach, CA	9.7
NA	Longmont, CO**	NA

RANK	CITY	% CHANGE	RANK	CITY	% CHANGE	RANK	CITY	% CHANGE
343	Longview, TX	(38.0)	187	Peoria, AZ	(2.4)	NA	Southfield, MI**	NA
196	Los Angeles, CA	(4.5)	NA	Peoria, IL**	NA	298	Sparks, NV	(23.7)
NA	Louisville, KY**	NA	278	Philadelphia, PA	(19.6)	303	Spokane Valley, WA	(25.0)
102	Lubbock, TX	11.8	124	Phoenix, AZ	7.9	283	Spokane, WA	(20.8)
254	Lynn, MA	(15.0)	256	Pittsburgh, PA	(15.3)	NA	Springfield, IL**	NA
321	Macon, GA	(31.6)	227	Plano, TX	(8.8)	185	Springfield, MA	(2.3)
353	Madison, WI	(44.9)	352	Plantation, FL	(43.5)	88	Springfield, MO	16.8
162	Manchester, NH	0.3	66	Pomona, CA	24.0	92	Stamford, CT	13.6
117	McAllen, TX	9.4	182	Pompano Beach, FL	(1.8)	NA	Sterling Heights, MI**	NA
239	McKinney, TX	(11.7)	52	Port St. Lucie, FL	30.7	312	Stockton, CA	(26.4)
295	Melbourne, FL	(23.2)	176	Portland, OR	(0.7)	338	St. George, UT	(36.1)
140	Memphis, TN	5.0	371	Portsmouth, VA	(65.9)	217	St. Joseph, MO	(7.6)
231	Merced, CA	(10.2)	95	Providence, RI	13.2	135	St. Louis, MO	5.9
308	Mesa, AZ	(25.9)	245	Provo, UT	(12.8)	109	St. Paul, MN	10.7
16	Mesquite, TX	70.7	NA	Pueblo, CO**	NA	154	St. Petersburg, FL	1.1
270	Miami Beach, FL	(18.6)	51	Quincy, MA	31.0	101	Suffolk, VA	12.1
332	Miami Gardens, FL	(34.4)	12	Racine, WI	84.4	75	Sugar Land, TX	19.7
24	Miami, FL	58.2	166	Raleigh, NC	0.0	341	Sunnyvale, CA	(36.2)
301	Midland, TX	(24.7)	334	Ramapo, NY	(35.0)	208	Sunrise, FL	(6.5)
185	Milwaukee, WI	(2.3)	85	Rancho Cucamon., CA	17.7	118	Surprise, AZ	8.9
108	Minneapolis, MN	10.8	325	Reading, PA	(32.8)	178	Syracuse, NY	(0.8)
300	Miramar, FL	(24.5)	308	Redding, CA	(25.9)	160	Tacoma, WA	0.4
20	Mission Viejo, CA	65.6	166	Reno, NV	0.0	242	Tallahassee, FL	(12.5)
306	Missouri City, TX	(25.5)	21	Rialto, CA	64.9	201	Tampa, FL	(5.7)
40	Mobile, AL	38.9	358	Richardson, TX	(48.9)	224	Temecula, CA	(8.6)
253	Modesto, CA	(14.9)	84	Richmond, CA	17.9	8	Tempe, AZ	92.7
14	Montgomery, AL	74.6	335	Richmond, VA	(35.1)	86	Thornton, CO	17.3
364	Moreno Valley, CA	(54.9)	174	Rio Rancho, NM	(0.3)	78	Thousand Oaks, CA	19.4
35	Murfreesboro, TN	43.7	231	Riverside, CA	(10.2)	43	Toledo, OH	36.3
37	Murrieta, CA	42.1	356	Roanoke, VA	(46.6)	366	Toms River Twnshp, NJ	(56.4)
348	Nampa, ID	(39.7)	NA	Rochester, MN**	NA	62	Topeka, KS	24.5
NA	Naperville, IL**	NA	179	Rochester, NY	(1.0)	76	Torrance, CA	19.6
NA	Nashua, NH**	NA	235	Rockford, IL	(10.8)	151	Tracy, CA	2.1
250	Nashville, TN	(14.2)	355	Roseville, CA	(45.9)	98	Trenton, NJ	12.5
110	New Bedford, MA	10.5	287	Roswell, GA	(22.0)	NA	Troy, MI**	NA
NA	New Haven, CT**	NA	102	Round Rock, TX	11.8	280	Tucson, AZ	(20.0)
60	New Orleans, LA	26.0	136	Sacramento, CA	5.8	162	Tulsa, OK	0.3
216	New York, NY	(7.5)	71	Salem, OR	21.2	183	Tuscaloosa, AL	(1.9)
49	Newark, NJ	34.1	67	Salinas, CA	23.4	82	Tyler, TX	18.1
282	Newport Beach, CA	(20.6)	50	Salt Lake City, UT	33.3	129	Upper Darby Twnshp, PA	6.9
105	Newton, MA	11.5	153	San Angelo, TX	1.4	357	Vacaville, CA	(48.4)
81	Norfolk, VA	18.6	34	San Antonio, TX	45.5	64	Vallejo, CA	24.4
166	Norman, OK	0.0	203	San Bernardino, CA	(5.9)	111	Vancouver, WA	10.3
293	North Charleston, SC	(23.0)	268	San Diego, CA	(18.2)	289	Ventura, CA	(22.1)
240	North Las Vegas, NV	(12.4)	133	San Francisco, CA	6.3	38	Victorville, CA	41.9
47	Norwalk, CA	34.5	89	San Jose, CA	15.9	198	Virginia Beach, VA	(4.8)
261	Norwalk, CT	(16.7)	55	San Leandro, CA	29.2	96	Visalia, CA	13.0
195	Oakland, CA	(4.3)	7	San Marcos, CA	99.0	286	Vista, CA	(21.9)
156	Oceanside, CA	0.8	351	San Mateo, CA	(43.1)	336	Waco, TX	(35.6)
NA	Odessa, TX**	NA	100	Sandy Springs, GA	12.2	NA	Warren, MI**	NA
368	O'Fallon, MO	(58.4)	166	Sandy, UT	0.0	42	Warwick, RI	36.9
310	Ogden, UT	(26.0)	87	Santa Ana, CA	17.0	281	Washington, DC	(20.4)
223	Oklahoma City, OK	(8.3)	104	Santa Barbara, CA	11.6	284	Waterbury, CT	(20.9)
NA	Olathe, KS**	NA	175	Santa Clara, CA	(0.6)	207	West Covina, CA	(6.4)
139	Omaha, NE	5.1	138	Santa Clarita, CA	5.4	347	West Jordan, UT	(39.3)
291	Ontario, CA	(22.5)	314	Santa Maria, CA	(26.8)	236	West Palm Beach, FL	(10.9)
44	Orange, CA	35.6	330	Santa Monica, CA	(33.8)	224	West Valley, UT	(8.6)
338	Orem, UT	(36.1)	29	Santa Rosa, CA	51.6	NA	Westland, MI**	NA
243	Orlando, FL	(12.6)	67	Savannah, GA	23.4	59	Westminster, CA	26.6
285	Overland Park, KS	(21.1)	324	Scottsdale, AZ	(32.5)	345	Westminster, CO	(39.1)
94	Oxnard, CA	13.3	279	Seattle, WA	(19.9)	33	Whittier, CA	46.6
132	Palm Bay, FL	6.4	82	Shreveport, LA	18.1	160	Wichita Falls, TX	0.4
313	Palmdale, CA	(26.7)	297	Simi Valley, CA	(23.4)	230	Wichita, KS	(9.9)
73	Pasadena, CA	20.0	331	Sioux City, IA	(34.3)	152	Wilmington, NC	1.6
209	Pasadena, TX	(6.6)	166	Sioux Falls, SD	0.0	144	Winston-Salem, NC	3.7
70	Paterson, NJ	22.2	370	Somerville, MA	(65.6)	350	Woodbridge Twnshp, NJ	(41.8)
233	Pearland, TX	(10.3)	294	South Bend, IN	(23.1)	349	Worcester, MA	(40.9)
327	Pembroke Pines, FL	(33.0)	158	South Gate, CA	0.5	255	Yonkers, NY	(15.2)
						200	Yuma, AZ	(5.4)

Source: CQ Press using reported data from the F.B.I. "Crime in the United States 2009"

*Forcible rape is the carnal knowledge of a female forcibly and against her will. Assaults or attempts to commit rape by force or threat of force are included. However, statutory rape without force and other sex offenses are excluded. **Not available

55. Percent Change in Rape Rate: 2008 to 2009 (continued)
National Percent Change = 3.5% Decrease*

RANK	CITY	% CHANGE
1	Amherst, NY	250.0
2	Lee's Summit, MO	162.0
3	Avondale, AZ	121.4
4	Allentown, PA	118.6
5	Brick Twnshp, NJ	100.0
5	Coral Springs, FL	100.0
7	San Marcos, CA	99.0
8	Tempe, AZ	92.7
9	Allen, TX	91.7
10	Hawthorne, CA	89.2
11	Alhambra, CA	88.2
12	Racine, WI	84.4
13	Broken Arrow, OK	76.4
14	Montgomery, AL	74.6
15	Federal Way, WA	71.2
16	Mesquite, TX	70.7
17	Garden Grove, CA	69.4
18	Danbury, CT	67.0
19	Columbia, MO	66.0
20	Mission Viejo, CA	65.6
21	Rialto, CA	64.9
22	Greece, NY	61.6
23	Concord, CA	58.6
24	Miami, FL	58.2
25	Bellingham, WA	57.9
26	Boca Raton, FL	57.6
27	Elizabeth, NJ	57.1
28	Lakewood, CA	54.5
29	Santa Rosa, CA	51.6
30	Irvine, CA	51.2
31	Centennial, CO	48.6
32	Cambridge, MA	47.8
33	Whittier, CA	46.6
34	San Antonio, TX	45.5
35	Murfreesboro, TN	43.7
36	Livermore, CA	43.3
37	Murrieta, CA	42.1
38	Victorville, CA	41.9
39	Lawrence, KS	41.7
40	Mobile, AL	38.9
41	Antioch, CA	37.2
42	Warwick, RI	36.9
43	Toledo, OH	36.3
44	Hesperia, CA	35.6
44	Orange, CA	35.6
46	Escondido, CA	34.8
47	Norwalk, CA	34.5
48	Chico, CA	34.4
49	Newark, NJ	34.1
50	Salt Lake City, UT	33.3
51	Quincy, MA	31.0
52	Port St. Lucie, FL	30.7
53	Citrus Heights, CA	30.0
54	Burbank, CA	29.9
55	Abilene, TX	29.2
55	San Leandro, CA	29.2
57	Fayetteville, NC	28.6
58	Jacksonville, NC	27.9
59	Westminster, CA	26.6
60	New Orleans, LA	26.0
61	Cedar Rapids, IA	24.6
62	Cranston, RI	24.5
62	Topeka, KS	24.5
64	Vallejo, CA	24.4
65	Fayetteville, AR	24.3
66	Pomona, CA	24.0
67	Salinas, CA	23.4
67	Savannah, GA	23.4
69	Fullerton, CA	22.5
70	Paterson, NJ	22.2
71	Salem, OR	21.2
72	Eugene, OR	20.8
73	Pasadena, CA	20.0
74	Clovis, CA	19.8
75	Sugar Land, TX	19.7
76	Honolulu, HI	19.6
76	Torrance, CA	19.6
78	Thousand Oaks, CA	19.4
79	Columbia, SC	19.3
80	Denver, CO	19.1
81	Norfolk, VA	18.6
82	Shreveport, LA	18.1
82	Tyler, TX	18.1
84	Richmond, CA	17.9
85	Rancho Cucamon., CA	17.7
86	Thornton, CO	17.3
87	Santa Ana, CA	17.0
88	Springfield, MO	16.8
89	San Jose, CA	15.9
90	Baltimore, MD	14.4
91	Fort Collins, CO	13.8
92	Stamford, CT	13.6
93	Akron, OH	13.4
94	Oxnard, CA	13.3
95	Providence, RI	13.2
96	Visalia, CA	13.0
97	Clearwater, FL	12.7
98	Trenton, NJ	12.5
99	Aurora, CO	12.3
100	Sandy Springs, GA	12.2
101	Suffolk, VA	12.1
102	Lubbock, TX	11.8
102	Round Rock, TX	11.8
104	Santa Barbara, CA	11.6
105	Newton, MA	11.5
106	Clifton, NJ	11.3
107	Hamilton Twnshp, NJ	11.0
108	Minneapolis, MN	10.8
109	St. Paul, MN	10.7
110	New Bedford, MA	10.5
111	Vancouver, WA	10.3
112	Lincoln, NE	10.2
113	Corpus Christi, TX	10.0
114	Arvada, CO	9.9
114	Boston, MA	9.9
116	Long Beach, CA	9.7
117	McAllen, TX	9.4
118	Charlotte, NC	8.9
118	Surprise, AZ	8.9
120	High Point, NC	8.5
121	Irving, TX	8.4
122	Berkeley, CA	8.1
122	Houston, TX	8.1
124	Phoenix, AZ	7.9
125	Inglewood, CA	7.6
126	Carlsbad, CA	7.3
126	Chino, CA	7.3
126	Gainesville, FL	7.3
129	Arlington, TX	6.9
129	Upper Darby Twnshp, PA	6.9
131	Fresno, CA	6.5
132	Palm Bay, FL	6.4
133	San Francisco, CA	6.3
134	Anchorage, AK	6.0
135	St. Louis, MO	5.9
136	Sacramento, CA	5.8
137	Lawton, OK	5.7
138	Santa Clarita, CA	5.4
139	Omaha, NE	5.1
140	Grand Prairie, TX	5.0
140	Memphis, TN	5.0
142	Edmond, OK	4.8
143	Knoxville, TN	4.2
144	Winston-Salem, NC	3.7
145	Kansas City, MO	3.6
146	Atlanta, GA	3.4
147	Canton, OH	3.0
148	Fargo, ND	2.9
149	Albany, NY	2.7
150	Fort Worth, TX	2.4
151	Tracy, CA	2.1
152	Wilmington, NC	1.6
153	San Angelo, TX	1.4
154	St. Petersburg, FL	1.1
155	Baldwin Park, CA	0.9
156	Oceanside, CA	0.8
157	Bakersfield, CA	0.7
158	Killeen, TX	0.5
158	South Gate, CA	0.5
160	Tacoma, WA	0.4
160	Wichita Falls, TX	0.4
162	Manchester, NH	0.3
162	Tulsa, OK	0.3
164	Bridgeport, CT	0.2
164	Davenport, IA	0.2
166	Buena Park, CA	0.0
166	Colonie, NY	0.0
166	Jersey City, NJ	0.0
166	Norman, OK	0.0
166	Raleigh, NC	0.0
166	Reno, NV	0.0
166	Sandy, UT	0.0
166	Sioux Falls, SD	0.0
174	Rio Rancho, NM	(0.3)
175	Santa Clara, CA	(0.6)
176	El Paso, TX	(0.7)
176	Portland, OR	(0.7)
178	Syracuse, NY	(0.8)
179	Rochester, NY	(1.0)
180	Brownsville, TX	(1.4)
181	Kent, WA	(1.7)
182	Pompano Beach, FL	(1.8)
183	Denton, TX	(1.9)
183	Tuscaloosa, AL	(1.9)
185	Milwaukee, WI	(2.3)
185	Springfield, MA	(2.3)
187	Peoria, AZ	(2.4)
188	College Station, TX	(2.5)
189	Lakewood, CO	(2.9)
189	Lancaster, CA	(2.9)
191	Colorado Springs, CO	(3.2)
192	Beaumont, TX	(3.6)
193	Dallas, TX	(3.8)
194	Indianapolis, IN	(3.9)
195	Oakland, CA	(4.3)
196	Los Angeles, CA	(4.5)
197	Austin, TX	(4.7)
198	Virginia Beach, VA	(4.8)
199	Beaverton, OR	(5.0)
200	Yuma, AZ	(5.4)
201	Erie, PA	(5.7)
201	Tampa, FL	(5.7)
203	Las Vegas, NV	(5.9)
203	San Bernardino, CA	(5.9)
205	Birmingham, AL	(6.2)
206	Cary, NC	(6.3)

RANK	CITY	% CHANGE
207	West Covina, CA	(6.4)
208	Sunrise, FL	(6.5)
209	Fontana, CA	(6.6)
209	Indio, CA	(6.6)
209	Pasadena, TX	(6.6)
212	Carrollton, TX	(6.7)
213	Clarksville, TN	(7.0)
214	Gary, IN	(7.3)
215	Huntsville, AL	(7.4)
216	New York, NY	(7.5)
217	Columbus, OH	(7.6)
217	St. Joseph, MO	(7.6)
219	Jackson, MS	(7.7)
220	Evansville, IN	(7.8)
221	Frisco, TX	(7.9)
222	Laredo, TX	(8.0)
223	Oklahoma City, OK	(8.3)
224	Temecula, CA	(8.6)
224	West Valley, UT	(8.6)
226	Fremont, CA	(8.7)
227	Huntington Beach, CA	(8.8)
227	Plano, TX	(8.8)
229	Lakeland, FL	(9.8)
230	Wichita, KS	(9.9)
231	Merced, CA	(10.2)
231	Riverside, CA	(10.2)
233	Pearland, TX	(10.3)
234	Kenosha, WI	(10.4)
235	Rockford, IL	(10.8)
236	West Palm Beach, FL	(10.9)
237	Cleveland, OH	(11.0)
238	Chula Vista, CA	(11.4)
239	McKinney, TX	(11.7)
240	Albuquerque, NM	(12.4)
240	North Las Vegas, NV	(12.4)
242	Tallahassee, FL	(12.5)
243	Dayton, OH	(12.6)
243	Orlando, FL	(12.6)
245	Provo, UT	(12.8)
246	Cincinnati, OH	(12.9)
247	Green Bay, WI	(13.4)
248	Baton Rouge, LA	(14.0)
249	Anaheim, CA	(14.1)
250	Greeley, CO	(14.2)
250	Nashville, TN	(14.2)
252	Boise, ID	(14.8)
253	Modesto, CA	(14.9)
254	Lynn, MA	(15.0)
255	Yonkers, NY	(15.2)
256	Pittsburgh, PA	(15.3)
257	Hillsboro, OR	(15.7)
258	Cheektowaga, NY	(16.1)
259	Chattanooga, TN	(16.3)
260	Hialeah, FL	(16.4)
261	Norwalk, CT	(16.7)
262	Jacksonville, FL	(17.2)
263	Camden, NJ	(17.3)
264	El Cajon, CA	(17.4)
265	Glendale, AZ	(17.5)
266	Fairfield, CA	(17.6)
267	Durham, NC	(18.0)
268	San Diego, CA	(18.2)
269	Buffalo, NY	(18.5)
270	Chandler, AZ	(18.6)
270	Hammond, IN	(18.6)
270	Miami Beach, FL	(18.6)
273	Lewisville, TX	(19.0)
274	Independence, MO	(19.2)

RANK	CITY	% CHANGE
275	Amarillo, TX	(19.4)
275	Hartford, CT	(19.4)
277	Gilbert, AZ	(19.5)
278	Philadelphia, PA	(19.6)
279	Seattle, WA	(19.9)
280	Tucson, AZ	(20.0)
281	Washington, DC	(20.4)
282	Newport Beach, CA	(20.6)
283	Spokane, WA	(20.8)
284	Waterbury, CT	(20.9)
285	Overland Park, KS	(21.1)
286	Vista, CA	(21.9)
287	Fort Wayne, IN	(22.0)
287	Roswell, GA	(22.0)
289	Davie, FL	(22.1)
289	Ventura, CA	(22.1)
291	Ontario, CA	(22.5)
292	Athens-Clarke, GA	(22.6)
293	North Charleston, SC	(23.0)
294	South Bend, IN	(23.1)
295	Melbourne, FL	(23.2)
296	Fort Lauderdale, FL	(23.3)
297	Simi Valley, CA	(23.4)
298	Sparks, NV	(23.7)
299	Compton, CA	(24.4)
300	Miramar, FL	(24.5)
301	Midland, TX	(24.7)
302	Downey, CA	(24.8)
303	Hollywood, FL	(25.0)
303	Spokane Valley, WA	(25.0)
305	Boulder, CO	(25.2)
306	Missouri City, TX	(25.5)
307	Bellevue, WA	(25.7)
308	Mesa, AZ	(25.9)
308	Redding, CA	(25.9)
310	Carson, CA	(26.0)
310	Ogden, UT	(26.0)
312	Stockton, CA	(26.4)
313	Palmdale, CA	(26.7)
314	Santa Maria, CA	(26.8)
315	Daly City, CA	(28.5)
316	Glendale, CA	(29.0)
317	Fall River, MA	(30.0)
318	Billings, MT	(31.4)
318	Fort Smith, AR	(31.4)
318	Greensboro, NC	(31.4)
321	Costa Mesa, CA	(31.6)
321	Macon, GA	(31.6)
323	Elk Grove, CA	(32.3)
324	Scottsdale, AZ	(32.5)
325	Everett, WA	(32.8)
325	Reading, PA	(32.8)
327	Pembroke Pines, FL	(33.0)
328	Garland, TX	(33.2)
329	Edison Twnshp, NJ	(33.3)
330	Santa Monica, CA	(33.8)
331	Sioux City, IA	(34.3)
332	Miami Gardens, FL	(34.4)
333	Columbus, GA	(34.9)
334	Ramapo, NY	(35.0)
335	Richmond, VA	(35.1)
336	Waco, TX	(35.6)
337	Hampton, VA	(35.8)
338	Chesapeake, VA	(36.1)
338	Orem, UT	(36.1)
338	St. George, UT	(36.1)
341	Sunnyvale, CA	(36.2)
342	Lafayette, LA	(37.1)

RANK	CITY	% CHANGE
343	Longview, TX	(38.0)
344	Henderson, NV	(39.0)
345	Las Cruces, NM	(39.1)
345	Westminster, CO	(39.1)
347	West Jordan, UT	(39.3)
348	Nampa, ID	(39.7)
349	Worcester, MA	(40.9)
350	Woodbridge Twnshp, NJ	(41.8)
351	San Mateo, CA	(43.1)
352	Plantation, FL	(43.5)
353	Madison, WI	(44.9)
354	Bend, OR	(45.8)
355	Roseville, CA	(45.9)
356	Roanoke, VA	(46.6)
357	Vacaville, CA	(48.4)
358	Cape Coral, FL	(48.9)
358	Richardson, TX	(48.9)
360	Charleston, SC	(49.2)
361	Gresham, OR	(49.4)
362	Hayward, CA	(49.5)
363	Corona, CA	(51.5)
364	Moreno Valley, CA	(54.9)
365	El Monte, CA	(56.2)
366	Toms River Twnshp, NJ	(56.4)
367	Lake Forest, CA	(57.0)
368	O'Fallon, MO	(58.4)
369	Alexandria, VA	(61.5)
370	Somerville, MA	(65.6)
371	Portsmouth, VA	(65.9)
372	Clarkstown, NY	(66.7)
NA	Albany, GA**	NA
NA	Ann Arbor, MI**	NA
NA	Aurora, IL**	NA
NA	Bloomington, MN**	NA
NA	Brockton, MA**	NA
NA	Canton Twnshp, MI**	NA
NA	Chicago, IL**	NA
NA	Clinton Twnshp, MI**	NA
NA	Dearborn, MI**	NA
NA	Decatur, IL**	NA
NA	Des Moines, IA**	NA
NA	Detroit, MI**	NA
NA	Duluth, MN**	NA
NA	Elgin, IL**	NA
NA	Farmington Hills, MI**	NA
NA	Flint, MI**	NA
NA	Grand Rapids, MI**	NA
NA	Joliet, IL**	NA
NA	Kansas City, KS**	NA
NA	Lansing, MI**	NA
NA	Lexington, KY**	NA
NA	Little Rock, AR**	NA
NA	Livonia, MI**	NA
NA	Longmont, CO**	NA
NA	Louisville, KY**	NA
NA	Naperville, IL**	NA
NA	Nashua, NH**	NA
NA	New Haven, CT**	NA
NA	Odessa, TX**	NA
NA	Olathe, KS**	NA
NA	Peoria, IL**	NA
NA	Pueblo, CO**	NA
NA	Rochester, MN**	NA
NA	Southfield, MI**	NA
NA	Springfield, IL**	NA
NA	Sterling Heights, MI**	NA
NA	Troy, MI**	NA
NA	Warren, MI**	NA
NA	Westland, MI**	NA

Source: CQ Press using reported data from the F.B.I. "Crime in the United States 2009"
*Forcible rape is the carnal knowledge of a female forcibly and against her will. Assaults or attempts to commit rape by force or threat of force are included. However, statutory rape without force and other sex offenses are excluded. **Not available

56. Percent Change in Rape Rate: 2005 to 2009
National Percent Change = 9.8% Decrease*

RANK	CITY	% CHANGE
31	Abilene, TX	46.4
111	Akron, OH	6.1
69	Albany, GA	21.5
265	Albany, NY	(27.3)
113	Albuquerque, NM	5.7
334	Alexandria, VA	(51.5)
48	Alhambra, CA	29.6
20	Allentown, PA	59.4
71	Allen, TX	21.1
105	Amarillo, TX	9.4
138	Amherst, NY	0.0
188	Anaheim, CA	(11.2)
65	Anchorage, AK	22.7
NA	Ann Arbor, MI**	NA
35	Antioch, CA	43.1
220	Arlington, TX	(17.7)
60	Arvada, CO	25.8
163	Athens-Clarke, GA	(5.4)
338	Atlanta, GA	(52.9)
190	Aurora, CO	(11.5)
NA	Aurora, IL**	NA
253	Austin, TX	(23.3)
NA	Avondale, AZ**	NA
165	Bakersfield, CA	(5.7)
290	Baldwin Park, CA	(34.1)
145	Baltimore, MD	(2.4)
287	Baton Rouge, LA	(33.5)
246	Beaumont, TX	(22.1)
292	Beaverton, OR	(35.2)
229	Bellevue, WA	(18.4)
66	Bellingham, WA	22.0
322	Bend, OR	(47.1)
23	Berkeley, CA	51.7
254	Billings, MT	(23.3)
205	Birmingham, AL	(15.2)
NA	Bloomington, MN**	NA
30	Boca Raton, FL	48.4
316	Boise, ID	(44.9)
176	Boston, MA	(8.7)
273	Boulder, CO	(28.7)
NA	Brick Twnshp, NJ***	NA
174	Bridgeport, CT	(8.2)
98	Brockton, MA	10.7
5	Broken Arrow, OK	138.0
342	Brownsville, TX	(55.1)
196	Buena Park, CA	(13.7)
231	Buffalo, NY	(19.2)
14	Burbank, CA	71.8
83	Cambridge, MA	14.0
49	Camden, NJ	29.5
NA	Canton Twnshp, MI**	NA
73	Canton, OH	20.3
361	Cape Coral, FL	(71.8)
7	Carlsbad, CA	114.6
59	Carrollton, TX	26.0
259	Carson, CA	(24.9)
270	Cary, NC	(28.6)
178	Cedar Rapids, IA	(9.0)
295	Centennial, CO	(36.3)
249	Chandler, AZ	(22.7)
305	Charleston, SC	(40.8)
227	Charlotte, NC	(18.2)
351	Chattanooga, TN	(58.6)
33	Cheektowaga, NY	44.0
233	Chesapeake, VA	(19.7)
NA	Chicago, IL**	NA
101	Chico, CA	9.5
25	Chino, CA	50.0

RANK	CITY	% CHANGE
282	Chula Vista, CA	(31.9)
278	Cincinnati, OH	(29.6)
NA	Citrus Heights, CA**	NA
NA	Clarkstown, NY**	NA
158	Clarksville, TN	(4.2)
164	Clearwater, FL	(5.6)
212	Cleveland, OH	(16.6)
82	Clifton, NJ	14.3
NA	Clinton Twnshp, MI**	NA
160	Clovis, CA	(4.3)
154	College Station, TX	(3.5)
364	Colonie, NY	(88.9)
53	Colorado Springs, CO	27.9
29	Columbia, MO	48.6
93	Columbia, SC	12.0
9	Columbus, GA	96.9
110	Columbus, OH	6.6
169	Compton, CA	(7.0)
39	Concord, CA	40.2
339	Coral Springs, FL	(53.6)
358	Corona, CA	(64.9)
148	Corpus Christi, TX	(2.9)
180	Costa Mesa, CA	(9.3)
17	Cranston, RI	69.4
221	Dallas, TX	(17.7)
182	Daly City, CA	(9.6)
94	Danbury, CT	11.7
203	Davenport, IA	(15.0)
127	Davie, FL	3.6
281	Dayton, OH	(31.8)
NA	Dearborn, MI**	NA
NA	Decatur, IL**	NA
235	Denton, TX	(20.8)
146	Denver, CO	(2.4)
NA	Des Moines, IA**	NA
NA	Detroit, MI**	NA
299	Downey, CA	(38.1)
NA	Duluth, MN**	NA
294	Durham, NC	(36.2)
285	Edison Twnshp, NJ	(33.3)
313	Edmond, OK	(43.9)
263	El Cajon, CA	(25.8)
285	El Monte, CA	(33.3)
303	El Paso, TX	(40.0)
NA	Elgin, IL**	NA
4	Elizabeth, NJ	144.4
NA	Elk Grove, CA**	NA
97	Erie, PA	11.0
45	Escondido, CA	34.8
50	Eugene, OR	28.9
128	Evansville, IN	3.4
120	Everett, WA	5.1
302	Fairfield, CA	(39.4)
NA	Fall River, MA**	NA
62	Fargo, ND	25.2
NA	Farmington Hills, MI**	NA
230	Fayetteville, AR	(18.8)
32	Fayetteville, NC	46.3
179	Federal Way, WA	(9.1)
NA	Flint, MI**	NA
248	Fontana, CA	(22.7)
280	Fort Collins, CO	(31.5)
252	Fort Lauderdale, FL	(23.1)
297	Fort Smith, AR	(36.7)
243	Fort Wayne, IN	(21.8)
133	Fort Worth, TX	0.8
200	Fremont, CA	(14.3)
315	Fresno, CA	(44.6)
307	Frisco, TX	(41.4)

RANK	CITY	% CHANGE
72	Fullerton, CA	20.7
170	Gainesville, FL	(7.3)
21	Garden Grove, CA	56.5
46	Garland, TX	32.8
277	Gary, IN	(29.4)
311	Gilbert, AZ	(42.8)
300	Glendale, AZ	(38.6)
100	Glendale, CA	10.1
232	Grand Prairie, TX	(19.6)
NA	Grand Rapids, MI**	NA
103	Greece, NY	9.4
250	Greeley, CO	(22.9)
79	Green Bay, WI	14.7
216	Greensboro, NC	(16.9)
328	Gresham, OR	(49.4)
96	Hamilton Twnshp, NJ	11.0
114	Hammond, IN	5.6
308	Hampton, VA	(41.6)
107	Hartford, CT	7.3
11	Hawthorne, CA	94.7
244	Hayward, CA	(21.8)
63	Henderson, NV	24.4
43	Hesperia, CA	36.3
171	Hialeah, FL	(7.8)
95	High Point, NC	11.2
189	Hillsboro, OR	(11.3)
279	Hollywood, FL	(30.5)
124	Honolulu, HI	3.9
204	Houston, TX	(15.0)
159	Huntington Beach, CA	(4.3)
166	Huntsville, AL	(6.6)
126	Independence, MO	3.7
199	Indianapolis, IN	(14.1)
272	Indio, CA	(28.7)
240	Inglewood, CA	(21.5)
42	Irvine, CA	36.8
330	Irving, TX	(49.7)
89	Jacksonville, FL	13.0
NA	Jacksonville, NC**	NA
223	Jackson, MS	(18.0)
87	Jersey City, NJ	13.4
NA	Joliet, IL**	NA
224	Kansas City, KS	(18.0)
195	Kansas City, MO	(13.7)
140	Kenosha, WI	(0.5)
37	Kent, WA	41.1
288	Killeen, TX	(33.7)
34	Knoxville, TN	43.8
331	Lafayette, LA	(50.2)
354	Lake Forest, CA	(61.2)
68	Lakeland, FL	21.5
19	Lakewood, CA	60.4
173	Lakewood, CO	(8.0)
150	Lancaster, CA	(3.1)
NA	Lansing, MI**	NA
125	Laredo, TX	3.9
362	Las Cruces, NM	(79.4)
116	Las Vegas, NV	5.4
16	Lawrence, KS	70.4
10	Lawton, OK	95.2
64	Lee's Summit, MO	23.2
237	Lewisville, TX	(20.9)
NA	Lexington, KY**	NA
118	Lincoln, NE	5.1
NA	Little Rock, AR**	NA
168	Livermore, CA	(6.7)
NA	Livonia, MI**	NA
47	Long Beach, CA	30.0
NA	Longmont, CO**	NA

RANK	CITY	% CHANGE
352	Longview, TX	(58.7)
219	Los Angeles, CA	(17.5)
NA	Louisville, KY**	NA
210	Lubbock, TX	(16.1)
3	Lynn, MA	153.7
326	Macon, GA	(49.0)
360	Madison, WI	(67.0)
142	Manchester, NH	(1.5)
319	McAllen, TX	(45.5)
266	McKinney, TX	(27.3)
236	Melbourne, FL	(20.8)
147	Memphis, TN	(2.9)
122	Merced, CA	4.3
301	Mesa, AZ	(39.2)
91	Mesquite, TX	12.3
269	Miami Beach, FL	(28.4)
340	Miami Gardens, FL	(54.1)
150	Miami, FL	(3.1)
306	Midland, TX	(41.0)
61	Milwaukee, WI	25.3
132	Minneapolis, MN	1.0
157	Miramar, FL	(4.2)
15	Mission Viejo, CA	71.0
134	Missouri City, TX	0.5
327	Mobile, AL	(49.3)
197	Modesto, CA	(13.8)
247	Montgomery, AL	(22.3)
344	Moreno Valley, CA	(55.4)
130	Murfreesboro, TN	2.1
44	Murrieta, CA	35.0
NA	Nampa, ID**	NA
NA	Naperville, IL**	NA
57	Nashua, NH	27.3
274	Nashville, TN	(28.9)
52	New Bedford, MA	28.5
NA	New Haven, CT**	NA
NA	New Orleans, LA**	NA
312	New York, NY	(43.1)
217	Newark, NJ	(17.3)
359	Newport Beach, CA	(66.4)
28	Newton, MA	48.6
84	Norfolk, VA	13.9
70	Norman, OK	21.5
304	North Charleston, SC	(40.3)
293	North Las Vegas, NV	(35.8)
141	Norwalk, CA	(1.3)
88	Norwalk, CT	13.2
115	Oakland, CA	5.5
241	Oceanside, CA	(21.6)
2	Odessa, TX	184.3
350	O'Fallon, MO	(58.4)
257	Ogden, UT	(24.3)
239	Oklahoma City, OK	(21.5)
NA	Olathe, KS**	NA
184	Omaha, NE	(10.4)
194	Ontario, CA	(13.5)
1	Orange, CA	433.3
202	Orem, UT	(14.9)
296	Orlando, FL	(36.6)
192	Overland Park, KS	(12.5)
329	Oxnard, CA	(49.6)
321	Palm Bay, FL	(45.8)
251	Palmdale, CA	(23.1)
104	Pasadena, CA	9.4
102	Pasadena, TX	9.5
177	Paterson, NJ	(9.0)
357	Pearland, TX	(64.6)
347	Pembroke Pines, FL	(57.7)

RANK	CITY	% CHANGE
75	Peoria, AZ	16.2
NA	Peoria, IL**	NA
215	Philadelphia, PA	(16.7)
183	Phoenix, AZ	(10.2)
119	Pittsburgh, PA	5.1
255	Plano, TX	(23.6)
181	Plantation, FL	(9.3)
109	Pomona, CA	6.8
186	Pompano Beach, FL	(10.7)
6	Port St. Lucie, FL	122.1
260	Portland, OR	(25.3)
333	Portsmouth, VA	(51.4)
332	Providence, RI	(51.3)
317	Provo, UT	(45.1)
38	Pueblo, CO	40.7
271	Quincy, MA	(28.6)
99	Racine, WI	10.6
172	Raleigh, NC	(7.9)
12	Ramapo, NY	92.6
325	Rancho Cucamon., CA	(48.2)
345	Reading, PA	(56.6)
245	Redding, CA	(21.9)
276	Reno, NV	(29.2)
200	Rialto, CA	(14.3)
143	Richardson, TX	(1.7)
58	Richmond, CA	26.2
349	Richmond, VA	(58.0)
8	Rio Rancho, NM	101.4
209	Riverside, CA	(15.9)
335	Roanoke, VA	(52.5)
NA	Rochester, MN**	NA
135	Rochester, NY	0.4
NA	Rockford, IL**	NA
343	Roseville, CA	(55.2)
22	Roswell, GA	55.0
218	Round Rock, TX	(17.5)
129	Sacramento, CA	2.4
55	Salem, OR	27.7
86	Salinas, CA	13.5
36	Salt Lake City, UT	41.8
81	San Angelo, TX	14.7
152	San Antonio, TX	(3.2)
206	San Bernardino, CA	(15.3)
228	San Diego, CA	(18.2)
155	San Francisco, CA	(3.9)
167	San Jose, CA	(6.6)
144	San Leandro, CA	(2.1)
185	San Marcos, CA	(10.6)
264	San Mateo, CA	(27.2)
NA	Sandy Springs, GA**	NA
24	Sandy, UT	50.3
112	Santa Ana, CA	6.1
156	Santa Barbara, CA	(4.0)
121	Santa Clara, CA	4.7
80	Santa Clarita, CA	14.7
90	Santa Maria, CA	12.6
284	Santa Monica, CA	(33.2)
67	Santa Rosa, CA	21.6
314	Savannah, GA	(44.5)
356	Scottsdale, AZ	(64.4)
275	Seattle, WA	(29.0)
226	Shreveport, LA	(18.2)
309	Simi Valley, CA	(42.3)
337	Sioux City, IA	(52.9)
234	Sioux Falls, SD	(20.5)
138	Somerville, MA	0.0
213	South Bend, IN	(16.6)
123	South Gate, CA	4.2

RANK	CITY	% CHANGE
NA	Southfield, MI**	NA
291	Sparks, NV	(34.4)
318	Spokane Valley, WA	(45.4)
162	Spokane, WA	(5.4)
NA	Springfield, IL**	NA
117	Springfield, MA	5.1
54	Springfield, MO	27.7
13	Stamford, CT	73.8
NA	Sterling Heights, MI**	NA
267	Stockton, CA	(27.4)
225	St. George, UT	(18.1)
323	St. Joseph, MO	(47.8)
191	St. Louis, MO	(11.8)
261	St. Paul, MN	(25.3)
78	St. Petersburg, FL	15.1
187	Suffolk, VA	(11.2)
41	Sugar Land, TX	37.7
353	Sunnyvale, CA	(60.5)
289	Sunrise, FL	(34.0)
341	Surprise, AZ	(55.0)
137	Syracuse, NY	0.2
74	Tacoma, WA	19.9
211	Tallahassee, FL	(16.4)
355	Tampa, FL	(63.6)
268	Temecula, CA	(28.4)
198	Tempe, AZ	(14.1)
207	Thornton, CO	(15.7)
26	Thousand Oaks, CA	49.5
153	Toledo, OH	(3.4)
346	Toms River Twnshp, NJ	(56.8)
193	Topeka, KS	(13.0)
56	Torrance, CA	27.3
320	Tracy, CA	(45.6)
51	Trenton, NJ	28.6
NA	Troy, MI**	NA
324	Tucson, AZ	(47.9)
208	Tulsa, OK	(15.8)
298	Tuscaloosa, AL	(36.9)
149	Tyler, TX	(3.0)
76	Upper Darby Twnshp, PA	15.5
283	Vacaville, CA	(33.1)
NA	Vallejo, CA**	NA
136	Vancouver, WA	0.3
161	Ventura, CA	(4.4)
85	Victorville, CA	13.9
262	Virginia Beach, VA	(25.6)
77	Visalia, CA	15.4
40	Vista, CA	39.5
242	Waco, TX	(21.6)
NA	Warren, MI**	NA
26	Warwick, RI	49.5
214	Washington, DC	(16.7)
336	Waterbury, CT	(52.5)
256	West Covina, CA	(24.1)
NA	West Jordan, UT**	NA
310	West Palm Beach, FL	(42.7)
175	West Valley, UT	(8.5)
NA	Westland, MI**	NA
131	Westminster, CA	1.3
108	Westminster, CO	6.8
92	Whittier, CA	12.1
106	Wichita Falls, TX	8.8
NA	Wichita, KS**	NA
222	Wilmington, NC	(18.0)
238	Winston-Salem, NC	(21.5)
348	Woodbridge Twnshp, NJ	(57.7)
363	Worcester, MA	(82.8)
18	Yonkers, NY	67.9
258	Yuma, AZ	(24.7)

Source: CQ Press using reported data from the F.B.I. "Crime in the United States 2009"

*Forcible rape is the carnal knowledge of a female forcibly and against her will. **Not available. ***Brick Township had a rape rate of 0 in 2005 but had 8 rapes in 2009. Calculating percent increase from zero results in an infinite number. This is shown as "NA."

56. Percent Change in Rape Rate: 2005 to 2009 (continued)
National Percent Change = 9.8% Decrease*

RANK	CITY	% CHANGE
1	Orange, CA	433.3
2	Odessa, TX	184.3
3	Lynn, MA	153.7
4	Elizabeth, NJ	144.4
5	Broken Arrow, OK	138.0
6	Port St. Lucie, FL	122.1
7	Carlsbad, CA	114.6
8	Rio Rancho, NM	101.4
9	Columbus, GA	96.9
10	Lawton, OK	95.2
11	Hawthorne, CA	94.7
12	Ramapo, NY	92.6
13	Stamford, CT	73.8
14	Burbank, CA	71.8
15	Mission Viejo, CA	71.0
16	Lawrence, KS	70.4
17	Cranston, RI	69.4
18	Yonkers, NY	67.9
19	Lakewood, CA	60.4
20	Allentown, PA	59.4
21	Garden Grove, CA	56.5
22	Roswell, GA	55.0
23	Berkeley, CA	51.7
24	Sandy, UT	50.3
25	Chino, CA	50.0
26	Thousand Oaks, CA	49.5
26	Warwick, RI	49.5
28	Newton, MA	48.6
29	Columbia, MO	48.6
30	Boca Raton, FL	48.4
31	Abilene, TX	46.4
32	Fayetteville, NC	46.3
33	Cheektowaga, NY	44.0
34	Knoxville, TN	43.8
35	Antioch, CA	43.1
36	Salt Lake City, UT	41.8
37	Kent, WA	41.1
38	Pueblo, CO	40.7
39	Concord, CA	40.2
40	Vista, CA	39.5
41	Sugar Land, TX	37.7
42	Irvine, CA	36.8
43	Hesperia, CA	36.3
44	Murrieta, CA	35.0
45	Escondido, CA	34.8
46	Garland, TX	32.8
47	Long Beach, CA	30.0
48	Alhambra, CA	29.6
49	Camden, NJ	29.5
50	Eugene, OR	28.9
51	Trenton, NJ	28.6
52	New Bedford, MA	28.5
53	Colorado Springs, CO	27.9
54	Springfield, MO	27.7
55	Salem, OR	27.7
56	Torrance, CA	27.3
57	Nashua, NH	27.3
58	Richmond, CA	26.2
59	Carrollton, TX	26.0
60	Arvada, CO	25.8
61	Milwaukee, WI	25.3
62	Fargo, ND	25.2
63	Henderson, NV	24.4
64	Lee's Summit, MO	23.2
65	Anchorage, AK	22.7
66	Bellingham, WA	22.0
67	Santa Rosa, CA	21.6
68	Lakeland, FL	21.5
69	Albany, GA	21.5
70	Norman, OK	21.5
71	Allen, TX	21.1
72	Fullerton, CA	20.7
73	Canton, OH	20.3
74	Tacoma, WA	19.9
75	Peoria, AZ	16.2
76	Upper Darby Twnshp, PA	15.5
77	Visalia, CA	15.4
78	St. Petersburg, FL	15.1
79	Green Bay, WI	14.7
80	Santa Clarita, CA	14.7
81	San Angelo, TX	14.7
82	Clifton, NJ	14.3
83	Cambridge, MA	14.0
84	Norfolk, VA	13.9
85	Victorville, CA	13.9
86	Salinas, CA	13.5
87	Jersey City, NJ	13.4
88	Norwalk, CT	13.2
89	Jacksonville, FL	13.0
90	Santa Maria, CA	12.6
91	Mesquite, TX	12.3
92	Whittier, CA	12.1
93	Columbia, SC	12.0
94	Danbury, CT	11.7
95	High Point, NC	11.2
96	Hamilton Twnshp, NJ	11.0
97	Erie, PA	11.0
98	Brockton, MA	10.7
99	Racine, WI	10.6
100	Glendale, CA	10.1
101	Chico, CA	9.5
102	Pasadena, TX	9.5
103	Greece, NY	9.4
104	Pasadena, CA	9.4
105	Amarillo, TX	9.4
106	Wichita Falls, TX	8.8
107	Hartford, CT	7.3
108	Westminster, CO	6.8
109	Pomona, CA	6.8
110	Columbus, OH	6.6
111	Akron, OH	6.1
112	Santa Ana, CA	6.1
113	Albuquerque, NM	5.7
114	Hammond, IN	5.6
115	Oakland, CA	5.5
116	Las Vegas, NV	5.4
117	Springfield, MA	5.1
118	Lincoln, NE	5.1
119	Pittsburgh, PA	5.1
120	Everett, WA	5.1
121	Santa Clara, CA	4.7
122	Merced, CA	4.3
123	South Gate, CA	4.2
124	Honolulu, HI	3.9
125	Laredo, TX	3.9
126	Independence, MO	3.7
127	Davie, FL	3.6
128	Evansville, IN	3.4
129	Sacramento, CA	2.4
130	Murfreesboro, TN	2.1
131	Westminster, CA	1.3
132	Minneapolis, MN	1.0
133	Fort Worth, TX	0.8
134	Missouri City, TX	0.5
135	Rochester, NY	0.4
136	Vancouver, WA	0.3
137	Syracuse, NY	0.2
138	Amherst, NY	0.0
138	Somerville, MA	0.0
140	Kenosha, WI	(0.5)
141	Norwalk, CA	(1.3)
142	Manchester, NH	(1.5)
143	Richardson, TX	(1.7)
144	San Leandro, CA	(2.1)
145	Baltimore, MD	(2.4)
146	Denver, CO	(2.4)
147	Memphis, TN	(2.9)
148	Corpus Christi, TX	(2.9)
149	Tyler, TX	(3.0)
150	Lancaster, CA	(3.1)
150	Miami, FL	(3.1)
152	San Antonio, TX	(3.2)
153	Toledo, OH	(3.4)
154	College Station, TX	(3.5)
155	San Francisco, CA	(3.9)
156	Santa Barbara, CA	(4.0)
157	Miramar, FL	(4.2)
158	Clarksville, TN	(4.2)
159	Huntington Beach, CA	(4.3)
160	Clovis, CA	(4.3)
161	Ventura, CA	(4.4)
162	Spokane, WA	(5.4)
163	Athens-Clarke, GA	(5.4)
164	Clearwater, FL	(5.6)
165	Bakersfield, CA	(5.7)
166	Huntsville, AL	(6.6)
167	San Jose, CA	(6.6)
168	Livermore, CA	(6.7)
169	Compton, CA	(7.0)
170	Gainesville, FL	(7.3)
171	Hialeah, FL	(7.8)
172	Raleigh, NC	(7.9)
173	Lakewood, CO	(8.0)
174	Bridgeport, CT	(8.2)
175	West Valley, UT	(8.5)
176	Boston, MA	(8.7)
177	Paterson, NJ	(9.0)
178	Cedar Rapids, IA	(9.0)
179	Federal Way, WA	(9.1)
180	Costa Mesa, CA	(9.3)
181	Plantation, FL	(9.3)
182	Daly City, CA	(9.6)
183	Phoenix, AZ	(10.2)
184	Omaha, NE	(10.4)
185	San Marcos, CA	(10.6)
186	Pompano Beach, FL	(10.7)
187	Suffolk, VA	(11.2)
188	Anaheim, CA	(11.2)
189	Hillsboro, OR	(11.3)
190	Aurora, CO	(11.5)
191	St. Louis, MO	(11.8)
192	Overland Park, KS	(12.5)
193	Topeka, KS	(13.0)
194	Ontario, CA	(13.5)
195	Kansas City, MO	(13.7)
196	Buena Park, CA	(13.7)
197	Modesto, CA	(13.8)
198	Tempe, AZ	(14.1)
199	Indianapolis, IN	(14.1)
200	Fremont, CA	(14.3)
200	Rialto, CA	(14.3)
202	Orem, UT	(14.9)
203	Davenport, IA	(15.0)
204	Houston, TX	(15.0)
205	Birmingham, AL	(15.2)
206	San Bernardino, CA	(15.3)

RANK	CITY	% CHANGE
207	Thornton, CO	(15.7)
208	Tulsa, OK	(15.8)
209	Riverside, CA	(15.9)
210	Lubbock, TX	(16.1)
211	Tallahassee, FL	(16.4)
212	Cleveland, OH	(16.6)
213	South Bend, IN	(16.6)
214	Washington, DC	(16.7)
215	Philadelphia, PA	(16.7)
216	Greensboro, NC	(16.9)
217	Newark, NJ	(17.3)
218	Round Rock, TX	(17.5)
219	Los Angeles, CA	(17.5)
220	Arlington, TX	(17.7)
221	Dallas, TX	(17.7)
222	Wilmington, NC	(18.0)
223	Jackson, MS	(18.0)
224	Kansas City, KS	(18.0)
225	St. George, UT	(18.1)
226	Shreveport, LA	(18.2)
227	Charlotte, NC	(18.2)
228	San Diego, CA	(18.2)
229	Bellevue, WA	(18.4)
230	Fayetteville, AR	(18.8)
231	Buffalo, NY	(19.2)
232	Grand Prairie, TX	(19.6)
233	Chesapeake, VA	(19.7)
234	Sioux Falls, SD	(20.5)
235	Denton, TX	(20.8)
236	Melbourne, FL	(20.8)
237	Lewisville, TX	(20.9)
238	Winston-Salem, NC	(21.5)
239	Oklahoma City, OK	(21.5)
240	Inglewood, CA	(21.5)
241	Oceanside, CA	(21.6)
242	Waco, TX	(21.6)
243	Fort Wayne, IN	(21.8)
244	Hayward, CA	(21.8)
245	Redding, CA	(21.9)
246	Beaumont, TX	(22.1)
247	Montgomery, AL	(22.3)
248	Fontana, CA	(22.7)
249	Chandler, AZ	(22.7)
250	Greeley, CO	(22.9)
251	Palmdale, CA	(23.1)
252	Fort Lauderdale, FL	(23.1)
253	Austin, TX	(23.3)
254	Billings, MT	(23.3)
255	Plano, TX	(23.6)
256	West Covina, CA	(24.1)
257	Ogden, UT	(24.3)
258	Yuma, AZ	(24.7)
259	Carson, CA	(24.9)
260	Portland, OR	(25.3)
261	St. Paul, MN	(25.3)
262	Virginia Beach, VA	(25.6)
263	El Cajon, CA	(25.8)
264	San Mateo, CA	(27.2)
265	Albany, NY	(27.3)
266	McKinney, TX	(27.3)
267	Stockton, CA	(27.4)
268	Temecula, CA	(28.4)
269	Miami Beach, FL	(28.4)
270	Cary, NC	(28.6)
271	Quincy, MA	(28.6)
272	Indio, CA	(28.7)
273	Boulder, CO	(28.7)
274	Nashville, TN	(28.9)
275	Seattle, WA	(29.0)
276	Reno, NV	(29.2)
277	Gary, IN	(29.4)
278	Cincinnati, OH	(29.6)
279	Hollywood, FL	(30.5)
280	Fort Collins, CO	(31.5)
281	Dayton, OH	(31.8)
282	Chula Vista, CA	(31.9)
283	Vacaville, CA	(33.1)
284	Santa Monica, CA	(33.2)
285	Edison Twnshp, NJ	(33.3)
285	El Monte, CA	(33.3)
287	Baton Rouge, LA	(33.5)
288	Killeen, TX	(33.7)
289	Sunrise, FL	(34.0)
290	Baldwin Park, CA	(34.1)
291	Sparks, NV	(34.4)
292	Beaverton, OR	(35.2)
293	North Las Vegas, NV	(35.8)
294	Durham, NC	(36.2)
295	Centennial, CO	(36.3)
296	Orlando, FL	(36.6)
297	Fort Smith, AR	(36.7)
298	Tuscaloosa, AL	(36.9)
299	Downey, CA	(38.1)
300	Glendale, AZ	(38.6)
301	Mesa, AZ	(39.2)
302	Fairfield, CA	(39.4)
303	El Paso, TX	(40.0)
304	North Charleston, SC	(40.3)
305	Charleston, SC	(40.8)
306	Midland, TX	(41.0)
307	Frisco, TX	(41.4)
308	Hampton, VA	(41.6)
309	Simi Valley, CA	(42.3)
310	West Palm Beach, FL	(42.7)
311	Gilbert, AZ	(42.8)
312	New York, NY	(43.1)
313	Edmond, OK	(43.9)
314	Savannah, GA	(44.5)
315	Fresno, CA	(44.6)
316	Boise, ID	(44.9)
317	Provo, UT	(45.1)
318	Spokane Valley, WA	(45.4)
319	McAllen, TX	(45.5)
320	Tracy, CA	(45.6)
321	Palm Bay, FL	(45.8)
322	Bend, OR	(47.1)
323	St. Joseph, MO	(47.8)
324	Tucson, AZ	(47.9)
325	Rancho Cucamon., CA	(48.2)
326	Macon, GA	(49.0)
327	Mobile, AL	(49.3)
328	Gresham, OR	(49.4)
329	Oxnard, CA	(49.6)
330	Irving, TX	(49.7)
331	Lafayette, LA	(50.2)
332	Providence, RI	(51.3)
333	Portsmouth, VA	(51.4)
334	Alexandria, VA	(51.5)
335	Roanoke, VA	(52.5)
336	Waterbury, CT	(52.5)
337	Sioux City, IA	(52.9)
338	Atlanta, GA	(52.9)
339	Coral Springs, FL	(53.6)
340	Miami Gardens, FL	(54.1)
341	Surprise, AZ	(55.0)
342	Brownsville, TX	(55.1)
343	Roseville, CA	(55.2)
344	Moreno Valley, CA	(55.4)
345	Reading, PA	(56.6)
346	Toms River Twnshp, NJ	(56.8)
347	Pembroke Pines, FL	(57.7)
348	Woodbridge Twnshp, NJ	(57.7)
349	Richmond, VA	(58.0)
350	O'Fallon, MO	(58.4)
351	Chattanooga, TN	(58.6)
352	Longview, TX	(58.7)
353	Sunnyvale, CA	(60.5)
354	Lake Forest, CA	(61.2)
355	Tampa, FL	(63.6)
356	Scottsdale, AZ	(64.4)
357	Pearland, TX	(64.6)
358	Corona, CA	(64.9)
359	Newport Beach, CA	(66.4)
360	Madison, WI	(67.0)
361	Cape Coral, FL	(71.8)
362	Las Cruces, NM	(79.4)
363	Worcester, MA	(82.8)
364	Colonie, NY	(88.9)
NA	Ann Arbor, MI**	NA
NA	Aurora, IL**	NA
NA	Avondale, AZ**	NA
NA	Bloomington, MN**	NA
NA	Brick Twnshp, NJ***	NA
NA	Canton Twnshp, MI**	NA
NA	Chicago, IL**	NA
NA	Citrus Heights, CA**	NA
NA	Clarkstown, NY**	NA
NA	Clinton Twnshp, MI**	NA
NA	Dearborn, MI**	NA
NA	Decatur, IL**	NA
NA	Des Moines, IA**	NA
NA	Detroit, MI**	NA
NA	Duluth, MN**	NA
NA	Elgin, IL**	NA
NA	Elk Grove, CA**	NA
NA	Fall River, MA**	NA
NA	Farmington Hills, MI**	NA
NA	Flint, MI**	NA
NA	Grand Rapids, MI**	NA
NA	Jacksonville, NC**	NA
NA	Joliet, IL**	NA
NA	Lansing, MI**	NA
NA	Lexington, KY**	NA
NA	Little Rock, AR**	NA
NA	Livonia, MI**	NA
NA	Longmont, CO**	NA
NA	Louisville, KY**	NA
NA	Nampa, ID**	NA
NA	Naperville, IL**	NA
NA	New Haven, CT**	NA
NA	New Orleans, LA**	NA
NA	Olathe, KS**	NA
NA	Peoria, IL**	NA
NA	Rochester, MN**	NA
NA	Rockford, IL**	NA
NA	Sandy Springs, GA**	NA
NA	Southfield, MI**	NA
NA	Springfield, IL**	NA
NA	Sterling Heights, MI**	NA
NA	Troy, MI**	NA
NA	Vallejo, CA**	NA
NA	Warren, MI**	NA
NA	West Jordan, UT**	NA
NA	Westland, MI**	NA
NA	Wichita, KS**	NA

Source: CQ Press using reported data from the F.B.I. "Crime in the United States 2009"

*Forcible rape is the carnal knowledge of a female forcibly and against her will. **Not available. ***Brick Township had a rape rate of 0 in 2005 but had 8 rapes in 2009. Calculating percent increase from zero results in an infinite number. This is shown as "NA."

57. Robberies in 2009
National Total = 408,217 Robberies*

RANK	CITY	ROBBERY
255	Abilene, TX	137
71	Akron, OH	727
190	Albany, GA	221
149	Albany, NY	327
47	Albuquerque, NM	1,103
252	Alexandria, VA	141
257	Alhambra, CA	133
108	Allentown, PA	474
406	Allen, TX	15
139	Amarillo, TX	352
362	Amherst, NY	46
102	Anaheim, CA	504
97	Anchorage, AK	534
332	Ann Arbor, MI	63
154	Antioch, CA	315
78	Arlington, TX	672
382	Arvada, CO	36
240	Athens-Clarke, GA	155
19	Atlanta, GA	2,725
95	Aurora, CO	553
254	Aurora, IL	138
36	Austin, TX	1,415
281	Avondale, AZ	111
73	Bakersfield, CA	704
277	Baldwin Park, CA	112
13	Baltimore, MD	3,707
45	Baton Rouge, LA	1,135
148	Beaumont, TX	332
359	Beaverton, OR	47
336	Bellevue, WA	61
357	Bellingham, WA	48
403	Bend, OR	19
116	Berkeley, CA	444
325	Billings, MT	71
44	Birmingham, AL	1,150
356	Bloomington, MN	49
319	Boca Raton, FL	78
335	Boise, ID	62
24	Boston, MA	2,277
350	Boulder, CO	51
378	Brick Twnshp, NJ	37
76	Bridgeport, CT	680
176	Brockton, MA	262
379	Broken Arrow, OK	37
243	Brownsville, TX	152
264	Buena Park, CA	127
32	Buffalo, NY	1,636
301	Burbank, CA	93
219	Cambridge, MA	179
69	Camden, NJ	766
394	Canton Twnshp, MI	26
150	Canton, OH	324
303	Cape Coral, FL	92
349	Carlsbad, CA	53
267	Carrollton, TX	124
233	Carson, CA	164
357	Cary, NC	48
286	Cedar Rapids, IA	107
397	Centennial, CO	23
199	Chandler, AZ	205
194	Charleston, SC	218
23	Charlotte, NC	2,346
96	Chattanooga, TN	535
314	Cheektowaga, NY	81
185	Chesapeake, VA	229
2	Chicago, IL	15,877
267	Chico, CA	124
327	Chino, CA	69

RANK	CITY	ROBBERY
147	Chula Vista, CA	335
25	Cincinnati, OH	2,272
262	Citrus Heights, CA	128
395	Clarkstown, NY	25
289	Clarksville, TN	105
169	Clearwater, FL	275
14	Cleveland, OH	3,555
293	Clifton, NJ	101
353	Clinton Twnshp, MI	50
348	Clovis, CA	54
396	College Station, TX	24
393	Colonie, NY	29
99	Colorado Springs, CO	525
237	Columbia, MO	157
130	Columbia, SC	379
94	Columbus, GA	574
16	Columbus, OH	3,395
101	Compton, CA	509
197	Concord, CA	212
306	Coral Springs, FL	90
274	Corona, CA	117
111	Corpus Christi, TX	459
275	Costa Mesa, CA	114
380	Cranston, RI	37
7	Dallas, TX	5,501
291	Daly City, CA	102
353	Danbury, CT	50
190	Davenport, IA	221
305	Davie, FL	91
67	Dayton, OH	770
277	Dearborn, MI	112
247	Decatur, IL	149
317	Denton, TX	79
52	Denver, CO	946
181	Des Moines, IA	244
6	Detroit, MI	5,913
183	Downey, CA	234
271	Duluth, MN	122
72	Durham, NC	710
296	Edison Twnshp, NJ	97
404	Edmond, OK	18
188	El Cajon, CA	226
160	El Monte, CA	304
113	El Paso, TX	452
317	Elgin, IL	79
70	Elizabeth, NJ	761
243	Elk Grove, CA	152
272	Erie, PA	121
180	Escondido, CA	249
200	Eugene, OR	201
256	Evansville, IN	136
175	Everett, WA	263
206	Fairfield, CA	193
170	Fall River, MA	273
385	Fargo, ND	34
402	Farmington Hills, MI	20
374	Fayetteville, AR	38
103	Fayetteville, NC	491
201	Federal Way, WA	198
88	Flint, MI	590
163	Fontana, CA	299
329	Fort Collins, CO	68
75	Fort Lauderdale, FL	685
249	Fort Smith, AR	144
104	Fort Wayne, IN	485
35	Fort Worth, TX	1,449
195	Fremont, CA	217
48	Fresno, CA	1,085
407	Frisco, TX	13

RANK	CITY	ROBBERY
208	Fullerton, CA	189
182	Gainesville, FL	239
230	Garden Grove, CA	167
160	Garland, TX	304
165	Gary, IN	289
342	Gilbert, AZ	59
121	Glendale, AZ	420
265	Glendale, CA	126
205	Grand Prairie, TX	194
90	Grand Rapids, MI	581
370	Greece, NY	41
327	Greeley, CO	69
309	Green Bay, WI	87
55	Greensboro, NC	908
242	Gresham, OR	153
286	Hamilton Twnshp, NJ	107
184	Hammond, IN	233
203	Hampton, VA	195
86	Hartford, CT	600
138	Hawthorne, CA	354
115	Hayward, CA	446
178	Henderson, NV	257
312	Hesperia, CA	84
156	Hialeah, FL	309
170	High Point, NC	273
340	Hillsboro, OR	60
153	Hollywood, FL	317
60	Honolulu, HI	869
4	Houston, TX	11,367
262	Huntington Beach, CA	128
119	Huntsville, AL	433
230	Independence, MO	167
11	Indianapolis, IN	3,929
277	Indio, CA	112
104	Inglewood, CA	485
346	Irvine, CA	55
196	Irving, TX	214
22	Jacksonville, FL	2,359
353	Jacksonville, NC	50
51	Jackson, MS	958
59	Jersey City, NJ	871
251	Joliet, IL	142
152	Kansas City, KS	318
28	Kansas City, MO	1,970
291	Kenosha, WI	102
217	Kent, WA	180
219	Killeen, TX	179
80	Knoxville, TN	660
167	Lafayette, LA	286
391	Lake Forest, CA	30
229	Lakeland, FL	169
225	Lakewood, CA	173
227	Lakewood, CO	171
151	Lancaster, CA	322
179	Lansing, MI	255
156	Laredo, TX	309
297	Las Cruces, NM	96
8	Las Vegas, NV	4,495
320	Lawrence, KS	76
216	Lawton, OK	181
386	Lee's Summit, MO	34
321	Lewisville, TX	75
92	Lexington, KY	578
202	Lincoln, NE	197
66	Little Rock, AR	799
346	Livermore, CA	55
371	Livonia, MI	40
37	Long Beach, CA	1,381
365	Longmont, CO	44

RANK	CITY	ROBBERY
211	Longview, TX	185
3	Los Angeles, CA	12,217
34	Louisville, KY	1,570
155	Lubbock, TX	311
221	Lynn, MA	178
145	Macon, GA	342
136	Madison, WI	364
227	Manchester, NH	171
258	McAllen, TX	132
345	McKinney, TX	56
207	Melbourne, FL	192
9	Memphis, TN	4,139
235	Merced, CA	158
85	Mesa, AZ	611
193	Mesquite, TX	220
120	Miami Beach, FL	421
140	Miami Gardens, FL	351
26	Miami, FL	2,094
311	Midland, TX	85
17	Milwaukee, WI	3,122
31	Minneapolis, MN	1,663
223	Miramar, FL	174
375	Mission Viejo, CA	38
362	Missouri City, TX	46
62	Mobile, AL	857
134	Modesto, CA	369
112	Montgomery, AL	453
110	Moreno Valley, CA	467
210	Murfreesboro, TN	187
387	Murrieta, CA	34
401	Nampa, ID	21
399	Naperville, IL	22
376	Nashua, NH	38
27	Nashville, TN	1,971
146	New Bedford, MA	340
57	New Haven, CT	906
53	New Orleans, LA	932
1	New York, NY	18,597
39	Newark, NJ	1,319
388	Newport Beach, CA	32
405	Newton, MA	18
84	Norfolk, VA	630
359	Norman, OK	47
132	North Charleston, SC	376
89	North Las Vegas, NV	587
221	Norwalk, CA	178
237	Norwalk, CT	157
18	Oakland, CA	2,898
190	Oceanside, CA	221
208	Odessa, TX	189
411	O'Fallon, MO	11
286	Ogden, UT	107
41	Oklahoma City, OK	1,249
365	Olathe, KS	44
58	Omaha, NE	892
167	Ontario, CA	286
329	Orange, CA	68
400	Orem, UT	22
68	Orlando, FL	767
350	Overland Park, KS	51
129	Oxnard, CA	384
324	Palm Bay, FL	72
174	Palmdale, CA	264
215	Pasadena, CA	182
213	Pasadena, TX	184
83	Paterson, NJ	631
372	Pearland, TX	40
293	Pembroke Pines, FL	101

RANK	CITY	ROBBERY
307	Peoria, AZ	89
124	Peoria, IL	409
5	Philadelphia, PA	9,037
12	Phoenix, AZ	3,757
38	Pittsburgh, PA	1,367
250	Plano, TX	143
226	Plantation, FL	172
144	Pomona, CA	344
142	Pompano Beach, FL	348
340	Port St. Lucie, FL	60
49	Portland, OR	1,037
140	Portsmouth, VA	351
128	Providence, RI	395
389	Provo, UT	32
232	Pueblo, CO	165
297	Quincy, MA	96
186	Racine, WI	228
65	Raleigh, NC	832
408	Ramapo, NY	13
270	Rancho Cucamon., CA	123
134	Reading, PA	369
313	Redding, CA	83
124	Reno, NV	409
189	Rialto, CA	225
283	Richardson, TX	109
126	Richmond, CA	407
63	Richmond, VA	850
392	Rio Rancho, NM	30
79	Riverside, CA	667
213	Roanoke, VA	184
344	Rochester, MN	58
64	Rochester, NY	846
87	Rockford, IL	596
303	Roseville, CA	92
322	Roswell, GA	73
390	Round Rock, TX	32
33	Sacramento, CA	1,606
272	Salem, OR	121
130	Salinas, CA	379
123	Salt Lake City, UT	411
364	San Angelo, TX	45
21	San Antonio, TX	2,683
77	San Bernardino, CA	677
29	San Diego, CA	1,905
15	San Francisco, CA	3,423
50	San Jose, CA	1,025
177	San Leandro, CA	261
329	San Marcos, CA	68
282	San Mateo, CA	110
267	Sandy Springs, GA	124
398	Sandy, UT	23
60	Santa Ana, CA	869
283	Santa Barbara, CA	109
332	Santa Clara, CA	63
259	Santa Clarita, CA	129
322	Santa Maria, CA	73
234	Santa Monica, CA	162
217	Santa Rosa, CA	180
82	Savannah, GA	642
259	Scottsdale, AZ	129
30	Seattle, WA	1,792
104	Shreveport, LA	485
350	Simi Valley, CA	51
367	Sioux City, IA	43
359	Sioux Falls, SD	47
290	Somerville, MA	104
143	South Bend, IN	346
137	South Gate, CA	360

RANK	CITY	ROBBERY
259	Southfield, MI	129
277	Sparks, NV	112
332	Spokane Valley, WA	63
117	Spokane, WA	443
173	Springfield, IL	268
90	Springfield, MA	581
163	Springfield, MO	299
246	Stamford, CT	151
384	Sterling Heights, MI	35
40	Stockton, CA	1,259
409	St. George, UT	13
283	St. Joseph, MO	109
20	St. Louis, MO	2,721
74	St. Paul, MN	694
56	St. Petersburg, FL	907
314	Suffolk, VA	81
336	Sugar Land, TX	61
325	Sunnyvale, CA	71
276	Sunrise, FL	113
381	Surprise, AZ	37
127	Syracuse, NY	403
81	Tacoma, WA	648
108	Tallahassee, FL	474
54	Tampa, FL	909
342	Temecula, CA	59
158	Tempe, AZ	306
336	Thornton, CO	61
373	Thousand Oaks, CA	40
43	Toledo, OH	1,222
367	Toms River Twnshp, NJ	43
162	Topeka, KS	301
253	Torrance, CA	139
316	Tracy, CA	80
100	Trenton, NJ	512
410	Troy, MI	13
42	Tucson, AZ	1,246
46	Tulsa, OK	1,117
203	Tuscaloosa, AL	195
308	Tyler, TX	88
172	Upper Darby Twnshp, PA	270
297	Vacaville, CA	96
118	Vallejo, CA	439
235	Vancouver, WA	158
266	Ventura, CA	125
165	Victorville, CA	289
113	Virginia Beach, VA	452
211	Visalia, CA	185
248	Vista, CA	145
186	Waco, TX	228
198	Warren, MI	209
377	Warwick, RI	38
10	Washington, DC	3,998
223	Waterbury, CT	174
243	West Covina, CA	152
383	West Jordan, UT	36
132	West Palm Beach, FL	376
240	West Valley, UT	155
295	Westland, MI	98
301	Westminster, CA	93
369	Westminster, CO	42
300	Whittier, CA	94
237	Wichita Falls, TX	157
98	Wichita, KS	527
158	Wilmington, NC	306
93	Winston-Salem, NC	575
336	Woodbridge Twnshp, NJ	61
122	Worcester, MA	414
107	Yonkers, NY	475
310	Yuma, AZ	86

Source: Reported data from the F.B.I. "Crime in the United States 2009"

*Robbery is the taking of anything of value by force or threat of force. Attempts are included.

57. Robberies in 2009 (continued)
National Total = 408,217 Robberies*

RANK	CITY	ROBBERY
1	New York, NY	18,597
2	Chicago, IL	15,877
3	Los Angeles, CA	12,217
4	Houston, TX	11,367
5	Philadelphia, PA	9,037
6	Detroit, MI	5,913
7	Dallas, TX	5,501
8	Las Vegas, NV	4,495
9	Memphis, TN	4,139
10	Washington, DC	3,998
11	Indianapolis, IN	3,929
12	Phoenix, AZ	3,757
13	Baltimore, MD	3,707
14	Cleveland, OH	3,555
15	San Francisco, CA	3,423
16	Columbus, OH	3,395
17	Milwaukee, WI	3,122
18	Oakland, CA	2,898
19	Atlanta, GA	2,725
20	St. Louis, MO	2,721
21	San Antonio, TX	2,683
22	Jacksonville, FL	2,359
23	Charlotte, NC	2,346
24	Boston, MA	2,277
25	Cincinnati, OH	2,272
26	Miami, FL	2,094
27	Nashville, TN	1,971
28	Kansas City, MO	1,970
29	San Diego, CA	1,905
30	Seattle, WA	1,792
31	Minneapolis, MN	1,663
32	Buffalo, NY	1,636
33	Sacramento, CA	1,606
34	Louisville, KY	1,570
35	Fort Worth, TX	1,449
36	Austin, TX	1,415
37	Long Beach, CA	1,381
38	Pittsburgh, PA	1,367
39	Newark, NJ	1,319
40	Stockton, CA	1,259
41	Oklahoma City, OK	1,249
42	Tucson, AZ	1,246
43	Toledo, OH	1,222
44	Birmingham, AL	1,150
45	Baton Rouge, LA	1,135
46	Tulsa, OK	1,117
47	Albuquerque, NM	1,103
48	Fresno, CA	1,085
49	Portland, OR	1,037
50	San Jose, CA	1,025
51	Jackson, MS	958
52	Denver, CO	946
53	New Orleans, LA	932
54	Tampa, FL	909
55	Greensboro, NC	908
56	St. Petersburg, FL	907
57	New Haven, CT	906
58	Omaha, NE	892
59	Jersey City, NJ	871
60	Honolulu, HI	869
60	Santa Ana, CA	869
62	Mobile, AL	857
63	Richmond, VA	850
64	Rochester, NY	846
65	Raleigh, NC	832
66	Little Rock, AR	799
67	Dayton, OH	770
68	Orlando, FL	767
69	Camden, NJ	766
70	Elizabeth, NJ	761
71	Akron, OH	727
72	Durham, NC	710
73	Bakersfield, CA	704
74	St. Paul, MN	694
75	Fort Lauderdale, FL	685
76	Bridgeport, CT	680
77	San Bernardino, CA	677
78	Arlington, TX	672
79	Riverside, CA	667
80	Knoxville, TN	660
81	Tacoma, WA	648
82	Savannah, GA	642
83	Paterson, NJ	631
84	Norfolk, VA	630
85	Mesa, AZ	611
86	Hartford, CT	600
87	Rockford, IL	596
88	Flint, MI	590
89	North Las Vegas, NV	587
90	Grand Rapids, MI	581
90	Springfield, MA	581
92	Lexington, KY	578
93	Winston-Salem, NC	575
94	Columbus, GA	574
95	Aurora, CO	553
96	Chattanooga, TN	535
97	Anchorage, AK	534
98	Wichita, KS	527
99	Colorado Springs, CO	525
100	Trenton, NJ	512
101	Compton, CA	509
102	Anaheim, CA	504
103	Fayetteville, NC	491
104	Fort Wayne, IN	485
104	Inglewood, CA	485
104	Shreveport, LA	485
107	Yonkers, NY	475
108	Allentown, PA	474
108	Tallahassee, FL	474
110	Moreno Valley, CA	467
111	Corpus Christi, TX	459
112	Montgomery, AL	453
113	El Paso, TX	452
113	Virginia Beach, VA	452
115	Hayward, CA	446
116	Berkeley, CA	444
117	Spokane, WA	443
118	Vallejo, CA	439
119	Huntsville, AL	433
120	Miami Beach, FL	421
121	Glendale, AZ	420
122	Worcester, MA	414
123	Salt Lake City, UT	411
124	Peoria, IL	409
124	Reno, NV	409
126	Richmond, CA	407
127	Syracuse, NY	403
128	Providence, RI	395
129	Oxnard, CA	384
130	Columbia, SC	379
130	Salinas, CA	379
132	North Charleston, SC	376
132	West Palm Beach, FL	376
134	Modesto, CA	369
134	Reading, PA	369
136	Madison, WI	364
137	South Gate, CA	360
138	Hawthorne, CA	354
139	Amarillo, TX	352
140	Miami Gardens, FL	351
140	Portsmouth, VA	351
142	Pompano Beach, FL	348
143	South Bend, IN	346
144	Pomona, CA	344
145	Macon, GA	342
146	New Bedford, MA	340
147	Chula Vista, CA	335
148	Beaumont, TX	332
149	Albany, NY	327
150	Canton, OH	324
151	Lancaster, CA	322
152	Kansas City, KS	318
153	Hollywood, FL	317
154	Antioch, CA	315
155	Lubbock, TX	311
156	Hialeah, FL	309
156	Laredo, TX	309
158	Tempe, AZ	306
158	Wilmington, NC	306
160	El Monte, CA	304
160	Garland, TX	304
162	Topeka, KS	301
163	Fontana, CA	299
163	Springfield, MO	299
165	Gary, IN	289
165	Victorville, CA	289
167	Lafayette, LA	286
167	Ontario, CA	286
169	Clearwater, FL	275
170	Fall River, MA	273
170	High Point, NC	273
172	Upper Darby Twnshp, PA	270
173	Springfield, IL	268
174	Palmdale, CA	264
175	Everett, WA	263
176	Brockton, MA	262
177	San Leandro, CA	261
178	Henderson, NV	257
179	Lansing, MI	255
180	Escondido, CA	249
181	Des Moines, IA	244
182	Gainesville, FL	239
183	Downey, CA	234
184	Hammond, IN	233
185	Chesapeake, VA	229
186	Racine, WI	228
186	Waco, TX	228
188	El Cajon, CA	226
189	Rialto, CA	225
190	Albany, GA	221
190	Davenport, IA	221
190	Oceanside, CA	221
193	Mesquite, TX	220
194	Charleston, SC	218
195	Fremont, CA	217
196	Irving, TX	214
197	Concord, CA	212
198	Warren, MI	209
199	Chandler, AZ	205
200	Eugene, OR	201
201	Federal Way, WA	198
202	Lincoln, NE	197
203	Hampton, VA	195
203	Tuscaloosa, AL	195
205	Grand Prairie, TX	194
206	Fairfield, CA	193

RANK	CITY	ROBBERY
207	Melbourne, FL	192
208	Fullerton, CA	189
208	Odessa, TX	189
210	Murfreesboro, TN	187
211	Longview, TX	185
211	Visalia, CA	185
213	Pasadena, TX	184
213	Roanoke, VA	184
215	Pasadena, CA	182
216	Lawton, OK	181
217	Kent, WA	180
217	Santa Rosa, CA	180
219	Cambridge, MA	179
219	Killeen, TX	179
221	Lynn, MA	178
221	Norwalk, CA	178
223	Miramar, FL	174
223	Waterbury, CT	174
225	Lakewood, CA	173
226	Plantation, FL	172
227	Lakewood, CO	171
227	Manchester, NH	171
229	Lakeland, FL	169
230	Garden Grove, CA	167
230	Independence, MO	167
232	Pueblo, CO	165
233	Carson, CA	164
234	Santa Monica, CA	162
235	Merced, CA	158
235	Vancouver, WA	158
237	Columbia, MO	157
237	Norwalk, CT	157
237	Wichita Falls, TX	157
240	Athens-Clarke, GA	155
240	West Valley, UT	155
242	Gresham, OR	153
243	Brownsville, TX	152
243	Elk Grove, CA	152
243	West Covina, CA	152
246	Stamford, CT	151
247	Decatur, IL	149
248	Vista, CA	145
249	Fort Smith, AR	144
250	Plano, TX	143
251	Joliet, IL	142
252	Alexandria, VA	141
253	Torrance, CA	139
254	Aurora, IL	138
255	Abilene, TX	137
256	Evansville, IN	136
257	Alhambra, CA	133
258	McAllen, TX	132
259	Santa Clarita, CA	129
259	Scottsdale, AZ	129
259	Southfield, MI	129
262	Citrus Heights, CA	128
262	Huntington Beach, CA	128
264	Buena Park, CA	127
265	Glendale, CA	126
266	Ventura, CA	125
267	Carrollton, TX	124
267	Chico, CA	124
267	Sandy Springs, GA	124
270	Rancho Cucamon., CA	123
271	Duluth, MN	122
272	Erie, PA	121
272	Salem, OR	121
274	Corona, CA	117

RANK	CITY	ROBBERY
275	Costa Mesa, CA	114
276	Sunrise, FL	113
277	Baldwin Park, CA	112
277	Dearborn, MI	112
277	Indio, CA	112
277	Sparks, NV	112
281	Avondale, AZ	111
282	San Mateo, CA	110
283	Richardson, TX	109
283	Santa Barbara, CA	109
283	St. Joseph, MO	109
286	Cedar Rapids, IA	107
286	Hamilton Twnshp, NJ	107
286	Ogden, UT	107
289	Clarksville, TN	105
290	Somerville, MA	104
291	Daly City, CA	102
291	Kenosha, WI	102
293	Clifton, NJ	101
293	Pembroke Pines, FL	101
295	Westland, MI	98
296	Edison Twnshp, NJ	97
297	Las Cruces, NM	96
297	Quincy, MA	96
297	Vacaville, CA	96
300	Whittier, CA	94
301	Burbank, CA	93
301	Westminster, CA	93
303	Cape Coral, FL	92
303	Roseville, CA	92
305	Davie, FL	91
306	Coral Springs, FL	90
307	Peoria, AZ	89
308	Tyler, TX	88
309	Green Bay, WI	87
310	Yuma, AZ	86
311	Midland, TX	85
312	Hesperia, CA	84
313	Redding, CA	83
314	Cheektowaga, NY	81
314	Suffolk, VA	81
316	Tracy, CA	80
317	Denton, TX	79
317	Elgin, IL	79
319	Boca Raton, FL	78
320	Lawrence, KS	76
321	Lewisville, TX	75
322	Roswell, GA	73
322	Santa Maria, CA	73
324	Palm Bay, FL	72
325	Billings, MT	71
325	Sunnyvale, CA	71
327	Chino, CA	69
327	Greeley, CO	69
329	Fort Collins, CO	68
329	Orange, CA	68
329	San Marcos, CA	68
332	Ann Arbor, MI	63
332	Santa Clara, CA	63
332	Spokane Valley, WA	63
335	Boise, ID	62
336	Bellevue, WA	61
336	Sugar Land, TX	61
336	Thornton, CO	61
336	Woodbridge Twnshp, NJ	61
340	Hillsboro, OR	60
340	Port St. Lucie, FL	60
342	Gilbert, AZ	59

Source: Reported data from the F.B.I. "Crime in the United States 2009"
*Robbery is the taking of anything of value by force or threat of force. Attempts are included.

RANK	CITY	ROBBERY
342	Temecula, CA	59
344	Rochester, MN	58
345	McKinney, TX	56
346	Irvine, CA	55
346	Livermore, CA	55
348	Clovis, CA	54
349	Carlsbad, CA	53
350	Boulder, CO	51
350	Overland Park, KS	51
350	Simi Valley, CA	51
353	Clinton Twnshp, MI	50
353	Danbury, CT	50
353	Jacksonville, NC	50
356	Bloomington, MN	49
357	Bellingham, WA	48
357	Cary, NC	48
359	Beaverton, OR	47
359	Norman, OK	47
359	Sioux Falls, SD	47
362	Amherst, NY	46
362	Missouri City, TX	46
364	San Angelo, TX	45
365	Longmont, CO	44
365	Olathe, KS	44
367	Sioux City, IA	43
367	Toms River Twnshp, NJ	43
369	Westminster, CO	42
370	Greece, NY	41
371	Livonia, MI	40
372	Pearland, TX	40
373	Thousand Oaks, CA	40
374	Fayetteville, AR	38
375	Mission Viejo, CA	38
376	Nashua, NH	38
377	Warwick, RI	38
378	Brick Twnshp, NJ	37
379	Broken Arrow, OK	37
380	Cranston, RI	37
381	Surprise, AZ	37
382	Arvada, CO	36
383	West Jordan, UT	36
384	Sterling Heights, MI	35
385	Fargo, ND	34
386	Lee's Summit, MO	34
387	Murrieta, CA	34
388	Newport Beach, CA	32
389	Provo, UT	32
390	Round Rock, TX	32
391	Lake Forest, CA	30
392	Rio Rancho, NM	30
393	Colonie, NY	29
394	Canton Twnshp, MI	26
395	Clarkstown, NY	25
396	College Station, TX	24
397	Centennial, CO	23
398	Sandy, UT	23
399	Naperville, IL	22
400	Orem, UT	22
401	Nampa, ID	21
402	Farmington Hills, MI	20
403	Bend, OR	19
404	Edmond, OK	18
405	Newton, MA	18
406	Allen, TX	15
407	Frisco, TX	13
408	Ramapo, NY	13
409	St. George, UT	13
410	Troy, MI	13
411	O'Fallon, MO	11

58. Robbery Rate in 2009
National Rate = 133.0 Robberies per 100,000 Population*

RANK	CITY	RATE
257	Abilene, TX	117.5
65	Akron, OH	352.1
98	Albany, GA	291.8
66	Albany, NY	349.9
153	Albuquerque, NM	207.9
285	Alexandria, VA	96.5
209	Alhambra, CA	154.7
33	Allentown, PA	441.6
405	Allen, TX	17.3
173	Amarillo, TX	186.5
368	Amherst, NY	41.7
213	Anaheim, CA	150.0
172	Anchorage, AK	188.5
340	Ann Arbor, MI	55.1
83	Antioch, CA	311.1
184	Arlington, TX	177.3
383	Arvada, CO	33.4
232	Athens-Clarke, GA	135.3
27	Atlanta, GA	492.9
192	Aurora, CO	170.7
306	Aurora, IL	78.8
177	Austin, TX	184.0
248	Avondale, AZ	125.0
151	Bakersfield, CA	212.8
222	Baldwin Park, CA	144.4
14	Baltimore, MD	580.3
20	Baton Rouge, LA	508.5
91	Beaumont, TX	301.2
351	Beaverton, OR	50.4
355	Bellevue, WA	48.8
333	Bellingham, WA	59.8
400	Bend, OR	23.6
34	Berkeley, CA	438.8
324	Billings, MT	67.3
21	Birmingham, AL	505.8
332	Bloomington, MN	60.6
293	Boca Raton, FL	90.7
388	Boise, ID	30.0
60	Boston, MA	364.8
349	Boulder, CO	51.0
357	Brick Twnshp, NJ	47.0
24	Bridgeport, CT	499.8
105	Brockton, MA	271.6
373	Broken Arrow, OK	39.2
298	Brownsville, TX	84.7
199	Buena Park, CA	159.7
12	Buffalo, NY	609.0
294	Burbank, CA	90.1
188	Cambridge, MA	174.0
1	Camden, NJ	969.9
387	Canton Twnshp, MI	31.5
46	Canton, OH	414.9
339	Cape Coral, FL	56.0
343	Carlsbad, CA	53.8
284	Carrollton, TX	97.3
185	Carson, CA	177.0
379	Cary, NC	35.9
300	Cedar Rapids, IA	83.1
402	Centennial, CO	23.1
305	Chandler, AZ	80.0
168	Charleston, SC	191.8
89	Charlotte, NC	301.7
84	Chattanooga, TN	310.1
269	Cheektowaga, NY	104.2
273	Chesapeake, VA	102.6
15	Chicago, IL	557.4
219	Chico, CA	146.4
304	Chino, CA	81.5

RANK	CITY	RATE
215	Chula Vista, CA	149.0
6	Cincinnati, OH	681.1
211	Citrus Heights, CA	151.8
386	Clarkstown, NY	31.7
296	Clarksville, TN	86.3
111	Clearwater, FL	261.0
2	Cleveland, OH	828.2
239	Clifton, NJ	129.3
346	Clinton Twnshp, MI	52.1
337	Clovis, CA	56.7
392	College Station, TX	27.9
375	Colonie, NY	37.2
236	Colorado Springs, CO	130.7
210	Columbia, MO	153.0
96	Columbia, SC	296.4
85	Columbus, GA	308.2
32	Columbus, OH	447.1
17	Compton, CA	542.2
187	Concord, CA	175.1
319	Coral Springs, FL	71.6
311	Corona, CA	76.8
200	Corpus Christi, TX	159.6
272	Costa Mesa, CA	103.5
358	Cranston, RI	46.1
40	Dallas, TX	426.3
276	Daly City, CA	100.7
329	Danbury, CT	62.7
146	Davenport, IA	218.6
275	Davie, FL	100.9
22	Dayton, OH	503.4
235	Dearborn, MI	131.3
163	Decatur, IL	197.0
328	Denton, TX	63.6
206	Denver, CO	156.4
250	Des Moines, IA	124.0
8	Detroit, MI	650.9
148	Downey, CA	217.5
220	Duluth, MN	145.1
82	Durham, NC	312.1
282	Edison Twnshp, NJ	97.6
403	Edmond, OK	22.3
121	El Cajon, CA	244.4
117	El Monte, CA	248.3
316	El Paso, TX	73.0
315	Elgin, IL	73.4
11	Elizabeth, NJ	609.2
262	Elk Grove, CA	108.1
259	Erie, PA	116.5
180	Escondido, CA	181.2
234	Eugene, OR	132.8
257	Evansville, IN	117.5
107	Everett, WA	267.2
176	Fairfield, CA	184.7
95	Fall River, MA	297.1
377	Fargo, ND	36.2
395	Farmington Hills, MI	25.6
350	Fayetteville, AR	50.6
101	Fayetteville, NC	282.2
128	Federal Way, WA	235.1
18	Flint, MI	528.4
203	Fontana, CA	157.1
354	Fort Collins, CO	49.1
54	Fort Lauderdale, FL	374.4
193	Fort Smith, AR	169.1
167	Fort Wayne, IN	192.8
161	Fort Worth, TX	200.3
264	Fremont, CA	107.0
136	Fresno, CA	225.4
411	Frisco, TX	12.0

RANK	CITY	RATE
225	Fullerton, CA	142.7
154	Gainesville, FL	207.3
276	Garden Grove, CA	100.7
228	Garland, TX	138.9
87	Gary, IN	303.5
396	Gilbert, AZ	25.5
196	Glendale, AZ	164.7
327	Glendale, CA	63.8
256	Grand Prairie, TX	117.7
91	Grand Rapids, MI	301.2
363	Greece, NY	44.0
313	Greeley, CO	74.1
296	Green Bay, WI	86.3
62	Greensboro, NC	358.6
214	Gresham, OR	149.3
255	Hamilton Twnshp, NJ	118.2
86	Hammond, IN	306.2
233	Hampton, VA	133.6
28	Hartford, CT	483.7
43	Hawthorne, CA	419.9
81	Hayward, CA	313.6
281	Henderson, NV	98.1
289	Hesperia, CA	94.5
218	Hialeah, FL	147.9
109	High Point, NC	263.3
331	Hillsboro, OR	62.1
140	Hollywood, FL	223.9
286	Honolulu, HI	95.8
23	Houston, TX	499.9
325	Huntington Beach, CA	66.4
124	Huntsville, AL	242.4
230	Independence, MO	136.7
29	Indianapolis, IN	483.0
246	Indio, CA	125.2
39	Inglewood, CA	430.3
397	Irvine, CA	25.5
266	Irving, TX	105.7
99	Jacksonville, FL	291.2
326	Jacksonville, NC	64.5
16	Jackson, MS	554.4
61	Jersey City, NJ	361.6
291	Joliet, IL	94.0
141	Kansas City, KS	223.8
48	Kansas City, MO	406.5
267	Kenosha, WI	104.4
150	Kent, WA	213.4
217	Killeen, TX	148.3
64	Knoxville, TN	355.1
114	Lafayette, LA	251.2
371	Lake Forest, CA	39.7
183	Lakeland, FL	179.2
145	Lakewood, CA	220.8
252	Lakewood, CO	121.6
149	Lancaster, CA	216.5
137	Lansing, MI	224.9
231	Laredo, TX	136.2
274	Las Cruces, NM	102.1
76	Las Vegas, NV	326.4
301	Lawrence, KS	82.9
158	Lawton, OK	201.5
372	Lee's Summit, MO	39.6
318	Lewisville, TX	71.7
166	Lexington, KY	195.0
310	Lincoln, NE	77.4
42	Little Rock, AR	420.1
323	Livermore, CA	68.0
362	Livonia, MI	44.3
93	Long Beach, CA	297.6
352	Longmont, CO	50.2

RANK	CITY	RATE
125	Longview, TX	238.2
80	Los Angeles, CA	317.4
116	Louisville, KY	248.7
227	Lubbock, TX	139.5
164	Lynn, MA	195.3
57	Macon, GA	370.5
208	Madison, WI	155.2
202	Manchester, NH	157.4
278	McAllen, TX	99.5
366	McKinney, TX	42.4
120	Melbourne, FL	246.6
9	Memphis, TN	620.1
160	Merced, CA	200.8
237	Mesa, AZ	129.8
194	Mesquite, TX	165.5
25	Miami Beach, FL	499.6
79	Miami Gardens, FL	318.1
26	Miami, FL	499.5
306	Midland, TX	78.8
19	Milwaukee, WI	516.3
37	Minneapolis, MN	434.6
198	Miramar, FL	160.6
369	Mission Viejo, CA	40.2
334	Missouri City, TX	59.3
67	Mobile, AL	348.1
181	Modesto, CA	180.5
142	Montgomery, AL	223.4
126	Moreno Valley, CA	236.9
186	Murfreesboro, TN	176.6
384	Murrieta, CA	32.3
398	Nampa, ID	25.0
409	Naperville, IL	15.2
364	Nashua, NH	43.9
78	Nashville, TN	323.0
59	New Bedford, MA	367.1
4	New Haven, CT	732.7
103	New Orleans, LA	277.0
144	New York, NY	221.4
30	Newark, NJ	472.4
370	Newport Beach, CA	40.0
404	Newton, MA	21.3
106	Norfolk, VA	268.0
365	Norman, OK	43.5
50	North Charleston, SC	391.7
113	North Las Vegas, NV	252.3
189	Norwalk, CA	173.1
171	Norwalk, CT	188.7
5	Oakland, CA	716.3
238	Oceanside, CA	129.6
170	Odessa, TX	189.4
410	O'Fallon, MO	13.7
240	Ogden, UT	128.9
139	Oklahoma City, OK	224.3
380	Olathe, KS	35.7
159	Omaha, NE	201.3
195	Ontario, CA	165.1
353	Orange, CA	49.6
401	Orem, UT	23.5
77	Orlando, FL	326.2
390	Overland Park, KS	29.4
156	Oxnard, CA	205.0
320	Palm Bay, FL	69.6
182	Palmdale, CA	180.4
244	Pasadena, CA	126.3
246	Pasadena, TX	125.2
36	Paterson, NJ	435.3
359	Pearland, TX	45.2
322	Pembroke Pines, FL	69.4

RANK	CITY	RATE
341	Peoria, AZ	54.1
63	Peoria, IL	358.0
13	Philadelphia, PA	583.9
127	Phoenix, AZ	235.2
35	Pittsburgh, PA	437.8
345	Plano, TX	52.4
155	Plantation, FL	205.9
138	Pomona, CA	224.5
70	Pompano Beach, FL	341.7
376	Port St. Lucie, FL	36.6
175	Portland, OR	184.9
68	Portsmouth, VA	347.6
131	Providence, RI	230.1
394	Provo, UT	26.8
204	Pueblo, CO	156.7
279	Quincy, MA	99.4
102	Racine, WI	277.3
157	Raleigh, NC	204.9
407	Ramapo, NY	17.0
320	Rancho Cucamon., CA	69.6
31	Reading, PA	458.9
292	Redding, CA	91.0
174	Reno, NV	185.1
135	Rialto, CA	226.4
265	Richardson, TX	106.2
49	Richmond, CA	396.8
45	Richmond, VA	418.2
378	Rio Rancho, NM	36.0
143	Riverside, CA	222.4
162	Roanoke, VA	197.6
336	Rochester, MN	56.9
47	Rochester, NY	411.6
53	Rockford, IL	377.4
308	Roseville, CA	78.7
303	Roswell, GA	82.6
391	Round Rock, TX	29.0
71	Sacramento, CA	341.5
309	Salem, OR	77.9
108	Salinas, CA	263.8
132	Salt Lake City, UT	227.4
355	San Angelo, TX	48.8
164	San Antonio, TX	195.3
72	San Bernardino, CA	339.0
221	San Diego, CA	144.9
41	San Francisco, CA	422.7
263	San Jose, CA	107.4
73	San Leandro, CA	336.0
302	San Marcos, CA	82.7
254	San Mateo, CA	119.3
212	Sandy Springs, GA	150.4
399	Sandy, UT	23.7
112	Santa Ana, CA	256.2
241	Santa Barbara, CA	127.2
337	Santa Clara, CA	56.7
312	Santa Clarita, CA	75.4
299	Santa Maria, CA	83.5
177	Santa Monica, CA	184.0
260	Santa Rosa, CA	115.0
88	Savannah, GA	301.8
342	Scottsdale, AZ	53.9
94	Seattle, WA	297.4
123	Shreveport, LA	243.0
367	Simi Valley, CA	42.0
346	Sioux City, IA	52.1
389	Sioux Falls, SD	29.6
229	Somerville, MA	138.5
74	South Bend, IN	334.9
56	South Gate, CA	372.5

RANK	CITY	RATE
191	Southfield, MI	171.8
251	Sparks, NV	122.5
317	Spokane Valley, WA	72.6
147	Spokane, WA	218.3
134	Springfield, IL	227.2
52	Springfield, MA	378.4
169	Springfield, MO	190.9
243	Stamford, CT	126.4
393	Sterling Heights, MI	27.5
38	Stockton, CA	430.9
406	St. George, UT	17.2
226	St. Joseph, MO	142.6
3	St. Louis, MO	766.0
118	St. Paul, MN	247.7
58	St. Petersburg, FL	370.3
288	Suffolk, VA	95.4
314	Sugar Land, TX	73.8
344	Sunnyvale, CA	53.7
242	Sunrise, FL	127.1
381	Surprise, AZ	35.3
97	Syracuse, NY	293.7
75	Tacoma, WA	328.0
104	Tallahassee, FL	272.1
109	Tampa, FL	263.3
335	Temecula, CA	58.5
190	Tempe, AZ	172.4
348	Thornton, CO	52.0
385	Thousand Oaks, CA	32.3
44	Toledo, OH	419.8
361	Toms River Twnshp, NJ	44.5
122	Topeka, KS	243.8
280	Torrance, CA	98.5
283	Tracy, CA	97.5
10	Trenton, NJ	619.8
408	Troy, MI	16.2
132	Tucson, AZ	227.4
100	Tulsa, OK	290.2
152	Tuscaloosa, AL	212.7
295	Tyler, TX	88.6
69	Upper Darby Twnshp, PA	345.8
270	Vacaville, CA	103.7
51	Vallejo, CA	383.6
287	Vancouver, WA	95.7
253	Ventura, CA	120.2
119	Victorville, CA	246.7
271	Virginia Beach, VA	103.6
216	Visalia, CA	148.9
201	Vista, CA	158.9
179	Waco, TX	182.3
205	Warren, MI	156.6
360	Warwick, RI	45.0
7	Washington, DC	666.7
197	Waterbury, CT	162.6
223	West Covina, CA	143.6
382	West Jordan, UT	33.6
55	West Palm Beach, FL	373.2
249	West Valley, UT	124.5
245	Westland, MI	125.4
267	Westminster, CA	104.4
374	Westminster, CO	39.0
261	Whittier, CA	114.5
207	Wichita Falls, TX	155.6
224	Wichita, KS	143.3
89	Wilmington, NC	301.7
115	Winston-Salem, NC	248.9
330	Woodbridge Twnshp, NJ	62.2
130	Worcester, MA	232.0
129	Yonkers, NY	234.9
290	Yuma, AZ	94.1

Source: CQ Press using reported data from the F.B.I. "Crime in the United States 2009"
*Robbery is the taking of anything of value by force or threat of force. Attempts are included.

58. Robbery Rate in 2009 (continued)
National Rate = 133.0 Robberies per 100,000 Population*

RANK	CITY	RATE
1	Camden, NJ	969.9
2	Cleveland, OH	828.2
3	St. Louis, MO	766.0
4	New Haven, CT	732.7
5	Oakland, CA	716.3
6	Cincinnati, OH	681.1
7	Washington, DC	666.7
8	Detroit, MI	650.9
9	Memphis, TN	620.1
10	Trenton, NJ	619.8
11	Elizabeth, NJ	609.2
12	Buffalo, NY	609.0
13	Philadelphia, PA	583.9
14	Baltimore, MD	580.3
15	Chicago, IL	557.4
16	Jackson, MS	554.4
17	Compton, CA	542.2
18	Flint, MI	528.4
19	Milwaukee, WI	516.3
20	Baton Rouge, LA	508.5
21	Birmingham, AL	505.8
22	Dayton, OH	503.4
23	Houston, TX	499.9
24	Bridgeport, CT	499.8
25	Miami Beach, FL	499.6
26	Miami, FL	499.5
27	Atlanta, GA	492.9
28	Hartford, CT	483.7
29	Indianapolis, IN	483.0
30	Newark, NJ	472.4
31	Reading, PA	458.9
32	Columbus, OH	447.1
33	Allentown, PA	441.6
34	Berkeley, CA	438.8
35	Pittsburgh, PA	437.8
36	Paterson, NJ	435.3
37	Minneapolis, MN	434.6
38	Stockton, CA	430.9
39	Inglewood, CA	430.3
40	Dallas, TX	426.3
41	San Francisco, CA	422.7
42	Little Rock, AR	420.1
43	Hawthorne, CA	419.9
44	Toledo, OH	419.8
45	Richmond, VA	418.2
46	Canton, OH	414.9
47	Rochester, NY	411.6
48	Kansas City, MO	406.5
49	Richmond, CA	396.8
50	North Charleston, SC	391.7
51	Vallejo, CA	383.6
52	Springfield, MA	378.4
53	Rockford, IL	377.4
54	Fort Lauderdale, FL	374.4
55	West Palm Beach, FL	373.2
56	South Gate, CA	372.5
57	Macon, GA	370.5
58	St. Petersburg, FL	370.3
59	New Bedford, MA	367.1
60	Boston, MA	364.8
61	Jersey City, NJ	361.6
62	Greensboro, NC	358.6
63	Peoria, IL	358.0
64	Knoxville, TN	355.1
65	Akron, OH	352.1
66	Albany, NY	349.9
67	Mobile, AL	348.1
68	Portsmouth, VA	347.6
69	Upper Darby Twnshp, PA	345.8
70	Pompano Beach, FL	341.7
71	Sacramento, CA	341.5
72	San Bernardino, CA	339.0
73	San Leandro, CA	336.0
74	South Bend, IN	334.9
75	Tacoma, WA	328.0
76	Las Vegas, NV	326.4
77	Orlando, FL	326.2
78	Nashville, TN	323.0
79	Miami Gardens, FL	318.1
80	Los Angeles, CA	317.4
81	Hayward, CA	313.6
82	Durham, NC	312.1
83	Antioch, CA	311.1
84	Chattanooga, TN	310.1
85	Columbus, GA	308.2
86	Hammond, IN	306.2
87	Gary, IN	303.5
88	Savannah, GA	301.8
89	Charlotte, NC	301.7
89	Wilmington, NC	301.7
91	Beaumont, TX	301.2
91	Grand Rapids, MI	301.2
93	Long Beach, CA	297.6
94	Seattle, WA	297.4
95	Fall River, MA	297.1
96	Columbia, SC	296.4
97	Syracuse, NY	293.7
98	Albany, GA	291.8
99	Jacksonville, FL	291.2
100	Tulsa, OK	290.2
101	Fayetteville, NC	282.2
102	Racine, WI	277.3
103	New Orleans, LA	277.0
104	Tallahassee, FL	272.1
105	Brockton, MA	271.6
106	Norfolk, VA	268.0
107	Everett, WA	267.2
108	Salinas, CA	263.8
109	High Point, NC	263.3
109	Tampa, FL	263.3
111	Clearwater, FL	261.0
112	Santa Ana, CA	256.2
113	North Las Vegas, NV	252.3
114	Lafayette, LA	251.2
115	Winston-Salem, NC	248.9
116	Louisville, KY	248.7
117	El Monte, CA	248.3
118	St. Paul, MN	247.7
119	Victorville, CA	246.7
120	Melbourne, FL	246.6
121	El Cajon, CA	244.4
122	Topeka, KS	243.8
123	Shreveport, LA	243.0
124	Huntsville, AL	242.4
125	Longview, TX	238.2
126	Moreno Valley, CA	236.9
127	Phoenix, AZ	235.2
128	Federal Way, WA	235.1
129	Yonkers, NY	234.9
130	Worcester, MA	232.0
131	Providence, RI	230.1
132	Salt Lake City, UT	227.4
132	Tucson, AZ	227.4
134	Springfield, IL	227.2
135	Rialto, CA	226.4
136	Fresno, CA	225.4
137	Lansing, MI	224.9
138	Pomona, CA	224.5
139	Oklahoma City, OK	224.3
140	Hollywood, FL	223.9
141	Kansas City, KS	223.8
142	Montgomery, AL	223.4
143	Riverside, CA	222.4
144	New York, NY	221.4
145	Lakewood, CA	220.8
146	Davenport, IA	218.6
147	Spokane, WA	218.3
148	Downey, CA	217.5
149	Lancaster, CA	216.5
150	Kent, WA	213.4
151	Bakersfield, CA	212.8
152	Tuscaloosa, AL	212.7
153	Albuquerque, NM	207.9
154	Gainesville, FL	207.3
155	Plantation, FL	205.9
156	Oxnard, CA	205.0
157	Raleigh, NC	204.9
158	Lawton, OK	201.5
159	Omaha, NE	201.3
160	Merced, CA	200.8
161	Fort Worth, TX	200.3
162	Roanoke, VA	197.6
163	Decatur, IL	197.0
164	Lynn, MA	195.3
164	San Antonio, TX	195.3
166	Lexington, KY	195.0
167	Fort Wayne, IN	192.8
168	Charleston, SC	191.8
169	Springfield, MO	190.9
170	Odessa, TX	189.4
171	Norwalk, CT	188.7
172	Anchorage, AK	188.5
173	Amarillo, TX	186.5
174	Reno, NV	185.1
175	Portland, OR	184.9
176	Fairfield, CA	184.7
177	Austin, TX	184.0
177	Santa Monica, CA	184.0
179	Waco, TX	182.3
180	Escondido, CA	181.2
181	Modesto, CA	180.5
182	Palmdale, CA	180.4
183	Lakeland, FL	179.2
184	Arlington, TX	177.3
185	Carson, CA	177.0
186	Murfreesboro, TN	176.6
187	Concord, CA	175.1
188	Cambridge, MA	174.0
189	Norwalk, CA	173.1
190	Tempe, AZ	172.4
191	Southfield, MI	171.8
192	Aurora, CO	170.7
193	Fort Smith, AR	169.1
194	Mesquite, TX	165.5
195	Ontario, CA	165.1
196	Glendale, AZ	164.7
197	Waterbury, CT	162.6
198	Miramar, FL	160.6
199	Buena Park, CA	159.7
200	Corpus Christi, TX	159.6
201	Vista, CA	158.9
202	Manchester, NH	157.4
203	Fontana, CA	157.1
204	Pueblo, CO	156.7
205	Warren, MI	156.6
206	Denver, CO	156.4

RANK	CITY	RATE
207	Wichita Falls, TX	155.6
208	Madison, WI	155.2
209	Alhambra, CA	154.7
210	Columbia, MO	153.0
211	Citrus Heights, CA	151.8
212	Sandy Springs, GA	150.4
213	Anaheim, CA	150.0
214	Gresham, OR	149.3
215	Chula Vista, CA	149.0
216	Visalia, CA	148.9
217	Killeen, TX	148.3
218	Hialeah, FL	147.9
219	Chico, CA	146.4
220	Duluth, MN	145.1
221	San Diego, CA	144.9
222	Baldwin Park, CA	144.4
223	West Covina, CA	143.6
224	Wichita, KS	143.3
225	Fullerton, CA	142.7
226	St. Joseph, MO	142.6
227	Lubbock, TX	139.5
228	Garland, TX	138.9
229	Somerville, MA	138.5
230	Independence, MO	136.7
231	Laredo, TX	136.2
232	Athens-Clarke, GA	135.3
233	Hampton, VA	133.6
234	Eugene, OR	132.8
235	Dearborn, MI	131.3
236	Colorado Springs, CO	130.7
237	Mesa, AZ	129.8
238	Oceanside, CA	129.6
239	Clifton, NJ	129.3
240	Ogden, UT	128.9
241	Santa Barbara, CA	127.2
242	Sunrise, FL	127.1
243	Stamford, CT	126.4
244	Pasadena, CA	126.3
245	Westland, MI	125.4
246	Indio, CA	125.2
246	Pasadena, TX	125.2
248	Avondale, AZ	125.0
249	West Valley, UT	124.5
250	Des Moines, IA	124.0
251	Sparks, NV	122.5
252	Lakewood, CO	121.6
253	Ventura, CA	120.2
254	San Mateo, CA	119.3
255	Hamilton Twnshp, NJ	118.2
256	Grand Prairie, TX	117.7
257	Abilene, TX	117.5
257	Evansville, IN	117.5
259	Erie, PA	116.5
260	Santa Rosa, CA	115.0
261	Whittier, CA	114.5
262	Elk Grove, CA	108.1
263	San Jose, CA	107.4
264	Fremont, CA	107.0
265	Richardson, TX	106.2
266	Irving, TX	105.7
267	Kenosha, WI	104.4
267	Westminster, CA	104.4
269	Cheektowaga, NY	104.2
270	Vacaville, CA	103.7
271	Virginia Beach, VA	103.6
272	Costa Mesa, CA	103.5
273	Chesapeake, VA	102.6
274	Las Cruces, NM	102.1

RANK	CITY	RATE
275	Davie, FL	100.9
276	Daly City, CA	100.7
276	Garden Grove, CA	100.7
278	McAllen, TX	99.5
279	Quincy, MA	99.4
280	Torrance, CA	98.5
281	Henderson, NV	98.1
282	Edison Twnshp, NJ	97.6
283	Tracy, CA	97.5
284	Carrollton, TX	97.3
285	Alexandria, VA	96.5
286	Honolulu, HI	95.8
287	Vancouver, WA	95.7
288	Suffolk, VA	95.4
289	Hesperia, CA	94.5
290	Yuma, AZ	94.1
291	Joliet, IL	94.0
292	Redding, CA	91.0
293	Boca Raton, FL	90.7
294	Burbank, CA	90.1
295	Tyler, TX	88.6
296	Clarksville, TN	86.3
296	Green Bay, WI	86.3
298	Brownsville, TX	84.7
299	Santa Maria, CA	83.5
300	Cedar Rapids, IA	83.1
301	Lawrence, KS	82.9
302	San Marcos, CA	82.7
303	Roswell, GA	82.6
304	Chino, CA	81.5
305	Chandler, AZ	80.0
306	Aurora, IL	78.8
306	Midland, TX	78.8
308	Roseville, CA	78.7
309	Salem, OR	77.9
310	Lincoln, NE	77.4
311	Corona, CA	76.8
312	Santa Clarita, CA	75.4
313	Greeley, CO	74.1
314	Sugar Land, TX	73.8
315	Elgin, IL	73.4
316	El Paso, TX	73.0
317	Spokane Valley, WA	72.6
318	Lewisville, TX	71.7
319	Coral Springs, FL	71.6
320	Palm Bay, FL	69.6
320	Rancho Cucamon., CA	69.6
322	Pembroke Pines, FL	69.4
323	Livermore, CA	68.0
324	Billings, MT	67.3
325	Huntington Beach, CA	66.4
326	Jacksonville, NC	64.5
327	Glendale, CA	63.8
328	Denton, TX	63.6
329	Danbury, CT	62.7
330	Woodbridge Twnshp, NJ	62.2
331	Hillsboro, OR	62.1
332	Bloomington, MN	60.6
333	Bellingham, WA	59.8
334	Missouri City, TX	59.3
335	Temecula, CA	58.5
336	Rochester, MN	56.9
337	Clovis, CA	56.7
337	Santa Clara, CA	56.7
339	Cape Coral, FL	56.0
340	Ann Arbor, MI	55.1
341	Peoria, AZ	54.1
342	Scottsdale, AZ	53.9

RANK	CITY	RATE
343	Carlsbad, CA	53.8
344	Sunnyvale, CA	53.7
345	Plano, TX	52.4
346	Clinton Twnshp, MI	52.1
346	Sioux City, IA	52.1
348	Thornton, CO	52.0
349	Boulder, CO	51.0
350	Fayetteville, AR	50.6
351	Beaverton, OR	50.4
352	Longmont, CO	50.2
353	Orange, CA	49.6
354	Fort Collins, CO	49.1
355	Bellevue, WA	48.8
355	San Angelo, TX	48.8
357	Brick Twnshp, NJ	47.0
358	Cranston, RI	46.1
359	Pearland, TX	45.2
360	Warwick, RI	45.0
361	Toms River Twnshp, NJ	44.5
362	Livonia, MI	44.3
363	Greece, NY	44.0
364	Nashua, NH	43.9
365	Norman, OK	43.5
366	McKinney, TX	42.4
367	Simi Valley, CA	42.0
368	Amherst, NY	41.7
369	Mission Viejo, CA	40.2
370	Newport Beach, CA	40.0
371	Lake Forest, CA	39.7
372	Lee's Summit, MO	39.6
373	Broken Arrow, OK	39.2
374	Westminster, CO	39.0
375	Colonie, NY	37.2
376	Port St. Lucie, FL	36.6
377	Fargo, ND	36.2
378	Rio Rancho, NM	36.0
379	Cary, NC	35.9
380	Olathe, KS	35.7
381	Surprise, AZ	35.3
382	West Jordan, UT	33.6
383	Arvada, CO	33.4
384	Murrieta, CA	32.3
385	Thousand Oaks, CA	32.3
386	Clarkstown, NY	31.7
387	Canton Twnshp, MI	31.5
388	Boise, ID	30.0
389	Sioux Falls, SD	29.6
390	Overland Park, KS	29.4
391	Round Rock, TX	29.0
392	College Station, TX	27.9
393	Sterling Heights, MI	27.5
394	Provo, UT	26.8
395	Farmington Hills, MI	25.6
396	Gilbert, AZ	25.5
397	Irvine, CA	25.5
398	Nampa, ID	25.0
399	Sandy, UT	23.7
400	Bend, OR	23.6
401	Orem, UT	23.5
402	Centennial, CO	23.1
403	Edmond, OK	22.3
404	Newton, MA	21.3
405	Allen, TX	17.3
406	St. George, UT	17.2
407	Ramapo, NY	17.0
408	Troy, MI	16.2
409	Naperville, IL	15.2
410	O'Fallon, MO	13.7
411	Frisco, TX	12.0

Source: CQ Press using reported data from the F.B.I. "Crime in the United States 2009"

*Robbery is the taking of anything of value by force or threat of force. Attempts are included.

59. Percent Change in Robbery Rate: 2008 to 2009
National Percent Change = 8.8% Decrease*

RANK	CITY	% CHANGE
338	Abilene, TX	(24.1)
213	Akron, OH	(9.1)
NA	Albany, GA**	NA
206	Albany, NY	(8.7)
302	Albuquerque, NM	(18.8)
208	Alexandria, VA	(8.8)
262	Alhambra, CA	(14.3)
159	Allentown, PA	(4.6)
54	Allen, TX	10.9
68	Amarillo, TX	8.1
99	Amherst, NY	2.2
247	Anaheim, CA	(12.6)
135	Anchorage, AK	(2.9)
NA	Ann Arbor, MI**	NA
320	Antioch, CA	(21.3)
149	Arlington, TX	(4.0)
374	Arvada, CO	(42.4)
340	Athens-Clarke, GA	(24.4)
315	Atlanta, GA	(20.6)
134	Aurora, CO	(2.7)
230	Aurora, IL	(10.8)
83	Austin, TX	4.0
349	Avondale, AZ	(27.4)
126	Bakersfield, CA	(2.0)
74	Baldwin Park, CA	6.3
201	Baltimore, MD	(8.5)
47	Baton Rouge, LA	11.8
116	Beaumont, TX	(0.7)
42	Beaverton, OR	13.3
285	Bellevue, WA	(17.0)
310	Bellingham, WA	(20.2)
377	Bend, OR	(47.4)
226	Berkeley, CA	(10.5)
16	Billings, MT	28.7
333	Birmingham, AL	(23.0)
145	Bloomington, MN	(3.8)
85	Boca Raton, FL	3.8
156	Boise, ID	(4.5)
198	Boston, MA	(8.0)
9	Boulder, CO	44.5
3	Brick Twnshp, NJ	93.4
195	Bridgeport, CT	(7.5)
NA	Brockton, MA**	NA
112	Broken Arrow, OK	0.3
252	Brownsville, TX	(13.4)
31	Buena Park, CA	19.7
72	Buffalo, NY	7.0
64	Burbank, CA	8.6
40	Cambridge, MA	13.8
215	Camden, NJ	(9.3)
NA	Canton Twnshp, MI**	NA
225	Canton, OH	(10.4)
123	Cape Coral, FL	(1.6)
92	Carlsbad, CA	3.1
208	Carrollton, TX	(8.8)
334	Carson, CA	(23.3)
152	Cary, NC	(4.3)
328	Cedar Rapids, IA	(22.4)
18	Centennial, CO	26.9
277	Chandler, AZ	(16.0)
343	Charleston, SC	(25.7)
334	Charlotte, NC	(23.3)
82	Chattanooga, TN	4.1
47	Cheektowaga, NY	11.8
371	Chesapeake, VA	(37.6)
165	Chicago, IL	(5.3)
27	Chico, CA	21.9
336	Chino, CA	(23.4)
87	Chula Vista, CA	3.7
178	Cincinnati, OH	(6.4)
203	Citrus Heights, CA	(8.6)
147	Clarkstown, NY	(3.9)
378	Clarksville, TN	(49.9)
257	Clearwater, FL	(13.8)
168	Cleveland, OH	(5.6)
29	Clifton, NJ	20.4
NA	Clinton Twnshp, MI**	NA
81	Clovis, CA	4.4
380	College Station, TX	(58.4)
239	Colonie, NY	(11.8)
156	Colorado Springs, CO	(4.5)
46	Columbia, MO	12.0
51	Columbia, SC	11.3
217	Columbus, GA	(9.6)
178	Columbus, OH	(6.4)
258	Compton, CA	(13.9)
130	Concord, CA	(2.2)
206	Coral Springs, FL	(8.7)
236	Corona, CA	(11.5)
185	Corpus Christi, TX	(6.7)
173	Costa Mesa, CA	(6.1)
365	Cranston, RI	(33.0)
275	Dallas, TX	(15.9)
355	Daly City, CA	(29.2)
26	Danbury, CT	22.0
62	Davenport, IA	8.8
356	Davie, FL	(29.4)
147	Dayton, OH	(3.9)
NA	Dearborn, MI**	NA
NA	Decatur, IL**	NA
291	Denton, TX	(17.7)
132	Denver, CO	(2.5)
NA	Des Moines, IA**	NA
NA	Detroit, MI**	NA
183	Downey, CA	(6.6)
159	Duluth, MN	(4.6)
323	Durham, NC	(21.9)
28	Edison Twnshp, NJ	21.4
306	Edmond, OK	(19.5)
55	El Cajon, CA	10.5
37	El Monte, CA	15.3
126	El Paso, TX	(2.0)
197	Elgin, IL	(7.8)
105	Elizabeth, NJ	1.5
108	Elk Grove, CA	1.1
381	Erie, PA	(61.8)
18	Escondido, CA	26.9
226	Eugene, OR	(10.5)
60	Evansville, IN	9.6
34	Everett, WA	18.1
300	Fairfield, CA	(18.6)
43	Fall River, MA	12.4
22	Fargo, ND	24.4
NA	Farmington Hills, MI**	NA
268	Fayetteville, AR	(15.0)
345	Fayetteville, NC	(25.9)
35	Federal Way, WA	17.3
NA	Flint, MI**	NA
77	Fontana, CA	5.4
6	Fort Collins, CO	71.1
304	Fort Lauderdale, FL	(19.2)
11	Fort Smith, AR	34.1
108	Fort Wayne, IN	1.1
289	Fort Worth, TX	(17.6)
190	Fremont, CA	(7.3)
61	Fresno, CA	9.0
68	Frisco, TX	8.1
14	Fullerton, CA	30.7
113	Gainesville, FL	0.0
360	Garden Grove, CA	(32.7)
177	Garland, TX	(6.3)
39	Gary, IN	14.4
230	Gilbert, AZ	(10.8)
352	Glendale, AZ	(28.1)
283	Glendale, CA	(16.7)
235	Grand Prairie, TX	(11.4)
NA	Grand Rapids, MI**	NA
213	Greece, NY	(9.1)
121	Greeley, CO	(1.3)
282	Green Bay, WI	(16.6)
224	Greensboro, NC	(10.3)
141	Gresham, OR	(3.4)
38	Hamilton Twnshp, NJ	14.8
110	Hammond, IN	1.0
196	Hampton, VA	(7.6)
151	Hartford, CT	(4.2)
175	Hawthorne, CA	(6.2)
263	Hayward, CA	(14.5)
33	Henderson, NV	18.5
169	Hesperia, CA	(5.7)
337	Hialeah, FL	(23.9)
251	High Point, NC	(13.1)
167	Hillsboro, OR	(5.5)
308	Hollywood, FL	(19.8)
178	Honolulu, HI	(6.4)
76	Houston, TX	5.6
63	Huntington Beach, CA	8.7
102	Huntsville, AL	1.7
192	Independence, MO	(7.4)
136	Indianapolis, IN	(3.0)
172	Indio, CA	(5.9)
119	Inglewood, CA	(1.2)
119	Irvine, CA	(1.2)
233	Irving, TX	(11.0)
309	Jacksonville, FL	(20.1)
376	Jacksonville, NC	(45.1)
95	Jackson, MS	2.8
358	Jersey City, NJ	(30.2)
273	Joliet, IL	(15.8)
NA	Kansas City, KS**	NA
244	Kansas City, MO	(12.2)
322	Kenosha, WI	(21.5)
75	Kent, WA	6.0
314	Killeen, TX	(20.4)
125	Knoxville, TN	(1.9)
188	Lafayette, LA	(6.9)
173	Lake Forest, CA	(6.1)
281	Lakeland, FL	(16.5)
330	Lakewood, CA	(22.6)
245	Lakewood, CO	(12.4)
223	Lancaster, CA	(10.1)
NA	Lansing, MI**	NA
131	Laredo, TX	(2.4)
29	Las Cruces, NM	20.4
226	Las Vegas, NV	(10.5)
139	Lawrence, KS	(3.2)
199	Lawton, OK	(8.3)
124	Lee's Summit, MO	(1.7)
307	Lewisville, TX	(19.6)
NA	Lexington, KY**	NA
203	Lincoln, NE	(8.6)
NA	Little Rock, AR**	NA
51	Livermore, CA	11.3
NA	Livonia, MI**	NA
181	Long Beach, CA	(6.5)
NA	Longmont, CO**	NA

RANK	CITY	% CHANGE
275	Longview, TX	(15.9)
211	Los Angeles, CA	(8.9)
NA	Louisville, KY**	NA
95	Lubbock, TX	2.8
141	Lynn, MA	(3.4)
190	Macon, GA	(7.3)
132	Madison, WI	(2.5)
90	Manchester, NH	3.4
150	McAllen, TX	(4.1)
17	McKinney, TX	27.7
260	Melbourne, FL	(14.1)
250	Memphis, TN	(12.9)
92	Merced, CA	3.1
217	Mesa, AZ	(9.6)
15	Mesquite, TX	29.1
92	Miami Beach, FL	3.1
370	Miami Gardens, FL	(37.3)
236	Miami, FL	(11.5)
242	Midland, TX	(12.0)
137	Milwaukee, WI	(3.1)
298	Minneapolis, MN	(18.3)
203	Miramar, FL	(8.6)
162	Mission Viejo, CA	(4.7)
319	Missouri City, TX	(21.2)
114	Mobile, AL	(0.1)
252	Modesto, CA	(13.4)
122	Montgomery, AL	(1.4)
258	Moreno Valley, CA	(13.9)
47	Murfreesboro, TN	11.8
10	Murrieta, CA	36.3
87	Nampa, ID	3.7
154	Naperville, IL	(4.4)
NA	Nashua, NH**	NA
299	Nashville, TN	(18.4)
50	New Bedford, MA	11.5
NA	New Haven, CT**	NA
352	New Orleans, LA	(28.1)
283	New York, NY	(16.7)
162	Newark, NJ	(4.7)
349	Newport Beach, CA	(27.4)
183	Newton, MA	(6.6)
373	Norfolk, VA	(40.0)
263	Norman, OK	(14.5)
369	North Charleston, SC	(36.3)
83	North Las Vegas, NV	4.0
261	Norwalk, CA	(14.2)
21	Norwalk, CT	26.1
252	Oakland, CA	(13.4)
40	Oceanside, CA	13.8
1	Odessa, TX	153.2
128	O'Fallon, MO	(2.1)
270	Ogden, UT	(15.4)
301	Oklahoma City, OK	(18.7)
NA	Olathe, KS**	NA
189	Omaha, NE	(7.2)
342	Ontario, CA	(24.9)
366	Orange, CA	(33.2)
2	Orem, UT	144.8
375	Orlando, FL	(43.2)
273	Overland Park, KS	(15.8)
270	Oxnard, CA	(15.4)
152	Palm Bay, FL	(4.3)
263	Palmdale, CA	(14.5)
357	Pasadena, CA	(29.8)
45	Pasadena, TX	12.3
292	Paterson, NJ	(17.8)
5	Pearland, TX	79.4
362	Pembroke Pines, FL	(32.8)

RANK	CITY	% CHANGE
320	Peoria, AZ	(21.3)
NA	Peoria, IL**	NA
246	Philadelphia, PA	(12.5)
331	Phoenix, AZ	(22.7)
242	Pittsburgh, PA	(12.0)
140	Plano, TX	(3.3)
58	Plantation, FL	10.2
343	Pomona, CA	(25.7)
289	Pompano Beach, FL	(17.6)
12	Port St. Lucie, FL	33.1
219	Portland, OR	(9.7)
102	Portsmouth, VA	1.7
318	Providence, RI	(21.0)
7	Provo, UT	52.3
NA	Pueblo, CO**	NA
222	Quincy, MA	(10.0)
326	Racine, WI	(22.2)
327	Raleigh, NC	(22.3)
359	Ramapo, NY	(32.5)
285	Rancho Cucamon., CA	(17.0)
294	Reading, PA	(17.9)
57	Redding, CA	10.3
287	Reno, NV	(17.1)
128	Rialto, CA	(2.1)
159	Richardson, TX	(4.6)
332	Richmond, CA	(22.9)
71	Richmond, VA	7.2
296	Rio Rancho, NM	(18.0)
199	Riverside, CA	(8.3)
266	Roanoke, VA	(14.7)
240	Rochester, MN	(11.9)
310	Rochester, NY	(20.2)
101	Rockford, IL	2.0
18	Roseville, CA	26.9
347	Roswell, GA	(26.5)
118	Round Rock, TX	(1.0)
216	Sacramento, CA	(9.4)
240	Salem, OR	(11.9)
43	Salinas, CA	12.4
272	Salt Lake City, UT	(15.5)
364	San Angelo, TX	(32.9)
145	San Antonio, TX	(3.8)
248	San Bernardino, CA	(12.7)
208	San Diego, CA	(8.8)
294	San Francisco, CA	(17.9)
219	San Jose, CA	(9.7)
348	San Leandro, CA	(26.9)
24	San Marcos, CA	22.9
192	San Mateo, CA	(7.4)
329	Sandy Springs, GA	(22.5)
368	Sandy, UT	(36.1)
91	Santa Ana, CA	3.3
185	Santa Barbara, CA	(6.7)
340	Santa Clara, CA	(24.4)
107	Santa Clarita, CA	1.2
351	Santa Maria, CA	(27.6)
346	Santa Monica, CA	(26.1)
32	Santa Rosa, CA	19.5
315	Savannah, GA	(20.6)
117	Scottsdale, AZ	(0.9)
56	Seattle, WA	10.4
99	Shreveport, LA	2.2
252	Simi Valley, CA	(13.4)
323	Sioux City, IA	(21.9)
115	Sioux Falls, SD	(0.3)
201	Somerville, MA	(8.5)
269	South Bend, IN	(15.2)
78	South Gate, CA	5.2

RANK	CITY	% CHANGE
NA	Southfield, MI**	NA
267	Sparks, NV	(14.9)
170	Spokane Valley, WA	(5.8)
154	Spokane, WA	(4.4)
NA	Springfield, IL**	NA
111	Springfield, MA	0.9
97	Springfield, MO	2.5
249	Stamford, CT	(12.8)
NA	Sterling Heights, MI**	NA
303	Stockton, CA	(18.9)
379	St. George, UT	(50.9)
23	St. Joseph, MO	23.8
89	St. Louis, MO	3.6
229	St. Paul, MN	(10.6)
292	St. Petersburg, FL	(17.8)
236	Suffolk, VA	(11.5)
13	Sugar Land, TX	31.1
67	Sunnyvale, CA	8.3
372	Sunrise, FL	(39.1)
317	Surprise, AZ	(20.7)
137	Syracuse, NY	(3.1)
85	Tacoma, WA	3.8
354	Tallahassee, FL	(28.4)
277	Tampa, FL	(16.0)
73	Temecula, CA	6.9
170	Tempe, AZ	(5.8)
305	Thornton, CO	(19.3)
66	Thousand Oaks, CA	8.4
143	Toledo, OH	(3.6)
252	Toms River Twnshp, NJ	(13.4)
64	Topeka, KS	8.6
310	Torrance, CA	(20.2)
36	Tracy, CA	17.2
187	Trenton, NJ	(6.8)
NA	Troy, MI**	NA
287	Tucson, AZ	(17.1)
106	Tulsa, OK	1.4
143	Tuscaloosa, AL	(3.6)
360	Tyler, TX	(32.7)
79	Upper Darby Twnshp, PA	4.9
297	Vacaville, CA	(18.1)
102	Vallejo, CA	1.7
234	Vancouver, WA	(11.1)
310	Ventura, CA	(20.2)
53	Victorville, CA	11.0
280	Virginia Beach, VA	(16.2)
181	Visalia, CA	(6.5)
175	Vista, CA	(6.2)
232	Waco, TX	(10.9)
NA	Warren, MI**	NA
4	Warwick, RI	80.7
164	Washington, DC	(5.0)
97	Waterbury, CT	2.5
211	West Covina, CA	(8.9)
25	West Jordan, UT	22.6
277	West Palm Beach, FL	(16.0)
192	West Valley, UT	(7.4)
NA	Westland, MI**	NA
166	Westminster, CA	(5.4)
362	Westminster, CO	(32.8)
221	Whittier, CA	(9.8)
339	Wichita Falls, TX	(24.2)
70	Wichita, KS	7.8
156	Wilmington, NC	(4.5)
325	Winston-Salem, NC	(22.0)
367	Woodbridge Twnshp, NJ	(35.1)
58	Worcester, MA	10.2
79	Yonkers, NY	4.9
8	Yuma, AZ	51.5

Source: CQ Press using reported data from the F.B.I. "Crime in the United States 2009"

*Robbery is the taking of anything of value by force or threat of force. Attempts are included.

**Not available.

59. Percent Change in Robbery Rate: 2008 to 2009 (continued)
National Percent Change = 8.8% Decrease*

RANK	CITY	% CHANGE
1	Odessa, TX	153.2
2	Orem, UT	144.8
3	Brick Twnshp, NJ	93.4
4	Warwick, RI	80.7
5	Pearland, TX	79.4
6	Fort Collins, CO	71.1
7	Provo, UT	52.3
8	Yuma, AZ	51.5
9	Boulder, CO	44.5
10	Murrieta, CA	36.3
11	Fort Smith, AR	34.1
12	Port St. Lucie, FL	33.1
13	Sugar Land, TX	31.1
14	Fullerton, CA	30.7
15	Mesquite, TX	29.1
16	Billings, MT	28.7
17	McKinney, TX	27.7
18	Centennial, CO	26.9
18	Escondido, CA	26.9
18	Roseville, CA	26.9
21	Norwalk, CT	26.1
22	Fargo, ND	24.4
23	St. Joseph, MO	23.8
24	San Marcos, CA	22.9
25	West Jordan, UT	22.6
26	Danbury, CT	22.0
27	Chico, CA	21.9
28	Edison Twnshp, NJ	21.4
29	Clifton, NJ	20.4
29	Las Cruces, NM	20.4
31	Buena Park, CA	19.7
32	Santa Rosa, CA	19.5
33	Henderson, NV	18.5
34	Everett, WA	18.1
35	Federal Way, WA	17.3
36	Tracy, CA	17.2
37	El Monte, CA	15.3
38	Hamilton Twnshp, NJ	14.8
39	Gary, IN	14.4
40	Cambridge, MA	13.8
40	Oceanside, CA	13.8
42	Beaverton, OR	13.3
43	Fall River, MA	12.4
43	Salinas, CA	12.4
45	Pasadena, TX	12.3
46	Columbia, MO	12.0
47	Baton Rouge, LA	11.8
47	Cheektowaga, NY	11.8
47	Murfreesboro, TN	11.8
50	New Bedford, MA	11.5
51	Columbia, SC	11.3
51	Livermore, CA	11.3
53	Victorville, CA	11.0
54	Allen, TX	10.9
55	El Cajon, CA	10.5
56	Seattle, WA	10.4
57	Redding, CA	10.3
58	Plantation, FL	10.2
58	Worcester, MA	10.2
60	Evansville, IN	9.6
61	Fresno, CA	9.0
62	Davenport, IA	8.8
63	Huntington Beach, CA	8.7
64	Burbank, CA	8.6
64	Topeka, KS	8.6
66	Thousand Oaks, CA	8.4
67	Sunnyvale, CA	8.3
68	Amarillo, TX	8.1

RANK	CITY	% CHANGE
68	Frisco, TX	8.1
70	Wichita, KS	7.8
71	Richmond, VA	7.2
72	Buffalo, NY	7.0
73	Temecula, CA	6.9
74	Baldwin Park, CA	6.3
75	Kent, WA	6.0
76	Houston, TX	5.6
77	Fontana, CA	5.4
78	South Gate, CA	5.2
79	Upper Darby Twnshp, PA	4.9
79	Yonkers, NY	4.9
81	Clovis, CA	4.4
82	Chattanooga, TN	4.1
83	Austin, TX	4.0
83	North Las Vegas, NV	4.0
85	Boca Raton, FL	3.8
85	Tacoma, WA	3.8
87	Chula Vista, CA	3.7
87	Nampa, ID	3.7
89	St. Louis, MO	3.6
90	Manchester, NH	3.4
91	Santa Ana, CA	3.3
92	Carlsbad, CA	3.1
92	Merced, CA	3.1
92	Miami Beach, FL	3.1
95	Jackson, MS	2.8
95	Lubbock, TX	2.8
97	Springfield, MO	2.5
97	Waterbury, CT	2.5
99	Amherst, NY	2.2
99	Shreveport, LA	2.2
101	Rockford, IL	2.0
102	Huntsville, AL	1.7
102	Portsmouth, VA	1.7
102	Vallejo, CA	1.7
105	Elizabeth, NJ	1.5
106	Tulsa, OK	1.4
107	Santa Clarita, CA	1.2
108	Elk Grove, CA	1.1
108	Fort Wayne, IN	1.1
110	Hammond, IN	1.0
111	Springfield, MA	0.9
112	Broken Arrow, OK	0.3
113	Gainesville, FL	0.0
114	Mobile, AL	(0.1)
115	Sioux Falls, SD	(0.3)
116	Beaumont, TX	(0.7)
117	Scottsdale, AZ	(0.9)
118	Round Rock, TX	(1.0)
119	Inglewood, CA	(1.2)
119	Irvine, CA	(1.2)
121	Greeley, CO	(1.3)
122	Montgomery, AL	(1.4)
123	Cape Coral, FL	(1.6)
124	Lee's Summit, MO	(1.7)
125	Knoxville, TN	(1.9)
126	Bakersfield, CA	(2.0)
126	El Paso, TX	(2.0)
128	O'Fallon, MO	(2.1)
128	Rialto, CA	(2.1)
130	Concord, CA	(2.2)
131	Laredo, TX	(2.4)
132	Denver, CO	(2.5)
132	Madison, WI	(2.5)
134	Aurora, CO	(2.7)
135	Anchorage, AK	(2.9)
136	Indianapolis, IN	(3.0)
137	Milwaukee, WI	(3.1)

RANK	CITY	% CHANGE
137	Syracuse, NY	(3.1)
139	Lawrence, KS	(3.2)
140	Plano, TX	(3.3)
141	Gresham, OR	(3.4)
141	Lynn, MA	(3.4)
143	Toledo, OH	(3.6)
143	Tuscaloosa, AL	(3.6)
145	Bloomington, MN	(3.8)
145	San Antonio, TX	(3.8)
147	Clarkstown, NY	(3.9)
147	Dayton, OH	(3.9)
149	Arlington, TX	(4.0)
150	McAllen, TX	(4.1)
151	Hartford, CT	(4.2)
152	Cary, NC	(4.3)
152	Palm Bay, FL	(4.3)
154	Naperville, IL	(4.4)
154	Spokane, WA	(4.4)
156	Boise, ID	(4.5)
156	Colorado Springs, CO	(4.5)
156	Wilmington, NC	(4.5)
159	Allentown, PA	(4.6)
159	Duluth, MN	(4.6)
159	Richardson, TX	(4.6)
162	Mission Viejo, CA	(4.7)
162	Newark, NJ	(4.7)
164	Washington, DC	(5.0)
165	Chicago, IL	(5.3)
166	Westminster, CA	(5.4)
167	Hillsboro, OR	(5.5)
168	Cleveland, OH	(5.6)
169	Hesperia, CA	(5.7)
170	Spokane Valley, WA	(5.8)
170	Tempe, AZ	(5.8)
172	Indio, CA	(5.9)
173	Costa Mesa, CA	(6.1)
173	Lake Forest, CA	(6.1)
175	Hawthorne, CA	(6.2)
175	Vista, CA	(6.2)
177	Garland, TX	(6.3)
178	Cincinnati, OH	(6.4)
178	Columbus, OH	(6.4)
178	Honolulu, HI	(6.4)
181	Long Beach, CA	(6.5)
181	Visalia, CA	(6.5)
183	Downey, CA	(6.6)
183	Newton, MA	(6.6)
185	Corpus Christi, TX	(6.7)
185	Santa Barbara, CA	(6.7)
187	Trenton, NJ	(6.8)
188	Lafayette, LA	(6.9)
189	Omaha, NE	(7.2)
190	Fremont, CA	(7.3)
190	Macon, GA	(7.3)
192	Independence, MO	(7.4)
192	San Mateo, CA	(7.4)
192	West Valley, UT	(7.4)
195	Bridgeport, CT	(7.5)
196	Hampton, VA	(7.6)
197	Elgin, IL	(7.8)
198	Boston, MA	(8.0)
199	Lawton, OK	(8.3)
199	Riverside, CA	(8.3)
201	Baltimore, MD	(8.5)
201	Somerville, MA	(8.5)
203	Citrus Heights, CA	(8.6)
203	Lincoln, NE	(8.6)
203	Miramar, FL	(8.6)
206	Albany, NY	(8.7)

RANK	CITY	% CHANGE
206	Coral Springs, FL	(8.7)
208	Alexandria, VA	(8.8)
208	Carrollton, TX	(8.8)
208	San Diego, CA	(8.8)
211	Los Angeles, CA	(8.9)
211	West Covina, CA	(8.9)
213	Akron, OH	(9.1)
213	Greece, NY	(9.1)
215	Camden, NJ	(9.3)
216	Sacramento, CA	(9.4)
217	Columbus, GA	(9.6)
217	Mesa, AZ	(9.6)
219	Portland, OR	(9.7)
219	San Jose, CA	(9.7)
221	Whittier, CA	(9.8)
222	Quincy, MA	(10.0)
223	Lancaster, CA	(10.1)
224	Greensboro, NC	(10.3)
225	Canton, OH	(10.4)
226	Berkeley, CA	(10.5)
226	Eugene, OR	(10.5)
226	Las Vegas, NV	(10.5)
229	St. Paul, MN	(10.6)
230	Aurora, IL	(10.8)
230	Gilbert, AZ	(10.8)
232	Waco, TX	(10.9)
233	Irving, TX	(11.0)
234	Vancouver, WA	(11.1)
235	Grand Prairie, TX	(11.4)
236	Corona, CA	(11.5)
236	Miami, FL	(11.5)
236	Suffolk, VA	(11.5)
239	Colonie, NY	(11.8)
240	Rochester, MN	(11.9)
240	Salem, OR	(11.9)
242	Midland, TX	(12.0)
242	Pittsburgh, PA	(12.0)
244	Kansas City, MO	(12.2)
245	Lakewood, CO	(12.4)
246	Philadelphia, PA	(12.5)
247	Anaheim, CA	(12.6)
248	San Bernardino, CA	(12.7)
249	Stamford, CT	(12.8)
250	Memphis, TN	(12.9)
251	High Point, NC	(13.1)
252	Brownsville, TX	(13.4)
252	Modesto, CA	(13.4)
252	Oakland, CA	(13.4)
252	Simi Valley, CA	(13.4)
252	Toms River Twnshp, NJ	(13.4)
257	Clearwater, FL	(13.8)
258	Compton, CA	(13.9)
258	Moreno Valley, CA	(13.9)
260	Melbourne, FL	(14.1)
261	Norwalk, CA	(14.2)
262	Alhambra, CA	(14.3)
263	Hayward, CA	(14.5)
263	Norman, OK	(14.5)
263	Palmdale, CA	(14.5)
266	Roanoke, VA	(14.7)
267	Sparks, NV	(14.9)
268	Fayetteville, AR	(15.0)
269	South Bend, IN	(15.2)
270	Ogden, UT	(15.4)
270	Oxnard, CA	(15.4)
272	Salt Lake City, UT	(15.5)
273	Joliet, IL	(15.8)
273	Overland Park, KS	(15.8)

RANK	CITY	% CHANGE
275	Dallas, TX	(15.9)
275	Longview, TX	(15.9)
277	Chandler, AZ	(16.0)
277	Tampa, FL	(16.0)
277	West Palm Beach, FL	(16.0)
280	Virginia Beach, VA	(16.2)
281	Lakeland, FL	(16.5)
282	Green Bay, WI	(16.6)
283	Glendale, CA	(16.7)
283	New York, NY	(16.7)
285	Bellevue, WA	(17.0)
285	Rancho Cucamon., CA	(17.0)
287	Reno, NV	(17.1)
287	Tucson, AZ	(17.1)
289	Fort Worth, TX	(17.6)
289	Pompano Beach, FL	(17.6)
291	Denton, TX	(17.7)
292	Paterson, NJ	(17.8)
292	St. Petersburg, FL	(17.8)
294	Reading, PA	(17.9)
294	San Francisco, CA	(17.9)
296	Rio Rancho, NM	(18.0)
297	Vacaville, CA	(18.1)
298	Minneapolis, MN	(18.3)
299	Nashville, TN	(18.4)
300	Fairfield, CA	(18.6)
301	Oklahoma City, OK	(18.7)
302	Albuquerque, NM	(18.8)
303	Stockton, CA	(18.9)
304	Fort Lauderdale, FL	(19.2)
305	Thornton, CO	(19.3)
306	Edmond, OK	(19.5)
307	Lewisville, TX	(19.6)
308	Hollywood, FL	(19.8)
309	Jacksonville, FL	(20.1)
310	Bellingham, WA	(20.2)
310	Rochester, NY	(20.2)
310	Torrance, CA	(20.2)
310	Ventura, CA	(20.2)
314	Killeen, TX	(20.4)
315	Atlanta, GA	(20.6)
315	Savannah, GA	(20.6)
317	Surprise, AZ	(20.7)
318	Providence, RI	(21.0)
319	Missouri City, TX	(21.2)
320	Antioch, CA	(21.3)
320	Peoria, AZ	(21.3)
322	Kenosha, WI	(21.5)
323	Durham, NC	(21.9)
323	Sioux City, IA	(21.9)
325	Winston-Salem, NC	(22.0)
326	Racine, WI	(22.2)
327	Raleigh, NC	(22.3)
328	Cedar Rapids, IA	(22.4)
329	Sandy Springs, GA	(22.5)
330	Lakewood, CA	(22.6)
331	Phoenix, AZ	(22.7)
332	Richmond, CA	(22.9)
333	Birmingham, AL	(23.0)
334	Carson, CA	(23.3)
334	Charlotte, NC	(23.3)
336	Chino, CA	(23.4)
337	Hialeah, FL	(23.9)
338	Abilene, TX	(24.1)
339	Wichita Falls, TX	(24.2)
340	Athens-Clarke, GA	(24.4)
340	Santa Clara, CA	(24.4)
342	Ontario, CA	(24.9)

RANK	CITY	% CHANGE
343	Charleston, SC	(25.7)
343	Pomona, CA	(25.7)
345	Fayetteville, NC	(25.9)
346	Santa Monica, CA	(26.1)
347	Roswell, GA	(26.5)
348	San Leandro, CA	(26.9)
349	Avondale, AZ	(27.4)
349	Newport Beach, CA	(27.4)
351	Santa Maria, CA	(27.6)
352	Glendale, AZ	(28.1)
352	New Orleans, LA	(28.1)
354	Tallahassee, FL	(28.4)
355	Daly City, CA	(29.2)
356	Davie, FL	(29.4)
357	Pasadena, CA	(29.8)
358	Jersey City, NJ	(30.2)
359	Ramapo, NY	(32.5)
360	Garden Grove, CA	(32.7)
360	Tyler, TX	(32.7)
362	Pembroke Pines, FL	(32.8)
362	Westminster, CO	(32.8)
364	San Angelo, TX	(32.9)
365	Cranston, RI	(33.0)
366	Orange, CA	(33.2)
367	Woodbridge Twnshp, NJ	(35.1)
368	Sandy, UT	(36.1)
369	North Charleston, SC	(36.3)
370	Miami Gardens, FL	(37.3)
371	Chesapeake, VA	(37.6)
372	Sunrise, FL	(39.1)
373	Norfolk, VA	(40.0)
374	Arvada, CO	(42.4)
375	Orlando, FL	(43.2)
376	Jacksonville, NC	(45.1)
377	Bend, OR	(47.4)
378	Clarksville, TN	(49.9)
379	St. George, UT	(50.9)
380	College Station, TX	(58.4)
381	Erie, PA	(61.8)
NA	Albany, GA**	NA
NA	Ann Arbor, MI**	NA
NA	Brockton, MA**	NA
NA	Canton Twnshp, MI**	NA
NA	Clinton Twnshp, MI**	NA
NA	Dearborn, MI**	NA
NA	Decatur, IL**	NA
NA	Des Moines, IA**	NA
NA	Detroit, MI**	NA
NA	Farmington Hills, MI**	NA
NA	Flint, MI**	NA
NA	Grand Rapids, MI**	NA
NA	Kansas City, KS**	NA
NA	Lansing, MI**	NA
NA	Lexington, KY**	NA
NA	Little Rock, AR**	NA
NA	Livonia, MI**	NA
NA	Longmont, CO**	NA
NA	Louisville, KY**	NA
NA	Nashua, NH**	NA
NA	New Haven, CT**	NA
NA	Olathe, KS**	NA
NA	Peoria, IL**	NA
NA	Pueblo, CO**	NA
NA	Southfield, MI**	NA
NA	Springfield, IL**	NA
NA	Sterling Heights, MI**	NA
NA	Troy, MI**	NA
NA	Warren, MI**	NA
NA	Westland, MI**	NA

Source: CQ Press using reported data from the F.B.I. "Crime in the United States 2009"
*Robbery is the taking of anything of value by force or threat of force. Attempts are included.
**Not available.

60. Percent Change in Robbery Rate: 2005 to 2009
National Percent Change = 5.6% Decrease*

RANK	CITY	% CHANGE
213	Abilene, TX	(6.1)
77	Akron, OH	19.6
144	Albany, GA	5.8
320	Albany, NY	(24.8)
245	Albuquerque, NM	(11.3)
358	Alexandria, VA	(36.9)
244	Alhambra, CA	(11.0)
223	Allentown, PA	(7.8)
279	Allen, TX	(16.8)
181	Amarillo, TX	(1.2)
127	Amherst, NY	7.8
230	Anaheim, CA	(9.0)
45	Anchorage, AK	35.5
NA	Ann Arbor, MI**	NA
44	Antioch, CA	36.2
270	Arlington, TX	(15.7)
348	Arvada, CO	(33.2)
142	Athens-Clarke, GA	6.0
328	Atlanta, GA	(25.8)
303	Aurora, CO	(21.6)
323	Aurora, IL	(25.1)
126	Austin, TX	7.9
NA	Avondale, AZ**	NA
94	Bakersfield, CA	14.8
95	Baldwin Park, CA	14.7
203	Baltimore, MD	(4.9)
92	Baton Rouge, LA	15.0
160	Beaumont, TX	2.0
183	Beaverton, OR	(1.6)
84	Bellevue, WA	17.9
277	Bellingham, WA	(16.5)
300	Bend, OR	(20.8)
59	Berkeley, CA	26.7
51	Billings, MT	31.7
282	Birmingham, AL	(17.0)
NA	Bloomington, MN**	NA
43	Boca Raton, FL	36.6
344	Boise, ID	(32.0)
306	Boston, MA	(21.8)
37	Boulder, CO	40.1
1	Brick Twnshp, NJ	518.4
124	Bridgeport, CT	8.1
69	Brockton, MA	22.0
24	Broken Arrow, OK	51.4
120	Brownsville, TX	8.5
153	Buena Park, CA	2.9
149	Buffalo, NY	3.5
35	Burbank, CA	41.0
334	Cambridge, MA	(26.8)
108	Camden, NJ	10.7
NA	Canton Twnshp, MI**	NA
257	Canton, OH	(12.9)
178	Cape Coral, FL	(0.9)
361	Carlsbad, CA	(38.9)
67	Carrollton, TX	22.7
318	Carson, CA	(24.4)
331	Cary, NC	(26.1)
270	Cedar Rapids, IA	(15.7)
363	Centennial, CO	(39.4)
221	Chandler, AZ	(7.4)
340	Charleston, SC	(29.7)
368	Charlotte, NC	(44.0)
112	Chattanooga, TN	9.8
215	Cheektowaga, NY	(6.4)
322	Chesapeake, VA	(25.0)
169	Chicago, IL	0.3
52	Chico, CA	30.9
279	Chino, CA	(16.8)

RANK	CITY	% CHANGE
233	Chula Vista, CA	(9.1)
222	Cincinnati, OH	(7.7)
NA	Citrus Heights, CA**	NA
NA	Clarkstown, NY**	NA
341	Clarksville, TN	(31.1)
39	Clearwater, FL	38.0
164	Cleveland, OH	1.5
70	Clifton, NJ	21.9
NA	Clinton Twnshp, MI**	NA
172	Clovis, CA	0.0
370	College Station, TX	(46.1)
258	Colonie, NY	(13.1)
104	Colorado Springs, CO	11.5
73	Columbia, MO	21.2
226	Columbia, SC	(8.3)
53	Columbus, GA	29.8
260	Columbus, OH	(13.6)
106	Compton, CA	10.8
105	Concord, CA	11.2
17	Coral Springs, FL	62.0
294	Corona, CA	(19.7)
207	Corpus Christi, TX	(5.2)
195	Costa Mesa, CA	(3.4)
303	Cranston, RI	(21.6)
314	Dallas, TX	(23.8)
275	Daly City, CA	(16.4)
269	Danbury, CT	(15.3)
298	Davenport, IA	(20.6)
75	Davie, FL	20.0
205	Dayton, OH	(5.1)
NA	Dearborn, MI**	NA
NA	Decatur, IL**	NA
275	Denton, TX	(16.4)
360	Denver, CO	(38.4)
NA	Des Moines, IA**	NA
NA	Detroit, MI**	NA
195	Downey, CA	(3.4)
NA	Duluth, MN**	NA
157	Durham, NC	2.1
39	Edison Twnshp, NJ	38.0
230	Edmond, OK	(9.0)
46	El Cajon, CA	35.3
59	El Monte, CA	26.7
187	El Paso, TX	(1.9)
NA	Elgin, IL**	NA
36	Elizabeth, NJ	40.8
NA	Elk Grove, CA**	NA
363	Erie, PA	(39.4)
49	Escondido, CA	32.8
18	Eugene, OR	61.4
302	Evansville, IN	(21.4)
26	Everett, WA	50.5
245	Fairfield, CA	(11.3)
NA	Fall River, MA**	NA
2	Fargo, ND	201.7
NA	Farmington Hills, MI**	NA
176	Fayetteville, AR	(0.6)
274	Fayetteville, NC	(16.2)
59	Federal Way, WA	26.7
NA	Flint, MI**	NA
122	Fontana, CA	8.2
106	Fort Collins, CO	10.8
268	Fort Lauderdale, FL	(15.0)
78	Fort Smith, AR	19.4
99	Fort Wayne, IN	13.4
242	Fort Worth, TX	(10.9)
89	Fremont, CA	15.9
289	Fresno, CA	(18.5)
317	Frisco, TX	(24.1)

RANK	CITY	% CHANGE
55	Fullerton, CA	28.7
41	Gainesville, FL	37.4
330	Garden Grove, CA	(25.9)
57	Garland, TX	28.3
177	Gary, IN	(0.8)
80	Gilbert, AZ	18.1
157	Glendale, AZ	2.1
203	Glendale, CA	(4.9)
182	Grand Prairie, TX	(1.3)
NA	Grand Rapids, MI**	NA
136	Greece, NY	6.8
139	Greeley, CO	6.2
71	Green Bay, WI	21.7
130	Greensboro, NC	7.3
191	Gresham, OR	(2.5)
88	Hamilton Twnshp, NJ	16.0
250	Hammond, IN	(11.7)
338	Hampton, VA	(28.3)
256	Hartford, CT	(12.6)
16	Hawthorne, CA	62.1
28	Hayward, CA	47.6
8	Henderson, NV	71.5
261	Hesperia, CA	(13.9)
254	Hialeah, FL	(12.3)
96	High Point, NC	14.5
285	Hillsboro, OR	(18.3)
169	Hollywood, FL	0.3
149	Honolulu, HI	3.5
225	Houston, TX	(8.1)
34	Huntington Beach, CA	41.9
295	Huntsville, AL	(19.9)
64	Independence, MO	24.4
80	Indianapolis, IN	18.1
281	Indio, CA	(16.9)
234	Inglewood, CA	(10.0)
117	Irvine, CA	9.0
309	Irving, TX	(22.6)
155	Jacksonville, FL	2.8
NA	Jacksonville, NC**	NA
14	Jackson, MS	63.4
372	Jersey City, NJ	(47.2)
270	Joliet, IL	(15.7)
305	Kansas City, KS	(21.7)
230	Kansas City, MO	(9.0)
298	Kenosha, WI	(20.6)
133	Kent, WA	7.0
353	Killeen, TX	(34.8)
87	Knoxville, TN	17.3
4	Lafayette, LA	99.8
218	Lake Forest, CA	(6.8)
90	Lakeland, FL	15.6
217	Lakewood, CA	(6.6)
218	Lakewood, CO	(6.8)
293	Lancaster, CA	(19.0)
NA	Lansing, MI**	NA
97	Laredo, TX	14.4
290	Las Cruces, NM	(18.6)
76	Las Vegas, NV	19.7
9	Lawrence, KS	66.1
50	Lawton, OK	32.6
189	Lee's Summit, MO	(2.0)
80	Lewisville, TX	18.1
NA	Lexington, KY**	NA
285	Lincoln, NE	(18.3)
NA	Little Rock, AR**	NA
5	Livermore, CA	97.7
NA	Livonia, MI**	NA
161	Long Beach, CA	1.7
NA	Longmont, CO**	NA

RANK	CITY	% CHANGE
31	Longview, TX	43.6
242	Los Angeles, CA	(10.9)
NA	Louisville, KY**	NA
202	Lubbock, TX	(4.6)
354	Lynn, MA	(35.5)
118	Macon, GA	8.9
148	Madison, WI	4.4
65	Manchester, NH	23.8
208	McAllen, TX	(5.3)
220	McKinney, TX	(7.0)
22	Melbourne, FL	53.3
212	Memphis, TN	(5.7)
254	Merced, CA	(12.3)
58	Mesa, AZ	27.6
54	Mesquite, TX	29.1
249	Miami Beach, FL	(11.6)
362	Miami Gardens, FL	(39.2)
199	Miami, FL	(3.9)
20	Midland, TX	57.0
151	Milwaukee, WI	3.4
357	Minneapolis, MN	(36.7)
113	Miramar, FL	9.6
124	Mission Viejo, CA	8.1
369	Missouri City, TX	(45.0)
30	Mobile, AL	45.6
194	Modesto, CA	(3.2)
371	Montgomery, AL	(46.7)
91	Moreno Valley, CA	15.3
55	Murfreesboro, TN	28.7
346	Murrieta, CA	(32.7)
NA	Nampa, ID**	NA
264	Naperville, IL	(14.6)
38	Nashua, NH	38.1
333	Nashville, TN	(26.3)
48	New Bedford, MA	33.9
NA	New Haven, CT**	NA
NA	New Orleans, LA**	NA
336	New York, NY	(27.3)
139	Newark, NJ	6.2
65	Newport Beach, CA	23.8
79	Newton, MA	19.0
335	Norfolk, VA	(27.0)
110	Norman, OK	10.4
354	North Charleston, SC	(35.5)
164	North Las Vegas, NV	1.5
183	Norwalk, CA	(1.6)
7	Norwalk, CT	73.4
129	Oakland, CA	7.4
283	Oceanside, CA	(17.2)
3	Odessa, TX	148.2
152	O'Fallon, MO	3.0
259	Ogden, UT	(13.5)
172	Oklahoma City, OK	0.0
NA	Olathe, KS**	NA
72	Omaha, NE	21.6
198	Ontario, CA	(3.8)
348	Orange, CA	(33.2)
10	Orem, UT	65.5
367	Orlando, FL	(43.0)
314	Overland Park, KS	(23.8)
187	Oxnard, CA	(1.9)
296	Palm Bay, FL	(20.0)
323	Palmdale, CA	(25.1)
356	Pasadena, CA	(35.7)
63	Pasadena, TX	25.7
103	Paterson, NJ	11.9
114	Pearland, TX	9.4
102	Pembroke Pines, FL	12.1

RANK	CITY	% CHANGE
130	Peoria, AZ	7.3
138	Peoria, IL	6.6
264	Philadelphia, PA	(14.6)
290	Phoenix, AZ	(18.6)
236	Pittsburgh, PA	(10.4)
111	Plano, TX	9.9
19	Plantation, FL	57.9
229	Pomona, CA	(8.7)
331	Pompano Beach, FL	(26.1)
12	Port St. Lucie, FL	64.1
252	Portland, OR	(12.1)
200	Portsmouth, VA	(4.3)
197	Providence, RI	(3.7)
15	Provo, UT	62.4
163	Pueblo, CO	1.6
193	Quincy, MA	(3.1)
223	Racine, WI	(7.8)
240	Raleigh, NC	(10.7)
93	Ramapo, NY	14.9
278	Rancho Cucamon., CA	(16.6)
175	Reading, PA	(0.2)
122	Redding, CA	8.2
234	Reno, NV	(10.0)
141	Rialto, CA	6.1
114	Richardson, TX	9.4
307	Richmond, CA	(22.3)
343	Richmond, VA	(31.7)
25	Rio Rancho, NM	50.6
200	Riverside, CA	(4.3)
292	Roanoke, VA	(18.8)
319	Rochester, MN	(24.7)
264	Rochester, NY	(14.6)
128	Rockford, IL	7.6
211	Roseville, CA	(5.6)
161	Roswell, GA	1.7
167	Round Rock, TX	0.7
309	Sacramento, CA	(22.6)
261	Salem, OR	(13.9)
86	Salinas, CA	17.5
167	Salt Lake City, UT	0.7
116	San Angelo, TX	9.2
98	San Antonio, TX	13.9
328	San Bernardino, CA	(25.8)
179	San Diego, CA	(1.0)
153	San Francisco, CA	2.9
109	San Jose, CA	10.6
100	San Leandro, CA	13.0
174	San Marcos, CA	(0.1)
214	San Mateo, CA	(6.3)
NA	Sandy Springs, GA**	NA
285	Sandy, UT	(18.3)
42	Santa Ana, CA	37.2
29	Santa Barbara, CA	47.2
73	Santa Clara, CA	21.2
83	Santa Clarita, CA	18.0
313	Santa Maria, CA	(23.5)
345	Santa Monica, CA	(32.5)
143	Santa Rosa, CA	5.9
227	Savannah, GA	(8.4)
180	Scottsdale, AZ	(1.1)
132	Seattle, WA	7.2
312	Shreveport, LA	(23.0)
134	Simi Valley, CA	6.9
273	Sioux City, IA	(15.8)
366	Sioux Falls, SD	(42.6)
321	Somerville, MA	(24.9)
157	South Bend, IN	2.1
68	South Gate, CA	22.5

RANK	CITY	% CHANGE
NA	Southfield, MI**	NA
134	Sparks, NV	6.9
119	Spokane Valley, WA	8.7
23	Spokane, WA	52.2
166	Springfield, IL	1.4
326	Springfield, MA	(25.6)
32	Springfield, MO	42.9
192	Stamford, CT	(3.0)
NA	Sterling Heights, MI**	NA
237	Stockton, CA	(10.5)
245	St. George, UT	(11.3)
6	St. Joseph, MO	73.9
239	St. Louis, MO	(10.6)
245	St. Paul, MN	(11.3)
183	St. Petersburg, FL	(1.6)
359	Suffolk, VA	(37.7)
241	Sugar Land, TX	(10.8)
205	Sunnyvale, CA	(5.1)
227	Sunrise, FL	(8.4)
27	Surprise, AZ	47.7
316	Syracuse, NY	(24.0)
209	Tacoma, WA	(5.5)
101	Tallahassee, FL	12.9
325	Tampa, FL	(25.3)
351	Temecula, CA	(33.7)
252	Tempe, AZ	(12.1)
250	Thornton, CO	(11.7)
337	Thousand Oaks, CA	(27.4)
209	Toledo, OH	(5.5)
171	Toms River Twnshp, NJ	0.2
121	Topeka, KS	8.4
347	Torrance, CA	(32.9)
62	Tracy, CA	25.8
352	Trenton, NJ	(34.1)
NA	Troy, MI**	NA
339	Tucson, AZ	(28.6)
156	Tulsa, OK	2.3
263	Tuscaloosa, AL	(14.2)
373	Tyler, TX	(53.1)
11	Upper Darby Twnshp, PA	64.9
33	Vacaville, CA	42.6
NA	Vallejo, CA**	NA
216	Vancouver, WA	(6.5)
85	Ventura, CA	17.7
47	Victorville, CA	34.4
326	Virginia Beach, VA	(25.6)
285	Visalia, CA	(18.3)
311	Vista, CA	(22.9)
267	Waco, TX	(14.9)
NA	Warren, MI**	NA
13	Warwick, RI	63.6
145	Washington, DC	4.8
284	Waterbury, CT	(17.5)
146	West Covina, CA	4.7
NA	West Jordan, UT**	NA
341	West Palm Beach, FL	(31.1)
21	West Valley, UT	56.0
NA	Westland, MI**	NA
183	Westminster, CA	(1.6)
365	Westminster, CO	(42.5)
301	Whittier, CA	(21.1)
348	Wichita Falls, TX	(33.2)
NA	Wichita, KS**	NA
189	Wilmington, NC	(2.0)
297	Winston-Salem, NC	(20.3)
308	Woodbridge Twnshp, NJ	(22.4)
147	Worcester, MA	4.6
237	Yonkers, NY	(10.5)
137	Yuma, AZ	6.7

Source: CQ Press using reported data from the F.B.I. "Crime in the United States 2009"

*Robbery is the taking of anything of value by force or threat of force. Attempts are included.

**Not available.

60. Percent Change in Robbery Rate: 2005 to 2009 (continued)
National Percent Change = 5.6% Decrease*

RANK	CITY	% CHANGE
1	Brick Twnshp, NJ	518.4
2	Fargo, ND	201.7
3	Odessa, TX	148.2
4	Lafayette, LA	99.8
5	Livermore, CA	97.7
6	St. Joseph, MO	73.9
7	Norwalk, CT	73.4
8	Henderson, NV	71.5
9	Lawrence, KS	66.1
10	Orem, UT	65.5
11	Upper Darby Twnshp, PA	64.9
12	Port St. Lucie, FL	64.1
13	Warwick, RI	63.6
14	Jackson, MS	63.4
15	Provo, UT	62.4
16	Hawthorne, CA	62.1
17	Coral Springs, FL	62.0
18	Eugene, OR	61.4
19	Plantation, FL	57.9
20	Midland, TX	57.0
21	West Valley, UT	56.0
22	Melbourne, FL	53.3
23	Spokane, WA	52.2
24	Broken Arrow, OK	51.4
25	Rio Rancho, NM	50.6
26	Everett, WA	50.5
27	Surprise, AZ	47.7
28	Hayward, CA	47.6
29	Santa Barbara, CA	47.2
30	Mobile, AL	45.6
31	Longview, TX	43.6
32	Springfield, MO	42.9
33	Vacaville, CA	42.6
34	Huntington Beach, CA	41.9
35	Burbank, CA	41.0
36	Elizabeth, NJ	40.8
37	Boulder, CO	40.1
38	Nashua, NH	38.1
39	Clearwater, FL	38.0
39	Edison Twnshp, NJ	38.0
41	Gainesville, FL	37.4
42	Santa Ana, CA	37.2
43	Boca Raton, FL	36.6
44	Antioch, CA	36.2
45	Anchorage, AK	35.5
46	El Cajon, CA	35.3
47	Victorville, CA	34.4
48	New Bedford, MA	33.9
49	Escondido, CA	32.8
50	Lawton, OK	32.6
51	Billings, MT	31.7
52	Chico, CA	30.9
53	Columbus, GA	29.8
54	Mesquite, TX	29.1
55	Fullerton, CA	28.7
55	Murfreesboro, TN	28.7
57	Garland, TX	28.3
58	Mesa, AZ	27.6
59	Berkeley, CA	26.7
59	El Monte, CA	26.7
59	Federal Way, WA	26.7
62	Tracy, CA	25.8
63	Pasadena, TX	25.7
64	Independence, MO	24.4
65	Manchester, NH	23.8
65	Newport Beach, CA	23.8
67	Carrollton, TX	22.7
68	South Gate, CA	22.5
69	Brockton, MA	22.0
70	Clifton, NJ	21.9
71	Green Bay, WI	21.7
72	Omaha, NE	21.6
73	Columbia, MO	21.2
73	Santa Clara, CA	21.2
75	Davie, FL	20.0
76	Las Vegas, NV	19.7
77	Akron, OH	19.6
78	Fort Smith, AR	19.4
79	Newton, MA	19.0
80	Gilbert, AZ	18.1
80	Indianapolis, IN	18.1
80	Lewisville, TX	18.1
83	Santa Clarita, CA	18.0
84	Bellevue, WA	17.9
85	Ventura, CA	17.7
86	Salinas, CA	17.5
87	Knoxville, TN	17.3
88	Hamilton Twnshp, NJ	16.0
89	Fremont, CA	15.9
90	Lakeland, FL	15.6
91	Moreno Valley, CA	15.3
92	Baton Rouge, LA	15.0
93	Ramapo, NY	14.9
94	Bakersfield, CA	14.8
95	Baldwin Park, CA	14.7
96	High Point, NC	14.5
97	Laredo, TX	14.4
98	San Antonio, TX	13.9
99	Fort Wayne, IN	13.4
100	San Leandro, CA	13.0
101	Tallahassee, FL	12.9
102	Pembroke Pines, FL	12.1
103	Paterson, NJ	11.9
104	Colorado Springs, CO	11.5
105	Concord, CA	11.2
106	Compton, CA	10.8
106	Fort Collins, CO	10.8
108	Camden, NJ	10.7
109	San Jose, CA	10.6
110	Norman, OK	10.4
111	Plano, TX	9.9
112	Chattanooga, TN	9.8
113	Miramar, FL	9.6
114	Pearland, TX	9.4
114	Richardson, TX	9.4
116	San Angelo, TX	9.2
117	Irvine, CA	9.0
118	Macon, GA	8.9
119	Spokane Valley, WA	8.7
120	Brownsville, TX	8.5
121	Topeka, KS	8.4
122	Fontana, CA	8.2
122	Redding, CA	8.2
124	Bridgeport, CT	8.1
124	Mission Viejo, CA	8.1
126	Austin, TX	7.9
127	Amherst, NY	7.8
128	Rockford, IL	7.6
129	Oakland, CA	7.4
130	Greensboro, NC	7.3
130	Peoria, AZ	7.3
132	Seattle, WA	7.2
133	Kent, WA	7.0
134	Simi Valley, CA	6.9
134	Sparks, NV	6.9
136	Greece, NY	6.8
137	Yuma, AZ	6.7
138	Peoria, IL	6.6
139	Greeley, CO	6.2
139	Newark, NJ	6.2
141	Rialto, CA	6.1
142	Athens-Clarke, GA	6.0
143	Santa Rosa, CA	5.9
144	Albany, GA	5.8
145	Washington, DC	4.8
146	West Covina, CA	4.7
147	Worcester, MA	4.6
148	Madison, WI	4.4
149	Buffalo, NY	3.5
149	Honolulu, HI	3.5
151	Milwaukee, WI	3.4
152	O'Fallon, MO	3.0
153	Buena Park, CA	2.9
153	San Francisco, CA	2.9
155	Jacksonville, FL	2.8
156	Tulsa, OK	2.3
157	Durham, NC	2.1
157	Glendale, AZ	2.1
157	South Bend, IN	2.1
160	Beaumont, TX	2.0
161	Long Beach, CA	1.7
161	Roswell, GA	1.7
163	Pueblo, CO	1.6
164	Cleveland, OH	1.5
164	North Las Vegas, NV	1.5
166	Springfield, IL	1.4
167	Round Rock, TX	0.7
167	Salt Lake City, UT	0.7
169	Chicago, IL	0.3
169	Hollywood, FL	0.3
171	Toms River Twnshp, NJ	0.2
172	Clovis, CA	0.0
172	Oklahoma City, OK	0.0
174	San Marcos, CA	(0.1)
175	Reading, PA	(0.2)
176	Fayetteville, AR	(0.6)
177	Gary, IN	(0.8)
178	Cape Coral, FL	(0.9)
179	San Diego, CA	(1.0)
180	Scottsdale, AZ	(1.1)
181	Amarillo, TX	(1.2)
182	Grand Prairie, TX	(1.3)
183	Beaverton, OR	(1.6)
183	Norwalk, CA	(1.6)
183	St. Petersburg, FL	(1.6)
183	Westminster, CA	(1.6)
187	El Paso, TX	(1.9)
187	Oxnard, CA	(1.9)
189	Lee's Summit, MO	(2.0)
189	Wilmington, NC	(2.0)
191	Gresham, OR	(2.5)
192	Stamford, CT	(3.0)
193	Quincy, MA	(3.1)
194	Modesto, CA	(3.2)
195	Costa Mesa, CA	(3.4)
195	Downey, CA	(3.4)
197	Providence, RI	(3.7)
198	Ontario, CA	(3.8)
199	Miami, FL	(3.9)
200	Portsmouth, VA	(4.3)
200	Riverside, CA	(4.3)
202	Lubbock, TX	(4.6)
203	Baltimore, MD	(4.9)
203	Glendale, CA	(4.9)
205	Dayton, OH	(5.1)
205	Sunnyvale, CA	(5.1)

RANK	CITY	% CHANGE
207	Corpus Christi, TX	(5.2)
208	McAllen, TX	(5.3)
209	Tacoma, WA	(5.5)
209	Toledo, OH	(5.5)
211	Roseville, CA	(5.6)
212	Memphis, TN	(5.7)
213	Abilene, TX	(6.1)
214	San Mateo, CA	(6.3)
215	Cheektowaga, NY	(6.4)
216	Vancouver, WA	(6.5)
217	Lakewood, CA	(6.6)
218	Lake Forest, CA	(6.8)
218	Lakewood, CO	(6.8)
220	McKinney, TX	(7.0)
221	Chandler, AZ	(7.4)
222	Cincinnati, OH	(7.7)
223	Allentown, PA	(7.8)
223	Racine, WI	(7.8)
225	Houston, TX	(8.1)
226	Columbia, SC	(8.3)
227	Savannah, GA	(8.4)
227	Sunrise, FL	(8.4)
229	Pomona, CA	(8.7)
230	Anaheim, CA	(9.0)
230	Edmond, OK	(9.0)
230	Kansas City, MO	(9.0)
233	Chula Vista, CA	(9.1)
234	Inglewood, CA	(10.0)
234	Reno, NV	(10.0)
236	Pittsburgh, PA	(10.4)
237	Stockton, CA	(10.5)
237	Yonkers, NY	(10.5)
239	St. Louis, MO	(10.6)
240	Raleigh, NC	(10.7)
241	Sugar Land, TX	(10.8)
242	Fort Worth, TX	(10.9)
242	Los Angeles, CA	(10.9)
244	Alhambra, CA	(11.0)
245	Albuquerque, NM	(11.3)
245	Fairfield, CA	(11.3)
245	St. George, UT	(11.3)
245	St. Paul, MN	(11.3)
249	Miami Beach, FL	(11.6)
250	Hammond, IN	(11.7)
250	Thornton, CO	(11.7)
252	Portland, OR	(12.1)
252	Tempe, AZ	(12.1)
254	Hialeah, FL	(12.3)
254	Merced, CA	(12.3)
256	Hartford, CT	(12.6)
257	Canton, OH	(12.9)
258	Colonie, NY	(13.1)
259	Ogden, UT	(13.5)
260	Columbus, OH	(13.6)
261	Hesperia, CA	(13.9)
261	Salem, OR	(13.9)
263	Tuscaloosa, AL	(14.2)
264	Naperville, IL	(14.6)
264	Philadelphia, PA	(14.6)
264	Rochester, NY	(14.6)
267	Waco, TX	(14.9)
268	Fort Lauderdale, FL	(15.0)
269	Danbury, CT	(15.3)
270	Arlington, TX	(15.7)
270	Cedar Rapids, IA	(15.7)
270	Joliet, IL	(15.7)
273	Sioux City, IA	(15.8)
274	Fayetteville, NC	(16.2)

RANK	CITY	% CHANGE
275	Daly City, CA	(16.4)
275	Denton, TX	(16.4)
277	Bellingham, WA	(16.5)
278	Rancho Cucamon., CA	(16.6)
279	Allen, TX	(16.8)
279	Chino, CA	(16.8)
281	Indio, CA	(16.9)
282	Birmingham, AL	(17.0)
283	Oceanside, CA	(17.2)
284	Waterbury, CT	(17.5)
285	Hillsboro, OR	(18.3)
285	Lincoln, NE	(18.3)
285	Sandy, UT	(18.3)
285	Visalia, CA	(18.3)
289	Fresno, CA	(18.5)
290	Las Cruces, NM	(18.6)
290	Phoenix, AZ	(18.6)
292	Roanoke, VA	(18.8)
293	Lancaster, CA	(19.0)
294	Corona, CA	(19.7)
295	Huntsville, AL	(19.9)
296	Palm Bay, FL	(20.0)
297	Winston-Salem, NC	(20.3)
298	Davenport, IA	(20.6)
298	Kenosha, WI	(20.6)
300	Bend, OR	(20.8)
301	Whittier, CA	(21.1)
302	Evansville, IN	(21.4)
303	Aurora, CO	(21.6)
303	Cranston, RI	(21.6)
305	Kansas City, KS	(21.7)
306	Boston, MA	(21.8)
307	Richmond, CA	(22.3)
308	Woodbridge Twnshp, NJ	(22.4)
309	Irving, TX	(22.6)
309	Sacramento, CA	(22.6)
311	Vista, CA	(22.9)
312	Shreveport, LA	(23.0)
313	Santa Maria, CA	(23.5)
314	Dallas, TX	(23.8)
314	Overland Park, KS	(23.8)
316	Syracuse, NY	(24.0)
317	Frisco, TX	(24.1)
318	Carson, CA	(24.4)
319	Rochester, MN	(24.7)
320	Albany, NY	(24.8)
321	Somerville, MA	(24.9)
322	Chesapeake, VA	(25.0)
323	Aurora, IL	(25.1)
323	Palmdale, CA	(25.1)
325	Tampa, FL	(25.3)
326	Springfield, MA	(25.6)
326	Virginia Beach, VA	(25.6)
328	Atlanta, GA	(25.8)
328	San Bernardino, CA	(25.8)
330	Garden Grove, CA	(25.9)
331	Cary, NC	(26.1)
331	Pompano Beach, FL	(26.1)
333	Nashville, TN	(26.3)
334	Cambridge, MA	(26.8)
335	Norfolk, VA	(27.0)
336	New York, NY	(27.3)
337	Thousand Oaks, CA	(27.4)
338	Hampton, VA	(28.3)
339	Tucson, AZ	(28.6)
340	Charleston, SC	(29.7)
341	Clarksville, TN	(31.1)
341	West Palm Beach, FL	(31.1)

RANK	CITY	% CHANGE
343	Richmond, VA	(31.7)
344	Boise, ID	(32.0)
345	Santa Monica, CA	(32.5)
346	Murrieta, CA	(32.7)
347	Torrance, CA	(32.9)
348	Arvada, CO	(33.2)
348	Orange, CA	(33.2)
348	Wichita Falls, TX	(33.2)
351	Temecula, CA	(33.7)
352	Trenton, NJ	(34.1)
353	Killeen, TX	(34.8)
354	Lynn, MA	(35.5)
354	North Charleston, SC	(35.5)
356	Pasadena, CA	(35.7)
357	Minneapolis, MN	(36.7)
358	Alexandria, VA	(36.9)
359	Suffolk, VA	(37.7)
360	Denver, CO	(38.4)
361	Carlsbad, CA	(38.9)
362	Miami Gardens, FL	(39.2)
363	Centennial, CO	(39.4)
363	Erie, PA	(39.4)
365	Westminster, CO	(42.5)
366	Sioux Falls, SD	(42.6)
367	Orlando, FL	(43.0)
368	Charlotte, NC	(44.0)
369	Missouri City, TX	(45.0)
370	College Station, TX	(46.1)
371	Montgomery, AL	(46.7)
372	Jersey City, NJ	(47.2)
373	Tyler, TX	(53.1)
NA	Ann Arbor, MI**	NA
NA	Avondale, AZ**	NA
NA	Bloomington, MN**	NA
NA	Canton Twnshp, MI**	NA
NA	Citrus Heights, CA**	NA
NA	Clarkstown, NY**	NA
NA	Clinton Twnshp, MI**	NA
NA	Dearborn, MI**	NA
NA	Decatur, IL**	NA
NA	Des Moines, IA**	NA
NA	Detroit, MI**	NA
NA	Duluth, MN**	NA
NA	Elgin, IL**	NA
NA	Elk Grove, CA**	NA
NA	Fall River, MA**	NA
NA	Farmington Hills, MI**	NA
NA	Flint, MI**	NA
NA	Grand Rapids, MI**	NA
NA	Jacksonville, NC**	NA
NA	Lansing, MI**	NA
NA	Lexington, KY**	NA
NA	Little Rock, AR**	NA
NA	Livonia, MI**	NA
NA	Longmont, CO**	NA
NA	Louisville, KY**	NA
NA	Nampa, ID**	NA
NA	New Haven, CT**	NA
NA	New Orleans, LA**	NA
NA	Olathe, KS**	NA
NA	Sandy Springs, GA**	NA
NA	Southfield, MI**	NA
NA	Sterling Heights, MI**	NA
NA	Troy, MI**	NA
NA	Vallejo, CA**	NA
NA	Warren, MI**	NA
NA	West Jordan, UT**	NA
NA	Westland, MI**	NA
NA	Wichita, KS**	NA

Source: CQ Press using reported data from the F.B.I. "Crime in the United States 2009"
*Robbery is the taking of anything of value by force or threat of force. Attempts are included.
**Not available.

61. Aggravated Assaults in 2009
National Total = 806,843 Aggravated Assaults*

RANK	CITY	ASSAULTS
188	Abilene, TX	400
89	Akron, OH	980
153	Albany, GA	536
131	Albany, NY	622
28	Albuquerque, NM	2,597
333	Alexandria, VA	129
354	Alhambra, CA	100
293	Allentown, PA	190
405	Allen, TX	47
78	Amarillo, TX	1,119
376	Amherst, NY	75
136	Anaheim, CA	599
52	Anchorage, AK	1,658
303	Ann Arbor, MI	177
152	Antioch, CA	537
58	Arlington, TX	1,494
336	Arvada, CO	122
249	Athens-Clarke, GA	265
22	Atlanta, GA	3,419
116	Aurora, CO	733
154	Aurora, IL	531
33	Austin, TX	2,322
280	Avondale, AZ	212
65	Bakersfield, CA	1,319
308	Baldwin Park, CA	170
9	Baltimore, MD	5,561
56	Baton Rouge, LA	1,558
140	Beaumont, TX	592
339	Beaverton, OR	117
377	Bellevue, WA	74
365	Bellingham, WA	84
339	Bend, OR	117
331	Berkeley, CA	138
319	Billings, MT	158
62	Birmingham, AL	1,399
386	Bloomington, MN	66
344	Boca Raton, FL	113
189	Boise, ID	399
19	Boston, MA	3,596
322	Boulder, CO	157
369	Brick Twnshp, NJ	78
107	Bridgeport, CT	777
98	Brockton, MA	870
345	Broken Arrow, OK	112
243	Brownsville, TX	272
349	Buena Park, CA	106
40	Buffalo, NY	2,083
332	Burbank, CA	137
227	Cambridge, MA	295
87	Camden, NJ	1,020
360	Canton Twnshp, MI	90
239	Canton, OH	279
271	Cape Coral, FL	221
285	Carlsbad, CA	203
349	Carrollton, TX	106
215	Carson, CA	317
379	Cary, NC	72
255	Cedar Rapids, IA	252
351	Centennial, CO	103
165	Chandler, AZ	484
206	Charleston, SC	337
25	Charlotte, NC	2,918
72	Chattanooga, TN	1,187
343	Cheektowaga, NY	114
147	Chesapeake, VA	548
2	Chicago, IL	15,727
328	Chico, CA	141
365	Chino, CA	84

RANK	CITY	ASSAULTS
201	Chula Vista, CA	359
59	Cincinnati, OH	1,414
252	Citrus Heights, CA	261
391	Clarkstown, NY	63
129	Clarksville, TN	629
135	Clearwater, FL	603
42	Cleveland, OH	1,976
363	Clifton, NJ	86
286	Clinton Twnshp, MI	202
391	Clovis, CA	63
354	College Station, TX	100
410	Colonie, NY	31
79	Colorado Springs, CO	1,084
220	Columbia, MO	309
96	Columbia, SC	878
156	Columbus, GA	519
66	Columbus, OH	1,288
97	Compton, CA	876
314	Concord, CA	164
264	Coral Springs, FL	242
372	Corona, CA	77
50	Corpus Christi, TX	1,682
315	Costa Mesa, CA	162
394	Cranston, RI	61
16	Dallas, TX	4,069
338	Daly City, CA	119
398	Danbury, CT	53
168	Davenport, IA	468
211	Davie, FL	321
128	Dayton, OH	642
283	Dearborn, MI	208
185	Decatur, IL	415
323	Denton, TX	154
37	Denver, CO	2,165
124	Des Moines, IA	664
4	Detroit, MI	11,255
295	Downey, CA	188
287	Duluth, MN	201
105	Durham, NC	797
315	Edison Twnshp, NJ	162
402	Edmond, OK	51
284	El Cajon, CA	204
191	El Monte, CA	395
36	El Paso, TX	2,184
313	Elgin, IL	167
167	Elizabeth, NJ	478
178	Elk Grove, CA	437
250	Erie, PA	264
207	Escondido, CA	334
290	Eugene, OR	195
268	Evansville, IN	233
229	Everett, WA	294
275	Fairfield, CA	215
111	Fall River, MA	763
279	Fargo, ND	213
372	Farmington Hills, MI	77
266	Fayetteville, AR	237
125	Fayetteville, NC	662
342	Federal Way, WA	115
57	Flint, MI	1,527
157	Fontana, CA	508
195	Fort Collins, CO	378
117	Fort Lauderdale, FL	727
161	Fort Smith, AR	503
226	Fort Wayne, IN	298
30	Fort Worth, TX	2,369
266	Fremont, CA	237
49	Fresno, CA	1,720
369	Frisco, TX	78

RANK	CITY	ASSAULTS
232	Fullerton, CA	291
104	Gainesville, FL	819
207	Garden Grove, CA	334
263	Garland, TX	243
240	Gary, IN	276
347	Gilbert, AZ	109
126	Glendale, AZ	655
319	Glendale, CA	158
245	Grand Prairie, TX	271
92	Grand Rapids, MI	936
408	Greece, NY	43
210	Greeley, CO	329
212	Green Bay, WI	319
93	Greensboro, NC	932
291	Gresham, OR	192
362	Hamilton Twnshp, NJ	88
170	Hammond, IN	467
271	Hampton, VA	221
94	Hartford, CT	921
222	Hawthorne, CA	308
253	Hayward, CA	259
227	Henderson, NV	295
300	Hesperia, CA	180
142	Hialeah, FL	576
198	High Point, NC	369
399	Hillsboro, OR	52
209	Hollywood, FL	332
60	Honolulu, HI	1,411
3	Houston, TX	13,116
274	Huntington Beach, CA	218
129	Huntsville, AL	629
155	Independence, MO	528
10	Indianapolis, IN	5,271
236	Indio, CA	283
164	Inglewood, CA	495
384	Irvine, CA	67
203	Irving, TX	352
15	Jacksonville, FL	4,096
325	Jacksonville, NC	145
190	Jackson, MS	396
101	Jersey City, NJ	843
217	Joliet, IL	316
158	Kansas City, KS	507
17	Kansas City, MO	3,957
334	Kenosha, WI	128
262	Kent, WA	244
163	Killeen, TX	497
75	Knoxville, TN	1,137
108	Lafayette, LA	776
375	Lake Forest, CA	76
238	Lakeland, FL	280
305	Lakewood, CA	172
181	Lakewood, CO	429
141	Lancaster, CA	584
100	Lansing, MI	845
95	Laredo, TX	895
205	Las Cruces, NM	341
7	Las Vegas, NV	7,735
232	Lawrence, KS	291
103	Lawton, OK	827
397	Lee's Summit, MO	55
357	Lewisville, TX	98
83	Lexington, KY	1,062
102	Lincoln, NE	838
48	Little Rock, AR	1,793
372	Livermore, CA	77
339	Livonia, MI	117
53	Long Beach, CA	1,609
248	Longmont, CO	269

RANK	CITY	ASSAULTS	RANK	CITY	ASSAULTS	RANK	CITY	ASSAULTS
165	Longview, TX	484	307	Peoria, AZ	171	261	Southfield, MI	246
5	Los Angeles, CA	10,638	145	Peoria, IL	554	264	Sparks, NV	242
44	Louisville, KY	1,907	6	Philadelphia, PA	8,928	298	Spokane Valley, WA	182
51	Lubbock, TX	1,662	13	Phoenix, AZ	4,329	115	Spokane, WA	745
134	Lynn, MA	606	55	Pittsburgh, PA	1,565	80	Springfield, IL	1,076
217	Macon, GA	316	243	Plano, TX	272	70	Springfield, MA	1,216
175	Madison, WI	457	297	Plantation, FL	184	106	Springfield, MO	780
230	Manchester, NH	293	143	Pomona, CA	561	309	Stamford, CT	169
291	McAllen, TX	192	132	Pompano Beach, FL	616	324	Sterling Heights, MI	150
326	McKinney, TX	142	220	Port St. Lucie, FL	309	32	Stockton, CA	2,329
121	Melbourne, FL	684	47	Portland, OR	1,797	386	St. George, UT	66
8	Memphis, TN	7,402	212	Portsmouth, VA	319	215	St. Joseph, MO	317
150	Merced, CA	541	118	Providence, RI	714	14	St. Louis, MO	4,239
68	Mesa, AZ	1,252	356	Provo, UT	99	67	St. Paul, MN	1,265
231	Mesquite, TX	292	120	Pueblo, CO	688	35	St. Petersburg, FL	2,304
178	Miami Beach, FL	437	251	Quincy, MA	263	309	Suffolk, VA	169
123	Miami Gardens, FL	666	298	Racine, WI	182	406	Sugar Land, TX	46
27	Miami, FL	2,765	84	Raleigh, NC	1,056	363	Sunnyvale, CA	86
234	Midland, TX	287	407	Ramapo, NY	45	318	Sunrise, FL	161
24	Milwaukee, WI	3,186	288	Rancho Cucamon., CA	198	389	Surprise, AZ	64
38	Minneapolis, MN	2,148	199	Reading, PA	363	99	Syracuse, NY	852
222	Miramar, FL	308	151	Redding, CA	539	73	Tacoma, WA	1,145
399	Mission Viejo, CA	52	91	Reno, NV	971	85	Tallahassee, FL	1,047
394	Missouri City, TX	61	236	Rialto, CA	283	54	Tampa, FL	1,588
80	Mobile, AL	1,076	347	Richardson, TX	109	399	Temecula, CA	52
90	Modesto, CA	974	138	Richmond, CA	597	147	Tempe, AZ	548
225	Montgomery, AL	302	119	Richmond, VA	709	312	Thornton, CO	168
184	Moreno Valley, CA	418	302	Rio Rancho, NM	178	352	Thousand Oaks, CA	102
172	Murfreesboro, TN	459	113	Riverside, CA	755	46	Toledo, OH	1,831
384	Murrieta, CA	67	183	Roanoke, VA	420	393	Toms River Twnshp, NJ	62
277	Nampa, ID	214	326	Rochester, MN	142	200	Topeka, KS	360
369	Naperville, IL	78	82	Rochester, NY	1,071	358	Torrance, CA	94
345	Nashua, NH	112	64	Rockford, IL	1,332	389	Tracy, CA	64
11	Nashville, TN	4,649	275	Roseville, CA	215	136	Trenton, NJ	599
110	New Bedford, MA	769	377	Roswell, GA	74	404	Troy, MI	49
71	New Haven, CT	1,206	379	Round Rock, TX	72	41	Tucson, AZ	2,075
61	New Orleans, LA	1,410	31	Sacramento, CA	2,350	26	Tulsa, OK	2,856
1	New York, NY	26,457	193	Salem, OR	379	293	Tuscaloosa, AL	190
77	Newark, NJ	1,130	122	Salinas, CA	678	193	Tyler, TX	379
361	Newport Beach, CA	89	112	Salt Lake City, UT	762	281	Upper Darby Twnshp, PA	210
386	Newton, MA	66	257	San Angelo, TX	250	315	Vacaville, CA	162
108	Norfolk, VA	776	12	San Antonio, TX	4,434	158	Vallejo, CA	507
381	Norman, OK	71	74	San Bernardino, CA	1,138	196	Vancouver, WA	375
146	North Charleston, SC	552	18	San Diego, CA	3,667	273	Ventura, CA	220
88	North Las Vegas, NV	1,013	34	San Francisco, CA	2,310	180	Victorville, CA	436
258	Norwalk, CA	249	39	San Jose, CA	2,128	197	Virginia Beach, VA	370
254	Norwalk, CT	257	335	San Leandro, CA	124	187	Visalia, CA	401
21	Oakland, CA	3,465	330	San Marcos, CA	140	217	Vista, CA	316
171	Oceanside, CA	462	281	San Mateo, CA	210	138	Waco, TX	597
144	Odessa, TX	557	409	Sandy Springs, GA	42	162	Warren, MI	498
403	O'Fallon, MO	50	337	Sandy, UT	120	396	Warwick, RI	57
258	Ogden, UT	249	113	Santa Ana, CA	755	23	Washington, DC	3,295
20	Oklahoma City, OK	3,573	234	Santa Barbara, CA	287	300	Waterbury, CT	180
305	Olathe, KS	172	367	Santa Clara, CA	79	328	West Covina, CA	141
69	Omaha, NE	1,249	241	Santa Clarita, CA	273	353	West Jordan, UT	101
192	Ontario, CA	392	133	Santa Maria, CA	615	168	West Palm Beach, FL	468
367	Orange, CA	79	277	Santa Monica, CA	214	214	West Valley, UT	318
411	Orem, UT	13	149	Santa Rosa, CA	546	260	Westland, MI	248
45	Orlando, FL	1,902	186	Savannah, GA	410	319	Westminster, CA	158
269	Overland Park, KS	226	255	Scottsdale, AZ	252	309	Westminster, CO	169
204	Oxnard, CA	350	43	Seattle, WA	1,945	270	Whittier, CA	224
181	Palm Bay, FL	429	76	Shreveport, LA	1,136	224	Wichita Falls, TX	306
160	Palmdale, CA	505	359	Simi Valley, CA	92	29	Wichita, KS	2,439
245	Pasadena, CA	271	245	Sioux City, IA	271	176	Wilmington, NC	454
173	Pasadena, TX	458	241	Sioux Falls, SD	273	86	Winston-Salem, NC	1,039
127	Paterson, NJ	644	288	Somerville, MA	198	382	Woodbridge Twnshp, NJ	70
383	Pearland, TX	69	202	South Bend, IN	353	63	Worcester, MA	1,344
296	Pembroke Pines, FL	185	303	South Gate, CA	177	177	Yonkers, NY	446
						173	Yuma, AZ	458

Source: Reported data from the F.B.I. "Crime in the United States 2009"

*Aggravated assault is an attack for the purpose of inflicting severe bodily injury.

61. Aggravated Assaults in 2009 (continued)
National Total = 806,843 Aggravated Assaults*

RANK	CITY	ASSAULTS
1	New York, NY	26,457
2	Chicago, IL	15,727
3	Houston, TX	13,116
4	Detroit, MI	11,255
5	Los Angeles, CA	10,638
6	Philadelphia, PA	8,928
7	Las Vegas, NV	7,735
8	Memphis, TN	7,402
9	Baltimore, MD	5,561
10	Indianapolis, IN	5,271
11	Nashville, TN	4,649
12	San Antonio, TX	4,434
13	Phoenix, AZ	4,329
14	St. Louis, MO	4,239
15	Jacksonville, FL	4,096
16	Dallas, TX	4,069
17	Kansas City, MO	3,957
18	San Diego, CA	3,667
19	Boston, MA	3,596
20	Oklahoma City, OK	3,573
21	Oakland, CA	3,465
22	Atlanta, GA	3,419
23	Washington, DC	3,295
24	Milwaukee, WI	3,186
25	Charlotte, NC	2,918
26	Tulsa, OK	2,856
27	Miami, FL	2,765
28	Albuquerque, NM	2,597
29	Wichita, KS	2,439
30	Fort Worth, TX	2,369
31	Sacramento, CA	2,350
32	Stockton, CA	2,329
33	Austin, TX	2,322
34	San Francisco, CA	2,310
35	St. Petersburg, FL	2,304
36	El Paso, TX	2,184
37	Denver, CO	2,165
38	Minneapolis, MN	2,148
39	San Jose, CA	2,128
40	Buffalo, NY	2,083
41	Tucson, AZ	2,075
42	Cleveland, OH	1,976
43	Seattle, WA	1,945
44	Louisville, KY	1,907
45	Orlando, FL	1,902
46	Toledo, OH	1,831
47	Portland, OR	1,797
48	Little Rock, AR	1,793
49	Fresno, CA	1,720
50	Corpus Christi, TX	1,682
51	Lubbock, TX	1,662
52	Anchorage, AK	1,658
53	Long Beach, CA	1,609
54	Tampa, FL	1,588
55	Pittsburgh, PA	1,565
56	Baton Rouge, LA	1,558
57	Flint, MI	1,527
58	Arlington, TX	1,494
59	Cincinnati, OH	1,414
60	Honolulu, HI	1,411
61	New Orleans, LA	1,410
62	Birmingham, AL	1,399
63	Worcester, MA	1,344
64	Rockford, IL	1,332
65	Bakersfield, CA	1,319
66	Columbus, OH	1,288
67	St. Paul, MN	1,265
68	Mesa, AZ	1,252
69	Omaha, NE	1,249
70	Springfield, MA	1,216
71	New Haven, CT	1,206
72	Chattanooga, TN	1,187
73	Tacoma, WA	1,145
74	San Bernardino, CA	1,138
75	Knoxville, TN	1,137
76	Shreveport, LA	1,136
77	Newark, NJ	1,130
78	Amarillo, TX	1,119
79	Colorado Springs, CO	1,084
80	Mobile, AL	1,076
80	Springfield, IL	1,076
82	Rochester, NY	1,071
83	Lexington, KY	1,062
84	Raleigh, NC	1,056
85	Tallahassee, FL	1,047
86	Winston-Salem, NC	1,039
87	Camden, NJ	1,020
88	North Las Vegas, NV	1,013
89	Akron, OH	980
90	Modesto, CA	974
91	Reno, NV	971
92	Grand Rapids, MI	936
93	Greensboro, NC	932
94	Hartford, CT	921
95	Laredo, TX	895
96	Columbia, SC	878
97	Compton, CA	876
98	Brockton, MA	870
99	Syracuse, NY	852
100	Lansing, MI	845
101	Jersey City, NJ	843
102	Lincoln, NE	838
103	Lawton, OK	827
104	Gainesville, FL	819
105	Durham, NC	797
106	Springfield, MO	780
107	Bridgeport, CT	777
108	Lafayette, LA	776
108	Norfolk, VA	776
110	New Bedford, MA	769
111	Fall River, MA	763
112	Salt Lake City, UT	762
113	Riverside, CA	755
113	Santa Ana, CA	755
115	Spokane, WA	745
116	Aurora, CO	733
117	Fort Lauderdale, FL	727
118	Providence, RI	714
119	Richmond, VA	709
120	Pueblo, CO	688
121	Melbourne, FL	684
122	Salinas, CA	678
123	Miami Gardens, FL	666
124	Des Moines, IA	664
125	Fayetteville, NC	662
126	Glendale, AZ	655
127	Paterson, NJ	644
128	Dayton, OH	642
129	Clarksville, TN	629
129	Huntsville, AL	629
131	Albany, NY	622
132	Pompano Beach, FL	616
133	Santa Maria, CA	615
134	Lynn, MA	606
135	Clearwater, FL	603
136	Anaheim, CA	599
136	Trenton, NJ	599
138	Richmond, CA	597
138	Waco, TX	597
140	Beaumont, TX	592
141	Lancaster, CA	584
142	Hialeah, FL	576
143	Pomona, CA	561
144	Odessa, TX	557
145	Peoria, IL	554
146	North Charleston, SC	552
147	Chesapeake, VA	548
147	Tempe, AZ	548
149	Santa Rosa, CA	546
150	Merced, CA	541
151	Redding, CA	539
152	Antioch, CA	537
153	Albany, GA	536
154	Aurora, IL	531
155	Independence, MO	528
156	Columbus, GA	519
157	Fontana, CA	508
158	Kansas City, KS	507
158	Vallejo, CA	507
160	Palmdale, CA	505
161	Fort Smith, AR	503
162	Warren, MI	498
163	Killeen, TX	497
164	Inglewood, CA	495
165	Chandler, AZ	484
165	Longview, TX	484
167	Elizabeth, NJ	478
168	Davenport, IA	468
168	West Palm Beach, FL	468
170	Hammond, IN	467
171	Oceanside, CA	462
172	Murfreesboro, TN	459
173	Pasadena, TX	458
173	Yuma, AZ	458
175	Madison, WI	457
176	Wilmington, NC	454
177	Yonkers, NY	446
178	Elk Grove, CA	437
178	Miami Beach, FL	437
180	Victorville, CA	436
181	Lakewood, CO	429
181	Palm Bay, FL	429
183	Roanoke, VA	420
184	Moreno Valley, CA	418
185	Decatur, IL	415
186	Savannah, GA	410
187	Visalia, CA	401
188	Abilene, TX	400
189	Boise, ID	399
190	Jackson, MS	396
191	El Monte, CA	395
192	Ontario, CA	392
193	Salem, OR	379
193	Tyler, TX	379
195	Fort Collins, CO	378
196	Vancouver, WA	375
197	Virginia Beach, VA	370
198	High Point, NC	369
199	Reading, PA	363
200	Topeka, KS	360
201	Chula Vista, CA	359
202	South Bend, IN	353
203	Irving, TX	352
204	Oxnard, CA	350
205	Las Cruces, NM	341
206	Charleston, SC	337

RANK	CITY	ASSAULTS
207	Escondido, CA	334
207	Garden Grove, CA	334
209	Hollywood, FL	332
210	Greeley, CO	329
211	Davie, FL	321
212	Green Bay, WI	319
212	Portsmouth, VA	319
214	West Valley, UT	318
215	Carson, CA	317
215	St. Joseph, MO	317
217	Joliet, IL	316
217	Macon, GA	316
217	Vista, CA	316
220	Columbia, MO	309
220	Port St. Lucie, FL	309
222	Hawthorne, CA	308
222	Miramar, FL	308
224	Wichita Falls, TX	306
225	Montgomery, AL	302
226	Fort Wayne, IN	298
227	Cambridge, MA	295
227	Henderson, NV	295
229	Everett, WA	294
230	Manchester, NH	293
231	Mesquite, TX	292
232	Fullerton, CA	291
232	Lawrence, KS	291
234	Midland, TX	287
234	Santa Barbara, CA	287
236	Indio, CA	283
236	Rialto, CA	283
238	Lakeland, FL	280
239	Canton, OH	279
240	Gary, IN	276
241	Santa Clarita, CA	273
241	Sioux Falls, SD	273
243	Brownsville, TX	272
243	Plano, TX	272
245	Grand Prairie, TX	271
245	Pasadena, CA	271
245	Sioux City, IA	271
248	Longmont, CO	269
249	Athens-Clarke, GA	265
250	Erie, PA	264
251	Quincy, MA	263
252	Citrus Heights, CA	261
253	Hayward, CA	259
254	Norwalk, CT	257
255	Cedar Rapids, IA	252
255	Scottsdale, AZ	252
257	San Angelo, TX	250
258	Norwalk, CA	249
258	Ogden, UT	249
260	Westland, MI	248
261	Southfield, MI	246
262	Kent, WA	244
263	Garland, TX	243
264	Coral Springs, FL	242
264	Sparks, NV	242
266	Fayetteville, AR	237
266	Fremont, CA	237
268	Evansville, IN	233
269	Overland Park, KS	226
270	Whittier, CA	224
271	Cape Coral, FL	221
271	Hampton, VA	221
273	Ventura, CA	220
274	Huntington Beach, CA	218
275	Fairfield, CA	215
275	Roseville, CA	215
277	Nampa, ID	214
277	Santa Monica, CA	214
279	Fargo, ND	213
280	Avondale, AZ	212
281	San Mateo, CA	210
281	Upper Darby Twnshp, PA	210
283	Dearborn, MI	208
284	El Cajon, CA	204
285	Carlsbad, CA	203
286	Clinton Twnshp, MI	202
287	Duluth, MN	201
288	Rancho Cucamon., CA	198
288	Somerville, MA	198
290	Eugene, OR	195
291	Gresham, OR	192
291	McAllen, TX	192
293	Allentown, PA	190
293	Tuscaloosa, AL	190
295	Downey, CA	188
296	Pembroke Pines, FL	185
297	Plantation, FL	184
298	Racine, WI	182
298	Spokane Valley, WA	182
300	Hesperia, CA	180
300	Waterbury, CT	180
302	Rio Rancho, NM	178
303	Ann Arbor, MI	177
303	South Gate, CA	177
305	Lakewood, CA	172
305	Olathe, KS	172
307	Peoria, AZ	171
308	Baldwin Park, CA	170
309	Stamford, CT	169
309	Suffolk, VA	169
309	Westminster, CO	169
312	Thornton, CO	168
313	Elgin, IL	167
314	Concord, CA	164
315	Costa Mesa, CA	162
315	Edison Twnshp, NJ	162
315	Vacaville, CA	162
318	Sunrise, FL	161
319	Billings, MT	158
319	Glendale, CA	158
319	Westminster, CA	158
322	Boulder, CO	157
323	Denton, TX	154
324	Sterling Heights, MI	150
325	Jacksonville, NC	145
326	McKinney, TX	142
326	Rochester, MN	142
328	Chico, CA	141
328	West Covina, CA	141
330	San Marcos, CA	140
331	Berkeley, CA	138
332	Burbank, CA	137
333	Alexandria, VA	129
334	Kenosha, WI	128
335	San Leandro, CA	124
336	Arvada, CO	122
337	Sandy, UT	120
338	Daly City, CA	119
339	Beaverton, OR	117
339	Bend, OR	117
339	Livonia, MI	117
342	Federal Way, WA	115
343	Cheektowaga, NY	114
344	Boca Raton, FL	113
345	Broken Arrow, OK	112
345	Nashua, NH	112
347	Gilbert, AZ	109
347	Richardson, TX	109
349	Buena Park, CA	106
349	Carrollton, TX	106
351	Centennial, CO	103
352	Thousand Oaks, CA	102
353	West Jordan, UT	101
354	Alhambra, CA	100
354	College Station, TX	100
356	Provo, UT	99
357	Lewisville, TX	98
358	Torrance, CA	94
359	Simi Valley, CA	92
360	Canton Twnshp, MI	90
361	Newport Beach, CA	89
362	Hamilton Twnshp, NJ	88
363	Clifton, NJ	86
363	Sunnyvale, CA	86
365	Bellingham, WA	84
365	Chino, CA	84
367	Orange, CA	79
367	Santa Clara, CA	79
369	Brick Twnshp, NJ	78
369	Frisco, TX	78
369	Naperville, IL	78
372	Corona, CA	77
372	Farmington Hills, MI	77
372	Livermore, CA	77
375	Lake Forest, CA	76
376	Amherst, NY	75
377	Bellevue, WA	74
377	Roswell, GA	74
379	Cary, NC	72
379	Round Rock, TX	72
381	Norman, OK	71
382	Woodbridge Twnshp, NJ	70
383	Pearland, TX	69
384	Irvine, CA	67
384	Murrieta, CA	67
386	Bloomington, MN	66
386	Newton, MA	66
386	St. George, UT	66
389	Surprise, AZ	64
389	Tracy, CA	64
391	Clarkstown, NY	63
391	Clovis, CA	63
393	Toms River Twnshp, NJ	62
394	Cranston, RI	61
394	Missouri City, TX	61
396	Warwick, RI	57
397	Lee's Summit, MO	55
398	Danbury, CT	53
399	Hillsboro, OR	52
399	Mission Viejo, CA	52
399	Temecula, CA	52
402	Edmond, OK	51
403	O'Fallon, MO	50
404	Troy, MI	49
405	Allen, TX	47
406	Sugar Land, TX	46
407	Ramapo, NY	45
408	Greece, NY	43
409	Sandy Springs, GA	42
410	Colonie, NY	31
411	Orem, UT	13

Source: Reported data from the F.B.I. "Crime in the United States 2009"

*Aggravated assault is an attack for the purpose of inflicting severe bodily injury.

62. Aggravated Assault Rate in 2009
National Rate = 262.8 Aggravated Assaults per 100,000 Population*

RANK	CITY	RATE
155	Abilene, TX	343.2
93	Akron, OH	474.6
32	Albany, GA	707.7
39	Albany, NY	665.6
88	Albuquerque, NM	489.4
361	Alexandria, VA	88.3
336	Alhambra, CA	116.3
283	Allentown, PA	177.0
400	Allen, TX	54.1
56	Amarillo, TX	592.8
380	Amherst, NY	67.9
281	Anaheim, CA	178.3
59	Anchorage, AK	585.2
301	Ann Arbor, MI	154.8
78	Antioch, CA	530.4
124	Arlington, TX	394.1
338	Arvada, CO	113.0
236	Athens-Clarke, GA	231.4
49	Atlanta, GA	618.4
242	Aurora, CO	226.2
187	Aurora, IL	303.2
189	Austin, TX	302.0
234	Avondale, AZ	238.8
121	Bakersfield, CA	398.6
252	Baldwin Park, CA	219.2
14	Baltimore, MD	870.6
34	Baton Rouge, LA	698.1
77	Beaumont, TX	537.0
328	Beaverton, OR	125.5
395	Bellevue, WA	59.2
349	Bellingham, WA	104.7
308	Bend, OR	145.3
315	Berkeley, CA	136.4
304	Billings, MT	149.9
50	Birmingham, AL	615.3
368	Bloomington, MN	81.6
321	Boca Raton, FL	131.5
268	Boise, ID	193.3
65	Boston, MA	576.1
297	Boulder, CO	156.9
355	Brick Twnshp, NJ	99.2
68	Bridgeport, CT	571.1
12	Brockton, MA	901.8
331	Broken Arrow, OK	118.6
302	Brownsville, TX	151.5
318	Buena Park, CA	133.3
23	Buffalo, NY	775.3
320	Burbank, CA	132.7
198	Cambridge, MA	286.8
2	Camden, NJ	1,291.5
345	Canton Twnshp, MI	108.9
140	Canton, OH	357.3
317	Cape Coral, FL	134.5
260	Carlsbad, CA	206.1
365	Carrollton, TX	83.2
157	Carson, CA	342.2
403	Cary, NC	53.8
266	Cedar Rapids, IA	195.7
351	Centennial, CO	103.6
271	Chandler, AZ	189.0
194	Charleston, SC	296.4
130	Charlotte, NC	375.2
35	Chattanooga, TN	688.0
307	Cheektowaga, NY	146.6
227	Chesapeake, VA	245.5
74	Chicago, IL	552.1
291	Chico, CA	166.4
354	Chino, CA	99.3
294	Chula Vista, CA	159.7
112	Cincinnati, OH	423.9
181	Citrus Heights, CA	309.5
370	Clarkstown, NY	79.8
82	Clarksville, TN	517.0
67	Clearwater, FL	572.2
97	Cleveland, OH	460.4
344	Clifton, NJ	110.1
256	Clinton Twnshp, MI	210.5
384	Clovis, CA	66.2
337	College Station, TX	116.2
409	Colonie, NY	39.7
213	Colorado Springs, CO	269.9
190	Columbia, MO	301.2
37	Columbia, SC	686.6
204	Columbus, GA	278.7
289	Columbus, OH	169.6
9	Compton, CA	933.2
316	Concord, CA	135.5
270	Coral Springs, FL	192.6
406	Corona, CA	50.5
60	Corpus Christi, TX	585.0
306	Costa Mesa, CA	147.1
375	Cranston, RI	76.0
177	Dallas, TX	315.4
334	Daly City, CA	117.5
383	Danbury, CT	66.5
96	Davenport, IA	462.8
143	Davie, FL	356.1
114	Dayton, OH	419.7
229	Dearborn, MI	243.8
76	Decatur, IL	548.6
329	Denton, TX	123.9
139	Denver, CO	358.0
159	Des Moines, IA	337.4
3	Detroit, MI	1,238.9
285	Downey, CA	174.7
233	Duluth, MN	239.1
148	Durham, NC	350.3
293	Edison Twnshp, NJ	163.1
391	Edmond, OK	63.0
246	El Cajon, CA	220.6
169	El Monte, CA	322.6
146	El Paso, TX	352.9
300	Elgin, IL	155.1
126	Elizabeth, NJ	382.7
180	Elk Grove, CA	310.9
225	Erie, PA	254.2
231	Escondido, CA	243.0
326	Eugene, OR	128.8
264	Evansville, IN	201.3
192	Everett, WA	298.7
261	Fairfield, CA	205.8
18	Fall River, MA	830.2
240	Fargo, ND	227.0
356	Farmington Hills, MI	98.5
176	Fayetteville, AR	315.5
128	Fayetteville, NC	380.5
314	Federal Way, WA	136.5
1	Flint, MI	1,367.6
216	Fontana, CA	266.9
207	Fort Collins, CO	272.9
122	Fort Lauderdale, FL	397.4
58	Fort Smith, AR	590.5
332	Fort Wayne, IN	118.4
165	Fort Worth, TX	327.5
335	Fremont, CA	116.9
140	Fresno, CA	357.3
377	Frisco, TX	72.1
249	Fullerton, CA	219.7
31	Gainesville, FL	710.5
263	Garden Grove, CA	201.4
343	Garland, TX	111.0
196	Gary, IN	289.9
407	Gilbert, AZ	47.0
222	Glendale, AZ	256.8
369	Glendale, CA	80.0
292	Grand Prairie, TX	164.5
89	Grand Rapids, MI	485.2
408	Greece, NY	46.1
145	Greeley, CO	353.5
173	Green Bay, WI	316.4
133	Greensboro, NC	368.1
274	Gresham, OR	187.4
357	Hamilton Twnshp, NJ	97.2
51	Hammond, IN	613.8
303	Hampton, VA	151.4
28	Hartford, CT	742.4
136	Hawthorne, CA	365.3
279	Hayward, CA	182.1
340	Henderson, NV	112.6
262	Hesperia, CA	202.5
206	Hialeah, FL	275.8
144	High Point, NC	355.9
401	Hillsboro, OR	53.9
235	Hollywood, FL	234.5
299	Honolulu, HI	155.5
64	Houston, TX	576.8
338	Huntington Beach, CA	113.0
147	Huntsville, AL	352.2
111	Independence, MO	432.2
44	Indianapolis, IN	648.0
174	Indio, CA	316.3
107	Inglewood, CA	439.2
410	Irvine, CA	31.1
286	Irving, TX	173.9
83	Jacksonville, FL	505.6
275	Jacksonville, NC	187.1
237	Jackson, MS	229.2
149	Jersey City, NJ	350.0
258	Joliet, IL	209.1
142	Kansas City, KS	356.8
19	Kansas City, MO	816.4
322	Kenosha, WI	131.1
197	Kent, WA	289.2
119	Killeen, TX	411.9
52	Knoxville, TN	611.8
38	Lafayette, LA	681.5
352	Lake Forest, CA	100.7
193	Lakeland, FL	296.9
250	Lakewood, CA	219.6
185	Lakewood, CO	305.1
125	Lancaster, CA	392.6
27	Lansing, MI	745.2
123	Laredo, TX	394.4
137	Las Cruces, NM	362.7
71	Las Vegas, NV	561.6
171	Lawrence, KS	317.3
10	Lawton, OK	920.6
389	Lee's Summit, MO	64.1
360	Lewisville, TX	93.7
138	Lexington, KY	358.3
162	Lincoln, NE	329.4
7	Little Rock, AR	942.7
358	Livermore, CA	95.2
324	Livonia, MI	129.7
152	Long Beach, CA	346.8
184	Longmont, CO	307.0

RANK	CITY	RATE
47	Longview, TX	623.2
205	Los Angeles, CA	276.4
188	Louisville, KY	302.1
26	Lubbock, TX	745.7
40	Lynn, MA	664.8
156	Macon, GA	342.4
267	Madison, WI	194.9
214	Manchester, NH	269.6
309	McAllen, TX	144.8
346	McKinney, TX	107.5
13	Melbourne, FL	878.6
5	Memphis, TN	1,109.0
36	Merced, CA	687.5
217	Mesa, AZ	265.9
250	Mesquite, TX	219.6
81	Miami Beach, FL	518.6
54	Miami Gardens, FL	603.6
42	Miami, FL	659.6
217	Midland, TX	265.9
79	Milwaukee, WI	526.9
72	Minneapolis, MN	561.4
201	Miramar, FL	284.2
399	Mission Viejo, CA	55.0
371	Missouri City, TX	78.7
108	Mobile, AL	437.1
92	Modesto, CA	476.3
305	Montgomery, AL	148.9
254	Moreno Valley, CA	212.1
110	Murfreesboro, TN	433.4
390	Murrieta, CA	63.7
224	Nampa, ID	255.1
402	Naperville, IL	53.9
325	Nashua, NH	129.4
24	Nashville, TN	761.9
17	New Bedford, MA	830.3
6	New Haven, CT	975.3
115	New Orleans, LA	419.1
178	New York, NY	314.9
120	Newark, NJ	404.7
342	Newport Beach, CA	111.4
372	Newton, MA	78.2
161	Norfolk, VA	330.1
385	Norman, OK	65.6
66	North Charleston, SC	575.1
109	North Las Vegas, NV	435.5
232	Norwalk, CA	242.2
182	Norwalk, CT	308.9
15	Oakland, CA	856.5
212	Oceanside, CA	270.8
73	Odessa, TX	558.3
392	O'Fallon, MO	62.1
191	Ogden, UT	299.9
45	Oklahoma City, OK	641.5
312	Olathe, KS	139.5
202	Omaha, NE	281.9
241	Ontario, CA	226.3
397	Orange, CA	57.6
411	Orem, UT	13.9
20	Orlando, FL	809.0
323	Overland Park, KS	130.1
276	Oxnard, CA	186.8
118	Palm Bay, FL	414.6
154	Palmdale, CA	345.0
273	Pasadena, CA	188.1
179	Pasadena, TX	311.6
104	Paterson, NJ	444.3
374	Pearland, TX	77.9
327	Pembroke Pines, FL	127.1
350	Peoria, AZ	104.0
90	Peoria, IL	484.9
63	Philadelphia, PA	576.9
210	Phoenix, AZ	271.0
84	Pittsburgh, PA	501.2
353	Plano, TX	99.7
248	Plantation, FL	220.2
135	Pomona, CA	366.1
53	Pompano Beach, FL	604.9
272	Port St. Lucie, FL	188.3
170	Portland, OR	320.4
175	Portsmouth, VA	315.9
116	Providence, RI	415.9
366	Provo, UT	82.9
43	Pueblo, CO	653.6
209	Quincy, MA	272.3
245	Racine, WI	221.3
221	Raleigh, NC	260.1
396	Ramapo, NY	58.7
341	Rancho Cucamon., CA	112.1
100	Reading, PA	451.4
57	Redding, CA	590.7
106	Reno, NV	439.3
200	Rialto, CA	284.7
347	Richardson, TX	106.2
61	Richmond, CA	582.1
150	Richmond, VA	348.9
253	Rio Rancho, NM	213.4
226	Riverside, CA	251.8
101	Roanoke, VA	451.1
313	Rochester, MN	139.4
80	Rochester, NY	521.1
16	Rockford, IL	843.3
277	Roseville, CA	184.0
364	Roswell, GA	83.7
386	Round Rock, TX	65.1
86	Sacramento, CA	499.7
228	Salem, OR	244.0
94	Salinas, CA	471.9
113	Salt Lake City, UT	421.6
211	San Angelo, TX	270.9
167	San Antonio, TX	322.7
69	San Bernardino, CA	569.9
203	San Diego, CA	278.9
199	San Francisco, CA	285.3
243	San Jose, CA	223.1
295	San Leandro, CA	159.6
288	San Marcos, CA	170.2
238	San Mateo, CA	227.7
405	Sandy Springs, GA	50.9
330	Sandy, UT	123.7
244	Santa Ana, CA	222.6
160	Santa Barbara, CA	334.8
379	Santa Clara, CA	71.1
296	Santa Clarita, CA	159.5
33	Santa Maria, CA	703.8
230	Santa Monica, CA	243.1
151	Santa Rosa, CA	348.8
269	Savannah, GA	192.7
348	Scottsdale, AZ	105.4
166	Seattle, WA	322.8
70	Shreveport, LA	569.1
376	Simi Valley, CA	75.7
163	Sioux City, IA	328.2
287	Sioux Falls, SD	172.1
220	Somerville, MA	263.6
158	South Bend, IN	341.6
278	South Gate, CA	183.1
164	Southfield, MI	327.7
219	Sparks, NV	264.7
257	Spokane Valley, WA	209.8
134	Spokane, WA	367.1
11	Springfield, IL	912.1
22	Springfield, MA	792.0
87	Springfield, MO	497.9
311	Stamford, CT	141.4
333	Sterling Heights, MI	117.7
21	Stockton, CA	797.0
362	St. George, UT	87.5
117	St. Joseph, MO	414.7
4	St. Louis, MO	1,193.4
99	St. Paul, MN	451.5
8	St. Petersburg, FL	940.7
265	Suffolk, VA	199.0
398	Sugar Land, TX	55.6
387	Sunnyvale, CA	65.1
280	Sunrise, FL	181.0
393	Surprise, AZ	61.1
48	Syracuse, NY	621.0
62	Tacoma, WA	579.6
55	Tallahassee, FL	601.1
98	Tampa, FL	460.0
404	Temecula, CA	51.5
183	Tempe, AZ	308.8
310	Thornton, CO	143.1
367	Thousand Oaks, CA	82.4
46	Toledo, OH	629.1
388	Toms River Twnshp, NJ	64.2
195	Topeka, KS	291.6
382	Torrance, CA	66.6
373	Tracy, CA	78.0
30	Trenton, NJ	725.1
394	Troy, MI	61.1
129	Tucson, AZ	378.7
29	Tulsa, OK	742.1
259	Tuscaloosa, AL	207.2
127	Tyler, TX	381.8
215	Upper Darby Twnshp, PA	268.9
284	Vacaville, CA	175.1
105	Vallejo, CA	443.0
239	Vancouver, WA	227.1
255	Ventura, CA	211.5
132	Victorville, CA	372.2
363	Virginia Beach, VA	84.8
167	Visalia, CA	322.7
153	Vista, CA	346.3
91	Waco, TX	477.2
131	Warren, MI	373.1
381	Warwick, RI	67.5
75	Washington, DC	549.5
290	Waterbury, CT	168.2
319	West Covina, CA	133.2
359	West Jordan, UT	94.3
95	West Palm Beach, FL	464.5
223	West Valley, UT	255.5
171	Westland, MI	317.3
282	Westminster, CA	177.4
297	Westminster, CO	156.9
207	Whittier, CA	272.9
186	Wichita Falls, TX	303.3
41	Wichita, KS	663.4
103	Wilmington, NC	447.6
102	Winston-Salem, NC	449.8
378	Woodbridge Twnshp, NJ	71.4
25	Worcester, MA	753.1
246	Yonkers, NY	220.6
85	Yuma, AZ	500.9

Source: CQ Press using reported data from the F.B.I. "Crime in the United States 2009"

*Aggravated assault is an attack for the purpose of inflicting severe bodily injury.

62. Aggravated Assault Rate in 2009 (continued)
National Rate = 262.8 Aggravated Assaults per 100,000 Population*

RANK	CITY	RATE	RANK	CITY	RATE	RANK	CITY	RATE
1	Flint, MI	1,367.6	69	San Bernardino, CA	569.9	138	Lexington, KY	358.3
2	Camden, NJ	1,291.5	70	Shreveport, LA	569.1	139	Denver, CO	358.0
3	Detroit, MI	1,238.9	71	Las Vegas, NV	561.6	140	Canton, OH	357.3
4	St. Louis, MO	1,193.4	72	Minneapolis, MN	561.4	140	Fresno, CA	357.3
5	Memphis, TN	1,109.0	73	Odessa, TX	558.3	142	Kansas City, KS	356.8
6	New Haven, CT	975.3	74	Chicago, IL	552.1	143	Davie, FL	356.1
7	Little Rock, AR	942.7	75	Washington, DC	549.5	144	High Point, NC	355.9
8	St. Petersburg, FL	940.7	76	Decatur, IL	548.6	145	Greeley, CO	353.5
9	Compton, CA	933.2	77	Beaumont, TX	537.0	146	El Paso, TX	352.9
10	Lawton, OK	920.6	78	Antioch, CA	530.4	147	Huntsville, AL	352.2
11	Springfield, IL	912.1	79	Milwaukee, WI	526.9	148	Durham, NC	350.3
12	Brockton, MA	901.8	80	Rochester, NY	521.1	149	Jersey City, NJ	350.0
13	Melbourne, FL	878.6	81	Miami Beach, FL	518.6	150	Richmond, VA	348.9
14	Baltimore, MD	870.6	82	Clarksville, TN	517.0	151	Santa Rosa, CA	348.8
15	Oakland, CA	856.5	83	Jacksonville, FL	505.6	152	Long Beach, CA	346.8
16	Rockford, IL	843.3	84	Pittsburgh, PA	501.2	153	Vista, CA	346.3
17	New Bedford, MA	830.3	85	Yuma, AZ	500.9	154	Palmdale, CA	345.0
18	Fall River, MA	830.2	86	Sacramento, CA	499.7	155	Abilene, TX	343.2
19	Kansas City, MO	816.4	87	Springfield, MO	497.9	156	Macon, GA	342.4
20	Orlando, FL	809.0	88	Albuquerque, NM	489.4	157	Carson, CA	342.2
21	Stockton, CA	797.0	89	Grand Rapids, MI	485.2	158	South Bend, IN	341.6
22	Springfield, MA	792.0	90	Peoria, IL	484.9	159	Des Moines, IA	337.4
23	Buffalo, NY	775.3	91	Waco, TX	477.2	160	Santa Barbara, CA	334.8
24	Nashville, TN	761.9	92	Modesto, CA	476.3	161	Norfolk, VA	330.1
25	Worcester, MA	753.1	93	Akron, OH	474.6	162	Lincoln, NE	329.4
26	Lubbock, TX	745.7	94	Salinas, CA	471.9	163	Sioux City, IA	328.2
27	Lansing, MI	745.2	95	West Palm Beach, FL	464.5	164	Southfield, MI	327.7
28	Hartford, CT	742.4	96	Davenport, IA	462.8	165	Fort Worth, TX	327.5
29	Tulsa, OK	742.1	97	Cleveland, OH	460.4	166	Seattle, WA	322.8
30	Trenton, NJ	725.1	98	Tampa, FL	460.0	167	San Antonio, TX	322.7
31	Gainesville, FL	710.5	99	St. Paul, MN	451.5	167	Visalia, CA	322.7
32	Albany, GA	707.7	100	Reading, PA	451.4	169	El Monte, CA	322.6
33	Santa Maria, CA	703.8	101	Roanoke, VA	451.1	170	Portland, OR	320.4
34	Baton Rouge, LA	698.1	102	Winston-Salem, NC	449.8	171	Lawrence, KS	317.3
35	Chattanooga, TN	688.0	103	Wilmington, NC	447.6	171	Westland, MI	317.3
36	Merced, CA	687.5	104	Paterson, NJ	444.3	173	Green Bay, WI	316.4
37	Columbia, SC	686.6	105	Vallejo, CA	443.0	174	Indio, CA	316.3
38	Lafayette, LA	681.5	106	Reno, NV	439.3	175	Portsmouth, VA	315.9
39	Albany, NY	665.6	107	Inglewood, CA	439.2	176	Fayetteville, AR	315.5
40	Lynn, MA	664.8	108	Mobile, AL	437.1	177	Dallas, TX	315.4
41	Wichita, KS	663.4	109	North Las Vegas, NV	435.5	178	New York, NY	314.9
42	Miami, FL	659.6	110	Murfreesboro, TN	433.4	179	Pasadena, TX	311.6
43	Pueblo, CO	653.6	111	Independence, MO	432.2	180	Elk Grove, CA	310.9
44	Indianapolis, IN	648.0	112	Cincinnati, OH	423.9	181	Citrus Heights, CA	309.5
45	Oklahoma City, OK	641.5	113	Salt Lake City, UT	421.6	182	Norwalk, CT	308.9
46	Toledo, OH	629.1	114	Dayton, OH	419.7	183	Tempe, AZ	308.8
47	Longview, TX	623.2	115	New Orleans, LA	419.1	184	Longmont, CO	307.0
48	Syracuse, NY	621.0	116	Providence, RI	415.9	185	Lakewood, CO	305.1
49	Atlanta, GA	618.4	117	St. Joseph, MO	414.7	186	Wichita Falls, TX	303.3
50	Birmingham, AL	615.3	118	Palm Bay, FL	414.6	187	Aurora, IL	303.2
51	Hammond, IN	613.8	119	Killeen, TX	411.9	188	Louisville, KY	302.1
52	Knoxville, TN	611.8	120	Newark, NJ	404.7	189	Austin, TX	302.0
53	Pompano Beach, FL	604.9	121	Bakersfield, CA	398.6	190	Columbia, MO	301.2
54	Miami Gardens, FL	603.6	122	Fort Lauderdale, FL	397.4	191	Ogden, UT	299.9
55	Tallahassee, FL	601.1	123	Laredo, TX	394.4	192	Everett, WA	298.7
56	Amarillo, TX	592.8	124	Arlington, TX	394.1	193	Lakeland, FL	296.9
57	Redding, CA	590.7	125	Lancaster, CA	392.6	194	Charleston, SC	296.4
58	Fort Smith, AR	590.5	126	Elizabeth, NJ	382.7	195	Topeka, KS	291.6
59	Anchorage, AK	585.2	127	Tyler, TX	381.8	196	Gary, IN	289.9
60	Corpus Christi, TX	585.0	128	Fayetteville, NC	380.5	197	Kent, WA	289.2
61	Richmond, CA	582.1	129	Tucson, AZ	378.7	198	Cambridge, MA	286.8
62	Tacoma, WA	579.6	130	Charlotte, NC	375.2	199	San Francisco, CA	285.3
63	Philadelphia, PA	576.9	131	Warren, MI	373.1	200	Rialto, CA	284.7
64	Houston, TX	576.8	132	Victorville, CA	372.2	201	Miramar, FL	284.2
65	Boston, MA	576.1	133	Greensboro, NC	368.1	202	Omaha, NE	281.9
66	North Charleston, SC	575.1	134	Spokane, WA	367.1	203	San Diego, CA	278.9
67	Clearwater, FL	572.2	135	Pomona, CA	366.1	204	Columbus, GA	278.7
68	Bridgeport, CT	571.1	136	Hawthorne, CA	365.3	205	Los Angeles, CA	276.4
			137	Las Cruces, NM	362.7	206	Hialeah, FL	275.8

RANK	CITY	RATE
207	Fort Collins, CO	272.9
207	Whittier, CA	272.9
209	Quincy, MA	272.3
210	Phoenix, AZ	271.0
211	San Angelo, TX	270.9
212	Oceanside, CA	270.8
213	Colorado Springs, CO	269.9
214	Manchester, NH	269.6
215	Upper Darby Twnshp, PA	268.9
216	Fontana, CA	266.9
217	Mesa, AZ	265.9
217	Midland, TX	265.9
219	Sparks, NV	264.7
220	Somerville, MA	263.6
221	Raleigh, NC	260.1
222	Glendale, AZ	256.8
223	West Valley, UT	255.5
224	Nampa, ID	255.1
225	Erie, PA	254.2
226	Riverside, CA	251.8
227	Chesapeake, VA	245.5
228	Salem, OR	244.0
229	Dearborn, MI	243.8
230	Santa Monica, CA	243.1
231	Escondido, CA	243.0
232	Norwalk, CA	242.2
233	Duluth, MN	239.1
234	Avondale, AZ	238.8
235	Hollywood, FL	234.5
236	Athens-Clarke, GA	231.4
237	Jackson, MS	229.2
238	San Mateo, CA	227.7
239	Vancouver, WA	227.1
240	Fargo, ND	227.0
241	Ontario, CA	226.3
242	Aurora, CO	226.2
243	San Jose, CA	223.1
244	Santa Ana, CA	222.6
245	Racine, WI	221.3
246	El Cajon, CA	220.6
246	Yonkers, NY	220.6
248	Plantation, FL	220.2
249	Fullerton, CA	219.7
250	Lakewood, CA	219.6
250	Mesquite, TX	219.6
252	Baldwin Park, CA	219.2
253	Rio Rancho, NM	213.4
254	Moreno Valley, CA	212.1
255	Ventura, CA	211.5
256	Clinton Twnshp, MI	210.5
257	Spokane Valley, WA	209.8
258	Joliet, IL	209.1
259	Tuscaloosa, AL	207.2
260	Carlsbad, CA	206.1
261	Fairfield, CA	205.8
262	Hesperia, CA	202.5
263	Garden Grove, CA	201.4
264	Evansville, IN	201.3
265	Suffolk, VA	199.0
266	Cedar Rapids, IA	195.7
267	Madison, WI	194.9
268	Boise, ID	193.3
269	Savannah, GA	192.7
270	Coral Springs, FL	192.6
271	Chandler, AZ	189.0
272	Port St. Lucie, FL	188.3
273	Pasadena, CA	188.1
274	Gresham, OR	187.4
275	Jacksonville, NC	187.1
276	Oxnard, CA	186.8
277	Roseville, CA	184.0
278	South Gate, CA	183.1
279	Hayward, CA	182.1
280	Sunrise, FL	181.0
281	Anaheim, CA	178.3
282	Westminster, CA	177.4
283	Allentown, PA	177.0
284	Vacaville, CA	175.1
285	Downey, CA	174.7
286	Irving, TX	173.9
287	Sioux Falls, SD	172.1
288	San Marcos, CA	170.2
289	Columbus, OH	169.6
290	Waterbury, CT	168.2
291	Chico, CA	166.4
292	Grand Prairie, TX	164.5
293	Edison Twnshp, NJ	163.1
294	Chula Vista, CA	159.7
295	San Leandro, CA	159.6
296	Santa Clarita, CA	159.5
297	Boulder, CO	156.9
297	Westminster, CO	156.9
299	Honolulu, HI	155.5
300	Elgin, IL	155.1
301	Ann Arbor, MI	154.8
302	Brownsville, TX	151.5
303	Hampton, VA	151.4
304	Billings, MT	149.9
305	Montgomery, AL	148.9
306	Costa Mesa, CA	147.1
307	Cheektowaga, NY	146.6
308	Bend, OR	145.3
309	McAllen, TX	144.8
310	Thornton, CO	143.1
311	Stamford, CT	141.4
312	Olathe, KS	139.5
313	Rochester, MN	139.4
314	Federal Way, WA	136.5
315	Berkeley, CA	136.4
316	Concord, CA	135.5
317	Cape Coral, FL	134.5
318	Buena Park, CA	133.3
319	West Covina, CA	133.2
320	Burbank, CA	132.7
321	Boca Raton, FL	131.5
322	Kenosha, WI	131.1
323	Overland Park, KS	130.1
324	Livonia, MI	129.7
325	Nashua, NH	129.4
326	Eugene, OR	128.8
327	Pembroke Pines, FL	127.1
328	Beaverton, OR	125.5
329	Denton, TX	123.9
330	Sandy, UT	123.7
331	Broken Arrow, OK	118.6
332	Fort Wayne, IN	118.4
333	Sterling Heights, MI	117.7
334	Daly City, CA	117.5
335	Fremont, CA	116.9
336	Alhambra, CA	116.3
337	College Station, TX	116.2
338	Arvada, CO	113.0
338	Huntington Beach, CA	113.0
340	Henderson, NV	112.6
341	Rancho Cucamon., CA	112.1
342	Newport Beach, CA	111.4
343	Garland, TX	111.0
344	Clifton, NJ	110.1
345	Canton Twnshp, MI	108.9
346	McKinney, TX	107.5
347	Richardson, TX	106.2
348	Scottsdale, AZ	105.4
349	Bellingham, WA	104.7
350	Peoria, AZ	104.0
351	Centennial, CO	103.6
352	Lake Forest, CA	100.7
353	Plano, TX	99.7
354	Chino, CA	99.3
355	Brick Twnshp, NJ	99.2
356	Farmington Hills, MI	98.5
357	Hamilton Twnshp, NJ	97.2
358	Livermore, CA	95.2
359	West Jordan, UT	94.3
360	Lewisville, TX	93.7
361	Alexandria, VA	88.3
362	St. George, UT	87.5
363	Virginia Beach, VA	84.8
364	Roswell, GA	83.7
365	Carrollton, TX	83.2
366	Provo, UT	82.9
367	Thousand Oaks, CA	82.4
368	Bloomington, MN	81.6
369	Glendale, CA	80.0
370	Clarkstown, NY	79.8
371	Missouri City, TX	78.7
372	Newton, MA	78.2
373	Tracy, CA	78.0
374	Pearland, TX	77.9
375	Cranston, RI	76.0
376	Simi Valley, CA	75.7
377	Frisco, TX	72.1
378	Woodbridge Twnshp, NJ	71.4
379	Santa Clara, CA	71.1
380	Amherst, NY	67.9
381	Warwick, RI	67.5
382	Torrance, CA	66.6
383	Danbury, CT	66.5
384	Clovis, CA	66.2
385	Norman, OK	65.6
386	Round Rock, TX	65.1
387	Sunnyvale, CA	65.1
388	Toms River Twnshp, NJ	64.2
389	Lee's Summit, MO	64.1
390	Murrieta, CA	63.7
391	Edmond, OK	63.0
392	O'Fallon, MO	62.1
393	Surprise, AZ	61.1
394	Troy, MI	61.1
395	Bellevue, WA	59.2
396	Ramapo, NY	58.7
397	Orange, CA	57.6
398	Sugar Land, TX	55.6
399	Mission Viejo, CA	55.0
400	Allen, TX	54.1
401	Hillsboro, OR	53.9
402	Naperville, IL	53.9
403	Cary, NC	53.8
404	Temecula, CA	51.5
405	Sandy Springs, GA	50.9
406	Corona, CA	50.5
407	Gilbert, AZ	47.0
408	Greece, NY	46.1
409	Colonie, NY	39.7
410	Irvine, CA	31.1
411	Orem, UT	13.9

Source: CQ Press using reported data from the F.B.I. "Crime in the United States 2009"
*Aggravated assault is an attack for the purpose of inflicting severe bodily injury.

63. Percent Change in Aggravated Assault Rate: 2008 to 2009
National Percent Change = 5.0% Decrease*

RANK	CITY	% CHANGE
81	Abilene, TX	7.0
76	Akron, OH	7.6
NA	Albany, GA**	NA
114	Albany, NY	1.9
268	Albuquerque, NM	(12.8)
263	Alexandria, VA	(12.4)
229	Alhambra, CA	(9.5)
354	Allentown, PA	(26.6)
130	Allen, TX	0.0
69	Amarillo, TX	9.6
331	Amherst, NY	(20.3)
219	Anaheim, CA	(7.8)
243	Anchorage, AK	(10.4)
NA	Ann Arbor, MI**	NA
25	Antioch, CA	21.4
92	Arlington, TX	5.5
175	Arvada, CO	(3.4)
188	Athens-Clarke, GA	(4.1)
287	Atlanta, GA	(14.7)
304	Aurora, CO	(16.9)
150	Aurora, IL	(1.5)
145	Austin, TX	(1.3)
358	Avondale, AZ	(29.2)
128	Bakersfield, CA	0.3
31	Baldwin Park, CA	18.8
169	Baltimore, MD	(2.8)
101	Baton Rouge, LA	3.8
167	Beaumont, TX	(2.7)
281	Beaverton, OR	(14.3)
43	Bellevue, WA	15.2
291	Bellingham, WA	(14.9)
5	Bend, OR	43.3
53	Berkeley, CA	12.2
258	Billings, MT	(12.1)
180	Birmingham, AL	(3.5)
63	Bloomington, MN	10.1
214	Boca Raton, FL	(7.3)
169	Boise, ID	(2.8)
264	Boston, MA	(12.5)
48	Boulder, CO	14.5
198	Brick Twnshp, NJ	(5.3)
200	Bridgeport, CT	(5.4)
NA	Brockton, MA**	NA
318	Broken Arrow, OK	(18.5)
376	Brownsville, TX	(37.8)
351	Buena Park, CA	(25.4)
84	Buffalo, NY	6.6
88	Burbank, CA	5.8
30	Cambridge, MA	19.6
36	Camden, NJ	17.4
NA	Canton Twnshp, MI**	NA
96	Canton, OH	5.2
198	Cape Coral, FL	(5.3)
10	Carlsbad, CA	34.2
346	Carrollton, TX	(24.3)
145	Carson, CA	(1.3)
3	Cary, NC	49.9
230	Cedar Rapids, IA	(9.6)
59	Centennial, CO	11.2
186	Chandler, AZ	(4.0)
347	Charleston, SC	(24.4)
345	Charlotte, NC	(23.7)
219	Chattanooga, TN	(7.8)
154	Cheektowaga, NY	(1.9)
109	Chesapeake, VA	2.5
225	Chicago, IL	(8.3)
311	Chico, CA	(17.7)
230	Chino, CA	(9.6)
335	Chula Vista, CA	(20.7)
161	Cincinnati, OH	(2.3)
121	Citrus Heights, CA	1.2
216	Clarkstown, NY	(7.4)
218	Clarksville, TN	(7.6)
183	Clearwater, FL	(3.7)
80	Cleveland, OH	7.1
289	Clifton, NJ	(14.8)
NA	Clinton Twnshp, MI**	NA
317	Clovis, CA	(18.3)
372	College Station, TX	(35.2)
2	Colonie, NY	55.1
227	Colorado Springs, CO	(9.0)
13	Columbia, MO	32.3
19	Columbia, SC	27.5
175	Columbus, GA	(3.4)
295	Columbus, OH	(15.4)
306	Compton, CA	(17.3)
283	Concord, CA	(14.4)
36	Coral Springs, FL	17.4
374	Corona, CA	(36.1)
65	Corpus Christi, TX	9.9
299	Costa Mesa, CA	(15.7)
196	Cranston, RI	(5.0)
205	Dallas, TX	(6.1)
102	Daly City, CA	3.6
113	Danbury, CT	2.0
297	Davenport, IA	(15.6)
8	Davie, FL	36.2
243	Dayton, OH	(10.4)
NA	Dearborn, MI**	NA
NA	Decatur, IL**	NA
343	Denton, TX	(23.2)
117	Denver, CO	1.6
NA	Des Moines, IA**	NA
NA	Detroit, MI**	NA
65	Downey, CA	9.9
105	Duluth, MN	3.2
208	Durham, NC	(6.4)
61	Edison Twnshp, NJ	10.5
41	Edmond, OK	16.5
359	El Cajon, CA	(29.4)
321	El Monte, CA	(19.1)
139	El Paso, TX	(0.5)
132	Elgin, IL	(0.2)
6	Elizabeth, NJ	43.0
255	Elk Grove, CA	(11.4)
52	Erie, PA	12.8
151	Escondido, CA	(1.6)
225	Eugene, OR	(8.3)
275	Evansville, IN	(13.2)
102	Everett, WA	3.6
337	Fairfield, CA	(21.5)
175	Fall River, MA	(3.4)
72	Fargo, ND	8.7
NA	Farmington Hills, MI**	NA
212	Fayetteville, AR	(7.0)
350	Fayetteville, NC	(25.3)
127	Federal Way, WA	0.6
NA	Flint, MI**	NA
184	Fontana, CA	(3.8)
283	Fort Collins, CO	(14.4)
85	Fort Lauderdale, FL	6.1
72	Fort Smith, AR	8.7
7	Fort Wayne, IN	37.7
221	Fort Worth, TX	(8.0)
341	Fremont, CA	(22.7)
119	Fresno, CA	1.3
228	Frisco, TX	(9.2)
18	Fullerton, CA	28.5
56	Gainesville, FL	11.6
145	Garden Grove, CA	(1.3)
368	Garland, TX	(31.9)
380	Gary, IN	(48.2)
364	Gilbert, AZ	(30.5)
130	Glendale, AZ	0.0
243	Glendale, CA	(10.4)
156	Grand Prairie, TX	(2.0)
NA	Grand Rapids, MI**	NA
378	Greece, NY	(44.4)
319	Greeley, CO	(18.6)
140	Green Bay, WI	(0.6)
246	Greensboro, NC	(10.5)
356	Gresham, OR	(27.5)
27	Hamilton Twnshp, NJ	20.1
26	Hammond, IN	20.7
98	Hampton, VA	4.7
33	Hartford, CT	18.3
250	Hawthorne, CA	(10.8)
248	Hayward, CA	(10.6)
16	Henderson, NV	29.9
104	Hesperia, CA	3.4
314	Hialeah, FL	(18.0)
142	High Point, NC	(0.8)
334	Hillsboro, OR	(20.5)
167	Hollywood, FL	(2.7)
144	Honolulu, HI	(1.1)
152	Houston, TX	(1.7)
210	Huntington Beach, CA	(6.7)
270	Huntsville, AL	(12.9)
329	Independence, MO	(19.8)
111	Indianapolis, IN	2.2
32	Indio, CA	18.4
60	Inglewood, CA	11.0
42	Irvine, CA	16.0
340	Irving, TX	(21.8)
277	Jacksonville, FL	(13.6)
271	Jacksonville, NC	(13.0)
338	Jackson, MS	(21.6)
255	Jersey City, NJ	(11.4)
292	Joliet, IL	(15.0)
NA	Kansas City, KS**	NA
175	Kansas City, MO	(3.4)
352	Kenosha, WI	(25.6)
280	Kent, WA	(14.1)
324	Killeen, TX	(19.5)
161	Knoxville, TN	(2.3)
264	Lafayette, LA	(12.5)
54	Lake Forest, CA	12.0
169	Lakeland, FL	(2.8)
13	Lakewood, CA	32.3
180	Lakewood, CO	(3.5)
348	Lancaster, CA	(24.5)
NA	Lansing, MI**	NA
223	Laredo, TX	(8.2)
242	Las Cruces, NM	(10.3)
124	Las Vegas, NV	0.8
134	Lawrence, KS	(0.3)
35	Lawton, OK	17.6
314	Lee's Summit, MO	(18.0)
329	Lewisville, TX	(19.8)
NA	Lexington, KY**	NA
271	Lincoln, NE	(13.0)
NA	Little Rock, AR**	NA
367	Livermore, CA	(31.8)
NA	Livonia, MI**	NA
78	Long Beach, CA	7.2
NA	Longmont, CO**	NA

RANK	CITY	% CHANGE
232	Longview, TX	(9.7)
234	Los Angeles, CA	(9.8)
NA	Louisville, KY**	NA
191	Lubbock, TX	(4.2)
123	Lynn, MA	1.1
362	Macon, GA	(30.2)
166	Madison, WI	(2.6)
94	Manchester, NH	5.4
237	McAllen, TX	(9.9)
332	McKinney, TX	(20.4)
188	Melbourne, FL	(4.1)
164	Memphis, TN	(2.5)
17	Merced, CA	29.3
302	Mesa, AZ	(16.6)
203	Mesquite, TX	(5.8)
314	Miami Beach, FL	(18.0)
9	Miami Gardens, FL	36.1
257	Miami, FL	(11.5)
70	Midland, TX	9.1
311	Milwaukee, WI	(17.7)
250	Minneapolis, MN	(10.8)
78	Miramar, FL	7.2
239	Mission Viejo, CA	(10.1)
363	Missouri City, TX	(30.3)
1	Mobile, AL	321.9
90	Modesto, CA	5.7
266	Montgomery, AL	(12.6)
254	Moreno Valley, CA	(11.3)
140	Murfreesboro, TN	(0.6)
15	Murrieta, CA	31.9
58	Nampa, ID	11.4
296	Naperville, IL	(15.5)
NA	Nashua, NH**	NA
320	Nashville, TN	(18.7)
223	New Bedford, MA	(8.2)
NA	New Haven, CT**	NA
344	New Orleans, LA	(23.4)
88	New York, NY	5.8
156	Newark, NJ	(2.0)
268	Newport Beach, CA	(12.8)
357	Newton, MA	(27.7)
148	Norfolk, VA	(1.4)
77	Norman, OK	7.4
353	North Charleston, SC	(26.1)
134	North Las Vegas, NV	(0.3)
283	Norwalk, CA	(14.4)
209	Norwalk, CT	(6.5)
303	Oakland, CA	(16.7)
300	Oceanside, CA	(16.4)
222	Odessa, TX	(8.1)
71	O'Fallon, MO	8.8
36	Ogden, UT	17.4
121	Oklahoma City, OK	1.2
NA	Olathe, KS**	NA
300	Omaha, NE	(16.4)
241	Ontario, CA	(10.2)
361	Orange, CA	(30.0)
381	Orem, UT	(60.3)
332	Orlando, FL	(20.4)
81	Overland Park, KS	7.0
92	Oxnard, CA	5.5
175	Palm Bay, FL	(3.4)
172	Palmdale, CA	(2.9)
322	Pasadena, CA	(19.3)
55	Pasadena, TX	11.8
129	Paterson, NJ	0.2
134	Pearland, TX	(0.3)
326	Pembroke Pines, FL	(19.6)
106	Peoria, AZ	3.0
NA	Peoria, IL**	NA
292	Philadelphia, PA	(15.0)
278	Phoenix, AZ	(13.9)
180	Pittsburgh, PA	(3.5)
371	Plano, TX	(34.3)
90	Plantation, FL	5.7
258	Pomona, CA	(12.1)
283	Pompano Beach, FL	(14.4)
138	Port St. Lucie, FL	(0.4)
271	Portland, OR	(13.0)
75	Portsmouth, VA	8.3
39	Providence, RI	17.0
328	Provo, UT	(19.7)
NA	Pueblo, CO**	NA
44	Quincy, MA	15.0
306	Racine, WI	(17.3)
214	Raleigh, NC	(7.3)
289	Ramapo, NY	(14.8)
276	Rancho Cucamon., CA	(13.3)
159	Reading, PA	(2.1)
50	Redding, CA	14.0
118	Reno, NV	1.5
201	Rialto, CA	(5.6)
313	Richardson, TX	(17.8)
39	Richmond, CA	17.0
185	Richmond, VA	(3.9)
161	Rio Rancho, NM	(2.3)
359	Riverside, CA	(29.4)
262	Roanoke, VA	(12.3)
94	Rochester, MN	5.4
173	Rochester, NY	(3.0)
246	Rockford, IL	(10.5)
234	Roseville, CA	(9.8)
22	Roswell, GA	22.9
297	Round Rock, TX	(15.6)
271	Sacramento, CA	(13.0)
116	Salem, OR	1.7
100	Salinas, CA	4.2
239	Salt Lake City, UT	(10.1)
97	San Angelo, TX	5.0
369	San Antonio, TX	(32.0)
194	San Bernardino, CA	(4.6)
148	San Diego, CA	(1.4)
186	San Francisco, CA	(4.0)
212	San Jose, CA	(7.0)
252	San Leandro, CA	(11.0)
210	San Marcos, CA	(6.7)
156	San Mateo, CA	(2.0)
205	Sandy Springs, GA	(6.1)
29	Sandy, UT	20.0
188	Santa Ana, CA	(4.1)
305	Santa Barbara, CA	(17.2)
375	Santa Clara, CA	(36.5)
111	Santa Clarita, CA	2.2
11	Santa Maria, CA	33.9
355	Santa Monica, CA	(27.3)
143	Santa Rosa, CA	(0.9)
164	Savannah, GA	(2.5)
174	Scottsdale, AZ	(3.1)
45	Seattle, WA	14.9
258	Shreveport, LA	(12.1)
279	Simi Valley, CA	(14.0)
34	Sioux City, IA	18.1
339	Sioux Falls, SD	(21.7)
46	Somerville, MA	14.8
65	South Bend, IN	9.9
342	South Gate, CA	(23.0)
NA	Southfield, MI**	NA
114	Sparks, NV	1.9
124	Spokane Valley, WA	0.8
203	Spokane, WA	(5.8)
NA	Springfield, IL**	NA
132	Springfield, MA	(0.2)
49	Springfield, MO	14.4
234	Stamford, CT	(9.8)
NA	Sterling Heights, MI**	NA
253	Stockton, CA	(11.1)
377	St. George, UT	(42.9)
20	St. Joseph, MO	27.2
160	St. Louis, MO	(2.2)
153	St. Paul, MN	(1.8)
83	St. Petersburg, FL	6.7
249	Suffolk, VA	(10.7)
379	Sugar Land, TX	(47.7)
287	Sunnyvale, CA	(14.7)
349	Sunrise, FL	(24.6)
134	Surprise, AZ	(0.3)
126	Syracuse, NY	0.7
207	Tacoma, WA	(6.2)
232	Tallahassee, FL	(9.7)
281	Tampa, FL	(14.3)
373	Temecula, CA	(35.7)
61	Tempe, AZ	10.5
365	Thornton, CO	(30.9)
64	Thousand Oaks, CA	10.0
193	Toledo, OH	(4.4)
24	Toms River Twnshp, NJ	22.5
21	Topeka, KS	23.7
266	Torrance, CA	(12.6)
68	Tracy, CA	9.7
4	Trenton, NJ	48.5
NA	Troy, MI**	NA
326	Tucson, AZ	(19.6)
323	Tulsa, OK	(19.4)
324	Tuscaloosa, AL	(19.5)
336	Tyler, TX	(21.4)
202	Upper Darby Twnshp, PA	(5.7)
56	Vacaville, CA	11.6
306	Vallejo, CA	(17.3)
47	Vancouver, WA	14.6
119	Ventura, CA	1.3
74	Victorville, CA	8.5
258	Virginia Beach, VA	(12.1)
217	Visalia, CA	(7.5)
154	Vista, CA	(1.9)
294	Waco, TX	(15.2)
NA	Warren, MI**	NA
12	Warwick, RI	32.4
237	Washington, DC	(9.9)
197	Waterbury, CT	(5.1)
370	West Covina, CA	(33.1)
366	West Jordan, UT	(31.7)
110	West Palm Beach, FL	2.3
191	West Valley, UT	(4.2)
NA	Westland, MI**	NA
22	Westminster, CA	22.9
195	Westminster, CO	(4.8)
27	Whittier, CA	20.1
108	Wichita Falls, TX	2.7
99	Wichita, KS	4.5
51	Wilmington, NC	13.5
309	Winston-Salem, NC	(17.4)
310	Woodbridge Twnshp, NJ	(17.6)
107	Worcester, MA	2.9
87	Yonkers, NY	5.9
85	Yuma, AZ	6.1

Source: CQ Press using reported data from the F.B.I. "Crime in the United States 2009"
*Aggravated assault is an attack for the purpose of inflicting severe bodily injury.
**Not available.

63. Percent Change in Aggravated Assault Rate: 2008 to 2009 (continued)
National Percent Change = 5.0% Decrease*

RANK	CITY	% CHANGE
1	Mobile, AL	321.9
2	Colonie, NY	55.1
3	Cary, NC	49.9
4	Trenton, NJ	48.5
5	Bend, OR	43.3
6	Elizabeth, NJ	43.0
7	Fort Wayne, IN	37.7
8	Davie, FL	36.2
9	Miami Gardens, FL	36.1
10	Carlsbad, CA	34.2
11	Santa Maria, CA	33.9
12	Warwick, RI	32.4
13	Columbia, MO	32.3
13	Lakewood, CA	32.3
15	Murrieta, CA	31.9
16	Henderson, NV	29.9
17	Merced, CA	29.3
18	Fullerton, CA	28.5
19	Columbia, SC	27.5
20	St. Joseph, MO	27.2
21	Topeka, KS	23.7
22	Roswell, GA	22.9
22	Westminster, CA	22.9
24	Toms River Twnshp, NJ	22.5
25	Antioch, CA	21.4
26	Hammond, IN	20.7
27	Hamilton Twnshp, NJ	20.1
27	Whittier, CA	20.1
29	Sandy, UT	20.0
30	Cambridge, MA	19.6
31	Baldwin Park, CA	18.8
32	Indio, CA	18.4
33	Hartford, CT	18.3
34	Sioux City, IA	18.1
35	Lawton, OK	17.6
36	Camden, NJ	17.4
36	Coral Springs, FL	17.4
36	Ogden, UT	17.4
39	Providence, RI	17.0
39	Richmond, CA	17.0
41	Edmond, OK	16.5
42	Irvine, CA	16.0
43	Bellevue, WA	15.2
44	Quincy, MA	15.0
45	Seattle, WA	14.9
46	Somerville, MA	14.8
47	Vancouver, WA	14.6
48	Boulder, CO	14.5
49	Springfield, MO	14.4
50	Redding, CA	14.0
51	Wilmington, NC	13.5
52	Erie, PA	12.8
53	Berkeley, CA	12.2
54	Lake Forest, CA	12.0
55	Pasadena, TX	11.8
56	Gainesville, FL	11.6
56	Vacaville, CA	11.6
58	Nampa, ID	11.4
59	Centennial, CO	11.2
60	Inglewood, CA	11.0
61	Edison Twnshp, NJ	10.5
61	Tempe, AZ	10.5
63	Bloomington, MN	10.1
64	Thousand Oaks, CA	10.0
65	Corpus Christi, TX	9.9
65	Downey, CA	9.9
65	South Bend, IN	9.9
68	Tracy, CA	9.7
69	Amarillo, TX	9.6
70	Midland, TX	9.1
71	O'Fallon, MO	8.8
72	Fargo, ND	8.7
72	Fort Smith, AR	8.7
74	Victorville, CA	8.5
75	Portsmouth, VA	8.3
76	Akron, OH	7.6
77	Norman, OK	7.4
78	Long Beach, CA	7.2
78	Miramar, FL	7.2
80	Cleveland, OH	7.1
81	Abilene, TX	7.0
81	Overland Park, KS	7.0
83	St. Petersburg, FL	6.7
84	Buffalo, NY	6.6
85	Fort Lauderdale, FL	6.1
85	Yuma, AZ	6.1
87	Yonkers, NY	5.9
88	Burbank, CA	5.8
88	New York, NY	5.8
90	Modesto, CA	5.7
90	Plantation, FL	5.7
92	Arlington, TX	5.5
92	Oxnard, CA	5.5
94	Manchester, NH	5.4
94	Rochester, MN	5.4
96	Canton, OH	5.2
97	San Angelo, TX	5.0
98	Hampton, VA	4.7
99	Wichita, KS	4.5
100	Salinas, CA	4.2
101	Baton Rouge, LA	3.8
102	Daly City, CA	3.6
102	Everett, WA	3.6
104	Hesperia, CA	3.4
105	Duluth, MN	3.2
106	Peoria, AZ	3.0
107	Worcester, MA	2.9
108	Wichita Falls, TX	2.7
109	Chesapeake, VA	2.5
110	West Palm Beach, FL	2.3
111	Indianapolis, IN	2.2
111	Santa Clarita, CA	2.2
113	Danbury, CT	2.0
114	Albany, NY	1.9
114	Sparks, NV	1.9
116	Salem, OR	1.7
117	Denver, CO	1.6
118	Reno, NV	1.5
119	Fresno, CA	1.3
119	Ventura, CA	1.3
121	Citrus Heights, CA	1.2
121	Oklahoma City, OK	1.2
123	Lynn, MA	1.1
124	Las Vegas, NV	0.8
124	Spokane Valley, WA	0.8
126	Syracuse, NY	0.7
127	Federal Way, WA	0.6
128	Bakersfield, CA	0.3
129	Paterson, NJ	0.2
130	Allen, TX	0.0
130	Glendale, AZ	0.0
132	Elgin, IL	(0.2)
132	Springfield, MA	(0.2)
134	Lawrence, KS	(0.3)
134	North Las Vegas, NV	(0.3)
134	Pearland, TX	(0.3)
134	Surprise, AZ	(0.3)
138	Port St. Lucie, FL	(0.4)
139	El Paso, TX	(0.5)
140	Green Bay, WI	(0.6)
140	Murfreesboro, TN	(0.6)
142	High Point, NC	(0.8)
143	Santa Rosa, CA	(0.9)
144	Honolulu, HI	(1.1)
145	Austin, TX	(1.3)
145	Carson, CA	(1.3)
145	Garden Grove, CA	(1.3)
148	Norfolk, VA	(1.4)
148	San Diego, CA	(1.4)
150	Aurora, IL	(1.5)
151	Escondido, CA	(1.6)
152	Houston, TX	(1.7)
153	St. Paul, MN	(1.8)
154	Cheektowaga, NY	(1.9)
154	Vista, CA	(1.9)
156	Grand Prairie, TX	(2.0)
156	Newark, NJ	(2.0)
156	San Mateo, CA	(2.0)
159	Reading, PA	(2.1)
160	St. Louis, MO	(2.2)
161	Cincinnati, OH	(2.3)
161	Knoxville, TN	(2.3)
161	Rio Rancho, NM	(2.3)
164	Memphis, TN	(2.5)
164	Savannah, GA	(2.5)
166	Madison, WI	(2.6)
167	Beaumont, TX	(2.7)
167	Hollywood, FL	(2.7)
169	Baltimore, MD	(2.8)
169	Boise, ID	(2.8)
169	Lakeland, FL	(2.8)
172	Palmdale, CA	(2.9)
173	Rochester, NY	(3.0)
174	Scottsdale, AZ	(3.1)
175	Arvada, CO	(3.4)
175	Columbus, GA	(3.4)
175	Fall River, MA	(3.4)
175	Kansas City, MO	(3.4)
175	Palm Bay, FL	(3.4)
180	Birmingham, AL	(3.5)
180	Lakewood, CO	(3.5)
180	Pittsburgh, PA	(3.5)
183	Clearwater, FL	(3.7)
184	Fontana, CA	(3.8)
185	Richmond, VA	(3.9)
186	Chandler, AZ	(4.0)
186	San Francisco, CA	(4.0)
188	Athens-Clarke, GA	(4.1)
188	Melbourne, FL	(4.1)
188	Santa Ana, CA	(4.1)
191	Lubbock, TX	(4.2)
191	West Valley, UT	(4.2)
193	Toledo, OH	(4.4)
194	San Bernardino, CA	(4.6)
195	Westminster, CO	(4.8)
196	Cranston, RI	(5.0)
197	Waterbury, CT	(5.1)
198	Brick Twnshp, NJ	(5.3)
198	Cape Coral, FL	(5.3)
200	Bridgeport, CT	(5.4)
201	Rialto, CA	(5.6)
202	Upper Darby Twnshp, PA	(5.7)
203	Mesquite, TX	(5.8)
203	Spokane, WA	(5.8)
205	Dallas, TX	(6.1)
205	Sandy Springs, GA	(6.1)

RANK	CITY	% CHANGE
207	Tacoma, WA	(6.2)
208	Durham, NC	(6.4)
209	Norwalk, CT	(6.5)
210	Huntington Beach, CA	(6.7)
210	San Marcos, CA	(6.7)
212	Fayetteville, AR	(7.0)
212	San Jose, CA	(7.0)
214	Boca Raton, FL	(7.3)
214	Raleigh, NC	(7.3)
216	Clarkstown, NY	(7.4)
217	Visalia, CA	(7.5)
218	Clarksville, TN	(7.6)
219	Anaheim, CA	(7.8)
219	Chattanooga, TN	(7.8)
221	Fort Worth, TX	(8.0)
222	Odessa, TX	(8.1)
223	Laredo, TX	(8.2)
223	New Bedford, MA	(8.2)
225	Chicago, IL	(8.3)
225	Eugene, OR	(8.3)
227	Colorado Springs, CO	(9.0)
228	Frisco, TX	(9.2)
229	Alhambra, CA	(9.5)
230	Cedar Rapids, IA	(9.6)
230	Chino, CA	(9.6)
232	Longview, TX	(9.7)
232	Tallahassee, FL	(9.7)
234	Los Angeles, CA	(9.8)
234	Roseville, CA	(9.8)
234	Stamford, CT	(9.8)
237	McAllen, TX	(9.9)
237	Washington, DC	(9.9)
239	Mission Viejo, CA	(10.1)
239	Salt Lake City, UT	(10.1)
241	Ontario, CA	(10.2)
242	Las Cruces, NM	(10.3)
243	Anchorage, AK	(10.4)
243	Dayton, OH	(10.4)
243	Glendale, CA	(10.4)
246	Greensboro, NC	(10.5)
246	Rockford, IL	(10.5)
248	Hayward, CA	(10.6)
249	Suffolk, VA	(10.7)
250	Hawthorne, CA	(10.8)
250	Minneapolis, MN	(10.8)
252	San Leandro, CA	(11.0)
253	Stockton, CA	(11.1)
254	Moreno Valley, CA	(11.3)
255	Elk Grove, CA	(11.4)
255	Jersey City, NJ	(11.4)
257	Miami, FL	(11.5)
258	Billings, MT	(12.1)
258	Pomona, CA	(12.1)
258	Shreveport, LA	(12.1)
258	Virginia Beach, VA	(12.1)
262	Roanoke, VA	(12.3)
263	Alexandria, VA	(12.4)
264	Boston, MA	(12.5)
264	Lafayette, LA	(12.5)
266	Montgomery, AL	(12.6)
266	Torrance, CA	(12.6)
268	Albuquerque, NM	(12.8)
268	Newport Beach, CA	(12.8)
270	Huntsville, AL	(12.9)
271	Jacksonville, NC	(13.0)
271	Lincoln, NE	(13.0)
271	Portland, OR	(13.0)
271	Sacramento, CA	(13.0)

RANK	CITY	% CHANGE
275	Evansville, IN	(13.2)
276	Rancho Cucamon., CA	(13.3)
277	Jacksonville, FL	(13.6)
278	Phoenix, AZ	(13.9)
279	Simi Valley, CA	(14.0)
280	Kent, WA	(14.1)
281	Beaverton, OR	(14.3)
281	Tampa, FL	(14.3)
283	Concord, CA	(14.4)
283	Fort Collins, CO	(14.4)
283	Norwalk, CA	(14.4)
283	Pompano Beach, FL	(14.4)
287	Atlanta, GA	(14.7)
287	Sunnyvale, CA	(14.7)
289	Clifton, NJ	(14.8)
289	Ramapo, NY	(14.8)
291	Bellingham, WA	(14.9)
292	Joliet, IL	(15.0)
292	Philadelphia, PA	(15.0)
294	Waco, TX	(15.2)
295	Columbus, OH	(15.4)
296	Naperville, IL	(15.5)
297	Davenport, IA	(15.6)
297	Round Rock, TX	(15.6)
299	Costa Mesa, CA	(15.7)
300	Oceanside, CA	(16.4)
300	Omaha, NE	(16.4)
302	Mesa, AZ	(16.6)
303	Oakland, CA	(16.7)
304	Aurora, CO	(16.9)
305	Santa Barbara, CA	(17.2)
306	Compton, CA	(17.3)
306	Racine, WI	(17.3)
306	Vallejo, CA	(17.3)
309	Winston-Salem, NC	(17.4)
310	Woodbridge Twnshp, NJ	(17.6)
311	Chico, CA	(17.7)
311	Milwaukee, WI	(17.7)
313	Richardson, TX	(17.8)
314	Hialeah, FL	(18.0)
314	Lee's Summit, MO	(18.0)
314	Miami Beach, FL	(18.0)
317	Clovis, CA	(18.3)
318	Broken Arrow, OK	(18.5)
319	Greeley, CO	(18.6)
320	Nashville, TN	(18.7)
321	El Monte, CA	(19.1)
322	Pasadena, CA	(19.3)
323	Tulsa, OK	(19.4)
324	Killeen, TX	(19.5)
324	Tuscaloosa, AL	(19.5)
326	Pembroke Pines, FL	(19.6)
326	Tucson, AZ	(19.6)
328	Provo, UT	(19.7)
329	Independence, MO	(19.8)
329	Lewisville, TX	(19.8)
331	Amherst, NY	(20.3)
332	McKinney, TX	(20.4)
332	Orlando, FL	(20.4)
334	Hillsboro, OR	(20.5)
335	Chula Vista, CA	(20.7)
336	Tyler, TX	(21.4)
337	Fairfield, CA	(21.5)
338	Jackson, MS	(21.6)
339	Sioux Falls, SD	(21.7)
340	Irving, TX	(21.8)
341	Fremont, CA	(22.7)
342	South Gate, CA	(23.0)

RANK	CITY	% CHANGE
343	Denton, TX	(23.2)
344	New Orleans, LA	(23.4)
345	Charlotte, NC	(23.7)
346	Carrollton, TX	(24.3)
347	Charleston, SC	(24.4)
348	Lancaster, CA	(24.5)
349	Sunrise, FL	(24.6)
350	Fayetteville, NC	(25.3)
351	Buena Park, CA	(25.4)
352	Kenosha, WI	(25.6)
353	North Charleston, SC	(26.1)
354	Allentown, PA	(26.6)
355	Santa Monica, CA	(27.3)
356	Gresham, OR	(27.5)
357	Newton, MA	(27.7)
358	Avondale, AZ	(29.2)
359	El Cajon, CA	(29.4)
359	Riverside, CA	(29.4)
361	Orange, CA	(30.0)
362	Macon, GA	(30.2)
363	Missouri City, TX	(30.3)
364	Gilbert, AZ	(30.5)
365	Thornton, CO	(30.9)
366	West Jordan, UT	(31.7)
367	Livermore, CA	(31.8)
368	Garland, TX	(31.9)
369	San Antonio, TX	(32.0)
370	West Covina, CA	(33.1)
371	Plano, TX	(34.3)
372	College Station, TX	(35.2)
373	Temecula, CA	(35.7)
374	Corona, CA	(36.1)
375	Santa Clara, CA	(36.5)
376	Brownsville, TX	(37.8)
377	St. George, UT	(42.9)
378	Greece, NY	(44.4)
379	Sugar Land, TX	(47.7)
380	Gary, IN	(48.2)
381	Orem, UT	(60.3)
NA	Albany, GA**	NA
NA	Ann Arbor, MI**	NA
NA	Brockton, MA**	NA
NA	Canton Twnshp, MI**	NA
NA	Clinton Twnshp, MI**	NA
NA	Dearborn, MI**	NA
NA	Decatur, IL**	NA
NA	Des Moines, IA**	NA
NA	Detroit, MI**	NA
NA	Farmington Hills, MI**	NA
NA	Flint, MI**	NA
NA	Grand Rapids, MI**	NA
NA	Kansas City, KS**	NA
NA	Lansing, MI**	NA
NA	Lexington, KY**	NA
NA	Little Rock, AR**	NA
NA	Livonia, MI**	NA
NA	Longmont, CO**	NA
NA	Louisville, KY**	NA
NA	Nashua, NH**	NA
NA	New Haven, CT**	NA
NA	Olathe, KS**	NA
NA	Peoria, IL**	NA
NA	Pueblo, CO**	NA
NA	Southfield, MI**	NA
NA	Springfield, IL**	NA
NA	Sterling Heights, MI**	NA
NA	Troy, MI**	NA
NA	Warren, MI**	NA
NA	Westland, MI**	NA

Source: CQ Press using reported data from the F.B.I. "Crime in the United States 2009"

*Aggravated assault is an attack for the purpose of inflicting severe bodily injury.

**Not available.

64. Percent Change in Aggravated Assault Rate: 2005 to 2009
National Percent Change = 9.6% Decrease*

RANK	CITY	% CHANGE
63	Abilene, TX	15.4
6	Akron, OH	134.3
8	Albany, GA	120.1
217	Albany, NY	(17.4)
257	Albuquerque, NM	(24.5)
359	Alexandria, VA	(51.7)
315	Alhambra, CA	(33.1)
319	Allentown, PA	(33.6)
54	Allen, TX	21.6
125	Amarillo, TX	(0.2)
20	Amherst, NY	47.9
341	Anaheim, CA	(38.3)
65	Anchorage, AK	14.8
NA	Ann Arbor, MI**	NA
12	Antioch, CA	90.4
106	Arlington, TX	2.9
135	Arvada, CO	(1.2)
28	Athens-Clarke, GA	39.0
321	Atlanta, GA	(34.1)
283	Aurora, CO	(28.9)
91	Aurora, IL	5.6
73	Austin, TX	11.7
NA	Avondale, AZ**	NA
102	Bakersfield, CA	3.7
262	Baldwin Park, CA	(25.6)
227	Baltimore, MD	(19.2)
126	Baton Rouge, LA	(0.4)
176	Beaumont, TX	(10.5)
161	Beaverton, OR	(6.8)
250	Bellevue, WA	(23.7)
195	Bellingham, WA	(14.0)
109	Bend, OR	1.8
279	Berkeley, CA	(28.5)
37	Billings, MT	31.0
194	Birmingham, AL	(13.8)
NA	Bloomington, MN**	NA
344	Boca Raton, FL	(39.3)
290	Boise, ID	(29.8)
271	Boston, MA	(27.2)
94	Boulder, CO	4.7
10	Brick Twnshp, NJ	105.4
103	Bridgeport, CT	3.2
NA	Brockton, MA**	NA
326	Broken Arrow, OK	(35.0)
370	Brownsville, TX	(65.4)
331	Buena Park, CA	(35.9)
86	Buffalo, NY	8.1
200	Burbank, CA	(14.7)
53	Cambridge, MA	23.1
64	Camden, NJ	15.2
NA	Canton Twnshp, MI**	NA
46	Canton, OH	26.4
264	Cape Coral, FL	(25.7)
69	Carlsbad, CA	12.6
353	Carrollton, TX	(47.0)
226	Carson, CA	(19.1)
236	Cary, NC	(20.9)
147	Cedar Rapids, IA	(4.0)
275	Centennial, CO	(27.9)
243	Chandler, AZ	(22.4)
360	Charleston, SC	(51.8)
323	Charlotte, NC	(34.5)
169	Chattanooga, TN	(8.2)
189	Cheektowaga, NY	(12.5)
287	Chesapeake, VA	(29.1)
183	Chicago, IL	(11.6)
204	Chico, CA	(15.4)
342	Chino, CA	(38.7)
334	Chula Vista, CA	(36.4)
36	Cincinnati, OH	31.9
NA	Citrus Heights, CA**	NA
NA	Clarkstown, NY**	NA
215	Clarksville, TN	(17.0)
189	Clearwater, FL	(12.5)
113	Cleveland, OH	1.3
55	Clifton, NJ	20.9
NA	Clinton Twnshp, MI**	NA
296	Clovis, CA	(30.5)
316	College Station, TX	(33.4)
201	Colonie, NY	(15.0)
164	Colorado Springs, CO	(7.3)
228	Columbia, MO	(19.3)
155	Columbia, SC	(5.8)
94	Columbus, GA	4.7
274	Columbus, OH	(27.7)
238	Compton, CA	(21.5)
347	Concord, CA	(42.7)
18	Coral Springs, FL	61.0
355	Corona, CA	(48.7)
51	Corpus Christi, TX	24.6
90	Costa Mesa, CA	6.1
229	Cranston, RI	(19.4)
357	Dallas, TX	(50.1)
207	Daly City, CA	(16.2)
77	Danbury, CT	11.0
362	Davenport, IA	(53.8)
21	Davie, FL	45.9
35	Dayton, OH	32.0
NA	Dearborn, MI**	NA
NA	Decatur, IL**	NA
351	Denton, TX	(45.0)
255	Denver, CO	(24.4)
NA	Des Moines, IA**	NA
NA	Detroit, MI**	NA
57	Downey, CA	20.5
NA	Duluth, MN**	NA
132	Durham, NC	(1.0)
88	Edison Twnshp, NJ	6.3
290	Edmond, OK	(29.8)
304	El Cajon, CA	(31.6)
179	El Monte, CA	(10.9)
66	El Paso, TX	14.4
NA	Elgin, IL**	NA
11	Elizabeth, NJ	93.7
NA	Elk Grove, CA**	NA
29	Erie, PA	38.6
292	Escondido, CA	(30.0)
52	Eugene, OR	24.1
119	Evansville, IN	0.9
163	Everett, WA	(7.0)
313	Fairfield, CA	(32.7)
NA	Fall River, MA**	NA
1	Fargo, ND	323.5
NA	Farmington Hills, MI**	NA
173	Fayetteville, AR	(9.9)
267	Fayetteville, NC	(26.8)
75	Federal Way, WA	11.4
NA	Flint, MI**	NA
144	Fontana, CA	(3.5)
34	Fort Collins, CO	32.5
138	Fort Lauderdale, FL	(1.7)
260	Fort Smith, AR	(24.7)
92	Fort Wayne, IN	5.3
165	Fort Worth, TX	(7.4)
223	Fremont, CA	(18.4)
309	Fresno, CA	(32.1)
151	Frisco, TX	(4.8)
23	Fullerton, CA	44.6
68	Gainesville, FL	12.8
296	Garden Grove, CA	(30.5)
316	Garland, TX	(33.4)
108	Gary, IN	2.1
358	Gilbert, AZ	(50.2)
302	Glendale, AZ	(31.5)
175	Glendale, CA	(10.4)
82	Grand Prairie, TX	9.7
NA	Grand Rapids, MI**	NA
3	Greece, NY	211.5
307	Greeley, CO	(31.8)
178	Green Bay, WI	(10.7)
210	Greensboro, NC	(16.6)
330	Gresham, OR	(35.3)
37	Hamilton Twnshp, NJ	31.0
50	Hammond, IN	25.3
197	Hampton, VA	(14.1)
30	Hartford, CT	36.8
59	Hawthorne, CA	18.8
186	Hayward, CA	(12.2)
94	Henderson, NV	4.7
56	Hesperia, CA	20.6
299	Hialeah, FL	(30.8)
166	High Point, NC	(7.7)
322	Hillsboro, OR	(34.3)
167	Hollywood, FL	(8.1)
149	Honolulu, HI	(4.5)
113	Houston, TX	1.3
325	Huntington Beach, CA	(34.8)
150	Huntsville, AL	(4.7)
242	Independence, MO	(22.2)
43	Indianapolis, IN	28.4
58	Indio, CA	19.3
60	Inglewood, CA	17.5
340	Irvine, CA	(37.9)
345	Irving, TX	(39.9)
133	Jacksonville, FL	(1.1)
NA	Jacksonville, NC**	NA
130	Jackson, MS	(0.8)
346	Jersey City, NJ	(40.6)
185	Joliet, IL	(12.0)
203	Kansas City, KS	(15.3)
180	Kansas City, MO	(11.1)
25	Kenosha, WI	42.0
155	Kent, WA	(5.8)
215	Killeen, TX	(17.0)
100	Knoxville, TN	4.0
109	Lafayette, LA	1.8
123	Lake Forest, CA	0.1
116	Lakeland, FL	1.2
85	Lakewood, CA	8.7
67	Lakewood, CO	13.3
320	Lancaster, CA	(33.7)
NA	Lansing, MI**	NA
71	Laredo, TX	12.2
76	Las Cruces, NM	11.1
31	Las Vegas, NV	36.4
43	Lawrence, KS	28.4
17	Lawton, OK	67.9
348	Lee's Summit, MO	(42.9)
281	Lewisville, TX	(28.6)
NA	Lexington, KY**	NA
249	Lincoln, NE	(23.5)
NA	Little Rock, AR**	NA
192	Livermore, CA	(13.1)
NA	Livonia, MI**	NA
174	Long Beach, CA	(10.1)
NA	Longmont, CO**	NA

RANK	CITY	% CHANGE
265	Longview, TX	(25.9)
324	Los Angeles, CA	(34.7)
NA	Louisville, KY**	NA
187	Lubbock, TX	(12.3)
253	Lynn, MA	(24.2)
218	Macon, GA	(17.7)
120	Madison, WI	0.8
2	Manchester, NH	226.4
283	McAllen, TX	(28.9)
308	McKinney, TX	(32.0)
45	Melbourne, FL	28.0
136	Memphis, TN	(1.3)
32	Merced, CA	35.2
260	Mesa, AZ	(24.7)
199	Mesquite, TX	(14.6)
234	Miami Beach, FL	(20.3)
361	Miami Gardens, FL	(52.3)
333	Miami, FL	(36.0)
148	Midland, TX	(4.3)
79	Milwaukee, WI	10.2
193	Minneapolis, MN	(13.4)
126	Miramar, FL	(0.4)
247	Mission Viejo, CA	(22.8)
310	Missouri City, TX	(32.6)
5	Mobile, AL	137.9
62	Modesto, CA	15.9
363	Montgomery, AL	(54.1)
106	Moreno Valley, CA	2.9
272	Murfreesboro, TN	(27.3)
338	Murrieta, CA	(37.1)
NA	Nampa, ID**	NA
16	Naperville, IL	68.4
124	Nashua, NH	0.0
296	Nashville, TN	(30.5)
80	New Bedford, MA	10.1
NA	New Haven, CT**	NA
NA	New Orleans, LA**	NA
170	New York, NY	(8.6)
222	Newark, NJ	(18.2)
78	Newport Beach, CA	10.7
285	Newton, MA	(29.0)
131	Norfolk, VA	(0.9)
366	Norman, OK	(57.0)
348	North Charleston, SC	(42.9)
221	North Las Vegas, NV	(18.0)
112	Norwalk, CA	1.6
40	Norwalk, CT	30.6
39	Oakland, CA	30.9
276	Oceanside, CA	(28.0)
94	Odessa, TX	4.7
140	O'Fallon, MO	(2.5)
71	Ogden, UT	12.2
61	Oklahoma City, OK	16.3
NA	Olathe, KS**	NA
220	Omaha, NE	(17.9)
248	Ontario, CA	(23.1)
331	Orange, CA	(35.9)
369	Orem, UT	(64.6)
289	Orlando, FL	(29.4)
352	Overland Park, KS	(46.8)
171	Oxnard, CA	(8.7)
93	Palm Bay, FL	4.8
301	Palmdale, CA	(31.1)
350	Pasadena, CA	(44.2)
89	Pasadena, TX	6.2
209	Paterson, NJ	(16.4)
24	Pearland, TX	43.2
197	Pembroke Pines, FL	(14.1)
237	Peoria, AZ	(21.3)
101	Peoria, IL	3.9
207	Philadelphia, PA	(16.2)
295	Phoenix, AZ	(30.3)
99	Pittsburgh, PA	4.4
365	Plano, TX	(54.5)
9	Plantation, FL	107.0
269	Pomona, CA	(27.0)
343	Pompano Beach, FL	(38.9)
155	Port St. Lucie, FL	(5.8)
270	Portland, OR	(27.1)
310	Portsmouth, VA	(32.6)
70	Providence, RI	12.3
233	Provo, UT	(20.2)
26	Pueblo, CO	40.4
74	Quincy, MA	11.5
13	Racine, WI	74.7
268	Raleigh, NC	(26.9)
191	Ramapo, NY	(12.6)
176	Rancho Cucamon., CA	(10.5)
262	Reading, PA	(25.6)
33	Redding, CA	34.0
167	Reno, NV	(8.1)
354	Rialto, CA	(47.7)
277	Richardson, TX	(28.1)
98	Richmond, CA	4.6
318	Richmond, VA	(33.5)
254	Rio Rancho, NM	(24.3)
336	Riverside, CA	(36.8)
287	Roanoke, VA	(29.1)
159	Rochester, MN	(5.9)
27	Rochester, NY	39.5
15	Rockford, IL	68.9
246	Roseville, CA	(22.6)
87	Roswell, GA	7.6
279	Round Rock, TX	(28.5)
255	Sacramento, CA	(24.4)
292	Salem, OR	(30.0)
83	Salinas, CA	9.1
128	Salt Lake City, UT	(0.7)
184	San Angelo, TX	(11.8)
240	San Antonio, TX	(21.6)
245	San Bernardino, CA	(22.5)
219	San Diego, CA	(17.8)
225	San Francisco, CA	(19.0)
188	San Jose, CA	(12.4)
335	San Leandro, CA	(36.7)
285	San Marcos, CA	(29.0)
230	San Mateo, CA	(19.5)
NA	Sandy Springs, GA**	NA
142	Sandy, UT	(3.3)
299	Santa Ana, CA	(30.8)
326	Santa Barbara, CA	(35.0)
337	Santa Clara, CA	(36.9)
49	Santa Clarita, CA	26.0
48	Santa Maria, CA	26.2
259	Santa Monica, CA	(24.6)
306	Santa Rosa, CA	(31.7)
278	Savannah, GA	(28.2)
202	Scottsdale, AZ	(15.2)
232	Seattle, WA	(20.1)
235	Shreveport, LA	(20.8)
206	Simi Valley, CA	(16.1)
153	Sioux City, IA	(5.6)
160	Sioux Falls, SD	(6.4)
14	Somerville, MA	72.9
128	South Bend, IN	(0.7)
161	South Gate, CA	(6.8)
NA	Southfield, MI**	NA
81	Sparks, NV	9.8
282	Spokane Valley, WA	(28.7)
137	Spokane, WA	(1.5)
231	Springfield, IL	(19.6)
314	Springfield, MA	(33.0)
47	Springfield, MO	26.3
151	Stamford, CT	(4.8)
NA	Sterling Heights, MI**	NA
213	Stockton, CA	(16.7)
371	St. George, UT	(72.7)
7	St. Joseph, MO	130.0
210	St. Louis, MO	(16.6)
182	St. Paul, MN	(11.5)
205	St. Petersburg, FL	(15.8)
356	Suffolk, VA	(49.1)
210	Sugar Land, TX	(16.6)
326	Sunnyvale, CA	(35.0)
273	Sunrise, FL	(27.4)
302	Surprise, AZ	(31.5)
145	Syracuse, NY	(3.7)
142	Tacoma, WA	(3.3)
195	Tallahassee, FL	(14.0)
364	Tampa, FL	(54.4)
372	Temecula, CA	(75.8)
241	Tempe, AZ	(22.0)
339	Thornton, CO	(37.5)
121	Thousand Oaks, CA	0.7
181	Toledo, OH	(11.2)
252	Toms River Twnshp, NJ	(24.1)
109	Topeka, KS	1.8
84	Torrance, CA	8.8
266	Tracy, CA	(26.3)
154	Trenton, NJ	(5.7)
NA	Troy, MI**	NA
304	Tucson, AZ	(31.6)
224	Tulsa, OK	(18.9)
329	Tuscaloosa, AL	(35.2)
118	Tyler, TX	1.0
4	Upper Darby Twnshp, PA	142.0
133	Vacaville, CA	(1.1)
NA	Vallejo, CA**	NA
105	Vancouver, WA	3.1
41	Ventura, CA	30.3
42	Victorville, CA	29.2
155	Virginia Beach, VA	(5.8)
367	Visalia, CA	(58.2)
113	Vista, CA	1.3
116	Waco, TX	1.2
NA	Warren, MI**	NA
243	Warwick, RI	(22.4)
238	Washington, DC	(21.5)
122	Waterbury, CT	0.4
214	West Covina, CA	(16.8)
NA	West Jordan, UT**	NA
257	West Palm Beach, FL	(24.5)
172	West Valley, UT	(9.0)
NA	Westland, MI**	NA
310	Westminster, CA	(32.6)
251	Westminster, CO	(23.9)
22	Whittier, CA	45.0
294	Wichita Falls, TX	(30.1)
NA	Wichita, KS**	NA
141	Wilmington, NC	(2.9)
139	Winston-Salem, NC	(2.4)
368	Woodbridge Twnshp, NJ	(64.5)
19	Worcester, MA	55.1
103	Yonkers, NY	3.2
146	Yuma, AZ	(3.9)

Source: CQ Press using reported data from the F.B.I. "Crime in the United States 2009"

*Aggravated assault is an attack for the purpose of inflicting severe bodily injury.

**Not available.

64. Percent Change in Aggravated Assault Rate: 2005 to 2009 (continued)
National Percent Change = 9.6% Decrease*

RANK	CITY	% CHANGE
1	Fargo, ND	323.5
2	Manchester, NH	226.4
3	Greece, NY	211.5
4	Upper Darby Twnshp, PA	142.0
5	Mobile, AL	137.9
6	Akron, OH	134.3
7	St. Joseph, MO	130.0
8	Albany, GA	120.1
9	Plantation, FL	107.0
10	Brick Twnshp, NJ	105.4
11	Elizabeth, NJ	93.7
12	Antioch, CA	90.4
13	Racine, WI	74.7
14	Somerville, MA	72.9
15	Rockford, IL	68.9
16	Naperville, IL	68.4
17	Lawton, OK	67.9
18	Coral Springs, FL	61.0
19	Worcester, MA	55.1
20	Amherst, NY	47.9
21	Davie, FL	45.9
22	Whittier, CA	45.0
23	Fullerton, CA	44.6
24	Pearland, TX	43.2
25	Kenosha, WI	42.0
26	Pueblo, CO	40.4
27	Rochester, NY	39.5
28	Athens-Clarke, GA	39.0
29	Erie, PA	38.6
30	Hartford, CT	36.8
31	Las Vegas, NV	36.4
32	Merced, CA	35.2
33	Redding, CA	34.0
34	Fort Collins, CO	32.5
35	Dayton, OH	32.0
36	Cincinnati, OH	31.9
37	Billings, MT	31.0
37	Hamilton Twnshp, NJ	31.0
39	Oakland, CA	30.9
40	Norwalk, CT	30.6
41	Ventura, CA	30.3
42	Victorville, CA	29.2
43	Indianapolis, IN	28.4
43	Lawrence, KS	28.4
45	Melbourne, FL	28.0
46	Canton, OH	26.4
47	Springfield, MO	26.3
48	Santa Maria, CA	26.2
49	Santa Clarita, CA	26.0
50	Hammond, IN	25.3
51	Corpus Christi, TX	24.6
52	Eugene, OR	24.1
53	Cambridge, MA	23.1
54	Allen, TX	21.6
55	Clifton, NJ	20.9
56	Hesperia, CA	20.6
57	Downey, CA	20.5
58	Indio, CA	19.3
59	Hawthorne, CA	18.8
60	Inglewood, CA	17.5
61	Oklahoma City, OK	16.3
62	Modesto, CA	15.9
63	Abilene, TX	15.4
64	Camden, NJ	15.2
65	Anchorage, AK	14.8
66	El Paso, TX	14.4
67	Lakewood, CO	13.3
68	Gainesville, FL	12.8
69	Carlsbad, CA	12.6
70	Providence, RI	12.3
71	Laredo, TX	12.2
71	Ogden, UT	12.2
73	Austin, TX	11.7
74	Quincy, MA	11.5
75	Federal Way, WA	11.4
76	Las Cruces, NM	11.1
77	Danbury, CT	11.0
78	Newport Beach, CA	10.7
79	Milwaukee, WI	10.2
80	New Bedford, MA	10.1
81	Sparks, NV	9.8
82	Grand Prairie, TX	9.7
83	Salinas, CA	9.1
84	Torrance, CA	8.8
85	Lakewood, CA	8.7
86	Buffalo, NY	8.1
87	Roswell, GA	7.6
88	Edison Twnshp, NJ	6.3
89	Pasadena, TX	6.2
90	Costa Mesa, CA	6.1
91	Aurora, IL	5.6
92	Fort Wayne, IN	5.3
93	Palm Bay, FL	4.8
94	Boulder, CO	4.7
94	Columbus, GA	4.7
94	Henderson, NV	4.7
94	Odessa, TX	4.7
98	Richmond, CA	4.6
99	Pittsburgh, PA	4.4
100	Knoxville, TN	4.0
101	Peoria, IL	3.9
102	Bakersfield, CA	3.7
103	Bridgeport, CT	3.2
103	Yonkers, NY	3.2
105	Vancouver, WA	3.1
106	Arlington, TX	2.9
106	Moreno Valley, CA	2.9
108	Gary, IN	2.1
109	Bend, OR	1.8
109	Lafayette, LA	1.8
109	Topeka, KS	1.8
112	Norwalk, CA	1.6
113	Cleveland, OH	1.3
113	Houston, TX	1.3
113	Vista, CA	1.3
116	Lakeland, FL	1.2
116	Waco, TX	1.2
118	Tyler, TX	1.0
119	Evansville, IN	0.9
120	Madison, WI	0.8
121	Thousand Oaks, CA	0.7
122	Waterbury, CT	0.4
123	Lake Forest, CA	0.1
124	Nashua, NH	0.0
125	Amarillo, TX	(0.2)
126	Baton Rouge, LA	(0.4)
126	Miramar, FL	(0.4)
128	Salt Lake City, UT	(0.7)
128	South Bend, IN	(0.7)
130	Jackson, MS	(0.8)
131	Norfolk, VA	(0.9)
132	Durham, NC	(1.0)
133	Jacksonville, FL	(1.1)
133	Vacaville, CA	(1.1)
135	Arvada, CO	(1.2)
136	Memphis, TN	(1.3)
137	Spokane, WA	(1.5)
138	Fort Lauderdale, FL	(1.7)
139	Winston-Salem, NC	(2.4)
140	O'Fallon, MO	(2.5)
141	Wilmington, NC	(2.9)
142	Sandy, UT	(3.3)
142	Tacoma, WA	(3.3)
144	Fontana, CA	(3.5)
145	Syracuse, NY	(3.7)
146	Yuma, AZ	(3.9)
147	Cedar Rapids, IA	(4.0)
148	Midland, TX	(4.3)
149	Honolulu, HI	(4.5)
150	Huntsville, AL	(4.7)
151	Frisco, TX	(4.8)
151	Stamford, CT	(4.8)
153	Sioux City, IA	(5.6)
154	Trenton, NJ	(5.7)
155	Columbia, SC	(5.8)
155	Kent, WA	(5.8)
155	Port St. Lucie, FL	(5.8)
155	Virginia Beach, VA	(5.8)
159	Rochester, MN	(5.9)
160	Sioux Falls, SD	(6.4)
161	Beaverton, OR	(6.8)
161	South Gate, CA	(6.8)
163	Everett, WA	(7.0)
164	Colorado Springs, CO	(7.3)
165	Fort Worth, TX	(7.4)
166	High Point, NC	(7.7)
167	Hollywood, FL	(8.1)
167	Reno, NV	(8.1)
169	Chattanooga, TN	(8.2)
170	New York, NY	(8.6)
171	Oxnard, CA	(8.7)
172	West Valley, UT	(9.0)
173	Fayetteville, AR	(9.9)
174	Long Beach, CA	(10.1)
175	Glendale, CA	(10.4)
176	Beaumont, TX	(10.5)
176	Rancho Cucamon., CA	(10.5)
178	Green Bay, WI	(10.7)
179	El Monte, CA	(10.9)
180	Kansas City, MO	(11.1)
181	Toledo, OH	(11.2)
182	St. Paul, MN	(11.5)
183	Chicago, IL	(11.6)
184	San Angelo, TX	(11.8)
185	Joliet, IL	(12.0)
186	Hayward, CA	(12.2)
187	Lubbock, TX	(12.3)
188	San Jose, CA	(12.4)
189	Cheektowaga, NY	(12.5)
189	Clearwater, FL	(12.5)
191	Ramapo, NY	(12.6)
192	Livermore, CA	(13.1)
193	Minneapolis, MN	(13.4)
194	Birmingham, AL	(13.8)
195	Bellingham, WA	(14.0)
195	Tallahassee, FL	(14.0)
197	Hampton, VA	(14.1)
197	Pembroke Pines, FL	(14.1)
199	Mesquite, TX	(14.6)
200	Burbank, CA	(14.7)
201	Colonie, NY	(15.0)
202	Scottsdale, AZ	(15.2)
203	Kansas City, KS	(15.3)
204	Chico, CA	(15.4)
205	St. Petersburg, FL	(15.8)
206	Simi Valley, CA	(16.1)

RANK	CITY	% CHANGE
207	Daly City, CA	(16.2)
207	Philadelphia, PA	(16.2)
209	Paterson, NJ	(16.4)
210	Greensboro, NC	(16.6)
210	St. Louis, MO	(16.6)
210	Sugar Land, TX	(16.6)
213	Stockton, CA	(16.7)
214	West Covina, CA	(16.8)
215	Clarksville, TN	(17.0)
215	Killeen, TX	(17.0)
217	Albany, NY	(17.4)
218	Macon, GA	(17.7)
219	San Diego, CA	(17.8)
220	Omaha, NE	(17.9)
221	North Las Vegas, NV	(18.0)
222	Newark, NJ	(18.2)
223	Fremont, CA	(18.4)
224	Tulsa, OK	(18.9)
225	San Francisco, CA	(19.0)
226	Carson, CA	(19.1)
227	Baltimore, MD	(19.2)
228	Columbia, MO	(19.3)
229	Cranston, RI	(19.4)
230	San Mateo, CA	(19.5)
231	Springfield, IL	(19.6)
232	Seattle, WA	(20.1)
233	Provo, UT	(20.2)
234	Miami Beach, FL	(20.3)
235	Shreveport, LA	(20.8)
236	Cary, NC	(20.9)
237	Peoria, AZ	(21.3)
238	Compton, CA	(21.5)
238	Washington, DC	(21.5)
240	San Antonio, TX	(21.6)
241	Tempe, AZ	(22.0)
242	Independence, MO	(22.2)
243	Chandler, AZ	(22.4)
243	Warwick, RI	(22.4)
245	San Bernardino, CA	(22.5)
246	Roseville, CA	(22.6)
247	Mission Viejo, CA	(22.8)
248	Ontario, CA	(23.1)
249	Lincoln, NE	(23.5)
250	Bellevue, WA	(23.7)
251	Westminster, CO	(23.9)
252	Toms River Twnshp, NJ	(24.1)
253	Lynn, MA	(24.2)
254	Rio Rancho, NM	(24.3)
255	Denver, CO	(24.4)
255	Sacramento, CA	(24.4)
257	Albuquerque, NM	(24.5)
257	West Palm Beach, FL	(24.5)
259	Santa Monica, CA	(24.6)
260	Fort Smith, AR	(24.7)
260	Mesa, AZ	(24.7)
262	Baldwin Park, CA	(25.6)
262	Reading, PA	(25.6)
264	Cape Coral, FL	(25.7)
265	Longview, TX	(25.9)
266	Tracy, CA	(26.3)
267	Fayetteville, NC	(26.8)
268	Raleigh, NC	(26.9)
269	Pomona, CA	(27.0)
270	Portland, OR	(27.1)
271	Boston, MA	(27.2)
272	Murfreesboro, TN	(27.3)
273	Sunrise, FL	(27.4)
274	Columbus, OH	(27.7)
275	Centennial, CO	(27.9)
276	Oceanside, CA	(28.0)
277	Richardson, TX	(28.1)
278	Savannah, GA	(28.2)
279	Berkeley, CA	(28.5)
279	Round Rock, TX	(28.5)
281	Lewisville, TX	(28.6)
282	Spokane Valley, WA	(28.7)
283	Aurora, CO	(28.9)
283	McAllen, TX	(28.9)
285	Newton, MA	(29.0)
285	San Marcos, CA	(29.0)
287	Chesapeake, VA	(29.1)
287	Roanoke, VA	(29.1)
289	Orlando, FL	(29.4)
290	Boise, ID	(29.8)
290	Edmond, OK	(29.8)
292	Escondido, CA	(30.0)
292	Salem, OR	(30.0)
294	Wichita Falls, TX	(30.1)
295	Phoenix, AZ	(30.3)
296	Clovis, CA	(30.5)
296	Garden Grove, CA	(30.5)
296	Nashville, TN	(30.5)
299	Hialeah, FL	(30.8)
299	Santa Ana, CA	(30.8)
301	Palmdale, CA	(31.1)
302	Glendale, AZ	(31.5)
302	Surprise, AZ	(31.5)
304	El Cajon, CA	(31.6)
304	Tucson, AZ	(31.6)
306	Santa Rosa, CA	(31.7)
307	Greeley, CO	(31.8)
308	McKinney, TX	(32.0)
309	Fresno, CA	(32.1)
310	Missouri City, TX	(32.6)
310	Portsmouth, VA	(32.6)
310	Westminster, CA	(32.6)
313	Fairfield, CA	(32.7)
314	Springfield, MA	(33.0)
315	Alhambra, CA	(33.1)
316	College Station, TX	(33.4)
316	Garland, TX	(33.4)
318	Richmond, VA	(33.5)
319	Allentown, PA	(33.6)
320	Lancaster, CA	(33.7)
321	Atlanta, GA	(34.1)
322	Hillsboro, OR	(34.3)
323	Charlotte, NC	(34.5)
324	Los Angeles, CA	(34.7)
325	Huntington Beach, CA	(34.8)
326	Broken Arrow, OK	(35.0)
326	Santa Barbara, CA	(35.0)
326	Sunnyvale, CA	(35.0)
329	Tuscaloosa, AL	(35.2)
330	Gresham, OR	(35.3)
331	Buena Park, CA	(35.9)
331	Orange, CA	(35.9)
333	Miami, FL	(36.0)
334	Chula Vista, CA	(36.4)
335	San Leandro, CA	(36.7)
336	Riverside, CA	(36.8)
337	Santa Clara, CA	(36.9)
338	Murrieta, CA	(37.1)
339	Thornton, CO	(37.5)
340	Irvine, CA	(37.9)
341	Anaheim, CA	(38.3)
342	Chino, CA	(38.7)
343	Pompano Beach, FL	(38.9)
344	Boca Raton, FL	(39.3)
345	Irving, TX	(39.9)
346	Jersey City, NJ	(40.6)
347	Concord, CA	(42.7)
348	Lee's Summit, MO	(42.9)
348	North Charleston, SC	(42.9)
350	Pasadena, CA	(44.2)
351	Denton, TX	(45.0)
352	Overland Park, KS	(46.8)
353	Carrollton, TX	(47.0)
354	Rialto, CA	(47.7)
355	Corona, CA	(48.7)
356	Suffolk, VA	(49.1)
357	Dallas, TX	(50.1)
358	Gilbert, AZ	(50.2)
359	Alexandria, VA	(51.7)
360	Charleston, SC	(51.8)
361	Miami Gardens, FL	(52.3)
362	Davenport, IA	(53.8)
363	Montgomery, AL	(54.1)
364	Tampa, FL	(54.4)
365	Plano, TX	(54.5)
366	Norman, OK	(57.0)
367	Visalia, CA	(58.2)
368	Woodbridge Twnshp, NJ	(64.5)
369	Orem, UT	(64.6)
370	Brownsville, TX	(65.4)
371	St. George, UT	(72.7)
372	Temecula, CA	(75.8)
NA	Ann Arbor, MI**	NA
NA	Avondale, AZ**	NA
NA	Bloomington, MN**	NA
NA	Brockton, MA**	NA
NA	Canton Twnshp, MI**	NA
NA	Citrus Heights, CA**	NA
NA	Clarkstown, NY**	NA
NA	Clinton Twnshp, MI**	NA
NA	Dearborn, MI**	NA
NA	Decatur, IL**	NA
NA	Des Moines, IA**	NA
NA	Detroit, MI**	NA
NA	Duluth, MN**	NA
NA	Elgin, IL**	NA
NA	Elk Grove, CA**	NA
NA	Fall River, MA**	NA
NA	Farmington Hills, MI**	NA
NA	Flint, MI**	NA
NA	Grand Rapids, MI**	NA
NA	Jacksonville, NC**	NA
NA	Lansing, MI**	NA
NA	Lexington, KY**	NA
NA	Little Rock, AR**	NA
NA	Livonia, MI**	NA
NA	Longmont, CO**	NA
NA	Louisville, KY**	NA
NA	Nampa, ID**	NA
NA	New Haven, CT**	NA
NA	New Orleans, LA**	NA
NA	Olathe, KS**	NA
NA	Sandy Springs, GA**	NA
NA	Southfield, MI**	NA
NA	Sterling Heights, MI**	NA
NA	Troy, MI**	NA
NA	Vallejo, CA**	NA
NA	Warren, MI**	NA
NA	West Jordan, UT**	NA
NA	Westland, MI**	NA
NA	Wichita, KS**	NA

Source: CQ Press using reported data from the F.B.I. "Crime in the United States 2009"
*Aggravated assault is an attack for the purpose of inflicting severe bodily injury.
**Not available.

65. Property Crimes in 2009
National Total = 9,320,971 Property Crimes*

RANK	CITY	CRIMES
190	Abilene, TX	4,830
87	Akron, OH	10,485
191	Albany, GA	4,788
209	Albany, NY	4,264
28	Albuquerque, NM	29,140
274	Alexandria, VA	3,296
380	Alhambra, CA	1,874
172	Allentown, PA	5,270
397	Allen, TX	1,535
84	Amarillo, TX	11,039
360	Amherst, NY	2,130
115	Anaheim, CA	7,993
90	Anchorage, AK	10,316
302	Ann Arbor, MI	2,950
322	Antioch, CA	2,653
41	Arlington, TX	20,516
320	Arvada, CO	2,696
157	Athens-Clarke, GA	5,644
21	Atlanta, GA	34,349
93	Aurora, CO	10,037
215	Aurora, IL	4,222
11	Austin, TX	48,026
206	Avondale, AZ	4,389
54	Bakersfield, CA	15,605
393	Baldwin Park, CA	1,661
26	Baltimore, MD	29,163
67	Baton Rouge, LA	13,656
142	Beaumont, TX	6,331
394	Beaverton, OR	1,592
227	Bellevue, WA	3,950
207	Bellingham, WA	4,341
368	Bend, OR	2,036
139	Berkeley, CA	6,467
194	Billings, MT	4,597
47	Birmingham, AL	18,159
281	Bloomington, MN	3,235
289	Boca Raton, FL	3,087
156	Boise, ID	5,757
40	Boston, MA	20,749
315	Boulder, CO	2,776
403	Brick Twnshp, NJ	1,382
161	Bridgeport, CT	5,615
283	Brockton, MA	3,207
369	Broken Arrow, OK	2,017
96	Brownsville, TX	9,778
374	Buena Park, CA	1,982
60	Buffalo, NY	14,481
321	Burbank, CA	2,663
285	Cambridge, MA	3,149
229	Camden, NJ	3,935
400	Canton Twnshp, MI	1,506
213	Canton, OH	4,241
214	Cape Coral, FL	4,233
376	Carlsbad, CA	1,908
220	Carrollton, TX	4,061
345	Carson, CA	2,331
371	Cary, NC	2,005
163	Cedar Rapids, IA	5,588
402	Centennial, CO	1,401
124	Chandler, AZ	7,458
223	Charleston, SC	3,991
16	Charlotte, NC	38,533
76	Chattanooga, TN	12,849
331	Cheektowaga, NY	2,570
121	Chesapeake, VA	7,731
3	Chicago, IL	120,407
343	Chico, CA	2,352
361	Chino, CA	2,122
173	Chula Vista, CA	5,263
42	Cincinnati, OH	20,357
252	Citrus Heights, CA	3,627
377	Clarkstown, NY	1,898
199	Clarksville, TN	4,551
192	Clearwater, FL	4,720
33	Cleveland, OH	24,128
390	Clifton, NJ	1,693
347	Clinton Twnshp, MI	2,303
275	Clovis, CA	3,289
278	College Station, TX	3,267
348	Colonie, NY	2,284
57	Colorado Springs, CO	14,723
231	Columbia, MO	3,906
122	Columbia, SC	7,689
58	Columbus, GA	14,684
10	Columbus, OH	48,813
294	Compton, CA	3,051
235	Concord, CA	3,870
304	Coral Springs, FL	2,918
242	Corona, CA	3,810
51	Corpus Christi, TX	16,112
271	Costa Mesa, CA	3,321
366	Cranston, RI	2,077
6	Dallas, TX	71,364
388	Daly City, CA	1,753
396	Danbury, CT	1,536
176	Davenport, IA	5,155
236	Davie, FL	3,869
102	Dayton, OH	8,949
210	Dearborn, MI	4,255
291	Decatur, IL	3,079
277	Denton, TX	3,271
38	Denver, CO	20,879
106	Des Moines, IA	8,688
9	Detroit, MI	50,578
257	Downey, CA	3,575
211	Duluth, MN	4,253
81	Durham, NC	11,763
354	Edison Twnshp, NJ	2,192
386	Edmond, OK	1,762
327	El Cajon, CA	2,609
314	El Monte, CA	2,810
45	El Paso, TX	18,528
349	Elgin, IL	2,244
179	Elizabeth, NJ	5,113
266	Elk Grove, CA	3,443
297	Erie, PA	3,018
233	Escondido, CA	3,880
107	Eugene, OR	8,627
168	Evansville, IN	5,376
131	Everett, WA	6,948
280	Fairfield, CA	3,246
272	Fall River, MA	3,312
284	Fargo, ND	3,187
398	Farmington Hills, MI	1,520
305	Fayetteville, AR	2,908
68	Fayetteville, NC	13,506
200	Federal Way, WA	4,533
140	Flint, MI	6,397
204	Fontana, CA	4,391
196	Fort Collins, CO	4,586
89	Fort Lauderdale, FL	10,374
183	Fort Smith, AR	4,992
98	Fort Wayne, IN	9,379
17	Fort Worth, TX	35,884
184	Fremont, CA	4,978
36	Fresno, CA	21,030
367	Frisco, TX	2,058
240	Fullerton, CA	3,824
141	Gainesville, FL	6,384
273	Garden Grove, CA	3,306
100	Garland, TX	9,098
267	Gary, IN	3,408
197	Gilbert, AZ	4,571
78	Glendale, AZ	12,489
248	Glendale, CA	3,755
118	Grand Prairie, TX	7,948
103	Grand Rapids, MI	8,835
325	Greece, NY	2,612
287	Greeley, CO	3,130
318	Green Bay, WI	2,742
56	Greensboro, NC	15,303
224	Gresham, OR	3,988
391	Hamilton Twnshp, NJ	1,693
249	Hammond, IN	3,754
174	Hampton, VA	5,226
148	Hartford, CT	6,189
365	Hawthorne, CA	2,104
203	Hayward, CA	4,405
175	Henderson, NV	5,171
392	Hesperia, CA	1,673
113	Hialeah, FL	8,213
171	High Point, NC	5,326
378	Hillsboro, OR	1,886
132	Hollywood, FL	6,841
23	Honolulu, HI	33,375
2	Houston, TX	120,933
197	Huntington Beach, CA	4,571
95	Huntsville, AL	9,790
127	Independence, MO	7,165
13	Indianapolis, IN	47,419
313	Indio, CA	2,821
295	Inglewood, CA	3,030
299	Irvine, CA	2,996
111	Irving, TX	8,427
15	Jacksonville, FL	41,781
329	Jacksonville, NC	2,598
70	Jackson, MS	13,182
151	Jersey City, NJ	5,984
234	Joliet, IL	3,878
120	Kansas City, KS	7,742
31	Kansas City, MO	26,695
298	Kenosha, WI	3,017
241	Kent, WA	3,820
164	Killeen, TX	5,513
79	Knoxville, TN	11,821
125	Lafayette, LA	7,451
408	Lake Forest, CA	964
182	Lakeland, FL	5,030
363	Lakewood, CA	2,117
143	Lakewood, CO	6,314
261	Lancaster, CA	3,507
232	Lansing, MI	3,882
66	Laredo, TX	13,725
195	Las Cruces, NM	4,591
12	Las Vegas, NV	47,668
205	Lawrence, KS	4,390
187	Lawton, OK	4,922
355	Lee's Summit, MO	2,179
253	Lewisville, TX	3,619
92	Lexington, KY	10,124
94	Lincoln, NE	10,007
53	Little Rock, AR	15,828
389	Livermore, CA	1,727
352	Livonia, MI	2,232
77	Long Beach, CA	12,643
340	Longmont, CO	2,388

RANK	CITY	CRIMES
165	Longview, TX	5,498
4	Los Angeles, CA	94,240
30	Louisville, KY	26,907
72	Lubbock, TX	13,010
307	Lynn, MA	2,884
128	Macon, GA	7,118
119	Madison, WI	7,884
250	Manchester, NH	3,714
114	McAllen, TX	8,020
270	McKinney, TX	3,339
225	Melbourne, FL	3,980
14	Memphis, TN	47,195
310	Merced, CA	2,850
52	Mesa, AZ	16,079
135	Mesquite, TX	6,739
109	Miami Beach, FL	8,439
146	Miami Gardens, FL	6,231
39	Miami, FL	20,778
230	Midland, TX	3,925
19	Milwaukee, WI	34,791
48	Minneapolis, MN	17,859
256	Miramar, FL	3,591
406	Mission Viejo, CA	1,164
405	Missouri City, TX	1,300
61	Mobile, AL	14,123
91	Modesto, CA	10,269
83	Montgomery, AL	11,065
152	Moreno Valley, CA	5,958
189	Murfreesboro, TN	4,851
399	Murrieta, CA	1,509
373	Nampa, ID	1,996
339	Naperville, IL	2,404
336	Nashua, NH	2,443
27	Nashville, TN	29,156
281	New Bedford, MA	3,235
130	New Haven, CT	7,043
74	New Orleans, LA	12,940
1	New York, NY	142,000
104	Newark, NJ	8,822
350	Newport Beach, CA	2,239
407	Newton, MA	971
74	Norfolk, VA	12,940
246	Norman, OK	3,783
149	North Charleston, SC	6,140
138	North Las Vegas, NV	6,515
358	Norwalk, CA	2,151
384	Norwalk, CT	1,786
43	Oakland, CA	20,173
222	Oceanside, CA	3,995
218	Odessa, TX	4,109
404	O'Fallon, MO	1,323
221	Ogden, UT	4,040
22	Oklahoma City, OK	33,964
327	Olathe, KS	2,609
46	Omaha, NE	18,291
177	Ontario, CA	5,146
323	Orange, CA	2,625
332	Orem, UT	2,520
49	Orlando, FL	17,357
201	Overland Park, KS	4,507
219	Oxnard, CA	4,087
337	Palm Bay, FL	2,426
255	Palmdale, CA	3,598
216	Pasadena, CA	4,158
162	Pasadena, TX	5,610
238	Paterson, NJ	3,836
370	Pearland, TX	2,006
167	Pembroke Pines, FL	5,386

RANK	CITY	CRIMES
188	Peoria, AZ	4,872
170	Peoria, IL	5,333
8	Philadelphia, PA	55,888
7	Phoenix, AZ	65,617
80	Pittsburgh, PA	11,775
115	Plano, TX	7,993
251	Plantation, FL	3,638
217	Pomona, CA	4,134
181	Pompano Beach, FL	5,066
259	Port St. Lucie, FL	3,552
32	Portland, OR	26,495
158	Portsmouth, VA	5,643
117	Providence, RI	7,990
303	Provo, UT	2,919
268	Pueblo, CO	3,392
387	Quincy, MA	1,759
260	Racine, WI	3,521
64	Raleigh, NC	13,817
409	Ramapo, NY	669
247	Rancho Cucamon., CA	3,765
244	Reading, PA	3,788
300	Redding, CA	2,979
105	Reno, NV	8,810
309	Rialto, CA	2,862
257	Richardson, TX	3,575
202	Richmond, CA	4,440
112	Richmond, VA	8,349
385	Rio Rancho, NM	1,774
97	Riverside, CA	9,590
185	Roanoke, VA	4,975
311	Rochester, MN	2,845
85	Rochester, NY	10,991
108	Rockford, IL	8,606
236	Roseville, CA	3,869
344	Roswell, GA	2,349
316	Round Rock, TX	2,772
37	Sacramento, CA	21,001
147	Salem, OR	6,213
186	Salinas, CA	4,966
59	Salt Lake City, UT	14,503
212	San Angelo, TX	4,247
5	San Antonio, TX	91,651
99	San Bernardino, CA	9,245
24	San Diego, CA	32,246
20	San Francisco, CA	34,509
35	San Jose, CA	22,755
265	San Leandro, CA	3,445
401	San Marcos, CA	1,416
356	San Mateo, CA	2,172
301	Sandy Springs, GA	2,975
263	Sandy, UT	3,456
133	Santa Ana, CA	6,798
306	Santa Barbara, CA	2,885
296	Santa Clara, CA	3,028
293	Santa Clarita, CA	3,067
382	Santa Maria, CA	1,826
269	Santa Monica, CA	3,354
208	Santa Rosa, CA	4,265
86	Savannah, GA	10,654
133	Scottsdale, AZ	6,798
18	Seattle, WA	35,090
88	Shreveport, LA	10,425
372	Simi Valley, CA	1,997
312	Sioux City, IA	2,833
193	Sioux Falls, SD	4,609
375	Somerville, MA	1,955
150	South Bend, IN	6,113
330	South Gate, CA	2,571

RANK	CITY	CRIMES
290	Southfield, MI	3,082
288	Sparks, NV	3,105
279	Spokane Valley, WA	3,262
71	Spokane, WA	13,166
126	Springfield, IL	7,181
123	Springfield, MA	7,518
62	Springfield, MO	14,012
359	Stamford, CT	2,143
326	Sterling Heights, MI	2,611
55	Stockton, CA	15,427
395	St. George, UT	1,540
243	St. Joseph, MO	3,794
25	St. Louis, MO	29,595
82	St. Paul, MN	11,431
50	St. Petersburg, FL	17,198
353	Suffolk, VA	2,200
381	Sugar Land, TX	1,854
317	Sunnyvale, CA	2,769
226	Sunrise, FL	3,963
338	Surprise, AZ	2,405
155	Syracuse, NY	5,779
63	Tacoma, WA	13,977
110	Tallahassee, FL	8,438
73	Tampa, FL	12,960
342	Temecula, CA	2,370
101	Tempe, AZ	8,986
239	Thornton, CO	3,832
383	Thousand Oaks, CA	1,793
NA	Toledo, OH**	NA
335	Toms River Twnshp, NJ	2,467
136	Topeka, KS	6,702
308	Torrance, CA	2,874
333	Tracy, CA	2,507
324	Trenton, NJ	2,624
379	Troy, MI	1,880
NA	Tucson, AZ**	NA
34	Tulsa, OK	23,220
180	Tuscaloosa, AL	5,082
154	Tyler, TX	5,835
357	Upper Darby Twnshp, PA	2,154
361	Vacaville, CA	2,122
166	Vallejo, CA	5,478
153	Vancouver, WA	5,944
292	Ventura, CA	3,068
228	Victorville, CA	3,939
69	Virginia Beach, VA	13,359
178	Visalia, CA	5,135
351	Vista, CA	2,238
129	Waco, TX	7,110
245	Warren, MI	3,785
319	Warwick, RI	2,725
29	Washington, DC	27,007
159	Waterbury, CT	5,635
276	West Covina, CA	3,282
254	West Jordan, UT	3,617
169	West Palm Beach, FL	5,365
144	West Valley, UT	6,263
334	Westland, MI	2,489
345	Westminster, CA	2,331
264	Westminster, CO	3,446
364	Whittier, CA	2,105
160	Wichita Falls, TX	5,618
44	Wichita, KS	19,597
145	Wilmington, NC	6,236
65	Winston-Salem, NC	13,788
341	Woodbridge Twnshp, NJ	2,377
137	Worcester, MA	6,691
286	Yonkers, NY	3,145
262	Yuma, AZ	3,471

Source: Reported data from the F.B.I. "Crime in the United States 2009"

*Property crimes are offenses of burglary, larceny-theft, and motor vehicle theft. Attempts are included.

65. Property Crimes in 2009 (continued)
National Total = 9,320,971 Property Crimes*

RANK	CITY	CRIMES
1	New York, NY	142,000
2	Houston, TX	120,933
3	Chicago, IL	120,407
4	Los Angeles, CA	94,240
5	San Antonio, TX	91,651
6	Dallas, TX	71,364
7	Phoenix, AZ	65,617
8	Philadelphia, PA	55,888
9	Detroit, MI	50,578
10	Columbus, OH	48,813
11	Austin, TX	48,026
12	Las Vegas, NV	47,668
13	Indianapolis, IN	47,419
14	Memphis, TN	47,195
15	Jacksonville, FL	41,781
16	Charlotte, NC	38,533
17	Fort Worth, TX	35,884
18	Seattle, WA	35,090
19	Milwaukee, WI	34,791
20	San Francisco, CA	34,509
21	Atlanta, GA	34,349
22	Oklahoma City, OK	33,964
23	Honolulu, HI	33,375
24	San Diego, CA	32,246
25	St. Louis, MO	29,595
26	Baltimore, MD	29,163
27	Nashville, TN	29,156
28	Albuquerque, NM	29,140
29	Washington, DC	27,007
30	Louisville, KY	26,907
31	Kansas City, MO	26,695
32	Portland, OR	26,495
33	Cleveland, OH	24,128
34	Tulsa, OK	23,220
35	San Jose, CA	22,755
36	Fresno, CA	21,030
37	Sacramento, CA	21,001
38	Denver, CO	20,879
39	Miami, FL	20,778
40	Boston, MA	20,749
41	Arlington, TX	20,516
42	Cincinnati, OH	20,357
43	Oakland, CA	20,173
44	Wichita, KS	19,597
45	El Paso, TX	18,528
46	Omaha, NE	18,291
47	Birmingham, AL	18,159
48	Minneapolis, MN	17,859
49	Orlando, FL	17,357
50	St. Petersburg, FL	17,198
51	Corpus Christi, TX	16,112
52	Mesa, AZ	16,079
53	Little Rock, AR	15,828
54	Bakersfield, CA	15,605
55	Stockton, CA	15,427
56	Greensboro, NC	15,303
57	Colorado Springs, CO	14,723
58	Columbus, GA	14,684
59	Salt Lake City, UT	14,503
60	Buffalo, NY	14,481
61	Mobile, AL	14,123
62	Springfield, MO	14,012
63	Tacoma, WA	13,977
64	Raleigh, NC	13,817
65	Winston-Salem, NC	13,788
66	Laredo, TX	13,725
67	Baton Rouge, LA	13,656
68	Fayetteville, NC	13,506

RANK	CITY	CRIMES
69	Virginia Beach, VA	13,359
70	Jackson, MS	13,182
71	Spokane, WA	13,166
72	Lubbock, TX	13,010
73	Tampa, FL	12,960
74	New Orleans, LA	12,940
74	Norfolk, VA	12,940
76	Chattanooga, TN	12,849
77	Long Beach, CA	12,643
78	Glendale, AZ	12,489
79	Knoxville, TN	11,821
80	Pittsburgh, PA	11,775
81	Durham, NC	11,763
82	St. Paul, MN	11,431
83	Montgomery, AL	11,065
84	Amarillo, TX	11,039
85	Rochester, NY	10,991
86	Savannah, GA	10,654
87	Akron, OH	10,485
88	Shreveport, LA	10,425
89	Fort Lauderdale, FL	10,374
90	Anchorage, AK	10,316
91	Modesto, CA	10,269
92	Lexington, KY	10,124
93	Aurora, CO	10,037
94	Lincoln, NE	10,007
95	Huntsville, AL	9,790
96	Brownsville, TX	9,778
97	Riverside, CA	9,590
98	Fort Wayne, IN	9,379
99	San Bernardino, CA	9,245
100	Garland, TX	9,098
101	Tempe, AZ	8,986
102	Dayton, OH	8,949
103	Grand Rapids, MI	8,835
104	Newark, NJ	8,822
105	Reno, NV	8,810
106	Des Moines, IA	8,688
107	Eugene, OR	8,627
108	Rockford, IL	8,606
109	Miami Beach, FL	8,439
110	Tallahassee, FL	8,438
111	Irving, TX	8,427
112	Richmond, VA	8,349
113	Hialeah, FL	8,213
114	McAllen, TX	8,020
115	Anaheim, CA	7,993
115	Plano, TX	7,993
117	Providence, RI	7,990
118	Grand Prairie, TX	7,948
119	Madison, WI	7,884
120	Kansas City, KS	7,742
121	Chesapeake, VA	7,731
122	Columbia, SC	7,689
123	Springfield, MA	7,518
124	Chandler, AZ	7,458
125	Lafayette, LA	7,451
126	Springfield, IL	7,181
127	Independence, MO	7,165
128	Macon, GA	7,118
129	Waco, TX	7,110
130	New Haven, CT	7,043
131	Everett, WA	6,948
132	Hollywood, FL	6,841
133	Santa Ana, CA	6,798
133	Scottsdale, AZ	6,798
135	Mesquite, TX	6,739
136	Topeka, KS	6,702
137	Worcester, MA	6,691

RANK	CITY	CRIMES
138	North Las Vegas, NV	6,515
139	Berkeley, CA	6,467
140	Flint, MI	6,397
141	Gainesville, FL	6,384
142	Beaumont, TX	6,331
143	Lakewood, CO	6,314
144	West Valley, UT	6,263
145	Wilmington, NC	6,236
146	Miami Gardens, FL	6,231
147	Salem, OR	6,213
148	Hartford, CT	6,189
149	North Charleston, SC	6,140
150	South Bend, IN	6,113
151	Jersey City, NJ	5,984
152	Moreno Valley, CA	5,958
153	Vancouver, WA	5,944
154	Tyler, TX	5,835
155	Syracuse, NY	5,779
156	Boise, ID	5,757
157	Athens-Clarke, GA	5,644
158	Portsmouth, VA	5,643
159	Waterbury, CT	5,635
160	Wichita Falls, TX	5,618
161	Bridgeport, CT	5,615
162	Pasadena, TX	5,610
163	Cedar Rapids, IA	5,588
164	Killeen, TX	5,513
165	Longview, TX	5,498
166	Vallejo, CA	5,478
167	Pembroke Pines, FL	5,386
168	Evansville, IN	5,376
169	West Palm Beach, FL	5,365
170	Peoria, IL	5,333
171	High Point, NC	5,326
172	Allentown, PA	5,270
173	Chula Vista, CA	5,263
174	Hampton, VA	5,226
175	Henderson, NV	5,171
176	Davenport, IA	5,155
177	Ontario, CA	5,146
178	Visalia, CA	5,135
179	Elizabeth, NJ	5,113
180	Tuscaloosa, AL	5,082
181	Pompano Beach, FL	5,066
182	Lakeland, FL	5,030
183	Fort Smith, AR	4,992
184	Fremont, CA	4,978
185	Roanoke, VA	4,975
186	Salinas, CA	4,966
187	Lawton, OK	4,922
188	Peoria, AZ	4,872
189	Murfreesboro, TN	4,851
190	Abilene, TX	4,830
191	Albany, GA	4,788
192	Clearwater, FL	4,720
193	Sioux Falls, SD	4,609
194	Billings, MT	4,597
195	Las Cruces, NM	4,591
196	Fort Collins, CO	4,586
197	Gilbert, AZ	4,571
197	Huntington Beach, CA	4,571
199	Clarksville, TN	4,551
200	Federal Way, WA	4,533
201	Overland Park, KS	4,507
202	Richmond, CA	4,440
203	Hayward, CA	4,405
204	Fontana, CA	4,391
205	Lawrence, KS	4,390
206	Avondale, AZ	4,389

RANK	CITY	CRIMES
207	Bellingham, WA	4,341
208	Santa Rosa, CA	4,265
209	Albany, NY	4,264
210	Dearborn, MI	4,255
211	Duluth, MN	4,253
212	San Angelo, TX	4,247
213	Canton, OH	4,241
214	Cape Coral, FL	4,233
215	Aurora, IL	4,222
216	Pasadena, CA	4,158
217	Pomona, CA	4,134
218	Odessa, TX	4,109
219	Oxnard, CA	4,087
220	Carrollton, TX	4,061
221	Ogden, UT	4,040
222	Oceanside, CA	3,995
223	Charleston, SC	3,991
224	Gresham, OR	3,988
225	Melbourne, FL	3,980
226	Sunrise, FL	3,963
227	Bellevue, WA	3,950
228	Victorville, CA	3,939
229	Camden, NJ	3,935
230	Midland, TX	3,925
231	Columbia, MO	3,906
232	Lansing, MI	3,882
233	Escondido, CA	3,880
234	Joliet, IL	3,878
235	Concord, CA	3,870
236	Davie, FL	3,869
236	Roseville, CA	3,869
238	Paterson, NJ	3,836
239	Thornton, CO	3,832
240	Fullerton, CA	3,824
241	Kent, WA	3,820
242	Corona, CA	3,810
243	St. Joseph, MO	3,794
244	Reading, PA	3,788
245	Warren, MI	3,785
246	Norman, OK	3,783
247	Rancho Cucamon., CA	3,765
248	Glendale, CA	3,755
249	Hammond, IN	3,754
250	Manchester, NH	3,714
251	Plantation, FL	3,638
252	Citrus Heights, CA	3,627
253	Lewisville, TX	3,619
254	West Jordan, UT	3,617
255	Palmdale, CA	3,598
256	Miramar, FL	3,591
257	Downey, CA	3,575
257	Richardson, TX	3,575
259	Port St. Lucie, FL	3,552
260	Racine, WI	3,521
261	Lancaster, CA	3,507
262	Yuma, AZ	3,471
263	Sandy, UT	3,456
264	Westminster, CO	3,446
265	San Leandro, CA	3,445
266	Elk Grove, CA	3,443
267	Gary, IN	3,408
268	Pueblo, CO	3,392
269	Santa Monica, CA	3,354
270	McKinney, TX	3,339
271	Costa Mesa, CA	3,321
272	Fall River, MA	3,312
273	Garden Grove, CA	3,306
274	Alexandria, VA	3,296
275	Clovis, CA	3,289
276	West Covina, CA	3,282
277	Denton, TX	3,271
278	College Station, TX	3,267
279	Spokane Valley, WA	3,262
280	Fairfield, CA	3,246
281	Bloomington, MN	3,235
281	New Bedford, MA	3,235
283	Brockton, MA	3,207
284	Fargo, ND	3,187
285	Cambridge, MA	3,149
286	Yonkers, NY	3,145
287	Greeley, CO	3,130
288	Sparks, NV	3,105
289	Boca Raton, FL	3,087
290	Southfield, MI	3,082
291	Decatur, IL	3,079
292	Ventura, CA	3,068
293	Santa Clarita, CA	3,067
294	Compton, CA	3,051
295	Inglewood, CA	3,030
296	Santa Clara, CA	3,028
297	Erie, PA	3,018
298	Kenosha, WI	3,017
299	Irvine, CA	2,996
300	Redding, CA	2,979
301	Sandy Springs, GA	2,975
302	Ann Arbor, MI	2,950
303	Provo, UT	2,919
304	Coral Springs, FL	2,918
305	Fayetteville, AR	2,908
306	Santa Barbara, CA	2,885
307	Lynn, MA	2,884
308	Torrance, CA	2,874
309	Rialto, CA	2,862
310	Merced, CA	2,850
311	Rochester, MN	2,845
312	Sioux City, IA	2,833
313	Indio, CA	2,821
314	El Monte, CA	2,810
315	Boulder, CO	2,776
316	Round Rock, TX	2,772
317	Sunnyvale, CA	2,769
318	Green Bay, WI	2,742
319	Warwick, RI	2,725
320	Arvada, CO	2,696
321	Burbank, CA	2,663
322	Antioch, CA	2,653
323	Orange, CA	2,625
324	Trenton, NJ	2,624
325	Greece, NY	2,612
326	Sterling Heights, MI	2,611
327	El Cajon, CA	2,609
327	Olathe, KS	2,609
329	Jacksonville, NC	2,598
330	South Gate, CA	2,571
331	Cheektowaga, NY	2,570
332	Orem, UT	2,520
333	Tracy, CA	2,507
334	Westland, MI	2,489
335	Toms River Twnshp, NJ	2,467
336	Nashua, NH	2,443
337	Palm Bay, FL	2,426
338	Surprise, AZ	2,405
339	Naperville, IL	2,404
340	Longmont, CO	2,388
341	Woodbridge Twnshp, NJ	2,377
342	Temecula, CA	2,370
343	Chico, CA	2,352
344	Roswell, GA	2,349
345	Carson, CA	2,331
345	Westminster, CA	2,331
347	Clinton Twnshp, MI	2,303
348	Colonie, NY	2,284
349	Elgin, IL	2,244
350	Newport Beach, CA	2,239
351	Vista, CA	2,238
352	Livonia, MI	2,232
353	Suffolk, VA	2,200
354	Edison Twnshp, NJ	2,192
355	Lee's Summit, MO	2,179
356	San Mateo, CA	2,172
357	Upper Darby Twnshp, PA	2,154
358	Norwalk, CA	2,151
359	Stamford, CT	2,143
360	Amherst, NY	2,130
361	Chino, CA	2,122
361	Vacaville, CA	2,122
363	Lakewood, CA	2,117
364	Whittier, CA	2,105
365	Hawthorne, CA	2,104
366	Cranston, RI	2,077
367	Frisco, TX	2,058
368	Bend, OR	2,036
369	Broken Arrow, OK	2,017
370	Pearland, TX	2,006
371	Cary, NC	2,005
372	Simi Valley, CA	1,997
373	Nampa, ID	1,996
374	Buena Park, CA	1,982
375	Somerville, MA	1,955
376	Carlsbad, CA	1,908
377	Clarkstown, NY	1,898
378	Hillsboro, OR	1,886
379	Troy, MI	1,880
380	Alhambra, CA	1,874
381	Sugar Land, TX	1,854
382	Santa Maria, CA	1,826
383	Thousand Oaks, CA	1,793
384	Norwalk, CT	1,786
385	Rio Rancho, NM	1,774
386	Edmond, OK	1,762
387	Quincy, MA	1,759
388	Daly City, CA	1,753
389	Livermore, CA	1,727
390	Clifton, NJ	1,693
391	Hamilton Twnshp, NJ	1,693
392	Hesperia, CA	1,673
393	Baldwin Park, CA	1,661
394	Beaverton, OR	1,592
395	St. George, UT	1,540
396	Danbury, CT	1,536
397	Allen, TX	1,535
398	Farmington Hills, MI	1,520
399	Murrieta, CA	1,509
400	Canton Twnshp, MI	1,506
401	San Marcos, CA	1,416
402	Centennial, CO	1,401
403	Brick Twnshp, NJ	1,382
404	O'Fallon, MO	1,323
405	Missouri City, TX	1,300
406	Mission Viejo, CA	1,164
407	Newton, MA	971
408	Lake Forest, CA	964
409	Ramapo, NY	669
NA	Toledo, OH**	NA
NA	Tucson, AZ**	NA

Source: Reported data from the F.B.I. "Crime in the United States 2009"
*Property crimes are offenses of burglary, larceny-theft, and motor vehicle theft. Attempts are included.

66. Property Crime Rate in 2009
National Rate = 3,036.1 Property Crimes per 100,000 Population*

RANK	CITY	RATE
160	Abilene, TX	4,143.9
94	Akron, OH	5,077.6
25	Albany, GA	6,322.1
137	Albany, NY	4,563.1
67	Albuquerque, NM	5,491.5
350	Alexandria, VA	2,255.3
354	Alhambra, CA	2,180.2
113	Allentown, PA	4,910.3
390	Allen, TX	1,766.4
44	Amarillo, TX	5,848.0
379	Amherst, NY	1,929.4
335	Anaheim, CA	2,379.1
193	Anchorage, AK	3,641.4
304	Ann Arbor, MI	2,579.4
298	Antioch, CA	2,620.4
76	Arlington, TX	5,411.7
317	Arvada, CO	2,497.6
112	Athens-Clarke, GA	4,927.5
27	Atlanta, GA	6,212.5
252	Aurora, CO	3,097.7
330	Aurora, IL	2,410.7
26	Austin, TX	6,245.5
110	Avondale, AZ	4,944.1
125	Bakersfield, CA	4,716.0
359	Baldwin Park, CA	2,142.1
136	Baltimore, MD	4,565.6
29	Baton Rouge, LA	6,118.6
49	Beaumont, TX	5,743.1
394	Beaverton, OR	1,707.8
248	Bellevue, WA	3,158.6
77	Bellingham, WA	5,409.8
311	Bend, OR	2,527.6
23	Berkeley, CA	6,390.9
147	Billings, MT	4,360.4
6	Birmingham, AL	7,986.4
171	Bloomington, MN	4,000.5
200	Boca Raton, FL	3,591.4
281	Boise, ID	2,788.7
229	Boston, MA	3,324.0
283	Boulder, CO	2,775.0
391	Brick Twnshp, NJ	1,756.8
163	Bridgeport, CT	4,127.2
228	Brockton, MA	3,324.3
360	Broken Arrow, OK	2,136.3
73	Brownsville, TX	5,447.6
319	Buena Park, CA	2,492.3
78	Buffalo, NY	5,390.2
305	Burbank, CA	2,579.2
256	Cambridge, MA	3,061.3
104	Camden, NJ	4,982.3
386	Canton Twnshp, MI	1,822.5
74	Canton, OH	5,431.3
306	Cape Coral, FL	2,575.7
378	Carlsbad, CA	1,937.4
243	Carrollton, TX	3,186.8
313	Carson, CA	2,516.3
401	Cary, NC	1,499.0
149	Cedar Rapids, IA	4,339.2
404	Centennial, CO	1,409.7
266	Chandler, AZ	2,912.2
204	Charleston, SC	3,510.7
109	Charlotte, NC	4,954.7
11	Chattanooga, TN	7,447.1
234	Cheektowaga, NY	3,304.5
208	Chesapeake, VA	3,462.8
156	Chicago, IL	4,227.1
282	Chico, CA	2,776.1
315	Chino, CA	2,507.5
343	Chula Vista, CA	2,340.8
30	Cincinnati, OH	6,102.8
151	Citrus Heights, CA	4,300.8
331	Clarkstown, NY	2,405.6
188	Clarksville, TN	3,740.7
141	Clearwater, FL	4,478.9
57	Cleveland, OH	5,621.1
356	Clifton, NJ	2,167.1
332	Clinton Twnshp, MI	2,400.1
212	Clovis, CA	3,453.8
183	College Station, TX	3,795.7
265	Colonie, NY	2,928.1
192	Colorado Springs, CO	3,665.8
181	Columbia, MO	3,807.5
37	Columbia, SC	6,012.5
7	Columbus, GA	7,885.1
21	Columbus, OH	6,427.9
237	Compton, CA	3,250.2
242	Concord, CA	3,197.2
344	Coral Springs, FL	2,322.2
316	Corona, CA	2,499.4
58	Corpus Christi, TX	5,604.0
259	Costa Mesa, CA	3,015.0
303	Cranston, RI	2,589.0
64	Dallas, TX	5,531.0
392	Daly City, CA	1,730.8
380	Danbury, CT	1,926.5
93	Davenport, IA	5,098.1
152	Davie, FL	4,291.9
43	Dayton, OH	5,850.4
102	Dearborn, MI	4,988.0
170	Decatur, IL	4,070.0
297	Denton, TX	2,631.4
213	Denver, CO	3,452.9
145	Des Moines, IA	4,414.8
61	Detroit, MI	5,567.6
230	Downey, CA	3,322.6
97	Duluth, MN	5,058.8
89	Durham, NC	5,170.7
352	Edison Twnshp, NJ	2,206.2
355	Edmond, OK	2,178.3
276	El Cajon, CA	2,821.6
347	El Monte, CA	2,295.2
260	El Paso, TX	2,994.1
368	Elgin, IL	2,083.8
168	Elizabeth, NJ	4,093.3
326	Elk Grove, CA	2,449.2
267	Erie, PA	2,906.5
274	Escondido, CA	2,823.2
52	Eugene, OR	5,698.8
130	Evansville, IN	4,643.7
16	Everett, WA	7,058.8
250	Fairfield, CA	3,106.9
198	Fall River, MA	3,603.9
220	Fargo, ND	3,396.6
377	Farmington Hills, MI	1,945.2
177	Fayetteville, AR	3,871.1
8	Fayetteville, NC	7,762.3
79	Federal Way, WA	5,382.4
51	Flint, MI	5,729.2
345	Fontana, CA	2,307.4
232	Fort Collins, CO	3,311.5
55	Fort Lauderdale, FL	5,670.6
42	Fort Smith, AR	5,860.9
189	Fort Wayne, IN	3,728.0
107	Fort Worth, TX	4,960.1
323	Fremont, CA	2,455.7
146	Fresno, CA	4,368.8
383	Frisco, TX	1,901.3
269	Fullerton, CA	2,886.5
63	Gainesville, FL	5,538.5
373	Garden Grove, CA	1,993.5
159	Garland, TX	4,156.8
202	Gary, IN	3,579.1
375	Gilbert, AZ	1,972.0
115	Glendale, AZ	4,896.1
382	Glendale, CA	1,902.4
120	Grand Prairie, TX	4,823.8
134	Grand Rapids, MI	4,580.1
279	Greece, NY	2,800.4
224	Greeley, CO	3,363.1
289	Green Bay, WI	2,719.3
35	Greensboro, NC	6,044.1
176	Gresham, OR	3,892.1
385	Hamilton Twnshp, NJ	1,870.9
111	Hammond, IN	4,934.0
201	Hampton, VA	3,581.1
101	Hartford, CT	4,989.2
318	Hawthorne, CA	2,495.4
253	Hayward, CA	3,097.2
374	Henderson, NV	1,974.5
384	Hesperia, CA	1,881.8
175	Hialeah, FL	3,932.0
91	High Point, NC	5,137.2
376	Hillsboro, OR	1,953.1
119	Hollywood, FL	4,831.3
191	Honolulu, HI	3,679.2
85	Houston, TX	5,318.6
336	Huntington Beach, CA	2,369.5
68	Huntsville, AL	5,481.5
41	Independence, MO	5,864.6
46	Indianapolis, IN	5,829.2
249	Indio, CA	3,153.4
292	Inglewood, CA	2,688.3
405	Irvine, CA	1,389.1
158	Irving, TX	4,162.6
90	Jacksonville, FL	5,157.7
227	Jacksonville, NC	3,351.9
10	Jackson, MS	7,628.5
320	Jersey City, NJ	2,484.5
307	Joliet, IL	2,566.5
72	Kansas City, KS	5,448.2
65	Kansas City, MO	5,507.7
254	Kenosha, WI	3,089.4
138	Kent, WA	4,528.1
135	Killeen, TX	4,568.7
24	Knoxville, TN	6,360.5
19	Lafayette, LA	6,543.5
406	Lake Forest, CA	1,276.7
82	Lakeland, FL	5,332.8
290	Lakewood, CA	2,702.5
140	Lakewood, CO	4,490.2
337	Lancaster, CA	2,357.8
215	Lansing, MI	3,423.5
34	Laredo, TX	6,047.7
116	Las Cruces, NM	4,882.8
209	Las Vegas, NV	3,461.0
121	Lawrence, KS	4,787.2
69	Lawton, OK	5,478.9
310	Lee's Summit, MO	2,539.9
210	Lewisville, TX	3,459.8
217	Lexington, KY	3,415.6
174	Lincoln, NE	3,933.0
4	Little Rock, AR	8,321.5
361	Livermore, CA	2,134.3
321	Livonia, MI	2,473.6
287	Long Beach, CA	2,725.0
285	Longmont, CO	2,725.7

RANK	CITY	RATE	RANK	CITY	RATE	RANK	CITY	RATE
13	Longview, TX	7,079.3	262	Peoria, AZ	2,964.1	167	Southfield, MI	4,105.3
327	Los Angeles, CA	2,448.6	127	Peoria, IL	4,668.2	221	Sparks, NV	3,396.4
154	Louisville, KY	4,262.4	196	Philadelphia, PA	3,611.3	185	Spokane Valley, WA	3,760.0
45	Lubbock, TX	5,837.1	166	Phoenix, AZ	4,107.7	20	Spokane, WA	6,487.9
246	Lynn, MA	3,164.1	184	Pittsburgh, PA	3,771.2	32	Springfield, IL	6,087.0
9	Macon, GA	7,711.9	264	Plano, TX	2,930.6	114	Springfield, MA	4,896.7
225	Madison, WI	3,362.6	148	Plantation, FL	4,354.6	2	Springfield, MO	8,944.3
216	Manchester, NH	3,417.7	291	Pomona, CA	2,698.1	388	Stamford, CT	1,793.2
33	McAllen, TX	6,048.4	105	Pompano Beach, FL	4,974.5	369	Sterling Heights, MI	2,048.8
312	McKinney, TX	2,526.8	357	Port St. Lucie, FL	2,164.9	86	Stockton, CA	5,279.4
92	Melbourne, FL	5,112.1	124	Portland, OR	4,723.6	370	St. George, UT	2,042.7
15	Memphis, TN	7,071.2	59	Portsmouth, VA	5,588.8	106	St. Joseph, MO	4,963.6
195	Merced, CA	3,621.7	129	Providence, RI	4,654.4	3	St. Louis, MO	8,331.7
218	Mesa, AZ	3,415.0	328	Provo, UT	2,443.3	169	St. Paul, MN	4,079.7
95	Mesquite, TX	5,069.2	239	Pueblo, CO	3,222.2	17	St. Petersburg, FL	7,021.5
1	Miami Beach, FL	10,015.4	387	Quincy, MA	1,821.3	302	Suffolk, VA	2,590.4
56	Miami Gardens, FL	5,646.8	153	Racine, WI	4,281.8	351	Sugar Land, TX	2,241.9
108	Miami, FL	4,956.5	219	Raleigh, NC	3,403.2	365	Sunnyvale, CA	2,095.4
194	Midland, TX	3,636.5	409	Ramapo, NY	873.2	143	Sunrise, FL	4,456.0
48	Milwaukee, WI	5,753.7	362	Rancho Cucamon., CA	2,131.0	346	Surprise, AZ	2,297.2
128	Minneapolis, MN	4,667.6	126	Reading, PA	4,710.4	157	Syracuse, NY	4,211.9
231	Miramar, FL	3,313.5	235	Redding, CA	3,264.9	14	Tacoma, WA	7,074.9
407	Mission Viejo, CA	1,231.1	173	Reno, NV	3,986.2	118	Tallahassee, FL	4,844.3
396	Missouri City, TX	1,676.5	271	Rialto, CA	2,879.7	186	Tampa, FL	3,754.0
50	Mobile, AL	5,737.1	207	Richardson, TX	3,481.9	339	Temecula, CA	2,348.3
99	Modesto, CA	5,022.2	150	Richmond, CA	4,328.9	96	Tempe, AZ	5,062.9
70	Montgomery, AL	5,455.6	165	Richmond, VA	4,108.1	236	Thornton, CO	3,263.6
258	Moreno Valley, CA	3,022.6	363	Rio Rancho, NM	2,126.7	402	Thousand Oaks, CA	1,449.1
133	Murfreesboro, TN	4,580.3	241	Riverside, CA	3,198.0	NA	Toledo, OH**	NA
403	Murrieta, CA	1,433.9	81	Roanoke, VA	5,343.1	309	Toms River Twnshp, NJ	2,553.5
334	Nampa, ID	2,379.7	280	Rochester, MN	2,792.4	75	Topeka, KS	5,429.0
397	Naperville, IL	1,661.0	80	Rochester, NY	5,347.5	371	Torrance, CA	2,036.7
275	Nashua, NH	2,822.5	71	Rockford, IL	5,448.8	257	Tracy, CA	3,056.6
123	Nashville, TN	4,778.3	233	Roseville, CA	3,311.2	245	Trenton, NJ	3,176.4
206	New Bedford, MA	3,492.7	295	Roswell, GA	2,658.1	340	Troy, MI	2,344.7
53	New Haven, CT	5,695.5	314	Round Rock, TX	2,507.9	NA	Tucson, AZ**	NA
178	New Orleans, LA	3,846.3	142	Sacramento, CA	4,465.4	36	Tulsa, OK	6,033.5
395	New York, NY	1,690.3	172	Salem, OR	3,999.9	62	Tuscaloosa, AL	5,542.7
247	Newark, NJ	3,159.7	211	Salinas, CA	3,456.8	40	Tyler, TX	5,877.4
277	Newport Beach, CA	2,801.8	5	Salt Lake City, UT	8,024.9	284	Upper Darby Twnshp, PA	2,758.4
408	Newton, MA	1,150.1	132	San Angelo, TX	4,602.8	348	Vacaville, CA	2,293.1
66	Norfolk, VA	5,504.1	18	San Antonio, TX	6,670.7	122	Vallejo, CA	4,786.7
205	Norman, OK	3,497.9	131	San Bernardino, CA	4,629.8	199	Vancouver, WA	3,599.2
22	North Charleston, SC	6,397.0	324	San Diego, CA	2,452.6	263	Ventura, CA	2,950.1
278	North Las Vegas, NV	2,800.6	155	San Francisco, CA	4,261.7	226	Victorville, CA	3,362.4
366	Norwalk, CA	2,092.3	333	San Jose, CA	2,385.2	255	Virginia Beach, VA	3,062.8
358	Norwalk, CT	2,146.7	144	San Leandro, CA	4,435.1	161	Visalia, CA	4,132.4
103	Oakland, CA	4,986.5	393	San Marcos, CA	1,721.4	325	Vista, CA	2,452.5
342	Oceanside, CA	2,342.0	338	San Mateo, CA	2,355.5	54	Waco, TX	5,683.5
164	Odessa, TX	4,118.5	197	Sandy Springs, GA	3,608.9	273	Warren, MI	2,835.5
399	O'Fallon, MO	1,642.9	203	Sandy, UT	3,561.7	238	Warwick, RI	3,225.3
117	Ogden, UT	4,866.5	372	Santa Ana, CA	2,004.2	139	Washington, DC	4,503.7
31	Oklahoma City, OK	6,098.3	223	Santa Barbara, CA	3,365.8	87	Waterbury, CT	5,266.0
364	Olathe, KS	2,115.6	286	Santa Clara, CA	2,725.3	251	West Covina, CA	3,100.7
162	Omaha, NE	4,128.5	389	Santa Clarita, CA	1,792.4	222	West Jordan, UT	3,376.8
261	Ontario, CA	2,970.9	367	Santa Maria, CA	2,089.7	84	West Palm Beach, FL	5,324.4
381	Orange, CA	1,914.2	180	Santa Monica, CA	3,809.7	98	West Valley, UT	5,031.7
293	Orem, UT	2,687.0	288	Santa Rosa, CA	2,724.5	244	Westland, MI	3,184.9
12	Orlando, FL	7,382.5	100	Savannah, GA	5,008.7	299	Westminster, CA	2,617.4
301	Overland Park, KS	2,594.9	272	Scottsdale, AZ	2,843.0	240	Westminster, CO	3,199.5
353	Oxnard, CA	2,181.4	47	Seattle, WA	5,823.8	308	Whittier, CA	2,564.1
341	Palm Bay, FL	2,344.5	88	Shreveport, LA	5,222.2	60	Wichita Falls, TX	5,568.8
322	Palmdale, CA	2,458.0	398	Simi Valley, CA	1,643.1	83	Wichita, KS	5,330.6
270	Pasadena, CA	2,886.2	214	Sioux City, IA	3,430.9	28	Wilmington, NC	6,147.6
179	Pasadena, TX	3,817.3	268	Sioux Falls, SD	2,904.7	38	Winston-Salem, NC	5,969.4
296	Paterson, NJ	2,646.6	300	Somerville, MA	2,602.8	329	Woodbridge Twnshp, NJ	2,425.2
349	Pearland, TX	2,265.9	39	South Bend, IN	5,916.2	187	Worcester, MA	3,749.0
190	Pembroke Pines, FL	3,701.4	294	South Gate, CA	2,660.1	400	Yonkers, NY	1,555.5
						182	Yuma, AZ	3,796.2

Source: CQ Press using reported data from the F.B.I. "Crime in the United States 2009"

*Property crimes are offenses of burglary, larceny-theft, and motor vehicle theft. Attempts are included.

**Not available.

66. Property Crime Rate in 2009 (continued)
National Rate = 3,036.1 Property Crimes per 100,000 Population*

RANK	CITY	RATE
1	Miami Beach, FL	10,015.4
2	Springfield, MO	8,944.3
3	St. Louis, MO	8,331.7
4	Little Rock, AR	8,321.5
5	Salt Lake City, UT	8,024.9
6	Birmingham, AL	7,986.4
7	Columbus, GA	7,885.1
8	Fayetteville, NC	7,762.3
9	Macon, GA	7,711.9
10	Jackson, MS	7,628.5
11	Chattanooga, TN	7,447.1
12	Orlando, FL	7,382.5
13	Longview, TX	7,079.3
14	Tacoma, WA	7,074.9
15	Memphis, TN	7,071.2
16	Everett, WA	7,058.8
17	St. Petersburg, FL	7,021.5
18	San Antonio, TX	6,670.7
19	Lafayette, LA	6,543.5
20	Spokane, WA	6,487.9
21	Columbus, OH	6,427.9
22	North Charleston, SC	6,397.0
23	Berkeley, CA	6,390.9
24	Knoxville, TN	6,360.5
25	Albany, GA	6,322.1
26	Austin, TX	6,245.5
27	Atlanta, GA	6,212.5
28	Wilmington, NC	6,147.6
29	Baton Rouge, LA	6,118.6
30	Cincinnati, OH	6,102.8
31	Oklahoma City, OK	6,098.3
32	Springfield, IL	6,087.0
33	McAllen, TX	6,048.4
34	Laredo, TX	6,047.7
35	Greensboro, NC	6,044.1
36	Tulsa, OK	6,033.5
37	Columbia, SC	6,012.5
38	Winston-Salem, NC	5,969.4
39	South Bend, IN	5,916.2
40	Tyler, TX	5,877.4
41	Independence, MO	5,864.6
42	Fort Smith, AR	5,860.9
43	Dayton, OH	5,850.4
44	Amarillo, TX	5,848.0
45	Lubbock, TX	5,837.1
46	Indianapolis, IN	5,829.2
47	Seattle, WA	5,823.8
48	Milwaukee, WI	5,753.7
49	Beaumont, TX	5,743.1
50	Mobile, AL	5,737.1
51	Flint, MI	5,729.2
52	Eugene, OR	5,698.8
53	New Haven, CT	5,695.5
54	Waco, TX	5,683.5
55	Fort Lauderdale, FL	5,670.6
56	Miami Gardens, FL	5,646.8
57	Cleveland, OH	5,621.1
58	Corpus Christi, TX	5,604.0
59	Portsmouth, VA	5,588.8
60	Wichita Falls, TX	5,568.8
61	Detroit, MI	5,567.6
62	Tuscaloosa, AL	5,542.7
63	Gainesville, FL	5,538.5
64	Dallas, TX	5,531.0
65	Kansas City, MO	5,507.7
66	Norfolk, VA	5,504.1
67	Albuquerque, NM	5,491.5
68	Huntsville, AL	5,481.5
69	Lawton, OK	5,478.9
70	Montgomery, AL	5,455.6
71	Rockford, IL	5,448.8
72	Kansas City, KS	5,448.2
73	Brownsville, TX	5,447.6
74	Canton, OH	5,431.3
75	Topeka, KS	5,429.0
76	Arlington, TX	5,411.7
77	Bellingham, WA	5,409.8
78	Buffalo, NY	5,390.2
79	Federal Way, WA	5,382.4
80	Rochester, NY	5,347.5
81	Roanoke, VA	5,343.1
82	Lakeland, FL	5,332.8
83	Wichita, KS	5,330.6
84	West Palm Beach, FL	5,324.4
85	Houston, TX	5,318.6
86	Stockton, CA	5,279.4
87	Waterbury, CT	5,266.0
88	Shreveport, LA	5,222.2
89	Durham, NC	5,170.7
90	Jacksonville, FL	5,157.7
91	High Point, NC	5,137.2
92	Melbourne, FL	5,112.1
93	Davenport, IA	5,098.1
94	Akron, OH	5,077.6
95	Mesquite, TX	5,069.2
96	Tempe, AZ	5,062.9
97	Duluth, MN	5,058.8
98	West Valley, UT	5,031.7
99	Modesto, CA	5,022.2
100	Savannah, GA	5,008.7
101	Hartford, CT	4,989.2
102	Dearborn, MI	4,988.0
103	Oakland, CA	4,986.5
104	Camden, NJ	4,982.3
105	Pompano Beach, FL	4,974.5
106	St. Joseph, MO	4,963.6
107	Fort Worth, TX	4,960.1
108	Miami, FL	4,956.5
109	Charlotte, NC	4,954.7
110	Avondale, AZ	4,944.1
111	Hammond, IN	4,934.0
112	Athens-Clarke, GA	4,927.5
113	Allentown, PA	4,910.3
114	Springfield, MA	4,896.7
115	Glendale, AZ	4,896.1
116	Las Cruces, NM	4,882.8
117	Ogden, UT	4,866.5
118	Tallahassee, FL	4,844.3
119	Hollywood, FL	4,831.3
120	Grand Prairie, TX	4,823.8
121	Lawrence, KS	4,787.2
122	Vallejo, CA	4,786.7
123	Nashville, TN	4,778.3
124	Portland, OR	4,723.6
125	Bakersfield, CA	4,716.0
126	Reading, PA	4,710.4
127	Peoria, IL	4,668.2
128	Minneapolis, MN	4,667.6
129	Providence, RI	4,654.4
130	Evansville, IN	4,643.7
131	San Bernardino, CA	4,629.8
132	San Angelo, TX	4,602.8
133	Murfreesboro, TN	4,580.3
134	Grand Rapids, MI	4,580.1
135	Killeen, TX	4,568.7
136	Baltimore, MD	4,565.6
137	Albany, NY	4,563.1
138	Kent, WA	4,528.1
139	Washington, DC	4,503.7
140	Lakewood, CO	4,490.2
141	Clearwater, FL	4,478.9
142	Sacramento, CA	4,465.4
143	Sunrise, FL	4,456.0
144	San Leandro, CA	4,435.1
145	Des Moines, IA	4,414.8
146	Fresno, CA	4,368.8
147	Billings, MT	4,360.4
148	Plantation, FL	4,354.6
149	Cedar Rapids, IA	4,339.2
150	Richmond, CA	4,328.9
151	Citrus Heights, CA	4,300.8
152	Davie, FL	4,291.9
153	Racine, WI	4,281.8
154	Louisville, KY	4,262.4
155	San Francisco, CA	4,261.7
156	Chicago, IL	4,227.1
157	Syracuse, NY	4,211.9
158	Irving, TX	4,162.6
159	Garland, TX	4,156.8
160	Abilene, TX	4,143.9
161	Visalia, CA	4,132.4
162	Omaha, NE	4,128.5
163	Bridgeport, CT	4,127.2
164	Odessa, TX	4,118.5
165	Richmond, VA	4,108.1
166	Phoenix, AZ	4,107.7
167	Southfield, MI	4,105.3
168	Elizabeth, NJ	4,093.3
169	St. Paul, MN	4,079.7
170	Decatur, IL	4,070.0
171	Bloomington, MN	4,000.5
172	Salem, OR	3,999.9
173	Reno, NV	3,986.2
174	Lincoln, NE	3,933.0
175	Hialeah, FL	3,932.0
176	Gresham, OR	3,892.1
177	Fayetteville, AR	3,871.1
178	New Orleans, LA	3,846.3
179	Pasadena, TX	3,817.3
180	Santa Monica, CA	3,809.7
181	Columbia, MO	3,807.5
182	Yuma, AZ	3,796.2
183	College Station, TX	3,795.7
184	Pittsburgh, PA	3,771.2
185	Spokane Valley, WA	3,760.0
186	Tampa, FL	3,754.0
187	Worcester, MA	3,749.0
188	Clarksville, TN	3,740.7
189	Fort Wayne, IN	3,728.0
190	Pembroke Pines, FL	3,701.4
191	Honolulu, HI	3,679.2
192	Colorado Springs, CO	3,665.8
193	Anchorage, AK	3,641.4
194	Midland, TX	3,636.5
195	Merced, CA	3,621.7
196	Philadelphia, PA	3,611.3
197	Sandy Springs, GA	3,608.9
198	Fall River, MA	3,603.9
199	Vancouver, WA	3,599.2
200	Boca Raton, FL	3,591.4
201	Hampton, VA	3,581.1
202	Gary, IN	3,579.1
203	Sandy, UT	3,561.7
204	Charleston, SC	3,510.7
205	Norman, OK	3,497.9
206	New Bedford, MA	3,492.7

RANK	CITY	RATE
207	Richardson, TX	3,481.9
208	Chesapeake, VA	3,462.8
209	Las Vegas, NV	3,461.0
210	Lewisville, TX	3,459.8
211	Salinas, CA	3,456.8
212	Clovis, CA	3,453.8
213	Denver, CO	3,452.9
214	Sioux City, IA	3,430.9
215	Lansing, MI	3,423.5
216	Manchester, NH	3,417.7
217	Lexington, KY	3,415.6
218	Mesa, AZ	3,415.0
219	Raleigh, NC	3,403.2
220	Fargo, ND	3,396.6
221	Sparks, NV	3,396.4
222	West Jordan, UT	3,376.8
223	Santa Barbara, CA	3,365.8
224	Greeley, CO	3,363.1
225	Madison, WI	3,362.6
226	Victorville, CA	3,362.4
227	Jacksonville, NC	3,351.9
228	Brockton, MA	3,324.3
229	Boston, MA	3,324.0
230	Downey, CA	3,322.6
231	Miramar, FL	3,313.5
232	Fort Collins, CO	3,311.5
233	Roseville, CA	3,311.2
234	Cheektowaga, NY	3,304.5
235	Redding, CA	3,264.9
236	Thornton, CO	3,263.6
237	Compton, CA	3,250.2
238	Warwick, RI	3,225.3
239	Pueblo, CO	3,222.2
240	Westminster, CO	3,199.5
241	Riverside, CA	3,198.0
242	Concord, CA	3,197.2
243	Carrollton, TX	3,186.8
244	Westland, MI	3,184.9
245	Trenton, NJ	3,176.4
246	Lynn, MA	3,164.1
247	Newark, NJ	3,159.7
248	Bellevue, WA	3,158.6
249	Indio, CA	3,153.4
250	Fairfield, CA	3,106.9
251	West Covina, CA	3,100.7
252	Aurora, CO	3,097.7
253	Hayward, CA	3,097.2
254	Kenosha, WI	3,089.4
255	Virginia Beach, VA	3,062.8
256	Cambridge, MA	3,061.3
257	Tracy, CA	3,056.6
258	Moreno Valley, CA	3,022.6
259	Costa Mesa, CA	3,015.0
260	El Paso, TX	2,994.1
261	Ontario, CA	2,970.9
262	Peoria, AZ	2,964.1
263	Ventura, CA	2,950.1
264	Plano, TX	2,930.6
265	Colonie, NY	2,928.1
266	Chandler, AZ	2,912.2
267	Erie, PA	2,906.5
268	Sioux Falls, SD	2,904.7
269	Fullerton, CA	2,886.5
270	Pasadena, CA	2,886.2
271	Rialto, CA	2,879.7
272	Scottsdale, AZ	2,843.0
273	Warren, MI	2,835.5
274	Escondido, CA	2,823.2
275	Nashua, NH	2,822.5
276	El Cajon, CA	2,821.6
277	Newport Beach, CA	2,801.8
278	North Las Vegas, NV	2,800.6
279	Greece, NY	2,800.4
280	Rochester, MN	2,792.4
281	Boise, ID	2,788.7
282	Chico, CA	2,776.1
283	Boulder, CO	2,775.0
284	Upper Darby Twnshp, PA	2,758.4
285	Longmont, CO	2,725.7
286	Santa Clara, CA	2,725.3
287	Long Beach, CA	2,725.0
288	Santa Rosa, CA	2,724.5
289	Green Bay, WI	2,719.3
290	Lakewood, CA	2,702.5
291	Pomona, CA	2,698.1
292	Inglewood, CA	2,688.3
293	Orem, UT	2,687.0
294	South Gate, CA	2,660.1
295	Roswell, GA	2,658.1
296	Paterson, NJ	2,646.6
297	Denton, TX	2,631.4
298	Antioch, CA	2,620.4
299	Westminster, CA	2,617.4
300	Somerville, MA	2,602.8
301	Overland Park, KS	2,594.9
302	Suffolk, VA	2,590.4
303	Cranston, RI	2,589.0
304	Ann Arbor, MI	2,579.4
305	Burbank, CA	2,579.2
306	Cape Coral, FL	2,575.7
307	Joliet, IL	2,566.5
308	Whittier, CA	2,564.1
309	Toms River Twnshp, NJ	2,553.5
310	Lee's Summit, MO	2,539.9
311	Bend, OR	2,527.6
312	McKinney, TX	2,526.8
313	Carson, CA	2,516.3
314	Round Rock, TX	2,507.9
315	Chino, CA	2,507.5
316	Corona, CA	2,499.4
317	Arvada, CO	2,497.6
318	Hawthorne, CA	2,495.4
319	Buena Park, CA	2,492.3
320	Jersey City, NJ	2,484.5
321	Livonia, MI	2,473.6
322	Palmdale, CA	2,458.0
323	Fremont, CA	2,455.7
324	San Diego, CA	2,452.6
325	Vista, CA	2,452.5
326	Elk Grove, CA	2,449.2
327	Los Angeles, CA	2,448.6
328	Provo, UT	2,443.3
329	Woodbridge Twnshp, NJ	2,425.2
330	Aurora, IL	2,410.7
331	Clarkstown, NY	2,405.6
332	Clinton Twnshp, MI	2,400.1
333	San Jose, CA	2,385.2
334	Nampa, ID	2,379.7
335	Anaheim, CA	2,379.1
336	Huntington Beach, CA	2,369.5
337	Lancaster, CA	2,357.8
338	San Mateo, CA	2,355.5
339	Temecula, CA	2,348.3
340	Troy, MI	2,344.7
341	Palm Bay, FL	2,344.5
342	Oceanside, CA	2,342.0
343	Chula Vista, CA	2,340.8
344	Coral Springs, FL	2,322.2
345	Fontana, CA	2,307.4
346	Surprise, AZ	2,297.2
347	El Monte, CA	2,295.2
348	Vacaville, CA	2,293.1
349	Pearland, TX	2,265.9
350	Alexandria, VA	2,255.3
351	Sugar Land, TX	2,241.9
352	Edison Twnshp, NJ	2,206.2
353	Oxnard, CA	2,181.4
354	Alhambra, CA	2,180.2
355	Edmond, OK	2,178.3
356	Clifton, NJ	2,167.1
357	Port St. Lucie, FL	2,164.9
358	Norwalk, CT	2,146.7
359	Baldwin Park, CA	2,142.1
360	Broken Arrow, OK	2,136.3
361	Livermore, CA	2,134.3
362	Rancho Cucamon., CA	2,131.0
363	Rio Rancho, NM	2,126.7
364	Olathe, KS	2,115.6
365	Sunnyvale, CA	2,095.4
366	Norwalk, CA	2,092.3
367	Santa Maria, CA	2,089.7
368	Elgin, IL	2,083.8
369	Sterling Heights, MI	2,048.8
370	St. George, UT	2,042.7
371	Torrance, CA	2,036.7
372	Santa Ana, CA	2,004.2
373	Garden Grove, CA	1,993.5
374	Henderson, NV	1,974.5
375	Gilbert, AZ	1,972.0
376	Hillsboro, OR	1,953.1
377	Farmington Hills, MI	1,945.2
378	Carlsbad, CA	1,937.4
379	Amherst, NY	1,929.4
380	Danbury, CT	1,926.5
381	Orange, CA	1,914.2
382	Glendale, CA	1,902.4
383	Frisco, TX	1,901.3
384	Hesperia, CA	1,881.8
385	Hamilton Twnshp, NJ	1,870.9
386	Canton Twnshp, MI	1,822.5
387	Quincy, MA	1,821.3
388	Stamford, CT	1,793.2
389	Santa Clarita, CA	1,792.4
390	Allen, TX	1,766.4
391	Brick Twnshp, NJ	1,756.8
392	Daly City, CA	1,730.8
393	San Marcos, CA	1,721.4
394	Beaverton, OR	1,707.8
395	New York, NY	1,690.3
396	Missouri City, TX	1,676.5
397	Naperville, IL	1,661.0
398	Simi Valley, CA	1,643.1
399	O'Fallon, MO	1,642.9
400	Yonkers, NY	1,555.5
401	Cary, NC	1,499.0
402	Thousand Oaks, CA	1,449.1
403	Murrieta, CA	1,433.9
404	Centennial, CO	1,409.7
405	Irvine, CA	1,389.1
406	Lake Forest, CA	1,276.7
407	Mission Viejo, CA	1,231.1
408	Newton, MA	1,150.1
409	Ramapo, NY	873.2
NA	Toledo, OH**	NA
NA	Tucson, AZ**	NA

Source: CQ Press using reported data from the F.B.I. "Crime in the United States 2009"

*Property crimes are offenses of burglary, larceny-theft, and motor vehicle theft. Attempts are included.

**Not available.

67. Percent Change in Property Crime Rate: 2008 to 2009
National Percent Change = 5.5% Decrease*

RANK	CITY	% CHANGE
30	Abilene, TX	7.1
131	Akron, OH	(2.0)
NA	Albany, GA**	NA
140	Albany, NY	(2.5)
272	Albuquerque, NM	(9.5)
212	Alexandria, VA	(6.2)
272	Alhambra, CA	(9.5)
226	Allentown, PA	(6.8)
112	Allen, TX	(0.9)
34	Amarillo, TX	6.5
65	Amherst, NY	2.3
178	Anaheim, CA	(4.7)
20	Anchorage, AK	10.7
NA	Ann Arbor, MI**	NA
238	Antioch, CA	(7.4)
82	Arlington, TX	0.9
117	Arvada, CO	(1.3)
320	Athens-Clarke, GA	(12.9)
340	Atlanta, GA	(15.0)
253	Aurora, CO	(8.1)
153	Aurora, IL	(3.2)
49	Austin, TX	5.0
283	Avondale, AZ	(10.2)
183	Bakersfield, CA	(4.9)
185	Baldwin Park, CA	(5.0)
189	Baltimore, MD	(5.2)
16	Baton Rouge, LA	11.4
134	Beaumont, TX	(2.2)
374	Beaverton, OR	(24.0)
278	Bellevue, WA	(9.8)
134	Bellingham, WA	(2.2)
369	Bend, OR	(21.6)
193	Berkeley, CA	(5.4)
43	Billings, MT	5.6
265	Birmingham, AL	(9.1)
84	Bloomington, MN	0.8
224	Boca Raton, FL	(6.6)
162	Boise, ID	(3.6)
285	Boston, MA	(10.4)
292	Boulder, CO	(11.0)
340	Brick Twnshp, NJ	(15.0)
261	Bridgeport, CT	(8.9)
NA	Brockton, MA**	NA
263	Broken Arrow, OK	(9.0)
185	Brownsville, TX	(5.0)
238	Buena Park, CA	(7.4)
201	Buffalo, NY	(5.8)
265	Burbank, CA	(9.1)
115	Cambridge, MA	(1.1)
371	Camden, NJ	(22.7)
NA	Canton Twnshp, MI**	NA
366	Canton, OH	(20.0)
351	Cape Coral, FL	(16.8)
363	Carlsbad, CA	(19.8)
71	Carrollton, TX	1.7
234	Carson, CA	(7.3)
363	Cary, NC	(19.8)
238	Cedar Rapids, IA	(7.4)
288	Centennial, CO	(10.6)
247	Chandler, AZ	(7.7)
328	Charleston, SC	(13.6)
365	Charlotte, NC	(19.9)
109	Chattanooga, TN	(0.7)
102	Cheektowaga, NY	(0.3)
17	Chesapeake, VA	11.3
258	Chicago, IL	(8.7)
327	Chico, CA	(13.5)
255	Chino, CA	(8.4)
362	Chula Vista, CA	(19.7)
93	Cincinnati, OH	0.2
130	Citrus Heights, CA	(1.8)
33	Clarkstown, NY	6.7
153	Clarksville, TN	(3.2)
128	Clearwater, FL	(1.7)
151	Cleveland, OH	(2.8)
316	Clifton, NJ	(12.5)
NA	Clinton Twnshp, MI**	NA
78	Clovis, CA	1.0
62	College Station, TX	3.2
111	Colonie, NY	(0.8)
329	Colorado Springs, CO	(13.7)
146	Columbia, MO	(2.6)
21	Columbia, SC	10.5
78	Columbus, GA	1.0
94	Columbus, OH	0.1
248	Compton, CA	(7.8)
324	Concord, CA	(13.3)
107	Coral Springs, FL	(0.6)
219	Corona, CA	(6.5)
263	Corpus Christi, TX	(9.0)
140	Costa Mesa, CA	(2.5)
189	Cranston, RI	(5.2)
226	Dallas, TX	(6.8)
339	Daly City, CA	(14.9)
195	Danbury, CT	(5.5)
311	Davenport, IA	(12.1)
13	Davie, FL	13.3
178	Dayton, OH	(4.7)
NA	Dearborn, MI**	NA
NA	Decatur, IL**	NA
185	Denton, TX	(5.0)
37	Denver, CO	6.0
NA	Des Moines, IA**	NA
NA	Detroit, MI**	NA
277	Downey, CA	(9.7)
76	Duluth, MN	1.1
171	Durham, NC	(4.1)
84	Edison Twnshp, NJ	0.8
147	Edmond, OK	(2.7)
370	El Cajon, CA	(22.4)
40	El Monte, CA	5.9
230	El Paso, TX	(6.9)
219	Elgin, IL	(6.5)
292	Elizabeth, NJ	(11.0)
183	Elk Grove, CA	(4.9)
340	Erie, PA	(15.0)
248	Escondido, CA	(7.8)
318	Eugene, OR	(12.8)
116	Evansville, IN	(1.2)
248	Everett, WA	(7.8)
358	Fairfield, CA	(19.0)
234	Fall River, MA	(7.3)
26	Fargo, ND	8.6
NA	Farmington Hills, MI**	NA
58	Fayetteville, AR	3.9
121	Fayetteville, NC	(1.4)
91	Federal Way, WA	0.3
NA	Flint, MI**	NA
136	Fontana, CA	(2.3)
139	Fort Collins, CO	(2.4)
104	Fort Lauderdale, FL	(0.4)
43	Fort Smith, AR	5.6
270	Fort Wayne, IN	(9.2)
123	Fort Worth, TX	(1.5)
82	Fremont, CA	0.9
201	Fresno, CA	(5.8)
375	Frisco, TX	(25.9)
242	Fullerton, CA	(7.5)
47	Gainesville, FL	5.3
336	Garden Grove, CA	(14.2)
121	Garland, TX	(1.4)
355	Gary, IN	(17.4)
304	Gilbert, AZ	(11.9)
219	Glendale, AZ	(6.5)
257	Glendale, CA	(8.6)
59	Grand Prairie, TX	3.7
NA	Grand Rapids, MI**	NA
11	Greece, NY	13.4
272	Greeley, CO	(9.5)
308	Green Bay, WI	(12.0)
177	Greensboro, NC	(4.6)
78	Gresham, OR	1.0
282	Hamilton Twnshp, NJ	(10.1)
164	Hammond, IN	(3.7)
67	Hampton, VA	1.9
140	Hartford, CT	(2.5)
147	Hawthorne, CA	(2.7)
166	Hayward, CA	(3.8)
322	Henderson, NV	(13.0)
360	Hesperia, CA	(19.6)
347	Hialeah, FL	(16.2)
334	High Point, NC	(14.0)
376	Hillsboro, OR	(27.3)
162	Hollywood, FL	(3.6)
50	Honolulu, HI	4.9
27	Houston, TX	7.5
41	Huntington Beach, CA	5.8
292	Huntsville, AL	(11.0)
366	Independence, MO	(20.0)
172	Indianapolis, IN	(4.2)
97	Indio, CA	(0.2)
113	Inglewood, CA	(1.0)
272	Irvine, CA	(9.5)
140	Irving, TX	(2.5)
281	Jacksonville, FL	(10.0)
97	Jacksonville, NC	(0.2)
65	Jackson, MS	2.3
360	Jersey City, NJ	(19.6)
155	Joliet, IL	(3.3)
NA	Kansas City, KS**	NA
311	Kansas City, MO	(12.1)
64	Kenosha, WI	2.6
354	Kent, WA	(17.2)
17	Killeen, TX	11.3
164	Knoxville, TN	(3.7)
22	Lafayette, LA	10.0
51	Lake Forest, CA	4.8
205	Lakeland, FL	(5.9)
63	Lakewood, CA	2.7
47	Lakewood, CO	5.3
373	Lancaster, CA	(23.5)
NA	Lansing, MI**	NA
207	Laredo, TX	(6.0)
73	Las Cruces, NM	1.6
304	Las Vegas, NV	(11.9)
214	Lawrence, KS	(6.3)
4	Lawton, OK	18.0
210	Lee's Summit, MO	(6.1)
32	Lewisville, TX	6.8
NA	Lexington, KY**	NA
147	Lincoln, NE	(2.7)
NA	Little Rock, AR**	NA
288	Livermore, CA	(10.6)
NA	Livonia, MI**	NA
131	Long Beach, CA	(2.0)
NA	Longmont, CO**	NA

RANK	CITY	% CHANGE
29	Longview, TX	7.2
219	Los Angeles, CA	(6.5)
NA	Louisville, KY**	NA
53	Lubbock, TX	4.5
195	Lynn, MA	(5.5)
252	Macon, GA	(8.0)
201	Madison, WI	(5.8)
46	Manchester, NH	5.4
96	McAllen, TX	(0.1)
5	McKinney, TX	16.6
207	Melbourne, FL	(6.0)
300	Memphis, TN	(11.7)
356	Merced, CA	(17.6)
291	Mesa, AZ	(10.9)
23	Mesquite, TX	9.7
67	Miami Beach, FL	1.9
231	Miami Gardens, FL	(7.0)
175	Miami, FL	(4.5)
24	Midland, TX	9.6
189	Milwaukee, WI	(5.2)
343	Minneapolis, MN	(15.4)
104	Miramar, FL	(0.4)
155	Mission Viejo, CA	(3.3)
28	Missouri City, TX	7.3
57	Mobile, AL	4.0
185	Modesto, CA	(5.0)
297	Montgomery, AL	(11.1)
197	Moreno Valley, CA	(5.6)
41	Murfreesboro, TN	5.8
91	Murrieta, CA	0.3
353	Nampa, ID	(16.9)
123	Naperville, IL	(1.5)
NA	Nashua, NH**	NA
292	Nashville, TN	(11.0)
178	New Bedford, MA	(4.7)
NA	New Haven, CT**	NA
377	New Orleans, LA	(27.3)
207	New York, NY	(6.0)
271	Newark, NJ	(9.3)
69	Newport Beach, CA	1.8
332	Newton, MA	(13.9)
35	Norfolk, VA	6.1
14	Norman, OK	12.4
299	North Charleston, SC	(11.5)
330	North Las Vegas, NV	(13.8)
304	Norwalk, CA	(11.9)
217	Norwalk, CT	(6.4)
226	Oakland, CA	(6.8)
182	Oceanside, CA	(4.8)
75	Odessa, TX	1.3
343	O'Fallon, MO	(15.4)
158	Ogden, UT	(3.4)
61	Oklahoma City, OK	3.5
NA	Olathe, KS**	NA
168	Omaha, NE	(3.9)
212	Ontario, CA	(6.2)
338	Orange, CA	(14.6)
131	Orem, UT	(2.0)
332	Orlando, FL	(13.9)
25	Overland Park, KS	9.0
193	Oxnard, CA	(5.4)
126	Palm Bay, FL	(1.6)
280	Palmdale, CA	(9.9)
97	Pasadena, CA	(0.2)
11	Pasadena, TX	13.4
345	Paterson, NJ	(15.5)
53	Pearland, TX	4.5
231	Pembroke Pines, FL	(7.0)
346	Peoria, AZ	(15.9)
NA	Peoria, IL**	NA
351	Philadelphia, PA	(16.8)
368	Phoenix, AZ	(21.2)
242	Pittsburgh, PA	(7.5)
172	Plano, TX	(4.2)
304	Plantation, FL	(11.9)
348	Pomona, CA	(16.3)
292	Pompano Beach, FL	(11.0)
320	Port St. Lucie, FL	(12.9)
290	Portland, OR	(10.7)
86	Portsmouth, VA	0.7
313	Providence, RI	(12.2)
147	Provo, UT	(2.7)
NA	Pueblo, CO**	NA
242	Quincy, MA	(7.5)
285	Racine, WI	(10.4)
94	Raleigh, NC	0.1
260	Ramapo, NY	(8.8)
117	Rancho Cucamon., CA	(1.3)
272	Reading, PA	(9.5)
214	Redding, CA	(6.3)
284	Reno, NV	(10.3)
2	Rialto, CA	28.3
59	Richardson, TX	3.7
298	Richmond, CA	(11.3)
86	Richmond, VA	0.7
349	Rio Rancho, NM	(16.5)
325	Riverside, CA	(13.4)
158	Roanoke, VA	(3.4)
123	Rochester, MN	(1.5)
117	Rochester, NY	(1.3)
323	Rockford, IL	(13.1)
261	Roseville, CA	(8.9)
197	Roswell, GA	(5.6)
175	Round Rock, TX	(4.5)
234	Sacramento, CA	(7.3)
336	Salem, OR	(14.2)
217	Salinas, CA	(6.4)
285	Salt Lake City, UT	(10.4)
225	San Angelo, TX	(6.7)
245	San Antonio, TX	(7.6)
126	San Bernardino, CA	(1.6)
372	San Diego, CA	(22.7)
214	San Francisco, CA	(6.3)
76	San Jose, CA	1.1
301	San Leandro, CA	(11.8)
317	San Marcos, CA	(12.6)
197	San Mateo, CA	(5.6)
169	Sandy Springs, GA	(4.0)
248	Sandy, UT	(7.8)
140	Santa Ana, CA	(2.5)
6	Santa Barbara, CA	15.0
97	Santa Clara, CA	(0.2)
128	Santa Clarita, CA	(1.7)
379	Santa Maria, CA	(30.0)
7	Santa Monica, CA	14.9
8	Santa Rosa, CA	14.6
201	Savannah, GA	(5.8)
335	Scottsdale, AZ	(14.1)
35	Seattle, WA	6.1
117	Shreveport, LA	(1.3)
90	Simi Valley, CA	0.6
51	Sioux City, IA	4.8
9	Sioux Falls, SD	14.4
350	Somerville, MA	(16.7)
308	South Bend, IN	(12.0)
226	South Gate, CA	(6.8)
NA	Southfield, MI**	NA
325	Sparks, NV	(13.4)
210	Spokane Valley, WA	(6.1)
3	Spokane, WA	18.6
NA	Springfield, IL**	NA
78	Springfield, MA	1.0
174	Springfield, MO	(4.4)
97	Stamford, CT	(0.2)
NA	Sterling Heights, MI**	NA
330	Stockton, CA	(13.8)
378	St. George, UT	(27.8)
56	St. Joseph, MO	4.3
140	St. Louis, MO	(2.5)
136	St. Paul, MN	(2.3)
19	St. Petersburg, FL	10.8
86	Suffolk, VA	0.7
37	Sugar Land, TX	6.0
37	Sunnyvale, CA	6.0
69	Sunrise, FL	1.8
265	Surprise, AZ	(9.1)
197	Syracuse, NY	(5.6)
245	Tacoma, WA	(7.6)
258	Tallahassee, FL	(8.7)
357	Tampa, FL	(18.4)
178	Temecula, CA	(4.7)
318	Tempe, AZ	(12.8)
86	Thornton, CO	0.7
71	Thousand Oaks, CA	1.7
NA	Toledo, OH**	NA
169	Toms River Twnshp, NJ	(4.0)
265	Topeka, KS	(9.1)
205	Torrance, CA	(5.9)
166	Tracy, CA	(3.8)
113	Trenton, NJ	(1.0)
NA	Troy, MI**	NA
NA	Tucson, AZ**	NA
74	Tulsa, OK	1.5
238	Tuscaloosa, AL	(7.4)
1	Tyler, TX	29.1
265	Upper Darby Twnshp, PA	(9.1)
104	Vacaville, CA	(0.4)
136	Vallejo, CA	(2.3)
219	Vancouver, WA	(6.5)
233	Ventura, CA	(7.2)
254	Victorville, CA	(8.2)
45	Virginia Beach, VA	5.5
308	Visalia, CA	(12.0)
301	Vista, CA	(11.8)
192	Waco, TX	(5.3)
NA	Warren, MI**	NA
107	Warwick, RI	(0.6)
234	Washington, DC	(7.3)
102	Waterbury, CT	(0.3)
315	West Covina, CA	(12.3)
15	West Jordan, UT	11.6
256	West Palm Beach, FL	(8.5)
160	West Valley, UT	(3.5)
NA	Westland, MI**	NA
301	Westminster, CA	(11.8)
155	Westminster, CO	(3.3)
152	Whittier, CA	(3.1)
359	Wichita Falls, TX	(19.2)
160	Wichita, KS	(3.5)
10	Wilmington, NC	13.9
278	Winston-Salem, NC	(9.8)
313	Woodbridge Twnshp, NJ	(12.2)
53	Worcester, MA	4.5
109	Yonkers, NY	(0.7)
31	Yuma, AZ	7.0

Source: CQ Press using reported data from the F.B.I. "Crime in the United States 2009"

*Property crimes are offenses of burglary, larceny-theft, and motor vehicle theft. Attempts are included.

**Not available.

67. Percent Change in Property Crime Rate: 2008 to 2009 (continued)
National Percent Change = 5.5% Decrease*

RANK	CITY	% CHANGE
1	Tyler, TX	29.1
2	Rialto, CA	28.3
3	Spokane, WA	18.6
4	Lawton, OK	18.0
5	McKinney, TX	16.6
6	Santa Barbara, CA	15.0
7	Santa Monica, CA	14.9
8	Santa Rosa, CA	14.6
9	Sioux Falls, SD	14.4
10	Wilmington, NC	13.9
11	Greece, NY	13.4
11	Pasadena, TX	13.4
13	Davie, FL	13.3
14	Norman, OK	12.4
15	West Jordan, UT	11.6
16	Baton Rouge, LA	11.4
17	Chesapeake, VA	11.3
17	Killeen, TX	11.3
19	St. Petersburg, FL	10.8
20	Anchorage, AK	10.7
21	Columbia, SC	10.5
22	Lafayette, LA	10.0
23	Mesquite, TX	9.7
24	Midland, TX	9.6
25	Overland Park, KS	9.0
26	Fargo, ND	8.6
27	Houston, TX	7.5
28	Missouri City, TX	7.3
29	Longview, TX	7.2
30	Abilene, TX	7.1
31	Yuma, AZ	7.0
32	Lewisville, TX	6.8
33	Clarkstown, NY	6.7
34	Amarillo, TX	6.5
35	Norfolk, VA	6.1
35	Seattle, WA	6.1
37	Denver, CO	6.0
37	Sugar Land, TX	6.0
37	Sunnyvale, CA	6.0
40	El Monte, CA	5.9
41	Huntington Beach, CA	5.8
41	Murfreesboro, TN	5.8
43	Billings, MT	5.6
43	Fort Smith, AR	5.6
45	Virginia Beach, VA	5.5
46	Manchester, NH	5.4
47	Gainesville, FL	5.3
47	Lakewood, CO	5.3
49	Austin, TX	5.0
50	Honolulu, HI	4.9
51	Lake Forest, CA	4.8
51	Sioux City, IA	4.8
53	Lubbock, TX	4.5
53	Pearland, TX	4.5
53	Worcester, MA	4.5
56	St. Joseph, MO	4.3
57	Mobile, AL	4.0
58	Fayetteville, AR	3.9
59	Grand Prairie, TX	3.7
59	Richardson, TX	3.7
61	Oklahoma City, OK	3.5
62	College Station, TX	3.2
63	Lakewood, CA	2.7
64	Kenosha, WI	2.6
65	Amherst, NY	2.3
65	Jackson, MS	2.3
67	Hampton, VA	1.9
67	Miami Beach, FL	1.9
69	Newport Beach, CA	1.8
69	Sunrise, FL	1.8
71	Carrollton, TX	1.7
71	Thousand Oaks, CA	1.7
73	Las Cruces, NM	1.6
74	Tulsa, OK	1.5
75	Odessa, TX	1.3
76	Duluth, MN	1.1
76	San Jose, CA	1.1
78	Clovis, CA	1.0
78	Columbus, GA	1.0
78	Gresham, OR	1.0
78	Springfield, MA	1.0
82	Arlington, TX	0.9
82	Fremont, CA	0.9
84	Bloomington, MN	0.8
84	Edison Twnshp, NJ	0.8
86	Portsmouth, VA	0.7
86	Richmond, VA	0.7
86	Suffolk, VA	0.7
86	Thornton, CO	0.7
90	Simi Valley, CA	0.6
91	Federal Way, WA	0.3
91	Murrieta, CA	0.3
93	Cincinnati, OH	0.2
94	Columbus, OH	0.1
94	Raleigh, NC	0.1
96	McAllen, TX	(0.1)
97	Indio, CA	(0.2)
97	Jacksonville, NC	(0.2)
97	Pasadena, CA	(0.2)
97	Santa Clara, CA	(0.2)
97	Stamford, CT	(0.2)
102	Cheektowaga, NY	(0.3)
102	Waterbury, CT	(0.3)
104	Fort Lauderdale, FL	(0.4)
104	Miramar, FL	(0.4)
104	Vacaville, CA	(0.4)
107	Coral Springs, FL	(0.6)
107	Warwick, RI	(0.6)
109	Chattanooga, TN	(0.7)
109	Yonkers, NY	(0.7)
111	Colonie, NY	(0.8)
112	Allen, TX	(0.9)
113	Inglewood, CA	(1.0)
113	Trenton, NJ	(1.0)
115	Cambridge, MA	(1.1)
116	Evansville, IN	(1.2)
117	Arvada, CO	(1.3)
117	Rancho Cucamon., CA	(1.3)
117	Rochester, NY	(1.3)
117	Shreveport, LA	(1.3)
121	Fayetteville, NC	(1.4)
121	Garland, TX	(1.4)
123	Fort Worth, TX	(1.5)
123	Naperville, IL	(1.5)
123	Rochester, MN	(1.5)
126	Palm Bay, FL	(1.6)
126	San Bernardino, CA	(1.6)
128	Clearwater, FL	(1.7)
128	Santa Clarita, CA	(1.7)
130	Citrus Heights, CA	(1.8)
131	Akron, OH	(2.0)
131	Long Beach, CA	(2.0)
131	Orem, UT	(2.0)
134	Beaumont, TX	(2.2)
134	Bellingham, WA	(2.2)
136	Fontana, CA	(2.3)
136	St. Paul, MN	(2.3)
136	Vallejo, CA	(2.3)
139	Fort Collins, CO	(2.4)
140	Albany, NY	(2.5)
140	Costa Mesa, CA	(2.5)
140	Hartford, CT	(2.5)
140	Irving, TX	(2.5)
140	Santa Ana, CA	(2.5)
140	St. Louis, MO	(2.5)
146	Columbia, MO	(2.6)
147	Edmond, OK	(2.7)
147	Hawthorne, CA	(2.7)
147	Lincoln, NE	(2.7)
147	Provo, UT	(2.7)
151	Cleveland, OH	(2.8)
152	Whittier, CA	(3.1)
153	Aurora, IL	(3.2)
153	Clarksville, TN	(3.2)
155	Joliet, IL	(3.3)
155	Mission Viejo, CA	(3.3)
155	Westminster, CO	(3.3)
158	Ogden, UT	(3.4)
158	Roanoke, VA	(3.4)
160	West Valley, UT	(3.5)
160	Wichita, KS	(3.5)
162	Boise, ID	(3.6)
162	Hollywood, FL	(3.6)
164	Hammond, IN	(3.7)
164	Knoxville, TN	(3.7)
166	Hayward, CA	(3.8)
166	Tracy, CA	(3.8)
168	Omaha, NE	(3.9)
169	Sandy Springs, GA	(4.0)
169	Toms River Twnshp, NJ	(4.0)
171	Durham, NC	(4.1)
172	Indianapolis, IN	(4.2)
172	Plano, TX	(4.2)
174	Springfield, MO	(4.4)
175	Miami, FL	(4.5)
175	Round Rock, TX	(4.5)
177	Greensboro, NC	(4.6)
178	Anaheim, CA	(4.7)
178	Dayton, OH	(4.7)
178	New Bedford, MA	(4.7)
178	Temecula, CA	(4.7)
182	Oceanside, CA	(4.8)
183	Bakersfield, CA	(4.9)
183	Elk Grove, CA	(4.9)
185	Baldwin Park, CA	(5.0)
185	Brownsville, TX	(5.0)
185	Denton, TX	(5.0)
185	Modesto, CA	(5.0)
189	Baltimore, MD	(5.2)
189	Cranston, RI	(5.2)
189	Milwaukee, WI	(5.2)
192	Waco, TX	(5.3)
193	Berkeley, CA	(5.4)
193	Oxnard, CA	(5.4)
195	Danbury, CT	(5.5)
195	Lynn, MA	(5.5)
197	Moreno Valley, CA	(5.6)
197	Roswell, GA	(5.6)
197	San Mateo, CA	(5.6)
197	Syracuse, NY	(5.6)
201	Buffalo, NY	(5.8)
201	Fresno, CA	(5.8)
201	Madison, WI	(5.8)
201	Savannah, GA	(5.8)
205	Lakeland, FL	(5.9)
205	Torrance, CA	(5.9)

RANK	CITY	% CHANGE
207	Laredo, TX	(6.0)
207	Melbourne, FL	(6.0)
207	New York, NY	(6.0)
210	Lee's Summit, MO	(6.1)
210	Spokane Valley, WA	(6.1)
212	Alexandria, VA	(6.2)
212	Ontario, CA	(6.2)
214	Lawrence, KS	(6.3)
214	Redding, CA	(6.3)
214	San Francisco, CA	(6.3)
217	Norwalk, CT	(6.4)
217	Salinas, CA	(6.4)
219	Corona, CA	(6.5)
219	Elgin, IL	(6.5)
219	Glendale, AZ	(6.5)
219	Los Angeles, CA	(6.5)
219	Vancouver, WA	(6.5)
224	Boca Raton, FL	(6.6)
225	San Angelo, TX	(6.7)
226	Allentown, PA	(6.8)
226	Dallas, TX	(6.8)
226	Oakland, CA	(6.8)
226	South Gate, CA	(6.8)
230	El Paso, TX	(6.9)
231	Miami Gardens, FL	(7.0)
231	Pembroke Pines, FL	(7.0)
233	Ventura, CA	(7.2)
234	Carson, CA	(7.3)
234	Fall River, MA	(7.3)
234	Sacramento, CA	(7.3)
234	Washington, DC	(7.3)
238	Antioch, CA	(7.4)
238	Buena Park, CA	(7.4)
238	Cedar Rapids, IA	(7.4)
238	Tuscaloosa, AL	(7.4)
242	Fullerton, CA	(7.5)
242	Pittsburgh, PA	(7.5)
242	Quincy, MA	(7.5)
245	San Antonio, TX	(7.6)
245	Tacoma, WA	(7.6)
247	Chandler, AZ	(7.7)
248	Compton, CA	(7.8)
248	Escondido, CA	(7.8)
248	Everett, WA	(7.8)
248	Sandy, UT	(7.8)
252	Macon, GA	(8.0)
253	Aurora, CO	(8.1)
254	Victorville, CA	(8.2)
255	Chino, CA	(8.4)
256	West Palm Beach, FL	(8.5)
257	Glendale, CA	(8.6)
258	Chicago, IL	(8.7)
258	Tallahassee, FL	(8.7)
260	Ramapo, NY	(8.8)
261	Bridgeport, CT	(8.9)
261	Roseville, CA	(8.9)
263	Broken Arrow, OK	(9.0)
263	Corpus Christi, TX	(9.0)
265	Birmingham, AL	(9.1)
265	Burbank, CA	(9.1)
265	Surprise, AZ	(9.1)
265	Topeka, KS	(9.1)
265	Upper Darby Twnshp, PA	(9.1)
270	Fort Wayne, IN	(9.2)
271	Newark, NJ	(9.3)
272	Albuquerque, NM	(9.5)
272	Alhambra, CA	(9.5)
272	Greeley, CO	(9.5)
272	Irvine, CA	(9.5)
272	Reading, PA	(9.5)
277	Downey, CA	(9.7)
278	Bellevue, WA	(9.8)
278	Winston-Salem, NC	(9.8)
280	Palmdale, CA	(9.9)
281	Jacksonville, FL	(10.0)
282	Hamilton Twnshp, NJ	(10.1)
283	Avondale, AZ	(10.2)
284	Reno, NV	(10.3)
285	Boston, MA	(10.4)
285	Racine, WI	(10.4)
285	Salt Lake City, UT	(10.4)
288	Centennial, CO	(10.6)
288	Livermore, CA	(10.6)
290	Portland, OR	(10.7)
291	Mesa, AZ	(10.9)
292	Boulder, CO	(11.0)
292	Elizabeth, NJ	(11.0)
292	Huntsville, AL	(11.0)
292	Nashville, TN	(11.0)
292	Pompano Beach, FL	(11.0)
297	Montgomery, AL	(11.1)
298	Richmond, CA	(11.3)
299	North Charleston, SC	(11.5)
300	Memphis, TN	(11.7)
301	San Leandro, CA	(11.8)
301	Vista, CA	(11.8)
301	Westminster, CA	(11.8)
304	Gilbert, AZ	(11.9)
304	Las Vegas, NV	(11.9)
304	Norwalk, CA	(11.9)
304	Plantation, FL	(11.9)
308	Green Bay, WI	(12.0)
308	South Bend, IN	(12.0)
308	Visalia, CA	(12.0)
311	Davenport, IA	(12.1)
311	Kansas City, MO	(12.1)
313	Providence, RI	(12.2)
313	Woodbridge Twnshp, NJ	(12.2)
315	West Covina, CA	(12.3)
316	Clifton, NJ	(12.5)
317	San Marcos, CA	(12.6)
318	Eugene, OR	(12.8)
318	Tempe, AZ	(12.8)
320	Athens-Clarke, GA	(12.9)
320	Port St. Lucie, FL	(12.9)
322	Henderson, NV	(13.0)
323	Rockford, IL	(13.1)
324	Concord, CA	(13.3)
325	Riverside, CA	(13.4)
325	Sparks, NV	(13.4)
327	Chico, CA	(13.5)
328	Charleston, SC	(13.6)
329	Colorado Springs, CO	(13.7)
330	North Las Vegas, NV	(13.8)
330	Stockton, CA	(13.8)
332	Newton, MA	(13.9)
332	Orlando, FL	(13.9)
334	High Point, NC	(14.0)
335	Scottsdale, AZ	(14.1)
336	Garden Grove, CA	(14.2)
336	Salem, OR	(14.2)
338	Orange, CA	(14.6)
339	Daly City, CA	(14.9)
340	Atlanta, GA	(15.0)
340	Brick Twnshp, NJ	(15.0)
340	Erie, PA	(15.0)
343	Minneapolis, MN	(15.4)
343	O'Fallon, MO	(15.4)
345	Paterson, NJ	(15.5)
346	Peoria, AZ	(15.9)
347	Hialeah, FL	(16.2)
348	Pomona, CA	(16.3)
349	Rio Rancho, NM	(16.5)
350	Somerville, MA	(16.7)
351	Cape Coral, FL	(16.8)
351	Philadelphia, PA	(16.8)
353	Nampa, ID	(16.9)
354	Kent, WA	(17.2)
355	Gary, IN	(17.4)
356	Merced, CA	(17.6)
357	Tampa, FL	(18.4)
358	Fairfield, CA	(19.0)
359	Wichita Falls, TX	(19.2)
360	Hesperia, CA	(19.6)
360	Jersey City, NJ	(19.6)
362	Chula Vista, CA	(19.7)
363	Carlsbad, CA	(19.8)
363	Cary, NC	(19.8)
365	Charlotte, NC	(19.9)
366	Canton, OH	(20.0)
366	Independence, MO	(20.0)
368	Phoenix, AZ	(21.2)
369	Bend, OR	(21.6)
370	El Cajon, CA	(22.4)
371	Camden, NJ	(22.7)
372	San Diego, CA	(22.7)
373	Lancaster, CA	(23.5)
374	Beaverton, OR	(24.0)
375	Frisco, TX	(25.9)
376	Hillsboro, OR	(27.3)
377	New Orleans, LA	(27.3)
378	St. George, UT	(27.8)
379	Santa Maria, CA	(30.0)
NA	Albany, GA**	NA
NA	Ann Arbor, MI**	NA
NA	Brockton, MA**	NA
NA	Canton Twnshp, MI**	NA
NA	Clinton Twnshp, MI**	NA
NA	Dearborn, MI**	NA
NA	Decatur, IL**	NA
NA	Des Moines, IA**	NA
NA	Detroit, MI**	NA
NA	Farmington Hills, MI**	NA
NA	Flint, MI**	NA
NA	Grand Rapids, MI**	NA
NA	Kansas City, KS**	NA
NA	Lansing, MI**	NA
NA	Lexington, KY**	NA
NA	Little Rock, AR**	NA
NA	Livonia, MI**	NA
NA	Longmont, CO**	NA
NA	Louisville, KY**	NA
NA	Nashua, NH**	NA
NA	New Haven, CT**	NA
NA	Olathe, KS**	NA
NA	Peoria, IL**	NA
NA	Pueblo, CO**	NA
NA	Southfield, MI**	NA
NA	Springfield, IL**	NA
NA	Sterling Heights, MI**	NA
NA	Toledo, OH**	NA
NA	Troy, MI**	NA
NA	Tucson, AZ**	NA
NA	Warren, MI**	NA
NA	Westland, MI**	NA

Source: CQ Press using reported data from the F.B.I. "Crime in the United States 2009"

*Property crimes are offenses of burglary, larceny-theft, and motor vehicle theft. Attempts are included.

**Not available.

68. Percent Change in Property Crime Rate: 2005 to 2009
National Percent Change = 11.5% Decrease*

RANK	CITY	% CHANGE
171	Abilene, TX	(12.1)
156	Akron, OH	(10.5)
78	Albany, GA	(0.8)
164	Albany, NY	(11.8)
157	Albuquerque, NM	(10.9)
165	Alexandria, VA	(11.9)
298	Alhambra, CA	(25.9)
142	Allentown, PA	(9.0)
263	Allen, TX	(22.0)
143	Amarillo, TX	(9.3)
23	Amherst, NY	12.0
204	Anaheim, CA	(16.0)
162	Anchorage, AK	(11.5)
NA	Ann Arbor, MI**	NA
139	Antioch, CA	(8.8)
88	Arlington, TX	(3.1)
343	Arvada, CO	(33.0)
122	Athens-Clarke, GA	(6.9)
190	Atlanta, GA	(14.8)
358	Aurora, CO	(37.7)
208	Aurora, IL	(16.6)
49	Austin, TX	3.9
NA	Avondale, AZ**	NA
223	Bakersfield, CA	(18.0)
232	Baldwin Park, CA	(19.1)
165	Baltimore, MD	(11.9)
101	Baton Rouge, LA	(4.5)
254	Beaumont, TX	(21.2)
368	Beaverton, OR	(51.5)
238	Bellevue, WA	(19.8)
310	Bellingham, WA	(28.2)
367	Bend, OR	(49.0)
224	Berkeley, CA	(18.1)
269	Billings, MT	(22.7)
80	Birmingham, AL	(1.0)
NA	Bloomington, MN**	NA
68	Boca Raton, FL	0.8
303	Boise, ID	(27.3)
289	Boston, MA	(25.1)
314	Boulder, CO	(28.4)
52	Brick Twnshp, NJ	3.4
229	Bridgeport, CT	(18.7)
195	Brockton, MA	(15.0)
173	Broken Arrow, OK	(12.3)
36	Brownsville, TX	7.4
52	Buena Park, CA	3.4
138	Buffalo, NY	(8.7)
86	Burbank, CA	(2.5)
124	Cambridge, MA	(7.0)
126	Camden, NJ	(7.3)
NA	Canton Twnshp, MI**	NA
310	Canton, OH	(28.2)
183	Cape Coral, FL	(13.6)
308	Carlsbad, CA	(28.0)
119	Carrollton, TX	(6.7)
81	Carson, CA	(1.2)
256	Cary, NC	(21.4)
211	Cedar Rapids, IA	(16.7)
328	Centennial, CO	(30.6)
231	Chandler, AZ	(19.0)
259	Charleston, SC	(21.5)
308	Charlotte, NC	(28.0)
129	Chattanooga, TN	(7.6)
36	Cheektowaga, NY	7.4
98	Chesapeake, VA	(4.2)
127	Chicago, IL	(7.4)
300	Chico, CA	(26.5)
284	Chino, CA	(24.4)
351	Chula Vista, CA	(35.5)
188	Cincinnati, OH	(14.4)
NA	Citrus Heights, CA**	NA
NA	Clarkstown, NY**	NA
75	Clarksville, TN	(0.2)
85	Clearwater, FL	(2.0)
147	Cleveland, OH	(9.6)
134	Clifton, NJ	(8.1)
NA	Clinton Twnshp, MI**	NA
175	Clovis, CA	(12.8)
105	College Station, TX	(4.9)
264	Colonie, NY	(22.2)
324	Colorado Springs, CO	(30.0)
22	Columbia, MO	12.2
130	Columbia, SC	(7.7)
19	Columbus, GA	12.9
181	Columbus, OH	(13.3)
9	Compton, CA	20.4
355	Concord, CA	(36.0)
12	Coral Springs, FL	15.4
222	Corona, CA	(17.8)
244	Corpus Christi, TX	(20.4)
175	Costa Mesa, CA	(12.8)
60	Cranston, RI	2.0
279	Dallas, TX	(23.5)
230	Daly City, CA	(18.8)
99	Danbury, CT	(4.3)
317	Davenport, IA	(28.9)
14	Davie, FL	14.7
225	Dayton, OH	(18.2)
NA	Dearborn, MI**	NA
NA	Decatur, IL**	NA
355	Denton, TX	(36.0)
365	Denver, CO	(42.5)
NA	Des Moines, IA**	NA
NA	Detroit, MI**	NA
46	Downey, CA	4.5
NA	Duluth, MN**	NA
165	Durham, NC	(11.9)
152	Edison Twnshp, NJ	(9.8)
208	Edmond, OK	(16.6)
346	El Cajon, CA	(34.0)
232	El Monte, CA	(19.1)
137	El Paso, TX	(8.4)
NA	Elgin, IL**	NA
57	Elizabeth, NJ	2.4
NA	Elk Grove, CA**	NA
43	Erie, PA	5.6
260	Escondido, CA	(21.6)
212	Eugene, OR	(16.8)
140	Evansville, IN	(8.9)
145	Everett, WA	(9.5)
302	Fairfield, CA	(27.1)
NA	Fall River, MA**	NA
2	Fargo, ND	32.2
NA	Farmington Hills, MI**	NA
190	Fayetteville, AR	(14.8)
116	Fayetteville, NC	(6.3)
307	Federal Way, WA	(27.9)
NA	Flint, MI**	NA
72	Fontana, CA	0.1
95	Fort Collins, CO	(3.9)
193	Fort Lauderdale, FL	(14.9)
161	Fort Smith, AR	(11.3)
278	Fort Wayne, IN	(23.4)
226	Fort Worth, TX	(18.3)
48	Fremont, CA	4.2
254	Fresno, CA	(21.2)
370	Frisco, TX	(52.6)
199	Fullerton, CA	(15.4)
6	Gainesville, FL	26.6
294	Garden Grove, CA	(25.5)
24	Garland, TX	11.8
341	Gary, IN	(32.6)
310	Gilbert, AZ	(28.2)
95	Glendale, AZ	(3.9)
62	Glendale, CA	1.7
131	Grand Prairie, TX	(7.9)
NA	Grand Rapids, MI**	NA
1	Greece, NY	33.4
366	Greeley, CO	(47.2)
113	Green Bay, WI	(5.7)
79	Greensboro, NC	(0.9)
323	Gresham, OR	(29.7)
73	Hamilton Twnshp, NJ	0.0
178	Hammond, IN	(12.9)
83	Hampton, VA	(1.6)
348	Hartford, CT	(34.4)
82	Hawthorne, CA	(1.3)
238	Hayward, CA	(19.8)
331	Henderson, NV	(31.0)
334	Hesperia, CA	(31.6)
54	Hialeah, FL	2.9
228	High Point, NC	(18.6)
371	Hillsboro, OR	(55.6)
28	Hollywood, FL	9.9
250	Honolulu, HI	(21.1)
147	Houston, TX	(9.6)
17	Huntington Beach, CA	13.5
256	Huntsville, AL	(21.4)
240	Independence, MO	(19.9)
120	Indianapolis, IN	(6.8)
332	Indio, CA	(31.3)
65	Inglewood, CA	1.0
269	Irvine, CA	(22.7)
185	Irving, TX	(13.8)
113	Jacksonville, FL	(5.7)
NA	Jacksonville, NC**	NA
15	Jackson, MS	14.6
335	Jersey City, NJ	(31.8)
250	Joliet, IL	(21.1)
297	Kansas City, KS	(25.8)
319	Kansas City, MO	(29.2)
69	Kenosha, WI	0.5
360	Kent, WA	(39.1)
276	Killeen, TX	(23.2)
50	Knoxville, TN	3.5
11	Lafayette, LA	15.7
61	Lake Forest, CA	1.9
101	Lakeland, FL	(4.5)
248	Lakewood, CA	(20.9)
271	Lakewood, CO	(22.8)
350	Lancaster, CA	(35.0)
NA	Lansing, MI**	NA
71	Laredo, TX	0.2
76	Las Cruces, NM	(0.4)
315	Las Vegas, NV	(28.5)
20	Lawrence, KS	12.6
45	Lawton, OK	4.6
155	Lee's Summit, MO	(10.0)
213	Lewisville, TX	(16.9)
NA	Lexington, KY**	NA
299	Lincoln, NE	(26.4)
NA	Little Rock, AR**	NA
65	Livermore, CA	1.0
NA	Livonia, MI**	NA
89	Long Beach, CA	(3.2)
NA	Longmont, CO**	NA

RANK	CITY	% CHANGE
27	Longview, TX	10.0
234	Los Angeles, CA	(19.2)
NA	Louisville, KY**	NA
90	Lubbock, TX	(3.5)
90	Lynn, MA	(3.5)
226	Macon, GA	(18.3)
94	Madison, WI	(3.8)
39	Manchester, NH	7.0
143	McAllen, TX	(9.3)
26	McKinney, TX	10.3
34	Melbourne, FL	7.7
199	Memphis, TN	(15.4)
357	Merced, CA	(36.9)
354	Mesa, AZ	(35.8)
7	Mesquite, TX	21.3
21	Miami Beach, FL	12.4
163	Miami Gardens, FL	(11.7)
218	Miami, FL	(17.5)
92	Midland, TX	(3.7)
55	Milwaukee, WI	2.8
261	Minneapolis, MN	(21.7)
38	Miramar, FL	7.1
109	Mission Viejo, CA	(5.3)
165	Missouri City, TX	(11.9)
74	Mobile, AL	(0.1)
240	Modesto, CA	(19.9)
196	Montgomery, AL	(15.1)
234	Moreno Valley, CA	(19.2)
115	Murfreesboro, TN	(6.2)
364	Murrieta, CA	(40.7)
NA	Nampa, ID**	NA
112	Naperville, IL	(5.5)
8	Nashua, NH	20.7
295	Nashville, TN	(25.6)
44	New Bedford, MA	5.0
NA	New Haven, CT**	NA
NA	New Orleans, LA**	NA
201	New York, NY	(15.6)
326	Newark, NJ	(30.2)
150	Newport Beach, CA	(9.7)
174	Newton, MA	(12.5)
62	Norfolk, VA	1.7
25	Norman, OK	10.6
293	North Charleston, SC	(25.4)
362	North Las Vegas, NV	(39.3)
246	Norwalk, CA	(20.6)
322	Norwalk, CT	(29.6)
180	Oakland, CA	(13.2)
326	Oceanside, CA	(30.2)
46	Odessa, TX	4.5
362	O'Fallon, MO	(39.3)
240	Ogden, UT	(19.9)
274	Oklahoma City, OK	(23.1)
NA	Olathe, KS**	NA
272	Omaha, NE	(22.9)
286	Ontario, CA	(24.6)
286	Orange, CA	(24.6)
320	Orem, UT	(29.3)
190	Orlando, FL	(14.8)
125	Overland Park, KS	(7.1)
133	Oxnard, CA	(8.0)
349	Palm Bay, FL	(34.9)
250	Palmdale, CA	(21.1)
104	Pasadena, CA	(4.6)
16	Pasadena, TX	13.8
150	Paterson, NJ	(9.7)
171	Pearland, TX	(12.1)
5	Pembroke Pines, FL	27.1
336	Peoria, AZ	(32.1)
320	Peoria, IL	(29.3)
169	Philadelphia, PA	(12.0)
351	Phoenix, AZ	(35.5)
243	Pittsburgh, PA	(20.2)
203	Plano, TX	(15.8)
32	Plantation, FL	8.5
245	Pomona, CA	(20.5)
186	Pompano Beach, FL	(13.9)
87	Port St. Lucie, FL	(2.8)
337	Portland, OR	(32.2)
30	Portsmouth, VA	9.0
145	Providence, RI	(9.5)
280	Provo, UT	(23.7)
368	Pueblo, CO	(51.5)
13	Quincy, MA	14.8
284	Racine, WI	(24.4)
152	Raleigh, NC	(9.8)
109	Ramapo, NY	(5.3)
264	Rancho Cucamon., CA	(22.2)
290	Reading, PA	(25.2)
318	Redding, CA	(29.0)
296	Reno, NV	(25.7)
215	Rialto, CA	(17.2)
65	Richardson, TX	1.0
276	Richmond, CA	(23.2)
359	Richmond, VA	(37.8)
99	Rio Rancho, NM	(4.3)
329	Riverside, CA	(30.8)
256	Roanoke, VA	(21.4)
41	Rochester, MN	6.3
221	Rochester, NY	(17.7)
218	Rockford, IL	(17.5)
303	Roseville, CA	(27.3)
77	Roswell, GA	(0.7)
108	Round Rock, TX	(5.2)
261	Sacramento, CA	(21.7)
347	Salem, OR	(34.2)
281	Salinas, CA	(23.9)
118	Salt Lake City, UT	(6.6)
274	San Angelo, TX	(23.1)
50	San Antonio, TX	3.5
220	San Bernardino, CA	(17.6)
340	San Diego, CA	(32.5)
120	San Francisco, CA	(6.8)
109	San Jose, CA	(5.3)
179	San Leandro, CA	(13.1)
303	San Marcos, CA	(27.3)
264	San Mateo, CA	(22.2)
NA	Sandy Springs, GA**	NA
59	Sandy, UT	2.2
342	Santa Ana, CA	(32.8)
69	Santa Barbara, CA	0.5
208	Santa Clara, CA	(16.6)
206	Santa Clarita, CA	(16.3)
290	Santa Maria, CA	(25.2)
92	Santa Monica, CA	(3.7)
187	Santa Rosa, CA	(14.0)
136	Savannah, GA	(8.3)
202	Scottsdale, AZ	(15.7)
267	Seattle, WA	(22.4)
236	Shreveport, LA	(19.3)
196	Simi Valley, CA	(15.1)
237	Sioux City, IA	(19.7)
116	Sioux Falls, SD	(6.3)
10	Somerville, MA	17.3
106	South Bend, IN	(5.1)
131	South Gate, CA	(7.9)
NA	Southfield, MI**	NA
169	Sparks, NV	(12.0)
247	Spokane Valley, WA	(20.7)
41	Spokane, WA	6.3
101	Springfield, IL	(4.5)
189	Springfield, MA	(14.7)
40	Springfield, MO	6.8
147	Stamford, CT	(9.6)
NA	Sterling Heights, MI**	NA
250	Stockton, CA	(21.1)
339	St. George, UT	(32.3)
183	St. Joseph, MO	(13.6)
286	St. Louis, MO	(24.6)
214	St. Paul, MN	(17.0)
29	St. Petersburg, FL	9.6
301	Suffolk, VA	(26.6)
134	Sugar Land, TX	(8.1)
64	Sunnyvale, CA	1.5
3	Sunrise, FL	30.6
268	Surprise, AZ	(22.6)
122	Syracuse, NY	(6.9)
206	Tacoma, WA	(16.3)
140	Tallahassee, FL	(8.9)
360	Tampa, FL	(39.1)
330	Temecula, CA	(30.9)
337	Tempe, AZ	(32.2)
324	Thornton, CO	(30.0)
58	Thousand Oaks, CA	2.3
NA	Toledo, OH**	NA
4	Toms River Twnshp, NJ	30.5
332	Topeka, KS	(31.3)
158	Torrance, CA	(11.0)
313	Tracy, CA	(28.3)
283	Trenton, NJ	(24.0)
NA	Troy, MI**	NA
NA	Tucson, AZ**	NA
127	Tulsa, OK	(7.4)
160	Tuscaloosa, AL	(11.2)
18	Tyler, TX	13.2
31	Upper Darby Twnshp, PA	8.7
182	Vacaville, CA	(13.5)
NA	Vallejo, CA**	NA
316	Vancouver, WA	(28.8)
249	Ventura, CA	(21.0)
345	Victorville, CA	(33.7)
56	Virginia Beach, VA	2.5
353	Visalia, CA	(35.6)
281	Vista, CA	(23.9)
272	Waco, TX	(22.9)
NA	Warren, MI**	NA
34	Warwick, RI	7.7
83	Washington, DC	(1.6)
106	Waterbury, CT	(5.1)
205	West Covina, CA	(16.2)
NA	West Jordan, UT**	NA
306	West Palm Beach, FL	(27.7)
216	West Valley, UT	(17.3)
NA	Westland, MI**	NA
217	Westminster, CA	(17.4)
344	Westminster, CO	(33.5)
193	Whittier, CA	(14.9)
290	Wichita Falls, TX	(25.2)
NA	Wichita, KS**	NA
159	Wilmington, NC	(11.1)
97	Winston-Salem, NC	(4.1)
175	Woodbridge Twnshp, NJ	(12.8)
33	Worcester, MA	8.2
152	Yonkers, NY	(9.8)
198	Yuma, AZ	(15.3)

Source: CQ Press using reported data from the F.B.I. "Crime in the United States 2009"

*Property crimes are offenses of burglary, larceny-theft, and motor vehicle theft. Attempts are included.

**Not available.

68. Percent Change in Property Crime Rate: 2005 to 2009 (continued)
National Percent Change = 11.5% Decrease*

RANK	CITY	% CHANGE
1	Greece, NY	33.4
2	Fargo, ND	32.2
3	Sunrise, FL	30.6
4	Toms River Twnshp, NJ	30.5
5	Pembroke Pines, FL	27.1
6	Gainesville, FL	26.6
7	Mesquite, TX	21.3
8	Nashua, NH	20.7
9	Compton, CA	20.4
10	Somerville, MA	17.3
11	Lafayette, LA	15.7
12	Coral Springs, FL	15.4
13	Quincy, MA	14.8
14	Davie, FL	14.7
15	Jackson, MS	14.6
16	Pasadena, TX	13.8
17	Huntington Beach, CA	13.5
18	Tyler, TX	13.2
19	Columbus, GA	12.9
20	Lawrence, KS	12.6
21	Miami Beach, FL	12.4
22	Columbia, MO	12.2
23	Amherst, NY	12.0
24	Garland, TX	11.8
25	Norman, OK	10.6
26	McKinney, TX	10.3
27	Longview, TX	10.0
28	Hollywood, FL	9.9
29	St. Petersburg, FL	9.6
30	Portsmouth, VA	9.0
31	Upper Darby Twnshp, PA	8.7
32	Plantation, FL	8.5
33	Worcester, MA	8.2
34	Melbourne, FL	7.7
34	Warwick, RI	7.7
36	Brownsville, TX	7.4
36	Cheektowaga, NY	7.4
38	Miramar, FL	7.1
39	Manchester, NH	7.0
40	Springfield, MO	6.8
41	Rochester, MN	6.3
41	Spokane, WA	6.3
43	Erie, PA	5.6
44	New Bedford, MA	5.0
45	Lawton, OK	4.6
46	Downey, CA	4.5
46	Odessa, TX	4.5
48	Fremont, CA	4.2
49	Austin, TX	3.9
50	Knoxville, TN	3.5
50	San Antonio, TX	3.5
52	Brick Twnshp, NJ	3.4
52	Buena Park, CA	3.4
54	Hialeah, FL	2.9
55	Milwaukee, WI	2.8
56	Virginia Beach, VA	2.5
57	Elizabeth, NJ	2.4
58	Thousand Oaks, CA	2.3
59	Sandy, UT	2.2
60	Cranston, RI	2.0
61	Lake Forest, CA	1.9
62	Glendale, CA	1.7
62	Norfolk, VA	1.7
64	Sunnyvale, CA	1.5
65	Inglewood, CA	1.0
65	Livermore, CA	1.0
65	Richardson, TX	1.0
68	Boca Raton, FL	0.8

RANK	CITY	% CHANGE
69	Kenosha, WI	0.5
69	Santa Barbara, CA	0.5
71	Laredo, TX	0.2
72	Fontana, CA	0.1
73	Hamilton Twnshp, NJ	0.0
74	Mobile, AL	(0.1)
75	Clarksville, TN	(0.2)
76	Las Cruces, NM	(0.4)
77	Roswell, GA	(0.7)
78	Albany, GA	(0.8)
79	Greensboro, NC	(0.9)
80	Birmingham, AL	(1.0)
81	Carson, CA	(1.2)
82	Hawthorne, CA	(1.3)
83	Hampton, VA	(1.6)
83	Washington, DC	(1.6)
85	Clearwater, FL	(2.0)
86	Burbank, CA	(2.5)
87	Port St. Lucie, FL	(2.8)
88	Arlington, TX	(3.1)
89	Long Beach, CA	(3.2)
90	Lubbock, TX	(3.5)
90	Lynn, MA	(3.5)
92	Midland, TX	(3.7)
92	Santa Monica, CA	(3.7)
94	Madison, WI	(3.8)
95	Fort Collins, CO	(3.9)
95	Glendale, AZ	(3.9)
97	Winston-Salem, NC	(4.1)
98	Chesapeake, VA	(4.2)
99	Danbury, CT	(4.3)
99	Rio Rancho, NM	(4.3)
101	Baton Rouge, LA	(4.5)
101	Lakeland, FL	(4.5)
101	Springfield, IL	(4.5)
104	Pasadena, CA	(4.6)
105	College Station, TX	(4.9)
106	South Bend, IN	(5.1)
106	Waterbury, CT	(5.1)
108	Round Rock, TX	(5.2)
109	Mission Viejo, CA	(5.3)
109	Ramapo, NY	(5.3)
109	San Jose, CA	(5.3)
112	Naperville, IL	(5.5)
113	Green Bay, WI	(5.7)
113	Jacksonville, FL	(5.7)
115	Murfreesboro, TN	(6.2)
116	Fayetteville, NC	(6.3)
116	Sioux Falls, SD	(6.3)
118	Salt Lake City, UT	(6.6)
119	Carrollton, TX	(6.7)
120	Indianapolis, IN	(6.8)
120	San Francisco, CA	(6.8)
122	Athens-Clarke, GA	(6.9)
122	Syracuse, NY	(6.9)
124	Cambridge, MA	(7.0)
125	Overland Park, KS	(7.1)
126	Camden, NJ	(7.3)
127	Chicago, IL	(7.4)
127	Tulsa, OK	(7.4)
129	Chattanooga, TN	(7.6)
130	Columbia, SC	(7.7)
131	Grand Prairie, TX	(7.9)
131	South Gate, CA	(7.9)
133	Oxnard, CA	(8.0)
134	Clifton, NJ	(8.1)
134	Sugar Land, TX	(8.1)
136	Savannah, GA	(8.3)
137	El Paso, TX	(8.4)

RANK	CITY	% CHANGE
138	Buffalo, NY	(8.7)
139	Antioch, CA	(8.8)
140	Evansville, IN	(8.9)
140	Tallahassee, FL	(8.9)
142	Allentown, PA	(9.0)
143	Amarillo, TX	(9.3)
143	McAllen, TX	(9.3)
145	Everett, WA	(9.5)
145	Providence, RI	(9.5)
147	Cleveland, OH	(9.6)
147	Houston, TX	(9.6)
147	Stamford, CT	(9.6)
150	Newport Beach, CA	(9.7)
150	Paterson, NJ	(9.7)
152	Edison Twnshp, NJ	(9.8)
152	Raleigh, NC	(9.8)
152	Yonkers, NY	(9.8)
155	Lee's Summit, MO	(10.0)
156	Akron, OH	(10.5)
157	Albuquerque, NM	(10.9)
158	Torrance, CA	(11.0)
159	Wilmington, NC	(11.1)
160	Tuscaloosa, AL	(11.2)
161	Fort Smith, AR	(11.3)
162	Anchorage, AK	(11.5)
163	Miami Gardens, FL	(11.7)
164	Albany, NY	(11.8)
165	Alexandria, VA	(11.9)
165	Baltimore, MD	(11.9)
165	Durham, NC	(11.9)
165	Missouri City, TX	(11.9)
169	Philadelphia, PA	(12.0)
169	Sparks, NV	(12.0)
171	Abilene, TX	(12.1)
171	Pearland, TX	(12.1)
173	Broken Arrow, OK	(12.3)
174	Newton, MA	(12.5)
175	Clovis, CA	(12.8)
175	Costa Mesa, CA	(12.8)
175	Woodbridge Twnshp, NJ	(12.8)
178	Hammond, IN	(12.9)
179	San Leandro, CA	(13.1)
180	Oakland, CA	(13.2)
181	Columbus, OH	(13.3)
182	Vacaville, CA	(13.5)
183	Cape Coral, FL	(13.6)
183	St. Joseph, MO	(13.6)
185	Irving, TX	(13.8)
186	Pompano Beach, FL	(13.9)
187	Santa Rosa, CA	(14.0)
188	Cincinnati, OH	(14.4)
189	Springfield, MA	(14.7)
190	Atlanta, GA	(14.8)
190	Fayetteville, AR	(14.8)
190	Orlando, FL	(14.8)
193	Fort Lauderdale, FL	(14.9)
193	Whittier, CA	(14.9)
195	Brockton, MA	(15.0)
196	Montgomery, AL	(15.1)
196	Simi Valley, CA	(15.1)
198	Yuma, AZ	(15.3)
199	Fullerton, CA	(15.4)
199	Memphis, TN	(15.4)
201	New York, NY	(15.6)
202	Scottsdale, AZ	(15.7)
203	Plano, TX	(15.8)
204	Anaheim, CA	(16.0)
205	West Covina, CA	(16.2)
206	Santa Clarita, CA	(16.3)

RANK	CITY	% CHANGE
206	Tacoma, WA	(16.3)
208	Aurora, IL	(16.6)
208	Edmond, OK	(16.6)
208	Santa Clara, CA	(16.6)
211	Cedar Rapids, IA	(16.7)
212	Eugene, OR	(16.8)
213	Lewisville, TX	(16.9)
214	St. Paul, MN	(17.0)
215	Rialto, CA	(17.2)
216	West Valley, UT	(17.3)
217	Westminster, CA	(17.4)
218	Miami, FL	(17.5)
218	Rockford, IL	(17.5)
220	San Bernardino, CA	(17.6)
221	Rochester, NY	(17.7)
222	Corona, CA	(17.8)
223	Bakersfield, CA	(18.0)
224	Berkeley, CA	(18.1)
225	Dayton, OH	(18.2)
226	Fort Worth, TX	(18.3)
226	Macon, GA	(18.3)
228	High Point, NC	(18.6)
229	Bridgeport, CT	(18.7)
230	Daly City, CA	(18.8)
231	Chandler, AZ	(19.0)
232	Baldwin Park, CA	(19.1)
232	El Monte, CA	(19.1)
234	Los Angeles, CA	(19.2)
234	Moreno Valley, CA	(19.2)
236	Shreveport, LA	(19.3)
237	Sioux City, IA	(19.7)
238	Bellevue, WA	(19.8)
238	Hayward, CA	(19.8)
240	Independence, MO	(19.9)
240	Modesto, CA	(19.9)
240	Ogden, UT	(19.9)
243	Pittsburgh, PA	(20.2)
244	Corpus Christi, TX	(20.4)
245	Pomona, CA	(20.5)
246	Norwalk, CA	(20.6)
247	Spokane Valley, WA	(20.7)
248	Lakewood, CA	(20.9)
249	Ventura, CA	(21.0)
250	Honolulu, HI	(21.1)
250	Joliet, IL	(21.1)
250	Palmdale, CA	(21.1)
250	Stockton, CA	(21.1)
254	Beaumont, TX	(21.2)
254	Fresno, CA	(21.2)
256	Cary, NC	(21.4)
256	Huntsville, AL	(21.4)
256	Roanoke, VA	(21.4)
259	Charleston, SC	(21.5)
260	Escondido, CA	(21.6)
261	Minneapolis, MN	(21.7)
261	Sacramento, CA	(21.7)
263	Allen, TX	(22.0)
264	Colonie, NY	(22.2)
264	Rancho Cucamon., CA	(22.2)
264	San Mateo, CA	(22.2)
267	Seattle, WA	(22.4)
268	Surprise, AZ	(22.6)
269	Billings, MT	(22.7)
269	Irvine, CA	(22.7)
271	Lakewood, CO	(22.8)
272	Omaha, NE	(22.9)
272	Waco, TX	(22.9)
274	Oklahoma City, OK	(23.1)

RANK	CITY	% CHANGE
274	San Angelo, TX	(23.1)
276	Killeen, TX	(23.2)
276	Richmond, CA	(23.2)
278	Fort Wayne, IN	(23.4)
279	Dallas, TX	(23.5)
280	Provo, UT	(23.7)
281	Salinas, CA	(23.9)
281	Vista, CA	(23.9)
283	Trenton, NJ	(24.0)
284	Chino, CA	(24.4)
284	Racine, WI	(24.4)
286	Ontario, CA	(24.6)
286	Orange, CA	(24.6)
286	St. Louis, MO	(24.6)
289	Boston, MA	(25.1)
290	Reading, PA	(25.2)
290	Santa Maria, CA	(25.2)
290	Wichita Falls, TX	(25.2)
293	North Charleston, SC	(25.4)
294	Garden Grove, CA	(25.5)
295	Nashville, TN	(25.6)
296	Reno, NV	(25.7)
297	Kansas City, KS	(25.8)
298	Alhambra, CA	(25.9)
299	Lincoln, NE	(26.4)
300	Chico, CA	(26.5)
301	Suffolk, VA	(26.6)
302	Fairfield, CA	(27.1)
303	Boise, ID	(27.3)
303	Roseville, CA	(27.3)
303	San Marcos, CA	(27.3)
306	West Palm Beach, FL	(27.7)
307	Federal Way, WA	(27.9)
308	Carlsbad, CA	(28.0)
308	Charlotte, NC	(28.0)
310	Bellingham, WA	(28.2)
310	Canton, OH	(28.2)
310	Gilbert, AZ	(28.2)
313	Tracy, CA	(28.3)
314	Boulder, CO	(28.4)
315	Las Vegas, NV	(28.5)
316	Vancouver, WA	(28.8)
317	Davenport, IA	(28.9)
318	Redding, CA	(29.0)
319	Kansas City, MO	(29.2)
320	Orem, UT	(29.3)
320	Peoria, IL	(29.3)
322	Norwalk, CT	(29.6)
323	Gresham, OR	(29.7)
324	Colorado Springs, CO	(30.0)
324	Thornton, CO	(30.0)
326	Newark, NJ	(30.2)
326	Oceanside, CA	(30.2)
328	Centennial, CO	(30.6)
329	Riverside, CA	(30.8)
330	Temecula, CA	(30.9)
331	Henderson, NV	(31.0)
332	Indio, CA	(31.3)
332	Topeka, KS	(31.3)
334	Hesperia, CA	(31.6)
335	Jersey City, NJ	(31.8)
336	Peoria, AZ	(32.1)
337	Portland, OR	(32.2)
337	Tempe, AZ	(32.2)
339	St. George, UT	(32.3)
340	San Diego, CA	(32.5)
341	Gary, IN	(32.6)
342	Santa Ana, CA	(32.8)

RANK	CITY	% CHANGE
343	Arvada, CO	(33.0)
344	Westminster, CO	(33.5)
345	Victorville, CA	(33.7)
346	El Cajon, CA	(34.0)
347	Salem, OR	(34.2)
348	Hartford, CT	(34.4)
349	Palm Bay, FL	(34.9)
350	Lancaster, CA	(35.0)
351	Chula Vista, CA	(35.5)
351	Phoenix, AZ	(35.5)
353	Visalia, CA	(35.6)
354	Mesa, AZ	(35.8)
355	Concord, CA	(36.0)
355	Denton, TX	(36.0)
357	Merced, CA	(36.9)
358	Aurora, CO	(37.7)
359	Richmond, VA	(37.8)
360	Kent, WA	(39.1)
360	Tampa, FL	(39.1)
362	North Las Vegas, NV	(39.3)
362	O'Fallon, MO	(39.3)
364	Murrieta, CA	(40.7)
365	Denver, CO	(42.5)
366	Greeley, CO	(47.2)
367	Bend, OR	(49.0)
368	Beaverton, OR	(51.5)
368	Pueblo, CO	(51.5)
370	Frisco, TX	(52.6)
371	Hillsboro, OR	(55.6)
NA	Ann Arbor, MI**	NA
NA	Avondale, AZ**	NA
NA	Bloomington, MN**	NA
NA	Canton Twnshp, MI**	NA
NA	Citrus Heights, CA**	NA
NA	Clarkstown, NY**	NA
NA	Clinton Twnshp, MI**	NA
NA	Dearborn, MI**	NA
NA	Decatur, IL**	NA
NA	Des Moines, IA**	NA
NA	Detroit, MI**	NA
NA	Duluth, MN**	NA
NA	Elgin, IL**	NA
NA	Elk Grove, CA**	NA
NA	Fall River, MA**	NA
NA	Farmington Hills, MI**	NA
NA	Flint, MI**	NA
NA	Grand Rapids, MI**	NA
NA	Jacksonville, NC**	NA
NA	Lansing, MI**	NA
NA	Lexington, KY**	NA
NA	Little Rock, AR**	NA
NA	Livonia, MI**	NA
NA	Longmont, CO**	NA
NA	Louisville, KY**	NA
NA	Nampa, ID**	NA
NA	New Haven, CT**	NA
NA	New Orleans, LA**	NA
NA	Olathe, KS**	NA
NA	Sandy Springs, GA**	NA
NA	Southfield, MI**	NA
NA	Sterling Heights, MI**	NA
NA	Toledo, OH**	NA
NA	Troy, MI**	NA
NA	Tucson, AZ**	NA
NA	Vallejo, CA**	NA
NA	Warren, MI**	NA
NA	West Jordan, UT**	NA
NA	Westland, MI**	NA
NA	Wichita, KS**	NA

Source: CQ Press using reported data from the F.B.I. "Crime in the United States 2009"
*Property crimes are offenses of burglary, larceny-theft, and motor vehicle theft. Attempts are included.
**Not available.

69. Burglaries in 2009
National Total = 2,199,125 Burglaries*

RANK	CITY	BURGLARY
165	Abilene, TX	1,301
58	Akron, OH	3,759
146	Albany, GA	1,451
226	Albany, NY	876
30	Albuquerque, NM	6,376
374	Alexandria, VA	347
372	Alhambra, CA	360
149	Allentown, PA	1,414
395	Allen, TX	273
87	Amarillo, TX	2,561
399	Amherst, NY	238
145	Anaheim, CA	1,457
131	Anchorage, AK	1,613
299	Ann Arbor, MI	609
234	Antioch, CA	824
38	Arlington, TX	4,891
355	Arvada, CO	402
113	Athens-Clarke, GA	1,917
19	Atlanta, GA	9,112
105	Aurora, CO	2,051
253	Aurora, IL	755
20	Austin, TX	8,753
206	Avondale, AZ	1,012
54	Bakersfield, CA	3,888
369	Baldwin Park, CA	365
22	Baltimore, MD	7,798
50	Baton Rouge, LA	4,268
126	Beaumont, TX	1,665
402	Beaverton, OR	226
290	Bellevue, WA	621
283	Bellingham, WA	651
383	Bend, OR	316
197	Berkeley, CA	1,079
254	Billings, MT	752
37	Birmingham, AL	5,019
393	Bloomington, MN	277
308	Boca Raton, FL	554
200	Boise, ID	1,046
77	Boston, MA	2,955
307	Boulder, CO	564
385	Brick Twnshp, NJ	315
169	Bridgeport, CT	1,276
246	Brockton, MA	772
348	Broken Arrow, OK	423
133	Brownsville, TX	1,576
342	Buena Park, CA	441
53	Buffalo, NY	3,954
323	Burbank, CA	499
343	Cambridge, MA	434
202	Camden, NJ	1,035
389	Canton Twnshp, MI	294
156	Canton, OH	1,369
170	Cape Coral, FL	1,267
339	Carlsbad, CA	446
193	Carrollton, TX	1,085
333	Carson, CA	475
337	Cary, NC	469
167	Cedar Rapids, IA	1,279
397	Centennial, CO	269
155	Chandler, AZ	1,376
305	Charleston, SC	566
17	Charlotte, NC	9,817
75	Chattanooga, TN	2,987
377	Cheektowaga, NY	334
163	Chesapeake, VA	1,317
2	Chicago, IL	26,494
272	Chico, CA	685
311	Chino, CA	543

RANK	CITY	BURGLARY
220	Chula Vista, CA	912
32	Cincinnati, OH	6,287
268	Citrus Heights, CA	702
410	Clarkstown, NY	136
134	Clarksville, TN	1,569
238	Clearwater, FL	802
18	Cleveland, OH	9,226
390	Clifton, NJ	294
319	Clinton Twnshp, MI	518
264	Clovis, CA	705
295	College Station, TX	613
406	Colonie, NY	205
66	Colorado Springs, CO	3,305
269	Columbia, MO	692
125	Columbia, SC	1,678
56	Columbus, GA	3,792
10	Columbus, OH	14,583
249	Compton, CA	768
237	Concord, CA	808
312	Coral Springs, FL	541
296	Corona, CA	612
76	Corpus Christi, TX	2,976
320	Costa Mesa, CA	516
350	Cranston, RI	415
3	Dallas, TX	19,428
382	Daly City, CA	317
405	Danbury, CT	219
190	Davenport, IA	1,097
271	Davie, FL	686
67	Dayton, OH	3,244
261	Dearborn, MI	712
158	Decatur, IL	1,344
276	Denton, TX	681
42	Denver, CO	4,763
119	Des Moines, IA	1,830
4	Detroit, MI	18,993
317	Downey, CA	524
288	Duluth, MN	632
64	Durham, NC	3,643
348	Edison Twnshp, NJ	423
366	Edmond, OK	373
325	El Cajon, CA	487
284	El Monte, CA	644
109	El Paso, TX	1,991
340	Elgin, IL	445
208	Elizabeth, NJ	1,002
228	Elk Grove, CA	859
205	Erie, PA	1,013
242	Escondido, CA	779
117	Eugene, OR	1,868
186	Evansville, IN	1,110
189	Everett, WA	1,099
242	Fairfield, CA	779
245	Fall River, MA	775
285	Fargo, ND	639
398	Farmington Hills, MI	256
327	Fayetteville, AR	483
49	Fayetteville, NC	4,289
259	Federal Way, WA	741
74	Flint, MI	3,057
199	Fontana, CA	1,060
254	Fort Collins, CO	752
79	Fort Lauderdale, FL	2,907
185	Fort Smith, AR	1,119
97	Fort Wayne, IN	2,269
16	Fort Worth, TX	10,188
179	Fremont, CA	1,190
46	Fresno, CA	4,423
373	Frisco, TX	357

RANK	CITY	BURGLARY
242	Fullerton, CA	779
139	Gainesville, FL	1,487
270	Garden Grove, CA	687
98	Garland, TX	2,206
138	Gary, IN	1,493
207	Gilbert, AZ	1,010
88	Glendale, AZ	2,551
287	Glendale, CA	635
102	Grand Prairie, TX	2,082
91	Grand Rapids, MI	2,454
375	Greece, NY	345
301	Greeley, CO	585
286	Green Bay, WI	637
41	Greensboro, NC	4,789
304	Gresham, OR	572
381	Hamilton Twnshp, NJ	320
216	Hammond, IN	938
232	Hampton, VA	835
183	Hartford, CT	1,135
281	Hawthorne, CA	654
211	Hayward, CA	979
150	Henderson, NV	1,411
331	Hesperia, CA	476
191	Hialeah, FL	1,093
144	High Point, NC	1,463
400	Hillsboro, OR	235
124	Hollywood, FL	1,687
33	Honolulu, HI	5,999
1	Houston, TX	29,279
266	Huntington Beach, CA	704
89	Huntsville, AL	2,520
161	Independence, MO	1,328
9	Indianapolis, IN	15,217
217	Indio, CA	927
272	Inglewood, CA	685
328	Irvine, CA	481
114	Irving, TX	1,913
13	Jacksonville, FL	11,306
292	Jacksonville, NC	618
44	Jackson, MS	4,569
152	Jersey City, NJ	1,400
223	Joliet, IL	899
112	Kansas City, KS	1,918
23	Kansas City, MO	7,231
300	Kenosha, WI	593
233	Kent, WA	828
122	Killeen, TX	1,735
85	Knoxville, TN	2,589
151	Lafayette, LA	1,407
408	Lake Forest, CA	179
173	Lakeland, FL	1,247
384	Lakewood, CA	316
222	Lakewood, CO	901
178	Lancaster, CA	1,206
159	Lansing, MI	1,340
100	Laredo, TX	2,164
215	Las Cruces, NM	964
12	Las Vegas, NV	13,512
274	Lawrence, KS	683
147	Lawton, OK	1,448
363	Lee's Summit, MO	378
280	Lewisville, TX	657
92	Lexington, KY	2,427
130	Lincoln, NE	1,618
47	Little Rock, AR	4,412
360	Livermore, CA	393
376	Livonia, MI	341
71	Long Beach, CA	3,116
350	Longmont, CO	415

RANK	CITY	BURGLARY	RANK	CITY	BURGLARY	RANK	CITY	BURGLARY
175	Longview, TX	1,217	184	Peoria, AZ	1,120	282	Southfield, MI	653
6	Los Angeles, CA	18,435	132	Peoria, IL	1,606	230	Sparks, NV	850
24	Louisville, KY	7,085	14	Philadelphia, PA	10,969	293	Spokane Valley, WA	616
60	Lubbock, TX	3,730	8	Phoenix, AZ	16,281	86	Spokane, WA	2,565
247	Lynn, MA	771	82	Pittsburgh, PA	2,811	123	Springfield, IL	1,711
121	Macon, GA	1,814	143	Plano, TX	1,477	104	Springfield, MA	2,068
136	Madison, WI	1,523	278	Plantation, FL	674	95	Springfield, MO	2,314
252	Manchester, NH	760	229	Pomona, CA	854	367	Stamford, CT	370
240	McAllen, TX	796	212	Pompano Beach, FL	971	369	Sterling Heights, MI	365
262	McKinney, TX	711	188	Port St. Lucie, FL	1,102	52	Stockton, CA	3,980
260	Melbourne, FL	737	62	Portland, OR	3,696	379	St. George, UT	322
11	Memphis, TN	13,943	180	Portsmouth, VA	1,184	213	St. Joseph, MO	970
277	Merced, CA	679	120	Providence, RI	1,825	25	St. Louis, MO	6,834
73	Mesa, AZ	3,076	353	Provo, UT	407	78	St. Paul, MN	2,929
153	Mesquite, TX	1,390	164	Pueblo, CO	1,311	48	St. Petersburg, FL	4,366
177	Miami Beach, FL	1,207	330	Quincy, MA	478	338	Suffolk, VA	465
127	Miami Gardens, FL	1,663	187	Racine, WI	1,108	396	Sugar Land, TX	270
39	Miami, FL	4,856	69	Raleigh, NC	3,187	344	Sunnyvale, CA	431
221	Midland, TX	909	411	Ramapo, NY	94	258	Sunrise, FL	742
29	Milwaukee, WI	6,534	227	Rancho Cucamon., CA	860	314	Surprise, AZ	532
43	Minneapolis, MN	4,741	162	Reading, PA	1,321	111	Syracuse, NY	1,946
204	Miramar, FL	1,020	241	Redding, CA	783	80	Tacoma, WA	2,905
403	Mission Viejo, CA	221	118	Reno, NV	1,848	70	Tallahassee, FL	3,125
368	Missouri City, TX	366	239	Rialto, CA	801	65	Tampa, FL	3,501
61	Mobile, AL	3,716	218	Richardson, TX	919	303	Temecula, CA	576
96	Modesto, CA	2,291	140	Richmond, CA	1,486	142	Tempe, AZ	1,478
72	Montgomery, AL	3,092	135	Richmond, VA	1,555	274	Thornton, CO	683
107	Moreno Valley, CA	2,020	346	Rio Rancho, NM	430	378	Thousand Oaks, CA	323
157	Murfreesboro, TN	1,346	107	Riverside, CA	2,020	21	Toledo, OH	8,064
334	Murrieta, CA	471	219	Roanoke, VA	913	326	Toms River Twnshp, NJ	485
335	Nampa, ID	470	357	Rochester, MN	398	127	Topeka, KS	1,663
388	Naperville, IL	296	81	Rochester, NY	2,899	341	Torrance, CA	442
362	Nashua, NH	379	90	Rockford, IL	2,459	331	Tracy, CA	476
31	Nashville, TN	6,318	316	Roseville, CA	525	234	Trenton, NJ	824
182	New Bedford, MA	1,144	302	Roswell, GA	584	401	Troy, MI	231
148	New Haven, CT	1,430	352	Round Rock, TX	412	36	Tucson, AZ	5,062
55	New Orleans, LA	3,821	35	Sacramento, CA	5,135	28	Tulsa, OK	6,626
5	New York, NY	18,780	214	Salem, OR	967	137	Tuscaloosa, AL	1,507
110	Newark, NJ	1,947	154	Salinas, CA	1,382	201	Tyler, TX	1,044
321	Newport Beach, CA	512	99	Salt Lake City, UT	2,173	391	Upper Darby Twnshp, PA	278
407	Newton, MA	187	209	San Angelo, TX	996	357	Vacaville, CA	398
103	Norfolk, VA	2,078	7	San Antonio, TX	18,164	93	Vallejo, CA	2,358
251	Norman, OK	765	94	San Bernardino, CA	2,349	225	Vancouver, WA	886
203	North Charleston, SC	1,024	27	San Diego, CA	6,693	294	Ventura, CA	615
114	North Las Vegas, NV	1,913	34	San Francisco, CA	5,197	172	Victorville, CA	1,253
359	Norwalk, CA	396	59	San Jose, CA	3,741	106	Virginia Beach, VA	2,043
386	Norwalk, CT	314	310	San Leandro, CA	547	171	Visalia, CA	1,261
40	Oakland, CA	4,798	387	San Marcos, CA	307	318	Vista, CA	519
249	Oceanside, CA	768	394	San Mateo, CA	274	116	Waco, TX	1,897
194	Odessa, TX	1,084	231	Sandy Springs, GA	848	224	Warren, MI	887
409	O'Fallon, MO	144	306	Sandy, UT	565	371	Warwick, RI	361
247	Ogden, UT	771	181	Santa Ana, CA	1,160	62	Washington, DC	3,696
15	Oklahoma City, OK	10,594	298	Santa Barbara, CA	610	256	Waterbury, CT	749
380	Olathe, KS	321	347	Santa Clara, CA	428	335	West Covina, CA	470
68	Omaha, NE	3,228	264	Santa Clarita, CA	705	314	West Jordan, UT	532
210	Ontario, CA	986	308	Santa Maria, CA	554	166	West Palm Beach, FL	1,291
344	Orange, CA	431	321	Santa Monica, CA	512	198	West Valley, UT	1,068
404	Orem, UT	220	263	Santa Rosa, CA	710	297	Westland, MI	611
57	Orlando, FL	3,770	84	Savannah, GA	2,652	354	Westminster, CA	406
313	Overland Park, KS	534	160	Scottsdale, AZ	1,337	328	Westminster, CO	481
266	Oxnard, CA	704	26	Seattle, WA	6,709	356	Whittier, CA	400
279	Palm Bay, FL	664	83	Shreveport, LA	2,730	168	Wichita Falls, TX	1,277
196	Palmdale, CA	1,080	365	Simi Valley, CA	375	51	Wichita, KS	4,045
234	Pasadena, CA	824	289	Sioux City, IA	625	129	Wilmington, NC	1,626
176	Pasadena, TX	1,213	257	Sioux Falls, SD	748	45	Winston-Salem, NC	4,532
174	Paterson, NJ	1,241	324	Somerville, MA	494	392	Woodbridge Twnshp, NJ	278
361	Pearland, TX	387	101	South Bend, IN	2,086	141	Worcester, MA	1,485
192	Pembroke Pines, FL	1,091	364	South Gate, CA	377	291	Yonkers, NY	620
						195	Yuma, AZ	1,082

Source: Reported data from the F.B.I. "Crime in the United States 2009"

*Burglary is the unlawful entry of a structure to commit a felony or theft. Attempts are included.

69. Burglaries in 2009 (continued)
National Total = 2,199,125 Burglaries*

RANK	CITY	BURGLARY
1	Houston, TX	29,279
2	Chicago, IL	26,494
3	Dallas, TX	19,428
4	Detroit, MI	18,993
5	New York, NY	18,780
6	Los Angeles, CA	18,435
7	San Antonio, TX	18,164
8	Phoenix, AZ	16,281
9	Indianapolis, IN	15,217
10	Columbus, OH	14,583
11	Memphis, TN	13,943
12	Las Vegas, NV	13,512
13	Jacksonville, FL	11,306
14	Philadelphia, PA	10,969
15	Oklahoma City, OK	10,594
16	Fort Worth, TX	10,188
17	Charlotte, NC	9,817
18	Cleveland, OH	9,226
19	Atlanta, GA	9,112
20	Austin, TX	8,753
21	Toledo, OH	8,064
22	Baltimore, MD	7,798
23	Kansas City, MO	7,231
24	Louisville, KY	7,085
25	St. Louis, MO	6,834
26	Seattle, WA	6,709
27	San Diego, CA	6,693
28	Tulsa, OK	6,626
29	Milwaukee, WI	6,534
30	Albuquerque, NM	6,376
31	Nashville, TN	6,318
32	Cincinnati, OH	6,287
33	Honolulu, HI	5,999
34	San Francisco, CA	5,197
35	Sacramento, CA	5,135
36	Tucson, AZ	5,062
37	Birmingham, AL	5,019
38	Arlington, TX	4,891
39	Miami, FL	4,856
40	Oakland, CA	4,798
41	Greensboro, NC	4,789
42	Denver, CO	4,763
43	Minneapolis, MN	4,741
44	Jackson, MS	4,569
45	Winston-Salem, NC	4,532
46	Fresno, CA	4,423
47	Little Rock, AR	4,412
48	St. Petersburg, FL	4,366
49	Fayetteville, NC	4,289
50	Baton Rouge, LA	4,268
51	Wichita, KS	4,045
52	Stockton, CA	3,980
53	Buffalo, NY	3,954
54	Bakersfield, CA	3,888
55	New Orleans, LA	3,821
56	Columbus, GA	3,792
57	Orlando, FL	3,770
58	Akron, OH	3,759
59	San Jose, CA	3,741
60	Lubbock, TX	3,730
61	Mobile, AL	3,716
62	Portland, OR	3,696
62	Washington, DC	3,696
64	Durham, NC	3,643
65	Tampa, FL	3,501
66	Colorado Springs, CO	3,305
67	Dayton, OH	3,244
68	Omaha, NE	3,228
69	Raleigh, NC	3,187
70	Tallahassee, FL	3,125
71	Long Beach, CA	3,116
72	Montgomery, AL	3,092
73	Mesa, AZ	3,076
74	Flint, MI	3,057
75	Chattanooga, TN	2,987
76	Corpus Christi, TX	2,976
77	Boston, MA	2,955
78	St. Paul, MN	2,929
79	Fort Lauderdale, FL	2,907
80	Tacoma, WA	2,905
81	Rochester, NY	2,899
82	Pittsburgh, PA	2,811
83	Shreveport, LA	2,730
84	Savannah, GA	2,652
85	Knoxville, TN	2,589
86	Spokane, WA	2,565
87	Amarillo, TX	2,561
88	Glendale, AZ	2,551
89	Huntsville, AL	2,520
90	Rockford, IL	2,459
91	Grand Rapids, MI	2,454
92	Lexington, KY	2,427
93	Vallejo, CA	2,358
94	San Bernardino, CA	2,349
95	Springfield, MO	2,314
96	Modesto, CA	2,291
97	Fort Wayne, IN	2,269
98	Garland, TX	2,206
99	Salt Lake City, UT	2,173
100	Laredo, TX	2,164
101	South Bend, IN	2,086
102	Grand Prairie, TX	2,082
103	Norfolk, VA	2,078
104	Springfield, MA	2,068
105	Aurora, CO	2,051
106	Virginia Beach, VA	2,043
107	Moreno Valley, CA	2,020
107	Riverside, CA	2,020
109	El Paso, TX	1,991
110	Newark, NJ	1,947
111	Syracuse, NY	1,946
112	Kansas City, KS	1,918
113	Athens-Clarke, GA	1,917
114	Irving, TX	1,913
114	North Las Vegas, NV	1,913
116	Waco, TX	1,897
117	Eugene, OR	1,868
118	Reno, NV	1,848
119	Des Moines, IA	1,830
120	Providence, RI	1,825
121	Macon, GA	1,814
122	Killeen, TX	1,735
123	Springfield, IL	1,711
124	Hollywood, FL	1,687
125	Columbia, SC	1,678
126	Beaumont, TX	1,665
127	Miami Gardens, FL	1,663
127	Topeka, KS	1,663
129	Wilmington, NC	1,626
130	Lincoln, NE	1,618
131	Anchorage, AK	1,613
132	Peoria, IL	1,606
133	Brownsville, TX	1,576
134	Clarksville, TN	1,569
135	Richmond, VA	1,555
136	Madison, WI	1,523
137	Tuscaloosa, AL	1,507
138	Gary, IN	1,493
139	Gainesville, FL	1,487
140	Richmond, CA	1,486
141	Worcester, MA	1,485
142	Tempe, AZ	1,478
143	Plano, TX	1,477
144	High Point, NC	1,463
145	Anaheim, CA	1,457
146	Albany, GA	1,451
147	Lawton, OK	1,448
148	New Haven, CT	1,430
149	Allentown, PA	1,414
150	Henderson, NV	1,411
151	Lafayette, LA	1,407
152	Jersey City, NJ	1,400
153	Mesquite, TX	1,390
154	Salinas, CA	1,382
155	Chandler, AZ	1,376
156	Canton, OH	1,369
157	Murfreesboro, TN	1,346
158	Decatur, IL	1,344
159	Lansing, MI	1,340
160	Scottsdale, AZ	1,337
161	Independence, MO	1,328
162	Reading, PA	1,321
163	Chesapeake, VA	1,317
164	Pueblo, CO	1,311
165	Abilene, TX	1,301
166	West Palm Beach, FL	1,291
167	Cedar Rapids, IA	1,279
168	Wichita Falls, TX	1,277
169	Bridgeport, CT	1,276
170	Cape Coral, FL	1,267
171	Visalia, CA	1,261
172	Victorville, CA	1,253
173	Lakeland, FL	1,247
174	Paterson, NJ	1,241
175	Longview, TX	1,217
176	Pasadena, TX	1,213
177	Miami Beach, FL	1,207
178	Lancaster, CA	1,206
179	Fremont, CA	1,190
180	Portsmouth, VA	1,184
181	Santa Ana, CA	1,160
182	New Bedford, MA	1,144
183	Hartford, CT	1,135
184	Peoria, AZ	1,120
185	Fort Smith, AR	1,119
186	Evansville, IN	1,110
187	Racine, WI	1,108
188	Port St. Lucie, FL	1,102
189	Everett, WA	1,099
190	Davenport, IA	1,097
191	Hialeah, FL	1,093
192	Pembroke Pines, FL	1,091
193	Carrollton, TX	1,085
194	Odessa, TX	1,084
195	Yuma, AZ	1,082
196	Palmdale, CA	1,080
197	Berkeley, CA	1,079
198	West Valley, UT	1,068
199	Fontana, CA	1,060
200	Boise, ID	1,046
201	Tyler, TX	1,044
202	Camden, NJ	1,035
203	North Charleston, SC	1,024
204	Miramar, FL	1,020
205	Erie, PA	1,013
206	Avondale, AZ	1,012

RANK	CITY	BURGLARY	RANK	CITY	BURGLARY	RANK	CITY	BURGLARY
207	Gilbert, AZ	1,010	274	Thornton, CO	683	343	Cambridge, MA	434
208	Elizabeth, NJ	1,002	276	Denton, TX	681	344	Orange, CA	431
209	San Angelo, TX	996	277	Merced, CA	679	344	Sunnyvale, CA	431
210	Ontario, CA	986	278	Plantation, FL	674	346	Rio Rancho, NM	430
211	Hayward, CA	979	279	Palm Bay, FL	664	347	Santa Clara, CA	428
212	Pompano Beach, FL	971	280	Lewisville, TX	657	348	Broken Arrow, OK	423
213	St. Joseph, MO	970	281	Hawthorne, CA	654	348	Edison Twnshp, NJ	423
214	Salem, OR	967	282	Southfield, MI	653	350	Cranston, RI	415
215	Las Cruces, NM	964	283	Bellingham, WA	651	350	Longmont, CO	415
216	Hammond, IN	938	284	El Monte, CA	644	352	Round Rock, TX	412
217	Indio, CA	927	285	Fargo, ND	639	353	Provo, UT	407
218	Richardson, TX	919	286	Green Bay, WI	637	354	Westminster, CA	406
219	Roanoke, VA	913	287	Glendale, CA	635	355	Arvada, CO	402
220	Chula Vista, CA	912	288	Duluth, MN	632	356	Whittier, CA	400
221	Midland, TX	909	289	Sioux City, IA	625	357	Rochester, MN	398
222	Lakewood, CO	901	290	Bellevue, WA	621	357	Vacaville, CA	398
223	Joliet, IL	899	291	Yonkers, NY	620	359	Norwalk, CA	396
224	Warren, MI	887	292	Jacksonville, NC	618	360	Livermore, CA	393
225	Vancouver, WA	886	293	Spokane Valley, WA	616	361	Pearland, TX	387
226	Albany, NY	876	294	Ventura, CA	615	362	Nashua, NH	379
227	Rancho Cucamon., CA	860	295	College Station, TX	613	363	Lee's Summit, MO	378
228	Elk Grove, CA	859	296	Corona, CA	612	364	South Gate, CA	377
229	Pomona, CA	854	297	Westland, MI	611	365	Simi Valley, CA	375
230	Sparks, NV	850	298	Santa Barbara, CA	610	366	Edmond, OK	373
231	Sandy Springs, GA	848	299	Ann Arbor, MI	609	367	Stamford, CT	370
232	Hampton, VA	835	300	Kenosha, WI	593	368	Missouri City, TX	366
233	Kent, WA	828	301	Greeley, CO	585	369	Baldwin Park, CA	365
234	Antioch, CA	824	302	Roswell, GA	584	369	Sterling Heights, MI	365
234	Pasadena, CA	824	303	Temecula, CA	576	371	Warwick, RI	361
234	Trenton, NJ	824	304	Gresham, OR	572	372	Alhambra, CA	360
237	Concord, CA	808	305	Charleston, SC	566	373	Frisco, TX	357
238	Clearwater, FL	802	306	Sandy, UT	565	374	Alexandria, VA	347
239	Rialto, CA	801	307	Boulder, CO	564	375	Greece, NY	345
240	McAllen, TX	796	308	Boca Raton, FL	554	376	Livonia, MI	341
241	Redding, CA	783	308	Santa Maria, CA	554	377	Cheektowaga, NY	334
242	Escondido, CA	779	310	San Leandro, CA	547	378	Thousand Oaks, CA	323
242	Fairfield, CA	779	311	Chino, CA	543	379	St. George, UT	322
242	Fullerton, CA	779	312	Coral Springs, FL	541	380	Olathe, KS	321
245	Fall River, MA	775	313	Overland Park, KS	534	381	Hamilton Twnshp, NJ	320
246	Brockton, MA	772	314	Surprise, AZ	532	382	Daly City, CA	317
247	Lynn, MA	771	314	West Jordan, UT	532	383	Bend, OR	316
247	Ogden, UT	771	316	Roseville, CA	525	384	Lakewood, CA	316
249	Compton, CA	768	317	Downey, CA	524	385	Brick Twnshp, NJ	315
249	Oceanside, CA	768	318	Vista, CA	519	386	Norwalk, CT	314
251	Norman, OK	765	319	Clinton Twnshp, MI	518	387	San Marcos, CA	307
252	Manchester, NH	760	320	Costa Mesa, CA	516	388	Naperville, IL	296
253	Aurora, IL	755	321	Newport Beach, CA	512	389	Canton Twnshp, MI	294
254	Billings, MT	752	321	Santa Monica, CA	512	390	Clifton, NJ	294
254	Fort Collins, CO	752	323	Burbank, CA	499	391	Upper Darby Twnshp, PA	278
256	Waterbury, CT	749	324	Somerville, MA	494	392	Woodbridge Twnshp, NJ	278
257	Sioux Falls, SD	748	325	El Cajon, CA	487	393	Bloomington, MN	277
258	Sunrise, FL	742	326	Toms River Twnshp, NJ	485	394	San Mateo, CA	274
259	Federal Way, WA	741	327	Fayetteville, AR	483	395	Allen, TX	273
260	Melbourne, FL	737	328	Irvine, CA	481	396	Sugar Land, TX	270
261	Dearborn, MI	712	328	Westminster, CO	481	397	Centennial, CO	269
262	McKinney, TX	711	330	Quincy, MA	478	398	Farmington Hills, MI	256
263	Santa Rosa, CA	710	331	Hesperia, CA	476	399	Amherst, NY	238
264	Clovis, CA	705	331	Tracy, CA	476	400	Hillsboro, OR	235
264	Santa Clarita, CA	705	333	Carson, CA	475	401	Troy, MI	231
266	Huntington Beach, CA	704	334	Murrieta, CA	471	402	Beaverton, OR	226
266	Oxnard, CA	704	335	Nampa, ID	470	403	Mission Viejo, CA	221
268	Citrus Heights, CA	702	335	West Covina, CA	470	404	Orem, UT	220
269	Columbia, MO	692	337	Cary, NC	469	405	Danbury, CT	219
270	Garden Grove, CA	687	338	Suffolk, VA	465	406	Colonie, NY	205
271	Davie, FL	686	339	Carlsbad, CA	446	407	Newton, MA	187
272	Chico, CA	685	340	Elgin, IL	445	408	Lake Forest, CA	179
272	Inglewood, CA	685	341	Torrance, CA	442	409	O'Fallon, MO	144
274	Lawrence, KS	683	342	Buena Park, CA	441	410	Clarkstown, NY	136
						411	Ramapo, NY	94

Source: Reported data from the F.B.I. "Crime in the United States 2009"

*Burglary is the unlawful entry of a structure to commit a felony or theft. Attempts are included.

70. Burglary Rate in 2009
National Rate = 716.3 Burglaries per 100,000 Population*

RANK	CITY	RATE
116	Abilene, TX	1,116.2
24	Akron, OH	1,820.4
18	Albany, GA	1,915.9
157	Albany, NY	937.4
100	Albuquerque, NM	1,201.6
400	Alexandria, VA	237.4
345	Alhambra, CA	418.8
75	Allentown, PA	1,317.5
382	Allen, TX	314.2
68	Amarillo, TX	1,356.7
407	Amherst, NY	215.6
336	Anaheim, CA	433.7
273	Anchorage, AK	569.4
294	Ann Arbor, MI	532.5
191	Antioch, CA	813.9
79	Arlington, TX	1,290.1
365	Arvada, CO	372.4
31	Athens-Clarke, GA	1,673.7
33	Atlanta, GA	1,648.0
250	Aurora, CO	633.0
337	Aurora, IL	431.1
111	Austin, TX	1,138.3
110	Avondale, AZ	1,140.0
106	Bakersfield, CA	1,175.0
319	Baldwin Park, CA	470.7
98	Baltimore, MD	1,220.8
19	Baton Rouge, LA	1,912.3
46	Beaumont, TX	1,510.4
399	Beaverton, OR	242.4
307	Bellevue, WA	496.6
192	Bellingham, WA	811.3
353	Bend, OR	392.3
127	Berkeley, CA	1,066.3
216	Billings, MT	713.3
6	Birmingham, AL	2,207.4
372	Bloomington, MN	342.6
241	Boca Raton, FL	644.5
303	Boise, ID	506.7
316	Boston, MA	473.4
277	Boulder, CO	563.8
352	Brick Twnshp, NJ	400.4
156	Bridgeport, CT	937.9
198	Brockton, MA	800.2
328	Broken Arrow, OK	448.0
170	Brownsville, TX	878.0
283	Buena Park, CA	554.5
52	Buffalo, NY	1,471.8
313	Burbank, CA	483.3
344	Cambridge, MA	421.9
78	Camden, NJ	1,310.5
369	Canton Twnshp, MI	355.8
28	Canton, OH	1,753.2
204	Cape Coral, FL	770.9
325	Carlsbad, CA	452.9
176	Carrollton, TX	851.4
300	Carson, CA	512.8
371	Cary, NC	350.6
144	Cedar Rapids, IA	993.2
394	Centennial, CO	270.7
291	Chandler, AZ	537.3
305	Charleston, SC	497.9
90	Charlotte, NC	1,262.3
29	Chattanooga, TN	1,731.2
340	Cheektowaga, NY	429.5
262	Chesapeake, VA	589.9
158	Chicago, IL	930.1
194	Chico, CA	808.5
245	Chino, CA	641.6
349	Chula Vista, CA	405.6
22	Cincinnati, OH	1,884.8
184	Citrus Heights, CA	832.4
410	Clarkstown, NY	172.4
81	Clarksville, TN	1,289.6
206	Clearwater, FL	761.0
7	Cleveland, OH	2,149.4
361	Clifton, NJ	376.3
288	Clinton Twnshp, MI	539.8
213	Clovis, CA	740.3
217	College Station, TX	712.2
395	Colonie, NY	262.8
187	Colorado Springs, CO	822.9
229	Columbia, MO	674.5
77	Columbia, SC	1,312.1
12	Columbus, GA	2,036.3
17	Columbus, OH	1,920.4
190	Compton, CA	818.1
233	Concord, CA	667.5
338	Coral Springs, FL	430.5
351	Corona, CA	401.5
134	Corpus Christi, TX	1,035.1
320	Costa Mesa, CA	468.5
298	Cranston, RI	517.3
49	Dallas, TX	1,505.7
384	Daly City, CA	313.0
393	Danbury, CT	274.7
122	Davenport, IA	1,084.9
206	Davie, FL	761.0
8	Dayton, OH	2,120.7
181	Dearborn, MI	834.7
27	Decatur, IL	1,776.6
284	Denton, TX	547.8
200	Denver, CO	787.7
159	Des Moines, IA	929.9
9	Detroit, MI	2,090.7
310	Downey, CA	487.0
209	Duluth, MN	751.7
39	Durham, NC	1,601.4
343	Edison Twnshp, NJ	425.7
322	Edmond, OK	461.1
295	El Cajon, CA	526.7
296	El Monte, CA	526.0
379	El Paso, TX	321.7
347	Elgin, IL	413.2
197	Elizabeth, NJ	802.2
256	Elk Grove, CA	611.1
148	Erie, PA	975.6
276	Escondido, CA	566.8
96	Eugene, OR	1,234.0
150	Evansville, IN	958.8
115	Everett, WA	1,116.5
211	Fairfield, CA	745.6
178	Fall River, MA	843.3
228	Fargo, ND	681.0
376	Farmington Hills, MI	327.6
242	Fayetteville, AR	643.0
4	Fayetteville, NC	2,465.0
169	Federal Way, WA	879.8
2	Flint, MI	2,737.8
282	Fontana, CA	557.0
286	Fort Collins, CO	543.0
40	Fort Lauderdale, FL	1,589.0
76	Fort Smith, AR	1,313.8
165	Fort Wayne, IN	901.9
62	Fort Worth, TX	1,408.2
264	Fremont, CA	587.0
163	Fresno, CA	918.8
375	Frisco, TX	329.8
263	Fullerton, CA	588.0
79	Gainesville, FL	1,290.1
346	Garden Grove, CA	414.3
141	Garland, TX	1,007.9
41	Gary, IN	1,568.0
335	Gilbert, AZ	435.7
142	Glendale, AZ	1,000.1
380	Glendale, CA	321.7
89	Grand Prairie, TX	1,263.6
84	Grand Rapids, MI	1,272.2
366	Greece, NY	369.9
252	Greeley, CO	628.6
251	Green Bay, WI	631.7
21	Greensboro, NC	1,891.5
280	Gresham, OR	558.3
370	Hamilton Twnshp, NJ	353.6
97	Hammond, IN	1,232.8
270	Hampton, VA	572.2
164	Hartford, CT	915.0
203	Hawthorne, CA	775.7
226	Hayward, CA	688.3
289	Henderson, NV	538.8
293	Hesperia, CA	535.4
297	Hialeah, FL	523.3
59	High Point, NC	1,411.1
398	Hillsboro, OR	243.4
101	Hollywood, FL	1,191.4
235	Honolulu, HI	661.3
82	Houston, TX	1,287.7
367	Huntington Beach, CA	364.9
60	Huntsville, AL	1,411.0
120	Independence, MO	1,087.0
23	Indianapolis, IN	1,870.6
132	Indio, CA	1,036.2
257	Inglewood, CA	607.7
405	Irvine, CA	223.0
154	Irving, TX	944.9
64	Jacksonville, FL	1,395.7
199	Jacksonville, NC	797.3
3	Jackson, MS	2,644.1
268	Jersey City, NJ	581.3
260	Joliet, IL	595.0
69	Kansas City, KS	1,349.7
50	Kansas City, MO	1,491.9
258	Kenosha, WI	607.2
145	Kent, WA	981.5
56	Killeen, TX	1,437.8
65	Knoxville, TN	1,393.1
94	Lafayette, LA	1,235.6
401	Lake Forest, CA	237.1
73	Lakeland, FL	1,322.1
350	Lakewood, CA	403.4
246	Lakewood, CO	640.7
193	Lancaster, CA	810.8
104	Lansing, MI	1,181.7
151	Laredo, TX	953.5
136	Las Cruces, NM	1,025.3
146	Las Vegas, NV	981.1
212	Lawrence, KS	744.8
36	Lawton, OK	1,611.8
332	Lee's Summit, MO	440.6
253	Lewisville, TX	628.1
189	Lexington, KY	818.8
248	Lincoln, NE	635.9
5	Little Rock, AR	2,319.6
312	Livermore, CA	485.7
359	Livonia, MI	377.9
232	Long Beach, CA	671.6
315	Longmont, CO	473.7

RANK	CITY	RATE
42	Longview, TX	1,567.0
314	Los Angeles, CA	479.0
113	Louisville, KY	1,122.4
32	Lubbock, TX	1,673.5
177	Lynn, MA	845.9
14	Macon, GA	1,965.4
240	Madison, WI	649.6
224	Manchester, NH	699.4
259	McAllen, TX	600.3
290	McKinney, TX	538.0
153	Melbourne, FL	946.6
10	Memphis, TN	2,089.1
172	Merced, CA	862.8
239	Mesa, AZ	653.3
130	Mesquite, TX	1,045.6
57	Miami Beach, FL	1,432.5
48	Miami Gardens, FL	1,507.1
108	Miami, FL	1,158.4
179	Midland, TX	842.2
123	Milwaukee, WI	1,080.6
93	Minneapolis, MN	1,239.1
155	Miramar, FL	941.2
403	Mission Viejo, CA	233.7
317	Missouri City, TX	472.0
47	Mobile, AL	1,509.5
114	Modesto, CA	1,120.4
44	Montgomery, AL	1,524.5
137	Moreno Valley, CA	1,024.8
85	Murfreesboro, TN	1,270.9
329	Murrieta, CA	447.6
278	Nampa, ID	560.4
408	Naperville, IL	204.5
333	Nashua, NH	437.9
133	Nashville, TN	1,035.4
95	New Bedford, MA	1,235.1
109	New Haven, CT	1,156.4
112	New Orleans, LA	1,135.8
404	New York, NY	223.5
225	Newark, NJ	697.3
246	Newport Beach, CA	640.7
406	Newton, MA	221.5
168	Norfolk, VA	883.9
221	Norman, OK	707.3
126	North Charleston, SC	1,066.9
188	North Las Vegas, NV	822.3
357	Norwalk, CA	385.2
360	Norwalk, CT	377.4
102	Oakland, CA	1,186.0
326	Oceanside, CA	450.2
121	Odessa, TX	1,086.5
409	O'Fallon, MO	178.8
161	Ogden, UT	928.7
20	Oklahoma City, OK	1,902.2
397	Olathe, KS	260.3
215	Omaha, NE	728.6
274	Ontario, CA	569.2
381	Orange, CA	314.3
402	Orem, UT	234.6
37	Orlando, FL	1,603.5
387	Overland Park, KS	307.4
362	Oxnard, CA	375.8
244	Palm Bay, FL	641.7
214	Palmdale, CA	737.8
271	Pasadena, CA	572.0
186	Pasadena, TX	825.4
175	Paterson, NJ	856.2
334	Pearland, TX	437.1
210	Pembroke Pines, FL	749.8

RANK	CITY	RATE
227	Peoria, AZ	681.4
63	Peoria, IL	1,405.8
220	Philadelphia, PA	708.8
138	Phoenix, AZ	1,019.2
166	Pittsburgh, PA	900.3
287	Plano, TX	541.5
195	Plantation, FL	806.8
281	Pomona, CA	557.4
151	Pompano Beach, FL	953.5
231	Port St. Lucie, FL	671.7
237	Portland, OR	658.9
107	Portsmouth, VA	1,172.6
128	Providence, RI	1,063.1
374	Provo, UT	340.7
92	Pueblo, CO	1,245.4
308	Quincy, MA	494.9
70	Racine, WI	1,347.4
201	Raleigh, NC	785.0
411	Ramapo, NY	122.7
311	Rancho Cucamon., CA	486.8
35	Reading, PA	1,642.7
173	Redding, CA	858.2
180	Reno, NV	836.2
196	Rialto, CA	805.9
167	Richardson, TX	895.1
55	Richmond, CA	1,448.8
205	Richmond, VA	765.1
299	Rio Rancho, NM	515.5
230	Riverside, CA	673.6
147	Roanoke, VA	980.6
355	Rochester, MN	390.6
61	Rochester, NY	1,410.5
43	Rockford, IL	1,556.9
327	Roseville, CA	449.3
236	Roswell, GA	660.9
364	Round Rock, TX	372.7
119	Sacramento, CA	1,091.8
254	Salem, OR	622.5
149	Salinas, CA	962.0
99	Salt Lake City, UT	1,202.4
124	San Angelo, TX	1,079.5
74	San Antonio, TX	1,322.0
105	San Bernardino, CA	1,176.4
301	San Diego, CA	509.1
243	San Francisco, CA	641.8
354	San Jose, CA	392.1
222	San Leandro, CA	704.2
363	San Marcos, CA	373.2
389	San Mateo, CA	297.2
135	Sandy Springs, GA	1,028.7
265	Sandy, UT	582.3
373	Santa Ana, CA	342.0
218	Santa Barbara, CA	711.7
357	Santa Clara, CA	385.2
348	Santa Clarita, CA	412.0
249	Santa Maria, CA	634.0
267	Santa Monica, CA	581.6
324	Santa Rosa, CA	453.6
91	Savannah, GA	1,246.8
279	Scottsdale, AZ	559.1
117	Seattle, WA	1,113.5
66	Shreveport, LA	1,367.5
386	Simi Valley, CA	308.5
208	Sioux City, IA	756.9
318	Sioux Falls, SD	471.4
238	Somerville, MA	657.7
13	South Bend, IN	2,018.9
356	South Gate, CA	390.1

RANK	CITY	RATE
171	Southfield, MI	869.8
160	Sparks, NV	929.8
219	Spokane Valley, WA	710.0
88	Spokane, WA	1,264.0
54	Springfield, IL	1,450.3
72	Springfield, MA	1,346.9
51	Springfield, MO	1,477.1
385	Stamford, CT	309.6
391	Sterling Heights, MI	286.4
67	Stockton, CA	1,362.0
342	St. George, UT	427.1
86	St. Joseph, MO	1,269.0
16	St. Louis, MO	1,923.9
131	St. Paul, MN	1,045.3
26	St. Petersburg, FL	1,782.5
285	Suffolk, VA	547.5
377	Sugar Land, TX	326.5
378	Sunnyvale, CA	326.2
182	Sunrise, FL	834.3
302	Surprise, AZ	508.2
58	Syracuse, NY	1,418.3
53	Tacoma, WA	1,470.5
25	Tallahassee, FL	1,794.1
140	Tampa, FL	1,014.1
272	Temecula, CA	570.7
183	Tempe, AZ	832.7
266	Thornton, CO	581.7
396	Thousand Oaks, CA	261.0
1	Toledo, OH	2,770.5
304	Toms River Twnshp, NJ	502.0
71	Topeka, KS	1,347.1
383	Torrance, CA	313.2
269	Tracy, CA	580.4
143	Trenton, NJ	997.5
390	Troy, MI	288.1
162	Tucson, AZ	923.8
30	Tulsa, OK	1,721.7
34	Tuscaloosa, AL	1,643.6
129	Tyler, TX	1,051.6
368	Upper Darby Twnshp, PA	356.0
339	Vacaville, CA	430.1
11	Vallejo, CA	2,060.4
292	Vancouver, WA	536.5
261	Ventura, CA	591.4
125	Victorville, CA	1,069.6
321	Virginia Beach, VA	468.4
139	Visalia, CA	1,014.8
275	Vista, CA	568.8
45	Waco, TX	1,516.4
234	Warren, MI	664.5
341	Warwick, RI	427.3
255	Washington, DC	616.4
223	Waterbury, CT	700.0
331	West Covina, CA	444.0
306	West Jordan, UT	496.7
83	West Palm Beach, FL	1,281.2
174	West Valley, UT	858.0
202	Westland, MI	781.8
323	Westminster, CA	455.9
330	Westminster, CO	446.6
309	Whittier, CA	487.2
87	Wichita Falls, TX	1,265.8
118	Wichita, KS	1,100.3
38	Wilmington, NC	1,602.9
15	Winston-Salem, NC	1,962.1
392	Woodbridge Twnshp, NJ	283.6
185	Worcester, MA	832.1
388	Yonkers, NY	306.6
103	Yuma, AZ	1,183.4

Source: CQ Press using reported data from the F.B.I. "Crime in the United States 2009"

*Burglary is the unlawful entry of a structure to commit a felony or theft. Attempts are included.

70. Burglary Rate in 2009 (continued)
National Rate = 716.3 Burglaries per 100,000 Population*

RANK	CITY	RATE
1	Toledo, OH	2,770.5
2	Flint, MI	2,737.8
3	Jackson, MS	2,644.1
4	Fayetteville, NC	2,465.0
5	Little Rock, AR	2,319.6
6	Birmingham, AL	2,207.4
7	Cleveland, OH	2,149.4
8	Dayton, OH	2,120.7
9	Detroit, MI	2,090.7
10	Memphis, TN	2,089.1
11	Vallejo, CA	2,060.4
12	Columbus, GA	2,036.3
13	South Bend, IN	2,018.9
14	Macon, GA	1,965.4
15	Winston-Salem, NC	1,962.1
16	St. Louis, MO	1,923.9
17	Columbus, OH	1,920.4
18	Albany, GA	1,915.9
19	Baton Rouge, LA	1,912.3
20	Oklahoma City, OK	1,902.2
21	Greensboro, NC	1,891.5
22	Cincinnati, OH	1,884.8
23	Indianapolis, IN	1,870.6
24	Akron, OH	1,820.4
25	Tallahassee, FL	1,794.1
26	St. Petersburg, FL	1,782.5
27	Decatur, IL	1,776.6
28	Canton, OH	1,753.2
29	Chattanooga, TN	1,731.2
30	Tulsa, OK	1,721.7
31	Athens-Clarke, GA	1,673.7
32	Lubbock, TX	1,673.5
33	Atlanta, GA	1,648.0
34	Tuscaloosa, AL	1,643.6
35	Reading, PA	1,642.7
36	Lawton, OK	1,611.8
37	Orlando, FL	1,603.5
38	Wilmington, NC	1,602.9
39	Durham, NC	1,601.4
40	Fort Lauderdale, FL	1,589.0
41	Gary, IN	1,568.0
42	Longview, TX	1,567.0
43	Rockford, IL	1,556.9
44	Montgomery, AL	1,524.5
45	Waco, TX	1,516.4
46	Beaumont, TX	1,510.4
47	Mobile, AL	1,509.5
48	Miami Gardens, FL	1,507.1
49	Dallas, TX	1,505.7
50	Kansas City, MO	1,491.9
51	Springfield, MO	1,477.1
52	Buffalo, NY	1,471.8
53	Tacoma, WA	1,470.5
54	Springfield, IL	1,450.3
55	Richmond, CA	1,448.8
56	Killeen, TX	1,437.8
57	Miami Beach, FL	1,432.5
58	Syracuse, NY	1,418.3
59	High Point, NC	1,411.1
60	Huntsville, AL	1,411.0
61	Rochester, NY	1,410.5
62	Fort Worth, TX	1,408.2
63	Peoria, IL	1,405.8
64	Jacksonville, FL	1,395.7
65	Knoxville, TN	1,393.1
66	Shreveport, LA	1,367.5
67	Stockton, CA	1,362.0
68	Amarillo, TX	1,356.7
69	Kansas City, KS	1,349.7
70	Racine, WI	1,347.4
71	Topeka, KS	1,347.1
72	Springfield, MA	1,346.9
73	Lakeland, FL	1,322.1
74	San Antonio, TX	1,322.0
75	Allentown, PA	1,317.5
76	Fort Smith, AR	1,313.8
77	Columbia, SC	1,312.1
78	Camden, NJ	1,310.5
79	Arlington, TX	1,290.1
79	Gainesville, FL	1,290.1
81	Clarksville, TN	1,289.6
82	Houston, TX	1,287.7
83	West Palm Beach, FL	1,281.2
84	Grand Rapids, MI	1,272.2
85	Murfreesboro, TN	1,270.9
86	St. Joseph, MO	1,269.0
87	Wichita Falls, TX	1,265.8
88	Spokane, WA	1,264.0
89	Grand Prairie, TX	1,263.6
90	Charlotte, NC	1,262.3
91	Savannah, GA	1,246.8
92	Pueblo, CO	1,245.4
93	Minneapolis, MN	1,239.1
94	Lafayette, LA	1,235.6
95	New Bedford, MA	1,235.1
96	Eugene, OR	1,234.0
97	Hammond, IN	1,232.8
98	Baltimore, MD	1,220.8
99	Salt Lake City, UT	1,202.4
100	Albuquerque, NM	1,201.6
101	Hollywood, FL	1,191.4
102	Oakland, CA	1,186.0
103	Yuma, AZ	1,183.4
104	Lansing, MI	1,181.7
105	San Bernardino, CA	1,176.4
106	Bakersfield, CA	1,175.0
107	Portsmouth, VA	1,172.6
108	Miami, FL	1,158.4
109	New Haven, CT	1,156.4
110	Avondale, AZ	1,140.0
111	Austin, TX	1,138.3
112	New Orleans, LA	1,135.8
113	Louisville, KY	1,122.4
114	Modesto, CA	1,120.4
115	Everett, WA	1,116.5
116	Abilene, TX	1,116.2
117	Seattle, WA	1,113.5
118	Wichita, KS	1,100.3
119	Sacramento, CA	1,091.8
120	Independence, MO	1,087.0
121	Odessa, TX	1,086.5
122	Davenport, IA	1,084.9
123	Milwaukee, WI	1,080.6
124	San Angelo, TX	1,079.5
125	Victorville, CA	1,069.6
126	North Charleston, SC	1,066.9
127	Berkeley, CA	1,066.3
128	Providence, RI	1,063.1
129	Tyler, TX	1,051.6
130	Mesquite, TX	1,045.6
131	St. Paul, MN	1,045.3
132	Indio, CA	1,036.2
133	Nashville, TN	1,035.4
134	Corpus Christi, TX	1,035.1
135	Sandy Springs, GA	1,028.7
136	Las Cruces, NM	1,025.3
137	Moreno Valley, CA	1,024.8
138	Phoenix, AZ	1,019.2
139	Visalia, CA	1,014.8
140	Tampa, FL	1,014.1
141	Garland, TX	1,007.9
142	Glendale, AZ	1,000.1
143	Trenton, NJ	997.5
144	Cedar Rapids, IA	993.2
145	Kent, WA	981.5
146	Las Vegas, NV	981.1
147	Roanoke, VA	980.6
148	Erie, PA	975.6
149	Salinas, CA	962.0
150	Evansville, IN	958.8
151	Laredo, TX	953.5
151	Pompano Beach, FL	953.5
153	Melbourne, FL	946.6
154	Irving, TX	944.9
155	Miramar, FL	941.2
156	Bridgeport, CT	937.9
157	Albany, NY	937.4
158	Chicago, IL	930.1
159	Des Moines, IA	929.9
160	Sparks, NV	929.8
161	Ogden, UT	928.7
162	Tucson, AZ	923.8
163	Fresno, CA	918.8
164	Hartford, CT	915.0
165	Fort Wayne, IN	901.9
166	Pittsburgh, PA	900.3
167	Richardson, TX	895.1
168	Norfolk, VA	883.9
169	Federal Way, WA	879.8
170	Brownsville, TX	878.0
171	Southfield, MI	869.8
172	Merced, CA	862.8
173	Redding, CA	858.2
174	West Valley, UT	858.0
175	Paterson, NJ	856.2
176	Carrollton, TX	851.4
177	Lynn, MA	845.9
178	Fall River, MA	843.3
179	Midland, TX	842.2
180	Reno, NV	836.2
181	Dearborn, MI	834.7
182	Sunrise, FL	834.3
183	Tempe, AZ	832.7
184	Citrus Heights, CA	832.4
185	Worcester, MA	832.1
186	Pasadena, TX	825.4
187	Colorado Springs, CO	822.9
188	North Las Vegas, NV	822.3
189	Lexington, KY	818.8
190	Compton, CA	818.1
191	Antioch, CA	813.9
192	Bellingham, WA	811.3
193	Lancaster, CA	810.8
194	Chico, CA	808.5
195	Plantation, FL	806.8
196	Rialto, CA	805.9
197	Elizabeth, NJ	802.2
198	Brockton, MA	800.2
199	Jacksonville, NC	797.3
200	Denver, CO	787.7
201	Raleigh, NC	785.0
202	Westland, MI	781.8
203	Hawthorne, CA	775.7
204	Cape Coral, FL	770.9
205	Richmond, VA	765.1
206	Clearwater, FL	761.0

RANK	CITY	RATE
206	Davie, FL	761.0
208	Sioux City, IA	756.9
209	Duluth, MN	751.7
210	Pembroke Pines, FL	749.8
211	Fairfield, CA	745.6
212	Lawrence, KS	744.8
213	Clovis, CA	740.3
214	Palmdale, CA	737.8
215	Omaha, NE	728.6
216	Billings, MT	713.3
217	College Station, TX	712.2
218	Santa Barbara, CA	711.7
219	Spokane Valley, WA	710.0
220	Philadelphia, PA	708.8
221	Norman, OK	707.3
222	San Leandro, CA	704.2
223	Waterbury, CT	700.0
224	Manchester, NH	699.4
225	Newark, NJ	697.3
226	Hayward, CA	688.3
227	Peoria, AZ	681.4
228	Fargo, ND	681.0
229	Columbia, MO	674.5
230	Riverside, CA	673.6
231	Port St. Lucie, FL	671.7
232	Long Beach, CA	671.6
233	Concord, CA	667.5
234	Warren, MI	664.5
235	Honolulu, HI	661.3
236	Roswell, GA	660.9
237	Portland, OR	658.9
238	Somerville, MA	657.7
239	Mesa, AZ	653.3
240	Madison, WI	649.6
241	Boca Raton, FL	644.5
242	Fayetteville, AR	643.0
243	San Francisco, CA	641.8
244	Palm Bay, FL	641.7
245	Chino, CA	641.6
246	Lakewood, CO	640.7
246	Newport Beach, CA	640.7
248	Lincoln, NE	635.9
249	Santa Maria, CA	634.0
250	Aurora, CO	633.0
251	Green Bay, WI	631.7
252	Greeley, CO	628.6
253	Lewisville, TX	628.1
254	Salem, OR	622.5
255	Washington, DC	616.4
256	Elk Grove, CA	611.1
257	Inglewood, CA	607.7
258	Kenosha, WI	607.2
259	McAllen, TX	600.3
260	Joliet, IL	595.0
261	Ventura, CA	591.4
262	Chesapeake, VA	589.9
263	Fullerton, CA	588.0
264	Fremont, CA	587.0
265	Sandy, UT	582.3
266	Thornton, CO	581.7
267	Santa Monica, CA	581.6
268	Jersey City, NJ	581.3
269	Tracy, CA	580.4
270	Hampton, VA	572.2
271	Pasadena, CA	572.0
272	Temecula, CA	570.7
273	Anchorage, AK	569.4
274	Ontario, CA	569.2

RANK	CITY	RATE
275	Vista, CA	568.8
276	Escondido, CA	566.8
277	Boulder, CO	563.8
278	Nampa, ID	560.4
279	Scottsdale, AZ	559.1
280	Gresham, OR	558.3
281	Pomona, CA	557.4
282	Fontana, CA	557.0
283	Buena Park, CA	554.5
284	Denton, TX	547.8
285	Suffolk, VA	547.5
286	Fort Collins, CO	543.0
287	Plano, TX	541.5
288	Clinton Twnshp, MI	539.8
289	Henderson, NV	538.8
290	McKinney, TX	538.0
291	Chandler, AZ	537.3
292	Vancouver, WA	536.5
293	Hesperia, CA	535.4
294	Ann Arbor, MI	532.5
295	El Cajon, CA	526.7
296	El Monte, CA	526.0
297	Hialeah, FL	523.3
298	Cranston, RI	517.3
299	Rio Rancho, NM	515.5
300	Carson, CA	512.8
301	San Diego, CA	509.1
302	Surprise, AZ	508.2
303	Boise, ID	506.7
304	Toms River Twnshp, NJ	502.0
305	Charleston, SC	497.9
306	West Jordan, UT	496.7
307	Bellevue, WA	496.6
308	Quincy, MA	494.9
309	Whittier, CA	487.2
310	Downey, CA	487.0
311	Rancho Cucamon., CA	486.8
312	Livermore, CA	485.7
313	Burbank, CA	483.3
314	Los Angeles, CA	479.0
315	Longmont, CO	473.7
316	Boston, MA	473.4
317	Missouri City, TX	472.0
318	Sioux Falls, SD	471.4
319	Baldwin Park, CA	470.7
320	Costa Mesa, CA	468.5
321	Virginia Beach, VA	468.4
322	Edmond, OK	461.1
323	Westminster, CA	455.9
324	Santa Rosa, CA	453.6
325	Carlsbad, CA	452.9
326	Oceanside, CA	450.2
327	Roseville, CA	449.3
328	Broken Arrow, OK	448.0
329	Murrieta, CA	447.6
330	Westminster, CO	446.6
331	West Covina, CA	444.0
332	Lee's Summit, MO	440.6
333	Nashua, NH	437.9
334	Pearland, TX	437.1
335	Gilbert, AZ	435.7
336	Anaheim, CA	433.7
337	Aurora, IL	431.1
338	Coral Springs, FL	430.5
339	Vacaville, CA	430.1
340	Cheektowaga, NY	429.5
341	Warwick, RI	427.3
342	St. George, UT	427.1

RANK	CITY	RATE
343	Edison Twnshp, NJ	425.7
344	Cambridge, MA	421.9
345	Alhambra, CA	418.8
346	Garden Grove, CA	414.3
347	Elgin, IL	413.2
348	Santa Clarita, CA	412.0
349	Chula Vista, CA	405.6
350	Lakewood, CA	403.4
351	Corona, CA	401.5
352	Brick Twnshp, NJ	400.4
353	Bend, OR	392.3
354	San Jose, CA	392.1
355	Rochester, MN	390.6
356	South Gate, CA	390.1
357	Norwalk, CA	385.2
357	Santa Clara, CA	385.2
359	Livonia, MI	377.9
360	Norwalk, CT	377.4
361	Clifton, NJ	376.3
362	Oxnard, CA	375.8
363	San Marcos, CA	373.2
364	Round Rock, TX	372.7
365	Arvada, CO	372.4
366	Greece, NY	369.9
367	Huntington Beach, CA	364.9
368	Upper Darby Twnshp, PA	356.0
369	Canton Twnshp, MI	355.8
370	Hamilton Twnshp, NJ	353.6
371	Cary, NC	350.6
372	Bloomington, MN	342.6
373	Santa Ana, CA	342.0
374	Provo, UT	340.7
375	Frisco, TX	329.8
376	Farmington Hills, MI	327.6
377	Sugar Land, TX	326.5
378	Sunnyvale, CA	326.2
379	El Paso, TX	321.7
380	Glendale, CA	321.7
381	Orange, CA	314.3
382	Allen, TX	314.2
383	Torrance, CA	313.2
384	Daly City, CA	313.0
385	Stamford, CT	309.6
386	Simi Valley, CA	308.5
387	Overland Park, KS	307.4
388	Yonkers, NY	306.6
389	San Mateo, CA	297.2
390	Troy, MI	288.1
391	Sterling Heights, MI	286.4
392	Woodbridge Twnshp, NJ	283.6
393	Danbury, CT	274.7
394	Centennial, CO	270.7
395	Colonie, NY	262.8
396	Thousand Oaks, CA	261.0
397	Olathe, KS	260.3
398	Hillsboro, OR	243.4
399	Beaverton, OR	242.4
400	Alexandria, VA	237.4
401	Lake Forest, CA	237.1
402	Orem, UT	234.6
403	Mission Viejo, CA	233.7
404	New York, NY	223.5
405	Irvine, CA	223.0
406	Newton, MA	221.5
407	Amherst, NY	215.6
408	Naperville, IL	204.5
409	O'Fallon, MO	178.8
410	Clarkstown, NY	172.4
411	Ramapo, NY	122.7

Source: CQ Press using reported data from the F.B.I. "Crime in the United States 2009"

*Burglary is the unlawful entry of a structure to commit a felony or theft. Attempts are included.

71. Percent Change in Burglary Rate: 2008 to 2009
National Percent Change = 2.2% Decrease*

RANK	CITY	% CHANGE
79	Abilene, TX	7.6
162	Akron, OH	(0.1)
NA	Albany, GA**	NA
314	Albany, NY	(14.1)
143	Albuquerque, NM	1.8
46	Alexandria, VA	13.8
342	Alhambra, CA	(19.0)
169	Allentown, PA	(0.6)
297	Allen, TX	(12.2)
108	Amarillo, TX	5.3
38	Amherst, NY	15.5
274	Anaheim, CA	(9.8)
8	Anchorage, AK	33.9
NA	Ann Arbor, MI**	NA
287	Antioch, CA	(11.2)
68	Arlington, TX	8.7
212	Arvada, CO	(4.3)
53	Athens-Clarke, GA	11.8
296	Atlanta, GA	(12.1)
271	Aurora, CO	(9.6)
315	Aurora, IL	(14.4)
162	Austin, TX	(0.1)
216	Avondale, AZ	(4.6)
256	Bakersfield, CA	(8.1)
129	Baldwin Park, CA	3.2
174	Baltimore, MD	(1.1)
40	Baton Rouge, LA	14.7
315	Beaumont, TX	(14.4)
364	Beaverton, OR	(24.5)
291	Bellevue, WA	(11.5)
166	Bellingham, WA	(0.3)
380	Bend, OR	(35.1)
180	Berkeley, CA	(1.5)
27	Billings, MT	19.1
188	Birmingham, AL	(2.2)
66	Bloomington, MN	8.8
198	Boca Raton, FL	(3.3)
241	Boise, ID	(6.6)
339	Boston, MA	(18.1)
72	Boulder, CO	8.4
51	Brick Twnshp, NJ	12.3
154	Bridgeport, CT	0.8
NA	Brockton, MA**	NA
302	Broken Arrow, OK	(13.3)
190	Brownsville, TX	(2.3)
107	Buena Park, CA	5.4
198	Buffalo, NY	(3.3)
322	Burbank, CA	(15.0)
76	Cambridge, MA	8.0
340	Camden, NJ	(18.2)
NA	Canton Twnshp, MI**	NA
333	Canton, OH	(16.5)
244	Cape Coral, FL	(6.9)
301	Carlsbad, CA	(12.8)
109	Carrollton, TX	5.2
81	Carson, CA	7.4
299	Cary, NC	(12.7)
156	Cedar Rapids, IA	0.7
251	Centennial, CO	(7.5)
210	Chandler, AZ	(3.8)
360	Charleston, SC	(23.2)
345	Charlotte, NC	(19.7)
117	Chattanooga, TN	4.5
337	Cheektowaga, NY	(17.6)
83	Chesapeake, VA	7.1
151	Chicago, IL	1.1
357	Chico, CA	(22.2)
140	Chino, CA	2.0
277	Chula Vista, CA	(10.1)
172	Cincinnati, OH	(1.0)
111	Citrus Heights, CA	5.1
42	Clarkstown, NY	14.2
49	Clarksville, TN	12.9
242	Clearwater, FL	(6.7)
134	Cleveland, OH	2.4
170	Clifton, NJ	(0.9)
NA	Clinton Twnshp, MI**	NA
117	Clovis, CA	4.5
246	College Station, TX	(7.1)
311	Colonie, NY	(13.9)
261	Colorado Springs, CO	(8.5)
341	Columbia, MO	(18.5)
3	Columbia, SC	39.3
36	Columbus, GA	15.9
183	Columbus, OH	(1.8)
305	Compton, CA	(13.7)
157	Concord, CA	0.4
172	Coral Springs, FL	(1.0)
271	Corona, CA	(9.6)
315	Corpus Christi, TX	(14.4)
174	Costa Mesa, CA	(1.1)
17	Cranston, RI	25.0
269	Dallas, TX	(9.1)
43	Daly City, CA	14.0
348	Danbury, CT	(20.3)
329	Davenport, IA	(16.2)
33	Davie, FL	17.2
153	Dayton, OH	1.0
NA	Dearborn, MI**	NA
NA	Decatur, IL**	NA
177	Denton, TX	(1.2)
273	Denver, CO	(9.7)
NA	Des Moines, IA**	NA
NA	Detroit, MI**	NA
368	Downey, CA	(26.0)
19	Duluth, MN	21.7
143	Durham, NC	1.8
222	Edison Twnshp, NJ	(5.2)
89	Edmond, OK	6.3
321	El Cajon, CA	(14.9)
134	El Monte, CA	2.4
222	El Paso, TX	(5.2)
255	Elgin, IL	(7.8)
117	Elizabeth, NJ	4.5
200	Elk Grove, CA	(3.4)
268	Erie, PA	(8.8)
309	Escondido, CA	(13.8)
66	Eugene, OR	8.8
157	Evansville, IN	0.4
295	Everett, WA	(12.0)
89	Fairfield, CA	6.3
269	Fall River, MA	(9.1)
2	Fargo, ND	43.1
NA	Farmington Hills, MI**	NA
329	Fayetteville, AR	(16.2)
77	Fayetteville, NC	7.8
243	Federal Way, WA	(6.8)
NA	Flint, MI**	NA
114	Fontana, CA	4.8
233	Fort Collins, CO	(6.0)
60	Fort Lauderdale, FL	10.4
122	Fort Smith, AR	4.4
233	Fort Wayne, IN	(6.0)
65	Fort Worth, TX	9.5
80	Fremont, CA	7.5
116	Fresno, CA	4.7
379	Frisco, TX	(34.9)
212	Fullerton, CA	(4.3)
100	Gainesville, FL	5.8
336	Garden Grove, CA	(17.1)
193	Garland, TX	(2.5)
86	Gary, IN	6.7
305	Gilbert, AZ	(13.7)
207	Glendale, AZ	(3.7)
282	Glendale, CA	(10.4)
37	Grand Prairie, TX	15.7
NA	Grand Rapids, MI**	NA
12	Greece, NY	29.2
359	Greeley, CO	(22.8)
193	Green Bay, WI	(2.5)
215	Greensboro, NC	(4.5)
346	Gresham, OR	(19.8)
374	Hamilton Twnshp, NJ	(30.6)
251	Hammond, IN	(7.5)
64	Hampton, VA	9.7
43	Hartford, CT	14.0
34	Hawthorne, CA	16.8
277	Hayward, CA	(10.1)
283	Henderson, NV	(10.5)
218	Hesperia, CA	(4.9)
378	Hialeah, FL	(33.0)
369	High Point, NC	(26.1)
355	Hillsboro, OR	(21.6)
143	Hollywood, FL	1.8
231	Honolulu, HI	(5.9)
84	Houston, TX	7.0
231	Huntington Beach, CA	(5.9)
132	Huntsville, AL	2.9
324	Independence, MO	(15.1)
94	Indianapolis, IN	6.0
95	Indio, CA	5.9
196	Inglewood, CA	(2.9)
129	Irvine, CA	3.2
126	Irving, TX	4.1
236	Jacksonville, FL	(6.3)
24	Jacksonville, NC	19.6
87	Jackson, MS	6.6
365	Jersey City, NJ	(24.9)
105	Joliet, IL	5.5
NA	Kansas City, KS**	NA
274	Kansas City, MO	(9.8)
165	Kenosha, WI	(0.2)
366	Kent, WA	(25.0)
195	Killeen, TX	(2.6)
200	Knoxville, TN	(3.4)
174	Lafayette, LA	(1.1)
154	Lake Forest, CA	0.8
27	Lakeland, FL	19.1
148	Lakewood, CA	1.7
180	Lakewood, CO	(1.5)
362	Lancaster, CA	(23.7)
NA	Lansing, MI**	NA
149	Laredo, TX	1.6
70	Las Cruces, NM	8.5
285	Las Vegas, NV	(10.9)
325	Lawrence, KS	(15.3)
140	Lawton, OK	2.0
293	Lee's Summit, MO	(11.7)
128	Lewisville, TX	3.6
NA	Lexington, KY**	NA
140	Lincoln, NE	2.0
NA	Little Rock, AR**	NA
248	Livermore, CA	(7.2)
NA	Livonia, MI**	NA
143	Long Beach, CA	1.8
NA	Longmont, CO**	NA

RANK	CITY	% CHANGE
95	Longview, TX	5.9
240	Los Angeles, CA	(6.5)
NA	Louisville, KY**	NA
32	Lubbock, TX	18.2
377	Lynn, MA	(32.8)
249	Macon, GA	(7.3)
370	Madison, WI	(26.3)
11	Manchester, NH	32.2
216	McAllen, TX	(4.6)
4	McKinney, TX	35.5
367	Melbourne, FL	(25.1)
292	Memphis, TN	(11.6)
229	Merced, CA	(5.8)
126	Mesa, AZ	4.1
6	Mesquite, TX	34.7
238	Miami Beach, FL	(6.4)
221	Miami Gardens, FL	(5.0)
159	Miami, FL	0.3
100	Midland, TX	5.8
150	Milwaukee, WI	1.5
333	Minneapolis, MN	(16.5)
134	Miramar, FL	2.4
70	Mission Viejo, CA	8.5
23	Missouri City, TX	19.7
40	Mobile, AL	14.7
207	Modesto, CA	(3.7)
289	Montgomery, AL	(11.3)
261	Moreno Valley, CA	(8.5)
13	Murfreesboro, TN	26.6
104	Murrieta, CA	5.6
249	Nampa, ID	(7.3)
259	Naperville, IL	(8.4)
NA	Nashua, NH**	NA
178	Nashville, TN	(1.4)
84	New Bedford, MA	7.0
NA	New Haven, CT**	NA
373	New Orleans, LA	(30.4)
235	New York, NY	(6.1)
191	Newark, NJ	(2.4)
50	Newport Beach, CA	12.6
170	Newton, MA	(0.9)
55	Norfolk, VA	11.2
111	Norman, OK	5.1
338	North Charleston, SC	(17.7)
322	North Las Vegas, NV	(15.0)
342	Norwalk, CA	(19.0)
56	Norwalk, CT	11.0
93	Oakland, CA	6.1
266	Oceanside, CA	(8.7)
30	Odessa, TX	18.8
375	O'Fallon, MO	(30.6)
59	Ogden, UT	10.7
45	Oklahoma City, OK	13.9
NA	Olathe, KS**	NA
159	Omaha, NE	0.3
183	Ontario, CA	(1.8)
167	Orange, CA	(0.5)
277	Orem, UT	(10.1)
311	Orlando, FL	(13.9)
123	Overland Park, KS	4.2
356	Oxnard, CA	(21.7)
305	Palm Bay, FL	(13.7)
132	Palmdale, CA	2.9
204	Pasadena, CA	(3.6)
15	Pasadena, TX	25.1
348	Paterson, NJ	(20.3)
117	Pearland, TX	4.5
25	Pembroke Pines, FL	19.5
309	Peoria, AZ	(13.8)
NA	Peoria, IL**	NA
350	Philadelphia, PA	(20.5)
311	Phoenix, AZ	(13.9)
281	Pittsburgh, PA	(10.3)
246	Plano, TX	(7.1)
254	Plantation, FL	(7.6)
358	Pomona, CA	(22.4)
353	Pompano Beach, FL	(21.2)
207	Port St. Lucie, FL	(3.7)
326	Portland, OR	(15.4)
89	Portsmouth, VA	6.3
197	Providence, RI	(3.1)
276	Provo, UT	(10.0)
NA	Pueblo, CO**	NA
354	Quincy, MA	(21.3)
320	Racine, WI	(14.7)
178	Raleigh, NC	(1.4)
361	Ramapo, NY	(23.5)
73	Rancho Cucamon., CA	8.2
114	Reading, PA	4.8
111	Redding, CA	5.1
251	Reno, NV	(7.5)
20	Rialto, CA	21.5
95	Richardson, TX	5.9
21	Richmond, CA	20.6
318	Richmond, VA	(14.5)
117	Rio Rancho, NM	4.5
266	Riverside, CA	(8.7)
257	Roanoke, VA	(8.2)
371	Rochester, MN	(26.4)
131	Rochester, NY	3.1
319	Rockford, IL	(14.6)
344	Roseville, CA	(19.4)
63	Roswell, GA	10.2
204	Round Rock, TX	(3.6)
188	Sacramento, CA	(2.2)
298	Salem, OR	(12.5)
191	Salinas, CA	(2.4)
92	Salt Lake City, UT	6.2
238	San Angelo, TX	(6.4)
228	San Antonio, TX	(5.5)
88	San Bernardino, CA	6.5
332	San Diego, CA	(16.4)
222	San Francisco, CA	(5.2)
82	San Jose, CA	7.2
331	San Leandro, CA	(16.3)
363	San Marcos, CA	(24.0)
35	San Mateo, CA	16.4
204	Sandy Springs, GA	(3.6)
211	Sandy, UT	(4.1)
95	Santa Ana, CA	5.9
15	Santa Barbara, CA	25.1
222	Santa Clara, CA	(5.2)
56	Santa Clarita, CA	11.0
123	Santa Maria, CA	4.2
265	Santa Monica, CA	(8.6)
287	Santa Rosa, CA	(11.2)
289	Savannah, GA	(11.3)
280	Scottsdale, AZ	(10.2)
134	Seattle, WA	2.4
69	Shreveport, LA	8.6
244	Simi Valley, CA	(6.9)
25	Sioux City, IA	19.5
58	Sioux Falls, SD	10.9
73	Somerville, MA	8.2
261	South Bend, IN	(8.5)
350	South Gate, CA	(20.5)
NA	Southfield, MI**	NA
259	Sparks, NV	(8.4)
212	Spokane Valley, WA	(4.3)
52	Spokane, WA	12.2
NA	Springfield, IL**	NA
143	Springfield, MA	1.8
78	Springfield, MO	7.7
48	Stamford, CT	13.0
NA	Sterling Heights, MI**	NA
258	Stockton, CA	(8.3)
372	St. George, UT	(28.0)
14	St. Joseph, MO	25.9
229	St. Louis, MO	(5.8)
182	St. Paul, MN	(1.7)
134	St. Petersburg, FL	2.4
31	Suffolk, VA	18.4
105	Sugar Land, TX	5.5
18	Sunnyvale, CA	22.1
202	Sunrise, FL	(3.5)
304	Surprise, AZ	(13.5)
151	Syracuse, NY	1.1
161	Tacoma, WA	0.2
75	Tallahassee, FL	8.1
335	Tampa, FL	(16.6)
347	Temecula, CA	(20.0)
218	Tempe, AZ	(4.9)
167	Thornton, CO	(0.5)
109	Thousand Oaks, CA	5.2
5	Toledo, OH	34.8
103	Toms River Twnshp, NJ	5.7
100	Topeka, KS	5.8
299	Torrance, CA	(12.7)
29	Tracy, CA	18.9
47	Trenton, NJ	13.2
NA	Troy, MI**	NA
227	Tucson, AZ	(5.3)
185	Tulsa, OK	(2.0)
186	Tuscaloosa, AL	(2.1)
7	Tyler, TX	34.4
328	Upper Darby Twnshp, PA	(15.5)
8	Vacaville, CA	33.9
62	Vallejo, CA	10.3
123	Vancouver, WA	4.2
261	Ventura, CA	(8.5)
293	Victorville, CA	(11.7)
95	Virginia Beach, VA	5.9
162	Visalia, CA	(0.1)
376	Vista, CA	(31.7)
284	Waco, TX	(10.6)
NA	Warren, MI**	NA
22	Warwick, RI	20.1
202	Washington, DC	(3.5)
39	Waterbury, CT	15.2
305	West Covina, CA	(13.7)
53	West Jordan, UT	11.8
286	West Palm Beach, FL	(11.0)
10	West Valley, UT	32.5
NA	Westland, MI**	NA
350	Westminster, CA	(20.5)
139	Westminster, CO	2.2
222	Whittier, CA	(5.2)
326	Wichita Falls, TX	(15.4)
186	Wichita, KS	(2.1)
60	Wilmington, NC	10.4
218	Winston-Salem, NC	(4.9)
381	Woodbridge Twnshp, NJ	(37.7)
302	Worcester, MA	(13.3)
236	Yonkers, NY	(6.3)
1	Yuma, AZ	67.4

Source: CQ Press using reported data from the F.B.I. "Crime in the United States 2009"
*Burglary is the unlawful entry of a structure to commit a felony or theft. Attempts are included.
**Not available.

71. Percent Change in Burglary Rate: 2008 to 2009 (continued)
National Percent Change = 2.2% Decrease*

RANK	CITY	% CHANGE
1	Yuma, AZ	67.4
2	Fargo, ND	43.1
3	Columbia, SC	39.3
4	McKinney, TX	35.5
5	Toledo, OH	34.8
6	Mesquite, TX	34.7
7	Tyler, TX	34.4
8	Anchorage, AK	33.9
8	Vacaville, CA	33.9
10	West Valley, UT	32.5
11	Manchester, NH	32.2
12	Greece, NY	29.2
13	Murfreesboro, TN	26.6
14	St. Joseph, MO	25.9
15	Pasadena, TX	25.1
15	Santa Barbara, CA	25.1
17	Cranston, RI	25.0
18	Sunnyvale, CA	22.1
19	Duluth, MN	21.7
20	Rialto, CA	21.5
21	Richmond, CA	20.6
22	Warwick, RI	20.1
23	Missouri City, TX	19.7
24	Jacksonville, NC	19.6
25	Pembroke Pines, FL	19.5
25	Sioux City, IA	19.5
27	Billings, MT	19.1
27	Lakeland, FL	19.1
29	Tracy, CA	18.9
30	Odessa, TX	18.8
31	Suffolk, VA	18.4
32	Lubbock, TX	18.2
33	Davie, FL	17.2
34	Hawthorne, CA	16.8
35	San Mateo, CA	16.4
36	Columbus, GA	15.9
37	Grand Prairie, TX	15.7
38	Amherst, NY	15.5
39	Waterbury, CT	15.2
40	Baton Rouge, LA	14.7
40	Mobile, AL	14.7
42	Clarkstown, NY	14.2
43	Daly City, CA	14.0
43	Hartford, CT	14.0
45	Oklahoma City, OK	13.9
46	Alexandria, VA	13.8
47	Trenton, NJ	13.2
48	Stamford, CT	13.0
49	Clarksville, TN	12.9
50	Newport Beach, CA	12.6
51	Brick Twnshp, NJ	12.3
52	Spokane, WA	12.2
53	Athens-Clarke, GA	11.8
53	West Jordan, UT	11.8
55	Norfolk, VA	11.2
56	Norwalk, CT	11.0
56	Santa Clarita, CA	11.0
58	Sioux Falls, SD	10.9
59	Ogden, UT	10.7
60	Fort Lauderdale, FL	10.4
60	Wilmington, NC	10.4
62	Vallejo, CA	10.3
63	Roswell, GA	10.2
64	Hampton, VA	9.7
65	Fort Worth, TX	9.5
66	Bloomington, MN	8.8
66	Eugene, OR	8.8
68	Arlington, TX	8.7
69	Shreveport, LA	8.6
70	Las Cruces, NM	8.5
70	Mission Viejo, CA	8.5
72	Boulder, CO	8.4
73	Rancho Cucamon., CA	8.2
73	Somerville, MA	8.2
75	Tallahassee, FL	8.1
76	Cambridge, MA	8.0
77	Fayetteville, NC	7.8
78	Springfield, MO	7.7
79	Abilene, TX	7.6
80	Fremont, CA	7.5
81	Carson, CA	7.4
82	San Jose, CA	7.2
83	Chesapeake, VA	7.1
84	Houston, TX	7.0
84	New Bedford, MA	7.0
86	Gary, IN	6.7
87	Jackson, MS	6.6
88	San Bernardino, CA	6.5
89	Edmond, OK	6.3
89	Fairfield, CA	6.3
89	Portsmouth, VA	6.3
92	Salt Lake City, UT	6.2
93	Oakland, CA	6.1
94	Indianapolis, IN	6.0
95	Indio, CA	5.9
95	Longview, TX	5.9
95	Richardson, TX	5.9
95	Santa Ana, CA	5.9
95	Virginia Beach, VA	5.9
100	Gainesville, FL	5.8
100	Midland, TX	5.8
100	Topeka, KS	5.8
103	Toms River Twnshp, NJ	5.7
104	Murrieta, CA	5.6
105	Joliet, IL	5.5
105	Sugar Land, TX	5.5
107	Buena Park, CA	5.4
108	Amarillo, TX	5.3
109	Carrollton, TX	5.2
109	Thousand Oaks, CA	5.2
111	Citrus Heights, CA	5.1
111	Norman, OK	5.1
111	Redding, CA	5.1
114	Fontana, CA	4.8
114	Reading, PA	4.8
116	Fresno, CA	4.7
117	Chattanooga, TN	4.5
117	Clovis, CA	4.5
117	Elizabeth, NJ	4.5
117	Pearland, TX	4.5
117	Rio Rancho, NM	4.5
122	Fort Smith, AR	4.4
123	Overland Park, KS	4.2
123	Santa Maria, CA	4.2
123	Vancouver, WA	4.2
126	Irving, TX	4.1
126	Mesa, AZ	4.1
128	Lewisville, TX	3.6
129	Baldwin Park, CA	3.2
129	Irvine, CA	3.2
131	Rochester, NY	3.1
132	Huntsville, AL	2.9
132	Palmdale, CA	2.9
134	Cleveland, OH	2.4
134	El Monte, CA	2.4
134	Miramar, FL	2.4
134	Seattle, WA	2.4
134	St. Petersburg, FL	2.4
139	Westminster, CO	2.2
140	Chino, CA	2.0
140	Lawton, OK	2.0
140	Lincoln, NE	2.0
143	Albuquerque, NM	1.8
143	Durham, NC	1.8
143	Hollywood, FL	1.8
143	Long Beach, CA	1.8
143	Springfield, MA	1.8
148	Lakewood, CA	1.7
149	Laredo, TX	1.6
150	Milwaukee, WI	1.5
151	Chicago, IL	1.1
151	Syracuse, NY	1.1
153	Dayton, OH	1.0
154	Bridgeport, CT	0.8
154	Lake Forest, CA	0.8
156	Cedar Rapids, IA	0.7
157	Concord, CA	0.4
157	Evansville, IN	0.4
159	Miami, FL	0.3
159	Omaha, NE	0.3
161	Tacoma, WA	0.2
162	Akron, OH	(0.1)
162	Austin, TX	(0.1)
162	Visalia, CA	(0.1)
165	Kenosha, WI	(0.2)
166	Bellingham, WA	(0.3)
167	Orange, CA	(0.5)
167	Thornton, CO	(0.5)
169	Allentown, PA	(0.6)
170	Clifton, NJ	(0.9)
170	Newton, MA	(0.9)
172	Cincinnati, OH	(1.0)
172	Coral Springs, FL	(1.0)
174	Baltimore, MD	(1.1)
174	Costa Mesa, CA	(1.1)
174	Lafayette, LA	(1.1)
177	Denton, TX	(1.2)
178	Nashville, TN	(1.4)
178	Raleigh, NC	(1.4)
180	Berkeley, CA	(1.5)
180	Lakewood, CO	(1.5)
182	St. Paul, MN	(1.7)
183	Columbus, OH	(1.8)
183	Ontario, CA	(1.8)
185	Tulsa, OK	(2.0)
186	Tuscaloosa, AL	(2.1)
186	Wichita, KS	(2.1)
188	Birmingham, AL	(2.2)
188	Sacramento, CA	(2.2)
190	Brownsville, TX	(2.3)
191	Newark, NJ	(2.4)
191	Salinas, CA	(2.4)
193	Garland, TX	(2.5)
193	Green Bay, WI	(2.5)
195	Killeen, TX	(2.6)
196	Inglewood, CA	(2.9)
197	Providence, RI	(3.1)
198	Boca Raton, FL	(3.3)
198	Buffalo, NY	(3.3)
200	Elk Grove, CA	(3.4)
200	Knoxville, TN	(3.4)
202	Sunrise, FL	(3.5)
202	Washington, DC	(3.5)
204	Pasadena, CA	(3.6)
204	Round Rock, TX	(3.6)
204	Sandy Springs, GA	(3.6)

RANK	CITY	% CHANGE
207	Glendale, AZ	(3.7)
207	Modesto, CA	(3.7)
207	Port St. Lucie, FL	(3.7)
210	Chandler, AZ	(3.8)
211	Sandy, UT	(4.1)
212	Arvada, CO	(4.3)
212	Fullerton, CA	(4.3)
212	Spokane Valley, WA	(4.3)
215	Greensboro, NC	(4.5)
216	Avondale, AZ	(4.6)
216	McAllen, TX	(4.6)
218	Hesperia, CA	(4.9)
218	Tempe, AZ	(4.9)
218	Winston-Salem, NC	(4.9)
221	Miami Gardens, FL	(5.0)
222	Edison Twnshp, NJ	(5.2)
222	El Paso, TX	(5.2)
222	San Francisco, CA	(5.2)
222	Santa Clara, CA	(5.2)
222	Whittier, CA	(5.2)
227	Tucson, AZ	(5.3)
228	San Antonio, TX	(5.5)
229	Merced, CA	(5.8)
229	St. Louis, MO	(5.8)
231	Honolulu, HI	(5.9)
231	Huntington Beach, CA	(5.9)
233	Fort Collins, CO	(6.0)
233	Fort Wayne, IN	(6.0)
235	New York, NY	(6.1)
236	Jacksonville, FL	(6.3)
236	Yonkers, NY	(6.3)
238	Miami Beach, FL	(6.4)
238	San Angelo, TX	(6.4)
240	Los Angeles, CA	(6.5)
241	Boise, ID	(6.6)
242	Clearwater, FL	(6.7)
243	Federal Way, WA	(6.8)
244	Cape Coral, FL	(6.9)
244	Simi Valley, CA	(6.9)
246	College Station, TX	(7.1)
246	Plano, TX	(7.1)
248	Livermore, CA	(7.2)
249	Macon, GA	(7.3)
249	Nampa, ID	(7.3)
251	Centennial, CO	(7.5)
251	Hammond, IN	(7.5)
251	Reno, NV	(7.5)
254	Plantation, FL	(7.6)
255	Elgin, IL	(7.8)
256	Bakersfield, CA	(8.1)
257	Roanoke, VA	(8.2)
258	Stockton, CA	(8.3)
259	Naperville, IL	(8.4)
259	Sparks, NV	(8.4)
261	Colorado Springs, CO	(8.5)
261	Moreno Valley, CA	(8.5)
261	South Bend, IN	(8.5)
261	Ventura, CA	(8.5)
265	Santa Monica, CA	(8.6)
266	Oceanside, CA	(8.7)
266	Riverside, CA	(8.7)
268	Erie, PA	(8.8)
269	Dallas, TX	(9.1)
269	Fall River, MA	(9.1)
271	Aurora, CO	(9.6)
271	Corona, CA	(9.6)
273	Denver, CO	(9.7)
274	Anaheim, CA	(9.8)
274	Kansas City, MO	(9.8)
276	Provo, UT	(10.0)
277	Chula Vista, CA	(10.1)
277	Hayward, CA	(10.1)
277	Orem, UT	(10.1)
280	Scottsdale, AZ	(10.2)
281	Pittsburgh, PA	(10.3)
282	Glendale, CA	(10.4)
283	Henderson, NV	(10.5)
284	Waco, TX	(10.6)
285	Las Vegas, NV	(10.9)
286	West Palm Beach, FL	(11.0)
287	Antioch, CA	(11.2)
287	Santa Rosa, CA	(11.2)
289	Montgomery, AL	(11.3)
289	Savannah, GA	(11.3)
291	Bellevue, WA	(11.5)
292	Memphis, TN	(11.6)
293	Lee's Summit, MO	(11.7)
293	Victorville, CA	(11.7)
295	Everett, WA	(12.0)
296	Atlanta, GA	(12.1)
297	Allen, TX	(12.2)
298	Salem, OR	(12.5)
299	Cary, NC	(12.7)
299	Torrance, CA	(12.7)
301	Carlsbad, CA	(12.8)
302	Broken Arrow, OK	(13.3)
302	Worcester, MA	(13.3)
304	Surprise, AZ	(13.5)
305	Compton, CA	(13.7)
305	Gilbert, AZ	(13.7)
305	Palm Bay, FL	(13.7)
305	West Covina, CA	(13.7)
309	Escondido, CA	(13.8)
309	Peoria, AZ	(13.8)
311	Colonie, NY	(13.9)
311	Orlando, FL	(13.9)
311	Phoenix, AZ	(13.9)
314	Albany, NY	(14.1)
315	Aurora, IL	(14.4)
315	Beaumont, TX	(14.4)
315	Corpus Christi, TX	(14.4)
318	Richmond, VA	(14.5)
319	Rockford, IL	(14.6)
320	Racine, WI	(14.7)
321	El Cajon, CA	(14.9)
322	Burbank, CA	(15.0)
322	North Las Vegas, NV	(15.0)
324	Independence, MO	(15.1)
325	Lawrence, KS	(15.3)
326	Portland, OR	(15.4)
326	Wichita Falls, TX	(15.4)
328	Upper Darby Twnshp, PA	(15.5)
329	Davenport, IA	(16.2)
329	Fayetteville, AR	(16.2)
331	San Leandro, CA	(16.3)
332	San Diego, CA	(16.4)
333	Canton, OH	(16.5)
333	Minneapolis, MN	(16.5)
335	Tampa, FL	(16.6)
336	Garden Grove, CA	(17.1)
337	Cheektowaga, NY	(17.6)
338	North Charleston, SC	(17.7)
339	Boston, MA	(18.1)
340	Camden, NJ	(18.2)
341	Columbia, MO	(18.5)
342	Alhambra, CA	(19.0)
342	Norwalk, CA	(19.0)
344	Roseville, CA	(19.4)
345	Charlotte, NC	(19.7)
346	Gresham, OR	(19.8)
347	Temecula, CA	(20.0)
348	Danbury, CT	(20.3)
348	Paterson, NJ	(20.3)
350	Philadelphia, PA	(20.5)
350	South Gate, CA	(20.5)
350	Westminster, CA	(20.5)
353	Pompano Beach, FL	(21.2)
354	Quincy, MA	(21.3)
355	Hillsboro, OR	(21.6)
356	Oxnard, CA	(21.7)
357	Chico, CA	(22.2)
358	Pomona, CA	(22.4)
359	Greeley, CO	(22.8)
360	Charleston, SC	(23.2)
361	Ramapo, NY	(23.5)
362	Lancaster, CA	(23.7)
363	San Marcos, CA	(24.0)
364	Beaverton, OR	(24.5)
365	Jersey City, NJ	(24.9)
366	Kent, WA	(25.0)
367	Melbourne, FL	(25.1)
368	Downey, CA	(26.0)
369	High Point, NC	(26.1)
370	Madison, WI	(26.3)
371	Rochester, MN	(26.4)
372	St. George, UT	(28.0)
373	New Orleans, LA	(30.4)
374	Hamilton Twnshp, NJ	(30.6)
375	O'Fallon, MO	(30.6)
376	Vista, CA	(31.7)
377	Lynn, MA	(32.8)
378	Hialeah, FL	(33.0)
379	Frisco, TX	(34.9)
380	Bend, OR	(35.1)
381	Woodbridge Twnshp, NJ	(37.7)
NA	Albany, GA**	NA
NA	Ann Arbor, MI**	NA
NA	Brockton, MA**	NA
NA	Canton Twnshp, MI**	NA
NA	Clinton Twnshp, MI**	NA
NA	Dearborn, MI**	NA
NA	Decatur, IL**	NA
NA	Des Moines, IA**	NA
NA	Detroit, MI**	NA
NA	Farmington Hills, MI**	NA
NA	Flint, MI**	NA
NA	Grand Rapids, MI**	NA
NA	Kansas City, KS**	NA
NA	Lansing, MI**	NA
NA	Lexington, KY**	NA
NA	Little Rock, AR**	NA
NA	Livonia, MI**	NA
NA	Longmont, CO**	NA
NA	Louisville, KY**	NA
NA	Nashua, NH**	NA
NA	New Haven, CT**	NA
NA	Olathe, KS**	NA
NA	Peoria, IL**	NA
NA	Pueblo, CO**	NA
NA	Southfield, MI**	NA
NA	Springfield, IL**	NA
NA	Sterling Heights, MI**	NA
NA	Troy, MI**	NA
NA	Warren, MI**	NA
NA	Westland, MI**	NA

Source: CQ Press using reported data from the F.B.I. "Crime in the United States 2009"
*Burglary is the unlawful entry of a structure to commit a felony or theft. Attempts are included.
**Not available.

72. Percent Change in Burglary Rate: 2005 to 2009
National Percent Change = 1.5% Decrease*

RANK	CITY	% CHANGE
258	Abilene, TX	(14.4)
65	Akron, OH	13.3
229	Albany, GA	(11.9)
345	Albany, NY	(33.4)
123	Albuquerque, NM	2.6
111	Alexandria, VA	5.0
351	Alhambra, CA	(35.5)
128	Allentown, PA	1.1
313	Allen, TX	(25.9)
153	Amarillo, TX	(2.2)
42	Amherst, NY	22.3
309	Anaheim, CA	(24.5)
227	Anchorage, AK	(11.8)
NA	Ann Arbor, MI**	NA
68	Antioch, CA	12.8
50	Arlington, TX	18.3
315	Arvada, CO	(26.1)
1	Athens-Clarke, GA	69.0
100	Atlanta, GA	6.8
308	Aurora, CO	(24.3)
285	Aurora, IL	(18.3)
96	Austin, TX	8.3
NA	Avondale, AZ**	NA
215	Bakersfield, CA	(10.3)
262	Baldwin Park, CA	(14.9)
101	Baltimore, MD	6.7
92	Baton Rouge, LA	9.0
268	Beaumont, TX	(16.2)
361	Beaverton, OR	(40.1)
141	Bellevue, WA	(1.1)
266	Bellingham, WA	(15.3)
370	Bend, OR	(50.9)
225	Berkeley, CA	(11.3)
53	Billings, MT	16.8
111	Birmingham, AL	5.0
NA	Bloomington, MN**	NA
243	Boca Raton, FL	(12.9)
323	Boise, ID	(27.2)
362	Boston, MA	(40.7)
162	Boulder, CO	(4.4)
3	Brick Twnshp, NJ	64.0
173	Bridgeport, CT	(4.9)
85	Brockton, MA	10.4
197	Broken Arrow, OK	(8.3)
54	Brownsville, TX	16.4
145	Buena Park, CA	(1.4)
148	Buffalo, NY	(1.7)
252	Burbank, CA	(13.6)
337	Cambridge, MA	(31.9)
120	Camden, NJ	2.9
NA	Canton Twnshp, MI**	NA
217	Canton, OH	(10.5)
148	Cape Coral, FL	(1.7)
299	Carlsbad, CA	(21.5)
78	Carrollton, TX	11.3
222	Carson, CA	(10.9)
271	Cary, NC	(16.4)
62	Cedar Rapids, IA	14.2
353	Centennial, CO	(36.1)
249	Chandler, AZ	(13.5)
346	Charleston, SC	(34.7)
343	Charlotte, NC	(33.1)
40	Chattanooga, TN	23.7
249	Cheektowaga, NY	(13.5)
210	Chesapeake, VA	(9.9)
104	Chicago, IL	5.6
295	Chico, CA	(20.5)
184	Chino, CA	(5.7)
340	Chula Vista, CA	(32.3)
91	Cincinnati, OH	9.1
NA	Citrus Heights, CA**	NA
NA	Clarkstown, NY**	NA
23	Clarksville, TN	32.6
222	Clearwater, FL	(10.9)
59	Cleveland, OH	14.7
142	Clifton, NJ	(1.2)
NA	Clinton Twnshp, MI**	NA
162	Clovis, CA	(4.4)
185	College Station, TX	(5.8)
358	Colonie, NY	(37.9)
268	Colorado Springs, CO	(16.2)
46	Columbia, MO	20.4
55	Columbia, SC	16.1
11	Columbus, GA	42.7
160	Columbus, OH	(4.0)
38	Compton, CA	24.2
312	Concord, CA	(25.0)
22	Coral Springs, FL	33.3
354	Corona, CA	(36.5)
229	Corpus Christi, TX	(11.9)
237	Costa Mesa, CA	(12.6)
26	Cranston, RI	31.2
275	Dallas, TX	(17.2)
35	Daly City, CA	26.3
157	Danbury, CT	(3.4)
316	Davenport, IA	(26.2)
56	Davie, FL	15.6
106	Dayton, OH	5.3
NA	Dearborn, MI**	NA
NA	Decatur, IL**	NA
292	Denton, TX	(20.0)
360	Denver, CO	(39.6)
NA	Des Moines, IA**	NA
NA	Detroit, MI**	NA
186	Downey, CA	(6.6)
NA	Duluth, MN**	NA
115	Durham, NC	4.0
202	Edison Twnshp, NJ	(9.1)
242	Edmond, OK	(12.8)
349	El Cajon, CA	(35.2)
194	El Monte, CA	(7.9)
211	El Paso, TX	(10.0)
NA	Elgin, IL**	NA
5	Elizabeth, NJ	55.0
NA	Elk Grove, CA**	NA
4	Erie, PA	60.7
158	Escondido, CA	(3.5)
78	Eugene, OR	11.3
211	Evansville, IN	(10.0)
259	Everett, WA	(14.5)
114	Fairfield, CA	4.3
NA	Fall River, MA**	NA
12	Fargo, ND	42.1
NA	Farmington Hills, MI**	NA
201	Fayetteville, AR	(9.0)
39	Fayetteville, NC	24.0
205	Federal Way, WA	(9.3)
NA	Flint, MI**	NA
63	Fontana, CA	13.8
200	Fort Collins, CO	(8.5)
113	Fort Lauderdale, FL	4.7
74	Fort Smith, AR	11.8
222	Fort Wayne, IN	(10.9)
137	Fort Worth, TX	(0.6)
49	Fremont, CA	18.5
126	Fresno, CA	1.5
373	Frisco, TX	(65.6)
151	Fullerton, CA	(1.9)
43	Gainesville, FL	21.9
245	Garden Grove, CA	(13.1)
82	Garland, TX	10.6
146	Gary, IN	(1.5)
324	Gilbert, AZ	(27.5)
319	Glendale, AZ	(26.9)
209	Glendale, CA	(9.8)
37	Grand Prairie, TX	25.2
NA	Grand Rapids, MI**	NA
10	Greece, NY	45.3
371	Greeley, CO	(53.0)
103	Green Bay, WI	6.1
70	Greensboro, NC	12.6
359	Gresham, OR	(38.8)
277	Hamilton Twnshp, NJ	(17.5)
179	Hammond, IN	(5.3)
165	Hampton, VA	(4.5)
284	Hartford, CT	(18.1)
254	Hawthorne, CA	(14.2)
263	Hayward, CA	(15.0)
289	Henderson, NV	(19.5)
285	Hesperia, CA	(18.3)
302	Hialeah, FL	(22.1)
342	High Point, NC	(32.4)
372	Hillsboro, OR	(57.3)
20	Hollywood, FL	34.0
156	Honolulu, HI	(3.2)
162	Houston, TX	(4.4)
202	Huntington Beach, CA	(9.1)
168	Huntsville, AL	(4.7)
187	Independence, MO	(6.7)
30	Indianapolis, IN	29.6
280	Indio, CA	(17.6)
254	Inglewood, CA	(14.2)
365	Irvine, CA	(43.5)
97	Irving, TX	8.0
41	Jacksonville, FL	23.3
NA	Jacksonville, NC**	NA
8	Jackson, MS	52.0
357	Jersey City, NJ	(37.1)
117	Joliet, IL	3.8
102	Kansas City, KS	6.6
213	Kansas City, MO	(10.1)
136	Kenosha, WI	(0.5)
335	Kent, WA	(31.6)
335	Killeen, TX	(31.6)
126	Knoxville, TN	1.5
72	Lafayette, LA	12.4
190	Lake Forest, CA	(7.2)
28	Lakeland, FL	31.0
297	Lakewood, CA	(21.2)
321	Lakewood, CO	(27.1)
273	Lancaster, CA	(16.5)
NA	Lansing, MI**	NA
34	Laredo, TX	26.9
87	Las Cruces, NM	10.2
235	Las Vegas, NV	(12.5)
73	Lawrence, KS	12.3
110	Lawton, OK	5.1
134	Lee's Summit, MO	(0.2)
76	Lewisville, TX	11.6
NA	Lexington, KY**	NA
293	Lincoln, NE	(20.1)
NA	Little Rock, AR**	NA
207	Livermore, CA	(9.7)
NA	Livonia, MI**	NA
92	Long Beach, CA	9.0
NA	Longmont, CO**	NA

RANK	CITY	% CHANGE
86	Longview, TX	10.3
282	Los Angeles, CA	(17.9)
NA	Louisville, KY**	NA
27	Lubbock, TX	31.1
192	Lynn, MA	(7.5)
180	Macon, GA	(5.4)
138	Madison, WI	(0.7)
81	Manchester, NH	11.2
133	McAllen, TX	0.4
99	McKinney, TX	7.2
277	Melbourne, FL	(17.5)
217	Memphis, TN	(10.5)
207	Merced, CA	(9.7)
274	Mesa, AZ	(17.0)
2	Mesquite, TX	64.7
221	Miami Beach, FL	(10.8)
77	Miami Gardens, FL	11.5
270	Miami, FL	(16.3)
98	Midland, TX	7.8
16	Milwaukee, WI	38.7
267	Minneapolis, MN	(15.8)
115	Miramar, FL	4.0
131	Mission Viejo, CA	0.6
191	Missouri City, TX	(7.4)
147	Mobile, AL	(1.6)
21	Modesto, CA	33.9
237	Montgomery, AL	(12.6)
69	Moreno Valley, CA	12.7
24	Murfreesboro, TN	32.5
332	Murrieta, CA	(31.3)
NA	Nampa, ID**	NA
139	Naperville, IL	(0.8)
36	Nashua, NH	25.3
219	Nashville, TN	(10.6)
25	New Bedford, MA	32.0
NA	New Haven, CT**	NA
NA	New Orleans, LA**	NA
301	New York, NY	(21.9)
168	Newark, NJ	(4.7)
234	Newport Beach, CA	(12.4)
331	Newton, MA	(31.2)
45	Norfolk, VA	20.6
89	Norman, OK	9.9
344	North Charleston, SC	(33.2)
325	North Las Vegas, NV	(27.6)
313	Norwalk, CA	(25.9)
237	Norwalk, CT	(12.6)
281	Oakland, CA	(17.8)
327	Oceanside, CA	(28.8)
18	Odessa, TX	35.6
350	O'Fallon, MO	(35.4)
180	Ogden, UT	(5.4)
65	Oklahoma City, OK	13.3
NA	Olathe, KS**	NA
178	Omaha, NE	(5.1)
148	Ontario, CA	(1.7)
296	Orange, CA	(21.1)
368	Orem, UT	(45.2)
245	Orlando, FL	(13.1)
121	Overland Park, KS	2.8
316	Oxnard, CA	(26.2)
366	Palm Bay, FL	(43.6)
130	Palmdale, CA	0.7
106	Pasadena, CA	5.3
63	Pasadena, TX	13.8
199	Paterson, NJ	(8.4)
352	Pearland, TX	(36.0)
6	Pembroke Pines, FL	54.9

RANK	CITY	% CHANGE
275	Peoria, AZ	(17.2)
249	Peoria, IL	(13.5)
168	Philadelphia, PA	(4.7)
196	Phoenix, AZ	(8.1)
144	Pittsburgh, PA	(1.3)
140	Plano, TX	(1.0)
47	Plantation, FL	20.2
235	Pomona, CA	(12.5)
206	Pompano Beach, FL	(9.5)
104	Port St. Lucie, FL	5.6
364	Portland, OR	(41.8)
70	Portsmouth, VA	12.6
121	Providence, RI	2.8
369	Provo, UT	(47.9)
254	Pueblo, CO	(14.2)
59	Quincy, MA	14.7
84	Racine, WI	10.5
254	Raleigh, NC	(14.2)
320	Ramapo, NY	(27.0)
125	Rancho Cucamon., CA	1.7
232	Reading, PA	(12.1)
288	Redding, CA	(18.9)
219	Reno, NV	(10.6)
67	Rialto, CA	13.1
51	Richardson, TX	18.2
13	Richmond, CA	40.5
363	Richmond, VA	(40.9)
290	Rio Rancho, NM	(19.9)
300	Riverside, CA	(21.7)
202	Roanoke, VA	(9.1)
243	Rochester, MN	(12.9)
95	Rochester, NY	8.8
132	Rockford, IL	0.5
367	Roseville, CA	(45.0)
29	Roswell, GA	30.7
82	Round Rock, TX	10.6
259	Sacramento, CA	(14.5)
298	Salem, OR	(21.3)
7	Salinas, CA	53.5
124	Salt Lake City, UT	2.2
263	San Angelo, TX	(15.0)
56	San Antonio, TX	15.6
188	San Bernardino, CA	(7.0)
247	San Diego, CA	(13.2)
304	San Francisco, CA	(22.5)
227	San Jose, CA	(11.8)
290	San Leandro, CA	(19.9)
326	San Marcos, CA	(28.5)
305	San Mateo, CA	(23.1)
NA	Sandy Springs, GA**	NA
61	Sandy, UT	14.3
142	Santa Ana, CA	(1.2)
195	Santa Barbara, CA	(8.0)
321	Santa Clara, CA	(27.1)
287	Santa Clarita, CA	(18.4)
14	Santa Maria, CA	39.6
346	Santa Monica, CA	(34.7)
237	Santa Rosa, CA	(12.6)
106	Savannah, GA	5.3
333	Scottsdale, AZ	(31.4)
166	Seattle, WA	(4.6)
197	Shreveport, LA	(8.3)
356	Simi Valley, CA	(36.7)
294	Sioux City, IA	(20.2)
173	Sioux Falls, SD	(4.9)
172	Somerville, MA	(4.8)
32	South Bend, IN	27.6
229	South Gate, CA	(11.9)

RANK	CITY	% CHANGE
NA	Southfield, MI**	NA
106	Sparks, NV	5.3
189	Spokane Valley, WA	(7.1)
118	Spokane, WA	3.5
155	Springfield, IL	(2.8)
166	Springfield, MA	(4.6)
32	Springfield, MO	27.6
241	Stamford, CT	(12.7)
NA	Sterling Heights, MI**	NA
75	Stockton, CA	11.7
333	St. George, UT	(31.4)
44	St. Joseph, MO	21.7
193	St. Louis, MO	(7.7)
271	St. Paul, MN	(16.4)
31	St. Petersburg, FL	28.5
152	Suffolk, VA	(2.0)
253	Sugar Land, TX	(14.1)
265	Sunnyvale, CA	(15.1)
15	Sunrise, FL	38.9
88	Surprise, AZ	10.0
94	Syracuse, NY	8.9
214	Tacoma, WA	(10.2)
89	Tallahassee, FL	9.9
339	Tampa, FL	(32.1)
330	Temecula, CA	(31.1)
310	Tempe, AZ	(24.6)
216	Thornton, CO	(10.4)
248	Thousand Oaks, CA	(13.3)
48	Toledo, OH	19.0
9	Toms River Twnshp, NJ	50.2
161	Topeka, KS	(4.2)
328	Torrance, CA	(29.7)
176	Tracy, CA	(5.0)
225	Trenton, NJ	(11.3)
NA	Troy, MI**	NA
168	Tucson, AZ	(4.7)
129	Tulsa, OK	0.9
78	Tuscaloosa, AL	11.3
259	Tyler, TX	(14.5)
135	Upper Darby Twnshp, PA	(0.3)
56	Vacaville, CA	15.6
NA	Vallejo, CA**	NA
329	Vancouver, WA	(30.8)
307	Ventura, CA	(24.0)
119	Victorville, CA	3.1
182	Virginia Beach, VA	(5.5)
232	Visalia, CA	(12.1)
338	Vista, CA	(32.0)
310	Waco, TX	(24.6)
NA	Warren, MI**	NA
19	Warwick, RI	34.7
176	Washington, DC	(5.0)
354	Waterbury, CT	(36.5)
346	West Covina, CA	(34.7)
NA	West Jordan, UT**	NA
303	West Palm Beach, FL	(22.2)
159	West Valley, UT	(3.8)
NA	Westland, MI**	NA
318	Westminster, CA	(26.5)
340	Westminster, CO	(32.3)
153	Whittier, CA	(2.2)
306	Wichita Falls, TX	(23.7)
NA	Wichita, KS**	NA
283	Wilmington, NC	(18.0)
173	Winston-Salem, NC	(4.9)
277	Woodbridge Twnshp, NJ	(17.5)
52	Worcester, MA	17.0
183	Yonkers, NY	(5.6)
17	Yuma, AZ	36.1

Source: CQ Press using reported data from the F.B.I. "Crime in the United States 2009"
*Burglary is the unlawful entry of a structure to commit a felony or theft. Attempts are included.
**Not available.

72. Percent Change in Burglary Rate: 2005 to 2009 (continued)
National Percent Change = 1.5% Decrease*

RANK	CITY	% CHANGE
1	Athens-Clarke, GA	69.0
2	Mesquite, TX	64.7
3	Brick Twnshp, NJ	64.0
4	Erie, PA	60.7
5	Elizabeth, NJ	55.0
6	Pembroke Pines, FL	54.9
7	Salinas, CA	53.5
8	Jackson, MS	52.0
9	Toms River Twnshp, NJ	50.2
10	Greece, NY	45.3
11	Columbus, GA	42.7
12	Fargo, ND	42.1
13	Richmond, CA	40.5
14	Santa Maria, CA	39.6
15	Sunrise, FL	38.9
16	Milwaukee, WI	38.7
17	Yuma, AZ	36.1
18	Odessa, TX	35.6
19	Warwick, RI	34.7
20	Hollywood, FL	34.0
21	Modesto, CA	33.9
22	Coral Springs, FL	33.3
23	Clarksville, TN	32.6
24	Murfreesboro, TN	32.5
25	New Bedford, MA	32.0
26	Cranston, RI	31.2
27	Lubbock, TX	31.1
28	Lakeland, FL	31.0
29	Roswell, GA	30.7
30	Indianapolis, IN	29.6
31	St. Petersburg, FL	28.5
32	South Bend, IN	27.6
32	Springfield, MO	27.6
34	Laredo, TX	26.9
35	Daly City, CA	26.3
36	Nashua, NH	25.3
37	Grand Prairie, TX	25.2
38	Compton, CA	24.2
39	Fayetteville, NC	24.0
40	Chattanooga, TN	23.7
41	Jacksonville, FL	23.3
42	Amherst, NY	22.3
43	Gainesville, FL	21.9
44	St. Joseph, MO	21.7
45	Norfolk, VA	20.6
46	Columbia, MO	20.4
47	Plantation, FL	20.2
48	Toledo, OH	19.0
49	Fremont, CA	18.5
50	Arlington, TX	18.3
51	Richardson, TX	18.2
52	Worcester, MA	17.0
53	Billings, MT	16.8
54	Brownsville, TX	16.4
55	Columbia, SC	16.1
56	Davie, FL	15.6
56	San Antonio, TX	15.6
56	Vacaville, CA	15.6
59	Cleveland, OH	14.7
59	Quincy, MA	14.7
61	Sandy, UT	14.3
62	Cedar Rapids, IA	14.2
63	Fontana, CA	13.8
63	Pasadena, TX	13.8
65	Akron, OH	13.3
65	Oklahoma City, OK	13.3
67	Rialto, CA	13.1
68	Antioch, CA	12.8
69	Moreno Valley, CA	12.7
70	Greensboro, NC	12.6
70	Portsmouth, VA	12.6
72	Lafayette, LA	12.4
73	Lawrence, KS	12.3
74	Fort Smith, AR	11.8
75	Stockton, CA	11.7
76	Lewisville, TX	11.6
77	Miami Gardens, FL	11.5
78	Carrollton, TX	11.3
78	Eugene, OR	11.3
78	Tuscaloosa, AL	11.3
81	Manchester, NH	11.2
82	Garland, TX	10.6
82	Round Rock, TX	10.6
84	Racine, WI	10.5
85	Brockton, MA	10.4
86	Longview, TX	10.3
87	Las Cruces, NM	10.2
88	Surprise, AZ	10.0
89	Norman, OK	9.9
89	Tallahassee, FL	9.9
91	Cincinnati, OH	9.1
92	Baton Rouge, LA	9.0
92	Long Beach, CA	9.0
94	Syracuse, NY	8.9
95	Rochester, NY	8.8
96	Austin, TX	8.3
97	Irving, TX	8.0
98	Midland, TX	7.8
99	McKinney, TX	7.2
100	Atlanta, GA	6.8
101	Baltimore, MD	6.7
102	Kansas City, KS	6.6
103	Green Bay, WI	6.1
104	Chicago, IL	5.6
104	Port St. Lucie, FL	5.6
106	Dayton, OH	5.3
106	Pasadena, CA	5.3
106	Savannah, GA	5.3
106	Sparks, NV	5.3
110	Lawton, OK	5.1
111	Alexandria, VA	5.0
111	Birmingham, AL	5.0
113	Fort Lauderdale, FL	4.7
114	Fairfield, CA	4.3
115	Durham, NC	4.0
115	Miramar, FL	4.0
117	Joliet, IL	3.8
118	Spokane, WA	3.5
119	Victorville, CA	3.1
120	Camden, NJ	2.9
121	Overland Park, KS	2.8
121	Providence, RI	2.8
123	Albuquerque, NM	2.6
124	Salt Lake City, UT	2.2
125	Rancho Cucamon., CA	1.7
126	Fresno, CA	1.5
126	Knoxville, TN	1.5
128	Allentown, PA	1.1
129	Tulsa, OK	0.9
130	Palmdale, CA	0.7
131	Mission Viejo, CA	0.6
132	Rockford, IL	0.5
133	McAllen, TX	0.4
134	Lee's Summit, MO	(0.2)
135	Upper Darby Twnshp, PA	(0.3)
136	Kenosha, WI	(0.5)
137	Fort Worth, TX	(0.6)
138	Madison, WI	(0.7)
139	Naperville, IL	(0.8)
140	Plano, TX	(1.0)
141	Bellevue, WA	(1.1)
142	Clifton, NJ	(1.2)
142	Santa Ana, CA	(1.2)
144	Pittsburgh, PA	(1.3)
145	Buena Park, CA	(1.4)
146	Gary, IN	(1.5)
147	Mobile, AL	(1.6)
148	Buffalo, NY	(1.7)
148	Cape Coral, FL	(1.7)
148	Ontario, CA	(1.7)
151	Fullerton, CA	(1.9)
152	Suffolk, VA	(2.0)
153	Amarillo, TX	(2.2)
153	Whittier, CA	(2.2)
155	Springfield, IL	(2.8)
156	Honolulu, HI	(3.2)
157	Danbury, CT	(3.4)
158	Escondido, CA	(3.5)
159	West Valley, UT	(3.8)
160	Columbus, OH	(4.0)
161	Topeka, KS	(4.2)
162	Boulder, CO	(4.4)
162	Clovis, CA	(4.4)
162	Houston, TX	(4.4)
165	Hampton, VA	(4.5)
166	Seattle, WA	(4.6)
166	Springfield, MA	(4.6)
168	Huntsville, AL	(4.7)
168	Newark, NJ	(4.7)
168	Philadelphia, PA	(4.7)
168	Tucson, AZ	(4.7)
172	Somerville, MA	(4.8)
173	Bridgeport, CT	(4.9)
173	Sioux Falls, SD	(4.9)
173	Winston-Salem, NC	(4.9)
176	Tracy, CA	(5.0)
176	Washington, DC	(5.0)
178	Omaha, NE	(5.1)
179	Hammond, IN	(5.3)
180	Macon, GA	(5.4)
180	Ogden, UT	(5.4)
182	Virginia Beach, VA	(5.5)
183	Yonkers, NY	(5.6)
184	Chino, CA	(5.7)
185	College Station, TX	(5.8)
186	Downey, CA	(6.6)
187	Independence, MO	(6.7)
188	San Bernardino, CA	(7.0)
189	Spokane Valley, WA	(7.1)
190	Lake Forest, CA	(7.2)
191	Missouri City, TX	(7.4)
192	Lynn, MA	(7.5)
193	St. Louis, MO	(7.7)
194	El Monte, CA	(7.9)
195	Santa Barbara, CA	(8.0)
196	Phoenix, AZ	(8.1)
197	Broken Arrow, OK	(8.3)
197	Shreveport, LA	(8.3)
199	Paterson, NJ	(8.4)
200	Fort Collins, CO	(8.5)
201	Fayetteville, AR	(9.0)
202	Edison Twnshp, NJ	(9.1)
202	Huntington Beach, CA	(9.1)
202	Roanoke, VA	(9.1)
205	Federal Way, WA	(9.3)
206	Pompano Beach, FL	(9.5)

RANK	CITY	% CHANGE
207	Livermore, CA	(9.7)
207	Merced, CA	(9.7)
209	Glendale, CA	(9.8)
210	Chesapeake, VA	(9.9)
211	El Paso, TX	(10.0)
211	Evansville, IN	(10.0)
213	Kansas City, MO	(10.1)
214	Tacoma, WA	(10.2)
215	Bakersfield, CA	(10.3)
216	Thornton, CO	(10.4)
217	Canton, OH	(10.5)
217	Memphis, TN	(10.5)
219	Nashville, TN	(10.6)
219	Reno, NV	(10.6)
221	Miami Beach, FL	(10.8)
222	Carson, CA	(10.9)
222	Clearwater, FL	(10.9)
222	Fort Wayne, IN	(10.9)
225	Berkeley, CA	(11.3)
225	Trenton, NJ	(11.3)
227	Anchorage, AK	(11.8)
227	San Jose, CA	(11.8)
229	Albany, GA	(11.9)
229	Corpus Christi, TX	(11.9)
229	South Gate, CA	(11.9)
232	Reading, PA	(12.1)
232	Visalia, CA	(12.1)
234	Newport Beach, CA	(12.4)
235	Las Vegas, NV	(12.5)
235	Pomona, CA	(12.5)
237	Costa Mesa, CA	(12.6)
237	Montgomery, AL	(12.6)
237	Norwalk, CT	(12.6)
237	Santa Rosa, CA	(12.6)
241	Stamford, CT	(12.7)
242	Edmond, OK	(12.8)
243	Boca Raton, FL	(12.9)
243	Rochester, MN	(12.9)
245	Garden Grove, CA	(13.1)
245	Orlando, FL	(13.1)
247	San Diego, CA	(13.2)
248	Thousand Oaks, CA	(13.3)
249	Chandler, AZ	(13.5)
249	Cheektowaga, NY	(13.5)
249	Peoria, IL	(13.5)
252	Burbank, CA	(13.6)
253	Sugar Land, TX	(14.1)
254	Hawthorne, CA	(14.2)
254	Inglewood, CA	(14.2)
254	Pueblo, CO	(14.2)
254	Raleigh, NC	(14.2)
258	Abilene, TX	(14.4)
259	Everett, WA	(14.5)
259	Sacramento, CA	(14.5)
259	Tyler, TX	(14.5)
262	Baldwin Park, CA	(14.9)
263	Hayward, CA	(15.0)
263	San Angelo, TX	(15.0)
265	Sunnyvale, CA	(15.1)
266	Bellingham, WA	(15.3)
267	Minneapolis, MN	(15.8)
268	Beaumont, TX	(16.2)
268	Colorado Springs, CO	(16.2)
270	Miami, FL	(16.3)
271	Cary, NC	(16.4)
271	St. Paul, MN	(16.4)
273	Lancaster, CA	(16.5)
274	Mesa, AZ	(17.0)

RANK	CITY	% CHANGE
275	Dallas, TX	(17.2)
275	Peoria, AZ	(17.2)
277	Hamilton Twnshp, NJ	(17.5)
277	Melbourne, FL	(17.5)
277	Woodbridge Twnshp, NJ	(17.5)
280	Indio, CA	(17.6)
281	Oakland, CA	(17.8)
282	Los Angeles, CA	(17.9)
283	Wilmington, NC	(18.0)
284	Hartford, CT	(18.1)
285	Aurora, IL	(18.3)
285	Hesperia, CA	(18.3)
287	Santa Clarita, CA	(18.4)
288	Redding, CA	(18.9)
289	Henderson, NV	(19.5)
290	Rio Rancho, NM	(19.9)
290	San Leandro, CA	(19.9)
292	Denton, TX	(20.0)
293	Lincoln, NE	(20.1)
294	Sioux City, IA	(20.2)
295	Chico, CA	(20.5)
296	Orange, CA	(21.1)
297	Lakewood, CA	(21.2)
298	Salem, OR	(21.3)
299	Carlsbad, CA	(21.5)
300	Riverside, CA	(21.7)
301	New York, NY	(21.9)
302	Hialeah, FL	(22.1)
303	West Palm Beach, FL	(22.2)
304	San Francisco, CA	(22.5)
305	San Mateo, CA	(23.1)
306	Wichita Falls, TX	(23.7)
307	Ventura, CA	(24.0)
308	Aurora, CO	(24.3)
309	Anaheim, CA	(24.5)
310	Tempe, AZ	(24.6)
310	Waco, TX	(24.6)
312	Concord, CA	(25.0)
313	Allen, TX	(25.9)
313	Norwalk, CA	(25.9)
315	Arvada, CO	(26.1)
316	Davenport, IA	(26.2)
316	Oxnard, CA	(26.2)
318	Westminster, CA	(26.5)
319	Glendale, AZ	(26.9)
320	Ramapo, NY	(27.0)
321	Lakewood, CO	(27.1)
321	Santa Clara, CA	(27.1)
323	Boise, ID	(27.2)
324	Gilbert, AZ	(27.5)
325	North Las Vegas, NV	(27.6)
326	San Marcos, CA	(28.5)
327	Oceanside, CA	(28.8)
328	Torrance, CA	(29.7)
329	Vancouver, WA	(30.8)
330	Temecula, CA	(31.1)
331	Newton, MA	(31.2)
332	Murrieta, CA	(31.3)
333	Scottsdale, AZ	(31.4)
333	St. George, UT	(31.4)
335	Kent, WA	(31.6)
335	Killeen, TX	(31.6)
337	Cambridge, MA	(31.9)
338	Vista, CA	(32.0)
339	Tampa, FL	(32.1)
340	Chula Vista, CA	(32.3)
340	Westminster, CO	(32.3)
342	High Point, NC	(32.4)

RANK	CITY	% CHANGE
343	Charlotte, NC	(33.1)
344	North Charleston, SC	(33.2)
345	Albany, NY	(33.4)
346	Charleston, SC	(34.7)
346	Santa Monica, CA	(34.7)
346	West Covina, CA	(34.7)
349	El Cajon, CA	(35.2)
350	O'Fallon, MO	(35.4)
351	Alhambra, CA	(35.5)
352	Pearland, TX	(36.0)
353	Centennial, CO	(36.1)
354	Corona, CA	(36.5)
354	Waterbury, CT	(36.5)
356	Simi Valley, CA	(36.7)
357	Jersey City, NJ	(37.1)
358	Colonie, NY	(37.9)
359	Gresham, OR	(38.8)
360	Denver, CO	(39.6)
361	Beaverton, OR	(40.1)
362	Boston, MA	(40.7)
363	Richmond, VA	(40.9)
364	Portland, OR	(41.8)
365	Irvine, CA	(43.5)
366	Palm Bay, FL	(43.6)
367	Roseville, CA	(45.0)
368	Orem, UT	(45.2)
369	Provo, UT	(47.9)
370	Bend, OR	(50.9)
371	Greeley, CO	(53.0)
372	Hillsboro, OR	(57.3)
373	Frisco, TX	(65.6)
NA	Ann Arbor, MI**	NA
NA	Avondale, AZ**	NA
NA	Bloomington, MN**	NA
NA	Canton Twnshp, MI**	NA
NA	Citrus Heights, CA**	NA
NA	Clarkstown, NY**	NA
NA	Clinton Twnshp, MI**	NA
NA	Dearborn, MI**	NA
NA	Decatur, IL**	NA
NA	Des Moines, IA**	NA
NA	Detroit, MI**	NA
NA	Duluth, MN**	NA
NA	Elgin, IL**	NA
NA	Elk Grove, CA**	NA
NA	Fall River, MA**	NA
NA	Farmington Hills, MI**	NA
NA	Flint, MI**	NA
NA	Grand Rapids, MI**	NA
NA	Jacksonville, NC**	NA
NA	Lansing, MI**	NA
NA	Lexington, KY**	NA
NA	Little Rock, AR**	NA
NA	Livonia, MI**	NA
NA	Longmont, CO**	NA
NA	Louisville, KY**	NA
NA	Nampa, ID**	NA
NA	New Haven, CT**	NA
NA	New Orleans, LA**	NA
NA	Olathe, KS**	NA
NA	Sandy Springs, GA**	NA
NA	Southfield, MI**	NA
NA	Sterling Heights, MI**	NA
NA	Troy, MI**	NA
NA	Vallejo, CA**	NA
NA	Warren, MI**	NA
NA	West Jordan, UT**	NA
NA	Westland, MI**	NA
NA	Wichita, KS**	NA

Source: CQ Press using reported data from the F.B.I. "Crime in the United States 2009"
*Burglary is the unlawful entry of a structure to commit a felony or theft. Attempts are included.
**Not available.

73. Larceny-Thefts in 2009
National Total = 6,327,230 Larceny-Thefts*

RANK	CITY	THEFTS
192	Abilene, TX	3,267
111	Akron, OH	5,763
207	Albany, GA	3,048
201	Albany, NY	3,149
25	Albuquerque, NM	19,365
238	Alexandria, VA	2,613
382	Alhambra, CA	1,209
183	Allentown, PA	3,385
384	Allen, TX	1,198
81	Amarillo, TX	7,768
321	Amherst, NY	1,844
116	Anaheim, CA	5,591
80	Anchorage, AK	7,835
276	Ann Arbor, MI	2,216
394	Antioch, CA	1,082
36	Arlington, TX	14,186
294	Arvada, CO	2,057
179	Athens-Clarke, GA	3,453
24	Atlanta, GA	19,511
90	Aurora, CO	6,820
191	Aurora, IL	3,272
9	Austin, TX	37,054
220	Avondale, AZ	2,831
64	Bakersfield, CA	9,341
406	Baldwin Park, CA	760
31	Baltimore, MD	16,741
72	Baton Rouge, LA	8,459
144	Beaumont, TX	4,385
379	Beaverton, OR	1,230
200	Bellevue, WA	3,150
176	Bellingham, WA	3,547
336	Bend, OR	1,642
131	Berkeley, CA	4,661
171	Billings, MT	3,592
48	Birmingham, AL	11,546
217	Bloomington, MN	2,846
255	Boca Raton, FL	2,375
137	Boise, ID	4,537
33	Boston, MA	15,507
290	Boulder, CO	2,093
399	Brick Twnshp, NJ	1,025
185	Bridgeport, CT	3,375
296	Brockton, MA	2,042
358	Broken Arrow, OK	1,486
79	Brownsville, TX	7,865
388	Buena Park, CA	1,145
67	Buffalo, NY	8,947
323	Burbank, CA	1,829
243	Cambridge, MA	2,524
271	Camden, NJ	2,251
393	Canton Twnshp, MI	1,120
237	Canton, OH	2,627
223	Cape Coral, FL	2,792
374	Carlsbad, CA	1,327
235	Carrollton, TX	2,633
368	Carson, CA	1,389
360	Cary, NC	1,454
150	Cedar Rapids, IA	4,068
398	Centennial, CO	1,053
115	Chandler, AZ	5,599
199	Charleston, SC	3,152
14	Charlotte, NC	25,379
66	Chattanooga, TN	8,949
287	Cheektowaga, NY	2,134
107	Chesapeake, VA	5,985
2	Chicago, IL	78,444
370	Chico, CA	1,359
372	Chino, CA	1,346
207	Chula Vista, CA	3,048
44	Cincinnati, OH	12,513
247	Citrus Heights, CA	2,447
330	Clarkstown, NY	1,710
226	Clarksville, TN	2,767
169	Clearwater, FL	3,617
51	Cleveland, OH	10,871
380	Clifton, NJ	1,219
352	Clinton Twnshp, MI	1,553
270	Clovis, CA	2,254
239	College Station, TX	2,580
297	Colonie, NY	2,037
55	Colorado Springs, CO	10,357
205	Columbia, MO	3,082
117	Columbia, SC	5,321
63	Columbus, GA	9,374
10	Columbus, OH	30,044
371	Compton, CA	1,355
277	Concord, CA	2,202
274	Coral Springs, FL	2,222
236	Corona, CA	2,632
43	Corpus Christi, TX	12,538
241	Costa Mesa, CA	2,557
359	Cranston, RI	1,466
6	Dallas, TX	41,481
392	Daly City, CA	1,126
381	Danbury, CT	1,219
158	Davenport, IA	3,866
221	Davie, FL	2,828
124	Dayton, OH	4,932
212	Dearborn, MI	2,961
345	Decatur, IL	1,580
250	Denton, TX	2,403
42	Denver, CO	12,628
102	Des Moines, IA	6,146
26	Detroit, MI	18,574
289	Downey, CA	2,105
181	Duluth, MN	3,431
82	Durham, NC	7,366
344	Edison Twnshp, NJ	1,585
375	Edmond, OK	1,319
351	El Cajon, CA	1,562
364	El Monte, CA	1,407
34	El Paso, TX	14,647
334	Elgin, IL	1,683
198	Elizabeth, NJ	3,164
284	Elk Grove, CA	2,152
320	Erie, PA	1,853
251	Escondido, CA	2,402
109	Eugene, OR	5,871
152	Evansville, IN	4,038
122	Everett, WA	5,070
291	Fairfield, CA	2,077
286	Fall River, MA	2,144
264	Fargo, ND	2,302
391	Farmington Hills, MI	1,134
263	Fayetteville, AR	2,306
73	Fayetteville, NC	8,455
195	Federal Way, WA	3,231
233	Flint, MI	2,664
249	Fontana, CA	2,430
170	Fort Collins, CO	3,604
92	Fort Lauderdale, FL	6,780
165	Fort Smith, AR	3,670
95	Fort Wayne, IN	6,683
19	Fort Worth, TX	23,564
194	Fremont, CA	3,237
40	Fresno, CA	13,359
339	Frisco, TX	1,627
232	Fullerton, CA	2,684
142	Gainesville, FL	4,457
285	Garden Grove, CA	2,145
103	Garland, TX	6,139
396	Gary, IN	1,069
188	Gilbert, AZ	3,337
75	Glendale, AZ	8,214
230	Glendale, CA	2,723
129	Grand Prairie, TX	4,743
106	Grand Rapids, MI	6,010
279	Greece, NY	2,190
256	Greeley, CO	2,373
305	Green Bay, WI	1,980
60	Greensboro, NC	9,668
227	Gresham, OR	2,747
377	Hamilton Twnshp, NJ	1,275
262	Hammond, IN	2,314
154	Hampton, VA	4,001
151	Hartford, CT	4,061
397	Hawthorne, CA	1,062
306	Hayward, CA	1,974
202	Henderson, NV	3,141
400	Hesperia, CA	907
108	Hialeah, FL	5,957
168	High Point, NC	3,619
354	Hillsboro, OR	1,527
141	Hollywood, FL	4,481
18	Honolulu, HI	23,647
3	Houston, TX	77,058
173	Huntington Beach, CA	3,571
99	Huntsville, AL	6,375
120	Independence, MO	5,134
13	Indianapolis, IN	27,717
363	Indio, CA	1,408
340	Inglewood, CA	1,615
259	Irvine, CA	2,365
112	Irving, TX	5,730
12	Jacksonville, FL	27,754
317	Jacksonville, NC	1,869
88	Jackson, MS	6,994
162	Jersey City, NJ	3,744
216	Joliet, IL	2,853
128	Kansas City, KS	4,744
32	Kansas City, MO	15,937
265	Kenosha, WI	2,296
254	Kent, WA	2,381
174	Killeen, TX	3,566
71	Knoxville, TN	8,553
114	Lafayette, LA	5,612
408	Lake Forest, CA	721
177	Lakeland, FL	3,515
365	Lakewood, CA	1,401
126	Lakewood, CO	4,788
323	Lancaster, CA	1,829
261	Lansing, MI	2,341
57	Laredo, TX	10,077
182	Las Cruces, NM	3,387
15	Las Vegas, NV	25,229
175	Lawrence, KS	3,551
193	Lawton, OK	3,240
335	Lee's Summit, MO	1,665
242	Lewisville, TX	2,526
84	Lexington, KY	7,154
78	Lincoln, NE	8,095
56	Little Rock, AR	10,253
385	Livermore, CA	1,191
345	Livonia, MI	1,580
83	Long Beach, CA	7,166
321	Longmont, CO	1,844

RANK	CITY	THEFTS
159	Longview, TX	3,842
5	Los Angeles, CA	57,414
27	Louisville, KY	18,094
70	Lubbock, TX	8,754
333	Lynn, MA	1,687
130	Macon, GA	4,679
105	Madison, WI	6,015
224	Manchester, NH	2,791
91	McAllen, TX	6,783
244	McKinney, TX	2,518
206	Melbourne, FL	3,058
11	Memphis, TN	29,059
314	Merced, CA	1,906
47	Mesa, AZ	11,700
131	Mesquite, TX	4,661
97	Miami Beach, FL	6,567
157	Miami Gardens, FL	3,921
39	Miami, FL	13,386
218	Midland, TX	2,845
20	Milwaukee, WI	23,397
49	Minneapolis, MN	11,320
273	Miramar, FL	2,227
402	Mission Viejo, CA	899
404	Missouri City, TX	877
61	Mobile, AL	9,457
96	Modesto, CA	6,637
86	Montgomery, AL	7,113
204	Moreno Valley, CA	3,086
189	Murfreesboro, TN	3,321
403	Murrieta, CA	884
362	Nampa, ID	1,423
295	Naperville, IL	2,047
309	Nashua, NH	1,962
21	Nashville, TN	21,113
325	New Bedford, MA	1,806
138	New Haven, CT	4,533
98	New Orleans, LA	6,507
1	New York, NY	112,526
160	Newark, NJ	3,781
342	Newport Beach, CA	1,600
407	Newton, MA	753
58	Norfolk, VA	9,912
215	Norman, OK	2,874
140	North Charleston, SC	4,510
180	North Las Vegas, NV	3,436
387	Norwalk, CA	1,146
378	Norwalk, CT	1,269
69	Oakland, CA	8,833
225	Oceanside, CA	2,786
219	Odessa, TX	2,834
386	O'Fallon, MO	1,154
213	Ogden, UT	2,955
23	Oklahoma City, OK	19,544
288	Olathe, KS	2,126
41	Omaha, NE	12,938
196	Ontario, CA	3,207
311	Orange, CA	1,959
280	Orem, UT	2,184
45	Orlando, FL	12,332
167	Overland Park, KS	3,628
214	Oxnard, CA	2,929
341	Palm Bay, FL	1,602
301	Palmdale, CA	2,031
209	Pasadena, CA	3,023
155	Pasadena, TX	3,955
307	Paterson, NJ	1,966
355	Pearland, TX	1,514
156	Pembroke Pines, FL	3,954

RANK	CITY	THEFTS
190	Peoria, AZ	3,303
184	Peoria, IL	3,378
8	Philadelphia, PA	37,941
7	Phoenix, AZ	39,643
76	Pittsburgh, PA	8,134
104	Plano, TX	6,047
228	Plantation, FL	2,729
267	Pomona, CA	2,273
164	Pompano Beach, FL	3,698
253	Port St. Lucie, FL	2,389
22	Portland, OR	19,624
147	Portsmouth, VA	4,163
121	Providence, RI	5,088
258	Provo, UT	2,367
327	Pueblo, CO	1,736
389	Quincy, MA	1,145
268	Racine, WI	2,266
59	Raleigh, NC	9,834
409	Ramapo, NY	542
248	Rancho Cucamon., CA	2,445
316	Reading, PA	1,872
304	Redding, CA	1,992
101	Reno, NV	6,209
367	Rialto, CA	1,391
257	Richardson, TX	2,372
353	Richmond, CA	1,533
110	Richmond, VA	5,822
383	Rio Rancho, NM	1,209
100	Riverside, CA	6,239
161	Roanoke, VA	3,774
260	Rochester, MN	2,343
85	Rochester, NY	7,130
113	Rockford, IL	5,697
210	Roseville, CA	3,020
336	Roswell, GA	1,642
269	Round Rock, TX	2,255
46	Sacramento, CA	11,720
134	Salem, OR	4,617
246	Salinas, CA	2,463
50	Salt Lake City, UT	10,888
203	San Angelo, TX	3,092
4	San Antonio, TX	67,684
127	San Bernardino, CA	4,775
28	San Diego, CA	18,057
17	San Francisco, CA	24,399
38	San Jose, CA	13,635
307	San Leandro, CA	1,966
401	San Marcos, CA	901
328	San Mateo, CA	1,720
318	Sandy Springs, GA	1,865
231	Sandy, UT	2,685
146	Santa Ana, CA	4,165
283	Santa Barbara, CA	2,176
281	Santa Clara, CA	2,182
299	Santa Clarita, CA	2,035
405	Santa Maria, CA	864
240	Santa Monica, CA	2,578
197	Santa Rosa, CA	3,165
89	Savannah, GA	6,867
119	Scottsdale, AZ	5,155
16	Seattle, WA	25,095
87	Shreveport, LA	7,054
356	Simi Valley, CA	1,508
297	Sioux City, IA	2,037
172	Sioux Falls, SD	3,584
376	Somerville, MA	1,301
163	South Bend, IN	3,702
395	South Gate, CA	1,070

RANK	CITY	THEFTS
310	Southfield, MI	1,960
303	Sparks, NV	2,007
252	Spokane Valley, WA	2,393
68	Spokane, WA	8,864
118	Springfield, IL	5,206
135	Springfield, MA	4,615
52	Springfield, MO	10,859
342	Stamford, CT	1,600
293	Sterling Heights, MI	2,061
65	Stockton, CA	9,274
390	St. George, UT	1,143
234	St. Joseph, MO	2,639
30	St. Louis, MO	17,799
93	St. Paul, MN	6,713
54	St. Petersburg, FL	10,575
338	Suffolk, VA	1,641
357	Sugar Land, TX	1,506
302	Sunnyvale, CA	2,026
211	Sunrise, FL	3,004
331	Surprise, AZ	1,706
178	Syracuse, NY	3,495
62	Tacoma, WA	9,395
123	Tallahassee, FL	4,975
77	Tampa, FL	8,098
347	Temecula, CA	1,574
94	Tempe, AZ	6,692
228	Thornton, CO	2,729
369	Thousand Oaks, CA	1,386
NA	Toledo, OH**	NA
312	Toms River Twnshp, NJ	1,944
133	Topeka, KS	4,632
300	Torrance, CA	2,034
329	Tracy, CA	1,719
366	Trenton, NJ	1,399
350	Troy, MI	1,564
NA	Tucson, AZ**	NA
35	Tulsa, OK	14,521
186	Tuscaloosa, AL	3,355
136	Tyler, TX	4,549
326	Upper Darby Twnshp, PA	1,748
348	Vacaville, CA	1,567
319	Vallejo, CA	1,854
148	Vancouver, WA	4,159
266	Ventura, CA	2,276
275	Victorville, CA	2,219
53	Virginia Beach, VA	10,751
187	Visalia, CA	3,346
373	Vista, CA	1,341
125	Waco, TX	4,879
315	Warren, MI	1,897
272	Warwick, RI	2,242
29	Washington, DC	18,012
143	Waterbury, CT	4,422
278	West Covina, CA	2,199
222	West Jordan, UT	2,807
166	West Palm Beach, FL	3,645
145	West Valley, UT	4,377
349	Westland, MI	1,566
332	Westminster, CA	1,701
245	Westminster, CO	2,511
361	Whittier, CA	1,435
153	Wichita Falls, TX	4,011
37	Wichita, KS	13,886
149	Wilmington, NC	4,119
74	Winston-Salem, NC	8,429
313	Woodbridge Twnshp, NJ	1,919
139	Worcester, MA	4,522
281	Yonkers, NY	2,182
292	Yuma, AZ	2,075

Source: Reported data from the F.B.I. "Crime in the United States 2009"

*Larceny-theft is the unlawful taking of property. Attempts are included.

**Not available.

73. Larceny-Thefts in 2009 (continued)
National Total = 6,327,230 Larceny-Thefts*

RANK	CITY	THEFTS
1	New York, NY	112,526
2	Chicago, IL	78,444
3	Houston, TX	77,058
4	San Antonio, TX	67,684
5	Los Angeles, CA	57,414
6	Dallas, TX	41,481
7	Phoenix, AZ	39,643
8	Philadelphia, PA	37,941
9	Austin, TX	37,054
10	Columbus, OH	30,044
11	Memphis, TN	29,059
12	Jacksonville, FL	27,754
13	Indianapolis, IN	27,717
14	Charlotte, NC	25,379
15	Las Vegas, NV	25,229
16	Seattle, WA	25,095
17	San Francisco, CA	24,399
18	Honolulu, HI	23,647
19	Fort Worth, TX	23,564
20	Milwaukee, WI	23,397
21	Nashville, TN	21,113
22	Portland, OR	19,624
23	Oklahoma City, OK	19,544
24	Atlanta, GA	19,511
25	Albuquerque, NM	19,365
26	Detroit, MI	18,574
27	Louisville, KY	18,094
28	San Diego, CA	18,057
29	Washington, DC	18,012
30	St. Louis, MO	17,799
31	Baltimore, MD	16,741
32	Kansas City, MO	15,937
33	Boston, MA	15,507
34	El Paso, TX	14,647
35	Tulsa, OK	14,521
36	Arlington, TX	14,186
37	Wichita, KS	13,886
38	San Jose, CA	13,635
39	Miami, FL	13,386
40	Fresno, CA	13,359
41	Omaha, NE	12,938
42	Denver, CO	12,628
43	Corpus Christi, TX	12,538
44	Cincinnati, OH	12,513
45	Orlando, FL	12,332
46	Sacramento, CA	11,720
47	Mesa, AZ	11,700
48	Birmingham, AL	11,546
49	Minneapolis, MN	11,320
50	Salt Lake City, UT	10,888
51	Cleveland, OH	10,871
52	Springfield, MO	10,859
53	Virginia Beach, VA	10,751
54	St. Petersburg, FL	10,575
55	Colorado Springs, CO	10,357
56	Little Rock, AR	10,253
57	Laredo, TX	10,077
58	Norfolk, VA	9,912
59	Raleigh, NC	9,834
60	Greensboro, NC	9,668
61	Mobile, AL	9,457
62	Tacoma, WA	9,395
63	Columbus, GA	9,374
64	Bakersfield, CA	9,341
65	Stockton, CA	9,274
66	Chattanooga, TN	8,949
67	Buffalo, NY	8,947
68	Spokane, WA	8,864
69	Oakland, CA	8,833
70	Lubbock, TX	8,754
71	Knoxville, TN	8,553
72	Baton Rouge, LA	8,459
73	Fayetteville, NC	8,455
74	Winston-Salem, NC	8,429
75	Glendale, AZ	8,214
76	Pittsburgh, PA	8,134
77	Tampa, FL	8,098
78	Lincoln, NE	8,095
79	Brownsville, TX	7,865
80	Anchorage, AK	7,835
81	Amarillo, TX	7,768
82	Durham, NC	7,366
83	Long Beach, CA	7,166
84	Lexington, KY	7,154
85	Rochester, NY	7,130
86	Montgomery, AL	7,113
87	Shreveport, LA	7,054
88	Jackson, MS	6,994
89	Savannah, GA	6,867
90	Aurora, CO	6,820
91	McAllen, TX	6,783
92	Fort Lauderdale, FL	6,780
93	St. Paul, MN	6,713
94	Tempe, AZ	6,692
95	Fort Wayne, IN	6,683
96	Modesto, CA	6,637
97	Miami Beach, FL	6,567
98	New Orleans, LA	6,507
99	Huntsville, AL	6,375
100	Riverside, CA	6,239
101	Reno, NV	6,209
102	Des Moines, IA	6,146
103	Garland, TX	6,139
104	Plano, TX	6,047
105	Madison, WI	6,015
106	Grand Rapids, MI	6,010
107	Chesapeake, VA	5,985
108	Hialeah, FL	5,957
109	Eugene, OR	5,871
110	Richmond, VA	5,822
111	Akron, OH	5,763
112	Irving, TX	5,730
113	Rockford, IL	5,697
114	Lafayette, LA	5,612
115	Chandler, AZ	5,599
116	Anaheim, CA	5,591
117	Columbia, SC	5,321
118	Springfield, IL	5,206
119	Scottsdale, AZ	5,155
120	Independence, MO	5,134
121	Providence, RI	5,088
122	Everett, WA	5,070
123	Tallahassee, FL	4,975
124	Dayton, OH	4,932
125	Waco, TX	4,879
126	Lakewood, CO	4,788
127	San Bernardino, CA	4,775
128	Kansas City, KS	4,744
129	Grand Prairie, TX	4,743
130	Macon, GA	4,679
131	Berkeley, CA	4,661
131	Mesquite, TX	4,661
133	Topeka, KS	4,632
134	Salem, OR	4,617
135	Springfield, MA	4,615
136	Tyler, TX	4,549
137	Boise, ID	4,537
138	New Haven, CT	4,533
139	Worcester, MA	4,522
140	North Charleston, SC	4,510
141	Hollywood, FL	4,481
142	Gainesville, FL	4,457
143	Waterbury, CT	4,422
144	Beaumont, TX	4,385
145	West Valley, UT	4,377
146	Santa Ana, CA	4,165
147	Portsmouth, VA	4,163
148	Vancouver, WA	4,159
149	Wilmington, NC	4,119
150	Cedar Rapids, IA	4,068
151	Hartford, CT	4,061
152	Evansville, IN	4,038
153	Wichita Falls, TX	4,011
154	Hampton, VA	4,001
155	Pasadena, TX	3,955
156	Pembroke Pines, FL	3,954
157	Miami Gardens, FL	3,921
158	Davenport, IA	3,866
159	Longview, TX	3,842
160	Newark, NJ	3,781
161	Roanoke, VA	3,774
162	Jersey City, NJ	3,744
163	South Bend, IN	3,702
164	Pompano Beach, FL	3,698
165	Fort Smith, AR	3,670
166	West Palm Beach, FL	3,645
167	Overland Park, KS	3,628
168	High Point, NC	3,619
169	Clearwater, FL	3,617
170	Fort Collins, CO	3,604
171	Billings, MT	3,592
172	Sioux Falls, SD	3,584
173	Huntington Beach, CA	3,571
174	Killeen, TX	3,566
175	Lawrence, KS	3,551
176	Bellingham, WA	3,547
177	Lakeland, FL	3,515
178	Syracuse, NY	3,495
179	Athens-Clarke, GA	3,453
180	North Las Vegas, NV	3,436
181	Duluth, MN	3,431
182	Las Cruces, NM	3,387
183	Allentown, PA	3,385
184	Peoria, IL	3,378
185	Bridgeport, CT	3,375
186	Tuscaloosa, AL	3,355
187	Visalia, CA	3,346
188	Gilbert, AZ	3,337
189	Murfreesboro, TN	3,321
190	Peoria, AZ	3,303
191	Aurora, IL	3,272
192	Abilene, TX	3,267
193	Lawton, OK	3,240
194	Fremont, CA	3,237
195	Federal Way, WA	3,231
196	Ontario, CA	3,207
197	Santa Rosa, CA	3,165
198	Elizabeth, NJ	3,164
199	Charleston, SC	3,152
200	Bellevue, WA	3,150
201	Albany, NY	3,149
202	Henderson, NV	3,141
203	San Angelo, TX	3,092
204	Moreno Valley, CA	3,086
205	Columbia, MO	3,082
206	Melbourne, FL	3,058

RANK	CITY	THEFTS
207	Albany, GA	3,048
207	Chula Vista, CA	3,048
209	Pasadena, CA	3,023
210	Roseville, CA	3,020
211	Sunrise, FL	3,004
212	Dearborn, MI	2,961
213	Ogden, UT	2,955
214	Oxnard, CA	2,929
215	Norman, OK	2,874
216	Joliet, IL	2,853
217	Bloomington, MN	2,846
218	Midland, TX	2,845
219	Odessa, TX	2,834
220	Avondale, AZ	2,831
221	Davie, FL	2,828
222	West Jordan, UT	2,807
223	Cape Coral, FL	2,792
224	Manchester, NH	2,791
225	Oceanside, CA	2,786
226	Clarksville, TN	2,767
227	Gresham, OR	2,747
228	Plantation, FL	2,729
228	Thornton, CO	2,729
230	Glendale, CA	2,723
231	Sandy, UT	2,685
232	Fullerton, CA	2,684
233	Flint, MI	2,664
234	St. Joseph, MO	2,639
235	Carrollton, TX	2,633
236	Corona, CA	2,632
237	Canton, OH	2,627
238	Alexandria, VA	2,613
239	College Station, TX	2,580
240	Santa Monica, CA	2,578
241	Costa Mesa, CA	2,557
242	Lewisville, TX	2,526
243	Cambridge, MA	2,524
244	McKinney, TX	2,518
245	Westminster, CO	2,511
246	Salinas, CA	2,463
247	Citrus Heights, CA	2,447
248	Rancho Cucamon., CA	2,445
249	Fontana, CA	2,430
250	Denton, TX	2,403
251	Escondido, CA	2,402
252	Spokane Valley, WA	2,393
253	Port St. Lucie, FL	2,389
254	Kent, WA	2,381
255	Boca Raton, FL	2,375
256	Greeley, CO	2,373
257	Richardson, TX	2,372
258	Provo, UT	2,367
259	Irvine, CA	2,365
260	Rochester, MN	2,343
261	Lansing, MI	2,341
262	Hammond, IN	2,314
263	Fayetteville, AR	2,306
264	Fargo, ND	2,302
265	Kenosha, WI	2,296
266	Ventura, CA	2,276
267	Pomona, CA	2,273
268	Racine, WI	2,266
269	Round Rock, TX	2,255
270	Clovis, CA	2,254
271	Camden, NJ	2,251
272	Warwick, RI	2,242
273	Miramar, FL	2,227
274	Coral Springs, FL	2,222
275	Victorville, CA	2,219
276	Ann Arbor, MI	2,216
277	Concord, CA	2,202
278	West Covina, CA	2,199
279	Greece, NY	2,190
280	Orem, UT	2,184
281	Santa Clara, CA	2,182
281	Yonkers, NY	2,182
283	Santa Barbara, CA	2,176
284	Elk Grove, CA	2,152
285	Garden Grove, CA	2,145
286	Fall River, MA	2,144
287	Cheektowaga, NY	2,134
288	Olathe, KS	2,126
289	Downey, CA	2,105
290	Boulder, CO	2,093
291	Fairfield, CA	2,077
292	Yuma, AZ	2,075
293	Sterling Heights, MI	2,061
294	Arvada, CO	2,057
295	Naperville, IL	2,047
296	Brockton, MA	2,042
297	Colonie, NY	2,037
297	Sioux City, IA	2,037
299	Santa Clarita, CA	2,035
300	Torrance, CA	2,034
301	Palmdale, CA	2,031
302	Sunnyvale, CA	2,026
303	Sparks, NV	2,007
304	Redding, CA	1,992
305	Green Bay, WI	1,980
306	Hayward, CA	1,974
307	Paterson, NJ	1,966
307	San Leandro, CA	1,966
309	Nashua, NH	1,962
310	Southfield, MI	1,960
311	Orange, CA	1,959
312	Toms River Twnshp, NJ	1,944
313	Woodbridge Twnshp, NJ	1,919
314	Merced, CA	1,906
315	Warren, MI	1,897
316	Reading, PA	1,872
317	Jacksonville, NC	1,869
318	Sandy Springs, GA	1,865
319	Vallejo, CA	1,854
320	Erie, PA	1,853
321	Amherst, NY	1,844
321	Longmont, CO	1,844
323	Burbank, CA	1,829
323	Lancaster, CA	1,829
325	New Bedford, MA	1,806
326	Upper Darby Twnshp, PA	1,748
327	Pueblo, CO	1,736
328	San Mateo, CA	1,720
329	Tracy, CA	1,719
330	Clarkstown, NY	1,710
331	Surprise, AZ	1,706
332	Westminster, CA	1,701
333	Lynn, MA	1,687
334	Elgin, IL	1,683
335	Lee's Summit, MO	1,665
336	Bend, OR	1,642
336	Roswell, GA	1,642
338	Suffolk, VA	1,641
339	Frisco, TX	1,627
340	Inglewood, CA	1,615
341	Palm Bay, FL	1,602
342	Newport Beach, CA	1,600
342	Stamford, CT	1,600
344	Edison Twnshp, NJ	1,585
345	Decatur, IL	1,580
345	Livonia, MI	1,580
347	Temecula, CA	1,574
348	Vacaville, CA	1,567
349	Westland, MI	1,566
350	Troy, MI	1,564
351	El Cajon, CA	1,562
352	Clinton Twnshp, MI	1,553
353	Richmond, CA	1,533
354	Hillsboro, OR	1,527
355	Pearland, TX	1,514
356	Simi Valley, CA	1,508
357	Sugar Land, TX	1,506
358	Broken Arrow, OK	1,486
359	Cranston, RI	1,466
360	Cary, NC	1,454
361	Whittier, CA	1,435
362	Nampa, ID	1,423
363	Indio, CA	1,408
364	El Monte, CA	1,407
365	Lakewood, CA	1,401
366	Trenton, NJ	1,399
367	Rialto, CA	1,391
368	Carson, CA	1,389
369	Thousand Oaks, CA	1,386
370	Chico, CA	1,359
371	Compton, CA	1,355
372	Chino, CA	1,346
373	Vista, CA	1,341
374	Carlsbad, CA	1,327
375	Edmond, OK	1,319
376	Somerville, MA	1,301
377	Hamilton Twnshp, NJ	1,275
378	Norwalk, CT	1,269
379	Beaverton, OR	1,230
380	Clifton, NJ	1,219
381	Danbury, CT	1,219
382	Alhambra, CA	1,209
383	Rio Rancho, NM	1,209
384	Allen, TX	1,198
385	Livermore, CA	1,191
386	O'Fallon, MO	1,154
387	Norwalk, CA	1,146
388	Buena Park, CA	1,145
389	Quincy, MA	1,145
390	St. George, UT	1,143
391	Farmington Hills, MI	1,134
392	Daly City, CA	1,126
393	Canton Twnshp, MI	1,120
394	Antioch, CA	1,082
395	South Gate, CA	1,070
396	Gary, IN	1,069
397	Hawthorne, CA	1,062
398	Centennial, CO	1,053
399	Brick Twnshp, NJ	1,025
400	Hesperia, CA	907
401	San Marcos, CA	901
402	Mission Viejo, CA	899
403	Murrieta, CA	884
404	Missouri City, TX	877
405	Santa Maria, CA	864
406	Baldwin Park, CA	760
407	Newton, MA	753
408	Lake Forest, CA	721
409	Ramapo, NY	542
NA	Toledo, OH**	NA
NA	Tucson, AZ**	NA

Source: Reported data from the F.B.I. "Crime in the United States 2009"
*Larceny-theft is the unlawful taking of property. Attempts are included.
**Not available.

74. Larceny-Theft Rate in 2009
National Rate = 2,060.9 Larceny-Thefts per 100,000 Population*

RANK	CITY	RATE
156	Abilene, TX	2,802.9
157	Akron, OH	2,790.8
43	Albany, GA	4,024.6
101	Albany, NY	3,369.9
69	Albuquerque, NM	3,649.4
295	Alexandria, VA	1,788.0
363	Alhambra, CA	1,406.5
123	Allentown, PA	3,153.9
369	Allen, TX	1,378.6
38	Amarillo, TX	4,115.1
312	Amherst, NY	1,670.3
313	Anaheim, CA	1,664.1
161	Anchorage, AK	2,765.6
275	Ann Arbor, MI	1,937.6
400	Antioch, CA	1,068.7
64	Arlington, TX	3,742.0
280	Arvada, CO	1,905.6
130	Athens-Clarke, GA	3,014.7
81	Atlanta, GA	3,528.8
244	Aurora, CO	2,104.8
284	Aurora, IL	1,868.3
17	Austin, TX	4,818.7
118	Avondale, AZ	3,189.0
152	Bakersfield, CA	2,822.9
404	Baldwin Park, CA	980.2
177	Baltimore, MD	2,620.9
58	Baton Rouge, LA	3,790.1
44	Beaumont, TX	3,977.8
378	Beaverton, OR	1,319.4
195	Bellevue, WA	2,518.9
24	Bellingham, WA	4,420.3
259	Bend, OR	2,038.5
20	Berkeley, CA	4,606.2
97	Billings, MT	3,407.1
9	Birmingham, AL	5,078.0
82	Bloomington, MN	3,519.5
162	Boca Raton, FL	2,763.0
235	Boise, ID	2,197.8
199	Boston, MA	2,484.2
248	Boulder, CO	2,092.3
379	Brick Twnshp, NJ	1,303.0
201	Bridgeport, CT	2,480.7
243	Brockton, MA	2,116.7
326	Broken Arrow, OK	1,573.9
26	Brownsville, TX	4,381.8
354	Buena Park, CA	1,439.8
105	Buffalo, NY	3,330.3
297	Burbank, CA	1,771.5
204	Cambridge, MA	2,453.7
149	Camden, NJ	2,850.1
373	Canton Twnshp, MI	1,355.4
102	Canton, OH	3,364.3
307	Cape Coral, FL	1,698.9
375	Carlsbad, CA	1,347.5
254	Carrollton, TX	2,066.2
342	Carson, CA	1,499.4
398	Cary, NC	1,087.0
122	Cedar Rapids, IA	3,158.9
401	Centennial, CO	1,059.5
238	Chandler, AZ	2,186.3
159	Charleston, SC	2,772.7
109	Charlotte, NC	3,263.3
6	Chattanooga, TN	5,186.7
166	Cheektowaga, NY	2,743.9
172	Chesapeake, VA	2,680.7
165	Chicago, IL	2,753.9
321	Chico, CA	1,604.0
324	Chino, CA	1,590.5
372	Chula Vista, CA	1,355.6
63	Cincinnati, OH	3,751.3
143	Citrus Heights, CA	2,901.6
241	Clarkstown, NY	2,167.3
228	Clarksville, TN	2,274.4
94	Clearwater, FL	3,432.2
193	Cleveland, OH	2,532.6
331	Clifton, NJ	1,560.3
319	Clinton Twnshp, MI	1,618.5
216	Clovis, CA	2,366.9
135	College Station, TX	2,997.5
179	Colonie, NY	2,611.4
185	Colorado Springs, CO	2,578.8
133	Columbia, MO	3,004.3
35	Columbia, SC	4,160.8
11	Columbus, GA	5,033.7
46	Columbus, OH	3,956.3
352	Compton, CA	1,443.5
293	Concord, CA	1,819.2
298	Coral Springs, FL	1,768.3
303	Corona, CA	1,726.6
28	Corpus Christi, TX	4,360.9
225	Costa Mesa, CA	2,321.4
291	Cranston, RI	1,827.4
116	Dallas, TX	3,214.9
394	Daly City, CA	1,111.7
338	Danbury, CT	1,528.9
56	Davenport, IA	3,823.3
124	Davie, FL	3,137.1
114	Dayton, OH	3,224.3
90	Dearborn, MI	3,471.1
250	Decatur, IL	2,088.5
277	Denton, TX	1,933.1
251	Denver, CO	2,088.4
126	Des Moines, IA	3,123.1
257	Detroit, MI	2,044.6
271	Downey, CA	1,956.4
39	Duluth, MN	4,081.1
112	Durham, NC	3,237.9
323	Edison Twnshp, NJ	1,595.3
316	Edmond, OK	1,630.6
311	El Cajon, CA	1,689.3
389	El Monte, CA	1,149.2
215	El Paso, TX	2,367.0
330	Elgin, IL	1,562.9
192	Elizabeth, NJ	2,533.0
337	Elk Grove, CA	1,530.8
296	Erie, PA	1,784.5
301	Escondido, CA	1,747.8
50	Eugene, OR	3,878.2
89	Evansville, IN	3,488.0
7	Everett, WA	5,150.8
266	Fairfield, CA	1,988.0
220	Fall River, MA	2,332.9
205	Fargo, ND	2,453.4
350	Farmington Hills, MI	1,451.2
128	Fayetteville, AR	3,069.8
16	Fayetteville, NC	4,859.3
55	Federal Way, WA	3,836.4
214	Flint, MI	2,385.9
381	Fontana, CA	1,276.9
183	Fort Collins, CO	2,602.4
66	Fort Lauderdale, FL	3,706.1
31	Fort Smith, AR	4,308.8
174	Fort Wayne, IN	2,656.4
110	Fort Worth, TX	3,257.1
322	Fremont, CA	1,596.8
158	Fresno, CA	2,775.2
341	Frisco, TX	1,503.1
260	Fullerton, CA	2,026.0
53	Gainesville, FL	3,866.7
380	Garden Grove, CA	1,293.4
155	Garland, TX	2,804.8
391	Gary, IN	1,122.7
355	Gilbert, AZ	1,439.6
115	Glendale, AZ	3,220.2
368	Glendale, CA	1,379.5
144	Grand Prairie, TX	2,878.6
127	Grand Rapids, MI	3,115.6
218	Greece, NY	2,347.9
188	Greeley, CO	2,549.7
269	Green Bay, WI	1,963.6
57	Greensboro, NC	3,818.5
171	Gresham, OR	2,681.0
362	Hamilton Twnshp, NJ	1,409.0
129	Hammond, IN	3,041.3
167	Hampton, VA	2,741.7
107	Hartford, CT	3,273.7
382	Hawthorne, CA	1,259.6
365	Hayward, CA	1,387.9
386	Henderson, NV	1,199.4
402	Hesperia, CA	1,020.2
148	Hialeah, FL	2,852.0
88	High Point, NC	3,490.7
325	Hillsboro, OR	1,581.4
121	Hollywood, FL	3,164.6
181	Honolulu, HI	2,606.8
99	Houston, TX	3,389.0
288	Huntington Beach, CA	1,851.1
77	Huntsville, AL	3,569.4
33	Independence, MO	4,202.2
96	Indianapolis, IN	3,407.3
326	Indio, CA	1,573.9
357	Inglewood, CA	1,432.9
396	Irvine, CA	1,096.6
151	Irving, TX	2,830.4
95	Jacksonville, FL	3,426.1
211	Jacksonville, NC	2,411.4
42	Jackson, MS	4,047.5
333	Jersey City, NJ	1,554.4
283	Joliet, IL	1,888.1
104	Kansas City, KS	3,338.4
106	Kansas City, MO	3,288.1
217	Kenosha, WI	2,351.1
153	Kent, WA	2,822.3
140	Killeen, TX	2,955.2
21	Knoxville, TN	4,602.1
14	Lafayette, LA	4,928.5
405	Lake Forest, CA	954.9
65	Lakeland, FL	3,726.6
294	Lakewood, CA	1,788.5
98	Lakewood, CO	3,405.0
384	Lancaster, CA	1,229.6
255	Lansing, MI	2,064.5
23	Laredo, TX	4,440.3
75	Las Cruces, NM	3,602.3
290	Las Vegas, NV	1,831.8
51	Lawrence, KS	3,872.3
74	Lawton, OK	3,606.6
274	Lee's Summit, MO	1,940.7
209	Lewisville, TX	2,414.9
210	Lexington, KY	2,413.6
119	Lincoln, NE	3,181.5
4	Little Rock, AR	5,390.5
347	Livermore, CA	1,471.9
299	Livonia, MI	1,751.0
335	Long Beach, CA	1,544.5
244	Longmont, CO	2,104.8

RANK	CITY	RATE
13	Longview, TX	4,947.0
344	Los Angeles, CA	1,491.7
145	Louisville, KY	2,866.3
48	Lubbock, TX	3,927.6
289	Lynn, MA	1,850.8
10	Macon, GA	5,069.4
187	Madison, WI	2,565.5
186	Manchester, NH	2,568.3
8	McAllen, TX	5,115.5
281	McKinney, TX	1,905.5
47	Melbourne, FL	3,927.9
29	Memphis, TN	4,353.9
207	Merced, CA	2,422.1
198	Mesa, AZ	2,485.0
86	Mesquite, TX	3,506.1
1	Miami Beach, FL	7,793.7
79	Miami Gardens, FL	3,553.4
117	Miami, FL	3,193.2
176	Midland, TX	2,635.9
52	Milwaukee, WI	3,869.4
138	Minneapolis, MN	2,958.6
256	Miramar, FL	2,054.9
406	Mission Viejo, CA	950.8
390	Missouri City, TX	1,131.0
54	Mobile, AL	3,841.6
111	Modesto, CA	3,245.9
85	Montgomery, AL	3,507.1
328	Moreno Valley, CA	1,565.6
125	Murfreesboro, TN	3,135.7
408	Murrieta, CA	840.0
308	Nampa, ID	1,696.6
361	Naperville, IL	1,414.3
230	Nashua, NH	2,266.8
92	Nashville, TN	3,460.1
273	New Bedford, MA	1,949.9
67	New Haven, CT	3,665.7
276	New Orleans, LA	1,934.2
376	New York, NY	1,339.5
374	Newark, NJ	1,354.2
265	Newport Beach, CA	2,002.2
407	Newton, MA	891.9
32	Norfolk, VA	4,216.1
173	Norman, OK	2,657.4
19	North Charleston, SC	4,698.8
346	North Las Vegas, NV	1,477.0
393	Norwalk, CA	1,114.7
339	Norwalk, CT	1,525.3
239	Oakland, CA	2,183.4
315	Oceanside, CA	1,633.3
150	Odessa, TX	2,840.5
356	O'Fallon, MO	1,433.0
78	Ogden, UT	3,559.6
84	Oklahoma City, OK	3,509.2
304	Olathe, KS	1,724.0
142	Omaha, NE	2,920.3
287	Ontario, CA	1,851.5
359	Orange, CA	1,428.6
222	Orem, UT	2,328.7
5	Orlando, FL	5,245.2
249	Overland Park, KS	2,088.8
329	Oxnard, CA	1,563.3
334	Palm Bay, FL	1,548.2
366	Palmdale, CA	1,387.5
246	Pasadena, CA	2,098.4
170	Pasadena, TX	2,691.2
371	Paterson, NJ	1,356.4
306	Pearland, TX	1,710.2
168	Pembroke Pines, FL	2,717.3

RANK	CITY	RATE
263	Peoria, AZ	2,009.5
139	Peoria, IL	2,956.9
206	Philadelphia, PA	2,451.6
200	Phoenix, AZ	2,481.7
182	Pittsburgh, PA	2,605.1
234	Plano, TX	2,217.1
108	Plantation, FL	3,266.5
345	Pomona, CA	1,483.5
71	Pompano Beach, FL	3,631.2
349	Port St. Lucie, FL	1,456.1
87	Portland, OR	3,498.6
37	Portsmouth, VA	4,123.0
137	Providence, RI	2,963.9
267	Provo, UT	1,981.2
314	Pueblo, CO	1,649.1
388	Quincy, MA	1,185.5
164	Racine, WI	2,755.6
207	Raleigh, NC	2,422.1
409	Ramapo, NY	707.5
367	Rancho Cucamon., CA	1,383.9
223	Reading, PA	2,327.8
240	Redding, CA	2,183.2
154	Reno, NV	2,809.4
364	Rialto, CA	1,399.6
226	Richardson, TX	2,310.2
343	Richmond, CA	1,494.6
146	Richmond, VA	2,864.7
351	Rio Rancho, NM	1,449.3
252	Riverside, CA	2,080.6
41	Roanoke, VA	4,053.3
227	Rochester, MN	2,299.7
91	Rochester, NY	3,469.0
73	Rockford, IL	3,607.0
184	Roseville, CA	2,584.6
286	Roswell, GA	1,858.1
258	Round Rock, TX	2,040.2
197	Sacramento, CA	2,492.0
136	Salem, OR	2,972.4
305	Salinas, CA	1,714.5
3	Salt Lake City, UT	6,024.7
103	San Angelo, TX	3,351.1
15	San Antonio, TX	4,926.3
213	San Bernardino, CA	2,391.3
370	San Diego, CA	1,373.4
131	San Francisco, CA	3,013.1
358	San Jose, CA	1,429.2
194	San Leandro, CA	2,531.0
397	San Marcos, CA	1,095.3
285	San Mateo, CA	1,865.3
231	Sandy Springs, GA	2,262.4
160	Sandy, UT	2,767.2
385	Santa Ana, CA	1,227.9
190	Santa Barbara, CA	2,538.6
268	Santa Clara, CA	1,963.9
387	Santa Clarita, CA	1,189.3
403	Santa Maria, CA	988.8
141	Santa Monica, CA	2,928.3
261	Santa Rosa, CA	2,021.8
113	Savannah, GA	3,228.3
242	Scottsdale, AZ	2,155.9
34	Seattle, WA	4,164.9
80	Shreveport, LA	3,533.6
383	Simi Valley, CA	1,240.8
202	Sioux City, IA	2,466.9
232	Sioux Falls, SD	2,258.7
302	Somerville, MA	1,732.1
76	South Bend, IN	3,582.8
395	South Gate, CA	1,107.1

RANK	CITY	RATE
180	Southfield, MI	2,610.8
236	Sparks, NV	2,195.3
163	Spokane Valley, WA	2,758.3
27	Spokane, WA	4,368.0
25	Springfield, IL	4,412.9
132	Springfield, MA	3,005.9
2	Springfield, MO	6,931.6
377	Stamford, CT	1,338.8
320	Sterling Heights, MI	1,617.2
120	Stockton, CA	3,173.7
340	St. George, UT	1,516.1
93	St. Joseph, MO	3,452.6
12	St. Louis, MO	5,010.9
212	St. Paul, MN	2,395.8
30	St. Petersburg, FL	4,317.5
278	Suffolk, VA	1,932.2
292	Sugar Land, TX	1,821.1
336	Sunnyvale, CA	1,533.2
100	Sunrise, FL	3,377.7
317	Surprise, AZ	1,629.5
189	Syracuse, NY	2,547.2
18	Tacoma, WA	4,755.6
147	Tallahassee, FL	2,856.2
219	Tampa, FL	2,345.7
332	Temecula, CA	1,559.6
61	Tempe, AZ	3,770.4
224	Thornton, CO	2,324.2
392	Thousand Oaks, CA	1,120.1
NA	Toledo, OH**	NA
262	Toms River Twnshp, NJ	2,012.1
62	Topeka, KS	3,752.2
353	Torrance, CA	1,441.4
247	Tracy, CA	2,095.9
309	Trenton, NJ	1,693.5
272	Troy, MI	1,950.6
NA	Tucson, AZ**	NA
60	Tulsa, OK	3,773.1
68	Tuscaloosa, AL	3,659.1
22	Tyler, TX	4,582.0
233	Upper Darby Twnshp, PA	2,238.5
310	Vacaville, CA	1,693.4
318	Vallejo, CA	1,620.0
196	Vancouver, WA	2,518.4
237	Ventura, CA	2,188.5
282	Victorville, CA	1,894.2
203	Virginia Beach, VA	2,464.8
169	Visalia, CA	2,692.7
348	Vista, CA	1,469.6
49	Waco, TX	3,900.1
360	Warren, MI	1,421.1
175	Warwick, RI	2,653.6
134	Washington, DC	3,003.7
36	Waterbury, CT	4,132.4
253	West Covina, CA	2,077.5
178	West Jordan, UT	2,620.6
72	West Palm Beach, FL	3,617.4
83	West Valley, UT	3,516.5
264	Westland, MI	2,003.9
279	Westminster, CA	1,910.0
221	Westminster, CO	2,331.4
300	Whittier, CA	1,748.0
45	Wichita Falls, TX	3,975.9
59	Wichita, KS	3,777.1
40	Wilmington, NC	4,060.6
70	Winston-Salem, NC	3,649.3
270	Woodbridge Twnshp, NJ	1,957.9
191	Worcester, MA	2,533.7
399	Yonkers, NY	1,079.2
229	Yuma, AZ	2,269.4

Source: CQ Press using reported data from the F.B.I. "Crime in the United States 2009"

*Larceny-theft is the unlawful taking of property. Attempts are included.

**Not available.

74. Larceny-Theft Rate in 2009 (continued)
National Rate = 2,060.9 Larceny-Thefts per 100,000 Population*

RANK	CITY	RATE
1	Miami Beach, FL	7,793.7
2	Springfield, MO	6,931.6
3	Salt Lake City, UT	6,024.7
4	Little Rock, AR	5,390.5
5	Orlando, FL	5,245.2
6	Chattanooga, TN	5,186.7
7	Everett, WA	5,150.8
8	McAllen, TX	5,115.5
9	Birmingham, AL	5,078.0
10	Macon, GA	5,069.4
11	Columbus, GA	5,033.7
12	St. Louis, MO	5,010.9
13	Longview, TX	4,947.0
14	Lafayette, LA	4,928.5
15	San Antonio, TX	4,926.3
16	Fayetteville, NC	4,859.3
17	Austin, TX	4,818.7
18	Tacoma, WA	4,755.6
19	North Charleston, SC	4,698.8
20	Berkeley, CA	4,606.2
21	Knoxville, TN	4,602.1
22	Tyler, TX	4,582.0
23	Laredo, TX	4,440.3
24	Bellingham, WA	4,420.3
25	Springfield, IL	4,412.9
26	Brownsville, TX	4,381.8
27	Spokane, WA	4,368.0
28	Corpus Christi, TX	4,360.9
29	Memphis, TN	4,353.9
30	St. Petersburg, FL	4,317.5
31	Fort Smith, AR	4,308.8
32	Norfolk, VA	4,216.1
33	Independence, MO	4,202.2
34	Seattle, WA	4,164.9
35	Columbia, SC	4,160.8
36	Waterbury, CT	4,132.4
37	Portsmouth, VA	4,123.0
38	Amarillo, TX	4,115.1
39	Duluth, MN	4,081.1
40	Wilmington, NC	4,060.6
41	Roanoke, VA	4,053.3
42	Jackson, MS	4,047.5
43	Albany, GA	4,024.6
44	Beaumont, TX	3,977.8
45	Wichita Falls, TX	3,975.9
46	Columbus, OH	3,956.3
47	Melbourne, FL	3,927.9
48	Lubbock, TX	3,927.6
49	Waco, TX	3,900.1
50	Eugene, OR	3,878.2
51	Lawrence, KS	3,872.3
52	Milwaukee, WI	3,869.4
53	Gainesville, FL	3,866.7
54	Mobile, AL	3,841.6
55	Federal Way, WA	3,836.4
56	Davenport, IA	3,823.3
57	Greensboro, NC	3,818.5
58	Baton Rouge, LA	3,790.1
59	Wichita, KS	3,777.1
60	Tulsa, OK	3,773.1
61	Tempe, AZ	3,770.4
62	Topeka, KS	3,752.2
63	Cincinnati, OH	3,751.3
64	Arlington, TX	3,742.0
65	Lakeland, FL	3,726.6
66	Fort Lauderdale, FL	3,706.1
67	New Haven, CT	3,665.7
68	Tuscaloosa, AL	3,659.1
69	Albuquerque, NM	3,649.4
70	Winston-Salem, NC	3,649.3
71	Pompano Beach, FL	3,631.2
72	West Palm Beach, FL	3,617.4
73	Rockford, IL	3,607.0
74	Lawton, OK	3,606.6
75	Las Cruces, NM	3,602.3
76	South Bend, IN	3,582.8
77	Huntsville, AL	3,569.4
78	Ogden, UT	3,559.6
79	Miami Gardens, FL	3,553.4
80	Shreveport, LA	3,533.6
81	Atlanta, GA	3,528.8
82	Bloomington, MN	3,519.5
83	West Valley, UT	3,516.5
84	Oklahoma City, OK	3,509.2
85	Montgomery, AL	3,507.1
86	Mesquite, TX	3,506.1
87	Portland, OR	3,498.6
88	High Point, NC	3,490.7
89	Evansville, IN	3,488.0
90	Dearborn, MI	3,471.1
91	Rochester, NY	3,469.0
92	Nashville, TN	3,460.1
93	St. Joseph, MO	3,452.6
94	Clearwater, FL	3,432.2
95	Jacksonville, FL	3,426.1
96	Indianapolis, IN	3,407.3
97	Billings, MT	3,407.1
98	Lakewood, CO	3,405.0
99	Houston, TX	3,389.0
100	Sunrise, FL	3,377.7
101	Albany, NY	3,369.9
102	Canton, OH	3,364.3
103	San Angelo, TX	3,351.1
104	Kansas City, KS	3,338.4
105	Buffalo, NY	3,330.3
106	Kansas City, MO	3,288.1
107	Hartford, CT	3,273.7
108	Plantation, FL	3,266.5
109	Charlotte, NC	3,263.3
110	Fort Worth, TX	3,257.1
111	Modesto, CA	3,245.9
112	Durham, NC	3,237.9
113	Savannah, GA	3,228.3
114	Dayton, OH	3,224.3
115	Glendale, AZ	3,220.2
116	Dallas, TX	3,214.9
117	Miami, FL	3,193.2
118	Avondale, AZ	3,189.0
119	Lincoln, NE	3,181.5
120	Stockton, CA	3,173.7
121	Hollywood, FL	3,164.6
122	Cedar Rapids, IA	3,158.9
123	Allentown, PA	3,153.9
124	Davie, FL	3,137.1
125	Murfreesboro, TN	3,135.7
126	Des Moines, IA	3,123.1
127	Grand Rapids, MI	3,115.6
128	Fayetteville, AR	3,069.8
129	Hammond, IN	3,041.3
130	Athens-Clarke, GA	3,014.7
131	San Francisco, CA	3,013.1
132	Springfield, MA	3,005.9
133	Columbia, MO	3,004.3
134	Washington, DC	3,003.7
135	College Station, TX	2,997.5
136	Salem, OR	2,972.4
137	Providence, RI	2,963.9
138	Minneapolis, MN	2,958.6
139	Peoria, IL	2,956.9
140	Killeen, TX	2,955.2
141	Santa Monica, CA	2,928.3
142	Omaha, NE	2,920.3
143	Citrus Heights, CA	2,901.6
144	Grand Prairie, TX	2,878.6
145	Louisville, KY	2,866.3
146	Richmond, VA	2,864.7
147	Tallahassee, FL	2,856.2
148	Hialeah, FL	2,852.0
149	Camden, NJ	2,850.1
150	Odessa, TX	2,840.5
151	Irving, TX	2,830.4
152	Bakersfield, CA	2,822.9
153	Kent, WA	2,822.3
154	Reno, NV	2,809.4
155	Garland, TX	2,804.8
156	Abilene, TX	2,802.9
157	Akron, OH	2,790.8
158	Fresno, CA	2,775.2
159	Charleston, SC	2,772.7
160	Sandy, UT	2,767.2
161	Anchorage, AK	2,765.6
162	Boca Raton, FL	2,763.0
163	Spokane Valley, WA	2,758.3
164	Racine, WI	2,755.6
165	Chicago, IL	2,753.9
166	Cheektowaga, NY	2,743.9
167	Hampton, VA	2,741.7
168	Pembroke Pines, FL	2,717.3
169	Visalia, CA	2,692.7
170	Pasadena, TX	2,691.2
171	Gresham, OR	2,681.0
172	Chesapeake, VA	2,680.7
173	Norman, OK	2,657.4
174	Fort Wayne, IN	2,656.4
175	Warwick, RI	2,653.6
176	Midland, TX	2,635.9
177	Baltimore, MD	2,620.9
178	West Jordan, UT	2,620.6
179	Colonie, NY	2,611.4
180	Southfield, MI	2,610.8
181	Honolulu, HI	2,606.8
182	Pittsburgh, PA	2,605.1
183	Fort Collins, CO	2,602.4
184	Roseville, CA	2,584.6
185	Colorado Springs, CO	2,578.8
186	Manchester, NH	2,568.3
187	Madison, WI	2,565.5
188	Greeley, CO	2,549.7
189	Syracuse, NY	2,547.2
190	Santa Barbara, CA	2,538.6
191	Worcester, MA	2,533.7
192	Elizabeth, NJ	2,533.0
193	Cleveland, OH	2,532.6
194	San Leandro, CA	2,531.0
195	Bellevue, WA	2,518.9
196	Vancouver, WA	2,518.4
197	Sacramento, CA	2,492.0
198	Mesa, AZ	2,485.0
199	Boston, MA	2,484.2
200	Phoenix, AZ	2,481.7
201	Bridgeport, CT	2,480.7
202	Sioux City, IA	2,466.9
203	Virginia Beach, VA	2,464.8
204	Cambridge, MA	2,453.7
205	Fargo, ND	2,453.4
206	Philadelphia, PA	2,451.6

RANK	CITY	RATE
207	Merced, CA	2,422.1
207	Raleigh, NC	2,422.1
209	Lewisville, TX	2,414.9
210	Lexington, KY	2,413.6
211	Jacksonville, NC	2,411.4
212	St. Paul, MN	2,395.8
213	San Bernardino, CA	2,391.3
214	Flint, MI	2,385.9
215	El Paso, TX	2,367.0
216	Clovis, CA	2,366.9
217	Kenosha, WI	2,351.1
218	Greece, NY	2,347.9
219	Tampa, FL	2,345.7
220	Fall River, MA	2,332.9
221	Westminster, CO	2,331.4
222	Orem, UT	2,328.7
223	Reading, PA	2,327.8
224	Thornton, CO	2,324.2
225	Costa Mesa, CA	2,321.4
226	Richardson, TX	2,310.2
227	Rochester, MN	2,299.7
228	Clarksville, TN	2,274.4
229	Yuma, AZ	2,269.4
230	Nashua, NH	2,266.8
231	Sandy Springs, GA	2,262.4
232	Sioux Falls, SD	2,258.7
233	Upper Darby Twnshp, PA	2,238.5
234	Plano, TX	2,217.1
235	Boise, ID	2,197.8
236	Sparks, NV	2,195.3
237	Ventura, CA	2,188.5
238	Chandler, AZ	2,186.3
239	Oakland, CA	2,183.4
240	Redding, CA	2,183.2
241	Clarkstown, NY	2,167.3
242	Scottsdale, AZ	2,155.9
243	Brockton, MA	2,116.7
244	Aurora, CO	2,104.8
244	Longmont, CO	2,104.8
246	Pasadena, CA	2,098.4
247	Tracy, CA	2,095.9
248	Boulder, CO	2,092.3
249	Overland Park, KS	2,088.8
250	Decatur, IL	2,088.5
251	Denver, CO	2,088.4
252	Riverside, CA	2,080.6
253	West Covina, CA	2,077.5
254	Carrollton, TX	2,066.2
255	Lansing, MI	2,064.5
256	Miramar, FL	2,054.9
257	Detroit, MI	2,044.6
258	Round Rock, TX	2,040.2
259	Bend, OR	2,038.5
260	Fullerton, CA	2,026.0
261	Santa Rosa, CA	2,021.8
262	Toms River Twnshp, NJ	2,012.1
263	Peoria, AZ	2,009.5
264	Westland, MI	2,003.9
265	Newport Beach, CA	2,002.2
266	Fairfield, CA	1,988.0
267	Provo, UT	1,981.2
268	Santa Clara, CA	1,963.9
269	Green Bay, WI	1,963.6
270	Woodbridge Twnshp, NJ	1,957.9
271	Downey, CA	1,956.4
272	Troy, MI	1,950.6
273	New Bedford, MA	1,949.9
274	Lee's Summit, MO	1,940.7
275	Ann Arbor, MI	1,937.6
276	New Orleans, LA	1,934.2
277	Denton, TX	1,933.1
278	Suffolk, VA	1,932.2
279	Westminster, CA	1,910.0
280	Arvada, CO	1,905.6
281	McKinney, TX	1,905.5
282	Victorville, CA	1,894.2
283	Joliet, IL	1,888.1
284	Aurora, IL	1,868.3
285	San Mateo, CA	1,865.3
286	Roswell, GA	1,858.1
287	Ontario, CA	1,851.5
288	Huntington Beach, CA	1,851.1
289	Lynn, MA	1,850.8
290	Las Vegas, NV	1,831.8
291	Cranston, RI	1,827.4
292	Sugar Land, TX	1,821.1
293	Concord, CA	1,819.2
294	Lakewood, CA	1,788.5
295	Alexandria, VA	1,788.0
296	Erie, PA	1,784.5
297	Burbank, CA	1,771.5
298	Coral Springs, FL	1,768.3
299	Livonia, MI	1,751.0
300	Whittier, CA	1,748.0
301	Escondido, CA	1,747.8
302	Somerville, MA	1,732.1
303	Corona, CA	1,726.6
304	Olathe, KS	1,724.0
305	Salinas, CA	1,714.5
306	Pearland, TX	1,710.2
307	Cape Coral, FL	1,698.9
308	Nampa, ID	1,696.6
309	Trenton, NJ	1,693.5
310	Vacaville, CA	1,693.4
311	El Cajon, CA	1,689.3
312	Amherst, NY	1,670.3
313	Anaheim, CA	1,664.1
314	Pueblo, CO	1,649.1
315	Oceanside, CA	1,633.3
316	Edmond, OK	1,630.6
317	Surprise, AZ	1,629.5
318	Vallejo, CA	1,620.0
319	Clinton Twnshp, MI	1,618.5
320	Sterling Heights, MI	1,617.2
321	Chico, CA	1,604.0
322	Fremont, CA	1,596.8
323	Edison Twnshp, NJ	1,595.3
324	Chino, CA	1,590.5
325	Hillsboro, OR	1,581.4
326	Broken Arrow, OK	1,573.9
326	Indio, CA	1,573.9
328	Moreno Valley, CA	1,565.6
329	Oxnard, CA	1,563.3
330	Elgin, IL	1,562.9
331	Clifton, NJ	1,560.3
332	Temecula, CA	1,559.6
333	Jersey City, NJ	1,554.4
334	Palm Bay, FL	1,548.2
335	Long Beach, CA	1,544.5
336	Sunnyvale, CA	1,533.2
337	Elk Grove, CA	1,530.8
338	Danbury, CT	1,528.9
339	Norwalk, CT	1,525.3
340	St. George, UT	1,516.1
341	Frisco, TX	1,503.1
342	Carson, CA	1,499.4
343	Richmond, CA	1,494.6
344	Los Angeles, CA	1,491.7
345	Pomona, CA	1,483.5
346	North Las Vegas, NV	1,477.0
347	Livermore, CA	1,471.9
348	Vista, CA	1,469.6
349	Port St. Lucie, FL	1,456.1
350	Farmington Hills, MI	1,451.2
351	Rio Rancho, NM	1,449.3
352	Compton, CA	1,443.5
353	Torrance, CA	1,441.4
354	Buena Park, CA	1,439.8
355	Gilbert, AZ	1,439.6
356	O'Fallon, MO	1,433.0
357	Inglewood, CA	1,432.9
358	San Jose, CA	1,429.2
359	Orange, CA	1,428.6
360	Warren, MI	1,421.1
361	Naperville, IL	1,414.3
362	Hamilton Twnshp, NJ	1,409.0
363	Alhambra, CA	1,406.5
364	Rialto, CA	1,399.6
365	Hayward, CA	1,387.9
366	Palmdale, CA	1,387.5
367	Rancho Cucamon., CA	1,383.9
368	Glendale, CA	1,379.5
369	Allen, TX	1,378.6
370	San Diego, CA	1,373.4
371	Paterson, NJ	1,356.4
372	Chula Vista, CA	1,355.6
373	Canton Twnshp, MI	1,355.4
374	Newark, NJ	1,354.2
375	Carlsbad, CA	1,347.5
376	New York, NY	1,339.5
377	Stamford, CT	1,338.8
378	Beaverton, OR	1,319.4
379	Brick Twnshp, NJ	1,303.0
380	Garden Grove, CA	1,293.4
381	Fontana, CA	1,276.9
382	Hawthorne, CA	1,259.6
383	Simi Valley, CA	1,240.8
384	Lancaster, CA	1,229.6
385	Santa Ana, CA	1,227.9
386	Henderson, NV	1,199.4
387	Santa Clarita, CA	1,189.3
388	Quincy, MA	1,185.5
389	El Monte, CA	1,149.2
390	Missouri City, TX	1,131.0
391	Gary, IN	1,122.7
392	Thousand Oaks, CA	1,120.1
393	Norwalk, CA	1,114.7
394	Daly City, CA	1,111.7
395	South Gate, CA	1,107.1
396	Irvine, CA	1,096.6
397	San Marcos, CA	1,095.3
398	Cary, NC	1,087.0
399	Yonkers, NY	1,079.2
400	Antioch, CA	1,068.7
401	Centennial, CO	1,059.5
402	Hesperia, CA	1,020.2
403	Santa Maria, CA	988.8
404	Baldwin Park, CA	980.2
405	Lake Forest, CA	954.9
406	Mission Viejo, CA	950.8
407	Newton, MA	891.9
408	Murrieta, CA	840.0
409	Ramapo, NY	707.5
NA	Toledo, OH**	NA
NA	Tucson, AZ**	NA

Source: CQ Press using reported data from the F.B.I. "Crime in the United States 2009"

*Larceny-theft is the unlawful taking of property. Attempts are included.

**Not available.

75. Percent Change in Larceny-Theft Rate: 2008 to 2009
National Percent Change = 4.8% Decrease*

RANK	CITY	% CHANGE
49	Abilene, TX	6.5
194	Akron, OH	(3.8)
NA	Albany, GA**	NA
109	Albany, NY	0.6
271	Albuquerque, NM	(8.8)
254	Alexandria, VA	(7.1)
204	Alhambra, CA	(4.3)
283	Allentown, PA	(9.4)
103	Allen, TX	0.9
36	Amarillo, TX	8.0
95	Amherst, NY	1.3
149	Anaheim, CA	(1.4)
48	Anchorage, AK	6.8
NA	Ann Arbor, MI**	NA
328	Antioch, CA	(13.3)
130	Arlington, TX	(0.5)
122	Arvada, CO	(0.1)
367	Athens-Clarke, GA	(21.5)
345	Atlanta, GA	(16.4)
249	Aurora, CO	(6.8)
93	Aurora, IL	1.4
34	Austin, TX	8.1
252	Avondale, AZ	(7.0)
178	Bakersfield, CA	(2.9)
237	Baldwin Park, CA	(5.8)
192	Baltimore, MD	(3.5)
21	Baton Rouge, LA	11.5
68	Beaumont, TX	4.1
369	Beaverton, OR	(22.3)
258	Bellevue, WA	(7.3)
136	Bellingham, WA	(0.9)
347	Bend, OR	(17.0)
176	Berkeley, CA	(2.7)
66	Billings, MT	4.4
276	Birmingham, AL	(9.1)
84	Bloomington, MN	1.9
247	Boca Raton, FL	(6.7)
162	Boise, ID	(2.1)
278	Boston, MA	(9.2)
338	Boulder, CO	(15.2)
365	Brick Twnshp, NJ	(21.1)
295	Bridgeport, CT	(10.2)
NA	Brockton, MA**	NA
204	Broken Arrow, OK	(4.3)
231	Brownsville, TX	(5.5)
219	Buena Park, CA	(5.2)
221	Buffalo, NY	(5.3)
117	Burbank, CA	0.1
130	Cambridge, MA	(0.5)
358	Camden, NJ	(19.4)
NA	Canton Twnshp, MI**	NA
359	Canton, OH	(20.0)
361	Cape Coral, FL	(20.3)
364	Carlsbad, CA	(20.8)
91	Carrollton, TX	1.5
171	Carson, CA	(2.5)
370	Cary, NC	(22.7)
266	Cedar Rapids, IA	(7.9)
302	Centennial, CO	(10.9)
199	Chandler, AZ	(4.1)
274	Charleston, SC	(8.9)
346	Charlotte, NC	(16.7)
129	Chattanooga, TN	(0.4)
63	Cheektowaga, NY	4.9
15	Chesapeake, VA	13.3
283	Chicago, IL	(9.4)
317	Chico, CA	(12.4)
293	Chino, CA	(10.1)
281	Chula Vista, CA	(9.3)
99	Cincinnati, OH	1.2
75	Citrus Heights, CA	3.0
55	Clarkstown, NY	6.0
281	Clarksville, TN	(9.3)
160	Clearwater, FL	(2.0)
77	Cleveland, OH	2.7
341	Clifton, NJ	(15.6)
NA	Clinton Twnshp, MI**	NA
160	Clovis, CA	(2.0)
41	College Station, TX	7.6
109	Colonie, NY	0.6
340	Colorado Springs, CO	(15.4)
83	Columbia, MO	2.3
65	Columbia, SC	4.5
178	Columbus, GA	(2.9)
59	Columbus, OH	5.3
185	Compton, CA	(3.2)
351	Concord, CA	(17.7)
81	Coral Springs, FL	2.5
267	Corona, CA	(8.0)
260	Corpus Christi, TX	(7.5)
133	Costa Mesa, CA	(0.7)
274	Cranston, RI	(8.9)
185	Dallas, TX	(3.2)
368	Daly City, CA	(21.6)
149	Danbury, CT	(1.4)
271	Davenport, IA	(8.8)
17	Davie, FL	12.9
156	Dayton, OH	(1.7)
NA	Dearborn, MI**	NA
NA	Decatur, IL**	NA
255	Denton, TX	(7.2)
11	Denver, CO	17.4
NA	Des Moines, IA**	NA
NA	Detroit, MI**	NA
70	Downey, CA	3.9
171	Duluth, MN	(2.5)
221	Durham, NC	(5.3)
88	Edison Twnshp, NJ	1.6
221	Edmond, OK	(5.3)
354	El Cajon, CA	(18.2)
52	El Monte, CA	6.1
171	El Paso, TX	(2.5)
196	Elgin, IL	(3.9)
288	Elizabeth, NJ	(9.5)
288	Elk Grove, CA	(9.5)
356	Erie, PA	(18.7)
134	Escondido, CA	(0.8)
334	Eugene, OR	(14.5)
143	Evansville, IN	(1.2)
132	Everett, WA	(0.6)
371	Fairfield, CA	(22.8)
283	Fall River, MA	(9.4)
99	Fargo, ND	1.2
NA	Farmington Hills, MI**	NA
28	Fayetteville, AR	9.6
199	Fayetteville, NC	(4.1)
24	Federal Way, WA	10.9
NA	Flint, MI**	NA
38	Fontana, CA	7.9
145	Fort Collins, CO	(1.3)
165	Fort Lauderdale, FL	(2.3)
36	Fort Smith, AR	8.0
264	Fort Wayne, IN	(7.8)
180	Fort Worth, TX	(3.0)
74	Fremont, CA	3.5
245	Fresno, CA	(6.4)
373	Frisco, TX	(24.9)
268	Fullerton, CA	(8.3)
60	Gainesville, FL	5.2
319	Garden Grove, CA	(12.7)
151	Garland, TX	(1.5)
378	Gary, IN	(39.2)
260	Gilbert, AZ	(7.5)
151	Glendale, AZ	(1.5)
239	Glendale, CA	(5.9)
66	Grand Prairie, TX	4.4
NA	Grand Rapids, MI**	NA
17	Greece, NY	12.9
208	Greeley, CO	(4.8)
331	Green Bay, WI	(14.3)
170	Greensboro, NC	(2.4)
33	Gresham, OR	8.2
93	Hamilton Twnshp, NJ	1.4
180	Hammond, IN	(3.0)
103	Hampton, VA	0.9
106	Hartford, CT	0.8
95	Hawthorne, CA	1.3
259	Hayward, CA	(7.4)
301	Henderson, NV	(10.8)
375	Hesperia, CA	(26.9)
255	Hialeah, FL	(7.2)
210	High Point, NC	(4.9)
377	Hillsboro, OR	(28.2)
196	Hollywood, FL	(3.9)
26	Honolulu, HI	10.0
25	Houston, TX	10.6
28	Huntington Beach, CA	9.6
331	Huntsville, AL	(14.3)
366	Independence, MO	(21.4)
185	Indianapolis, IN	(3.2)
151	Indio, CA	(1.5)
44	Inglewood, CA	7.3
295	Irvine, CA	(10.2)
190	Irving, TX	(3.3)
269	Jacksonville, FL	(8.4)
210	Jacksonville, NC	(4.9)
99	Jackson, MS	1.2
338	Jersey City, NJ	(15.2)
226	Joliet, IL	(5.4)
NA	Kansas City, KS**	NA
290	Kansas City, MO	(9.8)
43	Kenosha, WI	7.4
307	Kent, WA	(11.3)
7	Killeen, TX	19.1
95	Knoxville, TN	1.3
12	Lafayette, LA	15.9
51	Lake Forest, CA	6.2
304	Lakeland, FL	(11.0)
88	Lakewood, CA	1.6
32	Lakewood, CO	8.4
374	Lancaster, CA	(26.7)
NA	Lansing, MI**	NA
239	Laredo, TX	(5.9)
120	Las Cruces, NM	0.0
262	Las Vegas, NV	(7.7)
192	Lawrence, KS	(3.5)
3	Lawton, OK	28.1
221	Lee's Summit, MO	(5.3)
64	Lewisville, TX	4.7
NA	Lexington, KY**	NA
180	Lincoln, NE	(3.0)
NA	Little Rock, AR**	NA
325	Livermore, CA	(13.1)
NA	Livonia, MI**	NA
81	Long Beach, CA	2.5
NA	Longmont, CO**	NA

RANK	CITY	% CHANGE
44	Longview, TX	7.3
157	Los Angeles, CA	(1.8)
NA	Louisville, KY**	NA
108	Lubbock, TX	0.7
9	Lynn, MA	18.4
234	Macon, GA	(5.6)
73	Madison, WI	3.7
70	Manchester, NH	3.9
106	McAllen, TX	0.8
16	McKinney, TX	13.0
91	Melbourne, FL	1.5
293	Memphis, TN	(10.1)
360	Merced, CA	(20.1)
292	Mesa, AZ	(9.9)
57	Mesquite, TX	5.7
52	Miami Beach, FL	6.1
199	Miami Gardens, FL	(4.1)
111	Miami, FL	0.5
23	Midland, TX	11.1
145	Milwaukee, WI	(1.3)
323	Minneapolis, MN	(12.8)
171	Miramar, FL	(2.5)
194	Mission Viejo, CA	(3.8)
39	Missouri City, TX	7.8
85	Mobile, AL	1.8
208	Modesto, CA	(4.8)
310	Montgomery, AL	(11.7)
113	Moreno Valley, CA	0.4
122	Murfreesboro, TN	(0.1)
138	Murrieta, CA	(1.0)
352	Nampa, ID	(17.8)
117	Naperville, IL	0.1
NA	Nashua, NH**	NA
315	Nashville, TN	(12.3)
290	New Bedford, MA	(9.8)
NA	New Haven, CT**	NA
372	New Orleans, LA	(23.1)
214	New York, NY	(5.0)
219	Newark, NJ	(5.2)
158	Newport Beach, CA	(1.9)
348	Newton, MA	(17.2)
41	Norfolk, VA	7.6
10	Norman, OK	17.9
262	North Charleston, SC	(7.7)
244	North Las Vegas, NV	(6.1)
302	Norwalk, CA	(10.9)
300	Norwalk, CT	(10.7)
154	Oakland, CA	(1.6)
140	Oceanside, CA	(1.1)
145	Odessa, TX	(1.3)
319	O'Fallon, MO	(12.7)
239	Ogden, UT	(5.9)
127	Oklahoma City, OK	(0.3)
NA	Olathe, KS**	NA
138	Omaha, NE	(1.0)
175	Ontario, CA	(2.6)
319	Orange, CA	(12.7)
143	Orem, UT	(1.2)
311	Orlando, FL	(12.0)
22	Overland Park, KS	11.3
95	Oxnard, CA	1.3
69	Palm Bay, FL	4.0
324	Palmdale, CA	(12.9)
78	Pasadena, CA	2.6
30	Pasadena, TX	8.8
165	Paterson, NJ	(2.3)
58	Pearland, TX	5.6
311	Pembroke Pines, FL	(12.0)

RANK	CITY	% CHANGE
337	Peoria, AZ	(14.8)
NA	Peoria, IL**	NA
327	Philadelphia, PA	(13.2)
357	Phoenix, AZ	(19.2)
165	Pittsburgh, PA	(2.3)
207	Plano, TX	(4.5)
329	Plantation, FL	(13.4)
335	Pomona, CA	(14.7)
226	Pompano Beach, FL	(5.4)
342	Port St. Lucie, FL	(15.7)
297	Portland, OR	(10.4)
116	Portsmouth, VA	0.3
305	Providence, RI	(11.1)
154	Provo, UT	(1.6)
NA	Pueblo, CO**	NA
140	Quincy, MA	(1.1)
249	Racine, WI	(6.8)
78	Raleigh, NC	2.6
251	Ramapo, NY	(6.9)
217	Rancho Cucamon., CA	(5.1)
318	Reading, PA	(12.5)
271	Redding, CA	(8.8)
276	Reno, NV	(9.1)
1	Rialto, CA	69.0
85	Richardson, TX	1.8
349	Richmond, CA	(17.6)
44	Richmond, VA	7.3
349	Rio Rancho, NM	(17.6)
330	Riverside, CA	(13.8)
163	Roanoke, VA	(2.2)
31	Rochester, MN	8.5
103	Rochester, NY	0.9
283	Rockford, IL	(9.4)
234	Roseville, CA	(5.6)
283	Roswell, GA	(9.4)
234	Round Rock, TX	(5.6)
239	Sacramento, CA	(5.9)
343	Salem, OR	(15.8)
252	Salinas, CA	(7.0)
308	Salt Lake City, UT	(11.5)
210	San Angelo, TX	(4.9)
237	San Antonio, TX	(5.8)
226	San Bernardino, CA	(5.4)
362	San Diego, CA	(20.4)
204	San Francisco, CA	(4.3)
134	San Jose, CA	(0.8)
313	San Leandro, CA	(12.1)
203	San Marcos, CA	(4.2)
185	San Mateo, CA	(3.2)
196	Sandy Springs, GA	(3.9)
264	Sandy, UT	(7.8)
199	Santa Ana, CA	(4.1)
14	Santa Barbara, CA	14.0
117	Santa Clara, CA	0.1
111	Santa Clarita, CA	0.5
379	Santa Maria, CA	(45.5)
5	Santa Monica, CA	21.9
4	Santa Rosa, CA	24.3
191	Savannah, GA	(3.4)
319	Scottsdale, AZ	(12.7)
26	Seattle, WA	10.0
158	Shreveport, LA	(1.9)
62	Simi Valley, CA	5.0
113	Sioux City, IA	0.4
13	Sioux Falls, SD	15.6
363	Somerville, MA	(20.6)
306	South Bend, IN	(11.2)
47	South Gate, CA	7.2

RANK	CITY	% CHANGE
NA	Southfield, MI**	NA
333	Sparks, NV	(14.4)
125	Spokane Valley, WA	(0.2)
5	Spokane, WA	21.9
NA	Springfield, IL**	NA
78	Springfield, MA	2.6
221	Springfield, MO	(5.3)
122	Stamford, CT	(0.1)
NA	Sterling Heights, MI**	NA
344	Stockton, CA	(16.2)
376	St. George, UT	(27.1)
125	St. Joseph, MO	(0.2)
75	St. Louis, MO	3.0
165	St. Paul, MN	(2.3)
34	St. Petersburg, FL	8.1
127	Suffolk, VA	(0.3)
39	Sugar Land, TX	7.8
52	Sunnyvale, CA	6.1
56	Sunrise, FL	5.9
243	Surprise, AZ	(6.0)
231	Syracuse, NY	(5.5)
140	Tacoma, WA	(1.1)
335	Tallahassee, FL	(14.7)
353	Tampa, FL	(18.1)
72	Temecula, CA	3.8
315	Tempe, AZ	(12.3)
113	Thornton, CO	0.4
87	Thousand Oaks, CA	1.7
NA	Toledo, OH**	NA
226	Toms River Twnshp, NJ	(5.4)
278	Topeka, KS	(9.2)
184	Torrance, CA	(3.1)
299	Tracy, CA	(10.6)
136	Trenton, NJ	(0.9)
NA	Troy, MI**	NA
NA	Tucson, AZ**	NA
61	Tulsa, OK	5.1
255	Tuscaloosa, AL	(7.2)
2	Tyler, TX	28.9
214	Upper Darby Twnshp, PA	(5.0)
145	Vacaville, CA	(1.3)
308	Vallejo, CA	(11.5)
180	Vancouver, WA	(3.0)
217	Ventura, CA	(5.1)
231	Victorville, CA	(5.5)
49	Virginia Beach, VA	6.5
325	Visalia, CA	(13.1)
99	Vista, CA	1.2
163	Waco, TX	(2.2)
NA	Warren, MI**	NA
165	Warwick, RI	(2.3)
226	Washington, DC	(5.4)
185	Waterbury, CT	(3.2)
314	West Covina, CA	(12.2)
20	West Jordan, UT	12.1
246	West Palm Beach, FL	(6.5)
278	West Valley, UT	(9.2)
NA	Westland, MI**	NA
210	Westminster, CA	(4.9)
214	Westminster, CO	(5.0)
120	Whittier, CA	0.0
355	Wichita Falls, TX	(18.4)
177	Wichita, KS	(2.8)
8	Wilmington, NC	18.7
298	Winston-Salem, NC	(10.5)
270	Woodbridge Twnshp, NJ	(8.7)
19	Worcester, MA	12.7
88	Yonkers, NY	1.6
247	Yuma, AZ	(6.7)

Source: CQ Press using reported data from the F.B.I. "Crime in the United States 2009"
*Larceny-theft is the unlawful taking of property. Attempts are included.
**Not available.

75. Percent Change in Larceny-Theft Rate: 2008 to 2009 (continued)
National Percent Change = 4.8% Decrease*

RANK	CITY	% CHANGE
1	Rialto, CA	69.0
2	Tyler, TX	28.9
3	Lawton, OK	28.1
4	Santa Rosa, CA	24.3
5	Santa Monica, CA	21.9
5	Spokane, WA	21.9
7	Killeen, TX	19.1
8	Wilmington, NC	18.7
9	Lynn, MA	18.4
10	Norman, OK	17.9
11	Denver, CO	17.4
12	Lafayette, LA	15.9
13	Sioux Falls, SD	15.6
14	Santa Barbara, CA	14.0
15	Chesapeake, VA	13.3
16	McKinney, TX	13.0
17	Davie, FL	12.9
17	Greece, NY	12.9
19	Worcester, MA	12.7
20	West Jordan, UT	12.1
21	Baton Rouge, LA	11.5
22	Overland Park, KS	11.3
23	Midland, TX	11.1
24	Federal Way, WA	10.9
25	Houston, TX	10.6
26	Honolulu, HI	10.0
26	Seattle, WA	10.0
28	Fayetteville, AR	9.6
28	Huntington Beach, CA	9.6
30	Pasadena, TX	8.8
31	Rochester, MN	8.5
32	Lakewood, CO	8.4
33	Gresham, OR	8.2
34	Austin, TX	8.1
34	St. Petersburg, FL	8.1
36	Amarillo, TX	8.0
36	Fort Smith, AR	8.0
38	Fontana, CA	7.9
39	Missouri City, TX	7.8
39	Sugar Land, TX	7.8
41	College Station, TX	7.6
41	Norfolk, VA	7.6
43	Kenosha, WI	7.4
44	Inglewood, CA	7.3
44	Longview, TX	7.3
44	Richmond, VA	7.3
47	South Gate, CA	7.2
48	Anchorage, AK	6.8
49	Abilene, TX	6.5
49	Virginia Beach, VA	6.5
51	Lake Forest, CA	6.2
52	El Monte, CA	6.1
52	Miami Beach, FL	6.1
52	Sunnyvale, CA	6.1
55	Clarkstown, NY	6.0
56	Sunrise, FL	5.9
57	Mesquite, TX	5.7
58	Pearland, TX	5.6
59	Columbus, OH	5.3
60	Gainesville, FL	5.2
61	Tulsa, OK	5.1
62	Simi Valley, CA	5.0
63	Cheektowaga, NY	4.9
64	Lewisville, TX	4.7
65	Columbia, SC	4.5
66	Billings, MT	4.4
66	Grand Prairie, TX	4.4
68	Beaumont, TX	4.1
69	Palm Bay, FL	4.0
70	Downey, CA	3.9
70	Manchester, NH	3.9
72	Temecula, CA	3.8
73	Madison, WI	3.7
74	Fremont, CA	3.5
75	Citrus Heights, CA	3.0
75	St. Louis, MO	3.0
77	Cleveland, OH	2.7
78	Pasadena, CA	2.6
78	Raleigh, NC	2.6
78	Springfield, MA	2.6
81	Coral Springs, FL	2.5
81	Long Beach, CA	2.5
83	Columbia, MO	2.3
84	Bloomington, MN	1.9
85	Mobile, AL	1.8
85	Richardson, TX	1.8
87	Thousand Oaks, CA	1.7
88	Edison Twnshp, NJ	1.6
88	Lakewood, CA	1.6
88	Yonkers, NY	1.6
91	Carrollton, TX	1.5
91	Melbourne, FL	1.5
93	Aurora, IL	1.4
93	Hamilton Twnshp, NJ	1.4
95	Amherst, NY	1.3
95	Hawthorne, CA	1.3
95	Knoxville, TN	1.3
95	Oxnard, CA	1.3
99	Cincinnati, OH	1.2
99	Fargo, ND	1.2
99	Jackson, MS	1.2
99	Vista, CA	1.2
103	Allen, TX	0.9
103	Hampton, VA	0.9
103	Rochester, NY	0.9
106	Hartford, CT	0.8
106	McAllen, TX	0.8
108	Lubbock, TX	0.7
109	Albany, NY	0.6
109	Colonie, NY	0.6
111	Miami, FL	0.5
111	Santa Clarita, CA	0.5
113	Moreno Valley, CA	0.4
113	Sioux City, IA	0.4
113	Thornton, CO	0.4
116	Portsmouth, VA	0.3
117	Burbank, CA	0.1
117	Naperville, IL	0.1
117	Santa Clara, CA	0.1
120	Las Cruces, NM	0.0
120	Whittier, CA	0.0
122	Arvada, CO	(0.1)
122	Murfreesboro, TN	(0.1)
122	Stamford, CT	(0.1)
125	Spokane Valley, WA	(0.2)
125	St. Joseph, MO	(0.2)
127	Oklahoma City, OK	(0.3)
127	Suffolk, VA	(0.3)
129	Chattanooga, TN	(0.4)
130	Arlington, TX	(0.5)
130	Cambridge, MA	(0.5)
132	Everett, WA	(0.6)
133	Costa Mesa, CA	(0.7)
134	Escondido, CA	(0.8)
134	San Jose, CA	(0.8)
136	Bellingham, WA	(0.9)
136	Trenton, NJ	(0.9)
138	Murrieta, CA	(1.0)
138	Omaha, NE	(1.0)
140	Oceanside, CA	(1.1)
140	Quincy, MA	(1.1)
140	Tacoma, WA	(1.1)
143	Evansville, IN	(1.2)
143	Orem, UT	(1.2)
145	Fort Collins, CO	(1.3)
145	Milwaukee, WI	(1.3)
145	Odessa, TX	(1.3)
145	Vacaville, CA	(1.3)
149	Anaheim, CA	(1.4)
149	Danbury, CT	(1.4)
151	Garland, TX	(1.5)
151	Glendale, AZ	(1.5)
151	Indio, CA	(1.5)
154	Oakland, CA	(1.6)
154	Provo, UT	(1.6)
156	Dayton, OH	(1.7)
157	Los Angeles, CA	(1.8)
158	Newport Beach, CA	(1.9)
158	Shreveport, LA	(1.9)
160	Clearwater, FL	(2.0)
160	Clovis, CA	(2.0)
162	Boise, ID	(2.1)
163	Roanoke, VA	(2.2)
163	Waco, TX	(2.2)
165	Fort Lauderdale, FL	(2.3)
165	Paterson, NJ	(2.3)
165	Pittsburgh, PA	(2.3)
165	St. Paul, MN	(2.3)
165	Warwick, RI	(2.3)
170	Greensboro, NC	(2.4)
171	Carson, CA	(2.5)
171	Duluth, MN	(2.5)
171	El Paso, TX	(2.5)
171	Miramar, FL	(2.5)
175	Ontario, CA	(2.6)
176	Berkeley, CA	(2.7)
177	Wichita, KS	(2.8)
178	Bakersfield, CA	(2.9)
178	Columbus, GA	(2.9)
180	Fort Worth, TX	(3.0)
180	Hammond, IN	(3.0)
180	Lincoln, NE	(3.0)
180	Vancouver, WA	(3.0)
184	Torrance, CA	(3.1)
185	Compton, CA	(3.2)
185	Dallas, TX	(3.2)
185	Indianapolis, IN	(3.2)
185	San Mateo, CA	(3.2)
185	Waterbury, CT	(3.2)
190	Irving, TX	(3.3)
191	Savannah, GA	(3.4)
192	Baltimore, MD	(3.5)
192	Lawrence, KS	(3.5)
194	Akron, OH	(3.8)
194	Mission Viejo, CA	(3.8)
196	Elgin, IL	(3.9)
196	Hollywood, FL	(3.9)
196	Sandy Springs, GA	(3.9)
199	Chandler, AZ	(4.1)
199	Fayetteville, NC	(4.1)
199	Miami Gardens, FL	(4.1)
199	Santa Ana, CA	(4.1)
203	San Marcos, CA	(4.2)
204	Alhambra, CA	(4.3)
204	Broken Arrow, OK	(4.3)
204	San Francisco, CA	(4.3)

RANK	CITY	% CHANGE
207	Plano, TX	(4.5)
208	Greeley, CO	(4.8)
208	Modesto, CA	(4.8)
210	High Point, NC	(4.9)
210	Jacksonville, NC	(4.9)
210	San Angelo, TX	(4.9)
210	Westminster, CA	(4.9)
214	New York, NY	(5.0)
214	Upper Darby Twnshp, PA	(5.0)
214	Westminster, CO	(5.0)
217	Rancho Cucamon., CA	(5.1)
217	Ventura, CA	(5.1)
219	Buena Park, CA	(5.2)
219	Newark, NJ	(5.2)
221	Buffalo, NY	(5.3)
221	Durham, NC	(5.3)
221	Edmond, OK	(5.3)
221	Lee's Summit, MO	(5.3)
221	Springfield, MO	(5.3)
226	Joliet, IL	(5.4)
226	Pompano Beach, FL	(5.4)
226	San Bernardino, CA	(5.4)
226	Toms River Twnshp, NJ	(5.4)
226	Washington, DC	(5.4)
231	Brownsville, TX	(5.5)
231	Syracuse, NY	(5.5)
231	Victorville, CA	(5.5)
234	Macon, GA	(5.6)
234	Roseville, CA	(5.6)
234	Round Rock, TX	(5.6)
237	Baldwin Park, CA	(5.8)
237	San Antonio, TX	(5.8)
239	Glendale, CA	(5.9)
239	Laredo, TX	(5.9)
239	Ogden, UT	(5.9)
239	Sacramento, CA	(5.9)
243	Surprise, AZ	(6.0)
244	North Las Vegas, NV	(6.1)
245	Fresno, CA	(6.4)
246	West Palm Beach, FL	(6.5)
247	Boca Raton, FL	(6.7)
247	Yuma, AZ	(6.7)
249	Aurora, CO	(6.8)
249	Racine, WI	(6.8)
251	Ramapo, NY	(6.9)
252	Avondale, AZ	(7.0)
252	Salinas, CA	(7.0)
254	Alexandria, VA	(7.1)
255	Denton, TX	(7.2)
255	Hialeah, FL	(7.2)
255	Tuscaloosa, AL	(7.2)
258	Bellevue, WA	(7.3)
259	Hayward, CA	(7.4)
260	Corpus Christi, TX	(7.5)
260	Gilbert, AZ	(7.5)
262	Las Vegas, NV	(7.7)
262	North Charleston, SC	(7.7)
264	Fort Wayne, IN	(7.8)
264	Sandy, UT	(7.8)
266	Cedar Rapids, IA	(7.9)
267	Corona, CA	(8.0)
268	Fullerton, CA	(8.3)
269	Jacksonville, FL	(8.4)
270	Woodbridge Twnshp, NJ	(8.7)
271	Albuquerque, NM	(8.8)
271	Davenport, IA	(8.8)
271	Redding, CA	(8.8)
274	Charleston, SC	(8.9)

RANK	CITY	% CHANGE
274	Cranston, RI	(8.9)
276	Birmingham, AL	(9.1)
276	Reno, NV	(9.1)
278	Boston, MA	(9.2)
278	Topeka, KS	(9.2)
278	West Valley, UT	(9.2)
281	Chula Vista, CA	(9.3)
281	Clarksville, TN	(9.3)
283	Allentown, PA	(9.4)
283	Chicago, IL	(9.4)
283	Fall River, MA	(9.4)
283	Rockford, IL	(9.4)
283	Roswell, GA	(9.4)
288	Elizabeth, NJ	(9.5)
288	Elk Grove, CA	(9.5)
290	Kansas City, MO	(9.8)
290	New Bedford, MA	(9.8)
292	Mesa, AZ	(9.9)
293	Chino, CA	(10.1)
293	Memphis, TN	(10.1)
295	Bridgeport, CT	(10.2)
295	Irvine, CA	(10.2)
297	Portland, OR	(10.4)
298	Winston-Salem, NC	(10.5)
299	Tracy, CA	(10.6)
300	Norwalk, CT	(10.7)
301	Henderson, NV	(10.8)
302	Centennial, CO	(10.9)
302	Norwalk, CA	(10.9)
304	Lakeland, FL	(11.0)
305	Providence, RI	(11.1)
306	South Bend, IN	(11.2)
307	Kent, WA	(11.3)
308	Salt Lake City, UT	(11.5)
308	Vallejo, CA	(11.5)
310	Montgomery, AL	(11.7)
311	Orlando, FL	(12.0)
311	Pembroke Pines, FL	(12.0)
313	San Leandro, CA	(12.1)
314	West Covina, CA	(12.2)
315	Nashville, TN	(12.3)
315	Tempe, AZ	(12.3)
317	Chico, CA	(12.4)
318	Reading, PA	(12.5)
319	Garden Grove, CA	(12.7)
319	O'Fallon, MO	(12.7)
319	Orange, CA	(12.7)
319	Scottsdale, AZ	(12.7)
323	Minneapolis, MN	(12.8)
324	Palmdale, CA	(12.9)
325	Livermore, CA	(13.1)
325	Visalia, CA	(13.1)
327	Philadelphia, PA	(13.2)
328	Antioch, CA	(13.3)
329	Plantation, FL	(13.4)
330	Riverside, CA	(13.8)
331	Green Bay, WI	(14.3)
331	Huntsville, AL	(14.3)
333	Sparks, NV	(14.4)
334	Eugene, OR	(14.5)
335	Pomona, CA	(14.7)
335	Tallahassee, FL	(14.7)
337	Peoria, AZ	(14.8)
338	Boulder, CO	(15.2)
338	Jersey City, NJ	(15.2)
340	Colorado Springs, CO	(15.4)
341	Clifton, NJ	(15.6)
342	Port St. Lucie, FL	(15.7)

RANK	CITY	% CHANGE
343	Salem, OR	(15.8)
344	Stockton, CA	(16.2)
345	Atlanta, GA	(16.4)
346	Charlotte, NC	(16.7)
347	Bend, OR	(17.0)
348	Newton, MA	(17.2)
349	Richmond, CA	(17.6)
349	Rio Rancho, NM	(17.6)
351	Concord, CA	(17.7)
352	Nampa, ID	(17.8)
353	Tampa, FL	(18.1)
354	El Cajon, CA	(18.2)
355	Wichita Falls, TX	(18.4)
356	Erie, PA	(18.7)
357	Phoenix, AZ	(19.2)
358	Camden, NJ	(19.4)
359	Canton, OH	(20.0)
360	Merced, CA	(20.1)
361	Cape Coral, FL	(20.3)
362	San Diego, CA	(20.4)
363	Somerville, MA	(20.6)
364	Carlsbad, CA	(20.8)
365	Brick Twnshp, NJ	(21.1)
366	Independence, MO	(21.4)
367	Athens-Clarke, GA	(21.5)
368	Daly City, CA	(21.6)
369	Beaverton, OR	(22.3)
370	Cary, NC	(22.7)
371	Fairfield, CA	(22.8)
372	New Orleans, LA	(23.1)
373	Frisco, TX	(24.9)
374	Lancaster, CA	(26.7)
375	Hesperia, CA	(26.9)
376	St. George, UT	(27.1)
377	Hillsboro, OR	(28.2)
378	Gary, IN	(39.2)
379	Santa Maria, CA	(45.5)
NA	Albany, GA**	NA
NA	Ann Arbor, MI**	NA
NA	Brockton, MA**	NA
NA	Canton Twnshp, MI**	NA
NA	Clinton Twnshp, MI**	NA
NA	Dearborn, MI**	NA
NA	Decatur, IL**	NA
NA	Des Moines, IA**	NA
NA	Detroit, MI**	NA
NA	Farmington Hills, MI**	NA
NA	Flint, MI**	NA
NA	Grand Rapids, MI**	NA
NA	Kansas City, KS**	NA
NA	Lansing, MI**	NA
NA	Lexington, KY**	NA
NA	Little Rock, AR**	NA
NA	Livonia, MI**	NA
NA	Longmont, CO**	NA
NA	Louisville, KY**	NA
NA	Nashua, NH**	NA
NA	New Haven, CT**	NA
NA	Olathe, KS**	NA
NA	Peoria, IL**	NA
NA	Pueblo, CO**	NA
NA	Southfield, MI**	NA
NA	Springfield, IL**	NA
NA	Sterling Heights, MI**	NA
NA	Toledo, OH**	NA
NA	Troy, MI**	NA
NA	Tucson, AZ**	NA
NA	Warren, MI**	NA
NA	Westland, MI**	NA

Source: CQ Press using reported data from the F.B.I. "Crime in the United States 2009"
*Larceny-theft is the unlawful taking of property. Attempts are included.
**Not available.

76. Percent Change in Larceny-Theft Rate: 2005 to 2009
National Percent Change = 9.9% Decrease*

RANK	CITY	% CHANGE
180	Abilene, TX	(11.2)
247	Akron, OH	(18.3)
66	Albany, GA	6.6
94	Albany, NY	(0.2)
195	Albuquerque, NM	(13.5)
164	Alexandria, VA	(9.5)
220	Alhambra, CA	(15.4)
196	Allentown, PA	(13.6)
273	Allen, TX	(21.8)
154	Amarillo, TX	(8.3)
48	Amherst, NY	10.5
88	Anaheim, CA	1.0
148	Anchorage, AK	(7.4)
NA	Ann Arbor, MI**	NA
206	Antioch, CA	(14.4)
139	Arlington, TX	(6.4)
328	Arvada, CO	(28.5)
291	Athens-Clarke, GA	(23.8)
257	Atlanta, GA	(20.0)
347	Aurora, CO	(34.5)
203	Aurora, IL	(14.2)
74	Austin, TX	4.9
NA	Avondale, AZ**	NA
256	Bakersfield, CA	(19.6)
302	Baldwin Park, CA	(24.9)
212	Baltimore, MD	(14.7)
127	Baton Rouge, LA	(4.9)
265	Beaumont, TX	(20.8)
368	Beaverton, OR	(51.8)
214	Bellevue, WA	(14.8)
325	Bellingham, WA	(28.2)
366	Bend, OR	(45.9)
210	Berkeley, CA	(14.5)
320	Billings, MT	(26.9)
95	Birmingham, AL	(0.4)
NA	Bloomington, MN**	NA
68	Boca Raton, FL	6.5
291	Boise, ID	(23.8)
181	Boston, MA	(11.6)
333	Boulder, CO	(30.7)
144	Brick Twnshp, NJ	(6.8)
274	Bridgeport, CT	(21.9)
185	Brockton, MA	(12.1)
165	Broken Arrow, OK	(9.9)
61	Brownsville, TX	8.0
49	Buena Park, CA	10.4
142	Buffalo, NY	(6.5)
53	Burbank, CA	9.9
84	Cambridge, MA	2.9
104	Camden, NJ	(2.1)
NA	Canton Twnshp, MI**	NA
341	Canton, OH	(31.7)
193	Cape Coral, FL	(13.4)
317	Carlsbad, CA	(26.7)
149	Carrollton, TX	(7.5)
47	Carson, CA	11.4
270	Cary, NC	(21.6)
282	Cedar Rapids, IA	(22.8)
301	Centennial, CO	(24.6)
173	Chandler, AZ	(10.9)
215	Charleston, SC	(14.9)
238	Charlotte, NC	(17.3)
191	Chattanooga, TN	(13.3)
30	Cheektowaga, NY	16.3
97	Chesapeake, VA	(1.1)
130	Chicago, IL	(5.1)
279	Chico, CA	(22.5)
282	Chino, CA	(22.8)
311	Chula Vista, CA	(25.6)
227	Cincinnati, OH	(16.0)
NA	Citrus Heights, CA**	NA
NA	Clarkstown, NY**	NA
172	Clarksville, TN	(10.6)
82	Clearwater, FL	3.2
181	Cleveland, OH	(11.6)
109	Clifton, NJ	(2.7)
NA	Clinton Twnshp, MI**	NA
183	Clovis, CA	(11.7)
117	College Station, TX	(4.0)
245	Colonie, NY	(18.0)
343	Colorado Springs, CO	(31.8)
38	Columbia, MO	13.7
176	Columbia, SC	(11.0)
62	Columbus, GA	7.9
158	Columbus, OH	(8.9)
2	Compton, CA	44.0
364	Concord, CA	(42.7)
23	Coral Springs, FL	17.5
106	Corona, CA	(2.3)
269	Corpus Christi, TX	(21.5)
118	Costa Mesa, CA	(4.2)
89	Cranston, RI	0.8
300	Dallas, TX	(24.4)
271	Daly City, CA	(21.7)
100	Danbury, CT	(1.7)
323	Davenport, IA	(27.6)
33	Davie, FL	15.5
204	Dayton, OH	(14.3)
NA	Dearborn, MI**	NA
NA	Decatur, IL**	NA
360	Denton, TX	(39.3)
354	Denver, CO	(36.3)
NA	Des Moines, IA**	NA
NA	Detroit, MI**	NA
25	Downey, CA	17.4
NA	Duluth, MN**	NA
231	Durham, NC	(16.4)
143	Edison Twnshp, NJ	(6.6)
239	Edmond, OK	(17.4)
305	El Cajon, CA	(25.3)
206	El Monte, CA	(14.4)
123	El Paso, TX	(4.6)
NA	Elgin, IL**	NA
57	Elizabeth, NJ	9.1
NA	Elk Grove, CA**	NA
188	Erie, PA	(12.7)
268	Escondido, CA	(21.4)
222	Eugene, OR	(15.6)
153	Evansville, IN	(8.1)
21	Everett, WA	18.2
324	Fairfield, CA	(27.7)
NA	Fall River, MA**	NA
6	Fargo, ND	32.1
NA	Farmington Hills, MI**	NA
215	Fayetteville, AR	(14.9)
210	Fayetteville, NC	(14.5)
231	Federal Way, WA	(16.4)
NA	Flint, MI**	NA
4	Fontana, CA	36.4
81	Fort Collins, CO	3.4
240	Fort Lauderdale, FL	(17.5)
202	Fort Smith, AR	(14.1)
305	Fort Wayne, IN	(25.3)
254	Fort Worth, TX	(19.5)
64	Fremont, CA	7.2
264	Fresno, CA	(20.5)
367	Frisco, TX	(48.5)
198	Fullerton, CA	(13.7)
7	Gainesville, FL	31.9
224	Garden Grove, CA	(15.9)
38	Garland, TX	13.7
370	Gary, IN	(56.0)
290	Gilbert, AZ	(23.6)
8	Glendale, AZ	31.2
37	Glendale, CA	14.0
240	Grand Prairie, TX	(17.5)
NA	Grand Rapids, MI**	NA
3	Greece, NY	37.7
365	Greeley, CO	(43.5)
128	Green Bay, WI	(5.0)
106	Greensboro, NC	(2.3)
254	Gresham, OR	(19.5)
42	Hamilton Twnshp, NJ	13.3
169	Hammond, IN	(10.3)
83	Hampton, VA	3.0
347	Hartford, CT	(34.5)
11	Hawthorne, CA	30.1
224	Hayward, CA	(15.9)
287	Henderson, NV	(23.5)
262	Hesperia, CA	(20.3)
34	Hialeah, FL	14.9
138	High Point, NC	(6.1)
369	Hillsboro, OR	(53.3)
65	Hollywood, FL	7.1
253	Honolulu, HI	(19.4)
120	Houston, TX	(4.3)
9	Huntington Beach, CA	30.8
316	Huntsville, AL	(26.1)
267	Independence, MO	(21.0)
150	Indianapolis, IN	(7.7)
345	Indio, CA	(32.2)
14	Inglewood, CA	23.5
176	Irvine, CA	(11.0)
224	Irving, TX	(15.9)
151	Jacksonville, FL	(7.9)
NA	Jacksonville, NC**	NA
74	Jackson, MS	4.9
257	Jersey City, NJ	(20.0)
314	Joliet, IL	(25.9)
245	Kansas City, KS	(18.0)
343	Kansas City, MO	(31.8)
80	Kenosha, WI	4.0
346	Kent, WA	(33.1)
260	Killeen, TX	(20.1)
45	Knoxville, TN	12.4
22	Lafayette, LA	17.8
55	Lake Forest, CA	9.7
169	Lakeland, FL	(10.3)
276	Lakewood, CA	(22.3)
198	Lakewood, CO	(13.7)
347	Lancaster, CA	(34.5)
NA	Lansing, MI**	NA
151	Laredo, TX	(7.9)
100	Las Cruces, NM	(1.7)
218	Las Vegas, NV	(15.2)
38	Lawrence, KS	13.7
79	Lawton, OK	4.1
190	Lee's Summit, MO	(13.1)
302	Lewisville, TX	(24.9)
NA	Lexington, KY**	NA
322	Lincoln, NE	(27.2)
NA	Little Rock, AR**	NA
34	Livermore, CA	14.9
NA	Livonia, MI**	NA
58	Long Beach, CA	8.8
NA	Longmont, CO**	NA

RANK	CITY	% CHANGE
32	Longview, TX	15.7
187	Los Angeles, CA	(12.5)
NA	Louisville, KY**	NA
173	Lubbock, TX	(10.9)
60	Lynn, MA	8.2
252	Macon, GA	(19.2)
93	Madison, WI	0.0
51	Manchester, NH	10.1
156	McAllen, TX	(8.7)
27	McKinney, TX	16.6
20	Melbourne, FL	18.4
162	Memphis, TN	(9.4)
361	Merced, CA	(40.2)
335	Mesa, AZ	(30.9)
27	Mesquite, TX	16.6
13	Miami Beach, FL	25.0
193	Miami Gardens, FL	(13.4)
176	Miami, FL	(11.0)
139	Midland, TX	(6.4)
73	Milwaukee, WI	5.0
204	Minneapolis, MN	(14.3)
29	Miramar, FL	16.5
112	Mission Viejo, CA	(3.3)
146	Missouri City, TX	(7.3)
85	Mobile, AL	2.1
250	Modesto, CA	(18.5)
228	Montgomery, AL	(16.1)
257	Moreno Valley, CA	(20.0)
198	Murfreesboro, TN	(13.7)
362	Murrieta, CA	(40.4)
NA	Nampa, ID**	NA
135	Naperville, IL	(5.6)
15	Nashua, NH	23.1
311	Nashville, TN	(25.6)
128	New Bedford, MA	(5.0)
NA	New Haven, CT**	NA
NA	New Orleans, LA**	NA
166	New York, NY	(10.1)
287	Newark, NJ	(23.5)
137	Newport Beach, CA	(6.0)
125	Newton, MA	(4.8)
91	Norfolk, VA	0.2
23	Norman, OK	17.5
262	North Charleston, SC	(20.3)
310	North Las Vegas, NV	(25.4)
206	Norwalk, CA	(14.4)
341	Norwalk, CT	(31.7)
69	Oakland, CA	6.3
327	Oceanside, CA	(28.4)
114	Odessa, TX	(3.7)
359	O'Fallon, MO	(39.0)
278	Ogden, UT	(22.4)
352	Oklahoma City, OK	(34.8)
NA	Olathe, KS**	NA
261	Omaha, NE	(20.2)
212	Ontario, CA	(14.7)
231	Orange, CA	(16.4)
317	Orem, UT	(26.7)
162	Orlando, FL	(9.4)
144	Overland Park, KS	(6.8)
63	Oxnard, CA	7.8
332	Palm Bay, FL	(29.7)
284	Palmdale, CA	(23.2)
92	Pasadena, CA	0.1
31	Pasadena, TX	16.1
109	Paterson, NJ	(2.7)
97	Pearland, TX	(1.1)
12	Pembroke Pines, FL	26.6

RANK	CITY	% CHANGE
313	Peoria, AZ	(25.8)
336	Peoria, IL	(31.0)
130	Philadelphia, PA	(5.1)
333	Phoenix, AZ	(30.7)
236	Pittsburgh, PA	(16.6)
243	Plano, TX	(17.7)
49	Plantation, FL	10.4
230	Pomona, CA	(16.3)
168	Pompano Beach, FL	(10.2)
97	Port St. Lucie, FL	(1.1)
317	Portland, OR	(26.7)
46	Portsmouth, VA	12.0
77	Providence, RI	4.6
222	Provo, UT	(15.6)
371	Pueblo, CO	(65.2)
19	Quincy, MA	20.4
337	Racine, WI	(31.4)
130	Raleigh, NC	(5.1)
105	Ramapo, NY	(2.2)
296	Rancho Cucamon., CA	(24.0)
305	Reading, PA	(25.3)
321	Redding, CA	(27.0)
291	Reno, NV	(23.8)
186	Rialto, CA	(12.4)
121	Richardson, TX	(4.4)
347	Richmond, CA	(34.5)
339	Richmond, VA	(31.5)
77	Rio Rancho, NM	4.6
315	Riverside, CA	(26.0)
281	Roanoke, VA	(22.7)
44	Rochester, MN	12.6
231	Rochester, NY	(16.4)
247	Rockford, IL	(18.3)
220	Roseville, CA	(15.4)
136	Roswell, GA	(5.8)
160	Round Rock, TX	(9.2)
206	Sacramento, CA	(14.4)
352	Salem, OR	(34.8)
363	Salinas, CA	(41.1)
118	Salt Lake City, UT	(4.2)
291	San Angelo, TX	(23.8)
85	San Antonio, TX	2.1
196	San Bernardino, CA	(13.6)
329	San Diego, CA	(29.0)
41	San Francisco, CA	13.5
109	San Jose, CA	(2.7)
191	San Leandro, CA	(13.3)
291	San Marcos, CA	(23.8)
276	San Mateo, CA	(22.3)
NA	Sandy Springs, GA**	NA
87	Sandy, UT	1.7
284	Santa Ana, CA	(23.2)
59	Santa Barbara, CA	8.4
237	Santa Clara, CA	(16.8)
169	Santa Clarita, CA	(10.3)
357	Santa Maria, CA	(37.9)
43	Santa Monica, CA	13.2
173	Santa Rosa, CA	(10.9)
161	Savannah, GA	(9.3)
72	Scottsdale, AZ	5.1
179	Seattle, WA	(11.1)
266	Shreveport, LA	(20.9)
103	Simi Valley, CA	(2.0)
251	Sioux City, IA	(19.1)
122	Sioux Falls, SD	(4.5)
1	Somerville, MA	56.8
189	South Bend, IN	(13.0)
123	South Gate, CA	(4.6)

RANK	CITY	% CHANGE
NA	Southfield, MI**	NA
166	Sparks, NV	(10.1)
229	Spokane Valley, WA	(16.2)
54	Spokane, WA	9.8
116	Springfield, IL	(3.9)
154	Springfield, MA	(8.3)
76	Springfield, MO	4.7
146	Stamford, CT	(7.3)
NA	Sterling Heights, MI**	NA
275	Stockton, CA	(22.2)
304	St. George, UT	(25.0)
244	St. Joseph, MO	(17.9)
297	St. Louis, MO	(24.2)
201	St. Paul, MN	(14.0)
71	St. Petersburg, FL	5.8
339	Suffolk, VA	(31.5)
125	Sugar Land, TX	(4.8)
51	Sunnyvale, CA	10.1
5	Sunrise, FL	36.2
284	Surprise, AZ	(23.2)
90	Syracuse, NY	0.3
134	Tacoma, WA	(5.4)
184	Tallahassee, FL	(11.9)
358	Tampa, FL	(38.6)
305	Temecula, CA	(25.3)
297	Tempe, AZ	(24.2)
331	Thornton, CO	(29.3)
56	Thousand Oaks, CA	9.4
NA	Toledo, OH**	NA
10	Toms River Twnshp, NJ	30.2
355	Topeka, KS	(36.7)
112	Torrance, CA	(3.3)
337	Tracy, CA	(31.4)
305	Trenton, NJ	(25.3)
NA	Troy, MI**	NA
NA	Tucson, AZ**	NA
102	Tulsa, OK	(1.8)
242	Tuscaloosa, AL	(17.6)
16	Tyler, TX	22.2
16	Upper Darby Twnshp, PA	22.2
219	Vacaville, CA	(15.3)
NA	Vallejo, CA**	NA
329	Vancouver, WA	(29.0)
215	Ventura, CA	(14.9)
356	Victorville, CA	(37.8)
70	Virginia Beach, VA	6.1
351	Visalia, CA	(34.7)
231	Vista, CA	(16.4)
249	Waco, TX	(18.4)
NA	Warren, MI**	NA
36	Warwick, RI	14.7
26	Washington, DC	16.8
66	Waterbury, CT	6.6
133	West Covina, CA	(5.2)
NA	West Jordan, UT**	NA
287	West Palm Beach, FL	(23.5)
271	West Valley, UT	(21.7)
NA	Westland, MI**	NA
106	Westminster, CA	(2.3)
326	Westminster, CO	(28.3)
159	Whittier, CA	(9.1)
299	Wichita Falls, TX	(24.3)
NA	Wichita, KS**	NA
114	Wilmington, NC	(3.7)
96	Winston-Salem, NC	(0.6)
157	Woodbridge Twnshp, NJ	(8.8)
18	Worcester, MA	21.1
139	Yonkers, NY	(6.4)
279	Yuma, AZ	(22.5)

Source: CQ Press using reported data from the F.B.I. "Crime in the United States 2009"
*Larceny-theft is the unlawful taking of property. Attempts are included.
**Not available.

76. Percent Change in Larceny-Theft Rate: 2005 to 2009 (continued)
National Percent Change = 9.9% Decrease*

RANK	CITY	% CHANGE	RANK	CITY	% CHANGE	RANK	CITY	% CHANGE
1	Somerville, MA	56.8	69	Oakland, CA	6.3	138	High Point, NC	(6.1)
2	Compton, CA	44.0	70	Virginia Beach, VA	6.1	139	Arlington, TX	(6.4)
3	Greece, NY	37.7	71	St. Petersburg, FL	5.8	139	Midland, TX	(6.4)
4	Fontana, CA	36.4	72	Scottsdale, AZ	5.1	139	Yonkers, NY	(6.4)
5	Sunrise, FL	36.2	73	Milwaukee, WI	5.0	142	Buffalo, NY	(6.5)
6	Fargo, ND	32.1	74	Austin, TX	4.9	143	Edison Twnshp, NJ	(6.6)
7	Gainesville, FL	31.9	74	Jackson, MS	4.9	144	Brick Twnshp, NJ	(6.8)
8	Glendale, AZ	31.2	76	Springfield, MO	4.7	144	Overland Park, KS	(6.8)
9	Huntington Beach, CA	30.8	77	Providence, RI	4.6	146	Missouri City, TX	(7.3)
10	Toms River Twnshp, NJ	30.2	77	Rio Rancho, NM	4.6	146	Stamford, CT	(7.3)
11	Hawthorne, CA	30.1	79	Lawton, OK	4.1	148	Anchorage, AK	(7.4)
12	Pembroke Pines, FL	26.6	80	Kenosha, WI	4.0	149	Carrollton, TX	(7.5)
13	Miami Beach, FL	25.0	81	Fort Collins, CO	3.4	150	Indianapolis, IN	(7.7)
14	Inglewood, CA	23.5	82	Clearwater, FL	3.2	151	Jacksonville, FL	(7.9)
15	Nashua, NH	23.1	83	Hampton, VA	3.0	151	Laredo, TX	(7.9)
16	Tyler, TX	22.2	84	Cambridge, MA	2.9	153	Evansville, IN	(8.1)
16	Upper Darby Twnshp, PA	22.2	85	Mobile, AL	2.1	154	Amarillo, TX	(8.3)
18	Worcester, MA	21.1	85	San Antonio, TX	2.1	154	Springfield, MA	(8.3)
19	Quincy, MA	20.4	87	Sandy, UT	1.7	156	McAllen, TX	(8.7)
20	Melbourne, FL	18.4	88	Anaheim, CA	1.0	157	Woodbridge Twnshp, NJ	(8.8)
21	Everett, WA	18.2	89	Cranston, RI	0.8	158	Columbus, OH	(8.9)
22	Lafayette, LA	17.8	90	Syracuse, NY	0.3	159	Whittier, CA	(9.1)
23	Coral Springs, FL	17.5	91	Norfolk, VA	0.2	160	Round Rock, TX	(9.2)
23	Norman, OK	17.5	92	Pasadena, CA	0.1	161	Savannah, GA	(9.3)
25	Downey, CA	17.4	93	Madison, WI	0.0	162	Memphis, TN	(9.4)
26	Washington, DC	16.8	94	Albany, NY	(0.2)	162	Orlando, FL	(9.4)
27	McKinney, TX	16.6	95	Birmingham, AL	(0.4)	164	Alexandria, VA	(9.5)
27	Mesquite, TX	16.6	96	Winston-Salem, NC	(0.6)	165	Broken Arrow, OK	(9.9)
29	Miramar, FL	16.5	97	Chesapeake, VA	(1.1)	166	New York, NY	(10.1)
30	Cheektowaga, NY	16.3	97	Pearland, TX	(1.1)	166	Sparks, NV	(10.1)
31	Pasadena, TX	16.1	97	Port St. Lucie, FL	(1.1)	168	Pompano Beach, FL	(10.2)
32	Longview, TX	15.7	100	Danbury, CT	(1.7)	169	Hammond, IN	(10.3)
33	Davie, FL	15.5	100	Las Cruces, NM	(1.7)	169	Lakeland, FL	(10.3)
34	Hialeah, FL	14.9	102	Tulsa, OK	(1.8)	169	Santa Clarita, CA	(10.3)
34	Livermore, CA	14.9	103	Simi Valley, CA	(2.0)	172	Clarksville, TN	(10.6)
36	Warwick, RI	14.7	104	Camden, NJ	(2.1)	173	Chandler, AZ	(10.9)
37	Glendale, CA	14.0	105	Ramapo, NY	(2.2)	173	Lubbock, TX	(10.9)
38	Columbia, MO	13.7	106	Corona, CA	(2.3)	173	Santa Rosa, CA	(10.9)
38	Garland, TX	13.7	106	Greensboro, NC	(2.3)	176	Columbia, SC	(11.0)
38	Lawrence, KS	13.7	106	Westminster, CA	(2.3)	176	Irvine, CA	(11.0)
41	San Francisco, CA	13.5	109	Clifton, NJ	(2.7)	176	Miami, FL	(11.0)
42	Hamilton Twnshp, NJ	13.3	109	Paterson, NJ	(2.7)	179	Seattle, WA	(11.1)
43	Santa Monica, CA	13.2	109	San Jose, CA	(2.7)	180	Abilene, TX	(11.2)
44	Rochester, MN	12.6	112	Mission Viejo, CA	(3.3)	181	Boston, MA	(11.6)
45	Knoxville, TN	12.4	112	Torrance, CA	(3.3)	181	Cleveland, OH	(11.6)
46	Portsmouth, VA	12.0	114	Odessa, TX	(3.7)	183	Clovis, CA	(11.7)
47	Carson, CA	11.4	114	Wilmington, NC	(3.7)	184	Tallahassee, FL	(11.9)
48	Amherst, NY	10.5	116	Springfield, IL	(3.9)	185	Brockton, MA	(12.1)
49	Buena Park, CA	10.4	117	College Station, TX	(4.0)	186	Rialto, CA	(12.4)
49	Plantation, FL	10.4	118	Costa Mesa, CA	(4.2)	187	Los Angeles, CA	(12.5)
51	Manchester, NH	10.1	118	Salt Lake City, UT	(4.2)	188	Erie, PA	(12.7)
51	Sunnyvale, CA	10.1	120	Houston, TX	(4.3)	189	South Bend, IN	(13.0)
53	Burbank, CA	9.9	121	Richardson, TX	(4.4)	190	Lee's Summit, MO	(13.1)
54	Spokane, WA	9.8	122	Sioux Falls, SD	(4.5)	191	Chattanooga, TN	(13.3)
55	Lake Forest, CA	9.7	123	El Paso, TX	(4.6)	191	San Leandro, CA	(13.3)
56	Thousand Oaks, CA	9.4	123	South Gate, CA	(4.6)	193	Cape Coral, FL	(13.4)
57	Elizabeth, NJ	9.1	125	Newton, MA	(4.8)	193	Miami Gardens, FL	(13.4)
58	Long Beach, CA	8.8	125	Sugar Land, TX	(4.8)	195	Albuquerque, NM	(13.5)
59	Santa Barbara, CA	8.4	127	Baton Rouge, LA	(4.9)	196	Allentown, PA	(13.6)
60	Lynn, MA	8.2	128	Green Bay, WI	(5.0)	196	San Bernardino, CA	(13.6)
61	Brownsville, TX	8.0	128	New Bedford, MA	(5.0)	198	Fullerton, CA	(13.7)
62	Columbus, GA	7.9	130	Chicago, IL	(5.1)	198	Lakewood, CO	(13.7)
63	Oxnard, CA	7.8	130	Philadelphia, PA	(5.1)	198	Murfreesboro, TN	(13.7)
64	Fremont, CA	7.2	130	Raleigh, NC	(5.1)	201	St. Paul, MN	(14.0)
65	Hollywood, FL	7.1	133	West Covina, CA	(5.2)	202	Fort Smith, AR	(14.1)
66	Albany, GA	6.6	134	Tacoma, WA	(5.4)	203	Aurora, IL	(14.2)
66	Waterbury, CT	6.6	135	Naperville, IL	(5.6)	204	Dayton, OH	(14.3)
68	Boca Raton, FL	6.5	136	Roswell, GA	(5.8)	204	Minneapolis, MN	(14.3)
			137	Newport Beach, CA	(6.0)	206	Antioch, CA	(14.4)

RANK	CITY	% CHANGE
206	El Monte, CA	(14.4)
206	Norwalk, CA	(14.4)
206	Sacramento, CA	(14.4)
210	Berkeley, CA	(14.5)
210	Fayetteville, NC	(14.5)
212	Baltimore, MD	(14.7)
212	Ontario, CA	(14.7)
214	Bellevue, WA	(14.8)
215	Charleston, SC	(14.9)
215	Fayetteville, AR	(14.9)
215	Ventura, CA	(14.9)
218	Las Vegas, NV	(15.2)
219	Vacaville, CA	(15.3)
220	Alhambra, CA	(15.4)
220	Roseville, CA	(15.4)
222	Eugene, OR	(15.6)
222	Provo, UT	(15.6)
224	Garden Grove, CA	(15.9)
224	Hayward, CA	(15.9)
224	Irving, TX	(15.9)
227	Cincinnati, OH	(16.0)
228	Montgomery, AL	(16.1)
229	Spokane Valley, WA	(16.2)
230	Pomona, CA	(16.3)
231	Durham, NC	(16.4)
231	Federal Way, WA	(16.4)
231	Orange, CA	(16.4)
231	Rochester, NY	(16.4)
231	Vista, CA	(16.4)
236	Pittsburgh, PA	(16.6)
237	Santa Clara, CA	(16.8)
238	Charlotte, NC	(17.3)
239	Edmond, OK	(17.4)
240	Fort Lauderdale, FL	(17.5)
240	Grand Prairie, TX	(17.5)
242	Tuscaloosa, AL	(17.6)
243	Plano, TX	(17.7)
244	St. Joseph, MO	(17.9)
245	Colonie, NY	(18.0)
245	Kansas City, KS	(18.0)
247	Akron, OH	(18.3)
247	Rockford, IL	(18.3)
249	Waco, TX	(18.4)
250	Modesto, CA	(18.5)
251	Sioux City, IA	(19.1)
252	Macon, GA	(19.2)
253	Honolulu, HI	(19.4)
254	Fort Worth, TX	(19.5)
254	Gresham, OR	(19.5)
256	Bakersfield, CA	(19.6)
257	Atlanta, GA	(20.0)
257	Jersey City, NJ	(20.0)
257	Moreno Valley, CA	(20.0)
260	Killeen, TX	(20.1)
261	Omaha, NE	(20.2)
262	Hesperia, CA	(20.3)
262	North Charleston, SC	(20.3)
264	Fresno, CA	(20.5)
265	Beaumont, TX	(20.8)
266	Shreveport, LA	(20.9)
267	Independence, MO	(21.0)
268	Escondido, CA	(21.4)
269	Corpus Christi, TX	(21.5)
270	Cary, NC	(21.6)
271	Daly City, CA	(21.7)
271	West Valley, UT	(21.7)
273	Allen, TX	(21.8)
274	Bridgeport, CT	(21.9)

RANK	CITY	% CHANGE
275	Stockton, CA	(22.2)
276	Lakewood, CA	(22.3)
276	San Mateo, CA	(22.3)
278	Ogden, UT	(22.4)
279	Chico, CA	(22.5)
279	Yuma, AZ	(22.5)
281	Roanoke, VA	(22.7)
282	Cedar Rapids, IA	(22.8)
282	Chino, CA	(22.8)
284	Palmdale, CA	(23.2)
284	Santa Ana, CA	(23.2)
284	Surprise, AZ	(23.2)
287	Henderson, NV	(23.5)
287	Newark, NJ	(23.5)
287	West Palm Beach, FL	(23.5)
290	Gilbert, AZ	(23.6)
291	Athens-Clarke, GA	(23.8)
291	Boise, ID	(23.8)
291	Reno, NV	(23.8)
291	San Angelo, TX	(23.8)
291	San Marcos, CA	(23.8)
296	Rancho Cucamon., CA	(24.0)
297	St. Louis, MO	(24.2)
297	Tempe, AZ	(24.2)
299	Wichita Falls, TX	(24.3)
300	Dallas, TX	(24.4)
301	Centennial, CO	(24.6)
302	Baldwin Park, CA	(24.9)
302	Lewisville, TX	(24.9)
304	St. George, UT	(25.0)
305	El Cajon, CA	(25.3)
305	Fort Wayne, IN	(25.3)
305	Reading, PA	(25.3)
305	Temecula, CA	(25.3)
305	Trenton, NJ	(25.3)
310	North Las Vegas, NV	(25.4)
311	Chula Vista, CA	(25.6)
311	Nashville, TN	(25.6)
313	Peoria, AZ	(25.8)
314	Joliet, IL	(25.9)
315	Riverside, CA	(26.0)
316	Huntsville, AL	(26.1)
317	Carlsbad, CA	(26.7)
317	Orem, UT	(26.7)
317	Portland, OR	(26.7)
320	Billings, MT	(26.9)
321	Redding, CA	(27.0)
322	Lincoln, NE	(27.2)
323	Davenport, IA	(27.6)
324	Fairfield, CA	(27.7)
325	Bellingham, WA	(28.2)
326	Westminster, CO	(28.3)
327	Oceanside, CA	(28.4)
328	Arvada, CO	(28.5)
329	San Diego, CA	(29.0)
329	Vancouver, WA	(29.0)
331	Thornton, CO	(29.3)
332	Palm Bay, FL	(29.7)
333	Boulder, CO	(30.7)
333	Phoenix, AZ	(30.7)
335	Mesa, AZ	(30.9)
336	Peoria, IL	(31.0)
337	Racine, WI	(31.4)
337	Tracy, CA	(31.4)
339	Richmond, VA	(31.5)
339	Suffolk, VA	(31.5)
341	Canton, OH	(31.7)
341	Norwalk, CT	(31.7)

RANK	CITY	% CHANGE
343	Colorado Springs, CO	(31.8)
343	Kansas City, MO	(31.8)
345	Indio, CA	(32.2)
346	Kent, WA	(33.1)
347	Aurora, CO	(34.5)
347	Hartford, CT	(34.5)
347	Lancaster, CA	(34.5)
347	Richmond, CA	(34.5)
351	Visalia, CA	(34.7)
352	Oklahoma City, OK	(34.8)
352	Salem, OR	(34.8)
354	Denver, CO	(36.3)
355	Topeka, KS	(36.7)
356	Victorville, CA	(37.8)
357	Santa Maria, CA	(37.9)
358	Tampa, FL	(38.6)
359	O'Fallon, MO	(39.0)
360	Denton, TX	(39.3)
361	Merced, CA	(40.2)
362	Murrieta, CA	(40.4)
363	Salinas, CA	(41.1)
364	Concord, CA	(42.7)
365	Greeley, CO	(43.5)
366	Bend, OR	(45.9)
367	Frisco, TX	(48.5)
368	Beaverton, OR	(51.8)
369	Hillsboro, OR	(53.3)
370	Gary, IN	(56.0)
371	Pueblo, CO	(65.2)
NA	Ann Arbor, MI**	NA
NA	Avondale, AZ**	NA
NA	Bloomington, MN**	NA
NA	Canton Twnshp, MI**	NA
NA	Citrus Heights, CA**	NA
NA	Clarkstown, NY**	NA
NA	Clinton Twnshp, MI**	NA
NA	Dearborn, MI**	NA
NA	Decatur, IL**	NA
NA	Des Moines, IA**	NA
NA	Detroit, MI**	NA
NA	Duluth, MN**	NA
NA	Elgin, IL**	NA
NA	Elk Grove, CA**	NA
NA	Fall River, MA**	NA
NA	Farmington Hills, MI**	NA
NA	Flint, MI**	NA
NA	Grand Rapids, MI**	NA
NA	Jacksonville, NC**	NA
NA	Lansing, MI**	NA
NA	Lexington, KY**	NA
NA	Little Rock, AR**	NA
NA	Livonia, MI**	NA
NA	Longmont, CO**	NA
NA	Louisville, KY**	NA
NA	Nampa, ID**	NA
NA	New Haven, CT**	NA
NA	New Orleans, LA**	NA
NA	Olathe, KS**	NA
NA	Sandy Springs, GA**	NA
NA	Southfield, MI**	NA
NA	Sterling Heights, MI**	NA
NA	Toledo, OH**	NA
NA	Troy, MI**	NA
NA	Tucson, AZ**	NA
NA	Vallejo, CA**	NA
NA	Warren, MI**	NA
NA	West Jordan, UT**	NA
NA	Westland, MI**	NA
NA	Wichita, KS**	NA

Source: CQ Press using reported data from the F.B.I. "Crime in the United States 2009"
*Larceny-theft is the unlawful taking of property. Attempts are included.
**Not available.

77. Motor Vehicle Thefts in 2009
National Total = 794,616 Motor Vehicle Thefts*

RANK	CITY	THEFTS
274	Abilene, TX	262
94	Akron, OH	963
260	Albany, GA	289
286	Albany, NY	239
30	Albuquerque, NM	3,399
236	Alexandria, VA	336
254	Alhambra, CA	305
182	Allentown, PA	471
398	Allen, TX	64
136	Amarillo, TX	710
404	Amherst, NY	48
101	Anaheim, CA	945
110	Anchorage, AK	868
362	Ann Arbor, MI	125
132	Antioch, CA	747
67	Arlington, TX	1,439
287	Arvada, CO	237
267	Athens-Clarke, GA	274
13	Atlanta, GA	5,726
77	Aurora, CO	1,166
309	Aurora, IL	195
43	Austin, TX	2,219
169	Avondale, AZ	546
39	Bakersfield, CA	2,376
171	Baldwin Park, CA	536
19	Baltimore, MD	4,624
103	Baton Rouge, LA	929
264	Beaumont, TX	281
350	Beaverton, OR	136
322	Bellevue, WA	179
348	Bellingham, WA	143
391	Bend, OR	78
134	Berkeley, CA	727
276	Billings, MT	253
59	Birmingham, AL	1,594
372	Bloomington, MN	112
337	Boca Raton, FL	158
325	Boise, ID	174
41	Boston, MA	2,287
367	Boulder, CO	119
406	Brick Twnshp, NJ	42
93	Bridgeport, CT	964
215	Brockton, MA	393
375	Broken Arrow, OK	108
235	Brownsville, TX	337
214	Buena Park, CA	396
60	Buffalo, NY	1,580
237	Burbank, CA	335
311	Cambridge, MA	191
149	Camden, NJ	649
386	Canton Twnshp, MI	92
281	Canton, OH	245
325	Cape Coral, FL	174
353	Carlsbad, CA	135
230	Carrollton, TX	343
185	Carson, CA	467
389	Cary, NC	82
284	Cedar Rapids, IA	241
390	Centennial, CO	79
178	Chandler, AZ	483
268	Charleston, SC	273
31	Charlotte, NC	3,337
105	Chattanooga, TN	913
380	Cheektowaga, NY	102
201	Chesapeake, VA	429
2	Chicago, IL	15,469
252	Chico, CA	308
291	Chino, CA	233
73	Chula Vista, CA	1,303
61	Cincinnati, OH	1,557
179	Citrus Heights, CA	478
403	Clarkstown, NY	52
300	Clarksville, TN	215
255	Clearwater, FL	301
24	Cleveland, OH	4,031
320	Clifton, NJ	180
292	Clinton Twnshp, MI	232
239	Clovis, CA	330
395	College Station, TX	74
407	Colonie, NY	42
88	Colorado Springs, CO	1,061
355	Columbia, MO	132
139	Columbia, SC	690
62	Columbus, GA	1,518
22	Columbus, OH	4,186
104	Compton, CA	928
111	Concord, CA	860
340	Coral Springs, FL	155
164	Corona, CA	566
161	Corpus Christi, TX	598
278	Costa Mesa, CA	248
308	Cranston, RI	196
6	Dallas, TX	10,455
251	Daly City, CA	310
383	Danbury, CT	98
310	Davenport, IA	192
224	Davie, FL	355
126	Dayton, OH	773
163	Dearborn, MI	582
340	Decatur, IL	155
314	Denton, TX	187
29	Denver, CO	3,488
135	Des Moines, IA	712
4	Detroit, MI	13,011
100	Downey, CA	946
313	Duluth, MN	190
129	Durham, NC	754
318	Edison Twnshp, NJ	184
397	Edmond, OK	70
167	El Cajon, CA	560
128	El Monte, CA	759
49	El Paso, TX	1,890
369	Elgin, IL	116
99	Elizabeth, NJ	947
199	Elk Grove, CA	432
343	Erie, PA	152
138	Escondido, CA	699
109	Eugene, OR	888
294	Evansville, IN	228
125	Everett, WA	779
217	Fairfield, CA	390
215	Fall River, MA	393
280	Fargo, ND	246
356	Farmington Hills, MI	130
367	Fayetteville, AR	119
127	Fayetteville, NC	762
166	Federal Way, WA	561
144	Flint, MI	676
106	Fontana, CA	901
293	Fort Collins, CO	230
141	Fort Lauderdale, FL	687
305	Fort Smith, AR	203
203	Fort Wayne, IN	427
45	Fort Worth, TX	2,132
168	Fremont, CA	551
33	Fresno, CA	3,248
396	Frisco, TX	74
223	Fullerton, CA	361
196	Gainesville, FL	440
180	Garden Grove, CA	474
130	Garland, TX	753
114	Gary, IN	846
295	Gilbert, AZ	224
55	Glendale, AZ	1,724
212	Glendale, CA	397
83	Grand Prairie, TX	1,123
222	Grand Rapids, MI	371
393	Greece, NY	77
328	Greeley, CO	172
362	Green Bay, WI	125
114	Greensboro, NC	846
147	Gresham, OR	669
384	Hamilton Twnshp, NJ	98
174	Hammond, IN	502
217	Hampton, VA	390
91	Hartford, CT	993
220	Hawthorne, CA	388
65	Hayward, CA	1,452
156	Henderson, NV	619
259	Hesperia, CA	290
79	Hialeah, FL	1,163
282	High Point, NC	244
364	Hillsboro, OR	124
145	Hollywood, FL	673
26	Honolulu, HI	3,729
3	Houston, TX	14,596
256	Huntington Beach, CA	296
108	Huntsville, AL	895
137	Independence, MO	703
20	Indianapolis, IN	4,485
177	Indio, CA	486
133	Inglewood, CA	730
344	Irvine, CA	150
124	Irving, TX	784
36	Jacksonville, FL	2,721
373	Jacksonville, NC	111
58	Jackson, MS	1,619
116	Jersey City, NJ	840
361	Joliet, IL	126
85	Kansas City, KS	1,080
28	Kansas City, MO	3,527
358	Kenosha, WI	128
158	Kent, WA	611
301	Killeen, TX	212
143	Knoxville, TN	679
199	Lafayette, LA	432
399	Lake Forest, CA	64
270	Lakeland, FL	268
210	Lakewood, CA	400
154	Lakewood, CO	625
181	Lancaster, CA	472
307	Lansing, MI	201
63	Laredo, TX	1,484
285	Las Cruces, NM	240
8	Las Vegas, NV	8,927
339	Lawrence, KS	156
290	Lawton, OK	234
350	Lee's Summit, MO	136
198	Lewisville, TX	436
170	Lexington, KY	543
258	Lincoln, NE	294
79	Little Rock, AR	1,163
348	Livermore, CA	143
249	Livonia, MI	311
40	Long Beach, CA	2,361
357	Longmont, CO	129

RANK	CITY	THEFTS
197	Longview, TX	439
1	Los Angeles, CA	18,391
53	Louisville, KY	1,728
173	Lubbock, TX	526
204	Lynn, MA	426
154	Macon, GA	625
226	Madison, WI	346
332	Manchester, NH	163
194	McAllen, TX	441
374	McKinney, TX	110
315	Melbourne, FL	185
21	Memphis, TN	4,193
271	Merced, CA	265
73	Mesa, AZ	1,303
140	Mesquite, TX	688
148	Miami Beach, FL	665
150	Miami Gardens, FL	647
38	Miami, FL	2,536
329	Midland, TX	171
18	Milwaukee, WI	4,860
50	Minneapolis, MN	1,798
229	Miramar, FL	344
405	Mission Viejo, CA	44
402	Missouri City, TX	57
97	Mobile, AL	950
70	Modesto, CA	1,341
111	Montgomery, AL	860
113	Moreno Valley, CA	852
318	Murfreesboro, TN	184
342	Murrieta, CA	154
379	Nampa, ID	103
400	Naperville, IL	61
381	Nashua, NH	102
54	Nashville, TN	1,725
262	New Bedford, MA	285
85	New Haven, CT	1,080
37	New Orleans, LA	2,612
5	New York, NY	10,694
35	Newark, NJ	3,094
360	Newport Beach, CA	127
410	Newton, MA	31
97	Norfolk, VA	950
347	Norman, OK	144
160	North Charleston, SC	606
77	North Las Vegas, NV	1,166
159	Norwalk, CA	609
305	Norwalk, CT	203
11	Oakland, CA	6,542
194	Oceanside, CA	441
311	Odessa, TX	191
411	O'Fallon, MO	25
244	Ogden, UT	314
25	Oklahoma City, OK	3,826
333	Olathe, KS	162
46	Omaha, NE	2,125
96	Ontario, CA	953
288	Orange, CA	235
369	Orem, UT	116
76	Orlando, FL	1,255
227	Overland Park, KS	345
189	Oxnard, CA	454
334	Palm Bay, FL	160
176	Palmdale, CA	487
249	Pasadena, CA	311
193	Pasadena, TX	442
152	Paterson, NJ	629
376	Pearland, TX	105
232	Pembroke Pines, FL	341
192	Peoria, AZ	449
225	Peoria, IL	349
10	Philadelphia, PA	6,978
7	Phoenix, AZ	9,693
119	Pittsburgh, PA	830
183	Plano, TX	469
288	Plantation, FL	235
89	Pomona, CA	1,007
212	Pompano Beach, FL	397
401	Port St. Lucie, FL	61
34	Portland, OR	3,175
256	Portsmouth, VA	296
87	Providence, RI	1,077
346	Provo, UT	145
227	Pueblo, CO	345
350	Quincy, MA	136
345	Racine, WI	147
123	Raleigh, NC	796
409	Ramapo, NY	33
188	Rancho Cucamon., CA	460
162	Reading, PA	595
304	Redding, CA	204
130	Reno, NV	753
146	Rialto, CA	670
263	Richardson, TX	284
68	Richmond, CA	1,421
92	Richmond, VA	972
353	Rio Rancho, NM	135
72	Riverside, CA	1,331
261	Roanoke, VA	288
378	Rochester, MN	104
95	Rochester, NY	962
191	Rockford, IL	450
243	Roseville, CA	324
365	Roswell, GA	123
377	Round Rock, TX	105
23	Sacramento, CA	4,146
152	Salem, OR	629
84	Salinas, CA	1,121
66	Salt Lake City, UT	1,442
336	San Angelo, TX	159
12	San Antonio, TX	5,803
47	San Bernardino, CA	2,121
9	San Diego, CA	7,496
17	San Francisco, CA	4,913
14	San Jose, CA	5,379
102	San Leandro, CA	932
302	San Marcos, CA	208
323	San Mateo, CA	178
274	Sandy Springs, GA	262
303	Sandy, UT	206
64	Santa Ana, CA	1,473
382	Santa Barbara, CA	99
206	Santa Clara, CA	418
241	Santa Clarita, CA	327
207	Santa Maria, CA	408
272	Santa Monica, CA	264
217	Santa Rosa, CA	390
81	Savannah, GA	1,135
253	Scottsdale, AZ	306
32	Seattle, WA	3,286
151	Shreveport, LA	641
371	Simi Valley, CA	114
329	Sioux City, IA	171
266	Sioux Falls, SD	277
334	Somerville, MA	160
242	South Bend, IN	325
82	South Gate, CA	1,124
183	Southfield, MI	469
278	Sparks, NV	248
276	Spokane Valley, WA	253
52	Spokane, WA	1,737
272	Springfield, IL	264
118	Springfield, MA	835
117	Springfield, MO	839
327	Stamford, CT	173
315	Sterling Heights, MI	185
44	Stockton, CA	2,173
394	St. George, UT	75
315	St. Joseph, MO	185
16	St. Louis, MO	4,962
51	St. Paul, MN	1,789
42	St. Petersburg, FL	2,257
385	Suffolk, VA	94
392	Sugar Land, TX	78
246	Sunnyvale, CA	312
299	Sunrise, FL	217
331	Surprise, AZ	167
233	Syracuse, NY	338
56	Tacoma, WA	1,677
233	Tallahassee, FL	338
69	Tampa, FL	1,361
297	Temecula, CA	220
122	Tempe, AZ	816
205	Thornton, CO	420
388	Thousand Oaks, CA	84
71	Toledo, OH	1,337
408	Toms River Twnshp, NJ	38
208	Topeka, KS	407
211	Torrance, CA	398
246	Tracy, CA	312
209	Trenton, NJ	401
387	Troy, MI	85
27	Tucson, AZ	3,564
48	Tulsa, OK	2,073
297	Tuscaloosa, AL	220
283	Tyler, TX	242
358	Upper Darby Twnshp, PA	128
338	Vacaville, CA	157
75	Vallejo, CA	1,266
107	Vancouver, WA	899
324	Ventura, CA	177
185	Victorville, CA	467
165	Virginia Beach, VA	565
172	Visalia, CA	528
221	Vista, CA	378
238	Waco, TX	334
90	Warren, MI	1,001
366	Warwick, RI	122
15	Washington, DC	5,299
187	Waterbury, CT	464
157	West Covina, CA	613
265	West Jordan, UT	278
201	West Palm Beach, FL	429
121	West Valley, UT	818
246	Westland, MI	312
295	Westminster, CA	224
189	Westminster, CO	454
269	Whittier, CA	270
239	Wichita Falls, TX	330
57	Wichita, KS	1,666
175	Wilmington, NC	491
120	Winston-Salem, NC	827
320	Woodbridge Twnshp, NJ	180
142	Worcester, MA	684
230	Yonkers, NY	343
244	Yuma, AZ	314

Source: Reported data from the F.B.I. "Crime in the United States 2009"

*Motor vehicle theft includes the theft or attempted theft of a self-propelled vehicle. Excludes motorboats, construction equipment, airplanes, and farming equipment.

77. Motor Vehicle Thefts in 2009 (continued)
National Total = 794,616 Motor Vehicle Thefts*

RANK	CITY	THEFTS
1	Los Angeles, CA	18,391
2	Chicago, IL	15,469
3	Houston, TX	14,596
4	Detroit, MI	13,011
5	New York, NY	10,694
6	Dallas, TX	10,455
7	Phoenix, AZ	9,693
8	Las Vegas, NV	8,927
9	San Diego, CA	7,496
10	Philadelphia, PA	6,978
11	Oakland, CA	6,542
12	San Antonio, TX	5,803
13	Atlanta, GA	5,726
14	San Jose, CA	5,379
15	Washington, DC	5,299
16	St. Louis, MO	4,962
17	San Francisco, CA	4,913
18	Milwaukee, WI	4,860
19	Baltimore, MD	4,624
20	Indianapolis, IN	4,485
21	Memphis, TN	4,193
22	Columbus, OH	4,186
23	Sacramento, CA	4,146
24	Cleveland, OH	4,031
25	Oklahoma City, OK	3,826
26	Honolulu, HI	3,729
27	Tucson, AZ	3,564
28	Kansas City, MO	3,527
29	Denver, CO	3,488
30	Albuquerque, NM	3,399
31	Charlotte, NC	3,337
32	Seattle, WA	3,286
33	Fresno, CA	3,248
34	Portland, OR	3,175
35	Newark, NJ	3,094
36	Jacksonville, FL	2,721
37	New Orleans, LA	2,612
38	Miami, FL	2,536
39	Bakersfield, CA	2,376
40	Long Beach, CA	2,361
41	Boston, MA	2,287
42	St. Petersburg, FL	2,257
43	Austin, TX	2,219
44	Stockton, CA	2,173
45	Fort Worth, TX	2,132
46	Omaha, NE	2,125
47	San Bernardino, CA	2,121
48	Tulsa, OK	2,073
49	El Paso, TX	1,890
50	Minneapolis, MN	1,798
51	St. Paul, MN	1,789
52	Spokane, WA	1,737
53	Louisville, KY	1,728
54	Nashville, TN	1,725
55	Glendale, AZ	1,724
56	Tacoma, WA	1,677
57	Wichita, KS	1,666
58	Jackson, MS	1,619
59	Birmingham, AL	1,594
60	Buffalo, NY	1,580
61	Cincinnati, OH	1,557
62	Columbus, GA	1,518
63	Laredo, TX	1,484
64	Santa Ana, CA	1,473
65	Hayward, CA	1,452
66	Salt Lake City, UT	1,442
67	Arlington, TX	1,439
68	Richmond, CA	1,421

RANK	CITY	THEFTS
69	Tampa, FL	1,361
70	Modesto, CA	1,341
71	Toledo, OH	1,337
72	Riverside, CA	1,331
73	Chula Vista, CA	1,303
73	Mesa, AZ	1,303
75	Vallejo, CA	1,266
76	Orlando, FL	1,255
77	Aurora, CO	1,166
77	North Las Vegas, NV	1,166
79	Hialeah, FL	1,163
79	Little Rock, AR	1,163
81	Savannah, GA	1,135
82	South Gate, CA	1,124
83	Grand Prairie, TX	1,123
84	Salinas, CA	1,121
85	Kansas City, KS	1,080
85	New Haven, CT	1,080
87	Providence, RI	1,077
88	Colorado Springs, CO	1,061
89	Pomona, CA	1,007
90	Warren, MI	1,001
91	Hartford, CT	993
92	Richmond, VA	972
93	Bridgeport, CT	964
94	Akron, OH	963
95	Rochester, NY	962
96	Ontario, CA	953
97	Mobile, AL	950
97	Norfolk, VA	950
99	Elizabeth, NJ	947
100	Downey, CA	946
101	Anaheim, CA	945
102	San Leandro, CA	932
103	Baton Rouge, LA	929
104	Compton, CA	928
105	Chattanooga, TN	913
106	Fontana, CA	901
107	Vancouver, WA	899
108	Huntsville, AL	895
109	Eugene, OR	888
110	Anchorage, AK	868
111	Concord, CA	860
111	Montgomery, AL	860
113	Moreno Valley, CA	852
114	Gary, IN	846
114	Greensboro, NC	846
116	Jersey City, NJ	840
117	Springfield, MO	839
118	Springfield, MA	835
119	Pittsburgh, PA	830
120	Winston-Salem, NC	827
121	West Valley, UT	818
122	Tempe, AZ	816
123	Raleigh, NC	796
124	Irving, TX	784
125	Everett, WA	779
126	Dayton, OH	773
127	Fayetteville, NC	762
128	El Monte, CA	759
129	Durham, NC	754
130	Garland, TX	753
130	Reno, NV	753
132	Antioch, CA	747
133	Inglewood, CA	730
134	Berkeley, CA	727
135	Des Moines, IA	712
136	Amarillo, TX	710
137	Independence, MO	703

RANK	CITY	THEFTS
138	Escondido, CA	699
139	Columbia, SC	690
140	Mesquite, TX	688
141	Fort Lauderdale, FL	687
142	Worcester, MA	684
143	Knoxville, TN	679
144	Flint, MI	676
145	Hollywood, FL	673
146	Rialto, CA	670
147	Gresham, OR	669
148	Miami Beach, FL	665
149	Camden, NJ	649
150	Miami Gardens, FL	647
151	Shreveport, LA	641
152	Paterson, NJ	629
152	Salem, OR	629
154	Lakewood, CO	625
154	Macon, GA	625
156	Henderson, NV	619
157	West Covina, CA	613
158	Kent, WA	611
159	Norwalk, CA	609
160	North Charleston, SC	606
161	Corpus Christi, TX	598
162	Reading, PA	595
163	Dearborn, MI	582
164	Corona, CA	566
165	Virginia Beach, VA	565
166	Federal Way, WA	561
167	El Cajon, CA	560
168	Fremont, CA	551
169	Avondale, AZ	546
170	Lexington, KY	543
171	Baldwin Park, CA	536
172	Visalia, CA	528
173	Lubbock, TX	526
174	Hammond, IN	502
175	Wilmington, NC	491
176	Palmdale, CA	487
177	Indio, CA	486
178	Chandler, AZ	483
179	Citrus Heights, CA	478
180	Garden Grove, CA	474
181	Lancaster, CA	472
182	Allentown, PA	471
183	Plano, TX	469
183	Southfield, MI	469
185	Carson, CA	467
185	Victorville, CA	467
187	Waterbury, CT	464
188	Rancho Cucamon., CA	460
189	Oxnard, CA	454
189	Westminster, CO	454
191	Rockford, IL	450
192	Peoria, AZ	449
193	Pasadena, TX	442
194	McAllen, TX	441
194	Oceanside, CA	441
196	Gainesville, FL	440
197	Longview, TX	439
198	Lewisville, TX	436
199	Elk Grove, CA	432
199	Lafayette, LA	432
201	Chesapeake, VA	429
201	West Palm Beach, FL	429
203	Fort Wayne, IN	427
204	Lynn, MA	426
205	Thornton, CO	420
206	Santa Clara, CA	418

RANK	CITY	THEFTS
207	Santa Maria, CA	408
208	Topeka, KS	407
209	Trenton, NJ	401
210	Lakewood, CA	400
211	Torrance, CA	398
212	Glendale, CA	397
212	Pompano Beach, FL	397
214	Buena Park, CA	396
215	Brockton, MA	393
215	Fall River, MA	393
217	Fairfield, CA	390
217	Hampton, VA	390
217	Santa Rosa, CA	390
220	Hawthorne, CA	388
221	Vista, CA	378
222	Grand Rapids, MI	371
223	Fullerton, CA	361
224	Davie, FL	355
225	Peoria, IL	349
226	Madison, WI	346
227	Overland Park, KS	345
227	Pueblo, CO	345
229	Miramar, FL	344
230	Carrollton, TX	343
230	Yonkers, NY	343
232	Pembroke Pines, FL	341
233	Syracuse, NY	338
233	Tallahassee, FL	338
235	Brownsville, TX	337
236	Alexandria, VA	336
237	Burbank, CA	335
238	Waco, TX	334
239	Clovis, CA	330
239	Wichita Falls, TX	330
241	Santa Clarita, CA	327
242	South Bend, IN	325
243	Roseville, CA	324
244	Ogden, UT	314
244	Yuma, AZ	314
246	Sunnyvale, CA	312
246	Tracy, CA	312
246	Westland, MI	312
249	Livonia, MI	311
249	Pasadena, CA	311
251	Daly City, CA	310
252	Chico, CA	308
253	Scottsdale, AZ	306
254	Alhambra, CA	305
255	Clearwater, FL	301
256	Huntington Beach, CA	296
256	Portsmouth, VA	296
258	Lincoln, NE	294
259	Hesperia, CA	290
260	Albany, GA	289
261	Roanoke, VA	288
262	New Bedford, MA	285
263	Richardson, TX	284
264	Beaumont, TX	281
265	West Jordan, UT	278
266	Sioux Falls, SD	277
267	Athens-Clarke, GA	274
268	Charleston, SC	273
269	Whittier, CA	270
270	Lakeland, FL	268
271	Merced, CA	265
272	Santa Monica, CA	264
272	Springfield, IL	264
274	Abilene, TX	262
274	Sandy Springs, GA	262
276	Billings, MT	253
276	Spokane Valley, WA	253
278	Costa Mesa, CA	248
278	Sparks, NV	248
280	Fargo, ND	246
281	Canton, OH	245
282	High Point, NC	244
283	Tyler, TX	242
284	Cedar Rapids, IA	241
285	Las Cruces, NM	240
286	Albany, NY	239
287	Arvada, CO	237
288	Orange, CA	235
288	Plantation, FL	235
290	Lawton, OK	234
291	Chino, CA	233
292	Clinton Twnshp, MI	232
293	Fort Collins, CO	230
294	Evansville, IN	228
295	Gilbert, AZ	224
295	Westminster, CA	224
297	Temecula, CA	220
297	Tuscaloosa, AL	220
299	Sunrise, FL	217
300	Clarksville, TN	215
301	Killeen, TX	212
302	San Marcos, CA	208
303	Sandy, UT	206
304	Redding, CA	204
305	Fort Smith, AR	203
305	Norwalk, CT	203
307	Lansing, MI	201
308	Cranston, RI	196
309	Aurora, IL	195
310	Davenport, IA	192
311	Cambridge, MA	191
311	Odessa, TX	191
313	Duluth, MN	190
314	Denton, TX	187
315	Melbourne, FL	185
315	Sterling Heights, MI	185
315	St. Joseph, MO	185
318	Edison Twnshp, NJ	184
318	Murfreesboro, TN	184
320	Clifton, NJ	180
320	Woodbridge Twnshp, NJ	180
322	Bellevue, WA	179
323	San Mateo, CA	178
324	Ventura, CA	177
325	Boise, ID	174
325	Cape Coral, FL	174
327	Stamford, CT	173
328	Greeley, CO	172
329	Midland, TX	171
329	Sioux City, IA	171
331	Surprise, AZ	167
332	Manchester, NH	163
333	Olathe, KS	162
334	Palm Bay, FL	160
334	Somerville, MA	160
336	San Angelo, TX	159
337	Boca Raton, FL	158
338	Vacaville, CA	157
339	Lawrence, KS	156
340	Coral Springs, FL	155
340	Decatur, IL	155
342	Murrieta, CA	154
343	Erie, PA	152
344	Irvine, CA	150
345	Racine, WI	147
346	Provo, UT	145
347	Norman, OK	144
348	Bellingham, WA	143
348	Livermore, CA	143
350	Beaverton, OR	136
350	Lee's Summit, MO	136
350	Quincy, MA	136
353	Carlsbad, CA	135
353	Rio Rancho, NM	135
355	Columbia, MO	132
356	Farmington Hills, MI	130
357	Longmont, CO	129
358	Kenosha, WI	128
358	Upper Darby Twnshp, PA	128
360	Newport Beach, CA	127
361	Joliet, IL	126
362	Ann Arbor, MI	125
362	Green Bay, WI	125
364	Hillsboro, OR	124
365	Roswell, GA	123
366	Warwick, RI	122
367	Boulder, CO	119
367	Fayetteville, AR	119
369	Elgin, IL	116
369	Orem, UT	116
371	Simi Valley, CA	114
372	Bloomington, MN	112
373	Jacksonville, NC	111
374	McKinney, TX	110
375	Broken Arrow, OK	108
376	Pearland, TX	105
377	Round Rock, TX	105
378	Rochester, MN	104
379	Nampa, ID	103
380	Cheektowaga, NY	102
381	Nashua, NH	102
382	Santa Barbara, CA	99
383	Danbury, CT	98
384	Hamilton Twnshp, NJ	98
385	Suffolk, VA	94
386	Canton Twnshp, MI	92
387	Troy, MI	85
388	Thousand Oaks, CA	84
389	Cary, NC	82
390	Centennial, CO	79
391	Bend, OR	78
392	Sugar Land, TX	78
393	Greece, NY	77
394	St. George, UT	75
395	College Station, TX	74
396	Frisco, TX	74
397	Edmond, OK	70
398	Allen, TX	64
399	Lake Forest, CA	64
400	Naperville, IL	61
401	Port St. Lucie, FL	61
402	Missouri City, TX	57
403	Clarkstown, NY	52
404	Amherst, NY	48
405	Mission Viejo, CA	44
406	Brick Twnshp, NJ	42
407	Colonie, NY	42
408	Toms River Twnshp, NJ	38
409	Ramapo, NY	33
410	Newton, MA	31
411	O'Fallon, MO	25

Source: Reported data from the F.B.I. "Crime in the United States 2009"

*Motor vehicle theft includes the theft or attempted theft of a self-propelled vehicle. Excludes motorboats, construction equipment, airplanes, and farming equipment.

78. Motor Vehicle Theft Rate in 2009
National Rate = 258.8 Motor Vehicle Thefts per 100,000 Population*

RANK	CITY	RATE
277	Abilene, TX	224.8
129	Akron, OH	466.4
166	Albany, GA	381.6
248	Albany, NY	255.8
66	Albuquerque, NM	640.6
274	Alexandria, VA	229.9
183	Alhambra, CA	354.8
137	Allentown, PA	438.8
395	Allen, TX	73.6
172	Amarillo, TX	376.1
405	Amherst, NY	43.5
227	Anaheim, CA	281.3
211	Anchorage, AK	306.4
375	Ann Arbor, MI	109.3
38	Antioch, CA	737.8
168	Arlington, TX	379.6
280	Arvada, CO	219.6
265	Athens-Clarke, GA	239.2
10	Atlanta, GA	1,035.6
180	Aurora, CO	359.9
372	Aurora, IL	111.3
220	Austin, TX	288.6
73	Avondale, AZ	615.1
43	Bakersfield, CA	718.0
47	Baldwin Park, CA	691.3
41	Baltimore, MD	723.9
151	Baton Rouge, LA	416.2
250	Beaumont, TX	254.9
341	Beaverton, OR	145.9
346	Bellevue, WA	143.1
309	Bellingham, WA	178.2
382	Bend, OR	96.8
42	Berkeley, CA	718.5
263	Billings, MT	240.0
46	Birmingham, AL	701.1
349	Bloomington, MN	138.5
305	Boca Raton, FL	183.8
390	Boise, ID	84.3
176	Boston, MA	366.4
366	Boulder, CO	119.0
403	Brick Twnshp, NJ	53.4
45	Bridgeport, CT	708.6
154	Brockton, MA	407.4
371	Broken Arrow, OK	114.4
300	Brownsville, TX	187.8
116	Buena Park, CA	498.0
81	Buffalo, NY	588.1
201	Burbank, CA	324.5
302	Cambridge, MA	185.7
23	Camden, NJ	821.7
373	Canton Twnshp, MI	111.3
207	Canton, OH	313.8
379	Cape Coral, FL	105.9
350	Carlsbad, CA	137.1
238	Carrollton, TX	269.2
113	Carson, CA	504.1
401	Cary, NC	61.3
301	Cedar Rapids, IA	187.1
394	Centennial, CO	79.5
299	Chandler, AZ	188.6
262	Charleston, SC	240.1
143	Charlotte, NC	429.1
107	Chattanooga, TN	529.2
353	Cheektowaga, NY	131.2
295	Chesapeake, VA	192.2
101	Chicago, IL	543.1
178	Chico, CA	363.5
232	Chino, CA	275.3

RANK	CITY	RATE
84	Chula Vista, CA	579.5
128	Cincinnati, OH	466.8
89	Citrus Heights, CA	566.8
400	Clarkstown, NY	65.9
311	Clarksville, TN	176.7
222	Clearwater, FL	285.6
13	Cleveland, OH	939.1
273	Clifton, NJ	230.4
261	Clinton Twnshp, MI	241.8
185	Clovis, CA	346.5
388	College Station, TX	86.0
402	Colonie, NY	53.8
242	Colorado Springs, CO	264.2
356	Columbia, MO	128.7
102	Columbia, SC	539.6
24	Columbus, GA	815.1
95	Columbus, OH	551.2
12	Compton, CA	988.6
44	Concord, CA	710.5
362	Coral Springs, FL	123.4
175	Corona, CA	371.3
285	Corpus Christi, TX	208.0
276	Costa Mesa, CA	225.1
255	Cranston, RI	244.3
25	Dallas, TX	810.3
212	Daly City, CA	306.1
363	Danbury, CT	122.9
298	Davenport, IA	189.9
160	Davie, FL	393.8
112	Dayton, OH	505.3
49	Dearborn, MI	682.3
287	Decatur, IL	204.9
335	Denton, TX	150.4
86	Denver, CO	576.8
179	Des Moines, IA	361.8
2	Detroit, MI	1,432.2
19	Downey, CA	879.2
275	Duluth, MN	226.0
195	Durham, NC	331.4
303	Edison Twnshp, NJ	185.2
387	Edmond, OK	86.5
77	El Cajon, CA	605.6
72	El Monte, CA	620.0
214	El Paso, TX	305.4
377	Elgin, IL	107.7
34	Elizabeth, NJ	758.1
210	Elk Grove, CA	307.3
339	Erie, PA	146.4
111	Escondido, CA	508.6
82	Eugene, OR	586.6
290	Evansville, IN	196.9
29	Everett, WA	791.4
174	Fairfield, CA	373.3
144	Fall River, MA	427.6
243	Fargo, ND	262.2
324	Farmington Hills, MI	166.4
331	Fayetteville, AR	158.4
138	Fayetteville, NC	437.9
55	Federal Way, WA	666.1
78	Flint, MI	605.4
123	Fontana, CA	473.5
325	Fort Collins, CO	166.1
173	Fort Lauderdale, FL	375.5
266	Fort Smith, AR	238.3
321	Fort Wayne, IN	169.7
217	Fort Worth, TX	294.7
236	Fremont, CA	271.8
53	Fresno, CA	674.7
398	Frisco, TX	68.4

RANK	CITY	RATE
235	Fullerton, CA	272.5
165	Gainesville, FL	381.7
221	Garden Grove, CA	285.8
187	Garland, TX	344.0
16	Gary, IN	888.5
383	Gilbert, AZ	96.6
52	Glendale, AZ	675.9
288	Glendale, CA	201.1
50	Grand Prairie, TX	681.6
294	Grand Rapids, MI	192.3
393	Greece, NY	82.6
304	Greeley, CO	184.8
360	Green Bay, WI	124.0
192	Greensboro, NC	334.1
61	Gresham, OR	652.9
376	Hamilton Twnshp, NJ	108.3
56	Hammond, IN	659.8
239	Hampton, VA	267.2
27	Hartford, CT	800.5
130	Hawthorne, CA	460.2
11	Hayward, CA	1,020.9
268	Henderson, NV	236.4
200	Hesperia, CA	326.2
93	Hialeah, FL	556.8
271	High Point, NC	235.4
357	Hillsboro, OR	128.4
122	Hollywood, FL	475.3
153	Honolulu, HI	411.1
65	Houston, TX	641.9
334	Huntington Beach, CA	153.4
115	Huntsville, AL	501.1
87	Independence, MO	575.4
94	Indianapolis, IN	551.3
100	Indio, CA	543.3
64	Inglewood, CA	647.7
397	Irvine, CA	69.5
162	Irving, TX	387.3
191	Jacksonville, FL	335.9
345	Jacksonville, NC	143.2
14	Jackson, MS	936.9
184	Jersey City, NJ	348.8
391	Joliet, IL	83.4
33	Kansas City, KS	760.0
39	Kansas City, MO	727.7
354	Kenosha, WI	131.1
40	Kent, WA	724.3
313	Killeen, TX	175.7
177	Knoxville, TN	365.3
169	Lafayette, LA	379.4
389	Lake Forest, CA	84.8
224	Lakeland, FL	284.1
109	Lakewood, CA	510.6
135	Lakewood, CO	444.5
205	Lancaster, CA	317.3
310	Lansing, MI	177.3
60	Laredo, TX	653.9
249	Las Cruces, NM	255.3
63	Las Vegas, NV	648.2
320	Lawrence, KS	170.1
244	Lawton, OK	260.5
330	Lee's Summit, MO	158.5
150	Lewisville, TX	416.8
307	Lexington, KY	183.2
369	Lincoln, NE	115.5
74	Little Rock, AR	611.4
311	Livermore, CA	176.7
186	Livonia, MI	344.7
110	Long Beach, CA	508.9
338	Longmont, CO	147.2

RANK	CITY	RATE
91	Longview, TX	565.3
121	Los Angeles, CA	477.8
233	Louisville, KY	273.7
270	Lubbock, TX	236.0
126	Lynn, MA	467.4
51	Macon, GA	677.1
337	Madison, WI	147.6
336	Manchester, NH	150.0
194	McAllen, TX	332.6
392	McKinney, TX	83.2
267	Melbourne, FL	237.6
69	Memphis, TN	628.2
190	Merced, CA	336.8
230	Mesa, AZ	276.7
108	Mesquite, TX	517.5
30	Miami Beach, FL	789.2
83	Miami Gardens, FL	586.3
79	Miami, FL	605.0
331	Midland, TX	158.4
26	Milwaukee, WI	803.7
124	Minneapolis, MN	469.9
204	Miramar, FL	317.4
404	Mission Viejo, CA	46.5
396	Missouri City, TX	73.5
163	Mobile, AL	385.9
59	Modesto, CA	655.8
147	Montgomery, AL	424.0
142	Moreno Valley, CA	432.2
315	Murfreesboro, TN	173.7
340	Murrieta, CA	146.3
364	Nampa, ID	122.8
407	Naperville, IL	42.1
368	Nashua, NH	117.8
225	Nashville, TN	282.7
209	New Bedford, MA	307.7
20	New Haven, CT	873.4
32	New Orleans, LA	776.4
359	New York, NY	127.3
7	Newark, NJ	1,108.2
329	Newport Beach, CA	158.9
410	Newton, MA	36.7
156	Norfolk, VA	404.1
351	Norman, OK	133.1
68	North Charleston, SC	631.4
114	North Las Vegas, NV	501.2
80	Norwalk, CA	592.4
256	Norwalk, CT	244.0
1	Oakland, CA	1,617.1
247	Oceanside, CA	258.5
296	Odessa, TX	191.4
411	O'Fallon, MO	31.0
170	Ogden, UT	378.2
48	Oklahoma City, OK	687.0
352	Olathe, KS	131.4
119	Omaha, NE	479.6
96	Ontario, CA	550.2
318	Orange, CA	171.4
361	Orem, UT	123.7
105	Orlando, FL	533.8
289	Overland Park, KS	198.6
259	Oxnard, CA	242.3
333	Palm Bay, FL	154.6
193	Palmdale, CA	332.7
282	Pasadena, CA	215.9
215	Pasadena, TX	300.8
140	Paterson, NJ	434.0
367	Pearland, TX	118.6
272	Pembroke Pines, FL	234.3

RANK	CITY	RATE
234	Peoria, AZ	273.2
213	Peoria, IL	305.5
134	Philadelphia, PA	450.9
75	Phoenix, AZ	606.8
241	Pittsburgh, PA	265.8
317	Plano, TX	172.0
227	Plantation, FL	281.3
57	Pomona, CA	657.2
161	Pompano Beach, FL	389.8
409	Port St. Lucie, FL	37.2
90	Portland, OR	566.0
218	Portsmouth, VA	293.2
70	Providence, RI	627.4
365	Provo, UT	121.4
198	Pueblo, CO	327.7
347	Quincy, MA	140.8
308	Racine, WI	178.8
291	Raleigh, NC	196.1
406	Ramapo, NY	43.1
245	Rancho Cucamon., CA	260.4
37	Reading, PA	739.9
279	Redding, CA	223.6
189	Reno, NV	340.7
54	Rialto, CA	674.1
231	Richardson, TX	276.6
4	Richmond, CA	1,385.4
120	Richmond, VA	478.3
327	Rio Rancho, NM	161.8
136	Riverside, CA	443.9
208	Roanoke, VA	309.3
380	Rochester, MN	102.1
125	Rochester, NY	468.0
223	Rockford, IL	284.9
229	Roseville, CA	277.3
348	Roswell, GA	139.2
384	Round Rock, TX	95.0
18	Sacramento, CA	881.5
155	Salem, OR	404.9
31	Salinas, CA	780.3
28	Salt Lake City, UT	797.9
316	San Angelo, TX	172.3
148	San Antonio, TX	422.4
9	San Bernardino, CA	1,062.2
88	San Diego, CA	570.1
76	San Francisco, CA	606.7
92	San Jose, CA	563.8
5	San Leandro, CA	1,199.9
251	San Marcos, CA	252.9
293	San Mateo, CA	193.0
203	Sandy Springs, GA	317.8
284	Sandy, UT	212.3
139	Santa Ana, CA	434.3
369	Santa Barbara, CA	115.5
171	Santa Clara, CA	376.2
297	Santa Clarita, CA	191.1
127	Santa Maria, CA	466.9
216	Santa Monica, CA	299.9
253	Santa Rosa, CA	249.1
106	Savannah, GA	533.6
358	Scottsdale, AZ	128.0
97	Seattle, WA	545.4
202	Shreveport, LA	321.1
386	Simi Valley, CA	93.8
286	Sioux City, IA	207.1
314	Sioux Falls, SD	174.6
283	Somerville, MA	213.0
206	South Bend, IN	314.5
6	South Gate, CA	1,162.9

RANK	CITY	RATE
71	Southfield, MI	624.7
237	Sparks, NV	271.3
219	Spokane Valley, WA	291.6
21	Spokane, WA	856.0
278	Springfield, IL	223.8
99	Springfield, MA	543.9
104	Springfield, MO	535.6
343	Stamford, CT	144.8
342	Sterling Heights, MI	145.2
36	Stockton, CA	743.6
381	St. George, UT	99.5
260	St. Joseph, MO	242.0
3	St. Louis, MO	1,396.9
67	St. Paul, MN	638.5
15	St. Petersburg, FL	921.5
374	Suffolk, VA	110.7
385	Sugar Land, TX	94.3
269	Sunnyvale, CA	236.1
256	Sunrise, FL	244.0
328	Surprise, AZ	159.5
254	Syracuse, NY	246.3
22	Tacoma, WA	848.9
292	Tallahassee, FL	194.0
159	Tampa, FL	394.2
281	Temecula, CA	218.0
131	Tempe, AZ	459.8
182	Thornton, CO	357.7
399	Thousand Oaks, CA	67.9
132	Toledo, OH	459.3
408	Toms River Twnshp, NJ	39.3
196	Topeka, KS	329.7
226	Torrance, CA	282.1
167	Tracy, CA	380.4
117	Trenton, NJ	485.4
378	Troy, MI	106.0
62	Tucson, AZ	650.4
103	Tulsa, OK	538.7
264	Tuscaloosa, AL	239.9
258	Tyler, TX	243.8
326	Upper Darby Twnshp, PA	163.9
321	Vacaville, CA	169.7
8	Vallejo, CA	1,106.2
98	Vancouver, WA	544.4
319	Ventura, CA	170.2
158	Victorville, CA	398.6
355	Virginia Beach, VA	129.5
146	Visalia, CA	424.9
152	Vista, CA	414.2
240	Waco, TX	267.0
35	Warren, MI	749.9
344	Warwick, RI	144.4
17	Washington, DC	883.7
141	Waterbury, CT	433.6
85	West Covina, CA	579.1
246	West Jordan, UT	259.5
145	West Palm Beach, FL	425.8
57	West Valley, UT	657.2
157	Westland, MI	399.2
252	Westminster, CA	251.5
149	Westminster, CO	421.5
197	Whittier, CA	328.9
199	Wichita Falls, TX	327.1
133	Wichita, KS	453.2
118	Wilmington, NC	484.0
181	Winston-Salem, NC	358.0
306	Woodbridge Twnshp, NJ	183.6
164	Worcester, MA	383.2
323	Yonkers, NY	169.6
188	Yuma, AZ	343.4

Source: CQ Press using reported data from the F.B.I. "Crime in the United States 2009"

*Motor vehicle theft includes the theft or attempted theft of a self-propelled vehicle. Excludes motorboats, construction equipment, airplanes, and farming equipment.

78. Motor Vehicle Theft Rate in 2009 (continued)
National Rate = 258.8 Motor Vehicle Thefts per 100,000 Population*

RANK	CITY	RATE
1	Oakland, CA	1,617.1
2	Detroit, MI	1,432.2
3	St. Louis, MO	1,396.9
4	Richmond, CA	1,385.4
5	San Leandro, CA	1,199.9
6	South Gate, CA	1,162.9
7	Newark, NJ	1,108.2
8	Vallejo, CA	1,106.2
9	San Bernardino, CA	1,062.2
10	Atlanta, GA	1,035.6
11	Hayward, CA	1,020.9
12	Compton, CA	988.6
13	Cleveland, OH	939.1
14	Jackson, MS	936.9
15	St. Petersburg, FL	921.5
16	Gary, IN	888.5
17	Washington, DC	883.7
18	Sacramento, CA	881.5
19	Downey, CA	879.2
20	New Haven, CT	873.4
21	Spokane, WA	856.0
22	Tacoma, WA	848.9
23	Camden, NJ	821.7
24	Columbus, GA	815.1
25	Dallas, TX	810.3
26	Milwaukee, WI	803.7
27	Hartford, CT	800.5
28	Salt Lake City, UT	797.9
29	Everett, WA	791.4
30	Miami Beach, FL	789.2
31	Salinas, CA	780.3
32	New Orleans, LA	776.4
33	Kansas City, KS	760.0
34	Elizabeth, NJ	758.1
35	Warren, MI	749.9
36	Stockton, CA	743.6
37	Reading, PA	739.9
38	Antioch, CA	737.8
39	Kansas City, MO	727.7
40	Kent, WA	724.3
41	Baltimore, MD	723.9
42	Berkeley, CA	718.5
43	Bakersfield, CA	718.0
44	Concord, CA	710.5
45	Bridgeport, CT	708.6
46	Birmingham, AL	701.1
47	Baldwin Park, CA	691.3
48	Oklahoma City, OK	687.0
49	Dearborn, MI	682.3
50	Grand Prairie, TX	681.6
51	Macon, GA	677.1
52	Glendale, AZ	675.9
53	Fresno, CA	674.7
54	Rialto, CA	674.1
55	Federal Way, WA	666.1
56	Hammond, IN	659.8
57	Pomona, CA	657.2
57	West Valley, UT	657.2
59	Modesto, CA	655.8
60	Laredo, TX	653.9
61	Gresham, OR	652.9
62	Tucson, AZ	650.4
63	Las Vegas, NV	648.2
64	Inglewood, CA	647.7
65	Houston, TX	641.9
66	Albuquerque, NM	640.6
67	St. Paul, MN	638.5
68	North Charleston, SC	631.4
69	Memphis, TN	628.2
70	Providence, RI	627.4
71	Southfield, MI	624.7
72	El Monte, CA	620.0
73	Avondale, AZ	615.1
74	Little Rock, AR	611.4
75	Phoenix, AZ	606.8
76	San Francisco, CA	606.7
77	El Cajon, CA	605.6
78	Flint, MI	605.4
79	Miami, FL	605.0
80	Norwalk, CA	592.4
81	Buffalo, NY	588.1
82	Eugene, OR	586.6
83	Miami Gardens, FL	586.3
84	Chula Vista, CA	579.5
85	West Covina, CA	579.1
86	Denver, CO	576.8
87	Independence, MO	575.4
88	San Diego, CA	570.1
89	Citrus Heights, CA	566.8
90	Portland, OR	566.0
91	Longview, TX	565.3
92	San Jose, CA	563.8
93	Hialeah, FL	556.8
94	Indianapolis, IN	551.3
95	Columbus, OH	551.2
96	Ontario, CA	550.2
97	Seattle, WA	545.4
98	Vancouver, WA	544.4
99	Springfield, MA	543.9
100	Indio, CA	543.3
101	Chicago, IL	543.1
102	Columbia, SC	539.6
103	Tulsa, OK	538.7
104	Springfield, MO	535.6
105	Orlando, FL	533.8
106	Savannah, GA	533.6
107	Chattanooga, TN	529.2
108	Mesquite, TX	517.5
109	Lakewood, CA	510.6
110	Long Beach, CA	508.9
111	Escondido, CA	508.6
112	Dayton, OH	505.3
113	Carson, CA	504.1
114	North Las Vegas, NV	501.2
115	Huntsville, AL	501.1
116	Buena Park, CA	498.0
117	Trenton, NJ	485.4
118	Wilmington, NC	484.0
119	Omaha, NE	479.6
120	Richmond, VA	478.3
121	Los Angeles, CA	477.8
122	Hollywood, FL	475.3
123	Fontana, CA	473.5
124	Minneapolis, MN	469.9
125	Rochester, NY	468.0
126	Lynn, MA	467.4
127	Santa Maria, CA	466.9
128	Cincinnati, OH	466.8
129	Akron, OH	466.4
130	Hawthorne, CA	460.2
131	Tempe, AZ	459.8
132	Toledo, OH	459.3
133	Wichita, KS	453.2
134	Philadelphia, PA	450.9
135	Lakewood, CO	444.5
136	Riverside, CA	443.9
137	Allentown, PA	438.8
138	Fayetteville, NC	437.9
139	Santa Ana, CA	434.3
140	Paterson, NJ	434.0
141	Waterbury, CT	433.6
142	Moreno Valley, CA	432.2
143	Charlotte, NC	429.1
144	Fall River, MA	427.6
145	West Palm Beach, FL	425.8
146	Visalia, CA	424.9
147	Montgomery, AL	424.0
148	San Antonio, TX	422.4
149	Westminster, CO	421.5
150	Lewisville, TX	416.8
151	Baton Rouge, LA	416.2
152	Vista, CA	414.2
153	Honolulu, HI	411.1
154	Brockton, MA	407.4
155	Salem, OR	404.9
156	Norfolk, VA	404.1
157	Westland, MI	399.2
158	Victorville, CA	398.6
159	Tampa, FL	394.2
160	Davie, FL	393.8
161	Pompano Beach, FL	389.8
162	Irving, TX	387.3
163	Mobile, AL	385.9
164	Worcester, MA	383.2
165	Gainesville, FL	381.7
166	Albany, GA	381.6
167	Tracy, CA	380.4
168	Arlington, TX	379.6
169	Lafayette, LA	379.4
170	Ogden, UT	378.2
171	Santa Clara, CA	376.2
172	Amarillo, TX	376.1
173	Fort Lauderdale, FL	375.5
174	Fairfield, CA	373.3
175	Corona, CA	371.3
176	Boston, MA	366.4
177	Knoxville, TN	365.3
178	Chico, CA	363.5
179	Des Moines, IA	361.8
180	Aurora, CO	359.9
181	Winston-Salem, NC	358.0
182	Thornton, CO	357.7
183	Alhambra, CA	354.8
184	Jersey City, NJ	348.8
185	Clovis, CA	346.5
186	Livonia, MI	344.7
187	Garland, TX	344.0
188	Yuma, AZ	343.4
189	Reno, NV	340.7
190	Merced, CA	336.8
191	Jacksonville, FL	335.9
192	Greensboro, NC	334.1
193	Palmdale, CA	332.7
194	McAllen, TX	332.6
195	Durham, NC	331.4
196	Topeka, KS	329.7
197	Whittier, CA	328.9
198	Pueblo, CO	327.7
199	Wichita Falls, TX	327.1
200	Hesperia, CA	326.2
201	Burbank, CA	324.5
202	Shreveport, LA	321.1
203	Sandy Springs, GA	317.8
204	Miramar, FL	317.4
205	Lancaster, CA	317.3
206	South Bend, IN	314.5

RANK	CITY	RATE
207	Canton, OH	313.8
208	Roanoke, VA	309.3
209	New Bedford, MA	307.7
210	Elk Grove, CA	307.3
211	Anchorage, AK	306.4
212	Daly City, CA	306.1
213	Peoria, IL	305.5
214	El Paso, TX	305.4
215	Pasadena, TX	300.8
216	Santa Monica, CA	299.9
217	Fort Worth, TX	294.7
218	Portsmouth, VA	293.2
219	Spokane Valley, WA	291.6
220	Austin, TX	288.6
221	Garden Grove, CA	285.8
222	Clearwater, FL	285.6
223	Rockford, IL	284.9
224	Lakeland, FL	284.1
225	Nashville, TN	282.7
226	Torrance, CA	282.1
227	Anaheim, CA	281.3
227	Plantation, FL	281.3
229	Roseville, CA	277.3
230	Mesa, AZ	276.7
231	Richardson, TX	276.6
232	Chino, CA	275.3
233	Louisville, KY	273.7
234	Peoria, AZ	273.2
235	Fullerton, CA	272.5
236	Fremont, CA	271.8
237	Sparks, NV	271.3
238	Carrollton, TX	269.2
239	Hampton, VA	267.2
240	Waco, TX	267.0
241	Pittsburgh, PA	265.8
242	Colorado Springs, CO	264.2
243	Fargo, ND	262.2
244	Lawton, OK	260.5
245	Rancho Cucamon., CA	260.4
246	West Jordan, UT	259.5
247	Oceanside, CA	258.5
248	Albany, NY	255.8
249	Las Cruces, NM	255.3
250	Beaumont, TX	254.9
251	San Marcos, CA	252.9
252	Westminster, CA	251.5
253	Santa Rosa, CA	249.1
254	Syracuse, NY	246.3
255	Cranston, RI	244.3
256	Norwalk, CT	244.0
256	Sunrise, FL	244.0
258	Tyler, TX	243.8
259	Oxnard, CA	242.3
260	St. Joseph, MO	242.0
261	Clinton Twnshp, MI	241.8
262	Charleston, SC	240.1
263	Billings, MT	240.0
264	Tuscaloosa, AL	239.9
265	Athens-Clarke, GA	239.2
266	Fort Smith, AR	238.3
267	Melbourne, FL	237.6
268	Henderson, NV	236.4
269	Sunnyvale, CA	236.1
270	Lubbock, TX	236.0
271	High Point, NC	235.4
272	Pembroke Pines, FL	234.3
273	Clifton, NJ	230.4
274	Alexandria, VA	229.9
275	Duluth, MN	226.0
276	Costa Mesa, CA	225.1
277	Abilene, TX	224.8
278	Springfield, IL	223.8
279	Redding, CA	223.6
280	Arvada, CO	219.6
281	Temecula, CA	218.0
282	Pasadena, CA	215.9
283	Somerville, MA	213.0
284	Sandy, UT	212.3
285	Corpus Christi, TX	208.0
286	Sioux City, IA	207.1
287	Decatur, IL	204.9
288	Glendale, CA	201.1
289	Overland Park, KS	198.6
290	Evansville, IN	196.9
291	Raleigh, NC	196.1
292	Tallahassee, FL	194.0
293	San Mateo, CA	193.0
294	Grand Rapids, MI	192.3
295	Chesapeake, VA	192.2
296	Odessa, TX	191.4
297	Santa Clarita, CA	191.1
298	Davenport, IA	189.9
299	Chandler, AZ	188.6
300	Brownsville, TX	187.8
301	Cedar Rapids, IA	187.1
302	Cambridge, MA	185.7
303	Edison Twnshp, NJ	185.2
304	Greeley, CO	184.8
305	Boca Raton, FL	183.8
306	Woodbridge Twnshp, NJ	183.6
307	Lexington, KY	183.2
308	Racine, WI	178.8
309	Bellingham, WA	178.2
310	Lansing, MI	177.3
311	Clarksville, TN	176.7
311	Livermore, CA	176.7
313	Killeen, TX	175.7
314	Sioux Falls, SD	174.6
315	Murfreesboro, TN	173.7
316	San Angelo, TX	172.3
317	Plano, TX	172.0
318	Orange, CA	171.4
319	Ventura, CA	170.2
320	Lawrence, KS	170.1
321	Fort Wayne, IN	169.7
321	Vacaville, CA	169.7
323	Yonkers, NY	169.6
324	Farmington Hills, MI	166.4
325	Fort Collins, CO	166.1
326	Upper Darby Twnshp, PA	163.9
327	Rio Rancho, NM	161.8
328	Surprise, AZ	159.5
329	Newport Beach, CA	158.9
330	Lee's Summit, MO	158.5
331	Fayetteville, AR	158.4
331	Midland, TX	158.4
333	Palm Bay, FL	154.6
334	Huntington Beach, CA	153.4
335	Denton, TX	150.4
336	Manchester, NH	150.0
337	Madison, WI	147.6
338	Longmont, CO	147.2
339	Erie, PA	146.4
340	Murrieta, CA	146.3
341	Beaverton, OR	145.9
342	Sterling Heights, MI	145.2
343	Stamford, CT	144.8
344	Warwick, RI	144.4
345	Jacksonville, NC	143.2
346	Bellevue, WA	143.1
347	Quincy, MA	140.8
348	Roswell, GA	139.2
349	Bloomington, MN	138.5
350	Carlsbad, CA	137.1
351	Norman, OK	133.1
352	Olathe, KS	131.4
353	Cheektowaga, NY	131.2
354	Kenosha, WI	131.1
355	Virginia Beach, VA	129.5
356	Columbia, MO	128.7
357	Hillsboro, OR	128.4
358	Scottsdale, AZ	128.0
359	New York, NY	127.3
360	Green Bay, WI	124.0
361	Orem, UT	123.7
362	Coral Springs, FL	123.4
363	Danbury, CT	122.9
364	Nampa, ID	122.8
365	Provo, UT	121.4
366	Boulder, CO	119.0
367	Pearland, TX	118.6
368	Nashua, NH	117.8
369	Lincoln, NE	115.5
369	Santa Barbara, CA	115.5
371	Broken Arrow, OK	114.4
372	Aurora, IL	111.3
373	Canton Twnshp, MI	111.3
374	Suffolk, VA	110.7
375	Ann Arbor, MI	109.3
376	Hamilton Twnshp, NJ	108.3
377	Elgin, IL	107.7
378	Troy, MI	106.0
379	Cape Coral, FL	105.9
380	Rochester, MN	102.1
381	St. George, UT	99.5
382	Bend, OR	96.8
383	Gilbert, AZ	96.6
384	Round Rock, TX	95.0
385	Sugar Land, TX	94.3
386	Simi Valley, CA	93.8
387	Edmond, OK	86.5
388	College Station, TX	86.0
389	Lake Forest, CA	84.8
390	Boise, ID	84.3
391	Joliet, IL	83.4
392	McKinney, TX	83.2
393	Greece, NY	82.6
394	Centennial, CO	79.5
395	Allen, TX	73.6
396	Missouri City, TX	73.5
397	Irvine, CA	69.5
398	Frisco, TX	68.4
399	Thousand Oaks, CA	67.9
400	Clarkstown, NY	65.9
401	Cary, NC	61.3
402	Colonie, NY	53.8
403	Brick Twnshp, NJ	53.4
404	Mission Viejo, CA	46.5
405	Amherst, NY	43.5
406	Ramapo, NY	43.1
407	Naperville, IL	42.1
408	Toms River Twnshp, NJ	39.3
409	Port St. Lucie, FL	37.2
410	Newton, MA	36.7
411	O'Fallon, MO	31.0

Source: CQ Press using reported data from the F.B.I. "Crime in the United States 2009"

*Motor vehicle theft includes the theft or attempted theft of a self-propelled vehicle. Excludes motorboats, construction equipment, airplanes, and farming equipment.

79. Percent Change in Motor Vehicle Theft Rate: 2008 to 2009
National Percent Change = 17.8% Decrease*

RANK	CITY	% CHANGE
19	Abilene, TX	12.2
59	Akron, OH	1.5
NA	Albany, GA**	NA
38	Albany, NY	7.0
295	Albuquerque, NM	(27.7)
181	Alexandria, VA	(15.2)
191	Alhambra, CA	(16.0)
85	Allentown, PA	(4.3)
4	Allen, TX	25.0
88	Amarillo, TX	(4.7)
188	Amherst, NY	(15.9)
166	Anaheim, CA	(14.2)
21	Anchorage, AK	12.0
NA	Ann Arbor, MI**	NA
32	Antioch, CA	8.3
117	Arlington, TX	(7.8)
92	Arvada, CO	(5.4)
275	Athens-Clarke, GA	(25.3)
176	Atlanta, GA	(14.9)
152	Aurora, CO	(12.3)
253	Aurora, IL	(22.9)
210	Austin, TX	(17.4)
313	Avondale, AZ	(30.2)
109	Bakersfield, CA	(7.0)
123	Baldwin Park, CA	(8.7)
201	Baltimore, MD	(16.6)
76	Baton Rouge, LA	(3.0)
133	Beaumont, TX	(10.0)
345	Beaverton, OR	(36.0)
347	Bellevue, WA	(36.3)
317	Bellingham, WA	(30.5)
376	Bend, OR	(41.1)
258	Berkeley, CA	(23.6)
135	Billings, MT	(10.3)
274	Birmingham, AL	(25.2)
311	Bloomington, MN	(29.9)
188	Boca Raton, FL	(15.9)
232	Boise, ID	(20.1)
118	Boston, MA	(7.9)
126	Boulder, CO	(8.9)
128	Brick Twnshp, NJ	(9.2)
178	Bridgeport, CT	(15.0)
NA	Brockton, MA**	NA
362	Broken Arrow, OK	(38.4)
80	Brownsville, TX	(3.4)
257	Buena Park, CA	(23.2)
170	Buffalo, NY	(14.5)
340	Burbank, CA	(35.1)
247	Cambridge, MA	(22.2)
355	Camden, NJ	(37.3)
NA	Canton Twnshp, MI**	NA
343	Canton, OH	(35.4)
249	Cape Coral, FL	(22.4)
306	Carlsbad, CA	(29.1)
104	Carrollton, TX	(6.6)
295	Carson, CA	(27.7)
73	Cary, NC	(1.6)
320	Cedar Rapids, IA	(30.9)
198	Centennial, CO	(16.5)
371	Chandler, AZ	(40.5)
337	Charleston, SC	(34.9)
359	Charlotte, NC	(38.2)
195	Chattanooga, TN	(16.2)
287	Cheektowaga, NY	(26.6)
67	Chesapeake, VA	(0.6)
222	Chicago, IL	(19.0)
39	Chico, CA	6.9
224	Chino, CA	(19.1)
369	Chula Vista, CA	(40.3)
78	Cincinnati, OH	(3.3)
282	Citrus Heights, CA	(26.3)
15	Clarkstown, NY	13.0
215	Clarksville, TN	(18.1)
9	Clearwater, FL	19.4
253	Cleveland, OH	(22.9)
110	Clifton, NJ	(7.1)
NA	Clinton Twnshp, MI**	NA
10	Clovis, CA	17.4
315	College Station, TX	(30.3)
34	Colonie, NY	8.0
140	Colorado Springs, CO	(11.0)
146	Columbia, MO	(11.5)
46	Columbia, SC	5.0
98	Columbus, GA	(5.7)
245	Columbus, OH	(22.0)
127	Compton, CA	(9.1)
154	Concord, CA	(12.4)
313	Coral Springs, FL	(30.2)
42	Corona, CA	5.7
160	Corpus Christi, TX	(13.0)
226	Costa Mesa, CA	(19.4)
237	Cranston, RI	(21.2)
184	Dallas, TX	(15.3)
137	Daly City, CA	(10.5)
164	Danbury, CT	(14.0)
367	Davenport, IA	(39.5)
29	Davie, FL	9.1
331	Dayton, OH	(33.3)
NA	Dearborn, MI**	NA
NA	Decatur, IL**	NA
14	Denton, TX	13.8
89	Denver, CO	(4.9)
NA	Des Moines, IA**	NA
NA	Detroit, MI**	NA
251	Downey, CA	(22.7)
13	Duluth, MN	13.9
206	Durham, NC	(16.9)
29	Edison Twnshp, NJ	9.1
55	Edmond, OK	2.7
350	El Cajon, CA	(36.5)
31	El Monte, CA	8.8
323	El Paso, TX	(32.1)
310	Elgin, IL	(29.8)
289	Elizabeth, NJ	(26.9)
5	Elk Grove, CA	22.7
105	Erie, PA	(6.7)
236	Escondido, CA	(21.0)
326	Eugene, OR	(32.3)
112	Evansville, IN	(7.4)
334	Everett, WA	(34.1)
331	Fairfield, CA	(33.3)
24	Fall River, MA	11.2
12	Fargo, ND	14.9
NA	Farmington Hills, MI**	NA
66	Fayetteville, AR	0.2
193	Fayetteville, NC	(16.1)
318	Federal Way, WA	(30.8)
NA	Flint, MI**	NA
289	Fontana, CA	(26.9)
102	Fort Collins, CO	(6.4)
221	Fort Lauderdale, FL	(18.9)
238	Fort Smith, AR	(21.3)
345	Fort Wayne, IN	(36.0)
270	Fort Worth, TX	(24.7)
242	Fremont, CA	(21.6)
178	Fresno, CA	(15.0)
7	Frisco, TX	21.5
115	Fullerton, CA	(7.7)
48	Gainesville, FL	4.5
196	Garden Grove, CA	(16.4)
54	Garland, TX	2.8
159	Gary, IN	(12.9)
381	Gilbert, AZ	(45.5)
292	Glendale, AZ	(27.1)
242	Glendale, CA	(21.6)
181	Grand Prairie, TX	(15.2)
NA	Grand Rapids, MI**	NA
229	Greece, NY	(20.0)
212	Greeley, CO	(17.6)
217	Green Bay, WI	(18.5)
271	Greensboro, NC	(24.8)
81	Gresham, OR	(3.7)
370	Hamilton Twnshp, NJ	(40.4)
63	Hammond, IN	0.5
78	Hampton, VA	(3.3)
271	Hartford, CT	(24.8)
312	Hawthorne, CA	(30.0)
37	Hayward, CA	7.2
291	Henderson, NV	(27.0)
170	Hesperia, CA	(14.5)
330	Hialeah, FL	(33.2)
368	High Point, NC	(39.8)
281	Hillsboro, OR	(26.1)
161	Hollywood, FL	(13.3)
92	Honolulu, HI	(5.4)
94	Houston, TX	(5.5)
95	Huntington Beach, CA	(5.6)
229	Huntsville, AL	(20.0)
217	Independence, MO	(18.5)
318	Indianapolis, IN	(30.8)
105	Indio, CA	(6.7)
165	Inglewood, CA	(14.1)
303	Irvine, CA	(28.4)
142	Irving, TX	(11.2)
328	Jacksonville, FL	(32.8)
124	Jacksonville, NC	(8.8)
85	Jackson, MS	(4.3)
295	Jersey City, NJ	(27.7)
151	Joliet, IL	(12.1)
NA	Kansas City, KS**	NA
266	Kansas City, MO	(24.4)
364	Kenosha, WI	(38.6)
282	Kent, WA	(26.3)
8	Killeen, TX	20.5
374	Knoxville, TN	(41.0)
173	Lafayette, LA	(14.7)
58	Lake Forest, CA	1.8
252	Lakeland, FL	(22.8)
35	Lakewood, CA	7.7
99	Lakewood, CO	(5.8)
114	Lancaster, CA	(7.6)
NA	Lansing, MI**	NA
186	Laredo, TX	(15.6)
71	Las Cruces, NM	(1.3)
256	Las Vegas, NV	(23.1)
247	Lawrence, KS	(22.2)
51	Lawton, OK	4.0
62	Lee's Summit, MO	0.6
3	Lewisville, TX	27.9
NA	Lexington, KY**	NA
198	Lincoln, NE	(16.5)
NA	Little Rock, AR**	NA
45	Livermore, CA	5.1
NA	Livonia, MI**	NA
208	Long Beach, CA	(17.2)
NA	Longmont, CO**	NA

RANK	CITY	% CHANGE
26	Longview, TX	10.6
219	Los Angeles, CA	(18.7)
NA	Louisville, KY**	NA
161	Lubbock, TX	(13.3)
140	Lynn, MA	(11.0)
260	Macon, GA	(23.8)
321	Madison, WI	(31.5)
359	Manchester, NH	(38.2)
95	McAllen, TX	(5.6)
65	McKinney, TX	0.4
240	Melbourne, FL	(21.5)
246	Memphis, TN	(22.1)
267	Merced, CA	(24.6)
361	Mesa, AZ	(38.3)
74	Mesquite, TX	(1.7)
205	Miami Beach, FL	(16.7)
275	Miami Gardens, FL	(25.3)
309	Miami, FL	(29.4)
43	Midland, TX	5.3
280	Milwaukee, WI	(26.0)
285	Minneapolis, MN	(26.5)
40	Miramar, FL	6.2
331	Mission Viejo, CA	(33.3)
357	Missouri City, TX	(37.8)
130	Mobile, AL	(9.5)
119	Modesto, CA	(8.0)
91	Montgomery, AL	(5.3)
207	Moreno Valley, CA	(17.1)
115	Murfreesboro, TN	(7.7)
107	Murrieta, CA	(6.9)
354	Nampa, ID	(37.1)
186	Naperville, IL	(15.6)
NA	Nashua, NH**	NA
267	Nashville, TN	(24.6)
149	New Bedford, MA	(11.8)
NA	New Haven, CT**	NA
322	New Orleans, LA	(31.9)
172	New York, NY	(14.6)
210	Newark, NJ	(17.4)
23	Newport Beach, CA	11.3
44	Newton, MA	5.2
174	Norfolk, VA	(14.8)
299	Norman, OK	(28.1)
273	North Charleston, SC	(25.1)
308	North Las Vegas, NV	(29.2)
122	Norwalk, CA	(8.5)
67	Norwalk, CT	(0.6)
228	Oakland, CA	(19.7)
216	Oceanside, CA	(18.2)
315	Odessa, TX	(30.3)
299	O'Fallon, MO	(28.1)
128	Ogden, UT	(9.2)
75	Oklahoma City, OK	(2.7)
NA	Olathe, KS**	NA
255	Omaha, NE	(23.0)
229	Ontario, CA	(20.0)
372	Orange, CA	(40.6)
63	Orem, UT	0.5
306	Orlando, FL	(29.1)
90	Overland Park, KS	(5.2)
169	Oxnard, CA	(14.4)
53	Palm Bay, FL	3.5
233	Palmdale, CA	(20.3)
178	Pasadena, CA	(15.0)
2	Pasadena, TX	29.0
342	Paterson, NJ	(35.3)
130	Pearland, TX	(9.5)
150	Pembroke Pines, FL	(12.0)

RANK	CITY	% CHANGE
294	Peoria, AZ	(27.4)
NA	Peoria, IL**	NA
302	Philadelphia, PA	(28.3)
352	Phoenix, AZ	(36.8)
336	Pittsburgh, PA	(34.6)
25	Plano, TX	11.0
103	Plantation, FL	(6.5)
168	Pomona, CA	(14.3)
299	Pompano Beach, FL	(28.1)
358	Port St. Lucie, FL	(38.1)
101	Portland, OR	(6.3)
163	Portsmouth, VA	(13.5)
298	Providence, RI	(27.9)
56	Provo, UT	1.9
NA	Pueblo, CO**	NA
69	Quincy, MA	(0.8)
285	Racine, WI	(26.5)
227	Raleigh, NC	(19.5)
11	Ramapo, NY	16.2
50	Rancho Cucamon., CA	4.1
265	Reading, PA	(24.3)
222	Redding, CA	(19.0)
263	Reno, NV	(24.2)
137	Rialto, CA	(10.5)
17	Richardson, TX	12.7
278	Richmond, CA	(25.7)
111	Richmond, VA	(7.3)
380	Rio Rancho, NM	(45.2)
214	Riverside, CA	(18.0)
83	Roanoke, VA	(3.9)
379	Rochester, MN	(44.8)
261	Rochester, NY	(23.9)
366	Rockford, IL	(38.9)
213	Roseville, CA	(17.9)
176	Roswell, GA	(14.9)
6	Round Rock, TX	21.6
193	Sacramento, CA	(16.1)
85	Salem, OR	(4.3)
130	Salinas, CA	(9.5)
244	Salt Lake City, UT	(21.9)
327	San Angelo, TX	(32.6)
304	San Antonio, TX	(28.7)
70	San Bernardino, CA	(0.9)
323	San Diego, CA	(32.1)
188	San Francisco, CA	(15.9)
56	San Jose, CA	1.9
121	San Leandro, CA	(8.1)
267	San Marcos, CA	(24.6)
364	San Mateo, CA	(38.6)
99	Sandy Springs, GA	(5.8)
201	Sandy, UT	(16.6)
83	Santa Ana, CA	(3.9)
152	Santa Barbara, CA	(12.3)
52	Santa Clara, CA	3.6
305	Santa Clarita, CA	(28.8)
209	Santa Maria, CA	(17.3)
33	Santa Monica, CA	8.1
49	Santa Rosa, CA	4.3
107	Savannah, GA	(6.9)
375	Scottsdale, AZ	(41.0)
142	Seattle, WA	(11.2)
277	Shreveport, LA	(25.4)
239	Simi Valley, CA	(21.4)
22	Sioux City, IA	11.5
28	Sioux Falls, SD	9.2
351	Somerville, MA	(36.7)
340	South Bend, IN	(35.1)
156	South Gate, CA	(12.6)

RANK	CITY	% CHANGE
NA	Southfield, MI**	NA
235	Sparks, NV	(20.6)
377	Spokane Valley, WA	(41.3)
20	Spokane, WA	12.1
NA	Springfield, IL**	NA
124	Springfield, MA	(8.8)
225	Springfield, MO	(19.3)
234	Stamford, CT	(20.5)
NA	Sterling Heights, MI**	NA
158	Stockton, CA	(12.8)
352	St. George, UT	(36.8)
196	St. Joseph, MO	(16.4)
174	St. Louis, MO	(14.8)
76	St. Paul, MN	(3.0)
1	St. Petersburg, FL	53.3
344	Suffolk, VA	(35.8)
220	Sugar Land, TX	(18.8)
139	Sunnyvale, CA	(10.6)
259	Sunrise, FL	(23.7)
250	Surprise, AZ	(22.5)
325	Syracuse, NY	(32.2)
363	Tacoma, WA	(38.5)
339	Tallahassee, FL	(35.0)
263	Tampa, FL	(24.2)
156	Temecula, CA	(12.6)
292	Tempe, AZ	(27.1)
47	Thornton, CO	4.9
135	Thousand Oaks, CA	(10.3)
71	Toledo, OH	(1.3)
329	Toms River Twnshp, NJ	(33.0)
378	Topeka, KS	(41.3)
147	Torrance, CA	(11.7)
27	Tracy, CA	10.4
240	Trenton, NJ	(21.5)
NA	Troy, MI**	NA
373	Tucson, AZ	(40.8)
134	Tulsa, OK	(10.2)
335	Tuscaloosa, AL	(34.5)
16	Tyler, TX	12.8
347	Upper Darby Twnshp, PA	(36.3)
347	Vacaville, CA	(36.3)
119	Vallejo, CA	(8.0)
282	Vancouver, WA	(26.3)
262	Ventura, CA	(24.1)
145	Victorville, CA	(11.4)
154	Virginia Beach, VA	(12.4)
288	Visalia, CA	(26.8)
198	Vista, CA	(16.5)
181	Waco, TX	(15.2)
NA	Warren, MI**	NA
201	Warwick, RI	(16.6)
185	Washington, DC	(15.5)
36	Waterbury, CT	7.6
142	West Covina, CA	(11.2)
41	West Jordan, UT	6.0
201	West Palm Beach, FL	(16.6)
95	West Valley, UT	(5.6)
NA	Westland, MI**	NA
337	Westminster, CA	(34.9)
60	Westminster, CO	1.2
166	Whittier, CA	(14.2)
356	Wichita Falls, TX	(37.4)
147	Wichita, KS	(11.7)
113	Wilmington, NC	(7.5)
278	Winston-Salem, NC	(25.7)
18	Woodbridge Twnshp, NJ	12.6
61	Worcester, MA	1.0
82	Yonkers, NY	(3.8)
191	Yuma, AZ	(16.0)

Source: CQ Press using reported data from the F.B.I. "Crime in the United States 2009"
*Motor vehicle theft includes the theft or attempted theft of a self-propelled vehicle. Excludes motorboats, construction equipment, airplanes, and farming equipment. **Not available.

79. Percent Change in Motor Vehicle Theft Rate: 2008 to 2009 (continued)
National Percent Change = 17.8% Decrease*

RANK	CITY	% CHANGE
1	St. Petersburg, FL	53.3
2	Pasadena, TX	29.0
3	Lewisville, TX	27.9
4	Allen, TX	25.0
5	Elk Grove, CA	22.7
6	Round Rock, TX	21.6
7	Frisco, TX	21.5
8	Killeen, TX	20.5
9	Clearwater, FL	19.4
10	Clovis, CA	17.4
11	Ramapo, NY	16.2
12	Fargo, ND	14.9
13	Duluth, MN	13.9
14	Denton, TX	13.8
15	Clarkstown, NY	13.0
16	Tyler, TX	12.8
17	Richardson, TX	12.7
18	Woodbridge Twnshp, NJ	12.6
19	Abilene, TX	12.2
20	Spokane, WA	12.1
21	Anchorage, AK	12.0
22	Sioux City, IA	11.5
23	Newport Beach, CA	11.3
24	Fall River, MA	11.2
25	Plano, TX	11.0
26	Longview, TX	10.6
27	Tracy, CA	10.4
28	Sioux Falls, SD	9.2
29	Davie, FL	9.1
29	Edison Twnshp, NJ	9.1
31	El Monte, CA	8.8
32	Antioch, CA	8.3
33	Santa Monica, CA	8.1
34	Colonie, NY	8.0
35	Lakewood, CA	7.7
36	Waterbury, CT	7.6
37	Hayward, CA	7.2
38	Albany, NY	7.0
39	Chico, CA	6.9
40	Miramar, FL	6.2
41	West Jordan, UT	6.0
42	Corona, CA	5.7
43	Midland, TX	5.3
44	Newton, MA	5.2
45	Livermore, CA	5.1
46	Columbia, SC	5.0
47	Thornton, CO	4.9
48	Gainesville, FL	4.5
49	Santa Rosa, CA	4.3
50	Rancho Cucamon., CA	4.1
51	Lawton, OK	4.0
52	Santa Clara, CA	3.6
53	Palm Bay, FL	3.5
54	Garland, TX	2.8
55	Edmond, OK	2.7
56	Provo, UT	1.9
56	San Jose, CA	1.9
58	Lake Forest, CA	1.8
59	Akron, OH	1.5
60	Westminster, CO	1.2
61	Worcester, MA	1.0
62	Lee's Summit, MO	0.6
63	Hammond, IN	0.5
63	Orem, UT	0.5
65	McKinney, TX	0.4
66	Fayetteville, AR	0.2
67	Chesapeake, VA	(0.6)
67	Norwalk, CT	(0.6)
69	Quincy, MA	(0.8)
70	San Bernardino, CA	(0.9)
71	Las Cruces, NM	(1.3)
71	Toledo, OH	(1.3)
73	Cary, NC	(1.6)
74	Mesquite, TX	(1.7)
75	Oklahoma City, OK	(2.7)
76	Baton Rouge, LA	(3.0)
76	St. Paul, MN	(3.0)
78	Cincinnati, OH	(3.3)
78	Hampton, VA	(3.3)
80	Brownsville, TX	(3.4)
81	Gresham, OR	(3.7)
82	Yonkers, NY	(3.8)
83	Roanoke, VA	(3.9)
83	Santa Ana, CA	(3.9)
85	Allentown, PA	(4.3)
85	Jackson, MS	(4.3)
85	Salem, OR	(4.3)
88	Amarillo, TX	(4.7)
89	Denver, CO	(4.9)
90	Overland Park, KS	(5.2)
91	Montgomery, AL	(5.3)
92	Arvada, CO	(5.4)
92	Honolulu, HI	(5.4)
94	Houston, TX	(5.5)
95	Huntington Beach, CA	(5.6)
95	McAllen, TX	(5.6)
95	West Valley, UT	(5.6)
98	Columbus, GA	(5.7)
99	Lakewood, CO	(5.8)
99	Sandy Springs, GA	(5.8)
101	Portland, OR	(6.3)
102	Fort Collins, CO	(6.4)
103	Plantation, FL	(6.5)
104	Carrollton, TX	(6.6)
105	Erie, PA	(6.7)
105	Indio, CA	(6.7)
107	Murrieta, CA	(6.9)
107	Savannah, GA	(6.9)
109	Bakersfield, CA	(7.0)
110	Clifton, NJ	(7.1)
111	Richmond, VA	(7.3)
112	Evansville, IN	(7.4)
113	Wilmington, NC	(7.5)
114	Lancaster, CA	(7.6)
115	Fullerton, CA	(7.7)
115	Murfreesboro, TN	(7.7)
117	Arlington, TX	(7.8)
118	Boston, MA	(7.9)
119	Modesto, CA	(8.0)
119	Vallejo, CA	(8.0)
121	San Leandro, CA	(8.1)
122	Norwalk, CA	(8.5)
123	Baldwin Park, CA	(8.7)
124	Jacksonville, NC	(8.8)
124	Springfield, MA	(8.8)
126	Boulder, CO	(8.9)
127	Compton, CA	(9.1)
128	Brick Twnshp, NJ	(9.2)
128	Ogden, UT	(9.2)
130	Mobile, AL	(9.5)
130	Pearland, TX	(9.5)
130	Salinas, CA	(9.5)
133	Beaumont, TX	(10.0)
134	Tulsa, OK	(10.2)
135	Billings, MT	(10.3)
135	Thousand Oaks, CA	(10.3)
137	Daly City, CA	(10.5)
137	Rialto, CA	(10.5)
139	Sunnyvale, CA	(10.6)
140	Colorado Springs, CO	(11.0)
140	Lynn, MA	(11.0)
142	Irving, TX	(11.2)
142	Seattle, WA	(11.2)
142	West Covina, CA	(11.2)
145	Victorville, CA	(11.4)
146	Columbia, MO	(11.5)
147	Torrance, CA	(11.7)
147	Wichita, KS	(11.7)
149	New Bedford, MA	(11.8)
150	Pembroke Pines, FL	(12.0)
151	Joliet, IL	(12.1)
152	Aurora, CO	(12.3)
152	Santa Barbara, CA	(12.3)
154	Concord, CA	(12.4)
154	Virginia Beach, VA	(12.4)
156	South Gate, CA	(12.6)
156	Temecula, CA	(12.6)
158	Stockton, CA	(12.8)
159	Gary, IN	(12.9)
160	Corpus Christi, TX	(13.0)
161	Hollywood, FL	(13.3)
161	Lubbock, TX	(13.3)
163	Portsmouth, VA	(13.5)
164	Danbury, CT	(14.0)
165	Inglewood, CA	(14.1)
166	Anaheim, CA	(14.2)
166	Whittier, CA	(14.2)
168	Pomona, CA	(14.3)
169	Oxnard, CA	(14.4)
170	Buffalo, NY	(14.5)
170	Hesperia, CA	(14.5)
172	New York, NY	(14.6)
173	Lafayette, LA	(14.7)
174	Norfolk, VA	(14.8)
174	St. Louis, MO	(14.8)
176	Atlanta, GA	(14.9)
176	Roswell, GA	(14.9)
178	Bridgeport, CT	(15.0)
178	Fresno, CA	(15.0)
178	Pasadena, CA	(15.0)
181	Alexandria, VA	(15.2)
181	Grand Prairie, TX	(15.2)
181	Waco, TX	(15.2)
184	Dallas, TX	(15.3)
185	Washington, DC	(15.5)
186	Laredo, TX	(15.6)
186	Naperville, IL	(15.6)
188	Amherst, NY	(15.9)
188	Boca Raton, FL	(15.9)
188	San Francisco, CA	(15.9)
191	Alhambra, CA	(16.0)
191	Yuma, AZ	(16.0)
193	Fayetteville, NC	(16.1)
193	Sacramento, CA	(16.1)
195	Chattanooga, TN	(16.2)
196	Garden Grove, CA	(16.4)
196	St. Joseph, MO	(16.4)
198	Centennial, CO	(16.5)
198	Lincoln, NE	(16.5)
198	Vista, CA	(16.5)
201	Baltimore, MD	(16.6)
201	Sandy, UT	(16.6)
201	Warwick, RI	(16.6)
201	West Palm Beach, FL	(16.6)
205	Miami Beach, FL	(16.7)
206	Durham, NC	(16.9)

RANK	CITY	% CHANGE
207	Moreno Valley, CA	(17.1)
208	Long Beach, CA	(17.2)
209	Santa Maria, CA	(17.3)
210	Austin, TX	(17.4)
210	Newark, NJ	(17.4)
212	Greeley, CO	(17.6)
213	Roseville, CA	(17.9)
214	Riverside, CA	(18.0)
215	Clarksville, TN	(18.1)
216	Oceanside, CA	(18.2)
217	Green Bay, WI	(18.5)
217	Independence, MO	(18.5)
219	Los Angeles, CA	(18.7)
220	Sugar Land, TX	(18.8)
221	Fort Lauderdale, FL	(18.9)
222	Chicago, IL	(19.0)
222	Redding, CA	(19.0)
224	Chino, CA	(19.1)
225	Springfield, MO	(19.3)
226	Costa Mesa, CA	(19.4)
227	Raleigh, NC	(19.5)
228	Oakland, CA	(19.7)
229	Greece, NY	(20.0)
229	Huntsville, AL	(20.0)
229	Ontario, CA	(20.0)
232	Boise, ID	(20.1)
233	Palmdale, CA	(20.3)
234	Stamford, CT	(20.5)
235	Sparks, NV	(20.6)
236	Escondido, CA	(21.0)
237	Cranston, RI	(21.2)
238	Fort Smith, AR	(21.3)
239	Simi Valley, CA	(21.4)
240	Melbourne, FL	(21.5)
240	Trenton, NJ	(21.5)
242	Fremont, CA	(21.6)
242	Glendale, CA	(21.6)
244	Salt Lake City, UT	(21.9)
245	Columbus, OH	(22.0)
246	Memphis, TN	(22.1)
247	Cambridge, MA	(22.2)
247	Lawrence, KS	(22.2)
249	Cape Coral, FL	(22.4)
250	Surprise, AZ	(22.5)
251	Downey, CA	(22.7)
252	Lakeland, FL	(22.8)
253	Aurora, IL	(22.9)
253	Cleveland, OH	(22.9)
255	Omaha, NE	(23.0)
256	Las Vegas, NV	(23.1)
257	Buena Park, CA	(23.2)
258	Berkeley, CA	(23.6)
259	Sunrise, FL	(23.7)
260	Macon, GA	(23.8)
261	Rochester, NY	(23.9)
262	Ventura, CA	(24.1)
263	Reno, NV	(24.2)
263	Tampa, FL	(24.2)
265	Reading, PA	(24.3)
266	Kansas City, MO	(24.4)
267	Merced, CA	(24.6)
267	Nashville, TN	(24.6)
267	San Marcos, CA	(24.6)
270	Fort Worth, TX	(24.7)
271	Greensboro, NC	(24.8)
271	Hartford, CT	(24.8)
273	North Charleston, SC	(25.1)
274	Birmingham, AL	(25.2)
275	Athens-Clarke, GA	(25.3)
275	Miami Gardens, FL	(25.3)
277	Shreveport, LA	(25.4)
278	Richmond, CA	(25.7)
278	Winston-Salem, NC	(25.7)
280	Milwaukee, WI	(26.0)
281	Hillsboro, OR	(26.1)
282	Citrus Heights, CA	(26.3)
282	Kent, WA	(26.3)
282	Vancouver, WA	(26.3)
285	Minneapolis, MN	(26.5)
285	Racine, WI	(26.5)
287	Cheektowaga, NY	(26.6)
288	Visalia, CA	(26.8)
289	Elizabeth, NJ	(26.9)
289	Fontana, CA	(26.9)
291	Henderson, NV	(27.0)
292	Glendale, AZ	(27.1)
292	Tempe, AZ	(27.1)
294	Peoria, AZ	(27.4)
295	Albuquerque, NM	(27.7)
295	Carson, CA	(27.7)
295	Jersey City, NJ	(27.7)
298	Providence, RI	(27.9)
299	Norman, OK	(28.1)
299	O'Fallon, MO	(28.1)
299	Pompano Beach, FL	(28.1)
302	Philadelphia, PA	(28.3)
303	Irvine, CA	(28.4)
304	San Antonio, TX	(28.7)
305	Santa Clarita, CA	(28.8)
306	Carlsbad, CA	(29.1)
306	Orlando, FL	(29.1)
308	North Las Vegas, NV	(29.2)
309	Miami, FL	(29.4)
310	Elgin, IL	(29.8)
311	Bloomington, MN	(29.9)
312	Hawthorne, CA	(30.0)
313	Avondale, AZ	(30.2)
313	Coral Springs, FL	(30.2)
315	College Station, TX	(30.3)
315	Odessa, TX	(30.3)
317	Bellingham, WA	(30.5)
318	Federal Way, WA	(30.8)
318	Indianapolis, IN	(30.8)
320	Cedar Rapids, IA	(30.9)
321	Madison, WI	(31.5)
322	New Orleans, LA	(31.9)
323	El Paso, TX	(32.1)
323	San Diego, CA	(32.1)
325	Syracuse, NY	(32.2)
326	Eugene, OR	(32.3)
327	San Angelo, TX	(32.6)
328	Jacksonville, FL	(32.8)
329	Toms River Twnshp, NJ	(33.0)
330	Hialeah, FL	(33.2)
331	Dayton, OH	(33.3)
331	Fairfield, CA	(33.3)
331	Mission Viejo, CA	(33.3)
334	Everett, WA	(34.1)
335	Tuscaloosa, AL	(34.5)
336	Pittsburgh, PA	(34.6)
337	Charleston, SC	(34.9)
337	Westminster, CA	(34.9)
339	Tallahassee, FL	(35.0)
340	Burbank, CA	(35.1)
340	South Bend, IN	(35.1)
342	Paterson, NJ	(35.3)
343	Canton, OH	(35.4)
344	Suffolk, VA	(35.8)
345	Beaverton, OR	(36.0)
345	Fort Wayne, IN	(36.0)
347	Bellevue, WA	(36.3)
347	Upper Darby Twnshp, PA	(36.3)
347	Vacaville, CA	(36.3)
350	El Cajon, CA	(36.5)
351	Somerville, MA	(36.7)
352	Phoenix, AZ	(36.8)
352	St. George, UT	(36.8)
354	Nampa, ID	(37.1)
355	Camden, NJ	(37.3)
356	Wichita Falls, TX	(37.4)
357	Missouri City, TX	(37.8)
358	Port St. Lucie, FL	(38.1)
359	Charlotte, NC	(38.2)
359	Manchester, NH	(38.2)
361	Mesa, AZ	(38.3)
362	Broken Arrow, OK	(38.4)
363	Tacoma, WA	(38.5)
364	Kenosha, WI	(38.6)
364	San Mateo, CA	(38.6)
366	Rockford, IL	(38.9)
367	Davenport, IA	(39.5)
368	High Point, NC	(39.8)
369	Chula Vista, CA	(40.3)
370	Hamilton Twnshp, NJ	(40.4)
371	Chandler, AZ	(40.5)
372	Orange, CA	(40.6)
373	Tucson, AZ	(40.8)
374	Knoxville, TN	(41.0)
375	Scottsdale, AZ	(41.0)
376	Bend, OR	(41.1)
377	Spokane Valley, WA	(41.3)
378	Topeka, KS	(41.3)
379	Rochester, MN	(44.8)
380	Rio Rancho, NM	(45.2)
381	Gilbert, AZ	(45.5)
NA	Albany, GA**	NA
NA	Ann Arbor, MI**	NA
NA	Brockton, MA**	NA
NA	Canton Twnshp, MI**	NA
NA	Clinton Twnshp, MI**	NA
NA	Dearborn, MI**	NA
NA	Decatur, IL**	NA
NA	Des Moines, IA**	NA
NA	Detroit, MI**	NA
NA	Farmington Hills, MI**	NA
NA	Flint, MI**	NA
NA	Grand Rapids, MI**	NA
NA	Kansas City, KS**	NA
NA	Lansing, MI**	NA
NA	Lexington, KY**	NA
NA	Little Rock, AR**	NA
NA	Livonia, MI**	NA
NA	Longmont, CO**	NA
NA	Louisville, KY**	NA
NA	Nashua, NH**	NA
NA	New Haven, CT**	NA
NA	Olathe, KS**	NA
NA	Peoria, IL**	NA
NA	Pueblo, CO**	NA
NA	Southfield, MI**	NA
NA	Springfield, IL**	NA
NA	Sterling Heights, MI**	NA
NA	Troy, MI**	NA
NA	Warren, MI**	NA
NA	Westland, MI**	NA

Source: CQ Press using reported data from the F.B.I. "Crime in the United States 2009"

*Motor vehicle theft includes the theft or attempted theft of a self-propelled vehicle. Excludes motorboats, construction equipment, airplanes, and farming equipment. **Not available.

80. Percent Change in Motor Vehicle Theft Rate: 2005 to 2009
National Percent Change = 37.9% Decrease*

RANK	CITY	% CHANGE
42	Abilene, TX	(12.0)
117	Akron, OH	(28.2)
35	Albany, GA	(9.1)
160	Albany, NY	(34.6)
56	Albuquerque, NM	(17.2)
178	Alexandria, VA	(36.0)
235	Alhambra, CA	(43.9)
17	Allentown, PA	(0.8)
31	Allen, TX	(8.1)
158	Amarillo, TX	(34.5)
5	Amherst, NY	27.2
299	Anaheim, CA	(53.8)
182	Anchorage, AK	(36.6)
NA	Ann Arbor, MI**	NA
58	Antioch, CA	(18.3)
81	Arlington, TX	(23.4)
346	Arvada, CO	(60.7)
129	Athens-Clarke, GA	(29.9)
75	Atlanta, GA	(22.5)
347	Aurora, CO	(61.2)
200	Aurora, IL	(39.3)
72	Austin, TX	(21.5)
NA	Avondale, AZ**	NA
78	Bakersfield, CA	(22.8)
43	Baldwin Park, CA	(12.6)
93	Baltimore, MD	(25.3)
188	Baton Rouge, LA	(37.3)
244	Beaumont, TX	(44.9)
347	Beaverton, OR	(61.2)
368	Bellevue, WA	(70.1)
323	Bellingham, WA	(57.3)
373	Bend, OR	(75.2)
208	Berkeley, CA	(41.0)
160	Billings, MT	(34.6)
61	Birmingham, AL	(18.9)
NA	Bloomington, MN**	NA
63	Boca Raton, FL	(19.4)
365	Boise, ID	(67.1)
317	Boston, MA	(55.9)
317	Boulder, CO	(55.9)
26	Brick Twnshp, NJ	(6.6)
76	Bridgeport, CT	(22.6)
262	Brockton, MA	(47.7)
229	Broken Arrow, OK	(43.1)
121	Brownsville, TX	(28.4)
33	Buena Park, CA	(8.5)
134	Buffalo, NY	(30.6)
139	Burbank, CA	(31.3)
173	Cambridge, MA	(35.7)
137	Camden, NJ	(31.1)
NA	Canton Twnshp, MI**	NA
301	Canton, OH	(54.1)
307	Cape Coral, FL	(54.9)
279	Carlsbad, CA	(50.1)
170	Carrollton, TX	(35.4)
62	Carson, CA	(19.2)
197	Cary, NC	(38.7)
88	Cedar Rapids, IA	(24.0)
344	Centennial, CO	(60.4)
356	Chandler, AZ	(63.6)
259	Charleston, SC	(47.0)
332	Charlotte, NC	(59.1)
71	Chattanooga, TN	(21.2)
208	Cheektowaga, NY	(41.0)
74	Chesapeake, VA	(22.3)
134	Chicago, IL	(30.6)
261	Chico, CA	(47.6)
290	Chino, CA	(52.3)
289	Chula Vista, CA	(52.1)
281	Cincinnati, OH	(50.3)
NA	Citrus Heights, CA**	NA
NA	Clarkstown, NY**	NA
88	Clarksville, TN	(24.0)
105	Clearwater, FL	(26.8)
182	Cleveland, OH	(36.6)
194	Clifton, NJ	(38.3)
NA	Clinton Twnshp, MI**	NA
142	Clovis, CA	(31.9)
79	College Station, TX	(23.1)
360	Colonie, NY	(64.9)
239	Colorado Springs, CO	(44.4)
145	Columbia, MO	(32.8)
88	Columbia, SC	(24.0)
34	Columbus, GA	(8.9)
270	Columbus, OH	(48.5)
23	Compton, CA	(4.8)
83	Concord, CA	(23.5)
150	Coral Springs, FL	(33.3)
220	Corona, CA	(41.9)
157	Corpus Christi, TX	(34.4)
307	Costa Mesa, CA	(54.9)
100	Cranston, RI	(26.4)
132	Dallas, TX	(30.2)
154	Daly City, CA	(33.7)
123	Danbury, CT	(29.1)
307	Davenport, IA	(54.9)
12	Davie, FL	6.9
355	Dayton, OH	(63.3)
NA	Dearborn, MI**	NA
NA	Decatur, IL**	NA
198	Denton, TX	(38.9)
338	Denver, CO	(59.4)
NA	Des Moines, IA**	NA
NA	Detroit, MI**	NA
40	Downey, CA	(11.4)
NA	Duluth, MN**	NA
113	Durham, NC	(27.4)
140	Edison Twnshp, NJ	(31.4)
68	Edmond, OK	(20.4)
276	El Cajon, CA	(49.6)
145	El Monte, CA	(32.8)
127	El Paso, TX	(29.3)
NA	Elgin, IL**	NA
158	Elizabeth, NJ	(34.5)
NA	Elk Grove, CA**	NA
2	Erie, PA	43.8
173	Escondido, CA	(35.7)
273	Eugene, OR	(48.9)
58	Evansville, IN	(18.3)
354	Everett, WA	(63.0)
294	Fairfield, CA	(53.3)
NA	Fall River, MA**	NA
8	Fargo, ND	12.5
NA	Farmington Hills, MI**	NA
137	Fayetteville, AR	(31.1)
123	Fayetteville, NC	(29.1)
361	Federal Way, WA	(65.1)
NA	Flint, MI**	NA
250	Fontana, CA	(46.1)
282	Fort Collins, CO	(50.4)
225	Fort Lauderdale, FL	(42.4)
225	Fort Smith, AR	(42.4)
229	Fort Wayne, IN	(43.1)
288	Fort Worth, TX	(51.4)
107	Fremont, CA	(27.1)
211	Fresno, CA	(41.2)
268	Frisco, TX	(48.4)
216	Fullerton, CA	(41.6)
19	Gainesville, FL	(1.2)
321	Garden Grove, CA	(56.7)
14	Garland, TX	1.2
81	Gary, IN	(23.4)
353	Gilbert, AZ	(62.9)
258	Glendale, AZ	(46.9)
153	Glendale, CA	(33.6)
28	Grand Prairie, TX	(7.4)
NA	Grand Rapids, MI**	NA
211	Greece, NY	(41.2)
359	Greeley, CO	(64.5)
242	Green Bay, WI	(44.5)
166	Greensboro, NC	(34.9)
274	Gresham, OR	(49.5)
248	Hamilton Twnshp, NJ	(45.4)
142	Hammond, IN	(31.9)
127	Hampton, VA	(29.3)
253	Hartford, CT	(46.2)
129	Hawthorne, CA	(29.9)
110	Hayward, CA	(27.2)
351	Henderson, NV	(62.2)
341	Hesperia, CA	(60.0)
53	Hialeah, FL	(16.6)
295	High Point, NC	(53.5)
370	Hillsboro, OR	(71.0)
45	Hollywood, FL	(14.1)
246	Honolulu, HI	(45.1)
173	Houston, TX	(35.7)
231	Huntington Beach, CA	(43.2)
87	Huntsville, AL	(23.9)
136	Independence, MO	(30.8)
286	Indianapolis, IN	(50.9)
250	Indio, CA	(46.1)
60	Inglewood, CA	(18.5)
332	Irvine, CA	(59.1)
155	Irving, TX	(34.0)
249	Jacksonville, FL	(45.9)
NA	Jacksonville, NC**	NA
41	Jackson, MS	(11.5)
307	Jersey City, NJ	(54.9)
182	Joliet, IL	(36.6)
350	Kansas City, KS	(62.0)
233	Kansas City, MO	(43.7)
179	Kenosha, WI	(36.3)
335	Kent, WA	(59.3)
6	Killeen, TX	17.8
253	Knoxville, TN	(46.2)
13	Lafayette, LA	1.8
147	Lake Forest, CA	(32.9)
144	Lakeland, FL	(32.1)
47	Lakewood, CA	(14.9)
312	Lakewood, CO	(55.2)
335	Lancaster, CA	(59.3)
NA	Lansing, MI**	NA
3	Laredo, TX	41.1
50	Las Cruces, NM	(16.0)
330	Las Vegas, NV	(58.4)
29	Lawrence, KS	(7.5)
9	Lawton, OK	8.6
11	Lee's Summit, MO	7.4
10	Lewisville, TX	8.2
NA	Lexington, KY**	NA
166	Lincoln, NE	(34.9)
NA	Little Rock, AR**	NA
204	Livermore, CA	(40.0)
NA	Livonia, MI**	NA
164	Long Beach, CA	(34.8)
NA	Longmont, CO**	NA

RANK	CITY	% CHANGE
84	Longview, TX	(23.7)
172	Los Angeles, CA	(35.6)
NA	Louisville, KY**	NA
176	Lubbock, TX	(35.8)
120	Lynn, MA	(28.3)
192	Macon, GA	(37.9)
250	Madison, WI	(46.1)
169	Manchester, NH	(35.2)
123	McAllen, TX	(29.1)
253	McKinney, TX	(46.2)
48	Melbourne, FL	(15.2)
271	Memphis, TN	(48.6)
301	Merced, CA	(54.1)
369	Mesa, AZ	(70.5)
22	Mesquite, TX	(3.8)
100	Miami Beach, FL	(26.4)
190	Miami Gardens, FL	(37.5)
215	Miami, FL	(41.5)
39	Midland, TX	(11.3)
122	Milwaukee, WI	(28.9)
305	Minneapolis, MN	(54.6)
95	Miramar, FL	(25.5)
239	Mission Viejo, CA	(44.4)
325	Missouri City, TX	(57.5)
44	Mobile, AL	(14.0)
306	Modesto, CA	(54.7)
49	Montgomery, AL	(15.9)
283	Moreno Valley, CA	(50.6)
202	Murfreesboro, TN	(39.6)
332	Murrieta, CA	(59.1)
NA	Nampa, ID**	NA
66	Naperville, IL	(20.0)
69	Nashua, NH	(20.8)
303	Nashville, TN	(54.3)
32	New Bedford, MA	(8.4)
NA	New Haven, CT**	NA
NA	New Orleans, LA**	NA
234	New York, NY	(43.8)
247	Newark, NJ	(45.3)
152	Newport Beach, CA	(33.4)
150	Newton, MA	(33.3)
46	Norfolk, VA	(14.4)
263	Norman, OK	(48.0)
222	North Charleston, SC	(42.0)
362	North Las Vegas, NV	(66.6)
110	Norwalk, CA	(27.2)
179	Norwalk, CT	(36.3)
117	Oakland, CA	(28.2)
216	Oceanside, CA	(41.6)
15	Odessa, TX	0.9
345	O'Fallon, MO	(60.5)
93	Ogden, UT	(25.3)
67	Oklahoma City, OK	(20.3)
NA	Olathe, KS**	NA
265	Omaha, NE	(48.2)
299	Ontario, CA	(53.8)
343	Orange, CA	(60.3)
191	Orem, UT	(37.7)
265	Orlando, FL	(48.2)
70	Overland Park, KS	(20.9)
211	Oxnard, CA	(41.2)
208	Palm Bay, FL	(41.0)
228	Palmdale, CA	(42.5)
236	Pasadena, CA	(44.1)
21	Pasadena, TX	(2.9)
116	Paterson, NJ	(28.1)
117	Pearland, TX	(28.2)
54	Pembroke Pines, FL	(16.9)
366	Peoria, AZ	(67.4)
316	Peoria, IL	(55.8)
218	Philadelphia, PA	(41.8)
357	Phoenix, AZ	(63.7)
349	Pittsburgh, PA	(61.3)
107	Plano, TX	(27.1)
104	Plantation, FL	(26.6)
148	Pomona, CA	(33.0)
223	Pompano Beach, FL	(42.3)
367	Port St. Lucie, FL	(68.7)
256	Portland, OR	(46.6)
113	Portsmouth, VA	(27.4)
285	Providence, RI	(50.8)
203	Provo, UT	(39.9)
115	Pueblo, CO	(28.0)
54	Quincy, MA	(16.9)
328	Racine, WI	(57.7)
170	Raleigh, NC	(35.4)
4	Ramapo, NY	39.5
206	Rancho Cucamon., CA	(40.7)
232	Reading, PA	(43.6)
339	Redding, CA	(59.6)
303	Reno, NV	(54.3)
223	Rialto, CA	(42.3)
16	Richardson, TX	0.8
205	Richmond, CA	(40.4)
326	Richmond, VA	(57.6)
51	Rio Rancho, NM	(16.1)
295	Riverside, CA	(53.5)
168	Roanoke, VA	(35.0)
91	Rochester, MN	(24.5)
315	Rochester, NY	(55.6)
313	Rockford, IL	(55.4)
335	Roseville, CA	(59.3)
131	Roswell, GA	(30.1)
1	Round Rock, TX	55.2
218	Sacramento, CA	(41.8)
243	Salem, OR	(44.6)
76	Salinas, CA	(22.6)
123	Salt Lake City, UT	(29.1)
244	San Angelo, TX	(44.9)
38	San Antonio, TX	(11.1)
149	San Bernardino, CA	(33.2)
272	San Diego, CA	(48.7)
239	San Francisco, CA	(44.4)
27	San Jose, CA	(6.8)
30	San Leandro, CA	(8.0)
194	San Marcos, CA	(38.3)
63	San Mateo, CA	(19.4)
NA	Sandy Springs, GA**	NA
52	Sandy, UT	(16.3)
329	Santa Ana, CA	(58.2)
280	Santa Barbara, CA	(50.2)
17	Santa Clara, CA	(0.8)
194	Santa Clarita, CA	(38.3)
189	Santa Maria, CA	(37.4)
187	Santa Monica, CA	(37.2)
160	Santa Rosa, CA	(34.6)
98	Savannah, GA	(25.9)
372	Scottsdale, AZ	(74.7)
364	Seattle, WA	(67.0)
186	Shreveport, LA	(37.1)
267	Simi Valley, CA	(48.3)
92	Sioux City, IA	(24.7)
106	Sioux Falls, SD	(27.0)
276	Somerville, MA	(49.6)
214	South Bend, IN	(41.3)
36	South Gate, CA	(9.5)
NA	Southfield, MI**	NA
274	Sparks, NV	(49.5)
324	Spokane Valley, WA	(57.4)
24	Spokane, WA	(5.3)
84	Springfield, IL	(23.7)
264	Springfield, MA	(48.1)
37	Springfield, MO	(10.0)
73	Stamford, CT	(21.8)
NA	Sterling Heights, MI**	NA
257	Stockton, CA	(46.8)
371	St. George, UT	(73.4)
287	St. Joseph, MO	(51.1)
206	St. Louis, MO	(40.7)
112	St. Paul, MN	(27.3)
20	St. Petersburg, FL	(2.0)
103	Suffolk, VA	(26.5)
176	Sugar Land, TX	(35.8)
57	Sunnyvale, CA	(18.2)
100	Sunrise, FL	(26.4)
331	Surprise, AZ	(58.5)
358	Syracuse, NY	(64.0)
291	Tacoma, WA	(52.6)
320	Tallahassee, FL	(56.5)
297	Tampa, FL	(53.6)
307	Temecula, CA	(54.9)
363	Tempe, AZ	(66.9)
284	Thornton, CO	(50.7)
99	Thousand Oaks, CA	(26.3)
319	Toledo, OH	(56.2)
268	Toms River Twnshp, NJ	(48.4)
225	Topeka, KS	(42.4)
65	Torrance, CA	(19.7)
179	Tracy, CA	(36.3)
193	Trenton, NJ	(38.2)
NA	Troy, MI**	NA
260	Tucson, AZ	(47.2)
237	Tulsa, OK	(44.2)
96	Tuscaloosa, AL	(25.6)
7	Tyler, TX	12.7
292	Upper Darby Twnshp, PA	(53.1)
201	Vacaville, CA	(39.4)
NA	Vallejo, CA**	NA
97	Vancouver, WA	(25.7)
314	Ventura, CA	(55.5)
340	Victorville, CA	(59.9)
80	Virginia Beach, VA	(23.2)
352	Visalia, CA	(62.8)
155	Vista, CA	(34.0)
298	Waco, TX	(53.7)
NA	Warren, MI**	NA
342	Warwick, RI	(60.1)
164	Washington, DC	(34.8)
84	Waterbury, CT	(23.7)
132	West Covina, CA	(30.2)
NA	West Jordan, UT**	NA
322	West Palm Beach, FL	(57.1)
25	West Valley, UT	(6.0)
NA	Westland, MI**	NA
326	Westminster, CA	(57.6)
292	Westminster, CO	(53.1)
238	Whittier, CA	(44.3)
199	Wichita Falls, TX	(39.2)
NA	Wichita, KS**	NA
163	Wilmington, NC	(34.7)
107	Winston-Salem, NC	(27.1)
185	Woodbridge Twnshp, NJ	(36.9)
220	Worcester, MA	(41.9)
140	Yonkers, NY	(31.4)
278	Yuma, AZ	(49.9)

Source: CQ Press using reported data from the F.B.I. "Crime in the United States 2009"

*Motor vehicle theft includes the theft or attempted theft of a self-propelled vehicle. Excludes motorboats, construction equipment, airplanes, and farming equipment. **Not available.

80. Percent Change in Motor Vehicle Theft Rate: 2005 to 2009 (continued)
National Percent Change = 37.9% Decrease*

RANK	CITY	% CHANGE
1	Round Rock, TX	55.2
2	Erie, PA	43.8
3	Laredo, TX	41.1
4	Ramapo, NY	39.5
5	Amherst, NY	27.2
6	Killeen, TX	17.8
7	Tyler, TX	12.7
8	Fargo, ND	12.5
9	Lawton, OK	8.6
10	Lewisville, TX	8.2
11	Lee's Summit, MO	7.4
12	Davie, FL	6.9
13	Lafayette, LA	1.8
14	Garland, TX	1.2
15	Odessa, TX	0.9
16	Richardson, TX	0.8
17	Allentown, PA	(0.8)
17	Santa Clara, CA	(0.8)
19	Gainesville, FL	(1.2)
20	St. Petersburg, FL	(2.0)
21	Pasadena, TX	(2.9)
22	Mesquite, TX	(3.8)
23	Compton, CA	(4.8)
24	Spokane, WA	(5.3)
25	West Valley, UT	(6.0)
26	Brick Twnshp, NJ	(6.6)
27	San Jose, CA	(6.8)
28	Grand Prairie, TX	(7.4)
29	Lawrence, KS	(7.5)
30	San Leandro, CA	(8.0)
31	Allen, TX	(8.1)
32	New Bedford, MA	(8.4)
33	Buena Park, CA	(8.5)
34	Columbus, GA	(8.9)
35	Albany, GA	(9.1)
36	South Gate, CA	(9.5)
37	Springfield, MO	(10.0)
38	San Antonio, TX	(11.1)
39	Midland, TX	(11.3)
40	Downey, CA	(11.4)
41	Jackson, MS	(11.5)
42	Abilene, TX	(12.0)
43	Baldwin Park, CA	(12.6)
44	Mobile, AL	(14.0)
45	Hollywood, FL	(14.1)
46	Norfolk, VA	(14.4)
47	Lakewood, CA	(14.9)
48	Melbourne, FL	(15.2)
49	Montgomery, AL	(15.9)
50	Las Cruces, NM	(16.0)
51	Rio Rancho, NM	(16.1)
52	Sandy, UT	(16.3)
53	Hialeah, FL	(16.6)
54	Pembroke Pines, FL	(16.9)
54	Quincy, MA	(16.9)
56	Albuquerque, NM	(17.2)
57	Sunnyvale, CA	(18.2)
58	Antioch, CA	(18.3)
58	Evansville, IN	(18.3)
60	Inglewood, CA	(18.5)
61	Birmingham, AL	(18.9)
62	Carson, CA	(19.2)
63	Boca Raton, FL	(19.4)
63	San Mateo, CA	(19.4)
65	Torrance, CA	(19.7)
66	Naperville, IL	(20.0)
67	Oklahoma City, OK	(20.3)
68	Edmond, OK	(20.4)
69	Nashua, NH	(20.8)
70	Overland Park, KS	(20.9)
71	Chattanooga, TN	(21.2)
72	Austin, TX	(21.5)
73	Stamford, CT	(21.8)
74	Chesapeake, VA	(22.3)
75	Atlanta, GA	(22.5)
76	Bridgeport, CT	(22.6)
76	Salinas, CA	(22.6)
78	Bakersfield, CA	(22.8)
79	College Station, TX	(23.1)
80	Virginia Beach, VA	(23.2)
81	Arlington, TX	(23.4)
81	Gary, IN	(23.4)
83	Concord, CA	(23.5)
84	Longview, TX	(23.7)
84	Springfield, IL	(23.7)
84	Waterbury, CT	(23.7)
87	Huntsville, AL	(23.9)
88	Cedar Rapids, IA	(24.0)
88	Clarksville, TN	(24.0)
88	Columbia, SC	(24.0)
91	Rochester, MN	(24.5)
92	Sioux City, IA	(24.7)
93	Baltimore, MD	(25.3)
93	Ogden, UT	(25.3)
95	Miramar, FL	(25.5)
96	Tuscaloosa, AL	(25.6)
97	Vancouver, WA	(25.7)
98	Savannah, GA	(25.9)
99	Thousand Oaks, CA	(26.3)
100	Cranston, RI	(26.4)
100	Miami Beach, FL	(26.4)
100	Sunrise, FL	(26.4)
103	Suffolk, VA	(26.5)
104	Plantation, FL	(26.6)
105	Clearwater, FL	(26.8)
106	Sioux Falls, SD	(27.0)
107	Fremont, CA	(27.1)
107	Plano, TX	(27.1)
107	Winston-Salem, NC	(27.1)
110	Hayward, CA	(27.2)
110	Norwalk, CA	(27.2)
112	St. Paul, MN	(27.3)
113	Durham, NC	(27.4)
113	Portsmouth, VA	(27.4)
115	Pueblo, CO	(28.0)
116	Paterson, NJ	(28.1)
117	Akron, OH	(28.2)
117	Oakland, CA	(28.2)
117	Pearland, TX	(28.2)
120	Lynn, MA	(28.3)
121	Brownsville, TX	(28.4)
122	Milwaukee, WI	(28.9)
123	Danbury, CT	(29.1)
123	Fayetteville, NC	(29.1)
123	McAllen, TX	(29.1)
123	Salt Lake City, UT	(29.1)
127	El Paso, TX	(29.3)
127	Hampton, VA	(29.3)
129	Athens-Clarke, GA	(29.9)
129	Hawthorne, CA	(29.9)
131	Roswell, GA	(30.1)
132	Dallas, TX	(30.2)
132	West Covina, CA	(30.2)
134	Buffalo, NY	(30.6)
134	Chicago, IL	(30.6)
136	Independence, MO	(30.8)
137	Camden, NJ	(31.1)
137	Fayetteville, AR	(31.1)
139	Burbank, CA	(31.3)
140	Edison Twnshp, NJ	(31.4)
140	Yonkers, NY	(31.4)
142	Clovis, CA	(31.9)
142	Hammond, IN	(31.9)
144	Lakeland, FL	(32.1)
145	Columbia, MO	(32.8)
145	El Monte, CA	(32.8)
147	Lake Forest, CA	(32.9)
148	Pomona, CA	(33.0)
149	San Bernardino, CA	(33.2)
150	Coral Springs, FL	(33.3)
150	Newton, MA	(33.3)
152	Newport Beach, CA	(33.4)
153	Glendale, CA	(33.6)
154	Daly City, CA	(33.7)
155	Irving, TX	(34.0)
155	Vista, CA	(34.0)
157	Corpus Christi, TX	(34.4)
158	Amarillo, TX	(34.5)
158	Elizabeth, NJ	(34.5)
160	Albany, NY	(34.6)
160	Billings, MT	(34.6)
160	Santa Rosa, CA	(34.6)
163	Wilmington, NC	(34.7)
164	Long Beach, CA	(34.8)
164	Washington, DC	(34.8)
166	Greensboro, NC	(34.9)
166	Lincoln, NE	(34.9)
168	Roanoke, VA	(35.0)
169	Manchester, NH	(35.2)
170	Carrollton, TX	(35.4)
170	Raleigh, NC	(35.4)
172	Los Angeles, CA	(35.6)
173	Cambridge, MA	(35.7)
173	Escondido, CA	(35.7)
173	Houston, TX	(35.7)
176	Lubbock, TX	(35.8)
176	Sugar Land, TX	(35.8)
178	Alexandria, VA	(36.0)
179	Kenosha, WI	(36.3)
179	Norwalk, CT	(36.3)
179	Tracy, CA	(36.3)
182	Anchorage, AK	(36.6)
182	Cleveland, OH	(36.6)
182	Joliet, IL	(36.6)
185	Woodbridge Twnshp, NJ	(36.9)
186	Shreveport, LA	(37.1)
187	Santa Monica, CA	(37.2)
188	Baton Rouge, LA	(37.3)
189	Santa Maria, CA	(37.4)
190	Miami Gardens, FL	(37.5)
191	Orem, UT	(37.7)
192	Macon, GA	(37.9)
193	Trenton, NJ	(38.2)
194	Clifton, NJ	(38.3)
194	San Marcos, CA	(38.3)
194	Santa Clarita, CA	(38.3)
197	Cary, NC	(38.7)
198	Denton, TX	(38.9)
199	Wichita Falls, TX	(39.2)
200	Aurora, IL	(39.3)
201	Vacaville, CA	(39.4)
202	Murfreesboro, TN	(39.6)
203	Provo, UT	(39.9)
204	Livermore, CA	(40.0)
205	Richmond, CA	(40.4)
206	Rancho Cucamon., CA	(40.7)

RANK	CITY	% CHANGE	RANK	CITY	% CHANGE	RANK	CITY	% CHANGE
206	St. Louis, MO	(40.7)	274	Sparks, NV	(49.5)	343	Orange, CA	(60.3)
208	Berkeley, CA	(41.0)	276	El Cajon, CA	(49.6)	344	Centennial, CO	(60.4)
208	Cheektowaga, NY	(41.0)	276	Somerville, MA	(49.6)	345	O'Fallon, MO	(60.5)
208	Palm Bay, FL	(41.0)	278	Yuma, AZ	(49.9)	346	Arvada, CO	(60.7)
211	Fresno, CA	(41.2)	279	Carlsbad, CA	(50.1)	347	Aurora, CO	(61.2)
211	Greece, NY	(41.2)	280	Santa Barbara, CA	(50.2)	347	Beaverton, OR	(61.2)
211	Oxnard, CA	(41.2)	281	Cincinnati, OH	(50.3)	349	Pittsburgh, PA	(61.3)
214	South Bend, IN	(41.3)	282	Fort Collins, CO	(50.4)	350	Kansas City, KS	(62.0)
215	Miami, FL	(41.5)	283	Moreno Valley, CA	(50.6)	351	Henderson, NV	(62.2)
216	Fullerton, CA	(41.6)	284	Thornton, CO	(50.7)	352	Visalia, CA	(62.8)
216	Oceanside, CA	(41.6)	285	Providence, RI	(50.8)	353	Gilbert, AZ	(62.9)
218	Philadelphia, PA	(41.8)	286	Indianapolis, IN	(50.9)	354	Everett, WA	(63.0)
218	Sacramento, CA	(41.8)	287	St. Joseph, MO	(51.1)	355	Dayton, OH	(63.3)
220	Corona, CA	(41.9)	288	Fort Worth, TX	(51.4)	356	Chandler, AZ	(63.6)
220	Worcester, MA	(41.9)	289	Chula Vista, CA	(52.1)	357	Phoenix, AZ	(63.7)
222	North Charleston, SC	(42.0)	290	Chino, CA	(52.3)	358	Syracuse, NY	(64.0)
223	Pompano Beach, FL	(42.3)	291	Tacoma, WA	(52.6)	359	Greeley, CO	(64.5)
223	Rialto, CA	(42.3)	292	Upper Darby Twnshp, PA	(53.1)	360	Colonie, NY	(64.9)
225	Fort Lauderdale, FL	(42.4)	292	Westminster, CO	(53.1)	361	Federal Way, WA	(65.1)
225	Fort Smith, AR	(42.4)	294	Fairfield, CA	(53.3)	362	North Las Vegas, NV	(66.6)
225	Topeka, KS	(42.4)	295	High Point, NC	(53.5)	363	Tempe, AZ	(66.9)
228	Palmdale, CA	(42.5)	295	Riverside, CA	(53.5)	364	Seattle, WA	(67.0)
229	Broken Arrow, OK	(43.1)	297	Tampa, FL	(53.6)	365	Boise, ID	(67.1)
229	Fort Wayne, IN	(43.1)	298	Waco, TX	(53.7)	366	Peoria, AZ	(67.4)
231	Huntington Beach, CA	(43.2)	299	Anaheim, CA	(53.8)	367	Port St. Lucie, FL	(68.7)
232	Reading, PA	(43.6)	299	Ontario, CA	(53.8)	368	Bellevue, WA	(70.1)
233	Kansas City, MO	(43.7)	301	Canton, OH	(54.1)	369	Mesa, AZ	(70.5)
234	New York, NY	(43.8)	301	Merced, CA	(54.1)	370	Hillsboro, OR	(71.0)
235	Alhambra, CA	(43.9)	303	Nashville, TN	(54.3)	371	St. George, UT	(73.4)
236	Pasadena, CA	(44.1)	303	Reno, NV	(54.3)	372	Scottsdale, AZ	(74.7)
237	Tulsa, OK	(44.2)	305	Minneapolis, MN	(54.6)	373	Bend, OR	(75.2)
238	Whittier, CA	(44.3)	306	Modesto, CA	(54.7)	NA	Ann Arbor, MI**	NA
239	Colorado Springs, CO	(44.4)	307	Cape Coral, FL	(54.9)	NA	Avondale, AZ**	NA
239	Mission Viejo, CA	(44.4)	307	Costa Mesa, CA	(54.9)	NA	Bloomington, MN**	NA
239	San Francisco, CA	(44.4)	307	Davenport, IA	(54.9)	NA	Canton Twnshp, MI**	NA
242	Green Bay, WI	(44.5)	307	Jersey City, NJ	(54.9)	NA	Citrus Heights, CA**	NA
243	Salem, OR	(44.6)	307	Temecula, CA	(54.9)	NA	Clarkstown, NY**	NA
244	Beaumont, TX	(44.9)	312	Lakewood, CO	(55.2)	NA	Clinton Twnshp, MI**	NA
244	San Angelo, TX	(44.9)	313	Rockford, IL	(55.4)	NA	Dearborn, MI**	NA
246	Honolulu, HI	(45.1)	314	Ventura, CA	(55.5)	NA	Decatur, IL**	NA
247	Newark, NJ	(45.3)	315	Rochester, NY	(55.6)	NA	Des Moines, IA**	NA
248	Hamilton Twnshp, NJ	(45.4)	316	Peoria, IL	(55.8)	NA	Detroit, MI**	NA
249	Jacksonville, FL	(45.9)	317	Boston, MA	(55.9)	NA	Duluth, MN**	NA
250	Fontana, CA	(46.1)	317	Boulder, CO	(55.9)	NA	Elgin, IL**	NA
250	Indio, CA	(46.1)	319	Toledo, OH	(56.2)	NA	Elk Grove, CA**	NA
250	Madison, WI	(46.1)	320	Tallahassee, FL	(56.5)	NA	Fall River, MA**	NA
253	Hartford, CT	(46.2)	321	Garden Grove, CA	(56.7)	NA	Farmington Hills, MI**	NA
253	Knoxville, TN	(46.2)	322	West Palm Beach, FL	(57.1)	NA	Flint, MI**	NA
253	McKinney, TX	(46.2)	323	Bellingham, WA	(57.3)	NA	Grand Rapids, MI**	NA
256	Portland, OR	(46.6)	324	Spokane Valley, WA	(57.4)	NA	Jacksonville, NC**	NA
257	Stockton, CA	(46.8)	325	Missouri City, TX	(57.5)	NA	Lansing, MI**	NA
258	Glendale, AZ	(46.9)	326	Richmond, VA	(57.6)	NA	Lexington, KY**	NA
259	Charleston, SC	(47.0)	326	Westminster, CA	(57.6)	NA	Little Rock, AR**	NA
260	Tucson, AZ	(47.2)	328	Racine, WI	(57.7)	NA	Livonia, MI**	NA
261	Chico, CA	(47.6)	329	Santa Ana, CA	(58.2)	NA	Longmont, CO**	NA
262	Brockton, MA	(47.7)	330	Las Vegas, NV	(58.4)	NA	Louisville, KY**	NA
263	Norman, OK	(48.0)	331	Surprise, AZ	(58.5)	NA	Nampa, ID**	NA
264	Springfield, MA	(48.1)	332	Charlotte, NC	(59.1)	NA	New Haven, CT**	NA
265	Omaha, NE	(48.2)	332	Irvine, CA	(59.1)	NA	New Orleans, LA**	NA
265	Orlando, FL	(48.2)	332	Murrieta, CA	(59.1)	NA	Olathe, KS**	NA
267	Simi Valley, CA	(48.3)	335	Kent, WA	(59.3)	NA	Sandy Springs, GA**	NA
268	Frisco, TX	(48.4)	335	Lancaster, CA	(59.3)	NA	Southfield, MI**	NA
268	Toms River Twnshp, NJ	(48.4)	335	Roseville, CA	(59.3)	NA	Sterling Heights, MI**	NA
270	Columbus, OH	(48.5)	338	Denver, CO	(59.4)	NA	Troy, MI**	NA
271	Memphis, TN	(48.6)	339	Redding, CA	(59.6)	NA	Vallejo, CA**	NA
272	San Diego, CA	(48.7)	340	Victorville, CA	(59.9)	NA	Warren, MI**	NA
273	Eugene, OR	(48.9)	341	Hesperia, CA	(60.0)	NA	West Jordan, UT**	NA
274	Gresham, OR	(49.5)	342	Warwick, RI	(60.1)	NA	Westland, MI**	NA
						NA	Wichita, KS**	NA

Source: CQ Press using reported data from the F.B.I. "Crime in the United States 2009"
*Motor vehicle theft includes the theft or attempted theft of a self-propelled vehicle. Excludes motorboats, construction equipment, airplanes, and farming equipment. **Not available.

81. Police Officers in 2009
National Total = 706,866 Officers*

RANK	CITY	OFFICERS
226	Abilene, TX	181
82	Akron, OH	460
252	Albany, GA	166
125	Albany, NY	327
38	Albuquerque, NM	1,087
130	Alexandria, VA	316
384	Alhambra, CA	83
199	Allentown, PA	203
359	Allen, TX	106
133	Amarillo, TX	308
281	Amherst, NY	152
98	Anaheim, CA	405
104	Anchorage, AK	383
326	Ann Arbor, MI	124
340	Antioch, CA	114
64	Arlington, TX	623
268	Arvada, CO	159
177	Athens-Clarke, GA	230
26	Atlanta, GA	1,506
63	Aurora, CO	627
135	Aurora, IL	300
24	Austin, TX	1,564
362	Avondale, AZ	102
121	Bakersfield, CA	339
387	Baldwin Park, CA	75
9	Baltimore, MD	3,013
NA	Baton Rouge, LA**	NA
154	Beaumont, TX	261
301	Beaverton, OR	134
237	Bellevue, WA	175
351	Bellingham, WA	110
380	Bend, OR	88
229	Berkeley, CA	180
292	Billings, MT	143
47	Birmingham, AL	854
344	Bloomington, MN	113
213	Boca Raton, FL	192
142	Boise, ID	288
15	Boston, MA	2,177
252	Boulder, CO	166
313	Brick Twnshp, NJ	127
97	Bridgeport, CT	409
229	Brockton, MA	180
328	Broken Arrow, OK	122
167	Brownsville, TX	244
376	Buena Park, CA	90
51	Buffalo, NY	796
265	Burbank, CA	160
150	Cambridge, MA	272
111	Camden, NJ	361
382	Canton Twnshp, MI	86
268	Canton, OH	159
173	Cape Coral, FL	236
354	Carlsbad, CA	109
262	Carrollton, TX	161
NA	Carson, CA**	NA
258	Cary, NC	163
201	Cedar Rapids, IA	202
340	Centennial, CO	114
124	Chandler, AZ	329
100	Charleston, SC	390
22	Charlotte, NC	1,635
89	Chattanooga, TN	432
313	Cheektowaga, NY	127
107	Chesapeake, VA	371
2	Chicago, IL	13,088
372	Chico, CA	95
369	Chino, CA	97
175	Chula Vista, CA	232
37	Cincinnati, OH	1,113
381	Citrus Heights, CA	87
248	Clarkstown, NY	169
170	Clarksville, TN	239
163	Clearwater, FL	248
21	Cleveland, OH	1,642
291	Clifton, NJ	144
358	Clinton Twnshp, MI	107
373	Clovis, CA	93
351	College Station, TX	110
356	Colonie, NY	108
61	Colorado Springs, CO	660
281	Columbia, MO	152
118	Columbia, SC	345
81	Columbus, GA	462
19	Columbus, OH	1,878
NA	Compton, CA**	NA
281	Concord, CA	152
216	Coral Springs, FL	190
240	Corona, CA	174
87	Corpus Christi, TX	446
265	Costa Mesa, CA	160
293	Cranston, RI	141
7	Dallas, TX	3,577
354	Daly City, CA	109
285	Danbury, CT	147
262	Davenport, IA	161
256	Davie, FL	164
99	Dayton, OH	398
212	Dearborn, MI	193
259	Decatur, IL	162
278	Denton, TX	154
25	Denver, CO	1,510
105	Des Moines, IA	373
10	Detroit, MI	2,930
332	Downey, CA	119
288	Duluth, MN	145
82	Durham, NC	460
214	Edison Twnshp, NJ	191
340	Edmond, OK	114
336	El Cajon, CA	117
313	El Monte, CA	127
36	El Paso, TX	1,117
229	Elgin, IL	180
123	Elizabeth, NJ	335
313	Elk Grove, CA	127
251	Erie, PA	168
274	Escondido, CA	158
214	Eugene, OR	191
148	Evansville, IN	275
203	Everett, WA	199
328	Fairfield, CA	122
196	Fall River, MA	204
303	Fargo, ND	133
337	Farmington Hills, MI	116
332	Fayetteville, AR	119
116	Fayetteville, NC	347
305	Federal Way, WA	132
221	Flint, MI	186
207	Fontana, CA	197
248	Fort Collins, CO	169
77	Fort Lauderdale, FL	489
259	Fort Smith, AR	162
84	Fort Wayne, IN	452
27	Fort Worth, TX	1,502
234	Fremont, CA	177
48	Fresno, CA	827
303	Frisco, TX	133
277	Fullerton, CA	156
139	Gainesville, FL	292
252	Garden Grove, CA	166
128	Garland, TX	319
176	Gary, IN	231
180	Gilbert, AZ	225
95	Glendale, AZ	419
157	Glendale, CA	258
189	Grand Prairie, TX	217
126	Grand Rapids, MI	325
385	Greece, NY	82
288	Greeley, CO	145
226	Green Bay, WI	181
68	Greensboro, NC	602
326	Gresham, OR	124
235	Hamilton Twnshp, NJ	176
193	Hammond, IN	206
147	Hampton, VA	277
86	Hartford, CT	448
367	Hawthorne, CA	99
222	Hayward, CA	185
112	Henderson, NV	360
NA	Hesperia, CA**	NA
120	Hialeah, FL	343
186	High Point, NC	219
319	Hillsboro, OR	126
130	Hollywood, FL	316
16	Honolulu, HI	2,105
5	Houston, TX	5,371
180	Huntington Beach, CA	225
95	Huntsville, AL	419
196	Independence, MO	204
23	Indianapolis, IN	1,619
388	Indio, CA	72
217	Inglewood, CA	189
210	Irvine, CA	195
119	Irving, TX	344
20	Jacksonville, FL	1,746
346	Jacksonville, NC	112
79	Jackson, MS	485
46	Jersey City, NJ	885
152	Joliet, IL	269
NA	Kansas City, KS**	NA
30	Kansas City, MO	1,392
203	Kenosha, WI	199
313	Kent, WA	127
191	Killeen, TX	213
102	Knoxville, TN	388
159	Lafayette, LA	253
NA	Lake Forest, CA**	NA
184	Lakeland, FL	221
NA	Lakewood, CA**	NA
148	Lakewood, CO	275
NA	Lancaster, CA**	NA
164	Lansing, MI	246
89	Laredo, TX	432
235	Las Cruces, NM	176
11	Las Vegas, NV	2,735
300	Lawrence, KS	137
259	Lawton, OK	162
307	Lee's Summit, MO	131
301	Lewisville, TX	134
70	Lexington, KY	552
128	Lincoln, NE	319
73	Little Rock, AR	531
376	Livermore, CA	90
284	Livonia, MI	148
43	Long Beach, CA	955
298	Longmont, CO	138

RANK	CITY	OFFICERS
245	Longview, TX	170
3	Los Angeles, CA	9,980
34	Louisville, KY	1,206
114	Lubbock, TX	354
241	Lynn, MA	173
136	Macon, GA	295
88	Madison, WI	443
191	Manchester, NH	213
154	McAllen, TX	261
268	McKinney, TX	159
252	Melbourne, FL	166
14	Memphis, TN	2,202
367	Merced, CA	99
50	Mesa, AZ	801
182	Mesquite, TX	224
110	Miami Beach, FL	365
207	Miami Gardens, FL	197
35	Miami, FL	1,124
245	Midland, TX	170
17	Milwaukee, WI	1,921
45	Minneapolis, MN	888
217	Miramar, FL	189
NA	Mission Viejo, CA**	NA
386	Missouri City, TX	76
71	Mobile, AL	543
166	Modesto, CA	245
76	Montgomery, AL	501
NA	Moreno Valley, CA**	NA
188	Murfreesboro, TN	218
376	Murrieta, CA	90
328	Nampa, ID	122
222	Naperville, IL	185
245	Nashua, NH	170
28	Nashville, TN	1,433
154	New Bedford, MA	261
93	New Haven, CT	423
NA	New Orleans, LA**	NA
1	New York, NY	35,071
33	Newark, NJ	1,297
295	Newport Beach, CA	139
298	Newton, MA	138
56	Norfolk, VA	755
268	Norman, OK	159
132	North Charleston, SC	313
133	North Las Vegas, NV	308
NA	Norwalk, CA**	NA
237	Norwalk, CT	175
52	Oakland, CA	793
193	Oceanside, CA	206
278	Odessa, TX	154
351	O'Fallon, MO	110
310	Ogden, UT	130
39	Oklahoma City, OK	1,048
NA	Olathe, KS**	NA
55	Omaha, NE	769
185	Ontario, CA	220
268	Orange, CA	159
376	Orem, UT	90
57	Orlando, FL	725
161	Overland Park, KS	251
174	Oxnard, CA	233
265	Palm Bay, FL	160
NA	Palmdale, CA**	NA
167	Pasadena, CA	244
151	Pasadena, TX	270
78	Paterson, NJ	488
319	Pearland, TX	126
178	Pembroke Pines, FL	229

RANK	CITY	OFFICERS
224	Peoria, AZ	184
172	Peoria, IL	238
4	Philadelphia, PA	6,722
8	Phoenix, AZ	3,279
44	Pittsburgh, PA	914
122	Plano, TX	337
237	Plantation, FL	175
233	Pomona, CA	178
NA	Pompano Beach, FL**	NA
170	Port St. Lucie, FL	239
42	Portland, OR	957
169	Portsmouth, VA	241
80	Providence, RI	471
366	Provo, UT	100
202	Pueblo, CO	200
220	Quincy, MA	187
203	Racine, WI	199
59	Raleigh, NC	704
332	Ramapo, NY	119
NA	Rancho Cucamon., CA**	NA
209	Reading, PA	196
346	Redding, CA	112
109	Reno, NV	369
348	Rialto, CA	111
285	Richardson, TX	147
232	Richmond, CA	179
58	Richmond, VA	724
323	Rio Rancho, NM	125
108	Riverside, CA	370
160	Roanoke, VA	252
323	Rochester, MN	125
54	Rochester, NY	773
143	Rockford, IL	284
328	Roseville, CA	122
295	Roswell, GA	139
293	Round Rock, TX	141
60	Sacramento, CA	700
193	Salem, OR	206
256	Salinas, CA	164
91	Salt Lake City, UT	427
274	San Angelo, TX	158
13	San Antonio, TX	2,259
127	San Bernardino, CA	324
18	San Diego, CA	1,894
12	San Francisco, CA	2,367
31	San Jose, CA	1,371
374	San Leandro, CA	92
NA	San Marcos, CA**	NA
340	San Mateo, CA	114
362	Sandy Springs, GA	102
339	Sandy, UT	115
115	Santa Ana, CA	353
307	Santa Barbara, CA	131
288	Santa Clara, CA	145
NA	Santa Clarita, CA**	NA
348	Santa Maria, CA	111
199	Santa Monica, CA	203
248	Santa Rosa, CA	169
69	Savannah, GA	599
92	Scottsdale, AZ	426
32	Seattle, WA	1,351
NA	Shreveport, LA**	NA
332	Simi Valley, CA	119
313	Sioux City, IA	127
186	Sioux Falls, SD	219
311	Somerville, MA	128
162	South Bend, IN	249
383	South Gate, CA	84

RANK	CITY	OFFICERS
285	Southfield, MI	147
356	Sparks, NV	108
365	Spokane Valley, WA	101
140	Spokane, WA	291
153	Springfield, IL	268
85	Springfield, MA	450
136	Springfield, MO	295
143	Stamford, CT	284
244	Sterling Heights, MI	171
103	Stockton, CA	384
362	St. George, UT	102
337	St. Joseph, MO	116
29	St. Louis, MO	1,408
66	St. Paul, MN	614
72	St. Petersburg, FL	540
226	Suffolk, VA	181
295	Sugar Land, TX	139
190	Sunnyvale, CA	215
241	Sunrise, FL	173
319	Surprise, AZ	126
75	Syracuse, NY	505
101	Tacoma, WA	389
116	Tallahassee, FL	347
41	Tampa, FL	964
NA	Temecula, CA**	NA
113	Tempe, AZ	356
276	Thornton, CO	157
NA	Thousand Oaks, CA**	NA
67	Toledo, OH	604
268	Toms River Twnshp, NJ	159
145	Topeka, KS	283
179	Torrance, CA	226
375	Tracy, CA	91
106	Trenton, NJ	372
311	Troy, MI	128
40	Tucson, AZ	1,012
49	Tulsa, OK	812
146	Tuscaloosa, AL	279
225	Tyler, TX	183
319	Upper Darby Twnshp, PA	126
359	Vacaville, CA	106
348	Vallejo, CA	111
203	Vancouver, WA	199
307	Ventura, CA	131
NA	Victorville, CA**	NA
53	Virginia Beach, VA	780
305	Visalia, CA	132
NA	Vista, CA**	NA
164	Waco, TX	246
182	Warren, MI	224
262	Warwick, RI	161
6	Washington, DC	4,052
140	Waterbury, CT	291
344	West Covina, CA	113
361	West Jordan, UT	103
138	West Palm Beach, FL	294
219	West Valley, UT	188
370	Westland, MI	96
370	Westminster, CA	96
241	Westminster, CO	173
323	Whittier, CA	125
211	Wichita Falls, TX	194
62	Wichita, KS	643
158	Wilmington, NC	255
74	Winston-Salem, NC	519
196	Woodbridge Twnshp, NJ	204
93	Worcester, MA	423
65	Yonkers, NY	615
280	Yuma, AZ	153

Source: Reported data from the F.B.I. "Crime in the United States 2009"

*Sworn officers only, does not include civilian employees.

**Not available

81. Police Officers in 2009 (continued)
National Total = 706,866 Officers*

RANK	CITY	OFFICERS
1	New York, NY	35,071
2	Chicago, IL	13,088
3	Los Angeles, CA	9,980
4	Philadelphia, PA	6,722
5	Houston, TX	5,371
6	Washington, DC	4,052
7	Dallas, TX	3,577
8	Phoenix, AZ	3,279
9	Baltimore, MD	3,013
10	Detroit, MI	2,930
11	Las Vegas, NV	2,735
12	San Francisco, CA	2,367
13	San Antonio, TX	2,259
14	Memphis, TN	2,202
15	Boston, MA	2,177
16	Honolulu, HI	2,105
17	Milwaukee, WI	1,921
18	San Diego, CA	1,894
19	Columbus, OH	1,878
20	Jacksonville, FL	1,746
21	Cleveland, OH	1,642
22	Charlotte, NC	1,635
23	Indianapolis, IN	1,619
24	Austin, TX	1,564
25	Denver, CO	1,510
26	Atlanta, GA	1,506
27	Fort Worth, TX	1,502
28	Nashville, TN	1,433
29	St. Louis, MO	1,408
30	Kansas City, MO	1,392
31	San Jose, CA	1,371
32	Seattle, WA	1,351
33	Newark, NJ	1,297
34	Louisville, KY	1,206
35	Miami, FL	1,124
36	El Paso, TX	1,117
37	Cincinnati, OH	1,113
38	Albuquerque, NM	1,087
39	Oklahoma City, OK	1,048
40	Tucson, AZ	1,012
41	Tampa, FL	964
42	Portland, OR	957
43	Long Beach, CA	955
44	Pittsburgh, PA	914
45	Minneapolis, MN	888
46	Jersey City, NJ	885
47	Birmingham, AL	854
48	Fresno, CA	827
49	Tulsa, OK	812
50	Mesa, AZ	801
51	Buffalo, NY	796
52	Oakland, CA	793
53	Virginia Beach, VA	780
54	Rochester, NY	773
55	Omaha, NE	769
56	Norfolk, VA	755
57	Orlando, FL	725
58	Richmond, VA	724
59	Raleigh, NC	704
60	Sacramento, CA	700
61	Colorado Springs, CO	660
62	Wichita, KS	643
63	Aurora, CO	627
64	Arlington, TX	623
65	Yonkers, NY	615
66	St. Paul, MN	614
67	Toledo, OH	604
68	Greensboro, NC	602
69	Savannah, GA	599
70	Lexington, KY	552
71	Mobile, AL	543
72	St. Petersburg, FL	540
73	Little Rock, AR	531
74	Winston-Salem, NC	519
75	Syracuse, NY	505
76	Montgomery, AL	501
77	Fort Lauderdale, FL	489
78	Paterson, NJ	488
79	Jackson, MS	485
80	Providence, RI	471
81	Columbus, GA	462
82	Akron, OH	460
82	Durham, NC	460
84	Fort Wayne, IN	452
85	Springfield, MA	450
86	Hartford, CT	448
87	Corpus Christi, TX	446
88	Madison, WI	443
89	Chattanooga, TN	432
89	Laredo, TX	432
91	Salt Lake City, UT	427
92	Scottsdale, AZ	426
93	New Haven, CT	423
93	Worcester, MA	423
95	Glendale, AZ	419
95	Huntsville, AL	419
97	Bridgeport, CT	409
98	Anaheim, CA	405
99	Dayton, OH	398
100	Charleston, SC	390
101	Tacoma, WA	389
102	Knoxville, TN	388
103	Stockton, CA	384
104	Anchorage, AK	383
105	Des Moines, IA	373
106	Trenton, NJ	372
107	Chesapeake, VA	371
108	Riverside, CA	370
109	Reno, NV	369
110	Miami Beach, FL	365
111	Camden, NJ	361
112	Henderson, NV	360
113	Tempe, AZ	356
114	Lubbock, TX	354
115	Santa Ana, CA	353
116	Fayetteville, NC	347
116	Tallahassee, FL	347
118	Columbia, SC	345
119	Irving, TX	344
120	Hialeah, FL	343
121	Bakersfield, CA	339
122	Plano, TX	337
123	Elizabeth, NJ	335
124	Chandler, AZ	329
125	Albany, NY	327
126	Grand Rapids, MI	325
127	San Bernardino, CA	324
128	Garland, TX	319
128	Lincoln, NE	319
130	Alexandria, VA	316
130	Hollywood, FL	316
132	North Charleston, SC	313
133	Amarillo, TX	308
133	North Las Vegas, NV	308
135	Aurora, IL	300
136	Macon, GA	295
136	Springfield, MO	295
138	West Palm Beach, FL	294
139	Gainesville, FL	292
140	Spokane, WA	291
140	Waterbury, CT	291
142	Boise, ID	288
143	Rockford, IL	284
143	Stamford, CT	284
145	Topeka, KS	283
146	Tuscaloosa, AL	279
147	Hampton, VA	277
148	Evansville, IN	275
148	Lakewood, CO	275
150	Cambridge, MA	272
151	Pasadena, TX	270
152	Joliet, IL	269
153	Springfield, IL	268
154	Beaumont, TX	261
154	McAllen, TX	261
154	New Bedford, MA	261
157	Glendale, CA	258
158	Wilmington, NC	255
159	Lafayette, LA	253
160	Roanoke, VA	252
161	Overland Park, KS	251
162	South Bend, IN	249
163	Clearwater, FL	248
164	Lansing, MI	246
164	Waco, TX	246
166	Modesto, CA	245
167	Brownsville, TX	244
167	Pasadena, CA	244
169	Portsmouth, VA	241
170	Clarksville, TN	239
170	Port St. Lucie, FL	239
172	Peoria, IL	238
173	Cape Coral, FL	236
174	Oxnard, CA	233
175	Chula Vista, CA	232
176	Gary, IN	231
177	Athens-Clarke, GA	230
178	Pembroke Pines, FL	229
179	Torrance, CA	226
180	Gilbert, AZ	225
180	Huntington Beach, CA	225
182	Mesquite, TX	224
182	Warren, MI	224
184	Lakeland, FL	221
185	Ontario, CA	220
186	High Point, NC	219
186	Sioux Falls, SD	219
188	Murfreesboro, TN	218
189	Grand Prairie, TX	217
190	Sunnyvale, CA	215
191	Killeen, TX	213
191	Manchester, NH	213
193	Hammond, IN	206
193	Oceanside, CA	206
193	Salem, OR	206
196	Fall River, MA	204
196	Independence, MO	204
196	Woodbridge Twnshp, NJ	204
199	Allentown, PA	203
199	Santa Monica, CA	203
201	Cedar Rapids, IA	202
202	Pueblo, CO	200
203	Everett, WA	199
203	Kenosha, WI	199
203	Racine, WI	199
203	Vancouver, WA	199

RANK	CITY	OFFICERS
207	Fontana, CA	197
207	Miami Gardens, FL	197
209	Reading, PA	196
210	Irvine, CA	195
211	Wichita Falls, TX	194
212	Dearborn, MI	193
213	Boca Raton, FL	192
214	Edison Twnshp, NJ	191
214	Eugene, OR	191
216	Coral Springs, FL	190
217	Inglewood, CA	189
217	Miramar, FL	189
219	West Valley, UT	188
220	Quincy, MA	187
221	Flint, MI	186
222	Hayward, CA	185
222	Naperville, IL	185
224	Peoria, AZ	184
225	Tyler, TX	183
226	Abilene, TX	181
226	Green Bay, WI	181
226	Suffolk, VA	181
229	Berkeley, CA	180
229	Brockton, MA	180
229	Elgin, IL	180
232	Richmond, CA	179
233	Pomona, CA	178
234	Fremont, CA	177
235	Hamilton Twnshp, NJ	176
235	Las Cruces, NM	176
237	Bellevue, WA	175
237	Norwalk, CT	175
237	Plantation, FL	175
240	Corona, CA	174
241	Lynn, MA	173
241	Sunrise, FL	173
241	Westminster, CO	173
244	Sterling Heights, MI	171
245	Longview, TX	170
245	Midland, TX	170
245	Nashua, NH	170
248	Clarkstown, NY	169
248	Fort Collins, CO	169
248	Santa Rosa, CA	169
251	Erie, PA	168
252	Albany, GA	166
252	Boulder, CO	166
252	Garden Grove, CA	166
252	Melbourne, FL	166
256	Davie, FL	164
256	Salinas, CA	164
258	Cary, NC	163
259	Decatur, IL	162
259	Fort Smith, AR	162
259	Lawton, OK	162
262	Carrollton, TX	161
262	Davenport, IA	161
262	Warwick, RI	161
265	Burbank, CA	160
265	Costa Mesa, CA	160
265	Palm Bay, FL	160
268	Arvada, CO	159
268	Canton, OH	159
268	McKinney, TX	159
268	Norman, OK	159
268	Orange, CA	159
268	Toms River Twnshp, NJ	159
274	Escondido, CA	158

RANK	CITY	OFFICERS
274	San Angelo, TX	158
276	Thornton, CO	157
277	Fullerton, CA	156
278	Denton, TX	154
278	Odessa, TX	154
280	Yuma, AZ	153
281	Amherst, NY	152
281	Columbia, MO	152
281	Concord, CA	152
284	Livonia, MI	148
285	Danbury, CT	147
285	Richardson, TX	147
285	Southfield, MI	147
288	Duluth, MN	145
288	Greeley, CO	145
288	Santa Clara, CA	145
291	Clifton, NJ	144
292	Billings, MT	143
293	Cranston, RI	141
293	Round Rock, TX	141
295	Newport Beach, CA	139
295	Roswell, GA	139
295	Sugar Land, TX	139
298	Longmont, CO	138
298	Newton, MA	138
300	Lawrence, KS	137
301	Beaverton, OR	134
301	Lewisville, TX	134
303	Fargo, ND	133
303	Frisco, TX	133
305	Federal Way, WA	132
305	Visalia, CA	132
307	Lee's Summit, MO	131
307	Santa Barbara, CA	131
307	Ventura, CA	131
310	Ogden, UT	130
311	Somerville, MA	128
311	Troy, MI	128
313	Brick Twnshp, NJ	127
313	Cheektowaga, NY	127
313	El Monte, CA	127
313	Elk Grove, CA	127
313	Kent, WA	127
313	Sioux City, IA	127
319	Hillsboro, OR	126
319	Pearland, TX	126
319	Surprise, AZ	126
319	Upper Darby Twnshp, PA	126
323	Rio Rancho, NM	125
323	Rochester, MN	125
323	Whittier, CA	125
326	Ann Arbor, MI	124
326	Gresham, OR	124
328	Broken Arrow, OK	122
328	Fairfield, CA	122
328	Nampa, ID	122
328	Roseville, CA	122
332	Downey, CA	119
332	Fayetteville, AR	119
332	Ramapo, NY	119
332	Simi Valley, CA	119
336	El Cajon, CA	117
337	Farmington Hills, MI	116
337	St. Joseph, MO	116
339	Sandy, UT	115
340	Antioch, CA	114
340	Centennial, CO	114
340	Edmond, OK	114

RANK	CITY	OFFICERS
340	San Mateo, CA	114
344	Bloomington, MN	113
344	West Covina, CA	113
346	Jacksonville, NC	112
346	Redding, CA	112
348	Rialto, CA	111
348	Santa Maria, CA	111
348	Vallejo, CA	111
351	Bellingham, WA	110
351	College Station, TX	110
351	O'Fallon, MO	110
354	Carlsbad, CA	109
354	Daly City, CA	109
356	Colonie, NY	108
356	Sparks, NV	108
358	Clinton Twnshp, MI	107
359	Allen, TX	106
359	Vacaville, CA	106
361	West Jordan, UT	103
362	Avondale, AZ	102
362	Sandy Springs, GA	102
362	St. George, UT	102
365	Spokane Valley, WA	101
366	Provo, UT	100
367	Hawthorne, CA	99
367	Merced, CA	99
369	Chino, CA	97
370	Westland, MI	96
370	Westminster, CA	96
372	Chico, CA	95
373	Clovis, CA	93
374	San Leandro, CA	92
375	Tracy, CA	91
376	Buena Park, CA	90
376	Livermore, CA	90
376	Murrieta, CA	90
376	Orem, UT	90
380	Bend, OR	88
381	Citrus Heights, CA	87
382	Canton Twnshp, MI	86
383	South Gate, CA	84
384	Alhambra, CA	83
385	Greece, NY	82
386	Missouri City, TX	76
387	Baldwin Park, CA	75
388	Indio, CA	72
NA	Baton Rouge, LA**	NA
NA	Carson, CA**	NA
NA	Compton, CA**	NA
NA	Hesperia, CA**	NA
NA	Kansas City, KS**	NA
NA	Lake Forest, CA**	NA
NA	Lakewood, CA**	NA
NA	Lancaster, CA**	NA
NA	Mission Viejo, CA**	NA
NA	Moreno Valley, CA**	NA
NA	New Orleans, LA**	NA
NA	Norwalk, CA**	NA
NA	Olathe, KS**	NA
NA	Palmdale, CA**	NA
NA	Pompano Beach, FL**	NA
NA	Rancho Cucamon., CA**	NA
NA	San Marcos, CA**	NA
NA	Santa Clarita, CA**	NA
NA	Shreveport, LA**	NA
NA	Temecula, CA**	NA
NA	Thousand Oaks, CA**	NA
NA	Victorville, CA**	NA
NA	Vista, CA**	NA

Source: Reported data from the F.B.I. "Crime in the United States 2009"

*Sworn officers only, does not include civilian employees.

**Not available

82. Rate of Police Officers in 2009
National Rate = 244 Officers per 100,000 Population*

RANK	CITY	RATE
235	Abilene, TX	155
89	Akron, OH	223
96	Albany, GA	219
18	Albany, NY	350
118	Albuquerque, NM	205
100	Alexandria, VA	216
375	Alhambra, CA	97
154	Allentown, PA	189
319	Allen, TX	122
213	Amarillo, TX	163
274	Amherst, NY	138
322	Anaheim, CA	121
282	Anchorage, AK	135
357	Ann Arbor, MI	108
346	Antioch, CA	113
207	Arlington, TX	164
254	Arvada, CO	147
125	Athens-Clarke, GA	201
47	Atlanta, GA	272
141	Aurora, CO	194
187	Aurora, IL	171
122	Austin, TX	203
339	Avondale, AZ	115
370	Bakersfield, CA	102
376	Baldwin Park, CA	97
2	Baltimore, MD	472
NA	Baton Rouge, LA**	NA
73	Beaumont, TX	237
262	Beaverton, OR	144
271	Bellevue, WA	140
277	Bellingham, WA	137
356	Bend, OR	109
174	Berkeley, CA	178
280	Billings, MT	136
12	Birmingham, AL	376
271	Bloomington, MN	140
89	Boca Raton, FL	223
271	Boise, ID	140
19	Boston, MA	349
204	Boulder, CO	166
219	Brick Twnshp, NJ	161
33	Bridgeport, CT	301
158	Brockton, MA	187
294	Broken Arrow, OK	129
280	Brownsville, TX	136
346	Buena Park, CA	113
34	Buffalo, NY	296
235	Burbank, CA	155
55	Cambridge, MA	264
5	Camden, NJ	457
363	Canton Twnshp, MI	104
120	Canton, OH	204
262	Cape Coral, FL	144
352	Carlsbad, CA	111
303	Carrollton, TX	126
NA	Carson, CA**	NA
319	Cary, NC	122
229	Cedar Rapids, IA	157
339	Centennial, CO	115
295	Chandler, AZ	128
20	Charleston, SC	343
108	Charlotte, NC	210
60	Chattanooga, TN	250
213	Cheektowaga, NY	163
204	Chesapeake, VA	166
4	Chicago, IL	459
348	Chico, CA	112
339	Chino, CA	115
368	Chula Vista, CA	103
23	Cincinnati, OH	334
368	Citrus Heights, CA	103
102	Clarkstown, NY	214
134	Clarksville, TN	196
77	Clearwater, FL	235
11	Cleveland, OH	383
162	Clifton, NJ	184
348	Clinton Twnshp, MI	112
372	Clovis, CA	98
295	College Station, TX	128
274	Colonie, NY	138
207	Colorado Springs, CO	164
252	Columbia, MO	148
51	Columbia, SC	270
62	Columbus, GA	248
63	Columbus, OH	247
NA	Compton, CA**	NA
303	Concord, CA	126
246	Coral Springs, FL	151
344	Corona, CA	114
235	Corpus Christi, TX	155
258	Costa Mesa, CA	145
178	Cranston, RI	176
45	Dallas, TX	277
357	Daly City, CA	108
162	Danbury, CT	184
224	Davenport, IA	159
166	Davie, FL	182
56	Dayton, OH	260
86	Dearborn, MI	226
102	Decatur, IL	214
309	Denton, TX	124
60	Denver, CO	250
148	Des Moines, IA	190
26	Detroit, MI	323
352	Downey, CA	111
185	Duluth, MN	172
123	Durham, NC	202
144	Edison Twnshp, NJ	192
270	Edmond, OK	141
300	El Cajon, CA	127
363	El Monte, CA	104
167	El Paso, TX	181
199	Elgin, IL	167
52	Elizabeth, NJ	268
381	Elk Grove, CA	90
217	Erie, PA	162
339	Escondido, CA	115
303	Eugene, OR	126
70	Evansville, IN	238
123	Everett, WA	202
333	Fairfield, CA	117
92	Fall River, MA	222
268	Fargo, ND	142
252	Farmington Hills, MI	148
226	Fayetteville, AR	158
127	Fayetteville, NC	199
229	Federal Way, WA	157
199	Flint, MI	167
363	Fontana, CA	104
319	Fort Collins, CO	122
54	Fort Lauderdale, FL	267
148	Fort Smith, AR	190
168	Fort Wayne, IN	180
112	Fort Worth, TX	208
384	Fremont, CA	87
185	Fresno, CA	172
314	Frisco, TX	123
330	Fullerton, CA	118
58	Gainesville, FL	253
371	Garden Grove, CA	100
256	Garland, TX	146
66	Gary, IN	243
377	Gilbert, AZ	97
207	Glendale, AZ	164
289	Glendale, CA	131
287	Grand Prairie, TX	132
194	Grand Rapids, MI	168
383	Greece, NY	88
234	Greeley, CO	156
171	Green Bay, WI	179
70	Greensboro, NC	238
322	Gresham, OR	121
141	Hamilton Twnshp, NJ	194
49	Hammond, IN	271
148	Hampton, VA	190
16	Hartford, CT	361
333	Hawthorne, CA	117
292	Hayward, CA	130
277	Henderson, NV	137
NA	Hesperia, CA**	NA
207	Hialeah, FL	164
106	High Point, NC	211
292	Hillsboro, OR	130
89	Hollywood, FL	223
81	Honolulu, HI	232
75	Houston, TX	236
333	Huntington Beach, CA	117
77	Huntsville, AL	235
199	Independence, MO	167
127	Indianapolis, IN	199
388	Indio, CA	80
194	Inglewood, CA	168
382	Irvine, CA	90
190	Irving, TX	170
100	Jacksonville, FL	216
258	Jacksonville, NC	145
42	Jackson, MS	281
15	Jersey City, NJ	367
174	Joliet, IL	178
NA	Kansas City, KS**	NA
39	Kansas City, MO	287
120	Kenosha, WI	204
246	Kent, WA	151
177	Killeen, TX	177
110	Knoxville, TN	209
92	Lafayette, LA	222
NA	Lake Forest, CA**	NA
80	Lakeland, FL	234
NA	Lakewood, CA**	NA
134	Lakewood, CO	196
NA	Lancaster, CA**	NA
99	Lansing, MI	217
148	Laredo, TX	190
158	Las Cruces, NM	187
127	Las Vegas, NV	199
250	Lawrence, KS	149
168	Lawton, OK	180
242	Lee's Summit, MO	153
295	Lewisville, TX	128
160	Lexington, KY	186
308	Lincoln, NE	125
43	Little Rock, AR	279
352	Livermore, CA	111
207	Livonia, MI	164
116	Long Beach, CA	206
226	Longmont, CO	158

RANK	CITY	RATE
96	Longview, TX	219
57	Los Angeles, CA	259
146	Louisville, KY	191
224	Lubbock, TX	159
148	Lynn, MA	190
28	Macon, GA	320
154	Madison, WI	189
134	Manchester, NH	196
131	McAllen, TX	197
325	McKinney, TX	120
104	Melbourne, FL	213
24	Memphis, TN	330
303	Merced, CA	126
190	Mesa, AZ	170
194	Mesquite, TX	168
8	Miami Beach, FL	433
171	Miami Gardens, FL	179
52	Miami, FL	268
226	Midland, TX	158
29	Milwaukee, WI	318
81	Minneapolis, MN	232
181	Miramar, FL	174
NA	Mission Viejo, CA**	NA
373	Missouri City, TX	98
94	Mobile, AL	221
325	Modesto, CA	120
63	Montgomery, AL	247
NA	Moreno Valley, CA**	NA
116	Murfreesboro, TN	206
386	Murrieta, CA	86
258	Nampa, ID	145
295	Naperville, IL	128
134	Nashua, NH	196
77	Nashville, TN	235
40	New Bedford, MA	282
21	New Haven, CT	342
NA	New Orleans, LA**	NA
9	New York, NY	417
3	Newark, NJ	465
181	Newport Beach, CA	174
213	Newton, MA	163
27	Norfolk, VA	321
254	Norman, OK	147
25	North Charleston, SC	326
287	North Las Vegas, NV	132
NA	Norwalk, CA**	NA
108	Norwalk, CT	210
134	Oakland, CA	196
322	Oceanside, CA	121
240	Odessa, TX	154
277	O'Fallon, MO	137
229	Ogden, UT	157
156	Oklahoma City, OK	188
NA	Olathe, KS**	NA
181	Omaha, NE	174
300	Ontario, CA	127
336	Orange, CA	116
379	Orem, UT	96
30	Orlando, FL	308
258	Overland Park, KS	145
309	Oxnard, CA	124
235	Palm Bay, FL	155
NA	Palmdale, CA**	NA
193	Pasadena, CA	169
162	Pasadena, TX	184
22	Paterson, NJ	337
268	Pearland, TX	142
229	Pembroke Pines, FL	157

RANK	CITY	RATE
348	Peoria, AZ	112
112	Peoria, IL	208
7	Philadelphia, PA	434
118	Phoenix, AZ	205
35	Pittsburgh, PA	293
309	Plano, TX	124
110	Plantation, FL	209
336	Pomona, CA	116
NA	Pompano Beach, FL**	NA
256	Port St. Lucie, FL	146
187	Portland, OR	171
69	Portsmouth, VA	239
46	Providence, RI	274
387	Provo, UT	84
148	Pueblo, CO	190
141	Quincy, MA	194
67	Racine, WI	242
184	Raleigh, NC	173
235	Ramapo, NY	155
NA	Rancho Cucamon., CA**	NA
65	Reading, PA	244
314	Redding, CA	123
199	Reno, NV	167
348	Rialto, CA	112
266	Richardson, TX	143
179	Richmond, CA	175
17	Richmond, VA	356
249	Rio Rancho, NM	150
314	Riverside, CA	123
49	Roanoke, VA	271
314	Rochester, MN	123
12	Rochester, NY	376
168	Rockford, IL	180
363	Roseville, CA	104
229	Roswell, GA	157
295	Round Rock, TX	128
250	Sacramento, CA	149
286	Salem, OR	133
344	Salinas, CA	114
75	Salt Lake City, UT	236
187	San Angelo, TX	171
207	San Antonio, TX	164
217	San Bernardino, CA	162
262	San Diego, CA	144
37	San Francisco, CA	292
262	San Jose, CA	144
330	San Leandro, CA	118
NA	San Marcos, CA**	NA
309	San Mateo, CA	124
309	Sandy Springs, GA	124
329	Sandy, UT	119
363	Santa Ana, CA	104
242	Santa Barbara, CA	153
289	Santa Clara, CA	131
NA	Santa Clarita, CA**	NA
300	Santa Maria, CA	127
83	Santa Monica, CA	231
357	Santa Rosa, CA	108
40	Savannah, GA	282
174	Scottsdale, AZ	178
88	Seattle, WA	224
NA	Shreveport, LA**	NA
374	Simi Valley, CA	98
240	Sioux City, IA	154
274	Sioux Falls, SD	138
190	Somerville, MA	170
68	South Bend, IN	241
385	South Gate, CA	87

RANK	CITY	RATE
134	Southfield, MI	196
330	Sparks, NV	118
336	Spokane Valley, WA	116
266	Spokane, WA	143
85	Springfield, IL	227
35	Springfield, MA	293
156	Springfield, MO	188
70	Stamford, CT	238
284	Sterling Heights, MI	134
289	Stockton, CA	131
282	St. George, UT	135
244	St. Joseph, MO	152
10	St. Louis, MO	396
96	St. Paul, MN	219
95	St. Petersburg, FL	220
104	Suffolk, VA	213
194	Sugar Land, TX	168
213	Sunnyvale, CA	163
140	Sunrise, FL	195
325	Surprise, AZ	120
14	Syracuse, NY	368
131	Tacoma, WA	197
127	Tallahassee, FL	199
43	Tampa, FL	279
NA	Temecula, CA**	NA
125	Tempe, AZ	201
284	Thornton, CO	134
NA	Thousand Oaks, CA**	NA
112	Toledo, OH	208
206	Toms River Twnshp, NJ	165
84	Topeka, KS	229
222	Torrance, CA	160
352	Tracy, CA	111
6	Trenton, NJ	450
222	Troy, MI	160
161	Tucson, AZ	185
106	Tulsa, OK	211
31	Tuscaloosa, AL	304
162	Tyler, TX	184
219	Upper Darby Twnshp, PA	161
339	Vacaville, CA	115
378	Vallejo, CA	97
325	Vancouver, WA	120
303	Ventura, CA	126
NA	Victorville, CA**	NA
171	Virginia Beach, VA	179
362	Visalia, CA	106
NA	Vista, CA**	NA
131	Waco, TX	197
194	Warren, MI	168
146	Warwick, RI	191
1	Washington, DC	676
47	Waterbury, CT	272
361	West Covina, CA	107
380	West Jordan, UT	96
37	West Palm Beach, FL	292
246	West Valley, UT	151
314	Westland, MI	123
357	Westminster, CA	108
219	Westminster, CO	161
244	Whittier, CA	152
144	Wichita Falls, TX	192
179	Wichita, KS	175
59	Wilmington, NC	251
87	Winston-Salem, NC	225
112	Woodbridge Twnshp, NJ	208
73	Worcester, MA	237
31	Yonkers, NY	304
199	Yuma, AZ	167

Source: CQ Press using reported data from the F.B.I. "Crime in the United States 2009"
*Sworn officers only, does not include civilian employees.
**Not available

82. Rate of Police Officers in 2009 (continued)
National Rate = 244 Officers per 100,000 Population*

RANK	CITY	RATE
1	Washington, DC	676
2	Baltimore, MD	472
3	Newark, NJ	465
4	Chicago, IL	459
5	Camden, NJ	457
6	Trenton, NJ	450
7	Philadelphia, PA	434
8	Miami Beach, FL	433
9	New York, NY	417
10	St. Louis, MO	396
11	Cleveland, OH	383
12	Birmingham, AL	376
12	Rochester, NY	376
14	Syracuse, NY	368
15	Jersey City, NJ	367
16	Hartford, CT	361
17	Richmond, VA	356
18	Albany, NY	350
19	Boston, MA	349
20	Charleston, SC	343
21	New Haven, CT	342
22	Paterson, NJ	337
23	Cincinnati, OH	334
24	Memphis, TN	330
25	North Charleston, SC	326
26	Detroit, MI	323
27	Norfolk, VA	321
28	Macon, GA	320
29	Milwaukee, WI	318
30	Orlando, FL	308
31	Tuscaloosa, AL	304
31	Yonkers, NY	304
33	Bridgeport, CT	301
34	Buffalo, NY	296
35	Pittsburgh, PA	293
35	Springfield, MA	293
37	San Francisco, CA	292
37	West Palm Beach, FL	292
39	Kansas City, MO	287
40	New Bedford, MA	282
40	Savannah, GA	282
42	Jackson, MS	281
43	Little Rock, AR	279
43	Tampa, FL	279
45	Dallas, TX	277
46	Providence, RI	274
47	Atlanta, GA	272
47	Waterbury, CT	272
49	Hammond, IN	271
49	Roanoke, VA	271
51	Columbia, SC	270
52	Elizabeth, NJ	268
52	Miami, FL	268
54	Fort Lauderdale, FL	267
55	Cambridge, MA	264
56	Dayton, OH	260
57	Los Angeles, CA	259
58	Gainesville, FL	253
59	Wilmington, NC	251
60	Chattanooga, TN	250
60	Denver, CO	250
62	Columbus, GA	248
63	Columbus, OH	247
63	Montgomery, AL	247
65	Reading, PA	244
66	Gary, IN	243
67	Racine, WI	242
68	South Bend, IN	241
69	Portsmouth, VA	239
70	Evansville, IN	238
70	Greensboro, NC	238
70	Stamford, CT	238
73	Beaumont, TX	237
73	Worcester, MA	237
75	Houston, TX	236
75	Salt Lake City, UT	236
77	Clearwater, FL	235
77	Huntsville, AL	235
77	Nashville, TN	235
80	Lakeland, FL	234
81	Honolulu, HI	232
81	Minneapolis, MN	232
83	Santa Monica, CA	231
84	Topeka, KS	229
85	Springfield, IL	227
86	Dearborn, MI	226
87	Winston-Salem, NC	225
88	Seattle, WA	224
89	Akron, OH	223
89	Boca Raton, FL	223
89	Hollywood, FL	223
92	Fall River, MA	222
92	Lafayette, LA	222
94	Mobile, AL	221
95	St. Petersburg, FL	220
96	Albany, GA	219
96	Longview, TX	219
96	St. Paul, MN	219
99	Lansing, MI	217
100	Alexandria, VA	216
100	Jacksonville, FL	216
102	Clarkstown, NY	214
102	Decatur, IL	214
104	Melbourne, FL	213
104	Suffolk, VA	213
106	High Point, NC	211
106	Tulsa, OK	211
108	Charlotte, NC	210
108	Norwalk, CT	210
110	Knoxville, TN	209
110	Plantation, FL	209
112	Fort Worth, TX	208
112	Peoria, IL	208
112	Toledo, OH	208
112	Woodbridge Twnshp, NJ	208
116	Long Beach, CA	206
116	Murfreesboro, TN	206
118	Albuquerque, NM	205
118	Phoenix, AZ	205
120	Canton, OH	204
120	Kenosha, WI	204
122	Austin, TX	203
123	Durham, NC	202
123	Everett, WA	202
125	Athens-Clarke, GA	201
125	Tempe, AZ	201
127	Fayetteville, NC	199
127	Indianapolis, IN	199
127	Las Vegas, NV	199
127	Tallahassee, FL	199
131	McAllen, TX	197
131	Tacoma, WA	197
131	Waco, TX	197
134	Clarksville, TN	196
134	Lakewood, CO	196
134	Manchester, NH	196
134	Nashua, NH	196
134	Oakland, CA	196
134	Southfield, MI	196
140	Sunrise, FL	195
141	Aurora, CO	194
141	Hamilton Twnshp, NJ	194
141	Quincy, MA	194
144	Edison Twnshp, NJ	192
144	Wichita Falls, TX	192
146	Louisville, KY	191
146	Warwick, RI	191
148	Des Moines, IA	190
148	Fort Smith, AR	190
148	Hampton, VA	190
148	Laredo, TX	190
148	Lynn, MA	190
148	Pueblo, CO	190
154	Allentown, PA	189
154	Madison, WI	189
156	Oklahoma City, OK	188
156	Springfield, MO	188
158	Brockton, MA	187
158	Las Cruces, NM	187
160	Lexington, KY	186
161	Tucson, AZ	185
162	Clifton, NJ	184
162	Danbury, CT	184
162	Pasadena, TX	184
162	Tyler, TX	184
166	Davie, FL	182
167	El Paso, TX	181
168	Fort Wayne, IN	180
168	Lawton, OK	180
168	Rockford, IL	180
171	Green Bay, WI	179
171	Miami Gardens, FL	179
171	Virginia Beach, VA	179
174	Berkeley, CA	178
174	Joliet, IL	178
174	Scottsdale, AZ	178
177	Killeen, TX	177
178	Cranston, RI	176
179	Richmond, CA	175
179	Wichita, KS	175
181	Miramar, FL	174
181	Newport Beach, CA	174
181	Omaha, NE	174
184	Raleigh, NC	173
185	Duluth, MN	172
185	Fresno, CA	172
187	Aurora, IL	171
187	Portland, OR	171
187	San Angelo, TX	171
190	Irving, TX	170
190	Mesa, AZ	170
190	Somerville, MA	170
193	Pasadena, CA	169
194	Grand Rapids, MI	168
194	Inglewood, CA	168
194	Mesquite, TX	168
194	Sugar Land, TX	168
194	Warren, MI	168
199	Elgin, IL	167
199	Flint, MI	167
199	Independence, MO	167
199	Reno, NV	167
199	Yuma, AZ	167
204	Boulder, CO	166
204	Chesapeake, VA	166
206	Toms River Twnshp, NJ	165

RANK	CITY	RATE
207	Arlington, TX	164
207	Colorado Springs, CO	164
207	Glendale, AZ	164
207	Hialeah, FL	164
207	Livonia, MI	164
207	San Antonio, TX	164
213	Amarillo, TX	163
213	Cheektowaga, NY	163
213	Newton, MA	163
213	Sunnyvale, CA	163
217	Erie, PA	162
217	San Bernardino, CA	162
219	Brick Twnshp, NJ	161
219	Upper Darby Twnshp, PA	161
219	Westminster, CO	161
222	Torrance, CA	160
222	Troy, MI	160
224	Davenport, IA	159
224	Lubbock, TX	159
226	Fayetteville, AR	158
226	Longmont, CO	158
226	Midland, TX	158
229	Cedar Rapids, IA	157
229	Federal Way, WA	157
229	Ogden, UT	157
229	Pembroke Pines, FL	157
229	Roswell, GA	157
234	Greeley, CO	156
235	Abilene, TX	155
235	Burbank, CA	155
235	Corpus Christi, TX	155
235	Palm Bay, FL	155
235	Ramapo, NY	155
240	Odessa, TX	154
240	Sioux City, IA	154
242	Lee's Summit, MO	153
242	Santa Barbara, CA	153
244	St. Joseph, MO	152
244	Whittier, CA	152
246	Coral Springs, FL	151
246	Kent, WA	151
246	West Valley, UT	151
249	Rio Rancho, NM	150
250	Lawrence, KS	149
250	Sacramento, CA	149
252	Columbia, MO	148
252	Farmington Hills, MI	148
254	Arvada, CO	147
254	Norman, OK	147
256	Garland, TX	146
256	Port St. Lucie, FL	146
258	Costa Mesa, CA	145
258	Jacksonville, NC	145
258	Nampa, ID	145
258	Overland Park, KS	145
262	Beaverton, OR	144
262	Cape Coral, FL	144
262	San Diego, CA	144
262	San Jose, CA	144
266	Richardson, TX	143
266	Spokane, WA	143
268	Fargo, ND	142
268	Pearland, TX	142
270	Edmond, OK	141
271	Bellevue, WA	140
271	Bloomington, MN	140
271	Boise, ID	140
274	Amherst, NY	138
274	Colonie, NY	138
274	Sioux Falls, SD	138
277	Bellingham, WA	137
277	Henderson, NV	137
277	O'Fallon, MO	137
280	Billings, MT	136
280	Brownsville, TX	136
282	Anchorage, AK	135
282	St. George, UT	135
284	Sterling Heights, MI	134
284	Thornton, CO	134
286	Salem, OR	133
287	Grand Prairie, TX	132
287	North Las Vegas, NV	132
289	Glendale, CA	131
289	Santa Clara, CA	131
289	Stockton, CA	131
292	Hayward, CA	130
292	Hillsboro, OR	130
294	Broken Arrow, OK	129
295	Chandler, AZ	128
295	College Station, TX	128
295	Lewisville, TX	128
295	Naperville, IL	128
295	Round Rock, TX	128
300	El Cajon, CA	127
300	Ontario, CA	127
300	Santa Maria, CA	127
303	Carrollton, TX	126
303	Concord, CA	126
303	Eugene, OR	126
303	Merced, CA	126
303	Ventura, CA	126
308	Lincoln, NE	125
309	Denton, TX	124
309	Oxnard, CA	124
309	Plano, TX	124
309	San Mateo, CA	124
309	Sandy Springs, GA	124
314	Frisco, TX	123
314	Redding, CA	123
314	Riverside, CA	123
314	Rochester, MN	123
314	Westland, MI	123
319	Allen, TX	122
319	Cary, NC	122
319	Fort Collins, CO	122
322	Anaheim, CA	121
322	Gresham, OR	121
322	Oceanside, CA	121
325	McKinney, TX	120
325	Modesto, CA	120
325	Surprise, AZ	120
325	Vancouver, WA	120
329	Sandy, UT	119
330	Fullerton, CA	118
330	San Leandro, CA	118
330	Sparks, NV	118
333	Fairfield, CA	117
333	Hawthorne, CA	117
333	Huntington Beach, CA	117
336	Orange, CA	116
336	Pomona, CA	116
336	Spokane Valley, WA	116
339	Avondale, AZ	115
339	Centennial, CO	115
339	Chino, CA	115
339	Escondido, CA	115
339	Vacaville, CA	115
344	Corona, CA	114
344	Salinas, CA	114
346	Antioch, CA	113
346	Buena Park, CA	113
348	Chico, CA	112
348	Clinton Twnshp, MI	112
348	Peoria, AZ	112
348	Rialto, CA	112
352	Carlsbad, CA	111
352	Downey, CA	111
352	Livermore, CA	111
352	Tracy, CA	111
356	Bend, OR	109
357	Ann Arbor, MI	108
357	Daly City, CA	108
357	Santa Rosa, CA	108
357	Westminster, CA	108
361	West Covina, CA	107
362	Visalia, CA	106
363	Canton Twnshp, MI	104
363	El Monte, CA	104
363	Fontana, CA	104
363	Roseville, CA	104
363	Santa Ana, CA	104
368	Chula Vista, CA	103
368	Citrus Heights, CA	103
370	Bakersfield, CA	102
371	Garden Grove, CA	100
372	Clovis, CA	98
373	Missouri City, TX	98
374	Simi Valley, CA	98
375	Alhambra, CA	97
376	Baldwin Park, CA	97
377	Gilbert, AZ	97
378	Vallejo, CA	97
379	Orem, UT	96
380	West Jordan, UT	96
381	Elk Grove, CA	90
382	Irvine, CA	90
383	Greece, NY	88
384	Fremont, CA	87
385	South Gate, CA	87
386	Murrieta, CA	86
387	Provo, UT	84
388	Indio, CA	80
NA	Baton Rouge, LA**	NA
NA	Carson, CA**	NA
NA	Compton, CA**	NA
NA	Hesperia, CA**	NA
NA	Kansas City, KS**	NA
NA	Lake Forest, CA**	NA
NA	Lakewood, CA**	NA
NA	Lancaster, CA**	NA
NA	Mission Viejo, CA**	NA
NA	Moreno Valley, CA**	NA
NA	New Orleans, LA**	NA
NA	Norwalk, CA**	NA
NA	Olathe, KS**	NA
NA	Palmdale, CA**	NA
NA	Pompano Beach, FL**	NA
NA	Rancho Cucamon., CA**	NA
NA	San Marcos, CA**	NA
NA	Santa Clarita, CA**	NA
NA	Shreveport, LA**	NA
NA	Temecula, CA**	NA
NA	Thousand Oaks, CA**	NA
NA	Victorville, CA**	NA
NA	Vista, CA**	NA

Source: CQ Press using reported data from the F.B.I. "Crime in the United States 2009"
*Sworn officers only, does not include civilian employees.
**Not available

83. Percent Change in Rate of Police Officers: 2008 to 2009
National Percent Change = 1.6% Decrease*

RANK	CITY	% CHANGE
105	Abilene, TX	1.3
231	Akron, OH	(2.2)
348	Albany, GA	(6.4)
178	Albany, NY	(0.8)
35	Albuquerque, NM	5.1
329	Alexandria, VA	(5.3)
134	Alhambra, CA	0.0
89	Allentown, PA	2.2
211	Allen, TX	(1.6)
167	Amarillo, TX	(0.6)
175	Amherst, NY	(0.7)
318	Anaheim, CA	(4.7)
203	Anchorage, AK	(1.5)
384	Ann Arbor, MI	(16.3)
277	Antioch, CA	(3.4)
121	Arlington, TX	0.6
118	Arvada, CO	0.7
27	Athens-Clarke, GA	5.8
374	Atlanta, GA	(10.5)
203	Aurora, CO	(1.5)
121	Aurora, IL	0.6
51	Austin, TX	4.1
77	Avondale, AZ	2.7
336	Bakersfield, CA	(5.6)
63	Baldwin Park, CA	3.2
134	Baltimore, MD	0.0
NA	Baton Rouge, LA**	NA
27	Beaumont, TX	5.8
54	Beaverton, OR	3.6
343	Bellevue, WA	(6.0)
258	Bellingham, WA	(2.8)
42	Bend, OR	4.8
286	Berkeley, CA	(3.8)
88	Billings, MT	2.3
11	Birmingham, AL	8.7
175	Bloomington, MN	(0.7)
17	Boca Raton, FL	7.2
331	Boise, ID	(5.4)
313	Boston, MA	(4.6)
297	Boulder, CO	(4.0)
241	Brick Twnshp, NJ	(2.4)
265	Bridgeport, CT	(2.9)
248	Brockton, MA	(2.6)
326	Broken Arrow, OK	(5.1)
70	Brownsville, TX	3.0
277	Buena Park, CA	(3.4)
134	Buffalo, NY	0.0
60	Burbank, CA	3.3
248	Cambridge, MA	(2.6)
381	Camden, NJ	(12.1)
35	Canton Twnshp, MI	5.1
366	Canton, OH	(8.1)
277	Cape Coral, FL	(3.4)
353	Carlsbad, CA	(6.7)
134	Carrollton, TX	0.0
NA	Carson, CA**	NA
292	Cary, NC	(3.9)
105	Cedar Rapids, IA	1.3
134	Centennial, CO	0.0
286	Chandler, AZ	(3.8)
121	Charleston, SC	0.6
258	Charlotte, NC	(2.8)
160	Chattanooga, TN	(0.4)
194	Cheektowaga, NY	(1.2)
297	Chesapeake, VA	(4.0)
258	Chicago, IL	(2.8)
43	Chico, CA	4.7
134	Chino, CA	0.0
348	Chula Vista, CA	(6.4)
83	Cincinnati, OH	2.5
35	Citrus Heights, CA	5.1
186	Clarkstown, NY	(0.9)
203	Clarksville, TN	(1.5)
275	Clearwater, FL	(3.3)
70	Cleveland, OH	3.0
369	Clifton, NJ	(8.9)
223	Clinton Twnshp, MI	(1.8)
379	Clovis, CA	(11.7)
286	College Station, TX	(3.8)
134	Colonie, NY	0.0
360	Colorado Springs, CO	(7.3)
228	Columbia, MO	(2.0)
57	Columbia, SC	3.4
3	Columbus, GA	14.8
NA	Columbus, OH**	NA
NA	Compton, CA**	NA
364	Concord, CA	(8.0)
272	Coral Springs, FL	(3.2)
217	Corona, CA	(1.7)
167	Corpus Christi, TX	(0.6)
254	Costa Mesa, CA	(2.7)
231	Cranston, RI	(2.2)
51	Dallas, TX	4.1
282	Daly City, CA	(3.6)
248	Danbury, CT	(2.6)
282	Davenport, IA	(3.6)
89	Davie, FL	2.2
308	Dayton, OH	(4.4)
134	Dearborn, MI	0.0
223	Decatur, IL	(1.8)
268	Denton, TX	(3.1)
286	Denver, CO	(3.8)
248	Des Moines, IA	(2.6)
282	Detroit, MI	(3.6)
6	Downey, CA	12.1
54	Duluth, MN	3.6
163	Durham, NC	(0.5)
110	Edison Twnshp, NJ	1.1
277	Edmond, OK	(3.4)
268	El Cajon, CA	(3.1)
382	El Monte, CA	(12.6)
211	El Paso, TX	(1.6)
281	Elgin, IL	(3.5)
292	Elizabeth, NJ	(3.9)
231	Elk Grove, CA	(2.2)
45	Erie, PA	4.5
186	Escondido, CA	(0.9)
19	Eugene, OR	6.8
178	Evansville, IN	(0.8)
127	Everett, WA	0.5
134	Fairfield, CA	0.0
383	Fall River, MA	(15.9)
118	Fargo, ND	0.7
197	Farmington Hills, MI	(1.3)
167	Fayetteville, AR	(0.6)
93	Fayetteville, NC	2.1
60	Federal Way, WA	3.3
336	Flint, MI	(5.6)
190	Fontana, CA	(1.0)
83	Fort Collins, CO	2.5
117	Fort Lauderdale, FL	0.8
163	Fort Smith, AR	(0.5)
110	Fort Wayne, IN	1.1
225	Fort Worth, TX	(1.9)
231	Fremont, CA	(2.2)
167	Fresno, CA	(0.6)
367	Frisco, TX	(8.2)
178	Fullerton, CA	(0.8)
4	Gainesville, FL	14.0
265	Garden Grove, CA	(2.9)
134	Garland, TX	0.0
NA	Gary, IN**	NA
321	Gilbert, AZ	(4.9)
5	Glendale, AZ	13.1
134	Glendale, CA	0.0
178	Grand Prairie, TX	(0.8)
121	Grand Rapids, MI	0.6
372	Greece, NY	(9.3)
385	Greeley, CO	(24.3)
73	Green Bay, WI	2.9
134	Greensboro, NC	0.0
100	Gresham, OR	1.7
203	Hamilton Twnshp, NJ	(1.5)
203	Hammond, IN	(1.5)
127	Hampton, VA	0.5
24	Hartford, CT	6.5
45	Hawthorne, CA	4.5
285	Hayward, CA	(3.7)
333	Henderson, NV	(5.5)
NA	Hesperia, CA**	NA
107	Hialeah, FL	1.2
57	High Point, NC	3.4
23	Hillsboro, OR	6.6
134	Hollywood, FL	0.0
186	Honolulu, HI	(0.9)
41	Houston, TX	4.9
114	Huntington Beach, CA	0.9
89	Huntsville, AL	2.2
377	Independence, MO	(11.2)
113	Indianapolis, IN	1.0
342	Indio, CA	(5.9)
167	Inglewood, CA	(0.6)
57	Irvine, CA	3.4
167	Irving, TX	(0.6)
73	Jacksonville, FL	2.9
103	Jacksonville, NC	1.4
7	Jackson, MS	11.5
133	Jersey City, NJ	0.3
380	Joliet, IL	(11.9)
NA	Kansas City, KS**	NA
228	Kansas City, MO	(2.0)
95	Kenosha, WI	2.0
197	Kent, WA	(1.3)
12	Killeen, TX	8.6
70	Knoxville, TN	3.0
76	Lafayette, LA	2.8
NA	Lake Forest, CA**	NA
217	Lakeland, FL	(1.7)
NA	Lakewood, CA**	NA
292	Lakewood, CO	(3.9)
NA	Lancaster, CA**	NA
60	Lansing, MI	3.3
127	Laredo, TX	0.5
31	Las Cruces, NM	5.6
25	Las Vegas, NV	6.4
292	Lawrence, KS	(3.9)
134	Lawton, OK	0.0
15	Lee's Summit, MO	7.7
358	Lewisville, TX	(7.2)
313	Lexington, KY	(4.6)
134	Lincoln, NE	0.0
132	Little Rock, AR	0.4
305	Livermore, CA	(4.3)
83	Livonia, MI	2.5
134	Long Beach, CA	0.0
121	Longmont, CO	0.6

RANK	CITY	% CHANGE
49	Longview, TX	4.3
86	Los Angeles, CA	2.4
163	Louisville, KY	(0.5)
245	Lubbock, TX	(2.5)
297	Lynn, MA	(4.0)
26	Macon, GA	6.3
134	Madison, WI	0.0
245	Manchester, NH	(2.5)
228	McAllen, TX	(2.0)
211	McKinney, TX	(1.6)
272	Melbourne, FL	(3.2)
27	Memphis, TN	5.8
310	Merced, CA	(4.5)
352	Mesa, AZ	(6.6)
238	Mesquite, TX	(2.3)
211	Miami Beach, FL	(1.6)
33	Miami Gardens, FL	5.3
19	Miami, FL	6.8
9	Midland, TX	9.0
326	Milwaukee, WI	(5.1)
217	Minneapolis, MN	(1.7)
10	Miramar, FL	8.8
NA	Mission Viejo, CA**	NA
190	Missouri City, TX	(1.0)
13	Mobile, AL	8.3
333	Modesto, CA	(5.5)
107	Montgomery, AL	1.2
NA	Moreno Valley, CA**	NA
313	Murfreesboro, TN	(4.6)
86	Murrieta, CA	2.4
350	Nampa, ID	(6.5)
178	Naperville, IL	(0.8)
190	Nashua, NH	(1.0)
2	Nashville, TN	15.2
375	New Bedford, MA	(10.5)
8	New Haven, CT	9.3
NA	New Orleans, LA**	NA
258	New York, NY	(2.8)
197	Newark, NJ	(1.3)
231	Newport Beach, CA	(2.2)
241	Newton, MA	(2.4)
159	Norfolk, VA	(0.3)
1	Norman, OK	24.6
241	North Charleston, SC	(2.4)
203	North Las Vegas, NV	(1.5)
NA	Norwalk, CA**	NA
39	Norwalk, CT	5.0
80	Oakland, CA	2.6
178	Oceanside, CA	(0.8)
32	Odessa, TX	5.5
118	O'Fallon, MO	0.7
268	Ogden, UT	(3.1)
163	Oklahoma City, OK	(0.5)
NA	Olathe, KS**	NA
97	Omaha, NE	1.8
286	Ontario, CA	(3.8)
217	Orange, CA	(1.7)
63	Orem, UT	3.2
305	Orlando, FL	(4.3)
254	Overland Park, KS	(2.7)
211	Oxnard, CA	(1.6)
268	Palm Bay, FL	(3.1)
NA	Palmdale, CA**	NA
167	Pasadena, CA	(0.6)
35	Pasadena, TX	5.1
77	Paterson, NJ	2.7
89	Pearland, TX	2.2
197	Pembroke Pines, FL	(1.3)

RANK	CITY	% CHANGE
369	Peoria, AZ	(8.9)
333	Peoria, IL	(5.5)
362	Philadelphia, PA	(7.5)
258	Phoenix, AZ	(2.8)
18	Pittsburgh, PA	6.9
292	Plano, TX	(3.9)
301	Plantation, FL	(4.1)
321	Pomona, CA	(4.9)
NA	Pompano Beach, FL**	NA
313	Port St. Lucie, FL	(4.6)
310	Portland, OR	(4.5)
48	Portsmouth, VA	4.4
272	Providence, RI	(3.2)
194	Provo, UT	(1.2)
77	Pueblo, CO	2.7
353	Quincy, MA	(6.7)
93	Racine, WI	2.1
238	Raleigh, NC	(2.3)
NA	Ramapo, NY**	NA
NA	Rancho Cucamon., CA**	NA
178	Reading, PA	(0.8)
331	Redding, CA	(5.4)
134	Reno, NV	0.0
53	Rialto, CA	3.7
73	Richardson, TX	2.9
21	Richmond, CA	6.7
267	Richmond, VA	(3.0)
286	Rio Rancho, NM	(3.8)
318	Riverside, CA	(4.7)
321	Roanoke, VA	(4.9)
134	Rochester, MN	0.0
101	Rochester, NY	1.6
346	Rockford, IL	(6.3)
364	Roseville, CA	(8.0)
13	Roswell, GA	8.3
358	Round Rock, TX	(7.2)
248	Sacramento, CA	(2.6)
43	Salem, OR	4.7
360	Salinas, CA	(7.3)
160	Salt Lake City, UT	(0.4)
16	San Angelo, TX	7.5
67	San Antonio, TX	3.1
329	San Bernardino, CA	(5.3)
363	San Diego, CA	(7.7)
254	San Francisco, CA	(2.7)
201	San Jose, CA	(1.4)
245	San Leandro, CA	(2.5)
NA	San Marcos, CA**	NA
134	San Mateo, CA	0.0
376	Sandy Springs, GA	(10.8)
80	Sandy, UT	2.6
258	Santa Ana, CA	(2.8)
308	Santa Barbara, CA	(4.4)
231	Santa Clara, CA	(2.2)
NA	Santa Clarita, CA**	NA
134	Santa Maria, CA	0.0
134	Santa Monica, CA	0.0
344	Santa Rosa, CA	(6.1)
103	Savannah, GA	1.4
110	Scottsdale, AZ	1.1
97	Seattle, WA	1.8
NA	Shreveport, LA**	NA
341	Simi Valley, CA	(5.8)
134	Sioux City, IA	0.0
201	Sioux Falls, SD	(1.4)
217	Somerville, MA	(1.7)
258	South Bend, IN	(2.8)
378	South Gate, CA	(11.2)

RANK	CITY	% CHANGE
203	Southfield, MI	(1.5)
336	Sparks, NV	(5.6)
217	Spokane Valley, WA	(1.7)
254	Spokane, WA	(2.7)
160	Springfield, IL	(0.4)
328	Springfield, MA	(5.2)
313	Springfield, MO	(4.6)
178	Stamford, CT	(0.8)
67	Sterling Heights, MI	3.1
357	Stockton, CA	(7.1)
203	St. George, UT	(1.5)
95	St. Joseph, MO	2.0
127	St. Louis, MO	0.5
114	St. Paul, MN	0.9
33	St. Petersburg, FL	5.3
114	Suffolk, VA	0.9
97	Sugar Land, TX	1.8
301	Sunnyvale, CA	(4.1)
134	Sunrise, FL	0.0
371	Surprise, AZ	(9.1)
67	Syracuse, NY	3.1
102	Tacoma, WA	1.5
340	Tallahassee, FL	(5.7)
301	Tampa, FL	(4.1)
NA	Temecula, CA**	NA
190	Tempe, AZ	(1.0)
231	Thornton, CO	(2.2)
NA	Thousand Oaks, CA**	NA
56	Toledo, OH	3.5
167	Toms River Twnshp, NJ	(0.6)
186	Topeka, KS	(0.9)
194	Torrance, CA	(1.2)
30	Tracy, CA	5.7
63	Trenton, NJ	3.2
320	Troy, MI	(4.8)
336	Tucson, AZ	(5.6)
225	Tulsa, OK	(1.9)
45	Tuscaloosa, AL	4.5
248	Tyler, TX	(2.6)
121	Upper Darby Twnshp, PA	0.6
325	Vacaville, CA	(5.0)
297	Vallejo, CA	(4.0)
241	Vancouver, WA	(2.4)
353	Ventura, CA	(6.7)
NA	Victorville, CA**	NA
305	Virginia Beach, VA	(4.3)
310	Visalia, CA	(4.5)
NA	Vista, CA**	NA
80	Waco, TX	2.6
238	Warren, MI	(2.3)
368	Warwick, RI	(8.6)
175	Washington, DC	(0.7)
39	Waterbury, CT	5.0
356	West Covina, CA	(7.0)
49	West Jordan, UT	4.3
275	West Palm Beach, FL	(3.3)
134	West Valley, UT	0.0
211	Westland, MI	(1.6)
344	Westminster, CA	(6.1)
304	Westminster, CO	(4.2)
225	Whittier, CA	(1.9)
21	Wichita Falls, TX	6.7
107	Wichita, KS	1.2
321	Wilmington, NC	(4.9)
63	Winston-Salem, NC	3.2
127	Woodbridge Twnshp, NJ	0.5
346	Worcester, MA	(6.3)
350	Yonkers, NY	(6.5)
373	Yuma, AZ	(9.7)

Source: CQ Press using reported data from the F.B.I. "Crime in the United States 2009"
*Sworn officers only, does not include civilian employees.
**Not available

83. Percent Change in Rate of Police Officers: 2008 to 2009 (continued)
National Percent Change = 1.6% Decrease*

RANK	CITY	% CHANGE
1	Norman, OK	24.6
2	Nashville, TN	15.2
3	Columbus, GA	14.8
4	Gainesville, FL	14.0
5	Glendale, AZ	13.1
6	Downey, CA	12.1
7	Jackson, MS	11.5
8	New Haven, CT	9.3
9	Midland, TX	9.0
10	Miramar, FL	8.8
11	Birmingham, AL	8.7
12	Killeen, TX	8.6
13	Mobile, AL	8.3
13	Roswell, GA	8.3
15	Lee's Summit, MO	7.7
16	San Angelo, TX	7.5
17	Boca Raton, FL	7.2
18	Pittsburgh, PA	6.9
19	Eugene, OR	6.8
19	Miami, FL	6.8
21	Richmond, CA	6.7
21	Wichita Falls, TX	6.7
23	Hillsboro, OR	6.6
24	Hartford, CT	6.5
25	Las Vegas, NV	6.4
26	Macon, GA	6.3
27	Athens-Clarke, GA	5.8
27	Beaumont, TX	5.8
27	Memphis, TN	5.8
30	Tracy, CA	5.7
31	Las Cruces, NM	5.6
32	Odessa, TX	5.5
33	Miami Gardens, FL	5.3
33	St. Petersburg, FL	5.3
35	Albuquerque, NM	5.1
35	Canton Twnshp, MI	5.1
35	Citrus Heights, CA	5.1
35	Pasadena, TX	5.1
39	Norwalk, CT	5.0
39	Waterbury, CT	5.0
41	Houston, TX	4.9
42	Bend, OR	4.8
43	Chico, CA	4.7
43	Salem, OR	4.7
45	Erie, PA	4.5
45	Hawthorne, CA	4.5
45	Tuscaloosa, AL	4.5
48	Portsmouth, VA	4.4
49	Longview, TX	4.3
49	West Jordan, UT	4.3
51	Austin, TX	4.1
51	Dallas, TX	4.1
53	Rialto, CA	3.7
54	Beaverton, OR	3.6
54	Duluth, MN	3.6
56	Toledo, OH	3.5
57	Columbia, SC	3.4
57	High Point, NC	3.4
57	Irvine, CA	3.4
60	Burbank, CA	3.3
60	Federal Way, WA	3.3
60	Lansing, MI	3.3
63	Baldwin Park, CA	3.2
63	Orem, UT	3.2
63	Trenton, NJ	3.2
63	Winston-Salem, NC	3.2
67	San Antonio, TX	3.1
67	Sterling Heights, MI	3.1
67	Syracuse, NY	3.1
70	Brownsville, TX	3.0
70	Cleveland, OH	3.0
70	Knoxville, TN	3.0
73	Green Bay, WI	2.9
73	Jacksonville, FL	2.9
73	Richardson, TX	2.9
76	Lafayette, LA	2.8
77	Avondale, AZ	2.7
77	Paterson, NJ	2.7
77	Pueblo, CO	2.7
80	Oakland, CA	2.6
80	Sandy, UT	2.6
80	Waco, TX	2.6
83	Cincinnati, OH	2.5
83	Fort Collins, CO	2.5
83	Livonia, MI	2.5
86	Los Angeles, CA	2.4
86	Murrieta, CA	2.4
88	Billings, MT	2.3
89	Allentown, PA	2.2
89	Davie, FL	2.2
89	Huntsville, AL	2.2
89	Pearland, TX	2.2
93	Fayetteville, NC	2.1
93	Racine, WI	2.1
95	Kenosha, WI	2.0
95	St. Joseph, MO	2.0
97	Omaha, NE	1.8
97	Seattle, WA	1.8
97	Sugar Land, TX	1.8
100	Gresham, OR	1.7
101	Rochester, NY	1.6
102	Tacoma, WA	1.5
103	Jacksonville, NC	1.4
103	Savannah, GA	1.4
105	Abilene, TX	1.3
105	Cedar Rapids, IA	1.3
107	Hialeah, FL	1.2
107	Montgomery, AL	1.2
107	Wichita, KS	1.2
110	Edison Twnshp, NJ	1.1
110	Fort Wayne, IN	1.1
110	Scottsdale, AZ	1.1
113	Indianapolis, IN	1.0
114	Huntington Beach, CA	0.9
114	St. Paul, MN	0.9
114	Suffolk, VA	0.9
117	Fort Lauderdale, FL	0.8
118	Arvada, CO	0.7
118	Fargo, ND	0.7
118	O'Fallon, MO	0.7
121	Arlington, TX	0.6
121	Aurora, IL	0.6
121	Charleston, SC	0.6
121	Grand Rapids, MI	0.6
121	Longmont, CO	0.6
121	Upper Darby Twnshp, PA	0.6
127	Everett, WA	0.5
127	Hampton, VA	0.5
127	Laredo, TX	0.5
127	St. Louis, MO	0.5
127	Woodbridge Twnshp, NJ	0.5
132	Little Rock, AR	0.4
133	Jersey City, NJ	0.3
134	Alhambra, CA	0.0
134	Baltimore, MD	0.0
134	Buffalo, NY	0.0
134	Carrollton, TX	0.0
134	Centennial, CO	0.0
134	Chino, CA	0.0
134	Colonie, NY	0.0
134	Dearborn, MI	0.0
134	Fairfield, CA	0.0
134	Garland, TX	0.0
134	Glendale, CA	0.0
134	Greensboro, NC	0.0
134	Hollywood, FL	0.0
134	Lawton, OK	0.0
134	Lincoln, NE	0.0
134	Long Beach, CA	0.0
134	Madison, WI	0.0
134	Reno, NV	0.0
134	Rochester, MN	0.0
134	San Mateo, CA	0.0
134	Santa Maria, CA	0.0
134	Santa Monica, CA	0.0
134	Sioux City, IA	0.0
134	Sunrise, FL	0.0
134	West Valley, UT	0.0
159	Norfolk, VA	(0.3)
160	Chattanooga, TN	(0.4)
160	Salt Lake City, UT	(0.4)
160	Springfield, IL	(0.4)
163	Durham, NC	(0.5)
163	Fort Smith, AR	(0.5)
163	Louisville, KY	(0.5)
163	Oklahoma City, OK	(0.5)
167	Amarillo, TX	(0.6)
167	Corpus Christi, TX	(0.6)
167	Fayetteville, AR	(0.6)
167	Fresno, CA	(0.6)
167	Inglewood, CA	(0.6)
167	Irving, TX	(0.6)
167	Pasadena, CA	(0.6)
167	Toms River Twnshp, NJ	(0.6)
175	Amherst, NY	(0.7)
175	Bloomington, MN	(0.7)
175	Washington, DC	(0.7)
178	Albany, NY	(0.8)
178	Evansville, IN	(0.8)
178	Fullerton, CA	(0.8)
178	Grand Prairie, TX	(0.8)
178	Naperville, IL	(0.8)
178	Oceanside, CA	(0.8)
178	Reading, PA	(0.8)
178	Stamford, CT	(0.8)
186	Clarkstown, NY	(0.9)
186	Escondido, CA	(0.9)
186	Honolulu, HI	(0.9)
186	Topeka, KS	(0.9)
190	Fontana, CA	(1.0)
190	Missouri City, TX	(1.0)
190	Nashua, NH	(1.0)
190	Tempe, AZ	(1.0)
194	Cheektowaga, NY	(1.2)
194	Provo, UT	(1.2)
194	Torrance, CA	(1.2)
197	Farmington Hills, MI	(1.3)
197	Kent, WA	(1.3)
197	Newark, NJ	(1.3)
197	Pembroke Pines, FL	(1.3)
201	San Jose, CA	(1.4)
201	Sioux Falls, SD	(1.4)
203	Anchorage, AK	(1.5)
203	Aurora, CO	(1.5)
203	Clarksville, TN	(1.5)
203	Hamilton Twnshp, NJ	(1.5)

RANK	CITY	% CHANGE
203	Hammond, IN	(1.5)
203	North Las Vegas, NV	(1.5)
203	Southfield, MI	(1.5)
203	St. George, UT	(1.5)
211	Allen, TX	(1.6)
211	El Paso, TX	(1.6)
211	McKinney, TX	(1.6)
211	Miami Beach, FL	(1.6)
211	Oxnard, CA	(1.6)
211	Westland, MI	(1.6)
217	Corona, CA	(1.7)
217	Lakeland, FL	(1.7)
217	Minneapolis, MN	(1.7)
217	Orange, CA	(1.7)
217	Somerville, MA	(1.7)
217	Spokane Valley, WA	(1.7)
223	Clinton Twnshp, MI	(1.8)
223	Decatur, IL	(1.8)
225	Fort Worth, TX	(1.9)
225	Tulsa, OK	(1.9)
225	Whittier, CA	(1.9)
228	Columbia, MO	(2.0)
228	Kansas City, MO	(2.0)
228	McAllen, TX	(2.0)
231	Akron, OH	(2.2)
231	Cranston, RI	(2.2)
231	Elk Grove, CA	(2.2)
231	Fremont, CA	(2.2)
231	Newport Beach, CA	(2.2)
231	Santa Clara, CA	(2.2)
231	Thornton, CO	(2.2)
238	Mesquite, TX	(2.3)
238	Raleigh, NC	(2.3)
238	Warren, MI	(2.3)
241	Brick Twnshp, NJ	(2.4)
241	Newton, MA	(2.4)
241	North Charleston, SC	(2.4)
241	Vancouver, WA	(2.4)
245	Lubbock, TX	(2.5)
245	Manchester, NH	(2.5)
245	San Leandro, CA	(2.5)
248	Brockton, MA	(2.6)
248	Cambridge, MA	(2.6)
248	Danbury, CT	(2.6)
248	Des Moines, IA	(2.6)
248	Sacramento, CA	(2.6)
248	Tyler, TX	(2.6)
254	Costa Mesa, CA	(2.7)
254	Overland Park, KS	(2.7)
254	San Francisco, CA	(2.7)
254	Spokane, WA	(2.7)
258	Bellingham, WA	(2.8)
258	Charlotte, NC	(2.8)
258	Chicago, IL	(2.8)
258	New York, NY	(2.8)
258	Phoenix, AZ	(2.8)
258	Santa Ana, CA	(2.8)
258	South Bend, IN	(2.8)
265	Bridgeport, CT	(2.9)
265	Garden Grove, CA	(2.9)
267	Richmond, VA	(3.0)
268	Denton, TX	(3.1)
268	El Cajon, CA	(3.1)
268	Ogden, UT	(3.1)
268	Palm Bay, FL	(3.1)
272	Coral Springs, FL	(3.2)
272	Melbourne, FL	(3.2)
272	Providence, RI	(3.2)
275	Clearwater, FL	(3.3)
275	West Palm Beach, FL	(3.3)
277	Antioch, CA	(3.4)
277	Buena Park, CA	(3.4)
277	Cape Coral, FL	(3.4)
277	Edmond, OK	(3.4)
281	Elgin, IL	(3.5)
282	Daly City, CA	(3.6)
282	Davenport, IA	(3.6)
282	Detroit, MI	(3.6)
285	Hayward, CA	(3.7)
286	Berkeley, CA	(3.8)
286	Chandler, AZ	(3.8)
286	College Station, TX	(3.8)
286	Denver, CO	(3.8)
286	Ontario, CA	(3.8)
286	Rio Rancho, NM	(3.8)
292	Cary, NC	(3.9)
292	Elizabeth, NJ	(3.9)
292	Lakewood, CO	(3.9)
292	Lawrence, KS	(3.9)
292	Plano, TX	(3.9)
297	Boulder, CO	(4.0)
297	Chesapeake, VA	(4.0)
297	Lynn, MA	(4.0)
297	Vallejo, CA	(4.0)
301	Plantation, FL	(4.1)
301	Sunnyvale, CA	(4.1)
301	Tampa, FL	(4.1)
304	Westminster, CO	(4.2)
305	Livermore, CA	(4.3)
305	Orlando, FL	(4.3)
305	Virginia Beach, VA	(4.3)
308	Dayton, OH	(4.4)
308	Santa Barbara, CA	(4.4)
310	Merced, CA	(4.5)
310	Portland, OR	(4.5)
310	Visalia, CA	(4.5)
313	Boston, MA	(4.6)
313	Lexington, KY	(4.6)
313	Murfreesboro, TN	(4.6)
313	Port St. Lucie, FL	(4.6)
313	Springfield, MO	(4.6)
318	Anaheim, CA	(4.7)
318	Riverside, CA	(4.7)
320	Troy, MI	(4.8)
321	Gilbert, AZ	(4.9)
321	Pomona, CA	(4.9)
321	Roanoke, VA	(4.9)
321	Wilmington, NC	(4.9)
325	Vacaville, CA	(5.0)
326	Broken Arrow, OK	(5.1)
326	Milwaukee, WI	(5.1)
328	Springfield, MA	(5.2)
329	Alexandria, VA	(5.3)
329	San Bernardino, CA	(5.3)
331	Boise, ID	(5.4)
331	Redding, CA	(5.4)
333	Henderson, NV	(5.5)
333	Modesto, CA	(5.5)
333	Peoria, IL	(5.5)
336	Bakersfield, CA	(5.6)
336	Flint, MI	(5.6)
336	Sparks, NV	(5.6)
336	Tucson, AZ	(5.6)
340	Tallahassee, FL	(5.7)
341	Simi Valley, CA	(5.8)
342	Indio, CA	(5.9)
343	Bellevue, WA	(6.0)
344	Santa Rosa, CA	(6.1)
344	Westminster, CA	(6.1)
346	Rockford, IL	(6.3)
346	Worcester, MA	(6.3)
348	Albany, GA	(6.4)
348	Chula Vista, CA	(6.4)
350	Nampa, ID	(6.5)
350	Yonkers, NY	(6.5)
352	Mesa, AZ	(6.6)
353	Carlsbad, CA	(6.7)
353	Quincy, MA	(6.7)
353	Ventura, CA	(6.7)
356	West Covina, CA	(7.0)
357	Stockton, CA	(7.1)
358	Lewisville, TX	(7.2)
358	Round Rock, TX	(7.2)
360	Colorado Springs, CO	(7.3)
360	Salinas, CA	(7.3)
362	Philadelphia, PA	(7.5)
363	San Diego, CA	(7.7)
364	Concord, CA	(8.0)
364	Roseville, CA	(8.0)
366	Canton, OH	(8.1)
367	Frisco, TX	(8.2)
368	Warwick, RI	(8.6)
369	Clifton, NJ	(8.9)
369	Peoria, AZ	(8.9)
371	Surprise, AZ	(9.1)
372	Greece, NY	(9.3)
373	Yuma, AZ	(9.7)
374	Atlanta, GA	(10.5)
375	New Bedford, MA	(10.5)
376	Sandy Springs, GA	(10.8)
377	Independence, MO	(11.2)
378	South Gate, CA	(11.2)
379	Clovis, CA	(11.7)
380	Joliet, IL	(11.9)
381	Camden, NJ	(12.1)
382	El Monte, CA	(12.6)
383	Fall River, MA	(15.9)
384	Ann Arbor, MI	(16.3)
385	Greeley, CO	(24.3)
NA	Baton Rouge, LA**	NA
NA	Carson, CA**	NA
NA	Columbus, OH**	NA
NA	Compton, CA**	NA
NA	Gary, IN**	NA
NA	Hesperia, CA**	NA
NA	Kansas City, KS**	NA
NA	Lake Forest, CA**	NA
NA	Lakewood, CA**	NA
NA	Lancaster, CA**	NA
NA	Mission Viejo, CA**	NA
NA	Moreno Valley, CA**	NA
NA	New Orleans, LA**	NA
NA	Norwalk, CA**	NA
NA	Olathe, KS**	NA
NA	Palmdale, CA**	NA
NA	Pompano Beach, FL**	NA
NA	Ramapo, NY**	NA
NA	Rancho Cucamon., CA**	NA
NA	San Marcos, CA**	NA
NA	Santa Clarita, CA**	NA
NA	Shreveport, LA**	NA
NA	Temecula, CA**	NA
NA	Thousand Oaks, CA**	NA
NA	Victorville, CA**	NA
NA	Vista, CA**	NA

Source: CQ Press using reported data from the F.B.I. "Crime in the United States 2009"
*Sworn officers only, does not include civilian employees.
**Not available

84. Percent Change in Rate of Police Officers: 2005 to 2009
National Percent Change = 1.2% Increase*

RANK	CITY	% CHANGE
154	Abilene, TX	2.0
176	Akron, OH	0.9
62	Albany, GA	7.4
224	Albany, NY	(1.1)
134	Albuquerque, NM	3.0
351	Alexandria, VA	(10.4)
76	Alhambra, CA	6.6
5	Allentown, PA	20.4
292	Allen, TX	(4.7)
131	Amarillo, TX	3.2
218	Amherst, NY	(0.7)
146	Anaheim, CA	2.5
53	Anchorage, AK	8.0
375	Ann Arbor, MI	(19.4)
122	Antioch, CA	3.7
27	Arlington, TX	10.1
8	Arvada, CO	16.7
292	Athens-Clarke, GA	(4.7)
380	Atlanta, GA	(29.9)
238	Aurora, CO	(2.0)
170	Aurora, IL	1.2
123	Austin, TX	3.6
60	Avondale, AZ	7.5
328	Bakersfield, CA	(7.3)
174	Baldwin Park, CA	1.0
205	Baltimore, MD	(0.2)
NA	Baton Rouge, LA**	NA
80	Beaumont, TX	6.3
187	Beaverton, OR	0.7
267	Bellevue, WA	(3.4)
256	Bellingham, WA	(2.8)
365	Bend, OR	(14.2)
189	Berkeley, CA	0.6
69	Billings, MT	7.1
45	Birmingham, AL	8.4
229	Bloomington, MN	(1.4)
235	Boca Raton, FL	(1.8)
149	Boise, ID	2.2
291	Boston, MA	(4.6)
322	Boulder, CO	(6.7)
189	Brick Twnshp, NJ	0.6
193	Bridgeport, CT	0.3
330	Brockton, MA	(7.4)
301	Broken Arrow, OK	(5.1)
271	Brownsville, TX	(3.5)
220	Buena Park, CA	(0.9)
67	Buffalo, NY	7.2
106	Burbank, CA	4.7
73	Cambridge, MA	6.9
358	Camden, NJ	(11.9)
24	Canton Twnshp, MI	10.6
246	Canton, OH	(2.4)
29	Cape Coral, FL	9.9
301	Carlsbad, CA	(5.1)
195	Carrollton, TX	0.0
NA	Carson, CA**	NA
359	Cary, NC	(12.2)
189	Cedar Rapids, IA	0.6
NA	Centennial, CO**	NA
195	Chandler, AZ	0.0
147	Charleston, SC	2.4
314	Charlotte, NC	(5.8)
348	Chattanooga, TN	(9.7)
NA	Cheektowaga, NY**	NA
214	Chesapeake, VA	(0.6)
214	Chicago, IL	(0.6)
351	Chico, CA	(10.4)
359	Chino, CA	(12.2)
277	Chula Vista, CA	(3.7)
257	Cincinnati, OH	(2.9)
NA	Citrus Heights, CA**	NA
101	Clarkstown, NY	4.9
314	Clarksville, TN	(5.8)
88	Clearwater, FL	5.9
42	Cleveland, OH	8.8
285	Clifton, NJ	(4.2)
138	Clinton Twnshp, MI	2.8
372	Clovis, CA	(17.6)
316	College Station, TX	(5.9)
240	Colonie, NY	(2.1)
346	Colorado Springs, CO	(8.9)
251	Columbia, MO	(2.6)
88	Columbia, SC	5.9
2	Columbus, GA	28.5
181	Columbus, OH	0.8
NA	Compton, CA**	NA
160	Concord, CA	1.6
128	Coral Springs, FL	3.4
141	Corona, CA	2.7
45	Corpus Christi, TX	8.4
150	Costa Mesa, CA	2.1
195	Cranston, RI	0.0
14	Dallas, TX	14.9
307	Daly City, CA	(5.3)
138	Danbury, CT	2.8
225	Davenport, IA	(1.2)
336	Davie, FL	(8.1)
181	Dayton, OH	0.8
9	Dearborn, MI	16.5
136	Decatur, IL	2.9
349	Denton, TX	(10.1)
271	Denver, CO	(3.5)
223	Des Moines, IA	(1.0)
361	Detroit, MI	(12.5)
7	Downey, CA	18.1
134	Duluth, MN	3.0
292	Durham, NC	(4.7)
341	Edison Twnshp, NJ	(8.6)
86	Edmond, OK	6.0
357	El Cajon, CA	(11.8)
379	El Monte, CA	(20.6)
211	El Paso, TX	(0.5)
337	Elgin, IL	(8.2)
241	Elizabeth, NJ	(2.2)
NA	Elk Grove, CA**	NA
307	Erie, PA	(5.3)
285	Escondido, CA	(4.2)
181	Eugene, OR	0.8
192	Evansville, IN	0.4
16	Everett, WA	14.1
65	Fairfield, CA	7.3
341	Fall River, MA	(8.6)
164	Fargo, ND	1.4
92	Farmington Hills, MI	5.7
355	Fayetteville, AR	(11.7)
376	Fayetteville, NC	(19.4)
10	Federal Way, WA	16.3
374	Flint, MI	(18.1)
48	Fontana, CA	8.3
157	Fort Collins, CO	1.7
241	Fort Lauderdale, FL	(2.2)
211	Fort Smith, AR	(0.5)
337	Fort Wayne, IN	(8.2)
300	Fort Worth, TX	(5.0)
241	Fremont, CA	(2.2)
214	Fresno, CA	(0.6)
337	Frisco, TX	(8.2)
126	Fullerton, CA	3.5
154	Gainesville, FL	2.0
114	Garden Grove, CA	4.2
91	Garland, TX	5.8
353	Gary, IN	(10.7)
369	Gilbert, AZ	(15.7)
36	Glendale, AZ	9.3
232	Glendale, CA	(1.5)
312	Grand Prairie, TX	(5.7)
225	Grand Rapids, MI	(1.2)
350	Greece, NY	(10.2)
48	Greeley, CO	8.3
296	Green Bay, WI	(4.8)
32	Greensboro, NC	9.7
157	Gresham, OR	1.7
271	Hamilton Twnshp, NJ	(3.5)
141	Hammond, IN	2.7
110	Hampton, VA	4.4
45	Hartford, CT	8.4
144	Hawthorne, CA	2.6
259	Hayward, CA	(3.0)
54	Henderson, NV	7.9
NA	Hesperia, CA**	NA
27	Hialeah, FL	10.1
364	High Point, NC	(13.9)
245	Hillsboro, OR	(2.3)
208	Hollywood, FL	(0.4)
100	Honolulu, HI	5.0
176	Houston, TX	0.9
36	Huntington Beach, CA	9.3
80	Huntsville, AL	6.3
301	Independence, MO	(5.1)
211	Indianapolis, IN	(0.5)
370	Indio, CA	(16.7)
267	Inglewood, CA	(3.4)
128	Irvine, CA	3.4
101	Irving, TX	4.9
33	Jacksonville, FL	9.6
62	Jacksonville, NC	7.4
101	Jackson, MS	4.9
101	Jersey City, NJ	4.9
373	Joliet, IL	(17.6)
NA	Kansas City, KS**	NA
171	Kansas City, MO	1.1
99	Kenosha, WI	5.2
54	Kent, WA	7.9
29	Killeen, TX	9.9
195	Knoxville, TN	0.0
34	Lafayette, LA	9.4
NA	Lake Forest, CA**	NA
325	Lakeland, FL	(7.1)
NA	Lakewood, CA**	NA
48	Lakewood, CO	8.3
NA	Lancaster, CA**	NA
112	Lansing, MI	4.3
275	Laredo, TX	(3.6)
347	Las Cruces, NM	(9.2)
4	Las Vegas, NV	24.4
335	Lawrence, KS	(8.0)
31	Lawton, OK	9.8
12	Lee's Summit, MO	15.9
341	Lewisville, TX	(8.6)
251	Lexington, KY	(2.6)
317	Lincoln, NE	(6.0)
144	Little Rock, AR	2.6
176	Livermore, CA	0.9
44	Livonia, MI	8.6
25	Long Beach, CA	10.2
11	Longmont, CO	16.2

RANK	CITY	% CHANGE
16	Longview, TX	14.1
72	Los Angeles, CA	7.0
120	Louisville, KY	3.8
320	Lubbock, TX	(6.5)
310	Lynn, MA	(5.5)
NA	Macon, GA**	NA
62	Madison, WI	7.4
69	Manchester, NH	7.1
334	McAllen, TX	(7.5)
112	McKinney, TX	4.3
164	Melbourne, FL	1.4
19	Memphis, TN	13.4
88	Merced, CA	5.9
282	Mesa, AZ	(4.0)
92	Mesquite, TX	5.7
NA	Miami Beach, FL**	NA
3	Miami Gardens, FL	27.9
141	Miami, FL	2.7
236	Midland, TX	(1.9)
259	Milwaukee, WI	(3.0)
34	Minneapolis, MN	9.4
42	Miramar, FL	8.8
NA	Mission Viejo, CA**	NA
40	Missouri City, TX	8.9
80	Mobile, AL	6.3
282	Modesto, CA	(4.0)
54	Montgomery, AL	7.9
NA	Moreno Valley, CA**	NA
162	Murfreesboro, TN	1.5
310	Murrieta, CA	(5.5)
187	Nampa, ID	0.7
181	Naperville, IL	0.8
77	Nashua, NH	6.5
95	Nashville, TN	5.4
267	New Bedford, MA	(3.4)
193	New Haven, CT	0.3
NA	New Orleans, LA**	NA
312	New York, NY	(5.7)
214	Newark, NJ	(0.6)
297	Newport Beach, CA	(4.9)
340	Newton, MA	(8.4)
23	Norfolk, VA	10.7
1	Norman, OK	31.3
206	North Charleston, SC	(0.3)
354	North Las Vegas, NV	(11.4)
NA	Norwalk, CA**	NA
117	Norwalk, CT	4.0
58	Oakland, CA	7.7
39	Oceanside, CA	9.0
261	Odessa, TX	(3.1)
345	O'Fallon, MO	(8.7)
277	Ogden, UT	(3.7)
171	Oklahoma City, OK	1.1
NA	Olathe, KS**	NA
330	Omaha, NE	(7.4)
195	Ontario, CA	0.0
108	Orange, CA	4.5
150	Orem, UT	2.1
322	Orlando, FL	(6.7)
266	Overland Park, KS	(3.3)
160	Oxnard, CA	1.6
195	Palm Bay, FL	0.0
NA	Palmdale, CA**	NA
147	Pasadena, CA	2.4
79	Pasadena, TX	6.4
15	Paterson, NJ	14.6
371	Pearland, TX	(17.0)
130	Pembroke Pines, FL	3.3

RANK	CITY	% CHANGE
267	Peoria, AZ	(3.4)
229	Peoria, IL	(1.4)
279	Philadelphia, PA	(3.8)
126	Phoenix, AZ	3.5
25	Pittsburgh, PA	10.2
307	Plano, TX	(5.3)
229	Plantation, FL	(1.4)
176	Pomona, CA	0.9
NA	Pompano Beach, FL**	NA
319	Port St. Lucie, FL	(6.4)
321	Portland, OR	(6.6)
208	Portsmouth, VA	(0.4)
171	Providence, RI	1.1
290	Provo, UT	(4.5)
110	Pueblo, CO	4.4
365	Quincy, MA	(14.2)
208	Racine, WI	(0.4)
368	Raleigh, NC	(15.6)
250	Ramapo, NY	(2.5)
NA	Rancho Cucamon., CA**	NA
301	Reading, PA	(5.1)
261	Redding, CA	(3.1)
271	Reno, NV	(3.5)
176	Rialto, CA	0.9
48	Richardson, TX	8.3
12	Richmond, CA	15.9
195	Richmond, VA	0.0
367	Rio Rancho, NM	(15.3)
280	Riverside, CA	(3.9)
195	Roanoke, VA	0.0
280	Rochester, MN	(3.9)
6	Rochester, NY	18.2
341	Rockford, IL	(8.6)
362	Roseville, CA	(12.6)
85	Roswell, GA	6.1
NA	Round Rock, TX**	NA
150	Sacramento, CA	2.1
94	Salem, OR	5.6
123	Salinas, CA	3.6
80	Salt Lake City, UT	6.3
123	San Angelo, TX	3.6
108	San Antonio, TX	4.5
65	San Bernardino, CA	7.3
355	San Diego, CA	(11.7)
206	San Francisco, CA	(0.3)
255	San Jose, CA	(2.7)
95	San Leandro, CA	5.4
NA	San Marcos, CA**	NA
114	San Mateo, CA	4.2
NA	Sandy Springs, GA**	NA
97	Sandy, UT	5.3
174	Santa Ana, CA	1.0
154	Santa Barbara, CA	2.0
117	Santa Clara, CA	4.0
NA	Santa Clarita, CA**	NA
181	Santa Maria, CA	0.8
132	Santa Monica, CA	3.1
38	Santa Rosa, CA	9.1
22	Savannah, GA	11.0
106	Scottsdale, AZ	4.7
164	Seattle, WA	1.4
NA	Shreveport, LA**	NA
297	Simi Valley, CA	(4.9)
58	Sioux City, IA	7.7
330	Sioux Falls, SD	(7.4)
16	Somerville, MA	14.1
246	South Bend, IN	(2.4)
195	South Gate, CA	0.0

RANK	CITY	% CHANGE
150	Southfield, MI	2.1
325	Sparks, NV	(7.1)
297	Spokane Valley, WA	(4.9)
164	Spokane, WA	1.4
251	Springfield, IL	(2.6)
218	Springfield, MA	(0.7)
363	Springfield, MO	(13.8)
289	Stamford, CT	(4.4)
181	Sterling Heights, MI	0.8
301	Stockton, CA	(5.1)
287	St. George, UT	(4.3)
263	St. Joseph, MO	(3.2)
119	St. Louis, MO	3.9
74	St. Paul, MN	6.8
57	St. Petersburg, FL	7.8
263	Suffolk, VA	(3.2)
21	Sugar Land, TX	11.3
292	Sunnyvale, CA	(4.7)
40	Sunrise, FL	8.9
378	Surprise, AZ	(20.5)
52	Syracuse, NY	8.2
97	Tacoma, WA	5.3
330	Tallahassee, FL	(7.4)
322	Tampa, FL	(6.7)
NA	Temecula, CA**	NA
162	Tempe, AZ	1.5
257	Thornton, CO	(2.9)
NA	Thousand Oaks, CA**	NA
318	Toledo, OH	(6.3)
132	Toms River Twnshp, NJ	3.1
234	Topeka, KS	(1.7)
195	Torrance, CA	0.0
20	Tracy, CA	12.1
69	Trenton, NJ	7.1
246	Troy, MI	(2.4)
251	Tucson, AZ	(2.6)
164	Tulsa, OK	1.4
120	Tuscaloosa, AL	3.8
233	Tyler, TX	(1.6)
169	Upper Darby Twnshp, PA	1.3
60	Vacaville, CA	7.5
377	Vallejo, CA	(19.8)
263	Vancouver, WA	(3.2)
116	Ventura, CA	4.1
NA	Victorville, CA**	NA
157	Virginia Beach, VA	1.7
275	Visalia, CA	(3.6)
NA	Vista, CA**	NA
77	Waco, TX	6.5
282	Warren, MI	(4.0)
328	Warwick, RI	(7.3)
220	Washington, DC	(0.9)
80	Waterbury, CT	6.3
220	West Covina, CA	(0.9)
238	West Jordan, UT	(2.0)
138	West Palm Beach, FL	2.8
228	West Valley, UT	(1.3)
86	Westland, MI	6.0
136	Westminster, CA	2.9
246	Westminster, CO	(2.4)
105	Whittier, CA	4.8
75	Wichita Falls, TX	6.7
241	Wichita, KS	(2.2)
225	Wilmington, NC	(1.2)
287	Winston-Salem, NC	(4.3)
67	Woodbridge Twnshp, NJ	7.2
325	Worcester, MA	(7.1)
236	Yonkers, NY	(1.9)
301	Yuma, AZ	(5.1)

Source: CQ Press using reported data from the F.B.I. "Crime in the United States 2009"
*Sworn officers only, does not include civilian employees.
**Not available

84. Percent Change in Rate of Police Officers: 2005 to 2009 (continued)
National Percent Change = 1.2% Increase*

RANK	CITY	% CHANGE
1	Norman, OK	31.3
2	Columbus, GA	28.5
3	Miami Gardens, FL	27.9
4	Las Vegas, NV	24.4
5	Allentown, PA	20.4
6	Rochester, NY	18.2
7	Downey, CA	18.1
8	Arvada, CO	16.7
9	Dearborn, MI	16.5
10	Federal Way, WA	16.3
11	Longmont, CO	16.2
12	Lee's Summit, MO	15.9
12	Richmond, CA	15.9
14	Dallas, TX	14.9
15	Paterson, NJ	14.6
16	Everett, WA	14.1
16	Longview, TX	14.1
16	Somerville, MA	14.1
19	Memphis, TN	13.4
20	Tracy, CA	12.1
21	Sugar Land, TX	11.3
22	Savannah, GA	11.0
23	Norfolk, VA	10.7
24	Canton Twnshp, MI	10.6
25	Long Beach, CA	10.2
25	Pittsburgh, PA	10.2
27	Arlington, TX	10.1
27	Hialeah, FL	10.1
29	Cape Coral, FL	9.9
29	Killeen, TX	9.9
31	Lawton, OK	9.8
32	Greensboro, NC	9.7
33	Jacksonville, FL	9.6
34	Lafayette, LA	9.4
34	Minneapolis, MN	9.4
36	Glendale, AZ	9.3
36	Huntington Beach, CA	9.3
38	Santa Rosa, CA	9.1
39	Oceanside, CA	9.0
40	Missouri City, TX	8.9
40	Sunrise, FL	8.9
42	Cleveland, OH	8.8
42	Miramar, FL	8.8
44	Livonia, MI	8.6
45	Birmingham, AL	8.4
45	Corpus Christi, TX	8.4
45	Hartford, CT	8.4
48	Fontana, CA	8.3
48	Greeley, CO	8.3
48	Lakewood, CO	8.3
48	Richardson, TX	8.3
52	Syracuse, NY	8.2
53	Anchorage, AK	8.0
54	Henderson, NV	7.9
54	Kent, WA	7.9
54	Montgomery, AL	7.9
57	St. Petersburg, FL	7.8
58	Oakland, CA	7.7
58	Sioux City, IA	7.7
60	Avondale, AZ	7.5
60	Vacaville, CA	7.5
62	Albany, GA	7.4
62	Jacksonville, NC	7.4
62	Madison, WI	7.4
65	Fairfield, CA	7.3
65	San Bernardino, CA	7.3
67	Buffalo, NY	7.2
67	Woodbridge Twnshp, NJ	7.2
69	Billings, MT	7.1
69	Manchester, NH	7.1
69	Trenton, NJ	7.1
72	Los Angeles, CA	7.0
73	Cambridge, MA	6.9
74	St. Paul, MN	6.8
75	Wichita Falls, TX	6.7
76	Alhambra, CA	6.6
77	Nashua, NH	6.5
77	Waco, TX	6.5
79	Pasadena, TX	6.4
80	Beaumont, TX	6.3
80	Huntsville, AL	6.3
80	Mobile, AL	6.3
80	Salt Lake City, UT	6.3
80	Waterbury, CT	6.3
85	Roswell, GA	6.1
86	Edmond, OK	6.0
86	Westland, MI	6.0
88	Clearwater, FL	5.9
88	Columbia, SC	5.9
88	Merced, CA	5.9
91	Garland, TX	5.8
92	Farmington Hills, MI	5.7
92	Mesquite, TX	5.7
94	Salem, OR	5.6
95	Nashville, TN	5.4
95	San Leandro, CA	5.4
97	Sandy, UT	5.3
97	Tacoma, WA	5.3
99	Kenosha, WI	5.2
100	Honolulu, HI	5.0
101	Clarkstown, NY	4.9
101	Irving, TX	4.9
101	Jackson, MS	4.9
101	Jersey City, NJ	4.9
105	Whittier, CA	4.8
106	Burbank, CA	4.7
106	Scottsdale, AZ	4.7
108	Orange, CA	4.5
108	San Antonio, TX	4.5
110	Hampton, VA	4.4
110	Pueblo, CO	4.4
112	Lansing, MI	4.3
112	McKinney, TX	4.3
114	Garden Grove, CA	4.2
114	San Mateo, CA	4.2
116	Ventura, CA	4.1
117	Norwalk, CT	4.0
117	Santa Clara, CA	4.0
119	St. Louis, MO	3.9
120	Louisville, KY	3.8
120	Tuscaloosa, AL	3.8
122	Antioch, CA	3.7
123	Austin, TX	3.6
123	Salinas, CA	3.6
123	San Angelo, TX	3.6
126	Fullerton, CA	3.5
126	Phoenix, AZ	3.5
128	Coral Springs, FL	3.4
128	Irvine, CA	3.4
130	Pembroke Pines, FL	3.3
131	Amarillo, TX	3.2
132	Santa Monica, CA	3.1
132	Toms River Twnshp, NJ	3.1
134	Albuquerque, NM	3.0
134	Duluth, MN	3.0
136	Decatur, IL	2.9
136	Westminster, CA	2.9
138	Clinton Twnshp, MI	2.8
138	Danbury, CT	2.8
138	West Palm Beach, FL	2.8
141	Corona, CA	2.7
141	Hammond, IN	2.7
141	Miami, FL	2.7
144	Hawthorne, CA	2.6
144	Little Rock, AR	2.6
146	Anaheim, CA	2.5
147	Charleston, SC	2.4
147	Pasadena, CA	2.4
149	Boise, ID	2.2
150	Costa Mesa, CA	2.1
150	Orem, UT	2.1
150	Sacramento, CA	2.1
150	Southfield, MI	2.1
154	Abilene, TX	2.0
154	Gainesville, FL	2.0
154	Santa Barbara, CA	2.0
157	Fort Collins, CO	1.7
157	Gresham, OR	1.7
157	Virginia Beach, VA	1.7
160	Concord, CA	1.6
160	Oxnard, CA	1.6
162	Murfreesboro, TN	1.5
162	Tempe, AZ	1.5
164	Fargo, ND	1.4
164	Melbourne, FL	1.4
164	Seattle, WA	1.4
164	Spokane, WA	1.4
164	Tulsa, OK	1.4
169	Upper Darby Twnshp, PA	1.3
170	Aurora, IL	1.2
171	Kansas City, MO	1.1
171	Oklahoma City, OK	1.1
171	Providence, RI	1.1
174	Baldwin Park, CA	1.0
174	Santa Ana, CA	1.0
176	Akron, OH	0.9
176	Houston, TX	0.9
176	Livermore, CA	0.9
176	Pomona, CA	0.9
176	Rialto, CA	0.9
181	Columbus, OH	0.8
181	Dayton, OH	0.8
181	Eugene, OR	0.8
181	Naperville, IL	0.8
181	Santa Maria, CA	0.8
181	Sterling Heights, MI	0.8
187	Beaverton, OR	0.7
187	Nampa, ID	0.7
189	Berkeley, CA	0.6
189	Brick Twnshp, NJ	0.6
189	Cedar Rapids, IA	0.6
192	Evansville, IN	0.4
193	Bridgeport, CT	0.3
193	New Haven, CT	0.3
195	Carrollton, TX	0.0
195	Chandler, AZ	0.0
195	Cranston, RI	0.0
195	Knoxville, TN	0.0
195	Ontario, CA	0.0
195	Palm Bay, FL	0.0
195	Richmond, VA	0.0
195	Roanoke, VA	0.0
195	South Gate, CA	0.0
195	Torrance, CA	0.0
205	Baltimore, MD	(0.2)
206	North Charleston, SC	(0.3)

RANK	CITY	% CHANGE
206	San Francisco, CA	(0.3)
208	Hollywood, FL	(0.4)
208	Portsmouth, VA	(0.4)
208	Racine, WI	(0.4)
211	El Paso, TX	(0.5)
211	Fort Smith, AR	(0.5)
211	Indianapolis, IN	(0.5)
214	Chesapeake, VA	(0.6)
214	Chicago, IL	(0.6)
214	Fresno, CA	(0.6)
214	Newark, NJ	(0.6)
218	Amherst, NY	(0.7)
218	Springfield, MA	(0.7)
220	Buena Park, CA	(0.9)
220	Washington, DC	(0.9)
220	West Covina, CA	(0.9)
223	Des Moines, IA	(1.0)
224	Albany, NY	(1.1)
225	Davenport, IA	(1.2)
225	Grand Rapids, MI	(1.2)
225	Wilmington, NC	(1.2)
228	West Valley, UT	(1.3)
229	Bloomington, MN	(1.4)
229	Peoria, IL	(1.4)
229	Plantation, FL	(1.4)
232	Glendale, CA	(1.5)
233	Tyler, TX	(1.6)
234	Topeka, KS	(1.7)
235	Boca Raton, FL	(1.8)
236	Midland, TX	(1.9)
236	Yonkers, NY	(1.9)
238	Aurora, CO	(2.0)
238	West Jordan, UT	(2.0)
240	Colonie, NY	(2.1)
241	Elizabeth, NJ	(2.2)
241	Fort Lauderdale, FL	(2.2)
241	Fremont, CA	(2.2)
241	Wichita, KS	(2.2)
245	Hillsboro, OR	(2.3)
246	Canton, OH	(2.4)
246	South Bend, IN	(2.4)
246	Troy, MI	(2.4)
246	Westminster, CO	(2.4)
250	Ramapo, NY	(2.5)
251	Columbia, MO	(2.6)
251	Lexington, KY	(2.6)
251	Springfield, IL	(2.6)
251	Tucson, AZ	(2.6)
255	San Jose, CA	(2.7)
256	Bellingham, WA	(2.8)
257	Cincinnati, OH	(2.9)
257	Thornton, CO	(2.9)
259	Hayward, CA	(3.0)
259	Milwaukee, WI	(3.0)
261	Odessa, TX	(3.1)
261	Redding, CA	(3.1)
263	St. Joseph, MO	(3.2)
263	Suffolk, VA	(3.2)
263	Vancouver, WA	(3.2)
266	Overland Park, KS	(3.3)
267	Bellevue, WA	(3.4)
267	Inglewood, CA	(3.4)
267	New Bedford, MA	(3.4)
267	Peoria, AZ	(3.4)
271	Brownsville, TX	(3.5)
271	Denver, CO	(3.5)
271	Hamilton Twnshp, NJ	(3.5)
271	Reno, NV	(3.5)

RANK	CITY	% CHANGE
275	Laredo, TX	(3.6)
275	Visalia, CA	(3.6)
277	Chula Vista, CA	(3.7)
277	Ogden, UT	(3.7)
279	Philadelphia, PA	(3.8)
280	Riverside, CA	(3.9)
280	Rochester, MN	(3.9)
282	Mesa, AZ	(4.0)
282	Modesto, CA	(4.0)
282	Warren, MI	(4.0)
285	Clifton, NJ	(4.2)
285	Escondido, CA	(4.2)
287	St. George, UT	(4.3)
287	Winston-Salem, NC	(4.3)
289	Stamford, CT	(4.4)
290	Provo, UT	(4.5)
291	Boston, MA	(4.6)
292	Allen, TX	(4.7)
292	Athens-Clarke, GA	(4.7)
292	Durham, NC	(4.7)
292	Sunnyvale, CA	(4.7)
296	Green Bay, WI	(4.8)
297	Newport Beach, CA	(4.9)
297	Simi Valley, CA	(4.9)
297	Spokane Valley, WA	(4.9)
300	Fort Worth, TX	(5.0)
301	Broken Arrow, OK	(5.1)
301	Carlsbad, CA	(5.1)
301	Independence, MO	(5.1)
301	Reading, PA	(5.1)
301	Stockton, CA	(5.1)
301	Yuma, AZ	(5.1)
307	Daly City, CA	(5.3)
307	Erie, PA	(5.3)
307	Plano, TX	(5.3)
310	Lynn, MA	(5.5)
310	Murrieta, CA	(5.5)
312	Grand Prairie, TX	(5.7)
312	New York, NY	(5.7)
314	Charlotte, NC	(5.8)
314	Clarksville, TN	(5.8)
316	College Station, TX	(5.9)
317	Lincoln, NE	(6.0)
318	Toledo, OH	(6.3)
319	Port St. Lucie, FL	(6.4)
320	Lubbock, TX	(6.5)
321	Portland, OR	(6.6)
322	Boulder, CO	(6.7)
322	Orlando, FL	(6.7)
322	Tampa, FL	(6.7)
325	Lakeland, FL	(7.1)
325	Sparks, NV	(7.1)
325	Worcester, MA	(7.1)
328	Bakersfield, CA	(7.3)
328	Warwick, RI	(7.3)
330	Brockton, MA	(7.4)
330	Omaha, NE	(7.4)
330	Sioux Falls, SD	(7.4)
330	Tallahassee, FL	(7.4)
334	McAllen, TX	(7.5)
335	Lawrence, KS	(8.0)
336	Davie, FL	(8.1)
337	Elgin, IL	(8.2)
337	Fort Wayne, IN	(8.2)
337	Frisco, TX	(8.2)
340	Newton, MA	(8.4)
341	Edison Twnshp, NJ	(8.6)
341	Fall River, MA	(8.6)

RANK	CITY	% CHANGE
341	Lewisville, TX	(8.6)
341	Rockford, IL	(8.6)
345	O'Fallon, MO	(8.7)
346	Colorado Springs, CO	(8.9)
347	Las Cruces, NM	(9.2)
348	Chattanooga, TN	(9.7)
349	Denton, TX	(10.1)
350	Greece, NY	(10.2)
351	Alexandria, VA	(10.4)
351	Chico, CA	(10.4)
353	Gary, IN	(10.7)
354	North Las Vegas, NV	(11.4)
355	Fayetteville, AR	(11.7)
355	San Diego, CA	(11.7)
357	El Cajon, CA	(11.8)
358	Camden, NJ	(11.9)
359	Cary, NC	(12.2)
359	Chino, CA	(12.2)
361	Detroit, MI	(12.5)
362	Roseville, CA	(12.6)
363	Springfield, MO	(13.8)
364	High Point, NC	(13.9)
365	Bend, OR	(14.2)
365	Quincy, MA	(14.2)
367	Rio Rancho, NM	(15.3)
368	Raleigh, NC	(15.6)
369	Gilbert, AZ	(15.7)
370	Indio, CA	(16.7)
371	Pearland, TX	(17.0)
372	Clovis, CA	(17.6)
373	Joliet, IL	(17.6)
374	Flint, MI	(18.1)
375	Ann Arbor, MI	(19.4)
376	Fayetteville, NC	(19.4)
377	Vallejo, CA	(19.8)
378	Surprise, AZ	(20.5)
379	El Monte, CA	(20.6)
380	Atlanta, GA	(29.9)
NA	Baton Rouge, LA**	NA
NA	Carson, CA**	NA
NA	Centennial, CO**	NA
NA	Cheektowaga, NY**	NA
NA	Citrus Heights, CA**	NA
NA	Compton, CA**	NA
NA	Elk Grove, CA**	NA
NA	Hesperia, CA**	NA
NA	Kansas City, KS**	NA
NA	Lake Forest, CA**	NA
NA	Lakewood, CA**	NA
NA	Lancaster, CA**	NA
NA	Macon, GA**	NA
NA	Miami Beach, FL**	NA
NA	Mission Viejo, CA**	NA
NA	Moreno Valley, CA**	NA
NA	New Orleans, LA**	NA
NA	Norwalk, CA**	NA
NA	Olathe, KS**	NA
NA	Palmdale, CA**	NA
NA	Pompano Beach, FL**	NA
NA	Rancho Cucamon., CA**	NA
NA	Round Rock, TX**	NA
NA	San Marcos, CA**	NA
NA	Sandy Springs, GA**	NA
NA	Santa Clarita, CA**	NA
NA	Shreveport, LA**	NA
NA	Temecula, CA**	NA
NA	Thousand Oaks, CA**	NA
NA	Victorville, CA**	NA
NA	Vista, CA**	NA

Source: CQ Press using reported data from the F.B.I. "Crime in the United States 2009"
*Sworn officers only, does not include civilian employees.
**Not available

III. Metropolitan and City Populations

85. Metropolitan Population in 2009
National Total = 307,006,550*

RANK	METROPOLITAN AREA	POP
254	Abilene, TX	159,632
96	Akron, OH	700,932
78	Albany-Schenectady-Troy, NY	856,725
245	Albany, GA	165,165
77	Albuquerque, NM	862,190
259	Alexandria, LA	154,999
81	Allentown, PA-NJ	817,689
305	Altoona, PA	125,069
197	Amarillo, TX	246,040
360	Ames, IA	87,399
170	Anchorage, AK	305,284
295	Anderson, IN	131,524
234	Anderson, SC	185,794
162	Ann Arbor, MI	348,606
323	Anniston-Oxford, AL	114,155
208	Appleton, WI	221,608
141	Asheville, NC	413,556
231	Athens-Clarke County, GA	191,096
9	Atlanta, GA	5,494,398
184	Atlantic City, NJ	272,593
286	Auburn, AL	135,710
118	Augusta, GA-SC	537,765
52	Austin-Round Rock, TX	1,705,541
82	Bakersfield, CA	814,516
26	Baltimore-Towson, MD	2,693,099
268	Bangor, ME	148,774
207	Barnstable Town, MA	224,302
87	Baton Rouge, LA	787,715
289	Battle Creek, MI	135,076
337	Bay City, MI	106,777
154	Beaumont-Port Arthur, TX	377,984
221	Bellingham, WA	201,195
248	Bend, OR	163,637
64	Bethesda-Frederick, MD M.D.	1,194,257
260	Billings, MT	153,443
198	Binghamton, NY	244,367
66	Birmingham-Hoover, AL	1,130,745
336	Bismarck, ND	106,952
252	Blacksburg, VA	159,705
236	Bloomington, IN	185,191
106	Boise City-Nampa, ID	614,020
11	Boston (greater), MA-NH	4,586,485
44	Boston-Quincy, MA M.D.	1,912,393
176	Boulder, CO	296,153
315	Bowling Green, KY	119,746
201	Bremerton-Silverdale, WA	242,027
76	Bridgeport-Stamford, CT	878,051
150	Brownsville-Harlingen, TX	399,958
342	Brunswick, GA	103,525
69	Buffalo-Niagara Falls, NY	1,119,104
213	Burlington-South Burlington, VT	209,200
266	Burlington, NC	150,252
56	Cambridge-Newton, MA M.D.	1,504,293
60	Camden, NJ M.D.	1,257,180
108	Cape Coral-Fort Myers, FL	607,216
354	Cape Girardeau, MO-IL	93,713
369	Carson City, NV	54,462
366	Casper, WY	74,856
192	Cedar Rapids, IA	257,120
102	Charleston-North Charleston, SC	659,704
172	Charleston, WV	303,984
49	Charlotte-Gastonia, NC-SC	1,752,202
227	Charlottesville, VA	197,483
120	Chattanooga, TN-GA	523,787
357	Cheyenne, WY	89,355
209	Chico, CA	221,473
35	Cincinnati-Middletown, OH-KY-IN	2,178,158
187	Clarksville, TN-KY	265,303
39	Cleveland-Elyria-Mentor, OH	2,093,232
326	Cleveland, TN	113,409
281	Coeur d'Alene, ID	140,410
211	College Station-Bryan, TX	210,281
105	Colorado Springs, CO	628,075
243	Columbia, MO	166,465
92	Columbia, SC	741,623
179	Columbus, GA-AL	287,607
365	Columbus, IN	75,902
47	Columbus, OH	1,797,471
139	Corpus Christi, TX	417,198
362	Corvallis, OR	82,116
239	Crestview-Fort Walton Beach, FL	179,103
348	Cumberland, MD-WV	99,133
5	Dallas (greater), TX	6,449,790
14	Dallas-Plano-Irving, TX M.D.	4,330,070
288	Dalton, GA	135,102
363	Danville, IL	80,017
338	Danville, VA	105,723
80	Dayton, OH	837,876
264	Decatur, AL	151,260
334	Decatur, IL	107,232
124	Deltona-Daytona Beach, FL	499,859
28	Denver-Aurora, CO	2,550,871
111	Des Moines-West Des Moines, IA	564,422
12	Detroit (greater), MI	4,404,383
43	Detroit-Livonia-Dearborn, MI M.D.	1,930,388
280	Dothan, AL	142,752
255	Dover, DE	159,218
356	Dubuque, IA	92,984
182	Duluth, MN-WI	274,899
125	Durham-Chapel Hill, NC	498,273
251	Eau Claire, WI	159,822
33	Edison, NJ M.D.	2,340,627
244	El Centro, CA	165,988
89	El Paso, TX	749,958
328	Elizabethtown, KY	112,967
220	Elkhart-Goshen, IN	201,289
359	Elmira, NY	87,431
181	Erie, PA	279,714
163	Eugene-Springfield, OR	348,528
161	Evansville, IN-KY	351,684
223	Fargo, ND-MN	199,348
309	Farmington, NM	123,809
130	Fayetteville, AR-MO	457,820
158	Fayetteville, NC	358,986
301	Flagstaff, AZ	128,458
136	Flint, MI	426,176
275	Florence-Muscle Shoals, AL	144,517
219	Florence, SC	201,707
346	Fond du Lac, WI	99,634
175	Fort Collins-Loveland, CO	298,107
50	Fort Lauderdale, FL M.D.	1,749,470
177	Fort Smith, AR-OK	294,314
140	Fort Wayne, IN	414,144
38	Fort Worth-Arlington, TX M.D.	2,119,720
74	Fresno, CA	918,710
341	Gadsden, AL	103,760
190	Gainesville, FL	259,242
232	Gainesville, GA	189,639
300	Glens Falls, NY	129,238
324	Goldsboro, NC	113,890
350	Grand Forks, ND-MN	97,848
272	Grand Junction, CO	146,602
88	Grand Rapids-Wyoming, MI	777,531
361	Great Falls, MT	82,193
191	Greeley, CO	259,011
171	Green Bay, WI	305,045
93	Greensboro-High Point, NC	713,890
203	Gulfport-Biloxi, MS	233,616
185	Hagerstown-Martinsburg, MD-WV	269,769
119	Harrisburg-Carlisle, PA	534,951
313	Harrisonburg, VA	120,036
72	Hartford, CT	1,007,503
279	Hattiesburg, MS	142,822
157	Hickory, NC	365,928
367	Hinesville, GA	69,456
189	Holland-Grand Haven, MI	261,736
75	Honolulu, HI	907,124
349	Hot Springs, AR	98,925
217	Houma, LA	203,180
7	Houston, TX	5,858,967
149	Huntsville, AL	403,661
306	Idaho Falls, ID	125,056
51	Indianapolis, IN	1,742,101
263	Iowa City, IA	151,283
344	Ithaca, NY	101,616
57	Jacksonville, FL	1,324,985
241	Jacksonville, NC	168,113
253	Jackson, MI	159,695
115	Jackson, MS	542,259
325	Jackson, TN	113,615
250	Janesville, WI	161,011
269	Jefferson City, MO	147,055
226	Johnson City, TN	198,071
317	Jonesboro, AR	118,932
166	Kalamazoo-Portage, MI	323,342
42	Kansas City, MO-KS	2,060,705
199	Kennewick-Pasco-Richland, WA	242,824
153	Killeen-Temple-Fort Hood, TX	385,136
169	Kingsport, TN-VA	306,401
237	Kingston, NY	182,041
95	Knoxville, TN	702,038
347	Kokomo, IN	99,224
294	La Crosse, WI-MN	132,407
229	Lafayette, IN	194,848
188	Lafayette, LA	263,042
230	Lake Charles, LA	194,066
224	Lake Havasu City-Kingman, AZ	199,041
109	Lakeland, FL	587,062
123	Lancaster, PA	507,174
132	Lansing-East Lansing, MI	452,842

Note: All listings are for Metropolitan Statistical Areas (M.S.A.s) except for those ending with "M.D." Listings with "M.D." are Metropolitan Divisions which are smaller parts of eleven large M.S.A.s. See explanatory note at beginning of metropolitan area section.

Alpha Order - Metro Area (continued)

RANK	METROPOLITAN AREA	POP
200	Laredo, TX	242,446
215	Las Cruces, NM	205,347
45	Las Vegas-Paradise, NV	1,903,935
319	Lawrence, KS	116,602
329	Lawton, OK	112,142
299	Lebanon, PA	130,248
335	Lewiston-Auburn, ME	107,004
368	Lewiston, ID-WA	60,637
127	Lexington-Fayette, KY	470,843
339	Lima, OH	105,110
174	Lincoln, NE	299,461
99	Little Rock, AR	685,389
302	Logan, UT-ID	127,116
214	Longview, TX	206,197
343	Longview, WA	102,816
4	Los Angeles County, CA M.D.	9,863,786
2	Los Angeles (greater), CA	12,881,669
61	Louisville, KY-IN	1,256,252
183	Lubbock, TX	273,291
196	Lynchburg, VA	248,706
205	Macon, GA	230,750
265	Madera, CA	150,856
110	Madison, WI	568,019
148	Manchester-Nashua, NH	404,309
310	Manhattan, KS	123,597
355	Mankato-North Mankato, MN	93,372
307	Mansfield, OH	124,956
91	McAllen-Edinburg-Mission, TX	746,767
218	Medford, OR	203,007
58	Memphis, TN-MS-AR	1,299,027
195	Merced, CA	249,432
8	Miami (greater), FL	5,501,220
30	Miami-Dade County, FL M.D.	2,482,417
330	Michigan City-La Porte, IN	111,155
298	Midland, TX	131,294
55	Milwaukee, WI	1,553,875
20	Minneapolis-St. Paul, MN-WI	3,266,869
333	Missoula, MT	108,586
143	Mobile, AL	408,816
121	Modesto, CA	516,191
262	Monroe, MI	153,073
155	Montgomery, AL	369,848
316	Morgantown, WV	119,585
284	Morristown, TN	137,792
312	Mount Vernon-Anacortes, WA	120,438
322	Muncie, IN	114,435
240	Muskegon-Norton Shores, MI	174,071
291	Napa, CA	133,996
167	Naples-Marco Island, FL	320,093
54	Nashville-Davidson, TN	1,584,715
23	Nassau-Suffolk, NY M.D.	2,874,918
86	New Haven-Milford, CT	794,705
65	New Orleans, LA	1,179,206
1	New York (greater), NY-NJ-PA	19,075,412
3	New York-W. Plains NY-NJ M.D.	11,737,038
37	Newark-Union, NJ-PA M.D.	2,122,829
257	Niles-Benton Harbor, MI	158,501
98	North Port-Bradenton-Sarasota, FL	693,167
283	Norwich-New London, CT	138,611
29	Oakland-Fremont, CA M.D.	2,506,947
165	Ocala, FL	335,426
353	Ocean City, NJ	95,099
293	Odessa, TX	133,400

RANK	METROPOLITAN AREA	POP
116	Ogden-Clearfield, UT	539,260
63	Oklahoma City, OK	1,226,361
194	Olympia, WA	251,133
79	Omaha-Council Bluffs, NE-IA	847,725
40	Orlando, FL	2,087,292
249	Oshkosh-Neenah, WI	162,596
327	Owensboro, KY	113,253
84	Oxnard-Thousand Oaks, CA	799,696
117	Palm Bay-Melbourne, FL	538,696
351	Palm Coast, FL	96,615
246	Panama City-Lynn Haven, FL	164,328
261	Pascagoula, MS	153,415
90	Peabody, MA M.D.	747,294
131	Pensacola, FL	453,889
6	Philadelphia (greater) PA-NJ-MD-DI	5,970,355
18	Philadelphia, PA M.D.	4,011,029
13	Phoenix-Mesa-Scottsdale, AZ	4,362,725
345	Pine Bluff, AR	100,339
32	Pittsburgh, PA	2,348,787
297	Pittsfield, MA	131,299
358	Pocatello, ID	88,737
142	Port St. Lucie, FL	410,941
34	Portland-Vancouver, OR-WA	2,239,268
122	Portland, ME	515,866
101	Poughkeepsie, NY	677,974
210	Prescott, AZ	218,897
53	Providence-New Bedford, RI-MA	1,607,064
113	Provo-Orem, UT	559,579
256	Pueblo, CO	158,754
267	Punta Gorda, FL	149,640
222	Racine, WI	200,613
67	Raleigh-Cary, NC	1,127,897
308	Rapid City, SD	123,903
144	Reading, PA	407,999
238	Redding, CA	181,512
138	Reno-Sparks, NV	418,246
62	Richmond, VA	1,245,391
17	Riverside-San Bernardino, CA	4,208,217
173	Roanoke, VA	300,340
235	Rochester, MN	185,487
70	Rochester, NY	1,032,945
137	Rockingham County, NH M.D.	422,505
271	Rocky Mount, NC	146,985
352	Rome, GA	96,145
36	Sacramento, CA	2,139,517
225	Saginaw, MI	198,943
151	Salem, OR	396,094
145	Salinas, CA	407,403
311	Salisbury, MD	122,004
68	Salt Lake City, UT	1,126,937
331	San Angelo, TX	110,104
41	San Antonio, TX	2,072,016
22	San Diego, CA	3,010,824
15	San Francisco (greater), CA	4,275,475
48	San Francisco-S. Mateo, CA M.D.	1,768,528
46	San Jose, CA	1,821,945
186	San Luis Obispo, CA	266,382
364	Sandusky, OH	77,014
21	Santa Ana-Anaheim, CA M.D.	3,017,883
147	Santa Barbara-Santa Maria, CA	404,613
193	Santa Cruz-Watsonville, CA	251,964
274	Santa Fe, NM	145,984
129	Santa Rosa-Petaluma, CA	465,831

RANK	METROPOLITAN AREA	POP
164	Savannah, GA	337,908
114	Scranton--Wilkes-Barre, PA	549,402
27	Seattle-Bellevue-Everett, WA M.D.	2,598,918
19	Seattle-Tacoma-Bellevue, WA	3,398,863
292	Sebastian-Vero Beach, FL	133,420
321	Sheboygan, WI	114,705
314	Sherman-Denison, TX	119,831
152	Shreveport-Bossier City, LA	393,564
278	Sioux City, IA-NE-SD	143,132
202	Sioux Falls, SD	239,252
168	South Bend-Mishawaka, IN-MI	317,097
180	Spartanburg, SC	285,421
128	Spokane, WA	470,570
97	Springfield, MA	697,676
133	Springfield, MO	433,099
282	Springfield, OH	139,752
273	State College, PA	146,172
100	Stockton, CA	682,784
233	St. Cloud, MN	189,562
277	St. George, UT	143,274
303	St. Joseph, MO-KS	126,650
24	St. Louis, MO-IL	2,829,698
340	Sumter, SC	104,675
104	Syracuse, NY	642,939
83	Tacoma, WA M.D.	799,945
159	Tallahassee, FL	358,382
25	Tampa-St Petersburg, FL	2,750,962
285	Texarkana, TX-Texarkana, AR	136,443
103	Toledo, OH	649,954
206	Topeka, KS	230,405
156	Trenton-Ewing, NJ	366,219
71	Tucson, AZ	1,020,210
73	Tulsa, OK	928,117
212	Tuscaloosa, AL	209,255
216	Tyler, TX	204,582
178	Utica-Rome, NY	293,084
290	Valdosta, GA	134,375
146	Vallejo-Fairfield, CA	407,294
320	Victoria, TX	114,735
258	Vineland, NJ	157,963
134	Visalia-Porterville, CA	431,712
204	Waco, TX	232,320
287	Warner Robins, GA	135,248
31	Warren-Farmington Hills, MI M.D.	2,473,995
10	Washington (greater) DC-VA-MD-WV	5,452,184
16	Washington, DC-VA-MD-WV M.D.	4,257,927
247	Waterloo-Cedar Falls, IA	164,044
296	Wausau, WI	131,469
332	Wenatchee, WA	109,866
59	West Palm Beach, FL M.D.	1,269,333
276	Wheeling, WV-OH	144,342
270	Wichita Falls, TX	147,018
107	Wichita, KS	608,013
318	Williamsport, PA	116,606
94	Wilmington, DE-MD-NJ M.D.	702,146
160	Wilmington, NC	356,659
304	Winchester, VA-WV	125,112
126	Winston-Salem, NC	474,159
85	Worcester, MA	795,340
135	York-Hanover, PA	430,605
112	Youngstown, OH-PA	563,698
242	Yuba City, CA	167,852
228	Yuma, AZ	196,196

Source: Reported data from the F.B.I. "Crime in the United States 2009"
*Estimates as of July 2009 based on U.S. Bureau of the Census figures.

85. Metropolitan Population in 2009 (continued)
National Total = 307,006,550*

RANK	METROPOLITAN AREA	POP
1	New York (greater), NY-NJ-PA	19,075,412
2	Los Angeles (greater), CA	12,881,669
3	New York-W. Plains NY-NJ M.D.	11,737,038
4	Los Angeles County, CA M.D.	9,863,786
5	Dallas (greater), TX	6,449,790
6	Philadelphia (greater) PA-NJ-MD-DI	5,970,355
7	Houston, TX	5,858,967
8	Miami (greater), FL	5,501,220
9	Atlanta, GA	5,494,398
10	Washington (greater) DC-VA-MD-W	5,452,184
11	Boston (greater), MA-NH	4,586,485
12	Detroit (greater), MI	4,404,383
13	Phoenix-Mesa-Scottsdale, AZ	4,362,725
14	Dallas-Plano-Irving, TX M.D.	4,330,070
15	San Francisco (greater), CA	4,275,475
16	Washington, DC-VA-MD-WV M.D.	4,257,927
17	Riverside-San Bernardino, CA	4,208,217
18	Philadelphia, PA M.D.	4,011,029
19	Seattle-Tacoma-Bellevue, WA	3,398,863
20	Minneapolis-St. Paul, MN-WI	3,266,869
21	Santa Ana-Anaheim, CA M.D.	3,017,883
22	San Diego, CA	3,010,824
23	Nassau-Suffolk, NY M.D.	2,874,918
24	St. Louis, MO-IL	2,829,698
25	Tampa-St Petersburg, FL	2,750,962
26	Baltimore-Towson, MD	2,693,099
27	Seattle-Bellevue-Everett, WA M.D.	2,598,918
28	Denver-Aurora, CO	2,550,871
29	Oakland-Fremont, CA M.D.	2,506,947
30	Miami-Dade County, FL M.D.	2,482,417
31	Warren-Farmington Hills, MI M.D.	2,473,995
32	Pittsburgh, PA	2,348,787
33	Edison, NJ M.D.	2,340,627
34	Portland-Vancouver, OR-WA	2,239,268
35	Cincinnati-Middletown, OH-KY-IN	2,178,158
36	Sacramento, CA	2,139,517
37	Newark-Union, NJ-PA M.D.	2,122,829
38	Fort Worth-Arlington, TX M.D.	2,119,720
39	Cleveland-Elyria-Mentor, OH	2,093,232
40	Orlando, FL	2,087,292
41	San Antonio, TX	2,072,016
42	Kansas City, MO-KS	2,060,705
43	Detroit-Livonia-Dearborn, MI M.D.	1,930,388
44	Boston-Quincy, MA M.D.	1,912,393
45	Las Vegas-Paradise, NV	1,903,935
46	San Jose, CA	1,821,945
47	Columbus, OH	1,797,471
48	San Francisco-S. Mateo, CA M.D.	1,768,528
49	Charlotte-Gastonia, NC-SC	1,752,202
50	Fort Lauderdale, FL M.D.	1,749,470
51	Indianapolis, IN	1,742,101
52	Austin-Round Rock, TX	1,705,541
53	Providence-New Bedford, RI-MA	1,607,064
54	Nashville-Davidson, TN	1,584,715
55	Milwaukee, WI	1,553,875
56	Cambridge-Newton, MA M.D.	1,504,293
57	Jacksonville, FL	1,324,985
58	Memphis, TN-MS-AR	1,299,027
59	West Palm Beach, FL M.D.	1,269,333
60	Camden, NJ M.D.	1,257,180
61	Louisville, KY-IN	1,256,252
62	Richmond, VA	1,245,391
63	Oklahoma City, OK	1,226,361
64	Bethesda-Frederick, MD M.D.	1,194,257
65	New Orleans, LA	1,179,206
66	Birmingham-Hoover, AL	1,130,745
67	Raleigh-Cary, NC	1,127,897
68	Salt Lake City, UT	1,126,937
69	Buffalo-Niagara Falls, NY	1,119,104
70	Rochester, NY	1,032,945
71	Tucson, AZ	1,020,210
72	Hartford, CT	1,007,503
73	Tulsa, OK	928,117
74	Fresno, CA	918,710
75	Honolulu, HI	907,124
76	Bridgeport-Stamford, CT	878,051
77	Albuquerque, NM	862,190
78	Albany-Schenectady-Troy, NY	856,725
79	Omaha-Council Bluffs, NE-IA	847,725
80	Dayton, OH	837,876
81	Allentown, PA-NJ	817,689
82	Bakersfield, CA	814,516
83	Tacoma, WA M.D.	799,945
84	Oxnard-Thousand Oaks, CA	799,696
85	Worcester, MA	795,340
86	New Haven-Milford, CT	794,705
87	Baton Rouge, LA	787,715
88	Grand Rapids-Wyoming, MI	777,531
89	El Paso, TX	749,958
90	Peabody, MA M.D.	747,294
91	McAllen-Edinburg-Mission, TX	746,767
92	Columbia, SC	741,623
93	Greensboro-High Point, NC	713,890
94	Wilmington, DE-MD-NJ M.D.	702,146
95	Knoxville, TN	702,038
96	Akron, OH	700,932
97	Springfield, MA	697,676
98	North Port-Bradenton-Sarasota, FL	693,167
99	Little Rock, AR	685,389
100	Stockton, CA	682,784
101	Poughkeepsie, NY	677,974
102	Charleston-North Charleston, SC	659,704
103	Toledo, OH	649,954
104	Syracuse, NY	642,939
105	Colorado Springs, CO	628,075
106	Boise City-Nampa, ID	614,020
107	Wichita, KS	608,013
108	Cape Coral-Fort Myers, FL	607,216
109	Lakeland, FL	587,062
110	Madison, WI	568,019
111	Des Moines-West Des Moines, IA	564,422
112	Youngstown, OH-PA	563,698
113	Provo-Orem, UT	559,579
114	Scranton--Wilkes-Barre, PA	549,402
115	Jackson, MS	542,259
116	Ogden-Clearfield, UT	539,260
117	Palm Bay-Melbourne, FL	538,696
118	Augusta, GA-SC	537,765
119	Harrisburg-Carlisle, PA	534,951
120	Chattanooga, TN-GA	523,787
121	Modesto, CA	516,191
122	Portland, ME	515,866
123	Lancaster, PA	507,174
124	Deltona-Daytona Beach, FL	499,859
125	Durham-Chapel Hill, NC	498,273
126	Winston-Salem, NC	474,159
127	Lexington-Fayette, KY	470,843
128	Spokane, WA	470,570
129	Santa Rosa-Petaluma, CA	465,831
130	Fayetteville, AR-MO	457,820
131	Pensacola, FL	453,889
132	Lansing-East Lansing, MI	452,842
133	Springfield, MO	433,099
134	Visalia-Porterville, CA	431,712
135	York-Hanover, PA	430,605
136	Flint, MI	426,176
137	Rockingham County, NH M.D.	422,505
138	Reno-Sparks, NV	418,246
139	Corpus Christi, TX	417,198
140	Fort Wayne, IN	414,144
141	Asheville, NC	413,556
142	Port St. Lucie, FL	410,941
143	Mobile, AL	408,816
144	Reading, PA	407,999
145	Salinas, CA	407,403
146	Vallejo-Fairfield, CA	407,294
147	Santa Barbara-Santa Maria, CA	404,613
148	Manchester-Nashua, NH	404,309
149	Huntsville, AL	403,661
150	Brownsville-Harlingen, TX	399,958
151	Salem, OR	396,094
152	Shreveport-Bossier City, LA	393,564
153	Killeen-Temple-Fort Hood, TX	385,136
154	Beaumont-Port Arthur, TX	377,984
155	Montgomery, AL	369,848
156	Trenton-Ewing, NJ	366,219
157	Hickory, NC	365,928
158	Fayetteville, NC	358,986
159	Tallahassee, FL	358,382
160	Wilmington, NC	356,659
161	Evansville, IN-KY	351,684
162	Ann Arbor, MI	348,606
163	Eugene-Springfield, OR	348,528
164	Savannah, GA	337,908
165	Ocala, FL	335,426
166	Kalamazoo-Portage, MI	323,342
167	Naples-Marco Island, FL	320,093
168	South Bend-Mishawaka, IN-MI	317,097
169	Kingsport, TN-VA	306,401
170	Anchorage, AK	305,284
171	Green Bay, WI	305,045
172	Charleston, WV	303,984
173	Roanoke, VA	300,340
174	Lincoln, NE	299,461
175	Fort Collins-Loveland, CO	298,107
176	Boulder, CO	296,153
177	Fort Smith, AR-OK	294,314
178	Utica-Rome, NY	293,084
179	Columbus, GA-AL	287,607
180	Spartanburg, SC	285,421

Note: All listings are for Metropolitan Statistical Areas (M.S.A.s) except for those ending with "M.D." Listings with "M.D." are Metropolitan Divisions which are smaller parts of eleven large M.S.A.s. See explanatory note at beginning of metropolitan area section.

RANK	METROPOLITAN AREA	POP
181	Erie, PA	279,714
182	Duluth, MN-WI	274,899
183	Lubbock, TX	273,291
184	Atlantic City, NJ	272,593
185	Hagerstown-Martinsburg, MD-WV	269,769
186	San Luis Obispo, CA	266,382
187	Clarksville, TN-KY	265,303
188	Lafayette, LA	263,042
189	Holland-Grand Haven, MI	261,736
190	Gainesville, FL	259,242
191	Greeley, CO	259,011
192	Cedar Rapids, IA	257,120
193	Santa Cruz-Watsonville, CA	251,964
194	Olympia, WA	251,133
195	Merced, CA	249,432
196	Lynchburg, VA	248,706
197	Amarillo, TX	246,040
198	Binghamton, NY	244,367
199	Kennewick-Pasco-Richland, WA	242,824
200	Laredo, TX	242,446
201	Bremerton-Silverdale, WA	242,027
202	Sioux Falls, SD	239,252
203	Gulfport-Biloxi, MS	233,616
204	Waco, TX	232,320
205	Macon, GA	230,750
206	Topeka, KS	230,405
207	Barnstable Town, MA	224,302
208	Appleton, WI	221,608
209	Chico, CA	221,473
210	Prescott, AZ	218,897
211	College Station-Bryan, TX	210,281
212	Tuscaloosa, AL	209,255
213	Burlington-South Burlington, VT	209,200
214	Longview, TX	206,197
215	Las Cruces, NM	205,347
216	Tyler, TX	204,582
217	Houma, LA	203,180
218	Medford, OR	203,007
219	Florence, SC	201,707
220	Elkhart-Goshen, IN	201,289
221	Bellingham, WA	201,195
222	Racine, WI	200,613
223	Fargo, ND-MN	199,348
224	Lake Havasu City-Kingman, AZ	199,041
225	Saginaw, MI	198,943
226	Johnson City, TN	198,071
227	Charlottesville, VA	197,483
228	Yuma, AZ	196,196
229	Lafayette, IN	194,848
230	Lake Charles, LA	194,066
231	Athens-Clarke County, GA	191,096
232	Gainesville, GA	189,639
233	St. Cloud, MN	189,562
234	Anderson, SC	185,794
235	Rochester, MN	185,487
236	Bloomington, IN	185,191
237	Kingston, NY	182,041
238	Redding, CA	181,512
239	Crestview-Fort Walton Beach, FL	179,103
240	Muskegon-Norton Shores, MI	174,071
241	Jacksonville, NC	168,113
242	Yuba City, CA	167,852
243	Columbia, MO	166,465

RANK	METROPOLITAN AREA	POP
244	El Centro, CA	165,988
245	Albany, GA	165,165
246	Panama City-Lynn Haven, FL	164,328
247	Waterloo-Cedar Falls, IA	164,044
248	Bend, OR	163,637
249	Oshkosh-Neenah, WI	162,596
250	Janesville, WI	161,011
251	Eau Claire, WI	159,822
252	Blacksburg, VA	159,705
253	Jackson, MI	159,695
254	Abilene, TX	159,632
255	Dover, DE	159,218
256	Pueblo, CO	158,754
257	Niles-Benton Harbor, MI	158,501
258	Vineland, NJ	157,963
259	Alexandria, LA	154,999
260	Billings, MT	153,443
261	Pascagoula, MS	153,415
262	Monroe, MI	153,073
263	Iowa City, IA	151,283
264	Decatur, AL	151,260
265	Madera, CA	150,856
266	Burlington, NC	150,252
267	Punta Gorda, FL	149,640
268	Bangor, ME	148,774
269	Jefferson City, MO	147,055
270	Wichita Falls, TX	147,018
271	Rocky Mount, NC	146,985
272	Grand Junction, CO	146,602
273	State College, PA	146,172
274	Santa Fe, NM	145,984
275	Florence-Muscle Shoals, AL	144,517
276	Wheeling, WV-OH	144,342
277	St. George, UT	143,274
278	Sioux City, IA-NE-SD	143,132
279	Hattiesburg, MS	142,822
280	Dothan, AL	142,752
281	Coeur d'Alene, ID	140,410
282	Springfield, OH	139,752
283	Norwich-New London, CT	138,611
284	Morristown, TN	137,792
285	Texarkana, TX-Texarkana, AR	136,443
286	Auburn, AL	135,710
287	Warner Robins, GA	135,248
288	Dalton, GA	135,102
289	Battle Creek, MI	135,076
290	Valdosta, GA	134,375
291	Napa, CA	133,996
292	Sebastian-Vero Beach, FL	133,420
293	Odessa, TX	133,400
294	La Crosse, WI-MN	132,407
295	Anderson, IN	131,524
296	Wausau, WI	131,469
297	Pittsfield, MA	131,299
298	Midland, TX	131,294
299	Lebanon, PA	130,248
300	Glens Falls, NY	129,238
301	Flagstaff, AZ	128,458
302	Logan, UT-ID	127,116
303	St. Joseph, MO-KS	126,650
304	Winchester, VA-WV	125,112
305	Altoona, PA	125,069
306	Idaho Falls, ID	125,056

RANK	METROPOLITAN AREA	POP
307	Mansfield, OH	124,956
308	Rapid City, SD	123,903
309	Farmington, NM	123,809
310	Manhattan, KS	123,597
311	Salisbury, MD	122,004
312	Mount Vernon-Anacortes, WA	120,438
313	Harrisonburg, VA	120,036
314	Sherman-Denison, TX	119,831
315	Bowling Green, KY	119,746
316	Morgantown, WV	119,585
317	Jonesboro, AR	118,932
318	Williamsport, PA	116,606
319	Lawrence, KS	116,602
320	Victoria, TX	114,735
321	Sheboygan, WI	114,705
322	Muncie, IN	114,435
323	Anniston-Oxford, AL	114,155
324	Goldsboro, NC	113,890
325	Jackson, TN	113,615
326	Cleveland, TN	113,409
327	Owensboro, KY	113,253
328	Elizabethtown, KY	112,967
329	Lawton, OK	112,142
330	Michigan City-La Porte, IN	111,155
331	San Angelo, TX	110,104
332	Wenatchee, WA	109,866
333	Missoula, MT	108,586
334	Decatur, IL	107,232
335	Lewiston-Auburn, ME	107,004
336	Bismarck, ND	106,952
337	Bay City, MI	106,777
338	Danville, VA	105,723
339	Lima, OH	105,110
340	Sumter, SC	104,675
341	Gadsden, AL	103,760
342	Brunswick, GA	103,525
343	Longview, WA	102,816
344	Ithaca, NY	101,616
345	Pine Bluff, AR	100,339
346	Fond du Lac, WI	99,634
347	Kokomo, IN	99,224
348	Cumberland, MD-WV	99,133
349	Hot Springs, AR	98,925
350	Grand Forks, ND-MN	97,848
351	Palm Coast, FL	96,615
352	Rome, GA	96,145
353	Ocean City, NJ	95,099
354	Cape Girardeau, MO-IL	93,713
355	Mankato-North Mankato, MN	93,372
356	Dubuque, IA	92,984
357	Cheyenne, WY	89,355
358	Pocatello, ID	88,737
359	Elmira, NY	87,431
360	Ames, IA	87,399
361	Great Falls, MT	82,193
362	Corvallis, OR	82,116
363	Danville, IL	80,017
364	Sandusky, OH	77,014
365	Columbus, IN	75,902
366	Casper, WY	74,856
367	Hinesville, GA	69,456
368	Lewiston, ID-WA	60,637
369	Carson City, NV	54,462

Source: Reported data from the F.B.I. "Crime in the United States 2009"

*Estimates as of July 2009 based on U.S. Bureau of the Census figures.

86. Metropolitan Population in 2008
National Total = 304,374,846*

RANK	METROPOLITAN AREA	POP
234	Abilene, TX	159,257
85	Akron, OH	699,914
70	Albany-Schenectady-Troy, NY	856,504
NA	Albany, GA**	NA
71	Albuquerque, NM	846,731
NA	Alexandria, LA**	NA
74	Allentown, PA-NJ	811,166
278	Altoona, PA	125,036
185	Amarillo, TX	244,209
329	Ames, IA	85,516
161	Anchorage, AK	301,010
NA	Anderson, IN**	NA
220	Anderson, SC	182,566
150	Ann Arbor, MI	350,369
NA	Anniston-Oxford, AL**	NA
195	Appleton, WI	219,912
131	Asheville, NC	409,862
216	Athens-Clarke County, GA	189,226
8	Atlanta, GA	5,396,819
171	Atlantic City, NJ	271,795
266	Auburn, AL	132,798
107	Augusta, GA-SC	531,442
45	Austin-Round Rock, TX	1,646,660
75	Bakersfield, CA	804,287
24	Baltimore-Towson, MD	2,666,452
247	Bangor, ME	148,610
194	Barnstable Town, MA	223,304
78	Baton Rouge, LA	783,283
261	Battle Creek, MI	135,300
307	Bay City, MI	106,303
142	Beaumont-Port Arthur, TX	375,242
209	Bellingham, WA	196,614
233	Bend, OR	159,500
57	Bethesda-Frederick, MD M.D.	1,169,906
243	Billings, MT	151,343
183	Binghamton, NY	245,658
60	Birmingham-Hoover, AL	1,118,275
310	Bismarck, ND	104,611
237	Blacksburg, VA	157,811
218	Bloomington, IN	184,646
97	Boise City-Nampa, ID	603,185
11	Boston (greater), MA-NH	4,513,046
37	Boston-Quincy, MA M.D.	1,874,072
NA	Boulder, CO**	NA
290	Bowling Green, KY	117,583
188	Bremerton-Silverdale, WA	237,527
69	Bridgeport-Stamford, CT	878,111
138	Brownsville-Harlingen, TX	394,064
NA	Brunswick, GA**	NA
59	Buffalo-Niagara Falls, NY	1,122,844
NA	Burlington-South Burlington, VT**	NA
249	Burlington, NC	147,580
49	Cambridge-Newton, MA M.D.	1,482,271
53	Camden, NJ M.D.	1,248,666
96	Cape Coral-Fort Myers, FL	604,488
323	Cape Girardeau, MO-IL	93,556
337	Carson City, NV	54,316
334	Casper, WY	73,249
179	Cedar Rapids, IA	255,214
94	Charleston-North Charleston, SC	643,759
159	Charleston, WV	303,474
44	Charlotte-Gastonia, NC-SC	1,701,049
213	Charlottesville, VA	194,483
109	Chattanooga, TN-GA	518,576
327	Cheyenne, WY	87,931
196	Chico, CA	219,628
31	Cincinnati-Middletown, OH-KY-IN	2,150,520
173	Clarksville, TN-KY	265,686
NA	Cleveland-Elyria-Mentor, OH**	NA
301	Cleveland, TN	111,956
NA	Coeur d'Alene, ID**	NA
199	College Station-Bryan, TX	205,756
95	Colorado Springs, CO	618,723
226	Columbia, MO	164,226
83	Columbia, SC	728,119
167	Columbus, GA-AL	282,227
333	Columbus, IN	75,091
40	Columbus, OH	1,773,358
128	Corpus Christi, TX	415,807
331	Corvallis, OR	81,844
NA	Crestview-Fort Walton Beach, FL**	NA
318	Cumberland, MD-WV	98,503
5	Dallas (greater), TX	6,286,760
14	Dallas-Plano-Irving, TX M.D.	4,210,336
262	Dalton, GA	135,123
NA	Danville, IL**	NA
308	Danville, VA	104,868
73	Dayton, OH	834,203
244	Decatur, AL	150,005
NA	Decatur, IL**	NA
114	Deltona-Daytona Beach, FL	501,508
25	Denver-Aurora, CO	2,505,132
102	Des Moines-West Des Moines, IA	556,378
NA	Detroit (greater), MI**	NA
NA	Detroit-Livonia-Dearborn, MI M.D.*	NA
258	Dothan, AL	140,899
239	Dover, DE	155,344
324	Dubuque, IA	92,937
170	Duluth, MN-WI	273,527
115	Durham-Chapel Hill, NC	488,133
235	Eau Claire, WI	158,895
29	Edison, NJ M.D.	2,327,779
228	El Centro, CA	163,673
80	El Paso, TX	741,662
300	Elizabethtown, KY	112,156
206	Elkhart-Goshen, IN	199,699
328	Elmira, NY	87,619
169	Erie, PA	278,759
152	Eugene-Springfield, OR	346,191
149	Evansville, IN-KY	350,434
212	Fargo, ND-MN	194,942
281	Farmington, NM	123,156
122	Fayetteville, AR-MO	447,732
148	Fayetteville, NC	351,539
275	Flagstaff, AZ	128,071
123	Flint, MI	430,816
253	Florence-Muscle Shoals, AL	143,463
205	Florence, SC	200,297
317	Fond du Lac, WI	99,281
165	Fort Collins-Loveland, CO	292,381
41	Fort Lauderdale, FL M.D.	1,754,213
166	Fort Smith, AR-OK	291,712
129	Fort Wayne, IN	412,265
34	Fort Worth-Arlington, TX M.D.	2,076,424
67	Fresno, CA	907,820
312	Gadsden, AL	103,419
178	Gainesville, FL	257,041
NA	Gainesville, GA**	NA
273	Glens Falls, NY	129,422
297	Goldsboro, NC	113,923
319	Grand Forks, ND-MN	97,825
257	Grand Junction, CO	142,140
79	Grand Rapids-Wyoming, MI	774,538
330	Great Falls, MT	82,142
180	Greeley, CO	252,815
160	Green Bay, WI	303,250
84	Greensboro-High Point, NC	707,329
NA	Gulfport-Biloxi, MS**	NA
174	Hagerstown-Martinsburg, MD-WV	265,492
108	Harrisburg-Carlisle, PA	531,150
288	Harrisonburg, VA	118,335
65	Hartford, CT	1,006,641
NA	Hattiesburg, MS**	NA
146	Hickory, NC	363,694
335	Hinesville, GA	71,471
177	Holland-Grand Haven, MI	259,600
68	Honolulu, HI	906,349
320	Hot Springs, AR	97,366
201	Houma, LA	203,144
7	Houston, TX	5,752,684
139	Huntsville, AL	393,173
284	Idaho Falls, ID	121,458
43	Indianapolis, IN	1,717,530
245	Iowa City, IA	149,310
313	Ithaca, NY	101,591
50	Jacksonville, FL	1,308,904
225	Jacksonville, NC	164,774
231	Jackson, MI	162,183
104	Jackson, MS	540,558
299	Jackson, TN	113,254
232	Janesville, WI	160,438
NA	Jefferson City, MO**	NA
211	Johnson City, TN	194,959
291	Jonesboro, AR	117,434
155	Kalamazoo-Portage, MI	321,552
NA	Kansas City, MO-KS**	NA
189	Kennewick-Pasco-Richland, WA	234,413
143	Killeen-Temple-Fort Hood, TX	375,230
158	Kingsport, TN-VA	303,904
221	Kingston, NY	182,305
87	Knoxville, TN	689,656
316	Kokomo, IN	99,575
268	La Crosse, WI-MN	131,303
214	Lafayette, IN	193,802
176	Lafayette, LA	260,236
NA	Lake Charles, LA**	NA
208	Lake Havasu City-Kingman, AZ	199,207
99	Lakeland, FL	579,765
113	Lancaster, PA	501,669
119	Lansing-East Lansing, MI	453,640

Note: All listings are for Metropolitan Statistical Areas (M.S.A.s) except for those ending with "M.D." Listings with "M.D." are Metropolitan Divisions which are smaller parts of eleven large M.S.A.s. See explanatory note at beginning of metropolitan area section.

RANK	METROPOLITAN AREA	POP
187	Laredo, TX	238,490
204	Las Cruces, NM	201,390
38	Las Vegas-Paradise, NV	1,868,909
293	Lawrence, KS	115,531
298	Lawton, OK	113,817
274	Lebanon, PA	128,795
306	Lewiston-Auburn, ME	106,715
336	Lewiston, ID-WA	60,233
121	Lexington-Fayette, KY	452,390
309	Lima, OH	104,842
163	Lincoln, NE	295,470
91	Little Rock, AR	673,330
279	Logan, UT-ID	124,922
200	Longview, TX	204,851
314	Longview, WA	101,545
4	Los Angeles County, CA M.D.	9,872,263
2	Los Angeles (greater), CA	12,872,427
54	Louisville, KY-IN	1,243,209
172	Lubbock, TX	269,446
184	Lynchburg, VA	244,588
193	Macon, GA	229,719
246	Madera, CA	148,935
101	Madison, WI	562,105
NA	Manchester-Nashua, NH**	NA
287	Manhattan, KS	119,523
325	Mankato-North Mankato, MN	91,966
277	Mansfield, OH	125,317
82	McAllen-Edinburg-Mission, TX	729,820
203	Medford, OR	201,601
51	Memphis, TN-MS-AR	1,290,901
182	Merced, CA	248,898
9	Miami (greater), FL	5,395,910
27	Miami-Dade County, FL M.D.	2,373,744
302	Michigan City-La Porte, IN	109,674
276	Midland, TX	127,849
48	Milwaukee, WI	1,548,830
18	Minneapolis-St. Paul, MN-WI	3,231,521
305	Missoula, MT	107,119
135	Mobile, AL	405,797
110	Modesto, CA	516,995
240	Monroe, MI	153,241
144	Montgomery, AL	369,292
NA	Morgantown, WV**	NA
260	Morristown, TN	135,979
289	Mount Vernon-Anacortes, WA	118,241
294	Muncie, IN	114,943
223	Muskegon-Norton Shores, MI	173,418
265	Napa, CA	132,946
156	Naples-Marco Island, FL	320,551
47	Nashville-Davidson, TN	1,548,974
21	Nassau-Suffolk, NY M.D.	2,877,560
NA	New Haven-Milford, CT**	NA
61	New Orleans, LA	1,114,055
1	New York (greater), NY-NJ-PA	19,004,225
3	New York-W. Plains NY-NJ M.D.	11,675,083
32	Newark-Union, NJ-PA M.D.	2,123,803
236	Niles-Benton Harbor, MI	157,892
NA	North Port-Bradenton-Sarasota, FL**	NA
255	Norwich-New London, CT	142,186
26	Oakland-Fremont, CA M.D.	2,481,921
154	Ocala, FL	329,862
321	Ocean City, NJ	95,311
270	Odessa, TX	130,731

RANK	METROPOLITAN AREA	POP
106	Ogden-Clearfield, UT	535,090
56	Oklahoma City, OK	1,206,660
186	Olympia, WA	242,881
72	Omaha-Council Bluffs, NE-IA	838,325
35	Orlando, FL	2,060,706
230	Oshkosh-Neenah, WI	162,698
NA	Owensboro, KY**	NA
76	Oxnard-Thousand Oaks, CA	799,817
105	Palm Bay-Melbourne, FL	537,212
322	Palm Coast, FL	93,654
227	Panama City-Lynn Haven, FL	164,007
241	Pascagoula, MS	152,652
81	Peabody, MA M.D.	738,226
120	Pensacola, FL	453,297
6	Philadelphia (greater) PA-NJ-MD-DI	5,836,682
17	Philadelphia, PA M.D.	3,891,020
12	Phoenix-Mesa-Scottsdale, AZ	4,283,537
315	Pine Bluff, AR	100,732
28	Pittsburgh, PA	2,345,727
272	Pittsfield, MA	129,918
326	Pocatello, ID	87,959
133	Port St. Lucie, FL	406,587
30	Portland-Vancouver, OR-WA	2,207,851
112	Portland, ME	513,868
90	Poughkeepsie, NY	675,735
197	Prescott, AZ	217,520
46	Providence-New Bedford, RI-MA	1,597,765
111	Provo-Orem, UT	516,198
NA	Pueblo, CO**	NA
242	Punta Gorda, FL	152,292
210	Racine, WI	195,756
62	Raleigh-Cary, NC	1,085,760
283	Rapid City, SD	121,526
136	Reading, PA	405,335
222	Redding, CA	180,598
130	Reno-Sparks, NV	412,231
55	Richmond, VA	1,223,648
16	Riverside-San Bernardino, CA	4,175,614
162	Roanoke, VA	296,477
219	Rochester, MN	182,815
63	Rochester, NY	1,029,201
127	Rockingham County, NH M.D.	418,477
NA	Rocky Mount, NC**	NA
NA	Rome, GA**	NA
33	Sacramento, CA	2,119,553
207	Saginaw, MI	199,649
140	Salem, OR	391,860
134	Salinas, CA	406,198
285	Salisbury, MD	120,076
58	Salt Lake City, UT	1,131,292
303	San Angelo, TX	108,373
36	San Antonio, TX	2,027,812
20	San Diego, CA	2,979,368
13	San Francisco (greater), CA	4,230,321
42	San Francisco-S. Mateo, CA M.D.	1,748,400
39	San Jose, CA	1,802,847
175	San Luis Obispo, CA	263,017
332	Sandusky, OH	77,057
19	Santa Ana-Anaheim, CA M.D.	3,000,164
137	Santa Barbara-Santa Maria, CA	402,753
181	Santa Cruz-Watsonville, CA	250,002
252	Santa Fe, NM	144,261
117	Santa Rosa-Petaluma, CA	462,650

RANK	METROPOLITAN AREA	POP
153	Savannah, GA	332,641
103	Scranton--Wilkes-Barre, PA	547,925
NA	Seattle-Bellevue-Everett, WA M.D.**	NA
NA	Seattle-Tacoma-Bellevue, WA**	NA
267	Sebastian-Vero Beach, FL	132,682
295	Sheboygan, WI	114,653
286	Sherman-Denison, TX	119,673
141	Shreveport-Bossier City, LA	391,302
254	Sioux City, IA-NE-SD	143,016
190	Sioux Falls, SD	233,355
157	South Bend-Mishawaka, IN-MI	316,014
168	Spartanburg, SC	279,521
118	Spokane, WA	461,536
88	Springfield, MA	686,794
125	Springfield, MO	426,242
259	Springfield, OH	139,989
250	State College, PA	145,722
89	Stockton, CA	681,786
217	St. Cloud, MN	187,379
256	St. George, UT	142,153
282	St. Joseph, MO-KS	123,101
22	St. Louis, MO-IL	2,820,831
311	Sumter, SC	104,311
93	Syracuse, NY	644,461
NA	Tacoma, WA M.D.**	NA
147	Tallahassee, FL	352,043
23	Tampa-St Petersburg, FL	2,734,761
263	Texarkana, TX-Texarkana, AR	134,769
92	Toledo, OH	650,080
192	Topeka, KS	229,726
145	Trenton-Ewing, NJ	365,688
64	Tucson, AZ	1,010,650
66	Tulsa, OK	912,415
198	Tuscaloosa, AL	207,198
202	Tyler, TX	201,817
164	Utica-Rome, NY	294,181
269	Valdosta, GA	130,908
132	Vallejo-Fairfield, CA	408,066
296	Victoria, TX	114,072
238	Vineland, NJ	156,078
124	Visalia-Porterville, CA	426,568
191	Waco, TX	229,941
264	Warner Robins, GA	133,071
NA	Warren-Farmington Hills, MI M.D.**	NA
10	Washington (greater) DC-VA-MD-WV	5,363,413
15	Washington, DC-VA-MD-WV M.D.	4,193,507
229	Waterloo-Cedar Falls, IA	163,606
271	Wausau, WI	130,393
304	Wenatchee, WA	108,298
52	West Palm Beach, FL M.D.	1,267,953
251	Wheeling, WV-OH	144,612
248	Wichita Falls, TX	147,728
98	Wichita, KS	601,018
292	Williamsport, PA	116,368
86	Wilmington, DE-MD-NJ M.D.	696,996
151	Wilmington, NC	349,460
280	Winchester, VA-WV	123,259
116	Winston-Salem, NC	469,651
77	Worcester, MA	789,453
126	York-Hanover, PA	425,908
100	Youngstown, OH-PA	566,927
224	Yuba City, CA	166,703
215	Yuma, AZ	193,473

Source: Reported data from the F.B.I. "Crime in the United States 2008"
*Estimates as of July 2008 based on U.S. Bureau of the Census figures.
**Not available (comparable metro area not included in 2008 crime statistics).

86. Metropolitan Population in 2008 (continued)
National Total = 304,374,846*

RANK	METROPOLITAN AREA	POP	RANK	METROPOLITAN AREA	POP	RANK	METROPOLITAN AREA	POP
1	New York (greater), NY-NJ-PA	19,004,225	61	New Orleans, LA	1,114,055	121	Lexington-Fayette, KY	452,390
2	Los Angeles (greater), CA	12,872,427	62	Raleigh-Cary, NC	1,085,760	122	Fayetteville, AR-MO	447,732
3	New York-W. Plains NY-NJ M.D.	11,675,083	63	Rochester, NY	1,029,201	123	Flint, MI	430,816
4	Los Angeles County, CA M.D.	9,872,263	64	Tucson, AZ	1,010,650	124	Visalia-Porterville, CA	426,568
5	Dallas (greater), TX	6,286,760	65	Hartford, CT	1,006,641	125	Springfield, MO	426,242
6	Philadelphia (greater) PA-NJ-MD-DI	5,836,682	66	Tulsa, OK	912,415	126	York-Hanover, PA	425,908
7	Houston, TX	5,752,684	67	Fresno, CA	907,820	127	Rockingham County, NH M.D.	418,477
8	Atlanta, GA	5,396,819	68	Honolulu, HI	906,349	128	Corpus Christi, TX	415,807
9	Miami (greater), FL	5,395,910	69	Bridgeport-Stamford, CT	878,111	129	Fort Wayne, IN	412,265
10	Washington (greater) DC-VA-MD-W	5,363,413	70	Albany-Schenectady-Troy, NY	856,504	130	Reno-Sparks, NV	412,231
11	Boston (greater), MA-NH	4,513,046	71	Albuquerque, NM	846,731	131	Asheville, NC	409,862
12	Phoenix-Mesa-Scottsdale, AZ	4,283,537	72	Omaha-Council Bluffs, NE-IA	838,325	132	Vallejo-Fairfield, CA	408,066
13	San Francisco (greater), CA	4,230,321	73	Dayton, OH	834,203	133	Port St. Lucie, FL	406,587
14	Dallas-Plano-Irving, TX M.D.	4,210,336	74	Allentown, PA-NJ	811,166	134	Salinas, CA	406,198
15	Washington, DC-VA-MD-WV M.D.	4,193,507	75	Bakersfield, CA	804,287	135	Mobile, AL	405,797
16	Riverside-San Bernardino, CA	4,175,614	76	Oxnard-Thousand Oaks, CA	799,817	136	Reading, PA	405,335
17	Philadelphia, PA M.D.	3,891,020	77	Worcester, MA	789,453	137	Santa Barbara-Santa Maria, CA	402,753
18	Minneapolis-St. Paul, MN-WI	3,231,521	78	Baton Rouge, LA	783,283	138	Brownsville-Harlingen, TX	394,064
19	Santa Ana-Anaheim, CA M.D.	3,000,164	79	Grand Rapids-Wyoming, MI	774,538	139	Huntsville, AL	393,173
20	San Diego, CA	2,979,368	80	El Paso, TX	741,662	140	Salem, OR	391,860
21	Nassau-Suffolk, NY M.D.	2,877,560	81	Peabody, MA M.D.	738,226	141	Shreveport-Bossier City, LA	391,302
22	St. Louis, MO-IL	2,820,831	82	McAllen-Edinburg-Mission, TX	729,820	142	Beaumont-Port Arthur, TX	375,242
23	Tampa-St Petersburg, FL	2,734,761	83	Columbia, SC	728,119	143	Killeen-Temple-Fort Hood, TX	375,230
24	Baltimore-Towson, MD	2,666,452	84	Greensboro-High Point, NC	707,329	144	Montgomery, AL	369,292
25	Denver-Aurora, CO	2,505,132	85	Akron, OH	699,914	145	Trenton-Ewing, NJ	365,688
26	Oakland-Fremont, CA M.D.	2,481,921	86	Wilmington, DE-MD-NJ M.D.	696,996	146	Hickory, NC	363,694
27	Miami-Dade County, FL M.D.	2,373,744	87	Knoxville, TN	689,656	147	Tallahassee, FL	352,043
28	Pittsburgh, PA	2,345,727	88	Springfield, MA	686,794	148	Fayetteville, NC	351,539
29	Edison, NJ M.D.	2,327,779	89	Stockton, CA	681,786	149	Evansville, IN-KY	350,434
30	Portland-Vancouver, OR-WA	2,207,851	90	Poughkeepsie, NY	675,735	150	Ann Arbor, MI	350,369
31	Cincinnati-Middletown, OH-KY-IN	2,150,520	91	Little Rock, AR	673,330	151	Wilmington, NC	349,460
32	Newark-Union, NJ-PA M.D.	2,123,803	92	Toledo, OH	650,080	152	Eugene-Springfield, OR	346,191
33	Sacramento, CA	2,119,553	93	Syracuse, NY	644,461	153	Savannah, GA	332,641
34	Fort Worth-Arlington, TX M.D.	2,076,424	94	Charleston-North Charleston, SC	643,759	154	Ocala, FL	329,862
35	Orlando, FL	2,060,706	95	Colorado Springs, CO	618,723	155	Kalamazoo-Portage, MI	321,552
36	San Antonio, TX	2,027,812	96	Cape Coral-Fort Myers, FL	604,488	156	Naples-Marco Island, FL	320,551
37	Boston-Quincy, MA M.D.	1,874,072	97	Boise City-Nampa, ID	603,185	157	South Bend-Mishawaka, IN-MI	316,014
38	Las Vegas-Paradise, NV	1,868,909	98	Wichita, KS	601,018	158	Kingsport, TN-VA	303,904
39	San Jose, CA	1,802,847	99	Lakeland, FL	579,765	159	Charleston, WV	303,474
40	Columbus, OH	1,773,358	100	Youngstown, OH-PA	566,927	160	Green Bay, WI	303,250
41	Fort Lauderdale, FL M.D.	1,754,213	101	Madison, WI	562,105	161	Anchorage, AK	301,010
42	San Francisco-S. Mateo, CA M.D.	1,748,400	102	Des Moines-West Des Moines, IA	556,378	162	Roanoke, VA	296,477
43	Indianapolis, IN	1,717,530	103	Scranton--Wilkes-Barre, PA	547,925	163	Lincoln, NE	295,470
44	Charlotte-Gastonia, NC-SC	1,701,049	104	Jackson, MS	540,558	164	Utica-Rome, NY	294,181
45	Austin-Round Rock, TX	1,646,660	105	Palm Bay-Melbourne, FL	537,212	165	Fort Collins-Loveland, CO	292,381
46	Providence-New Bedford, RI-MA	1,597,765	106	Ogden-Clearfield, UT	535,090	166	Fort Smith, AR-OK	291,712
47	Nashville-Davidson, TN	1,548,974	107	Augusta, GA-SC	531,442	167	Columbus, GA-AL	282,227
48	Milwaukee, WI	1,548,830	108	Harrisburg-Carlisle, PA	531,150	168	Spartanburg, SC	279,521
49	Cambridge-Newton, MA M.D.	1,482,271	109	Chattanooga, TN-GA	518,576	169	Erie, PA	278,759
50	Jacksonville, FL	1,308,904	110	Modesto, CA	516,995	170	Duluth, MN-WI	273,527
51	Memphis, TN-MS-AR	1,290,901	111	Provo-Orem, UT	516,198	171	Atlantic City, NJ	271,795
52	West Palm Beach, FL M.D.	1,267,953	112	Portland, ME	513,868	172	Lubbock, TX	269,446
53	Camden, NJ M.D.	1,248,666	113	Lancaster, PA	501,669	173	Clarksville, TN-KY	265,686
54	Louisville, KY-IN	1,243,209	114	Deltona-Daytona Beach, FL	501,508	174	Hagerstown-Martinsburg, MD-WV	265,492
55	Richmond, VA	1,223,648	115	Durham-Chapel Hill, NC	488,133	175	San Luis Obispo, CA	263,017
56	Oklahoma City, OK	1,206,660	116	Winston-Salem, NC	469,651	176	Lafayette, LA	260,236
57	Bethesda-Frederick, MD M.D.	1,169,906	117	Santa Rosa-Petaluma, CA	462,650	177	Holland-Grand Haven, MI	259,600
58	Salt Lake City, UT	1,131,292	118	Spokane, WA	461,536	178	Gainesville, FL	257,041
59	Buffalo-Niagara Falls, NY	1,122,844	119	Lansing-East Lansing, MI	453,640	179	Cedar Rapids, IA	255,214
60	Birmingham-Hoover, AL	1,118,275	120	Pensacola, FL	453,297	180	Greeley, CO	252,815

Note: All listings are for Metropolitan Statistical Areas (M.S.A.s) except for those ending with "M.D." Listings with "M.D." are Metropolitan Divisions which are smaller parts of eleven large M.S.A.s. See explanatory note at beginning of metropolitan area section.

RANK	METROPOLITAN AREA	POP
181	Santa Cruz-Watsonville, CA	250,002
182	Merced, CA	248,898
183	Binghamton, NY	245,658
184	Lynchburg, VA	244,588
185	Amarillo, TX	244,209
186	Olympia, WA	242,881
187	Laredo, TX	238,490
188	Bremerton-Silverdale, WA	237,527
189	Kennewick-Pasco-Richland, WA	234,413
190	Sioux Falls, SD	233,355
191	Waco, TX	229,941
192	Topeka, KS	229,726
193	Macon, GA	229,719
194	Barnstable Town, MA	223,304
195	Appleton, WI	219,912
196	Chico, CA	219,628
197	Prescott, AZ	217,520
198	Tuscaloosa, AL	207,198
199	College Station-Bryan, TX	205,756
200	Longview, TX	204,851
201	Houma, LA	203,144
202	Tyler, TX	201,817
203	Medford, OR	201,601
204	Las Cruces, NM	201,390
205	Florence, SC	200,297
206	Elkhart-Goshen, IN	199,699
207	Saginaw, MI	199,649
208	Lake Havasu City-Kingman, AZ	199,207
209	Bellingham, WA	196,614
210	Racine, WI	195,756
211	Johnson City, TN	194,959
212	Fargo, ND-MN	194,942
213	Charlottesville, VA	194,483
214	Lafayette, IN	193,802
215	Yuma, AZ	193,473
216	Athens-Clarke County, GA	189,226
217	St. Cloud, MN	187,379
218	Bloomington, IN	184,646
219	Rochester, MN	182,815
220	Anderson, SC	182,566
221	Kingston, NY	182,305
222	Redding, CA	180,598
223	Muskegon-Norton Shores, MI	173,418
224	Yuba City, CA	166,703
225	Jacksonville, NC	164,774
226	Columbia, MO	164,226
227	Panama City-Lynn Haven, FL	164,007
228	El Centro, CA	163,673
229	Waterloo-Cedar Falls, IA	163,606
230	Oshkosh-Neenah, WI	162,698
231	Jackson, MI	162,183
232	Janesville, WI	160,438
233	Bend, OR	159,500
234	Abilene, TX	159,257
235	Eau Claire, WI	158,895
236	Niles-Benton Harbor, MI	157,892
237	Blacksburg, VA	157,811
238	Vineland, NJ	156,078
239	Dover, DE	155,344
240	Monroe, MI	153,241
241	Pascagoula, MS	152,652
242	Punta Gorda, FL	152,292
243	Billings, MT	151,343
244	Decatur, AL	150,005
245	Iowa City, IA	149,310
246	Madera, CA	148,935
247	Bangor, ME	148,610
248	Wichita Falls, TX	147,728
249	Burlington, NC	147,580
250	State College, PA	145,722
251	Wheeling, WV-OH	144,612
252	Santa Fe, NM	144,261
253	Florence-Muscle Shoals, AL	143,463
254	Sioux City, IA-NE-SD	143,016
255	Norwich-New London, CT	142,186
256	St. George, UT	142,153
257	Grand Junction, CO	142,140
258	Dothan, AL	140,899
259	Springfield, OH	139,989
260	Morristown, TN	135,979
261	Battle Creek, MI	135,300
262	Dalton, GA	135,123
263	Texarkana, TX-Texarkana, AR	134,769
264	Warner Robins, GA	133,071
265	Napa, CA	132,946
266	Auburn, AL	132,798
267	Sebastian-Vero Beach, FL	132,682
268	La Crosse, WI-MN	131,303
269	Valdosta, GA	130,908
270	Odessa, TX	130,731
271	Wausau, WI	130,393
272	Pittsfield, MA	129,918
273	Glens Falls, NY	129,422
274	Lebanon, PA	128,795
275	Flagstaff, AZ	128,071
276	Midland, TX	127,849
277	Mansfield, OH	125,317
278	Altoona, PA	125,036
279	Logan, UT-ID	124,922
280	Winchester, VA-WV	123,259
281	Farmington, NM	123,156
282	St. Joseph, MO-KS	123,101
283	Rapid City, SD	121,526
284	Idaho Falls, ID	121,458
285	Salisbury, MD	120,076
286	Sherman-Denison, TX	119,673
287	Manhattan, KS	119,523
288	Harrisonburg, VA	118,335
289	Mount Vernon-Anacortes, WA	118,241
290	Bowling Green, KY	117,583
291	Jonesboro, AR	117,434
292	Williamsport, PA	116,368
293	Lawrence, KS	115,531
294	Muncie, IN	114,943
295	Sheboygan, WI	114,653
296	Victoria, TX	114,072
297	Goldsboro, NC	113,923
298	Lawton, OK	113,817
299	Jackson, TN	113,254
300	Elizabethtown, KY	112,156
301	Cleveland, TN	111,956
302	Michigan City-La Porte, IN	109,674
303	San Angelo, TX	108,373
304	Wenatchee, WA	108,298
305	Missoula, MT	107,119
306	Lewiston-Auburn, ME	106,715
307	Bay City, MI	106,303
308	Danville, VA	104,868
309	Lima, OH	104,842
310	Bismarck, ND	104,611
311	Sumter, SC	104,311
312	Gadsden, AL	103,419
313	Ithaca, NY	101,591
314	Longview, WA	101,545
315	Pine Bluff, AR	100,732
316	Kokomo, IN	99,575
317	Fond du Lac, WI	99,281
318	Cumberland, MD-WV	98,503
319	Grand Forks, ND-MN	97,825
320	Hot Springs, AR	97,366
321	Ocean City, NJ	95,311
322	Palm Coast, FL	93,654
323	Cape Girardeau, MO-IL	93,556
324	Dubuque, IA	92,937
325	Mankato-North Mankato, MN	91,966
326	Pocatello, ID	87,959
327	Cheyenne, WY	87,931
328	Elmira, NY	87,619
329	Ames, IA	85,516
330	Great Falls, MT	82,142
331	Corvallis, OR	81,844
332	Sandusky, OH	77,057
333	Columbus, IN	75,091
334	Casper, WY	73,249
335	Hinesville, GA	71,471
336	Lewiston, ID-WA	60,233
337	Carson City, NV	54,316
NA	Albany, GA**	NA
NA	Alexandria, LA**	NA
NA	Anderson, IN**	NA
NA	Anniston-Oxford, AL**	NA
NA	Boulder, CO**	NA
NA	Brunswick, GA**	NA
NA	Burlington-South Burlington, VT**	NA
NA	Cleveland-Elyria-Mentor, OH**	NA
NA	Coeur d'Alene, ID**	NA
NA	Crestview-Fort Walton Beach, FL**	NA
NA	Danville, IL**	NA
NA	Decatur, IL**	NA
NA	Detroit (greater), MI**	NA
NA	Detroit-Livonia-Dearborn, MI M.D.*	NA
NA	Gainesville, GA**	NA
NA	Gulfport-Biloxi, MS**	NA
NA	Hattiesburg, MS**	NA
NA	Jefferson City, MO**	NA
NA	Kansas City, MO-KS**	NA
NA	Lake Charles, LA**	NA
NA	Manchester-Nashua, NH**	NA
NA	Morgantown, WV**	NA
NA	New Haven-Milford, CT**	NA
NA	North Port-Bradenton-Sarasota, FL	NA
NA	Owensboro, KY**	NA
NA	Pueblo, CO**	NA
NA	Rocky Mount, NC**	NA
NA	Rome, GA**	NA
NA	Seattle-Bellevue-Everett, WA M.D.	NA
NA	Seattle-Tacoma-Bellevue, WA**	NA
NA	Tacoma, WA M.D.**	NA
NA	Warren-Farmington Hills, MI M.D.*	NA

Source: Reported data from the F.B.I. "Crime in the United States 2008"
*Estimates as of July 2008 based on U.S. Bureau of the Census figures.
**Not available (comparable metro area not included in 2008 crime statistics).

87. Metropolitan Population in 2005
National Total = 296,507,061*

RANK	METROPOLITAN AREA	POP
226	Abilene, TX	161,123
84	Akron, OH	702,386
72	Albany-Schenectady-Troy, NY	846,480
220	Albany, GA	167,284
76	Albuquerque, NM	791,750
244	Alexandria, LA	147,408
77	Allentown, PA-NJ	781,316
268	Altoona, PA	127,708
180	Amarillo, TX	239,998
327	Ames, IA	80,727
161	Anchorage, AK	291,624
262	Anderson, IN	131,322
218	Anderson, SC	175,907
147	Ann Arbor, MI	339,467
NA	Anniston-Oxford, AL**	NA
192	Appleton, WI	214,153
133	Asheville, NC	393,687
216	Athens-Clarke County, GA	178,545
10	Atlanta, GA	4,837,981
167	Atlantic City, NJ	269,281
279	Auburn, AL	121,450
102	Augusta, GA-SC	527,083
52	Austin-Round Rock, TX	1,435,502
81	Bakersfield, CA	739,726
24	Baltimore-Towson, MD	2,659,312
241	Bangor, ME	148,674
185	Barnstable Town, MA	228,050
82	Baton Rouge, LA	729,999
255	Battle Creek, MI	139,180
303	Bay City, MI	109,569
135	Beaumont-Port Arthur, TX	389,750
208	Bellingham, WA	182,606
257	Bend, OR	136,218
62	Bethesda-Frederick, MD M.D.	1,148,021
245	Billings, MT	145,842
173	Binghamton, NY	249,588
NA	Birmingham-Hoover, AL**	NA
318	Bismarck, ND	98,280
233	Blacksburg, VA	153,046
215	Bloomington, IN	178,566
NA	Boise City-Nampa, ID**	NA
12	Boston (greater), MA-NH	4,416,837
42	Boston-Quincy, MA M.D.	1,805,283
NA	Boulder, CO**	NA
301	Bowling Green, KY	109,812
178	Bremerton-Silverdale, WA	242,375
70	Bridgeport-Stamford, CT	886,621
137	Brownsville-Harlingen, TX	377,941
315	Brunswick, GA	100,737
60	Buffalo-Niagara Falls, NY	1,156,031
NA	Burlington-South Burlington, VT**	NA
251	Burlington, NC	140,764
51	Cambridge-Newton, MA M.D.	1,460,573
57	Camden, NJ M.D.	1,240,483
103	Cape Coral-Fort Myers, FL	525,904
NA	Cape Girardeau, MO-IL**	NA
335	Carson City, NV	57,893
333	Casper, WY	69,387
176	Cedar Rapids, IA	245,529
96	Charleston-North Charleston, SC	591,358
154	Charleston, WV	308,017
50	Charlotte-Gastonia, NC-SC	1,498,697
207	Charlottesville, VA	183,511
109	Chattanooga, TN-GA	497,125
325	Cheyenne, WY	85,764
191	Chico, CA	214,382
35	Cincinnati-Middletown, OH-KY-IN	2,061,977
179	Clarksville, TN-KY	241,081
NA	Cleveland-Elyria-Mentor, OH**	NA
NA	Cleveland, TN**	NA
275	Coeur d'Alene, ID	125,497
203	College Station-Bryan, TX	192,585
97	Colorado Springs, CO	584,237
235	Columbia, MO	152,508
86	Columbia, SC	688,684
162	Columbus, GA-AL	286,160
332	Columbus, IN	73,390
47	Columbus, OH	1,694,651
122	Corpus Christi, TX	416,481
329	Corvallis, OR	80,383
NA	Crestview-Fort Walton Beach, FL**	NA
313	Cumberland, MD-WV	101,601
6	Dallas (greater), TX	5,794,020
16	Dallas-Plano-Irving, TX M.D.	3,875,593
NA	Dalton, GA**	NA
NA	Danville, IL**	NA
302	Danville, VA	109,683
73	Dayton, OH	846,018
242	Decatur, AL	148,529
NA	Decatur, IL**	NA
NA	Deltona-Daytona Beach, FL**	NA
31	Denver-Aurora, CO	2,362,441
106	Des Moines-West Des Moines, IA	513,940
11	Detroit (greater), MI	4,496,826
37	Detroit-Livonia-Dearborn, MI M.D.	2,017,845
258	Dothan, AL	136,070
250	Dover, DE	140,951
323	Dubuque, IA	91,366
NA	Duluth, MN-WI**	NA
113	Durham-Chapel Hill, NC	458,714
231	Eau Claire, WI	153,906
32	Edison, NJ M.D.	2,296,411
232	El Centro, CA	153,460
83	El Paso, TX	724,856
300	Elizabethtown, KY	110,277
202	Elkhart-Goshen, IN	192,826
324	Elmira, NY	90,113
164	Erie, PA	282,886
149	Eugene-Springfield, OR	335,881
146	Evansville, IN-KY	350,443
210	Fargo, ND-MN	182,319
274	Farmington, NM	125,803
131	Fayetteville, AR-MO	394,610
144	Fayetteville, NC	353,533
270	Flagstaff, AZ	126,931
117	Flint, MI	444,309
NA	Florence-Muscle Shoals, AL**	NA
196	Florence, SC	199,935
317	Fond du Lac, WI	99,150
166	Fort Collins-Loveland, CO	272,598
43	Fort Lauderdale, FL M.D.	1,794,506
163	Fort Smith, AR-OK	284,640
125	Fort Wayne, IN	404,303
39	Fort Worth-Arlington, TX M.D.	1,918,427
71	Fresno, CA	872,528
310	Gadsden, AL	103,880
177	Gainesville, FL	244,512
221	Gainesville, GA	165,357
NA	Glens Falls, NY**	NA
284	Goldsboro, NC	116,145
321	Grand Forks, ND-MN	96,477
265	Grand Junction, CO	129,017
79	Grand Rapids-Wyoming, MI	768,164
328	Great Falls, MT	80,608
189	Greeley, CO	222,296
159	Green Bay, WI	296,931
88	Greensboro-High Point, NC	678,641
NA	Gulfport-Biloxi, MS**	NA
175	Hagerstown-Martinsburg, MD-WV	245,946
105	Harrisburg-Carlisle, PA	520,307
293	Harrisonburg, VA	112,890
65	Hartford, CT	1,002,799
NA	Hattiesburg, MS**	NA
142	Hickory, NC	358,599
331	Hinesville, GA	74,678
171	Holland-Grand Haven, MI	252,557
68	Honolulu, HI	908,521
322	Hot Springs, AR	93,029
197	Houma, LA	199,025
8	Houston, TX	5,265,657
141	Huntsville, AL	364,669
291	Idaho Falls, ID	113,276
48	Indianapolis, IN	1,630,558
256	Iowa City, IA	137,950
NA	Ithaca, NY**	NA
56	Jacksonville, FL	1,253,042
NA	Jacksonville, NC**	NA
223	Jackson, MI	163,106
104	Jackson, MS	520,502
297	Jackson, TN	111,328
229	Janesville, WI	157,284
247	Jefferson City, MO	143,579
205	Johnson City, TN	189,289
294	Jonesboro, AR	112,605
151	Kalamazoo-Portage, MI	319,525
38	Kansas City, MO-KS	1,936,981
190	Kennewick-Pasco-Richland, WA	218,379
145	Killeen-Temple-Fort Hood, TX	351,810
155	Kingsport, TN-VA	304,191
212	Kingston, NY	182,039
94	Knoxville, TN	653,969
312	Kokomo, IN	101,779
264	La Crosse, WI-MN	129,304
209	Lafayette, IN	182,513
174	Lafayette, LA	246,589
201	Lake Charles, LA	194,981
NA	Lake Havasu City-Kingman, AZ**	NA
99	Lakeland, FL	536,226
111	Lancaster, PA	488,248
114	Lansing-East Lansing, MI	456,300

Note: All listings are for Metropolitan Statistical Areas (M.S.A.s) except for those ending with "M.D." Listings with "M.D." are Metropolitan Divisions which are smaller parts of eleven large M.S.A.s. See explanatory note at beginning of metropolitan area section.

RANK	METROPOLITAN AREA	POP
188	Laredo, TX	223,074
206	Las Cruces, NM	188,549
45	Las Vegas-Paradise, NV	1,707,257
311	Lawrence, KS	103,131
298	Lawton, OK	111,277
276	Lebanon, PA	124,723
305	Lewiston-Auburn, ME	107,367
334	Lewiston, ID-WA	59,909
119	Lexington-Fayette, KY	427,476
307	Lima, OH	106,920
165	Lincoln, NE	280,043
95	Little Rock, AR	642,769
292	Logan, UT-ID	113,266
195	Longview, TX	203,701
319	Longview, WA	97,491
4	Los Angeles County, CA M.D.	10,003,731
2	Los Angeles (greater), CA	13,011,161
58	Louisville, KY-IN	1,208,545
169	Lubbock, TX	261,901
182	Lynchburg, VA	235,893
183	Macon, GA	234,455
254	Madera, CA	139,874
100	Madison, WI	534,388
129	Manchester-Nashua, NH	401,776
NA	Manhattan, KS**	NA
NA	Mankato-North Mankato, MN**	NA
267	Mansfield, OH	128,152
89	McAllen-Edinburg-Mission, TX	669,076
199	Medford, OR	195,487
55	Memphis, TN-MS-AR	1,262,520
181	Merced, CA	238,579
7	Miami (greater), FL	5,482,749
29	Miami-Dade County, FL M.D.	2,416,950
299	Michigan City-La Porte, IN	110,360
278	Midland, TX	122,324
49	Milwaukee, WI	1,523,217
NA	Minneapolis-St. Paul, MN-WI**	NA
316	Missoula, MT	99,959
127	Mobile, AL	402,968
108	Modesto, CA	501,664
234	Monroe, MI	152,676
143	Montgomery, AL	357,347
289	Morgantown, WV	113,868
263	Morristown, TN	130,365
295	Mount Vernon-Anacortes, WA	112,567
281	Muncie, IN	118,424
219	Muskegon-Norton Shores, MI	174,543
260	Napa, CA	133,218
156	Naples-Marco Island, FL	303,375
53	Nashville-Davidson, TN	1,410,545
22	Nassau-Suffolk, NY M.D.	2,819,162
NA	New Haven-Milford, CT**	NA
NA	New Orleans, LA**	NA
1	New York (greater), NY-NJ-PA	18,741,475
3	New York-W. Plains NY-NJ M.D.	11,468,310
33	Newark-Union, NJ-PA M.D.	2,157,592
222	Niles-Benton Harbor, MI	163,258
NA	North Port-Bradenton-Sarasota, FL**	NA
249	Norwich-New London, CT	141,228
26	Oakland-Fremont, CA M.D.	2,480,743
158	Ocala, FL	297,898
314	Ocean City, NJ	100,979
272	Odessa, TX	126,536

RANK	METROPOLITAN AREA	POP
110	Ogden-Clearfield, UT	493,553
61	Oklahoma City, OK	1,152,229
186	Olympia, WA	227,714
74	Omaha-Council Bluffs, NE-IA	808,810
40	Orlando, FL	1,903,731
228	Oshkosh-Neenah, WI	159,792
296	Owensboro, KY	111,764
75	Oxnard-Thousand Oaks, CA	802,996
101	Palm Bay-Melbourne, FL	531,111
NA	Palm Coast, FL**	NA
225	Panama City-Lynn Haven, FL	161,514
230	Pascagoula, MS	157,249
NA	Peabody, MA M.D.**	NA
116	Pensacola, FL	447,002
5	Philadelphia (greater) PA-NJ-MD-D	5,819,726
15	Philadelphia, PA M.D.	3,889,872
17	Phoenix-Mesa-Scottsdale, AZ	3,841,790
308	Pine Bluff, AR	106,885
30	Pittsburgh, PA	2,406,091
261	Pittsfield, MA	132,119
326	Pocatello, ID	85,293
139	Port St. Lucie, FL	373,006
34	Portland-Vancouver, OR-WA	2,091,269
107	Portland, ME	512,440
90	Poughkeepsie, NY	664,698
198	Prescott, AZ	197,115
NA	Providence-New Bedford, RI-MA**	NA
120	Provo-Orem, UT	426,264
237	Pueblo, CO	152,252
227	Punta Gorda, FL	160,681
200	Racine, WI	195,146
67	Raleigh-Cary, NC	929,889
282	Rapid City, SD	118,257
134	Reading, PA	392,376
214	Redding, CA	178,997
130	Reno-Sparks, NV	397,671
59	Richmond, VA	1,170,973
18	Riverside-San Bernardino, CA	3,818,268
160	Roanoke, VA	295,336
217	Rochester, MN	175,945
64	Rochester, NY	1,042,990
123	Rockingham County, NH M.D.	414,043
243	Rocky Mount, NC	147,841
320	Rome, GA	96,598
36	Sacramento, CA	2,030,094
193	Saginaw, MI	209,232
138	Salem, OR	374,181
121	Salinas, CA	417,382
285	Salisbury, MD	115,518
63	Salt Lake City, UT	1,053,174
306	San Angelo, TX	107,246
41	San Antonio, TX	1,884,548
21	San Diego, CA	2,951,182
13	San Francisco (greater), CA	4,181,453
46	San Francisco-S. Mateo, CA M.D.	1,700,710
44	San Jose, CA	1,752,994
170	San Luis Obispo, CA	256,256
330	Sandusky, OH	79,027
20	Santa Ana-Anaheim, CA M.D.	3,007,430
124	Santa Barbara-Santa Maria, CA	404,519
172	Santa Cruz-Watsonville, CA	252,297
253	Santa Fe, NM	140,534
112	Santa Rosa-Petaluma, CA	471,561

RANK	METROPOLITAN AREA	POP
152	Savannah, GA	319,272
98	Scranton--Wilkes-Barre, PA	552,568
28	Seattle-Bellevue-Everett, WA M.D.	2,454,192
19	Seattle-Tacoma-Bellevue, WA	3,209,692
271	Sebastian-Vero Beach, FL	126,916
287	Sheboygan, WI	114,520
283	Sherman-Denison, TX	117,840
136	Shreveport-Bossier City, LA	382,482
246	Sioux City, IA-NE-SD	143,872
194	Sioux Falls, SD	204,654
150	South Bend-Mishawaka, IN-MI	319,704
168	Spartanburg, SC	267,819
118	Spokane, WA	441,541
87	Springfield, MA	678,672
132	Springfield, MO	394,091
248	Springfield, OH	142,676
252	State College, PA	140,740
93	Stockton, CA	654,183
213	St. Cloud, MN	180,272
290	St. George, UT	113,630
277	St. Joseph, MO-KS	123,143
23	St. Louis, MO-IL	2,784,658
304	Sumter, SC	107,382
92	Syracuse, NY	654,925
80	Tacoma, WA M.D.	755,500
148	Tallahassee, FL	339,142
25	Tampa-St Petersburg, FL	2,646,385
259	Texarkana, TX-Texarkana, AR	134,610
91	Toledo, OH	658,525
184	Topeka, KS	228,584
140	Trenton-Ewing, NJ	366,071
66	Tucson, AZ	937,925
69	Tulsa, OK	887,903
NA	Tuscaloosa, AL**	NA
204	Tyler, TX	189,480
157	Utica-Rome, NY	299,248
273	Valdosta, GA	126,064
NA	Vallejo-Fairfield, CA**	NA
286	Victoria, TX	115,316
238	Vineland, NJ	151,514
126	Visalia-Porterville, CA	404,168
187	Waco, TX	226,098
269	Warner Robins, GA	127,162
27	Warren-Farmington Hills, MI M.D.	2,478,981
9	Washington (greater) DC-VA-MD-WV	5,187,049
14	Washington, DC-VA-MD-WV M.D.	4,039,028
224	Waterloo-Cedar Falls, IA	162,564
266	Wausau, WI	128,363
309	Wenatchee, WA	104,814
54	West Palm Beach, FL M.D.	1,271,293
240	Wheeling, WV-OH	149,595
239	Wichita Falls, TX	150,258
NA	Wichita, KS**	NA
280	Williamsport, PA	118,765
85	Wilmington, DE-MD-NJ M.D.	689,371
153	Wilmington, NC	308,288
288	Winchester, VA-WV	114,269
115	Winston-Salem, NC	448,950
78	Worcester, MA	777,330
128	York-Hanover, PA	402,368
NA	Youngstown, OH-PA**	NA
236	Yuba City, CA	152,396
211	Yuma, AZ	182,075

Source: Reported data from the F.B.I. "Crime in the United States 2005"
*Estimates as of July 2005 based on U.S. Bureau of the Census figures.
**Not available (comparable metro area not included in 2005 crime statistics).

87. Metropolitan Population in 2005 (continued)
National Total = 296,507,061*

RANK	METROPOLITAN AREA	POP
1	New York (greater), NY-NJ-PA	18,741,475
2	Los Angeles (greater), CA	13,011,161
3	New York-W. Plains NY-NJ M.D.	11,468,310
4	Los Angeles County, CA M.D.	10,003,731
5	Philadelphia (greater) PA-NJ-MD-DI	5,819,726
6	Dallas (greater), TX	5,794,020
7	Miami (greater), FL	5,482,749
8	Houston, TX	5,265,657
9	Washington (greater) DC-VA-MD-W	5,187,049
10	Atlanta, GA	4,837,981
11	Detroit (greater), MI	4,496,826
12	Boston (greater), MA-NH	4,416,837
13	San Francisco (greater), CA	4,181,453
14	Washington, DC-VA-MD-WV M.D.	4,039,028
15	Philadelphia, PA M.D.	3,889,872
16	Dallas-Plano-Irving, TX M.D.	3,875,593
17	Phoenix-Mesa-Scottsdale, AZ	3,841,790
18	Riverside-San Bernardino, CA	3,818,268
19	Seattle-Tacoma-Bellevue, WA	3,209,692
20	Santa Ana-Anaheim, CA M.D.	3,007,430
21	San Diego, CA	2,951,182
22	Nassau-Suffolk, NY M.D.	2,819,162
23	St. Louis, MO-IL	2,784,658
24	Baltimore-Towson, MD	2,659,312
25	Tampa-St Petersburg, FL	2,646,385
26	Oakland-Fremont, CA M.D.	2,480,743
27	Warren-Farmington Hills, MI M.D.	2,478,981
28	Seattle-Bellevue-Everett, WA M.D.	2,454,192
29	Miami-Dade County, FL M.D.	2,416,950
30	Pittsburgh, PA	2,406,091
31	Denver-Aurora, CO	2,362,441
32	Edison, NJ M.D.	2,296,411
33	Newark-Union, NJ-PA M.D.	2,157,592
34	Portland-Vancouver, OR-WA	2,091,269
35	Cincinnati-Middletown, OH-KY-IN	2,061,977
36	Sacramento, CA	2,030,094
37	Detroit-Livonia-Dearborn, MI M.D.	2,017,845
38	Kansas City, MO-KS	1,936,981
39	Fort Worth-Arlington, TX M.D.	1,918,427
40	Orlando, FL	1,903,731
41	San Antonio, TX	1,884,548
42	Boston-Quincy, MA M.D.	1,805,283
43	Fort Lauderdale, FL M.D.	1,794,506
44	San Jose, CA	1,752,994
45	Las Vegas-Paradise, NV	1,707,257
46	San Francisco-S. Mateo, CA M.D.	1,700,710
47	Columbus, OH	1,694,651
48	Indianapolis, IN	1,630,558
49	Milwaukee, WI	1,523,217
50	Charlotte-Gastonia, NC-SC	1,498,697
51	Cambridge-Newton, MA M.D.	1,460,573
52	Austin-Round Rock, TX	1,435,502
53	Nashville-Davidson, TN	1,410,545
54	West Palm Beach, FL M.D.	1,271,293
55	Memphis, TN-MS-AR	1,262,520
56	Jacksonville, FL	1,253,042
57	Camden, NJ M.D.	1,240,483
58	Louisville, KY-IN	1,208,545
59	Richmond, VA	1,170,973
60	Buffalo-Niagara Falls, NY	1,156,031
61	Oklahoma City, OK	1,152,229
62	Bethesda-Frederick, MD M.D.	1,148,021
63	Salt Lake City, UT	1,053,174
64	Rochester, NY	1,042,990
65	Hartford, CT	1,002,799
66	Tucson, AZ	937,925
67	Raleigh-Cary, NC	929,889
68	Honolulu, HI	908,521
69	Tulsa, OK	887,903
70	Bridgeport-Stamford, CT	886,621
71	Fresno, CA	872,528
72	Albany-Schenectady-Troy, NY	846,480
73	Dayton, OH	846,018
74	Omaha-Council Bluffs, NE-IA	808,810
75	Oxnard-Thousand Oaks, CA	802,996
76	Albuquerque, NM	791,750
77	Allentown, PA-NJ	781,316
78	Worcester, MA	777,330
79	Grand Rapids-Wyoming, MI	768,164
80	Tacoma, WA M.D.	755,500
81	Bakersfield, CA	739,726
82	Baton Rouge, LA	729,999
83	El Paso, TX	724,856
84	Akron, OH	702,386
85	Wilmington, DE-MD-NJ M.D.	689,371
86	Columbia, SC	688,684
87	Springfield, MA	678,672
88	Greensboro-High Point, NC	678,641
89	McAllen-Edinburg-Mission, TX	669,076
90	Poughkeepsie, NY	664,698
91	Toledo, OH	658,525
92	Syracuse, NY	654,925
93	Stockton, CA	654,183
94	Knoxville, TN	653,969
95	Little Rock, AR	642,769
96	Charleston-North Charleston, SC	591,358
97	Colorado Springs, CO	584,237
98	Scranton--Wilkes-Barre, PA	552,568
99	Lakeland, FL	536,226
100	Madison, WI	534,388
101	Palm Bay-Melbourne, FL	531,111
102	Augusta, GA-SC	527,083
103	Cape Coral-Fort Myers, FL	525,904
104	Jackson, MS	520,502
105	Harrisburg-Carlisle, PA	520,307
106	Des Moines-West Des Moines, IA	513,940
107	Portland, ME	512,440
108	Modesto, CA	501,664
109	Chattanooga, TN-GA	497,125
110	Ogden-Clearfield, UT	493,553
111	Lancaster, PA	488,248
112	Santa Rosa-Petaluma, CA	471,561
113	Durham-Chapel Hill, NC	458,714
114	Lansing-East Lansing, MI	456,300
115	Winston-Salem, NC	448,950
116	Pensacola, FL	447,002
117	Flint, MI	444,309
118	Spokane, WA	441,541
119	Lexington-Fayette, KY	427,476
120	Provo-Orem, UT	426,264
121	Salinas, CA	417,382
122	Corpus Christi, TX	416,481
123	Rockingham County, NH M.D.	414,043
124	Santa Barbara-Santa Maria, CA	404,519
125	Fort Wayne, IN	404,303
126	Visalia-Porterville, CA	404,168
127	Mobile, AL	402,968
128	York-Hanover, PA	402,368
129	Manchester-Nashua, NH	401,776
130	Reno-Sparks, NV	397,671
131	Fayetteville, AR-MO	394,610
132	Springfield, MO	394,091
133	Asheville, NC	393,687
134	Reading, PA	392,376
135	Beaumont-Port Arthur, TX	389,750
136	Shreveport-Bossier City, LA	382,482
137	Brownsville-Harlingen, TX	377,941
138	Salem, OR	374,181
139	Port St. Lucie, FL	373,006
140	Trenton-Ewing, NJ	366,071
141	Huntsville, AL	364,669
142	Hickory, NC	358,599
143	Montgomery, AL	357,347
144	Fayetteville, NC	353,533
145	Killeen-Temple-Fort Hood, TX	351,810
146	Evansville, IN-KY	350,443
147	Ann Arbor, MI	339,467
148	Tallahassee, FL	339,142
149	Eugene-Springfield, OR	335,881
150	South Bend-Mishawaka, IN-MI	319,704
151	Kalamazoo-Portage, MI	319,525
152	Savannah, GA	319,272
153	Wilmington, NC	308,288
154	Charleston, WV	308,017
155	Kingsport, TN-VA	304,191
156	Naples-Marco Island, FL	303,375
157	Utica-Rome, NY	299,248
158	Ocala, FL	297,898
159	Green Bay, WI	296,931
160	Roanoke, VA	295,336
161	Anchorage, AK	291,624
162	Columbus, GA-AL	286,160
163	Fort Smith, AR-OK	284,640
164	Erie, PA	282,886
165	Lincoln, NE	280,043
166	Fort Collins-Loveland, CO	272,598
167	Atlantic City, NJ	269,281
168	Spartanburg, SC	267,819
169	Lubbock, TX	261,901
170	San Luis Obispo, CA	256,256
171	Holland-Grand Haven, MI	252,557
172	Santa Cruz-Watsonville, CA	252,297
173	Binghamton, NY	249,588
174	Lafayette, LA	246,589
175	Hagerstown-Martinsburg, MD-WV	245,946
176	Cedar Rapids, IA	245,529
177	Gainesville, FL	244,512
178	Bremerton-Silverdale, WA	242,375
179	Clarksville, TN-KY	241,081
180	Amarillo, TX	239,998

Note: All listings are for Metropolitan Statistical Areas (M.S.A.s) except for those ending with "M.D." Listings with "M.D." are Metropolitan Divisions which are smaller parts of eleven large M.S.A.s. See explanatory note at beginning of metropolitan area section.

RANK	METROPOLITAN AREA	POP
181	Merced, CA	238,579
182	Lynchburg, VA	235,893
183	Macon, GA	234,455
184	Topeka, KS	228,584
185	Barnstable Town, MA	228,050
186	Olympia, WA	227,714
187	Waco, TX	226,098
188	Laredo, TX	223,074
189	Greeley, CO	222,296
190	Kennewick-Pasco-Richland, WA	218,379
191	Chico, CA	214,382
192	Appleton, WI	214,153
193	Saginaw, MI	209,232
194	Sioux Falls, SD	204,654
195	Longview, TX	203,701
196	Florence, SC	199,935
197	Houma, LA	199,025
198	Prescott, AZ	197,115
199	Medford, OR	195,487
200	Racine, WI	195,146
201	Lake Charles, LA	194,981
202	Elkhart-Goshen, IN	192,826
203	College Station-Bryan, TX	192,585
204	Tyler, TX	189,480
205	Johnson City, TN	189,289
206	Las Cruces, NM	188,549
207	Charlottesville, VA	183,511
208	Bellingham, WA	182,606
209	Lafayette, IN	182,513
210	Fargo, ND-MN	182,319
211	Yuma, AZ	182,075
212	Kingston, NY	182,039
213	St. Cloud, MN	180,272
214	Redding, CA	178,997
215	Bloomington, IN	178,566
216	Athens-Clarke County, GA	178,545
217	Rochester, MN	175,945
218	Anderson, SC	175,907
219	Muskegon-Norton Shores, MI	174,543
220	Albany, GA	167,284
221	Gainesville, GA	165,357
222	Niles-Benton Harbor, MI	163,258
223	Jackson, MI	163,106
224	Waterloo-Cedar Falls, IA	162,564
225	Panama City-Lynn Haven, FL	161,514
226	Abilene, TX	161,123
227	Punta Gorda, FL	160,681
228	Oshkosh-Neenah, WI	159,792
229	Janesville, WI	157,284
230	Pascagoula, MS	157,249
231	Eau Claire, WI	153,906
232	El Centro, CA	153,460
233	Blacksburg, VA	153,046
234	Monroe, MI	152,676
235	Columbia, MO	152,508
236	Yuba City, CA	152,396
237	Pueblo, CO	152,252
238	Vineland, NJ	151,514
239	Wichita Falls, TX	150,258
240	Wheeling, WV-OH	149,595
241	Bangor, ME	148,674
242	Decatur, AL	148,529
243	Rocky Mount, NC	147,841
244	Alexandria, LA	147,408
245	Billings, MT	145,842
246	Sioux City, IA-NE-SD	143,872
247	Jefferson City, MO	143,579
248	Springfield, OH	142,676
249	Norwich-New London, CT	141,228
250	Dover, DE	140,951
251	Burlington, NC	140,764
252	State College, PA	140,740
253	Santa Fe, NM	140,534
254	Madera, CA	139,874
255	Battle Creek, MI	139,180
256	Iowa City, IA	137,950
257	Bend, OR	136,218
258	Dothan, AL	136,070
259	Texarkana, TX-Texarkana, AR	134,610
260	Napa, CA	133,218
261	Pittsfield, MA	132,119
262	Anderson, IN	131,322
263	Morristown, TN	130,365
264	La Crosse, WI-MN	129,304
265	Grand Junction, CO	129,017
266	Wausau, WI	128,363
267	Mansfield, OH	128,152
268	Altoona, PA	127,708
269	Warner Robins, GA	127,162
270	Flagstaff, AZ	126,931
271	Sebastian-Vero Beach, FL	126,916
272	Odessa, TX	126,536
273	Valdosta, GA	126,064
274	Farmington, NM	125,803
275	Coeur d'Alene, ID	125,497
276	Lebanon, PA	124,723
277	St. Joseph, MO-KS	123,143
278	Midland, TX	122,324
279	Auburn, AL	121,450
280	Williamsport, PA	118,765
281	Muncie, IN	118,424
282	Rapid City, SD	118,257
283	Sherman-Denison, TX	117,840
284	Goldsboro, NC	116,145
285	Salisbury, MD	115,518
286	Victoria, TX	115,316
287	Sheboygan, WI	114,520
288	Winchester, VA-WV	114,269
289	Morgantown, WV	113,868
290	St. George, UT	113,630
291	Idaho Falls, ID	113,276
292	Logan, UT-ID	113,266
293	Harrisonburg, VA	112,890
294	Jonesboro, AR	112,605
295	Mount Vernon-Anacortes, WA	112,567
296	Owensboro, KY	111,764
297	Jackson, TN	111,328
298	Lawton, OK	111,277
299	Michigan City-La Porte, IN	110,360
300	Elizabethtown, KY	110,277
301	Bowling Green, KY	109,812
302	Danville, VA	109,683
303	Bay City, MI	109,569
304	Sumter, SC	107,382
305	Lewiston-Auburn, ME	107,367
306	San Angelo, TX	107,246
307	Lima, OH	106,920
308	Pine Bluff, AR	106,885
309	Wenatchee, WA	104,814
310	Gadsden, AL	103,880
311	Lawrence, KS	103,131
312	Kokomo, IN	101,779
313	Cumberland, MD-WV	101,601
314	Ocean City, NJ	100,979
315	Brunswick, GA	100,737
316	Missoula, MT	99,959
317	Fond du Lac, WI	99,150
318	Bismarck, ND	98,280
319	Longview, WA	97,491
320	Rome, GA	96,598
321	Grand Forks, ND-MN	96,477
322	Hot Springs, AR	93,029
323	Dubuque, IA	91,366
324	Elmira, NY	90,113
325	Cheyenne, WY	85,764
326	Pocatello, ID	85,293
327	Ames, IA	80,727
328	Great Falls, MT	80,608
329	Corvallis, OR	80,383
330	Sandusky, OH	79,027
331	Hinesville, GA	74,678
332	Columbus, IN	73,390
333	Casper, WY	69,387
334	Lewiston, ID-WA	59,909
335	Carson City, NV	57,893
NA	Anniston-Oxford, AL**	NA
NA	Birmingham-Hoover, AL**	NA
NA	Boise City-Nampa, ID**	NA
NA	Boulder, CO**	NA
NA	Burlington-South Burlington, VT**	NA
NA	Cape Girardeau, MO-IL**	NA
NA	Cleveland-Elyria-Mentor, OH**	NA
NA	Cleveland, TN**	NA
NA	Crestview-Fort Walton Beach, FL**	NA
NA	Dalton, GA**	NA
NA	Danville, IL**	NA
NA	Decatur, IL**	NA
NA	Deltona-Daytona Beach, FL**	NA
NA	Duluth, MN-WI**	NA
NA	Florence-Muscle Shoals, AL**	NA
NA	Glens Falls, NY**	NA
NA	Gulfport-Biloxi, MS**	NA
NA	Hattiesburg, MS**	NA
NA	Ithaca, NY**	NA
NA	Jacksonville, NC**	NA
NA	Lake Havasu City-Kingman, AZ**	NA
NA	Manhattan, KS**	NA
NA	Mankato-North Mankato, MN**	NA
NA	Minneapolis-St. Paul, MN-WI**	NA
NA	New Haven-Milford, CT**	NA
NA	New Orleans, LA**	NA
NA	North Port-Bradenton-Sarasota, FL	NA
NA	Palm Coast, FL**	NA
NA	Peabody, MA M.D.**	NA
NA	Providence-New Bedford, RI-MA**	NA
NA	Tuscaloosa, AL**	NA
NA	Vallejo-Fairfield, CA**	NA
NA	Wichita, KS**	NA
NA	Youngstown, OH-PA**	NA

Source: Reported data from the F.B.I. "Crime in the United States 2005"
*Estimates as of July 2005 based on U.S. Bureau of the Census figures.
**Not available (comparable metro area not included in 2005 crime statistics).

88. City Population in 2009
National Total = 307,006,550*

RANK	CITY	POP
213	Abilene, TX	116,557
99	Akron, OH	206,497
405	Albany, GA	75,734
303	Albany, NY	93,445
35	Albuquerque, NM	530,636
160	Alexandria, VA	146,145
341	Alhambra, CA	85,956
240	Allentown, PA	107,326
337	Allen, TX	86,901
119	Amarillo, TX	188,767
227	Amherst, NY	110,399
56	Anaheim, CA	335,970
66	Anchorage, AK	283,300
218	Ann Arbor, MI	114,367
268	Antioch, CA	101,243
50	Arlington, TX	379,104
235	Arvada, CO	107,943
216	Athens-Clarke, GA	114,540
33	Atlanta, GA	552,901
59	Aurora, CO	324,014
130	Aurora, IL	175,135
18	Austin, TX	768,970
331	Avondale, AZ	88,773
58	Bakersfield, CA	330,897
400	Baldwin Park, CA	77,539
22	Baltimore, MD	638,755
92	Baton Rouge, LA	223,187
229	Beaumont, TX	110,237
305	Beaverton, OR	93,221
191	Bellevue, WA	125,054
378	Bellingham, WA	80,243
375	Bend, OR	80,550
269	Berkeley, CA	101,190
245	Billings, MT	105,427
88	Birmingham, AL	227,373
374	Bloomington, MN	80,864
341	Boca Raton, FL	85,956
100	Boise, ID	206,437
24	Boston, MA	624,222
276	Boulder, CO	100,035
387	Brick Twnshp, NJ	78,666
177	Bridgeport, CT	136,049
291	Brockton, MA	96,471
297	Broken Arrow, OK	94,415
125	Brownsville, TX	179,491
383	Buena Park, CA	79,525
70	Buffalo, NY	268,655
257	Burbank, CA	103,248
258	Cambridge, MA	102,866
384	Camden, NJ	78,980
364	Canton Twnshp, MI	82,634
393	Canton, OH	78,085
144	Cape Coral, FL	164,344
282	Carlsbad, CA	98,482
188	Carrollton, TX	127,432
308	Carson, CA	92,635
178	Cary, NC	133,757
185	Cedar Rapids, IA	128,779
279	Centennial, CO	99,385
72	Chandler, AZ	256,091
221	Charleston, SC	113,681
17	Charlotte, NC	777,708
136	Chattanooga, TN	172,536
396	Cheektowaga, NY	77,772
91	Chesapeake, VA	223,261
3	Chicago, IL	2,848,431
348	Chico, CA	84,724
349	Chino, CA	84,626
90	Chula Vista, CA	224,841
57	Cincinnati, OH	333,568
353	Citrus Heights, CA	84,333
385	Clarkstown, NY	78,899
203	Clarksville, TN	121,661
246	Clearwater, FL	105,383
43	Cleveland, OH	429,238
391	Clifton, NJ	78,124
293	Clinton Twnshp, MI	95,956
294	Clovis, CA	95,229
340	College Station, TX	86,072
394	Colonie, NY	78,003
47	Colorado Springs, CO	401,626
261	Columbia, MO	102,588
186	Columbia, SC	127,884
121	Columbus, GA	186,224
19	Columbus, OH	759,391
300	Compton, CA	93,872
205	Concord, CA	121,042
189	Coral Springs, FL	125,656
154	Corona, CA	152,438
65	Corpus Christi, TX	287,507
230	Costa Mesa, CA	110,150
379	Cranston, RI	80,223
10	Dallas, TX	1,290,266
267	Daly City, CA	101,284
382	Danbury, CT	79,729
270	Davenport, IA	101,116
325	Davie, FL	90,147
153	Dayton, OH	152,965
345	Dearborn, MI	85,305
406	Decatur, IL	75,651
194	Denton, TX	124,308
27	Denver, CO	604,680
114	Des Moines, IA	196,794
12	Detroit, MI	908,441
239	Downey, CA	107,598
357	Duluth, MN	84,071
87	Durham, NC	227,492
280	Edison Twnshp, NJ	99,356
373	Edmond, OK	80,889
311	El Cajon, CA	92,466
201	El Monte, CA	122,428
25	El Paso, TX	618,812
238	Elgin, IL	107,686
192	Elizabeth, NJ	124,910
172	Elk Grove, CA	140,576
253	Erie, PA	103,837
174	Escondido, CA	137,432
155	Eugene, OR	151,383
214	Evansville, IN	115,770
283	Everett, WA	98,431
251	Fairfield, CA	104,478
315	Fall River, MA	91,901
301	Fargo, ND	93,830
390	Farmington Hills, MI	78,140
409	Fayetteville, AR	75,120
132	Fayetteville, NC	173,995
356	Federal Way, WA	84,219
224	Flint, MI	111,657
117	Fontana, CA	190,303
173	Fort Collins, CO	138,487
123	Fort Lauderdale, FL	182,942
346	Fort Smith, AR	85,175
76	Fort Wayne, IN	251,584
20	Fort Worth, TX	723,456
106	Fremont, CA	202,714
37	Fresno, CA	481,370
233	Frisco, TX	108,244
182	Fullerton, CA	132,478
215	Gainesville, FL	115,265
140	Garden Grove, CA	165,837
95	Garland, TX	218,872
295	Gary, IN	95,219
85	Gilbert, AZ	231,799
73	Glendale, AZ	255,080
112	Glendale, CA	197,384
142	Grand Prairie, TX	164,766
116	Grand Rapids, MI	192,901
304	Greece, NY	93,274
307	Greeley, CO	93,070
274	Green Bay, WI	100,836
75	Greensboro, NC	253,191
263	Gresham, OR	102,463
323	Hamilton Twnshp, NJ	90,491
404	Hammond, IN	76,085
161	Hampton, VA	145,932
196	Hartford, CT	124,049
354	Hawthorne, CA	84,314
167	Hayward, CA	142,227
71	Henderson, NV	261,883
330	Hesperia, CA	88,904
98	Hialeah, FL	208,874
254	High Point, NC	103,675
290	Hillsboro, OR	96,563
169	Hollywood, FL	141,597
13	Honolulu, HI	907,124
4	Houston, TX	2,273,771
115	Huntington Beach, CA	192,911
126	Huntsville, AL	178,601
202	Independence, MO	122,174
14	Indianapolis, IN	813,471
327	Indio, CA	89,459
223	Inglewood, CA	112,712
96	Irvine, CA	215,673
107	Irving, TX	202,447
15	Jacksonville, FL	810,064
401	Jacksonville, NC	77,508
135	Jackson, MS	172,799
79	Jersey City, NJ	240,858
156	Joliet, IL	151,103
168	Kansas City, KS	142,102
36	Kansas City, MO	484,684
285	Kenosha, WI	97,657
352	Kent, WA	84,363
206	Killeen, TX	120,670
122	Knoxville, TN	185,850
220	Lafayette, LA	113,868
407	Lake Forest, CA	75,509
298	Lakeland, FL	94,322
388	Lakewood, CA	78,334
171	Lakewood, CO	140,618
157	Lancaster, CA	148,742
222	Lansing, MI	113,392
89	Laredo, TX	226,944
299	Las Cruces, NM	94,024
7	Las Vegas, NV	1,377,282
316	Lawrence, KS	91,703
326	Lawton, OK	89,835
343	Lee's Summit, MO	85,792
250	Lewisville, TX	104,601
62	Lexington, KY	296,406
74	Lincoln, NE	254,438
118	Little Rock, AR	190,205
372	Livermore, CA	80,915
324	Livonia, MI	90,232
40	Long Beach, CA	463,969
335	Longmont, CO	87,611

RANK	CITY	POP
398	Longview, TX	77,663
2	Los Angeles, CA	3,848,776
23	Louisville, KY	631,260
93	Lubbock, TX	222,884
322	Lynn, MA	91,149
312	Macon, GA	92,299
83	Madison, WI	234,461
231	Manchester, NH	108,671
181	McAllen, TX	132,598
183	McKinney, TX	132,146
395	Melbourne, FL	77,854
21	Memphis, TN	667,421
386	Merced, CA	78,693
38	Mesa, AZ	470,833
180	Mesquite, TX	132,941
355	Miami Beach, FL	84,260
228	Miami Gardens, FL	110,346
44	Miami, FL	419,205
236	Midland, TX	107,933
28	Milwaukee, WI	604,673
49	Minneapolis, MN	382,618
232	Miramar, FL	108,375
296	Mission Viejo, CA	94,552
399	Missouri City, TX	77,543
77	Mobile, AL	246,171
102	Modesto, CA	204,474
105	Montgomery, AL	202,818
113	Moreno Valley, CA	197,114
243	Murfreesboro, TN	105,910
248	Murrieta, CA	105,238
358	Nampa, ID	83,875
164	Naperville, IL	144,731
339	Nashua, NH	86,554
26	Nashville, TN	610,176
309	New Bedford, MA	92,621
198	New Haven, CT	123,659
55	New Orleans, LA	336,425
1	New York, NY	8,400,907
68	Newark, NJ	279,203
381	Newport Beach, CA	79,912
351	Newton, MA	84,427
82	Norfolk, VA	235,097
234	Norman, OK	108,152
292	North Charleston, SC	95,982
84	North Las Vegas, NV	232,631
259	Norwalk, CA	102,807
361	Norwalk, CT	83,198
46	Oakland, CA	404,553
139	Oceanside, CA	170,579
277	Odessa, TX	99,770
376	O'Fallon, MO	80,528
362	Ogden, UT	83,016
32	Oklahoma City, OK	556,939
200	Olathe, KS	123,321
41	Omaha, NE	443,037
134	Ontario, CA	173,212
176	Orange, CA	137,132
302	Orem, UT	93,785
81	Orlando, FL	235,109
133	Overland Park, KS	173,688
120	Oxnard, CA	187,357
255	Palm Bay, FL	103,475
159	Palmdale, CA	146,377
165	Pasadena, CA	144,063
158	Pasadena, TX	146,963
163	Paterson, NJ	144,943
332	Pearland, TX	88,528
162	Pembroke Pines, FL	145,514

RANK	CITY	POP
143	Peoria, AZ	164,366
219	Peoria, IL	114,241
6	Philadelphia, PA	1,547,605
5	Phoenix, AZ	1,597,397
60	Pittsburgh, PA	312,232
69	Plano, TX	272,747
359	Plantation, FL	83,544
152	Pomona, CA	153,217
265	Pompano Beach, FL	101,840
145	Port St. Lucie, FL	164,069
31	Portland, OR	560,908
271	Portsmouth, VA	100,970
137	Providence, RI	171,664
208	Provo, UT	119,472
247	Pueblo, CO	105,271
289	Quincy, MA	96,580
369	Racine, WI	82,232
45	Raleigh, NC	406,005
402	Ramapo, NY	76,611
129	Rancho Cucamon., CA	176,676
377	Reading, PA	80,418
321	Redding, CA	91,242
94	Reno, NV	221,010
278	Rialto, CA	99,386
260	Richardson, TX	102,675
262	Richmond, CA	102,566
103	Richmond, VA	203,233
360	Rio Rancho, NM	83,417
61	Riverside, CA	299,871
306	Roanoke, VA	93,110
264	Rochester, MN	101,884
101	Rochester, NY	205,537
147	Rockford, IL	157,943
212	Roseville, CA	116,846
333	Roswell, GA	88,371
226	Round Rock, TX	110,531
39	Sacramento, CA	470,308
150	Salem, OR	155,329
166	Salinas, CA	143,660
124	Salt Lake City, UT	180,724
313	San Angelo, TX	92,269
8	San Antonio, TX	1,373,936
109	San Bernardino, CA	199,683
9	San Diego, CA	1,314,773
16	San Francisco, CA	809,755
11	San Jose, CA	954,009
397	San Leandro, CA	77,676
368	San Marcos, CA	82,258
314	San Mateo, CA	92,208
367	Sandy Springs, GA	82,435
286	Sandy, UT	97,031
54	Santa Ana, CA	339,196
344	Santa Barbara, CA	85,715
225	Santa Clara, CA	111,106
138	Santa Clarita, CA	171,112
336	Santa Maria, CA	87,381
334	Santa Monica, CA	88,038
149	Santa Rosa, CA	156,541
97	Savannah, GA	212,711
80	Scottsdale, AZ	239,115
29	Seattle, WA	602,531
110	Shreveport, LA	199,629
204	Simi Valley, CA	121,538
366	Sioux City, IA	82,573
146	Sioux Falls, SD	158,672
410	Somerville, MA	75,112
256	South Bend, IN	103,326
287	South Gate, CA	96,651

RANK	CITY	POP
411	Southfield, MI	75,074
319	Sparks, NV	91,421
338	Spokane Valley, WA	86,756
104	Spokane, WA	202,932
209	Springfield, IL	117,973
151	Springfield, MA	153,533
148	Springfield, MO	156,659
207	Stamford, CT	119,507
187	Sterling Heights, MI	127,440
63	Stockton, CA	292,212
408	St. George, UT	75,391
403	St. Joseph, MO	76,436
52	St. Louis, MO	355,208
67	St. Paul, MN	280,194
78	St. Petersburg, FL	244,933
347	Suffolk, VA	84,929
363	Sugar Land, TX	82,696
184	Sunnyvale, CA	132,144
329	Sunrise, FL	88,936
249	Surprise, AZ	104,692
175	Syracuse, NY	137,208
111	Tacoma, WA	197,557
131	Tallahassee, FL	174,183
53	Tampa, FL	345,233
272	Temecula, CA	100,922
128	Tempe, AZ	177,486
210	Thornton, CO	117,415
197	Thousand Oaks, CA	123,735
64	Toledo, OH	291,066
288	Toms River Twnshp, NJ	96,614
199	Topeka, KS	123,449
170	Torrance, CA	141,109
371	Tracy, CA	82,019
365	Trenton, NJ	82,609
380	Troy, MI	80,182
34	Tucson, AZ	547,981
48	Tulsa, OK	384,851
317	Tuscaloosa, AL	91,688
281	Tyler, TX	99,279
392	Upper Darby Twnshp, PA	78,088
310	Vacaville, CA	92,538
217	Vallejo, CA	114,443
141	Vancouver, WA	165,147
252	Ventura, CA	103,997
211	Victorville, CA	117,150
42	Virginia Beach, VA	436,175
195	Visalia, CA	124,263
320	Vista, CA	91,252
190	Waco, TX	125,098
179	Warren, MI	133,485
350	Warwick, RI	84,488
30	Washington, DC	599,657
242	Waterbury, CT	107,007
244	West Covina, CA	105,846
241	West Jordan, UT	107,113
275	West Palm Beach, FL	100,763
193	West Valley, UT	124,472
389	Westland, MI	78,149
328	Westminster, CA	89,057
237	Westminster, CO	107,705
370	Whittier, CA	82,096
273	Wichita Falls, TX	100,884
51	Wichita, KS	367,635
266	Wilmington, NC	101,438
86	Winston-Salem, NC	230,978
284	Woodbridge Twnshp, NJ	98,013
127	Worcester, MA	178,474
108	Yonkers, NY	202,192
318	Yuma, AZ	91,433

Source: Reported data from the F.B.I. "Crime in the United States 2009"

*Estimates as of July 2009 based on U.S. Bureau of the Census figures. Charlotte, Honolulu, Indianapolis, Las Vegas, Louisville, Mobile, and Savannah include areas under their police department but outside the city limits. All populations are for area covered by police department.

88. City Population in 2009 (continued)
National Total = 307,006,550*

RANK	CITY	POP
1	New York, NY	8,400,907
2	Los Angeles, CA	3,848,776
3	Chicago, IL	2,848,431
4	Houston, TX	2,273,771
5	Phoenix, AZ	1,597,397
6	Philadelphia, PA	1,547,605
7	Las Vegas, NV	1,377,282
8	San Antonio, TX	1,373,936
9	San Diego, CA	1,314,773
10	Dallas, TX	1,290,266
11	San Jose, CA	954,009
12	Detroit, MI	908,441
13	Honolulu, HI	907,124
14	Indianapolis, IN	813,471
15	Jacksonville, FL	810,064
16	San Francisco, CA	809,755
17	Charlotte, NC	777,708
18	Austin, TX	768,970
19	Columbus, OH	759,391
20	Fort Worth, TX	723,456
21	Memphis, TN	667,421
22	Baltimore, MD	638,755
23	Louisville, KY	631,260
24	Boston, MA	624,222
25	El Paso, TX	618,812
26	Nashville, TN	610,176
27	Denver, CO	604,680
28	Milwaukee, WI	604,673
29	Seattle, WA	602,531
30	Washington, DC	599,657
31	Portland, OR	560,908
32	Oklahoma City, OK	556,939
33	Atlanta, GA	552,901
34	Tucson, AZ	547,981
35	Albuquerque, NM	530,636
36	Kansas City, MO	484,684
37	Fresno, CA	481,370
38	Mesa, AZ	470,833
39	Sacramento, CA	470,308
40	Long Beach, CA	463,969
41	Omaha, NE	443,037
42	Virginia Beach, VA	436,175
43	Cleveland, OH	429,238
44	Miami, FL	419,205
45	Raleigh, NC	406,005
46	Oakland, CA	404,553
47	Colorado Springs, CO	401,626
48	Tulsa, OK	384,851
49	Minneapolis, MN	382,618
50	Arlington, TX	379,104
51	Wichita, KS	367,635
52	St. Louis, MO	355,208
53	Tampa, FL	345,233
54	Santa Ana, CA	339,196
55	New Orleans, LA	336,425
56	Anaheim, CA	335,970
57	Cincinnati, OH	333,568
58	Bakersfield, CA	330,897
59	Aurora, CO	324,014
60	Pittsburgh, PA	312,232
61	Riverside, CA	299,871
62	Lexington, KY	296,406
63	Stockton, CA	292,212
64	Toledo, OH	291,066
65	Corpus Christi, TX	287,507
66	Anchorage, AK	283,300
67	St. Paul, MN	280,194
68	Newark, NJ	279,203
69	Plano, TX	272,747
70	Buffalo, NY	268,655
71	Henderson, NV	261,883
72	Chandler, AZ	256,091
73	Glendale, AZ	255,080
74	Lincoln, NE	254,438
75	Greensboro, NC	253,191
76	Fort Wayne, IN	251,584
77	Mobile, AL	246,171
78	St. Petersburg, FL	244,933
79	Jersey City, NJ	240,858
80	Scottsdale, AZ	239,115
81	Orlando, FL	235,109
82	Norfolk, VA	235,097
83	Madison, WI	234,461
84	North Las Vegas, NV	232,631
85	Gilbert, AZ	231,799
86	Winston-Salem, NC	230,978
87	Durham, NC	227,492
88	Birmingham, AL	227,373
89	Laredo, TX	226,944
90	Chula Vista, CA	224,841
91	Chesapeake, VA	223,261
92	Baton Rouge, LA	223,187
93	Lubbock, TX	222,884
94	Reno, NV	221,010
95	Garland, TX	218,872
96	Irvine, CA	215,673
97	Savannah, GA	212,711
98	Hialeah, FL	208,874
99	Akron, OH	206,497
100	Boise, ID	206,437
101	Rochester, NY	205,537
102	Modesto, CA	204,474
103	Richmond, VA	203,233
104	Spokane, WA	202,932
105	Montgomery, AL	202,818
106	Fremont, CA	202,714
107	Irving, TX	202,447
108	Yonkers, NY	202,192
109	San Bernardino, CA	199,683
110	Shreveport, LA	199,629
111	Tacoma, WA	197,557
112	Glendale, CA	197,384
113	Moreno Valley, CA	197,114
114	Des Moines, IA	196,794
115	Huntington Beach, CA	192,911
116	Grand Rapids, MI	192,901
117	Fontana, CA	190,303
118	Little Rock, AR	190,205
119	Amarillo, TX	188,767
120	Oxnard, CA	187,357
121	Columbus, GA	186,224
122	Knoxville, TN	185,850
123	Fort Lauderdale, FL	182,942
124	Salt Lake City, UT	180,724
125	Brownsville, TX	179,491
126	Huntsville, AL	178,601
127	Worcester, MA	178,474
128	Tempe, AZ	177,486
129	Rancho Cucamon., CA	176,676
130	Aurora, IL	175,135
131	Tallahassee, FL	174,183
132	Fayetteville, NC	173,995
133	Overland Park, KS	173,688
134	Ontario, CA	173,212
135	Jackson, MS	172,799
136	Chattanooga, TN	172,536
137	Providence, RI	171,664
138	Santa Clarita, CA	171,112
139	Oceanside, CA	170,579
140	Garden Grove, CA	165,837
141	Vancouver, WA	165,147
142	Grand Prairie, TX	164,766
143	Peoria, AZ	164,366
144	Cape Coral, FL	164,344
145	Port St. Lucie, FL	164,069
146	Sioux Falls, SD	158,672
147	Rockford, IL	157,943
148	Springfield, MO	156,659
149	Santa Rosa, CA	156,541
150	Salem, OR	155,329
151	Springfield, MA	153,533
152	Pomona, CA	153,217
153	Dayton, OH	152,965
154	Corona, CA	152,438
155	Eugene, OR	151,383
156	Joliet, IL	151,103
157	Lancaster, CA	148,742
158	Pasadena, TX	146,963
159	Palmdale, CA	146,377
160	Alexandria, VA	146,145
161	Hampton, VA	145,932
162	Pembroke Pines, FL	145,514
163	Paterson, NJ	144,943
164	Naperville, IL	144,731
165	Pasadena, CA	144,063
166	Salinas, CA	143,660
167	Hayward, CA	142,227
168	Kansas City, KS	142,102
169	Hollywood, FL	141,597
170	Torrance, CA	141,109
171	Lakewood, CO	140,618
172	Elk Grove, CA	140,576
173	Fort Collins, CO	138,487
174	Escondido, CA	137,432
175	Syracuse, NY	137,208
176	Orange, CA	137,132
177	Bridgeport, CT	136,049
178	Cary, NC	133,757
179	Warren, MI	133,485
180	Mesquite, TX	132,941
181	McAllen, TX	132,598
182	Fullerton, CA	132,478
183	McKinney, TX	132,146
184	Sunnyvale, CA	132,144
185	Cedar Rapids, IA	128,779
186	Columbia, SC	127,884
187	Sterling Heights, MI	127,440
188	Carrollton, TX	127,432
189	Coral Springs, FL	125,656
190	Waco, TX	125,098
191	Bellevue, WA	125,054
192	Elizabeth, NJ	124,910
193	West Valley, UT	124,472
194	Denton, TX	124,308
195	Visalia, CA	124,263
196	Hartford, CT	124,049
197	Thousand Oaks, CA	123,735
198	New Haven, CT	123,659
199	Topeka, KS	123,449
200	Olathe, KS	123,321
201	El Monte, CA	122,428
202	Independence, MO	122,174
203	Clarksville, TN	121,661
204	Simi Valley, CA	121,538
205	Concord, CA	121,042
206	Killeen, TX	120,670

RANK	CITY	POP
207	Stamford, CT	119,507
208	Provo, UT	119,472
209	Springfield, IL	117,973
210	Thornton, CO	117,415
211	Victorville, CA	117,150
212	Roseville, CA	116,846
213	Abilene, TX	116,557
214	Evansville, IN	115,770
215	Gainesville, FL	115,265
216	Athens-Clarke, GA	114,540
217	Vallejo, CA	114,443
218	Ann Arbor, MI	114,367
219	Peoria, IL	114,241
220	Lafayette, LA	113,868
221	Charleston, SC	113,681
222	Lansing, MI	113,392
223	Inglewood, CA	112,712
224	Flint, MI	111,657
225	Santa Clara, CA	111,106
226	Round Rock, TX	110,531
227	Amherst, NY	110,399
228	Miami Gardens, FL	110,346
229	Beaumont, TX	110,237
230	Costa Mesa, CA	110,150
231	Manchester, NH	108,671
232	Miramar, FL	108,375
233	Frisco, TX	108,244
234	Norman, OK	108,152
235	Arvada, CO	107,943
236	Midland, TX	107,933
237	Westminster, CO	107,705
238	Elgin, IL	107,686
239	Downey, CA	107,598
240	Allentown, PA	107,326
241	West Jordan, UT	107,113
242	Waterbury, CT	107,007
243	Murfreesboro, TN	105,910
244	West Covina, CA	105,846
245	Billings, MT	105,427
246	Clearwater, FL	105,383
247	Pueblo, CO	105,271
248	Murrieta, CA	105,238
249	Surprise, AZ	104,692
250	Lewisville, TX	104,601
251	Fairfield, CA	104,478
252	Ventura, CA	103,997
253	Erie, PA	103,837
254	High Point, NC	103,675
255	Palm Bay, FL	103,475
256	South Bend, IN	103,326
257	Burbank, CA	103,248
258	Cambridge, MA	102,866
259	Norwalk, CA	102,807
260	Richardson, TX	102,675
261	Columbia, MO	102,588
262	Richmond, CA	102,566
263	Gresham, OR	102,463
264	Rochester, MN	101,884
265	Pompano Beach, FL	101,840
266	Wilmington, NC	101,438
267	Daly City, CA	101,284
268	Antioch, CA	101,243
269	Berkeley, CA	101,190
270	Davenport, IA	101,116
271	Portsmouth, VA	100,970
272	Temecula, CA	100,922
273	Wichita Falls, TX	100,884
274	Green Bay, WI	100,836

RANK	CITY	POP
275	West Palm Beach, FL	100,763
276	Boulder, CO	100,035
277	Odessa, TX	99,770
278	Rialto, CA	99,386
279	Centennial, CO	99,385
280	Edison Twnshp, NJ	99,356
281	Tyler, TX	99,279
282	Carlsbad, CA	98,482
283	Everett, WA	98,431
284	Woodbridge Twnshp, NJ	98,013
285	Kenosha, WI	97,657
286	Sandy, UT	97,031
287	South Gate, CA	96,651
288	Toms River Twnshp, NJ	96,614
289	Quincy, MA	96,580
290	Hillsboro, OR	96,563
291	Brockton, MA	96,471
292	North Charleston, SC	95,982
293	Clinton Twnshp, MI	95,956
294	Clovis, CA	95,229
295	Gary, IN	95,219
296	Mission Viejo, CA	94,552
297	Broken Arrow, OK	94,415
298	Lakeland, FL	94,322
299	Las Cruces, NM	94,024
300	Compton, CA	93,872
301	Fargo, ND	93,830
302	Orem, UT	93,785
303	Albany, NY	93,445
304	Greece, NY	93,274
305	Beaverton, OR	93,221
306	Roanoke, VA	93,110
307	Greeley, CO	93,070
308	Carson, CA	92,635
309	New Bedford, MA	92,621
310	Vacaville, CA	92,538
311	El Cajon, CA	92,466
312	Macon, GA	92,299
313	San Angelo, TX	92,269
314	San Mateo, CA	92,208
315	Fall River, MA	91,901
316	Lawrence, KS	91,703
317	Tuscaloosa, AL	91,688
318	Yuma, AZ	91,433
319	Sparks, NV	91,421
320	Vista, CA	91,252
321	Redding, CA	91,242
322	Lynn, MA	91,149
323	Hamilton Twnshp, NJ	90,491
324	Livonia, MI	90,232
325	Davie, FL	90,147
326	Lawton, OK	89,835
327	Indio, CA	89,459
328	Westminster, CA	89,057
329	Sunrise, FL	88,936
330	Hesperia, CA	88,904
331	Avondale, AZ	88,773
332	Pearland, TX	88,528
333	Roswell, GA	88,371
334	Santa Monica, CA	88,038
335	Longmont, CO	87,611
336	Santa Maria, CA	87,381
337	Allen, TX	86,901
338	Spokane Valley, WA	86,756
339	Nashua, NH	86,554
340	College Station, TX	86,072
341	Alhambra, CA	85,956
341	Boca Raton, FL	85,956

RANK	CITY	POP
343	Lee's Summit, MO	85,792
344	Santa Barbara, CA	85,715
345	Dearborn, MI	85,305
346	Fort Smith, AR	85,175
347	Suffolk, VA	84,929
348	Chico, CA	84,724
349	Chino, CA	84,626
350	Warwick, RI	84,488
351	Newton, MA	84,427
352	Kent, WA	84,363
353	Citrus Heights, CA	84,333
354	Hawthorne, CA	84,314
355	Miami Beach, FL	84,260
356	Federal Way, WA	84,219
357	Duluth, MN	84,071
358	Nampa, ID	83,875
359	Plantation, FL	83,544
360	Rio Rancho, NM	83,417
361	Norwalk, CT	83,198
362	Ogden, UT	83,016
363	Sugar Land, TX	82,696
364	Canton Twnshp, MI	82,634
365	Trenton, NJ	82,609
366	Sioux City, IA	82,573
367	Sandy Springs, GA	82,435
368	San Marcos, CA	82,258
369	Racine, WI	82,232
370	Whittier, CA	82,096
371	Tracy, CA	82,019
372	Livermore, CA	80,915
373	Edmond, OK	80,889
374	Bloomington, MN	80,864
375	Bend, OR	80,550
376	O'Fallon, MO	80,528
377	Reading, PA	80,418
378	Bellingham, WA	80,243
379	Cranston, RI	80,223
380	Troy, MI	80,182
381	Newport Beach, CA	79,912
382	Danbury, CT	79,729
383	Buena Park, CA	79,525
384	Camden, NJ	78,980
385	Clarkstown, NY	78,899
386	Merced, CA	78,693
387	Brick Twnshp, NJ	78,666
388	Lakewood, CA	78,334
389	Westland, MI	78,149
390	Farmington Hills, MI	78,140
391	Clifton, NJ	78,124
392	Upper Darby Twnshp, PA	78,088
393	Canton, OH	78,085
394	Colonie, NY	78,003
395	Melbourne, FL	77,854
396	Cheektowaga, NY	77,772
397	San Leandro, CA	77,676
398	Longview, TX	77,663
399	Missouri City, TX	77,543
400	Baldwin Park, CA	77,539
401	Jacksonville, NC	77,508
402	Ramapo, NY	76,611
403	St. Joseph, MO	76,436
404	Hammond, IN	76,085
405	Albany, GA	75,734
406	Decatur, IL	75,651
407	Lake Forest, CA	75,509
408	St. George, UT	75,391
409	Fayetteville, AR	75,120
410	Somerville, MA	75,112
411	Southfield, MI	75,074

Source: Reported data from the F.B.I. "Crime in the United States 2009"

*Estimates as of July 2009 based on U.S. Bureau of the Census figures. Charlotte, Honolulu, Indianapolis, Las Vegas, Louisville, Mobile, and Savannah include areas under their police department but outside the city limits. All populations are for area covered by police department.

89. City Population in 2008
National Total = 304,374,846*

RANK	CITY	POP
208	Abilene, TX	116,267
99	Akron, OH	206,845
405	Albany, GA	75,715
296	Albany, NY	94,152
35	Albuquerque, NM	527,464
170	Alexandria, VA	140,891
337	Alhambra, CA	86,404
234	Allentown, PA	107,335
358	Allen, TX	83,242
119	Amarillo, TX	187,674
227	Amherst, NY	110,351
55	Anaheim, CA	333,746
66	Anchorage, AK	280,068
212	Ann Arbor, MI	115,148
267	Antioch, CA	100,702
50	Arlington, TX	375,836
236	Arvada, CO	106,847
216	Athens-Clarke, GA	113,950
33	Atlanta, GA	533,016
59	Aurora, CO	316,323
130	Aurora, IL	174,488
18	Austin, TX	753,535
340	Avondale, AZ	85,376
57	Bakersfield, CA	326,046
393	Baldwin Park, CA	78,031
22	Baltimore, MD	634,549
86	Baton Rouge, LA	226,920
228	Beaumont, TX	109,103
308	Beaverton, OR	92,198
198	Bellevue, WA	122,459
385	Bellingham, WA	78,804
395	Bend, OR	77,898
261	Berkeley, CA	101,170
251	Billings, MT	103,196
85	Birmingham, AL	228,314
371	Bloomington, MN	80,996
344	Boca Raton, FL	84,630
103	Boise, ID	203,770
25	Boston, MA	604,465
298	Boulder, CO	93,410
391	Brick Twnshp, NJ	78,218
175	Bridgeport, CT	136,327
289	Brockton, MA	95,650
309	Broken Arrow, OK	92,075
126	Brownsville, TX	176,893
381	Buena Park, CA	79,431
69	Buffalo, NY	270,289
247	Burbank, CA	103,640
259	Cambridge, MA	101,362
402	Camden, NJ	76,182
346	Canton Twnshp, MI	84,506
394	Canton, OH	78,006
142	Cape Coral, FL	163,403
282	Carlsbad, CA	97,670
187	Carrollton, TX	125,607
299	Carson, CA	93,170
189	Cary, NC	125,277
184	Cedar Rapids, IA	126,984
277	Centennial, CO	98,749
73	Chandler, AZ	253,076
224	Charleston, SC	111,645
17	Charlotte, NC	758,769
135	Chattanooga, TN	171,611
389	Cheektowaga, NY	78,303
91	Chesapeake, VA	220,812
3	Chicago, IL	2,829,304
352	Chico, CA	84,086
345	Chino, CA	84,595
88	Chula Vista, CA	223,408
56	Cincinnati, OH	332,608
349	Citrus Heights, CA	84,361
383	Clarkstown, NY	78,869
202	Clarksville, TN	121,386
243	Clearwater, FL	104,986
43	Cleveland, OH	433,452
392	Clifton, NJ	78,180
287	Clinton Twnshp, MI	96,315
297	Clovis, CA	93,848
368	College Station, TX	81,925
390	Colonie, NY	78,272
48	Colorado Springs, CO	378,403
263	Columbia, MO	101,033
188	Columbia, SC	125,485
121	Columbus, GA	186,217
19	Columbus, OH	751,887
293	Compton, CA	94,519
203	Concord, CA	120,679
186	Coral Springs, FL	126,222
152	Corona, CA	153,193
63	Corpus Christi, TX	286,558
230	Costa Mesa, CA	108,898
375	Cranston, RI	79,987
9	Dallas, TX	1,276,214
270	Daly City, CA	100,542
378	Danbury, CT	79,753
276	Davenport, IA	99,070
322	Davie, FL	90,268
149	Dayton, OH	154,218
333	Dearborn, MI	87,482
403	Decatur, IL	76,044
204	Denton, TX	120,295
29	Denver, CO	592,881
113	Des Moines, IA	196,680
13	Detroit, MI	905,783
232	Downey, CA	108,184
351	Duluth, MN	84,171
90	Durham, NC	221,785
273	Edison Twnshp, NJ	99,562
380	Edmond, OK	79,529
307	El Cajon, CA	92,225
196	El Monte, CA	123,049
24	El Paso, TX	612,374
241	Elgin, IL	105,535
190	Elizabeth, NJ	124,823
172	Elk Grove, CA	139,395
246	Erie, PA	103,881
174	Escondido, CA	136,508
155	Eugene, OR	150,297
210	Evansville, IN	115,639
279	Everett, WA	98,552
244	Fairfield, CA	104,927
319	Fall River, MA	90,760
301	Fargo, ND	92,883
386	Farmington Hills, MI	78,602
411	Fayetteville, AR	73,999
136	Fayetteville, NC	171,457
343	Federal Way, WA	84,775
219	Flint, MI	113,462
117	Fontana, CA	189,253
176	Fort Collins, CO	135,785
123	Fort Lauderdale, FL	182,932
342	Fort Smith, AR	84,847
75	Fort Wayne, IN	251,194
20	Fort Worth, TX	701,345
105	Fremont, CA	200,964
36	Fresno, CA	475,723
275	Frisco, TX	99,472
179	Fullerton, CA	132,776
221	Gainesville, FL	113,286
140	Garden Grove, CA	165,629
94	Garland, TX	219,135
288	Gary, IN	95,699
92	Gilbert, AZ	220,373
71	Glendale, AZ	256,659
111	Glendale, CA	197,182
143	Grand Prairie, TX	162,706
116	Grand Rapids, MI	193,096
300	Greece, NY	92,932
312	Greeley, CO	91,900
271	Green Bay, WI	100,531
77	Greensboro, NC	249,561
266	Gresham, OR	100,935
321	Hamilton Twnshp, NJ	90,282
400	Hammond, IN	76,498
160	Hampton, VA	145,897
191	Hartford, CT	124,610
347	Hawthorne, CA	84,445
169	Hayward, CA	140,984
72	Henderson, NV	256,091
329	Hesperia, CA	88,853
98	Hialeah, FL	207,908
254	High Point, NC	102,298
294	Hillsboro, OR	94,373
168	Hollywood, FL	141,048
12	Honolulu, HI	906,349
4	Houston, TX	2,238,895
115	Huntington Beach, CA	193,241
131	Huntsville, AL	172,794
226	Independence, MO	110,376
14	Indianapolis, IN	808,329
326	Indio, CA	89,486
220	Inglewood, CA	113,454
97	Irvine, CA	209,278
107	Irving, TX	200,470
15	Jacksonville, FL	806,080
404	Jacksonville, NC	75,770
129	Jackson, MS	174,734
79	Jersey City, NJ	241,588
156	Joliet, IL	149,617
166	Kansas City, KS	142,231
40	Kansas City, MO	451,454
286	Kenosha, WI	96,977
341	Kent, WA	84,966
209	Killeen, TX	115,906
122	Knoxville, TN	184,559
217	Lafayette, LA	113,770
406	Lake Forest, CA	75,637
303	Lakeland, FL	92,669
382	Lakewood, CA	78,894
171	Lakewood, CO	139,803
158	Lancaster, CA	147,017
214	Lansing, MI	114,415
89	Laredo, TX	222,870
311	Las Cruces, NM	91,982
7	Las Vegas, NV	1,353,175
316	Lawrence, KS	91,089
315	Lawton, OK	91,459
348	Lee's Summit, MO	84,399
264	Lewisville, TX	100,947
64	Lexington, KY	281,473
74	Lincoln, NE	251,550
118	Little Rock, AR	187,978
374	Livermore, CA	80,258
306	Livonia, MI	92,329
38	Long Beach, CA	467,055
335	Longmont, CO	86,754

RANK	CITY	POP
398	Longview, TX	77,272
2	Los Angeles, CA	3,850,920
23	Louisville, KY	629,679
93	Lubbock, TX	219,594
325	Lynn, MA	90,042
304	Macon, GA	92,576
82	Madison, WI	231,231
229	Manchester, NH	109,083
182	McAllen, TX	130,039
185	McKinney, TX	126,659
397	Melbourne, FL	77,286
21	Memphis, TN	672,046
387	Merced, CA	78,598
39	Mesa, AZ	456,821
180	Mesquite, TX	132,600
353	Miami Beach, FL	83,609
231	Miami Gardens, FL	108,657
44	Miami, FL	427,740
242	Midland, TX	105,049
27	Milwaukee, WI	602,131
49	Minneapolis, MN	376,753
223	Miramar, FL	112,055
292	Mission Viejo, CA	94,702
399	Missouri City, TX	77,075
76	Mobile, AL	251,041
100	Modesto, CA	205,750
102	Montgomery, AL	204,398
114	Moreno Valley, CA	195,649
252	Murfreesboro, TN	102,536
240	Murrieta, CA	105,666
361	Nampa, ID	83,007
163	Naperville, IL	144,205
334	Nashua, NH	86,845
26	Nashville, TN	602,181
314	New Bedford, MA	91,473
194	New Haven, CT	123,953
65	New Orleans, LA	281,440
1	New York, NY	8,345,075
67	Newark, NJ	279,788
377	Newport Beach, CA	79,821
359	Newton, MA	83,191
81	Norfolk, VA	235,067
233	Norman, OK	108,016
302	North Charleston, SC	92,749
84	North Las Vegas, NV	228,363
248	Norwalk, CA	103,612
354	Norwalk, CT	83,503
45	Oakland, CA	401,587
138	Oceanside, CA	169,502
283	Odessa, TX	97,644
384	O'Fallon, MO	78,837
357	Ogden, UT	83,353
32	Oklahoma City, OK	552,452
201	Olathe, KS	121,472
41	Omaha, NE	437,238
132	Ontario, CA	172,543
177	Orange, CA	134,852
295	Orem, UT	94,228
83	Orlando, FL	229,808
133	Overland Park, KS	171,909
120	Oxnard, CA	186,434
257	Palm Bay, FL	101,759
164	Palmdale, CA	144,109
162	Pasadena, CA	144,545
157	Pasadena, TX	147,114
161	Paterson, NJ	145,542
360	Pearland, TX	83,185
159	Pembroke Pines, FL	146,108
153	Peoria, AZ	151,493
218	Peoria, IL	113,616
6	Philadelphia, PA	1,441,117
5	Phoenix, AZ	1,585,838
60	Pittsburgh, PA	309,757
70	Plano, TX	265,739
355	Plantation, FL	83,480
151	Pomona, CA	153,201
256	Pompano Beach, FL	101,769
144	Port St. Lucie, FL	159,735
31	Portland, OR	553,023
255	Portsmouth, VA	101,782
137	Providence, RI	170,965
205	Provo, UT	119,189
245	Pueblo, CO	104,017
291	Quincy, MA	95,061
366	Racine, WI	82,226
46	Raleigh, NC	388,661
407	Ramapo, NY	75,433
128	Rancho Cucamon., CA	176,307
372	Reading, PA	80,860
318	Redding, CA	90,881
95	Reno, NV	218,556
274	Rialto, CA	99,485
268	Richardson, TX	100,597
258	Richmond, CA	101,680
108	Richmond, VA	199,674
379	Rio Rancho, NM	79,647
61	Riverside, CA	299,384
310	Roanoke, VA	91,983
269	Rochester, MN	100,589
101	Rochester, NY	205,341
145	Rockford, IL	157,262
222	Roseville, CA	112,817
331	Roswell, GA	88,069
253	Round Rock, TX	102,411
37	Sacramento, CA	467,065
150	Salem, OR	153,831
165	Salinas, CA	143,520
124	Salt Lake City, UT	180,514
320	San Angelo, TX	90,739
8	San Antonio, TX	1,351,244
106	San Bernardino, CA	200,617
10	San Diego, CA	1,271,655
16	San Francisco, CA	798,144
11	San Jose, CA	945,197
396	San Leandro, CA	77,474
370	San Marcos, CA	81,683
313	San Mateo, CA	91,650
363	Sandy Springs, GA	82,953
285	Sandy, UT	96,998
53	Santa Ana, CA	339,674
338	Santa Barbara, CA	85,791
225	Santa Clara, CA	110,712
134	Santa Clarita, CA	171,821
336	Santa Maria, CA	86,744
332	Santa Monica, CA	87,572
148	Santa Rosa, CA	154,874
96	Savannah, GA	211,475
80	Scottsdale, AZ	238,905
28	Seattle, WA	598,077
110	Shreveport, LA	199,434
200	Simi Valley, CA	121,572
365	Sioux City, IA	82,404
146	Sioux Falls, SD	155,110
410	Somerville, MA	74,012
249	South Bend, IN	103,561
284	South Gate, CA	97,179
408	Southfield, MI	75,024
328	Sparks, NV	88,913
339	Spokane Valley, WA	85,551
104	Spokane, WA	201,491
207	Springfield, IL	117,762
154	Springfield, MA	151,249
147	Springfield, MO	155,106
206	Stamford, CT	118,597
183	Sterling Heights, MI	127,697
62	Stockton, CA	293,073
409	St. George, UT	74,356
401	St. Joseph, MO	76,377
52	St. Louis, MO	356,204
68	St. Paul, MN	276,083
78	St. Petersburg, FL	243,111
356	Suffolk, VA	83,470
369	Sugar Land, TX	81,763
181	Sunnyvale, CA	131,052
327	Sunrise, FL	89,139
262	Surprise, AZ	101,141
173	Syracuse, NY	138,211
112	Tacoma, WA	196,851
139	Tallahassee, FL	168,984
54	Tampa, FL	336,911
278	Temecula, CA	98,663
127	Tempe, AZ	176,388
213	Thornton, CO	114,923
193	Thousand Oaks, CA	124,106
58	Toledo, OH	317,401
290	Toms River Twnshp, NJ	95,410
197	Topeka, KS	122,554
167	Torrance, CA	141,819
362	Tracy, CA	82,960
367	Trenton, NJ	82,140
373	Troy, MI	80,491
34	Tucson, AZ	528,917
47	Tulsa, OK	382,954
324	Tuscaloosa, AL	90,157
281	Tyler, TX	98,042
388	Upper Darby Twnshp, PA	78,550
305	Vacaville, CA	92,424
211	Vallejo, CA	115,330
141	Vancouver, WA	163,574
250	Ventura, CA	103,483
215	Victorville, CA	114,305
42	Virginia Beach, VA	434,163
199	Visalia, CA	121,850
317	Vista, CA	90,919
195	Waco, TX	123,208
178	Warren, MI	133,721
350	Warwick, RI	84,326
30	Washington, DC	591,833
235	Waterbury, CT	107,157
238	West Covina, CA	106,524
239	West Jordan, UT	105,772
272	West Palm Beach, FL	100,434
192	West Valley, UT	124,128
376	Westland, MI	79,944
330	Westminster, CA	88,730
237	Westminster, CO	106,810
364	Whittier, CA	82,727
260	Wichita Falls, TX	101,279
51	Wichita, KS	362,602
265	Wilmington, NC	100,944
87	Winston-Salem, NC	226,460
280	Woodbridge Twnshp, NJ	98,154
125	Worcester, MA	177,151
109	Yonkers, NY	199,615
323	Yuma, AZ	90,245

Source: Reported data from the F.B.I. "Crime in the United States 2008"

*Updated estimates as of July 2008 based on U.S. Bureau of the Census figures. Charlotte, Honolulu, Indianapolis, Las Vegas, Louisville, Mobile, and Savannah include areas under their police department but outside the city limits.

89. City Population in 2008 (continued)
National Total = 304,374,846*

RANK	CITY	POP
1	New York, NY	8,345,075
2	Los Angeles, CA	3,850,920
3	Chicago, IL	2,829,304
4	Houston, TX	2,238,895
5	Phoenix, AZ	1,585,838
6	Philadelphia, PA	1,441,117
7	Las Vegas, NV	1,353,175
8	San Antonio, TX	1,351,244
9	Dallas, TX	1,276,214
10	San Diego, CA	1,271,655
11	San Jose, CA	945,197
12	Honolulu, HI	906,349
13	Detroit, MI	905,783
14	Indianapolis, IN	808,329
15	Jacksonville, FL	806,080
16	San Francisco, CA	798,144
17	Charlotte, NC	758,769
18	Austin, TX	753,535
19	Columbus, OH	751,887
20	Fort Worth, TX	701,345
21	Memphis, TN	672,046
22	Baltimore, MD	634,549
23	Louisville, KY	629,679
24	El Paso, TX	612,374
25	Boston, MA	604,465
26	Nashville, TN	602,181
27	Milwaukee, WI	602,131
28	Seattle, WA	598,077
29	Denver, CO	592,881
30	Washington, DC	591,833
31	Portland, OR	553,023
32	Oklahoma City, OK	552,452
33	Atlanta, GA	533,016
34	Tucson, AZ	528,917
35	Albuquerque, NM	527,464
36	Fresno, CA	475,723
37	Sacramento, CA	467,065
38	Long Beach, CA	467,055
39	Mesa, AZ	456,821
40	Kansas City, MO	451,454
41	Omaha, NE	437,238
42	Virginia Beach, VA	434,163
43	Cleveland, OH	433,452
44	Miami, FL	427,740
45	Oakland, CA	401,587
46	Raleigh, NC	388,661
47	Tulsa, OK	382,954
48	Colorado Springs, CO	378,403
49	Minneapolis, MN	376,753
50	Arlington, TX	375,836
51	Wichita, KS	362,602
52	St. Louis, MO	356,204
53	Santa Ana, CA	339,674
54	Tampa, FL	336,911
55	Anaheim, CA	333,746
56	Cincinnati, OH	332,608
57	Bakersfield, CA	326,046
58	Toledo, OH	317,401
59	Aurora, CO	316,323
60	Pittsburgh, PA	309,757
61	Riverside, CA	299,384
62	Stockton, CA	293,073
63	Corpus Christi, TX	286,558
64	Lexington, KY	281,473
65	New Orleans, LA	281,440
66	Anchorage, AK	280,068
67	Newark, NJ	279,788
68	St. Paul, MN	276,083
69	Buffalo, NY	270,289
70	Plano, TX	265,739
71	Glendale, AZ	256,659
72	Henderson, NV	256,091
73	Chandler, AZ	253,076
74	Lincoln, NE	251,550
75	Fort Wayne, IN	251,194
76	Mobile, AL	251,041
77	Greensboro, NC	249,561
78	St. Petersburg, FL	243,111
79	Jersey City, NJ	241,588
80	Scottsdale, AZ	238,905
81	Norfolk, VA	235,067
82	Madison, WI	231,231
83	Orlando, FL	229,808
84	North Las Vegas, NV	228,363
85	Birmingham, AL	228,314
86	Baton Rouge, LA	226,920
87	Winston-Salem, NC	226,460
88	Chula Vista, CA	223,408
89	Laredo, TX	222,870
90	Durham, NC	221,785
91	Chesapeake, VA	220,812
92	Gilbert, AZ	220,373
93	Lubbock, TX	219,594
94	Garland, TX	219,135
95	Reno, NV	218,556
96	Savannah, GA	211,475
97	Irvine, CA	209,278
98	Hialeah, FL	207,908
99	Akron, OH	206,845
100	Modesto, CA	205,750
101	Rochester, NY	205,341
102	Montgomery, AL	204,398
103	Boise, ID	203,770
104	Spokane, WA	201,491
105	Fremont, CA	200,964
106	San Bernardino, CA	200,617
107	Irving, TX	200,470
108	Richmond, VA	199,674
109	Yonkers, NY	199,615
110	Shreveport, LA	199,434
111	Glendale, CA	197,182
112	Tacoma, WA	196,851
113	Des Moines, IA	196,680
114	Moreno Valley, CA	195,649
115	Huntington Beach, CA	193,241
116	Grand Rapids, MI	193,096
117	Fontana, CA	189,253
118	Little Rock, AR	187,978
119	Amarillo, TX	187,674
120	Oxnard, CA	186,434
121	Columbus, GA	186,217
122	Knoxville, TN	184,559
123	Fort Lauderdale, FL	182,932
124	Salt Lake City, UT	180,514
125	Worcester, MA	177,151
126	Brownsville, TX	176,893
127	Tempe, AZ	176,388
128	Rancho Cucamon., CA	176,307
129	Jackson, MS	174,734
130	Aurora, IL	174,488
131	Huntsville, AL	172,794
132	Ontario, CA	172,543
133	Overland Park, KS	171,909
134	Santa Clarita, CA	171,821
135	Chattanooga, TN	171,611
136	Fayetteville, NC	171,457
137	Providence, RI	170,965
138	Oceanside, CA	169,502
139	Tallahassee, FL	168,984
140	Garden Grove, CA	165,629
141	Vancouver, WA	163,574
142	Cape Coral, FL	163,403
143	Grand Prairie, TX	162,706
144	Port St. Lucie, FL	159,735
145	Rockford, IL	157,262
146	Sioux Falls, SD	155,110
147	Springfield, MO	155,106
148	Santa Rosa, CA	154,874
149	Dayton, OH	154,218
150	Salem, OR	153,831
151	Pomona, CA	153,201
152	Corona, CA	153,193
153	Peoria, AZ	151,493
154	Springfield, MA	151,249
155	Eugene, OR	150,297
156	Joliet, IL	149,617
157	Pasadena, TX	147,114
158	Lancaster, CA	147,017
159	Pembroke Pines, FL	146,108
160	Hampton, VA	145,897
161	Paterson, NJ	145,542
162	Pasadena, CA	144,545
163	Naperville, IL	144,205
164	Palmdale, CA	144,109
165	Salinas, CA	143,520
166	Kansas City, KS	142,231
167	Torrance, CA	141,819
168	Hollywood, FL	141,048
169	Hayward, CA	140,984
170	Alexandria, VA	140,891
171	Lakewood, CO	139,803
172	Elk Grove, CA	139,395
173	Syracuse, NY	138,211
174	Escondido, CA	136,508
175	Bridgeport, CT	136,327
176	Fort Collins, CO	135,785
177	Orange, CA	134,852
178	Warren, MI	133,721
179	Fullerton, CA	132,776
180	Mesquite, TX	132,600
181	Sunnyvale, CA	131,052
182	McAllen, TX	130,039
183	Sterling Heights, MI	127,697
184	Cedar Rapids, IA	126,984
185	McKinney, TX	126,659
186	Coral Springs, FL	126,222
187	Carrollton, TX	125,607
188	Columbia, SC	125,485
189	Cary, NC	125,277
190	Elizabeth, NJ	124,823
191	Hartford, CT	124,610
192	West Valley, UT	124,128
193	Thousand Oaks, CA	124,106
194	New Haven, CT	123,953
195	Waco, TX	123,208
196	El Monte, CA	123,049
197	Topeka, KS	122,554
198	Bellevue, WA	122,459
199	Visalia, CA	121,850
200	Simi Valley, CA	121,572
201	Olathe, KS	121,472
202	Clarksville, TN	121,386
203	Concord, CA	120,679
204	Denton, TX	120,295
205	Provo, UT	119,189
206	Stamford, CT	118,597

RANK	CITY	POP
207	Springfield, IL	117,762
208	Abilene, TX	116,267
209	Killeen, TX	115,906
210	Evansville, IN	115,639
211	Vallejo, CA	115,330
212	Ann Arbor, MI	115,148
213	Thornton, CO	114,923
214	Lansing, MI	114,415
215	Victorville, CA	114,305
216	Athens-Clarke, GA	113,950
217	Lafayette, LA	113,770
218	Peoria, IL	113,616
219	Flint, MI	113,462
220	Inglewood, CA	113,454
221	Gainesville, FL	113,286
222	Roseville, CA	112,817
223	Miramar, FL	112,055
224	Charleston, SC	111,645
225	Santa Clara, CA	110,712
226	Independence, MO	110,376
227	Amherst, NY	110,351
228	Beaumont, TX	109,103
229	Manchester, NH	109,083
230	Costa Mesa, CA	108,898
231	Miami Gardens, FL	108,657
232	Downey, CA	108,184
233	Norman, OK	108,016
234	Allentown, PA	107,335
235	Waterbury, CT	107,157
236	Arvada, CO	106,847
237	Westminster, CO	106,810
238	West Covina, CA	106,524
239	West Jordan, UT	105,772
240	Murrieta, CA	105,666
241	Elgin, IL	105,535
242	Midland, TX	105,049
243	Clearwater, FL	104,986
244	Fairfield, CA	104,927
245	Pueblo, CO	104,017
246	Erie, PA	103,881
247	Burbank, CA	103,640
248	Norwalk, CA	103,612
249	South Bend, IN	103,561
250	Ventura, CA	103,483
251	Billings, MT	103,196
252	Murfreesboro, TN	102,536
253	Round Rock, TX	102,411
254	High Point, NC	102,298
255	Portsmouth, VA	101,782
256	Pompano Beach, FL	101,769
257	Palm Bay, FL	101,759
258	Richmond, CA	101,680
259	Cambridge, MA	101,362
260	Wichita Falls, TX	101,279
261	Berkeley, CA	101,170
262	Surprise, AZ	101,141
263	Columbia, MO	101,033
264	Lewisville, TX	100,947
265	Wilmington, NC	100,944
266	Gresham, OR	100,935
267	Antioch, CA	100,702
268	Richardson, TX	100,597
269	Rochester, MN	100,589
270	Daly City, CA	100,542
271	Green Bay, WI	100,531
272	West Palm Beach, FL	100,434
273	Edison Twnshp, NJ	99,562
274	Rialto, CA	99,485
275	Frisco, TX	99,472
276	Davenport, IA	99,070
277	Centennial, CO	98,749
278	Temecula, CA	98,663
279	Everett, WA	98,552
280	Woodbridge Twnshp, NJ	98,154
281	Tyler, TX	98,042
282	Carlsbad, CA	97,670
283	Odessa, TX	97,644
284	South Gate, CA	97,179
285	Sandy, UT	96,998
286	Kenosha, WI	96,977
287	Clinton Twnshp, MI	96,315
288	Gary, IN	95,699
289	Brockton, MA	95,650
290	Toms River Twnshp, NJ	95,410
291	Quincy, MA	95,061
292	Mission Viejo, CA	94,702
293	Compton, CA	94,519
294	Hillsboro, OR	94,373
295	Orem, UT	94,228
296	Albany, NY	94,152
297	Clovis, CA	93,848
298	Boulder, CO	93,410
299	Carson, CA	93,170
300	Greece, NY	92,932
301	Fargo, ND	92,883
302	North Charleston, SC	92,749
303	Lakeland, FL	92,669
304	Macon, GA	92,576
305	Vacaville, CA	92,424
306	Livonia, MI	92,329
307	El Cajon, CA	92,225
308	Beaverton, OR	92,198
309	Broken Arrow, OK	92,075
310	Roanoke, VA	91,983
311	Las Cruces, NM	91,982
312	Greeley, CO	91,900
313	San Mateo, CA	91,650
314	New Bedford, MA	91,473
315	Lawton, OK	91,459
316	Lawrence, KS	91,089
317	Vista, CA	90,919
318	Redding, CA	90,881
319	Fall River, MA	90,760
320	San Angelo, TX	90,739
321	Hamilton Twnshp, NJ	90,282
322	Davie, FL	90,268
323	Yuma, AZ	90,245
324	Tuscaloosa, AL	90,157
325	Lynn, MA	90,042
326	Indio, CA	89,486
327	Sunrise, FL	89,139
328	Sparks, NV	88,913
329	Hesperia, CA	88,853
330	Westminster, CA	88,730
331	Roswell, GA	88,069
332	Santa Monica, CA	87,572
333	Dearborn, MI	87,482
334	Nashua, NH	86,845
335	Longmont, CO	86,754
336	Santa Maria, CA	86,744
337	Alhambra, CA	86,404
338	Santa Barbara, CA	85,791
339	Spokane Valley, WA	85,551
340	Avondale, AZ	85,376
341	Kent, WA	84,966
342	Fort Smith, AR	84,847
343	Federal Way, WA	84,775
344	Boca Raton, FL	84,630
345	Chino, CA	84,595
346	Canton Twnshp, MI	84,506
347	Hawthorne, CA	84,445
348	Lee's Summit, MO	84,399
349	Citrus Heights, CA	84,361
350	Warwick, RI	84,326
351	Duluth, MN	84,171
352	Chico, CA	84,086
353	Miami Beach, FL	83,609
354	Norwalk, CT	83,503
355	Plantation, FL	83,480
356	Suffolk, VA	83,470
357	Ogden, UT	83,353
358	Allen, TX	83,242
359	Newton, MA	83,191
360	Pearland, TX	83,185
361	Nampa, ID	83,007
362	Tracy, CA	82,960
363	Sandy Springs, GA	82,953
364	Whittier, CA	82,727
365	Sioux City, IA	82,404
366	Racine, WI	82,226
367	Trenton, NJ	82,140
368	College Station, TX	81,925
369	Sugar Land, TX	81,763
370	San Marcos, CA	81,683
371	Bloomington, MN	80,996
372	Reading, PA	80,860
373	Troy, MI	80,491
374	Livermore, CA	80,258
375	Cranston, RI	79,987
376	Westland, MI	79,944
377	Newport Beach, CA	79,821
378	Danbury, CT	79,753
379	Rio Rancho, NM	79,647
380	Edmond, OK	79,529
381	Buena Park, CA	79,431
382	Lakewood, CA	78,894
383	Clarkstown, NY	78,869
384	O'Fallon, MO	78,837
385	Bellingham, WA	78,804
386	Farmington Hills, MI	78,602
387	Merced, CA	78,598
388	Upper Darby Twnshp, PA	78,550
389	Cheektowaga, NY	78,303
390	Colonie, NY	78,272
391	Brick Twnshp, NJ	78,218
392	Clifton, NJ	78,180
393	Baldwin Park, CA	78,031
394	Canton, OH	78,006
395	Bend, OR	77,898
396	San Leandro, CA	77,474
397	Melbourne, FL	77,286
398	Longview, TX	77,272
399	Missouri City, TX	77,075
400	Hammond, IN	76,498
401	St. Joseph, MO	76,377
402	Camden, NJ	76,182
403	Decatur, IL	76,044
404	Jacksonville, NC	75,770
405	Albany, GA	75,715
406	Lake Forest, CA	75,637
407	Ramapo, NY	75,433
408	Southfield, MI	75,024
409	St. George, UT	74,356
410	Somerville, MA	74,012
411	Fayetteville, AR	73,999

Source: Reported data from the F.B.I. "Crime in the United States 2008"

*Updated estimates as of July 2008 based on U.S. Bureau of the Census figures. Charlotte, Honolulu, Indianapolis, Las Vegas, Louisville, Mobile, and Savannah include areas under their police department but outside the city limits.

90. City Population in 2005
National Total = 296,507,061*

RANK	CITY	POP
198	Abilene, TX	116,695
88	Akron, OH	212,272
362	Albany, GA	78,353
275	Albany, NY	94,361
34	Albuquerque, NM	490,631
173	Alexandria, VA	130,056
304	Alhambra, CA	88,579
218	Allentown, PA	106,933
386	Allen, TX	67,432
115	Amarillo, TX	183,765
208	Amherst, NY	111,178
52	Anaheim, CA	335,992
66	Anchorage, AK	276,109
203	Ann Arbor, MI	113,660
242	Antioch, CA	101,593
49	Arlington, TX	365,380
231	Arvada, CO	103,983
222	Athens-Clarke, GA	105,727
42	Atlanta, GA	430,666
58	Aurora, CO	295,888
126	Aurora, IL	167,266
18	Austin, TX	693,019
NA	Avondale, AZ**	NA
60	Bakersfield, CA	285,821
357	Baldwin Park, CA	79,411
21	Baltimore, MD	641,097
81	Baton Rouge, LA	224,487
202	Beaumont, TX	114,141
324	Beaverton, OR	83,979
194	Bellevue, WA	118,496
375	Bellingham, WA	73,980
388	Bend, OR	63,751
239	Berkeley, CA	102,191
258	Billings, MT	97,898
76	Birmingham, AL	234,571
NA	Bloomington, MN**	NA
355	Boca Raton, FL	79,831
109	Boise, ID	195,012
27	Boston, MA	567,589
281	Boulder, CO	93,474
359	Brick Twnshp, NJ	78,646
162	Bridgeport, CT	140,177
269	Brockton, MA	94,746
318	Broken Arrow, OK	84,982
131	Brownsville, TX	163,877
354	Buena Park, CA	79,884
62	Buffalo, NY	283,269
225	Burbank, CA	104,805
247	Cambridge, MA	100,492
350	Camden, NJ	80,125
319	Canton Twnshp, MI	84,723
353	Canton, OH	79,940
172	Cape Coral, FL	130,874
299	Carlsbad, CA	89,633
192	Carrollton, TX	119,761
276	Carson, CA	94,355
237	Cary, NC	102,949
186	Cedar Rapids, IA	122,698
254	Centennial, CO	99,607
78	Chandler, AZ	231,613
219	Charleston, SC	106,307
20	Charlotte, NC	677,122
139	Chattanooga, TN	156,480
338	Cheektowaga, NY	81,793
85	Chesapeake, VA	217,823
3	Chicago, IL	2,873,441
382	Chico, CA	70,670
369	Chino, CA	76,547
93	Chula Vista, CA	206,239
56	Cincinnati, OH	314,292
NA	Citrus Heights, CA**	NA
NA	Clarkstown, NY**	NA
213	Clarksville, TN	110,117
210	Clearwater, FL	111,058
37	Cleveland, OH	458,885
351	Clifton, NJ	80,119
265	Clinton Twnshp, MI	96,028
329	Clovis, CA	82,921
379	College Station, TX	73,373
368	Colonie, NY	77,048
48	Colorado Springs, CO	374,482
295	Columbia, MO	90,304
195	Columbia, SC	117,911
111	Columbus, GA	187,886
17	Columbus, OH	730,329
263	Compton, CA	96,874
181	Concord, CA	125,154
171	Coral Springs, FL	131,252
152	Corona, CA	146,363
60	Corpus Christi, TX	285,821
209	Costa Mesa, CA	111,144
339	Cranston, RI	81,649
10	Dallas, TX	1,230,303
243	Daly City, CA	101,288
361	Danbury, CT	78,413
256	Davenport, IA	98,751
321	Davie, FL	84,443
135	Dayton, OH	160,363
266	Dearborn, MI	95,548
NA	Decatur, IL**	NA
252	Denton, TX	99,905
28	Denver, CO	564,552
108	Des Moines, IA	195,093
13	Detroit, MI	900,932
211	Downey, CA	111,051
NA	Duluth, MN**	NA
94	Durham, NC	205,080
248	Edison Twnshp, NJ	100,361
377	Edmond, OK	73,585
271	El Cajon, CA	94,611
184	El Monte, CA	122,934
24	El Paso, TX	601,839
NA	Elgin, IL**	NA
183	Elizabeth, NJ	124,997
NA	Elk Grove, CA**	NA
230	Erie, PA	104,120
165	Escondido, CA	136,362
155	Eugene, OR	144,526
196	Evansville, IN	117,802
261	Everett, WA	97,402
228	Fairfield, CA	104,639
NA	Fall River, MA**	NA
287	Fargo, ND	91,380
344	Farmington Hills, MI	80,853
387	Fayetteville, AR	64,809
179	Fayetteville, NC	127,323
334	Federal Way, WA	82,457
191	Flint, MI	119,814
137	Fontana, CA	159,769
177	Fort Collins, CO	128,727
124	Fort Lauderdale, FL	168,293
332	Fort Smith, AR	82,638
84	Fort Wayne, IN	220,561
23	Fort Worth, TX	613,261
96	Fremont, CA	203,717
36	Fresno, CA	460,758
390	Frisco, TX	63,398
168	Fullerton, CA	134,325
207	Gainesville, FL	111,313
123	Garden Grove, CA	168,458
83	Garland, TX	220,748
251	Gary, IN	100,065
133	Gilbert, AZ	162,257
71	Glendale, AZ	243,608
97	Glendale, CA	202,663
159	Grand Prairie, TX	142,628
106	Grand Rapids, MI	195,274
270	Greece, NY	94,688
315	Greeley, CO	85,991
241	Green Bay, WI	101,599
75	Greensboro, NC	235,393
264	Gresham, OR	96,609
296	Hamilton Twnshp, NJ	90,255
349	Hammond, IN	80,426
148	Hampton, VA	148,057
182	Hartford, CT	125,086
311	Hawthorne, CA	86,852
160	Hayward, CA	141,730
77	Henderson, NV	232,536
376	Hesperia, CA	73,863
79	Hialeah, FL	229,590
273	High Point, NC	94,401
330	Hillsboro, OR	82,912
150	Hollywood, FL	147,798
12	Honolulu, HI	908,521
4	Houston, TX	2,045,732
105	Huntington Beach, CA	196,602
129	Huntsville, AL	165,147
206	Independence, MO	111,905
14	Indianapolis, IN	800,304
389	Indio, CA	63,747
200	Inglewood, CA	116,079
118	Irvine, CA	179,501
103	Irving, TX	197,747
15	Jacksonville, FL	795,259
378	Jacksonville, NC	73,538
116	Jackson, MS	180,417
73	Jersey City, NJ	239,603
174	Joliet, IL	130,026
153	Kansas City, KS	145,491
40	Kansas City, MO	447,915
277	Kenosha, WI	94,261
331	Kent, WA	82,736
257	Killeen, TX	98,538
117	Knoxville, TN	179,989
205	Lafayette, LA	112,161
365	Lake Forest, CA	77,523
294	Lakeland, FL	90,351
340	Lakewood, CA	81,626
158	Lakewood, CO	143,259
175	Lancaster, CA	129,784
197	Lansing, MI	117,036
92	Laredo, TX	206,555
346	Las Cruces, NM	80,573
7	Las Vegas, NV	1,281,698
337	Lawrence, KS	82,148
303	Lawton, OK	88,823
358	Lee's Summit, MO	79,284
292	Lewisville, TX	90,608
67	Lexington, KY	268,124
74	Lincoln, NE	237,710
112	Little Rock, AR	185,855
360	Livermore, CA	78,501
255	Livonia, MI	99,017
35	Long Beach, CA	479,729
NA	Longmont, CO**	NA

RANK	CITY	POP
370	Longview, TX	76,545
2	Los Angeles, CA	3,871,077
22	Louisville, KY	623,735
89	Lubbock, TX	211,271
301	Lynn, MA	89,234
259	Macon, GA	97,606
82	Madison, WI	221,419
212	Manchester, NH	110,188
185	McAllen, TX	122,729
297	McKinney, TX	89,863
367	Melbourne, FL	77,067
19	Memphis, TN	678,988
381	Merced, CA	72,968
39	Mesa, AZ	452,340
170	Mesquite, TX	131,844
288	Miami Beach, FL	91,115
234	Miami Gardens, FL	103,164
45	Miami, FL	388,295
253	Midland, TX	99,695
25	Milwaukee, WI	586,500
47	Minneapolis, MN	376,277
232	Miramar, FL	103,777
262	Mission Viejo, CA	96,892
384	Missouri City, TX	67,682
69	Mobile, AL	249,798
91	Modesto, CA	208,142
98	Montgomery, AL	202,209
125	Moreno Valley, CA	167,394
335	Murfreesboro, TN	82,367
372	Murrieta, CA	75,008
NA	Nampa, ID**	NA
161	Naperville, IL	140,654
306	Nashua, NH	88,113
29	Nashville, TN	557,034
279	New Bedford, MA	93,720
NA	New Haven, CT**	NA
NA	New Orleans, LA**	NA
1	New York, NY	8,115,690
64	Newark, NJ	281,063
348	Newport Beach, CA	80,488
326	Newton, MA	83,570
72	Norfolk, VA	241,267
240	Norman, OK	101,620
317	North Charleston, SC	85,416
130	North Las Vegas, NV	164,190
217	Norwalk, CA	107,391
320	Norwalk, CT	84,562
44	Oakland, CA	400,619
122	Oceanside, CA	168,550
274	Odessa, TX	94,371
385	O'Fallon, MO	67,541
342	Ogden, UT	81,166
32	Oklahoma City, OK	531,688
215	Olathe, KS	108,754
43	Omaha, NE	412,128
121	Ontario, CA	171,186
167	Orange, CA	134,708
286	Orem, UT	91,607
90	Orlando, FL	210,290
132	Overland Park, KS	163,274
113	Oxnard, CA	184,806
291	Palm Bay, FL	90,762
169	Palmdale, CA	132,024
154	Pasadena, CA	145,025
151	Pasadena, TX	146,546
146	Paterson, NJ	151,200
394	Pearland, TX	53,264
142	Pembroke Pines, FL	153,492

RANK	CITY	POP
164	Peoria, AZ	136,995
204	Peoria, IL	113,161
5	Philadelphia, PA	1,472,915
6	Phoenix, AZ	1,466,296
54	Pittsburgh, PA	330,780
70	Plano, TX	249,448
308	Plantation, FL	87,427
139	Pomona, CA	156,480
290	Pompano Beach, FL	90,880
188	Port St. Lucie, FL	121,069
31	Portland, OR	540,389
246	Portsmouth, VA	100,724
119	Providence, RI	177,392
236	Provo, UT	102,983
224	Pueblo, CO	105,057
298	Quincy, MA	89,661
347	Racine, WI	80,503
53	Raleigh, NC	332,084
374	Ramapo, NY	74,388
134	Rancho Cucamon., CA	160,404
343	Reading, PA	80,879
302	Redding, CA	89,161
95	Reno, NV	204,749
249	Rialto, CA	100,321
245	Richardson, TX	100,896
235	Richmond, CA	102,997
107	Richmond, VA	195,271
391	Rio Rancho, NM	62,770
59	Riverside, CA	290,299
280	Roanoke, VA	93,685
278	Rochester, MN	93,866
87	Rochester, NY	212,785
143	Rockford, IL	153,048
229	Roseville, CA	104,297
309	Roswell, GA	87,386
327	Round Rock, TX	83,390
38	Sacramento, CA	457,347
149	Salem, OR	148,009
147	Salinas, CA	149,167
114	Salt Lake City, UT	184,627
300	San Angelo, TX	89,561
9	San Antonio, TX	1,256,584
99	San Bernardino, CA	199,723
8	San Diego, CA	1,272,148
16	San Francisco, CA	749,172
11	San Jose, CA	910,528
356	San Leandro, CA	79,709
383	San Marcos, CA	68,801
285	San Mateo, CA	91,881
NA	Sandy Springs, GA**	NA
282	Sandy, UT	93,013
51	Santa Ana, CA	344,991
307	Santa Barbara, CA	87,950
227	Santa Clara, CA	104,692
128	Santa Clarita, CA	165,894
322	Santa Maria, CA	84,312
305	Santa Monica, CA	88,406
141	Santa Rosa, CA	154,656
86	Savannah, GA	213,587
80	Scottsdale, AZ	229,339
26	Seattle, WA	579,215
101	Shreveport, LA	199,021
193	Simi Valley, CA	119,682
323	Sioux City, IA	84,017
163	Sioux Falls, SD	137,590
371	Somerville, MA	75,412
221	South Bend, IN	106,076
250	South Gate, CA	100,289

RANK	CITY	POP
364	Southfield, MI	77,554
325	Sparks, NV	83,791
336	Spokane Valley, WA	82,288
100	Spokane, WA	199,384
201	Springfield, IL	115,187
145	Springfield, MA	151,670
144	Springfield, MO	151,901
189	Stamford, CT	120,456
178	Sterling Heights, MI	127,580
63	Stockton, CA	281,747
393	St. George, UT	61,795
380	St. Joseph, MO	73,205
50	St. Louis, MO	346,005
65	St. Paul, MN	278,692
68	St. Petersburg, FL	254,713
363	Suffolk, VA	77,691
373	Sugar Land, TX	74,934
176	Sunnyvale, CA	128,862
283	Sunrise, FL	92,264
392	Surprise, AZ	62,751
157	Syracuse, NY	143,306
102	Tacoma, WA	198,748
136	Tallahassee, FL	160,147
55	Tampa, FL	329,035
333	Temecula, CA	82,628
127	Tempe, AZ	166,144
233	Thornton, CO	103,487
180	Thousand Oaks, CA	125,884
57	Toledo, OH	305,107
272	Toms River Twnshp, NJ	94,527
187	Topeka, KS	122,218
156	Torrance, CA	143,790
366	Tracy, CA	77,411
316	Trenton, NJ	85,566
341	Troy, MI	81,498
33	Tucson, AZ	529,447
46	Tulsa, OK	386,414
345	Tuscaloosa, AL	80,670
289	Tyler, TX	91,025
352	Upper Darby Twnshp, PA	80,104
267	Vacaville, CA	94,929
NA	Vallejo, CA**	NA
138	Vancouver, WA	157,152
226	Ventura, CA	104,759
328	Victorville, CA	83,340
41	Virginia Beach, VA	446,448
223	Visalia, CA	105,350
284	Vista, CA	92,193
190	Waco, TX	120,036
166	Warren, MI	136,229
310	Warwick, RI	87,322
30	Washington, DC	550,521
216	Waterbury, CT	108,636
214	West Covina, CA	109,390
NA	West Jordan, UT**	NA
260	West Palm Beach, FL	97,496
199	West Valley, UT	116,477
312	Westland, MI	86,386
293	Westminster, CA	90,452
220	Westminster, CO	106,211
314	Whittier, CA	86,077
238	Wichita Falls, TX	102,589
NA	Wichita, KS**	NA
268	Wilmington, NC	94,843
110	Winston-Salem, NC	194,708
244	Woodbridge Twnshp, NJ	100,998
120	Worcester, MA	175,479
104	Yonkers, NY	197,408
313	Yuma, AZ	86,157

Source: Reported data from the F.B.I. "Crime in the United States 2005"

*Updated estimates as of July 2005 based on U.S. Bureau of the Census figures. Charlotte, Honolulu, Indianapolis, Las Vegas, Louisville, Mobile, and Savannah include areas under their police department but outside the city limits. **Not available.

90. City Population in 2005 (continued)
National Total = 296,507,061*

RANK	CITY	POP
1	New York, NY	8,115,690
2	Los Angeles, CA	3,871,077
3	Chicago, IL	2,873,441
4	Houston, TX	2,045,732
5	Philadelphia, PA	1,472,915
6	Phoenix, AZ	1,466,296
7	Las Vegas, NV	1,281,698
8	San Diego, CA	1,272,148
9	San Antonio, TX	1,256,584
10	Dallas, TX	1,230,303
11	San Jose, CA	910,528
12	Honolulu, HI	908,521
13	Detroit, MI	900,932
14	Indianapolis, IN	800,304
15	Jacksonville, FL	795,259
16	San Francisco, CA	749,172
17	Columbus, OH	730,329
18	Austin, TX	693,019
19	Memphis, TN	678,988
20	Charlotte, NC	677,122
21	Baltimore, MD	641,097
22	Louisville, KY	623,735
23	Fort Worth, TX	613,261
24	El Paso, TX	601,839
25	Milwaukee, WI	586,500
26	Seattle, WA	579,215
27	Boston, MA	567,589
28	Denver, CO	564,552
29	Nashville, TN	557,034
30	Washington, DC	550,521
31	Portland, OR	540,389
32	Oklahoma City, OK	531,688
33	Tucson, AZ	529,447
34	Albuquerque, NM	490,631
35	Long Beach, CA	479,729
36	Fresno, CA	460,758
37	Cleveland, OH	458,885
38	Sacramento, CA	457,347
39	Mesa, AZ	452,340
40	Kansas City, MO	447,915
41	Virginia Beach, VA	446,448
42	Atlanta, GA	430,666
43	Omaha, NE	412,128
44	Oakland, CA	400,619
45	Miami, FL	388,295
46	Tulsa, OK	386,414
47	Minneapolis, MN	376,277
48	Colorado Springs, CO	374,482
49	Arlington, TX	365,380
50	St. Louis, MO	346,005
51	Santa Ana, CA	344,991
52	Anaheim, CA	335,992
53	Raleigh, NC	332,084
54	Pittsburgh, PA	330,780
55	Tampa, FL	329,035
56	Cincinnati, OH	314,292
57	Toledo, OH	305,107
58	Aurora, CO	295,888
59	Riverside, CA	290,299
60	Bakersfield, CA	285,821
60	Corpus Christi, TX	285,821
62	Buffalo, NY	283,269
63	Stockton, CA	281,747
64	Newark, NJ	281,063
65	St. Paul, MN	278,692
66	Anchorage, AK	276,109
67	Lexington, KY	268,124
68	St. Petersburg, FL	254,713
69	Mobile, AL	249,798
70	Plano, TX	249,448
71	Glendale, AZ	243,608
72	Norfolk, VA	241,267
73	Jersey City, NJ	239,603
74	Lincoln, NE	237,710
75	Greensboro, NC	235,393
76	Birmingham, AL	234,571
77	Henderson, NV	232,536
78	Chandler, AZ	231,613
79	Hialeah, FL	229,590
80	Scottsdale, AZ	229,339
81	Baton Rouge, LA	224,487
82	Madison, WI	221,419
83	Garland, TX	220,748
84	Fort Wayne, IN	220,561
85	Chesapeake, VA	217,823
86	Savannah, GA	213,587
87	Rochester, NY	212,785
88	Akron, OH	212,272
89	Lubbock, TX	211,271
90	Orlando, FL	210,290
91	Modesto, CA	208,142
92	Laredo, TX	206,555
93	Chula Vista, CA	206,239
94	Durham, NC	205,080
95	Reno, NV	204,749
96	Fremont, CA	203,717
97	Glendale, CA	202,663
98	Montgomery, AL	202,209
99	San Bernardino, CA	199,723
100	Spokane, WA	199,384
101	Shreveport, LA	199,021
102	Tacoma, WA	198,748
103	Irving, TX	197,747
104	Yonkers, NY	197,408
105	Huntington Beach, CA	196,602
106	Grand Rapids, MI	195,274
107	Richmond, VA	195,271
108	Des Moines, IA	195,093
109	Boise, ID	195,012
110	Winston-Salem, NC	194,708
111	Columbus, GA	187,886
112	Little Rock, AR	185,855
113	Oxnard, CA	184,806
114	Salt Lake City, UT	184,627
115	Amarillo, TX	183,765
116	Jackson, MS	180,417
117	Knoxville, TN	179,989
118	Irvine, CA	179,501
119	Providence, RI	177,392
120	Worcester, MA	175,479
121	Ontario, CA	171,186
122	Oceanside, CA	168,550
123	Garden Grove, CA	168,458
124	Fort Lauderdale, FL	168,293
125	Moreno Valley, CA	167,394
126	Aurora, IL	167,266
127	Tempe, AZ	166,144
128	Santa Clarita, CA	165,894
129	Huntsville, AL	165,147
130	North Las Vegas, NV	164,190
131	Brownsville, TX	163,877
132	Overland Park, KS	163,274
133	Gilbert, AZ	162,257
134	Rancho Cucamon., CA	160,404
135	Dayton, OH	160,363
136	Tallahassee, FL	160,147
137	Fontana, CA	159,769
138	Vancouver, WA	157,152
139	Chattanooga, TN	156,480
139	Pomona, CA	156,480
141	Santa Rosa, CA	154,656
142	Pembroke Pines, FL	153,492
143	Rockford, IL	153,048
144	Springfield, MO	151,901
145	Springfield, MA	151,670
146	Paterson, NJ	151,200
147	Salinas, CA	149,167
148	Hampton, VA	148,057
149	Salem, OR	148,009
150	Hollywood, FL	147,798
151	Pasadena, TX	146,546
152	Corona, CA	146,363
153	Kansas City, KS	145,491
154	Pasadena, CA	145,025
155	Eugene, OR	144,526
156	Torrance, CA	143,790
157	Syracuse, NY	143,306
158	Lakewood, CO	143,259
159	Grand Prairie, TX	142,628
160	Hayward, CA	141,730
161	Naperville, IL	140,654
162	Bridgeport, CT	140,177
163	Sioux Falls, SD	137,590
164	Peoria, AZ	136,995
165	Escondido, CA	136,362
166	Warren, MI	136,229
167	Orange, CA	134,708
168	Fullerton, CA	134,325
169	Palmdale, CA	132,024
170	Mesquite, TX	131,844
171	Coral Springs, FL	131,252
172	Cape Coral, FL	130,874
173	Alexandria, VA	130,056
174	Joliet, IL	130,026
175	Lancaster, CA	129,784
176	Sunnyvale, CA	128,862
177	Fort Collins, CO	128,727
178	Sterling Heights, MI	127,580
179	Fayetteville, NC	127,323
180	Thousand Oaks, CA	125,884
181	Concord, CA	125,154
182	Hartford, CT	125,086
183	Elizabeth, NJ	124,997
184	El Monte, CA	122,934
185	McAllen, TX	122,729
186	Cedar Rapids, IA	122,698
187	Topeka, KS	122,218
188	Port St. Lucie, FL	121,069
189	Stamford, CT	120,456
190	Waco, TX	120,036
191	Flint, MI	119,814
192	Carrollton, TX	119,761
193	Simi Valley, CA	119,682
194	Bellevue, WA	118,496
195	Columbia, SC	117,911
196	Evansville, IN	117,802
197	Lansing, MI	117,036
198	Abilene, TX	116,695
199	West Valley, UT	116,477
200	Inglewood, CA	116,079
201	Springfield, IL	115,187
202	Beaumont, TX	114,141
203	Ann Arbor, MI	113,660
204	Peoria, IL	113,161
205	Lafayette, LA	112,161
206	Independence, MO	111,905

RANK	CITY	POP
207	Gainesville, FL	111,313
208	Amherst, NY	111,178
209	Costa Mesa, CA	111,144
210	Clearwater, FL	111,058
211	Downey, CA	111,051
212	Manchester, NH	110,188
213	Clarksville, TN	110,117
214	West Covina, CA	109,390
215	Olathe, KS	108,754
216	Waterbury, CT	108,636
217	Norwalk, CA	107,391
218	Allentown, PA	106,933
219	Charleston, SC	106,307
220	Westminster, CO	106,211
221	South Bend, IN	106,076
222	Athens-Clarke, GA	105,727
223	Visalia, CA	105,350
224	Pueblo, CO	105,057
225	Burbank, CA	104,805
226	Ventura, CA	104,759
227	Santa Clara, CA	104,692
228	Fairfield, CA	104,639
229	Roseville, CA	104,297
230	Erie, PA	104,120
231	Arvada, CO	103,983
232	Miramar, FL	103,777
233	Thornton, CO	103,487
234	Miami Gardens, FL	103,164
235	Richmond, CA	102,997
236	Provo, UT	102,983
237	Cary, NC	102,949
238	Wichita Falls, TX	102,589
239	Berkeley, CA	102,191
240	Norman, OK	101,620
241	Green Bay, WI	101,599
242	Antioch, CA	101,593
243	Daly City, CA	101,288
244	Woodbridge Twnshp, NJ	100,998
245	Richardson, TX	100,896
246	Portsmouth, VA	100,724
247	Cambridge, MA	100,492
248	Edison Twnshp, NJ	100,361
249	Rialto, CA	100,321
250	South Gate, CA	100,289
251	Gary, IN	100,065
252	Denton, TX	99,905
253	Midland, TX	99,695
254	Centennial, CO	99,607
255	Livonia, MI	99,017
256	Davenport, IA	98,751
257	Killeen, TX	98,538
258	Billings, MT	97,898
259	Macon, GA	97,606
260	West Palm Beach, FL	97,496
261	Everett, WA	97,402
262	Mission Viejo, CA	96,892
263	Compton, CA	96,874
264	Gresham, OR	96,609
265	Clinton Twnshp, MI	96,028
266	Dearborn, MI	95,548
267	Vacaville, CA	94,929
268	Wilmington, NC	94,843
269	Brockton, MA	94,746
270	Greece, NY	94,688
271	El Cajon, CA	94,611
272	Toms River Twnshp, NJ	94,527
273	High Point, NC	94,401
274	Odessa, TX	94,371

RANK	CITY	POP
275	Albany, NY	94,361
276	Carson, CA	94,355
277	Kenosha, WI	94,261
278	Rochester, MN	93,866
279	New Bedford, MA	93,720
280	Roanoke, VA	93,685
281	Boulder, CO	93,474
282	Sandy, UT	93,013
283	Sunrise, FL	92,264
284	Vista, CA	92,193
285	San Mateo, CA	91,881
286	Orem, UT	91,607
287	Fargo, ND	91,380
288	Miami Beach, FL	91,115
289	Tyler, TX	91,025
290	Pompano Beach, FL	90,880
291	Palm Bay, FL	90,762
292	Lewisville, TX	90,608
293	Westminster, CA	90,452
294	Lakeland, FL	90,351
295	Columbia, MO	90,304
296	Hamilton Twnshp, NJ	90,255
297	McKinney, TX	89,863
298	Quincy, MA	89,661
299	Carlsbad, CA	89,633
300	San Angelo, TX	89,561
301	Lynn, MA	89,234
302	Redding, CA	89,161
303	Lawton, OK	88,823
304	Alhambra, CA	88,579
305	Santa Monica, CA	88,406
306	Nashua, NH	88,113
307	Santa Barbara, CA	87,950
308	Plantation, FL	87,427
309	Roswell, GA	87,386
310	Warwick, RI	87,322
311	Hawthorne, CA	86,852
312	Westland, MI	86,386
313	Yuma, AZ	86,157
314	Whittier, CA	86,077
315	Greeley, CO	85,991
316	Trenton, NJ	85,566
317	North Charleston, SC	85,416
318	Broken Arrow, OK	84,982
319	Canton Twnshp, MI	84,723
320	Norwalk, CT	84,562
321	Davie, FL	84,443
322	Santa Maria, CA	84,312
323	Sioux City, IA	84,017
324	Beaverton, OR	83,979
325	Sparks, NV	83,791
326	Newton, MA	83,570
327	Round Rock, TX	83,390
328	Victorville, CA	83,340
329	Clovis, CA	82,921
330	Hillsboro, OR	82,912
331	Kent, WA	82,736
332	Fort Smith, AR	82,638
333	Temecula, CA	82,628
334	Federal Way, WA	82,457
335	Murfreesboro, TN	82,367
336	Spokane Valley, WA	82,288
337	Lawrence, KS	82,148
338	Cheektowaga, NY	81,793
339	Cranston, RI	81,649
340	Lakewood, CA	81,626
341	Troy, MI	81,498
342	Ogden, UT	81,166

RANK	CITY	POP
343	Reading, PA	80,879
344	Farmington Hills, MI	80,853
345	Tuscaloosa, AL	80,670
346	Las Cruces, NM	80,573
347	Racine, WI	80,503
348	Newport Beach, CA	80,488
349	Hammond, IN	80,426
350	Camden, NJ	80,125
351	Clifton, NJ	80,119
352	Upper Darby Twnshp, PA	80,104
353	Canton, OH	79,940
354	Buena Park, CA	79,884
355	Boca Raton, FL	79,831
356	San Leandro, CA	79,709
357	Baldwin Park, CA	79,411
358	Lee's Summit, MO	79,284
359	Brick Twnshp, NJ	78,646
360	Livermore, CA	78,501
361	Danbury, CT	78,413
362	Albany, GA	78,353
363	Suffolk, VA	77,691
364	Southfield, MI	77,554
365	Lake Forest, CA	77,523
366	Tracy, CA	77,411
367	Melbourne, FL	77,067
368	Colonie, NY	77,048
369	Chino, CA	76,547
370	Longview, TX	76,545
371	Somerville, MA	75,412
372	Murrieta, CA	75,008
373	Sugar Land, TX	74,934
374	Ramapo, NY	74,388
375	Bellingham, WA	73,980
376	Hesperia, CA	73,863
377	Edmond, OK	73,585
378	Jacksonville, NC	73,538
379	College Station, TX	73,373
380	St. Joseph, MO	73,205
381	Merced, CA	72,968
382	Chico, CA	70,670
383	San Marcos, CA	68,801
384	Missouri City, TX	67,682
385	O'Fallon, MO	67,541
386	Allen, TX	67,432
387	Fayetteville, AR	64,809
388	Bend, OR	63,751
389	Indio, CA	63,747
390	Frisco, TX	63,398
391	Rio Rancho, NM	62,770
392	Surprise, AZ	62,751
393	St. George, UT	61,795
394	Pearland, TX	53,264
NA	Avondale, AZ**	NA
NA	Bloomington, MN**	NA
NA	Citrus Heights, CA**	NA
NA	Clarkstown, NY**	NA
NA	Decatur, IL**	NA
NA	Duluth, MN**	NA
NA	Elgin, IL**	NA
NA	Elk Grove, CA**	NA
NA	Fall River, MA**	NA
NA	Longmont, CO**	NA
NA	Nampa, ID**	NA
NA	New Haven, CT**	NA
NA	New Orleans, LA**	NA
NA	Sandy Springs, GA**	NA
NA	Vallejo, CA**	NA
NA	West Jordan, UT**	NA
NA	Wichita, KS**	NA

Source: Reported data from the F.B.I. "Crime in the United States 2005"

*Updated estimates as of July 2005 based on U.S. Bureau of the Census figures. Charlotte, Honolulu, Indianapolis, Las Vegas, Louisville, Mobile, and Savannah include areas under their police department but outside the city limits. **Not available.

Appendix

DESCRIPTIONS OF METROPOLITAN AREAS IN 2009

Abilene, TX includes Callahan, Jones and Taylor counties

Akron, OH includes Portage and Summit counties

Albany, GA includes Baker, Dougherty, Lee, Terrell and Worth counties

Albany-Schenectady-Troy, NY includes Albany, Rensselaer, Saratoga, Schenectady and Schoharie counties

Albuquerque, NM includes Bernalillo, Sandoval, Torrance and Valencia counties

Alexandria, LA includes Grant and Rapides parishes

Allentown-Bethlehem-Easton, PA-NJ includes Warren, NJ, Carbon, PA, Lehigh, PA and Northampton, PA counties

Altoona, PA includes Blair County

Amarillo, TX includes Armstrong, Carson, Potter and Randall counties

Ames, IA includes Story County

Anchorage, AK includes Anchorage Municipality and Matanuska-Susitna Borough

Anderson, IN includes Madison County

Anderson, SC includes Anderson County

Ann Arbor, MI includes Washtenaw County

Anniston-Oxford, AL includes Calhoun County

Appleton, WI includes Calumet and Outagamie counties

Asheville, NC includes Buncombe, Haywood, Henderson and Madison counties

Athens-Clarke, GA includes, Clarke, Madison, Oconee and Oglethorpe counties

Atlanta-Sandy Springs-Marietta, GA includes Barrow, Bartow, Butts, Carroll, Cherokee, Clayton, Cobb, Coweta, Dawson, DeKalb, Douglas, Fayette, Forsyth, Fulton, Gwinnett, Haralson, Heard, Henry, Jasper, Lamar, Meriwether, Newton, Paulding, Pickens, Pike, Rockdale, Spalding and Walton counties

Atlantic City, NJ includes Atlantic County

Auburn-Opelika, AL includes Lee County

Augusta-Richmond, GA-SC includes Burke, GA, Columbia, GA, McDuffie, GA, Richmond, GA and Aiken, SC and Edgefield, SC counties

Austin-Round Rock, TX includes Bastrop, Caldwell, Hays, Travis and Williamson counties

Bakersfield, CA includes Kern County

Baltimore-Towson, MD includes Anne Arundel, Baltimore, Carroll, Harford, Howard and Queen Anne's counties and Baltimore city

Bangor, ME includes Penobscot County

Barnstable Town, MA includes Barnstable County

Baton Rouge, LA includes Ascension, East Baton Rouge, East Feliciana, Iberville, Livingston, Pointe Coupee, St. Helena, West Baton Rouge and West Feliciana parishes

Battle Creek, MI includes Calhoun County

Bay City, MI includes Bay County

Beaumont-Port Arthur, TX includes Hardin, Jefferson and Orange counties

Bellingham, WA includes Whatcom County

Bend, OR includes Deschutes County

Bethesda, MD see Washington, DC

Billings, MT includes Carbon and Yellowstone counties

Binghamton, NY includes Broome and Tioga counties

Birmingham-Hoover, AL includes Bibb, Blount, Chilton, Jefferson, St. Clair, Shelby and Walker counties

Bismarck, ND includes Burleigh and Morton counties

Blacksburg-Christiansburg-Radford, VA includes Giles, Montgomery and Pulaski counties and Radford city

Bloomington, IN includes Greene, Monroe and Owen counties

Bloomington-Normal, IL includes McLean County

Boise City-Nampa, ID includes Ada, Boise, Canyon, Gem and Owyhee counties

Boston-Cambridge-Quincy, MA-NH includes:

- Boston-Quincy, MA Metropolitan Division includes Norfolk, Plymouth, and Suffolk counties
- Cambridge-Newton-Framingham, MA Metropolitan Division includes Middlesex County
- Essex Metropolitan Division, MA includes Essex County
- Rockingham County-Strafford Metropolitan Division includes Rockingham and Strafford counties

Boulder, CO includes Boulder County

Bowling Green, KY includes Edmonson and Warren counties

Bremerton-Silverdale, WA includes Kitsap County

Bridgeport-Stamford-Norwalk, CT includes Fairfield County

Brownsville-Harlingen, TX includes Cameron County

Brunswick, GA includes Brantley, Glynn and McIntosh counties

Buffalo-Niagara Falls, NY includes Erie and Niagara counties

Burlington, NC includes Alamance County

Burlington-South Burlington, VT includes Chittenden, Franklin and Grand Isle counties

Cambridge, MA see Boston, MA

Camden, NJ see Philadelphia, PA

Canton-Massillon, OH includes Carroll and Stark counties

Cape Coral-Fort Myers, FL includes Lee County

DESCRIPTIONS OF METROPOLITAN AREAS IN 2009 (continued)

Cape Girardeau-Jackson, MO-IL includes Alexander County, IL and Bollinger and Cape Girardeau Counties, MO

Carson City, NV includes Carson City

Casper, WY includes Natrona County

Cedar Rapids, IA includes Benton, Jones and Linn counties

Champaign-Urbana, IL includes Champaign, Ford and Piatt counties

Charleston, WV includes Boone, Clay, Kanawha, Lincoln and Putnam counties

Charleston-North Charleston, SC includes Berkeley, Charleston and Dorchester counties

Charlotte-Gastonia-Concord, NC-SC includes Anson, Cabarrus, Gaston, Mecklenburg, Union and York, SC counties

Charlottesville, VA includes Albemarle, Fluvanna, Greene and Nelson counties and Charlottesville city

Chattanooga, TN-GA includes Catoosa, GA, Dade, GA, Walker, GA, Hamilton, TN, Marion, TN and Sequatchie, TN counties

Cheyenne, WY includes Laramie County

Chicago-Naperville-Joliet, IL-IN-WI includes:

- Chicago-Naperville-Joliet, IL Metropolitan Division includes Cook, DeKalb, DuPage, Grundy, Kane, Kendall, McHenry and Will counties,
- Gary, IN Metropolitan Division includes Jasper, Lake, Newton and Porter counties, and
- Lake County-Kenosha-WI Metropolitan Division includes Lake, IL and Kenosha, WI counties

Chico, CA includes Butte County

Cincinnati-Middletown, OH-KY-IN includes Dearborn, IN, Franklin, IN, Ohio, IN, Boone KY, Bracken KY, Campbell, KY, Gallatin, KY, Grant, KY, Kenton, KY, Pendleton, KY, Brown, OH, Butler, OH, Clermont, OH, Hamilton, OH and Warren, OH counties

Clarksville, TN-KY includes Christian, KY, Trigg, KY, Montgomery, TN and Stewart, TN counties

Cleveland, TN includes Bradley and Polk counties

Cleveland-Elyria-Mentor, OH includes Cuyahoga, Geauga, Lake, Lorain and Medina counties

Coeur d'Alene, ID includes Kootenai County

College Station-Bryan, TX includes Brazos, Burleson and Robertson counties

Colorado Springs, CO includes El Paso and Teller counties

Columbia, MO includes Boone and Howard counties

Columbia, SC includes Calhoun, Fairfield, Kershaw, Lexington, Richland and Saluda counties

Columbus, GA-AL includes Russell, AL, Chattahoochee, GA, Harris, GA, Marion, GA and Muscogee, GA counties

Columbus, IN includes Bartholomew County

Columbus, OH includes Delaware, Fairfield, Franklin, Licking, Madison, Morrow, Pickaway and Union counties

Corpus Christi, TX includes Aransas, Nueces and San Patricio counties

Corvallis, OR includes Benton County

Crestview-Fort Walton Beach, FL includes Okaloosa County

Cumberland, MD-WV includes Allegany, MD and Mineral, WV counties

Dallas-Fort Worth-Arlington, TX includes:

- Dallas-Plano-Irving, TX Metropolitan Division includes Collin, Dallas, Delta, Denton, Ellis, Hunt, Kaufman and Rockwall counties and
- Fort Worth-Arlington, TX Metropolitan Division includes Johnson, Parker, Tarrant and Wise counties

Dalton, GA includes Murray and Whitfield counties

Danville, IL includes Vermilion County

Danville, VA includes Pittsylvania County and Danville city

Davenport-Moline-Rock Island, IA-IL includes Henry, IL, Mercer, IL, Rock Island, IL and Scott, IA counties

Dayton, OH includes Greene, Miami, Montgomery and Preble counties

Decatur, AL includes Lawrence and Morgan counties

Decatur, IL includes Macon County

Deltona-Daytona Beach-Ormond Beach, FL includes Volusia County

Denver-Aurora, CO includes Adams, Arapahoe, Broomfield, Clear Creek, Denver, Douglas, Elbert, Gilpin, Jefferson and Park counties

Des Moines, IA includes Dallas, Guthrie, Madison, Polk and Warren counties

Detroit-Warren-Livonia, MI includes:

- Detroit-Livonia-Dearborn, MI Metropolitan Division includes Wayne County and
- Warren-Farmington Hills-Troy, MI Metropolitan Division includes Lapeer, Livingston, Macomb, Oakland and St. Clair counties

Dothan, AL includes Geneva, Henry and Houston counties

Dover, DE includes Kent County

Dubuque, IA includes Dubuque County

Duluth, MN-WI includes Carlton, MN, St. Louis, MN and Douglas, WI counties

Durham-Chapel Hill, NC includes Chatham, Durham, Orange and Person counties

Eau Claire, WI includes Chippewa and Eau Claire counties

Edison, NJ see New York, NY

El Centro, CA includes Imperial County

Elizabethtown, KY includes Hardin and Larue counties

DESCRIPTIONS OF METROPOLITAN AREAS IN 2009 (continued)

Elkhart-Goshen, IN includes Elkhart County

Elmira, NY includes Chemung County

El Paso, TX includes El Paso County
Erie, PA includes Erie County

Essex County, MA see Boston, MA

Eugene-Springfield, OR includes Lane County

Evansville, IN-KY includes Gibson, IN, Posey, IN, Vanderburgh, IN, Warrick, IN, Henderson, KY and Webster, KY counties

Fairbanks, AK includes Fairbanks North Star Borough

Fargo, ND-MN includes Clay, MN and Cass, ND counties

Farmington, NM includes San Juan County

Fayetteville, NC includes Cumberland and Hoke counties

Fayetteville-Springdale-Rogers, AR-MO includes Benton, AR, Madison, AR, Washington, AR and McDonald, MO counties

Flagstaff, AZ includes Coconino County

Flint, MI includes Genesee County

Florence, SC includes Darlington and Florence counties

Florence-Muscle Shoals, AL includes Colbert and Lauderdale counties

Fond du Lac, WI includes Fond du Lac County

Fort Collins-Loveland, CO includes Larimer County

Fort Lauderdale, FL see Miami, FL

Fort Smith, AR-OK includes Crawford, AR, Franklin, AR, Sebastian, AR, Le Flore, OK and Sequoyah, OK counties

Fort Wayne, IN includes Allen, Wells and Whitley counties

Fort Worth, TX see Dallas, TX

Fresno, CA includes Fresno County

Gadsden, AL includes Etowah County

Gainesville, FL includes Alachua and Gilchrist counties

Gainesville, GA includes Hall County

Glens Falls, NY includes Warren and Washington counties

Goldsboro, NC includes Wayne County

Grand Forks, ND-MN includes Polk, MN and Grand Forks, ND counties

Grand Junction, CO includes Mesa County

Grand Rapids-Wyoming, MI includes Barry, Ionia, Kent and Newaygo counties

Great Falls, MT includes Cascade County

Greeley, CO includes Weld County

Green Bay, WI includes Brown, Kewaunee and Oconto counties

Greensboro-High Point, NC includes Guilford, Randolph and Rockingham counties

Greenville, NC includes Greene and Pitt counties

Greenville, SC includes Greenville, Laurens and Pickens counties

Gulfport-Biloxi, MS includes Hancock, Harrison and Stone counties

Hagerstown-Martinsburg, MD-WV includes Washington, MD, Berkeley, WV and Morgan, WV counties

Hanford-Corcoran, CA includes Kings County

Harrisburg-Carlisle, PA includes Cumberland, Dauphin and Perry counties

Harrisonburg, VA includes Rockingham County and Harrisonburg city

Hartford-West Hartford-East Hartford, CT includes Hartford, Middlesex and Tolland counties

Hattiesburg, MS includes Forrest, Lamar and Perry counties

Hickory-Lenoir-Morganton, NC includes Alexander, Burke, Caldwell and Catawba counties

Hinesville-Fort Stewart, GA includes Liberty and Long counties

Holland-Grand Haven, MI includes Ottawa County

Honolulu, HI includes Honolulu County

Hot Springs, AR includes Garland County

Houma-Bayou Cane-Thibodaux, LA includes Lafourche and Terrebonne parishes

Houston-Baytown-Sugar Land, TX includes Austin, Brazoria, Chambers, Fort Bend, Galveston, Harris, Liberty, Montgomery, San Jacinto and Waller counties

Huntington-Ashland, WV-KY-OH includes Boyd, KY, Greenup, KY, Lawrence, OH, Cabell, WV and Wayne, WV counties

Huntsville, AL includes Limestone and Madison counties

Idaho Falls, ID includes Bonneville and Jefferson counties

Indianapolis, IN includes Boone, Brown, Hamilton, Hancock, Hendricks, Johnson, Marion, Morgan, Putnam and Shelby counties

Iowa City, IA includes Johnson and Washington counties

Ithaca, NY includes Tompkins County

Jackson, MI includes Jackson County

Jackson, MS includes Copiah, Hinds, Madison, Rankin and Simpson counties

Jackson, TN includes Chester and Madison counties

Jacksonville, FL includes Baker, Clay, Duval, Nassau and St. Johns counties

Jacksonville, NC includes Onslow County

Janesville, WI includes Rock County

Jefferson City, MO includes Callaway, Cole, Moniteau and Osage counties

DESCRIPTIONS OF METROPOLITAN AREAS IN 2009 (continued)

Johnson City, TN includes Carter, Unicoi and Washington counties

Johnstown, PA includes Cambria County

Jonesboro, AR includes Craighead and Poinsett counties

Joplin, MO includes Jasper and Newton counties

Kalamazoo-Portage, MI includes Kalamazoo and Van Buren counties

Kankakee-Bradley, IL includes Kankakee County

Kansas City, MO-KS includes Franklin, KS, Johnson, KS, Leavenworth, KS, Linn, KS, Miami, KS, Wyandotte, KS, Bates, MO, Caldwell, MO, Cass, MO, Clay, MO, Clinton, MO, Jackson, MO, Lafayette, MO, Platte, MO and Ray, MO counties

Kennewick-Richland-Pasco, WA includes Benton and Franklin counties

Killeen-Temple-Fort Hood, TX includes Bell, Coryell and Lampasas counties

Kingsport-Bristol-Bristol, TN-VA includes Hawkins, TN, Sullivan, TN, Scott, VA, and Washington, VA counties and Bristol city, VA

Kingston, NY includes Ulster County

Knoxville, TN includes Anderson, Blount, Knox, Loudon and Union counties

Kokomo, IN includes Howard and Tipton counties

La Crosse, WI-MN includes Houston, MN and La Crosse, WI counties

Lafayette, IN includes Benton, Carroll and Tippecanoe counties

Lafayette, LA includes Lafayette and St. Martin parishes

Lake Charles, LA includes Calcasieu and Cameron parishes

Lake Havasu City-Kingman, AZ includes Mohave County

Lakeland, FL includes Polk County

Lancaster, PA includes Lancaster County

Lansing-East Lansing, MI includes Clinton, Eaton and Ingham counties

Laredo, TX includes Webb County

Las Cruces, NM includes Dona Ana County

Las Vegas-Paradise, NV includes Clark County

Lawrence, KS includes Douglas County

Lawton, OK includes Comanche County

Lebanon, PA includes Lebanon County

Lewiston, ID-WA includes Nez Perce, ID and Asotin, WA counties

Lewiston-Auburn, ME includes Androscoggin County

Lexington-Fayette, KY includes Bourbon, Clark, Fayette, Jessamine, Scott and Woodford counties

Lima, OH includes Allen County

Lincoln, NE includes Lancaster and Seward counties

Little Rock-North Little Rock, AR includes Faulkner, Grant, Lonoke, Perry, Pulaski and Saline counties

Logan, UT-ID includes Franklin, ID and Cache, UT counties

Longview, TX includes Gregg, Rusk and Upshur counties

Longview, WA includes Cowlitz County

Los Angeles-Long Beach-Santa Ana, CA includes:
- Los Angeles-Long Beach-Glendale, CA Metropolitan Division includes Los Angeles County and
- Santa Ana-Anaheim-Irvine, CA Metropolitan Division includes Orange County

Louisville, KY-IN includes Clark, IN, Floyd, IN, Harrison, IN, Washington, IN, Bullitt, KY, Henry, KY, Jefferson, KY, Meade, KY, Nelson, KY, Oldham, KY, Shelby, KY, Spencer, KY and Trimble, KY counties

Lubbock, TX includes Crosby and Lubbock counties

Lynchburg, VA includes Amherst, Appomattox, Bedford and Campbell counties and Bedford and Lynchburg cities

Macon, GA includes Bibb, Crawford, Jones, Monroe and Twiggs counties

Madera, CA includes Madera County

Madison, WI includes Columbia, Dane and Iowa counties

Manchester-Nashua, NH includes Hillsborough County

Manhattan, KS Includes Geary, Pottawatomie, and Riley Counties

Mankato-North Mankato, MN Includes Blue Earth and Nicollet Counties

Mansfield, OH includes Richland County

McAllen-Edinburg-Pharr, TX includes Hidalgo County

Medford, OR includes Jackson County

Memphis, TN-MS-AR includes Crittenden, AR, DeSoto, MS, Marshall, MS, Tate, MS, Tunica, MS, Fayette, TN, Shelby, TN and Tipton, TN counties

Merced, CA includes Merced County

Miami-Fort Lauderdale-Miami Beach, FL includes:
- Fort Lauderdale-Pompano Beach-Deerfield Beach, FL Metropolitan Division includes Broward County,
- Miami-Miami Beach-Kendall, FL Metropolitan Division includes Miami-Dade County and
- West Palm Beach-Boca Raton-Boynton Beach, FL Metropolitan Division includes Palm Beach County

Michigan City-La Porte, IN includes LaPorte County

Midland, TX includes Midland County

Milwaukee-Waukesha-West Allis, WI includes Milwaukee, Ozaukee, Washington and Waukesha counties

Minneapolis-St. Paul-Bloomington, MN-WI includes Anoka, MN, Carver, MN, Chisago, MN, Dakota, MN, Hennepin, MN, Isanti, MN, Ramsey, MN, Scott, MN, Sherburne, MN, Washington, MN, Wright, MN, Pierce, WI and St. Croix, WI counties

DESCRIPTIONS OF METROPOLITAN AREAS IN 2009 (continued)

Missoula, MT includes Missoula County

Mobile, AL includes Mobile County

Modesto, CA includes Stanislaus County

Monroe, LA includes Ouachita and Union parishes

Monroe, MI includes Monroe County

Montgomery, AL includes Autauga, Elmore, Lowndes and Montgomery counties

Morgantown, WV includes Monongalia and Preston counties

Morristown, TN includes Grainger, Hamblen and Jefferson counties

Mount Vernon-Anacortes, WA includes Skagit County

Muncie, IN includes Delaware County

Muskegon-Norton Shores, MI includes Muskegon County

Myrtle Beach-Conway-North Myrtle Beach, SC includes Horry County

Napa, CA includes Napa County

Naples-Marco Island, FL includes Collier County

Nashville-Davidson-Murfreesboro, TN includes Cannon, Cheatham, Davidson, Dickson, Hickman, Macon, Robertson, Rutherford, Smith, Sumner, Trousdale, Williamson and Wilson counties

Nassau, NY see New York, NY

New Haven-Milford, CT includes New Haven County

New Orleans-Metairie-Kenner, LA includes Jefferson, Orleans, Plaquemines, St. Bernard, St. Charles, St. John the Baptist and St. Tammany parishes

New York-Northern New Jersey-Long Island, NY-NJ-PA includes:
- Edison, NJ, Metropolitan Division includes Middlesex, Monmouth, Ocean and Somerset counties,
- Nassau-Suffolk, NY Metropolitan Division includes Nassau and Suffolk counties,
- New York-Wayne-White Plains, NY-NJ Metropolitan Division includes Bergen, NJ, Hudson, NJ, Passaic, NJ, Bronx, NY, Kings, NY, New York, NY, Putnam, NY, Queens, NY, Richmond, NY, Rockland, NY and Westchester, NY counties and
- Newark-Union, NJ-PA Metropolitan Division includes Essex, NJ, Hunterdon, NJ, Morris, NJ Sussex, NJ, Union, NJ and Pike, PA counties

Niles-Benton Harbor, MI includes Berrien County

North Port-Bradenton-Sarasota-Venice, FL includes Manatee and Sarasota counties

Norwich-New London, CT includes New London County

Oakland, CA see San Francisco, CA

Ocala, FL includes Marion County

Ocean City, NJ includes Cape May County

Odessa, TX includes Ector County

Ogden-Clearfield, UT includes Davis, Morgan and Weber counties

Oklahoma City, OK includes Canadian, Cleveland, Grady, Lincoln, Logan, McClain and Oklahoma counties

Olympia, WA includes Thurston County

Omaha-Council Bluffs, NE-IA includes Harrison, IA, Mills, IA, Pottawattamie, IA, Cass, NE, Douglas, NE, Sarpy, NE, Saunders, NE and Washington, NE counties

Orlando, FL includes Lake, Orange, Osceola and Seminole counties

Oshkosh-Neenah, WI includes Winnebago County

Owensboro, KY includes Daviess, Hancock and McLean counties

Oxnard-Thousand Oaks-Ventura, CA includes Ventura County

Palm Bay-Melbourne-Titusville, FL includes Brevard County

Palm Coast, FL includes Flagler County

Panama City-Lynn Haven, FL includes Bay County

Parkersburg-Marietta, WV-OH includes Washington, OH, Pleasants, WV, Wirt, WV and Wood, WV counties

Pascagoula, MS includes George and Jackson counties

Pensacola-Ferry Pass-Brent, FL includes Escambia and Santa Rosa counties

Peoria, IL includes Marshall, Peoria, Stark, Tazewell and Woodford counties

Philadelphia-Camden-Wilmington, PA-NJ-DE-MD includes:
- Camden, NJ Metropolitan Division includes Burlington, Camden, and Gloucester counties,
- Philadelphia, PA Metropolitan Division includes Bucks, Chester, Delaware, Montgomery and Philadelphia counties and
- Wilmington, DE-MD-NJ Metropolitan Division includes New Castle, DE, Cecil, MD and Salem, NJ counties

Phoenix-Mesa-Scottsdale, AZ includes Maricopa and Pinal counties

Pine Bluff, AR includes Cleveland, Jefferson and Lincoln counties

Pittsburgh, PA includes Allegheny, Armstrong, Beaver, Butler, Fayette, Washington and Westmoreland counties

Pittsfield, MA includes Berkshire County

Pocatello, ID includes Bannock and Power counties

Portland-South Portland-Biddeford, ME includes Cumberland, Sagadahoc and York counties

Portland-Vancouver-Beaverton, OR-WA includes Clackamas, Columbia, OR, Multnomah, OR, Washington, OR, Yamhill, OR, Clark, WA and Skamania, WA counties

Port St. Lucie-Fort Pierce, FL includes Martin and St. Lucie counties

Poughkeepsie-Newburgh-Middletown, NY includes Dutchess and Orange counties

Prescott, AZ includes Yavapai County

DESCRIPTIONS OF METROPOLITAN AREAS IN 2009 (continued)

Providence-New Bedford-Fall River, RI-MA includes Bristol, MA, Bristol, RI, Kent, RI, Newport, RI, Providence, RI and Washington, RI counties

Provo-Orem, UT includes Juab and Utah counties

Pueblo, CO includes Pueblo County

Punta Gorda, FL includes Charlotte County

Racine, WI includes Racine County

Raleigh-Cary, NC includes Franklin, Johnston and Wake counties

Rapid City, SD includes Meade and Pennington counties

Reading, PA includes Berks County

Redding, CA includes Shasta County

Reno-Sparks, NV includes Storey and Washoe counties

Richmond, VA includes Amelia, Caroline, Charles city, Chesterfield, Cumberland, Dinwiddie, Goochland, Hanover, Henrico, King and Queen, King William, Louisa, New, Kent, Powhatan, Prince George and Sussex counties and Colonial Heights, Hopewell, Petersburg and Richmond cities

Riverside-San Bernardino-Ontario, CA includes Riverside and San Bernardino counties

Roanoke, VA includes Botetourt, Craig, Franklin and Roanoke counties and Roanoke and Salem cities

Rochester, MN includes Dodge, Olmsted and Wabasha counties

Rochester, NY includes Livingston, Monroe, Ontario, Orleans and Wayne counties

Rockford, IL includes Boone and Winnebago counties

Rockingham County, NH see Boston, MA

Rocky Mount, NC includes Edgecombe and Nash counties

Rome, GA includes Floyd County

Sacramento-Arden-Arcade-Roseville, CA includes El Dorado, Placer, Sacramento and Yolo counties

Saginaw-Saginaw Township North, MI includes Saginaw County

St. Cloud, MN includes Benton and Stearns counties

St. George, UT includes Washington County

St. Joseph, MO-KS includes Doniphan, KS, Andrew, MO, Buchanan, MO and DeKalb, MO counties

St. Louis, MO-IL includes, Bond, IL, Calhoun, IL, Clinton, IL, Jersey, IL, Macoupin, IL, Madison, IL, Monroe, IL, St. Clair, IL, Crawford, MO (pt.), Franklin, MO, Jefferson, MO, Lincoln, MO, St. Charles, MO, St. Louis, MO, Warren, MO and Washington, MO counties and St. Louis city, MO

Salem, OR includes Marion and Polk counties

Salinas, CA includes Monterey County

Salisbury, MD includes Somerset and Wicomico counties

Salt Lake City, UT includes Salt Lake, Summit and Tooele counties

San Angelo, TX includes Irion and Tom Green counties

San Antonio, TX includes Atascosa, Bandera, Bexar, Comal, Guadalupe, Kendall, Medina and Wilson counties

San Diego-Carlsbad-San Marcos, CA includes San Diego County

Sandusky, OH includes Erie County

San Francisco-Oakland-Fremont, CA includes:

- Oakland-Fremont-Hayward, CA Metropolitan Division includes Alameda and Contra Costa counties and
- San Francisco-San Mateo-Redwood City, CA Metropolitan Division includes Marin, San Francisco and San Mateo counties

San Jose-Sunnyvale-Santa Clara, CA includes San Benito and Santa Clara counties

San Luis Obispo-Paso Robles, CA includes San Luis Obispo County

Santa Ana, CA see Los Angeles, CA

Santa Barbara-Santa Maria-Goleta, CA includes Santa Barbara County

Santa Cruz-Watsonville, CA includes Santa Cruz County

Santa Fe, NM includes Santa Fe County

Santa Rosa-Petaluma, CA includes Sonoma County

Savannah, GA includes Bryan, Chatham and Effingham counties

Scranton--Wilkes-Barre, PA includes Lackawanna, Luzerne, Wyoming counties

Seattle-Tacoma-Bellevue, WA includes:

- Seattle-Bellevue-Everett, WA Metropolitan Division includes King and Snohomish counties and
- Tacoma, WA Metropolitan Division includes Pierce County

Sebastian-Vero Beach, FL includes Indian River County

Sheboygan, WI includes Sheboygan County

Sherman-Denison, TX includes Grayson County

Shreveport-Bossier City, LA includes Bossier, Caddo and De Soto parishes

Sioux City, IA-NE-SD includes Woodbury, IA, Dakota, NE, Dixon, NE and Union, SD counties

Sioux Falls, SD includes Lincoln, McCook, Minnehaha and Turner counties

South Bend-Mishawaka, IN-MI includes St. Joseph, IN and Cass, MI counties

Spartanburg, SC includes Spartanburg County

Spokane, WA includes Spokane County

Springfield, IL includes Menard and Sangamon counties

Springfield, MA includes Franklin, Hampden and Hampshire counties

DESCRIPTIONS OF METROPOLITAN AREAS IN 2009 (continued)

Springfield, MO includes Christian, Dallas, Greene, Polk and Webster counties

Springfield, OH includes Clark County

State College, PA includes Centre County

Stockton, CA includes San Joaquin County

Sumter, SC includes Sumter County

Syracuse, NY includes Madison, Onondaga and Oswego counties

Tacoma, WA see Seattle, WA

Tallahassee, FL includes Gadsden, Jefferson, Leon and Wakulla counties

Tampa-St. Petersburg-Clearwater, FL includes Hernando, Hillsborough, Pasco and Pinellas counties

Terre Haute, IN includes Clay, Sullivan, Vermillion and Vigo counties

Texarkana, TX-Texarkana, AR includes Miller, AR and Bowie, TX counties

Toledo, OH includes Fulton, Lucas, Ottawa and Wood counties

Topeka, KS includes Jackson, Jefferson, Osage, Shawnee and Wabaunsee counties

Trenton-Ewing, NJ includes Mercer County

Tucson, AZ includes Pima County

Tulsa, OK includes Creek, Okmulgee, Osage, Pawnee, Rogers, Tulsa and Wagoner counties

Tuscaloosa, AL includes Greene, Hale and Tuscaloosa counties

Tyler, TX includes Smith County

Utica-Rome, NY includes Herkimer and Oneida counties

Valdosta, GA includes Brooks, Echols, Lanier and Lowndes counties

Vallejo-Fairfield, CA includes Solano County

Victoria, TX includes Calhoun, Goliad and Victoria counties

Vineland-Millville-Bridgeton, NJ includes Cumberland County

Virginia Beach-Norfolk-Newport News, VA-NC includes Currituck, NC, Gloucester, VA, Isle of Wight, VA, James city, VA, Mathews, VA, Surry, VA and York, VA counties and Chesapeake, VA, Hampton, VA, Newport News, VA, Norfolk, VA, Poquoson, VA, Portsmouth, VA, Suffolk, VA, Virginia Beach, VA and Williamsburg, VA cities

Visalia-Porterville, CA includes Tulare County

Waco, TX includes McLennan County

Warner Robins, GA includes Houston County

Warren, MI see Detroit, MI

Washington-Arlington-Alexandria, DC-VA-MD-WV includes:

- Bethesda-Frederick-Gaithersburg, MD Metropolitan Division includes Frederick and Montgomery counties,
- Washington-Arlington-Alexandria, DC-VA-MD-WV Metropolitan Division includes District of Columbia, DC and Calvert, MD, Charles, MD, Prince George's, MD, Arlington, VA, Clarke, VA, Fairfax, VA, Fauquier, VA, Loudoun, VA, Prince William, VA, Spotsylvania, VA, Stafford, VA and Warren, VA counties and Alexandria, VA, Fairfax, VA, Falls Church, VA, Fredericksburg, VA, Manassas, VA and Manassas Park, VA cities and Jefferson WV County

Waterloo-Cedar Falls, IA includes Black Hawk, Bremer and Grundy counties

Wausau, WI includes Marathon County

Weirton-Steubenville, WV-OH includes Jefferson, OH, Brooke, WV and Hancock, WV counties

Wenatchee, WA includes Chelan and Douglas counties

West Palm Beach, FL see Miami, FL

Wheeling, WV-OH includes Belmont, OH, Marshall, WV and Ohio, WV

Wichita, KS includes Butler, Harvey, Sedgwick and Sumner counties

Wichita Falls, TX includes Archer, Clay and Wichita counties

Williamsport, PA includes Lycoming County

Wilmington, DE see Philadelphia, PA

Wilmington, NC includes Brunswick, New Hanover and Pender counties

Winchester, VA-WV includes Frederick, VA County, Winchester city, VA and Hampshire, WV County

Winston-Salem, NC includes Davie, Forsyth, Stokes and Yadkin counties

Worcester, MA includes Worcester County

Yakima, WA includes Yakima County

York-Hanover, PA includes York County

Youngstown-Warren-Boardman, OH-PA includes Mahoning, OH, Trumbull, OH and Mercer, PA counties

Yuba City, CA includes Sutter and Yuba counties

Yuma, AZ includes Yuma County

COUNTY INDEX: 2009

COUNTY:	IS IN METROPOLITAN:
Adams, CO	Denver-Aurora, CO
Ada, ID	Boise City-Nampa, ID
Aiken, SC	Augusta-Richmond County, GA-SC
Alachua, FL	Gainesville, FL
Alamance, NC	Burlington, NC
Alameda, CA	San Francisco-Oakland-Fremont, CA
Albany, NY	Albany-Schenectady-Troy, NY
Albemarle, VA	Charlottesville, VA
Alexander, NC	Hickory-Lenoir-Morganton, NC
Alexander, IL	Cape Girardeau-Jackson, MO-IL
Alexandria city, VA	Washington, DC-VA-MD-WV
Allegany, MD	Cumberland, MD-WV
Allegheny, PA	Pittsburgh, PA
Allen, IN	Fort Wayne, IN
Allen, OH	Lima, OH
Amelia, VA	Richmond, VA
Amherst, VA	Lynchburg, VA
Anchorage city, AK	Anchorage, AK
Anderson, SC	Anderson, SC
Anderson, TN	Knoxville, TN
Andrew, MO	St. Joseph, MO-KS
Androscoggin, ME	Lewiston-Auburn, ME
Anne Arundel, MD	Baltimore-Towson, MD
Anoka, MN	Minneapolis-St. Paul-Bloomington, MN-WI
Anson, NC	Charlotte-Gastonia-Concord, NC-SC
Appomattox, VA	Lynchburg, VA
Aransas, TX	Corpus Christi, TX
Arapahoe, CO	Denver-Aurora, CO
Archer, TX	Wichita Falls, TX
Arlington, VA	Washington, DC-VA-MD-WV
Armstrong, PA	Pittsburgh, PA
Armstrong, TX	Amarillo, TX
Ascension, LA	Baton Rouge, LA
Asotin, WA	Lewiston, ID-WA
Atascosa, TX	San Antonio, TX
Atlantic, NJ	Atlantic City, NJ
Austin, TX	Houston-Baytown-Sugar Land, TX
Autauga, AL	Montgomery, AL
Baker, FL	Jacksonville, FL
Baker, GA	Albany, GA
Baltimore city, MD	Baltimore-Towson, MD
Baltimore, MD	Baltimore-Towson, MD
Bandera, TX	San Antonio, TX
Bannock, ID	Pocatello, ID
Barnstable, MA	Barnstable Town, MA
Barrow, GA	Atlanta-Sandy Springs-Marietta, GA
Barry, MI	Grand Rapids-Wyoming, MI
Bartholomew, IN	Columbus, IN
Bartow, GA	Atlanta-Sandy Springs-Marietta, GA
Bastrop, TX	Austin-Round Rock, TX
Bates, MO	Kansas City, MO-KS
Bay, FL	Panama City-Lynn Haven, FL
Bay, MI	Bay City, MI
Beaver, PA	Pittsburgh, PA
Bedford city, VA	Lynchburg, VA
Bedford, VA	Lynchburg, VA
Bell, TX	Killeen-Temple-Fort Hood, TX
Belmont, OH	Wheeling, WV-OH
Benton, AR	Fayetteville-Springdale-Rogers, AR-MO
Benton, IA	Cedar Rapids, IA
Benton, IN	Lafayette, IN
Benton, MN	St. Cloud, MN
Benton, OR	Corvallis, OR
Benton, WA	Kennewick-Richland-Pasco, WA
Bergen, NJ	New York, NY-NJ-PA
Berkeley, SC	Charleston-North Charleston, SC
Berkeley, WV	Hagerstown-Martinsburg, MD-WV
Berkshire, MA	Pittsfield, MA
Berks, PA	Reading, PA
Bernalillo, NM	Albuquerque, NM
Berrien, MI	Niles-Benton Harbor, MI
Bexar, TX	San Antonio, TX
Bibb, AL	Birmingham-Hoover, AL
Bibb, GA	Macon, GA
Black Hawk, IA	Waterloo-Cedar Falls, IA
Blair, PA	Altoona, PA
Blue Earth, MN	Mankato-North Mankato, MN
Blount, AL	Birmingham-Hoover, AL
Blount, TN	Knoxville, TN
Boise, ID	Boise City-Nampa, ID
Bollinger, MO	Cape Girardeau-Jackson, MO-IL
Bond, IL	St. Louis, MO-IL
Bonneville, ID	Idaho Falls, ID
Boone, IL	Rockford, IL
Boone, IN	Indianapolis, IN
Boone, KY	Cincinnati-Middletown, OH-KY-IN
Boone, MO	Columbia, MO
Boone, WV	Charleston, WV
Bossier, LA	Shreveport-Bossier City, LA
Botetourt, VA	Roanoke, VA
Boulder, CO	Boulder, CO
Bourbon, KY	Lexington-Fayette, KY
Bowie, TX	Texarkana, TX-Texarkana, AR
Boyd, KY	Huntington-Ashland, WV-KY-OH
Bracken, KY	Cincinnati-Middletown, OH-KY-IN
Bradley, TN	Cleveland, TN
Brantley, GA	Brunswick, GA
Brazoria, TX	Houston-Baytown-Sugar Land, TX
Brazos, TX	College Station-Bryan, TX
Bremer, IA	Waterloo-Cedar Falls, IA
Brevard, FL	Palm Bay-Melbourne-Titusville, FL
Bristol city, VA	Kingsport-Bristol-Bristol, TN-VA
Bristol, MA	Providence-New Bedford-Fall River, RI-MA
Bristol, RI	Providence-New Bedford-Fall River, RI-MA
Bronx, NY	New York, NY-NJ-PA
Brooke, WV	Weirton-Steubenville, WV-OH
Brooks, GA	Valdosta, GA
Broome, NY	Binghamton, NY
Broomfield, CO	Denver-Aurora, CO
Broward, FL	Miami-Fort Lauderdale-Miami Beach, FL
Brown, IN	Indianapolis, IN
Brown, OH	Cincinnati-Middletown, OH-KY-IN
Brown, WI	Green Bay, WI
Brunswick, NC	Wilmington, NC
Bryan, GA	Savannah, GA
Buchanan, MO	St. Joseph, MO-KS
Bucks, PA	Philadelphia, PA-NJ-DE-MD
Bullitt, KY	Louisville, KY-IN
Buncombe, NC	Asheville, NC
Burke, GA	Augusta-Richmond County, GA-SC
Burke, NC	Hickory-Lenoir-Morganton, NC
Burleigh, ND	Bismarck, ND
Burleson, TX	College Station-Bryan, TX
Burlington, NJ	Philadelphia, PA-NJ-DE-MD
Butler, KS	Wichita, KS
Butler, OH	Cincinnati-Middletown, OH-KY-IN
Butler, PA	Pittsburgh, PA
Butte, CA	Chico, CA
Butts, GA	Atlanta-Sandy Springs-Marietta, GA
Cabarrus, NC	Charlotte-Gastonia-Concord, NC-SC
Cabell, WV	Huntington-Ashland, WV-KY-OH
Cache, UT	Logan, UT-ID
Caddo, LA	Shreveport-Bossier City, LA
Calcasieu, LA	Lake Charles, LA
Caldwell, MO	Kansas City, MO-KS
Caldwell, NC	Hickory-Lenoir-Morganton, NC
Caldwell, TX	Austin-Round Rock, TX
Calhoun, AL	Anniston-Oxford, AL
Calhoun, IL	St. Louis, MO-IL
Calhoun, MI	Battle Creek, MI
Calhoun, SC	Columbia, SC
Calhoun, TX	Victoria, TX
Callahan, TX	Abilene, TX
Callaway, MO	Jefferson City, MO
Calumet, WI	Appleton, WI
Calvert, MD	Washington, DC-VA-MD-WV
Cambria, PA	Johnstown, PA
Camden, NJ	Philadelphia, PA-NJ-DE-MD
Cameron, LA	Lake Charles, LA
Cameron, TX	Brownsville-Harlingen, TX
Campbell, KY	Cincinnati-Middletown, OH-KY-IN
Campbell, VA	Lynchburg, VA
Canadian, OK	Oklahoma City, OK
Cannon, TN	Nashville-Davidson--Murfreesboro, TN
Canyon, ID	Boise City-Nampa, ID
Cape May, NJ	Ocean City, NJ
Cape Girardeau, MO	Cape Girardeau-Jackson, MO-IL
Carbon, MT	Billings, MT

COUNTY INDEX: 2009 (continued)

COUNTY:	IS IN METROPOLITAN:
Carbon, PA	Allentown-Bethlehem-Easton, PA-NJ
Carlton, MN	Duluth, MN-WI
Caroline, VA	Richmond, VA
Carroll, GA	Atlanta-Sandy Springs-Marietta, GA
Carroll, IN	Lafayette, IN
Carroll, MD	Baltimore-Towson, MD
Carroll, OH	Canton-Massillon, OH
Carson City, NV	Carson City, NV
Carson, TX	Amarillo, TX
Carter, TN	Johnson City, TN
Carver, MN	Minneapolis-St. Paul-Bloomington, MN-WI
Cascade, MT	Great Falls, MT
Cass, MI	South Bend-Mishawaka, IN-MI
Cass, MO	Kansas City, MO-KS
Cass, ND	Fargo, ND-MN
Cass, NE	Omaha-Council Bluffs, NE-IA
Catawba, NC	Hickory-Lenoir-Morganton, NC
Catoosa, GA	Chattanooga, TN-GA
Cecil, MD	Philadelphia, PA-NJ-DE-MD
Centre, PA	State College, PA
Chambers, TX	Houston-Baytown-Sugar Land, TX
Champaign, IL	Champaign-Urbana, IL
Charles City, VA	Richmond, VA
Charleston, SC	Charleston-North Charleston, SC
Charles, MD	Washington, DC-VA-MD-WV
Charlottesville city, VA	Charlottesville, VA
Charlotte, FL	Punta Gorda, FL
Chatham, GA	Savannah, GA
Chatham, NC	Durham-Chapel Hill, NC
Chattahoochee, GA	Columbus, GA-AL
Cheatham, TN	Nashville-Davidson--Murfreesboro, TN
Chelan, WA	Wenatchee, WA
Chemung, NY	Elmira, NY
Cherokee, GA	Atlanta-Sandy Springs-Marietta, GA
Chesapeake city, VA	Virginia Beach-Norfolk, VA-NC
Chesterfield, VA	Richmond, VA
Chester, PA	Philadelphia, PA-NJ-DE-MD
Chester, TN	Jackson, TN
Chilton, AL	Birmingham-Hoover, AL
Chippewa, WI	Eau Claire, WI
Chisago, MN	Minneapolis-St. Paul-Bloomington, MN-WI
Chittenden, VT	Burlington-South Burlington, VT
Christian, KY	Clarksville, TN-KY
Christian, MO	Springfield, MO
Clackamas, OR	Portland-Vancouver-Beaverton, OR-WA
Clarke, GA	Athens-Clarke County, GA
Clarke, VA	Washington, DC-VA-MD-WV
Clark, IN	Louisville, KY-IN
Clark, KY	Lexington-Fayette, KY
Clark, NV	Las Vegas-Paradise, NV
Clark, OH	Springfield, OH
Clark, WA	Portland-Vancouver-Beaverton, OR-WA
Clayton, GA	Atlanta-Sandy Springs-Marietta, GA
Clay, FL	Jacksonville, FL
Clay, IN	Terre Haute, IN
Clay, MN	Fargo, ND-MN
Clay, MO	Kansas City, MO-KS
Clay, TX	Wichita Falls, TX
Clay, WV	Charleston, WV
Clear Creek, CO	Denver-Aurora, CO
Clermont, OH	Cincinnati-Middletown, OH-KY-IN
Cleveland, AR	Pine Bluff, AR
Cleveland, OK	Oklahoma City, OK
Clinton, IL	St. Louis, MO-IL
Clinton, MI	Lansing-East Lansing, MI
Clinton, MO	Kansas City, MO-KS
Cobb, GA	Atlanta-Sandy Springs-Marietta, GA
Coconino, AZ	Flagstaff, AZ
Colbert, AL	Florence-Muscle Shoals, AL
Cole, MO	Jefferson City, MO
Collier, FL	Naples-Marco Island, FL
Collin, TX	Dallas-Fort Worth-Arlington, TX
Colonial Heights city, VA	Richmond, VA
Columbia, GA	Augusta-Richmond County, GA-SC
Columbia, OR	Portland-Vancouver-Beaverton, OR-WA
Columbia, WI	Madison, WI
Comal, TX	San Antonio, TX
Comanche, OK	Lawton, OK
Contra Costa, CA	San Francisco-Oakland-Fremont, CA

COUNTY:	IS IN METROPOLITAN:
Cook, IL	Chicago-Naperville-Joliet, IL-IN-WI
Copiah, MS	Jackson, MS
Coryell, TX	Killeen-Temple-Fort Hood, TX
Coweta, GA	Atlanta-Sandy Springs-Marietta, GA
Cowlitz, WA	Longview, WA
Craighead, AR	Jonesboro, AR
Craig, VA	Roanoke, VA
Crawford, AR	Fort Smith, AR-OK
Crawford, GA	Macon, GA
Creek, OK	Tulsa, OK
Crittenden, AR	Memphis, TN-MS-AR
Crosby, TX	Lubbock, TX
Cumberland, ME	Portland-South Portland-Biddeford, ME
Cumberland, NC	Fayetteville, NC
Cumberland, NJ	Vineland-Millville-Bridgeton, NJ
Cumberland, PA	Harrisburg-Carlisle, PA
Cumberland, VA	Richmond, VA
Currituck, NC	Virginia Beach-Norfolk, VA-NC
Cuyahoga, OH	Cleveland-Elyria-Mentor, OH
Dade, GA	Chattanooga, TN-GA
Dakota, MN	Minneapolis-St. Paul-Bloomington, MN-WI
Dakota, NE	Sioux City, IA-NE-SD
Dallas, IA	Des Moines, IA
Dallas, MO	Springfield, MO
Dallas, TX	Dallas-Fort Worth-Arlington, TX
Dane, WI	Madison, WI
Danville city, VA	Danville, VA
Darlington, SC	Florence, SC
Dauphin, PA	Harrisburg-Carlisle, PA
Davidson, TN	Nashville-Davidson--Murfreesboro, TN
Daviess, KY	Owensboro, KY
Davie, NC	Winston-Salem, NC
Davis, UT	Ogden-Clearfield, UT
Dawson, GA	Atlanta-Sandy Springs-Marietta, GA
De Soto, LA	Shreveport-Bossier City, LA
Dearborn, IN	Cincinnati-Middletown, OH-KY-IN
DeKalb, GA	Atlanta-Sandy Springs-Marietta, GA
DeKalb, IL	Chicago-Naperville-Joliet, IL-IN-WI
DeKalb, MO	St. Joseph, MO-KS
Delaware, IN	Muncie, IN
Delaware, OH	Columbus, OH
Delaware, PA	Philadelphia, PA-NJ-DE-MD
Delta, TX	Dallas-Fort Worth-Arlington, TX
Denton, TX	Dallas-Fort Worth-Arlington, TX
Denver, CO	Denver-Aurora, CO
Deschutes, OR	Bend, OR
DeSoto, MS	Memphis, TN-MS-AR
Dickson, TN	Nashville-Davidson--Murfreesboro, TN
Dinwiddie, VA	Richmond, VA
District of Columbia, DC	Washington, DC-VA-MD-WV
Dixon, NE	Sioux City, IA-NE-SD
Dodge, MN	Rochester, MN
Dona Ana, NM	Las Cruces, NM
Doniphan, KS	St. Joseph, MO-KS
Dorchester, SC	Charleston-North Charleston, SC
Dougherty, GA	Albany, GA
Douglas, CO	Denver-Aurora, CO
Douglas, GA	Atlanta-Sandy Springs-Marietta, GA
Douglas, KS	Lawrence, KS
Douglas, NE	Omaha-Council Bluffs, NE-IA
Douglas, WA	Wenatchee, WA
Douglas, WI	Duluth, MN-WI
Dubuque, IA	Dubuque, IA
DuPage, IL	Chicago-Naperville-Joliet, IL-IN-WI
Durham, NC	Durham-Chapel Hill, NC
Dutchess, NY	Poughkeepsie-Newburgh-Middletown, NY
Duval, FL	Jacksonville, FL
East Baton Rouge, LA	Baton Rouge, LA
East Feliciana, LA	Baton Rouge, LA
Eaton, MI	Lansing-East Lansing, MI
Eau Claire, WI	Eau Claire, WI
Echols, GA	Valdosta, GA
Ector, TX	Odessa, TX
Edgecombe, NC	Rocky Mount, NC
Edgefield, SC	Augusta-Richmond County, GA-SC
Edmonson, KY	Bowling Green, KY
Effingham, GA	Savannah, GA
El Dorado, CA	Sacramento--Arden-Arcade--Roseville, CA
El Paso, CO	Colorado Springs, CO

COUNTY INDEX: 2009 (continued)

COUNTY:	IS IN METROPOLITAN:	COUNTY:	IS IN METROPOLITAN:
El Paso, TX	El Paso, TX	Grant, LA	Alexandria, LA
Elbert, CO	Denver-Aurora, CO	Grayson, TX	Sherman-Denison, TX
Elkhart, IN	Elkhart-Goshen, IN	Greene, AL	Tuscaloosa, AL
Ellis, TX	Dallas-Fort Worth-Arlington, TX	Greene, IN	Bloomington, IN
Elmore, AL	Montgomery, AL	Greene, MO	Springfield, MO
Erie, NY	Buffalo-Niagara Falls, NY	Greene, NC	Greenville, NC
Erie, OH	Sandusky, OH	Greene, OH	Dayton, OH
Erie, PA	Erie, PA	Greene, VA	Charlottesville, VA
Escambia, FL	Pensacola-Ferry Pass-Brent, FL	Greenup, KY	Huntington-Ashland, WV-KY-OH
Essex, MA	Boston-Cambridge-Quincy, MA-NH	Greenville, SC	Greenville, SC
Essex, NJ	New York, NY-NJ-PA	Gregg, TX	Longview, TX
Etowah, AL	Gadsden, AL	Grundy, IA	Waterloo-Cedar Falls, IA
Fairbanks North Star, AK	Fairbanks, AK	Grundy, IL	Chicago-Naperville-Joliet, IL-IN-WI
Fairfax city, VA	Washington, DC-VA-MD-WV	Guadalupe, TX	San Antonio, TX
Fairfax, VA	Washington, DC-VA-MD-WV	Guilford, NC	Greensboro-High Point, NC
Fairfield, CT	Bridgeport-Stamford-Norwalk, CT	Guthrie, IA	Des Moines, IA
Fairfield, OH	Columbus, OH	Gwinnett, GA	Atlanta-Sandy Springs-Marietta, GA
Fairfield, SC	Columbia, SC	Hale, AL	Tuscaloosa, AL
Falls Church city, VA	Washington, DC-VA-MD-WV	Hall, GA	Gainesville, GA
Faulkner, AR	Little Rock-North Little Rock, AR	Hamblen, TN	Morristown, TN
Fauquier, VA	Washington, DC-VA-MD-WV	Hamilton, IN	Indianapolis, IN
Fayette, GA	Atlanta-Sandy Springs-Marietta, GA	Hamilton, OH	Cincinnati-Middletown, OH-KY-IN
Fayette, KY	Lexington-Fayette, KY	Hamilton, TN	Chattanooga, TN-GA
Fayette, PA	Pittsburgh, PA	Hampden, MA	Springfield, MA
Fayette, TN	Memphis, TN-MS-AR	Hampshire, MA	Springfield, MA
Flagler, FL	Palm Coast, FL	Hampshire, WV	Winchester, VA-WV
Florence, SC	Florence, SC	Hampton city, VA	Virginia Beach-Norfolk, VA-NC
Floyd, GA	Rome, GA	Hancock, IN	Indianapolis, IN
Floyd, IN	Louisville, KY-IN	Hancock, KY	Owensboro, KY
Fluvanna, VA	Charlottesville, VA	Hancock, MS	Gulfport-Biloxi, MS
Fond du Lac, WI	Fond du Lac, WI	Hancock, WV	Weirton-Steubenville, WV-OH
Ford, IL	Champaign-Urbana, IL	Hanover, VA	Richmond, VA
Forrest, MS	Hattiesburg, MS	Haralson, GA	Atlanta-Sandy Springs-Marietta, GA
Forsyth, GA	Atlanta-Sandy Springs-Marietta, GA	Hardin, KY	Elizabethtown, KY
Forsyth, NC	Winston-Salem, NC	Hardin, TX	Beaumont-Port Arthur, TX
Fort Bend, TX	Houston-Baytown-Sugar Land, TX	Harford, MD	Baltimore-Towson, MD
Franklin, AR	Fort Smith, AR-OK	Harrisonburg city, VA	Harrisonburg, VA
Franklin, ID	Logan, UT-ID	Harrison, IA	Omaha-Council Bluffs, NE-IA
Franklin, IN	Cincinnati-Middletown, OH-KY-IN	Harrison, IN	Louisville, KY-IN
Franklin, KS	Kansas City, MO-KS	Harrison, MS	Gulfport-Biloxi, MS
Franklin, MA	Springfield, MA	Harris, GA	Columbus, GA-AL
Franklin, MO	St. Louis, MO-IL	Harris, TX	Houston-Baytown-Sugar Land, TX
Franklin, NC	Raleigh-Cary, NC	Hartford, CT	Hartford-West Hartford-East Hartford, CT
Franklin, OH	Columbus, OH	Harvey, KS	Wichita, KS
Franklin, VA	Roanoke, VA	Hawkins, TN	Kingsport-Bristol-Bristol, TN-VA
Franklin, VT	Burlington-South Burlington, VT	Hays, TX	Austin-Round Rock, TX
Franklin, WA	Kennewick-Richland-Pasco, WA	Haywood, NC	Asheville, NC
Fredericksburg city, VA	Washington, DC-VA-MD-WV	Heard, GA	Atlanta-Sandy Springs-Marietta, GA
Frederick, MD	Washington, DC-VA-MD-WV	Henderson, KY	Evansville, IN-KY
Frederick, VA	Winchester, VA-WV	Henderson, NC	Asheville, NC
Fresno, CA	Fresno, CA	Hendricks, IN	Indianapolis, IN
Fulton, GA	Atlanta-Sandy Springs-Marietta, GA	Hennepin, MN	Minneapolis-St. Paul-Bloomington, MN-WI
Fulton, OH	Toledo, OH	Henrico, VA	Richmond, VA
Gadsden, FL	Tallahassee, FL	Henry, AL	Dothan, AL
Gallatin, KY	Cincinnati-Middletown, OH-KY-IN	Henry, GA	Atlanta-Sandy Springs-Marietta, GA
Galveston, TX	Houston-Baytown-Sugar Land, TX	Henry, IL	Davenport-Moline-Rock Island, IA-IL
Garland, AR	Hot Springs, AR	Henry, KY	Louisville, KY-IN
Gaston, NC	Charlotte-Gastonia-Concord, NC-SC	Herkimer, NY	Utica-Rome, NY
Geary, KS	Manhattan, KS	Hernando, FL	Tampa-St. Petersburg-Clearwater, FL
Geauga, OH	Cleveland-Elyria-Mentor, OH	Hickman, TN	Nashville-Davidson--Murfreesboro, TN
Gem, ID	Boise City-Nampa, ID	Hidalgo, TX	McAllen-Edinburg-Pharr, TX
Genesee, MI	Flint, MI	Hillsborough, FL	Tampa-St. Petersburg-Clearwater, FL
Geneva, AL	Dothan, AL	Hillsborough, NH	Manchester-Nashua, NH
George, MS	Pascagoula, MS	Hinds, MS	Jackson, MS
Gibson, IN	Evansville, IN-KY	Hoke, NC	Fayetteville, NC
Gilchrist, FL	Gainesville, FL	Honolulu, HI	Honolulu, HI
Giles, VA	Blacksburg-Christiansburg-Radford, VA	Hopewell city, VA	Richmond, VA
Gilpin, CO	Denver-Aurora, CO	Horry, SC	Myrtle Beach-Conway, SC
Gloucester, NJ	Philadelphia, PA-NJ-DE-MD	Houston, AL	Dothan, AL
Gloucester, VA	Virginia Beach-Norfolk, VA-NC	Houston, GA	Warner Robins, GA
Glynn, GA	Brunswick, GA	Houston, MN	La Crosse, WI-MN
Goliad, TX	Victoria, TX	Howard, IN	Kokomo, IN
Goochland, VA	Richmond, VA	Howard, MD	Baltimore-Towson, MD
Grady, OK	Oklahoma City, OK	Howard, MO	Columbia, MO
Grainger, TN	Morristown, TN	Hudson, NJ	New York, NY-NJ-PA
Grand Forks, ND	Grand Forks, ND-MN	Hunterdon, NJ	New York, NY-NJ-PA
Grand Isle, VT	Burlington-South Burlington, VT	Hunt, TX	Dallas-Fort Worth-Arlington, TX
Grant, AR	Little Rock-North Little Rock, AR	Iberville, LA	Baton Rouge, LA
Grant, KY	Cincinnati-Middletown, OH-KY-IN	Imperial, CA	El Centro, CA

COUNTY INDEX: 2009 (continued)

COUNTY:	IS IN METROPOLITAN:	COUNTY:	IS IN METROPOLITAN:
Indian River, FL	Sebastian-Vero Beach, FL	Lapeer, MI	Detroit-Warren-Livonia, MI
Ingham, MI	Lansing-East Lansing, MI	LaPorte, IN	Michigan City-La Porte, IN
Ionia, MI	Grand Rapids-Wyoming, MI	Laramie, WY	Cheyenne, WY
Iowa, WI	Madison, WI	Larimer, CO	Fort Collins-Loveland, CO
Irion, TX	San Angelo, TX	Larue, KY	Elizabethtown, KY
Isanti, MN	Minneapolis-St. Paul-Bloomington, MN-WI	Lauderdale, AL	Florence-Muscle Shoals, AL
Isle of Wight, VA	Virginia Beach-Norfolk, VA-NC	Laurens, SC	Greenville, SC
Jackson, KS	Topeka, KS	Lawrence, AL	Decatur, AL
Jackson, MI	Jackson, MI	Lawrence, OH	Huntington-Ashland, WV-KY-OH
Jackson, MO	Kansas City, MO-KS	Le Flore, OK	Fort Smith, AR-OK
Jackson, MS	Pascagoula, MS	Leavenworth, KS	Kansas City, MO-KS
Jackson, OR	Medford, OR	Lebanon, PA	Lebanon, PA
James City, VA	Virginia Beach-Norfolk, VA-NC	Lee, AL	Auburn-Opelika, AL
Jasper, GA	Atlanta-Sandy Springs-Marietta, GA	Lee, FL	Cape Coral-Fort Myers, FL
Jasper, IN	Chicago-Naperville-Joliet, IL-IN-WI	Lee, GA	Albany, GA
Jasper, MO	Joplin, MO	Lehigh, PA	Allentown-Bethlehem-Easton, PA-NJ
Jefferson, AL	Birmingham-Hoover, AL	Leon, FL	Tallahassee, FL
Jefferson, AR	Pine Bluff, AR	Lexington, SC	Columbia, SC
Jefferson, CO	Denver-Aurora, CO	Liberty, GA	Hinesville-Fort Stewart, GA
Jefferson, FL	Tallahassee, FL	Liberty, TX	Houston-Baytown-Sugar Land, TX
Jefferson, ID	Idaho Falls, ID	Licking, OH	Columbus, OH
Jefferson, KS	Topeka, KS	Limestone, AL	Huntsville, AL
Jefferson, KY	Louisville, KY-IN	Lincoln, AR	Pine Bluff, AR
Jefferson, LA	New Orleans-Metairie-Kenner, LA	Lincoln, MO	St. Louis, MO-IL
Jefferson, MO	St. Louis, MO-IL	Lincoln, OK	Oklahoma City, OK
Jefferson, OH	Weirton-Steubenville, WV-OH	Lincoln, SD	Sioux Falls, SD
Jefferson, TN	Morristown, TN	Lincoln, WV	Charleston, WV
Jefferson, TX	Beaumont-Port Arthur, TX	Linn, IA	Cedar Rapids, IA
Jefferson, WV	Washington, DC-VA-MD-WV	Linn, KS	Kansas City, MO-KS
Jersey, IL	St. Louis, MO-IL	Livingston, LA	Baton Rouge, LA
Jessamine, KY	Lexington-Fayette, KY	Livingston, MI	Detroit-Warren-Livonia, MI
Johnson, IA	Iowa City, IA	Livingston, NY	Rochester, NY
Johnson, IN	Indianapolis, IN	Logan, OK	Oklahoma City, OK
Johnson, KS	Kansas City, MO-KS	Long, GA	Hinesville-Fort Stewart, GA
Johnson, TX	Dallas-Fort Worth-Arlington, TX	Lonoke, AR	Little Rock-North Little Rock, AR
Johnston, NC	Raleigh-Cary, NC	Lorain, OH	Cleveland-Elyria-Mentor, OH
Jones, GA	Macon, GA	Los Angeles, CA	Los Angeles-Long Beach-Santa Ana, CA
Jones, IA	Cedar Rapids, IA	Loudon, TN	Knoxville, TN
Jones, TX	Abilene, TX	Loudoun, VA	Washington, DC-VA-MD-WV
Juab, UT	Provo-Orem, UT	Louisa, VA	Richmond, VA
Kalamazoo, MI	Kalamazoo-Portage, MI	Lowndes, AL	Montgomery, AL
Kanawha, WV	Charleston, WV	Lowndes, GA	Valdosta, GA
Kane, IL	Chicago-Naperville-Joliet, IL-IN-WI	Lubbock, TX	Lubbock, TX
Kankakee, IL	Kankakee-Bradley, IL	Lucas, OH	Toledo, OH
Kaufman, TX	Dallas-Fort Worth-Arlington, TX	Luzerne, PA	Scranton--Wilkes-Barre, PA
Kendall, IL	Chicago-Naperville-Joliet, IL-IN-WI	Lycoming, PA	Williamsport, PA
Kendall, TX	San Antonio, TX	Lynchburg city, VA	Lynchburg, VA
Kenosha, WI	Chicago-Naperville-Joliet, IL-IN-WI	Macomb, MI	Detroit-Warren-Livonia, MI
Kenton, KY	Cincinnati-Middletown, OH-KY-IN	Macon, IL	Decatur, IL
Kent, DE	Dover, DE	Macon, TN	Nashville-Davidson--Murfreesboro, TN
Kent, MI	Grand Rapids-Wyoming, MI	Macoupin, IL	St. Louis, MO-IL
Kent, RI	Providence-New Bedford-Fall River, RI-MA	Madera, CA	Madera, CA
Kern, CA	Bakersfield, CA	Madison, AL	Huntsville, AL
Kershaw, SC	Columbia, SC	Madison, AR	Fayetteville-Springdale-Rogers, AR-MO
Kewaunee, WI	Green Bay, WI	Madison, GA	Athens-Clarke County, GA
King and Queen, VA	Richmond, VA	Madison, IA	Des Moines, IA
King William, VA	Richmond, VA	Madison, IL	St. Louis, MO-IL
Kings, CA	Hanford-Corcoran, CA	Madison, IN	Anderson, IN
Kings, NY	New York, NY-NJ-PA	Madison, MS	Jackson, MS
King, WA	Seattle-Tacoma-Bellevue, WA	Madison, NC	Asheville, NC
Kitsap, WA	Bremerton-Silverdale, WA	Madison, NY	Syracuse, NY
Knox, TN	Knoxville, TN	Madison, OH	Columbus, OH
Kootenai, ID	Coeur d'Alene, ID	Madison, TN	Jackson, TN
La Crosse, WI	La Crosse, WI-MN	Mahoning, OH	Youngstown-Warren-Boardman, OH-PA
Lackawanna, PA	Scranton--Wilkes-Barre, PA	Manassas city, VA	Washington, DC-VA-MD-WV
Lafayette, LA	Lafayette, LA	Manassas Park city, VA	Washington, DC-VA-MD-WV
Lafayette, MO	Kansas City, MO-KS	Manatee, FL	North Port-Bradenton-Sarasota, FL
Lafourche, LA	Houma-Bayou Cane-Thibodaux, LA	Marathon, WI	Wausau, WI
Lake, FL	Orlando, FL	Maricopa, AZ	Phoenix-Mesa-Scottsdale, AZ
Lake, IL	Chicago-Naperville-Joliet, IL-IN-WI	Marin, CA	San Francisco-Oakland-Fremont, CA
Lake, IN	Chicago-Naperville-Joliet, IL-IN-WI	Marion, FL	Ocala, FL
Lake, OH	Cleveland-Elyria-Mentor, OH	Marion, GA	Columbus, GA-AL
Lamar, GA	Atlanta-Sandy Springs-Marietta, GA	Marion, IN	Indianapolis, IN
Lamar, MS	Hattiesburg, MS	Marion, OR	Salem, OR
Lampasas, TX	Killeen-Temple-Fort Hood, TX	Marion, TN	Chattanooga, TN-GA
Lancaster, NE	Lincoln, NE	Marshall, IL	Peoria, IL
Lancaster, PA	Lancaster, PA	Marshall, MS	Memphis, TN-MS-AR
Lane, OR	Eugene-Springfield, OR	Marshall, WV	Wheeling, WV-OH
Lanier, GA	Valdosta, GA	Martin, FL	Port St. Lucie-Fort Pierce, FL

COUNTY INDEX: 2009 (continued)

COUNTY:	IS IN METROPOLITAN:	COUNTY:	IS IN METROPOLITAN:
Matanuska-Susitna, AK	Anchorage, AK	Newport News city, VA	Virginia Beach-Norfolk, VA-NC
Mathews, VA	Virginia Beach-Norfolk, VA-NC	Newport, RI	Providence-New Bedford-Fall River, RI-MA
McClain, OK	Oklahoma City, OK	Newton, GA	Atlanta-Sandy Springs-Marietta, GA
McCook, SD	Sioux Falls, SD	Newton, IN	Chicago-Naperville-Joliet, IL-IN-WI
McDonald, MO	Fayetteville-Springdale-Rogers, AR-MO	Newton, MO	Joplin, MO
McDuffie, GA	Augusta-Richmond County, GA-SC	Nez Perce, ID	Lewiston, ID-WA
McHenry, IL	Chicago-Naperville-Joliet, IL-IN-WI	Niagara, NY	Buffalo-Niagara Falls, NY
McIntosh, GA	Brunswick, GA	Nicollet, MN	Mankato-North Mankato, MN
McLean, IL	Bloomington-Normal, IL	Norfolk city, VA	Virginia Beach-Norfolk, VA-NC
McLean, KY	Owensboro, KY	Norfolk, MA	Boston-Cambridge-Quincy, MA-NH
McLennan, TX	Waco, TX	Northampton, PA	Allentown-Bethlehem-Easton, PA-NJ
Meade, KY	Louisville, KY-IN	Nueces, TX	Corpus Christi, TX
Meade, SD	Rapid City, SD	Oakland, MI	Detroit-Warren-Livonia, MI
Mecklenburg, NC	Charlotte-Gastonia-Concord, NC-SC	Ocean, NJ	New York, NY-NJ-PA
Medina, OH	Cleveland-Elyria-Mentor, OH	Oconee, GA	Athens-Clarke County, GA
Medina, TX	San Antonio, TX	Oconto, WI	Green Bay, WI
Menard, IL	Springfield, IL	Oglethorpe, GA	Athens-Clarke County, GA
Merced, CA	Merced, CA	Ohio, IN	Cincinnati-Middletown, OH-KY-IN
Mercer, IL	Davenport-Moline-Rock Island, IA-IL	Ohio, WV	Wheeling, WV-OH
Mercer, NJ	Trenton-Ewing, NJ	Okaloosa, FL	Crestview-Fort Walton Beach, FL
Mercer, PA	Youngstown-Warren-Boardman, OH-PA	Oklahoma, OK	Oklahoma City, OK
Meriwether, GA	Atlanta-Sandy Springs-Marietta, GA	Okmulgee, OK	Tulsa, OK
Mesa, CO	Grand Junction, CO	Oldham, KY	Louisville, KY-IN
Miami-Dade, FL	Miami-Fort Lauderdale-Miami Beach, FL	Olmsted, MN	Rochester, MN
Miami, KS	Kansas City, MO-KS	Oneida, NY	Utica-Rome, NY
Miami, OH	Dayton, OH	Onondaga, NY	Syracuse, NY
Middlesex, CT	Hartford-West Hartford-East Hartford, CT	Onslow, NC	Jacksonville, NC
Middlesex, MA	Boston-Cambridge-Quincy, MA-NH	Ontario, NY	Rochester, NY
Middlesex, NJ	New York, NY-NJ-PA	Orange, CA	Los Angeles-Long Beach-Santa Ana, CA
Midland, TX	Midland, TX	Orange, FL	Orlando, FL
Miller, AR	Texarkana, TX-Texarkana, AR	Orange, NC	Durham-Chapel Hill, NC
Mills, IA	Omaha-Council Bluffs, NE-IA	Orange, NY	Poughkeepsie-Newburgh-Middletown, NY
Milwaukee, WI	Milwaukee-Waukesha-West Allis, WI	Orange, TX	Beaumont-Port Arthur, TX
Mineral, WV	Cumberland, MD-WV	Orleans, LA	New Orleans-Metairie-Kenner, LA
Minnehaha, SD	Sioux Falls, SD	Orleans, NY	Rochester, NY
Missoula, MT	Missoula, MT	Osage, KS	Topeka, KS
Mobile, AL	Mobile, AL	Osage, MO	Jefferson City, MO
Mohave, AZ	Lake Havasu City-Kingman, AZ	Osage, OK	Tulsa, OK
Moniteau, MO	Jefferson City, MO	Osceola, FL	Orlando, FL
Monmouth, NJ	New York, NY-NJ-PA	Oswego, NY	Syracuse, NY
Monongalia, WV	Morgantown, WV	Ottawa, MI	Holland-Grand Haven, MI
Monroe, GA	Macon, GA	Ottawa, OH	Toledo, OH
Monroe, IL	St. Louis, MO-IL	Ouachita, LA	Monroe, LA
Monroe, IN	Bloomington, IN	Outagamie, WI	Appleton, WI
Monroe, MI	Monroe, MI	Owen, IN	Bloomington, IN
Monroe, NY	Rochester, NY	Owyhee, ID	Boise City-Nampa, ID
Monterey, CA	Salinas, CA	Ozaukee, WI	Milwaukee-Waukesha-West Allis, WI
Montgomery, AL	Montgomery, AL	Palm Beach, FL	Miami-Fort Lauderdale-Miami Beach, FL
Montgomery, MD	Washington, DC-VA-MD-WV	Parker, TX	Dallas-Fort Worth-Arlington, TX
Montgomery, OH	Dayton, OH	Park, CO	Denver-Aurora, CO
Montgomery, PA	Philadelphia, PA-NJ-DE-MD	Pasco, FL	Tampa-St. Petersburg-Clearwater, FL
Montgomery, TN	Clarksville, TN-KY	Passaic, NJ	New York, NY-NJ-PA
Montgomery, TX	Houston-Baytown-Sugar Land, TX	Paulding, GA	Atlanta-Sandy Springs-Marietta, GA
Montgomery, VA	Blacksburg-Christiansburg-Radford, VA	Pawnee, OK	Tulsa, OK
Morgan, AL	Decatur, AL	Pender, NC	Wilmington, NC
Morgan, IN	Indianapolis, IN	Pendleton, KY	Cincinnati-Middletown, OH-KY-IN
Morgan, UT	Ogden-Clearfield, UT	Pennington, SD	Rapid City, SD
Morgan, WV	Hagerstown-Martinsburg, MD-WV	Penobscot, ME	Bangor, ME
Morris, NJ	New York, NY-NJ-PA	Peoria, IL	Peoria, IL
Morrow, OH	Columbus, OH	Perry, AR	Little Rock-North Little Rock, AR
Morton, ND	Bismarck, ND	Perry, MS	Hattiesburg, MS
Multnomah, OR	Portland-Vancouver-Beaverton, OR-WA	Perry, PA	Harrisburg-Carlisle, PA
Murray, GA	Dalton, GA	Person, NC	Durham-Chapel Hill, NC
Muscogee, GA	Columbus, GA-AL	Petersburg city, VA	Richmond, VA
Muskegon, MI	Muskegon-Norton Shores, MI	Philadelphia, PA	Philadelphia, PA-NJ-DE-MD
Napa, CA	Napa, CA	Piatt, IL	Champaign-Urbana, IL
Nash, NC	Rocky Mount, NC	Pickaway, OH	Columbus, OH
Nassau, FL	Jacksonville, FL	Pickens, GA	Atlanta-Sandy Springs-Marietta, GA
Nassau, NY	New York, NY-NJ-PA	Pickens, SC	Greenville, SC
Natrona, WY	Casper, WY	Pierce, WA	Seattle-Tacoma-Bellevue, WA
Nelson, KY	Louisville, KY-IN	Pierce, WI	Minneapolis-St. Paul-Bloomington, MN-WI
Nelson, VA	Charlottesville, VA	Pike, GA	Atlanta-Sandy Springs-Marietta, GA
New Castle, DE	Philadelphia, PA-NJ-DE-MD	Pike, PA	New York, NY-NJ-PA
New Hanover, NC	Wilmington, NC	Pima, AZ	Tucson, AZ
New Haven, CT	New Haven-Milford, CT	Pinal, AZ	Phoenix-Mesa-Scottsdale, AZ
New Kent, VA	Richmond, VA	Pinellas, FL	Tampa-St. Petersburg-Clearwater, FL
New London, CT	Norwich-New London, CT	Pittsylvania, VA	Danville, VA
New York, NY	New York, NY-NJ-PA	Pitt, NC	Greenville, NC
Newaygo, MI	Grand Rapids-Wyoming, MI	Placer, CA	Sacramento--Arden-Arcade--Roseville, CA

COUNTY INDEX: 2009 (continued)

COUNTY:	IS IN METROPOLITAN:
Plaquemines, LA	New Orleans-Metairie-Kenner, LA
Platte, MO	Kansas City, MO-KS
Pleasants, WV	Parkersburg-Marietta, WV-OH
Plymouth, MA	Boston-Cambridge-Quincy, MA-NH
Poinsett, AR	Jonesboro, AR
Pointe Coupee, LA	Baton Rouge, LA
Polk, FL	Lakeland, FL
Polk, IA	Des Moines, IA
Polk, MN	Grand Forks, ND-MN
Polk, MO	Springfield, MO
Polk, OR	Salem, OR
Polk, TN	Cleveland, TN
Poquoson city , VA	Virginia Beach-Norfolk, VA-NC
Portage, OH	Akron, OH
Porter, IN	Chicago-Naperville-Joliet, IL-IN-WI
Portsmouth city, VA	Virginia Beach-Norfolk, VA-NC
Posey, IN	Evansville, IN-KY
Pottawattamie, IA	Omaha-Council Bluffs, NE-IA
Pottawattamie, KS	Manhattan, KS
Potter, TX	Amarillo, TX
Power, ID	Pocatello, ID
Powhatan, VA	Richmond, VA
Preble, OH	Dayton, OH
Preston, WV	Morgantown, WV
Prince George's, MD	Washington, DC-VA-MD-WV
Prince George, VA	Richmond, VA
Prince William, VA	Washington, DC-VA-MD-WV
Providence, RI	Providence-New Bedford-Fall River, RI-MA
Pueblo, CO	Pueblo, CO
Pulaski, AR	Little Rock-North Little Rock, AR
Pulaski, VA	Blacksburg-Christiansburg-Radford, VA
Putnam, IN	Indianapolis, IN
Putnam, NY	New York, NY-NJ-PA
Putnam, WV	Charleston, WV
Queen Anne's, MD	Baltimore-Towson, MD
Queens, NY	New York, NY-NJ-PA
Racine, WI	Racine, WI
Radford city, VA	Blacksburg-Christiansburg-Radford, VA
Ramsey, MN	Minneapolis-St. Paul-Bloomington, MN-WI
Randall, TX	Amarillo, TX
Randolph, NC	Greensboro-High Point, NC
Rankin, MS	Jackson, MS
Rapides, LA	Alexandria, LA
Ray, MO	Kansas City, MO-KS
Rensselaer, NY	Albany-Schenectady-Troy, NY
Richland, OH	Mansfield, OH
Richland, SC	Columbia, SC
Richmond city, VA	Richmond, VA
Richmond, GA	Augusta-Richmond County, GA-SC
Richmond, NY	New York, NY-NJ-PA
Riley, KS	Manhattan, KS
Riverside, CA	Riverside-San Bernardino-Ontario, CA
Roanoke city, VA	Roanoke, VA
Roanoke, VA	Roanoke, VA
Robertson, TN	Nashville-Davidson--Murfreesboro, TN
Robertson, TX	College Station-Bryan, TX
Rock Island, IL	Davenport-Moline-Rock Island, IA-IL
Rockdale, GA	Atlanta-Sandy Springs-Marietta, GA
Rockingham, NC	Greensboro-High Point, NC
Rockingham, NH	Boston-Cambridge-Quincy, MA-NH
Rockingham, VA	Harrisonburg, VA
Rockland, NY	New York, NY-NJ-PA
Rockwall, TX	Dallas-Fort Worth-Arlington, TX
Rock, WI	Janesville, WI
Rogers, OK	Tulsa, OK
Rusk, TX	Longview, TX
Russell, AL	Columbus, GA-AL
Rutherford, TN	Nashville-Davidson--Murfreesboro, TN
Sacramento, CA	Sacramento--Arden-Arcade--Roseville, CA
Sagadahoc, ME	Portland-South Portland-Biddeford, ME
Saginaw, MI	Saginaw-Saginaw Township North, MI
Salem city, VA	Roanoke, VA
Salem, NJ	Philadelphia, PA-NJ-DE-MD
Saline, AR	Little Rock-North Little Rock, AR
Salt Lake, UT	Salt Lake City, UT
Saluda, SC	Columbia, SC
San Benito, CA	San Jose-Sunnyvale-Santa Clara, CA
San Bernardino, CA	Riverside-San Bernardino-Ontario, CA
San Diego, CA	San Diego-Carlsbad-San Marcos, CA
San Francisco, CA	San Francisco-Oakland-Fremont, CA
San Jacinto, TX	Houston-Baytown-Sugar Land, TX
San Joaquin, CA	Stockton, CA
San Juan, NM	Farmington, NM
San Luis Obispo, CA	San Luis Obispo-Paso Robles, CA
San Mateo, CA	San Francisco-Oakland-Fremont, CA
San Patricio, TX	Corpus Christi, TX
Sandoval, NM	Albuquerque, NM
Sangamon, IL	Springfield, IL
Santa Barbara, CA	Santa Barbara-Santa Maria-Goleta, CA
Santa Clara, CA	San Jose-Sunnyvale-Santa Clara, CA
Santa Cruz, CA	Santa Cruz-Watsonville, CA
Santa Fe, NM	Santa Fe, NM
Santa Rosa, FL	Pensacola-Ferry Pass-Brent, FL
Sarasota, FL	North Port-Bradenton-Sarasota, FL
Saratoga, NY	Albany-Schenectady-Troy, NY
Sarpy, NE	Omaha-Council Bluffs, NE-IA
Saunders, NE	Omaha-Council Bluffs, NE-IA
Schenectady, NY	Albany-Schenectady-Troy, NY
Schoharie, NY	Albany-Schenectady-Troy, NY
Scott, IA	Davenport-Moline-Rock Island, IA-IL
Scott, KY	Lexington-Fayette, KY
Scott, MN	Minneapolis-St. Paul-Bloomington, MN-WI
Scott, VA	Kingsport-Bristol-Bristol, TN-VA
Sebastian, AR	Fort Smith, AR-OK
Sedgwick, KS	Wichita, KS
Seminole, FL	Orlando, FL
Sequatchie, TN	Chattanooga, TN-GA
Sequoyah, OK	Fort Smith, AR-OK
Seward, NE	Lincoln, NE
Shasta, CA	Redding, CA
Shawnee, KS	Topeka, KS
Sheboygan, WI	Sheboygan, WI
Shelby, AL	Birmingham-Hoover, AL
Shelby, IN	Indianapolis, IN
Shelby, KY	Louisville, KY-IN
Shelby, TN	Memphis, TN-MS-AR
Sherburne, MN	Minneapolis-St. Paul-Bloomington, MN-WI
Simpson, MS	Jackson, MS
Skagit, WA	Mount Vernon-Anacortes, WA
Skamania, WA	Portland-Vancouver-Beaverton, OR-WA
Smith, TN	Nashville-Davidson--Murfreesboro, TN
Smith, TX	Tyler, TX
Snohomish, WA	Seattle-Tacoma-Bellevue, WA
Solano, CA	Vallejo-Fairfield, CA
Somerset, MD	Salisbury, MD
Somerset, NJ	New York, NY-NJ-PA
Sonoma, CA	Santa Rosa-Petaluma, CA
Spalding, GA	Atlanta-Sandy Springs-Marietta, GA
Spartanburg, SC	Spartanburg, SC
Spencer, KY	Louisville, KY-IN
Spokane, WA	Spokane, WA
Spotsylvania, VA	Washington, DC-VA-MD-WV
Stafford, VA	Washington, DC-VA-MD-WV
Stanislaus, CA	Modesto, CA
Stark, IL	Peoria, IL
Stark, OH	Canton-Massillon, OH
Stearns, MN	St. Cloud, MN
Stewart, TN	Clarksville, TN-KY
Stokes, NC	Winston-Salem, NC
Stone, MS	Gulfport-Biloxi, MS
Storey, NV	Reno-Sparks, NV
Story, IA	Ames, IA
Strafford, NH	Boston-Cambridge-Quincy, MA-NH
St. Bernard, LA	New Orleans-Metairie-Kenner, LA
St. Charles, LA	New Orleans-Metairie-Kenner, LA
St. Charles, MO	St. Louis, MO-IL
St. Clair, AL	Birmingham-Hoover, AL
St. Clair, IL	St. Louis, MO-IL
St. Clair, MI	Detroit-Warren-Livonia, MI
St. Croix, WI	Minneapolis-St. Paul-Bloomington, MN-WI
St. Helena, LA	Baton Rouge, LA
St. John the Baptist, LA	New Orleans-Metairie-Kenner, LA
St. Johns, FL	Jacksonville, FL
St. Joseph, IN	South Bend-Mishawaka, IN-MI
St. Louis city, MO	St. Louis, MO-IL
St. Louis, MN	Duluth, MN-WI
St. Louis, MO	St. Louis, MO-IL
St. Lucie, FL	Port St. Lucie-Fort Pierce, FL

COUNTY INDEX: 2009 (continued)

National Crime Trends: 1990 to 2009

In the 20 years from 1990 to 2009, crime rates in the United States fell significantly. The total crime rate dropped 40.3%: from 5,802.7 crimes per 100,000 population in 1990 to a rate of 3,465.5 in 2009. Violent crime rates also decreased, falling 41.1% from 1990 to 2009. In addition, property crime rates dropped 40.2%.

Among individual crime categories, each recorded declines from 1990 to 2009. The nation's motor vehicle theft rate posted the largest decrease, falling 60.5% from 1990 to 2009. The smallest decline was in the rape rate, which dropped 30.2% during that same 20-year time frame.

The table below shows rates for each category of crime for every year since 1990. Trends for each individual crime are shown in graphs on the following pages. Violent crimes are murder, rape, robbery, and aggravated assault. Property crimes consist of burglary, larceny-theft, and motor vehicle theft. The total crime rate is simply the sum of the seven specific crimes and was calculated by the editors. All rates are crimes per 100,000 population for the year shown.

Year	Crime	Violent Crime	Property Crime	Murder	Rape	Robbery	Assault	Burglary	Larceny-Theft	Motor Vehicle Theft
1990	5,802.7	729.6	5,073.1	9.4	41.1	256.3	422.9	1,232.2	3,185.1	655.8
1991	5,898.4	758.2	5,140.2	9.8	42.3	272.7	433.4	1,252.1	3,229.1	659.0
1992	5,661.4	757.7	4,903.7	9.3	42.8	263.7	441.9	1,168.4	3,103.6	631.6
1993	5,487.1	747.1	4,740.0	9.5	41.1	256.0	440.5	1,099.7	3,033.9	606.3
1994	5,373.8	713.6	4,660.2	9.0	39.3	237.8	427.6	1,042.1	3,026.9	591.3
1995	5,275.0	684.5	4,590.5	8.2	37.1	220.9	418.3	987.0	3,043.2	560.3
1996	5,087.6	636.6	4,451.0	7.4	36.3	201.9	391.0	945.0	2,980.3	525.7
1997	4,927.3	611.0	4,316.3	6.8	35.9	186.2	382.1	918.8	2,891.8	505.7
1998	4,620.1	567.6	4,052.5	6.3	34.5	165.5	361.4	863.2	2,729.5	459.9
1999	4,266.6	523.0	3,743.6	5.7	32.8	150.1	334.3	770.4	2,550.7	422.5
2000	4,124.8	506.5	3,618.3	5.5	32.0	145.0	324.0	728.8	2,477.3	412.2
2001	4,162.6	504.5	3,658.1	5.6	31.8	148.5	318.6	741.8	2,485.7	430.5
2002	4,125.0	494.4	3,630.6	5.6	33.1	146.1	309.5	747.0	2,450.7	432.9
2003	4,067.0	475.8	3,591.2	5.7	32.3	142.5	295.4	741.0	2,416.5	433.7
2004	3,977.3	463.2	3,514.1	5.5	32.4	136.7	288.6	730.3	2,362.3	421.5
2005	3,900.5	469.0	3,431.5	5.6	31.8	140.8	290.8	726.9	2,287.8	416.8
2006	3,838.3	480.6	3,357.7	5.8	31.7	150.6	292.6	735.2	2,221.4	401.1
2007	3,748.8	472.0	3,276.8	5.7	30.5	148.4	287.4	726.0	2,186.3	364.6
2008	3,669.0	457.5	3,211.5	5.4	29.7	145.7	276.7	732.1	2,164.5	315.0
2009	3,465.5	429.4	3,036.1	5.0	28.7	133.0	262.8	716.3	2,060.9	258.8

Source: Reported data from the F.B.I.
"Crime in the United States 2009" (Uniform Crime Reports, September 13, 2010)

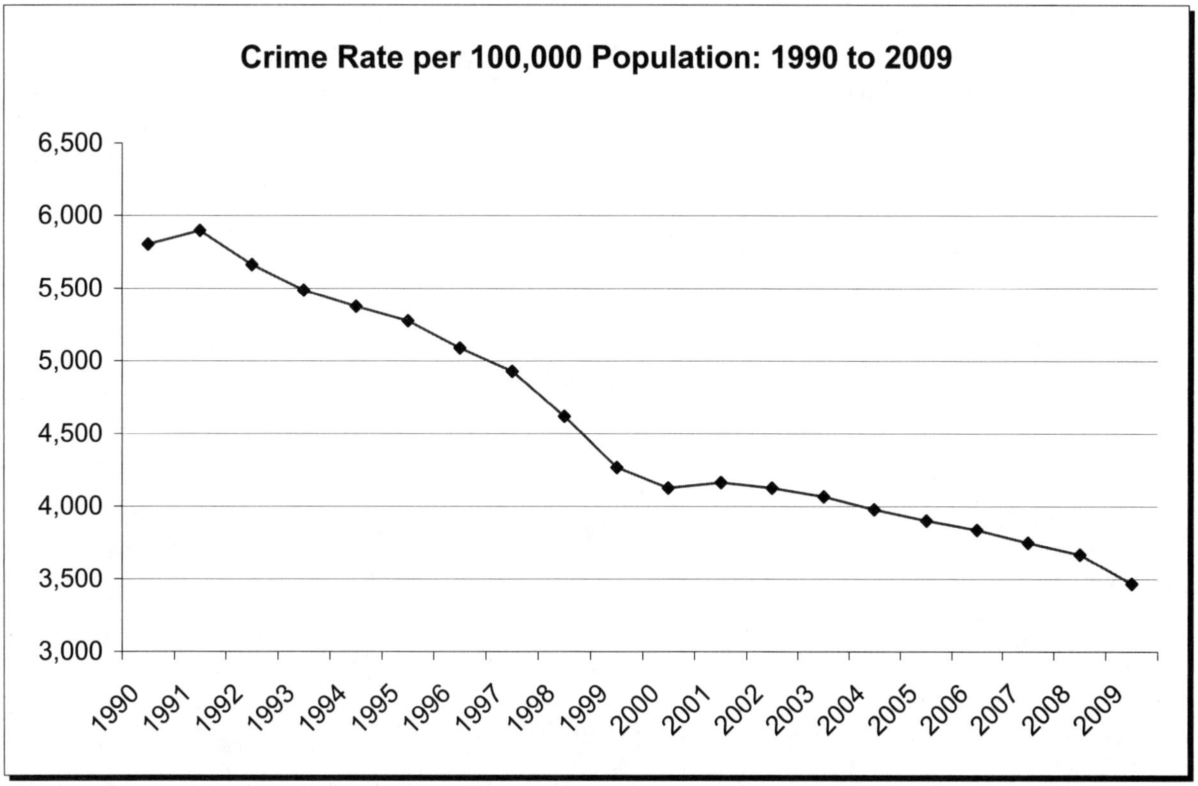

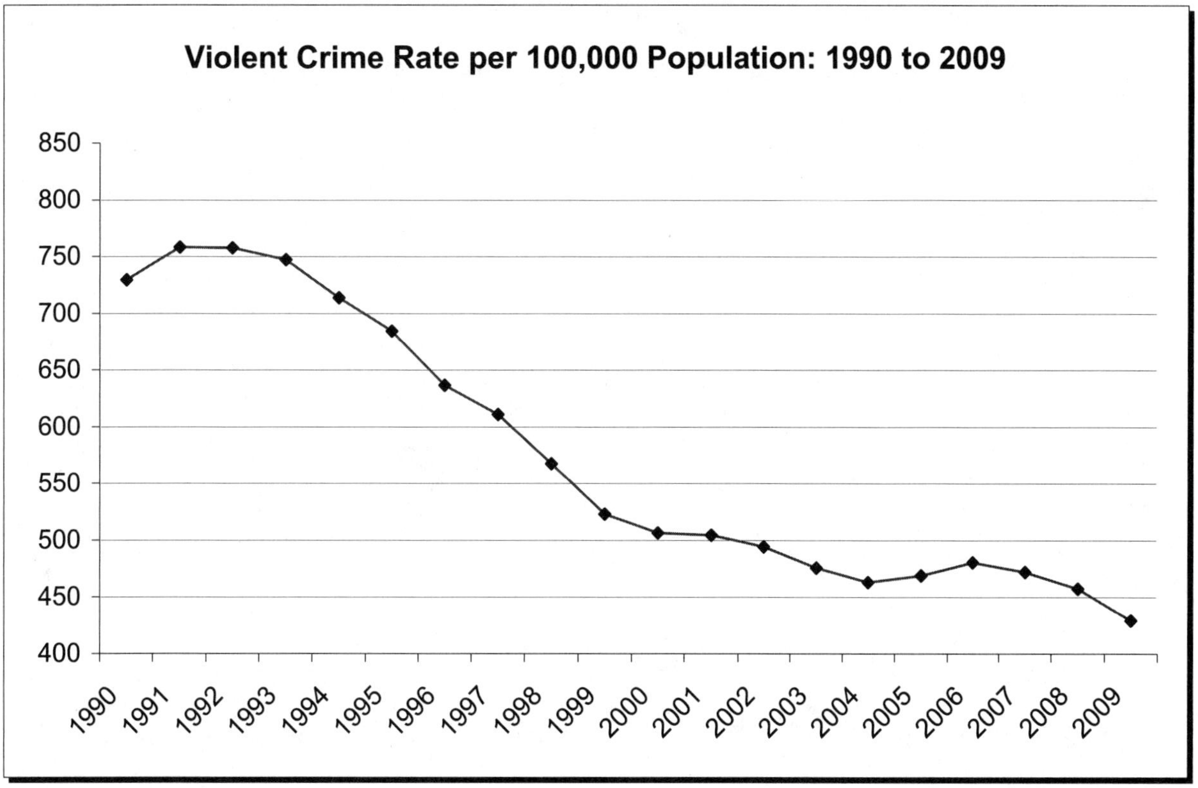

Source: Reported data from the F.B.I.
"Crime in the United States 2009" (Uniform Crime Reports, September 13, 2010)

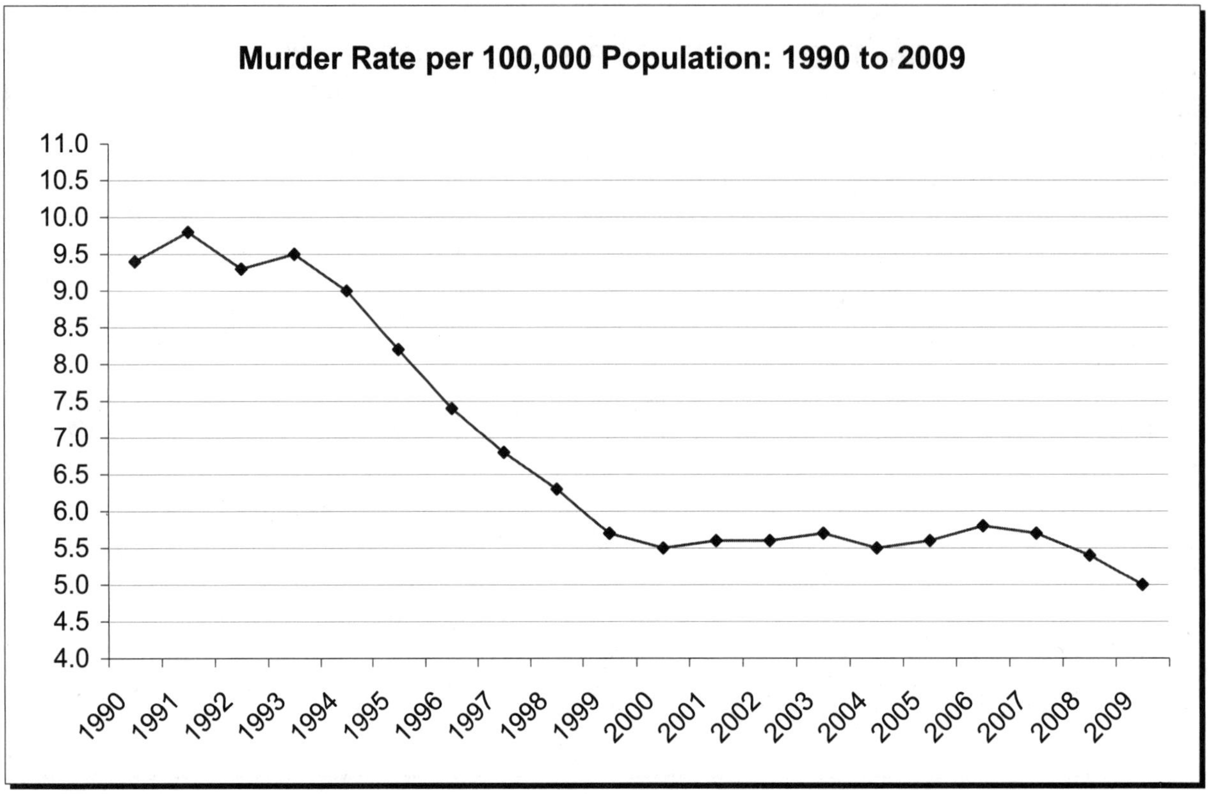

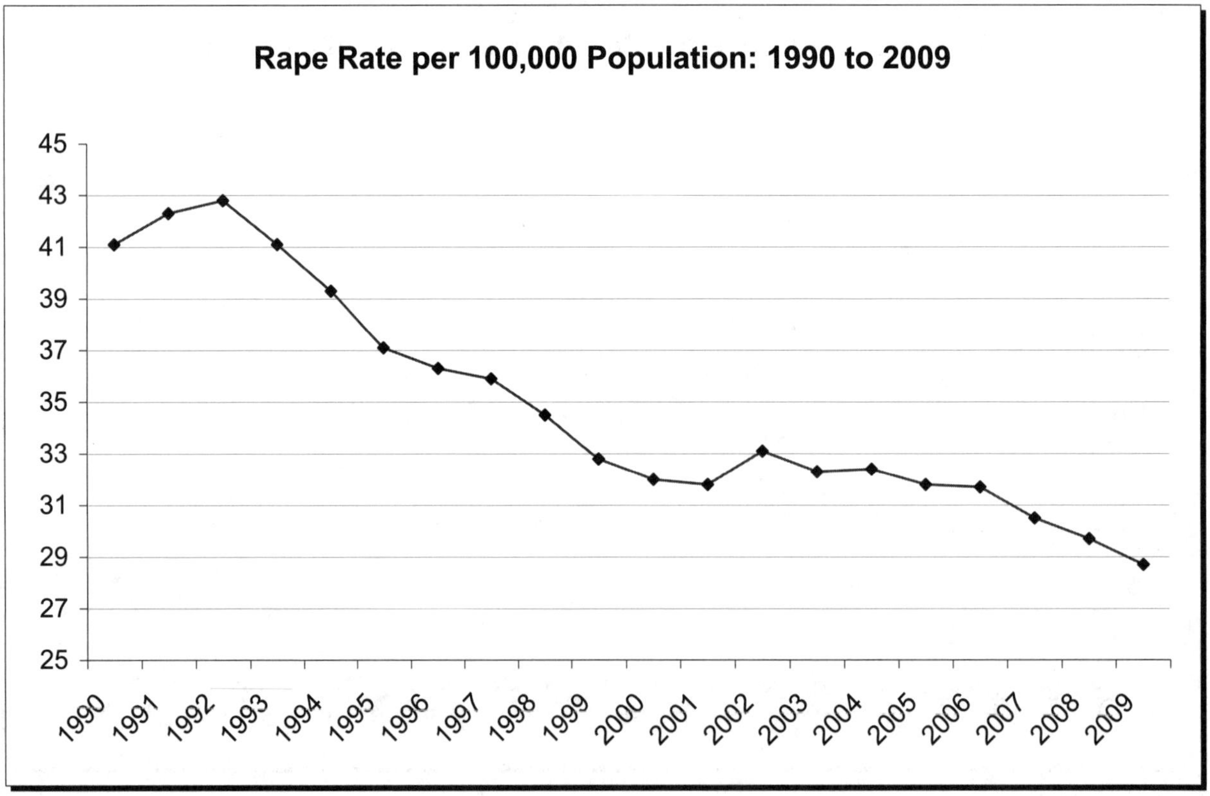

Source: Reported data from the F.B.I.
"Crime in the United States 2009" (Uniform Crime Reports, September 13, 2010)

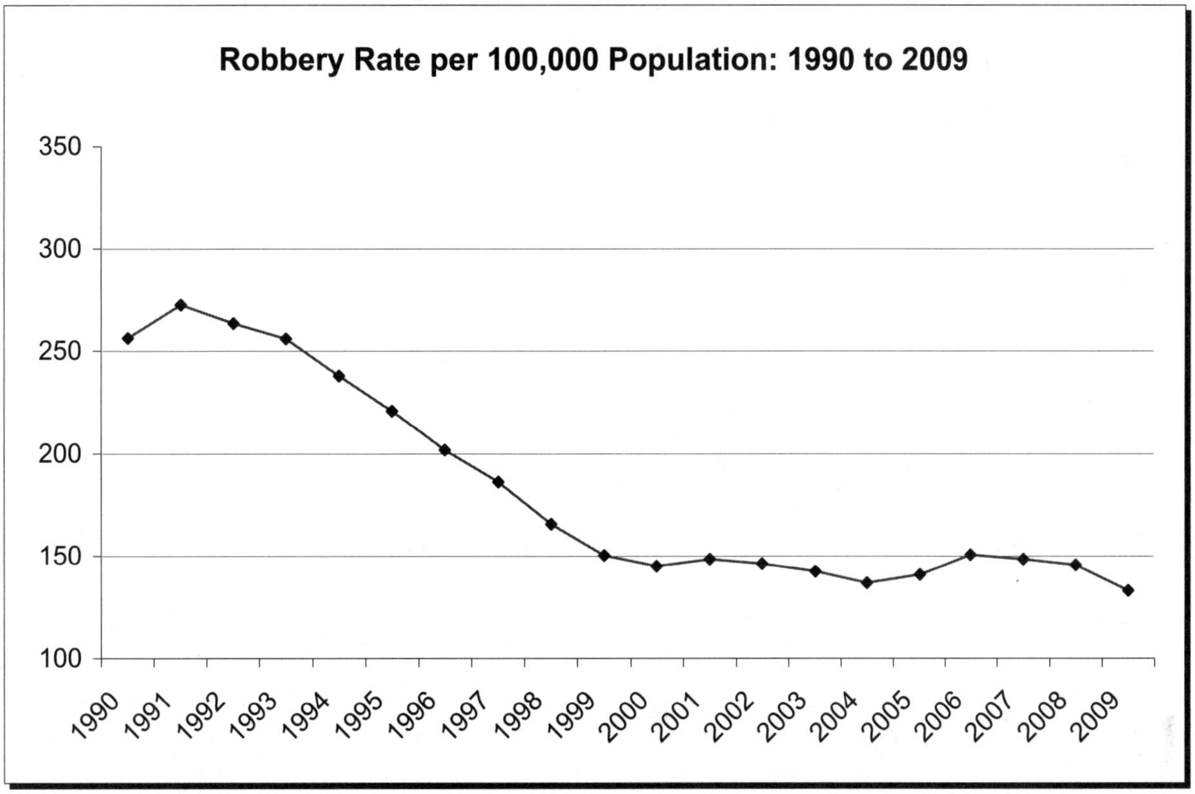

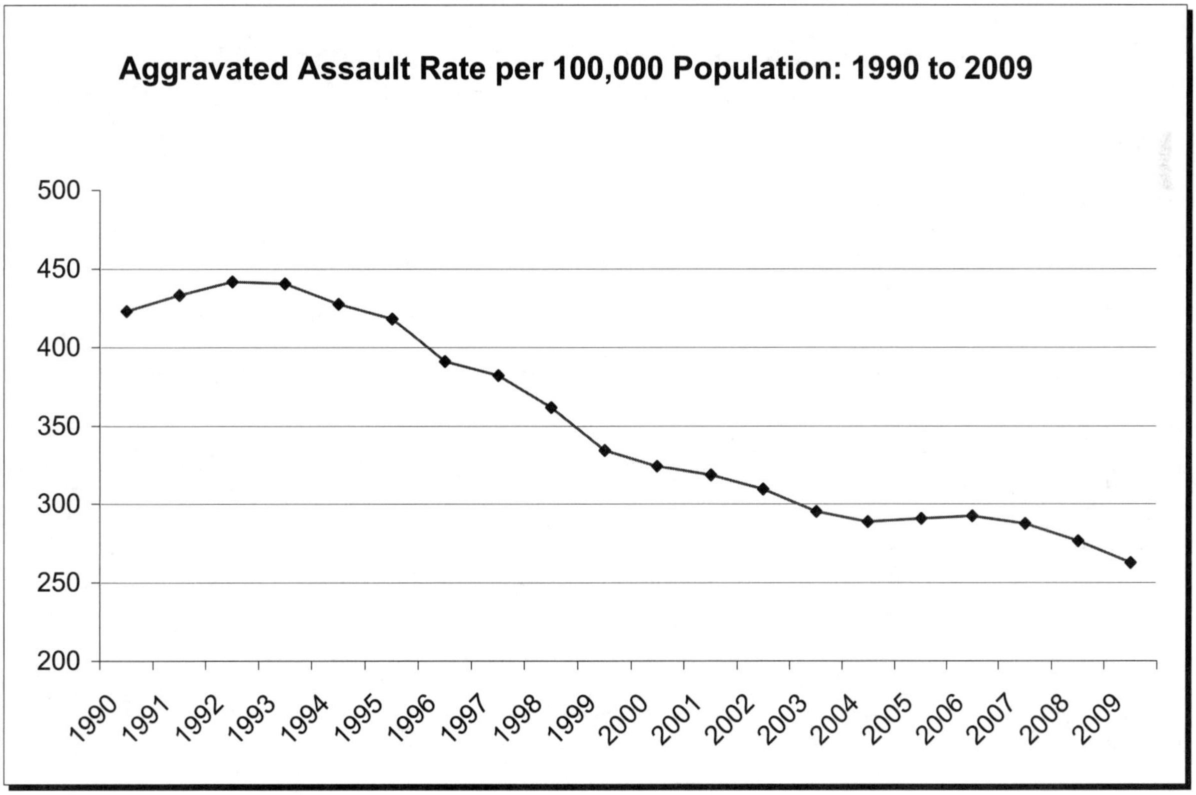

Source: Reported data from the F.B.I.
"Crime in the United States 2009" (Uniform Crime Reports, September 13, 2010)

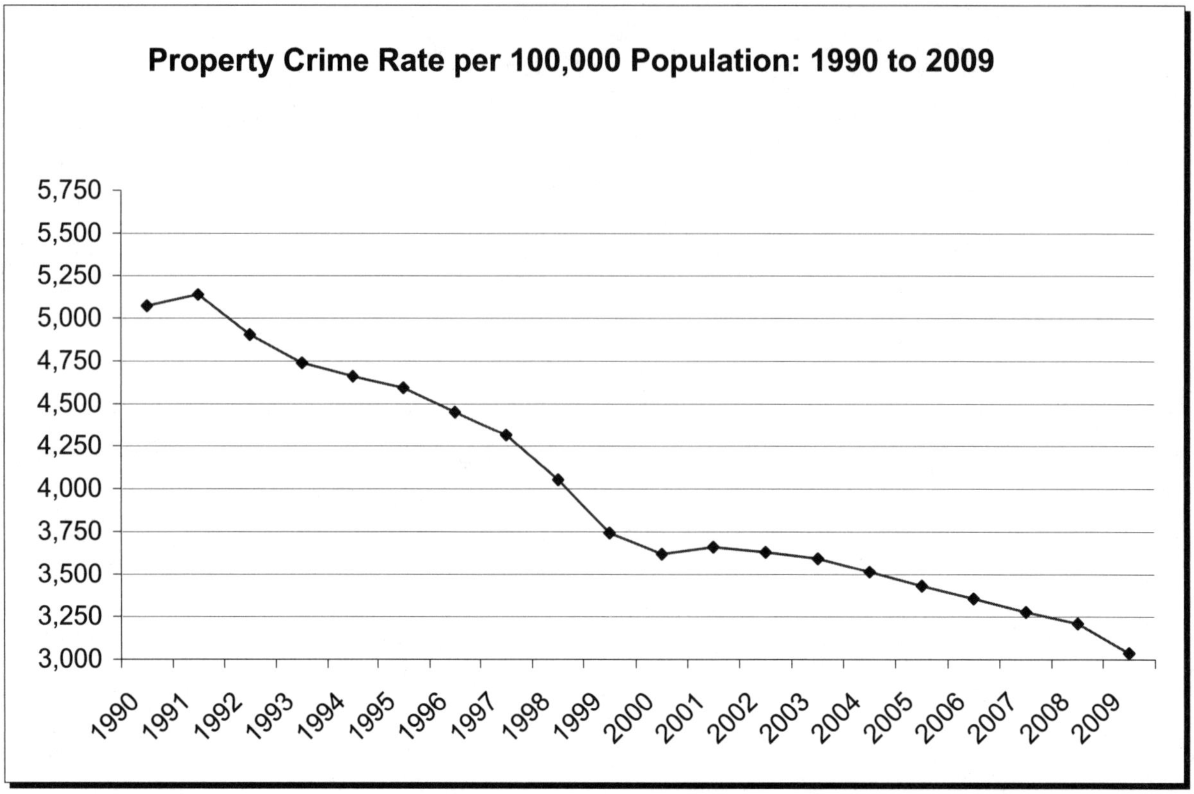

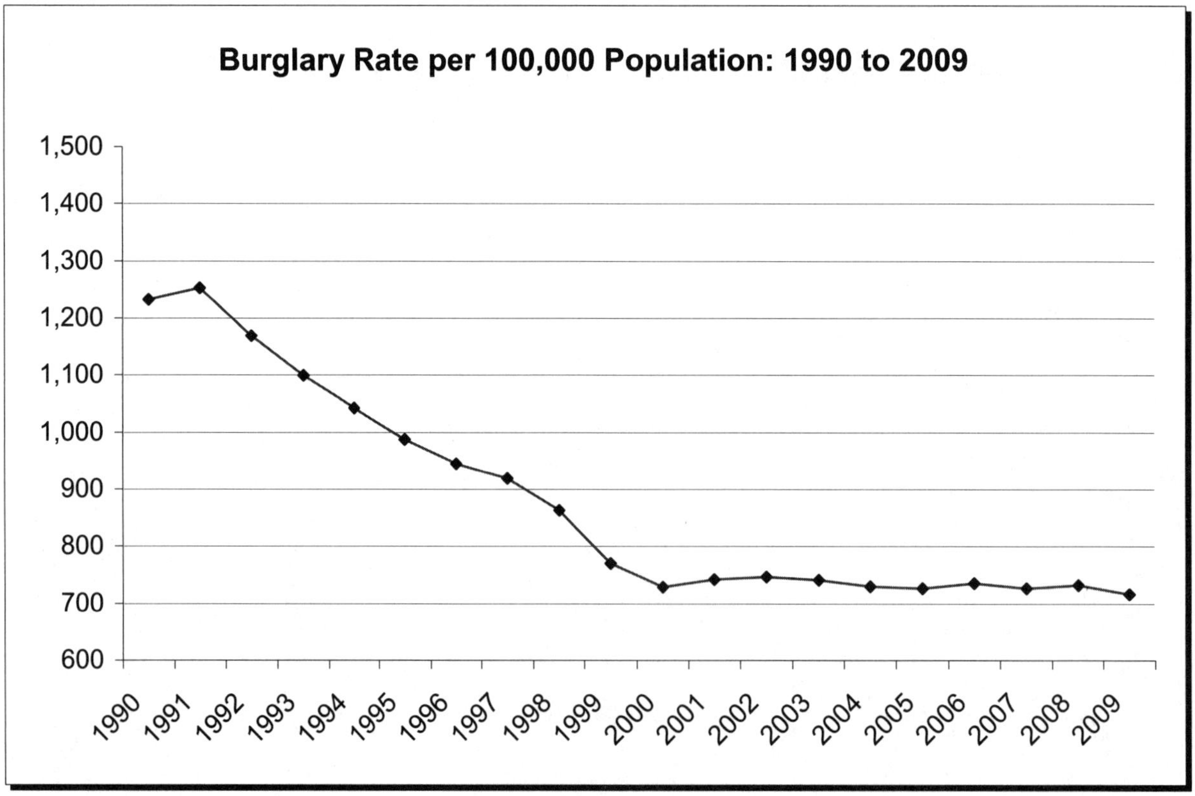

Source: Reported data from the F.B.I.
"Crime in the United States 2009" (Uniform Crime Reports, September 13, 2010)

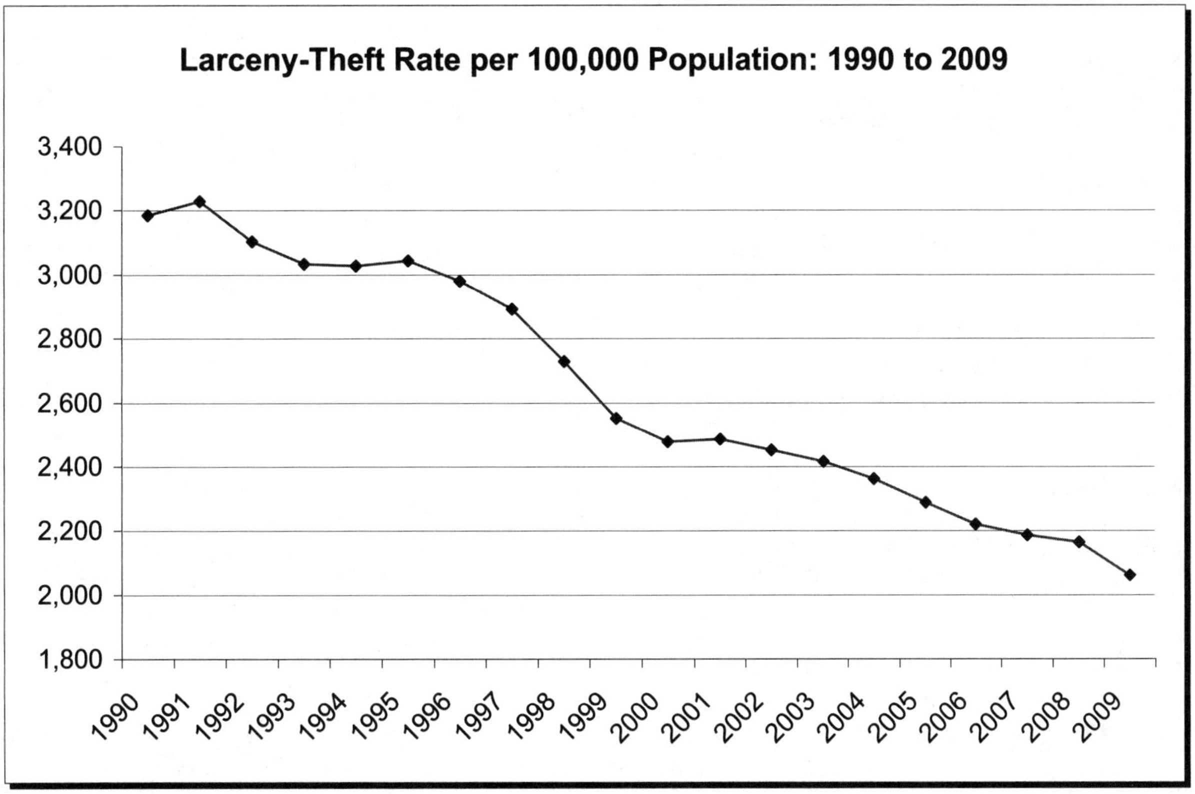

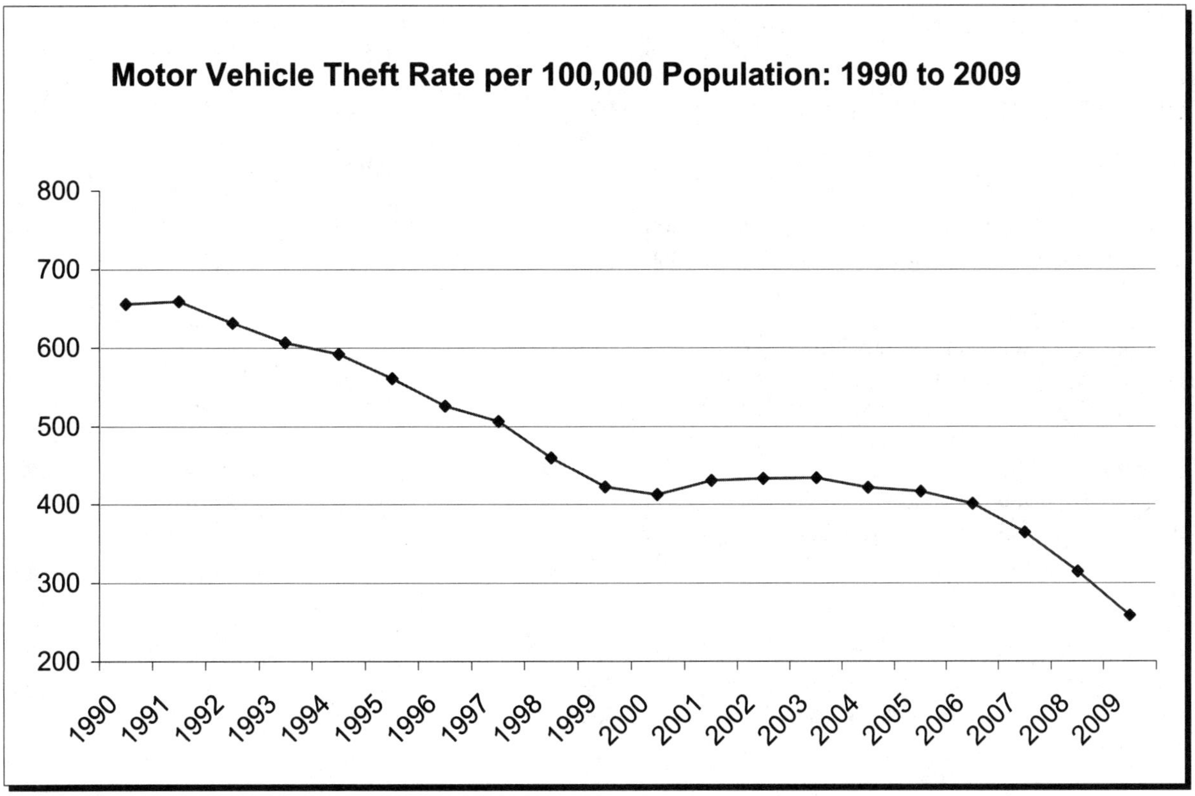

Source: Reported data from the F.B.I.
"Crime in the United States 2009" (Uniform Crime Reports, September 13, 2010)

I
84.75
6/11

NATIONAL, METROPOLITAN, AND CITY CRIME STATISTICS SUMMARY: 2009

	NATIONAL	METRO*	CITY*
Population 2009	307,006,550	256,734,191	84,785,447
Police (Sworn Officers)	706,886		208,315
Rate of Police Officers (per 100,000 Population)	244		246
Crimes in 2009	10,639,369	9,290,991	4,098,594
Crime Rate in 2009 (per 100,000 Population)	3,465.5	3,618.9	4,712.8
Percent Change in Crime Rate: 2008 to 2009	(5.5)	(5.8)	(6.1)
Percent Change in Crime Rate: 2005 to 2009	(11.2)	(11.9)	(14.4)
Violent Crimes in 2009	1,318,398	1,177,758	625,135
Violent Crime Rate in 2009 (per 100,000 Population)	429.4	458.7	718.8
Percent Change in Violent Crime Rate: 2008 to 2009	(6.1)	(6.2)	(7.2)
Percent Change in Violent Crime Rate: 2005 to 2009	(8.4)	(10.0)	(10.6)
Murders in 2009	15,241	13,408	7,816
Murder Rate in 2009 (per 100,000 Population)	5.0	5.2	9.0
Percent Change in Murder Rate: 2008 to 2009	(8.1)	(8.8)	(10.0)
Percent Change in Murder Rate: 2005 to 2009	(12.1)	(14.8)	(18.9)
Rapes in 2009	88,097	72,413	29,142
Rape Rate in 2009 (per 100,000 Population)	28.7	28.2	33.5
Percent Change in Rape Rate: 2008 to 2009	(3.5)	(3.8)	(2.6)
Percent Change in Rape Rate: 2005 to 2009	(9.8)	(11.3)	(13.0)
Robberies in 2009	408,217	390,483	244,453
Robbery Rate in 2009 (per 100,000 Population)	133.0	152.1	281.1
Percent Change in Robbery Rate: 2008 to 2009	(8.8)	(8.8)	(10.1)
Percent Change in Robbery Rate: 2005 to 2009	(5.6)	(6.7)	(10.6)
Aggravated Assaults in 2009	806,843	701,454	343,724
Aggravated Assault Rate in 2009 (per 100,000 Population)	262.8	273.2	395.2
Percent Change in Aggravated Assault Rate: 2008 to 2009	(5.0)	(4.9)	(5.4)
Percent Change in Aggravated Assault Rate: 2005 to 2009	(9.6)	(11.5)	(10.1)
Property Crimes in 2009	9,320,971	8,113,233	3,473,459
Property Crime Rate in 2009 (per 100,000 Population)	3,036.1	3,160.2	3,994.0
Percent Change in Property Crime Rate: 2008 to 2009	(5.5)	(5.7)	(5.9)
Percent Change in Property Crime Rate: 2005 to 2009	(11.5)	(12.2)	(15.0)
Burglaries in 2009	2,199,125	1,867,157	808,639
Burglary Rate in 2009 (per 100,000 Population)	716.3	727.3	929.8
Percent Change in Burglary Rate: 2008 to 2009	(2.2)	(2.5)	(2.5)
Percent Change in Burglary Rate: 2005 to 2009	(1.5)	(2.2)	(3.0)
Larceny-Thefts in 2009	6,327,230	5,511,868	2,270,305
Larceny-Theft Rate in 2009 (per 100,000 Population)	2,060.9	2,146.9	2,610.5
Percent Change in Larceny-Theft Rate: 2008 to 2009	(4.8)	(4.9)	(4.4)
Percent Change in Larceny-Theft Rate: 2005 to 2009	(9.9)	(10.0)	(11.8)
Motor Vehicle Thefts in 2009	794,616	734,208	394,515
Motor Vehicle Theft Rate in 2009 (per 100,000 Population)	258.8	286.0	453.6
Percent Change in Motor Vehicle Theft Rate: 2008 to 2009	(17.8)	(18.2)	(19.2)
Percent Change in Motor Vehicle Theft Rate: 2005 to 2009	(37.9)	(39.0)	(41.9)

Source: CQ Press using reported data from the F.B.I.
"Crime in the United States 2009" (Uniform Crime Reports, September 13, 2010)
*Metro includes population and crime for all metropolitan statistical areas. City statistics are for cities of 100,000 or more in population.